T0134704

Lecture Notes in Computer Science　14306

Founding Editors

Gerhard Goos
Juris Hartmanis

Editorial Board Members

The series Lecture Notes in Computer Science (LNCS), including its subseries Lecture Notes in Artificial Intelligence (LNAI) and Lecture Notes in Bioinformatics (LNBI), has established itself as a medium for the publication of new developments in computer science and information technology research, teaching, and education.

LNCS enjoys close cooperation with the computer science R & D community, the series counts many renowned academics among its volume editors and paper authors, and collaborates with prestigious societies. Its mission is to serve this international community by providing an invaluable service, mainly focused on the publication of conference and workshop proceedings and postproceedings. LNCS commenced publication in 1973.

Feng Zhang · Hua Wang · Mahmoud Barhamgi ·
Lu Chen · Rui Zhou
Editors

Web Information Systems Engineering – WISE 2023

24th International Conference
Melbourne, VIC, Australia, October 25–27, 2023
Proceedings

 Springer

Editors
Feng Zhang
Renmin University of China
Beijing, China

Hua Wang ⓘ
Victoria University
Footscray, VIC, Australia

Mahmoud Barhamgi
Qatar University
Doha, Qatar

Lu Chen
Swinburne University of Technology
Hawthorn, Australia

Rui Zhou
Swinburne University of Technology
Hawthorn, Australia

ISSN 0302-9743   ISSN 1611-3349 (electronic)
Lecture Notes in Computer Science
ISBN 978-981-99-7253-1   ISBN 978-981-99-7254-8 (eBook)
https://doi.org/10.1007/978-981-99-7254-8

This Springer imprint is published by the registered company Springer Nature Singapore Pte Ltd.
The registered company address is: 152 Beach Road, #21-01/04 Gateway East, Singapore 189721, Singapore

Paper in this product is recyclable.

Preface

Welcome to the proceedings of the 24th International Conference on Web Information Systems Engineering (WISE 2023), held in Melbourne, Australia, October 25–27, 2023.

The series of WISE conferences aims to provide an international forum for researchers, professionals, and industrial practitioners to share their knowledge in the rapidly growing area of web technologies, methodologies, and applications. The first WISE event took place in Hong Kong, China (2000). Then the trip continued to Kyoto, Japan (2001); Singapore (2002); Rome, Italy (2003); Brisbane, Australia (2004); New York, USA (2005); Wuhan, China (2006); Nancy, France (2007); Auckland, New Zealand (2008); Poznan, Poland (2009); Hong Kong, China (2010); Sydney, Australia (2011); Paphos, Cyprus (2012); Nanjing, China (2013); Thessaloniki, Greece (2014); Miami, USA (2015); Shanghai, China (2016); Puschino, Russia (2017); Dubai, UAE (2018); Hong Kong, China (2019); Amsterdam and Leiden, The Netherlands (2020), Australia – virtual event (2021), Biarritz, France (2022), and this year, WISE 2023 was held in Melbourne, Australia.

A total of 137 research papers were submitted to the conference for consideration, and each paper was reviewed by at least three reviewers. Finally, 33 submissions were selected as regular papers (an acceptance rate of 24% approximately), plus 40 as short papers. The research papers cover the areas of social networks, recommendation, text data, cyber security, web, prediction, natural language processing, optimization, streaming data, machine learning fundamentals, graph data, etc.

We would like to sincerely thank our keynote speakers:

- Jie Lu AO, University of Technology Sydney, Australia
- Shazia Sadiq, University of Queensland, Australia

In addition, special thanks are due to the members of the International Program Committee and the external reviewers for a rigorous and robust reviewing process. We are also grateful to Springer and the International WISE Society for supporting this conference.

We expect that the ideas that have emerged in WISE 2023 will result in the development of further innovations for the benefit of scientific, industrial, and social communities.

October 2023

Feng Zhang
Hua Wang
Mahmoud Barhamgi
Lu Chen
Rui Zhou

Organization

General Co-chairs

Athman Bouguettaya   University of Sydney, Australia
Richard Chbeir   University of Pau and the Adour Region, France
Xiaoyang Wang   Fudan University, China

PC Co-chairs

Feng Zhang   Renmin University of China, China
Hua Wang   Victoria University, Australia
Mahmoud Barhamgi   Qatar University, Qatar

Publicity Co-chairs

Djamal Benslimane   Lyon 1 University, France
Michael Mrissa   University of Primorska, Slovenia
Xiaohui Tao   University of Southern Queensland, Australia
Zhenying He   Fudan University, China

Publication Co-chairs

Lu Chen   Swinburne University of Technology, Australia
Rui Zhou   Swinburne University of Technology, Australia

Diversity and Inclusion Chair

Jinli Cao   La Trobe University, Australia

Industry Relationship Chair

Jian Yang   Macquarie University, Australia

Finance Chair

Jiao Yin   Victoria University, Australia

Website Co-chairs

Yong-Feng Ge   Victoria University, Australia
Mingshan You   Victoria University, Australia

Local Arrangement Co-chairs

Jiaying Kou   Australian Urban Research Infrastructure
                                      Network, University of Melbourne, Australia
Hui Zheng   Data61, Australia

Senior Program Committee

Yanchun Zhang   Victoria University, Australia
Qing Li   Hong Kong Polytechnic University, China
Xiaohua Jia   City University of Hong Kong, China
Elisa Bertino   Purdue University, USA
Xiaofang Zhou   Hong Kong University of Science and
                                      Technology, China

HIS Steering Committee Representatives

Yanchun Zhang   Victoria University, Australia
Qing Li   Hong Kong Polytechnic University, China

Program Committee

Toshiyuki Amagasa   University of Tsukuba, Japan
Mohamed-Amine Baazizi   Sorbonne Université, France
Luciano Baresi   Politecnico di Milano, Italy
Mahmoud Barhamgi   Qatar University, Qatar
Ladjel Bellatreche   LIAS/ENSMA, France
Boualem Benatallah   University of New South Wales, Australia

Devis Bianchini	University of Brescia, Italy
Mohamed Reda Bouadjenek	Deakin University, Australia
Khouloud Boukadi	University of Tunis, Tunisia
Javier Luis Canovas Izquierdo	IN3 - UOC, Spain
Bin Cao	Zhejiang University of Technology, China
Jinli Cao	La Trobe University, Australia
Xin Cao	University of New South Wales, Australia
Cinzia Cappiello	Politecnico di Milano, Italy
Sven Casteleyn	Universitat Jaume I, Spain
Barbara Catania	University of Genoa, Italy
Tsz Chan	Hong Kong Baptist University, China
Cindy Chen	UMass Lowell, USA
Lu Chen	Zhejiang University, China
Lu Chen	Swinburne University of Technology, Australia
Theodoros Chondrogiannis	University of Konstanz, Germany
Dario Colazzo	Paris-Dauphine University, France
Damiano Distante	University of Rome Unitelma Sapienza, Italy
Benslimane Djamal	Lyon 1 University, Italy
Francisco Jose Dominguez Mayo	University of Seville, Spain
Hai Dong	RMIT University, Australia
Schahram Dustdar	Vienna University of Technology, Austria
Nora Faci	Université Lyon 1, France
Flavius Frasincar	Erasmus University Rotterdam, The Netherlands
Yongfeng Ge	Victoria University, Australia
Azadeh Ghari Neiat	Deakin University, Australia
Xiangyang Gou	Peking University, China
Daniela Grigori	Paris-Dauphine University, France
Viswanath Gunturi	IIT Ropar, India
Allel Hadjali	LIAS/ENSMA, France
Armin Haller	Australian National University, Australia
Kongzhang Hao	University of New South Wales, Australia
Tanzima Hashem	Bangladesh University of Engineering and Technology, Bangladesh
Md Rafiul Hassan	King Fahd University of Petroleum and Minerals, Saudi Arabia
Zhenying He	Fudan University, China
Hao Huang	Wuhan University, China
Xiaodi Huang	Charles Sturt University, Australia
Peiquan Jin	University of Science and Technology of China, China
Guy-Vincent Jourdan	University of Ottawa, Canada

Eleanna Kafeza	Athens University of Economics and Business, Greece
Georgios Kambourakis	University of the Aegean, Greece
Verena Kantere	University of Ottawa, Canada
Epaminondas Kapetanios	University of Hertfordshire, UK
Georgia Kapitsaki	University of Cyprus, Cyprus
Kyoung-Sook Kim	National Institute of Advanced Industrial Science and Technology, Japan
Alexander Knapp	Universität Augsburg, Germany
Anne Laurent	University of Montpellier, France
Jiuyong Li	University of South Australia, Australia
Xiang Lian	Kent State University, USA
Kewen Liao	Australian Catholic University, Australia
Dan Lin	Vanderbilt University, USA
Guanfeng Liu	Macquarie University, Australia
Jiangang Ma	Federation University, Australia
Murali Mani	University of Michigan, USA
Santiago Melia	Universidad de Alicante, Spain
Xiaoye Miao	Zhejiang University, China
Sajib Mistry	Curtin University, Australia
Lourdes Moreno	Universidad Carlos III de Madrid, Spain
Nathalie Moreno	Universidad de Málaga, Spain
Amira Mouakher	Corvinus University of Budapest, Hungary
Michael Mrissa	InnoRenew CoE, University of Primorska, Slovenia
Mitsunori Ogihara	University of Miami, USA
Vincent Oria	New Jersey Institute of Technology, USA
George Pallis	University of Cyprus, Cyprus
Jose Ignacio Panach Navarrete	Universitat de València, Spain
George Papastefanatos	ATHENA Research Center, Greece
Peng Peng	Hunan University, China
Alfonso Pierantonio	University of L'Aquila, Italy
Dimitris Plexousakis	FORTH, Greece
Birgit Pröll	Johannes Kepler University Linz, Austria
Werner Retschitzegger	Johannes Kepler University Linz, Austria
Filippo Ricca	Università di Genova, Italy
Thomas Richter	Rhein-Waal University of Applied Sciences, Germany
Gustavo Rossi	UNLP, Argentina
Jarogniew Rykowski	Poznan University of Economics and Business, Poland
Heiko Schuldt	University of Basel, Switzerland

Wieland Schwinger	Johannes Kepler University Linz, Austria
Mohamed Sellami	Télécom SudParis, France
Wei Shen	Nankai University, China
Yain-Whar Si	University of Macau, China
Siuly Siuly	Victoria University, Australia
Qingqiang Sun	University of New South Wales, Australia
Kari Systä	Tampere University of Technology, Finland
Chaogang Tang	China University of Mining and Technology, China
Xiaohui Tao	University of Southern Queensland, Australia
Joe Tekli	Lebanese American University, Lebanon
Dimitri Theodoratos	New Jersey Institute of Technology, USA
Katerina Tzompanaki	CY Cergy Paris University, France
Leong Hou U.	University of Macau, China
Markel Vigo	University of Manchester, UK
Hanchen Wang	University of Technology Sydney, Australia
Hongzhi Wang	Harbin Institute of Technology, China
Hua Wang	Victoria University, Australia
Junhu Wang	Griffith University, Australia
Lizhen Wang	Yunnan University, China
Michael Weiss	Carleton University, Canada
Shiting Wen	Zhejiang University, China
Marco Winckler	Université Côte d'Azur, France
Dingming Wu	Shenzhen University, China
Adam Wójtowicz	Poznań University of Economics and Business, Poland
Hayato Yamana	Waseda University, Japan
Lei Yang	Peking University, China
Xun Yi	RMIT University, Australia
Hongzhi Yin	University of Queensland, Australia
Jiao Yin	Victoria University, Australia
Jianming Yong	University of Southern Queensland, Australia
Sira Yongchareon	Auckland University of Technology, New Zealand
Nicola Zannone	Eindhoven University of Technology, The Netherlands
Feng Zhang	Renmin University of China, China
Gefei Zhang	HTW Berlin, Germany
Jiujing Zhang	Guangzhou University, China
Wenjie Zhang	University of New South Wales, Australia
Rui Zhou	Swinburne University of Technology, Australia
Xiangmin Zhou	RMIT University, Australia
Jürgen Ziegler	University of Duisburg-Essen, Germany

Additional Reviewers

Baird, Cameron
Biswas, Punam
Foysal, Md. Ferdouse Ahmed
Hajj Hassan, Houssam
Han, Keqi
Hao, Kongzhang
Hashem, Tahsina
He, Chengkun
Islam, Md. Ashraful
Jerbi, Imen
Kelarev, Andrei
Li, Ke
Miller, Ian
Muhammad, Syed
Murturi, Ilir

Nicewarner, Tyler
Papadakos, Panagiotis
Papadopoulos, Panagiotis
Paschalides, Demetris
Saidani, Fayçal Rédha
Sana, Nadouri
Stefanidis, Dimosthenis
Tamzid, Tasmiah
Tang, Mingjian
Wen, Hechuan
Wu, Xiaoying
Wu, Yidu
Zhang, Boyu
Zhang, Yihong
Zhu, Zichen

Contents

Security and Privacy

Web Technologies

Graph Embeddings and Link Predictions

Predictive Analysis and Machine Learning

Recommendation Systems

Natural Language Processing (NLP) and Databases

Data Analysis and Optimization

Anomaly and Threat Detection:

Streaming Data

Miscellaneous

Explainability and Scalability in AI

Text and Sentiment Analysis

Ensemble Learning Model for Medical Text Classification

Ghada Ben Abdennour[1(✉)], Karim Gasmi[2], and Ridha Ejbali[1]

[1] Research Team in Intelligent Machines (RTIM), National School of Engineering of Gabes, Gabes University, Gabes, Tunisia
ghadabenabdennour@gmail.com, ridha_ejbali@ieee.org
[2] Research Laboratory on Development and Control of Distributed Applications (REDCAD), ENIS, Sfax University, Sfax, Tunisia
karim.gasmi@redcad.org

Abstract. Automatic text classification, in which textual data is categorized into specified categories based on its content, is a classic issue in the science of Natural Language Processing (NLP). These models have proven useful when applied to data with several dimensions, including sparse features. It would appear that machine learning and other statistical approaches, like those employed in medical text classification, are highly effective for these jobs. Yet a lot of manual labor is still needed to classify the massive dataset used for training. Pretrained language models, such as machine learning models, have been proven effective in recent studies, demonstrating their capacity to reduce the time and effort spent on feature engineering. Yet, there is no statistically significant improvement in performance when applying the machine learning model directly to the classification job. We present a RFSVM algorithm-based hybrid machine learning model to boost the accuracy of the machine learning prediction. The model has three steps: (1) medical text processing; (2) medical text feature extraction; and (3) ensemble learning model for text classification. Using the PubMed dataset, we conducted experiments demonstrating that the proposed strategy greatly improves the precision of the results.

Keywords: Medical Text · Classification · Ensemble learning · Hybridisation

1 Introduction

Over the past decade, more than 50 million academic publications have been published, with a growing yearly output [1]. Around half of these are medical papers cataloged in MEDLINE, overseen by the US National Library of Medicine [2]. Medical professionals rely on these texts for accurate diagnoses, but their workload is increasing. Text classification offers a solution to this issue, gaining prominence due to its relevance in healthcare research. Artificial Intelligence

K. Gasmi and R. Ejbali—These authors contributed equally to this work.

(AI), particularly Machine Learning (ML), supported by Natural Language Processing (NLP), has effectively addressed healthcare challenges. Text classification, a fundamental NLP task, finds applications in various domains like spam detection [3], language identification [4], and sentiment analysis [5].

Our focus is on medical literature classification, encompassing vast healthcare literature available online, including platforms like *PubMed* [6]. Given the burgeoning medical data, accurate classification and analysis of medical texts have become essential. Therefore, we propose an NLP-based text classification system to automatically categorize PubMed abstracts. We introduce data cleaning in this context. After preprocessing, we evaluate the impact of feature extraction and compare five classifiers. We employ an ensemble approach with the top three models, demonstrating the benefits of hybridization over single-model approaches. Additionally, we delve into weight parameter selection and optimization details.

The remainder of the paper is organized as follows: Sect. 2 shows the related literature about current medical text classification in the area of machine learning. The proposed method is described in detail in Sect. 3. The outcomes of the experiments are elaborated upon in Sect. 4. Finally, in Sect. 5, we make a conclusion to the paper.

2   Related Work

In recent years, diverse approaches for medical text classification using Machine Learning (ML) have been developed. In this section, we aim to provide an overview of the research efforts conducted on this topic. In [7], Kalra *et al.* had done a comparative study on three algorithms, namely KNN, Random Forest (RF), and DNN. This study discussed the automation of radiology protocols using CT and IRM datasets of radiological reports. RF model has achieved the best results in this classification task. Pilar *et al.* have made a comparison between different machine learning models based on NLP using CT and MRI datasets of radiological reports. As a consequence, SVM proven efficient in real scenarios by radiologists [8]. The authors of [9] have used the Random Forest algorithm for accurate identification of HCM patients from CMR reports.

Other studies have investigated the classification of medical texts using the same dataset used in our proposed approach. For example, a study by Anantharaman *et al.* has implemented tokenization, stemming, and lemmatization and removed stop words as a preprocessing step. After the preprocessing steps, they have presented a bag of words, TF-IDF, and topic modeling like the feature extraction step. Finally, Random Forest is the model for classification. In this study, they obtained an accuracy between 48.6% and 57.5% for PubMed 20K RCT dataset [10]. While a study by Mercadier has talked about abstract classification using the PubMed 200K RCT dataset, A comparative study between diverse models of machine learning is done and he achieved different values of accuracy, but the best is equal to 65.20% [11].

3 Ensemble Learning for Medical Text Classification

This section introduces our developed medical text classification model. The process, illustrated in Fig. 1, comprises three key stages: (1) Preprocessing, (2) Feature Extraction, and (3) Classification. The process begins with loading the PubMed dataset, followed by text cleaning. The subsequent focus is on text representation. In the testing phase, various models, utilizing single and hybrid strategies, are compared for accuracy, precision, and F1-score, ultimately determining the optimal classifier.

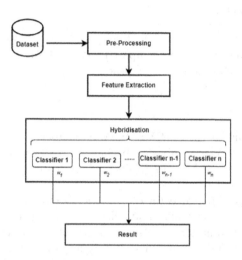

Fig. 1. Proposed model for medical text classification.

3.1 Pre-processing

Pre-processing is vital for NLP text classification, converting data into a suitable format for machine learning, thereby minimizing errors. This involves tokenization, converting text to lowercase, and eliminating stop words and punctuation.

3.2 Feature Extraction

After pre-processing and cleaning the data, the important task of text classification is feature extraction. This stage involves converting the text into numerical features that machine learning models can easily understand and process. Feature extractions used in this work are CountVectorizer (CV) and Term Frequency- Inverse Document Frequency (TF-IDF).

- **CountVectorizer (CV):** It converts the text document into a matrix where each row is a document and each column is a word (token), and the value inside the matrix corresponds to the number of each word in each document. This technique converts the text document into numeric features, which can be used as input for machine learning models [12].

- **Term Frequency- Inverse Document Frequency (TF-IDF):** The purpose of this task is to evaluate the importance of words in text documents or in a corpus. The term frequency (TF) measures the frequency of a word in a document. It is obtained by dividing the number of occurrences of a word in a document by the total number of words in the document. Next, the inverse document frequency (IDF) is computed as the logarithm of the total number of documents in the corpus divided by the number of documents that contain the word in question [12].

3.3   Model Selection

In this paper, the algorithms mentioned below are used in two strategies (simple and hybrid), and they have been compared with each other to conclude which, in terms of strategy and model, is the best.

3.3.1   Single Model

1. **Support Vector Machine (SVM):** SVM, a supervised learning method, is commonly used for classification, especially in text classification. Renowned for its effectiveness, SVM aims to find a hyperplane that clearly separates data into multiple classes [13].
2. **Naïve Bayes (NB):** Naïve Bayes is a widely employed text classification model, valued for its optimality and efficiency. Operating on the principles of Bayes Theorem, it functions as a probabilistic classifier [14].
3. **Decision Tree (DT):** A decision tree is a prevalent supervised machine learning technique for classification. Comprising nodes, branches, and leaf nodes, it employs internal nodes to test attributes, branches to show test outcomes, and leaf nodes for final class decisions [13].
4. **Random Forest (RF):** The Random Forest classifier is a favored machine learning approach for text classification, known for its effectiveness. It assembles multiple decision trees using random data subsets, with the final prediction often based on a majority vote from the ensemble [13].
5. **Logistic Regression (LR):** Logistic regression encompasses regression analyses that model outcome probabilities using predictor variables. Commonly applied in classification, it suits scenarios with binary output variables, taking two distinct values [5].

3.3.2   Ensemble Learning Model

This paragraph highlights the hybridization strategy commonly employed to enhance prediction accuracy and robustness by combining multiple algorithms. Various combination methods exist in the literature, and we will now introduce three popular techniques: voting, bagging and stacking.

1. **Voting:** A voting classifier can employ two types of voting techniques: hard and soft. In hard voting, each classifier votes for the output class, and thus the

majority-voted class is chosen. On the other hand, the soft voting classifier, which we used in our approach, combines the predictions of different individual classifiers to make a final prediction. Each classifier provides the probability about the output class, and the probabilities are weighted, summed up, and the best probable class is chosen as a prediction [13,14].

From the mathematical point of view;

$$S = \underset{i}{\mathrm{argmax}} \sum_{j=1}^{n} W_i * p_{ij} \qquad (1)$$

where S final prediction, argmax function return class with the highest probability, i the number of classes $i = \{1, 2, \ldots, m\}$, j the number of models $j = \{1, 2, \ldots, n\}$, W represents the weight and P probability from the classifiers

2. **Bagging:** Ensemble machine learning often involves the use of a sampling technique known as bagging, where subsets of the original training set are created. Each model within the ensemble is trained independently on one of these subsets. These models operate in parallel, making predictions individually. Finally, the ensemble combines the predictions from all the models to determine the final prediction [15].

3. **Stacking:** Stacking is an ensemble machine learning technique that involves training multiple models on the same dataset. The predictions made by these models are then used as input features to construct a new matrix. This matrix is utilized to train a final model, known as a meta-learner, which learns to combine the predictions from the individual models [16].

4   Result

To start with, we utilized the models outlined in Sect. 3 and carried out a series of experiments. Our investigation also encompassed a comparative analysis of multiple machine learning techniques, employing two distinct strategies: single and hybrid.

4.1   Dataset

As a first step in this research work, we used a **PubMed 20k RCT** [6]. This dataset was liberated in 2017 by Dernoncourt and Lee which it is based on PubMed for sentence classification in biomedical literature. This dataset contains 20,000 abstracts of randomized controlled trials. Each sentence of each abstract is labeled with its role in the abstract using one of five classes: **background, objective, method, result, and conclusion.**

4.2   Evaluation Metrics

In order to assess the effectiveness of our classification method, we employed widely recognized metrics such as Accuracy, Precision and F1-score [13] (Table 1).

Table 1. Dataset description

	Size	Sentence Length	Classes
PubMed 20K RCT	20000	210175	5

The equations of the different metrics are described below:

$$Accuracy = (TP + TN)/(TP + FP + TN + FN) \qquad (2)$$

$$Precision = TP/(TP + FP) \qquad (3)$$

$$F1\text{-}score = 2 * \text{Precision} * (TP/TP + FN)/\text{Precision} + (TP/TP + FN) \quad (4)$$

where TP, TN, FP and FN mean True Positive, True Negative, False Positive and False Negative, respectively.

4.3   Evaluation of the Feature Extraction Method

Beginning with an evaluation of different feature extraction techniques like TF-IDF and CountVectorizer. For each technique, we trained a classification model and evaluated its performance using various evaluation metrics.

The results showed that each feature extraction technique improved the performance of the classification models. However, we have noticed that a combination of these technologies can improve the performance of the model even more. Overall, these results indicate that combining different feature extraction techniques can be an effective approach to improving the performance of text classification models, but not for all classifiers. Table 2 presents the results of the evaluations of the different feature extraction techniques we discussed.

Table 2. Evaluation Feature Extraction techniques.

		Accuracy (%)	Precision (%)	F1-score (%)
SVM	CountVectorizer	74.478	74.652	74.468
	TF-IDF	77.194	76.926	76.953
	CountVectorizer + TF-IDF	**78.085**	**77.826**	**77.845**
DT	**CountVectorizer**	**67.577**	**66.920**	**67.176**
	TF-IDF	66.516	65.951	66.183
	CountVectorizer + TF-IDF	66.213	65.651	65.894
RF	CountVectorizer	74.766	73.932	73.514
	TF-IDF	75.281	74.418	74.148
	CountVectorizer + TF-IDF	**75.298**	**74.460**	**74.204**
NB	**CountVectorizer**	**74.308**	**74.534**	**74.276**
	TF-IDF	69.732	70.019	66.264
	CountVectorizer + TF-IDF	69.029	69.421	65.268
LR	CountVectorizer	77.008	76.610	76.744
	TF-IDF	77.798	77.284	77.406
	CountVectorizer + TF-IDF	**77.798**	**77.284**	**77.406**

4.4 Evaluation of the Classification Method

While our primary objective was to develop an optimal machine learning model to classify medical abstracts, Thus, we evaluated a variety of algorithms with single and hybrid strategies, including SVM, DT, RF, NB, and LR. Table 3 compares the different classification machine learning models as a single strategy on the PubMed 20K RCT dataset.

Table 3. Comparable result of different algorithms as single strategy.

	Accuracy (%)	Precision (%)	F1-score (%)
Support Vector Machine (SVM)	78.085	77.826	77.845
Decision Tree (DT)	66.213	65.651	65.894
Random Forest (RF)	75.298	74.460	74.204
Naïve Bayes (NB)	69.029	69.421	65.268
Logistic Regression (LR)	77.798	77.284	77.406

The idea of combining 2 classifiers in an ensemble approach proves highly effective in achieving a high-performing and stable model. This strategy leverages the individual strengths of each classifier to make optimal decisions based on the input instance. By capitalizing on the diverse capabilities of the classifiers, the ensemble model enhances the overall performance and reliability of the system. For this reason, we have used an ensemble of machine learning algorithms such as SVM, LR, and RF classifiers. The top three above-mentioned algorithms have been ensembled with a soft voting classifier. As shown in Table 4, comparing the accuracy, precision, and F1-score rates of the different models that utilize a hybrid strategy with a voting classifier.

Table 4. Comparable result of different models as hybrid strategy.

	Accuracy (%)	Precision (%)	F1-score (%)
RF-SVM	**83.574**	**83.123**	**83.195**
RF-LR	78.539	77.929	77.972
SVM-LR	82.453	82.278	82.302

According to the results presented in Table 4, RF-SVM achieved the highest accuracy rate with 83.574%, which is significantly better than any models including single to achieve the aim for the PubMed 20k RCT dataset.

4.5 Impact of the Weights Parameter in a Soft Voting Classifier for Ensemble Learning

From the mathematical function cited in the Sect. 3.3.2.1 the assigned weight for each classifier is a crucial factor that significantly affects the model's performance. Thus, in this discussion, we will examine the influence of the weights parameter on the performance of our model.

The model weights allocated in the soft voting classifier determine the significance of each individual model in the final prediction. Assigning equal weights to all models will result in equal contributions to the final prediction. However, in reality, some models may be more precise than others, and allocating equal weights may not be ideal. By allocating higher weights to more accurate models, we can enhance the overall performance of the soft voting classifier. In essence, assigning higher weights to more accurate models can lead to better overall performance.

To demonstrate the effect of assigning different weights to the soft voting classifier, we conducted experiments on a dataset utilizing our optimized model (RFSVM) to enhance efficiency. Table 5 shows the evaluation metrics values for each weight assigned in the soft voting classifier proposed.

Table 5. Weight Parameters Evaluation.

Weight of SVM	Weight of RF	Accuracy (%)	Precision (%)	F1-score (%)
0.1	0.9	81.304	80.691	80.647
0.2	0.8	82.192	81.624	81.633
0.3	0.7	83.017	82.488	82.541
0.4	0.6	83.336	82.864	82.930
0.5	0.5	83.574	83.123	83.195
0.6	0.4	83.636	83.325	83.311
0.7	0.3	83.782	83.442	83.501
0.8	0.2	83.939	83.634	83.690
0.9	0.1	83.828	83.551	83.602

At the outset, we systematically varied the weight parameters and evaluated the classifier's performance. We explored a range of weight values, spanning from 0.1 to 0.9, with increments of 0.1. We conducted the first experiment by assigning identical weights to all models in the soft voting classifier equal to 0.5 and running the initial experiment. As a result, the model achieved an accuracy rate of 83.574%. Assigning a weight of 0.8 to SVM and 0.2 to Random Forest resulted in a higher accuracy value of 83.939% indicating their meaningful contributions to the ensemble. This disparity implies that the predictions of the SVM had a stronger and more significant impact on the final decision made by the ensemble.

4.6   Ensemble Learning Models

Our primary objective was to construct an optimal hybrid model, taking into account its numerous benefits. To accomplish this, we explored various techniques such as bagging and stacking, excluding the previously discussed voting method. The comparison of bagging, stacking, and voting ensemble methods, as depicted in Table 6, offers valuable insights into their performance in terms of accuracy, precision, and F1-score.

The voting classifier stood out with an impressive 83.939% accuracy, surpassing bagging and stacking in accuracy, precision, and f1-score. Its skill in harnessing multiple model strengths for accurate predictions highlights its ensemble effectiveness. Our models outperformed existing approaches [10], affirming the hybrid classification's benefits that enhance accuracy, robustness, and forecast resilience by leveraging individual ensemble methods.

Table 6. Comparative analysis using state-of-art methods with the same dataset (PubMed 20k RCT).

	Accuracy (%)	Precision (%)	F1-score (%)
Voting	**83.939**	**83.634**	**83.690**
Bagging	82.349	82.806	81.973
Stacking	75.874	75.860	75.866
Anantharaman and al. [10]	57.5	50.5	44.4

5   Conclusion

In light of the escalating applications of text classification within healthcare, where a substantial volume of medical data exists in textual form, our focus was on classifying medical literature, specifically medical abstracts. Multiple models (SVM, DT, RF, NB, LR) and feature extraction techniques (TF-IDF, CountVectorizer) were evaluated. While each model exhibited strengths and weaknesses, their combination yielded notably superior outcomes compared to individual models. Notably, our hybrid model achieved an impressive 83.939% accuracy when applied to the PubMed 20k RCT dataset, highlighting the efficacy and robustness of model fusion in text classification-a parallel to outcomes achieved by other researchers. Future exploration may involve integrating diverse deep learning models for heightened efficiency, alongside investigating an adaptive optimization algorithm to fine-tune weight selection.

Acknowledgements. The authors would like to acknowledge the financial support of this work by grants from General Direction of Scientific Research (DGRST), Tunisia, under the ARUB program.

References

1. Larsen, P., Von Ins, M.: The rate of growth in scientific publication and the decline in coverage provided by science citation index. Scientometrics **84**(3), 575–603 (2010)
2. MEDLINE. https://www.nlm.nih.gov/databases/databases_medline.html

3. Heredia, B., Khoshgoftaar, T.M., Prusa, J., Crawford, M.: An investigation of ensemble techniques for detection of spam reviews. In: 2016 15th IEEE International Conference on Machine Learning and Applications (ICMLA), pp. 127–133. IEEE (2016)

4. Utomo, M.R.A., Sibaroni, Y.: Text classification of British English and American English using support vector machine. In: 2019 7th International Conference on Information and Communication Technology (ICoICT), pp. 1–6. IEEE (2019)

5. Prabhat, A., Khullar, V.: Sentiment classification on big data using Naïve Bayes and logistic regression. In: 2017 International Conference on Computer Communication and Informatics (ICCCI), pp. 1–5. IEEE (2017)

6. Lee, D.: Pubmed (2017). https://pubmed.ncbi.nlm.nih.gov/

7. Kalra, A., Chakraborty, A., Fine, B., Reicher, J.: Machine learning for automation of radiology protocols for quality and efficiency improvement. J. Am. Coll. Radiol. **17**(9), 1149–1158 (2020)

8. López-Úbeda, P., Díaz-Galiano, M.C., Martín-Noguerol, T., Luna, A., Ureña-López, L.A., Martín-Valdivia, M.T.: Automatic medical protocol classification using machine learning approaches. Comput. Methods Prog. Biomed. **200**, 105939 (2021)

9. Sundaram, D.S.B., et al.: Natural language processing based machine learning model using cardiac MRI reports to identify hypertrophic cardiomyopathy patients. In: Frontiers in Biomedical Devices, vol. 84812, p. V001T03A005. American Society of Mechanical Engineers (2021)

10. Anantharaman, A., Jadiya, A., Siri, C.T.S., Adikar, B.N., Mohan, B.: Performance evaluation of topic modeling algorithms for text classification. In: 2019 3rd International Conference on Trends in Electronics and Informatics (ICOEI), pp. 704–708. IEEE (2019)

11. Mercadier, Y.: Classification automatique de textes par réseaux de neurones profonds: application au domaine de la santé. Ph.D. thesis, Université Montpellier (2020)

12. Tripathy, A., Anand, A., Rath, S.K.: Document-level sentiment classification using hybrid machine learning approach. Knowl. Inf. Syst. **53**, 805–831 (2017). https://doi.org/10.1007/s10115-017-1055-z

13. Asif, M., et al.: Performance evaluation and comparative analysis of different machine learning algorithms in predicting cardiovascular disease. Eng. Lett. **29**(2), 731–741 (2021)

14. Kumari, S., Kumar, D., Mittal, M.: An ensemble approach for classification and prediction of diabetes mellitus using soft voting classifier. Int. J. Cogn. Comput. Eng. **2**, 40–46 (2021)

15. Sutton, C.D.: Classification and regression trees, bagging, and boosting. Handb. Stat. **24**, 303–329 (2005)

16. Sakkis, G., Androutsopoulos, I., Paliouras, G., Karkaletsis, V., Spyropoulos, C.D., Stamatopoulos, P.: Stacking classifiers for anti-spam filtering of E-Mail. arXiv preprint arXiv:cs/0106040 (2001)

Fuzzy Based Text Quality Assessment for Sentiment Analysis

Manel BenSassi[1]([✉]), Maher Abbes[1]([✉]), and Faten Atigui[2]([✉])

[1] Univ. Manouba, ENSI, RIADI LR99ES26, Campus universitaire,
2010 Manouba, Tunisia
{manel.bensassi,maher.abbes}@ensi.uma.tn
[2] CEDRIC, Conservatoire National des Arts et des Métiers (CNAM) PARIS,
Rue Saint Martin, 75003 Paris, France
faten.atigui@cnam.fr

Abstract. Practitioners have emphasized the importance of employing sentiment analysis techniques in decision-making. The data utilized in this process is typically gathered from social media, making it somewhat unreliable for decision-making. To address this issue, this study focuses on the Text Quality (TQ) aspect to capture the characteristics of Twitter data streams. Our objective is to develop an automated approach that assists the user in assessing the quality of textual data. This is accomplished through a fuzzified classifier, which automatically identifies ambiguous and unambiguous text at both the syntactic and semantic levels. We present a software tool that captures real-time and batch Twitter data streams. This tool calculates their TQ and presents the outcomes through diverse graphical depictions. It also empowers users to customize the weights allocated to individual quality dimensions and metrics used in computing the overall data quality of a tweet. This flexibility enables customization of weights according to different analysis contexts and user profiles. To demonstrate the usability and value of our contributions, we conducted a case study focusing on the Covid-19 vaccine. A preliminary analysis shows that by removing ambiguous text, the accuracy of the deployed algorithms enhances.

Keywords: Sentiment Analysis · Data Analytics · Data Quality · Big Data · Fuzzy Logic

1 Introduction

The literature provides evidence that furnishing decision-makers with trustworthy information has a positive impact on both tactical and strategic decisions. The growing need to discover and integrate reliable information from heterogeneous data sources, distributed in the Web, Social Networks, Cloud platforms or Data Lakes, makes Data Quality (DQ) an imperative topic. Becoming one of the most important elements in the decision-making process, sentiment analysis is concerned with gathering, analyzing, specifying and predicting user opinions

F. Zhang et al. (Eds.): WISE 2023, LNCS 14306, pp. 13–23, 2023.
https://doi.org/10.1007/978-981-99-7254-8_2

that are described in natural language for the most part. According to [1], there is a prevailing belief that the quality of social media data streams is commonly low and uncertain, which, to a certain extent, renders them unreliable for making decisions based on such data. Thus, to be used in decision-making scenarios, tweets should have a minimum quality to avoid deficient decisions. The main problem in extracting opinions from social media texts is that words in natural language are highly ambiguous.

Research Hypothesis. Our hypothesis is that errors introduced into sentiment analysis (and the consequent confidence decrease in decision making process based on sentiment analysis) are primarily attributed to the ambiguity present in the text. In our work, we use the term "ambiguity" in its more general sense: 1) The first aspect is "the capability of being understood in two or more possible senses or ways" [2] that derived from linguistic features such as poorly constructed sentences or syntactical errors [3] and, 2) "Uncertainty" [3] refers to the lack of semantic information and grounding between the writer and reader. Thus, with reference to the investigation done by [4] ambiguity could be classified into "syntactic" and "semantic" metrics. For this, our main research questions are the following:

- *How can we assess the TQ of streamed tweets in real and in batch time ?*
- *What are the relevant metrics and indicators to measure in order to ensure TQ?*

The aim of our research is to provide automated assistance for assessing the quality of textual data. To be used for different goals in different situations, context had to be given to data quality which means that data quality dimensions and metrics should be addressed differently in each case. Besides, we think that domain experts should be involved in the analysis process. Thus, it gives more flexibility to reuse our proposal in different contexts.

The research reported in this paper targets an automatic assessment of sentiment analysis text by means of a fuzzified classifier to automatically flag ambiguous and unambiguous text at syntactic and semantic level. Our approach considers textual data and consists of: (i) involving domain expert for a contextual analysis by allowing to change the weight of quality dimension metrics, (ii) evaluating tweets using text quality metrics especially ambiguity ones at real and batch time,(iii) and storing searches in a document-oriented database in order to ensure efficient information retrieval.

This paper is structured as follows. Section 2 gives an overview of sentiment analysis, and text quality related work. Section 3 presents our contribution for text quality dimensions and metrics. We present the experimental study in Sect. 4 before concluding in Sect. 5.

2   Related Work

Many issues have been highlighted, in the field of DQ and TQ in machine learning applications, such as the noisy nature of input data extracted from social media sites [5] or insufficiency [6]. Other research on mining tweets regarding the irrelevance of data [5] and on performing sentiment analysis to discover the user's feeling behind a tweet, have been done in crisis times [7].

A more comprehensive analysis from DQ point of view, [1] proposed a DQ evaluation system based on computing only higher DQ dimensions and metrics for data streamed in real time. A DQ approach based on three strategies for social media data retrieval by monitoring the crawling process, the profiling of social media users, and the involvement of domain experts in the analytical process is advanced by [8]. [9] enhanced TQ through data cleansing model for short text topic modeling. However, most of the previous studies advance the DQ assessment as a crisp process based on quantitative data or statistical function which can reinforce difficulties for interpreting quality measure.

Other studies have considered that textual data couldn't be processed as certain input data [10]. For this, to handle uncertain and imprecise data, fuzzy ontology to assess the quality of linked data [11] and fuzzy knowledge-based system that combines the domain knowledge of an expert with existing measurement metric [12] were advanced.

Nevertheless, these approaches do not dive into rudimentary DQ dimensions and metrics and are closely tied to their context making their reuse heavy. We think that the challenges of TQ assessment remain into proposing an automatic evaluation approach having these main features: (i) adaptable and reusable according to the context of deployment through expert's involvement, (ii) extensible allowing the mashup of multiple fuzzy data sources, (iii) visualizing results at real and batch time, (iv) and based on hierarchical definition of multi-level quality dimensions and metrics explained in the following section.

3   Fuzzy Based Text Quality Assessment for Sentiment Analysis Approach

This section introduces our innovative automatic assessment approach that relies on a fuzzy tree classifier explained in Sect. 3.2 and a hierarchical definition of TQ dimensions and metrics introduced in Sect. 3.1.

3.1   Underlying Quality Model

Based on the proposed hierarchical definition of quality and its indicators in [13], we suggest enriching data quality metrics definition with text ambiguity metrics and context management as shown in Fig. 1. When dealing with text quality assessment, three main levels could be identified: **word**, **sentence**, and **discourse level**. Quality evaluation needs to be spread over these abstraction levels and consider the decision-making context. Besides, the hierarchical decomposition of the ambiguity concept into quantifiable indicators affecting the quality of the text could be adapted and adjusted according to different viewpoints.

For this purpose, we had to identify the discriminating features of the text that characterize the quality of social network text from syntactic and semantic point of view. We propose in Table 1, a formal definition of adopted syntactic and semantic ambiguity metrics. These metrics should be weighted by domain experts. We think that this proposal would provide : (i) flexibility, since domain experts can adapt to context variations, (ii) generality, since they can include many particular context-dependent cases, and (iii) richness, leading to include more aspects to the metric.

3.2   Fuzzy Tree-Based Classifier for Text Quality Assessment

To be used for different goals in different situations, data quality dimensions and metrics should be addressed differently in each case. For this, domain experts should be involved in the analysis process. Thus, it gives more flexibility to reuse our proposal in different contexts. So, our TQ assessment approach is based on the computing of TQ weighted metrics regulated by activation factors considering the context of deployment.

The TQ assessment, as depicted in Fig. 2, involves a two-phase process. The first pre-processing phase is elementary to establish necessary data for the quality computing phase. Hence, the pre-processing phase aims to set up (1) the weighted and activation set for TQ parameters and, (2) the conflict resolution when more than one expert are involving in the analytical process.

Based on those pre-established configuration and parameters, the quality assessment phase is divided into two main steps which are:(1) the computing of fuzzy metric and, (2) the inference of fuzzy decision tree, detailed as follow.

3.2.1   Pre-processing Phase
This phase is elementary to establish necessary data and parameters for the run-time execution of the system. In this section, we present our approach for

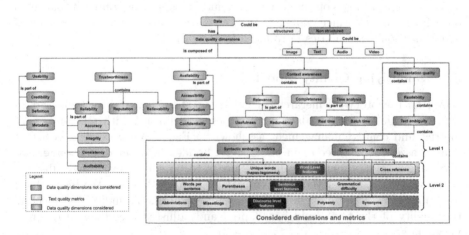

Fig. 1. Text quality dimensions

Table 1. Description of ambiguity text metrics

Level	Type	Metric	Formal definition	Formal description	Interpretation
Word	Synt	Unique words (hapax-legoma)	$\frac{1}{card(S)}\,card\left(\bigcup_{\substack{i=1\\w_i\neq w_j}}^{n} w_i\right)$	The percentage of unique words in the text	The more the number of words that have only one occurrence in a given corpus is high the more the text becomes ambiguous
	Sem	Cross reference	$\frac{1}{card(S)}\,card\left(\bigcup_{\substack{i=1\\w_i\in P}}^{n} w_i\right)$ $n \in N^*$	The percentage of words that references other information[a]	This discourse-level feature increases the text ambiguity because some words could reference the same object and algorithms will not detect this reference
Sentence	Synt	Words per sentence	$\frac{1}{card(D)}\,card(S)$	The percentage of words per sentence	The more words the sentence contains, the more ambiguous it becomes
		Parentheses	$\frac{1}{card(S)}\,card\left(\bigcup_{\substack{i=1\\w_i\in D}}^{n} w_i\right)$ $n \in N^*$	The percentage of parentheses per text	The more the sentence contains parentheses, the more it becomes ambiguous
	Sem	Grammatical difficulty	$\frac{1}{card(D)}\,card\left(\bigcup_{i=1}^{n}\bigcup_{j=1}^{k} p_{ij}\right)$ $n \in N^*$	The percentage of words that might have different positions in discourse. For example, the word "work" can be a noun or a verb in the sentence	The more words might have different positions in discourse, the more it becomes ambiguous
Discourse	Synt	Abbreviations	$abbreviation(W) = True \Longleftrightarrow$ $\forall x \in w, x \in C$	The percentage of abbreviations in text[b]	The more the discourse contains abbreviations, the more it becomes ambiguous
		Misspellings	$Misspellings(w) =$ $False \Longleftrightarrow w \in D$	The percentage of words spelled incorrectly	This indicator increases the ambiguity in texts and especially in models training
	Sem	Polysemy	$\frac{1}{card(D)}\,card\left(\bigcup_{i=1}^{n}\bigcup_{j=1}^{k} m_{ij}\right)$ $n \in N^*$	The percentage of words that have multiple related meanings	It presents the capacity of a word to have multiple related meanings and make it harder for prediction systems to realize that it is the same word
		Synonyms	$w\ has\ a\ synonym\ in\ S \Longleftrightarrow$ $\exists\, x \in S,\, \exists\, y \in E,\quad x = y$	The percentage of different words that can be synonyms in the text	This metric calculates the number of synonyms of every word in the discourse

[a] Cross reference is a notation to pertinent information at another place

[b] An abbreviation is a shortened form of a written word or phrase used to refer to names, places, companies, etc.

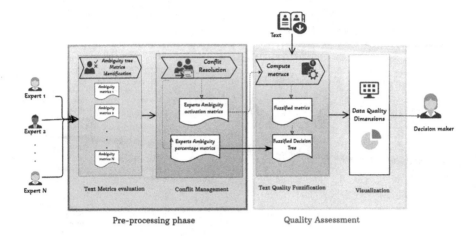

Fig. 2. Text quality evaluation approach

weighting the importance of text quality indicators. Our goal is to evaluate the importance of every indicator for the inference of a given text quality evaluation. This phase consists of two sub-phases. The first one, **"Text metrics evaluation"** is based on the knowledge of the domain experts; it deals with:

- First, the establishment of metrics' importance weighting and their relationship for high, intermediate and rudimentary levels. As the rudimentary metrics may not have the same importance for an intermediate metric for a given context, a weighting coefficient is used to reflect the relevance score of a given metric Mh,i to the intermediate metric $Mh+1,i$.
- Second, an activation function is defined to decide whether a metric should be activated or not. This function aims to transform the weighted metric into an output value to be fed to the next layer.

The second sub-phase is the **"Conflict management"**. Our approach is based on aggregating the weights accorded by several experts. Thus, in order to handle imprecise and conflicting experts' opinions, we apply the Evidence theory (also known as Dempster-Shafer Theory). It is a general framework for reasoning with uncertainty, with understood connections to other frameworks such as probability, possibility and imprecise probability theories. [14].

Given the problem of evaluating the text ambiguity associated with a given context, the universe of discourse Θ of the evidence theory would be seen as the set of all possible metrics for syntactic ambiguity evaluating (respectively semantic ambiguity).

The power set of Θ_{syn} noted as $2^{\Theta_{syn}}$, consists of all the subsets of Θ_{syn} such that: $\Theta_{syn} = \{\Theta_1^{syn}, \Theta_2^{syn}, \Theta_3^{syn}, \Theta_4^{syn}, \Theta_5^{syn}\}$.

Accorded weight and function activation for each metric per each expert Ei is expressed using evidence mass function $m_i^{syn}(x)$ known also as basic probability assignment such that:

$$m_i^{syn}(x) : 2^{\Theta_{syn}} \to [0,1] \times [0,1]$$

To access the percentage coefficient of the metric θ_i, we define the function $per(m_i)$ where:

$$per(m_i) : [0,1] \times [0,1] \to [0,1]$$
$$(x,y) \quad \mapsto \quad x$$

Moreover, to access the percentage coefficient of the metric θ_i, we define the function $act(m_i)$ where:

$$act(m_i) : [0,1] \times [0,1] \to [0,1]$$
$$(x,y) \quad \mapsto \quad y$$

$$\begin{cases} m_i^{syn}(\varnothing) = (0,0) \\ \sum_{A \in 2^{\Theta_{syn}}} per(m_i^{syn}(A)) = 1 \end{cases}$$

Then, each expert is objectively weighted according to the similarity of his/her opinions with others experts opinions by means of evidence distance as given in

$$m_{1,\dots,s}^{Aver}(X) = \frac{1}{s} \sum_{i=1}^{s} m_i(X) \tag{1}$$

where $m_i(X)$ are the representation of mass functions.

The measure of conflict between an expert Ei and all the other set of experts is:

$$conf(j,\varepsilon) = \frac{1}{n-1} \sum_{e=1}^{n} conf(j,e) \tag{2}$$

Finally, adjusted scores are combined to generate the weighting coefficient using the Dempster's combination rule for combining two or more belief functions [15].

3.2.2   Quality Assessment Based on Fuzzy Decision Tree Inference

To assess TQ ambiguity, we investigate the hierarchical representation of metrics and fuzzy logic inference. We need to extend different fuzzified values of rudimentary metrics (a subset U) to intermediate or high-level metrics (which are fuzzy subset). Thus, we chose the extension principle that is in fact a special case of the compositional rule of inference.

The extension principle, described by [14] is a general method for extending crisp mathematical concepts to address fuzzy quantities. It is particularly useful in connection with the computation of linguistic variables, the computing of linguistic probabilities, arithmetic of fuzzy numbers, etc. We applied this theory to deduce metrics value in the higher level of ambiguity tree. Thus, the extension principle is defined:

$$\mu_B(y) = sup\{min(\mu_\phi(x,y), \mu_A(x)/x \in E\} \tag{3}$$

where:

- A is the set which includes syntactic ambiguity metrics M_1, M_2, .., M_n, C is the set which includes semantic ambiguity metrics M_1, M_2, .., M_n for a given level.
- B is the set which includes fuzzy data type used to represent the text ambiguity degree of a given text A="Very High ambiguity", "High ambiguity", "Normal ambiguity", "Low ambiguity", "Very Low ambiguity".
- ϕ is a function that associates x $\in$ A to y $\in$ B, $\phi(x) = y$

To explain the fuzzification part, a metric M_i and a threshold value $M_{th,i}$ is fixed by experts for a text T in a given context. The max between $(M_i - M_{th,i})$ and 0 is considered. Then, the determined value is treated by a sigmoid function to compute the ambiguity level. For example, if $M_1 = 0.3$ and $M_{th_1} = 0.1$. The result is: $max(0.3 - 0.1, 0) = 0.2$. Finally, passing by the sigmoid function, the obtained result is $\mu_{M1}(T) = $ Very Low.

4   Experimental Study

This section presents the data collection and acquisition process and quality computing result before evaluating the quality model.

4.1   Data Collection and Acquisition

We leverage a meticulously curated dataset sourced from Kaggle [16] that is structured with two pivotal columns: "text", which contains the text of the tweets, and "sentiments", which indicates the sentiment of the tweets and ranges between −1, 0, and 1. To enrich our data repository, we seamlessly integrate the Tweepy Python library to our developed interface allowing experts to customize the weight of each metric and to choose the subject of scrapped data as shown in the Fig. 3.

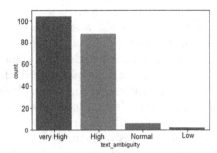

Fig. 3. Configuration interface   **Fig. 4.** Evaluation of text ambiguity

Table 2. Evaluation of forecasting models

Model	RMSE
Polynomial regression	0.0046
Holt's Linear	0.0032
AUTO ARIMA	0.00054

Table 3. Evaluation of sentiment analysis models

Model	Accuracy	f1-score
LSTM	84.65 %	0.845
XGBoost	84.03 %	0.836
Random Forest	80.09 %	0.797
Naive Bayes	70.46 %	0.685

Table 4. The effect of text quality on sentiment analysis models

Metrics	Before[a]		After[b]	
	Accuracy	F1-Score	Accuracy	F1-Score
Random Forest	40%	0.333	43.34%	0.351
Naive Bayes	48.5%	0.452	53%	0.472
XGBoost	32%	0.357	34.66 %	0.379

[a] Before eliminating very High ambiguous Data.
[b] After eliminating very High ambiguous Data.

4.2 Quality Computing Results

The goal of the experiment is to illustrate how the quality of a Twitter stream can be assessed using the dimension and metrics presented in Sect. 3. Sentiment analysis in Covid-19 vaccine is token as a case study to illustrate the usefulness of our approach.

Sentiment Analysis Models Evaluation. The Table 3 presents the evaluation results of 4 sentiment analysis models which show that LSTM has the best accuracy and f1-score.

Forecasting Models Evaluation. Three forecasting models with this data were trained and the evaluation results are shown in Table 2: AUTO ARIMA forecasting model has the lowest value of RMSE (Root Mean Square Error).

4.3 Quality Model Evaluation

We evaluated the quality of 200 texts which present more than 50% of very high ambiguity as shown in Fig. 4. We trained 3 ML algorithms with and without very high ambiguous data. The obtained results, shown in Table 4, ensure that TQ is one of necessary exigences to get better results. Despite the limited quantity of texts used for training sentiment analysis models (which accounts for the relatively low accuracy and F1-score values), the removal of high ambiguous data induce an improvement in the performance of the sentiment analysis models.

5   Conclusion and Future Directions

In light of the growing concern surrounding data quality in sentiment analysis for decision-making, this research presents an automatic text quality approach that can be scalable and applicable to machine learning applications within different contexts. By leveraging the principles of the data quality model, evidence theory, and fuzzy logic reasoning, we can improve the accuracy and reliability of sentiment analysis algorithms. The key contributions of this research are as follows: (1) a hierarchical decomposition of the text quality model tree to address both syntactic and semantic ambiguity, (2) contextual weighting of metrics by experts and conflict management, and (3) fuzzified quality inference by integrating weighted metrics evaluated at both low-level and high-level measurements. We believe that this proposal can be gradually enhanced by integrating additional DQ dimensions and metrics. Furthermore, the system architecture has the potential to be enriched with intelligent features and components that facilitate the derivation of contextual recommendations.

References

1. Arolfo, F., Rodriguez, K.C., Vaisman, A.: Analyzing the quality of twitter data streams. Inf. Syst. Front. 1–21 (2020)
2. Wand, Y., Wang, R.Y.: Anchoring data quality dimensions in ontological foundations. Commun. ACM **39**(11), 86–95 (1996)
3. Handbook, A.: From contract drafting to software specification: linguistic sources of ambiguity (2003)
4. Khezri, R.: Automated detection of syntactic ambiguity using shallow parsing and web data (2017)
5. Ali, K., Dong, H., Bouguettaya, A., Erradi, A., Hadjidj, R.: Sentiment analysis as a service: a social media based sentiment analysis framework. In: 2017 IEEE International Conference on Web Services (ICWS), pp. 660–667. IEEE (2017)
6. Pollacci, L., SSîrbu, A., Giannotti, F., Pedreschi, D., Lucchese, C., Muntean, C.I.: Sentiment spreading: an epidemic model for lexicon-based sentiment analysis on twitter. In: Esposito, F., Basili, R., Ferilli, S., Lisi, F. (eds.) AI*IA 2017. LNCS, vol. 10640, pp. 114–127. Springer, Cham (2017). https://doi.org/10.1007/978-3-319-70169-1_9
7. Alamoodi, A.H., et al.: Sentiment analysis and its applications in fighting COVID-19 and infectious diseases: a systematic review. Expert Syst. Appl. **167**, 114155 (2021)
8. Soto, A., et al.: Data quality challenges in twitter content analysis for informing policy making in health care (2018)
9. Murshed, B.A.H., Abawajy, J., Mallappa, S., Saif, M.A.N., Al-Ghuribi, S.M., Ghanem, F.A.: Enhancing big social media data quality for use in short-text topic modeling. IEEE Access **10**, 105328–105351 (2022)
10. Suanmali, L., Salim, N., Binwahlan, M.S.: Fuzzy logic based method for improving text summarization. arXiv preprint arXiv:0906.4690 (2009)
11. Arruda, N., et al.: A fuzzy approach for data quality assessment of linked datasets. In: International Conference on Enterprise Information Systems, vol. 1, pp. 399–406. SciTePress (2019)

12. Cichy, C., Rass, S.: Fuzzy expert systems for automated data quality assessment and improvement processes. In: EKAW (Posters & Demos), pp. 7–11 (2020)
13. Salvatore, C., Biffignandi, S., Bianchi, A.: Social Media and Twitter Data Quality for New Social Indicators. Soc. Indicat. Res. **156**(2), 601–630 (2021). ISSN 1573-0921
14. Zadeh, L.A., Klir, G.J., Yuan, B.: Fuzzy sets, fuzzy logic, and fuzzy systems. Adv. Fuzzy Syst. Appl. Theory **6** (1996)
15. Shafer, G.: Dempster's rule of combination. Int. J. Approximate Reasoning **79**, 26–40 (2016)
16. Nasreen Taj, M.B., Girisha, G.S.: Insights of strength and weakness of evolving methodologies of sentiment analysis. Glob. Transit. Proc. **2**(2), 157–162 (2021)

Prompt-Learning for Semi-supervised Text Classification

Chengzhe Yuan[1,4], Zekai Zhou[3], Feiyi Tang[2,4], Ronghua Lin[3,4],
Chengjie Mao[3,4], and Luyao Teng[2,4(✉)]

[1] School of Electronics and Information, Guangdong Polytechnic Normal University,
Guangzhou 510665, Guangdong, China
[2] School of Information Engineering, Guangzhou Panyu Polytechnic,
Guangzhou 511483, Guangdong, China
luna.teng@qq.com
[3] School of Computer Science, South China Normal University,
Guangzhou 510631, Guangdong, China
[4] Pazhou Lab, Guangzhou 510330, Guangdong, China

Abstract. In the Semi-Supervised Text Classification (SSTC) task, the performance of the SSTC-based models heavily rely on the accuracy of the pseudo-labels for unlabeled data, which is not practical in real-world scenarios. Prompt-learning has recently proved to be effective to alleviate the low accuracy problem caused by the limited label data in SSTC. In this paper, we present a **P**attern **E**xploiting **T**raining with **U**nsupervised **D**ata **A**ugmentation (PETUDA) method to address SSCT under limited labels setting. We first exploit the potential of the PLMs using prompt learning, convert the text classification task into a cloze-style task, and use the masked prediction ability of the PLMs to predict the categories. Then, we use a variety of data augmentation methods to enhance the model performance with unlabeled data, and introduce a consistency loss in the model training process to make full use of unlabeled data. Finally, we conduct extensive experiments on three text classification benchmark datasets. Empirical results show that PETUDA consistently outperforms the baselines in all cases.

Keywords: Text classification · Prompt-Learning · Pre-trained language models

1 Introduction

As a fundamental task in Natural Language Processing (NLP), text classification aims to automatically categorize a piece of text based on its content. With a great success of pre-trained language models (PLMs) in text classification [11]. These methods tend to apply deep representation learning on unlabeled texts followed by a fine-tuning step on labeled texts. However, high-quality labeled data is the key to the improvement of these methods, and limited labeled data leads to the risk of overfitting. To alleviate the problem of collecting labeled

F. Zhang et al. (Eds.): WISE 2023, LNCS 14306, pp. 24–34, 2023.
https://doi.org/10.1007/978-981-99-7254-8_3

data, SSTC-based models try to utilize large amount of unlabeled data for text classification.

Current SSTC-based methods tend to apply data augmentation techniques and PLMs fine-tuning to improve the performance of text classification task. The basic idea behind the fine-tuned PLMs is that by training on extensive corpora, these methods iteratively apply prediction on the unlabeled data as pseudo-labels for future training [6]. However, a drawback of the paradigm of fine-tuned PLMs is that the labeled and unlabeled data are trained separately, and the labeling information are not utilized for the deep representations, leading to potentially poor discriminative representations and worse performance [5].

In this paper, we propose a pattern exploiting training with unsupervised data augmentation (PETUDA) method to address SSTC with limited labels setting. In specific, we first exploit the potential of the PLMs using prompt learning, convert the text classification task into a cloze-style task, and use the masked prediction ability of the PLMs to predict the categories. Secondly, we use a variety of data augmentation methods from character-level, word-level and sentence-level to enhance the model performance with unlabeled data, and introduce a consistency loss in the model training process to make full use of unlabeled data. Finally, In the experiment, we conduct extensive experiments on three text classification benchmark datasets with different ratios of labeled data. In brief, the contributions of our paper are summarized as follows:

- We propose a pattern exploiting training with unsupervised data augmentation method, namely PETUDA, to address the semi-supervised text classification problem.
- We first uses a prompt learning based method to fine-tune the model in order to fully exploit the potential capabilities of PLMs. Then, we introduce a set of data augmentation methods and a consistency loss to fully utilize unlabeled data.
- We evaluate the proposed method on three text classification benchmark datasets. Extensive experiments show that PETUDA outperforms all the baseline methods.

2   Related Work

This section reviews two lines of works related to our research: semi-supervised text classification, and the prompt-based learning.

Semi-supervised Text Classification. Semi-supervised learning aims at improving model performance by making full use of limited labeled data and large amount of unlabeled data under certain applications. Recently, various data augmentation techniques have been applied to SSTC-based methods. For example, Xie et al. [9] show that better data augmentation can lead to significantly better semi-supervised learning. Chen et al. [3] introduce an interpolation-based augmentation and regularization technique to alleviate the dependencies of supervised models on labeled data. There are some works focus on exploiting pre-trained language models and consistency to improve the performance of the model. Murtadha et al. [6] proposed a self-training semi-supervised framework to address text classification problem in learning with noisy labels manner. Li et al. [5] proposed a self-training method to solve the margin bias problem caused by the large difference between representation distributions of labels in SSTC.

Prompt-Based Learning. Recent years have witnessed the success of the fine-tuned PLMs. Inspired by GPT-3 [1], prompt-learning has been proposed to convert text classification problem into cloze-style task [11]. A line of works are proposed to apply hand-crafted prompts in text classification. For example, Han et al. [4] proposed prompt tuning with rules (PTR) for many-class text classification tasks. Song et al. [8] designed a set of templates for multi-label text classification by integrating labels into the input of the pre-trained language model, and jointly optimizing by masked language models.

3   Methodology

In this section, we describe the proposed **P**attern **E**xploiting **T**raining with **U**nsupervised **D**ata **A**ugmentation method, namely PETUDA (see Fig. 1).

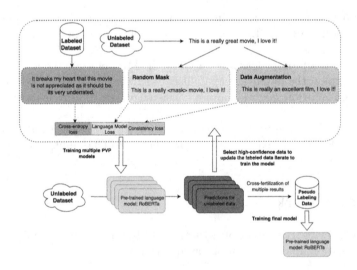

Fig. 1. Overview the framework of PETUDA.

3.1   Single Model Training

To fine-tune the pre-trained language model M on the small labeled text dataset X_l and the large unlabeled text dataset X_u, this paper utilizes techniques related to prompt learning and semi-supervised learning to fine-tune the model, using Eq. (1) as the loss function to optimize model parameters.

$$L = (1 - \alpha - \beta) * L_{CE} + \alpha * L_{MLM} + \beta * L_C \tag{1}$$

Here, L_{CE} represents the cross-entropy loss, L_{MLM} represents the masked language model loss, L_C represents the consistency loss, α is the weight of the masked language model loss, and β is the weight of the consistency loss.

Cross-Entropy Loss. When training on the labeled samples $X_l = \{(x_n^l, y_n^l)\}_{n=1}^N$, the pre-defined PVP is used to transform the samples into cloze-style questions, and the pre-trained language model M is used to predict the masks in these questions, calculating the cross-entropy loss between the prediction at each position and the actual label. For an input text x^l, the probability of its label $y^l \in Y$ is calculated as shown in Eq. (2).

$$s_p(y^l \mid x^l) = M(V(y^l) \mid P(x^l)) \tag{2}$$

Here, P represents the pattern in the PVP, V represents the mapping table in the PVP, $p = (P, V)$ represents the PVP, and $M(V(y^l) \mid P(x^l))$ represents the probability of the pre-trained language model M predicting the mask in the input text $P(x^l)$ as $V(y^l)$.

Then, the softmax function is used to normalize the above probability values to get a prediction probability distribution, as shown in Eq. (3).

$$q_p(y^l \mid x^l) = \frac{e^{s_p(y^l \mid x^l)}}{\sum\limits_{y' \in Y} e^{s_p(y' \mid x^l)}} \tag{3}$$

Finally, the cross-entropy loss between the prediction probability distribution $q_p(y \mid x^l)$ and the distribution of the actual labels is calculated, as shown in Eq. (4).

$$L_{CE} = -\sum_{j=1}^{C} y_j \, log(q_p(y \mid x^l)_j) \tag{4}$$

Here, C is the size of the label set, y is the distribution of the actual labels, y_j represents its j_{th} component, when the label of the labeled sample $y_j = 1$, $q_p(y \mid x^l)_j$ represents the j_{th} component of the prediction probability distribution.

Masked Language Model Loss. In a semi-supervised learning scenario, the shortage of training samples can lead to overfitting and forgetting in the pre-trained language model. In addition, the calculation of cross-entropy loss usually requires prediction of the mask to keep it consistent with the task during the pre-training stage, so the masked language task can be continued on the unlabeled corpus in the unsupervised learning scenario to maintain task consistency. The calculation formula for masked language model loss is as shown in Eq. (5).

$$L_{MLM} = - \sum_{x_t \in mask(x^u)} log(p(x_t \mid x^u_{mask(x^u)}))$$ (5)

Here, $mask(x^u)$ represents the set of masks in the input text x^u, $x^u_{mask(x^u)}$ represents the unmasked part of x^u, x_t is the mask word in $mask(x^u)$. A mask sequence is constructed by randomly extracting 15% of the words in the input sequence x^u for dynamic masking, and the masked language model loss L_{MLM} is calculated on this sequence. Among them, 80% of the masked words are replaced with [MASK], 10% of the masked words are replaced with random words, and 10% of the masked words remain the same.

Consistency Loss. To assess the consistency between the original samples and the augmented samples, the consistency loss between them can be calculated. If the consistency loss is small, it indicates that the difference between the augmented data and the original data is not large, and the model can be effectively trained with the augmented data.

By applying multiple data augmentation techniques on the unlabeled sample x^u and calculating the consistency loss between the original sample x^u and the augmented sample $\hat{x}^u$, the generalizability of the model can be improved. Through PVP, the original sample and the augmented sample are turned into a cloze test, and the pre-trained language model is used to predict the mask, respectively calculating the probability distributions $q_p(y \mid x^u)$ and $q_p(y \mid \hat{x}^u)$. The KL divergence is calculated on these two probability distributions as the consistency loss L_C, shown in Eq. (6).

$$L_C = \frac{1}{k} \sum_{i=1}^{k} q_p(y \mid x^u)_i log \frac{q_p(y \mid x^u)_i}{q_p(y \mid \hat{x}^u)_i}$$ (6)

Here, k is the size of the label set, $q_p(y \mid x^u)_i$ is the prediction probability of the original sample in the i_{th} category, and $q_p(y \mid \hat{x}^u)_i$ is the prediction probability of the augmented sample in the i_{th} category.

3.2   Multi-model Fusion

In practical applications of semi-supervised learning, the scarcity of labeled data leads to a lack of enough labeled data as a validation set, making the validation evaluation process difficult after model training. Although multiple PVPs are designed to modify the input sequences into different cloze-style questions, the performance of models trained with different PVPs varies, and a small amount of validation data can not evaluate the advantages and disadvantages of different models. To overcome the above problem, a model distillation-based ensemble strategy is proposed, which integrates models with varying performance to obtain a more accurate and stable ensemble model. The multi-model fusion strategy proposed in this paper is as follows.

(1) We use multiple models trained in the first phase to predict the unlabeled data X_u. Then, the prediction results of multiple models are weighted using Eq. (7), and finally normalized by the softmax function to get the prediction probability distribution $q_P(y \mid x^u)$.

$$s_P(y^u \mid x^u) = \frac{1}{z} \sum_{p \in P} w(p) * s_p(y^u \mid x^u) \tag{7}$$

Here, z represents the number of PVP, P represents the set of PVP and p is an element of P. $s_p(y^u \mid x^u)$ denotes the probability of predicting the label as y^u for the unlabeled sample x^u, $w(p)$ denotes the weight of p.

(2) A new pre-trained language model θ_{new} is fine-tuned through supervised learning using KL divergence to fit the prediction probability distribution q_P on unlabeled data. KL divergence is shown in Eq. (8).

$$KL(p_u, q_P) = \sum_{i=1}^{k} p_u(y \mid x^u)_i \, log \frac{p_u(y \mid x^u)_i}{q_P(y \mid x^u)_i} \tag{8}$$

Here, k denotes the size of the labeled set, x_u denotes the unlabeled sample and p_u denotes the predicted probability distribution of θ_{new} on x_u. By training the KL scatter as a loss function, the prediction results of multiple models on unlabeled data can be integrated into a new pre-trained language model.

3.3 Iterative Boosting Algorithm

Multiple PVPs are designed To increase the diversity of input sequences. However, different PVPs lead to variations in model performance. To prevent this, the iPETUDA iterative boosting algorithm is introduced in this paper, which distils multiple PVP corresponding models to a pre-trained language model. In the distillation training process, pseudo-labels of unlabeled samples are generated to expand labeled samples, and the model's performance is improved through multiple rounds of training.

By using the iterative boosting algorithm, a series of model generations is obtained, and model fusion is applied on the final generation M^k. The approach is consistent with the model fusion steps described earlier, using each model in M^k to make predictions on unlabeled data. Predictions from multiple models are aggregated, and KL divergence is used to make the model's prediction probabilities converge to the aggregated prediction probabilities.

4 Experimental Setup

In this section, we conduct comparative experiments on three datasets to demonstrate the effectiveness of the proposed methods.

4.1 Datasets

We evaluate the performance of the proposed methods on three text classification benchmark datasets: AG News [10], Yahoo [2] and Yelp [10]. These datasets consist of 4, 10, and 5 categories, respectively, with corresponding test sizes of 7.6k, 60k, and 5k. Besides, different template are set according to the content of the datasets.

4.2 Baseline Models

To evaluate the effectiveness of our proposed methods, we choose three strong semi-supervised learning methods for few-shot text classification.

- UDA [9]. This method uses a variety of training techniques, including training signal annealing, sharpening predictions, and domain-specific data filtering.
- MixText [3]. This method proposes a new data augmentation method TMix, which interpolates data in the hidden space of the input sample to expand the sample.
- PET [7]. This method organizes input samples in the form of cloze, using the ability of pre-trained language models to predict categories. In addition, iPET refers to PET that uses the iterative boosting algorithm.

5 Evaluation and Results

In this section, we describe the evaluation tasks and report the experimental results.

Comparing the performance of different semi-supervised text classification methods under different labeled sample number configurations. The experimental results are shown in Table 1. We can learn that the iPETUDA model achieved better classification accuracy on all three datasets under different labeled sample number configurations. When $|T| = 10$, iPETUDA improved by 0.72%, 0.86%, and 0.4% on the three datasets, respectively; when $|T| = 50$, iPETUDA improved by 0.64%, 0.43%, and 1.71% on the three datasets, respectively. Compared with other semi-supervised text classification methods, iPETUDA can achieve the best results in text classification in the semi-supervised learning scenario.

When $|T| = 10$, the RoBERTa model did not perform well, and its performance was close to randomly guessing the category. The performance of UDA and MixText was not as good as the prompt learning based methods (PET and PETUDA). The experimental results show that when the number of labeled samples is small, using promt learning to fine-tune the model can fully exploit the capabilities of the PLMs itself. When $|T| = 50$, the RoBERTa model used 50 labeled samples to train in a supervised manner and achieved certain text classification performance, indicating that the PLMs can alleviate the downstream task's demand for data volume through the PLMs fine-tuning. Compared with UDA, MixText, PET/iPET, and other semi-supervised learning methods, PETUDA/iPETUDA has relative advantages because PETUDA/iPETUDA digs into the ability of the PLMs at the "model" level and uses unlabeled data in various ways at the "data" level to improve the effectiveness of the model.

Table 1. The different labeled sample number on methods, whereas $|T|$ denotes the number of labeled samples, iPET and iPETUDA denote the iterative boosting algorithm based PET and PETUDA methods.

	Methods	AG News	Yahoo	Yelp		Methods	AG News	Yahoo	Yelp
$|T| = 10$	RoBERTa	0.25	0.101	0.211	$|T| = 50$	RoBERTa	0.821	0.525	0.448
	UDA	0.726	0.367	0.273		UDA	0.83	0.602	0.466
	MixText	0.811	0.206	0.204		MixText	0.848	0.615	0.313
	PET	0.8473	0.5990	0.5110		PET	0.8644	0.6342	0.5574
	iPET	0.8622	0.6639	0.5261		iPET	0.8692	0.6699	0.5681
	PETUDA	0.8555	0.6129	0.4775		PETUDA	0.8648	0.6389	0.5592
	iPETUDA	**0.8694**	**0.6725**	**0.5301**		iPETUDA	**0.8756**	**0.6742**	**0.5852**

5.1 Single Model Training and Multi-model Fusion

As mentioned previously, the proposed PETUDA method can be divided into two stages: single model training and multi-model fusion. The experimental results will be presented according to two stages.

Single Model Training Stage. Table 2 shows the single model experimental results of using prompt learning on three datasets.

As shown in Table 2, the prompt learning based fine-tuning methods have better performance than the supervised model. When $|T| = 10$, the prompt learning based fine-tuning methods can still make predictions for the samples, while the performance of the supervised method is close to random guessing. When $|T| = 50$, the performance obtained by different PVP templates is still higher than the supervised method. Different from supervised method, which only uses labeled data, semi-supervised learning methods can use unlabeled data to improve the effect. The comparison of different PVPs template indicates that appropriately increasing the number of labeled samples can help improve model performance.

Multi-model Fusion Stage. The multi-model fusion experiment results are shown in Table 3.

The experimental results show that the accuracy of PETUDA is higher than the average accuracy on different datasets, which shows that the fusion of different PVP models can improve accuracy. iPETUDA has varying degrees of improvement over PETUDA on different datasets, indicating that the accuracy of the model can be further improved by using iterative boosting algorithm.

In summary, the first stage can train a text classification model with certain classification performance, and the model fusion and iterative enhancement algorithm in the second stage both have a positive impact on model performance.

Table 2. The results of single model training, whereas Supervised means the supervised text classification method.

Template_id	AG News		Yahoo		Yelp	
	$|T| = 10$	$|T| = 50$	$|T| = 10$	$|T| = 50$	$|T| = 10$	$|T| = 50$
1	0.8339	0.8513	0.5612	0.6122	0.3366	0.5170
2	**0.8351**	0.8582	0.5714	0.6248	**0.4967**	0.5285
3	0.7979	**0.8599**	0.5052	0.6016	0.4108	**0.5301**
4	0.8237	0.8534	0.5441	0.6024	0.4660	0.5196
5	0.8188	0.8587	0.5781	0.6321	-	-
6	0.8097	0.8521	0.5644	0.6058	-	-
Supervised	0.25	0.8210	0.1010	0.5250	0.2110	0.4480

Table 3. The results of multi-model fusion, whereas Patterns Average denotes the average accuracy of multiple models with corresponding PVP templates.

	Methods	AG News	Yahoo	Yelp		Methods	AG News	Yahoo	Yelp
$|T| = 10$	Patterns Average	0.8199	0.5541	0.4275	$|T| = 50$	Patterns Average	0.8556	0.6131	0.5238
	PETUDA	0.8555	0.6129	0.4775		PETUDA	0.8648	0.6389	0.5592
	iPETUDA	**0.8694**	**0.6725**	**0.5301**		iPETUDA	**0.8756**	**0.6742**	**0.5852**

5.2 Ablation Study

In order to verify the effectiveness of the data augmentation methods and consistency loss function in our work, a set of experiments was carried out on the Yelp dataset. Table 4 describes the performances of multiple models with corresponding PVP templates with the consistency loss function enabled and disabled, and also showing the average accuracy over different methods. When $|T| = 10$, the introduction of the consistency loss function can increase the average accuracy by 1.83%, and when $|T| = 50$, the average accuracy increases by 0.57%. The improvement is relatively small, indicating that when the number of data is small, the introduction of a consistency loss function is more conducive to improving the performance of the model. For PETUDA and iPETUDA, when $|T| = 10$, they were improved by 1.39% and 0.86% respectively, and when $|T| = 50$, they were improved by 0.47% and 0.43% respectively, indicating that the introduction of consistency loss can improve the overall performance of the model. Overall,the experimental results verifying the effectiveness of data augmentation methods and consistency loss function.

Table 4. The effect of data augmentation methods and consistency loss function to the overall performance.

id	$|T| = 10$		$|T| = 50$	
	enable	disable	enable	disable
1	**0.5612**	0.5586	**0.6122**	0.6089
2	**0.5714**	0.5627	**0.6248**	0.6236
3	**0.5052**	0.4880	**0.6016**	0.5917
4	**0.5441**	0.4957	**0.6024**	0.5963
5	0.5781	**0.5842**	**0.6321**	0.6266
6	**0.5644**	0.5256	**0.6058**	0.5972
Average	**0.5541**	0.5358	**0.6131**	0.6074
PETUDA	**0.6129**	0.5990	**0.6389**	0.6342
iPETUDA	**0.6725**	0.6639	**0.6742**	0.6699

6   Conclusion

In this paper, we proposed a pattern exploiting training with unsupervised data augmentation model, namely PETUDA, to address the semi-supervised text classification problem. PETUDA first uses a method based on prompt learning to fine-tune the model, in order to fully exploit the potential capabilities of PLMs. Then, it uses a variety of data augmentation methods, and introduces a consistency loss to fully utilize unlabeled data. The extensive experiments have shown that PETUDA mostly outperformed baseline models. In future work, we will focus on visually analyzing the model parameters to enhance the interpretability of the model.

Acknowledgements. This work was supported in part by the National Natural Science Foundation of China under Grant U1811263, the Science and Technology Program of Guangzhou under Grant 2023A04J1728, the Talent Research Start-Up Foundation of Guangdong Polytechnic Normal University (No. 2021SDKYA098).

References

1. Brown, T., et al.: Language models are few-shot learners. In: NeurIPS 2020, pp. 1877–1901 (2020)
2. Chang, M., Ratinov, L., Roth, D., Srikumar, V.: Importance of semantic representation: dataless classification. In: AAAI 2008, pp. 830–835 (2008)
3. Chen, J., Yang, Z., Yang, D.: MixText: linguistically-informed interpolation of hidden space for semi-supervised text classification. In: ACL 2020, pp. 2147–2157 (2020)
4. Han, X., Zhao, W., Ding, N., Liu, Z., Sun, M.: PTR: prompt tuning with rules for text classification. AI Open **3**, 182–192 (2022)
5. Li, C., Li, X., Ouyang, J.: Semi-supervised text classification with balanced deep representation distributions. In: ACL 2021, pp. 5044–5053 (2021)

6. Murtadha, A., et al.: Rank-aware negative training for semi-supervised text classification. CoRR abs/2306.07621 (2023)
7. Schick, T., Schütze, H.: Exploiting cloze-questions for few-shot text classification and natural language inference. In: EACL 2021, pp. 255–269 (2021)
8. Song, R., et al.: Label prompt for multi-label text classification. Appl. Intell. **53**(8), 8761–8775 (2023)
9. Xie, Q., Dai, Z., Hovy, E., Luong, M.T., Le, Q.V.: Unsupervised data augmentation for consistency training. In: NeurIPS 2020, pp. 6256–6268 (2020)
10. Zhang, X., Zhao, J.J., LeCun, Y.: Character-level convolutional networks for text classification. In: (NIPS 2015), pp. 649–657 (2015)
11. Zhu, Y., Zhou, X., Qiang, J., Li, Y., Yuan, Y., Wu, X.: Prompt-learning for short text classification. CoRR abs/2202.11345 (2022)

Label-Dependent Hypergraph Neural Network for Enhanced Multi-label Text Classification

Xuqiang Xue[1,2], Xiaoming Wu[1,2], Shengnan Li[1,2], Xiangzhi Liu[1,2]([✉]),
and Man Li[3]

[1] Key Laboratory of Computing Power Network and Information Security, Ministry
of Education, Shandong Computer Science Center (National Supercomputer Center
in Jinan), Qilu University of Technology (Shandong Academy of Sciences), Jinan,
China
Liuxzh@sdas.org
[2] Shandong Provincial Key Laboratory of Computer Networks, Shandong
Fundamental Research Center for Computer Science, Jinan, China
[3] School of IT, Deakin University, Geelong, VIC 3220, Australia

Abstract. Multi-label text classification (MLTC) is a challenging task
in natural language processing. Improving the performance of MLTC
through building label dependencies remains a focus of current research.
Previous researches used label tree structure or label graph structure
to build label dependencies. However, these label dependency structure
building methods suffer from complexity and lack of interpretability of
label relationships. To solve these problems, we propose a new model
LHGN: Label-Dependent Hypergraph Neural Network for Enhanced
Multi-label Text Classification, which introduces hypergraph structure
to build label-dependent relationships, enhance the correlation between
labels, reduce graph complexity and improve the interpretability of label
relationships. In addition, we build hypergraph structures for each text
instance to capture its structural information, and use the BERT model
to capture the semantic information of texts. By integrating text information and combining the hypergraph label structure dependencies for
multi-label text classification. Experimental results on three benchmark
datasets demonstrate that the LHGN model outperforms state-of-the-art
baseline models.

Keywords: Label dependency graph · Hypergraph neural network ·
BERT · Multi-label text classification

1 Introduction

Multi-label text classification (MLTC) is a task in which a text is correlated with
one or more labels and there are some dependencies between the labels. MLTC
has essential applications in many practical scenarios, such as sentiment analysis

F. Zhang et al. (Eds.): WISE 2023, LNCS 14306, pp. 35–49, 2023.
https://doi.org/10.1007/978-981-99-7254-8_4

[1], recommendation system [2], etc. Unlike the single-label text classification task that assigns one text instance to one label, MLTC task allows a text instance to multiple labels, so it faces more challenges.

With the development of deep learning, many deep learning models such as Convolutional Neural Networks (CNN) [3], Recurrent Neural Networks (RNN) [1], and pre-trained language model BERT [4] have achieved significant results in MLTC tasks. However, these models only focus on extracting text features, ignoring the correlation between labels, which is not much different from solving single-label classification tasks. Recently, the introduction of graph-based models, such as graph convolutional networks (GCN) [5] and graph attention networks (GAT) [6], has made it possible to build dependencies between labels. These graph-based models can capture correlation information between labels using graph structure and achieve promising performance in MLTC tasks.

Currently, most approaches [7–9] build label-pair co-occurrence based on graph networks to build label dependencies. However, in the MLTC task, the number of labels assigned to a text is uncertain, and it is far from enough to only consider the co-occurrence between pairs of labels. Moreover, this method will lead to problems such as complex graph structure and weak interpretability. Therefore, we introduce a hypergraph structure to build label dependencies and use hyperedges to connect multiple co-occurring labels to reduce the complexity of the graph structure and enhance interpretability. Taking the labels (cs.LG, cs.AI, cs.SY, math.OC, stat.ML), (cs.NI, cs.SY, math.OC) of two texts in Fig. 1 as an example. Figure 1(a) shows the building method of the graph structure, i.e., the graph structure is built by the co-occurrence of pairs of labels. It can be seen that the nodes are intricately connected with a total of 12 edges used to build label dependencies, and it is difficult to determine their combination without showing which text corresponds to which labels. Figure 1(b) shows our proposed construction method of the hypergraph structure, where a hyperedge connects a label group. Using only two hyperedges, the dependencies between the labels are determined, and it is clear which label group those labels belong to.

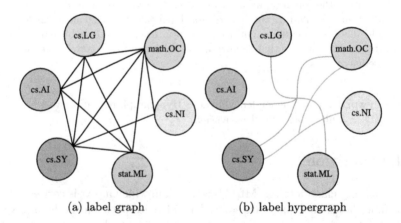

(a) label graph   (b) label hypergraph

Fig. 1. Example of two different label dependency graph constructions.

In addition to solving the above label structure problem, we construct text-level hypergraphs [10] and obtain their complex higher-order structural information about data relevance through hypergraph neural networks (HGNN) [11]. The text structure information obtained by the text hypergraph is combined with the text semantic information obtained by BERT to enrich the text representation.

In summary, the contributions of this paper are as follows:

- We propose a novel hypergraph multi-label dependency structure that uses hyperedges to connect multiple co-occurring labels, reducing the complexity and enhancing the interpretability of the label graph structure.
- We propose a novel multi-label text classification model: on the one hand, the text representation is enriched by combining the structural information of the text obtained from the hypergraph neural network and the semantic information of the text obtained from BERT. On the other hand, the enriched text representation is combined with hypergraph fusion of label dependencies to improve multi-label text classification performance.
- We evaluate our experiments on three benchmark datasets and compare them with multiple baseline models. We also performed ablation experiments to analyze the validity of our proposed model.

The rest of this paper is as follows: In Sect. 2, we summarize the existing MLTC methods and analyzes their strengths and weaknesses. In Sect. 3, details of our proposed model are presented. In Sect. 4, experiments are conducted to validate the effectiveness of our proposed model. In Sect. 5, we summarize the whole paper and describe the direction of future work.

2   Related Work

In recent years, a significant development and application of deep learning techniques have been witnessed in multi-label text classification. Existing multi-label text classification methods can be classified into document content based methods and label dependency based methods.

2.1   Document Content Based Methods

With the continuous development of deep learning, Attention methods are gradually replacing the use of CNN [12] and RNN [13] to extract sentence semantics. Hierarchical Attention Networks (HAN) [14] have a two-level attention mechanism applied at the word and sentence levels, enabling them to distinguish between more and less critical content when constructing document representations. Later, with the advent of the "Attention is all you need" Transformer model [15], attention was paid to BERT [16], a bi-directional Transformer encoder pre-trained language model trained from a large corpus and successfully applied to MLTC tasks with very competitive performance [4]. However, an approach based only on document content, missing the dependencies between labels, leads to information loss and performance degradation [9].

2.2 Label Dependency Based Methods

Since there are dependencies between labels in MLTC, many researchers have started to improve the performance of MLTC tasks by constructing dependencies between labels. [17] treated the MTLC task as a sequence generation problem to consider the correlations between labels. [18] is a deep learning model based on probabilistic label tree that captures the most relevant parts of the text with each label using attention mechanisms. [19] proposes to solve the multi-label text classification task by considering document content and labeled text through a label-specific attention network model. [20] proposed to jointly encode the representation of text and label mutual attention through a co-attention network with label embedding. Although the above approaches consider the use of labels to improve the performance of MLTC, they only combine label embedding with document embedding and do not fully consider the correlation between labels.

Recently, graph neural networks [5,21] have attracted a lot of attention in the field of MLTC. Since graph neural networks are suitable for processing data with inter-node correlations [22], more researchers have started using graph neural networks to extract inter-label dependencies and apply them to assist text classification tasks.

[7] proposed to build and capture dependencies between labels based on graph attention networks. [23] proposed an interpretable labeled graph convolutional network model to solve the MLTC problem by modeling tokens and labels as nodes in a heterogeneous graph. [24] constructs words and labels as heterogeneous graphs and learns label representation by metapath2vec. [9] constructs a label correlation matrix and uses GCN to learn label information and then combines it with the textual contextual representation learned by the BERT model to achieve multi-label text classification. The above methods for building graph structures for label dependencies mostly consider only homogeneous or heterogeneous graphs. They only build the relationship between label pairs and rarely consider the relationship of a group of labels. Therefore, we propose a method to build label dependencies using hypergraphs that consider the dependencies of groups of labels and combine them with the text representations generated by BERT and HGNN.

3 Method

In this section, we describe in detail the general framework of LHGN, as shown in Fig. 2. The model consists of four main modules: 1) Graph Construction, 2) HGNN Obtains Label Relevance Information and Document Structure Information, 3) Document Semantic Information Extraction and Fusion with Structural Information, and 4) Classification. Specifically, the label and text are constructed as hypergraph structures, respectively. The hypergraph neural network processes complex higher-order associations through the hypergraph structure for representation learning. Semantic features of the text are extracted by BERT and fused with structural features to form a text representation. The text representation is fused with the label structure for output to achieve classification.

3.1   Graph Construction

Hypergraph is defined as $\mathcal{G} = (\mathcal{V}, \mathcal{E}, W)$, which consists of a vertex set $\mathcal{V} = \{v_1, v_2, \ldots, v_n\}$ and a hyperedge set $\mathcal{E} = \{e_1, e_2, \ldots, e_m\}$. Each hyperedge is assigned a weight and W is a diagonal matrix of edge weights. For any hyperedge e, it can connect two or more vertices. The hypergraph $\mathcal{G}$ also can be represented by an association matrix A, which is defined as:

$$A_{ij} = \begin{cases} 1, if \ v_i \in e_j \\ 0, if \ v_i \notin e_j \end{cases} \tag{1}$$

In order to build complex relationships and dependencies between multiple labels, as introduced in Fig. 1(b), we use a hypergraph to build label dependencies. We consider labels as nodes in hypergraph and groups of labels as hyperedges in hypergraph with an association matrix defined as $A_{label} \in \mathbb{R}^{c \times m}$. c is the number of labels, and m is the number of label hyperedges, i.e., the number of label groups.

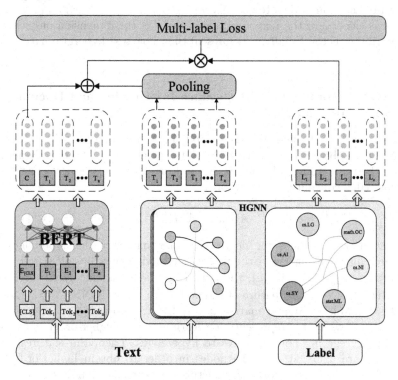

Fig. 2. The overall architecture of the proposed model.

By connecting groups of labels through hyperedges, we not only model the relationship between labels but also make the graph structure clearer and more interpretable. As for the node attributes of labels, we use the same way as in [9] to map each label to the Wikipedia corpus, and use sentence-bert[1] to encode the first two most relevant sentences of each label for enriching the semantic information of the label, and represent it as $X_{label} = [x_{label,1}, x_{label,2}, \ldots, x_{label,c}]^T \in \mathbb{R}^{c \times d}$, c is the number of labels and d is the dimension of each label node attribute vector. Finally, we represent the whole label hypergraph as $G_{label} = (A_{label}, X_{label})$.

In addition to using hypergraphs to model the dependencies between multiple labels, we also use hypergraphs to model the dependencies between each text word to construct text-level hypergraphs to obtain higher-order structural information of each text. For the text-level hypergraph, we use the words in each text vocabulary as nodes in the hypergraph and each sentence as a hyperedge. Its association matrix is defined as $A_{text} \in \mathbb{R}^{n \times s}$, n is the size of this text vocabulary and s is the number of text sentences.

Since we only build word dependencies using hypergraphs, we initialize the node representations of the text hypergraph by sampling random numbers from a normal distribution with a mean of 0 and a standard deviation of 0.01. The node representation is denoted as $X_{text} = [x_{text,1}, x_{text,2}, \ldots, x_{text,n}]^T \in \mathbb{R}^{n \times d}$, where n is the size of the text vocabulary and d is the dimension of each word node attribute vector. Finally, we represent the whole text hypergraph as $G_{text} = (A_{text}, X_{text})$.

3.2 HGNN Obtains Label Relevance Information and Document Structure Information

We input the label hypergraph G_{label} and the text hypergraph G_{text} into the HGNN [11] to obtain their higher-order data correlations. The HGNN network performs better learning of higher-order data correlation representations through the hyper-edge convolution operation:

$$X^{(l)} = \sigma \left(D_v^{-1/2} A W D_e^{-1} A^\top D_v^{-1/2} X^{(l-1)} \Theta^{(l-1)} \right) \qquad (2)$$

where D_e and D_v denote the degree diagonal matrix of the hyperedges and the degree diagonal matrix of the nodes. The node degree is calculated as follows: $d(v) = \sum_{e \in \mathcal{E}} \omega(e) A(v, e)$, the hyperedge degree is calculated as: $\delta(e) = \sum_{v \in \mathcal{V}} A(v, e)$. $X^{(l)}$ is the feature of the node's lth layer HGNN, $X^{(0)} = X$, and Θ is the trainable parameter matrix, σ is ReLU activation.

HGNN allows better representation learning using higher-order data correlation by aggregating node features to hyperedges. Then, the features of the hyperedges are aggregated to the nodes in order to obtain higher-order representations of the corresponding structures between label nodes in the label hypergraph and between word nodes in the text hypergraph.

To facilitate the conversion of the output text hypergraph node features when fusing them with subsequent BERT Semantic features, We use graph pooling for text hypergraph node features, which is the sum of the mean-pooling function and the max-pooling function:

---

[1] https://www.sbert.net/.

$$H_{text} = \frac{1}{n} \sum_{i \in n} x_{text,i}^{(l)} + Max \left(x_{text,1}^{(l)} \ldots x_{text,n}^{(l)} \right) \tag{3}$$

The mean-pooling function is used to average the word node features, and the max-pooling function is used to select the word features that contributed the most to the classification. The two are summed to make them fused into a complete information graph.

3.3   Document Semantic Information Extraction and Fusion with Structural Information

The content of texts is fed into the BERT model, which contains 12 hidden layers, each consisting of 768 hidden units, to obtain the corresponding word embeddings. We consider the feature $H_{bert,[cls]}$ of the last layer of the first token $[cls]$ of the text as a feature of the text and combine it with the text structure information generated in Sect. 3.2 by means of linear interpolation [25] to:

$$H = \beta H_{bert,[cls]} + (1 - \beta) H_{text} \tag{4}$$

where β is a hyperparameter to balance the text semantic features obtained by BERT and the text structural features obtained by HGNN, and add the two together to make the text content follow representation more abundant and multifaceted.

3.4   Classification

To facilitate the classification, we multiply the features incorporating semantic and structural information of the text with the label relevance features obtained from the label hypergraph by HGNN to obtain the final prediction scores.

$$\hat{Y} = H X_{label}^{(l)}{}^{T} \tag{5}$$

Finally, the loss function of LHGN is a binary cross-entropy loss:

$$\mathcal{L} = \sum_{c=1}^{c} Y^c \log \left(\sigma \left(\hat{Y}^c \right) \right) + (1 - Y^c) \log \left(1 - \sigma \left(\hat{Y}^c \right) \right) \tag{6}$$

where $Y \in \mathbb{R}^c$ is the true label of the text, $Y_i = \{0,1\}$, σ is sigmoid activation function.

4   Experiments

4.1   Dataset

We conducted our experiments on three benchmark datasets (Reuters-21578 [26], AAPD [17] and EUR-Lex [27]) and show the statistics for all datasets in Table 1.

Table 1. Dataset statistics.

Dataset	#Doc	#Train	#dev	#test	#class	#Class/Doc
Reuters-21578	10,788	7,769	–	3,019	90	1.24
AAPD	55,840	53,840	1,000	1,000	54	2.41
EUR-Lex	17,770	13,905	–	3,865	3,714	5.32

Reuters-21578: collected from Reuters News Network, with 90 categories and 10,778 texts, of which 8,630 are for training, and 2,158 are for testing.

Arxiv Academic Paper Dataset (AAPD): contains the abstract content of 55,840 academic papers, each belonging to one or more topics, in 54 categories, with 44,672 for training texts and 11,168 for testing texts.

EUR-Lex: contains 17,770 European Union law documents belonging to 3,956 categories, divided into 13,905 training samples and 3,865 test samples.

4.2 Experimental Settings

This experiment was implemented by PyTorch and trained and tested using an Nvidia Tesla A100 40 GB GPU. We use bert-base-uncased[2] to extract semantic information from the text. The learning rate is initialized to 5e−5 and gradually decreases during the training process. The dropout rate is 0.2 and the linear interpolation β is 0.8 using the Adam optimizer with a batch size of 16. Both the text hypergraph and the label hypergraph use a two-layer HGNN with hidden layer dimension of 768 dimensions.

4.3 Evaluation Indicators

Because different work evaluates different datasets with different evaluation metrics, we used Micro-F1 as an evaluation metric in the Reuters-2157 and AAPD datasets.

$$Micro - F1 = \frac{2Precision \times Recall}{Precision + Recall} \tag{7}$$

$$Precision = \frac{TP}{TP + FP} \tag{8}$$

$$Recall = \frac{TP}{TP + FN} \tag{9}$$

We used Precision at top k (P@K) and Normalized Discounted Cumulated Gains at top K (nDCG@K) as evaluation metrics in the AAPD and EUR-lex datasets.

$$P@k = \frac{1}{k} \sum_{l \in rank_k(\hat{Y})} Y_l \tag{10}$$

---

[2] https://huggingface.co/bert-base-uncased.

$$DCG@k = \sum_{l \in rank_k(\hat{Y})} \frac{Y_l}{\log(l+1)} \tag{11}$$

$$nDCG@k = \frac{DCG@k}{\sum_{l=1}^{\min(k,\|Y\|_0)} \frac{1}{\log(l+1)}} \tag{12}$$

where Y is the true label vector, $\hat{Y}$ is the prediction score of the model. $rank_k(\hat{Y})$ is the label index of the top k highest scores of the current prediction result. $\|Y\|_0$ counts the number of relevant labels in the true label vector Y.

4.4 Baseline

To verify the effectiveness of the model proposed in this paper, we choose to compare it with the following 11 multi-label text classification methods.

- TextCNN [12]: Assigning features to the split words as sentence matrix, and using CNN to extract text features for text classification.
- XML-CNN [28]: CNN-based model with dynamic maximum pooling scheme for Extreme multi-label text classification.
- HAN [14]: Two-level attention mechanism using word level and sentence level for document classification.
- SGM [17]: Consider the multi-label text classification task as a sequence generation problem to take into account the correlation between labels.
- AttentionXML [18]: Based on a probabilistic label tree, the most relevant parts of the text with each label are captured using attention mechanisms.
- DXML [29]: Introduction of label co-occurrence graphs for modeling large-scale label spaces for Extreme multi-label text classification.
- LSAN [19]: Consider document content and labeled text through label-specific attention network models to solve multi-label text classification task.
- MAGNET [7]: Building and capturing correlations between labels based on graph attention networks.
- CNLE [20]: Text and labels are jointly encoded into a representation of their mutual attention by a co-attention network with label embedding.
- HTTN [30]: Solving the long-tail problem in multi-label text classification using label dependencies between meta-knowledge and head and tail labels.
- LAHA [8]: Constructs a label-aware document representation by considering both the document content and the label structure.

4.5 Experimental Results and Analysis

We report the results for Micro-F1 in Table 2 for the Reuters-21578 and AAPD datasets, and the results for P@k and N@k (k = 1, 3, 5) in Table 3 for the AAPD and EUR-lex.

From the results in Table 2, the LHGN model outperforms the current document-based approach as well as the current label dependency based approach. It is 1.6% and 1.1% higher than the CNLE model that jointly encodes

Table 2. Micro-F1 (%) results on Reuters-21578 and AAPD.

Model	Reuters-21578	AAPD
TextCNN	86.3	66.4
XML-CNN	86.2	68.7
HAN	85.2	68.0
SGM	78.8	71.0
MAGNET	89.9	69.6
CNLE	89.9	71.7
LHGN	**91.5**	**72.8**

text and labels by using co-attention network. It is 1.6% and 3.2% higher than the MAGNET model that uses graph attention networks to construct and capture the correlation between labels. On the one hand, it is demonstrated that combining semantic and structural information of the text would make the text more distinctive in the document-based aspect, and on the other hand, it is demonstrated that building label dependencies in the hypergraph will make the relationships between labels much clearer, and the higher-order data correlations between labels can be better exploited by HGNN.

Table 3. P@k and nDCG@k results on AAPD and EUR-Lex.

Method	P@1 (%)	P@3 (%)	P@5 (%)	nDCG@3 (%)	nDCG@5 (%)
AAPD					
XML-CNN	74.38	53.84	37.79	71.12	75.93
SGM	75.67	56.75	35.65	72.36	75.35
DXML	80.54	56.30	39.16	77.23	80.99
AttentionXML	83.02	58.72	40.65	78.01	82.31
LSAN	<u>85.28</u>	61.12	41.84	80.84	84.78
LAHA	84.48	60.72	41.19	80.11	83.70
HTTN	83.84	59.92	40.79	79.27	82.67
LHGN	84.50	**61.90**	**41.98**	**81.44**	**85.06**
EUR-Lex					
XML-CNN	70.40	54.98	44.86	58.62	53.10
SGM	70.45	60.37	43.88	60.72	55.24
DXML	75.63	60.13	48.65	63.96	53.60
AttentionXML	74.28	60.17	48.92	63.78	57.68
LSAN	79.17	64.99	53.67	68.32	62.47
LAHA	78.34	64.62	53.08	68.15	62.27
HTTN	81.14	67.62	56.38	70.89	64.42
LHGN	**81.50**	**69.68**	**58.10**	**72.93**	**67.37**

From the results Table 3, XML-CNN is poor in several metrics on both datasets relative to other benchmarks, proving that multi-label text classification based only on documents and ignoring label dependencies is far from adequate. AttentionXML considers the label tree to obtain the correlation between labels and documents, but its main focus is on the document content, which makes the performance limited. LSAN makes the results competitive by identifying the correlation between labels and documents through the attention mechanism, but it still does not consider the dependency relationship between labels. LAHA considers both document content and label graph structure, but its results are not as good as LSAN, possibly due to the complexity of the label graph and the redundancy of label dependencies. LHGN is the optimal value for all evaluation metrics on the Eur-lex dataset, while the improvement on the AAPD dataset is not as obvious as on the Eur-lex dataset. We believe this is due to the fact that there are more label categories and more groupings of different labels in the Eur-lex dataset, which makes the graph structure complex, and there are redundant label relationships in other models that construct label co-occurrence graph structures, and the graph structure is not easily classified. This is not the case in our hypergraph structure, which further demonstrates the necessity of using hypergraphs to build label-dependent structures.

Ablation Study. To demonstrate the effectiveness of our proposed hypergraphs for constructing text representations and label dependencies, we conducted ablation experiments on the AAPD dataset to investigate the relative contributions of text hypergraphs and label hypergraph.

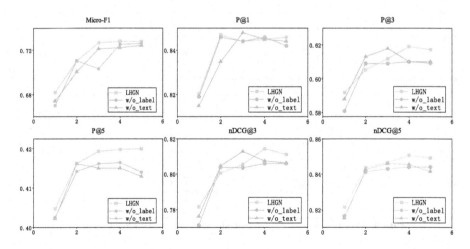

Fig. 3. Comparison of 5 iterations of hypergraphic structure ablation experiments.

Figure 3 shows the results of P@K and nDCG@K for LHGN with different hypergraph structures removed for 5 iterations on the AAPD dataset. It can be seen that LHGN basically works better than the model with the other hyper-graphs removed in each iteration. The second is to remove the text hypergraph w/o_text, and the last is to remove the label hypergraph w/o_label. The specific experimental results are shown in Table 4, and we can see that the LHGN model's performance is weakened after removing the text hypergraph and the label hypergraph, which implies that the text structure features and label dependencies are meaningful. We believe that the main reason why the reduction of multiple evaluation metrics in several evaluation of w/o_text is smaller than metrics that of w/o_label remains that the dependencies between labels are more important in multi-label text classification, and how to exploit the dependencies between labels is the key to improve the performance of multi-label text classification.

Table 4. Results of hypergraph structure ablation experiments.

Method	P@1 (%)	P@3 (%)	P@5 (%)	nDCG@3 (%)	nDCG@5 (%)
w/o_label	84.20	60.93	41.40	80.49	84.28
w/o_text	84.40	61.03	41.30	80.64	84.16
LHGN	**84.50**	**61.90**	**41.98**	**81.44**	**85.06**

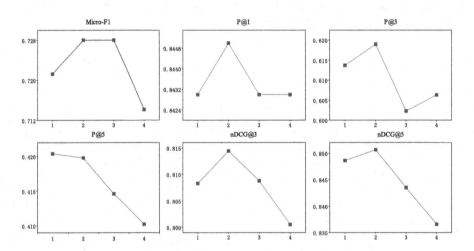

Fig. 4. Comparison of results for the number of HGNN layers.

In addition to studying the contribution of the graph structure to LHGN, we also analyzed the effect of the number of HGNN layers on the effect of the model. Figure 4 shows the effect of using HGNN with different numbers of layers, and it can be clearly seen that the effect is best at two layers, and the effect starts to decrease as the layers increase. We believe that the stacking of HGNN layers can lead to many labels learning unnecessary dependencies, thus leading to performance degradation. Second, the stacking of layers on the graph neural network leads to excessive smoothing [31].

5   Conclusion

In this paper, we propose the LHGN model for improving label dependencies in multi-label text classification tasks. We introduce hypergraphs to build the label dependency structure to reduce the complexity and enhance the interpretability of the graph structure. Besides, we also use hypergraphs to build text structure representations and use HGNN to obtain the higher-order data relevance of labels and text, respectively, and combine them with the semantic features of text obtained by the BERT model for classification. The experimental results demonstrate the effectiveness of the LHGN model and each of its submodules. In future work, we will research other ways of constructing label dependencies to improve the performance of multi-label text classification.

Acknowledgments.. This work is supported by "National Key Research and Development Project (No. 2021YFF0901300)", "Taishan Scholars Program (NO. tsqn202211203)".

References

1. Tang, D., Qin, B., Liu, T.: Document modeling with gated recurrent neural network for sentiment classification. In: Proceedings of the 2015 Conference on Empirical Methods in Natural Language Processing, pp. 1422–1432 (2015)
2. Guo, L., Jin, B., Yu, R., Yao, C., Sun, C., Huang, D.: Multi-label classification methods for green computing and application for mobile medical recommendations. IEEE Access **4**, 3201–3209 (2016)
3. Feng, S., Wang, Y., Song, K., Wang, D., Yu, G.: Detecting multiple coexisting emotions in microblogs with convolutional neural networks. Cogn. Comput. **10**, 136–155 (2018). https://doi.org/10.1007/s12559-017-9521-1
4. Li, R., Si, Q., Fu, P., Lin, Z., Wang, W., Shi, G.: A multi-channel neural network for imbalanced emotion recognition. In: 2019 IEEE 31st International Conference on Tools with Artificial Intelligence (ICTAI), pp. 353–360. IEEE (2019)
5. Kipf, T.N., Welling, M.: Semi-supervised classification with graph convolutional networks. arXiv preprint arXiv:1609.02907 (2016)
6. Veličković, P., Cucurull, G., Casanova, A., Romero, A., Lio, P., Bengio, Y.: Graph attention networks. arXiv preprint arXiv:1710.10903 (2017)
7. Pal, A., Selvakumar, M., Sankarasubbu, M.: Multi-label text classification using attention-based graph neural network. arXiv preprint arXiv:2003.11644 (2020)
8. Huang, X., Chen, B., Xiao, L., Yu, J., Jing, L.: Label-aware document representation via hybrid attention for extreme multi-label text classification. Neural Process. Lett. **54**, 3601–3617 (2022). https://doi.org/10.1007/s11063-021-10444-7

9. Vu, H.T., Nguyen, M.T., Nguyen, V.C., Pham, M.H., Nguyen, V.Q., Nguyen, V.H.: Label-representative graph convolutional network for multi-label text classification. Appl. Intell. **53**, 14759–14774 (2023). https://doi.org/10.1007/s10489-022-04106-x

10. Ding, K., Wang, J., Li, J., Li, D., Liu, H.: Be more with less: hypergraph attention networks for inductive text classification. arXiv preprint arXiv:2011.00387 (2020)

11. Feng, Y., You, H., Zhang, Z., Ji, R., Gao, Y.: Hypergraph neural networks. In: Proceedings of the AAAI Conference on Artificial Intelligence, vol. 33, pp. 3558–3565 (2019)

12. Kim, Y.: Convolutional neural networks for sentence classification. arXiv preprint arXiv:1408.5882 (2014)

13. Liu, P., Qiu, X., Huang, X.: Recurrent neural network for text classification with multi-task learning. arXiv preprint arXiv:1605.05101 (2016)

14. Yang, Z., Yang, D., Dyer, C., He, X., Smola, A., Hovy, E.: Hierarchical attention networks for document classification. In: Proceedings of the 2016 Conference of the North American Chapter of the Association for Computational Linguistics: Human Language Technologies, pp. 1480–1489 (2016)

15. Vaswani, A., et al.: Attention is all you need. In: Advances in Neural Information Processing Systems, vol. 30 (2017)

16. Devlin, J., Chang, M.W., Lee, K., Toutanova, K.: BERT: pre-training of deep bidirectional transformers for language understanding. arXiv preprint arXiv:1810.04805 (2018)

17. Yang, P., Sun, X., Li, W., Ma, S., Wu, W., Wang, H.: SGM: sequence generation model for multi-label classification. arXiv preprint arXiv:1806.04822 (2018)

18. You, R., Zhang, Z., Wang, Z., Dai, S., Mamitsuka, H., Zhu, S.: AttentionXML: label tree-based attention-aware deep model for high-performance extreme multi-label text classification. In: Advances in Neural Information Processing Systems, vol. 32 (2019)

19. Xiao, L., Huang, X., Chen, B., Jing, L.: Label-specific document representation for multi-label text classification. In: Proceedings of the 2019 Conference on Empirical Methods in Natural Language Processing and the 9th International Joint Conference on Natural Language Processing (EMNLP-IJCNLP), pp. 466–475 (2019)

20. Liu, M., Liu, L., Cao, J., Du, Q.: Co-attention network with label embedding for text classification. Neurocomputing **471**, 61–69 (2022)

21. Wang, X., et al.: Heterogeneous graph attention network. In: The World Wide Web Conference, pp. 2022–2032 (2019)

22. Zhu, X., Zhang, Y., Zhang, Z., Guo, D., Li, Q., Li, Z.: Interpretability evaluation of botnet detection model based on graph neural network. In: IEEE INFOCOM 2022-IEEE Conference on Computer Communications Workshops (INFOCOM WKSHPS), pp. 1–6. IEEE (2022)

23. Li, I., Feng, A., Wu, H., Li, T., Suzumura, T., Dong, R.: LiGCN: label-interpretable graph convolutional networks for multi-label text classification. arXiv preprint arXiv:2103.14620 (2021)

24. Guo, H., Li, X., Zhang, L., Liu, J., Chen, W.: Label-aware text representation for multi-label text classification. In: ICASSP 2021–2021 IEEE International Conference on Acoustics, Speech and Signal Processing (ICASSP), pp. 7728–7732. IEEE (2021)

25. Lin, Y., et al.: BertGCN: transductive text classification by combining GCN and BERT. arXiv preprint arXiv:2105.05727 (2021)

26. Apté, C., Damerau, F., Weiss, S.M.: Automated learning of decision rules for text categorization. ACM Trans. Inf. Syst. (TOIS) **12**(3), 233–251 (1994)

27. Loza Mencía, E., Fürnkranz, J.: Efficient pairwise multilabel classification for large-scale problems in the legal domain. In: Daelemans, W., Goethals, B., Morik, K. (eds.) ECML PKDD 2008. LNCS (LNAI), vol. 5212, pp. 50–65. Springer, Heidelberg (2008). https://doi.org/10.1007/978-3-540-87481-2_4

28. Liu, J., Chang, W.C., Wu, Y., Yang, Y.: Deep learning for extreme multi-label text classification. In: Proceedings of the 40th International ACM SIGIR Conference on Research and Development in Information Retrieval, pp. 115–124 (2017)

29. Zhang, W., Yan, J., Wang, X., Zha, H.: Deep extreme multi-label learning. In: Proceedings of the 2018 ACM on International Conference on Multimedia Retrieval, pp. 100–107 (2018)

30. Xiao, L., Zhang, X., Jing, L., Huang, C., Song, M.: Does head label help for long-tailed multi-label text classification. In: Proceedings of the AAAI Conference on Artificial Intelligence, vol. 35, pp. 14103–14111 (2021)

31. Yao, L., Mao, C., Luo, Y.: Graph convolutional networks for text classification. In: Proceedings of the AAAI Conference on Artificial Intelligence, vol. 33, pp. 7370–7377 (2019)

Fast Text Comparison Based on ElasticSearch and Dynamic Programming

Pengcheng Xiao, Peng Lu, Chunqi Luo, Zhousen Zhu, and Xuehua Liao[✉]

Sichuan Normal University, Chengdu, China
liaoxuehua@163.com

Abstract. Text comparison is a process of comparing and matching two or more texts to determine their similarities or differences. By calculating the similarity between two texts, tasks such as classification, clustering, retrieval, and comparison can be performed on texts. In this work, we have improved existing text matching methods based on ElasticSearch and dynamic programming. Leveraging the powerful indexing and search capabilities of ElasticSearch, our method enables fast retrieval and comparison of relevant documents. During the text comparison process, we utilize an improved LCS (Longest Common Subsequence) algorithm to calculate the matches between the texts. We conduct extensive experiments on real-world datasets to evaluate the performance and effectiveness of our method. The results demonstrate that our approach can accomplish text comparison tasks more efficiently while handling various types of text noise.

Keywords: Text comparison · ElasticSearch · Document similarity · Dynamic programming

1 Introduction

Text comparison is the process of comparing and matching two or more texts to determine their similarities or differences. This technique has a wide range of applications, including information retrieval, duplicate detection, copyright infringement detection, semantic analysis, and natural language processing. In the field of information retrieval, text comparison has become an essential technology. To accomplish this, various algorithms and techniques have been developed, such as string matching algorithms, sequence alignment, clustering, and machine learning. The success of text comparison depends on the ability to effectively handle various types of text variations and noise, including spelling mistakes, synonyms, abbreviations, and different language styles. However, the design of previous text matching models was inefficient in the field of information retrieval, and there were issues such as inaccurate reflection of word position information and difficulty in identifying new and popular words.

Text comparison is a common technique used for text analysis, which is widely used in fields such as text similarity analysis, copyright protection, and intelligence analysis [2]. Machine learning-based comparison algorithms have higher accuracy and can automatically learn the semantic features of text [25]. Additionally, Elasticsearch, a search engine based on Lucene, is commonly used for real-time data analysis, log analysis, and full-text search scenarios, supporting indexing of multiple data sources [20,26,27,30,32]. Furthermore, dynamic programming is an algorithm used to solve optimization problems in multi-stage decision-making processes, commonly used to solve problems such as longest common subsequence, knapsack problem, and shortest path [3].

In the past, traditional TF-IDF(Term Frequency-Inverse Document Frequency) algorithms were often improved by weighting the numerator and denominator in the TF-IDF formula or dividing the terms into different hierarchies with different weight calculation methods [11,16]. These methods ultimately improve text comparison performance. Neural network-based models have been introduced into text comparison, which can simultaneously learn semantic matching, word alignment, and synonym detection tasks [19,31]. However, these methods are still not accurate enough in large-scale data scenarios and have problems identifying new words, hot words, and synonyms.

To address the aforementioned issues, we have designed a text comparison model based on ElasticSearch and dynamic programming. In this model, we first utilize the inverted index structure of ElasticSearch and combine it with the Longest Common Subsequence (LCS) algorithm based on dynamic programming to achieve efficient text comparison. Secondly, we introduce a lexicon module to solve the problem of identifying new words, hot words, and synonyms. Finally, to visualize the weak similarity results of text comparison, we transform the weak similarity results. The model aims to provide a clear and accurate comparison of texts with high efficiency and precision, while also addressing issues related to the identification of new words, hot words, and synonyms.

In summary, this paper's main contributions can be summarized as follows:

- Designed a text comparison model based on ElasticSearch and dynamic programming, which improves the performance of text comparison.
- Introduced a vocabulary module into the text comparison model, which solves the problem of identifying new words, hot words, and synonyms in text comparison.
- Visualized the weak similarity results of text comparison and obtained intuitive results through normalization processing.

The organizational structure of this paper is as follows. We first expound the relevant work of text comparison in Sect. 2. The problem definition of text comparison is described in Sect. 3. In Sect. 4, we provide a detailed description of the modules of our proposed text comparison model. The model is experimentally evaluated in Sect. 5. Finally, we draw the conclusion of this paper in Sect. 6 and briefly describe future work.

2   Related Work

In this section, we provide an overview of existing work related to text comparison from three perspectives: 1) text similarity calculation; 2) LCS algorithm based on dynamic programming; 3) improved TF-IDF algorithm.

2.1   Text Similarity Calculation

There are three main categories of text similarity calculation methods. The first category is based on rule-based text matching, which uses predefined rules or patterns to match and compare text. Common methods include regular expression matching and string matching algorithms [24]. This method is suitable for text with clear structures and explicit rules. Nonetheless, it may be limited when dealing with complex or irregular text. The second category is based on statistical models, such as bag-of-words models, word embedding models, syntactic structure models, and deep learning models [1,4,14,17]. These methods have different characteristics and are suitable for different scenarios and tasks. The third category is based on machine learning, which utilizes machine learning algorithms to establish models by learning from large text corpora to calculate text similarity [10,13]. In contrast to traditional rule-based methods, the advantage of machine learning-based methods is their adaptability to different domains and languages, as well as their ability to discover potential semantics and features. However, the downside is that they require a large amount of training data and computing resources, and the models have weak robustness and interpretability. Therefore, it is necessary to adopt a more suitable method for text comparison to improve accuracy.

2.2   LCS Algorithm Based on Dynamic Programming

Dynamic programming-based LCS algorithm can also be used for text comparison [22]. Some of these methods improve existing data structures and propose new improved LCS algorithms, which achieve faster calculation speed and lower space complexity. Zhengyu Liu and Jianming Huang proposed the Line Segment Collaborative Segmentation (LCS) framework, where both vector extraction and semantic segmentation performance are simultaneously improved [7,15]. However, this algorithm requires preprocessing of the text and extra storage space during calculation, and its effectiveness is not significant for text that does not satisfy the block property. Debarati Das and Yoshifumi Sakai proposed a data structure that can be used to solve the longest common subsequence problem in linear time or certain related local variants of the problem [5,21]. However, this algorithm requires a larger memory space when processing texts, and its effectiveness is not significant for text that does not satisfy the Trie property. Therefore, it is necessary to combine it with a data structure that can quickly search for specific words in the text to improve the efficiency of text comparison.

2.3   Improved TF-IDF Algorithm

Improved variants of the TF-IDF algorithm have been proposed to enhance text matching accuracy [9, 23, 33]. For example, Jiaohua Qin, Zhuo Zhou, and Yun Tan developed a novel multi-level TF-IDF algorithm for text classification that considers both the term frequency within a document and the term frequency within the category, as well as the length of the document and the length of the category [18]. Their method was compared to traditional TF-IDF and other state-of-the-art methods, and showed better performance in accuracy and score. However, the paper lacked detailed explanation and analysis of the proposed method, making it difficult to understand and replicate. They evaluated their method on several datasets and compared it to traditional TF-IDF and other state-of-the-art methods, and showed better performance in precision, recall, and score. Nevertheless, the paper lacked detailed explanation and analysis of the proposed method, making it difficult to understand and replicate.

3   Problem Definition

Text comparison refers to finding the degree of similarity between two given texts A and B. Generally, a method called similarity calculation is used to quantify the similarity between texts, and one commonly used method is based on the TF-IDF algorithm, which is defined by the following formula:

$$similarity(A, B) = \frac{\sum_{t \in A \cap B} tf_{t,A} \times tf_{t,B} \times idf_t}{\sqrt{\sum_{t \in A}(tf_{t,A} \times idf_t)^2} \times \sqrt{\sum_{t \in B}(tf_{t,B} \times idf_t)^2}} \quad (1)$$

The Eq. (1) involves three terms: $tf_{t,A}$, $tf_{t,B}$, and idf_t, representing the term frequency of term t in text A, the term frequency of term t in text B, and the inverse document frequency of term t, respectively. The numerator of the formula represents the sum of the weights of term t that are shared by both text A and B, while the denominator represents the product of the square root of the sum of weights of term t in text A and the sum of weights of term t in text B.

In other words, the formula calculates the cosine similarity between two texts based on the term frequency and inverse document frequency of their shared terms. Specifically, it measures how similar the texts are in terms of the occurrence and rarity of their shared terms, where a larger cosine similarity score indicates a higher degree of similarity between the texts.

4   Methodology

In order to address the challenges of low efficiency and accuracy in text comparison, we propose a new approach that combines the dynamic programming-based LCS algorithm with ElasticSearch. This hybrid model is designed to enhance the performance and accuracy of text comparison. Figure 1 shows the flow chart of the model:

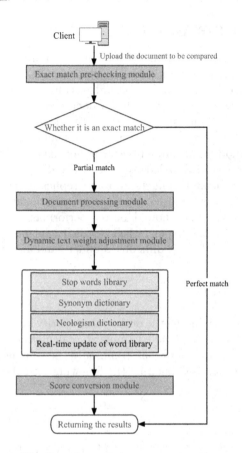

Fig. 1. The flow chart of the text comparison model.

4.1 Exact Match Pre-detection

The first part of our proposed text comparison model is the Exact Match Pre-processing module, which aims to conduct a preliminary check on the documents uploaded by users. This module filters out completely matched documents and sends partially matched documents to the next module for further processing. To efficiently handle documents, we conducted extensive research and decided to employ the Rabin-Karp algorithm for this task.

To be more specific, the Rabin-Karp algorithm is a more efficient algorithm when processing texts [28]. With this algorithm, the Exact Match Preprocessing module can quickly and accurately identify and filter out completely matched documents. As a result, the subsequent modules can focus on processing partially matched documents, thereby enhancing the overall efficiency of the text comparison model. Algorithm 1 describes the process of exact matching pre-scanning module.

Algorithm 1. Rabin-Karp algorithm

Require: s: The Text to be compared; *pattern*: The Pattern string
Ensure: The pattern *pattern* is found in the text s at index i
  $n \leftarrow \text{length}(s)$
  $m \leftarrow \text{length}(pattern)$
  $patternHash \leftarrow \text{hash}(pattern[1..m])$
  for $i \leftarrow 1$ to $n - m + 1$ **do**
    if $\text{hash}(s[i..i + m - 1]) == patternHash$ **then**
      if $s[i..i + m - 1] == pattern$ **then**
        return i
      end if
    end if
  end for
  return -1

4.2 Document Processing

Text keyword extraction refers to the process of identifying and extracting the most important and relevant keywords or phrases from a given text document. The document's title, main headings, subheadings, introductory sentences, and concluding sentences often express the meaning of the text, making it crucial to extract the key parts of the document. Text keyword extraction aims to identify and extract the most significant and relevant keywords or phrases from a given text document. The primary objective of this module is to extract the key portions of the document that can summarize its content.

There are several algorithms and tools available for document keyword extraction. TextRank is a text ranking algorithm that can extract keywords from a given text by leveraging the relationships between textual elements [6]. It has the advantage of utilizing the relationships between elements effectively. However, its drawback is that the extraction results are significantly influenced by word segmentation, including the inclusion or exclusion of certain stop words, which directly affects the final outcome. POI is a tool used for processing Microsoft Office documents such as Excel, Word, and PowerPoint. It supports various file formats and can handle different Microsoft Office file formats, including .doc, .docx, .xls, .xlsx, etc. In this module, we only need to extract the key parts of the document without considering the relationships between textual elements. Therefore, we utilize the POI tool to extract key information from the document, resulting in a collection of multi-level headings, paragraph starting and ending sentences, and document paragraphs. These collections will serve as input for the next module.

4.3 Dynamic Adjustment of Text Weight

Upon receiving the document collection data from the previous module, we will utilize a novel similarity calculation method to compare the similarity between texts. Traditional text similarity calculation often employs the LCS (Longest

Common Subsequence) algorithm based on dynamic programming [22]. However, this approach has two shortcomings. Firstly, it relies solely on surface-level character matching and does not encompass semantic matching. Secondly, it lacks efficiency in the comparison process. Therefore, it is necessary to introduce a data structure to enhance the efficiency of the comparison. ElasticSearch [29] is an open-source search engine with an internal structure as shown in the Fig. 2. First of all, ElasticSearch has high performance and scalability. It stores and retrieves data using an inverted index, which enables it to quickly respond to user queries. At the same time, it supports various types of queries, such as full-text search, fuzzy search, and aggregation queries, which can meet various complex query requirements. In addition, it can easily scale horizontally across multiple servers to meet the requirements of large-scale data storage and processing. Therefore, introducing ElasticSearch in text comparison can help us address performance issues in large data scenarios.

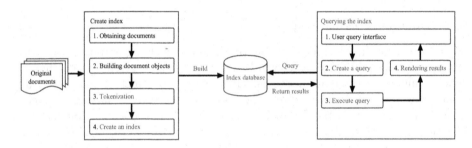

Fig. 2. The internal indexing process of ElasticSearch.

Meanwhile, we incorporate ElasticSearch to assist in calculating text similarity using the LCS (Longest Common Subsequence) algorithm [12]. This integration aims to enhance the computation of text similarity between documents by leveraging the capabilities of ElasticSearch. The main methods used in this module are as follows:

$$score(q,d) = qN(q) \cdot coord(q,d) \cdot \sum_{t \in q} (tf_{t,d} \cdot idf_t^2) \cdot \frac{t.getBoost() \cdot d.getBoost()}{norm_d} \quad (2)$$

Equation (2) represents the scoring method in ElasticSearch, where the parameter names and their meanings are as follows: q represents the query statement, d represents the document, $tf_{t,d}$ represents the frequency of term t in document d, idf_t represents the inverse document frequency of term t, $boost_t$ represents the weight of term t, and $norm_d$ represents the length normalization factor of document d. The scoring formula calculates the similarity between each term in the query statement and the document to obtain the final document score, thus achieving the text retrieval function. The meanings of each factor in the scoring formula are as follows: $qN(q)$ represents the normalization of the weight of each term in the query statement, making the comparison between different query statements more fair. $coord(q, d)$ represents the collaborative effect of the terms in the query statement in the document. If multiple terms in the query statement appear in the document at the same time, the document score will be increased. The product of the remaining factors represents the similarity score between each term in the query statement and the document. The sum of all term scores is used to obtain the final weight of the document.

$$c[i, j] = \begin{cases} 0, & i = 0 \text{ or } j = 0 \\ c[i-1, j-1], & i, j > 0 \text{ and } x_i = y_i \\ max(c[i, j-1], c[i-1, j]), & i, j > 0 \text{ and } x_i \neq y_i \end{cases} \quad (3)$$

$$sim = \frac{c[i, j] * 2}{len(X_m) + len(Y_n)} \quad (4)$$

Equation (3) and Eq. (4) are methods for calculating text similarity using the LCS algorithm. Here, $c[i, j]$ represents the length of the longest common subsequence between two known text sequences X_m and Y_n. After obtaining the length of the longest common subsequence using Eq. (3), text similarity is calculated using Eq. (4).

$$c = w_a * a + w_b * b \quad (5)$$

Finally, we take a weighted average of the similarity scores computed by ElasticSearch and LCS algorithms to obtain a weak similarity result for text comparison in Eq. (5). Here, a represents the score obtained by applying the weight boosting algorithm of ElasticSearch to enhance the weights of key parts such as first-level headings, second-level headings, etc., and calculating the score. b represents the score obtained by using the traditional LCS algorithm to compute the similarity of the paragraph parts in the document. w_a and w_b represent the weights assigned to w_a and w_b, and it is generally required that $w_a + w_b = 1$. The specific values of w_a and w_b are adjusted according to the contribution of a and b. c represents the result of the weighted average.

In summary, the main intention of this module is to combine the similarity calculation method of ElasSearch and the dynamic programming-based LCS algorithm through a weighted average, in order to obtain a weak similarity result for text comparison, followed by a series of further processing.

4.4   Lexicon Management

In the process of text comparison, we need to consider the influence of text semantics in addition to the comparison of word forms [8]. This experiment mainly considers three types of words that can affect text comparison: stop words, synonyms, and new words. Stop words refer to words that appear frequently in the text but usually do not carry much meaning, such as "the", "is", "in", etc. In text processing, we filter out these words to reduce the complexity of text processing. Synonyms refer to words with similar meanings. In text comparison, we can use a synonym library to replace keywords in user queries with their synonyms to improve the recall and accuracy of comparison results. New words refer to words that have not been included in the conventional word library, such as new vocabulary, new brands, new technologies, etc. In text processing, we need to update the word library in a timely manner, add these new words to the library, and delete outdated words or modify existing words to ensure the accuracy and completeness of text processing.

Therefore, in this module, we need to configure stop word libraries, synonym libraries, and new word libraries to improve the accuracy of text comparison. At the same time, we need to perform hot updates on the word library to ensure timely addition of new words, deletion of outdated words, or modification of existing words, making the system's word processing more accurate.

4.5   Conversion of Scoring Results

This module is the last one in the text matching model. Its ultimate goal is to transform weak similarity results into more intuitive text matching results through normalization scaling and score mapping. In this module, weak similarity results of text matching are first normalized to the same range for easy comparison and processing. Then, the results are transformed into different matching levels according to their score, where a higher score indicates a stronger text matching and a lower score indicates a weaker text similarity.

$$score_{norm} = \frac{score - score_{min}}{score_{max} - score_{min}} \tag{6}$$

Equation (6) is a Min-Max normalization method used to process the similarity scores into a range of $[0, 1]$, aiming to facilitate the transformation of scores into different matching levels based on their magnitudes. In this formula, $score$ represents the raw data, $score_{min}$ and $score_{max}$ denote the minimum and maximum values of the score, and $score_{norm}$ represents the normalized data. Finally, $score_{norm}$ is transformed into intuitive text matching results. Using different $score_{norm}$ to represent corresponding text similarity.

5   Experiment

5.1   Experiment Settings

Dataset: The test documents we used in our study were obtained from the CNKI database, consisting of 200 Chinese research papers. We filtered out irrelevant information such as abstracts, author information, and reference lists, and retained only the essential parts of the documents, including document titles, first-level headings, second-level headings, third-level headings, and the main body text. These selected parts were used as experimental data for text comparison. First and foremost, our study primarily focuses on text comparison of Chinese documents, hence the selection of Chinese texts. Additionally, we have employed an improved model that assigns certain weights to the key sections of the Chinese documents and combines it with the classical LCS algorithm to calculate text similarity. Therefore, it is necessary to preserve the key sections of the documents.

Experiment Environment: Tabel 1 shows the experiment environment. We employed a machine with 8 cores, 16GiB memory, and 500GiB storage to run our model.

Table 1. Experiment environment.

Item	Description
CPU	12 Cores
Memory	16 GiB
Storeage	500 GiB
Operation System	Windows 11
Network bandwidth	5 Mbps

5.2 Experiment Comparison Analysis

This experiment evaluates three aspects. The first aspect examines the impact of the presence or absence of the text matching pre-detection module on the efficiency of our proposed text alignment model. The second aspect compares our proposed method to the classical LCS algorithm in terms of model runtime within the dynamically adjusting text weighting module, showcasing the advantages of our approach. The third aspect compares our proposed LCS algorithm to the classical LCS algorithm within the dynamically adjusting text weighting module, highlighting the superiority of our model based on the quantity of text recall rate.

This test examines the impact of the text matching pre-detection module on the response time of the model. In this test, the response time of the proposed model will be evaluated using two approaches: one with the text matching pre-detection module enabled and another with the module disabled. The relationship between the number of texts and the system's response time under these two approaches is illustrated in Fig. 3.

The test results indicate that the system response time increases with an increase in the number of texts for both processing approaches. When the number of texts exceeds 100, the text matching pre-detection module demonstrates significantly lower time consumption compared to the same number of texts without the module. Therefore, incorporating this module can effectively enhance the performance of our model.

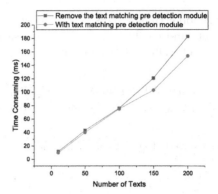

Fig. 3. The relationship between the number of texts and system response time under different processing approaches.

The second test aimed to assess the impact of using the improved LCS algorithm and the classical LCS algorithm within the dynamically adjusting text weighting module on the performance of the proposed model. The relationship between the number of texts and system response time under these two approaches is depicted in Fig. 4. The test results indicate that the improved LCS algorithm outperforms the classical LCS algorithm in terms of time consumption. Therefore, within this module, the improved LCS algorithm proves to enhance the performance of our model.

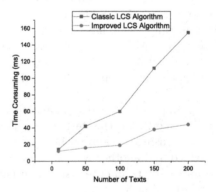

Fig. 4. The relationship between the number of texts and system response time under different algorithm.

The third test aimed to evaluate the impact of using the improved LCS algorithm and the classical LCS algorithm on the text recall rate.

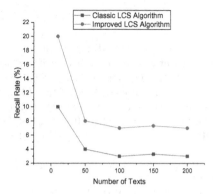

Fig. 5. The relationship between the number of texts and recall rate under different algorithm.

Figure 5 presents the experimental results in Sect. 4.3, where w_a is set to 0.8 and w_b is set to 0.2. Under these conditions, the improved LCS algorithm demonstrates a significantly higher recall rate compared to the recall rate of the classical LCS algorithm. The recall rate is calculated according to Eq. (7).

$$recall = \frac{number_{sim}}{number_{total}} \times 100\% \tag{7}$$

In this case, $number_{sim}$ represents the number of similar texts, and $number_{total}$ represents the total number of texts. A higher recall rate indicates a more precise text matching. Therefore, under these conditions, the improved LCS algorithm exhibits a higher level of accuracy compared to the classical LCS algorithm.

6   Conclusion and Future Work

This paper presents a text comparison model based on ElasticSearch and dynamic programming. The model consists of five modules: matching pre-detection, document processing, dynamic adjustment of text weights, lexicon management, and score result conversion. This model not only improves the performance of text comparison but also enhances its accuracy. The experimental results demonstrate that our proposed model outperforms traditional methods in terms of both performance and accuracy. However, we have identified some limitations that need further improvement: firstly, the system can only compare Chinese documents, and secondly, the security level is not high enough. In the future, we will continue our research based on this paper and incorporate other recently proposed algorithms to obtain more accurate results.

References

1. Alleman, M., Mamou, J., Rio, M.A.D., Tang, H., Kim, Y., Chung, S.: Syntactic perturbations reveal representational correlates of hierarchical phrase structure in pretrained language models (2021). https://doi.org/10.48550/arXiv.2104.07578
2. Atabuzzaman, M., Shajalal, M., Ahmed, M.E., Afjal, M.I., Aono, M.: Leveraging grammatical roles for measuring semantic similarity between texts. IEEE Access **9**, 62972–62983 (2021). https://doi.org/10.1109/ACCESS.2021.3074747
3. Cao, S., Yang, Y.: DP-BERT: dynamic programming BERT for text summarization. In: Fang, L., Chen, Y., Zhai, G., Wang, J., Wang, R., Dong, W. (eds.) CICAI 2021. LNCS, vol. 13070, pp. 285–296. Springer, Cham (2021). https://doi.org/10.1007/978-3-030-93049-3_24
4. Castro, A.P., Wainer, G.A., Calixto, W.P.: Weighting construction by bag-of-words with similarity-learning and supervised training for classification models in court text documents. Appl. Soft Comput. **124**, 108987 (2022). https://doi.org/10.1016/j.asoc.2022.108987
5. Das, D., Saha, B.: Approximating LCS and alignment distance over multiple sequences. CoRR abs/2110.12402 (2021). https://doi.org/10.48550/arXiv.2110.12402
6. Guo, W., Wang, Z., Han, F.: Multifeature fusion keyword extraction algorithm based on textrank. IEEE Access **10**, 71805–71813 (2022). https://doi.org/10.1109/ACCESS.2022.3188861
7. Huang, J., Fang, Z., Kasai, H.: LCS graph kernel based on Wasserstein distance in longest common subsequence metric space. Signal Process. **189**, 108281 (2021). https://doi.org/10.1016/j.sigpro.2021.108281
8. Inan, E.: Simit: a text similarity method using lexicon and dependency representations. New Gener. Comput. **38**(3), 509–530 (2020). https://doi.org/10.1007/s00354-020-00099-8
9. Jalilifard, A., Caridá, V.F., Mansano, A., Cristo, R.: Semantic sensitive TF-IDF to determine word relevance in documents. CoRR abs/2001.09896 (2020). https://doi.org/10.48550/arXiv.2001.09896
10. Kalbaliyev, E., Rustamov, S.: Text similarity detection using machine learning algorithms with character-based similarity measures. In: Biele, C., Kacprzyk, J., Owsiński, J.W., Romanowski, A., Sikorski, M. (eds.) MIDI 2020. AISC, vol. 1376, pp. 11–19. Springer, Cham (2021). https://doi.org/10.1007/978-3-030-74728-2_2
11. Koloski, B., Pollak, S., Škrlj, B., Martinc, M.: Extending neural keyword extraction with TF-IDF tagset matching. In: Proceedings of the EACL Hackashop on News Media Content Analysis and Automated Report Generation, pp. 22–29. Association for Computational Linguistics (2021). www.aclanthology.org/2021.hackashop-1.4
12. Korfhage, N., Mühling, M., Freisleben, B.: *ElasticHash*: semantic image similarity search by deep hashing with elasticsearch. In: Tsapatsoulis, N., Panayides, A., Theocharides, T., Lanitis, A., Pattichis, C., Vento, M. (eds.) CAIP 2021. LNCS, vol. 13053, pp. 14–23. Springer, Cham (2021). https://doi.org/10.1007/978-3-030-89131-2_2
13. Kuppili, V., Biswas, M., Edla, D.R., Prasad, K.J.R., Suri, J.S.: A mechanics-based similarity measure for text classification in machine learning paradigm. IEEE Trans. Emerg. Top. Comput. Intell. **4**(2), 180–200 (2020). https://doi.org/10.1109/TETCI.2018.2863728

14. Lim, J., Sa, I., Ahn, H.S., Gasteiger, N., Lee, S.J., MacDonald, B.: Subsentence extraction from text using coverage-based deep learning language models. Sensors **21**(8), 2712 (2021). https://doi.org/10.3390/s21082712
15. Liu, Z., Shi, Q., Ou, J.: LCS: a collaborative optimization framework of vector extraction and semantic segmentation for building extraction. IEEE Trans. Geosci. Remote Sens. **60**, 1–15 (2022). https://doi.org/10.1109/TGRS.2022.3215852
16. Marcińczuk, M., Gniewkowski, M., Walkowiak, T., Będkowski, M.: Text document clustering: Wordnet vs. TF-IDF vs. word embeddings. In: Proceedings of the 11th Global Wordnet Conference, pp. 207–214. Global Wordnet Association (2021). www.aclanthology.org/2021.gwc-1.24
17. Murakami, R., Chakraborty, B.: Investigating the efficient use of word embedding with neural-topic models for interpretable topics from short texts. Sensors **22**(3), 852 (2022). https://doi.org/10.3390/s22030852
18. Qin, J., Zhou, Z., Tan, Y., Xiang, X., He, Z.: A big data text coverless information hiding based on topic distribution and TF-IDF. Int. J. Digit. Crime Forensics **13**(4), 40–56 (2021). https://doi.org/10.4018/ijdcf.20210701.oa4
19. Romanov, A.S., Kurtukova, A.V., Sobolev, A.A., Shelupanov, A.A., Fedotova, A.M.: Determining the age of the author of the text based on deep neural network models. Information **11**(12), 589 (2020). https://doi.org/10.3390/info11120589
20. Rosenberg, J., Coronel, J.B., Meiring, J., Gray, S., Brown, T.: Leveraging elasticsearch to improve data discoverability in science gateways. In: Proceedings of the Practice and Experience in Advanced Research Computing on Rise of the Machines (learning), PEARC 2019, Chicago, IL, USA, 28 July–01 August 2019, pp. 19:1–19:5. ACM (2019). https://doi.org/10.1145/3332186.3332230
21. Sakai, Y.: A substring-substring LCS data structure. Theor. Comput. Sci. **753**, 16–34 (2019). https://doi.org/10.1016/j.tcs.2018.06.034
22. Sakai, Y.: A data structure for substring-substring LCS length queries. Theoret. Comput. Sci. **911**, 41–54 (2022). https://doi.org/10.1016/j.tcs.2022.02.004
23. Shang, W., Underwood, T.: Improving measures of text reuse in English poetry: A TF–IDF based method. In: Toeppe, K., Yan, H., Chu, S.K.W. (eds.) iConference 2021. LNCS, vol. 12645, pp. 469–477. Springer, Cham (2021). https://doi.org/10.1007/978-3-030-71292-1_36
24. Sheshasaayee, A., Thailambal, G.: Performance of multiple string matching algorithms in text mining. In: Satapathy, S.C., Bhateja, V., Udgata, S.K., Pattnaik, P.K. (eds.) Proceedings of the 5th International Conference on Frontiers in Intelligent Computing: Theory and Applications. AISC, vol. 516, pp. 671–681. Springer, Singapore (2017). https://doi.org/10.1007/978-981-10-3156-4_71
25. Sinha, A., Naskar, M.B., Pandey, M., Rautaray, S.S.: Text classification using machine learning techniques: comparative analysis. In: 2022 OITS International Conference on Information Technology (OCIT), pp. 102–107 (2022). https://doi.org/10.1109/OCIT56763.2022.00029
26. Sun, J., Nie, P., Xu, L., Zhang, H.: Design and implementation of analyzer management system based on elasticsearch. In: Zhao, X., Yang, S., Wang, X., Li, J. (eds.) WISA 2022. LNCS, vol. 13579, pp. 254–266. Springer, Cham (2022). https://doi.org/10.1007/978-3-031-20309-1_22
27. Van, D.N., Trung, S.N., Hong, A.P.T., Hoang, T.T., Thanh, T.M.: A novel approach to end-to-end facial recognition framework with virtual search engine elasticsearch. In: Gervasi, O., et al. (eds.) ICCSA 2021. LNCS, vol. 12951, pp. 454–470. Springer, Cham (2021). https://doi.org/10.1007/978-3-030-86970-0_32

28. Vishnupriya, G., Ramachandran, R.: Rabin-Karp algorithm based malevolent node detection and energy-efficient data gathering approach in wireless sensor network. Microprocess. Microsyst. **82**, 103829 (2021). https://doi.org/10.1016/j.micpro.2021.103829

29. Wei, B., Dai, J., Deng, L., Huang, H.: An optimization method for elasticsearch index shard number. In: 2020 16th International Conference on Computational Intelligence and Security (CIS), pp. 191–195 (2020). https://doi.org/10.1109/CIS52066.2020.00048

30. Yang, W., Li, H., Li, Y., Zou, Y., Zhao, H.: Design and implementation of intelligent warehouse platform based on elasticsearch. In: 6th International Conference on Software and e-Business, ICSEB 2022, Shenzhen, China, 9–11 December 2022, pp. 69–73. ACM (2022). https://doi.org/10.1145/3578997.3579016

31. Yao, J., Wang, K., Yan, J.: Incorporating label co-occurrence into neural network-based models for multi-label text classification. IEEE Access **7**, 183580–183588 (2019). https://doi.org/10.1109/ACCESS.2019.2960626

32. Zamfir, V., Carabas, M., Carabas, C., Tapus, N.: Systems monitoring and big data analysis using the elasticsearch system. In: 22nd International Conference on Control Systems and Computer Science, CSCS 2019, Bucharest, Romania, 28–30 May 2019, pp. 188–193. IEEE (2019). https://doi.org/10.1109/CSCS.2019.00039

33. Zandigohar, M., Dai, Y.: Information retrieval in single cell chromatin analysis using TF-IDF transformation methods. In: IEEE International Conference on Bioinformatics and Biomedicine, BIBM 2022, Las Vegas, NV, USA, 6–8 December 2022, pp. 877–882. IEEE (2022). https://doi.org/10.1109/BIBM55620.2022.9994949

Question Answering and Information Retrieval

User Context-Aware Attention Networks for Answer Selection

Yuyang He, Juntao Zhang⬥, Xiandi Yang, and Zhiyong Peng(✉)

School of Computer Science, Wuhan University, Wuhan, China
{yuyanghe,juntaozhang,xiandiy,peng}@whu.edu.cn

Abstract. Answer selection aims to find the most appropriate answer from a set of candidate answers, playing an increasingly important role in Community-based Question Answering. However, existing studies overlook the correlation among historical answers of users and simply summarize user contexts by concatenation or max-pooling when modeling user representations. In this paper, we propose a novel User Context-aware Attention Network (UCAN) for the answer selection task. Specifically, we apply the BERT model to encode representations of questions, answers, and user contexts. Then we use the CNN model to extract the n-gram features. Next, we model the user context as a graph and utilize the graph attention mechanism to capture the correlation among answers in the user context. We further use the Bi-LSTM to enhance the contextual representations. Finally, we adopt a multi-view attention mechanism to learn the context-based semantic representations. We conduct experiments on two widely used datasets, and the experimental results show that the UCAN outperforms all baselines.

Keywords: Answer selection · User context · Attention mechanism · Contextual representations

1 Introduction

Community-based Question Answering (CQA) has gained more and more attention in recent years, providing a way for users to share their insights, wisdom, and knowledge. Several popular CQA platforms, such as Quora and StackOverflow, enable users to ask questions and receive answers from others conveniently. It is critical for these platforms to provide users with high-quality answers based on their questions. Although the number of votes each answer receives can serve as a reference standard for evaluating the quality of answers, their accumulation often takes a relatively long time [25]. Therefore, finding high-quality answers quickly and automatically plays a pivotal role in enhancing user experience.

Traditional approaches for answer selection typically rely on feature engineerings, such as bag-of-words, n-grams, and syntactic and semantic features [12,24,26]. However, they have limitations in learning the complex semantic features and generalizing to other domains. Several studies [2,17,23] use deep neural

ⓒ The Author(s), under exclusive license to Springer Nature Singapore Pte Ltd. 2023
F. Zhang et al. (Eds.): WISE 2023, LNCS 14306, pp. 67–81, 2023.
https://doi.org/10.1007/978-981-99-7254-8_6

Table 1. An Example in CQA.

Question	hi, I work for a company and am on business visa. what are the rules company should follow under business visa to get workdone from me? pls tell your valuable answers ASAP
Good Answer	Victoria, do not mislead people. As I explained, if he/she is in Qatar less then 30 days, no need for exit permit
User Context	1. you have to get a visa prior to your arrival to UAE. Charge depends on duration. I think the shortest stay (few dys or so) is about \$250. Multi visa is \$1000
	2. You cannot "go on the process" yourself. You have to find a job first, and then the company will issue a work visa for you
Bad Answer	Yes, my business visa expired and they extended 3 times.......this third time they extended. can I go without exit permit? that's what my question is?

networks for answer selection, and they learn the representations of questions and answers (QA) and compute the matching degree of QA pairs to achieve high performance. These studies have achieved good performance, but they neglect the user context that can reveal available information about the user's expertise and interests. In fact, users whose expertise and interests are more relevant to the question are more likely to provide high-quality answers. An example from the QatarLiving forum[1] is shown in Table 1. Although the "Bad Answer" is more similar to the question than the "Good Answer" due to the similar words, such as "business" and "visa", the "Good Answer" provides more useful information relevant to the given question. Existing methods [16,22] that only consider the text matching between QA pairs may mistakenly classify the "Bad Answer" as "Good" based on text similarity. We observe that the user's expertise in "visa" reflected by the user context indicates the professionalism and reliability of the answer. Several previous studies [7,15,19,25] also utilize user information, whereas they overlook the correlation among past answers of users. As shown in Table 1, "visa" appears in multiple past answers in the user context and can reflect the user's expertise in "visa". Instead of concatenating past answers of users [15] or using max-pooling operation [19], we need to consider the correlation among historical answers of users to capture key features in the user context.

To address the problem above, we propose the User Context-aware Attention Network (UCAN) for answer selection, which exploits the correlation among answers in the user context and learns the hierarchical and attentive features of questions, answers, and user contexts. Unlike previous studies that may lose latent useful information by applying concatenation or max-pooling to the user context, we construct a graph to represent the user context. Each historical answer of the user is regarded as a node in the constructed graph and similar

---

[1] http://www.qatarliving.com/forum.

answers are connected by edges. Therefore, the relationship among historical answers in the user context can be reflected by the graph structure. The main contributions of our work can be summarized as follows:

1. We propose the User Context-aware Attention Network (UCAN) for answer selection. The UCAN model incorporates user contexts to model users and combines hierarchical features with attention mechanisms to learn the contextual representations of questions, answers, and user contexts.
2. We design the user context graph and encode the correlation among historical answers in the user context as user representations by employing Graph Attention Networks (GAT) on the constructed graph.
3. We develop an n-gram encoder to extract the multi-level features, capturing important semantic elements of sentences. We apply a multi-view attention mechanism to focus on the informative parts of questions, answers, and user contexts. Besides, we design an attention fusion method to effectively integrate the attention representations.
4. We conduct a series of experiments on SemEval-2015 and SemEval-2017 datasets. The results show that our method outperforms other state-of-the-art models for answer selection.

2   Related Work

Existing methods for answer selection are mainly divided into feature engineering-based methods and deep learning-based methods.

Feature Engineering-Based Methods. Early studies for answer selection in CQA mainly use artificial features, such as syntactic and novelty-based features. Tymoshenko et al. [12] proposed tree structures for representations of QA pairs. Omari et al. [10] measured the quality of answers by their novelty and relevance. Zhao et al. [26] considered user activities in QA and designed new features to express the expertise of users. However, these feature engineering-based methods require domain knowledge to design high-quality features. Besides, it is difficult for them to excavate potential semantic relevance in texts.

Deep Learning-Based Methods. Deep learning-based methods have significantly improved the performance of answer selection in recent years [1,2,23]. For example, Wu et al. [16] utilized the relationship between the subject and body of the question by question condensing networks. Gao et al. [5] proposed an attention-based sequence-to-sequence model to generate clarifying questions to supplement original questions. To incorporate the external knowledge into answer selection, Deng et al. [3] mapped the knowledge sequence of the sentence into the knowledge graph, and used a graph convolutional network to learn the contextualized knowledge representation. Yang et al. [22] used the BERT model [4] to enhance the representation of question subjects, question bodies, and answers. Then the interactive features of questions and answers are obtained by the cross-attention mechanism. By building CQA concept graphs for question-subject-answer pair and question-body-answer pair, Yang et al. [21] obtained more informative representations of questions and answers. However, these methods ignore user expertise, an important factor in CQA. Several recent studies focus on learning user representations to capture the expertise behind answers. Wen et al. [15] modeled user representations by calculating the attention between past answers of users and questions to attend to key parts of them. Xie et al. [19] applied an adversarial training module to filter the irrelevant content in users' past answers. Instead of capturing user expertise from historical answers of users, Lyu et al. [7] and Zhang et al. [25] regarded the user representations as learnable latent vectors. All the above-mentioned methods neglect the potential correlation among historical answers of users, which is helpful to model user expertise. Jing et al. [6] utilized matrix factorization to capture users' expertise and authority from past answers and social networks, respectively.

3   Proposed Model

In this section, we introduce our proposed UCAN for answer selection in CQA. The framework of UCAN consists of three layers, as shown in Fig. 1. Specifically, we first use BERT to obtain the representations of questions, answers, and user contexts in the encoding layer. To extract the n-gram features of sentences, we employ an n-gram encoder. Subsequently, we use Bi-LSTM to encode questions, answers, and user contexts, and learn the user representations by GAT. Then we adopt an attention mechanism to capture the contextual information in questions, answers, and user contexts in the attention layer. Finally, we feed obtained representations into the prediction layer to make predictions.

3.1   Problem Definition

Answer selection is the task of selecting the most appropriate answers from a set of possible answers for a given question. In this paper, we formulate it as a binary classification problem. Formally, given a question $Q = \{w_1^Q, w_2^Q, \ldots, w_{l_Q}^Q\}$, a candidate answer $A = \{w_1^A, w_2^A, \ldots, w_{l_A}^A\}$, and user context $U = \{U_1, U_2, \ldots, U_K\}$ of the user who gives the answer A, where l_Q and l_A represent the length of the question Q and the answer A, respectively. K denotes the number of historical answers in the user context U. The answer selection task of CQA is to learn a classification function $f(Q, A, U) \rightarrow \{Good, Bad\}$, which takes the question Q together with the answer A and users' historical answers U as input and outputs whether the answer A is the correct answer or not.

3.2   Encoding Layer

The encoding layer of UCAN consists of four modules: Pre-trained Encoder, N-gram Feature, Graph-based User Modeling, and Context Module.

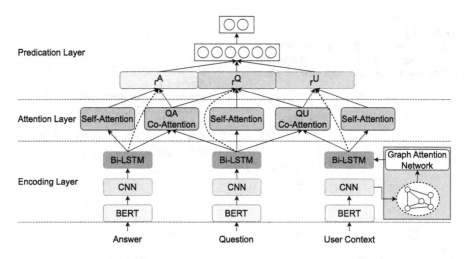

Fig. 1. The framework of UCAN.

Pre-trained Encoder. Give a question $Q = \{w_1^Q, \ldots, w_{l^Q}^Q\}$, an answer $A = \{w_1^A, \ldots, w_{l^A}^A\}$ and user context $U = \{U_1, \ldots, U_K\}$ with K historical answers, we adopt the BERT model [4], which is a pre-trained language model that uses a transformer architecture to learn contextual relationships between words in a given text corpus. We fine-tune it during training to obtain latent semantic representations of the question, the answer, and the user context:

$$H^Q = BERT(Q) = \{h_1^Q, \ldots, h_{l^Q}^Q\}, \tag{1}$$

$$H^A = BERT(A) = \{h_1^A, \ldots, h_{l^A}^A\}, \tag{2}$$

$$H^{U_i} = BERT(U_i) = \{h_1^{U_i}, \ldots, h_{l^{U_i}}^{U_i}\}, \tag{3}$$

where $H^Q \in \mathbb{R}^{l^Q \times d_h}$, $H^A \in \mathbb{R}^{l^A \times d_h}$, and $H^{U_i} \in \mathbb{R}^{l^{U_i} \times d_h}$. l^Q, l^A, and l^{U_i} denote the length of the question, the answer, and the historical answer i, respectively. d_h is the embedding size.

N-Gram Feature. A sentence usually contains multiple n-grams that reflect important features of the text. To capture the n-gram semantic features, we apply Convolutional Neural Network (CNN) to slide over the embedding matrix. Here we consider convolutional filters with sizes of 2 and 3 to explore the multi-level features of sentences. Formally, given the word-level representations of the question H^Q and the filter F_n of size n, the n-gram features of the question are calculated as follows:

$$P_n^Q = tanh(H^Q * F_n + b_n), \tag{4}$$

where $P_n^Q \in \mathbb{R}^{(l^Q - n + 1) \times m}$, $*$ is the convolution operator, b is the bias vector, m is the number of filters. We pad the input of the convolutional filters and

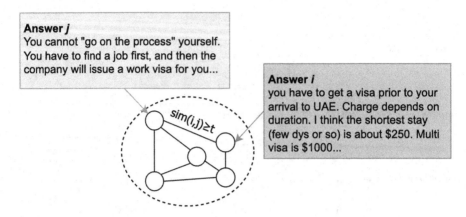

Fig. 2. The user context graph, where nodes denote historical answers of the same user.

concatenate the output of two convolutional filters to get the n-gram-based representations of the question:

$$P^Q = [P_2^Q; P_3^Q], \tag{5}$$

where $[;]$ denotes the column-wise concatenation. Similarly, we compute the n-gram-based representations P^A and P^U for the answer and the user context, respectively.

Graph-Based User Modeling. Intuitively, past answers of users can reflect their expertise and interests, thus contributing to the answer selection in CQA. Different from previous studies [15, 19] that also use the hidden context information from the past answers of users, we integrate user representations through modeling relationships among historical answers in user contexts.

Inspired by [20], we build a graph to represent the user context, where nodes are representations of historical answers in the user context, and edges are indicated by cosine similarity between representations of answers. An example of the user context graph is shown in Fig. 2. Given the threshold value t, the adjacency matrix A is given by:

$$A_{ij} = \begin{cases} 1, & sim(i,j) \geq t \\ 0, & sim(i,j) < t \end{cases}, \tag{6}$$

where $sim(i,j)$ denotes the cosine similarity between representations of answer i and answer j.

To model answer correlations effectively, we apply Graph Attention Networks (GAT) [13] to the user context graph. GAT introduces a self-attention mechanism in the propagation process, where the hidden states of each node are calculated by attending to its neighboring nodes. GAT treats nodes with different importance, thus being suitable for learning the correlations among nodes.

Specifically, we assume the n-gram representations of node i and its neighbourhood $j \in \mathcal{N}_i$ as $p_i \in \mathbb{R}^{l \times 2m}$ and $p_j \in \mathbb{R}^{l \times 2m}$, respectively. The attention weights α_{ij} is calculated as follows:

$$\alpha_{ij} = \frac{exp(LeakyReLU([p_iW; p_jW]W_a))}{\sum_{k \in \mathcal{N}_i} exp(LeakyReLU([p_iW; p_kW]W_a))}, \tag{7}$$

where $W_a \in \mathbb{R}^{2d_f}$ is a weight vector and d_f is the output dimension of GAT. $W \in \mathbb{R}^{2m \times d_f}$ is a weight matrix for linear transformation.

GAT incorporates multi-head attention to improve the model effect. We can obtain the representation g_i of node i by averaging the output of N attention heads. Then the representations of all nodes in the graph are aggregated to form the user representation G for the user:

$$g_i = \sigma(\frac{1}{N} \sum_{n=1}^{N} \sum_{j \in \mathcal{N}(i)} \alpha_{ij}^n W^n p_j), \tag{8}$$

$$G = \frac{1}{K} \sum_{i=1}^{K} g_i, \tag{9}$$

where σ denotes the activation function, α_{ij}^n and W^n are the attention weights and the linear transformation weight matrix of n-th attention head, respectively. K is the number of nodes in the user context graph (i.e., the number of historical answers in the user context).

Context Module. The context module further enhances the representations by taking advantage of contextual information. We use Bi-directional Long Short-Term Memory (Bi-LSTM) [14] which can process sequential data in both forward and backward directions to capture contextual information from the past and the future at the same time. Given the input representation P, the contextual representation M is computed by:

$$\overrightarrow{m}_t = \overrightarrow{LSTM}(\overrightarrow{m}_{t-1}, p_t), \tag{10}$$

$$\overleftarrow{m}_t = \overleftarrow{LSTM}(\overleftarrow{m}_{t+1}, p_t), \tag{11}$$

$$m_t = [\overrightarrow{m}_t, \overleftarrow{m}_t], \tag{12}$$

where $M \in \mathbb{R}^{l \times 2d_w}$ and d_w denotes the hidden dimension of Bi-LSTM. $\overrightarrow{m}_t$ represents the output from the forward LSTM, $\overleftarrow{m}_t$ represents the output from the backward LSTM, and p_t represents the t-th element of the input sequence P. The final output m_t is obtained by concatenating the output from both directions. Hence we obtain the contextual representations M^Q, M^A, and M^U for the question, the answer, and the user context, respectively.

3.3 Attention Layer

In the attention layer of UCAN, we adopt a multi-view attention mechanism to capture useful parts of sentences and interactive features among questions, answers, and user contexts.

Self-Attention. The self-attention mechanism aims to be aware of important parts of sentences by assigning different weights to different parts of sentences. Given the question representation M^Q, the question-view self-attention weights can be computed as follows:

$$\lambda^Q = softmax(tanh(M^Q W_s)u_s), \tag{13}$$

where $u_s \in \mathbb{R}^{d_s}$ and $W_s \in \mathbb{R}^{2d_w \times d_s}$ are trainable parameters. d_s is the attention dimension. Similarly, we can obtain the answer-view self-attention weights λ^A and the user-view self-attention weights λ^U.

Co-Attention. Since only parts of the question, the answer, and the user context are relevant to each other, we apply a co-attention mechanism to learn the interaction among them. First, we calculate the co-attention matrix $C \in \mathbb{R}^{l^Q \times l^A}$. Then we perform max-pooling on C by rows and columns to get attention weights. The question-answer-view co-attention mechanism is defined as:

$$C = M^Q U_c (M^A)^T, \tag{14}$$

$$\mu^{QA} = softmax(max\text{-}pooling(C)), \tag{15}$$

$$\mu^{AQ} = softmax(max\text{-}pooling(C^T)), \tag{16}$$

where $U_c \in \mathbb{R}^{2d_w \times 2d_w}$ is a trainable weight matrix and T denotes transpose. Similarly, we can obtain the question-user-view attention weights μ^{QU} and μ^{UQ} for the question and the user context separately.

Attention Fusion. After obtaining the self-attention and co-attention weights, we adopt the attention fusion to fuse the weights adaptively. The attention fusion is formulated as:

$$F^Q = [\lambda^Q, \mu^{QA}, \mu^{QU}], \tag{17}$$

$$\delta^Q = (F^Q)^T softmax(F^Q w^Q), \tag{18}$$

where $[,]$ denotes the row-wise concatenation and $w^Q \in \mathbb{R}^{l^Q}$ is a trainable parameter. We conduct the same operation to get the final attention weights δ^A and δ^U for the answer and the user context, respectively. Finally, the attention representations of the question, the answer, and the user context are given as:

$$r^Q = (\delta^Q)^T M^Q, r^A = (\delta^A)^T M^A, r^U = (\delta^U)^T M^U. \tag{19}$$

3.4   Prediction Layer

In the prediction layer of UCAN, we add a shortcut to facilitate the flow of information. In particular, we apply max-pooling to the output of the context module to capture the main semantic features, denoted as $\widetilde{r}^Q$, $\widetilde{r}^A$, and $\widetilde{r}^U$:

$$\widetilde{r}^Q = max\text{-}pooling(M^Q), \tag{20}$$

$$\widetilde{r}^A = max\text{-}pooling(M^A), \tag{21}$$

$$\widetilde{r}^U = max\text{-}pooling(M^U), \tag{22}$$

Then we concatenate them with the final representations of the question, the answer, and the user context. Therefore, the input of the prediction layer is expressed as $r = [r^Q; \widetilde{r}^Q; r^A; \widetilde{r}^A; r^U; \widetilde{r}^U]$. Then the input vector is passed to fully connected layers with Sigmoid activation to generate the predicted probability p:

$$p = Sigmoid(W_2(tanh(W_1 r) + b_1) + b_2), \tag{23}$$

where W_1 and W_2 are trainable weight matrices, b_1 and b_2 are bias vectors.

During the training process, our model is trained to minimize the binary cross-entropy loss function:

$$L = -\sum_{i=1}^{N}[y_i log p_i + (1 - y_i)log(1 - p_i)] + \lambda ||\theta||_{L_2}, \tag{24}$$

where y is the ground-truth label and p is the predicted probability. N is the size of the training data. $\lambda ||\theta||_{L_2}$ denotes the L_2 regularization.

4   Experiments

4.1   Datasets

We conduct experiments on two widely used CQA datasets from SemEval-2015 Task 3 [9] and SemEval-2017 Task 3 [8] to evaluate the UCAN model. These datasets are collected from the QatarLiving forum. We do not consider the SemEval-2016 dataset, because the SemEval-2017 dataset is the extended version of SemEval-2016 and they share the same evaluation metrics. The statistics of the datasets are shown in Table 2.

4.2   Evaluation Metrics

We adopt three metrics to evaluate our model: F1 Score, Accuracy, and Mean Average Precision (MAP). Following the official task and prior works [16], we adopt F1 Score and Accuracy for the SemEval-2015 dataset. For the SemEval-2017 dataset, MAP is used for evaluation in addition to F1 Score and Accuracy. In the perfect ranking, all *Good* answers are ranked higher than all *Bad* answers for each question.

Table 2. Statistics of SemEval-2015 and SemEval-2017 datasets.

	SemEval-2015			SemEval-2017		
	Train	Dev	Test	Train	Dev	Test
Number of Questions	2,376	266	300	5,124	327	293
Number of Answers	15,013	1,447	1,793	38,638	3,270	2,930
Average Length of Questions	39.37	39.69	39.64	43.14	48.10	54.19
Average Length of Answers	36.03	34.15	37.53	37.95	37.51	39.79

4.3 Baselines

We compare our model with several state-of-the-art models as follows:

- **JAIST** [11] combines multiple features and uses a regression model to predict the quality of answers.
- **BGMN** [17] updates the attention representation of questions and answers iteratively in two directions by memory mechanism and introduces a gate to determine the importance of questions and answers in each iteration.
- **CNN-LSTM-CRF** [18] combines CNN, LSTM, and Conditional Random Fields (CRF) in two different ways to validate the effectiveness of label dependency.
- **QCN** [16] treats the question subject as the primary part of the question, and reduces the redundancy in question representation by aggregating the question body based on similarity and disparity with the question subject.
- **UIA-LSTM-CNN** [15] proposes a hybrid attention mechanism to focus on the informative parts in QA pairs and model users from past answers.
- **AUANN** [19] adopts Generative Adversarial Network (GAN) to reduce the noise from user contexts and captures the contextual information in questions, answers, and user contexts by attention mechanism.
- **BERTDAN** [22] obtains representations of question subjects, question bodies, and answers via the pre-trained model. Besides, it leverages cross-attention and dual-attention fusion to filter noise and capture contextual features in questions and answers.

4.4 Implementation Details

We adopt the base variation of the BERT model as the pre-trained embeddings. The maximum length of the question, the answer, and the user's historical answer are set to 130, 100, and 90, respectively. We use the cosine similarity between the question embeddings and historical answer embeddings to select K historical answers in the user context that is most relevant to the question. The maximum number of answers in the user context K is set to 5 and the threshold t is set to 0.8. The number of convolutional filters is set to 200. The number of attention heads of GAT is set to 3. The hidden dimension of Bi-LSTM is set to 128, and the dimension of the hidden layer is set to 100. We use Adam optimizer to train our model. The batch size and the initial learning rate are set to 100 and 1×10^{-4}, respectively. To avoid overfitting, the dropout rate and L2 regularization are set to 0.3 and 1×10^{-5}, respectively.

4.5   Model Comparisons

The experimental results are shown in Table 3. We can observe that our model UCAN achieves the best performance compared to other baselines. Specifically, on the SemEval-2015 dataset, UCAN shows an improvement of approximately 0.17% and 0.88% over other models in Accuracy and F1 Score, respectively. On the SemEval-2017 dataset, UCAN outperforms other models by at least 0.28%, 3.71%, and 0.31% in Accuracy, F1 Score, and MAP, respectively. It's worth noting that UCAN demonstrates significantly better performance in F1 Score than all other baselines, thereby highlighting its strong classification ability.

Moreover, JAIST outperforms BGMN on the SemEval-2015 dataset, indicating the efficacy of feature engineering even when compared to deep learning models. QCN achieves better results than most models since it condenses question representations by considering the relationship between the question subject and body. AUANN performs better than UIA-LSTM-CNN by filtering noise in the user context using GAN. BERTDAN has an advantage over all other baselines, attributed to the pre-trained model and useful interactive features among the question subject, question body, and answer.

Compared with AUANN and BERTDAN, UCAN aggregates the correlation among historical answers of users into user representations and captures n-gram features by CNN, thus achieving better performance.

Table 3. The performance comparison on two datasets.

Dataset	Model	Accuracy	F1	MAP
SemEval-2015	JAIST	79.10	78.96	–
	BGMN	78.40	77.23	–
	CNN-LSTM-CRF	82.24	82.22	–
	QCN	85.65	83.91	–
	BERTDAN	85.84	84.96	–
	UCAN	**86.01**	**85.84**	–
SemEval-2017	QCN	80.71	78.11	88.51
	UIA-LSTM-CNN	77.13	76.45	87.96
	AUANN	78.46	79.81	89.59
	BERTDAN	82.35	79.39	90.26
	UCAN	**82.63**	**83.10**	**90.57**

4.6   Ablation Study

To analyze the effectiveness of each part in our model, we perform the ablation study by comparing our model with 6 variants:

– UCAN-RUC (Remove User Context) does not use the user context in UCAN.
– UCAN-RGC (Replace user context Graph with Concatenation) removes the user context graph and concatenates the historical answers of the user simply to model user representations.
– UCAN-RHF (Remove Hierarchical Features) discards n-gram features.

- UCAN-RSA (Remove Self-Attention) removes the self-attention mechanism.
- UCAN-RCA (Remove Co-Attention) removes the co-attention mechanism.
- UCAN-RAFC (Replace Attention Fusion with Concatenation) replaces the attention fusion with simple concatenation.

Table 4. Ablation study.

Model	SemEval-2015		SemEval-2017		
	Acc	F1	Acc	F1	MAP
UCAN-RUC	83.71	83.21	81.16	82.34	88.83
UCAN-RGC	82.82	83.64	81.43	81.38	88.37
UCAN-RHF	82.49	83.06	79.25	78.64	87.89
UCAN-RSA	82.32	83.26	80.89	80.86	87.39
UCAN-RCA	82.15	82.49	80.85	81.17	87.48
UCAN-RAFC	84.77	84.29	80.51	80.73	88.49
UCAN	**86.01**	**85.84**	**82.63**	**83.10**	**90.57**

As shown in Table 4, UCAN achieves the best results, thereby validating the effectiveness of each component in our model. Concretely, we can observe that our model outperforms UCAN-RUC, demonstrating the importance of user context in CQA. However, no distinct advantage is observed for UCAN-RGC as compared to UCAN-RUC, suggesting that unintegrated user contexts may introduce irrelevant noise. Comparison between our model and UCAN-RGC indicates that encoding the correlation among historical answers of users by GAT improves performance. Additionally, the results of UCAN-RHF reveal the effectiveness of incorporating n-gram features as a complement to word-level features.

Furthermore, without self-attention or co-attention mechanisms, UCAN-RSA and UCAN-RCA fail to capture the interior or exterior contextual information in the text, resulting in underperformance as compared to our model. Finally, our model outperforms UCAN-RAFC, indicating that failure to adaptively aggregate the multi-view attention reduces effectiveness.

4.7   Case Study

To intuitively understand how our model works, we present an example from the SemEval-2017 dataset and visualize the attention scores of the question and the answer. Figure 3 illustrates the visualization results of self-attention and co-attention mechanisms.

As shown in Fig. 3(a) and Fig. 3(b), the attention mechanism can effectively focus on important words in the question and answer, such as "service", "gratuity", and "contract". While the self-attention mechanism attends only to the text's own information, the co-attention mechanism provides a more informative perspective. Specifically, the self-attention mechanism tends to emphasize some words that are irrelevant to the context, such as "Hi" and "exact". On the other hand, the co-attention mechanism captures the interactive parts, such as "service gratuity" and "contract".

In contrast to the attention visualization on the question in Fig. 3(b), the attention visualization in Fig. 3(c) highlights the words "service", "worked", and "personal", which are more relevant to the user's expertise. Hence, our model is capable of encoding user context to provide useful information.

Question:
Hi all, I would to ask if i can get my end of service gratuity even though i did not finish my contract for 2 years. I worked for 21 months to be exact. I was urged to resign for personal reason.

Answer:
with cause, you are not entitled. But if it is a mutual consent, then you are entitled to all what's mentioned in your contract!

(a) Self-attention of the question and answer.

Question:
Hi all, I would to ask if i can get my end of service gratuity even though i did not finish my contract for 2 years. I worked for 21 months to be exact. I was urged to resign for personal reason.

Answer:
with cause, you are not entitled. But if it is a mutual consent, then you are entitled to all what's mentioned in your contract!

(b) Co-attention between the question and answer.

Question:
Hi all, I would to ask if i can get my end of service gratuity even though i did not finish my contract for 2 years. I worked for 21 months to be exact. I was urged to resign for personal reason.

(c) Co-attention of the question over the user context.

Fig. 3. Visualization of attention on the question and answer.

5 Conclusion and Future Work

In this paper, we propose a new model UCAN for answer selection in CQA. First, we obtain word-level representations of questions, answers, and user contexts by pre-trained BERT. To extract hierarchical features from texts, we apply CNN to learn the n-gram representations. In order to capture the expertise and interests of users effectively, we build a graph and use a graph attention layer to model the correlation among answers in the user context. Furthermore, we learn the contextual representations via Bi-LSTM. Finally, we use a multi-view attention mechanism to comprehensively fetch the interior and exterior semantic features. Experiments on two real-world datasets demonstrate the superiority of our model over state-of-the-art baselines. The quality of user historical answers is uneven and the constructed user context graph is relatively simple. In the future, we will incorporate the entity/keyword and knowledge graph into the user context graph to enhance the user representation.

Acknowledgments. This work is partially supported by National Natural Science Foundation of China Nos. U1811263, 62072349, National Key Research and Development Project of China No. 2020YFC1522602.

References

1. Chen, Q., Wang, J., Lan, X., Zheng, N.: Preference relationship-based CrossCMN scheme for answer ranking in community QA. In: 2019 IEEE International Conference on Data Mining (ICDM), pp. 81–90. IEEE (2019)
2. Deng, Y., et al.: Multi-task learning with multi-view attention for answer selection and knowledge base question answering. In: Proceedings of the AAAI Conference on Artificial Intelligence, vol. 33, pp. 6318–6325 (2019)
3. Deng, Y., Xie, Y., Li, Y., Yang, M., Lam, W., Shen, Y.: Contextualized knowledge-aware attentive neural network: enhancing answer selection with knowledge. ACM Trans. Inf. Syst. (TOIS) **40**(1), 1–33 (2021)
4. Devlin, J., Chang, M., Lee, K., Toutanova, K.: Bert: pre-training of deep bidirectional transformers for language understanding. In: Proceedings of naacL-HLT, pp. 4171–4186 (2019)
5. Gao, Z., Xia, X., Lo, D., Grundy, J.: Technical Q&A site answer recommendation via question boosting. ACM Trans. Softw. Eng. Methodol. (TOSEM) **30**(1), 1–34 (2020)
6. Jing, F., Ren, H., Cheng, W., Wang, X., Zhang, Q.: Knowledge-enhanced attentive learning for answer selection in community question answering systems. Knowl.-Based Syst. **250**, 109117 (2022)
7. Lyu, S., Ouyang, W., Wang, Y., Shen, H., Cheng, X.: What we vote for? Answer selection from user expertise view in community question answering. In: The World Wide Web Conference, pp. 1198–1209 (2019)
8. Nakov, P., et al.: SemEval-2017 task 3: community question answering. In: Proceedings of the 11th International Workshop on Semantic Evaluation (SemEval-2017), pp. 27–48. Association for Computational Linguistics (2017)
9. Nakov, P., Màrquez, L., Magdy, W., Moschitti, A., Glass, J., Randeree, B.: SemEval-2015 task 3: answer selection in community question answering. In: Proceedings of the 9th International Workshop on Semantic Evaluation (SemEval 2015), pp. 269–281. Association for Computational Linguistics (2015)
10. Omari, A., Carmel, D., Rokhlenko, O., Szpektor, I.: Novelty based ranking of human answers for community questions. In: Proceedings of the 39th International ACM SIGIR Conference on Research and Development in Information Retrieval, pp. 215–224. SIGIR '16, Association for Computing Machinery (2016)
11. Tran, Q.H., Tran, D.V., Vu, T., Le Nguyen, M., Pham, S.B.: JAIST: combining multiple features for answer selection in community question answering. In: Proceedings of the 9th International Workshop on Semantic Evaluation (SemEval 2015), pp. 215–219 (2015)
12. Tymoshenko, K., Moschitti, A.: Assessing the impact of syntactic and semantic structures for answer passages reranking. In: Proceedings of the 24th ACM International on Conference on Information and Knowledge Management, pp. 1451–1460 (2015)
13. Veličković, P., Cucurull, G., Casanova, A., Romero, A., Lió, P., Bengio, Y.: Graph attention networks. In: International Conference on Learning Representations (2018). https://openreview.net/forum?id=rJXMpikCZ

14. Wang, D., Nyberg, E.: A long short-term memory model for answer sentence selection in question answering. In: Proceedings of the 53rd Annual Meeting of the Association for Computational Linguistics and the 7th International Joint Conference on Natural Language Processing, pp. 707–712 (2015)

15. Wen, J., Ma, J., Feng, Y., Zhong, M.: Hybrid attentive answer selection in CQA with deep users modelling. In: Proceedings of the AAAI Conference on Artificial Intelligence, vol. 32 (2018)

16. Wu, W., Sun, X., Wang, H.: Question condensing networks for answer selection in community question answering. In: Proceedings of the 56th Annual Meeting of the Association for Computational Linguistics, pp. 1746–1755 (2018)

17. Wu, W., Wang, H., Li, S.: Bi-directional gated memory networks for answer selection. In: Sun, M., Wang, X., Chang, B., Xiong, D. (eds.) CCL/NLP-NABD -2017. LNCS (LNAI), vol. 10565, pp. 251–262. Springer, Cham (2017). https://doi.org/10.1007/978-3-319-69005-6_21

18. Xiang, Y., et al.: Incorporating label dependency for answer quality tagging in community question answering via CNN-LSTM-CRF. In: Proceedings of COLING 2016, the 26th International Conference on Computational Linguistics: Technical Papers, pp. 1231–1241 (2016)

19. Xie, Y., Shen, Y., Li, Y., Yang, M., Lei, K.: Attentive user-engaged adversarial neural network for community question answering. In: Proceedings of the AAAI conference on artificial intelligence, vol. 34, pp. 9322–9329 (2020)

20. Xu, Z., Zheng, H.T., Zhai, S., Wang, D.: Knowledge and cross-pair pattern guided semantic matching for question answering. In: Proceedings of the AAAI Conference on Artificial Intelligence, vol. 34, pp. 9370–9377 (2020)

21. Yang, H., Zhao, X., Wang, Y., Li, M., Chen, W., Huang, W.: DGQAN: dual graph question-answer attention networks for answer selection. In: Proceedings of the 45th International ACM SIGIR Conference on Research and Development in Information Retrieval, pp. 1230–1239 (2022)

22. Yang, H., et al.: BERTDAN: question-answer dual attention fusion networks with pre-trained models for answer selection. In: Mantoro, T., Lee, M., Ayu, M.A., Wong, K.W., Hidayanto, A.N. (eds.) ICONIP 2021. LNCS, vol. 13110, pp. 520–531. Springer, Cham (2021). https://doi.org/10.1007/978-3-030-92238-2_43

23. Yang, M., Chen, L., Lyu, Z., Liu, J., Shen, Y., Wu, Q.: Hierarchical fusion of common sense knowledge and classifier decisions for answer selection in community question answering. Neural Netw. **132**, 53–65 (2020)

24. Yih, S.W.T., Chang, M.W., Meek, C., Pastusiak, A.: Question answering using enhanced lexical semantic models. In: Proceedings of the 51st Annual Meeting of the Association for Computational Linguistics (2013)

25. Zhang, W., Chen, Z., Dong, C., Wang, W., Zha, H., Wang, J.: Graph-based tri-attention network for answer ranking in CQA. In: Proceedings of the AAAI Conference on Artificial Intelligence, vol. 35, pp. 14463–14471 (2021)

26. Zhao, C., Xu, L., Huang, H.: Exploiting user activities for answer ranking in Q&A forums. In: Romdhani, I., Shu, L., Takahiro, H., Zhou, Z., Gordon, T., Zeng, D. (eds.) CollaborateCom 2017. LNICST, vol. 252, pp. 693–703. Springer, Cham (2018). https://doi.org/10.1007/978-3-030-00916-8_63

Towards Robust Token Embeddings for Extractive Question Answering

Xun Yao[1], Junlong Ma[1], Xinrong Hu[1], Jie Yang[2(✉)], Yi Guo[3],
and Junping Liu[1]

[1] School of Computer Science and Artificial Intelligence, Wuhan Textile University,
Wuhan, China
{yaoxun,2015363059,hxr,jpliu}@wtu.edu.cn
[2] School of Computing and Information Technology, University of Wollongong,
Wollongong, Australia
jiey@uow.edu.au
[3] School of Computer, Data and Mathematical Sciences, Western Sydney University,
Penrith, Australia
y.guo@westernsydney.edu.au

Abstract. Extractive Question Answering (EQA) tasks have gained intensive attention in recent years, while Pre-trained Language Models (PLMs) have been widely adopted for encoding purposes. Yet, PLMs typically take as initial input token embeddings and rely on attention mechanisms to extract contextual representations. In this paper, a simple yet comprehensive framework, termed perturbation for alignment (PFA), is proposed to investigate variations towards token embeddings. A robust encoder is further formed being tolerant against the embedding variation and hence beneficial to subsequent EQA tasks. Specifically, PFA consists of two general modules, including the embedding perturbation (a transformation to produce embedding variations) and the semantic alignment (to ensure the representation similarity from original and perturbed embeddings). Furthermore, the framework is flexible to allow several alignment strategies with different interpretations. Our framework is evaluated on four highly-competitive EQA benchmarks, and PFA consistently improves state-of-the-art models.

Keywords: Extractive Question Answering · Token embedding · Contextual representation · Wasserstein distances · Divergence

1 Introduction

Extractive Question Answering (EQA) is a fundamental task for Machine Reading Comprehension (MRC), that aims to identify the answer span (a sequence of continuous words) over the given question and passage. Recent years have witnessed a remarkable success in utilizing Pre-trained Language Models (PLMs) to address EQA [2,6,9]. Approaches usually consist of a three-step process. In the first step, each input token is linked with an **embedding** vector via a predetermined lookup table. The second step is to further utilize those token embeddings and estimate their contextual **representation**, followed by a decision layer

F. Zhang et al. (Eds.): WISE 2023, LNCS 14306, pp. 82–96, 2023.
https://doi.org/10.1007/978-981-99-7254-8_7

(*i.e.*, a binary classifier to identify the start and end position of the answer span) as the last step. Without explicitly mentioned, we refer token **embeddings** as vectors obtained directly from the lookup table, while token **representations** as those obtained using attention mechanisms after the lookup.

The majority research on EQA has focused on extracting contextual-aware representation (the second step) using a variety of attention mechanisms, ranging from the standard self-attention [2], block based [10,12], gated adapter [16], and hierarchical flow [14,18], *etc.* While the contextual representation has been tremendously critical, token embeddings (from the first step) still remain fundamentally significant: (1) as the input to the second step, embeddings have a direct impact on forming the subsequent contextual representation; (2) each token has one initial and fixed embedding (regardless of surrounding context), while the variation of token embeddings towards the downstream task is underexplored.

To alleviate the aforementioned gap, a simple yet comprehensive framework, termed Perturbation for Alignment (PFA), is proposed in this paper (illustrated in Fig. 1). Our framework consists of two main modules, including embeddings perturbation and semantic alignment. The former takes as input the original token embedding to produce its perturbed version.

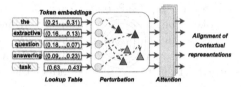

Fig. 1. PFA perturbs initial token embeddings (circles) to form their variations (triangles), and later align their semantic to increase the model robustness and generalizability.

With the presence of perturbed embeddings, the latter module is then enforced to form perturbation-invariant representation via flexible alignment strategies of the Wasserstein distances or other divergence.

Our work differs from existing methods in the following perspectives: (1) PFA strengthens the model generalizability via tolerating variations of token embeddings, which is neglected by the majority of existing work (focusing on subsequent contextual representations). (2) a few studies apply the noise addition ([8], requires the prior knowledge) and dropout mask ([13], depends on the hyperparameter setting) to distort token embedding. Yet, our work offers a more general framework for the embedding perturbation and the representation alignment, embracing previous methods as special cases. The main contributions of our proposed work are summarized as follows, and the source code is available at https://anonymous.4open.science/r/Perturbation4EQA-1BC5:

- Our study introduces a unified framework (Perturbation for Alignment, PFA) to investigate the variation of token embeddings and its influence towards the subsequent Extractive Question Answering task.
- PFA is characterized by embeddings perturbation and semantic alignment modules, while the former perturbs original embeddings and the latter ensures contextual representations (from perturbed embeddings) remain semantically close to original ones.

- The framework is flexible to accommodate many metrics. Specifically, exploiting the Wasserstein distance used in the optimal-transport theory, PFA can be also cast as a general min-max optimization.
- Empirically, PFA outperforms recent-strong baselines on four standard EQA benchmarks, advancing the best state-of-the-arts by on average 1.43 absolute point in accuracy. Moreover, PFA also demonstrates a strong capability in the setting of low-resource fine-tuning and out-of-domain generalizability.

2 Related Work

Given the input pair of question (q) and passage (p), Extractive Question Answering (EQA) aims to identify the start and end positions of the answer span ($a_{s/e}$) from p. Specifically, the input of EQA is a tokenized sequence, *i.e.*, [CLS] $p_1 p_2 \cdots p_{|p|}$ [SEP] $q_1 q_2 \cdots q_{|q|}$ [SEP], where p_i and q_j represent the i-th and j-th token from p and q, respectively. At first, individual tokens (say p_i) are represented by their own static embeddings (say $\mathcal{S}(p_i)$) from a preset lookup table. Then the encoder ($\mathcal{F}$, a Pre-trained Language Model (PLM) such as BERT [2] or RoBERTa [9]) is applied to induce the following probability distribution:

$$p(p_i = a_{s/e}) \triangleq \frac{\exp(\mathcal{F}(\mathcal{S}(p_i))^T w_{s/e})}{\sum_j^{|p|} \exp(\mathcal{F}(\mathcal{S}(p_j))^T w_{s/e})}, \tag{1}$$

where $w_{s/e}$ is the learnable parameter from a decision layer (usually performed as a multilayer perceptron (MLP)). Accordingly, the loss function is defined as follows:

$$\mathcal{L}_{EQA} \triangleq -\sum_i^{|p|} \mathbb{1}(p_i = a_{s/e}) \log p(p_i = a_{s/e}), \tag{2}$$

where $\mathbb{1}(\cdot)$ is the indicator function that returns 1 if the condition is true and returns 0 otherwise. Notably, the majority of existing models focus on utilizing PLMs to form contextual-aware representations via different enhancement strategies. For instance, a block-based attention method is proposed in [12], which predicts answers and supporting words (*i.e.*, contexts highly-relevant to answers). Another similar work is found in [10]. In [14], different-level attention mechanisms are implemented to simulate the process of back-and-forth reading, highlighting, and self-assessment, while [18] simulates the human-reading strategy of reading-attending-excluding to train PLMs. In addition, the work [16] integrates a gated-attention adapter with PLMs to identify answers. More recently, KALA [7] is proposed to integrate the contextual representation of intermediate PLM layers with related entity and relational representations (from the external Knowledge Graph). With knowledge-augmented representations, KALA improves the performance of the vanilla PLM on various EQA tasks.

On the other hand, another line of work considers the embedding-focused strategy. Typically, input tokens are manipulated to produce crafted examples (including token deletion [17] or replacement [11]), which is equivalent to modifying input embeddings. Additionally, Srivastava *et al.* consider to apply the dropout mask on embeddings [13], and SWEP [8] augments them with adjustable noises. The subsequent EQA model is further trained using both original and perturbed embeddings simultaneously. Yet, token manipulation methods could decrease the model accuracy due to over-fitting crafted examples, while other methods require the prior knowledge to select the dropout masking rate [13] or to follow a multivariate Gaussian distribution [8]. In contrast, our work provides a hyperparameter-free transformation framework to perturb token embeddings and later align their semantic to improve the robustness of the encoder.

3   Methodology

The proposed perturbation-for-alignment (PFA) framework is detailed in this section via introducing two general modules: embedding perturbation (EP) and semantic alignment (SA). Specifically, the EP module perturbs input embeddings, while the SA module ensures the semantic-representation similarity from original and perturbed embeddings. Proposed modules are integrated into a unified framework and are fully end-to-end trainable (shown in Fig. 2).

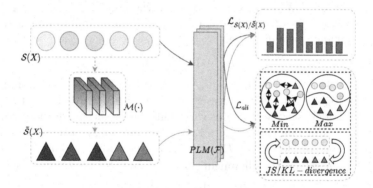

Fig. 2. Illustration of the proposed PFA framework for EQA. Original inputs are distorted via a embedding perturbation module, while their representation similarity is later maximized via a semantic alignment module.

3.1   PFA

Embedding Perturbation. Let $\mathcal{S}(\boldsymbol{X})$ be the embedding for the tokenized passage sequence $\boldsymbol{X}(=\boldsymbol{p}_1\boldsymbol{p}_2\cdots\boldsymbol{p}_{|p|})$. The traditional perturbation mainly involves adding the noise element-wisely ($i.e.$ $\tilde{\mathcal{S}}(\boldsymbol{X}) = \mathcal{S}(\boldsymbol{X}) + \text{noise}$) or sampling with a dropout mask ($i.e.$ $\tilde{\mathcal{S}}(\boldsymbol{X}) = \text{dropout}(\mathcal{S}(\boldsymbol{X}))$). In contrast, this paper introduces a more-general transformation to produce $\tilde{\mathcal{S}}(\boldsymbol{X})$. Specifically, a multilayer perceptron (MLP), written as $\mathcal{M}(\cdot)$, with one-hidden layer is employed. Accordingly, the proposed embedding perturbation is formulated as follows:

$$\tilde{\mathcal{S}}(\boldsymbol{X}) = \mathcal{M}(\mathcal{S}(\boldsymbol{X})). \tag{3}$$

Note that $\mathcal{M}(\cdot)$ can be any function, for example the existing dropout or noise superimposition, which effectively makes the previous methods special cases. The application of MLP here however, provides a family of transformations due to its functional form and well known universal approximation capability.

Additionally, to avoid triviality, *i.e.*, $\mathcal{M}(\cdot)$ being an identity mapping, we employ the bottleneck-structure technique to implement the MLP [4,5], *i.e.*, from which the hidden layer has a smaller size than its adjacent layers. However, we point out that it might not be necessary due to the complex nature of the loss function landscape, especially the non-convexity. Interestingly, the size of the bottleneck becomes a controllable factor, towards generating a better performing $\mathcal{F}$ (which is evaluated in our ablation study). Overall, different from the additive noise or the random dropout, $\mathcal{M}(\cdot)$ offers much greater flexibility to program the perturbed (embedding) distribution within the same space.

Semantic Alignment. With perturbed embeddings, the semantic alignment module is further employed to robustify the encoder $\mathcal{F}$ via tolerating perturbed signals conveyed in $\tilde{\mathcal{S}}(X)$. This is done by explicitly encouraging the representation similarity after encoding original and perturbed embeddings. Let $\mathbf{C}$ and $\tilde{\mathbf{C}}$ represent latent representation associated with original and perturbed embeddings, *i.e.*, $\mathbf{C} = \mathcal{F}(\mathcal{S}(X))$ and $\tilde{\mathbf{C}} = \mathcal{F}(\tilde{\mathcal{S}}(X))$, where $\mathbf{C}/\tilde{\mathbf{C}} \in \mathbb{R}^{|X| \times l}$ and l is the hidden dimension. The alignment objective can be formulated as minimizing the following `instance`-wise distance:

$$\mathcal{L}_{ali}^{i} = \text{dist}(\mathbf{C}, \tilde{\mathbf{C}}), \tag{4}$$

where $\text{dist}(\cdot, \cdot)$ is a distance function. As such, this proposed loss minimization ensures the original semantic is preserved even with perturbations, to further improve the model tolerance to input variations. Moreover, in addition to matching collections of instances as in Eq. (4), one can also align their representations at the `distribution` level. Let $P_{\mathbf{C}}$ and $P_{\tilde{\mathbf{C}}}$ be the corresponding distributions of $\mathbf{C}$ and $\tilde{\mathbf{C}}$. Therefore, the alignment objective can also be reformulated as:

$$\mathcal{L}_{ali}^{d} = \text{dist}(P_{\mathbf{C}}, P_{\tilde{\mathbf{C}}}). \tag{5}$$

The analysis of alternative implementations (including the distance function) will be detailed in Sect. 3.2.

Overall Objective Function. In summary, the following joint loss is utilized for the proposed Perturbation-for-Alignment (PFA) framework:

$$\mathcal{L} = \mathcal{L}_{\mathcal{S}(X)} + \mathcal{L}_{\tilde{\mathcal{S}}(X)} + \mathcal{L}_{ali}^{i/d}, \tag{6}$$

where $\mathcal{L}_{\mathcal{S}(X)}$ represents the standard (cross-entropy) loss using the original embeddings (followed by Eq. (2)), while $\mathcal{L}_{\tilde{\mathcal{S}}(X)}$ is the loss obtained by swapping $\mathcal{S}(\cdot)$ with $\tilde{\mathcal{S}}(\cdot)$ in Eq. (1) and further inferring answers as Eq. (2). The last term then ensures that perturbed embeddings remain semantically close to the original ones. During inference, the EP and SA modules are discarded, and testing samples follow the traditional three steps to: (1) lookup token embeddings, (2) extract latent representation via the trained encoder, (3) apply the trained decision layer to identify the start and end position of answers.

3.2 Analysis

There are many choices for aligning original and perturbed representations, either from the instance (Eq. (4)) or distribution level (Eq. (5)). For instance, the matrix Frobenius Norm and cosine similarity can be leveraged for the instance alignment, *e.g.* forcing representation vectors being similar. In this paper, we are particularly interested in the distribution-level alignment, for which the Wasserstein distance [15] is employed as a measurement:

Definition 1 (Wasserstein distance[15]). *Let $(\mathcal{X},\ d)$ be a Polish metric space, and $p \in [1, \infty]$. For any two probability measures μ, ν on $\mathcal{X}$, the Wasserstein distance of order p between μ and ν is defined by*

$$W_p(\mu, \nu) = \left(\inf_{\pi \in \Pi(\mu,\nu)} \int_{\mathcal{X}} d(x,y)^p d\pi(x,y) \right)^{\frac{1}{p}}, \tag{7}$$

$$s.t. \int_{\mathcal{X}} \pi(x,y)dy = \mu, \quad \int_{\mathcal{X}} \pi(x,y)dx = \nu.$$

where $\Pi(\mu, \nu)$ is the set of all couplings of μ and ν.

It is metrized version of the optimal transportation (OT) cost, where $d(x, y)$ is replaced by a cost function $c(x, y) \geq 0$ that is not necessarily a metric. The one we are particularly interested in is W_1, *i.e.*, when $p = 1$, usually called Kantorovich-Rubinstein distance. In a nutshell, the Wasserstein distance or OT cost is measuring the dissimilarity of two sets exhausting all possible joint probabilities given that the marginal probabilities are fixed. This is an ideal choice towards our purpose of aligning representations from original and perturbed embeddings. Notably, there are many variants for the OT cost, for example the Sinkhorn distance [1], defined for discrete observations. Therefore, the proposed SA module is not limited to a particular measure but open to vast possibilities. One interesting extension comes from the dual form of Eq. (7) [15]:

$$W_1(\mu, \nu) = \sup_{f, \|f\|_{\text{Lip}} \leq 1} \left\{ \int_{\mathcal{X}} f d\mu - \int_{\mathcal{X}} f d\nu \right\}, \tag{8}$$

where f is a measurable function defined from $\mathcal{X}$ to $\mathbb{R}$ and $\|f\|_{\text{Lip}}$ is the Lipschitz constant of f, *a.k.a* $\|f\|_{\text{Lip}} = \inf\{c : cd(x,y) \geq |f(x) - f(y)|\}, \forall x, y \in \mathcal{X}$. The dual form of W_1 distance indicates that one can maximize Eq. (8) over all nicely smooth functions defined on $\mathcal{X}$ to obtain its value. In our context, if we choose μ and ν to be probability measures of embeddings, *i.e.*, $\mathcal{S}(\boldsymbol{X})$ and $\tilde{\mathcal{S}}(\boldsymbol{X})$, then Eq. (8) shows that W_1 distances between these two distributions is the largest mode differences under all smooth transformations as the integrals are exactly the expectations of f. This not only gives us the interpretation of the distribution alignment, but also provides a way to compute the W_1 distance approximately, for example, via a regularization

$$W_1(\mu, \nu) \approx \max_f \int_{\mathcal{X}} f d\mu - \int_{\mathcal{X}} f d\nu - \gamma \int_{\mathcal{X}} \|\nabla f\|^2 d\xi, \tag{9}$$

for a hyperparameter $\gamma \geq 0$ (*e.g.* $\gamma = 1$). Note that the regularization term, the last term in Eq. (9), which is an integral with respect to some Radon measure ξ, is to clamp f roughly to be 1-Lipschitz. To further simplify the computation, we choose

$$\xi = (1 - \alpha)\mu + \alpha\nu, \qquad (10)$$

for any $\alpha \in (0, 1)$. Accordingly, Eq. (9) can be effectively rewritten as the following

$$W_1(\mu, \nu) \approx \max_f \int_{\mathcal{X}} (f - \gamma(1 - \alpha)\|\nabla f\|^2)d\mu - \int_{\mathcal{X}} (f + \gamma\alpha\|\nabla f\|^2)d\nu, \qquad (11)$$

where the integrals can be computed easily by evaluating expectation. We point out that the value of α is not critical as we minimize this distance so that μ and ν become more or less the same.

Additionally, although f is nothing more than a dummy function in Eq. (9), one can have a preference on its structure and hence assign some meaning to it at the cost of further restricting the approximation capacity to the original W_1 distance. Specifically, in this paper we consider

$$f = \mathcal{H} \circ \mathcal{F}, \qquad (12)$$

where $\mathcal{H}$ is a function that maps the output of $\mathcal{F}$ to $\mathbb{R}$. If we set $\mathcal{H}$ to be a binary MLP classifying instances from either $\mathcal{S}(\boldsymbol{X})$ or $\tilde{\mathcal{S}}(\boldsymbol{X})$, which is the choice in our numerical experiments, then the proposed PFA can be cast as a **min-max** optimization, *i.e.*, combining Eq. (9) with the minimization of Eq. (6), such that f cannot differentiate two distributions. Based on this understanding, we reach to Eq. (5) that admits more choices, such as the Kullback-Leibler (KL) divergence and Jensen-Shannon (JS) divergence. These divergences also serve for the purpose of Eq. (5) exactly to align $P_{\mathbf{C}}$ and $P_{\tilde{\mathbf{C}}}$.

4   Experiment

4.1   Setup

Experiments and analysis are carried out on four benchmark datasets from MRQA 2019 [3], including SQuAD (1.1), HotpotQA, NewsQA, and NaturalQ. Their statistics are shown in Table 1.

Table 1. Employed datasets for the EQA task, where **Domain** represents the passage resource, and **#Train** and **#Test** is the number of training and test samples, respectively.

Dataset	Domain	#Train	#Test
SQuAD(1.1)	Wikipedia	86,588	10,507
HotpotQA	Wikipedia	72,928	5,904
NewsQA	News articles	74,160	4,212
NaturalQ	Wikipedia	104,071	12,836

Training Details. The RoBERTa-base model [9] is adopted as the contextual encoder, with the dropout rate of 0.1. The Adam optimizer with a dynamic learning rate is adopted, for which the learning rate is warmed up for 10 thousand steps to a maximum value of $1e^{-4}$ before decaying linearly to a minimum value of $2e^{-5}$ (by the cosine annealing). The training is performed with batches of 8 sequences of length 512. The maximal number of training epoch is 10. The F1-evaluation metric, measured by the number of overlapping tokens between the predicted and ground-truth answers, is adopted. At last, all models are performed using a machine of the NVIDIA A100 GPU server.

4.2 Main Results

Our proposed PFA method is compared with several baseline models:

- Base [9] is implemented via fine-tuning the RoBERTa-base model.
- BLANC [12] applies a block-attention strategy to predict answers and supporting contexts (spans surrounding around answers) simultaneously[1];
- SSMBA [11] randomly substitutes tokens with [Mask] to modify input embeddings, and then recovers them to produce new samples[2];
- SWEP [8] augments the data by perturbing the input embedding with an adjustable Gaussian noise[3];
- KALA [7] augments the original contextual representation using related entity and relational representation from the external Knowledge Graph[4].

Notably, SSMBA, SWEP and KALA can be cast as the data-augmentation methods, from the perspectives of either modifying input tokens or introducing external knowledge. Therefore, PFA is compared with them specifically to evaluate its capability on the data augmentation, as perturbed embeddings also play a role in bringing additional training samples. All contender methods are re-implemented using their released code packages and kept with the original configurations. Additionally, the embedding perturbation (EP) module is implemented using a one-hidden-layer MLP with the bottleneck structure, where the size for the input, hidden (or **bottleneck**) and output layer is 768, 500, and 768, respectively, and a LeakyReLU activation function. For the semantic alignment (SA) module, the W_1 distance is adopted together with a binary classifier for $\mathcal{H}$ (from Eq. (12)), and $\alpha = 0.5$.

The comparison from Table 2 provides the strong evidence for the proposed PFA in addressing the EQA task. The proposed method consistently improves the state-of-the-art models. For instance, PFA outperforms the strongest baseline (SWEP) by 1.4, 0.7, 1.6, and 2.0 absolute points with respect to the SQuAD, HotpotQA, NewsQA, and NaturalQ datasets, respectively. We also notice that the KALA method relies on the quality of the constructed Knowledge Graph,

---

[1] available from https://github.com/yeonsw/BLANC.
[2] available from https://github.com/nng555/ssmba.
[3] available from https://github.com/seanie12/SWEP.
[4] available from https://github.com/Nardien/KALA.

Table 2. Comparison among PFA and existing methods, in which the best result is **bolded**. Statistically significant gains achieved by the proposed method at p-values <0.01 are marked with †.

	SQuAD	HotpotQA	NewsQA	NaturalQ
Base	90.3 ± 0.2	78.7 ± 0.3	69.8 ± 0.4	79.6 ± 0.2
BLANC	91.1 ± 0.2	77.8 ± 0.1	70.7 ± 0.5	80.3 ± 0.1
SSMBA	90.1 ± 0.3	77.3 ± 0.4	69.2 ± 0.2	79.8 ± 0.2
SWEP	91.0 ± 0.1	78.6 ± 0.2	71.7 ± 0.1	80.2 ± 0.3
KALA	90.9 ± 0.4	77.3 ± 0.5	72.7 ± 0.3	80.1 ± 0.4
PFA	$\mathbf{92.4 \pm 0.2}$†	$\mathbf{79.3 \pm 0.1}$†	$\mathbf{73.3 \pm 0.4}$†	$\mathbf{82.2 \pm 0.3}$†

which leads to a notable performance variation. For instance, KALA achieves a even worse result than the Base model on the HotpotQA dataset. In addition, the significance test (*i.e.*, the one-sample T-test) is also implemented, and the p-values of our results being greater than relevant strongest baselines are $6.2e^{-6}$, $1.3e^{-7}$, $5.6e^{-7}$, and $4.9e^{-8}$, respectively. The results clearly verifies the effectiveness and stability of our proposed method.

On the other hand, in terms of the computational complexity, PFA has a similar scale of parameters as the vanilla model (RoBERTa-base). Specifically, during training PFA only needs additional parameters of two MLP classifiers for Eq. (3) and Eq. (12); that is, approximately 2.4M parameters are added (compared to the original 128.0M of RoBERTa-base). During inference, both the EP and SA modules are discarded as PFA only requires the trained encoder.

4.3 Ablation Study

Experiments are conducted using the SQuAD dataset, and all results are reported as an averaged F1 over 10 runs.

On the Encoder Flexibility. We first evaluate the impact from the fundamental encoder. Specifically, the BERT-base encoder [2] is employed as the **Base**, and the strongest baseline **SWEP** and **KALA** from Table 2 is also re-implemented. Most of the experimental settings, such as the batch size and the sequence length, are the same as RoBERTa, except the

Table 3. Impact analysis of the underlying encoder.

	Base	SWEP	KALA	PFA
SQuAD	88.6	89.4	89.2	89.7
HotpotQA	74.9	75.1	75.3	75.8
NewsQA	64.7	65.4	65.8	66.6
NaturalQ	77.1	77.7	77.5	78.8

learning rate is set as $3e^{-5}$. Comparison results are presented in Table 3, where PFA demonstrates highest F1 scores across all datasets. These findings highlight the stability/robustness of PFA on the underlying encodes (both RoBERTa and BERT), outperforming current best models. To maintain consistency, subsequent ablation studies are still conducted using RoBERTa.

On the Breakdown. We investigate individual aspects of EP and SA to manifest their efficacy. Specifically, for comparison purposes we take "Base" to represent the vanilla training; "Base+EP" applies both original and perturbed embeddings for fine-tuning the model; "Base+SA" considers to utilize original embeddings, without perturbed ones, for the model training, in addition to the semantic similarity of original-perturbed pairs. The EP is implemented using a MLP with a Bottleneck layer of the size 500 and the W_1 distance for SA.

The results are summarized in Table 4, while all variants stably improve F1 scores. Specifically, with both original and perturbed embeddings (*i.e.*, Base+EP), the model obtains 91.2, indicating the benefit of employing perturbation as a special data augmentation. Interestingly, we also observe that the Base+SA model achieves a even higher performance (91.7). Notably, the SA

Table 4. Effect of individual modules on F1.

	Base	Base+EP
F1	90.3	91.2

	Base+SA	Base+EP+SA
F1	91.7	92.4

module enforces the similarity representation of original-perturbed pairs. That is, the encoder is fine-tuned so that the presentation of perturbed embeddings is similar to that of original ones. The perturbation tolerance of the encoder is enhanced, leading to a better F1 score. Empirically, SA brings a larger performance boost, in comparison with EP, which indicates the importance of imposing the semantic alignment to the embedding perturbation.

On the EP module. In addition to the MLP generator in Eq. (3), we also consider to perturb embeddings via an element-wise noise addition and a dropout mask, respectively, while the SA module is fixed using the W_1 distance. Specifically, let $\Delta(> 0)$ be a pre-determined hyperparameter ($\Delta \in$

Table 5. Effect of different EP implementations including the noise addition and dropout mask.

Δ	0.1	0.3	0.5	0.7	0.9
Noise	91.1	91.4	91.4	91.2	91.3
Dropout	91.0	91.1	91.3	91.2	90.8

{0.1, 0.3, 0.5, 0.7, 0.9}). Accordingly, the noise is then introduced to follow a uniform distribution on $[-\Delta, \Delta]$ or applying a dropout rate as Δ. The comparison is shown in Table 5, while the performance from the noise and dropout perturbation is clearly worse than that of MLP (92.4). The reason could be the structural change as a perturbation introduced by the MLP is stronger than that of noise and dropout, and therefore better in robustifying the encoder $\mathcal{F}$ (to tolerate more variation).

On the other hand, as discussed in the *Analysis* section, the choice of α (from Eq. (10)) is not critical. Herein we also evaluate the impact from α empirically. The result from Table 6 illustrates that PFA is insensitive to α, as a stable performance (with *std.* of ±0.15) is achieved.

Table 6. Effect of α

α	0.1	0.3	0.5	0.7	0.9
F1	92.3	92.4	92.4	92.3	92.7

On the SA Module. Additionally, the SA's effect is also studied while fixing EP as the MLP. In other words, we simply replace the W_1 distance with

Table 7. Effect of the SA module with different implementations, including the instance-level (*cos*) and the distribution-level (KL, JS, and W_1) alignment.

	cos	KL	JS	W_1
SQuAD	92.2	92.4	92.3	92.4
HotpotQA	78.6	79.1	78.8	79.3
NewsQA	73.0	73.4	73.5	73.3
NaturalQ	82.1	82.2	82.2	82.2

the instance-level alignment (*i.e.*, *cos*ine similarity) and the distribution level of the Kullback-Leibler (KL) and Jensen-Shannon (JS) divergence, respectively; all other hyperparameters and structures are unchanged, although they might be suboptimal for those variants.

Comparisons are summarized in Table 7, and *cos* is associated with a lowest result, suggesting the rigidness of aligning from the instance level that slightly compromises the performance. Yet, the averaged performance from *cos* is still notably higher than that of Base (using the vanilla RoBERTa-base model). Other than that, both the KL and JS divergence lead to competitive performances as W_1, which empirically indicates the flexibility of the proposed SA module.

On the Bottleneck Layer. The EP module implements a bottleneck structure of MLP (as shown in Eq. (3)) to avoid the trivial solution (*i.e.*, an identity mapping), although it is very unlikely to happen in the optimization process (due to complex loss function landscapes in terms of model parameters). To investigate the impact from the structure, specifically, we vary the size of the hidden (or bot-

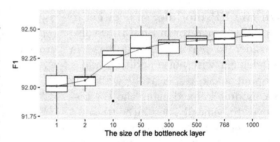

Fig. 3. Boxplot of F1 performance as the function of the size of the bottleneck layer in the EP module. The red curve shows the trend of the mean F1. (Color figure online)

tleneck) layer, in $\{1, 2, 10, 50, 300, 500, 768, 1000\}$, and the corresponding result, using the SQuAD dataset, as reported in Fig. 3. Clearly, we observed the larger size leads to the better performance in the statistical sense. Even with 1 hidden neuron, our method still achieves an averaged 91.95 F1 score (better than 90.30 of Base). We conjecture that more neurons increase the MLP modeling power, which may in turn give stronger perturbation and hence further improves the encoder's tolerance to the embedding variation.

On the Low-Resource Fine-Tuning. The following experiment validates PFA with the low-resource setting, as perturbed embeddings also play a role in providing additional (training) data. Accordingly, only a small amount (say k) of (randomly-selected) training samples are utilized for fine-tuning PFA, where $k = \{20\%, 40\%, 60\%, 80\%, 100\%\}$ (100% represents the full dataset). Fig. 4 shows the averaged F1-performance obtained with different percentages of training samples for the SQuAD dataset. Compared to the Base and SWEP (the strongest baseline from Table 2), PFA significantly improves the model performance with all percentages of the training samples. For instance, with only 40% of labeled data, PFA has achieved even higher accuracy than SWEP with 80% samples. Empirically, the result demonstrates the superiority of the proposed PFA on training robust encoders with the presence of perturbation samples; accordingly, the latent representation is strengthened thanks to the robustness of the encoder, and in turn enhances the downstream performance.

On Out-of-Domain Generalizability. At last, PFA is evaluated via the model generalizability. Specifically, following SSMBA and SWEP, the model is first trained on a single source dataset (SQuAD in this case), and further evaluated on unseen datasets (*i.e.*, HotpotQA, NewsQA, and NaturalQ) without further fine-tuning.

The averaged F1 scores obtained using the proposed and existing methods is presented in Fig. 5. Clearly, a direct application of the Base model to downstream dataset (the vanilla RoBERTa-base model trained from SQuAD) achieves the worst F1 (60.1 on average), which indicates the distribution difference from diverse datasets and the low model generalizability (from SQuAD to others). Additionally, SWEP is observed with a better F1 performance (61.3), while PFA scores the best performance (63.5) on average across three target datasets. Due to perturbed embeddings, PFA enforces the encoder to produce more perturbation-invariant (in comparison with original token embeddings) representation, which significantly contributes to the model flexibility and generalizability. The result further indicates that PFA offers a robust starting point for fine-tuning downstream tasks, that can also be regarded as a supplementary pre-training strategy.

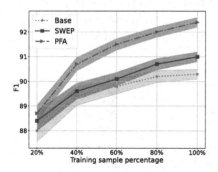

Fig. 4. Averaged F1-accuracy as a function of the training sample size.

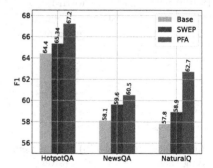

Fig. 5. Comparative F1-accuracy for the out-of-domain generalizability.

4.4 Qualitative Study

We further investigate the model characteristic via visualizing the iterative loss evolution and the formed embedding/representation space.

Loss Visualization. Figure 6 illustrates the iterative training loss obtained from the EQA loss (*i.e.* $\mathcal{L}_S + \mathcal{L}_{\tilde{S}}$ from Eq. (6)) against the semantic alignment (Wasserstein) loss (*i.e.* $\mathcal{L}_{ali}^d$ from Eq. (6)), for the SQuAD dataset. The learning curve shows that the EQA and alignment loss are well balanced, which justifies the simple choice of the weights for all loss components (currently all 1 for three losses).

On the other hand, one can also add weights during the loss formulation, for example, $\mathcal{L} = \mathcal{L}_{S(X)} + \lambda_1 \mathcal{L}_{\tilde{S}(X)} + \lambda_2 \mathcal{L}_{ali}^{i/d}$, to allow more control. However, a detailed study on the choice of λ_1 and λ_2 is required and we leave it as future research.

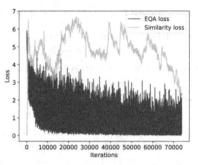

Token Embedding and Representation Visualization. We further visualize the latent space formed by the token embedding and subsequent representation, shown in Fig. 7. This 2D visualization is performed using the PCA to reduce the token embedding and representation dimension and visualize one passage sample from the SQuAD dataset.

Fig. 6. Loss visualization with the training iteration. The orange and blue curves are alignment and EQA loss respectively.

Clearly, the perturbation projects the initial token embeddings (Fig. 7(a)) to different locations (Fig. 7(b)). This comparison evidences the proposed embedding perturbation module via producing embedding variations. On the other hand, relevant contextualized representations obtained with/out the perturbation are still similar, shown in Fig. 7(c) and (d) respectively. That demonstrates the encoder robustness of being tolerant against embedding variations and generating similar representations, from the semantic alignment module.

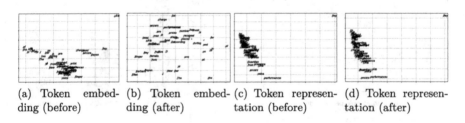

(a) Token embedding (before) (b) Token embedding (after) (c) Token representation (before) (d) Token representation (after)

Fig. 7. The 2D PCA visualization of token embedding and representation before and after the EP and SA module, using one SQuAD example (the first 70 tokens) with the ID of e5348d10-cd31-11ed-b387-97a8ff18f3ed.

5   Conclusion

This paper investigates the task of Extractive Question Answering (EQA), for which a span of passage tokens are identified as answers to the given question. Existing methods mainly focus on the contextual-aware representation, while the impact from input token embeddings is underexplored. In this paper, a Perturbation for Alignment (PFA) framework is introduced to bridge this gap. Concretely, an embedding perturbation module utilizes a general transformation to produce embedding variations, while a semantic aliment module ensures the representation similarity between the original and perturbed embeddings. The goal is to strengthen the encoder so that the generated representation is stable against the embedding variation and hence beneficial to subsequent EQA tasks. This framework is also versatile due to many interpretations in terms of the semantic alignment unified under the Wasserstein-distance dual form. Intensive experiments based on four benchmarking datasets are conducted, and PFA obtains notable improvements compared to state-of-the-arts. To our knowledge, this is the first work that explores the token-embedding variation and its impact on EQA, while existing work focus on the token representation aspect. We will continue exploring this idea for other downstream tasks as our future work.

Acknowledgments. This work was partially supported by the Australian Research Council Discovery Project (DP210101426) and AEGiS Advance Grant(888/008/268), University of Wollongong.

References

1. Cuturi, M.: Sinkhorn distances: lightspeed computation of optimal transport. In: Burges, C., Bottou, L., Welling, M., Ghahramani, Z., Weinberger, K. (eds.) Advances in Neural Information Processing Systems, vol. 26 (2013)
2. Devlin, J., Chang, M.W., Lee, K., Toutanova, K.: BERT: pre-training of deep bidirectional transformers for language understanding. In: Proceedings of the 2019 Conference of the North American Chapter of the Association for Computational Linguistics: Human Language Technologies, Volume 1 (Long and Short Papers), pp. 4171–4186. Association for Computational Linguistics, Minneapolis, Minnesota (2019)
3. Fisch, A., Talmor, A., Jia, R., Seo, M., Choi, E., Chen, D.: MRQA 2019 shared task: evaluating generalization in reading comprehension. In: Proceedings of the 2nd Workshop on Machine Reading for Question Answering, pp. 1–13. Association for Computational Linguistics, Hong Kong, China (2019)
4. Gehring, J., Miao, Y., Metze, F., Waibel, A.: Extracting deep bottleneck features using stacked auto-encoders. In: 2013 IEEE International Conference on Acoustics, Speech and Signal Processing, pp. 3377–3381 (2013)
5. Goodfellow, I., Bengio, Y., Courville, A.: Deep Learning. MIT Press, Cambridge (2016). http://www.deeplearningbook.org
6. Joshi, M., Chen, D., Liu, Y., Weld, D.S., Zettlemoyer, L., Levy, O.: SpanBERT: improving pre-training by representing and predicting spans, vol. 8, pp. 64–77. MIT Press, Cambridge, MA (2020)

7. Kang, M., Baek, J., Hwang, S.J.: KALA: knowledge-augmented language model adaptation. In: Proceedings of the 2022 Conference of the North American Chapter of the Association for Computational Linguistics: Human Language Technologies, pp. 5144–5167. Association for Computational Linguistics, Seattle, United States (2022). https://doi.org/10.18653/v1/2022.naacl-main.379, https://aclanthology.org/2022.naacl-main.379

8. Lee, S., Kang, M., Lee, J., Hwang, S.J.: Learning to perturb word embeddings for out-of-distribution QA. In: Proceedings of the 59th Annual Meeting of the Association for Computational Linguistics and the 11th International Joint Conference on Natural Language Processing (Volume 1: Long Papers), pp. 5583–5595. Association for Computational Linguistics (2021)

9. Liu, Y., et al.: RoBERTa: A robustly optimized BERT pretraining approach. ArXiv preprint abs/1907.11692. (019)

10. Luo, D., et al.: Evidence augment for multiple-choice machine reading comprehension by weak supervision. In: Farkaš, I., Masulli, P., Otte, S., Wermter, S. (eds.) ICANN 2021. LNCS, vol. 12895, pp. 357–368. Springer, Cham (2021). https://doi.org/10.1007/978-3-030-86383-8_29

11. Ng, N., Cho, K., Ghassemi, M.: SSMBA: self-supervised manifold based data augmentation for improving out-of-domain robustness. In: Proceedings of the 2020 Conference on Empirical Methods in Natural Language Processing (EMNLP), pp. 1268–1283. Association for Computational Linguistics (2020)

12. Seonwoo, Y., Kim, J.H., Ha, J.W., Oh, A.: Context-aware answer extraction in question answering. In: Proceedings of the 2020 Conference on Empirical Methods in Natural Language Processing (EMNLP), pp. 2418–2428. Association for Computational Linguistics (2020)

13. Srivastava, N., Hinton, G., Krizhevsky, A., Sutskever, I., Salakhutdinov, R.: Dropout: a simple way to prevent neural networks from overfitting. J. Mach. Learn. Res. **15**(56), 1929–1958 (2014)

14. Sun, K., Yu, D., Yu, D., Cardie, C.: Improving machine reading comprehension with general reading strategies. In: Proceedings of the 2019 Conference of the North American Chapter of the Association for Computational Linguistics: Human Language Technologies, Volume 1 (Long and Short Papers), pp. 2633–2643. Association for Computational Linguistics, Minneapolis, Minnesota (2019)

15. Villani, C.: Optimal Transport Old and New. Grundlehren der mathematischen Wissenschaften, vol. 338. Springer, Berlin (2009). https://doi.org/10.1007/978-3-540-71050-9

16. Wang, R., et al.: K-Adapter: infusing knowledge into pre-trained models with adapters. In: Findings of the Association for Computational Linguistics: ACL-IJCNLP 2021, pp. 1405–1418. Association for Computational Linguistics (2021)

17. Wei, J., Zou, K.: EDA: easy data augmentation techniques for boosting performance on text classification tasks. In: Proceedings of the 2019 Conference on Empirical Methods in Natural Language Processing and the 9th International Joint Conference on Natural Language Processing (EMNLP-IJCNLP), pp. 6382–6388. Association for Computational Linguistics, Hong Kong, China (2019)

18. Zhang, C., et al.: Read, attend, and exclude: multi-choice reading comprehension by mimicking human reasoning process. In: Proceedings of the 43rd International ACM SIGIR Conference on Research and Development in Information Retrieval, SIGIR 2020, pp. 1945–1948. Association for Computing Machinery, New York (2020)

Math Information Retrieval with Contrastive Learning of Formula Embeddings

Jingyi Wang[1,2,3] and Xuedong Tian[1,2,3(✉)]

[1] School of Cyber Security and Computer, Hebei University, Baoding 071002, China
jingyiwang571@126.com, Xuedong_tian@126.com
[2] Institute of Intelligent Image and Document Information Processing, Hebei University, Baoding 071002, China
[3] Hebei Machine Vision Engineering Research Center, Hebei University, Baoding 071002, China

Abstract. The core and hard part of Mathematical Information Retrieval (MathIR) is formula retrieval. The datasets used for formula retrieval are usually scientific documents containing formulas. However, there is a lack of labeled datasets specifically for formula similarity. Contrastive learning can learn general features of datasets from unlabeled data and autonomously discover latent structures in the data. Furthermore, dense retrieval methods based on bi-encoders have gained increasing attention. Therefore, we propose CLFE, a simple framework for contrastive learning of formula embeddings. It can learn the latent structure and content information of formulas from unlabeled formulas and generate formula embeddings for formula retrieval. We design two frameworks, Contrastive Presentation MathML-Content MathML Learning and Contrastive LaTeX-MathML Learning, which initialize the encoders using transformer-based models and can produce superior LaTeX, Presentation MathML, and Content MathML embeddings for each formula. The combination of these three embeddings results in the Add embedding and Concat embedding. Finally, the formula retrieval task is achieved by finding the k nearest formulas in the vector space through nearest neighbor search. Experimental results show that when applying our proposed method on the NTCIR-12 dataset to retrieve 20 non-wildcard formulas and scoring the top-10 results, the highest achieved scores for mean P@10, mean nDCG@10, and MAP@10 are 0.6250, 0.9792, and 0.9381.

Keywords: Information Retrieval · Math Information Retrieval · Contrastive Learning · Dense Retrieval · Formula Embedding

1 Introduction

In the information age, the doubling cycle of human knowledge is constantly shortening, and the amount of information is growing explosively. How to quickly and efficiently retrieve high-quality information from massive data has become

F. Zhang et al. (Eds.): WISE 2023, LNCS 14306, pp. 97–107, 2023.
https://doi.org/10.1007/978-981-99-7254-8_8

increasingly essential. Text-based information retrieval systems have been widely applied, providing great convenience for study and scientific research. However, mathematical formulas, as an important part of scientific documents, pose a more challenging retrieval task due to their unique two-dimensional structure. Additionally, the current formula datasets are mostly unlabeled, and the definition of similar formulas is relatively ambiguous, making it impossible to obtain corresponding formula encoding models through effective supervised learning.

Nowadays, structured documents are becoming increasingly accessible. Ar5iv offers HTML5 articles from arXiv as converted with latexml, where formulas are mainly represented in LaTeX and MathML. MathML is an XML-based markup language used to encode both the presentation of mathematical notation for high-quality visual display, and mathematical content. A formula can be represented in two ways: Presentation MathML (PMML), which uses tags to describe the appearance of the formula, and Content MathML (CMML), which uses semantic tags to provide mathematical meaning. Unlike MathML, LaTeX can also represent a formula, focusing on the symbol layout. In the NTCIR12 dataset [11], each formula has three representations: PMML, CMML, and LaTeX. In other words, PMML, CMML, and LaTeX are three distinct representations that can uniquely represent the same formula. Theoretically, these three representations should be embedded into the same point in the same vector space. From a sampling perspective, any two of them form natural positive sample pairs.

Recently, dense retrieval [3] has achieved good performance in text retrieval. It usually constructs a bi-encoder to encode the query and the document separately, where the encoder generally uses a transformer-based encoder, and finally outputs the corresponding fixed-length embeddings, namely dense vector. However, dense retrieval has not been widely used in MathIR.

In this paper, we present CLFE, a simple framework for contrastive learning of formula embeddings, which can learn general features of formulas from unlabeled formulas and generate formula embeddings for formula retrieval. Firstly, a siamese contrastive Presentation MathML-Content MathML learning framework is designed to train MathMLM, a Mathematical Markup Language Model to encode PMML and CMML. Secondly, a pseudo-siamese contrastive LaTeX-MathML learning framework is designed to train CLFE, which encodes LaTeX, PMML, and CMML of formulas into corresponding 768-dimensional embeddings. The idea behind formula retrieval is to embed all formulas from a formula collection into a vector space. During search, the query is embedded into the same vector space, and the closest embeddings from the collection are found.

2   Related Work

2.1   Formula Retrieval

Formula retrieval methods can be roughly categorized into three types: text-based methods, tree-based methods, and embedding-based methods.

Text-based methods typically involve transforming formulas into linearized text and then using traditional text retrieval models for searching. For instance,

Term Frequency and Inverse Document Frequency (TF-IDF) is used in MIaS [9] for indexing documents. Text-based retrieval methods cannot capture the hierarchical structure information of formulas well.

Tree-based methods usually represent formulas as trees and perform retrieval by comparing subtrees or paths. Approach0 [13] extracts leaf-root paths from operator trees to form path sets. It calculates both structural and symbolic similarity between queries and documents using the path set to find subtrees with the same structure and matching subexpressions. Tangent-S [1] obtains candidates by matching symbol tuples, then aligns queries and formulas by computing three structural similarity scores between queries and candidates, and combines the scores using linear regression. Finally, the results of Symbol Layout Tree (SLT) and Operator Tree (OPT) are combined to obtain the final similarity score.

Embedding-based methods convert various forms of formulas into vectors and returns retrieval results based on similarity measures. Mansouri et al. [7] propose an embedding model called Tangent-CFT for formulas represented by SLT and OPT. They linearize mathematical expressions to generate SLT and OPT tuples, tokenize the formula tuples, use FastText to embed formulas. Mansouri et al. [6] apply the Abstract Meaning Representation (AMR) to formula retrieval, resulting in MathAMR, which can be used to represent sentences containing formulas. MathAMR integrates AMR graphs and operator tree. In the retrieval phase, a linearized MathAMR graph is embedded using Sentence-BERT.

Here, we will introduce a novel formula embedding model that can directly encode formulas in the LaTeX, PMML, and CMML format into dense vectors.

2.2 Contrastive Learning

Contrastive learning learns general features of unlabeled datasets by distinguishing between similar and dissimilar data. ConVIRT [12] learns medical visual representations from naturally paired medical images and descriptive texts. By relying on a bidirectional objective between two modalities, ConVIRT contrasts the image representations with the paired text representations. Among PMML, CMML, and LaTeX, each pair also forms a natural pairing. We follow the contrastive learning approach used in SimCSE [2] and ConVIRT, and the training objective is based on the cross-entropy objective with in-batch negatives.

Alignment and Uniformity. Wang et al. [10] identify two key properties related to the contrastive loss: alignment and uniformity. Alignment measures the proximity between positive samples, while uniformity assesses the dispersion of embeddings in the vector space. These two properties are quantified as optimizable metrics $\mathcal{L}_{align}$ and $\mathcal{L}_{uniform}$. In the subsequent sections, we will apply these two properties to evaluate the formula embedding model during training.

3   Formula Embedding Model

3.1   Encoding MathML and LaTeX

For the MathML (including PMML and CMML) encoder f_m, we use MarkupLM [4] followed by a mean-pooling layer over all output vectors, since MathML is classed as markup languages. MarkupLM extracts the Document Object Model (DOM) tree and generates an XPath expression for each node in the markup-language-based document. Specifically, the tag dictionary of MarkupLM is replaced with MathML elements for the embedding model dedicated to formulas.

For the LaTeX encoder f_x, we use the Sentence-transformer [8], as LaTeX strings consist of a sequence of symbols. Specifically, we choose the pre-trained model "all-mpnet-base-v2" from the Sentence-transformer to initialize the LaTeX encoder, which maps sentences into a 768-dimensional dense vector.

3.2   Contrastive Presentation MathML-Content MathML Learning

The model in this section called MathMLM is expected to obtain four aspects of information: two formula embeddings, the meaning of MathML elements, the latent relation between PMML and CMML, as well as the structure and content information of formulas. MathMLM learns the representation of formulas by maximizing agreement between PMML and CMML of the same formula, while increasing the distance between different formulas within a minibatch. As illustrated in Fig. 1, this framework consists of the following four main components:

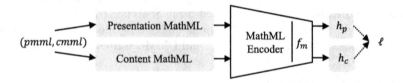

Fig. 1. Contrastive Presentation MathML-Content MathML Learning Framework.

Sampling. We randomly sample a minibatch of N $(pmml, cmml)$ pairs in the training set, where we assume that $(pmml_i,\ cmml_i)$ is a positive pair and $(pmml_i,\ cmml_j)$ for $i \neq j$ is a negative pair. For each $pmml_i$, it uses all other $cmml_j$ in a minibatch as negative samples.

Encoder. Both PMML and CMML belong to MathML. Figure 1 is a Siamese Bi-encoder, where the encoder shares weights, enabling the use of the same encoder to obtain $h_p = f_m(pmml) = MathMLM(pmml)$ and $h_c = f_m(cmml) = MathMLM(cmml)$ where $h_p \in R^{768}$ represents the embedding of PMML, and $h_c \in R^{768}$ represents the embedding of CMML.

Contrastive Loss Function. We consider each $(pmml_i,\ cmml_i)$ as a positive pair. After encoding them, we obtain h_i^p and h_i^c. Assuming that the batch size is N, τ is a temperature hyperparameter, and $\langle u, v \rangle = u^T v / \|u\| \|v\|$ represent the cosine similarity, the loss function of MathMLM becomes:

$$\ell_i = -\log \frac{e^{\langle h_i^p, h_i^c \rangle / \tau}}{\sum_{j=1}^{N} e^{\langle h_i^p, h_j^c \rangle / \tau}} \tag{1}$$

Evaluator. The evaluator by default uses the alignment and uniformity loss. Following the loss function used by Wang et al. [10] for the BOOKCORPUS, it is defined as $\mathcal{L} = 0.9\mathcal{L}_{align}\,(\alpha = 2) + 0.1\mathcal{L}_{uniform}\,(t = 5)$. These two metrics are applied to assess its performance and decide whether to store the trained formula embedding model obtained during the training process.

3.3   Contrastive LaTeX-MathML Learning

It is also desired for the model in this section called CLFE to acquire three types of information: three formula embeddings, the latent relation between LaTeX and MathML, and richer formula structure and content information. CLFE aims to learn the formula representation by maximizing agreement between the LaTeX and MathML of the same formula, while simultaneously increasing the dissimilarity between different formulas within a minibatch in the latent space. As illustrated in Fig. 2, the framework comprises five important components:

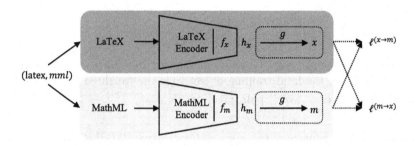

Fig. 2. Contrastive LaTeX-MathML Learning Framework.

Sampling. Like MathMLM, We also randomly sample a minibatch of N $(latex, mml)$ pairs in the training set, where mml represents $pmml$ or $cmml$. Similarly, in the minibatch, $(latex_i,\ mml_i)$ is considered as a positive pair, while $(latex_i,\ mml_j)$ for $i \neq j$ is treated as a negative pair.

Encoder. Since the formats of LaTeX and MathML are distinct, we choose to use different encoders to encode LaTeX and MathML separately, making it a pseudo-siamese bi-encoder configuration. Specifically, we utilize a pre-trained sentence-transformer to encode LaTeX to obtain h_x, and MathMLM to encode MathML to obtain h_m. Thus, the encoding process can be expressed as $h_x = f_x\,(latex) = SBERT\,(latex)$ and $h_m = f_m\,(mml) = MathMLM\,(mml)$ where $h_x \in R^{768}$ represents the embedding of LaTeX, and $h_c \in R^{768}$ represents the embedding of MathML.

Project Head. An extra MLP layer is added on top of encoder as project head, which maps h_x and h_m into a new space to obtain new LaTeX and MathML embeddings: x and m. The contrastive loss is computed in this new space, and such a project head is defined as $x = g(h_x) = \sigma(Wh_x)$ and $m = g(h_m) = \sigma(Wh_m)$ where $W \in R^{768 \times 768}$ is linear projection matrix and σ is a Tanh non-linearity. This introduces a non-linear projection between the representation and the contrastive loss, which further transforms h_x and h_m into vector x and m.

Contrastive Loss Function. Following the design of asymmetric contrastive loss in ConVIRT [12], the training objective of ConFE includes two loss functions. The first loss function is the LaTeX-to-MathML contrastive loss, defined as:

$$\ell_i^{(x \to m)} = -\log \frac{e^{\langle x_i, m_i \rangle / \tau}}{\sum_{j=1}^{N} e^{\langle x_i, m_j \rangle / \tau}} \tag{2}$$

The second loss function is the MathML-to-LaTeX contrastive loss, defined as:

$$\ell_i^{(m \to x)} = -\log \frac{e^{\langle m_i, x_i \rangle / \tau}}{\sum_{j=1}^{N} e^{\langle m_i, x_j \rangle / \tau}} \tag{3}$$

The two loss functions have the same numerator but different denominators. Assuming $\lambda \epsilon [0, 1]$, the final training objective is the weighted average of them for each positive $(latex, mml)$ pair, given by $\mathcal{L}_i = \lambda \ell_i^{(x \to m)} + (1 - \lambda) \ell_i^{(m \to x)}$.

Evaluator. The evaluator is the same as Contrastive PMML-CMML Learning.

3.4   Combining LaTeX, PMML and CMML Embeddings

LaTeX and PMML capture the structure of formulas, while CMML focuses on the semantic of formulas. Therefore, a further idea is to combine these three embeddings, resulting in a new embedding that can simultaneously incorporate both the structure and semantic information of a formula. To combine LaTeX, PMML, and CMML, two methods are employed. One is element-wise addition, where the corresponding dimensions of the LaTeX, PMML, and CMML embeddings for each formula are added together resulting in "Add embedding". They are all 768-dimensional dense vectors. The other is concatenation, where these three embeddings of the same formula are concatenated into a single vector. This process results in the "Concat embedding" which is a 2304-dimensional vector.

4   Experiment

4.1   Dataset and Preprocessing

Here, the proposed method is evaluated on the NTCIR-12 MathIR Task Wikipedia Corpus dataset. This dataset consists of 31,839 articles containing over half a million formulas and 20 concrete queries without wildcards for testing. During preprocessing, PMML, CMML, and LaTeX representations of each formula are extracted. For PMML and CMML, the tags are preserved while removing any attributes. After that, randomly sort the original example pairs, and then divide them into a training set, a development set and a test set in the ratio of 8:1:1.

4.2 Model Training

Experiments are conducted on Intel(R) Xeon(R) W-2295 CPU @ 3.00 GHz each core, DDR4 64 GB RAM, NVIDIA GeForce RTX 3080 devices. We train the formula embedding model for one epoch, evaluate the model performance during training on dev data every 10% of the training data, and use a batch-size of 4, $\lambda = 0.5$, Adam optimizer with learning rate 5e-5, a linear learning rate warm-up 10% of the training data. To test CLFE model, we select three formulas: $13 \times x$, $O\,(mn\log m)$, and $O\,(n\log m)$. The second and third formulas are highly similar. We produce LaTeX, PMML, and CMML embeddings for each formula and calculate the cosine similarity between them. Figure 3 indicates that CLFE is capable of effectively distinguishing between similar and dissimilar formulas.

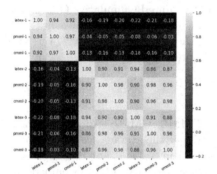
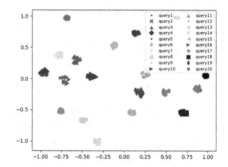

Fig. 3. latex-k, pmml-k, and cmml-k represent the LaTeX, PMML, and CMML of the k-th formula.

Fig. 4. Visualization of formula embeddings. Top-20 search results of 20 queries are visualized in 2-dimensional space.

4.3 Formula Retrieval Overview

Figure 5 illustrates the flow of formula retrieval. CLFE is used to encode the formulas in the NTCIR-12 dataset. The pre-encoded LaTeX, PMML, CMML, Add, and Concat embeddings of the formulas in the dataset are stored as a vector library, enabling efficient offline indexing. When a user inputs a query, CLFE encodes the query and produces its embeddings. Then, cosine similarity between query and candidate embeddings is calculated to retrieve the top-k results from the pre-stored embedding files. Finally, the retrieved results are sorted in descending order based on the cosine similarity and outputted.

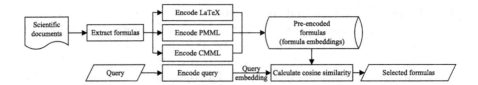

Fig. 5. Overview of formula retrieval.

4.4 Evaluation Measures

The relevance of formulas is classified into four categories: fully relevant, highly relevant, partially relevant, and irrelevant. The relevance score *rel* is assigned as 3 for fully relevant, 2 for highly relevant, 1 for partially relevant and 0 for irrelevant. Two human assessors scored the top-10 retrieval results of the 20 queries with scores from 2, 1 and 0 (higher scores indicating higher relevance). Then, the scores given by the two assessors are added, and a total score is 4 for fully relevant ($rel = 3$), 3 for highly relevant ($rel = 2$), 2 or 1 for partially relevant ($rel = 1$) and 0 for irrelevant ($rel = 1$).

The evaluation of retrieval results is based on P (Precision), MAP (Mean Average Precision), and nDCG (Normalized Discounted Cumulative Gain). The cutoff values are set at 5 and 10. nDCG produces a single-valued measure with graded relevance, while P and MAP are binary relevance metrics. For P and MAP, $rel = 3, 2$ *or* 1 are all regarded as relevant, while $rel = 0$ is irrelevant.

4.5 Retrieval Results and Analysis

Different Embedding Settings. LaTeX, PMML, CMML, Add and Concat embeddings are considered during retrieval. We get the average score and search time of 20 queries for each embedding, as shown in Table 1. For P, LaTeX and Concat embedding perform relatively well. The superiority of LaTeX embedding

Table 1. Retrieval results for different models and embeddings.

Model	Embedding		P@5	P@10	MAP @5	MAP @10	nDCG @5	nDCG @10	Search Time(/s)
w/o MLP	LaTeX		**0.7200**	**0.6250**	0.9669	0.9276	0.9880	0.9751	0.3966
	PMML		0.6500	0.5650	0.9486	0.9031	0.9818	0.9662	0.3962
	CMML		0.6900	0.5950	0.9738	0.9334	0.9891	0.9762	0.4040
	fusion	Add	0.6900	0.5900	0.9738	0.9057	0.9867	0.9698	0.4860
		Concat	0.7100	0.6000	0.9783	0.9370	0.9893	**0.9792**	1.1619
w/MLP	LaTeX		0.7000	0.5850	0.9564	0.9261	0.9851	0.9791	0.3692
	PMML		0.6400	0.5050	0.9769	0.9026	0.9899	0.9641	0.3628
	CMML		0.6400	0.5500	0.9519	0.9035	0.9834	0.9587	0.3701
	fusion	Add	0.6400	0.5200	0.9850	0.9102	0.9896	0.9656	0.4029
		Concat	0.6500	0.5400	**0.9875**	0.9211	0.9919	0.9630	1.0077
w/MLP(train)	LaTeX		0.7100	0.5900	0.9519	0.9314	0.9847	0.9778	0.3972
	PMML		0.6300	0.5200	0.9727	0.8733	0.9908	0.9561	0.3965
	CMML		0.6500	0.5550	0.9697	0.9129	0.9877	0.9655	0.4052
	fusion	Add	0.6400	0.5750	0.9728	0.9197	0.9925	0.9721	0.4949
		Concat	0.7000	0.5900	0.9753	**0.9381**	**0.9944**	0.9736	1.2335

may be attributed to more partially relevant results. The determination of partial relevance can be ambiguous, but it is uniformly considered as relevance. As for MAP and nDCG related to the ranking, Concat embedding is the best, probably because Concat embedding has more dimensions and contains most information.

Effectiveness of Project Head. In Sect. 3.3, project head is added on top of the encoder, which is an MLP layer. To investigate the role of MLP, three different models are considered to encode formulas: 1) no MLP layer; 2) using MLP layer; 3) using MLP layer during training but removing it during retrieval. Likewise, the results are also shown in Table 1. For P and nDCG@10, the first model performs the best. For MAP@5, the second model shows outstanding performance. The third model performs better in the MAP@10 and nDCG@5. By default, we take the w/ MLP (train) model and Concat embedding.

Different Evaluators During Training. To study the effectiveness of alignment and uniformity loss as an evaluator, we additionally set average cosine similarity for comparison. We use these two metrics separately to evaluate the model on the dev set and save the model with a higher average cosine similarity or a smaller alignment and uniformity loss. The performance of two models is shown in Table 2. Alignment and uniformity loss is better in all measures. This might be because it considers both the similarity and uniformity of their spatial distribution of formulas, while cosine similarity only focuses on similarity.

Table 2. Effect of different evaluators on formula embedding models during training.

Evaluator	P@5	P@10	MAP@5	MAP@10	nDCG@5	nDCG@10
Cosine similarity	0.6400	0.5300	0.9617	0.8888	0.9790	0.9587
Alignment and uniformity loss	**0.7000**	**0.5900**	**0.9753**	**0.9381**	**0.9944**	**0.9736**

Comparison with Others. Comparisons are made between Tangent-S, Tangent-CFT and our CLFE. Table 3 gives the results, and CLFE outperforms Tangent-S and Tangent-CFT in general. Particularly, CLFE demonstrates outstanding performance in metrics related to ranking, such as MAP and nDCG. For example, taking $O(mnlogm)$ as a query, we compared the top-5 retrieval results of them, as shown in Table 4. To better understand our CLFE, the top-20 retrieval results of the 20 queries are visualized in Fig. 4 using t-SNE [5]. It can be seen that the top-20 formulas retrieved for the same query are mapped to nearby positions.

Table 3. Retrieval results compared to Tangent-S and Tangent-CFT.

Model	P@5	P@10	MAP@5	MAP@10	nDCG@5	nDCG@10
Tangent-S	0.6400	0.5300	0.9211	0.8875	0.9486	0.9276
Tangent-CFT	**0.7100**	**0.5900**	0.9314	0.9026	0.9792	0.9587
CLFE	0.7000	**0.5900**	**0.9753**	**0.9381**	**0.9944**	**0.9736**

Table 4. Top-5 formulas results for $O(mnlogm)$.

Rank	Tangent-S	Tangent-CFT	CLFE
1	$O\left(mn \log m\right)$	$O\left(mn \log m\right)$	$O\left(mn \log m\right)$
2	$O\left(mn \log p\right) = O(n \log n)$	$O\left(m \log n\right)$	$O\left(mn \cdot \log\left(mn\right)\right)$
3	$O\left(M\ (m)\, log^2 m\right) = O\left(M\ (m) \log n\right)$	$O\left(n \log n\right)$	$O\left(n \log m\right)$
4	$O\left(mnr^2 \log \frac{1}{\epsilon}\right)$	$O\left(n \log m\right)$	$O\left(n \log m\right)$
5	$O\left(mn\right) = O\left(n^3 \log n\right)$	$O\left(nm\right)$	$O\left(n * m\right)$

5 Conclusion

In this paper, CLFE, a simple contrastive learning framework, is proposed to produce formula embeddings for formula retrieval tasks by training a formula embedding model with a large amount of formula data. Each formula has three types of embeddings: LaTeX embedding, PMML embedding, and CMML embedding. We also combine these three embeddings to obtain more informative embeddings: Add embedding and Concat embedding. These embeddings are applied to formula retrieval, which results in higher scores in some measures. In the future, we plan to incorporate textual information about formula context into the formula embedding model and explore broader applications of it.

Acknowledgment. This work is supported by the Natural Science Foundation of Hebei Province of China under Grant F2019201329.

References

1. Davila, K., Zanibbi, R.: Layout and semantics: combining representations for mathematical formula search. In: Proceedings of the 40th International ACM SIGIR Conference on Research and Development in Information Retrieval, pp. 1165–1168 (2017)
2. Gao, T., Yao, X., Chen, D.: SimCSE: simple contrastive learning of sentence embeddings. In: Proceedings of the 2021 Conference on Empirical Methods in Natural Language Processing, pp. 6894–6910 (2021)
3. Karpukhin, V., et al.: Dense passage retrieval for open-domain question answering. In: Proceedings of the 2020 Conference on Empirical Methods in Natural Language Processing (EMNLP). Association for Computational Linguistics (2020)

4. Li, J., Xu, Y., Cui, L., Wei, F.: MarkupLM: pre-training of text and markup language for visually-rich document understanding. arXiv preprint arXiv:2110.08518 (2021)

5. Van der Maaten, L., Hinton, G.: Visualizing data using t-SNE. J. Mach. Learn. Res. **9**(11) (2008)

6. Mansouri, B., Oard, D.W., Zanibbi, R.: Contextualized formula search using math abstract meaning representation. In: Proceedings of the 31st ACM International Conference on Information & Knowledge Management, pp. 4329–4333 (2022)

7. Mansouri, B., Rohatgi, S., Oard, D.W., Wu, J., Giles, C.L., Zanibbi, R.: Tangent-CFT: an embedding model for mathematical formulas (2019)

8. Reimers, N., Gurevych, I.: Sentence-BERT: sentence embeddings using siamese BERT-networks. arXiv preprint arXiv:1908.10084 (2019)

9. Sojka, P., Líška, M.: The art of mathematics retrieval. In: Proceedings of the 11th ACM Symposium on Document Engineering, pp. 57–60 (2011)

10. Wang, T., Isola, P.: Understanding contrastive representation learning through alignment and uniformity on the hypersphere. In: International Conference on Machine Learning, pp. 9929–9939. PMLR (2020)

11. Zanibbi, R., Aizawa, A., Kohlhase, M., Ounis, I., Topic, G., Davila, K.: NTCIR-12 MathIR task overview. In: NTCIR (2016)

12. Zhang, Y., Jiang, H., Miura, Y., Manning, C.D., Langlotz, C.P.: Contrastive learning of medical visual representations from paired images and text. In: Machine Learning for Healthcare Conference, pp. 2–25. PMLR (2022)

13. Zhong, W., Zanibbi, R.: Structural similarity search for formulas using leaf-root paths in operator subtrees. In: Azzopardi, L., Stein, B., Fuhr, N., Mayr, P., Hauff, C., Hiemstra, D. (eds.) ECIR 2019, Part I. LNCS, vol. 11437, pp. 116–129. Springer, Cham (2019). https://doi.org/10.1007/978-3-030-15712-8_8

Social Media and News Analysis

Influence Embedding from Incomplete Observations in Sina Weibo

Wei Huang, Guohao Sun$^{(\boxtimes)}$, Mei Wang, Weiliang Zhao, and Jian Yang

Donghua University, Shanghai, China
ghsun@dhu.edu.cn

Abstract. Online Social Networks (OSNs) such as Twitter, Sina Weibo, and Facebook play an important role in our daily life recently. The influence diffusion between users is a common phenomenon on OSNs, which has been applied in numerous applications such as rumor detection and product marketing. Most of the existing influence modeling methods are based on complete data. However, due to certain reasons like privacy protection, it is very hard to obtain complete history data in OSNs. In this paper, we propose a new method to estimate user influence based on incomplete data from user behaviors. Firstly, we apply the maximum likelihood estimator to estimate the user's missing behaviors. Then, we use direct interaction to get the influence of the sender and receiver. In addition, we apply different actions between users to improve the performance of our method. Empirical experiments on the Weibo dataset show that our method outperforms the existing methods.

Keywords: Social network · Influence embedding · Sina Weibo

1 Introduction

OSNs such as Twitter, Sina Weibo, and Facebook have been widely used in recent years, providing a new way for people to communicate with others. As many people are using these OSNs, a lot of application research has been carried out, such as product marketing [3] and rumor detection [21]. All of these applications are based on the influence diffusion characteristics in OSNs. In Sina Weibo, one user will influence others after posting/reposting/commenting a microblog, and the influence will spread in the same way. From this observation, we can clearly capture the influence diffusion between users and learn the influence relationship between users. However, there are still two challenges in building an influence model on Sina Weibo.

Challenge 1: How to estimate the comment number from incomplete data?

The calculation of influence probability is the premise of predicting influence diffusion. Given a social network, we can associate each link (u, v) with a probability $p(u, v)$, which represents the probability that a microblog posted by u will influence v [8]. Due to the importance of influence probability in influence diffusion prediction, many studies [1,2,4,8–11,15,17–19] have focused on how to

© The Author(s), under exclusive license to Springer Nature Singapore Pte Ltd. 2023
F. Zhang et al. (Eds.): WISE 2023, LNCS 14306, pp. 111–121, 2023.
https://doi.org/10.1007/978-981-99-7254-8_9

calculate the influence probability from historical data. All of these methods of calculating the influence probability rely on the complete data. However, in the real world, it is hard to get complete data [5, 7, 15, 22] due to the privacy restrictions [22] or API restrictions [5]. For example, although the comment data is very important to calculate the influence probability, in Sina Weibo, it's hard to get complete comment data.

Challenge 2: How to learn the influence probability from direct interactions?

User's direct interactions in the social network is an important characteristic for building influence relationship between users. Existing studies calculate the influence probability by observing the influence diffusion episodes (Fig. 1(b)) rather than the direct interaction (Fig. 1(c)) between users. By using direct interactions, we can easily obtain the first-order influence relationship. For example, in Fig. 1(a), user A initially posts a microblog at time t_0, user B and D repost/comment this microblog respectively, and then user C comments at t_2. Existing research believes that user C will be influenced by both A and B from the observation of diffusion episode (Fig. 1(b)). In Fig. 1(c), by using the direct interactions, and can know that user C is influenced by user B.

The main contribution of this paper can be summarized as follows:

1. We are the first to apply the Maximum Likelihood Estimator (MLE) to calculate the expected number of comments between users. By using this method, model can be established in the case of incomplete history data.
2. We propose a new embedding method to learn user's influence probability from direct interactions instead of diffusion episode.

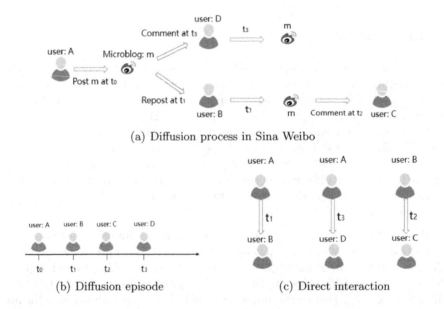

(a) Diffusion process in Sina Weibo

(b) Diffusion episode   (c) Direct interaction

Fig. 1. Diffusion process, diffusion episode and direct interaction in Sina Weibo

3. We use both comment and repost actions to capture the influence process between users, which can fully reflect the relationship between users.

2   Related Work

The research of learning influence relationship can be grouped into two groups: statistical method and embedding method.

2.1   Statistical Method

Many researchers directly learn the pairwise influence probability for IC (Independent Cascade) model [3] in a statistical method. Satio et al. [11] are the first to learn the pairwise influence probability by using the Expectation Maximization algorithm. However, this method is not suitable for large network data due to the time consumption. Goyal et al. [4] develop three methods (Bernoulli distribution, Jaccard Index and Partial Credits) to estimate the influence probability. These three methods can greatly reduce time consumption. However, they only consider the first-order diffusion in the network, which is not consistent with the diffusion process. All of these statistical methods suffer from over-fitting problems [2].

2.2   Embedding Method

In embedding methods, users are embedded into a continuous latent space and infer the relationship between users based on the relative distance in the latent space. Feng et at. [2] apply network structure and influence diffusion observation to learn network embedding and they are the first to capture the social influence by network representation. Sankar et al. [12] proposed Inf-VAE to jointly embed homophily and influence. However, these methods rely on network structure, and in real life, network structure changes dynamically in most cases. Wang et al. [14] proposed an encoder-decoder framework to predict influence diffusion. Xie et al. [20] proposed an asymmetric embedding method to embed each user into multiple latent susceptibility spaces. Wang et al. [16] distinguish the positive and negative information in social networks. Jin et al. [6] modeling influence diffusion based on the dynamics of user interest.

All the above-mentioned statistical and embedding methods are not applicable to Sina Weibo for the following reasons: **1.** The premise of these modeling methods is that there is no missing data, but the comment data of Sina Weibo is missing; **2.** These methods are based on diffusion episode data for modeling, rather than using direct interaction between users.

3   Preliminaries

Direct Interaction: In Sina Weibo social network, when user u posts microblog m and microblog m is commented/reposted by user v, there is a direct interaction between user u and user v.

Diffusion Episode: Each microblog m corresponds to one diffusion episode $D(m) = (u_i, t_i)$, which is a set of users who adopt action to m [2]. The difference between direct interaction and diffusion episode is shown in Fig. 1.

In the Sina Weibo dataset, the repost list records all the users who repost the microblog, and the comment list records partial users who comment on the microblog. Therefore, we can use the repost action directly, and we need to estimate the comment action before using it.

The symbols used in this paper are presented in Table 1.

Table 1. Symbol Description

Symbols	$\mathcal{G}$	$\mathcal{V}$	$\mathcal{E}$	$\mathcal{P}$	$\mathcal{M}$	T
Description	A graph of social network extracted from Sina Weibo	The nodes of the social network. Each node represents a user	The edges of the social network. An edge $(u,v) \in \mathcal{E}$ represents a directed influence tie from u to v	The set of influence probability between users. Also represents the weights of the edges	The microblogs posted by users in $\mathcal{V}$	The duration of the whole diffusion process
Symbols	t	$\mathcal{C}(m)$	$\mathcal{R}(m)$	$|\mathcal{C}(m)|$	$|\mathcal{R}(m)|$	
Description	The length of the time slot	The comment list of microblog m, which records the users who comment the microblog m	The repost list of microblog m, which records the users who repost the microblog m	The number of comments that microblog m received	The number of reposts that microblog m received	

4   Inf-Embedding

4.1   Overview

An overview of our proposed framework (Inf-embedding) is presented in Fig. 2, which consists of three parts. The first part is called data preprocessing, which aims to deal with the problem of missing comment data. The second part is called influence embedding. In the second part, we propose a new embedding algorithm, which can apply the comment data and repost data as input to learn the user's representation. The third part is called influence diffusion. In the third part, we simulate the influence diffusion process in social networks.

4.2   Data Preprocessing

Due to the missing data in social networks [5,15,22], we propose a method based on MLE to estimate the missing data. Specifically, in the Sina Weibo platform, the comment interaction is incomplete. For each microblog, we can know the number of comments that the microblog received and partial users who comment on the microblog.

For each user pair (u, v) in the network, we need to estimate the number that v has commented on u's microblogs. The actual received comment number of K microblogs posted by u is represented as $N(1), N(2), ...N(K)$, and the number of comment users we can see in each microblog is denoted as $n(1), n(2), ...n(K)$.

Preprocessing Method: For each microblog, we can calculate the proportion of the number of comment users in the comment list to the total number of comment users: $pro(i) = \frac{n(i)}{N(i)}$

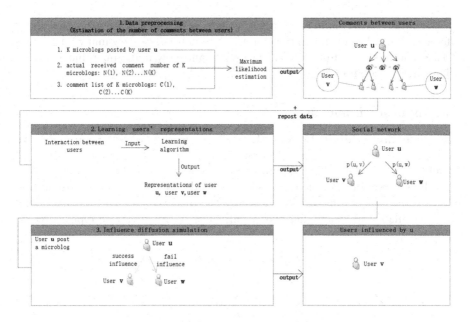

Fig. 2. The proposed Inf-embedding framework

If user v is in the comment list $C(m)$ of user u's microblog m, it must satisfy two requirements: 1) User v comments the user u's microblog m (the probability is $p_c(u,v)$); 2) User v belongs to the part of comment users obtained by microblog m, instead of the missing part (the probability is $pro(m)$). In this case, the likelihood function that user v is in the comment list $C(m)$ of user u's microblog m is: $L = pro(m) * p_c(u,v)$

If user v is not in the comment list $C(m)$ of user u's microblog m, it must satisfy one of the following requirements: 1) User v comments on user u's microblog m and user v belongs to the missing part of commented users (the probability is $(1 - pro(m)) * p_c(u,v)$); 2) User v does not comment on user u's microblog m (the probability is $1 - p_c(u,v)$). In this case, the likelihood function is: $L = (1 - pro(m)) * p_c(u,v) + (1 - p_c(u,v))$

The above calculation considers the condition of one microblog m of user u, and we extend it to all microblogs $\mathcal{M}(u)$ of user u:

$$L(u,v) = \prod_{i=1}^{K}((1-pro(i))*p_c(u,v)+(1-p_c(u,v)))^{1-I(i)} *(pro(i)*p_c(u,v))^{I(i)} \quad (1)$$

where $I(i)$ is the indicator function, indicating that if user v comment the microblog i. $p_c(u,v)$ is the comment probability from v to u, and K is the number of microblogs posted by u. For each user pair (u,v), we can infer the comment probability from $p_c(u,v)$ by maximizing Eq. 1.

Meeting the need for the following embedding method, we calculate the expected comment number from v to u: $num(u,v) = p_c(u,v) * K$

Where K is the number of microblogs posted by u. Based on the above inference, it can be concluded that for any user pair (u, v), how many microblogs of user u have successfully influenced user v, and how many microblogs of user u have not successfully influenced user v.

4.3   Influence Embedding

Influence Embedding. Because the social network is directed, we follow the work [1,2], to use two vectors to represent each user. User u has two vectors: $I_u \in \mathbb{R}^d$ and $S_u \in \mathbb{R}^d$. Here, d is the number of dimensions. The d-dimensional vector I_u is the representation of u as an influence sender, and S_u is the representation of u as a receiver of influence. We leverage the relative distance between I_u and S_v to calculate the probability that u influence v, which can be represented as follows:

$$f(I_u, S_v, I_{u_0}, S_{v_0}) = \frac{1}{1 + Z(I_u, S_v, I_{u_0}, S_{v_0})} \tag{2}$$

$$Z(I_u, S_v, I_{u_0}, S_{v_0}) = exp(\sum_{i=1}^{d}(I_u^i - S_v^i)^2 + I_{u_0} + S_{v_0}) \tag{3}$$

$$p(u, v) = f(I_u, S_v, I_{u_0}, S_{v_0}) \tag{4}$$

where I_{u_0} represents the global influence ability of user u, and S_{v_0} represents the global susceptibility of user v.

Learning Algorithm for Influence Embedding. Based on the above inference, we exploit an algorithm to learn representations of users. Considering the pairwise influence probability $\mathcal{P} = \{p(u, v)|(u, v) \in \mathcal{V}^2\}$, we can calculate the likelihood of the repost list and comment list of user u's microblog:

$$L(\mathcal{M}(u)|\mathcal{P}) = \prod_{m \in \mathcal{M}(u)} (\prod_{v \in C(m) \cup R(m)} p(u, v) \prod_{v \notin C(m) \cup R(m)} (1 - p(u, v))) \tag{5}$$

Equation 5 considers the condition of microblogs $M(u)$ posted by user u , and we extend it to all microblogs $\mathcal{M}$:

$$logL(\mathcal{M}|\mathcal{P}) = \sum_{u, m \in \mathcal{M}} (\sum_{v \in C(m) \cup R(m)} p(u, v) + \sum_{v \notin C(m) \cup R(m))} (1 - p(u, v))) \tag{6}$$

Equation 6 constructs the likelihood function of comment and repost among all users. Thus, the ultimate learning objective is to maximize the log-likelihood. We use the stochastic gradient to maximize the log-likelihood and use the negative sampling method to get the uninfluenced samples. The pseudo-code of learning is presented in Algorithm 1. The aim of this algorithm is to learn representations of users (the parameters sets I, S, I_0, S_0). Based on the learning method, we can get representations of users. Combining representations of users and Eq. 4, it's easy to obtain the pairwise influence probability.

4.4   Influence Diffusion

In this section, we aim to explain the influence diffusion process. In the real social network, the diffusion process is continuous. Due to the consumption of the continuous model, we use a discrete model which proceeds in discrete steps from one-time slot to the next. Once user u takes an action, then at each time slot i, user u has a chance to influence his neighbor v (influence probability $p^{t_i}(u, v)$) who have not been influenced. And the overall influence probability between u and v is $p(u, v)$ (calculated by Eq. 4) in the whole diffusion process. The relationship between the influence probability of each time slot and the overall influence probability is as follows:

$$p(u, v) = 1 - \prod_{i=1}^{N} (1 - p^{t_i}(u, v)) \tag{7}$$

In the previous section, according to the static vector of user u and user v, the direct influence probability $p(u, v)$ from user u to user v is obtained. However, the probability does not take into account other users and their interactions. In this paper, we consider how to simulate the diffusion process of influence based on the direct influence probability $p(u, v)$, and calculate the real influence of users. The solution is shown in Algorithm 2. After Algorithm 2, all influenced users can be obtained step by step from the direct influence probability of each time slot.

Algorithm 1. Learning Users' Representation

Input: learning rate $step^1, step^2, step^3, step^4$, user sets $\mathcal{V}$, negative sample number n, number of dimension d, the frequency of stop tests $freq$, comment list sets C, repost list sets R
output: user representation I, S, I_0, S_0

1: **for** $u \in \mathcal{V}$ **do**
2:    initializing representation of each user in standardized normal distribution: I_u, S_u, I_{0u}, S_{0u}
3: $it \leftarrow 0$
4: $oldL \leftarrow -\infty$
5: **while** True **do**
6:    $it \leftarrow it + 1$
7:    $\mathcal{V} \leftarrow shuffle(\mathcal{V})$
8:    **for** u in $\mathcal{V}$ **do**
9:       $\mathcal{M}(u) \leftarrow GetMicroblogs(u)$
10:       **for** m in $\mathcal{M}(u)$ **do**
11:          $V \leftarrow C(m) \cup R(m)$
12:          $V \leftarrow shuffle(V)$
13:          **for** v in V **do**
14:             $\Delta_u, \Delta_v, \Delta_{0u}, \Delta_{0v} \leftarrow \partial \frac{log(p(u,v))}{I_u}, \partial \frac{log(p(u,v))}{S_v}, \partial \frac{log(p(u,v))}{I_{0u}}, \partial \frac{log(p(u,v))}{S_{0v}}$
15:             $I_u, S_v, I_{0u}, S_{0v} \leftarrow I_u + step^1 * \Delta_u, S_v + step^1 * \Delta_v, I_{0u} + step^2 * \Delta_{0u}, S_{0v} + step^2 * \Delta_{0v}$
16:          $V \leftarrow SampleNotInfluenced(m, n)$
17:          $V \leftarrow shuffle(V)$
18:          **for** v in V **do**
19:             $\Delta_u, \Delta_v, \Delta_{0u}, \Delta_{0v} \leftarrow \partial \frac{log(1-p(u,v))}{I_u}, \partial \frac{log(1-p(u,v))}{S_v}, \partial \frac{log(1-p(u,v))}{I_{0u}}, \partial \frac{log(1-p(u,v))}{S_{0v}}$
20:             $I_u, S_v, I_{0u}, S_{0v} \leftarrow I_u + step^3 * \Delta_u, S_v + step^3 * \Delta_v, I_{0u} + step^4 * \Delta_{0u}, S_{0v} + step^4 * \Delta_{0v}$
21:    **if** it mod $freq = 0$ **then**
22:       $\mathcal{P} \leftarrow \{p(u,v)|(u,v) \in \mathcal{V}^2 \wedge p(u,v) = f(u,v)\}$
23:       $L \leftarrow$ Computation of log-likelihood using equation 6 with probabilities in $\mathcal{P}$
24:       **if** $L < oldL$ **then**
25:          return S, I, S_0, I_0
26:       $oldL \leftarrow L$

Algorithm 2. Influence Diffusion

Input: initial active user sets S, influence probability sets $\mathcal{P}$, user sets $\mathcal{V}$, number of time slot Nt
output: Influenced user sets $f(S)$

1: $f(S) \leftarrow S$
2: **for** $i \leftarrow 1, Nt$ **do**
3:     **for** $v \in \mathcal{V}$ **do**
4:         **for** $u \in f(S)$ **do**
5:             **if** $p(u, v) > 0$ **then**
6:                 random number $x \in (0, 1)$
7:                 calculate $p^{t_i}(u, v)$ by Eq. 7 and 8
8:                 **if** $x < p^{t_i}(u, v)$ **then**
9:                     $f(S) \leftarrow f(S) \cup v$
10: **return** $f(S)$

---

5   Experiments

5.1   Dataset

There are 6792 users in the dataset, and we collect the microblogs posted by these users from 2020/08/01 to 2020/08/04. We select the microblogs posted from 2020/08/01 to 2020/08/03 as the training set, and the rest of the microblogs posted as the testing set. The missing number of comments is 127519.

5.2   Parameter Setup

We set the length of each time slot t to $1\,\mathrm{min}$. And the learning rate $step^1$, $step^2$, $step^3$ and $step^4$ in algorithm is 0.01, 0.001, 0.2, and 0.005. The negative sample number n is 500. The frequency of stop tests $freq$ is 20. The number of dimension is 50.

5.3   Baseline

1. **DTIC-Jaccard** [4]: The discrete time independent cascade proposed in [4]. In this method, the Jaccard index is used to learn the parameter.
2. **DTIC-Credit** [4]: The discrete time independent cascade proposed in [4]. In this method, partial credit is used to learn the parameter. The influence probability is calculated by the user's credit.
3. **TopoLstm** [13]: In this method, Long Short Term Memory (LSTM) is used to predict diffusion.
4. **Inf2vec** [2]: This method combines both the local influence context and the global user similarity context.
5. **IAE** [20]: This method embeds each user into multiple latent susceptibility spaces.
6. **Inf-embedding:** The method proposed in this paper.

5.4   Evaluation

We will evaluate our model in two aspects: Influence relationship detection and influence diffusion prediction.

Influence Relationship Detection: The first aspect is the influence relationship detection [1]. The influence relationship is also called the influence probability in [22]. We further consider the strength of the influence relationship, not just the existence of the influence relationship. In our evaluation experiment, the influence probability for user pair (u, v) in the test set is calculated by the ratio idea $p(u, v) = \frac{A_{u2v}}{A_u}$, where A_{u2v} is the number of microblogs that successfully influence v posted by u, and the A_u is the number of microblogs posted by u.

We utilize the following metric to evaluate influence relationship detection: the Area Under Curve (AUC) value of the Receiver Operating Characteristic (ROC), the sum of squares errors (SSE), Precision, Recall and F1.

Table 2 presents the results of different methods in influence relationship detection. Inf-embedding can get the best performance in AUC, SSE, Recall and F1. The Precision of Inf-embedding is lower than TopoLstm because TopoLstm has a very low recall rate. TopoLstm is designed to predict influence diffusion in an end-to-end way. So the TopoLstm is not suitable for relationship detection, which is intuitively reflected in the imbalance between the precision and recall of TopoLstm in relationship detection. The good performance of Inf-embedding indicates that our method is suitable for influence relationship detection.

Table 2. The results of influence relationship detection

Method	AUC	SSE	Precision	Recall	F1	nbParams
Inf-embedding	**0.915**	**79.3**	0.137	**0.314**	**0.190**	**339650**
DTIC-Jaccard	0.650	83.3	0.114	0.300	0.166	46131264
DTIC-Credit	0.621	133.7	0.082	0.241	0.123	46131264
TopoLstm	0.504	151	**0.182**	0.035	0.059	869376
Inf2vec	0.909	79.8	0.132	0.292	0.182	339650
IAE	0.853	80.1	0.122	0.165	0.140	230656300

Influence Diffusion Prediction: The second aspect of evaluation is influence diffusion, which is significant for influence analysis. We model the diffusion process based on Monte Carlo simulation. We will compare the actual influenced users with the simulated influenced users. We utilize the following metric to evaluate influence diffusion prediction: NMSE (Normalise Mean Squared Error), precision, recall and F1. $NMSE = \frac{1}{n}(\sum_i \frac{s(u_i) - \hat{s}(u_i)}{s(u_i)})^2$, where $s(u_i)$ is the average number of users in the influence cascade of actions initiated by u_i according to the testing data, and $\hat{s}(u_i)$ is the predicted value.

Table 3 presents the results of different methods in influence diffusion prediction. Inf-embedding can get the best performance in NMSE, Precision, Recall, and F1. The good performance of Inf-embedding indicates that our method is suitable for influence diffusion prediction. The best performance in F1 means

Inf-embedding can predict whether a user will be influenced. And the best performance in NMSE indicates that our method can predict a user's influence accurately. Modeling diffusion of user influence is a very challenging work, such as the F1 of 0.013 in Twitter [1], and the average precision of 0.18 in the Digg [2]. The precision of the proposed method is 0.400, which is greatly improved compared with other models.

Table 3. The results of influence diffusion prediction

Method	NMSE	Precision	Recall	F1
Inf-embedding	**0.0107**	**0.400**	**0.142**	**0.209**
DTIC-Jaccard	0.0115	0.250	0.123	0.165
DTIC-Credit	0.1264	0.215	0.101	0.138
TopoLstm	0.1236	0.331	0.141	0.198
Inf2vec	0.0732	0.392	0.135	0.200
IAE	0.085	0.341	0.105	0.161

6 Conclusion

In this paper, we study the influence embedding problem on Sina Weibo. Different from other embedding methods, our method is based on incomplete observations. One of the main contributions of this paper is to estimate missing comment data. In addition, based on the estimated data, we propose a new embedding method, which utilizes direct interactions of users. Compared with other methods, this embedding method is more suitable for Sina Weibo.

Acknowledgments. This work was supported by Shanghai Science and Technology Commission (No. 22YF1401100), Fundamental Research Funds for the Central Universities (No. 22D111210, 22D111207), and National Science Fund for Young Scholars (No. 62202095).

References

1. Bourigault, S., Lamprier, S., Gallinari, P.: Representation learning for information diffusion through social networks: an embedded cascade model. In: Proceedings of the Ninth ACM International Conference on Web Search and Data Mining (2016)
2. Feng, S., Cong, G., Khan, A., Li, X., Liu, Y., Chee, M.Y.: Inf2vec: latent representation model for social influence embedding. In: ICDE, pp. 941–952 (2018)
3. Goldenberg, J., Libai, B., Muller, E.: Talk of the network: a complex systems look at the underlying process of word-of-mouth. Mark. Lett. **12**, 211–223 (2001)
4. Goyal, A., Bonchi, F., Lakshmanan, V.L.: Learning influence probabilities in social networks. In: WSDM, pp. 241–250 (2010)

5. He, X., Xu, K., Kempe, D., Liu, Y.: Learning influence functions from incomplete observations. In: Advances in Neural Information Processing Systems (NIPS 2016), vol. 29, pp. 2065–2073 (2016)
6. Jin, H., Wu, Y., Huang, H., Song, Y., Wei, H., Shi, X.: Modeling information diffusion with sequential interactive hypergraphs. IEEE Trans. Sustain. Comput. **7**, 644–655 (2022)
7. Kossinets, G.: Effects of missing data in social networks (2006)
8. Kutzkov, K., Bifet, A., Bonchi, F., Gionis, A.: STRIP: stream learning of influence probabilities. In: KDD, pp. 275–283 (2013)
9. Li, D., Zhang, S., Sun, X., Zhou, H., Li, S., Li, X.: Modeling information diffusion over social networks for temporal dynamic prediction. IEEE Trans. Knowl. Data Eng. 1985–1997 (2017)
10. Liu, S., Shen, H., Zheng, H., Cheng, X., Liao, X.: CT LIS: learning influences and susceptibilities through temporal behaviors. ACM Trans. Knowl. Discov. Data **13**, 1–21 (2019)
11. Saito, K., Nakano, R., Kimura, M.: Prediction of information diffusion probabilities for independent cascade model. In: Lovrek, I., Howlett, R.J., Jain, L.C. (eds.) KES 2008. LNCS (LNAI), vol. 5179, pp. 67–75. Springer, Heidelberg (2008). https://doi.org/10.1007/978-3-540-85567-5_9
12. Sankar, A., Zhang, X., Krishnan, A., Han, J.: Inf-VAE: a variational autoencoder framework to integrate homophily and influence in diffusion prediction (2020)
13. Wang, J., Zheng, V.W., Liu, Z., Chang, K.C.C.: Topological recurrent neural network for diffusion prediction. In: 2017 IEEE International Conference on Data Mining (ICDM), pp. 475–484. IEEE (2017)
14. Wang, R., Huang, Z., Liu, S., Shao, H., Abdelzaher, T.: DyDiff-VAE: a dynamic variational framework for information diffusion prediction (2021)
15. Wang, W., Yin, H., Du, X., Hua, W., Li, Y., Nguyen, V.H.Q.: Online user representation learning across heterogeneous social networks. In: Proceedings of the 42nd International ACM SIGIR Conference on Research and Development in Information Retrieval, pp. 545–554 (2019)
16. Wang, X., Wang, X., Min, G., Hao, F., Chen, C.L.P.: An efficient feedback control mechanism for positive/negative information spread in online social networks. IEEE Trans. Cybern. **52**(1), 87–100 (2022)
17. Wang, Y., Shen, H., Liu, S., Cheng, X.: Learning user-specific latent influence and susceptibility from information cascades. In: AAAI, pp. 477–484 (2015)
18. Wang, Z., Chen, C., Li, W.: Information diffusion prediction with network regularized role-based user representation learning. ACM Trans. Knowl. Discov. Data (TKDD) **13**, 1–23 (2019)
19. Wang, Z., Chen, C., Li, W.: Joint learning of user representation with diffusion sequence and network structure. IEEE Trans. Knowl. Data Eng. 1 (2020)
20. Xie, W., Wang, X., Jia, T.: Independent asymmetric embedding for information diffusion prediction on social networks. In: 2022 IEEE 25th International Conference on Computer Supported Cooperative Work in Design (CSCWD), pp. 190–195 (2022)
21. Yang, F., Liu, Y., Yu, X., Yang, M.: Automatic detection of rumor on sina weibo. In: Proceedings of the ACM SIGKDD Workshop on Mining Data Semantics (2012)
22. Zhang, D., Yin, J., Zhu, X., Zhang, C.: SINE: scalable incomplete network embedding. In: ICDM (2018)

Dissemination of Fact-Checked News Does Not Combat False News: Empirical Analysis

Ziyuan Jing[1], Basem Suleiman[1,2(✉)] ⬤, Waheeb Yaqub[1] ⬤,
and Manoranjan Mohanty[3]

[1] School of Computer Science, University of Sydney, Sydney, Australia
`b.suleiman@unsw.edu.au`
[2] School of Computer Science and Engineering, University of New South Wales,
Sydney, Australia
[3] University of Technology Sydney, Sydney, Australia

Abstract. This paper examines the impact of true news on the propagation of false news in social media networks. Due to the unavailability of real-world data, we present our methodological approach for collecting Twitter data using the Twitter API. Our dataset includes about five million tweets over six months, encompassing 400 false news stories with fact-checker labels, verified true news tweets, and related interactions (retweets, quoted tweets, replies). Our analysis investigates the influence of true news on curbing false news dissemination on Twitter and explores potential user network connections between false and true news. Statistical analysis on the dataset suggests that true news tweets have an insignificant impact on the spread of false news tweets. These results contribute to our understanding of the dynamics between true and false news within social media networks.

1 Introduction

Social media is widely used daily, enabling users to easily share information with a click of a button [1]. This process increases users' exposure to misleading and false news [23]. In this study, we investigate whether true news, an important tool for countering false news, can effectively impact the spread of false news on Twitter. Previous studies have demonstrated the effectiveness of fact-checked news interventions in reducing the dissemination of false news [20,22].

We collected real Twitter data and conducted statistical analysis to assess the impact of true news on the spread of false news. Consequently, we address the following research question: How does fact-checked news impact the spread of false news on Twitter?

This research question is crucial for understanding ways to combat the spread of false news. We observed a lack of real Twitter data for analyzing the impact of true news on the spread of false news [20]. As false news evolves on social platforms with time and technology [13], it becomes necessary to collect up-to-date data and analyze the actual impact of true news on false news. Our

F. Zhang et al. (Eds.): WISE 2023, LNCS 14306, pp. 122–133, 2023.
https://doi.org/10.1007/978-981-99-7254-8_10

research aims to uncover the current relationship between false news and true news, serving as inspiration and guidance for future research on the subject.

We focus on utilizing verified true news to combat false news on Twitter, also known as conflicting news [20] because verified news reduces sharing of false news [22]. Conflicting news occurs when someone responds to a false news tweet with an opposing view and shares compelling evidence, such as a fact-checking URL, to debunk the false news (see Fig. 1). These users, who fight against the spread of false news tweets, have been referred to as "Guardians" in some studies [18].

We provide a detailed description of our data collection method and outline the process used to collect tweet data for studying conflicting news and present the results of our data analysis. Then, we quantify the influence of fact-checked news insertion (true news) on the spread of false news. Finally, we conclude with a summary of the findings and provide suggestions for future research.

Fig. 1. A real-life conflicting news example where Twitter user @ericknoerdel combat false news tweet posted by user @RealTina40 in the comment after the false news tweet was posted one day later.

2   Related Work

Combating the spread of false news in online communities by spreading the truth has been a widely used and accepted method [21]. The previously mentioned verified news tweets with Fact-checking URLs are a manifestation of the truth. Although the use of verified news to combat false news has been around for a long time, recent research is divided on how effective it is.

Friggeri et al. found that users are more likely to delete a shared false news message when they see a fact-checked message [5]. Additionally, 95% of users do not investigate or seek more information about false news [3]. These findings suggest that the power of the masses has a significant counteractive influence on the spread of false news. Similarly, in the Twitter community, some research supports the use of moderators in order to self-censorship and rectify misinformation spread due to false news [18, 24].

Some studies challenge the aforementioned perspective. Firstly, false news spreads much faster than the truth on social media [19]. Moreover, people tend to believe in views aligned with their ideology and disregard opposing views and statements [12]. These viewpoints raise doubts about the effectiveness of verified news in curbing the spread of false news. In fact, up to 51.9% of retweets of false news occur even after fact-checking [9]. Several factors may contribute to this, such as users not reading all comments and comments of Guardians before sharing false news. Overall, it appears that verified news is not fulfilling its role. Additionally, some studies express concerns about the self-correction of false news behavior on social media, suggesting that relying on individual users to fight false news is a slow process [15]. For instance, one study found that 9 out of 10 Americans who read news on social media platforms do not fact-check what they read [7]. This could be one of the reasons why the dissemination of fact-checking URLs to combat false news has been slow to yield results.

However, the aforementioned studies and findings do not provide a comprehensive explanation of the impact of verified news on the spread of false news. Some of the studies are outdated and may not accurately reflect the current community network environment. On the other hand, there is a lack of strong evidence, specifically a substantial amount of real-world data and data analysis, to effectively summarize the relationship between verified news and false news. Therefore, this study aims to collect real-world tweet data to examine the true impact of verified news on false news.

3   Methodology

Twitter Data Collection: Studying false news is challenging due to the need for quality data and balancing the distribution of false and true news [2]. Online available datasets in literature do not meet our requirements because datasets are outdated as certain articles or tweets may have been deleted over time and focus on a single topic non-conflicting topic. Pennycook et al. [14] suggested methods to collect false news can be useful for non-conflicting news. However, Vosoughi et al. [19] adopted a useful approach by first identifying true news tweets containing URLs from fact-checking websites before locating corresponding false news tweets. We have implemented a similar approach to construct our data collection model.

Data Collection Method: Data collection method can be summarised in three main steps (see Fig. 2). **First,** collect the URLs of the articles on the fact-checking websites that are labeled as false news using a web crawler. The fact-check article about false news can be used as a basis for refuting false news tweets. The **second step** is to use the Twitter API to search for tweets that reference these URLs which are our true news tweet candidates. We look for tweets

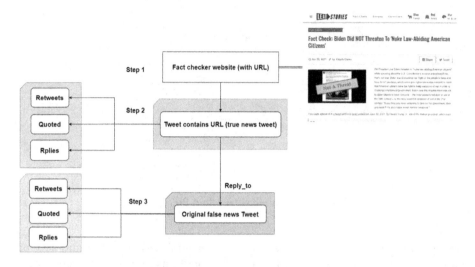

Fig. 2. Data collection flow chart

with the "reply to" attribute in the collected true news tweets and assume that the true news tweets are replying to the false news tweets. If a fact-checking website URL is referenced in a tweet, it means that the tweet is debunking false news. Finally, we collect all the tweets associated with true news tweets and false news tweets, including retweets, quoted tweets, and replies.

We also need to collect data from users. These include users who post false news tweets, users who post true news tweets, and their followers. This user data is used analyse whether the user groups of true news tweets and the target groups of false news tweets intersect.

We collected data on 404 false news stories from December 2020 to July 2021, which includes false news tweets, verified true news, and related interactions (retweets, quoted tweets, replies). This dataset has around 5 million tweets, including follower information of the tweet authors on Twitter. The collected dataset and its detailed structure is accessible online for further research experiments and studies. Interested researchers can access the dataset through[1].

Analysis Approach: We used two ways to analyse the data on whether true news tweets affect the spread of false news tweets: the first is to analyse the effect of true news tweets on the spread of false news tweets in the temporal dimension; the second is to visualise the data in terms of spread relationships, looking at the spread network dimension to see if there is a correlation between the spread of true news tweets and false news tweets (see Fig. 3).

Using time as an axis, we analysed how many times a false news tweet was retweeted, quoted and commented on. Now we have a time-based distribution history of false news tweets. Based on this record, the corresponding true news tweets are inserted. We then analyse whether the spread speed rate of false news tweets has decreased or increased during the time period in which the true news

---

[1] https://github.com/BasemSuleiman/Combacting-False-News-Twitter-Dataset.

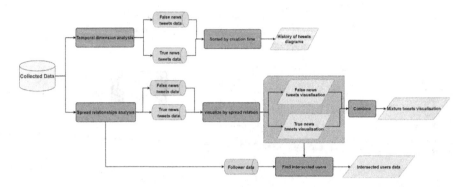

Fig. 3. Data analysis method flow chart

tweets appeared in the false news tweets comments section. If the majority of false news tweets have a significant drop in popularity during the time period when true news tweets appear, then it is highly likely that true news tweets impacted the rate of spread of false news tweets. This assumes that users, having seen the true news the comments section reduced spreading the false news tweets because of fact-check [22]. Conversely, if the spread of false news tweets is not affected by the appearance of true news tweets, then this means that true news tweets have no significant effect on the spread of false news.

To visualize spread relationships, we utilized tweet data to depict the interaction between false news tweets, true news tweets, and related content. Our approach linked retweeted or referenced tweets, constructing a graphical representation with lines indicating connections between nodes. This resulted in a tree diagram illustrating the dissemination and popularity of false and true news tweets. By contrasting the quantities of false and true news tweets, we measured whether true news had a notable presence to counteract false news. User relationships were then integrated into the diagram, facilitating a comparative assessment of their impact on the results. The visualization of tweet propagation was followed by graph statistics analysis, evaluating structural properties like degree, clusters, betweenness, harmonic centrality, eccentricity, closeness, Kleinberg's authority score, and Kleinberg's hub score for each vertex. This analysis examined the overlap of users between true and false news groups, identifying users who initially engaged with false news but later acknowledged it as false and supported truth. A substantial intersection of users suggests true news tweets' influence in users recognizing false news as rumors.

4   Results

Temporal Dimension Analysis: after analysing the data in the temporal dimension using the method described above, each group of combating news tweets has a time-based propagation history graph. See Figs. 4 and 5 as examples.

Fig. 4. Temporal dimension analysis of false news without fact-checked news

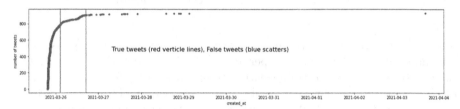

Fig. 5. Temporal dimension analysis of false news tweets when debunked by a fact-checked URL

The x-axis displays tweet creation time, and the y-axis shows tweet count. Blue dots represent tweets related to false news, notably prevalent and rapidly spreading, as seen in Figs. 4 and 5. Around 89% of false news, tweets spread rapidly in the initial one to two weeks before slowing. Graph points form a curve that flattens as propagation wanes, returning to individual points. Figure 5 features red lines denoting true news tweets, their thickness reflecting tweet volume per period. The absence of a red line in Fig. 4 indicates no or minimal true news response to the corresponding false news. If red lines coincide with the blue curve's turning point, where false news propagation decelerates, true news likely impacts it. This occurs in only 1.98% of time analysis plots. Certain false news retains propagation despite true news response (Fig. 6). True news occasionally affects low-popularity false news comments (Fig. 7).

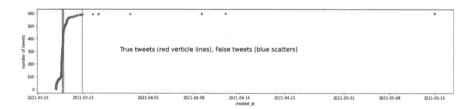

Fig. 6. Temporal dimension analysis of false news with fact-checked news. The propagation of false news despite true news debunk

For in-depth analysis, we statistically compared false news and true news tweets. A pretest-posttest approach was used to assess the impact of true news

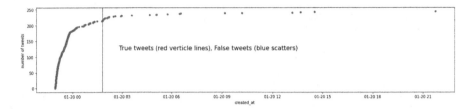

Fig. 7. Temporal dimension analysis of false news when debunked with fact-checked news. Fact-checked or true news occasionally affects low-popularity false news

comments on false news propagation on Twitter. Pretest-postest design is widely used in experimental and quasi-experimental studies to compare changes in test subjects before and after certain treatments [4]. Data was divided into treatment (false news with true news comments) and control groups (false news without corresponding true news). We observed over a two-week window as per [6], the treatment group's false news tweet diffusion was tallied a week before and after true news appearance. Control group's rates were calculated in the first and second week after false news creation. Data underwent two pretest and posttest ANCOVA analyses. Figure 8 displays the results of the first. We utilized the Difference (propagation rate change before/after true news) as dependent variable and Group (treatment/control) as fixed factor. Group's p-value (6.663 sum of squares, 1 degree of freedom, 6.663 mean square) is 0.989, well above 0.05. Therefore, no significant difference between treatment and control group data was found.

For the second pretest and posttest, post-speed (false news tweet propagation rate after true news appearance) was the dependent variable, group (treatment/control) the fixed factor, and pre-speed (false news tweet propagation rate before true news) the covariate. Figure 9 results reveal Group's p-value (5765.423 sum of squares, 1 degree of freedom, 5765.423 mean square, F = 0.169) as 0.682. Similar to the previous test, the p-value greatly exceeds 0.05. Both pretest and posttest analyses conclude that true news tweets had minimal impact on the majority of false news tweet propagation.

Tests of Between-Subjects Effects

Dependent Variable: Difference

Source	Type III Sum of Squares	df	Mean Square	F	Sig.	Partial Eta Squared
Corrected Model	6.663ª	1	6.663	.000	.989	.000
Intercept	88241.179	1	88241.179	2.444	.123	.036
Group	6.663	1	6.663	.000	.989	.000
Error	2382896.463	66	36104.492			
Total	2471144.305	68				
Corrected Total	2382903.126	67				

Fig. 8. Pretest and posttest with ANCOVA 1a

Tests of Between-Subjects Effects

Dependent Variable: Postspeed

Source	Type III Sum of Squares	df	Mean Square	F	Sig.
Corrected Model	28572989.847ᵃ	2	14286494.923	419.578	.000
Intercept	30467.999	1	30467.999	.895	.348
Prespeed	27682604.785	1	27682604.785	813.006	.000
Group	5765.423	1	5765.423	.169	.682
Error	2213229.862	65	34049.690		
Total	33540958.496	68			
Corrected Total	30786219.709	67			

Fig. 9. Pretest and posttest with ANCOVA 1b

Multivariate Testsᵃ

Effect		Value	F	Hypothesis df	Error df	Sig.
time	Pillai's Trace	.036	2.444ᵇ	1.000	66.000	.123
	Wilks' Lambda	.964	2.444ᵇ	1.000	66.000	.123
	Hotelling's Trace	.037	2.444ᵇ	1.000	66.000	.123
	Roy's Largest Root	.037	2.444ᵇ	1.000	66.000	.123
time * Group	Pillai's Trace	.000	.000ᵇ	1.000	66.000	.989
	Wilks' Lambda	1.000	.000ᵇ	1.000	66.000	.989
	Hotelling's Trace	.000	.000ᵇ	1.000	66.000	.989
	Roy's Largest Root	.000	.000ᵇ	1.000	66.000	.989

Fig. 10. Pretest and posttest with repeated measures ANOVA: Multivariate Tests

To enhance rigor and depth of analysis, the data underwent repeated measures ANOVA pretest and posttest. Within-subject factor "time" had two levels: pre-speed (false news tweet propagation before true news creation) and postspeed (false news tweet propagation after true news appearance). The between-subject factor was "group" (treatment/control) in the general linear model. Multivariate Tests' results (see Fig. 10) indicated p-values for time (p-value = 0.123) and time*group (p-value = 0.989) both exceeding 0.05. Similarly, Tests of Between-Subjects Effects (see Fig. 11) displayed Group's p-value (0.139) above 0.05. This implies that true news tweet emergence seemed to lack notable impact on false news tweet spread in terms of time-based dissemination.

4.1   Spread Relationships Analysis

Spread Relationships Analysis:
We present the tweet data into 3D visualisation of each false news tweet and true news tweet. For example, Fig. 12 is a tree diagram of the spread of a false news tweet The diagram consists of many different nodes connected by lines, with different coloured nodes representing different kinds of tweets. Light blue nodes represent retweets, dark blue represents replies, and green represent quoted tweets. A spherical group of many nodes can be seen in the diagram. At the centre of these spheres are false news quoted tweets or sources, which can be spread around to create a sphere, suggesting that the users posting them are the most influential on Twitter.

Tests of Between-Subjects Effects

Measure: MEASURE_1

Transformed Variable: Average

Source	Type III Sum of Squares	df	Mean Square	F	Sig.	Partial Eta Squared
Intercept	4567532.447	1	4567532.447	5.773	.019	.080
Group	1775902.066	1	1775902.066	2.244	.139	.033
Error	52222231.192	66	791245.927			

Fig. 11. Pretest and posttest with repeated measures ANOVA: Tests of Between-Subjects Effects

From network analysis, we found that 98% of true news has a smaller reach than false news tweets. In terms of influence, true news is less influential than false news tweets, and users do not follow true news tweets but retweet and quote false news tweets. Results showed that 49.1% of combating news had no common users, while 58.1% had just one intersect user; none had more. This suggests users that who engaged with false news tweets are not exposed to true news information content, indicating segregation between false and true news spreaders. This aligns with the tree diagram analysis, concluding true news struggles to influence false news spreaders and subsequent users, explaining their limited reach and impact on user engagement.

5   Discussion

The Emergence of True News Has No Significant Impact on the Spread of False News: Our findings indicate that true news tweets have minimal impact on false news tweet spread. Despite true news availability to counter false news misconceptions, the latter persists in spreading. False news tweets maintain high attention levels during their creation week, regardless of true news presence. The "echo chamber" phenomenon prevalent in social media creates homogeneity, diminishing fact-checking [16]. Data demonstrates false news tweets peak in spreading within a week (e.g., Fig. 6) while disproving evidence for true news necessitates time and resources [13]. By the time falseness is confirmed, false news tweets lose popularity and go viral (Fig. 7). Compared to false news' viral spread, the timing and frequency of true news tweets barely influence false news propagation. Effective false news prevention requires timely true news intervention within the false news-affected communities [8]. While earlier studies implied false news corrections could worsen belief [12], our study reveals no significant link between false news spread and true news correction. False news doesn't spread faster due to true news presence.

True News Cannot Reach People Who Previously Spread False News: True news tweets emerge only after false news tweets have already spread considerably, which means that people who previously disseminated false news may no longer follow the news. Users tend to favor news aligning with their beliefs [11], and the social media environment often diverts from accurate content sharing

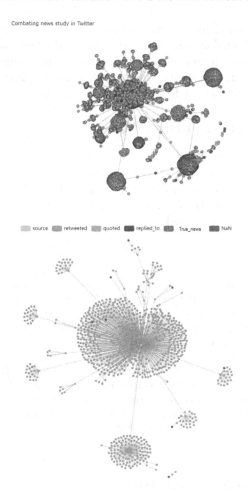

Fig. 12. 3D visualisation of the spread of a false news tweet

[13]. Network graph data analysis highlights the significant volume difference between true and false news tweets. Despite true news tweets linking to fact-checking sites, this suggests limited user engagement with such resources [16]. Beyond time constraints, identifying true news tweets amidst numerous retweets, quoted tweets, and replies to false news tweets is difficult, suggesting the need for better ways to inform users. Even if true news reaches its target audience, its efficacy in refuting false news dwindles over time [17].

People Tend to Focus on False News Rather than True News:
Distribution patterns and user networks of false news tweets reveal stark attention disparities between true and false news tweets. True news tweets get limited retweets and references, potentially due to false news' novel nature [19]. Moreover, followers of true news tweets are scarcely linked to followers of false

news tweets, resulting in near-complete segregation between the two groups. This underscores the minimal influence of true news on false news tweets. Such strong polarization signifies a larger false news believers' base compared to true news believers. Our data-driven finding aligns with the notion that deeply entrenched polarized communities hinder fact-checking's reach [10].

6   Conclusion and Future Work

Our findings indicate true news doesn't significantly affect false news spread, it doesn't rule out its use in combating misinformation. Current fact-checking methods are time-consuming [13], so finding ways to spotlight true news faster could be beneficial. The role of language and potential use of bots to spread true news also can also be considered.

References

1. Aldwairi, M., Alwahedi, A.: Detecting fake news in social media networks. Procedia Comput. Sci. **141**, 215–222 (2018). https://doi.org/10.1016/j.procs.2018.10.171. https://www.sciencedirect.com/science/article/pii/S1877050918318210
2. Asr, F., Taboada, M.: Big data and quality data for fake news and misinformation detection. Big Data Soc. **6**(1), 205395171984331 (2019). https://doi.org/10.1177/2053951719843310
3. CNN: How Facebook is combating spread of COVID-19 misinformation— CNN business (2020). https://edition.cnn.com/videos/tech/2020/04/17/mark-zuckerberg-facebook-limit-coronavirus-misinformation-cnn-town-hall-vpx.cnn
4. Dimitrov, D., Rumrill, P.: Pretest-posttest designs and measurement of change. Work (Reading Mass.) **20**, 159–65 (2003)
5. Friggeri, A., Adamic, L., Eckles, D., Cheng, J.: Rumor cascades. In: Proceedings of the 8th International Conference on Weblogs and Social Media, ICWSM 2014, pp. 101–110 (2014)
6. Goel, S., Watts, D.J., Goldstein, D.G.: The structure of online diffusion networks. In: Proceedings of the 13th ACM Conference on Electronic Commerce, pp. 623–638. Association for Computing Machinery, New York (2012)
7. Howells, T.: The fake news epidemic (2017). https://zignallabs.com/blog/fake-news-epidemic/
8. Kim, A., Moravec, P.L., Dennis, A.R.: Combating fake news on social media with source ratings: the effects of user and expert reputation ratings. J. Manag. Inf. Syst. **36**(3), 931–968 (2019)
9. Lewandowsky, S., Ecker, U., Seifert, C., Schwarz, N., Cook, J.: Misinformation and its correction continued influence and successful debiasing. Psychol. Sci. Public Interest **13**, 106–131 (2012)
10. Micallef, N., He, B., Kumar, S., Ahamad, M., Memon, N.: The Role of the crowd in countering misinformation: a case study of the COVID-19 infodemic, In: 2020 IEEE International Conference on Big Data (Big Data) pp. 748–757 (2020). https://doi.org/10.1109/BigData50022.2020.9377956
11. Moravec, P., Minas, R., Dennis, A.R.: Fake news on social media: people believe what they want to believe when it makes no sense at all, 9 august 2018. Kelley school of business research paper no. 18–87. SSRN: https://ssrn.com/abstract=3269541

12. Nyhan, B., Reifler, J.: When corrections fail: the persistence of political misperceptions. Polit. Behav. **32**, 303–330 (2010)
13. Pennycook, G.: The psychology of fake news. Trends Cogn. Sci. **25**, 388–402 (2021)
14. Pennycook, G., Binnendyk, J., Newton, C.: A practical guide to doing behavioral research on fake news and misinformation. Collabra Psychol. **7**, 25293 (2021)
15. Procter, R., Vis, F., Voss, A.: Reading the riots on twitter: methodological innovation for the analysis of big data. Int. J. Soc. Res. Methodol. **16**, 197–214 (2013)
16. Schuetz, S., Sykes, T.A., Venkatesh, V.: Combating COVID-19 fake news on social media through fact checking: antecedents and consequences. Eur. J. Inf. Syst. **30**, 376–388 (2021)
17. Swire-Thompson, B., Ecker, U., Lewandowsky, S.: The role of familiarity in correcting inaccurate information. J. Exp. Psychol. Learn. Mem. Cogn. **43**, 1948 (2017)
18. Vo, N., Lee, K.: Standing on the shoulders of guardians: novel methodologies to combat fake news (2019)
19. Vosoughi, S., Roy, D., Aral, S.: The spread of true and false news online. Science **359**, 1146–1151 (2018)
20. Wang, K., Yaqub, W., Lakhdari, A., Suleiman, B.: Combating fake news by empowering fact-checked news spread via topology-based interventions. arXiv preprint arXiv:2107.05016 (2021)
21. Wen, S., Sayad Haghighi, M., Chen, C., Xiang, Y., Zhou, W., Jia, W.: A sword with two edges: propagation studies on both positive and negative information in online social networks. IEEE Trans. Comput. **64**, 640–653 (2015)
22. Yaqub, W., Kakhidze, O., Brockman, M.L., Memon, N., Patil, S.: Effects of credibility indicators on social media news sharing intent, p. 1–14. Association for Computing Machinery, New York (2020)
23. Zhang, X., Ghorbani, A.: An overview of online fake news: characterization, detection, and discussion. Inf. Process. Manage. **57**, 102025 (2019)
24. Zubiaga, A., Aker, A., Bontcheva, K., Liakata, M., Procter, R.: Detection and resolution of rumours in social media: a survey. ACM Comput. Surv. **51**, 1–36 (2018)

Highly Applicable Linear Event Detection Algorithm on Social Media with Graph Stream

Lihua Liu[1], Mao Wang[1], Haiwei Jiang[3], Ziming Li[2], Peifan Shi[2], and Youhuan Li[2(✉)]

[1] National University of Defense Technology, Changsha, China
wangmao@nudt.edu.cn
[2] Hunan University, Changsha, China
{zimingli,spf,liyouhuan}@hnu.edu.cn
[3] Longyan Tobacco Industrial Co., Ltd., Changsha, China
jhw228800@fjtic.cn

Abstract. In this paper, we model social media with graph stream and propose an efficient event detection algorithm that costs only linear time and space. Different from existing work, we propose an LIS (longest increasing subsequence)-based edge weight to evaluate the importance of keywords co-occurrence with regard to an event. LIS-based measure conquers the limitations of existing metrics, such as ignoring the inherent correlations and sensitive to noises. More importantly, we propose a linear time and space stream algorithm to detect event subgraphs from social media. The elegant theoretical results indicate the high scalability of our graph stream solution in web-scale social media data. Extensive experiments over Tweets stream from Twitter confirms the efficiency and effectiveness of our solution.

Keywords: Graph Stream · Event Detection · Subgraph

1 Introduction

Event detection is one of the fundamental problems over social media [5,15,18,19], which can help us gather real time information and react much more quickly to public events, such as natural disasters, conflagration, traffic accident and so on. In this paper, we propose a general linear framework for event detection over social streams. Specifically, we do not require special data in our solutions, such as search records on Twitter, location information and so on. Instead, we only focus on the stream consisting of texts (posts) and the corresponding timestamps, which makes our method highly applicable. Also, we argue that the propose solution ct at most linear time and space in view of the large sc, ale of social data.

Many works are proposed for event detection on social medias. Most of them require special information or make specific assumptions in their methods, such as twitter search records [13], hashtag [6], user-following information [10,21,24] and short text distribution [11]. Some of them may also focus on detecting domain specific event such as earthquakes [18]. These methods with specific assumptions are not highly applicable.

F. Zhang et al. (Eds.): WISE 2023, LNCS 14306, pp. 134–143, 2023.
https://doi.org/10.1007/978-981-99-7254-8_11

In this paper, we are committed to build a event detection framework over text stream with timestamps. Information derived from these co-occurring keywords brings us an adequate understanding about relevant events. Furthermore, behaviors of keywords indicating events tends to be different from those normal ones, i.e., keywords related no events. For example, *"Kobe"* and *"crash"* co-occurred in an unusual frequency when Calabasas helicopter crash event happened. Therefore, it is feasible to detect sudden events based on behaviors of keywords and their co-occurrences. Apparently, this framework built over text stream is of great significance since it is promising on event detection but also highly applicable.

There are also some work on event detection focusing on text stream [3,7–9,14,17,22,23]. A part of them compute similarity between different keywords, which will be further clustered into groups, forming different events [7–9,14,17]. While, clustering based methods are usually difficult to update efficiently for expired information (posts related to outdated events). Angel et al. [3] propose to mine dense subgraphs as event subgraphs. They build a keyword graph G, in which each vertex represents a keyword and an edge denotes the keyword co-occurrence in the same post. An edge weight measures co-occurrence strength. The goal of event detection is to find subgraphs (of G) that reflect some important events. We often call these subgraphs as *event subgraphs*. However, these methods provide no performance guarantee. In view of the large scale of the social data, algorithm costing $O(n^2)$ time would be not applicable.

Some text stream based approaches consider the "burst" (i.e., sudden change of frequency) as a promising hint for sudden events [22,23], since some keywords tend to co-occur much more frequently when events happen, leading the burst of the co-occurrence frequency. These solutions can be efficiently computed and updated. While the simple assumption is reasonable, some bursts happen because of noises rather than events.

1.1 Our Solution and Contributions

Considering the above shortages in existing work, we propose a graph stream-based solution for event detection with *linear worst-case time and space complexity*. Also, our solution is highly applicable.

First, we propose an Longest Increasing Subsequence(LIS)-based edge weight, of which the most important benefits of LIS-based edge weight are robust to noises and considering the inherent correlation between keywords. LIS prefers to select an increasing subsequence that exhibits a long rising duration. We also need to measure the rising amplitude when defining edge weights. Intuitively, the high rising amplitude indicates the importance of an event. Thus, we use the relative rising amplitude of a LIS in defining edge weights, i.e., the ratio of the total increase to the first value of the sequence. The relative rising amplitude takes the inherent correlation between keyword pairs into account. Second, our graph stream-based algorithm has the worst case performance guarantee (linear time and space complexity in terms of the number of edges in the current time window). There are two tasks in our algorithm: computing and maintaining LIS-based edge weight and mining subgraphs corresponding to events. We design an algorithm with time complexity $O(|W|)$ to maintain LIS for each edge. More importantly, we utilize a linear algorithm $(O(|E|))$ to detect event subgraphs as G changes dynamically. We summarize our contributions as following:

1. To detect events in social media, we propose a novel edge weight (in keyword graph) that is robust to noises and considering the inherent correlation between keywords. The edge weight computation relies only on text stream with timestamps, which makes our method highly applicable.
2. We design linear algorithms on time and space for both edge weight maintenance and event subgraph mining. This is the first work that provides the worst-case performance guarantee for general graph stream-based event detection.
3. Extensive experiments on a large Twitter dataset confirm the superiority of our method in both effectiveness and efficiency.

2   Problem Formulation

A time window W consists of $|W|$ time intervals. We assume that there are $|V|$ keywords in total, each of which is represented as a vertex. A graph stream is defined by a continuously arriving sequences of edges. An edge $e = \overline{k_1 k_2}$ means that keywords k_1 and k_2 co-occur in some posts. In view that a keyword pair may co-occur multiple times, leading the repetitions of edges, we define e's edge frequency $F(e, T_i^{i+1})$ as the number of co-occurrences during time interval T_i^{i+1}. For the simplicity of notation, we often use T_i instead of T_i^{i+1} to refer to the corresponding time interval.

A temporal graph G_W over the time window W is defined in Definition 1. Obviously, G_W is consistently updating when the first time interval (in W) expires and a new time interval is inserted.

Definition 1 *(Temporal Graph). A temporal graph at the time window W is defined as $G_W = (V, E)$, where V denotes all keywords and E indicates all keyword co-occurrence during the time window W. Each edge $e \in E$ has a frequency sequence $\alpha(e, W) = \{F(e, T_s), F(e, T_{s+1}), ... F(e, T_{s+|W|-1})\}$.*

We consider two requirements in defining $w(e, W)$: *long rising duration* and *high rising amplitude*. When an important event happens, the related keyword pairs' frequencies should exhibit a long rising duration, since the burst of frequency in a short duration are likely to be noises. Also, we consider relative rising amplitude, i.e., the ratio of the total increase to the first value of the sequence (see $A(s)$ in Definition 3). The relative rising amplitude takes the inherent correlation between keyword pairs into account. Thus, we propose a LIS-based edge weight measurement as follows:

Definition 2 *(Longest Increasing Subsequence). Given a sequence $\alpha = \{a_1, a_2, ..., a_n\}$, an increasing subsequence s of α is a subsequence whose elements are in sorted order, lowest to highest. The head and the tail of s are denoted as s^h and s^t, respectively. $|s|$ denotes the length of s.*

An increasing subsequence s of α is called a Longest Increasing Subsequence (LIS) if and only if there exists no any increasing subsequence s', where $|s| < |s'|$.

A sequence α may contain multiple LIS. A collection of them is denoted as $LIS(\alpha)$.

Definition 4 defines edge weight, which has two parts $L(s)$ and $A(s)$. Obviously, if a keyword co-occurrence is related to an event, it should exhibit a clear rising trend, i.e., $L(s)$ in Definition 3. The burst of frequency in a short time is likely to be noise. Furthermore, the high rising amplitude means the importance of an event, i.e., $A(s)$ in Definition 3.

Definition 3 *(Edge Weight). Given an edge e in a temporal graph G_W at time window W, edge weight $w(e, W)$ is defined as follows:*

$$w(e, W) = \max_{s \in LIS(\alpha(e, W))} \{L(s) * A(s)\} \tag{1}$$

$$L(s) = \frac{|s|}{|W|}, A(s) = \frac{F(e, T_{s^t}) - F(e, T_{s^h})}{(1 + \varepsilon)^{F(e, T_{s^h})}}$$

where $F(e, T_{s^h})$ and $F(e, T_{s^t})$ denote the head frequency and the tail frequency of LIS s, respectively, and ϵ is a tunable parameter that is slightly larger than zero.

2.1 Rising Subgraph

According to "keyword co-occurrence assumption", if an edge $e = \overline{k_1, k_2}$ has a high weight $w(e, W)$, it indicates that an event concerning keywords k_1 and k_2 are happening in the time window W. An event may involve more than two keywords. Therefore, our event detection task is defined as follows:

Definition 4 *(Rising Subgraph). Given an temporal graph G_W over time window W, a connected subgraph H (in G_W) is called a rising subgraph if and only if the following conditions hold: ① each edge e of H has weight $w(e, W) \geq \theta$, a user specified threshold; ② there exists no any other connected subgraph H', where H is a subgraph of H' and H' also satisfies the first condition.*

Definition 5 *(Problem Definition). Given a temporal graph G_W over time window W, the goal is to detect all rising subgraphs $R(G_W)$ within a continuous period of time, while $G(w)$ are consistently updating.*

3 Rising Edge Identification

Given an edge e in temporal graph G_W, e is a *rising edge* if edge weight $w(e, W) \geq \theta$, where θ is a tunable parameter. Insertion and deletion of the frequency sequence $\alpha(e, w)$ lead to the update of the edge weight $w(e, W)$. Thus, the key issues in rising edge identification are how to compute edge weights and cope with frequency sequence updates in the stream model. Specifically, we design an efficient algorithm over a novel index, quadruple neighbor list (QN-list, for short), to support both edge weight computation and maintenance. QN-list is proposed in our previous work where we have discussed the corresponding definition, construction and maintenance (in stream scenario) [12]. We first briefly introduce QN-list (Sect. 3.1) and then we will present the edge weight computation over QN-list.

3.1   Quadruple Neighbor List (QN-List)

Let's consider an edge e and its corresponding frequency sequence $\alpha(e, W)$: $a_1, a_2, ...,$ a_w, where $w = |W|$. When the context is clear, we often use α to represent $\alpha(e, W)$. According to edge weight definition (Definition 3), we need to find a LIS (longest increasing subsequence, Definition 2) to maximize Eq. 1. To achieve that, we utilize a data structure $\mathbb{L}_\alpha$ for edge e, which is essentially a quadruple neighbor list: each item a_i ($i = 1, ..., w$) in $\mathbb{L}_\alpha$ has both left and right horizontal neighbors (denoted as $ln_\alpha(a_i)$ and $rn_\alpha(a_i)$, respectively) and up and down vertical neighbors (denoted as $un_\alpha(a_i)$ and $dn_\alpha(a_i)$, respectively). Before introducing the definition of QN-list, we present some important concepts which will be used in our algorithms. These definitions are also presented in our previous work [12].

We say that a_i is *compatible* with a_j if $i < j$ and $a_i \le a_j$ in α, denoted as $a_i \overset{\alpha}{\lessgtr} a_j$. Also, we define the *rising length* $RL_\alpha(a_i)$ of a_i as the maximum length of increasing subsequences that end with a_i. If $a_j \overset{\alpha}{\lessgtr} a_i$ and $RL_\alpha(a_j) = RL_\alpha(a_i) - 1$, we say that a_j is a *predecessor* of a_i, and the set of predecessors of a_i is denoted as $Pred_\alpha(a_i)$. With these concepts, we introduce the definition of QN-list in Definition 6.

Definition 6 (Quadruple Neighbor List (QN-list). *Given a sequence α, quadruple neighbor list of α, denoted as $\mathbb{L}_\alpha$, is a data structure where each item $a_i \in \alpha$ has at least four neighbors: left, right, up and down neighbors, denoted as $ln_\alpha(a_i)$, $rn_\alpha(a_i)$, $un_\alpha(a_i)$ and $dn_\alpha(a_i)$, respectively.*

1. *$ln_\alpha(a_i) = a_j$ if a_j is the nearest item before a_i such that $RL_\alpha(a_i) = RL_\alpha(a_j)$.*
2. *$rn_\alpha(a_i) = a_j$ if a_j is the nearest item after a_i such that $RL_\alpha(a_i) = RL_\alpha(a_j)$.*
3. *$un_\alpha(a_i) = a_j$ if a_j is the nearest item before a_i such that $RL_\alpha(a_j) = RL_\alpha(a_i) - 1$.*
4. *$dn_\alpha(a_i) = a_j$ if a_j is the nearest item before a_i such that $RL_\alpha(a_j) = RL_\alpha(a_i) + 1$.*

We use $\mathbb{L}_\alpha^k$ to denote the list formed by linking items of rising length k according to their horizontal neighbor relationships and we call the list as horizontal list. The QN-list over running example sequence $\{3, 9, 6, 2, 8, 5, 7\}$ is presented in Fig. 1. Apparently, up neighbor is the nearest predecessor of an item. For those who have no up neighbors, their rising length is 1 and they are in $\mathbb{L}_\alpha^1$.

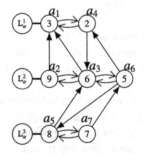

Fig. 1. QN-list over frequency sequence $\{3, 9, 6, 2, 8, 5, 7\}$

Also, the maximum rising length of items in the sequence is exactly the LIS length of the sequence (as well as the number of horizontal lists in the QN-list). Thus, the last item of each LIS must be in the last horizontal list of QN-list.

3.2 Edge Weight Computation over QN-List

In this subsection, we propose a $\mathbb{L}_\alpha$-based algorithm to compute edge weights. For an LIS $\{a_{i_1}, a_{i_j}, \ldots a_{i_t}\}$, $a_{i_{j-1}}$ must be a predecessor of a_{i_j} $(1 < j \le t)$, hence, to find LIS of α, we need to conduct a traverse starting from items in $\mathbb{L}_\alpha^{|\mathbb{L}_\alpha|}$ following the predecessor relationships recursively until the visited items constitute an sequence of length $|\mathbb{L}_\alpha|$. For example, in Fig. 1, if we first visit 7 in $\mathbb{L}_\alpha^3$, following the predecessor relationship to 5 and 3, we can find an LIS: $\{3, 5, 7\}$. Thus, a straightforward approach to computing edge weights is to enumerate all LIS in sequence α, finding one LIS s to maximize Eq. 1. To save computation cost, in the following, we propose an efficient algorithm to avoid enumerating all LIS.

We first introduce some important concepts. We use $un_\alpha^k(a_i)$ denote $un_\alpha(un_\alpha^{k-1}(a_i))$, and $un_\alpha^0(a_i) = a_i$. We define starting item of a_i, denoted as $ST_\alpha(a_i)$, as $un_\alpha^{RL_\alpha(a_i)-1}(a_i)$. In Fig. 1, $ST_\alpha(8) = ST_\alpha(6) = 3$, while $ST_\alpha(7) = ST_\alpha(5) = 2$. For $\forall a_i \in \alpha$, there may exist multiple increasing subsequences with the maximum length $RL_\alpha(a_i)$. For example, the lengths of both increasing subsequences $s_1 = \{3, 6, 7\}$ and $s_2 = \{2, 5, 7\}$ are 3, ending with 7. According to Eq. 1, $A(s_1) < A(s_2)$. Thus, only s_2 contributes to computing edge weight. However, the straightforward solution needs to enumerate all LIS in α.

Actually, Given $a_i \in \alpha = \{a_1, a_2, ..., a_w\}$, for any $s \in IS_\alpha(a_i)$ with the maximum length (i.e., $|s| = RL_\alpha(a_i)$, we have $ST_\alpha(a_i) \le s^h$. Also, for any sequence s^* where $s^* = \{un_\alpha^{RL_\alpha(a_i)-1}(a_i), un_\alpha^{RL_\alpha(a_i)-2}(a_i), \cdots, un_\alpha(a_i), a_i\}$, the following two claims hold: ① s^* is an increasing subsequence with the maximum length $RL_\alpha(a_i)$; ② for any increasing subsequence s ending with a_i with the longest length $RL_\alpha(a_i)$, we have:

$$\frac{a_i - s^h}{(1 + \epsilon)^{s^h}} \le \frac{a_i - s^{*h}}{(1 + \epsilon)^{s^{*h}}} = \frac{a_i - un_\alpha^{RL_\alpha(a_i)-1}(a_i)}{(1 + \epsilon)^{un_\alpha^{RL_\alpha(a_i)-1}(a_i)}} = \frac{a_i - ST_\alpha(a_i)}{(1 + \epsilon)^{ST_\alpha(a_i)}}$$

The above remark provides an efficient algorithm to compute edge weights. Specifically, for each a_i in the last horizontal list $\mathbb{L}_\alpha^{|\mathbb{L}_\alpha|}$, we can get the corresponding increasing subsequence s^* by computing its k-hop up neighbors. Then, we find the one to maximize $A(s) = \frac{a_i - ST_\alpha(a_i)}{(1+\epsilon)^{ST_\alpha(a_i)}}$, which is used to commute edge weights.

However, two different elements a_i and a_j in the last horizontal list $\mathbb{L}_\alpha^{|\mathbb{L}_\alpha|}$ may share the same x-hop up neighbors, resulting in the same k-hop up neighbors $(k \ge x)$. Thus, there is much room for sharing computation.

4 Rising Subgraph Detection

A rising subgraph is a maximal connected subgraph (in G_W), all of whose edge weights are larger than a threshold θ. We need to detect these rising subgraphs as edge weights are consistently changing. Actually, we can apply a connected component maintenance algorithm in the rising subgraph problem.

Given a threshold θ, we build a virtual un-weighted graph $G_W^u = (V, E^u, W)$, while V is exactly same with the vertex set in G_W and $e \in E^u$ if and only if e is an edge in G_W and $w(e, W) > \theta$. It can be easily understood that, for $u, v \in V$ the following statements are equivalent: ① u, v are connected by a path in G_W, while the weight of each constituting edge is larger than θ; ② u, v are connected in G_W^u. Hence, detecting rising subgraph in G_W can be solved directly by detecting the connected component in G_W^u. It is straightforward to design a BFS or DFS algorithm with the linear time complexity to find all connected components in G_W^u. There are also efficient algorithms to dynamically track the connected components of a graph as vertices and edges are updated. It is easy to understand that the time complexity of our event detection approach is $O(|W| \times |E(G_W)|)$, and the space complexity of our event detection approach is $O(|W| \times |E(G_W)|)$.

5   Experimental Results

We use a real-world Tweet data set of 5.34M tweets in our evaluation. All experiments are implemented with C++ and conducted on Intel(R) Xeon E5645, 4G mem (Figs. 2 and 4).

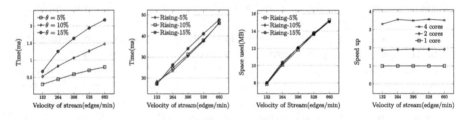

Fig. 2. Used Time   **Fig. 3.** Average Time   **Fig. 4.** Linear space   **Fig. 5.** Multi-thread

5.1   Efficiency

Figure 3 shows that our total running time is linear to edge stream velocity. It is straightforward to know that the number of edges in a time window is linear to edge stream velocity when time window size $|W|$ is given. Thus, Fig. 3 also confirms that our algorithm is linear in terms of the number of edges in a time window. Figure 5 shows that we can further optimize running time by parallelization. Considering a real Twitter environment, edge velocity may be faster than our experimental data. However, it is easy to speed up our method by a large "scale-out" computing cluster, which enables apply our approach in Web-scale social media data. Moreover, our approach has linear space complexity. Figure 7 also confirms our theoretical result.

We compare our algorithm with Dense [3]. We implement Dense using AVGWEIGHT definition of density on weighted dataset. There are three important parameter in Dense, namely *Nmax*, *T* and δ_{it}. We adopt all suggested parameter values in [3]. Since the time window of our method spans 30 min, we set the mean life in Dense as 30 min, too. Note that both our method and Dense are implemented using one core (single thread) in comparison. Figure 6 shows that our method outperforms Dense by almost two orders of magnitude.

5.2 Effectiveness

Effectiveness of Edge Weight. We compare our LIS-based rising edge weight with some classical measures for event detection, such as frequency-based, burst-based and the two measures used in [3]: one is a combination of the Chi-Square measure and the correlation coefficient [4], the other is the log-likelihood ratio [20]. We compute these five kinds of measure over the edge stream. At each time t, for any measure above, we retrieve the top $\tau \in \{20\%, 40\%, 60\%, 80\%, 100\%\}$ edges (ranked by the corresponding weight) and calculate the precision of these edges on reflecting some events. We compare these measures using their average precision of the whole stream in Fig. 8. We find that precision of rising edge weight is higher than that of other measures (Fig. 9).

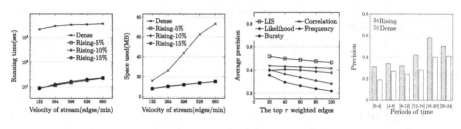

Fig. 6. Time Cost   **Fig. 7.** Space Cost   **Fig. 8.** Rising Edge   **Fig. 9.** Precision

Effectiveness of Rising Subgraph. We also compare our approach with Dense [3] on effectiveness. For every four hours since 00:00:00, March 7th, 2014, we manually extract some events with the help of the four kinds of measure (We check the top 100 edges weighted by each measure during that four hours and find the real events from related edges). Those extracted events are used as the benchmark of the corresponding period to examine the precision our approach and the dense subgraph maintenance. We can see that the event detected by our approach is more likely to reflect an real event than that by Dense.

6 Related Work

Many solutions on event detection are design for specific social media, such as Twitter and Weibo [1,6,10,11,13,16,18,21,24]. We omit discussions over these methods since their specific assumptions are not highly applicable.

There are also some work on event detection focusing on text stream only. *Keyword-based weight computation* detect events by finding keywords that reflect some important events in social media. [4] detects keyword clusters on blog stream, based on the association strength between keywords, measured through a way combining both χ^2 and correlated coefficient. [20] identifies coupled entities with strong entity associations measured by Likelihood Ratio statistical test. *Clustering based methods* retrieve important keywords indicating events and then cluster them into different groups forming detected events [7–9,14,17]. These methods usually cost square time w.r.t. keywords number and difficult to update when posts expired (i.e., deletion or decay of some keywords). *Subgraph mining based event detection* also attracted researchers' attentions [2,3]. Angel et al. identify real-time story by identifying and maintaining dense subgraph under streaming edge weight updates [3]. There are two problems that prohibit the scalability of their method in large scale social media data. First, the time complexity and space complexity of dense subgraph mining are both unbounded (i.e., exponential complexity). Charu et al. studied the dense pattern mining in graph streams [2], which can be borrowed to event detection problem. However, their method cannot eliminate expired data, which limits the usage of [2] in event detection problem, since events employ strong temporal components. *Burst based solutions* consider the "burst" (i.e., sudden change of frequency) as a promising hint for sudden events, since some keywords tend to co-occur much more frequently when events happen, leading the burst of the co-occurrence frequency. TwitterMonitor [13] detects bursty keywords and groups them with their co-occurrence. TopicSketch [22,23] maintains a sketch using acceleration to detect bursty topics. Although "bursty" is a promising tool to identify realtime events in social media, it has inevitable shortcomings in event detection, that is not robust to noises in social media.

7 Conclusions

In this paper, we propose a graph stream approach to detect realtime events from social media. We first propose a LIS (longest increasing subsequence)-based edge weight to evaluate the importance of keyword co-occurrences with regard to an event. We also propose an efficient index structure, an quadruble neighbor list $\mathbb{L}_\alpha$, to compute edge weight. Finally, we find rising subgraphs as reporting events. More importantly, we prove the linear time and space complexity in our approach. Extensive experiments confirm the efficiency and effectiveness of our approach.

References

1. Abel, F., Hauff, C., Houben, G.-J., Stronkman, R., Tao, K.: Twitcident: fighting fire with information from social web streams. In: Proceedings of the 21st International Conference Companion on World Wide Web, pp. 305–308. ACM (2012)
2. Aggarwal, C.C., Li, Y., Yu, P.S., Jin, R.: On dense pattern mining in graph streams. Proc. VLDB Endow. 3(1), 975–984 (2010)
3. Angel, A., Koudas, N., Sarkas, N., Srivastava, D.: Dense subgraph maintenance under streaming edge weight updates for real-time story identification. PVLDB 5(6), 574–585 (2012)
4. Bansal, N., Chiang, F., Koudas, N., Tompa, F.W.: Seeking stable clusters in the blogosphere. VLDB Endow. 806–817 (2007)
5. Becker, H., Naaman, M., Gravano, L.: Event identification in social media. In: WebDB (2009)
6. Boom, C.D., Canneyt, S.V., Dhoedt, B.: Semantics-driven event clustering in twitter feeds. In: Proceedings of the the 5th Workshop on Making Sense of Microposts Co-located with the 24th International World Wide Web Conference. CEUR Workshop Proceedings, vol. 1395, pp. 2–9 (2015)

7. Fedoryszak, M., Frederick, B., Rajaram, V., Zhong, C.: Real-time event detection on social data streams. In: Proceedings of the 25th ACM International Conference on Knowledge Discovery & Data Mining, pp. 2774–2782. ACM (2019)

8. Hasan, M., Orgun, M.A., Schwitter, R.: TwitterNews+: a framework for real time event detection from the twitter data stream. In: Spiro, E., Ahn, Y.-Y. (eds.) SocInfo 2016. LNCS, vol. 10046, pp. 224–239. Springer, Cham (2016). https://doi.org/10.1007/978-3-319-47880-7_14

9. Kaleel, S.B., Abhari, A.: Cluster-discovery of twitter messages for event detection and trending. J. Comput. Sci. **6**, 47–57 (2015)

10. Kwan, E., Hsu, P., Liang, J., Chen, Y.: Event identification for social streams using keyword-based evolving graph sequences. In: Advances in Social Networks Analysis and Mining, pp. 450–457. ACM (2013)

11. Li, J., Tai, Z., Zhang, R. Yu, W., Liu, L.: Online bursty event detection from microblog. In: Proceedings of the 7th IEEE/ACM International Conference on Utility and Cloud Computing, pp. 865–870. IEEE Computer Society (2014)

12. Li, Y., Zou, L., Zhang, H., Zhao, D.: Computing longest increasing subsequences over sequential data streams. Proc. VLDB Endow. **10**(3), 181–192 (2016)

13. Mathioudakis, M., Koudas, N.: TwitterMonitor: trend detection over the twitter stream. In: Proceedings of the 2010 ACM SIGMOD International Conference on Management of Data, pp. 1155–1158. ACM (2010)

14. McMinn, A.J., Jose, J.M.: Real-time entity-based event detection for twitter. In: Mothe, J., et al. (eds.) CLEF 2015. LNCS, vol. 9283, pp. 65–77. Springer, Cham (2015). https://doi.org/10.1007/978-3-319-24027-5_6

15. Olanrewaju, A.-S.T., Hossain, M.A., Whiteside, N., Mercieca, P.: Social media and entrepreneurship research: a literature review. Int. J. Inf. Manage. **50**, 90–110 (2020)

16. Osborne, M., Petrovic, S., McCreadie, R., Macdonald, C., Ounis, I.: Bieber no more: first story detection using twitter and Wikipedia. In: Proceedings of the Workshop on Time-aware Information Access. TAIA, vol. 12 (2012)

17. Parikh, R., Karlapalem, K.: ET: events from tweets. In: 22nd International World Wide Web Conference, pp. 613–620. ACM (2013)

18. Sakaki, T., Okazaki, M., Matsuo, Y.: Earthquake shakes twitter users: real-time event detection by social sensors. In: Proceedings of the 19th International Conference on World Wide Web, pp. 851–860. ACM (2010)

19. Sakaki, T., Okazaki, M., Matsuo, Y.: Tweet analysis for real-time event detection and earthquake reporting system development. IEEE Trans. Knowl. Data Eng. **25**(4), 919–931 (2013)

20. Sarkas, N., Angel, A., Koudas, N., Srivastava, D.: Efficient identification of coupled entities in document collections. In: IEEE 26th International Conference on Data Engineering, pp. 769–772. IEEE (2010)

21. Xie, R., Zhu, F., Ma, H., Xie, W., Lin, C.: CLEar: a real-time online observatory for bursty and viral events. Proc. VLDB Endow. **7**(13), 1637–1640 (2014)

22. Xie, W., Zhu, F. Jiang, J., Lim, E., Wang, K.: TopicSketch: real-time bursty topic detection from twitter. In: ICDM, pp. 837–846 (2013)

23. Xie, W., Zhu, F., Jiang, J., Lim, E., Wang, K.: TopicSketch: Real-time bursty topic detection from twitter. IEEE Trans. Knowl. Data Eng. **28**(8), 2216–2229 (2016)

24. Zhang, X., Chen, X., Chen, Y., Wang, S., Li, Z., Xia, J.: Event detection and popularity prediction in microblogging. Neurocomputing **149**, 1469–1480 (2015)

Leveraging Social Networks for Mergers and Acquisitions Forecasting

Alessandro Visintin$^{(\boxtimes)}$ and Mauro Conti

University of Padova, Via VIII Febbraio, 2, 35122 Padova, Italy
alevise.public@gmail.com

Abstract. Mergers and acquisitions are pivotal strategies employed by companies to maintain competitiveness, leading to enhanced production efficiency, scale, and market dominance. Due to their significant financial implications, predicting these operations has become a profitable area of study for both scholars and industry professionals. The accurate forecasting of mergers and acquisitions activities is a complex task, demanding advanced statistical tools and generating substantial returns for stakeholders and investors. Existing research in this field has proposed various methods encompassing econometric models, machine learning algorithms, and sentiment analysis. However, the effectiveness and accuracy of these approaches vary considerably, posing challenges for the development of robust and scalable models.

In this paper, we present a novel approach to forecast mergers and acquisitions activities by utilizing social network analysis. By examining temporal changes in social network graphs of the involved entities, potential transactions can be identified prior to public announcements, granting a significant advantage in the forecasting process. To validate our approach, we conduct a case study on three recent acquisitions made by Microsoft, leveraging the social network platform Twitter. Our methodology involves distinguishing employees from random users and subsequently analyzing the evolution of mutual connections over time. The results demonstrate a strong link between engaged firms, with the connections between Microsoft employees and acquired companies ranging from five to twenty times higher than those of baseline companies in the two years preceding the official announcement. These findings underscore the potential of social network analysis in accurately forecasting mergers and acquisitions activities and open avenues for the development of innovative methodologies.

Keywords: Social networks analysis · Merger and acquisition prediction · Twitter analysis

1 Introduction

Mergers and acquisitions (M&A) are strategic business activities that involve the integration of two or more firms into a single entity. These transactions can occur in several forms, including the acquisition of one company by another,

F. Zhang et al. (Eds.): WISE 2023, LNCS 14306, pp. 144–159, 2023.
https://doi.org/10.1007/978-981-99-7254-8_12

the merger of two organizations to create a new entity, or the purchase of a segment of a company's assets by another firm. M&A activities are motivated by a range of factors, such as expanding market shares, diversifying product offerings, reducing costs, or accessing new technologies. These transactions have far-reaching implications for the involved firms, their industries, and the broader economy. In the year 2022, the aggregate value of M&A transactions worldwide amounted to 3.8 trillion dollars [14], underlining the significant role of these activities in the global economy. Therefore, M&A transactions represent a substantial portion of the overall economic landscape and can have an immediate impact on the market value of the companies involved.

For these reasons, the development of predictive models for M&A transactions gained substantial attention from both scholars and stakeholders. Scholars may study M&A activity to gain insights into the underlying economic and strategic factors that drive these transactions. Stakeholders, on the other hand, may try to predict M&A activity to gain an edge in the stock market and potentially generate significant profits. Traditional techniques for the prediction are based on the analysis of numerical fundamentals such as company value, revenue, and profit [3,15,19,22,31]. Statistical methods like logistic regression or support vectors machine are then applied to perform the classification and generate a model. These studies reported promising results, revealing a systematic nature of such transactions. However, their practical application is limited by several factors. Financial data is often sparse and requires extensive manual work to build labeled datasets. Additionally, these datasets are heavily skewed towards negative samples, thus leading to generalization issues and over-fitting. The largest dataset used in the previous works only contained 2394 cases and 61 acquisitions [31]. These aspects hinder the successful creation of an automated method at scale. Methods based on topic modeling and natural language processing [18,32] tried to overcome these issue by leveraging the written text of news articles. These approaches extract valuable features from specialized articles and use machine learning techniques to infer potential players in a merger and acquisition transaction. However, data from articles is very sparse and biased towards larger, best-known companies.

This paper presents an analysis on social network relationship graphs as a valuable source of information regarding merger and acquisition transactions. Many companies maintain official accounts on social networks, and their followers typically include employees and individuals closely associated with the company. By monitoring the evolution of these followers' connections over time, it becomes possible to examine the ties between two companies. Specifically, in the context of a planned M&A, we expect to observe a higher degree of interconnectivity between the two firms relative to other, unrelated companies. In particular, we except these interactions to happen before the public announcement of the operation, thus becoming a crucial source of information to leverage.

To prove our point, we conducted a study on three major acquisitions made by Microsoft (*i.e.,* LinkedIn, GitHub, and Activision) using Twitter data. To determine the strength of the interconnections between the companies involved, we developed a methodology for recovering the timestamps of user-following events on the platform. We also devised a means of differentiating between employees and random users, and defined the time frame in which they worked for their respective companies. Our results provide evidence in support of our hypothesis, as Microsoft exhibited between five and twenty times more connections than our baseline reference of unrelated companies (*i.e.,* Google and Apple) in the two years preceding the announcement of the acquisition. Furthermore, these connections exhibited clear bursts in the same time period, further reinforcing the validity of our claim.

Contributions. The contributions of this article are five-fold:

- we develop a novel technique for extracting connection dates from Twitter, which allows us to precisely measure the strength and evolution of interconnections over time;
- we devise a methodology for discriminating between employees and random users, which enables us to isolate the relevant connections and analyze them more effectively;
- we develop a methodology for identifying the working period of the employees, which enables us to provide more precise results;
- we conduct a comprehensive analysis of three major acquisitions using Twitter data, which provides insights into the dynamics of these transactions and the interplay between the companies involved;
- we identify several potential avenues for further improving our methodology and expanding its applicability to other acquisition transactions.

Collectively, these contributions demonstrate the potential of social network graphs as a powerful tool for gaining a deeper understanding of M&A transactions and informing strategic decision-making.

Organization. This paper is structured as follows: Sect. 2 provides an overview of previous works and defines the current state of the art in the field of analyzing social network graphs for acquisition transactions. Section 3 introduces Twitter, the Snowflakes IDs, and the methodology employed for extracting timestamps from Twitter connections. Section 4 presents the case studies and describes the methodology used to identify employees and detect their working periods, as well as the results of our analysis. Section 5 discusses the current limitations of our work and potential avenues for future improvements. Finally, Sect. 6 offers concluding remarks.

2   Related Works

Several prior works modeled mergers and acquisitions with the usage of financial and managerial variables. Commonly used indicators are firm size [3,5,19, 22,26], market-to-book ratio [5,19,23,26], cash flow [3,23,26], and return on assets [19,22]. Researchers also investigated the forecasting power of patenting data [3] and bankruptcies [9,21,24]. These studies applied a variety of data mining and machine learning approaches: logistic regression [3,5,19,22,23], discriminant analysis [5,23], rule induction [23], decision tree [28], rough set approach [25], support vector machines [24], decision trees [9]. Adelaja et al. [2] built a two-logit model to explain merger and acquisition activities in US food manu-facturing. Using firm level data, they derived a target model for predicting the likelihood of a firm becoming a target for an acquisition, and a takeover model predicting the likelihood of a targeted firm being taken over. The reported predic-tive accuracy was of 74.5% and 62.9% respectively. Wei et al. [31] used ensemble learning algorithm on resampled data to solve the problem of data skewness, resulting in a TP rate of 46.43% on 2394 companies out of which 61 actually got acquired. Olson et al. [21] applied a variety of data mining tools to bankruptcy data, with the purpose of comparing accuracy and number of rules. Decision trees were relatively more accurate compared to neural networks and support vector machines. They reported a classification performance ranging from 0.661 of SVM to 0.948 of J48 decision tree.

More recent works explored the integration of different data sources to improve the scale and forecast capabilities. Xiang et al. [32] used public infor-mation available on news websites (*i.e.,* TechCrunch, CrunchBase) to build a topic modeling system. They collected firm information and news articles from these websites and organized them into 22 factual features and a varied num-ber of topic features. Their model achieved a true positive rate between 60% and 79.8%, and a false positive rate mostly between 0% and 8.3%. Li et al. [18] applied graph neural networks to the task at hand. They integrated the database from [32] with novel data points. They reported an improvement over the state of the art, with a true positive rate of 83% and a false positive rate of 7.8%.

3 Retrieving Connection Dates from Twitter

Twitter [30] utilizes the Snowflake ID generation system [4,11] to organize its data. The Snowflake IDs preserve their respective creation times, thereby enabling the recovery of this information. Consequently, this can be leveraged to construct a time series of profile-following activities.

3.1 Twitter and the Snowflake IDs

Twitter is a micro-blogging service that was launched in July of 2006. It has since become one of the major social media platforms, boasting an impressive active user base of approximately 230 million units [27]. The primary functionality of the service is the ability to post short text messages, known as *tweets*, which are limited to a maximum of 280 characters. These tweets allow users to share their thoughts and opinions with others on the platform. In addition to posting tweets, users have the option to create a short *biography* for their profile and upload a *profile image*, specify a *location* and a *birthday*. One unique feature of Twitter is its unidirectional friendship functionality, which allows users to follow other users without requiring a mutual connection. This results in a distinction between a user's *friends* and *followers*. Specifically, a user's *friends* are those who are followed by that user, while the user's *followers* are those who follow that user. Consequently, each user on the platform maintains two separate lists of *friends* and *followers* in their profile.

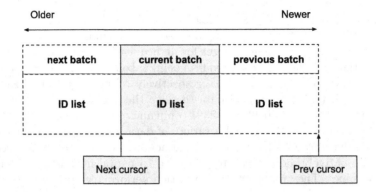

Fig. 1. Twitter employs pagination for organizing the friends and followers list, which are arranged in subsequent batches. Each batch comprises a list of profiles, a cursor to the previous batch, and a cursor to the next batch. The batches are chronologically ordered from the most recent to the oldest.

Twitter employs the Snowflake ID system to organize data within its platform. A Snowflake ID consists of a 64-bit number that includes a creation timestamp (42 bits), a machine code (10 bits), and a rolling sequence number (12 bits). Every object on Twitter is assigned with a unique ID in this format, including each entry in a user's *friends* and *followers* lists. This organization allows for chronological ordering and efficient pagination. Upon retrieving these lists, the data is arranged into batches of profiles. Each batch is enclosed by references to the previous and subsequent batches, known as the *previous cursor* and the *next cursor*. The list is consumed from the newest *followers* to the oldest ones with the *next cursor* pointing to an older batch of IDs. It is important to note that the *next cursor* correspond to the ID of the last profile in the batch. Figure 1 provides a visual representation of this scheme.

3.2   Regressing a Conversion Formula

As discussed in Sect. 3.1, Snowflake IDs are timestamp-based identifiers that are utilized to identify each object on Twitter. Specifically, each entry in a *followers* list is assigned an ID that is arranged in descending order, indicative of a chronological ordering of the list. In this context, the *next cursor* serves as a time pointer that aligns with the ID of the last entry in the current batch. To provide qualitative evidence supporting this observation, we conducted an experiment where we incremented and decremented the *next cursor* to observe how the returned batch would change. The results of this experiment are summarized in Fig. 2. Decrementing the *next cursor* (i.e., moving to an earlier time) yields the same batch profiles. Conversely, incrementing it (i.e., moving to a more recent time) also results in the same batch of profiles, but with the last profile of the current batch at the top. This behavior strongly suggests that the *followers* list is organized as a time series, with the *cursors* serving as convenient time

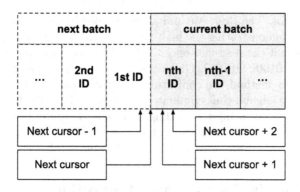

Fig. 2. The cursors within the followers list serve as time pointers. When a cursor retrieves a batch of profiles, the system returns a list starting from the profile that follows the cursor in time. Decreasing the cursor does not alter the output, whereas increasing it generates a list with the last profile of the current batch at the top.

pointers. When a batch of profiles is requested, the system employs the *next cursor* as a reference point and navigates the time series backward until a sufficient number of profiles are retrieved or the end of the list is reached. Due to this structural arrangement, two consecutive *cursors* can be leveraged to temporally delimit a batch of profiles. The temporal resolution of this frame is determined by the interval between the two *cursors*.

Given the above observations, it is feasible to acquire a conversion formula for *cursors* and UTC timestamps by establishing a mapping between these two values. This is achieved by repeatedly requesting a batch of length one from the top of a *followers* list and recording the time and *next cursor* values whenever a new *follower* is added. To estimate the actual UTC timestamp, we recorded the time interval between two consecutive requests. The average time difference between the measures was found to be 1.14s, with a standard deviation of 0.33s. We opted to employ the mean of the two values as an approximation of the actual UTC timestamp. The minor imprecision introduced, in the order of seconds, is negligible, particularly considering the time resolution used in this study, which is in the order of days and months. To expedite the data collection process, we monitored an influential Twitter account (*i.e.*, @Microsoft), which gains several hundred new followers within a few hours. We amassed a total of 732 data points between March 9th and March 12th, 2023. As described in Sect. 3.1, we utilized the 42 most significant bits of the *cursors* for estimating a regression line. We employed the RANSAC regressor provided by the *sklearn* package to determine the best-fit line, primarily due to its robustness against outliers. We found the formula for the fitted line to be:

$$utc = 0.004 * (cursor >> 22) - 1746 \tag{1}$$

The first 42 bits of the *cursors* were obtained by bit-shifting, denoted by $>>$. An excellent fit was achieved, with R^2 values close to 1 up to the tenth decimal place, indicating that almost all of the variability in the dependent variable had been accounted for. The Root Mean Squared Error ($RMSE$) was calculated to be 0.36, further demonstrating the high quality of the fit. The negative intercept value indicates that the reference epoch is half an hour prior to the Linux epoch (i.e. $1970 - 01 - 0100 : 00 : 00$). Given the broad time range and minimal error introduced by our method, we conjecture that the actual starting epoch aligns with the Linux epoch and thus eliminate the intercept from the formula. We can then state that incrementing the leading 42 bits by 1 results in a time increase of 0.004s. Put differently, the formula has a sensitivity of 4ms, which is more than adequate for the time resolution required in our study.

4   Analyzing the Mergers and Acquisitions

In section, we provide a thorough analysis of three acquisitions performed by Microsoft in recent years. After introducing the case studies (Sect. 4.1), we provide the methodology for detecting employees (Sect. 4.2) and their working period in a company (Sect. 4.3). We eventually leverage this information to plot a time series of companies interactions through time and analyze it (Sect. 4.4).

4.1   Case Studies

Our study delved into the analysis of three prominent mergers and acquisitions made by Microsoft [20] Corporation, a multinational technology company head-quartered in Redmond, Washington, USA. Founded on April 4, 1975, *Microsoft* initially aimed to develop and market personal computer software. Over time, the company diversified its business interests, expanding to various technology products and services such as computer software, gaming, hardware, and cloud computing. The rationale behind our choice to focus on Microsoft lies in its extensive presence on Twitter. Additionally, we were intrigued by the significant financial impact that Microsoft's acquisitions have had on the market.

Acquisition of Linkedin. On June 13, 2016 [6], Microsoft announced that it would acquire LinkedIn [13], the world's largest professional networking site, for 26.2 billion dollars in cash. The acquisition of LinkedIn was seen as a strategic move by Microsoft to expand its offerings in the professional services and social networking markets, and to create new opportunities and innovations for professionals and the broader technology industry. The announcement of the acquisition had a mixed impact on the market value of both companies. Microsoft's stock price decreased by around 3%, which represented a loss of approximately 9 billion dollars in market value. The decrease was likely due to concerns about the high price tag and the potential challenges of integrating LinkedIn's business with Microsoft's existing operations. LinkedIn's stock price, on the other hand, increased by around 47% on the day of the announcement, adding approximately 10 billion dollars to its market value. This increase was largely due to the fact that the price that Microsoft was offering for the company represented a significant premium over its previous stock price.

Acquisition of Github. On June 4, 2018 [7], Microsoft announced that it would acquire GitHub [13], a popular platform for software developers to collaborate and share code, for 7.5 billion dollars. The acquisition of GitHub was seen as a positive move by many in the developer community, as it brought the resources and expertise of Microsoft to one of the most important platforms for software development. After the announcement of the acquisition, Microsoft's stock price increased by around 1%, adding approximately 8 billion dolalrs to its market value. The increase was largely attributed to the potential benefits that the acquisition could bring to Microsoft's developer tools and cloud computing business. GitHub, as a private company, did not have a public market value at the time of the acquisition. However, its previous funding round in 2015 valued the company 2 billion dollars, thus determing an appreciation of 5.5 billion dollars.

Acquisition of Activision. On January 18, 2022 [8], Microsoft announced that it would acquire Activision Blizzard [1], one of the world's largest video game companies, for 68.7 billions. The acquisition of Activision is part of a larger strategy to expand Microsoft's presence in the gaming industry. Microsoft has been investing heavily in its gaming division, which includes the Xbox console and the Xbox Game Pass subscription service. The announcement had a significant impact on the market value of both companies. In the days following the announcement, Microsoft's stock price rose by about 8%, adding approximately 110 billion dollars to its market value. Activision's stock price, on the other hand, jumped by more than 40% on the day of the announcement, adding approximately 27 billion dollars to its market value. This increase was largely due to the fact that the price that Microsoft was offering for the company represented a significant premium over its previous stock price.

4.2 Detecting Employees on Twitter

At the heart of our methodology lies the fundamental process of distinguishing between employee profiles and those of random users. To achieve this objective, we rely on the intuition that employees active on Twitter are likely to follow the official account of their employer. As such, we procured the followers lists of the four accounts central to our analysis, in addition to two supplementary accounts for baseline comparison: @microsoft, @linkedin, @github, @activision, @google, and @apple. We used the official API service [29] provided by Twitter to collect the data. We opened 3 developer accounts and interacted with the API using the Python [12] programming language. The collection was performed between March, 12 2023 and March, 19 2023. The data was stored and organized using a *SQLite* [10] database. To detect the employees, we opted for a simple approach based on regular expressions. Regular expressions are a powerful tool for searching patterns in text using sequences of characters. Major programming languages already include a standard library for processing regular expressions (*e.g.*, *re* module for Python). We leveraged on the tendency of Twitter users to summarize their life experiences within the confines of the description field, often including comprehensive accounts of their professional backgrounds. The ensuing examples serve as prototypical illustrations of this practice.

"Principal Design Director @Microsoft"
"Information Technology Professional (currently at @Microsoft)"
"Program Manager @Meta. Ex-@Microsoft, @Twitter"

We created three regex expressions via a semi-automated inspection of a batch of descriptions. While the last two examples are simple variations of a common pattern (*e.g., formerly, former, ex, ex-*), the first one required to collect a list of working positions to prepend to the profile handle. For this purpose, we additionally built a list of 1102 jobs while inspecting the descriptions. Using this approach, we were able to find 4369 employees of Microsoft, 382 for LinkedIn, 408 for GitHub, 818 for Activision, 4115 for Google, and 804 for Apple. The details on the procedure and the regex used are provided in algorithm 1.

Algorithm 1. Detecting employees using regex expressions

```
 1: procedure CLEANDESCRIPTION(d)
 2:     # transform to lowercase
 3:     d ← d.lowercase()
 4:     # keep only alphanumeric chars, spaces, _, and @
 5:     d ← d.remove([^a-z0-9 _@])
 6:     # substitute multiple spaces with single ones
 7:     d ← d.substitute(\s+,\s)
 8:     return d
 9: procedure FINDCURRENTLY(d)
10:     # catch all variations of currently
11:     r ← current(?:ly)?(?: at| @)?((?: @\w+)+)
12:     return d.find(r)
13: procedure FINDPREVIOUSLY(d)
14:     # catch all variations of previously (splitted string due to length)
15:     r1 ← (?:former(?:ly)?|fmr|prev(?:ious(?:ly)?)?|ex)
16:     r2 ← (?: at| @)?((?: @\w+)+)
17:     r = concatenate(r1,r2)
18:     return d.find(r)
19: procedure FINDJOB(d, jobsList, profileHandle)
20:     # check presence of job + Twitter handle for each job
21:     for job in jobsList do
22:         s ← concatenate(job, profileHandle)
23:         if s in d then
24:             return True
25:     return False
26: procedure DETECTEMPLOYEE(d, jobsList, handlesList)
27:     d ← ClearDescription(d)
28:     if FindCurrently(d) then
29:         return True
30:     if FindPreviously(d) then
31:         return True
32:     # check jobs for each Twitter handle of interest
33:     for handle in handlesList do
34:         if FindJob(d, jobsList, handle) then
35:             return True
36:     return False
```

4.3 Determine the Working Period

The application of regex expressions facilitated the identification of employees on Twitter. Nevertheless, given the dynamic nature of the labor market, individuals may switch jobs or fail to update their employment status in their profile descriptions. To address this limitation and refine our results, we developed a methodology to determine the actual period in which an individual was employed by a specific company. We analyzed again the connection graph and examined the mutual links between employees to establish their overlapping tenure within the organization. In Fig. 3, we present an illustrative example of a Microsoft employee's activity on Twitter during the period spanning from December 2018 to December 2022. The dotted blue line represents the actual trend of the data, which is primarily concentrated within the individual's work period, as indicated by the vertical, solid black lines. To estimate the employee's tenure, we first applied a smoothing technique to the curve by utilizing an averaging filter with a window size of 360 days, which corresponds to approximately one year. This choice was guided by the common assumption that people generally do not switch jobs within this temporal frame. We then calculated the 10% highest density region (HDR [16]) on the smoothed curve. The HDR corresponds to the intervals in which the density of a function is mostly concentrated. Specifically, the 10% HDR represents the regions in which 90% of the density is found. In the context of our study, higher densities indicate a greater number of interactions between the employee in question and her colleagues on Twitter. The dashed black lines represent the estimated working period obtained through this methodology. The results demonstrate good accuracy, with a deviation of 11 months for the starting point and 6 months for the ending point. To ensure the reliability of our findings, we applied this methodology to all employees who had at least 5 mutual connections with other employees. Under that threshold the results became less reliable. By applying this technique, we were able to derive the working periods for a significant number of employees: 2309 for Microsoft, 2294 for Google, 244 for Apple, 496 for Activision, 327 for Github, and 144 for Linkedin.

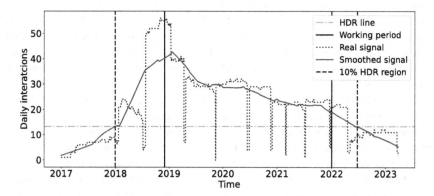

Fig. 3. Daily interactions of an employee with the others. The 10% HDR region provides a good approximation for the working period.

4.4   Results Analysis

In Fig. 4, we observe the monthly interactions between Microsoft employees and those of acquired companies, considering only the connections that occurred within the working periods detected in Sect. 4.1. To provide a reference baseline, we also included the interactions between employees of unrelated companies and those of the acquired ones, (*i.e.,* Google and Apple). Both the graph for Activision and Github show a larger number of connections with the acquirer before the public announcement of the deal. Notably, the graphs for Activision and Github exhibit a significantly larger number of connections with Microsoft before the public announcement of the acquisition deal. Specifically, in the case of Activision, Microsoft had respectively 5 times more and 20 times more connections with respect to Google and Apple in the two years preceding the announcement (515, 107, and 25 connections). A similar trend is observed for Github, where Microsoft had 6 and 17 times more connections than the reference companies (121, 18, and 7 connections). An interesting observation about these two graphs concerns the trend of the lines. In the case of Activision, the graph for Microsoft displays a positive trend that begins around 2018, with a sudden jump in the middle of 2020. This trend suggests that the acquiring firm's interest was steadily growing and peaked a couple of years before the public announcement of the acquisition. Conversely, in the case of Github, the graph for Microsoft exhibits a sudden jump in the first half of 2017, a year before the public announcement. This trend suggests that the decision to acquire Github was more sudden and less predictable than in the case of Activision.

A different perspective emerges from the graph of Linkedin, which does not display a clear burst of activity preceding the acquisition announcement, resulting in a false negative outcome. This finding may be attributed to the low resolution of our method, which may not be sufficient for detecting lower levels of interactions. Another possible explanation could be that the available data may not be sufficiently informative in certain cases. Our methodology relies on the data available on Twitter, which provides a partial view of the world and may not capture all the relevant interactions. Interestingly enough, an article presents a compelling argument that Google had also expressed an interest in acquiring LinkedIn but later retracted its offer [17]. According to the article, the involved companies presented their interest only a couple of months before the official announcement. This temporal proximity between the expression of interest and the public announcement may explain the relatively low signal observed for both the companies in the graph.

Overall, the findings of this study highlight the potential of our methodology, as evidenced by the observed trends. Specifically, our results demonstrate that companies engaged in the acquisition process tend to participate in a dense network of relationships well in advance of any official announcement. Furthermore, our analysis of social media graphs provides a means of detecting these connections. In Sect. 5, we will delve further into the implications of these results and explore potential avenues for improving the efficacy of our methodology.

5   Discussion

In this section, we provide some insights on the impacts of our work and potential improvements on the core features of our methodology.

Impacts of the Findings. Our developed methodology has significant implications for the research on mergers and acquisitions. One of its crucial advantages is its scalability. All of its components are automated except for the creation of a regex system, which was a one-time semi-automated task. In contrast, previous methods relied on well-formed financial databases of labeled entries, which require extensive manual work to create and maintain. The machine learning-based solutions that use article data also suffer from sparse data and bias towards larger companies. In contrast, our methodology only requires a company to have a presence on a social platform, making it more accessible and less biased. However, the speed at which data can be collected from the Twitter website poses a real challenge. For example, to time a connection date at the desired resolution, we used a bisection algorithm applied to the retrieval of batches. By iteratively halving the requested batches, we were able to diminish the distance between the previous cursor and the next cursor, thus reaching the desired resolution. While this operation is fundamental to our approach, it is also costly, as we were able to frame followers in the range of hundreds per hour. This aspect raises important questions about financial fairness and unfair competition, as Twitter has direct access to the data and can potentially harness this advantage point to gain an edge on the market.

Improving the Detection of Employees. In this work, we introduced a methodology for distinguishing employees from random users on Twitter. The proposed approach relies on the analysis of profile descriptions and the use of regular expression patterns. While the method is effective to a certain extent, it is approximative and may miss some employees due to unexpected text variations. To verify our claim, we checked the pool of common followers of the Microsoft employees we identified. Among the top 50 most followed, we found 11 employees who used either a variation of our regex or a different pattern. To address this limitation, one potential alternative could be to use more sophisticated methods, such as machine learning and artificial neural networks. However, we could not use existing Natural Language Processing (NLP) tools, as they are trained on general text and would not work on the specific syntax of Twitter. Furthermore, our task requires detecting a working position and the employer, rendering traditional NLP tools unsuitable. Therefore, a potential improvement to this work would be to develop a specialized NLP model capable of improving the detection of employees on social media platforms.

Improving the Detection of Working Periods. In addition to detecting employees, we also developed a methodology to identify the period in which an employee worked in a company. To achieve this, we leveraged the connections between employees of the same companies to frame a probable working period. Since the mobility of the labor market is high, this piece of data is fundamental in rendering the final results more reliable. However, our methodology is

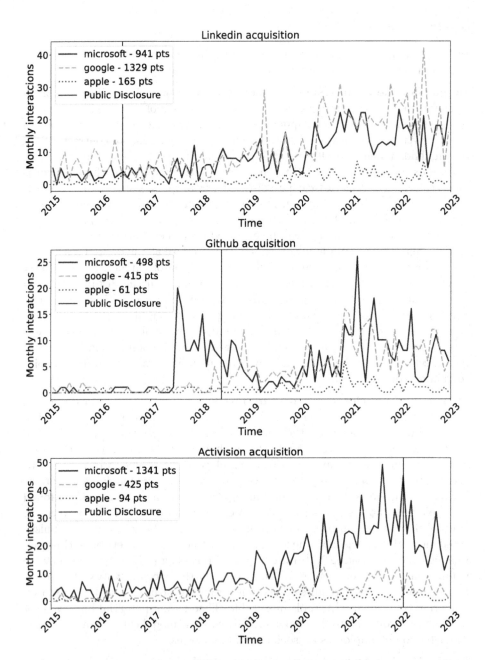

Fig. 4. Monthly interactions between companies over time. Each graph plots both the interactions between the players of an M&A operation and two baselines with the connections with unrelated companies. The trends for Activision and GitHub suggests that the interactions in a social graph can effectively help in the forecast of a M&A transaction.

approximative and only provides summary data on the actual working period. To ensure meaningful information, we set the minimum connection threshold at five. However, the goodness of the results for employees with a slightly higher number of connections still lacks precision. While the connections are usually created inside the actual working period, our measure may underestimate the real extent of the working period. One potential solution to this issue could be to improve the employee detection, which would provide more connection data points. Another approach would be to integrate working periods from external sources (*i.e.*, LinkedIn). This would require acquiring the data from the external website (either by collecting it or buying it) and then developing an algorithm for matching Twitter profiles with the specific entry on the external database. This improvement could be considered for future work.

6 Conclusion

In this paper, we presented a novel methodology for forecasting mergers and acquisitions using social networks. Our focus was on three acquisitions operated by Microsoft, which we analyzed through the Twitter platform. To achieve this, we retrieved the connection dates from the followers lists and developed a method for discerning employees from random users. The results of our methodology support our claims, with the connections between Microsoft employees and acquired companies being from five to twenty times higher than baseline companies in the two years preceding the announcement. These findings demonstrate the potential of social network analysis for forecasting mergers and acquisitions. However, our results also raise concerns about financial fairness and unfair competition from companies holding the data. The speed at which data can be collected from social media platforms, such as Twitter, poses challenges and highlights the need for better strategies for gathering data. Companies that have direct access to this data have an advantage over their competitors, which could lead to unfair competition. Overall, our methodology provides a valuable contribution to the field of forecasting mergers and acquisitions, and there is ample room for further research to improve its accuracy and effectiveness.

References

1. Activision Blizzard, Inc.: Activision homepage (2023). https://www.activision.com/. Accessed 08 Jan 2023
2. Adelaja, A., Nayga Jr, R., Farooq, Z.: Predicting mergers and acquisitions in the food industry. Agribusiness: Int. J. **15**(1), 1–23 (1999)
3. Ali-Yrkkö, J., Hyytinen, A., Pajarinen, M.: Does patenting increase the probability of being acquired? Evidence from cross-border and domestic acquisitions. Appl. Financ. Econ. **15**(14), 1007–1017 (2005)
4. Archive, T.: Snowflake GitHub repository (2023). https://github.com/twitter-archive/snowflake/tree/snowflake-2010. Accessed 01 Jan 2023

5. Barnes, P.: The identification of UK takeover targets using published historical cost accounting data some empirical evidence comparing logit with linear discriminant analysis and raw financial ratios with industry-relative ratios. Int. Rev. Financ. Anal. **9**(2), 147–162 (2000)
6. Center, M.N.: Microsoft to acquire Linkedin (2016). https://news.microsoft.com/2016/06/13/microsoft-to-acquire-linkedin/. Accessed 08 Jan 2023
7. Center, M.N.: Microsoft to acquire GitHub for $7.5 billion (2018). https://news.microsoft.com/2018/06/04/microsoft-to-acquire-github-for-7-5-billion/. Accessed 08 Jan 2023
8. Center, M.N.: Microsoft to acquire activision blizzard to bring the joy and community of gaming to everyone, across every device (2022). https://news.microsoft.com/2022/01/18/microsoft-to-acquire-activision-blizzard-to-bring-the-joy-and-community-of-gaming-to-everyone-across-every-device/. Accessed 08 Jan 2023
9. Cho, S., Hong, H., Ha, B.C.: A hybrid approach based on the combination of variable selection using decision trees and case-based reasoning using the Mahalanobis distance: For bankruptcy prediction. Expert Syst. Appl. **37**(4), 3482–3488 (2010)
10. Consortium, S.: SQLite homepage (2023). https://www.sqlite.org/index.html. Accessed 01 Jan 2023
11. Discord, I.: Discord API reference (2023). https://discord.com/developers/docs/reference#snowflakes. Accessed 01 Jan 2023
12. Foundation, P.: Python homepage. https://www.python.org/. Accessed 01 Jan 2023
13. GitHub, I.: GitHub homepage (2023). https://github.com/. Accessed 08 Jan 2023
14. GmbH, S.: Value of mergers and acquisition (m&a) transactions worldwide from 2000 to 2022 (2023). https://www.statista.com/statistics/267369/volume-of-mergers-and-acquisitions-worldwide/. Accessed 01 Jan 2023
15. Gugler, K., Konrad, K.A.: Merger target selection and financial structure. University of Vienna and Wissenschaftszentrum Berlin (WZB) (2002)
16. Hyndman, R.J.: Computing and graphing highest density regions. Am. Stat. **50**(2), 120–126 (1996). https://doi.org/10.1080/00031305.1996.10474359
17. Kuert, W., Mark, B.: Google and Facebook also looked at buying Linkedin. https://www.vox.com/2016/7/1/12085946/google-facebook-salesforce-linkedin-acquisition. Accessed 01 Jan 2023
18. Li, Y., Shou, J., Treleaven, P., Wang, J.: Graph neural network for merger and acquisition prediction. In: Proceedings of the Second ACM International Conference on AI in Finance, pp. 1–8 (2021)
19. Meador, A.L., Church, P.H., Rayburn, L.G.: Development of prediction models for horizontal and vertical mergers. J. Financ. Strateg. Decis. **9**(1), 11–23 (1996)
20. Microsoft, I.: Microsoft homepage. https://www.microsoft.com/. Accessed 08 Jan 2023
21. Olson, D.L., Delen, D., Meng, Y.: Comparative analysis of data mining methods for bankruptcy prediction. Decis. Support Syst. **52**(2), 464–473 (2012)
22. Pasiouras, F., Gaganis, C.: Financial characteristics of banks involved in acquisitions: evidence from Asia. Appl. Financ. Econ. **17**(4), 329–341 (2007)
23. Ragothaman, S., Naik, B., Ramakrishnan, K.: Predicting corporate acquisitions: an application of uncertain reasoning using rule induction. Inf. Syst. Front. **5**(4), 401–412 (2003)
24. Shin, K.S., Lee, T.S., Kim, H.J.: An application of support vector machines in bankruptcy prediction model. Expert Syst. Appl. **28**(1), 127–135 (2005)

25. Slowinski, R., Zopounidis, C., Dimitras, A.: Prediction of company acquisition in Greece by means of the rough set approach. Eur. J. Oper. Res. **100**(1), 1–15 (1997)
26. Song, X.L., Zhang, Q.S., Chu, Y.H., Song, E.Z.: A study on financial strategy for determining the target enterprise of merger and acquisition. In: 2009 IEEE/INFORMS International Conference on Service Operations, Logistics and Informatics, pp. 477–480. IEEE (2009)
27. Statista: Twitter global mDAU 2022. https://www.statista.com/statistics/970920/monetizable-daily-active-twitter-users-worldwide/. Accessed 01 Jan 2023
28. Tsagkanos, A., Georgopoulos, A., Siriopoulos, C.: Predicting Greek mergers and acquisitions: a new approach. Int. J. Financ. Serv. Manage. **2**(4), 289–303 (2007)
29. Twitter, I.: Twitter API homepage. https://developer.twitter.com/en/docs/twitter-api. Accessed 01 Jan 2023
30. Twitter, I.: Twitter homepage (2023). https://twitter.com/. Accessed 01 Jan 2023
31. Wei, C.-P., Jiang, Y.-S., Yang, C.-S.: Patent analysis for supporting merger and acquisition (M&A) prediction: a data mining approach. In: Weinhardt, C., Luckner, S., Stößer, J. (eds.) WEB 2008. LNBIP, vol. 22, pp. 187–200. Springer, Heidelberg (2009). https://doi.org/10.1007/978-3-642-01256-3_16
32. Xiang, G., Zheng, Z., Wen, M., Hong, J., Rose, C., Liu, C.: A supervised approach to predict company acquisition with factual and topic features using profiles and news articles on TechCrunch. In: Proceedings of the International AAAI Conference on Web and Social Media, vol. 6, pp. 607–610 (2012)

Enhancing Trust Prediction in Attributed Social Networks with Self-Supervised Learning

Hongjiao Liu$^{(\boxtimes)}$, Shan Xue, Jian Yang, and Jia Wu

School of Computing, Macquarie University, Sydney, NSW 2109, Australia
hongjiao.liu@hdr.mq.edu.au, {emma.xue,jian.yang,jia.wu}@mq.edu.au

Abstract. Predicting trust in Online Social Networks (OSNs) is essential for a range of applications including online marketing and decision-making. Traditional methods, while effective in some scenarios, encounter difficulties when attempting to handle the complexities of trust networks and the sparsity of trust relationships. Current techniques attempt to use user attributes such as ratings and reviews to fill these data gaps, although this approach can introduce noise and compromise prediction accuracy. A significant problem remains: most users do not explicitly state their trust relationships, making it difficult to infer trust from a vast amount of unlabelled data. This paper introduces a novel model, Trust Network Prediction (TNP), which employs self-supervised learning to address these issues within attributed trust networks. TNP learns efficiently from unlabelled data, enabling the inference of potential trust connections even without explicit trust relationships. It also minimises redundancy and the impact of abundant unlabelled data by generating comprehensive user representations based on existing trust relationships and reviewing behaviour. Through comprehensive testing on two real-world datasets, our proposed model demonstrates its effectiveness and reliability in trust prediction tasks, underscoring its potential utility in OSNs.

Keywords: Trust Prediction · Online Social Network · Self-supervised Learning · Network Representation

1 Introduction

Trust prediction aims to predict trust relationships between users within online social networks [6] and has been widely employed in many research areas [28]. For instance, trust prediction has been identified as a critical factor in improving reliable marketing [27,28], information dissemination [7,28], and recommendations within social networks [1,5,7,18,26]. An examination of currently popular social networks reveals that an increasing number of users are socialising online on these platforms [15]. However, building a precise user trust prediction model still remains an open and challenging problem.

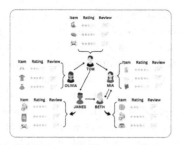

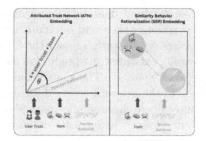

(a) Trust network with user attributes   (b) ATN and SBR module description

Fig. 1. An attributed trust network and an overview of the model

In real-world applications, trust networks are characterised by complex interactions that include user trust relationships and a set of associated attributes. A directed trust network with users as nodes and trust relationships as edges is presented in Fig. 1(a). Here, Tom trusts Mia and James, while Mia trusts Beth. Each user has a set of attributes, including ratings and reviews of items. For example, Tom rated and reviewed computers, mice, and gamepads, while Mia rated and reviewed two dresses and a book. Although Tom and Mia did not express any similar preferences for items, Tom still built a trust relationship with Mia. This indicates that user preferences could be composed of both item preferences and trusted social preferences reflected in the establishment of a trust relationship.

Establishing a trust relationship with another user in online social networks is more intricate than forming a relationship simply based around "likes" and "follows". In fact, a trust relationship is usually established after deeper analysis, as users typically consider a range of factors such as reputation [23] and past behaviour [16]. Consequently, the high sparsity of trust networks is well-documented. Trust relationships follow power law distribution rules [25], meaning that only a few users hold the majority of trusted relationships, while most users only make a few trust-based connections. As a result, most conventional trust prediction approaches, which explore trust links [21] and trust network structures [13] between users, inevitably suffer from significant problems with data sparsity. One of the primary obstacles to trust prediction is that the predictions are generally based on only a single, sparse trust network, which increases the complexity of the prediction, in turn negatively impacting accuracy.

According to sociological homogeneity theories [17,22], individuals tend to set up trust with others who have similar interests or backgrounds [27]. However, many existing trust prediction methods seem to prioritise the similarity of user content, such as shared interests derived from the user rating scores, review content, or item labels [25,31]. What they do not consider is the internal consistency of user behaviours. These online behaviours refer to the actions and habits of users in terms of how they create connections with other users or items. Specifically, trust behaviours are the actions taken and decisions made by users when establishing trust relations with other users. Similarly, review behaviours are the actions taken and decisions made when reviewing items. Both of these behaviours significantly impact the forecasting of trust relations between users.

Overall, existing trust prediction methodologies encounter various challenges: 1) Network Sparsity: The sparse connections or edges between numerous nodes or users in the network create difficulties in integrating trust networks and user attributes due to limited information about user trust relationships. 2) Excessive Attribute Noise: The intricate dynamics within the trust network, compounded by the vast number of attributes, complicates the establishment of reliable correlations between users and their attributes. 3) Difficult Inference from Unlabelled Data: The fact that the preponderance of users do not openly express their trust relationships makes identifying potential trust links within extensive unlabelled data exceptionally challenging. This necessitates a strategy to evaluate user attribute representation that promotes consistency and aggregation among like users, which is particularly challenging within online social trust prediction.

To mitigate these challenges, we introduce a self-supervised trust prediction model that aims to predict user trust relationships. This model trains on user-related online behavioural data (user trust and review behaviours), learning to identify underlying user patterns and representations. We first incorporate user attributes (reviews and items), disregarding the specific content of reviews and focusing on the user's item reviewing behaviour. This approach helps to supplement the sparse trust relationships with additional attributes, enriching the network's information content.

We then address the noise problem caused by the excess of attributes by integrating the trust network with the aforementioned attributes. This integration aids in exploring users' trust and item preferences, simplifying complex structural relationships and reducing data noise. Finally, to reduce the difficulty associated with making inferences from large quantities of unlabelled trust relationships, we examine how trust or item preferences influence users' review behaviours. We differentiate between review behaviours driven by personal preferences and those shaped by trust relationships. This distinction aids in calibrating user distances and facilitates the prediction of potential trust relationships within extensive unlabelled data. Our model employs a contrastive learning strategy in a self-supervised learning (SSL) framework, allowing the model to learn attribute similarities and filter out unnecessary or redundant data.

In summary, the primary contributions of our work include:

- Proposing an SSL-based TNP model that addresses the high sparsity and complexity of trust networks by integrating user attributes (item and review behaviour) and facilitating learning from unlabelled data for enhanced network representation learning.
- The Attributed Trust Network Embedding module first reduces network sparsity by integrating two attributes into the trust network. It then tackles the data noise issues arising from the inclusion of too many attributes, as depicted on the left side of Fig. 1(b). This module harmonises the relationship between

user attribute embedding and user trust embedding, generating user attribute embedding influenced by both item attributes and trust preferences.

- The Similarity Behaviour Rationalization Embedding module addresses the absence of an effective strategy for assessing user attribute representation, as depicted on the right side of Fig. 1(b). This module enables the model to capture a consistent and rationalised representation of user attributes (item preferences and review behaviour).

- Our model demonstrates adaptability to real-world datasets, having been rigorously tested on multiple datasets derived from various scenarios and settings.

2   Related Work

In this section, an overview of existing works on trust prediction is provided below.

2.1   Approaches Based on Network Structures

Approaches to prediction based on the structure of trust relation networks attempt to make predictions based on the data structures and key features of the network. For example, Guha et al. [11] constructed a framework incorporating distrust to assess the amount of trust between a given node and other nodes. These researchers found that even a tiny amount of information on distrust can be used to forecast the level of trust between users [11]. Building upon Guha et al. [11], Massa et al. [19] focused on contentious users - those who were trusted by many people but also receive significant amounts of distrustful or negative feedback. They introduced local trust measurements to increase the trustworthiness of users. These researchers argued that such contentious individuals are ubiquitous in society; accordingly, they predicted the reliability of users in a more personalised manner than global trust metrics by introducing local trust measurements [19]. Golbeck et al. [9] used the trust ratings in social networks as a foundation for similarity assessments. These authors introduced the idea of a binary user trust relationship (i.e., trust or distrust) to address the sparsity problem between rated items and users in traditional recommendation systems. Later, Golbeck et al. [8] employed a rating value of trust between users to infer binary trust results based on trust transitivity theory.

Despite the promise of these approaches, however, all consistently ignore user attribute information, which prevents them from achieving precise trust prediction.

2.2   Approaches Based on Attributes

The sparsity problem associated with most trust networks has led researchers to explore different methods of leveraging user characteristics or attributes to address the issue. For example, Beigi et al. [2] used changes in user emotions as an indicator for predicting trust relationships based on psychological and sociological principles. However, other studies suggested that user ratings can be used to supplement the sparsity of trust relationships [4,15,20,25,26,31]. For instance, Ziegler et al. [31] found that there was a relationship between trust and user similarity when a community's trusted network is strongly connected to a specific application. Matsuo and Yamamoto [20] developed a trust and rating model, which they used to explain community gravitation from theoretical and empirical perspectives. Borzymek and Sydow [4] used a C4.5 decision tree-based algorithm to explore the use of both graph-based and user rating-based features for trust prediction between pairs of users in social networks. Tang et al. [26] proposed a fine-grained method for combining inter-user trust networks with classic rating prediction algorithms where the goal was to capture complex trust connections. Korovaiko and Thomo [15] approached trust prediction as a classification problem, generating predictions by matching user ratings.

Recent works have also sought to leverage all available user attributes to support trust prediction, such as user reviews, ratings, and items purchased. For example, Wang et al. [27,28] attempted to solve the data sparsity problem by using a deep learning model to integrate a user trust network with all user attributes. The idea was to capture user characteristics and related attributes. However, while user attribute-based approaches generally yield more accurate trust predictions because they use some or all user attributes, they failed to take the specific relationships between individual entities into account, which may lead to inconsistencies and the accumulation of errors.

3   Preliminaries

This section sets out the problem definitions for the TNP model, and explains the terms and symbols used in the paper.

3.1   Problem Definition

The purpose of our study is to infer trust relationships in pairs of users who presently do not exist with such links. Therefore, we primarily concentrate on two categories of entities (users and items) and their interactions - that is, existing user trust relationships and user reviews of particular items. In pursuit of this goal, we present a self-supervised Trust Network Prediction (TNP) model consisting of two main components: an Attributed Trust Network Embedding Module and a Similarity Behaviour Rationalisation Embedding Module.

The Attribute Trust Network (ATN) Embedding Module: Consider a trust network G, where $G = (U, E)$. Here, U represents the set of users, called nodes, while E signifies the set of user trust relationships, known as edges. $t_{ij} \in 0,1$ represents the trust value between the users u_i and u_j. $X \in \mathbb{R}^{m \times n \times d}$ is the user attributes matrix, including item and review behaviour information, where m is the number of users, n is the number of items, and d is the dimensions associated with each review. The objective of the embedding function f is to explore the user attributes while preserving the trust network structure:

$$Z = f(X, G) \tag{1}$$

where $Z \in \mathbb{R}^{m \times k}$, m is the number of users, and k is the desired dimension of feature embedding.

The Similarity Behaviour Rationalisation (SBR) Embedding Module: Given the user attributes item $X_{it} \in \mathbb{R}^{m \times n \times d}$ and the review behaviour $X_{rb} \in \mathbb{R}^{m \times n \times d}$, the SBR module learns a joint representation of user attributes (items and review behaviour) $Y \in \mathbb{R}^{m \times n \times d}$:

$$Y = f_{CL}(X_{it}, X_{rb}) \tag{2}$$

where f_{CL} is a self-supervised contrastive learning functions, while d represents the dimension of the user attributes. This contrastive learning embedding function aims to capture a consistent and rationalised representation of user attributes (item preferences and review behaviour).

4   Methodology

In this section, we detailed introduce our proposed model. The TNP framework is illustrated in Fig. 2.

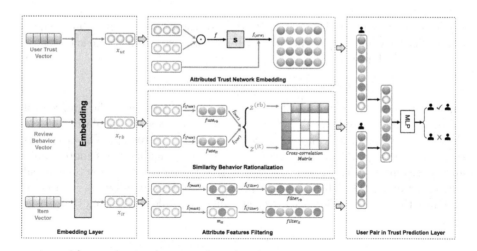

Fig. 2. TNP model framework

4.1   The Attributed Trust Network Embedding Module

Constructing the Adjacency Matrix: Using users and their attributes (items and reviews) construct adjacency matrices are built so as to study the interactions. (1) User-Item: Position (u,i) is 1 if user u reviews the item i, and 0 otherwise. (2) User-Review: Position (u,r) is 1 if user u posts a review r, and 0 otherwise. (3) Item-Review: Position (i,r) is 1 if the item i corresponds to the review r, and 0 otherwise.

Constructing the Feature Vectors: The vectors extracted include behaviour vectors for user trust relationships, items, and reviews. These vectors are embedded and then padded to match the user trust embedding length, to result in embedded features of a uniform dimension: x_{ut}, x_{rb}, and x_{it}.

Generating the Trust Network Embeddings: In the knowledge graph embedding *TransE* model [3], the nodes represent entities, while the different types of edges (head, label, and tail) are expressed as (h, l, t). In each triple of this kind, there exists a name-label relationship between its entity head and tail. Based on this idea, the embedded features of each user, $(x_{ut}, x_{rb}, \text{and } x_{it})$, are considered to be a triple similar to the above, while user-item connections (review behaviours) are regarded as a translation from user to item.

Hence, our attributed trust network embedding is based on the aforementioned triple representation (x_{ut}, x_{rb}, x_{it}). This tuple further combines the user trust and item embedding features to create a new representation (s), which allows the model to better integrate the information contained. The expression for s is as follows:

$$s = x_{ut} \odot x_{it} \tag{3}$$

where $\odot$ represents the Hadamard Product of the user trust and item embeddings. The loss function of the attribute network embeddings of each user i is represented as follows:

$$L_{ATN} = \mathbb{E}\left[\|x_{rb} - s\|^2 - \eta \cdot \cos(x_{rb}, s)\right] \tag{4}$$

where $\mathbb{E}$ represents the mean calculation. $\|x_{rb} - s\|^2$ calculates the squared difference between s and x_{rb}, bringing the embedding vector calculation of s as close as possible to the review behaviour embedding vector x_{rb}. The $\cos(x_{rb}, s)$ calculates the cosine similarity between s and x_{rb}, making the s more similar and consistent with the x_{rb} in the vector space. The constant η acts as a balancing factor between these two components. The loss function L_{ATN} aims to minimise the squared difference between s and x_{rb}, while maximising their cosine similarity.

4.2   The Similarity Behaviour Rationalisation Embedding Module

Fusing the Attribute Features: The two embedding features x_{rb} and x_{it} are separately processed through a linear layer with a weight matrix and an activation function, resulting in the following low-dimensional fused features:

$$fuse_{rb} = \tanh\left(\text{mean}\left(W_{rb} \cdot x_{rb} + b_{rb}, axis = 1\right)\right) \tag{5}$$

$$fuse_{it} = \tanh\left(\text{mean}\left(W_{it} \cdot x_{it} + b_{it}, \text{ axis } = 1\right)\right) \tag{6}$$

where W_{rb} and W_{it} are the weight matrices, b_{rb} and b_{it} are the corresponding biases, $tanh$ is the hyperbolic tangent activation function, and axis=1 indicates that the mean is computed along the sequence length dimension of x_{rb} and x_{it}.

The Barlow Twins Loss Function: Taking the fused features $fuse_{rb}$ and $fuse_{it}$ as inputs, the Barlow Twins loss function normalises both along the batch dimension:

$$z^{rb} = \frac{fuse_{rb} - \overline{fuse_{rb}}}{\sigma\left(fuse_{rb}\right)}, \quad z^{it} = \frac{fuse_{it} - \overline{fuse_{it}}}{\sigma\left(fuse_{it}\right)} \tag{7}$$

where $\sigma\left(fuse_{rb}\right)$ and $\sigma\left(fuse_{it}\right)$ denote the standard deviations, while $\overline{fuse_{rb}}$ and $\overline{fuse_{it}}$ represent the means of the fused features. The cross-correlation matrix between z^{rb} and z^{it} is then computed:

$$C_{ij} \triangleq \frac{\sum_b t z_{b,i}^{rb} z_{b,j}^{it}}{\sqrt{\sum_b t \left(z_{b,i}^{rb}\right)^2} \sqrt{\sum_i t \left(z_{b,j}^{it}\right)^2}} \tag{8}$$

where b denotes the index of the batch samples, while i and j represent the indices of the vector dimensions in the network outputs, i.e., the row and column indices of the cross-correlation matrix C. As C is a square matrix, its size is equal to the dimensions of the network output, and its values range between -1 (perfectly anti-correlated) and 1 (perfectly correlated). The loss function is:

$$L_{SBR} \triangleq \sum_i \left(1 - C_{ii}\right)^2 + \lambda \sum_i \sum_{j \neq i} C_{ij}^2 \tag{9}$$

where λ is a positive scalar that balances the importance of the invariance term $\sum_i \left(1 - C_{ii}\right)^2$ and the redundancy reduction term $\sum_i \sum_{j \neq i} C_{ij}^2$ in the loss function.

4.3 Comprehensive Feature Representation

Filtering the Attribute Features: To obtain the filtering features of the user attributes (items and review behaviours) embeddings, their respective embeddings x_{rb} and x_{it} are first taken as inputs. Taking x_{rb} as an example, mask processing is then performed as follows:

$$m_{rb} = \left(1 - m_{\text{expanded}}\right) \odot x_{rb} \tag{10}$$

where $m_{expanded}$ is the masking tensor expanded to the same dimensions as x_{rb}, while $\odot$ denotes element-wise multiplication. To exclude the influence of padding values during the computation in this process, the mask operation sets the value of all padded positions to 1 (the original value is 0) and that of all valid data positions to 0 (the original value is 1). And the filtering features are computed as follows:

$$filter_{rb} = \text{sigmoid} \left(\text{mean} \left(V_{rb} \cdot m_{rb} + b_{vrb}, axis = 1 \right) \right) \tag{11}$$

where V_{rb} is the weight matrix, and b_{vrb} is the bias vector. This formula performs weighted calculations on each element in the m_{rb}, computes the mean along the sequence length dimension $(axis = 1)$, and then passes it through a sigmoid activation function. The filtering features for the item embedding, denoted as $filter_{it}$, are obtained after the mask processing by following the same steps.

Generating the Feature Representations: A tanh activation function is applied directly to obtain the user trust integrated feature y_{ut} as follows:

$$y_{ut} = \tanh \left(x_{ut} \right) \tag{12}$$

where y_{ut} is in the range of values between -1 and 1. The fused features of the integrated representations of the item and review behaviour features y_{rb} and y_{it} and the filtering features are used in combination with the original user trust relationship embedding to obtain the following:

$$y_{rb} = (1 - filter_{rb}) \cdot fuse_{rb} + filter_r b \cdot x_{ut} \tag{13}$$

$$y_{it} = (1 - filter_{it}) \cdot fuse_{it} + filter_{it} \cdot x_{ut} \tag{14}$$

4.4   Generating the Trust Predictions

User Representation: A concatenated feature representation is generated for each user u_i:

$$u^i_{\text{concat}} = y^i_{ut} \oplus y^i_{rb} \oplus y^i_{it}, u^j_{\text{concat}} = y^j_{ut} \oplus y^j_{rb} \oplus y^i_{it} \tag{15}$$

In the same way, a concatenated feature representation of u_j, denoted as u^j_{concat}, is generated for each user pair (u_i, u_j) in which u_i is located. Consequently, the representations of each user pair are further connected as the input to a multi-layer perceptron (MLP) as follows:

$$y'_{ij} = \text{softmax} \left(W_{mlp} \times \left(u^i_{\text{concat}} \oplus u^j_{\text{concat}} \right) + b_{mlp} \right) \tag{16}$$

where $\oplus$ is the concatenation operation, while W_{mlp} and b_{mlp} represent the weight matrix and bias vector, respectively. y'_{ij} is the predicted probability of a trust or distrust relationship between the user pair (u_i, u_j). The loss function for the trust prediction is a cross entropy function:

$$L_{pre} = - \sum_{ij} y_{ij} \log \left(y'_{ij} \right) \tag{17}$$

The Reconstruction Embedding Loss: The respective total embedding loss of each user in the user pair (u_i, u_j) can be represented as:

$$L_i = L_{ATN_i} + \theta L_{SBR_i}, \; L_j = L_{ATN_j} + \theta L_{SBR_j} \tag{18}$$

where θ is a constant parameter that determines how much of L_{SBR} will be added to the total embedding loss of each user. And the overall reconstruction embedding loss of each user pair is then defined as the following:

$$L_{emb} = L_i + L_j \tag{19}$$

where L_{emb} provides a unified embedding representation for each user pair (u_i, u_j), prompting the model to simultaneously focus on user i and user j and learn the similarities and differences between these two users.

4.5 The Optimisation Objective

The ultimate optimisation goal of this model is to minimise the total losses for the reconstruction and trust evaluation:

$$L = L_{pre} + \beta L_{emb} \tag{20}$$

where the coefficient $\beta \geqslant 0$ balances two components.

5 Experiments

Our experiments with the TNP model were devised to provide answers to the following questions:

RQ1: How does TNP compare to conventional and state-of-the-art methods?
RQ2: What particular contributions does TNP provide to trust prediction?
RQ3: How can different parameter settings affect the model performance of TNP?

5.1 Datasets

We used two publicly accessible, real-world datasets, Epinions and Ciao, to verify the effectiveness of our method[1]. Epinions and Ciao are online platforms for sharing product reviews and facilitating knowledge exchange. The characteristics of these datasets are presented in Tables 1.

5.2 Evaluation Metrics

Since trust prediction is a classification issue, the model needs to decide whether a pair of users have a relationship is trust or not. Therefore, we use the AUC [12] and F1 [14] as evaluation metrics for this model and the baseline models. The model's performance is proportional to the values of these two metrics, i.e., the better the performance, the higher values of AUC and F1 metrics.

---

[1] https://www.cse.msu.edu/~tangjili/trust.html.

5.3   Implementation

We used the Pytorch framework[2] to develop TNP. To guarantee sufficient data for model training, we selected only users who had completed at least 15 reviews. Since both datasets only include positive linkages (trust relationships), we created negative instances by randomly sampling user pairs without trust relationships, maintaining a 1:2 ratio between the trust pairs and the unobserved negative pairs during training. To ensure a fair comparison, we used the recommended parameter settings for each baseline methods .

Table 1. Statistics of Datasets for TNP

Dataset	Epinions	Ciao
number of Users	17,230	4,457
number of Items	105,320	9,382
number of Reviews	1,032,232	267,396
number of Trust Relationships	137,354	34,165

5.4   Model Performance

In response to **RQ1**, we compared TNP to some baseline methods, including classic and state-of-the-art trust prediction techniques. A brief overview of the baseline models is provided below.

- **Trust Propagation (TP):** TP represents a typical structure-based approach to trust network prediction, where user trust relationships are assessed based on the propagation of trust along social paths [11].
- **MF:** This method relies on low-rank approximations, where factorization is conducted on a matrix of trust relationships to derive the trust values [30].
- **DeepTrust:** This model identifies the homophily effect in trust prediction by considering diverse user characteristics. It is an advanced user model that employs deep learning techniques to predict trust [27].
- **Node2Vec:** A method based on Skip-Gram that ensures node representations within the same community or that or play similar roles in different communities are close to each other [10].
- **LINE:** Embeds the corresponding node vectors by defining the graph's first-order and second-order similarities [24].
- **AtNE-Trust:** Embeds an attributed trust network to learn user representations for trust prediction [28].

From the model performance results presented in Table 2, we can draw the following conclusions:

- The results indicate that TNP outshines both the conventional and SOTA baselines in predicting user trust relationships. Further, TNP performs more effectively than the SOTA approach, AtNE-Trust.

---

[2] https://pytorch.org/.

- TNP, AtNE-Trust, and DeepTrust outperform the other approaches since they take user attributes into account.
- The performance of the MF, TP, Node2Vec, and LINE methods is hindered because they do not consider user attributes and are susceptible to the sparsity of trust relationship networks. Of these methods, MF delivers comparatively good results, while TP struggles with data sparsity issues. By contrast, AtNE-Trust achieves superior performance, only outdone by our model TNP.

Relative to the comparison approaches, TNP performs better for the following reasons. (1) Compared with the other models, ours only involves two user attributes – items and review behaviour. Hence, the model's focus is on the binary relationship between them and on reducing the noise and redundancy caused by introducing an overabundance of attributes and relationships. (2) Rather than processing the attributes separately and fusing them later, we directly integrated these attributes with the user trust feature and input them into the model for joint learning. As a result, the interactions between the attributes and the user trust features are fully exploited, which improves the model's representation ability and, in turn, its ability to generalise. (3) The self-supervised contrastive learning method Barlow Twins learns the fusion embedding of attributes, which encourages the model to learn the similarity between items and review behaviour. This facilitates a better understanding of the users' review behaviour across different items.

Table 2. TNP's performance vs. the baselines

Methods	Epinions		Ciao	
	AUC	F1	AUC	F1
TP	0.6502 ± 0.0013	0.7833 ± 0.0009	0.6418 ± 0.0008	0.7120 ± 0.0012
MF	0.8624 ± 0.0004	0.8798 ± 0.0012	0.8013 ± 0.0010	0.8107 ± 0.0013
DeepTrust	0.8709 ± 0.0009	0.8818 ± 0.0002	0.8037 ± 0.0012	0.8191 ± 0.0006
LINE	0.7936 ± 0.0005	0.8721 ± 0.0006	0.7667 ± 0.0015	0.7901 ± 0.0018
Node2Vec	0.8734 ± 0.0007	0.8936 ± 0.0004	0.7805 ± 0.0013	0.8017 ± 0.0014
AtNE-Trust	0.8938 ± 0.0021	0.9004 ± 0.0027	0.8176 ± 0.0026	0.8204 ± 0.0031
Our Model (TNP)	$\mathbf{0.9051 \pm 0.0015}$	$\mathbf{0.9177 \pm 0.0013}$	$\mathbf{0.8302 \pm 0.0019}$	$\mathbf{0.8492 \pm 0.0025}$

Table 3. TNP – Ablation study results

Methods	Epinions		Ciao	
	AUC	F1	AUC	F1
$TNP_{(mask)}$	0.8604 ± 0.0019	0.8714 ± 0.0017	0.7911 ± 0.0016	0.8049 ± 0.0022
$TNP_{(mask+ATN)}$	0.8745 ± 0.0012	0.8812 ± 0.0014	0.8077 ± 0.0014	0.8164 ± 0.0020
$TNP_{(mask+SBR)}$	0.8795 ± 0.0021	0.8911 ± 0.0019	0.8199 ± 0.0021	0.8211 ± 0.0027
TNP	$\mathbf{0.9051 \pm 0.0015}$	$\mathbf{0.9177 \pm 0.0013}$	$\mathbf{0.8302 \pm 0.0019}$	$\mathbf{0.8492 \pm 0.0025}$

5.5   Ablation Study

To answer **RQ2**, we evaluated the impact of various components of the TNP model on both datasets, as illustrated in Table 3. The $TNP_{(mask)}$ component includes the filtered features obtained from the mask processing, then filters and concatenates different embedded features to represent the users. $TNP_{(mask+ATN)}$ uses the ATN module to learn the relationship between users and attributes uniformly and applies mask processing to represent the users. $TNP_{(mask+SBR)}$ uses the mask processing and the SBR module, with the SBR module employed to learn fused attribute embedding features so as to obtain a more consistent and reasonable representation

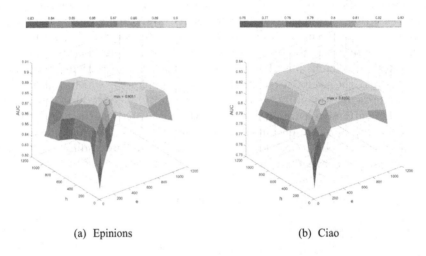

(a) Epinions   (b) Ciao

Fig. 3. AUC scores under the joint effect of parameters e and h

The results indicate that, on average, the AUC and F1 scores for the different model components decrease by approximately 4.4%, 3.1%, and 2.3%, respectively, in comparison to the complete TNP model. The SBR module makes the largest contribution by mining the similarity of the fusion features of items and review behaviours, capturing the user's item preferences and the internal logic of review behaviour. The ATN module in also makes an important contribution by integrating and unifying user trust and attribute embedding features. Although the contribution of $TNP_{(mask)}$ is the smallest of the three components, it eliminates the negative impact of padding through mask processing. Therefore, these three parts jointly promote better performance in the trust prediction model in different ways.

5.6   Impact of the Hyperparameters

To understand the effect of specific parameters on the model and answer **RQ3**, we conducted a sensitivity analysis for each of the parameters e (embedding dimension), h (hidden dimension), and n (number of epochs), as shown in Fig. 3.

Parameter e controls the embedding size of the input vectors. Here, the AUC scores improve as e increases, with optimal results at $e = 256$. Parameter h controls the size of the hidden layers in the model, with the AUC scores peaking when $h = 512$ with both datasets. The parameter n determines how many times the model traverses the training dataset. Here, the AUC scores no longer increase with the continued increase of n after the model reaches its best performance. The optimal performances of η, θ, and β : occur at $\eta = 0.5$, $\theta = 0.2$, and $\beta = 0.5$. To set λ, we followed the suggestion made by the authors of the Barlow Twins method and set it to 0.005 [29].

6   Conclusion

In this paper, we propose a novel trust prediction model intending to improve the accuracy of trust prediction between users in social networks. The proposed model TNP focuses solely on the binary relations between users and their attributes. It addresses three key challenges: sparsity in the user trust network, noisy data caused by the introduction of too many attributes, and complex inference from extensive unlabelled trust relationships between users. The results show that our proposed trust prediction model outperforms conventional and SOTA techniques by empirical evaluations of real-world datasets.

References

1. Ahmadian, S., Ahmadian, M., Jalili, M.: A deep learning based trust-and tag-aware recommender system. Neurocomputing **488**, 557–571 (2022)
2. Beigi, G., Tang, J., Wang, S., Liu, H.: Exploiting emotional information for trust/distrust prediction. In: Proceedings of the 2016 SIAM International Conference on Data Mining, pp. 81–89. SIAM (2016)
3. Bordes, A., Usunier, N., Garcia-Duran, A., Weston, J., Yakhnenko, O.: Translating embeddings for modeling multi-relational data. In: Advances in Neural Information Processing Systems, vol. 26 (2013)
4. Borzymek, P., Sydow, M.: Trust and distrust prediction in social network with combined graphical and review-based attributes. In: Jędrzejowicz, P., Nguyen, N.T., Howlet, R.J., Jain, L.C. (eds.) KES-AMSTA 2010. LNCS (LNAI), vol. 6070, pp. 122–131. Springer, Heidelberg (2010). https://doi.org/10.1007/978-3-642-13480-7_14
5. Gao, X., Xu, W., Liao, M., Chen, G.: Trust prediction for online social networks with integrated time-aware similarity. ACM Trans. Knowl. Discov. Data (TKDD) **15**(6), 1–30 (2021)
6. Ghafari, S.M., et al.: A survey on trust prediction in online social networks. IEEE Access **8**, 144292–144309 (2020)
7. Golbeck, J.: Trust and nuanced profile similarity in online social networks. ACM Trans. Web (TWEB) **3**(4), 1–33 (2009)
8. Golbeck, J., Hendler, J.: Inferring binary trust relationships in web-based social networks. ACM Trans. Internet Technol. (TOIT) **6**(4), 497–529 (2006)
9. Golbeck, J., Hendler, J.A., et al.: FilmTrust: movie recommendations using trust in web-based social networks. In: CCNC, vol. 2006, pp. 282–286 (2006)

10. Grover, A., Leskovec, J.: node2vec: scalable feature learning for networks. In: Proceedings of the 22nd ACM SIGKDD International Conference on Knowledge Discovery and Data Mining, pp. 855–864 (2016)

11. Guha, R., Kumar, R., Raghavan, P., Tomkins, A.: Propagation of trust and distrust. In: Proceedings of the 13th International Conference on World Wide Web, pp. 403–412 (2004)

12. Hanley, J.A., McNeil, B.J.: The meaning and use of the area under a receiver operating characteristic (ROC) curve. Radiology **143**(1), 29–36 (1982)

13. Huang, J., Nie, F., Huang, H., Tu, Y.C.: Trust prediction via aggregating heterogeneous social networks. In: Proceedings of the 21st ACM International Conference on Information and Knowledge Management, pp. 1774–1778 (2012)

14. Islam, M.R., Aditya Prakash, B., Ramakrishnan, N.: SIGNet: scalable embeddings for signed networks. In: Phung, D., Tseng, V.S., Webb, G.I., Ho, B., Ganji, M., Rashidi, L. (eds.) PAKDD 2018, Part II. LNCS (LNAI), vol. 10938, pp. 157–169. Springer, Cham (2018). https://doi.org/10.1007/978-3-319-93037-4_13

15. Korovaiko, N., Thomo, A.: Trust prediction from user-item ratings. Soc. Netw. Anal. Min. **3**(3), 749–759 (2013)

16. Lewicki, R.J., Bunker, B.B., et al.: Developing and maintaining trust in work relationships. Trust Organ.: Front. Theory Res. **114**, 139 (1996)

17. Liu, H., et al.: Predicting trusts among users of online communities: an epinions case study. In: Proceedings of the 9th ACM Conference on Electronic Commerce, pp. 310–319 (2008)

18. Ma, H., Zhou, D., Liu, C., Lyu, M.R., King, I.: Recommender systems with social regularization. In: Proceedings of the fourth ACM International Conference on Web Search and Data Mining, pp. 287–296 (2011)

19. Massa, P., Avesani, P.: Controversial users demand local trust metrics: an experimental study on epinions.com community. In: AAAI, vol. 1, pp. 121–126 (2005)

20. Matsuo, Y., Yamamoto, H.: Community gravity: measuring bidirectional effects by trust and rating on online social networks. In: Proceedings of the 18th International Conference on World Wide Web, pp. 751–760 (2009)

21. Matsutani, K., Kumano, M., Kimura, M., Saito, K., Ohara, K., Motoda, H.: Combining activity-evaluation information with NMF for trust-link prediction in social media. In: 2015 IEEE International Conference on Big Data (Big Data), pp. 2263–2272. IEEE (2015)

22. McPherson, M., Smith-Lovin, L., Cook, J.M.: Birds of a feather: homophily in social networks. Annu. Rev. Sociol. **27**, 415–444 (2001)

23. Moorman, C., Deshpande, R., Zaltman, G.: Factors affecting trust in market research relationships. J. Mark. **57**(1), 81–101 (1993)

24. Tang, J., Qu, M., Wang, M., Zhang, M., Yan, J., Mei, Q.: LINE: large-scale information network embedding. In: Proceedings of the 24th International Conference on World Wide Web, pp. 1067–1077 (2015)

25. Tang, J., Gao, H., Hu, X., Liu, H.: Exploiting homophily effect for trust prediction. In: Proceedings of the Sixth ACM International Conference on Web Search and Data Mining, pp. 53–62 (2013)

26. Tang, J., Gao, H., Liu, H.: mTrust: discerning multi-faceted trust in a connected world. In: Proceedings of the fifth ACM International Conference on Web Search and Data Mining, pp. 93–102 (2012)

27. Wang, Q., Zhao, W., Yang, J., Wu, J., Hu, W., Xing, Q.: DeepTrust: a deep user model of homophily effect for trust prediction. In: 2019 IEEE International Conference on Data Mining (ICDM), pp. 618–627. IEEE (2019)

28. Wang, Q., Zhao, W., Yang, J., Wu, J., Zhou, C., Xing, Q.: AtNE-trust: attributed trust network embedding for trust prediction in online social networks. In: 2020 IEEE International Conference on Data Mining (ICDM), pp. 601–610. IEEE (2020)
29. Zbontar, J., Jing, L., Misra, I., LeCun, Y., Deny, S.: Barlow twins: self-supervised learning via redundancy reduction. In: International Conference on Machine Learning, pp. 12310–12320. PMLR (2021)
30. Zhu, S., Yu, K., Chi, Y., Gong, Y.: Combining content and link for classification using matrix factorization. In: Proceedings of the 30th annual international ACM SIGIR Conference on Research and Development in Information Retrieval, pp. 487–494 (2007)
31. Ziegler, C.N., Golbeck, J.: Investigating interactions of trust and interest similarity. Decis. Support Syst. **43**(2), 460–475 (2007)

Security and Privacy

Bilateral Insider Threat Detection: Harnessing Standalone and Sequential Activities with Recurrent Neural Networks

Phavithra Manoharan[1], Wei Hong[1], Jiao Yin[1(✉)], Yanchun Zhang[1],
Wenjie Ye[1], and Jiangang Ma[2]

[1] Institute for Sustainable Industries and Liveable Cities, Victoria University,
Melbourne, VIC 3011, Australia
{phavithra.manoharan,wei.hong2}@live.vu.edu.au,
{jiao.yin,yanchun.Zhang,wenjie.ye}@vu.edu.au
[2] Institute of Innovation, Science and Sustainability, Federation University,
Berwick, VIC, Australia
j.ma@federation.edu.au

Abstract. Insider threats involving authorised individuals exploiting their access privileges within an organisation can yield substantial damage compared to external threats. Conventional detection approaches analyse user behaviours from logs, using binary classifiers to distinguish between malicious and non-malicious users. However, existing methods focus solely on standalone or sequential activities. To enhance the detection of malicious insiders, we propose a novel approach: bilateral insider threat detection combining RNNs to incorporate standalone and sequential activities. Initially, we extract behavioural traits from log files representing standalone activities. Subsequently, RNN models capture features of sequential activities. Concatenating these features, we employ binary classification to detect insider threats effectively. Experiments on the CERT 4.2 dataset showcase the approach's superiority, significantly enhancing insider threat detection using features from both standalone and sequential activities.

Keywords: Insider threats · Recurrent Neural Networks · Sequential activities · Standalone activities

1 Introduction

Recent global data breaches and computer sabotage incidents with severe user impacts highlight prioritising and improving cyber security measures to protect sensitive information and counter malicious threats [10,16,24]. The COVID-19 pandemic has significantly contributed to the rise of insider attacks, as the shift to remote work and increased reliance on digital platforms have created new opportunities for malicious insiders [3]. Organisations must remain vigilant and implement robust security measures to detect and prevent these insider threats in the evolving cybersecurity landscape [23].

According to the 2023 Insider Threat Report by Cybersecurity Insiders, a significant majority of organisations, approximately 74%, are deemed to have at least a moderate level of vulnerability to insider threats[1]. The insider threat involves risks from organisation-affiliated individuals accessing sensitive resources, causing concerns across industries [22]. These threats can lead to data breaches, intellectual property theft, and reputation damage [19,29]. Examining user device and application operation logs has gained prominence in detecting internal threats, currently regarded as a primary method for uncovering potential insider risks [1,8].

This paper proposes Bilateral Insider Threat Detection, which involves extracting standalone activities from domain expertise and sequential activities using the LSTM model. Using a binary classification approach, we combine the features extracted from the two activities and utilise them for insider threat detection. By merging the features, we enhance the detection capability and effectively distinguish between normal and malicious user behaviour. Our proposed contributions are in the following ways:

- We proposed a bilateral insider threat detection framework based on the daily behaviours of the user. It combines both standalone activities and sequential activities to increase the performance of insider threat detection.
- We developed a feature extraction method based on Recurrent Neural Networks (RNNs) and LSTM to extract the sequential features of the data.
- We conducted experiments on the CERT r4.2 dataset to compare the performance of bilateral features using different classifiers, including KNN, MLP, LR, and SVM classifiers. Additionally, we compared the performance of RNN and LSTM feature extractors using the same classifiers, namely KNN, MLP, LR, and SVM.

In the remaining sections of this paper, we will review related works in Sect. 2. Then, in Sect. 3, we will present the methodology used in this study. The proposed methodology will be implemented and discussed in Sect. 4. The experimental results on insider threat detection will be presented in Sect. 5, followed by the paper's conclusion in Sect. 6.

2   Related Work

Researchers have explored diverse techniques to counter insider threats [4,13, 21,25]. A new technique introduced an LSTM-based autoencoder for identifying insider threats through user behaviour analysis [16]. The article [17] serves as a tutorial that comprehensively explains fundamental LSTM and RNN concepts, covering topics like the derivation of conventional RNN from differential equations, LSTM equations, training challenges, enhancement strategies, and novel prospects in the field.

---

[1] https://www.cybersecurity-insiders.com/portfolio/2023-insider-threat-report-gurucul/.

Meng et al. [12] introduced an LSTM-RNN-based framework for insider threat detection via attribute classification. Outperforming k-NN, IF, SVM, and PCA techniques on CERT dataset v6.2, optimised hyperparameters enhance detection rates while reducing false alarms. In their study [2], the authors presented RADISH, a novel approach for efficient insider threat detection by identifying disparities across data streams to optimise organisational resources. However, complexities arise when detecting anomalies based on individual user behaviour.

The proposed multilayer framework in paper [1] combines misuse and anomaly detection methods for insider threat detection. Evaluated using performance metrics and computation time, it effectively identifies known and unknown insider threats. In paper [28], a novel method merges Deep Neural Networks (DNN) with user behaviour analysis for insider threat detection. Employing an LSTM-CNN architecture, relevant features are extracted to enable efficient threat detection via a Convolutional Neural Networks (CNN).

In paper [11], Lu et al. presented Insider Catcher, utilising deep neural networks with LSTM to analyse system logs as sequential data. The system distinguishes legitimate from malicious activities by identifying normal user behaviour patterns, enabling accurate insider threat detection based on learned sequential patterns. Tuor et al. introduced a supervised deep recurrent neural network framework in paper [20] for real-time insider threat detection using system logs. The framework decomposes anomaly scores into individual user behaviour features, enhancing interpretability in the detection process.

3   Methodology

In this section, we comprehensively demonstrate the complete workflow involved in the proposed bilateral insider threat detection framework to detect insider threats. Section 4 delves into the detailed extraction of standalone and sequential activity features, providing an in-depth exploration of the methodology.

Malicious users exhibit distinct behavioural patterns reflected in their daily activities [14,15,18]. To effectively detect insider threats, we extract standalone activity features from user behavioural log files, with the detailed method for extracting these behavioural features provided in Sect. 4.

Domain knowledge guides the selection of features for standalone activities on a user-day basis [4]. The standalone feature matrix, denoted as X_m, is extracted from the daily behaviours of isolated user-days, as depicted in Fig. 1. This matrix is derived from the daily behaviours of isolated user-days, where $X_m \in \mathbb{R}^{n \times d_m}$. Here, n represents the total number of user-days, and d_m represents the dimension of the manual features extracted from standalone activities. For each user-day, the extracted feature vector can be represented as $x_i^{(m)} \in \mathbb{R}^{d_m}$, where $i \in \{1, 2, \ldots, n\}$.

To handle sequential activities, deep learning models that specialized in processing sequences are designed to extract relevant features through a supervised training procedure. After training, the output for all user-days is used as the

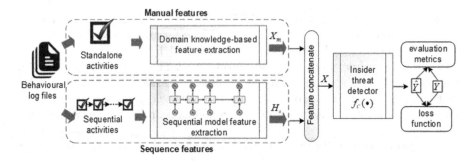

Fig. 1. Proposed Framework

feature matrix for sequential activities. Since those features are generated from the daily activity sequence, we denote them as H_s, where $H_s \in \mathbb{R}^{n \times d_s}$, with n representing the total number of user-days, and d_s denoting the dimension of sequential features. For each user-day, the sequential feature vector can be denoted as $x_i^{(s)} \in \mathbb{R}^{d_s}$, where $i \in \{1, 2, \ldots, n\}$.

$$H_s = f_{Seq}(Seq, \Theta_{Seq}) \tag{1}$$

The features extracted from the standalone and sequential methods are concatenated to form the final behavioural feature matrix, as illustrated in Eq. (2).

$$X = \text{concatenate}(X_m, H_s) \tag{2}$$

where the final user-day feature matrix for insider threat detection is denoted as $X \in \mathbb{R}^{n \times (d_m + d_s)}$, where the dimension of the final feature is equal to $d_m + d_s$.

4   Implementation

4.1   Dataset and Pre-processing

This study utilized the widely used synthetic CERT dataset to relief privacy concerns [5,6], which comprises over 20 GB of system log records spanning 500 days. It simulated 1,000 users, including 70 identified as malicious insiders. Curated by Carnegie Mellon University's CERT Insider Threat Center, the dataset encompasses diverse user behaviours, from investigations to case files and forensic analysis [7]. Our focus was explicitly on the CERT r4.2 version dataset, which features only 0.03% anomalous incidents; the remaining 99.7% represents normal activities, spanning logons, device usage, emails, HTTPS, files, and psychometric scores. The dataset's multiple CSV files provided rich user behaviour analysis and insider threat detection sources, each containing specific activity and attribute details. To address the class imbalance, we created a balanced dataset through downsampling normal users [26], resulting in a 70% training set and a 30% testing set.

4.2   Feature Extraction

This section provides detailed information on the construction of bilateral features following the method layed out in Sect. 3.

Manual Features. This feature utilizes two activity files, device.csv, and logon.csv, to extract five behavioural features from users' daily routines. Regarding data labeling, if a user is engaged in at least one malicious activity on a particular user-day, that user-day is labeled as an insider threat incident. The behavioural features are represented as F1, F2, F3, F4, and F5. In manual feature engineering, the selection of potential indicators heavily relies on domain knowledge. For each user-day sample, the following are the five standalone behavioural features listed:

1. F1, "First logon time", is extracted from logon.csv by mapping the initial login timestamp to $[0, 1]$ within a 24-h span.
2. F2, "Last logoff time", is derived from logon.csv by mapping the final logoff timestamp to $[0, 1]$ on a 24-h basis.
3. F3, "First device activity time", is obtained from device.csv, mapping the initial device activity timestamp to $[0, 1]$ over 24 h.
4. F4, "Last device activity time", comes from device.csv, mapping the final device activity timestamp to $[0, 1]$ in a 24-h span.
5. F5, "Number of off-hour device activities", from device.csv, counts device activities (connect or disconnect) between 18:00 PM and 8:00 AM.

Table 1. Sequential activities Encoding

Nature of the activity	Code for on-duty hours	Code for non-working hours
Logon a pc	1	13
Logoff a pc	2	14
Connect a usb drive	3	15
Disconnect a usb drive	4	16
Open a .doc file	5	17
Open a .exe file	6	18
Open a .jpg file	7	19
Open a .pdf file	8	20
Open a .text file	9	21
Open a .zip file	10	22
Send an email to internal address	11	23
Send an email to external address	12	24

Sequential Features. To automate feature engineering, the initial step involves encoding daily activities, assigning each activity a distinct numerical code. Subsequently, these encoded activities are organized into sequences based on their chronological occurrence. This sequential arrangement preserves the temporal order of activities, greatly aiding subsequent analysis and modeling. We adopted the activity encoding approach described in the referenced paper [9, 28]. We analyzed activity logs from files such as file.csv, logon.csv, device.csv, and email.csv. Each activity was assigned a code following predefined rules (see Table 1). Our study covered 12 activity types, further categorized into 24 types based on working or off-hours, each assigned a unique numerical identifier (1–24). The longest daily activity sequence in our dataset contained 74 activities, leading us to use a sequence length of 74 during sequential feature extraction for improved feature engineering. The resulting two-dimensional representation serves as the new feature for activity sequences.

5   Experiments

The effectiveness of the proposed bilateral framework was assessed through comparative experiments in the first part of this section against standalone activities. Following that, the feature extraction capabilities of RNN and LSTM models were compared in the second part of this section. All experiments were conducted using Python, with binary classifiers implemented using the scikit-learn library. SVM, LR, KNN, and MLP classifiers adhered to default parameters unless otherwise noted [27].

Comparison Between Standalone Activities and Bilateral for Different Classifiers. The binary classification was performed with KNN, MLP, SVM, and LR classifiers to assess sequential features' impact on bilateral insider threat detection. By comparing classifier performance using manual features versus those integrating sequential features from a plain RNN model, our goal was to gauge the value of daily activity sequences in bilateral insider threat detection, considering its classifier-independent nature. The comparison outcomes are detailed in Table 2.

Table 2. Performance improvements with bilateral features across classifiers

Classifier	Features	Acc	Pre	Rec	F1	ΔAcc	ΔPre	ΔRec	ΔF1
KNN	Manual	87.59	84.32	90.30	87.21	3.15	4.21	1.87	3.10
	Manual+RnnSeq	90.73	88.53	92.16	90.31				
MLP	Manual	89.51	85.14	94.03	89.36	2.97	5.19	0.00	2.78
	Manual+RnnSeq	92.48	90.32	94.03	92.14				
LR	Manual	90.03	86.51	93.28	89.77	2.97	4.80	0.75	2.88
	Manual+RnnSeq	93.01	91.30	94.03	92.65				
SVM	Manual	90.21	86.55	93.66	89.96	2.10	3.16	0.75	2.04
	Manual+RnnSeq	92.31	89.72	94.40	92.00				

Table 2 outlines the performance of different classifiers with varying feature sets, including Accuracy (Acc), Precision (Pre), Recall (Rec), and F1-score (F1)

and (Δ) represents the differences in metrics between manual features and features from daily activity sequences using a simple RNN model (referred to as "RnnSeq"). The results indicate a significant improvement in classifier performance when combining manual and RNN sequential features compared to manual features alone. For instance, in the KNN classifier, Acc improves by 3.15%, Pre by 4.21%, Rec by 1.87%, and F1 by 3.10%. Similar improvements are observed across other classifiers like MLP, LR, and SVM.

Figure 2 displays ROC curves for all classifiers. Combining manual features with RNN sequential features ("Manual+RnnSeq") outperforms using manual features alone. The AUC values, representing classifier discriminative power, are displayed. For instance, KNN's AUC improves from 0.916 to 0.940 with manual features and RNN sequential features together, while SVM's AUC increases from 0.914 to 0.966. These findings underscore the effectiveness of integrating RNN sequential features with manual ones, thereby enhancing discriminative performance.

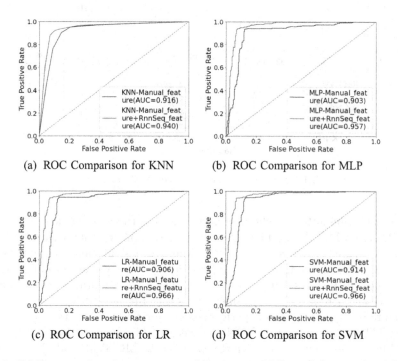

(a) ROC Comparison for KNN   (b) ROC Comparison for MLP

(c) ROC Comparison for LR   (d) ROC Comparison for SVM

Fig. 2. ROC comparison between manual feature and bilateral feature for different classifiers

Comparison Between RNN and LSTM Feature Extractor. In the preceding section, we observed performance enhancement through a basic sequential data-oriented model, prompting exploration for better results with a more advanced approach. We compare the sequential feature extraction capabilities of LSTM and RNN models in Table 3.

Table 3. Performance comparison between RNN and LSTM feature extractor

Classifier	Sequential feature extractor	Acc	Pre	Rec	F1	ΔAcc	ΔPre	ΔRec	ΔF1
KNN	RNN	90.73	88.53	92.16	90.31	4.37	6.92	1.87	4.43
	LSTM	95.10	95.45	94.03	94.74				
MLP	RNN	92.48	90.32	94.03	92.14	2.97	5.17	0.75	2.99
	LSTM	95.45	95.49	94.78	95.13				
LR	RNN	93.01	91.30	94.03	92.65	2.97	5.63	0.37	3.01
	LSTM	95.98	96.93	94.40	95.65				
SVM	RNN	92.31	89.72	94.40	92.00	3.32	6.13	0.37	3.31
	LSTM	95.63	95.85	94.78	95.31				

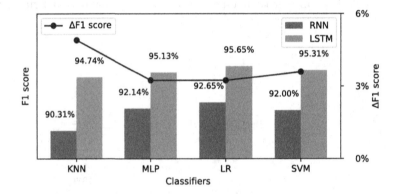

Fig. 3. F1-score comparison between RNN and LSTM

The table illustrates the classifier performance with sequential feature extractors, RNN and LSTM, and highlights significant improvements with LSTM features. For instance, the KNN classifier exhibited a significant Acc increase of 4.37% with LSTM, along with an impressive Pre improvement of 6.92% and a 1.87% boost in Rec, resulting in a 4.43% higher F1. Comparable enhancements are noticeable across various classifiers like MLP, LR, and SVM.

Figure 3 displays F1-score performance improvements between the RNN and LSTM feature extractor. KNN achieved a 4.43% higher F1-score with the LSTM feature extractor than with RNN. Similarly, LR, SVM, and MLP showed improvements of 3.01%, 3.31%, and 2.99%, respectively. These findings underscore the LSTM's effectiveness in elevating F1-scores across different classifiers.

6   Conclusion

This paper presents a bilateral insider threat detection approach integrating standalone and sequential activities, enhancing detection performance. Experimental results on the CERT 4.2 dataset show our Bilateral approach outperforms algorithms relying solely on standalone features. Combining manual and sequential features yields superior performance compared to using manual features alone. While LSTM outperforms RNN, acknowledging study limitations, future research can address challenges like imbalanced learning and develop strategies for real-world data imbalance issues.

References

1. Al-Mhiqani, M.N., et al.: A new intelligent multilayer framework for insider threat detection. Comput. Electr. Eng. **97**, 107597 (2022)
2. Böse, B., Avasarala, B., Tirthapura, S., Chung, Y.Y., Steiner, D.: Detecting insider threats using radish: a system for real-time anomaly detection in heterogeneous data streams. IEEE Syst. J. **11**(2), 471–482 (2017)
3. Deloitte: Impact of COVID-19 on cybersecurity (2023). https://www2.deloitte.com/ch/en/pages/risk/articles/impact-covid-cybersecurity.html
4. Fatima, M., Rehman, O., Rahman, I.M.: Impact of features reduction on machine learning based intrusion detection systems. EAI Endors. Trans. Scalable Inf. Syst. **9**(6), e9 (2022)
5. Ge, Y.F., Orlowska, M., Cao, J., Wang, H., Zhang, Y.: MDDE: multitasking distributed differential evolution for privacy-preserving database fragmentation. VLDB J. **31**(5), 957–975 (2022)
6. Ge, Y.F., Wang, H., Cao, J., Zhang, Y.: An information-driven genetic algorithm for privacy-preserving data publishing. In: Chbeir, R., Huang, H., Silvestri, F., Manolopoulos, Y., Zhang, Y. (eds.) WISE 2022. LNCS, vol. 13724, pp. 340–354. Springer, Cham (2022). https://doi.org/10.1007/978-3-031-20891-1_24
7. Glasser, J., Lindauer, B.: Bridging the gap: a pragmatic approach to generating insider threat data. In: 2013 IEEE Security and Privacy Workshops, pp. 98–104. IEEE (2013)
8. Hong, W., Yin, J., You, M., Wang, H., Cao, J., Li, J., Liu, M.: Graph intelligence enhanced bi-channel insider threat detection. In: Yuan, X., Bai, G., Alcaraz, C., Majumdar, S. (eds.) NSS 2022. LNCS, vol. 13787, pp. 86–102. Springer, Cham (2022). https://doi.org/10.1007/978-3-031-23020-2_5
9. Hong, W., et al.: A graph empowered insider threat detection framework based on daily activities. ISA Trans. (2023, in press). https://doi.org/10.1016/j.isatra.2023.06.030
10. Le, D.C., Zincir-Heywood, N., Heywood, M.I.: Analyzing data granularity levels for insider threat detection using machine learning. IEEE Trans. Netw. Serv. Manage. **17**(1), 30–44 (2020). https://doi.org/10.1109/TNSM.2020.2967721
11. Lu, J., Wong, R.K.: Insider threat detection with long short-term memory. In: Proceedings of the Australasian Computer Science Week Multiconference, pp. 1–10 (2019)
12. Meng, F., Lou, F., Fu, Y., Tian, Z.: Deep learning based attribute classification insider threat detection for data security. In: 2018 IEEE Third International Conference on Data Science in Cyberspace (DSC), pp. 576–581. IEEE (2018)
13. Patil, D.R., Pattewar, T.M.: Majority voting and feature selection based network intrusion detection system. EAI Endors. Trans. Scalable Inf. Syst. **9**(6), e6–e6 (2022)
14. Sarki, R., Ahmed, K., Wang, H., Zhang, Y., Wang, K.: Convolutional neural network for multi-class classification of diabetic eye disease. EAI Endors. Trans. Scalable Inf. Syst. **9**(4), e5–e5 (2022)

15. Shalini, R., Manoharan, R.: Trust model for effective consensus in blockchain. EAI Endors. Trans. Scalable Inf. Syst. **9**(5), 1–8 (2022). https://doi.org/10.4108/eai.1-2-2022.173294
16. Sharma, B., Pokharel, P., Joshi, B.: User behavior analytics for anomaly detection using LSTM autoencoder-insider threat detection. In: Proceedings of the 11th International Conference on Advances in Information Technology, pp. 1–9 (2020)
17. Sherstinsky, A.: Fundamentals of recurrent neural network (RNN) and long short-term memory (LSTM) network. Phys. D **404**, 132306 (2020)
18. Singh, R., et al.: Antisocial behavior identification from twitter feeds using traditional machine learning algorithms and deep learning. EAI Endors. Trans. Scalable Inf. Syst. **10**(4), e17–e17 (2023)
19. Sun, X., Wang, H., Li, J., Zhang, Y.: Satisfying privacy requirements before data anonymization. Comput. J. **55**(4), 422–437 (2012). https://doi.org/10.1093/comjnl/bxr028
20. Tuor, A., Kaplan, S., Hutchinson, B., Nichols, N., Robinson, S.: Deep learning for unsupervised insider threat detection in structured cybersecurity data streams. arXiv preprint arXiv:1710.00811 (2017)
21. Venkateswaran, N., Prabaharan, S.P.: An efficient neuro deep learning intrusion detection system for mobile adhoc networks. EAI Endors. Trans. Scalable Inf. Syst. **9**(6), e7 (2022)
22. Wang, H., Yi, X., Bertino, E., Sun, L.: Protecting outsourced data in cloud computing through access management. Concurr. Comput.: Pract. Exp. **28** (2014). https://doi.org/10.1002/cpe.3286
23. Yin, J., Tang, M.J., Cao, J., Wang, H., You, M., Lin, Y.: Adaptive online learning for vulnerability exploitation time prediction. In: Huang, Z., Beek, W., Wang, H., Zhou, R., Zhang, Y. (eds.) WISE 2020, Part II. LNCS, vol. 12343, pp. 252–266. Springer, Cham (2020). https://doi.org/10.1007/978-3-030-62008-0_18
24. Yin, J., Tang, M., Cao, J., You, M., Wang, H.: Cybersecurity applications in software: data-driven software vulnerability assessment and management. In: Daimi, K., Alsadoon, A., Peoples, C., El Madhoun, N. (eds.) Emerging Trends in Cybersecurity Applications, pp. 371–389. Springer, Cham (2022). https://doi.org/10.1007/978-3-031-09640-2_17
25. Yin, J., You, M., Cao, J., Wang, H., Tang, M.J., Ge, Y.-F.: Data-driven hierarchical neural network modeling for high-pressure feedwater heater group. In: Borovica-Gajic, R., Qi, J., Wang, W. (eds.) ADC 2020. LNCS, vol. 12008, pp. 225–233. Springer, Cham (2020). https://doi.org/10.1007/978-3-030-39469-1_19
26. You, M., Yin, J., Wang, H., Cao, J., Miao, Y.: A minority class boosted framework for adaptive access control decision-making. In: Zhang, W., Zou, L., Maamar, Z., Chen, L. (eds.) WISE 2021. LNCS, vol. 13080, pp. 143–157. Springer, Cham (2021). https://doi.org/10.1007/978-3-030-90888-1_12
27. You, M., et al.: A knowledge graph empowered online learning framework for access control decision-making. World Wide Web **26**(2), 827–848 (2023)
28. Yuan, F., Cao, Y., Shang, Y., Liu, Y., Tan, J., Fang, B.: Insider threat detection with deep neural network. In: Shi, Y., Fu, H., Tian, Y., Krzhizhanovskaya, V.V., Lees, M.H., Dongarra, J., Sloot, P.M.A. (eds.) ICCS 2018, Part I. LNCS, vol. 10860, pp. 43–54. Springer, Cham (2018). https://doi.org/10.1007/978-3-319-93698-7_4
29. Yuan, S., Wu, X.: Deep learning for insider threat detection: review, challenges and opportunities. Comput. Secur. **104**, 102221 (2021)

ATDG: An Automatic Cyber Threat Intelligence Extraction Model of DPCNN and BIGRU Combined with Attention Mechanism

Bo Cui[(⊠)], Jinling Li, and Wenhan Hou

Inner Mongolia Key Laboratory of Wireless Networking and Mobile Computing,
College of Computer Science, Inner Mongolia University, Hohhot, China
cscb@imu.edu.cn, {32109042,cshwh}@mail.imu.edu.cn

Abstract. With the situation of cyber security becoming more and more complex, the mining and analysis of Cyber Threat Intelligence (CTI) have become a prominent focus in the field of cyber security. Social media platforms like Twitter, due to their powerful timeliness and extensive coverage, have become valuable data sources for cyber security. However, these data often comprise a substantial amount of invalid and interfering data, posing challenges for existing deep learning models in identifying critical CTI. To address this issue, we propose a novel CTI automatic extraction model, called ATDG, designed for detecting cyber security text and extracting cyber threat entities. Specifically, our model utilizes a Deep Pyramid Convolutional Neural Network (DPCNN) and BIGRU to extract character-level and word-level features from the text, to better extract of semantic information at different levels, which effectively improved out of vocabulary (OOV) problem in threat intelligence. Additionally, we introduce a self-attention mechanism at the encoding layer to enable the model to focus on key features and enhance its performance, which dynamically adjusts the attention given to different features. Furthermore, to address the issue of imbalanced sample distribution, we have incorporated Focal Loss into ATDG, enhancing our model capability to effectively handle data imbalances. Experimental results demonstrate that ATDG (92.49% F1-score and 93.07% F1-score) outperforms the state-of-the-art methods in both tasks, and effectiveness of introducing self-attention mechanism and Focal Loss is also demonstrated.

Keywords: Cyber security · CTI · Social media · Twitter · Information extraction

1 Introduction

In recent years, advancements in network technologies have resulted in a significant increase in sophisticated cyberthreats, including data leakage, zero-day

F. Zhang et al. (Eds.): WISE 2023, LNCS 14306, pp. 189–204, 2023.
https://doi.org/10.1007/978-981-99-7254-8_15

vulnerabilities, and financial fraud [1]. These issues not only lead to substantial losses for individuals and enterprises but also pose a significant threat to national security. According to a report by Hackmageddon, an information security company, there were 713 cyber-attacks in the first quarter of 2021 alone, indicating a continuous increase in attack frequency [2]. To effectively address the covert challenges prevalent in network security, Gartner introduced the concept of Cyber Threat Intelligence (CTI) for network defense in 2013 [3].

CTI encompasses knowledge about existing or upcoming threats to assets, including scenarios, mechanisms, indicators, implications and actionable suggestions, etc., which can provide organizations with effective strategies against threats [4]. The collection of CTI greatly alleviates the heavy analytical workload of security analysts and effectively safeguards organizations from cyberattacks [5]. However, it is crucial to note that CTI primarily exists in the form of unstructured text. This data is characterized by its extensive scale, decentralization, fragmentation and hidden relationships [6]. Consequently, the timely and accurate analysis, processing and mining of this extensive data for potential valuable threat information remain significant challenge in the field of network security.

Social media platforms, including Twitter, hacker forums, and vendor advertisements (such as Microsoft and Cisco), have emerged as powerful mediums for the exchange and dissemination of network security information [7]. These platforms witness a significant influx of public events on a daily basis, with users frequently sharing information related to threats that often reveal new vulnerabilities [8]. As a result, these social media platforms have become valuable sources of data for cybersecurity. However, the structure of these data on social media platforms are concise (e.g., tweets limited to 140 characters) and users have different writing styles. Additionally, the field of cybersecurity encompasses a vast amount of specialized vocabulary and out-of-vocabulary (OOV) terms, leading to complex sentence structures and highly imbalanced label distributions within the data. Thus, a more advanced model is needed, which can overcome the complexity of these data on social media platforms and achieve higher performance in extracting CTI [9,10].

This paper proposes ATDG, a novel model to automatically extract CTI. By leveraging the proposed model, security analysts can gain valuable insights and strengthen their proactive defenses against emerging cyber threats. We utilize the multi-task method to design a shared model, which integrates two tasks: detecting cyber security text and extracting cyber threat entities. The main contributions of this paper are summarized as follows:

• We propose an optimized text representation method using an improved a Deep Pyramid Convolutional Neural Network (DPCNN) with a residual structure and BIGRU. This method extracts character-level and word-level features of text, capturing semantic information at various text levels, and effectively addressing OOV issues. • We introduce a self-attention mechanism in the encoding layer to better capture the global dependencies within the text sequence. This mechanism dynamically adjusts the attention allocated to different features, effectively resolving the challenge of long-range dependencies in the model and substantially enhancing its performance. Through experiments, we have demonstrated the indispensability of the self-attention mechanism. • To achieve a balanced sample distribution, we incorporated Focal Loss into ATDG and used balancing factors and modulation coefficients to decrease the weights of negative samples and easily classifiable samples. This enables the model to concentrate more on the entity parts and challenging samples during the training process, thereby enhancing its performance.

The rest of this paper is organized as follows: Sect. 2 will discuss recent work. In Sect. 3, we describe the task definition. Section 4 introduces our method. Section 5 shows the experimental results. Finally, we conclude this paper and outline future work in Sect. 6.

2 Related Work

In the following, we briefly review the previous work related to ATDG: researches on malicious information extraction based on machine learning and deep learning.

Machine Learning for Extracting CTI. Traditional information extraction methods based on statistical machine learning can achieve good results in general domains, Isuf Deliu et al. [11] explored machine learning methods to quickly screen specific IOCs in hacker forums. Sabottke et al. [12] proposed a Twitter-based vulnerability SVM detector that can detect whether the vulnerability has been exploited in the real world. In 2020, Zhao et al. [13] proposed a novel framework called TIMiner for automatic extraction and evaluation of OSCTI with domain labels based on social media data. The framework utilizes word embedding and syntactic dependency techniques to achieve personalized classification of OSCTI with domain labels. Zhu et al. [14] implemented a large-scale on-site data processing model that can automatically extract IOCs and associate them with corresponding activity stages. However, the model cannot automatically record IOC semantics and other information, so security personnel need to manually extract and report qualitative activity features, which is inefficient and not universally applicable. Alves et al. [15] proposed a Twitter network threat monitor based on SVM and multi-layer perceptron (MLP), which is used to generate threat information related to the monitored IT infrastructure. Liao et al. [16] proposed a system called iACE that automatically extracts IOCs from network security blogs. However, the extraction accuracy of iACE depends heavily on the construction of the context word bank and the performance of the syntactic parser and feature engineering.

Deep Learning for Extracting CTI. Compared to traditional machine learning, deep learning utilizes various feature extractors to uncover the deeper features of text. Ebrahimi et al. [17] applied deep traditional neural networks to capture malicious conversations in social media. Le Sceller et al. [18] proposed a self-learning framework called SONAR for Twitter streams, which can be used to detect, locate and classify network security events in real-time on Twitter. A team from the University of Lisbon [9] used CNN to determine whether the collected tweets contained security information related to the property of IT infrastructure, followed by extracting named entities with BILSTM to obtain security alerts. The University of Maryland [8] developed Cyber Twitter, a framework for identifying and analyzing OSCTI from social media information streams such as Twitter. The framework uses the Security Vulnerability Extractor to extract security vulnerability-related terms. Fang et al. [19] used IDCNN and BILSTM to extract text features for network threat detection, without considering incorporating text morphology information. Zhou et al. [20] proposed an end-to-end model based on neural network sequence labeling, which converts the problem of IOC extraction into a sequence labeling problem, labeling each word in the article and extracting words with IOC labels. The model combines artificial neural networks (ANN), bidirectional LSTM and CRF, but it has caused a large number of misjudgments due to spelling features and other issues. The team continued their work from the previous paper [21] by introducing context features into the ANN model. Although it had some effect, this work heavily relied on the completeness of manually established context keyword libraries. In paper [22], a model based on convolutional neural networks was proposed to preprocess semantic text and input it into a word embedding model for feature vector extraction.

Although the aforementioned research works can help security analysts identify and extract open-source threat intelligence from social media data while avoiding redundant work, there are still deficiencies in extraction performance.

3   Task Definition

As shown in Fig. 1, our first task is to detect cyber threat events from unstructured network text data. This task can be considered as a text classification problem in the field of natural language processing (NLP). If the text contains non-O entity information (as indicated in Table 1 of Sect. 5), it is labeled as 1; otherwise, it is labeled as 0.

Furthermore, the second task is extracting network security entities from the text. This task can be seen as a named entity recognition task within a specific domain, equivalent to a sequence labeling problem in the field of natural language processing. Performing named entity recognition on network threat entities helps security analysts quickly identify network threats and enables more comprehensive and in-depth analysis and understanding of potential threats.

In this paper, we take sentences in network security text as the basic unit and focus on any sentence $s = [x]^N = \{x_1, \cdots, x_i, \cdots, x_N\}$, where x_i is the i_{th} word in the sentence and N is the number of words in the sentence. We use the BIO tagging method to extract entities from the text, where B (Begin) represents the start position of an entity, I (Inside) represents the interior or end of an entity, and O (Outside) represents a non-entity word. Identifying security entities in sentence s is equivalent to providing a labeling sequence $L_s = [l]^N$, where l is the label for each word. For example, given the sentence s "SAP Patches Multiple XSS and Missing Authorization Vulnerabilities: SAP on Tuesday released its first set ... https://t.co/TWKcHIXz3L #infosec", this text is considered to contain cyber threat information and labels it as 1. The corresponding labeling sequence L_s is "B-ORG O B-VUL I-VUL O B-VUL I-VUL I-VUL B-ORG O O O O O O O". Here, VUL indicates that the entity is a threat information, and specific entity categories are shown in Table 1.

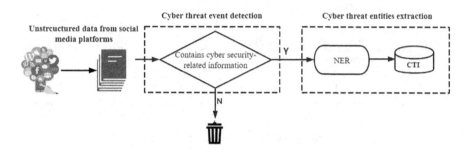

Fig. 1. Task processing flow.

4 ATDG

This section illustrates the design of ATDG, which consists of three major components as shown in Fig. 2: embedding layer, encoding layer and decoding layer. To begin with, we employ the *Word2vec* model to obtain word vectors. In contrast to the state-of-the-art models mentioned in paper [9,23], we employ DPCNN in the embedding layer to extract character-features and concatenate them with word vectors, resulting in low-dimensional word representations. This approach effectively addresses the OOV problem prevalent in CTI due to the presence of specialized vocabulary. Subsequently, we integrate BIGRU with a self-attention mechanism in the encoding layer to encode the word representations. Moreover, we abandon the conventional cross-entropy function and introduce Focal Loss to rebalance the sample distribution. This modification enhances the model's emphasis on entity labels within the text, thereby improving its focus on relevant information. The following details the descriptions of each component.

4.1 Embedding Layer

Natural language text cannot be directly encoded by neural networks. In ATDG, we extract word-features and character-features for each text and concatenate them, as shown in Fig. 2. The input to the embedding layer is a sequence of words, denoted as $S = \{x_1, x_2, \cdots, x_i, \cdots, x_m\}$, where S represents the input sentence, m represents the length of the sentence, and x_i represents the i_{th} word of the sentence. Each word consists of $x_i = \{c_1, c_2, \cdots, c_i, \cdots, c_p\}$, where c_i represents the i_{th} character of the word and p represents the length of the word. The following provides a detailed explanation of the process of word embedding and character embedding.

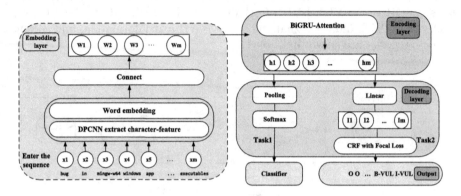

Fig. 2. The architecture of ATDG.

Word Embedding. In natural language processing (NLP), the way of word embedding largely determines the model's ability to understand the semantic meaning of text [12]. Traditional word representations such as one-hot vectors can easily result in the problems of disorder and high dimensionality. Compared with one-hot word embedding representations, distributed word embedding representations are more suitable and effective. We utilized the *Word2vec* model proposed by Bhatta et al. [24] to train on a large threat corpus, resulting in a *Word2vec* model specific to threat descriptions. We utilized *Skip-gram* method in *Word2vec* to predicts the contextual relationship of the target word, effectively capturing the semantic relationship between words. Thus, embedded word $W : word \rightarrow R^n$ is a parameterized function that maps words in text to vector of values. For example, the word *"cybersecurity"* corresponding vector W_{out} is:

$$Embedding(\text{"cybersecurity"}) = (0.1523, -0.1846, 0.2051, \cdots)$$

This vector can reflect the semantic relationship between words in the text and further enhance the performance and effectiveness of the model in network security event detection tasks.

Char-Embedding. Previous studies have shown [8,25] that adding character-level features can more effectively extract text morphological information (such as prefixes and suffixes of words). In this paper, ATDG utilizes the DPCNN to encode the characters in words into neural network representations, aiming to better extract the morphological information of the words. The core of DPCNN consists of equally-sized convolutional and 1/2 pooling layers. As the number of layers increases, the lengths are stacked up and eventually form a pyramid shape.

Since the text structure in social media is short and concise, we improve DPCNN by reducing two convolutional layers to preserve more text features and achieve better performance of the model [26]. Figure 3 shows our improved DPCNN structure. The initialized characters are input into DPCNN, and after passing through a convolutional layer, the data is concatenated with those that have not passed through a convolutional layer, and then input into the cyclic module. First, it passes through 1/2 pooling layer, and then through the convolutional layer, and concatenates the pooled data with the convolutional data, and circulates the module continuously. Finally, the final features were obtained by pooling the data once. Additionally, DPCNN introduces the residual network structure through the pyramid pool mechanism, which reduces the problem of disappearing gradient, makes the model easier to train, has faster convergence rate, and has higher generalization ability.

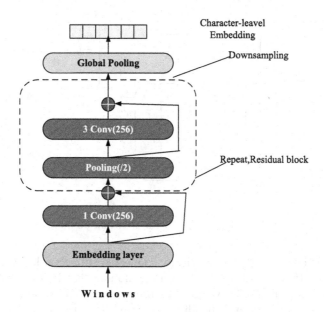

Fig. 3. Architecture of DPCNN model.

Finally, concatenating the word vector h_w with the character vector h_c as shown in Fig. 3. Assuming the input sequence is S the final word representation vector of S is $h = \{h_1, h_2, \cdots, h_i, \cdots, h_m\}$, and h_i represents the i_{th} word vector, as shown in the Eq. 1.

$$h_i = [C_{out} \oplus W_{out}] \tag{1}$$

4.2 Encoding Layer

Different from the traditional encoding layer using random word embedding, in this paper, BIGRU is introduced to obtain historical and future information about the current word. The previous work [27] demonstrated the effectiveness of BIGRU in capturing contextual semantic information. BIGRU is an improved version of bi-directional long short-term memory (BILSTM). Compared to BIL-STM, it has lower complexity and can effectively alleviate the problem of vanishing gradients in recurrent neural networks (RNNs). It also has the advantages of fewer parameters and reduced overfitting. In addition, training with BIGRU is easier and more efficient.

BIGRU consists of a forward two GRU layer, a backward GRU layer, and a connectivity layer, as shown in Fig. 4.

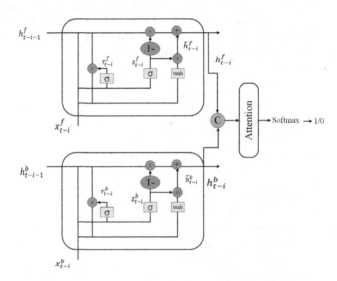

Fig. 4. BIGRU combined with attention mechanism.

Each GRU contains a set of cyclically connected subnetworks, called storage modules. Each time step is an GRU storage module that is obtained based on the previous moment hidden vector, the previous moment storage cell vector, and the current input word embedding operation. Feature vectors are obtained by inputting the word representation sequence of embedding layer into BIGRU.

$$B = BiGRU[c_1, \cdots, c_m] = [\overrightarrow{b_l} \circ \overleftarrow{b_r}, \cdots, \overrightarrow{b_l} \circ \overleftarrow{b_r}] \tag{2}$$

Then, motivated by the successful application of self-attention in many NLP tasks [12,24] and in order to obtain vector representations that are important for entities, our model integrates a multi-head self-attention mechanism after BIGRU. This mechanism can learn dependencies between any two words and assign different weights to each word representation to obtain key information. Multiple attention heads can be used to learn features in different representation subspaces, thus significantly improving the model performance. Specifically, in this paper, the output of BIGRU is used as input to the attention mechanism to obtain contextually significant embeddings of the current word.

Given the squence of embeddings e_i as input, and the output is defined as follows:

$$Attention(Q, K, V) = softmax(\frac{QK^T}{\sqrt{d_k}}) \tag{3}$$

$$MultiHead(Q, K, V) = (head_1; \cdots ; head_i),$$
$$where\ head_i = Attention(QW_i^Q, KW_i^K, VW_i^V) \tag{4}$$

where, QW_i^Q, KW_i^K, VW_i^V are parameter matrices for the projects of queries Q, keys K and values V in the i_{th} head, respectively. Here, Q, K, V are set as the input sequence $e_i(i = 1, \cdots, n)$. The $MultiHead(Q, K, V)$ is the given to the two convolutions and the output of multi-head self-attention $h_i^M (i = 1, \cdots, n)$ is obtained.

4.3 Decoding Layer

In the decoding layer, we design different decoding methods for the two tasks described in Sect. 3.

Detecing Cyber Security Events. We already know that this task is equivalent to a binary classification problem, so our model introduces maximum pooling operation in the decoding layer of the first task for further feature extraction and information filtering to achieve feature dimension reduction. The features after pooling are fully connected through the softmax function to obtain the probability of the final category, and further output the final result $\hat{y}$. The calculation process is shown in Eq. 5.

$$\hat{y} = max(softmax(\sigma(X \cdot W + b))) \tag{5}$$

Extracting CTI. The second task aims to extract cyber threat entities from texts that contain cybersecurity events. The CRF module takes into account the relationship between adjacent word labels, which is consistent with the non-independence of the relationships between word entity labels. This fully utilizes the contextual information of word entity labels, and only by jointly decoding label sequences can the model performance be effectively improved.

Assuming that the input sequence $X = (x_1, x_2, \cdots, x_n)$ corresponds to the predicted label sequence $y = (y_1, y_2, \cdots, y_n)$, the probability score of y with respect to x is defined as shown in Eq. 6.

$$score(X, y) = \sum_{i=1}^{n} P_{i,y_i} + \sum_{i=1}^{n} A_{y_i, y_{i+1}} \tag{6}$$

The matrix P is obtained by performing feature extraction on the output of the attention layer. P_{i,y_i} represents the probability of word i corresponding to label y_i. A represents the feature transition matrix parameter of CRF, which is obtained by learning the dependency relationship between labels through CRF.

$A_{y_i,y_{i+1}}$ represents the probability that the next label is y_{i+1} given the current label is y_i.

The final label prediction for each position in the input sequence will be jointly determined by the feature matrix P and the transition matrix A. According to the situation where each sentence sequence corresponds to multiple sets of label sequences, given an input sentence sequence $X = (x_1, x_2, \cdots, x_n)$, the conditional probability of generating a label sequence $y = (y_1, y_2, \cdots, y_n)$ for all possible sets of label sequences Y_x is shown in Eq. 7.

$$P(y|X) = \frac{exp(score(X, y))}{\sum_{y' \in Y_x} exp(score(X, y'))} \qquad (7)$$

Cyber threat intelligence typically consists of long texts, containing a large number of non-entity words (labeled as "O"). The binary cross-entropy loss function iterates slowly and may deviate from the correct optimization direction, making it unable to converge to the optimum. Additionally, in entity extraction tasks in the field of network security, there is a severe problem of imbalanced label distribution. Therefore, this paper introduces the Focal Loss function to optimize the model. It is a variant of the binary cross-entropy loss function that addresses the issue of class imbalance by altering the relative frequency of positive and negative samples and reducing the contribution weight of easy samples. This enables the model to focus more on challenging samples. The Focal Loss is defined as follows:

$$LOSS_{Focal} = -\alpha(1 - P(y|X))^\gamma ln(P(y|X)) \qquad (8)$$

Here, $\alpha \in [0, 1]$ is the balance factor used to balance the quantity of positive and negative samples. $\gamma \geq 0$ is the modulation coefficient used to reduce the loss of non-entity samples (easy samples) and direct the model's attention towards entity labels (difficult samples). $P(y|x)$ represents the probability of word x having the label y.

5   Experiment

5.1   Datasets

Table 1. Entities category.

Label	Description	Number
O	Does not contain useful information	59965
ORG	Company or organization	10051
PRO	A product or asset	18617
VER	A version number, possibly from the identified asset or product	7172
VUL	May be referencing the existence of a threat or a vulnerability	18095
ID	An identifier, either from a public repository or from an update or patch	7037

To evaluate the effectiveness of the threat intelligence extraction model proposed in this paper, we conducted experiments using the open cyber threat extracting dataset of Twitter [9]. The dataset consists of 31,218 tweets from security-related accounts. Each data contains timestamps, keywords, tweets, the preprocessed tweet, article-related tags (including cyber security event tags are 1, otherwise 0) and entity annotation sequence. Among them, there are 11780 tweets containing entities and 19438 tweets without entities (namely all words are labeled "O"). The "BIO" mode is adopted to mark the specific position of entities in the text. And there are six types of entities, among which we also count the number of each type of entity, as shown in Table 1.

5.2   Experiment Settings

In the experiment, for pre-trained word embedding, we apply Word2vec to all tweets. The Word2vec models are train with a window size of 8, a minimum vocabulary count of 1, and 15 iterations. The negative sampling number of Word2vec is set to 8 and the model type is skip-gram. The dimension of the output word embedding is set to 300. Additionally, the character embedding vector size was set to 100. To enhance the model's robustness, we adjusted the dropout rate accordingly, setting it to 0.2 for character embeddings and 0.3 for words. The number of BIGRU neurons is 300, with the one hidden layer.

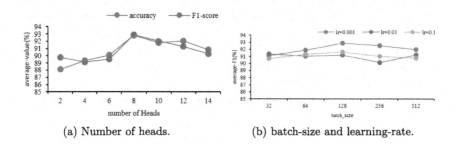

(a) Number of heads.   (b) batch-size and learning-rate.

Fig. 5. Parameters adjustment.

Additionally, it can be seen from Fig. 5(a) that when the number of attention head is 8, both the F1 score and accuracy reached the highest point, so *attention_head* = 8 was set. To achieve better performance, we also adjust *batch_size* and *learning_rate*, as shown in Fig. 5(b). Finally *batch_size* = 128 and *learning_rate* = 0.01. During our model training, we utilized the "patience" parameter to control the training iterations, setting it to 20. Additionally, in the results analysis, we employed this parameter to compare the efficiency of the models. Our model uses the Adam optimizer to improve the model convergence speed. All models were trained on Inter(R) Core(TM) i7-12700F CPU based on Pytorch 1.13.1.

5.3   Results Analysis

To further demonstrate the advantages of our model in this paper, we compared ATDG with the state-of-the-art models [9,19] and reproduced their code[1] to ensure a fair comparison.Table 2 presents a comparison of the results between ATDG and the baseline models on both tasks. We used accuracy(A), precision (P), recall rate (R)and F1 values (F1) as evaluation indicators of the models.

As shown in Table 2, compared with these state-of-the-art models, ATDG achieved 2.05% increase in accuracy and 3.21% increase in F1-score on the cyber threat event detection task. And the accuracy and F1-score of ATDG on extracting cyber threat entities task are increased by 1.43% and 1.19% respectively, and the other two indicators are also significantly improved. Additionally, we compared the training time of the models based on the number of iterations during the training process to illustrate the efficiency of the models.

Table 2. Comparison of models results.

Models	Task1				Task2			
	A(%)	P(%)	R(%)	F1(%)	A(%)	P(%)	R(%)	F1(%)
CNN+CNN [9]	82.88	91.87	87.61	89.69	91.61	92.15	91.61	91.18
CNN+BILSTM [9]	89.50	90.11	89.26	89.68	88.79	89.03	88.79	88.91
BILSTM+CNN [9]	89.50	90.11	89.26	89.68	88.79	89.03	88.79	88.91
BILSTM+BILSTM [9]	90.51	85.89	92.33	89.00	91.12	91.23	91.12	91.18
IDCNN+BILSTM [19]	89.93	91.30	88.55	89.91	89.91	90.34	89.91	90.13
DPCNN+BILSTM	90.46	93.12	89.41	91.23	92.28	92.40	92.28	92.34
No-DPCNN	91.89	88.40	93.26	90.77	90.69	90.85	90.69	90.77
No-attention	91.38	84.96	93.91	89.21	90.20	90.25	90.20	90.23
No-FL	91.00	87.64	92.40	89.86	92.04	92.08	92.04	92.06
ATDG	**92.56**	**92.30**	**92.67**	**92.49**	**93.04**	**93.09**	**93.04**	**93.07**

We use the value of patience to measure the time taken by the model, "patience" refers to a parameter that controls the number of consecutive epochs with no improvement on a specific evaluation metric before the training process is stopped. A lower number of patience indicates faster convergence, suggesting higher efficiency in terms of training time. The red line shown in Fig. 6 demonstrates that we replace BIGRU in ATDG with BILSTM, it required fewer iterations compared to BILSTM, resulting in shorter training time. This meets our initial expectations of achieving the same performance with less overhead and expense. Compared to other models, ATDG did not exhibit a significant improvement in terms of training time. However, our primary focus was on evaluating the model's F1 score and accuracy metrics. Therefore, improving the

---

[1] https://github.com/ndionysus/multitask-cyberthreat-detection.

training efficiency of the model will be an area of future research and development, as it is essential to strike a balance between model performance and training time.

In Fig. 6, we present the average values of the model on these two tasks, which demonstrate the high reliability of our model. In the ATDG, the four average metrics are nearly identical, indicating that our model effectively balances various metrics. It can capture positive instances well (high recall) while maintaining a low false positive rate (high precision). This balance implies that our model exhibits excellent performance and reliability in classification task.

5.4 Ablation Experiment

Ablation experiments were performed to analyze the effect of each module on the model performance, as shown in Table 2. First, the DPCNN was removed (labeled as No-DPCNN), and it was observed that F1 score of the two tasks were decreased by 1.72% and 2.30%. Particularly, according to the analysis, the advantage of DPCNN is that it can extract certain morphological features. Moreover, the words of cyber threat intelligence are relatively rare and the formats are diverse, so capturing the morphological information of words has a significant impact on the model performance.

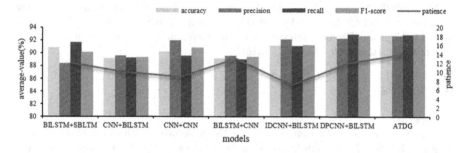

Fig. 6. Models performance comparison.

Then, the multi-head self-attention layer was removed (labeled as No-attention). It was observed that F1 score were decreased by 3.28% and 2.84% respectively. The experiment results indicate that the multi-head self-attention mechanism can help to locate vital context and capture long-distance interdependent features.

Finally, the Focal Loss was removed (labeled as No-FL), and using a cross-entropy loss function. It was observed that F1 score of the two tasks were decreased by 2.83% and 1.01%. The experiment results indicate that Focal Loss addressed the problem of unbalanced distribution of labels and improves model performance.

6 Conclusion

In this paper, we propose a novel automatic extract cyber security threat model, named ATDG. It performs two tasks concurrently, providing a significant advancement in the field of cyber security. The model enhances the word representation by incorporating an improved DPCNN that captures morphological information from the text. By connecting the enhanced representations with word embedding vectors, we effectively address the OOV issue commonly encountered in cybersecurity text. Furthermore, we introduce an attention-based BIGRU to capture contextual semantic information, highlighting key features from the vast feature space and improving the model's performance. Additionally, we employ Focal Loss to mitigate the problem of imbalanced data label distributions. The experimental results demonstrate substantial improvements over the baseline model, highlighting the necessity of each module in our proposed model.

In future work, we will further explore the problem of relationship extraction in threat intelligence, and optimize the model to consider more time consumption issue.

Acknowledgements.. This paper is supported by the National Natural Science Foundation of China (61962042) and Science and Technology Program of Inner Mongolia Autonomous Region (2020GG0188), and Natural Science Foundation of Inner Mongolia (2022MS06020), and the Central Government Guides Local Science and Technology Development Fund (2022ZY0064), and the University Youth Science and Technology Talent Development Project (Innovation Group Development Plan) of Inner Mongolia A. R. of China (Grant No. NMGIRT2318).

References

1. xxxxx
2. Gao, P., et al.: Enabling efficient cyber threat hunting with cyber threat intelligence. In: 2021 IEEE 37th International Conference on Data Engineering (ICDE), pp. 193–204. IEEE (2021)
3. Kurogome, Y., et al.: EIGER: automated IOC generation for accurate and interpretable endpoint malware detection. In: Proceedings of the 35th Annual Computer Security Applications Conference, pp. 687–701 (2019)
4. Khandpur, R.P., et al.: Crowdsourcing cybersecurity: cyber attack detection using social media. In: Proceedings of the 2017 ACM on Conference on Information and Knowledge Management, pp. 1049–1057 (2017)
5. Kim, E., et al.: CyTIME: cyber threat intelligence management framework for automatically generating security rules. In: Proceedings of the 13th International Conference on Future Internet Technologies, pp. 1–5 (2018)
6. Altalhi, S., Gutub, A.: A survey on predictions of cyber-attacks utilizing real-time twitter tracing recognition. J. Ambient Intell. Humanized Comput. **12**, 10209–10221 (2021)
7. Husari, G., et al.: Using entropy and mutual information to extract threat actions from cyber threat intelligence[. In: 2018 IEEE International Conference on Intelligence and Security Informatics (ISI), pp. 1–6. IEEE (2018)

8. Mittal, S., et al. CyberTwitter: using twitter to generate alerts for cybersecurity threats and vulnerabilities. In: 2016 IEEE/ACM International Conference on Advances in Social Networks Analysis and Mining (ASONAM), pp. 860–867. IEEE (2016)

9. Dionísio, N., et al.: Towards end-to-end cyberthreat detection from Twitter using multi-task learning. In: 2020 International Joint Conference on Neural Networks (IJCNN), pp. 1–8. IEEE (2020)

10. Wagner, C., et al.: MISP: the design and implementation of a collaborative threat intelligence sharing platform. In: Proceedings of the 2016 ACM on Workshop on Information Sharing and Collaborative Security, pp. 49–56 (2016)

11. Deliu, I., Leichter, C., Franke, K.: Extracting cyber threat intelligence from hacker forums: support vector machines versus convolutional neural networks. In: 2017 IEEE International Conference on Big Data (Big Data), pp. 3648–3656. IEEE (2017)

12. Sabottke, C., Suciu, O., Dumitras, T.: Vulnerability disclosure in the age of social media: exploiting Twitter for predicting real-world exploits. In: Proceedings of the 24th USENIX Security Symposium (USENIX Security 15). USENIX Association (2015)

13. Zhao, J., Yan, Q., Li, J., et al.: TIMiner: automatically extracting and analyzing categorized cyber threat intelligence from social data. Comput. Secur. **95**, 101867 (2020)

14. Zhu, Z., Dumitras, T.: ChainSmith: automatically learning the semantics of malicious campaigns by mining threat intelligence reports. In: 2018 IEEE European Symposium on Security and Privacy (EuroS&P), pp. 458–472. IEEE (2018)

15. Alves, F., Ferreira, P.M., Bessani, A.: Design of a classification model for a twitter-based streaming threat monitor. In: 2019 49th Annual IEEE/IFIP International Conference on Dependable Systems and Networks Workshops (DSN-W), pp. 9–14. IEEE (2019)

16. Liao, X., et al.: Acing the IOC game: toward automatic discovery and analysis of open-source cyber threat intelligence. In: Proceedings of the 2016 ACM SIGSAC Conference on Computer and Communications Security, pp. 755–766 (2016)

17. Ebrahimi, M., Suen, C.Y., Ormandjieva, O.: Detecting predatory conversations in social media by deep convolutional neural networks. Digit. Invest. **18**, 33–49 (2016)

18. Le Sceller, Q., et al.: SONAR: automatic detection of cyber security events over the twitter stream. In: Proceedings of the 12th International Conference on Availability, Reliability and Security, pp. 1–11 (2017)

19. Fang, Y., Gao, J., Liu, Z., Huang, C.: Detecting cyber threat event from twitter using IDCNN and BiLSTM. Appl. Sci. Sci. **10**(17), 5922 (2020)

20. Zhou, S., et al.: Automatic identification of indicators of compromise using neural-based sequence labelling. arXiv preprint arXiv:1810.10156 (2018)

21. Long, Z., et al.: Collecting indicators of compromise from unstructured text of cybersecurity articles using neural-based sequence labelling. In: 2019 International Joint Conference on Neural Networks (IJCNN), pp. 1–8. IEEE (2019)

22. Xun, S., Li, X., Gao, Y.: AITI: an automatic identification model of threat intelligence based on convolutional neural network. In: Proceedings of the 2020 the 4th International Conference on Innovation in Artificial Intelligence, pp. 20–24 (2020)

23. Dionísio, N., et al.: Cyberthreat detection from twitter using deep neural networks. In: 2019 International Joint Conference on Neural Networks (IJCNN), pp. 1–8. IEEE (2019)

24. Behzadan, V., et al.: Corpus and deep learning classifier for collection of cyber threat indicators in twitter stream. In: 2018 IEEE International Conference on Big Data (Big Data). IEEE (2018)
25. Ritter, A., et al.: Weakly Supervised Extraction of Computer Security Events from Twitter. In: International World Wide Web Conferences Steering Committee. International World Wide Web Conferences Steering Committee, pp. 896–905 (2015)
26. Trabelsi, S., et al.: Mining social networks for software vulnerabilities monitoring. In: International Conference on New Technologies. IEEE (2015)
27. Liu, X., Fu, J., Chen, Y.: Event evolution model for cybersecurity event mining in tweet streams. Inf. Sci. **524**(3), 254–276 (2020)

Blockchain-Empowered Resource Allocation and Data Security for Efficient Vehicular Edge Computing

Maojie Wang[1] , Shaodong Han[1] , Guihong Chen[1(⊠)] , Jiao Yin[2] ,
and Jinli Cao[3]

[1] School of Cyber Security, Guangdong Polytechnic Normal University,
Guangzhou 510635, China
chenguihong@gpnu.edu.cn
[2] Institute for Sustainable Industries and Liveable Cities, Victoria University,
Melbourne, Australia
jiao.yin@VU.edu.au
[3] Department of Computer Science and Information Technology,
La Trobe University, Melbourne, Australia
j.cao@latrobe.edu.au

Abstract. Vehicular networking technology is advancing rapidly, and one promising area of research is blockchain-based vehicular edge computing to enhance resource allocation and data security. This paper aims to optimize resource allocation and data security in vehicular edge computing by leveraging blockchain technology, thereby improving the overall system efficiency and reliability. By integrating the computational, storage, and communication capabilities of vehicles with blockchain, efficient utilization of edge computing and fair resource allocation are achieved. Additionally, data encryption techniques are introduced to ensure data security and privacy protection. Experimental results demonstrate that the system can automatically identify and allocate the most suitable edge computing nodes, thereby enhancing the responsiveness and quality of computational tasks. The blockchain-based vehicular edge offloading system not only optimizes the performance of vehicular networking systems and enhances user experience but also strengthens data security and privacy protection, providing a novel solution for the development of the vehicular networking industry.

Keywords: Blockchain · Vehicular network · Edge computing · Reinforcement learning

The work is supported in part by Key Research Projects of Universities in Guangdong Province under Grant 2022ZDZX1011. Guangdong Provincial Natural Science Fund Project under Grant 2023A1515011084 and Doctoral Program Construction Unit Research Capability Enhancement Project at Guangdong Polytechnic Normal University under Grant 22GPNUZDJS27.

1 Introduction

In the context of edge computing, vehicular edge computing has gained significant attention as one of its crucial application domains. In fields such as intelligent transportation and Internet of Vehicle (IoV), vehicles are not merely conventional means of transportation but also mobile data generators and consumers. However, challenges such as network latency, bandwidth constraints, and data security continue to hinder the development of intelligent vehicular applications [1,5,6]. Blockchain, as a distributed ledger technology, offers secure data storage and interaction mechanisms, effectively resolving concerns related to vehicular data security and privacy protection. By offloading computing tasks and data to edge nodes, the computational load on vehicles can be reduced, thereby improving computing performance and response speed. This further facilitates the development of intelligent vehicular applications [2,15].

While there have been studies in the field of vehicular edge computing offloading, research on blockchain-based intelligent vehicular edge computing offloading (BIVECO) remains relatively limited. Therefore, the objective of this paper is to build upon existing research and investigate in detail the mechanisms and optimization strategies for BIVECO, aiming to enhance the efficiency, reliability and security of intelligent vehicular applications [4]. Considering the dynamic vehicular environment, the offloading strategy should adapt to the state of the vehicular network. Therefore, in this study, we utilize the Multi-step Deep Q Network (MSDQN) reinforcement learning algorithm, as introduced in our previous work [13], to leverage the influence of multiple states for optimizing vehicle task allocation. MSDQN effectively addresses multi-objective optimization problems through Markov Decision Processes (MDP), determining the optimal multi-step value. However, the edge computing model employed in MSDQN establishes a one-to-one relationship between vehicles and Roadside Units (RSU) nodes, posing significant limitations in practical applications. Furthermore, the processing and transmission of edge computing data in MSDQN do not account for security and reliability aspects. Therefore, this paper adopts a multi-to-multi mode to better simulate real-world scenarios and incorporates blockchain technology to enhance data security and ensure privacy protection. The main contributions of this paper can be summarized as follows:

1) We introduce a blockchain framework for the vehicular networking system, where Mobile Edge Computing (MEC) servers maintain the blockchain. The blockchain is responsible for evaluating vehicle reliability based on reputation values and further incentivizes appropriate resource allocation by vehicles.
2) We propose a Blockchain-based Intelligent Vehicle Edge Computing Offloading algorithm, which employs the actor-critic algorithm to address the multi-objective optimization problem and derive an optimal offloading strategy. The security and reliability of the offloading process are guaranteed through node data processing and node consensus mechanisms.

3) Experimental results demonstrate that the proposed BIVECO algorithm enables vehicles to find the most efficient RSU node for task offloading by training, thereby reducing latency and energy consumption for subsequent edge computing offloading tasks, thus offering high practicality.

The rest of this paper is organized as follows. In Sect. 2, we review the related work, and in Sect. 3, we present the system model. In Sect. 4, we propose the blockchain-based deep vehicular edge computing offloading algorithm. Section 5 provides privacy and security analyses of simulation results and convergence performance. Finally, the conclusions are presented in Sect. 6.

2   Related Works

In [11], the authors proposed a novel blockchain-based framework with an adaptive block size for video streaming with mobile edge computing. For video analytics applications, Jiang et al. integrated multi-access edge computing and blockchain technologies into the Internet of Vehicles. This work aims to optimize transaction throughput while also reducing the latency of the MEC system. [7]. Fu et al. proposed a blockchain-enabled distributed framework to reach consensus among multiple systems where the computation tasks of the blockchain are processed with MEC [4]. Due to the dynamical variation environment of traffic system, the computing resource is quite difficult to be allocated. To solve the above problems, Xiao et al. proposed a deep reinforcement learning based algorithm for resource optimization in the blockchain-supported-IoV system [18]. Xu et al. proposed an integrated blockchain and MEC framework based on a space-structured ledger to meet the transaction demands for IoT applications [20]. IoV could assist the smart city to achieve flexible computing resource demand response via paid sharing the idle vehicle computing resources. Motivated by this, the authors in [9] proposed a peer-to-peer computing resource trading system to balance computing resource spatio-temporal dynamic demands in IoV-assisted smart city. Traditional cloud-based federated learning poses challenges to the communication overhead with the rapid increase of terminal equipment in IoV system. Ye et al. studied MEC and blockchain-enabled energy-efficient IoV based on Asynchronous Advantage Actor-Critic approach [21]. Blockchain technology is adopted to ensure reliable transmission and interaction of data. Liu et al. studied the interaction of MEC nodes and parked vehicles in blockchain-based parking vehicle edge computing and model it as a two-stage Stackelberg game to optimize the utility of MEC nodes and parked vehicles [10]. To this end, Samy et al. proposed a new blockchain-based framework for secure task offloading in MEC systems with guaranteed performance in terms of execution delay and energy consumption [12]. In blockchain-based scheme, all communication entities are registered, verified and thereafter validated using smart contract-based Practical Byzantine Fault Tolerance consensus algorithm [8]. In [16] and [17], the authors investigated the computational paradigms used to meet the stringent requirements of modern applications. The state-of-the-art approaches suffer from several drawbacks, including bottlenecks of the single cloud server model, high computational overhead of operations, excessive trust in cloud servers and RSUs, and leakage of vehicle trajectory privacy.

Although there have been numerous studies in the field of vehicle edge computing offloading, several crucial issues need to be addressed, including the security and privacy of data transmission, appropriate resource allocation for collaborative computing and caching, and more. Thus, in this article, we propose a blockchain-based Intelligent Vehicle Edge Computing Offloading algorithm to enhance the reliability of RSUs and service vehicles in task distribution, as well as to optimize edge resource allocation.

3   System Model

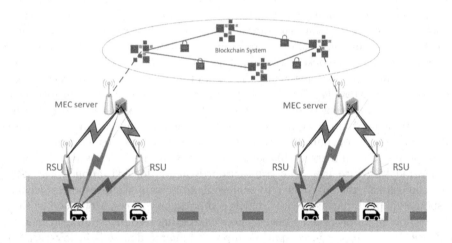

Fig. 1. Blockchain based Vehicle Trusted MEC system model.

3.1   Network Model

The proposed model encompasses three essential layers: the user layer, edge layer, and blockchain layer. It incorporates intelligent vehicles, RSUs, MEC servers, and a blockchain network, as shown in Fig. 1.

In this architecture, the system is composed of N vehicles, M RSUs, and H MEC servers. When vehicle V_i enters the communication range of an MEC server M_j, a wireless communication connection is established between the vehicle and the RSU associated with that MEC server, considering the reputation value of the vehicle. The offloading process is formulated as a MDP in our approach, where the state s is defined as $s = \{S, B_{ij}^k, G_{ij}^k\}$, representing the system variables including the signal-to-interference-plus-noise ratio (SINR) S, the bandwidth B_{ij}^k

and channel gain G_{ij}^k. The calculation of these variables follows the methodology established in our previous work [3,13]. To make decisions within the MDP, we define the action a as $a = \{o, p\}$, where o represents the offloading rate ranging from 0 to 1, and p signifies the transmission power between the vehicle and the RSU, which can vary between 0 and 100 mW.

The total size of the computation task for vehicle V_i is denoted by C. The total computation delay, denoted as d, is the larger of the local computation delay d_v and the sum of the RSU computation delay d_r and the RSU transmission delay d_t, which can be denoted as $d = max\{d_v, d_t + d_r\}$. The energy consumption E can be calculated as the sum of the local computation energy consumption E_v and the offloading transmission energy consumption E_o, expressed as $E = E_v + E_o$.

3.2   Blockchain Network Model

In contrast to the conventional architecture, the framework proposed in this paper introduces a blockchain network as a replacement for the centralized Certificate Authority institution [19]. The blockchain network assumes management and control functions for the underlying mobile MEC system. It records the identity of intelligent vehicles, computation offloading reputation values, and RSU data information within the IoV environment, as illustrated in Fig. 2. In this framework, both intelligent vehicles and RSUs actively participate in the construction of the blockchain network. Intelligent vehicles function as regular nodes, while the master node is generated by RSUs. The master node assumes responsibilities such as producing new blocks and achieving node consensus. When an intelligent vehicle selects an RSU node for a computation offloading request, the request is uploaded to the blockchain network as transaction information and managed by the block-generating node, which, in this paper, corresponds to an RSU.

Upon entering the communication range of an MEC server, a vehicle engages in simulation training for computation offloading with all RSUs. Based on the average training results, a specific RSU node is identified as the preferred choice for subsequent computation offloading. The blockchain network maintains a record of the identity of intelligent vehicles, their corresponding reputation values, and information of the selected RSU node. The initial reputation value for intelligent vehicles is assigned by the blockchain network and can be updated through subsequent training processes. Reputation values and corresponding identity information of intelligent vehicles are broadcasted to all participating nodes in the blockchain network. During computation offloading, RSUs authenticate the identity of intelligent vehicle through the blockchain network. Once authenticated, RSUs retrieve information of the intelligent vehicle from the blockchain network and formulate computing resource allocation strategies for the vehicle.

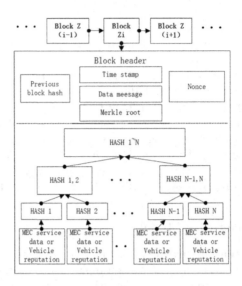

Fig. 2. Block service record diagram.

4   Blockchain-Based Intelligent Vehicle Edge Computing Offloading

We propose a blockchain-based Intelligent Vehicle Edge Computing Offloading to further improve the computing performance. This scheme combines MSDQN and actor-critic algorithms to handle continuous and high-dimensional offloading strategies for vehicles. Based on two online convolutional neural network [22], that is, the actor network selects RSU, transmission power and offloading rate based on the computation delay, energy consumption, SINR, and RSU radio bandwidth. The critic network is used to update the actor network weight. This algorithm uses two target networks to improve learning stability during the offloading strategy formulation process. The target actor network is used to generate actions and improve policies based on observed system states, while the target critic network is responsible for evaluating the policies provided by the actor network.

4.1   Actor-Critic Network Training

The main goal of BIVECO algorithm is to find an optimal strategy that maximizes the expected long-term return while maximizing the entropy of the strategy to improve robustness and exploration. In actor critic network [14], the strategy is random and represented as $\pi(\alpha|s)$. It represents the probability distribution of actions given a particular state s. The critic network, on the other hand, is responsible for evaluating the effectiveness of the strategy. To train the network, the RSU node samples a batch of experiences from the replay buffer B_u and proceeds with neural network training. The state parameters are fed into the actor network to generate the neural network's output value. Additionally, an identical target evaluation network is constructed based on the output value of the neural network. The weights of the neural network are updated using the Adam gradient descent algorithm. The same training steps are applied to train the critic network.

4.2   Node Data Processing

The RSU is selected based on factors such as bandwidth, channel gain, and distance to the vehicle. This selection process takes into account these parameters, which are then encrypted and stored in the blockchain network. The key generation method involves selecting two particularly large prime numbers, denoted as p and q, and calculating their product, represented as $n = p * q$. Additionally, Euler's totient function (1) is computed.

$$\phi(n) = (p - 1) * (q - 1) \tag{1}$$

Select an integer e that satisfies $1 < e < \phi(n)$ and that e and $\phi(n)$ are mutually prime. To obtain the public and private keys (pub_k, pri_k), we calculate the Modular multiplicative inverse of e. Let f represent the private key $(f = pri_k)$ and e the public key $(e = pub_k)$, as shown in Eq. (2).

$$(pub_k, pri_k) = 1(mod)\phi(n) \tag{2}$$

To digitally sign a message using a private key, first, encode the message using a registered codec for encoding. The string is encoded according to the specified codec. Then, perform digital signature encryption on the encoded data and private key, following the encryption formula described in Eq. (3).

$$E(x) = x^{e_{int}}(mod)n \tag{3}$$

Among them, x is the plaintext to be encrypted, n is the large positive integer in the public key, and e_{int} is the integer in the public key. $E(x)$ represents the encrypted ciphertext. Decryption formula is (4):

$$D(y) = y^{d_{int}}(mod)n \tag{4}$$

y is the encrypted ciphertext, d_{int} is an integer in the private key, and n is a large positive integer in the public key. $D(y)$ represents the decrypted plaintext.

The RSU uses its own private key to sign the message, and the vehicle can use the RSU's public key to verify the validity of the signature. $Sign = (r, u)$, where r is a random number during the signature process and u is the signature result, as shown in Eq. (5).

$$r = P_x(mod)G \tag{5}$$

P_x represents the value of point P on the horizontal axis. $P = KG$, K is a random number, where G is the coordinate of the point on the elliptic curve, as shown in Eq. (6).

$$s = K^{-1}(H(m) + d_{int})(mod)G \tag{6}$$

$H(m)$ is the hash value of message m, and d_{int} is an integer in the private key. Verification process is shown as (7).

$$R = \begin{cases} 0 & r \neq V_x (mod)G \\ 1 & r = V_x (mod)G \end{cases} \quad (7)$$

$R = 1$ represents the signature is valid, $R = 0$ represents invalid. V_x is expressed as (8).

$$V_x = ((H(m) \times w)(mod)G) \times G + ((r \times w)(mod)G) \times Q \quad (8)$$

Q is the point in the public key, w is expressed as (9).

$$w = u^{-1}(mod)G \quad (9)$$

Among them, r and u are the output results of the signature algorithm. $H(m)$ is the message digest calculated by the hash function, and K, d_{int}, G, and Q are the random numbers, private keys, points on the elliptic curve, and points in the public key used in the signature and verification processes, respectively. Through the above process, interactive authentication between the private key of the RSU and the public key of the vehicle has been achieved, ensuring the integrity and security of data transmission between the communication parties, while also not disclosing the sender's private information.

4.3   Node Consensus Process

When vehicles engage in task offloading training, they retrieve the corresponding RSU information from the blockchain and select an RSU node for the training process. Upon receiving an offloading request, an RSU node checks the reputation value of the vehicle on the blockchain. Only requests with reputation values exceeding a predetermined threshold are accepted for offloading participation. Once the offloading task training is completed, the vehicle selects the most appropriate RSU node to generate offload information based on the utilization of the RSU node. This information is recorded as a transaction in the blockchain system, containing the identity of the task vehicle, vehicle reputation value, service RSU ID, and timestamp. In each round of blockchain consensus, the Proof-of-Work (PoW) consensus algorithm is employed. PoW has the following requirements for the format of block B submitted by nodes: $H(B) <= target$, where H is the hash algorithm and $target$ is a fixed number. That is to say, the hash value of the entire block should be less than a given number target. A block is considered legal and can be accepted by other nodes only when it satisfies this condition. And when a node finds such a legitimate block, it will receive a certain numerical reward. This also solves the result decision-making problem of multi node without a center: the entire network uses the data of the node that first found the legal block. The value of the target is automatically adjusted every other period of time to ensure that the time for generating blocks is basically fixed, such as bitcoin ensuring that a new block is generated every ten minutes. The smaller the value of the target, the greater the difficulty in generating blocks. Assuming the maximum hash value is $HASH_{max}$, the probability of finding a valid block in each attempt is $target/HASH_{max}$. From this formula, it can be seen that the smaller the $target$, the smaller the probability of finding a valid block in each attempt.

The hash value generated by the hash function is random, and a small change to the original data can make the hash value completely different from the previous one. In order to obtain a valid block, we can add a redundant integer nonce to the block and find the valid block by constantly trying different nonces.

The verification process involves concatenating the proof-of-work of the previous block and the current block into a string and encoding it as a byte sequence. The SHA256 hash value of the byte sequence is then calculated, and the first four characters are extracted. If these characters are 0000, the PoW is considered valid. Otherwise, it is deemed invalid. Each newly generated block undergoes node verification, which includes the following steps: 1) Starting from the first genesis block, traverse the chain to verify if the previous hash of the current block matches the previously computed hash. If they are different, it indicates an invalid chain. 2) Check if the proof-of-work meets the requirements. If it does not, it is also considered an invalid chain. Validated nodes are permanently stored in the block, and the verified blocks contribute to assessing the reliability of vehicles and RSU.

The algorithm details are shown in Algorithm 1. The system state parameters and BIVECO learning parameters are initialized in line 1. After initialization, the node information is stored in the block and the block is updated in line 2. Then, when the vehicle enters the MEC service scope, the node information is obtained from the block and the vehicle reputation value is uploaded in line 5. Use the Markov decision formula to get the k-th state. Next, randomly choosing λ $(s - a)$ pairs from the experience buffer to develop s^λ and a^λ, which will be sent with $s^{(k)}$ into the actor network. The actor network outputs action $a^{(k)}$. For exploration, $O - U$ noise $\rho^{(k)}$ will be added to the action policy, as shown in lines 6–8. Then, the vehicle sends the computation task with transmitting power p to the selected RSU for computation in line 9. After a while, i.e., $t > Z$, Z experience samples will be sampled randomly from the experience buffer. The samples are used to train the actor network and critic network. Adam gradient descent algorithm is used in the network training process, as shown in lines 10–15. Lines 14–15 represent the update of the target actor network and the critic network parameters. After the vehicle completes training, the best node information for selecting the current vehicle is obtained according to the training results. Broadcast the current vehicle ID and select RSU node ID for block messages, then update the vehicle reputation value as shown in lines 18–20.

Algorithm 1. blockchain-based Intelligent Vehicle Edge Computing Offloading (BIVECO)

1: Initialize $\lambda, k, d, E, S, B, \delta, \gamma, \rho^{(k)}, Z, \varphi$;
2: Store node information in blocks and update blocks;
3: **for** c=1,2,3,$\cdots$ **do**
4:   **for** k=1,2,3,$\cdots$ **do**
5:       Obtaining node and vehicle information from blocks;
6:       Formulating state $s^{(k)} = \{B^{(k)}, d^{(k)}, E^{(k)}, S^{(k)}\}$ based on MDP;
7:       Input the state sequence $\left\{\mathbf{s}^\lambda, \mathbf{a}^\lambda, s^{(k)}\right\}_{(0<\lambda<k)}$ into the actor network;
8:       Obtaining action policy $a^{(k)}$ based on output of actor network γ and O-U noise $\rho^{(k)}$;
9:       Vehicle uses the transmission power p to send the computation task C to the RSU for computation;
10:       Saving $s^{(k)}, a^{(k)}, r^{(k)}$ into the experience pool;
11:       **if** k>Z **then**
12:           Randomly sampling Z experience samples from the experience buffer;
13:           Update actor network, critic network weights θ^μ, θ^Q using Adam gradient descent algorithm;
14:           $\theta^{\mu'} = \varphi\theta^\mu + (1-\varphi)\theta^{\mu'}$;
15:           $\theta^{Q'} = \varphi\theta^Q + (1-\varphi)\theta^{Q'}$;
16:       **end if**
17:   **end for**
18:   Obtain the best node for selecting the current vehicle based on the training results
19:   Current vehicle ID, select RSU node ID for block message broadcast
20:   Update vehicle reputation value
21: **end for**

---

5   Simulation Results and Analysis

5.1   Simulation Results

To evaluate the performance of the proposed BIVECO algorithm, simulation experiments is conducted in a 5G communication scenario. The setup includes three vehicles and six RSUs situated within the communication coverage of an existing MEC server.

Based on the experiments conducted in our previous work, it has been determined that the optimal number of multiple steps is $n = 8$ [13]. Wireless communication technology is used for communication between vehicles and RSUs, with a channel bandwidth ranging from 60 MHz to 100 MHz. The vehicles generated computation task data with a size of 1 Mbit. The local computation rate of the vehicles is 6.4 Mbits/s, and processing one bit of data requires 1000 CPU cycles. Once the offloading strategy is determined, the vehicles transmit the computation tasks to the RSUs using a power range of 0–100 mW. To simulate realistic communication interference, we randomly select interference power ranging from 8 to 12 mW. The RSUs perform calculations at a rate of 64 Mbits/s, and processing one bit of data also requires 1000 CPU cycles. The BIVECO employs an actor network and a critic network, each consisting of two convolutional layers and four fully connected layers. The first convolutional layer has 16 kernels of size 5 × 1, and the second convolutional layer has 32 kernels of size 3 × 1. The first three fully connected layers of both networks have 500, 200, and 150 neuron nodes, respectively. The fourth fully connected layer of the actor network has 3 neuron nodes, while the fourth fully connected layer of the critic network has 1 neuron node.

In the initial phase, we conduct experiments to determine the optimal RSU node. Figure 4 presents the average utility of different RSU nodes. Each vehicle undergoes 10,000 offloading training iterations with each RSU within the MEC server's communication range. The training results for each RSU are averaged. Figure 5–7 illustrate the variations in computation offloading utility, delay and energy consumption for different RSU nodes. The selected node exhibits significant advantages in terms of utility and delay compared to other nodes. For example in Fig. 6, considering Car1, the average computation delay with RSU0, RSU1, RSU2, RSU3, and RSU4 is 64 ms, 64 ms, 79 ms, 72 ms, and 74 ms, respectively. In contrast, the average computation delay with RSU5 as the selected node was only 35 ms. RSU5's average computation delay is 54% of RSU0, 54% of RSU1, 44% of RSU2, 48% of RSU3, and 47% of RSU4. Thus, RSU5 has the lowest average computation delay when selected. Similarly, in Fig. 7 RSU5 exhibits the lowest average computation energy consumption, with a value of only 32 mJ compared to other nodes. The utility also reaches its highest converged value at RSU5. As shown in Fig. 3, each time slot corresponds to the average utility computed every 100 iterations. With an increasing number of training iterations, compared with other RSU nodes, the utility of RSU5 is gradually increasing and converging at 75%, which aligned with the average utility of the current node.

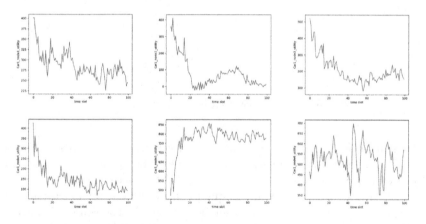

Fig. 3. Utilities of vehicle.

5.2 Privacy and Security Analysis

The privacy and security analysis can be summarized as follows.

Distributed storage: The blockchain system is being controlled by multiple MEC servers in a distributed manner. After reaching a consensus protocol, each MEC server is storing the blocks independently. This ensures fault tolerance and eliminates the risk of a single point of failure.

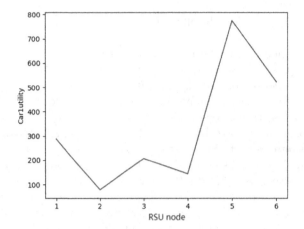

Fig. 4. Utility of selecting RSU nodes for vehicles 1.

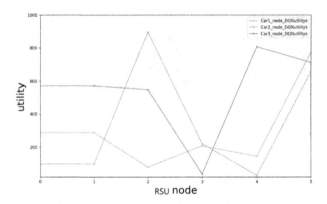

Fig. 5. Utility of selecting RSU nodes for vehicles.

Anonymity and identity authentication: Each vehicle and RSU node are required to register their identities on the blockchain and undergo identity authentication using public-private key pairs. When accessing information on the blockchain, nodes are utilizing unique public keys for communication verification, protecting their real identities and preventing malicious users from tracking them. Additionally, the private keys of nodes are being kept confidential and stored locally, ensuring resilience against node impersonation attacks.

Request confirmation: Each request submitted by vehicles is accompanied by a corresponding reputation value, which helps prevent malicious nodes from engaging in unauthorized or malicious request behavior. Moreover, reputation values can be used to mitigate flooding attacks involving forged requests. Therefore, vehicles need to update their reputation values after task execution to prevent malicious vehicles from rejecting the feedback on processing results.

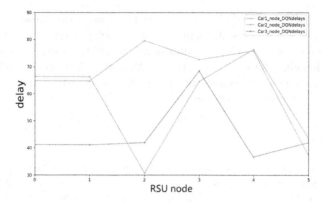

Fig. 6. Computing delay of selecting RSU nodes for vehicles.

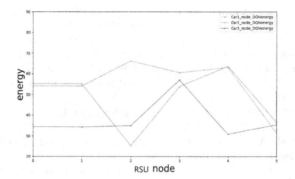

Fig. 7. Energy consumption of selecting RSU nodes for vehicles.

Computation verification: Verification of the processing results uploaded by RSUs is essential to ensure they meet the requirements of the serviced vehicles. Reputation values are playing a crucial role in defending against deceptive attacks from malicious vehicles that may attempt to upload misleading results.

6   Conclusion

In this paper, we propose a consortium blockchain approach for computation offloading in vehicular networks, aiming to ensure secure and efficient resource sharing between RSUs and vehicles. Our approach involves several key components, including identity verification, request issuance, task offloading, and computation verification. To achieve consensus among the blockchain nodes, we employ a PoW consensus mechanism. Furthermore, we introduce a BIVECO-based reinforcement learning algorithm that allows vehicles to derive an optimal offloading strategy and determine the target node for offloading. Based on the established offloading strategy, the RSU node with the highest offloading performance within the MEC server range is selected for subsequent offloading tasks. Experimental results demonstrate the effectiveness of our proposed solution in improving vehicle computational efficiency, ensuring local data privacy, and enhancing data sharing security. As part of our future work, we plan to focus on enhancing the consensus algorithm and smart contracts to address more complex requirements effectively.

References

1. Bukhari, M.M., et al.: An intelligent proposed model for task offloading in fog-cloud collaboration using logistics regression. Comput. Intell. Neurosci. **2022** (2022)
2. Cao, C., Su, M., Duan, S., Dai, M., Li, J., Li, Y.: QoS-aware joint task scheduling and resource allocation in vehicular edge computing. Sensors **22**(23), 9340 (2022)
3. Chen, Y., Han, S., Chen, G., Yin, J., Wang, K.N., Cao, J.: A deep reinforcement learning-based wireless body area network offloading optimization strategy for healthcare services. Health Inf. Sci. Syst. **11**(1), 8 (2023)
4. Fu, X., Yu, F.R., Wang, J., Qi, Q., Liao, J.: Performance optimization for blockchain-enabled distributed network function virtualization management and orchestration. IEEE Trans. Veh. Technol. **69**(6), 6670–6679 (2020)
5. Hong, W., et al.: Graph intelligence enhanced Bi-channel insider threat detection. In: Yuan, X., Bai, G., Alcaraz, C., Majumdar, S. (eds.) Network and System Security. NSS 2022. LNCS, vol. 13787, pp. 86–102. Springer, Cham (2022). https://doi.org/10.1007/978-3-031-23020-2_5
6. Hong, W., et al.: A graph empowered insider threat detection framework based on daily activities. ISA Transactions (2023)
7. Jiang, X., Ma, Z., Yu, F.R., Song, T., Boukerche, A.: Edge computing for video analytics in the internet of vehicles with blockchain. In: Proceedings of the 10th ACM Symposium on Design and Analysis of Intelligent Vehicular Networks and Applications, pp. 1–7 (2020)
8. Kumar, P., Kumar, R., Gupta, G.P., Tripathi, R.: BDEdge: blockchain and deep-learning for secure edge-envisioned green CAVs. IEEE Trans. Green Commun. Netw. **6**(3), 1330–1339 (2022)
9. Lin, X., Wu, J., Mumtaz, S., Garg, S., Li, J., Guizani, M.: Blockchain-based on-demand computing resource trading in IoV-assisted smart city. IEEE Trans. Emerg. Top. Comput. **9**(3), 1373–1385 (2020)
10. Liu, K., Xu, J., Yang, H., Lin, X.: Computing offloading of multi-MEC nodes in blockchain-based parked vehicle edge computing. In: Second International Conference on Advanced Algorithms and Signal Image Processing (AASIP 2022), vol. 12475, pp. 394–400. SPIE (2022)
11. Liu, M., Yu, F.R., Teng, Y., Leung, V.C., Song, M.: Distributed resource allocation in blockchain-based video streaming systems with mobile edge computing. IEEE Trans. Wirel. Commun. **18**(1), 695–708 (2018)
12. Samy, A., Elgendy, I.A., Yu, H., Zhang, W., Zhang, H.: Secure task offloading in blockchain-enabled mobile edge computing with deep reinforcement learning. IEEE Trans. Netw. Serv. Manag. (2022)
13. Shaodong, H., Yingqun, C., Guihong, C., Yin, J., Wang, H., Cao, J.: Multi-step reinforcement learning-based offloading for vehicle edge computing. In: 2023 15th International Conference on Advanced Computational Intelligence (ICACI), pp. 1–8. IEEE (2023)

14. Shi, J., Du, J., Shen, Y., Wang, J., Yuan, J., Han, Z.: DRL-based V2V computation offloading for blockchain-enabled vehicular networks. IEEE Trans. Mob. Comput. (2022)
15. Tang, C., Cheng, Y., Yin, J.: An optimized algorithm of grid calibration in WSN node deployment based on the energy consumption distribution model. J. Inf. Comput. Sci. **9**(4), 1035–1042 (2012)
16. Wang, R., Li, H., Liu, E.: Blockchain-based federated learning in mobile edge networks with application in internet of vehicles. arXiv preprint arXiv:2103.01116 (2021)
17. Wang, Y., Zhao, J.: Mobile edge computing, metaverse, 6G wireless communications, artificial intelligence, and blockchain: survey and their convergence. arXiv preprint arXiv:2209.14147 (2022)
18. Xiao, H., Qiu, C., Yang, Q., Huang, H., Wang, J., Su, C.: Deep reinforcement learning for optimal resource allocation in blockchain-based IoV secure systems. In: 2020 16th International Conference on Mobility, Sensing and Networking (MSN), pp. 137–144. IEEE (2020)
19. Xiao, L., et al.: A reinforcement learning and blockchain-based trust mechanism for edge networks. IEEE Trans. Commun. **68**(9), 5460–5470 (2020)
20. Xu, Y., Zhang, H., Ji, H., Yang, L., Li, X., Leung, V.C.: Transaction throughput optimization for integrated blockchain and MEC system in IoT. IEEE Trans. Wirel. Commun. **21**(2), 1022–1036 (2021)
21. Ye, X., Li, M., Yu, F.R., Si, P., Wang, Z., Zhang, Y.: MEC and blockchain-enabled energy-efficient internet of vehicles based on A3C approach. In: 2021 IEEE Global Communications Conference (GLOBECOM), pp. 01–06. IEEE (2021)
22. Yin, J., You, M., Cao, J., Wang, H., Tang, M.J., Ge, Y.-F.: Data-driven hierarchical neural network modeling for high-pressure feedwater heater group. In: Borovica-Gajic, R., Qi, J., Wang, W. (eds.) ADC 2020. LNCS, vol. 12008, pp. 225–233. Springer, Cham (2020). https://doi.org/10.1007/978-3-030-39469-1_19

Priv-S: Privacy-Sensitive Data Identification in Online Social Networks

Yuzi Yi, Nafei Zhu, Jingsha He$^{(\boxtimes)}$, Xiangjun Ma, and Yehong Luo

Faculty of Information Technology, Beijing University of Technology, Beijing 100124, China
jhe@bjut.edu.cn

Abstract. Privacy inference imposes a serious threat to user privacy in Online Social Networks (OSNs) as the vast amount of personal data and relationships in OSNs can be used not only to infer user privacy but also to enrich the training set of inference methods. Previous studies have mostly focused on privacy inference from the perspective of the adversary with the objective of tracking the accuracy of the inference results. However, countering privacy inference requires not only the analysis of the inference method but also the roles that data would play in the inference process, i.e., to determine the sensitivity of the data. To address this issue, in this paper, we propose a model for the identification of privacy-sensitive data in which we formulate the identification as an influence maximization problem to identify both the privacy-sensitive users and the privacy-sensitive attributes for privacy inference. In our model, a privacy-affected tree is first constructed based on the influence between users with respect to the concerned privacy. Then, privacy-sensitive users in the privacy-affected tree are identified along with their privacy-sensitive attributes based on their contribution to the inference result of the concerned privacy. Experiments show that the results of our proposed model can significantly affect the accuracy of privacy inference, which demonstrates that our model can identify the privacy-sensitive data. Meanwhile, the impact of privacy-sensitive users and privacy-sensitive attributes is analyzed to guide the design of effective privacy-enhancing technologies.

Keywords: privacy protection · privacy inference · targeted influence maximization · online social networks

1 Introduction

Online social networks (OSNs) provide the environments for people to communicate with others to satisfy their social needs. When using OSNs, users typically publish some profile information and share some daily information with their friends in real time. As the result, many different types of user generated data (UGD) get transmitted and processed in OSNs continuously among which there is a lot of sensitive information, imposing a threat to the privacy of users and thus causing a serious privacy concern [1] to users. Generally, UGD can be used to launch malicious attacks [2, 3] among which privacy inference [4] is typical for inferring the privacy of the concerned users. Therefore, reducing privacy risks while letting users enjoy the benefits offered by OSNs

© The Author(s), under exclusive license to Springer Nature Singapore Pte Ltd. 2023
F. Zhang et al. (Eds.): WISE 2023, LNCS 14306, pp. 220–234, 2023.
https://doi.org/10.1007/978-981-99-7254-8_17

is an important issue that needs to be addressed urgently. There have already been many methods of privacy inference designed from the viewpoint of the attackers that apply various kind of data collected from OSNs to infer the attributes of users that have not yet been exposed with the ultimate goal of improving the accuracy of the inference results [5, 6, 8–10].

Since it is not usually possible to identify the data to which user privacy is sensitive from simply applying the methods of privacy inference, most of the existing work is not enough for laying the foundation for the development of targeted privacy policies. Therefore, in addition to the inference results, it is necessary to pay some attention to the inference process to identify privacy-sensitive data for users. There are at least three main issues that need to be addressed in order to achieve privacy-sensitive data identification. The first issue is measurement of the contributions of the dimensional data since multi-dimensional data in OSNs can be used for privacy inference. The second issue is to characterize the users since the privacy-sensitive data of each user is different and then adapt privacy-sensitive data identification to the different characteristics of users. The third issue is to determine the scope of search to identify the privacy-sensitive data of the target user in the complex structure of OSNs along with various user attributes and large number of nodes and edges to improve the efficiency of identification.

In this paper, we propose a privacy-sensitive data identification model, called Priv-S, which can be used to identify the data (including OSN users and their attributes) to which user privacy is sensitive. To achieve the identification, a privacy-affected tree (PAT) is first constructed for target users to reflect the influence between users with respect to privacy inference. Then, a novel privacy inference method based on conditional random fields (CRF) [11] is proposed to evaluate the contribution of specific data in the PAT. By embedding privacy inference in the process of privacy-sensitive data identification, privacy-sensitive data can be identified, including privacy-sensitive users and privacy-sensitive attributes.

The main contributions of this paper can be summarized as follows:

1) We define the problem of privacy-sensitive data identification. Formulation of the problem allows us to develop a solution to identify users and their attributes that have the most influence on the privacy of users. In contrast to many current studies that focus mostly on pursuing privacy inference results with high accuracy from the viewpoint of the adversary, privacy-sensitive data identification could provide basis for targeted privacy protection.

2) We propose a model for the identification of privacy-sensitive data. In the model, a PAT is used to characterize the influence of users and their attributes on the privacy of the target users. Then, a novel privacy inference method based on CRF is developed to evaluate the contribution of data in the PAT for the purpose of identifying privacy-sensitive data. By constructing a PAT on the target user, privacy-sensitive data for the target user can be identified and the resulting privacy-sensitive data can be adapted to the user's characteristics.

3) We carry out some experiment to verify the effectiveness of the proposed model and to compare the privacy inference method to some similar methods using real datasets to demonstrate the advantages of our method. In addition, the impact of some key

factors of privacy inference is analyzed to provide some guidance to the design of privacy protection mechanisms.

The remainder of this paper is organized as follows. Section 2 reviews some related work. Section 3 introduces the problem of privacy-sensitive data identification. Section 4 describes the proposed model and method in details. Section 5 verifies the proposed method through some experiment along with some analysis. Finally, Sect. 6 concludes the paper.

2 Related Work

A lot of research has been conducted on privacy inference in OSNs in recent years. Heatherly et al. proposed a joint classification method [12] in which attributes of users and relationships among the users were utilized in privacy inference. The effect of deleting attributes and destructing relationships on the inference was also analyzed. It was shown that the joint use of user attributes and user relationships could help achieve more accurate results than the use of user attributes alone. Gong and Liu constructed an SBA (social-behavior-attribute) network to express attributes, behaviors, and relationships of users. Based on SBA network, a method called VIAL (vote distribution attack) inspired by the idea of the random walk algorithm was proposed for privacy inference [6]. In VIAL, after being assigned an initial voting weight, each node continuously updates the weight according to the walking rules. When the maximum number of iterations is reached or the voting weight reaches a stable probability of distribution, the node with the highest weight value is regarded as the inference result. Since this method adopts the random walk approach, a walking mechanism needs to be established for each target user, making it less likely to perform privacy inference on multiple users at the same time and thus less efficient. Mao et al. constructed a social-attribute network in which the relationships between users and attributes and between attributes and attributes were added based on the relationships between users [7]. Then, the random walk with restart algorithm was applied to perform privacy inference with the target user being the starting point and the attribute node with the highest proximity to the target user was taken as the inference result. Similar to the random walk mechanism, this method needs to establish a walking mechanism for each target user, thus suffering from the same shortcomings brought about by the inefficiency. Qian et al. applied knowledge graphs to studying de-anonymization and privacy inference in OSNs [13] in which the privacy inference problem was transformed into the link prediction problem in the knowledge graph. User privacy attributes could then be inferred by using the path ranking algorithm according to the background knowledge of the attacker. Since the accuracy of privacy inference depends on the quality of the knowledge graph, the selection and construction of the knowledge graph is crucial for achieving desired effectiveness. Luo et al. designed a privacy inference method based on graph embedding [10] where a deep neural network based on a multi-layer full connection was established to map the relationships between the embedding network and the attribute vector so that multiple attributes could be predicted simultaneously. Liu and Li took the friendships between users as the inference goal and designed a collusion attack method in which the function of user retrieval provided by OSNs was used to analyze the friendships between users without explicitly transforming the inference problem into a classification problem [14].

By analyzing the advantages and disadvantages of related research on privacy inference, we found that there is a lack of analysis of the roles that different data play in the process of privacy inference, which is crucial for privacy protection. Thus, we propose a privacy-sensitive identification model to fill this research gap. Our model can be seen as an extension of privacy inference.

3 Problem Formulation

3.1 Privacy Inference

To achieve the goal of privacy inference, an adversary can make use of both the public data collected from OSNs and some background knowledge previously acquired to infer user privacy. Since the amount of background knowledge can vary, it is not easy to determine the ability of different adversaries. In this paper, we assume that the adversary has the reasonably strong ability in the sense that the adversary has a complete view of the topology of the OSN and thus all the observable attributes of the OSN users. Under this assumption, the adversary can use all the OSN data for privacy inference. In our context, the OSN is defined as follows.

Definition 1 (Online Social Network). An OSN can be expressed as a graph $G = (V, E, O)$, where V is the set of users, $E \subseteq V \times V$ is the set of social relationships between users and O is the set of observable attributes of the users. For an undirected network, the social relationship $e_{u,v} \in E$ between users $u \in V$ and $v \in V$ satisfies $e_{u,v} = e_{v,u}$. For a directed network, however, $e_{u,v} \neq e_{v,u}$.

Based on Definition 1, the observable attribute set on which privacy inference relies and the private attribute set that privacy inference is concerned can be defined as follows.

Definition 2 (Observable Attribute Set). The set of observable attributes O contains all the attributes that have been shared by users in the OSN. For an arbitrary user $u \in V$, its observable attributes set $O^u \subseteq O$ can be expressed as $O^u = \{(c_1 : \{l_1^1, \ldots, l_k^1\}), (c_2 : \{l_1^2, \ldots, l_k^2\}), \ldots, (c_s : \{l_1^s, \ldots, l_k^s\})\}$, where $c_s \in C$ denotes the s-th attribute category and $\{l_1^s, \ldots, l_k^s\}$ denotes the corresponding k attribute values.

Definition 3 (Private Attribute Set). For any user $u \in V$ in OSN $G = (V, E, O)$, the private attribute set P^u of u refers to the set of attributes that have not been published in G, i.e., $P^u \bigcap O^u = \varnothing$. Given an attribute category set $A = \{c_1, c_2, \ldots, c_n\}$ consisting of n attribute categories, the private attribute set regarding u can be expressed as: $P^u = \{c_1, c_2, \ldots, c_j\} \backslash c \in O^u$.

Finally, privacy inference is defined as follows.

Definition 4 (Privacy inference). Privacy inference in OSNs aims to deduce the value x of a private attribute $p^t \in P^t$ for the target user $t \in T$ through an inference method $f(\cdot)$. Under the assumption that the adversary has reasonably strong ability, the privacy inference based on data in G can be formally defined as finding the attribute value with maximum probability that $p^t = x$ under $f(\cdot)$:

$$\Phi(t, p^t, f, G) := \arg \max_x \Pr[p^t = x | f(G)] \tag{1}$$

3.2 Problem of Privacy-Sensitive Data Identification

We now define the problem of privacy-sensitive identification as follows.

Definition 5 (Privacy-sensitive Data Identification). Privacy-sensitive data identification is to find the set of privacy-sensitive data $S = \{S_V \bigcup S_A\}$ that has the greatest influence on the privacy inference result $\Pr(p^t = x)$ towards a target user t in G, where S_V denotes the set of privacy-sensitive users and S_A denotes the set of privacy-sensitive attributes of $v \in S_V$. Without loss of generality, privacy-sensitive data identification based on a specific privacy inference method $f(\cdot)$ can be expressed as follows:

$$S = \underset{\substack{S = \{S_V \bigcup S_A\} \\ |S| = K}}{\arg\max} \left\{ \Pr\left[p^t = x | f(G)\right] - \Pr\left[p^t = x | f(G \backslash S)\right] \right\} \qquad (2)$$

where $|S| = K = K_V + K_A$ is the total number of privacy-sensitive data requests.

4 The Proposed Method

We now describe the proposed privacy-sensitive data identification model called Priv-S that can be used to identify privacy-sensitive data based on the influence among users along the paths of the OSN. Figure 1 illustrates the framework of Priv-S in which a privacy-affected tree (PAT) of a target user is first constructed through reverse influence sampling based on the connection structure of the OSN. Then, the contribution of data in the PAT to privacy inference towards the target user is evaluated and the K pieces of data that have the most contribution constitute the privacy-sensitive data.

4.1 Construction of the Privacy-Affected Tree

Reverse influence sampling (RIS) [15] is a common approach for generating reverse reachable (RR) sets for a given node in a graph to solve the influence maximization problem [15, 16] and the targeted influence maximization problem [17]. Through RR sets, the path of influence propagation can be determined. Then, methods such as the greedy selection can be applied to finding the K seed nodes that have the most influence on the target node in the graph. There is generally a high correlation between the privacy of the user and the data to which privacy is sensitive in privacy inference. Since OSN users with high homogeneity tend to gather together [18], RIS is suitable for sampling users who are related to the target user in the OSN along with the social relationships between them, which provides a viable approach for subsequent privacy-sensitive data identification.

To achieve the purpose, we propose to construct a PAT first through sampling using RIS to reflect the social relationships between the target user and other related users as well as the influence between them in terms of privacy inference. The PAT can be defined as follows:

Definition 6 (Privacy-Affected Tree). For a target user t of the privacy inference, the privacy-affected tree T_t is a tree with t as the root and the child nodes are the users each of which has a path to t along with observable attributes of the user. A path in T_t

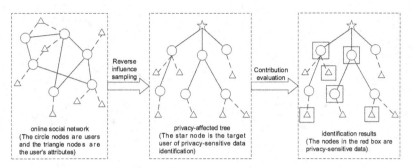

Fig. 1. The framework of Priv-S

from t to a user node n corresponding to a path from n to t in G. An attribute node a_n of user n is only directly connected to the owner n through the directed edge from n to a_n. Each edge $e(u, v)$ between the nodes in $\mathcal{T}_t$ is weighted according to the degree of influence $c(u, v)$ of u on v with respect to privacy inference towards t's privacy.

Note that if there are more than one path between n and t in G, we can create the exact number of copies of n as well as its attributes a_n in the PAT. There will then be multiple branches in $\mathcal{T}_t$ from t to each copy of n.

Since there are two types of child nodes in $\mathcal{T}_t$, namely, the user nodes and the attribute nodes, the influence of each type of nodes should be made explicit. In this study, the correlation between two users is used to derive the influence between the two user nodes by examining the proportion of common attributes between the two users [5, 6, 13]. Regarding the influence between an attribute node and a user node, we assess the influence of the attribute on its owner by the proportion of the number of neighbor nodes that have the attribute to the total number of neighbor nodes based on the homogeneity principle. Therefore, the influence of nodes in $\mathcal{T}_t$ is expressed as follows.

$$c(u, v) = \begin{cases} \frac{|O^u \cap O^v|}{|O^v|}, & if u \in V and v \in V \\ \frac{|N_u(v)|}{|N(v)|}, & if u \in O and v \in V \end{cases} \tag{3}$$

Figure 2 is an example of PAT in which the structure of the OSN as well as the attributes of users are shown in Fig. 2(a). As can be seen, all the edges between nodes in the OSN are weighted by the influence between nodes. The PAT of user t that is constructed accordingly is shown in Fig. 2(b). In the PAT, all the edges with influence of more than 0.3 are generated by RIS and a connection between an attribute and its owner user is established.

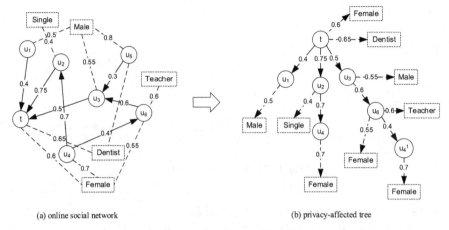

(a) online social network   (b) privacy-affected tree

Fig. 2. An example of PAT

Algorithm 1: PATGenerate

Input: OSN G, target user t, influence threshold η,

Output: privacy-affected tree $\mathcal{T}_t$

1   Create tree root t

2   **while** breadth-first traversal of $n \in \mathcal{T}_t$ does not reach the termination condition **do**

3   computing the influence $c(n, u)$ between t and u using equation (3)

4   **if** $c(n, u) \geq \eta$ **do**

5   Flip a coin with probability that equals $c(n, u)$

6   **if** decision is YES **do**

7   add u or a copy of u in $\mathcal{T}_t$ if u has been added before

8   place u's in-neighbors in the processing queue.

9   **else**

10   **continue**

11   **else**

12   **continue**

13   **for** each node n in the tree **do**

14   add attribute node a_n of n that $c(a_n, n)$ higher than η

15   Return $\mathcal{T}_t$

In this study, algorithm PATGenerate is designed based on Breadth-First Search (BFS) to generate $\mathcal{T}_t$ for target user t whose details are shown in Algorithm 1. In the algorithm, in-neighbors $u \in N^-(t)$ of t are first sampled by applying breadth-first traversal (line 1–2). Then, whether the correlation $c(t, u) \in [0, 1]$ between t and u is smaller than the pre-defined threshold η is checked (lines 3–4). If $c(t, u) \geq \eta$, we decide with a probability that is the same as the weight between t and u whether to add u in $\mathcal{T}_t$ (line 5). If the decision is yes, node u or a copy of u in $\mathcal{T}_t$ if u has been added before is created (lines 6–7). Meanwhile, an in-neighbors $v \in N^-(u)$ is placed in the processing queue (line 8). The traversal terminates when conditions of termination are reached, i.e., the maximum depth is reached or the processing queue becomes empty. Finally, the attributes a_n of node n in the tree that satisfy η are added to the tree as attribute nodes (lines 13–14).

After the PAT for a target user is generated, the next task is to identify the users with the most influence on the target user with respect to privacy inference.

4.2 Identification of Privacy-Sensitive Data

Recall that privacy-sensitive data identification aims to find the most K_V users along with their K_A attributes that have the most influence on the privacy of the target user t. According to the idea of targeted influence maximization, after generating the PAT set $\mathcal{T}$ for target user t, we should find K_V users that cover the largest number of PATs $\mathcal{T}_t \in \mathcal{T}$. To achieve the goal, it is essential to first assess the contribution of any node $n \in \mathcal{T}_t$ to the inference of t's privacy. In our context, the contribution of $n \in \mathcal{T}_t$ is described using Eq. (4) below.

$$Con(n, \mathcal{T}_t) = \begin{cases} f(x_t|n, \mathcal{T}_t) & S = \varnothing \\ f(x_t|S \bigcup\{n\}, \mathcal{T}_t) - f(x_t|S, \mathcal{T}_t) & \text{otherwise} \end{cases} \tag{4}$$

where $f(\cdot)$ denotes the privacy inference method and S denotes the seed set of users that are involved in $f(\cdot)$.

Equation (4) expresses the contribution of node n due to the existence of the seed nodes. Therefore, we need to apply a privacy inference method to reflect the common effect of all the users who contribute to the privacy inference and evaluates the specific contribution of each individual node in the inference. To address this issue, a privacy inference method based on Conditional Random Fields (CRF) is proposed to instantiate $f(\cdot)$. We now describe the privacy inference method.

Firstly, we analyze the correlation between the attributes of different users using the Naïve Bayes classifier. After the attribute category of t to be inferred is determined, $X = \{x_1, x_2, \ldots x_r\}$ is used to denote the r possible values of the attribute category. Based on the collected set of observable attributes $O = \{o_1, o_2, \ldots, o_k\}$ of users, the probability that t has the attribute value x is:

$$P(x|o_1, o_2, \ldots, o_k) \tag{5}$$

According to the Bayes Theorem and the attribute conditional independence assumption in the Naïve Bayes theory, i.e., the k observable attributes in attribute category x are independent of each other for, we have:

$$\frac{P(x) \times P(o_1|x) \times \cdots \times P(o_k|x)}{P(o_1, o_2, \ldots, o_k)} \tag{6}$$

where $P(o_1, o_2, \ldots, o_k)$ does not contain any parameter about x. Hence, $P(o_1, o_2, \ldots, o_k)$ is equal for arbitrary $x \in X$. Therefore, the posterior probability that t has x is:

$$\alpha_t = P(x) \propto [P(x) \times P(o_1|x) \times \cdots \times P(o_k|x)] \tag{7}$$

where the likelihood $P(o_k|x)$ indicates the probability of the occurrence of the k-th observable attribute o_k under the condition that the privacy is x.

According to the homogeneity theory [18], users who are directly connected are more likely to have similar attributes, which suggests that only considering the correlation between user attributes is not enough in privacy inference. Therefore, to reflect the common effect of all the users involved in privacy inference, we further construct the CRF for the target user based on the relationships between users in PAT T_t. The CRF of target user t can be expressed using Eq. (8) after integrating the correlation of user attributes.

$$P(x_t|O_S, T_t) = \frac{1}{Z} \prod_{Q \in \Theta} \exp\left\{ \sum_t \varphi_l(x_t, O_S, T_t) + \sum_{j \in S} \varphi_h(x_t, x_j, O_S, T_t) \right\} \qquad (8)$$

where Z is the normalization factor of the probability to make the sum of the probabilities equal to 1, $\Theta = \{Q_1, Q_2, \ldots, Q_q\}$ is the set of pairwise cliques which would have connections in T_t when two users are combined, $\varphi_l(x_t, O_S, T_t) = \alpha_t$ is the own state of the target user t obtained from the Naïve Bayes classifier, and $\varphi_h(x_t, x_j, O_S, T_t)$ represents the influence of user $j \in S$ on t.

In this study, $\varphi_h(x_t, x_j, O_S, T_t)$ is denoted by the correlation between t and j as expressed in Eq. (9).

$$\varphi_h(x_t, x_j, O_S, T_t) = e^{-\alpha \times l(t,j)} \times c(t, j) \qquad (9)$$

where $c(t, j)$ is the influence between t and j computed using Eq. (3), $e^{-\alpha \times l(t,j)}$ denotes the degree of attenuation of the path length $l(t, j)$ of t and j due to the correlation between them, and α is used to adjust the sensitivity of the degree of attenuation with path length.

Therefore, the contribution of node $n \in T_t$ can be instantiated by integrating Eq. (8) into Eq. (4), i.e.,

$$Con(n, T_t) = \begin{cases} P(x_t|O_n, T_t) & S = \varnothing \\ P(x_t|O_{S \cup \{n\}}, T_t) - P(x_t|O_S, T_t) & \text{otherwise} \end{cases} \qquad (10)$$

Using Eq. (10), the contribution of any node in PAT T_t can be calculated. At each iteration, we select the node with the highest contribution and put it in S_V. This process is repeated K_V times to get the complete privacy-sensitive user set S_V and to obtain privacy-sensitive attribute set S_A through the most K_A likelihood $P(o_k^t|x_t)$ in Eq. (7). Finally, the privacy-sensitive data is obtained, i.e., $S = S_V \cup S_A$.

The details of Priv-S are described in Algorithm 2. Specifically, after generating θ PATs (lines 1–3), we first identify K_V privacy-sensitive users S_V with the highest $\sum_{T_t \in T} con(n, T_t)$ in each iteration (lines 4–7). Then, we identify K_A privacy-sensitive attributes S_A of user $u \in S_V$ based on the highest likelihood of the occurrence of the k-th observable attribute o_k under the condition that the privacy is x (lines 8–11). Finally, we obtain the privacy-sensitive data $S = S_V \cup S_A$ (line 12).

Algorithm 2: Priv-S
Input: OSN G, target user t
Output: privacy-sensitive data S
1   Initiate $\mathcal{T} = \emptyset, S_V = \emptyset, S_A = \emptyset$
2   **while** $|\mathcal{T}| < \theta$ **do**
3      $\mathcal{T} = \mathcal{T} \cup$ PATGenerate()
4   **for** $i = 1$ to K_V **do**
5   identify $n \in \mathcal{T}_t$ with highest $\sum_{\mathcal{T}_t \in \mathcal{T}} con(n, \mathcal{T}_t)$
6        $S_V = S_V \cup n$
7   set contribution of any node copy of n to 0
8   **for** $j = 1$ to K_A **do**
9   identify attribute o of $u \in S_V$ with highest $\sum_{\mathcal{T}_t \in \mathcal{T}} con(n, \mathcal{T}_t)$
10      $S_A = S_A \cup o$
11   ignore o in subsequent steps
12   Return $S = S_V \cup S_A$

5 Experiment and Analysis

In this section, we first introduce the dataset used in the experiment and the experiment settings. Then, the results of privacy-sensitive data identification are shown through visualization. Moreover, based on the results of privacy-sensitive identification, the influence of attributes as well as users on privacy inference is analyzed.

5.1 Dataset Description and Experiment Setting

The dataset of the ego-Facebook [19], which has been widely used in related researches is used in our experiment. The statistics of ego-Facebook are consistent with key characteristics of complex networks and user attributes collected in ego-Facebook are explicit and understandable. Therefore, we can obtain straightforward, well-understood and easily interpreted experimental results by using ego-Facebook. Table 1 lists the main statistics of the dataset.

In the experiment, three categories of attributes were selected as the target attributes for privacy inference, namely, gender, education type, and work location, with the statistics being listed in Table 2. Since the characteristics of the three categories of attributes are distinctive, the analysis based on them could comprehensively and objectively reflect the performance as well as the advantages of the proposed privacy inference model.

5.2 Results and Analysis

Privacy inference methods are biased against privacy-sensitive data, i.e., different privacy-sensitive data may be obtained based on different privacy inference methods, Ideally, privacy-sensitive data obtained based on an attacker's specific privacy inference method will have the best results in defending against that attacker. In the case where the specific privacy inference method used by the attacker is not available, identifying

Table 1. The main statistics of the dataset of the ego-Facebook

Property of the ego-Facebook	Value
Total number of nodes	4039
Total number of edges	88234
Average clustering coefficient	0.6055
Diameter	8
Total number of categories of user attributes	18

Table 2. Statistics of the attributes to be inferred

attribute categories	number of users disclosing this attribute (%)	number of attribute values
gender	3955 (97.92%)	2
education type	3013 (74.60%)	3
work location	604 4.95%)	48

privacy-sensitive data based on the privacy inference method with the strongest inference capability is one of reasonable remedies. Since there are no other researches that can be used to compare the advantages of privacy-sensitive data identification algorithm and the proposed model is compatible with different privacy inference methods, the ability of privacy inference methods is used to demonstrate the advantages of our privacy-sensitive data identification model.

Results and Analysis of Privacy Inference.

In the demonstration of the performance of the proposed model, the following benchmark methods were selected as the methods to be compared.

AttrOnly: This method doesn't consider the homogeneity among users and infers privacy attributes based only on the observable attributes of users.

RelationOnly: In contrast to AttrOnly, this method considers the homogeneity between users as the basis for inferring user privacy attributes without considering the correlations between the attributes. Since the probability value is absent, we assign an average value to the probability of each attribute for unlabeled users, i.e., the n attribute values of any user satisfy $p_1 = p_2 = \cdots = p_n = 1/n$.

AttriInfer [5]: This method has received extensive attention in recent years, which applies the Markov Random Field (MRF) to determining whether a user has a certain attribute value. According to the setting in [5], the degree of homogeneity is set to be 0.7 in the experiment. The main difference between our approach and AttriInfer is that of a more fine-grained characterization of user homogeneity. Therefore, comparison with AttriInfer can better demonstrate the advantages of more fine-grained analysis of homogeneity among users on the inference results.

ReAl [7]: Besides the relationships between users and the attributes of users, this method uses the Kulczynski measure to quantify the relevance between user attributes, and the random walk with restart to achieve privacy inference for each target user. During the inference process, the node weight vector is updated iteratively and the process terminates after the node weight vectors converge.

In the experiment, all the methods selected the top 30% attribute values that have the highest degree of correlation with the target attribute as the training data to achieve high accuracy on the prediction. In addition, the ratio of the test set and the training set is 60% to 40%. Tables 3, 4 and 5 show the macro-precision, macro-recall, and macro-F1 of the four methods, respectively, which clearly demonstrate that our privacy inference method can more accurately predict the vast majority of target attributes of OSN users. Through fine-grained characterization of user homogeneity, it can be more flexible in adapting to the characteristics of different target attributes to improve the accuracy of prediction. In addition, our model can significantly reduce the number of classifiers compared to AttriInfer, thus improving the overall efficiency.

Table 3. Macro-precision (%) on different target attributes

Methods	gender	education type	work location
AttrOnly	64.99	52.55	13.69
RelationOnly	63.29	45.61	14.58
AttriInfer	66.45	55.07	2.10
ReAI	67.58	47.54	**23.44**
Ours	**79.66**	**55.95**	12.68

Table 4. Macro-recall (%) on different target attributes

Methods	gender	education type	work location
AttrOnly	65.53	40.61	17.64
RelationOnly	66.85	37.96	18.16
AttriInfer	67.28	40.86	4.23
ReAI	66.84	39.25	**25.34**
Ours	**79.98**	**42.50**	20.84

Results and Analysis of Privacy-Sensitive Data Identification.
The performance of greedy algorithm-based solutions for influence maximization problems has been extensively studied [15, 17, 20, 21]. However, there is currently no study as far as we know that focuses on the same issue as ours, making direct comparison infeasible. Therefore, we first show the results of privacy-sensitive data identification visibly as displayed in Fig. 3. The performance of privacy-sensitive data identification is reflected through the impact of the identification results on the accuracy of privacy inference, which will be described in the next section.

Table 5. Macro-F1 (%) on different target attributes

Methods	gender	education type	work location
AttrOnly	65.11	42.57	13.74
RelationOnly	66.23	41.42	14.03
AttriInfer	66.51	43.15	2.82
ReAI	66.21	42.43	**23.14**
Ours	**79.81**	**45.24**	19.71

In Fig. 3, the red star indicates the target user of privacy inference, circles represent other users and triangles with different colors represent different attribute values of the users. The size of a node indicates the degree of influence of the node on the inference result of the target node. In the experiment, the privacy is the gender of the target user. We set $K = 70$ which includes 50 user nodes and 20 attribute nodes.

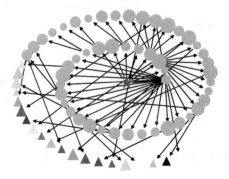

Fig. 3. Visualization of key node identification

In contrast to the classic influence maximization method [17], the homogeneity between users in OSNs is used to instantiate the influence between user nodes while sampling of the edges that have little influence is reduced. Therefore, the PAT construction process would be more suitable for our study and can help achieve the same efficiency as the WRRGenerate + method [17].

5.3 Factors that Influence Privacy Inference

The results of privacy-sensitive data identification are now used to analyze their impact on privacy inference. Meanwhile, since the more sensitive the data, the higher the impact of the data on the accuracy of privacy inference, changes in the accuracy of privacy inference based on the results of privacy-sensitive data identification can reflect the performance of the Priv-S model.

In the analysis of the factors that impact privacy inference, we select the top 20% attribute categories and the top 30% users that contribute the most to privacy inference in the analysis. We reduce the contribution of data by deleting the corresponding data in the PAT using four strategies, thus forming four groups. The first group, which is denoted as (0%, 0%), doesn't have any data deleted. The second group, which is denoted as (20%, 0), only deletes the user attributes. The third group, which is denoted as (0%, 30%), only deletes the social relationships. Lastly, the fourth group, which is denoted as (20%, 30%), deletes both the user attributes and the social relationships. The macro-precisions of the inference results corresponding to the four groups are shown in Fig. 4.

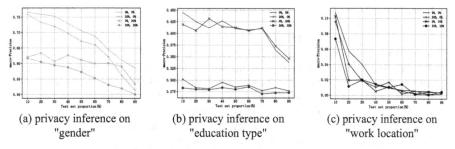

| (a) privacy inference on "gender" | (b) privacy inference on "education type" | (c) privacy inference on "work location" |

Fig. 4. Change of the macro-precisions of attributes and edges are deleted

We can see from the Fig. 4 that attributes and social relationships have different degrees of influence on different attributes. This indicates that attributes and social relationships have different degrees of influence on different hidden attributes. Therefore, the design of privacy protection mechanisms needs to consider the characteristics of the target attributes to be protected to improve the effectiveness privacy protection.

6 Conclusion

In this study, we proposed a privacy-sensitive data identification model to provide basis for targeted privacy protection. In our model, we first constructed a privacy-affected tree of a target user to express the influence of other users on the user. Then, we proposed a novel privacy inference method based on conditional random fields to evaluate the contribution of nodes in a privacy-affected tree. Finally, the privacy-sensitive data, which includes privacy-sensitive users and privacy-sensitive attributes, can be identified through greedy selection based on the contributions of nodes. Comparison study through experiments with other methods demonstrated that our method has a clear advantage in the evaluation of the contribution of nodes, making it possible to perform accurate identification of privacy-sensitive data. Meanwhile, by analyzing the main factors of privacy inference, we could see that privacy-sensitive data changes with context, illustrating the importance of data identification.

References

1. Sun, Q., Xu, Y.: Research on privacy concerns of social network users. In: 2019 IEEE 5th International Conference on Computer and Communications (ICCC), pp. 1453–1460 (2019)

2. Wang, Z., Zhu, H., Sun, L.: Social engineering in cybersecurity: effect mechanisms, human vulnerabilities and attack methods. IEEE Access **9**, 11895–11910 (2021)
3. Al-Dablan, D., Al-Hamad, A., Al-Bahlal, R., Badawi, M.A.: An analysis of various social engineering attack in social network using machine learning algorithm. Int. J. Distrib. Sens. Networks. **46** (2020)
4. Piao, Y., Ye, K., Cui, X.: Privacy inference attack against users in online social networks: a literature review. IEEE Access **9**, 40417–40431 (2021)
5. Jia, J., Wang, B., Zhang, L., Gong, N.Z.: AttriInfer: inferring user attributes in online social networks using Markov random fields (2017)
6. Gong, N.Z., Liu, B.: Attribute inference attacks in online social networks. ACM Trans. Priv. Secur. **21**, 3 (2018)
7. Mao, J., Tian, W., Yang, Y., Liu, J.: An efficient social attribute inference scheme based on social links and attribute relevance. IEEE Access **7**, 153074–153085 (2019)
8. Tian, Y., Niu, Y., Yan, J., Tian, F.: Inferring private attributes based on graph convolutional neural network in social networks. In: Proceedings of the 2019 International Conference on Networking and Network Applications. NaNA 2019, pp. 186–190 (2019)
9. Wu, Y., Lian, D., Jin, S., Chen, E.: Graph convolutional networks on user mobility heterogeneous graphs for social relationship inference. In: IJCAI International Joint Conference on Artificial Intelligence, 2019-August, pp. 3898–3904 (2019)
10. Luo, X., Xie, M., Zhang, K., Zhou, F., Zhong, T.: DeepAttr: inferring demographic attributes via social network embedding. IEEE Access **7**, 130270–130282 (2019)
11. Sutton, C., McCallum, A.: An introduction to conditional random fields. Found. Trends Mach. Learn. **4**, 267–373 (2011)
12. Heatherly, R., Kantarcioglu, M., Thuraisingham, B.: Preventing private information inference attacks on social networks. IEEE Trans. Knowl. Data Eng. **25**, 1849–1862 (2013)
13. Qian, J., Li, X.Y., Zhang, C., Chen, L., Jung, T., Han, J.: Social network de-anonymization and privacy inference with knowledge graph model. IEEE Trans. Dependable Secur. Comput. **16**, 679–692 (2019)
14. Liu, Y., Li, N.: Retrieving hidden friends: a collusion privacy attack against online friend search engine. IEEE Trans. Inf. Forensics Secur. **14**, 833–847 (2019)
15. Borgs, C., Brautbar, M., Chayes, J., Lucier, B.: Maximizing social influence in nearly optimal time. Soc. Ind. Appl. Math. (2014)
16. Wang, X., Zhang, Y., Zhang, W., Lin, X., Chen, C.: Bring order into the samples: a novel scalable method for influence maximization. IEEE Trans. Knowl. Data Eng. **29**, 243–256 (2017)
17. Song, C., Hsu, W., Lee, M.L.: Targeted influence maximization in social networks. In: Proceedings of the 25th ACM International on Conference on Information and Knowledge Management, pp. 1683–1692 (2016)
18. McPherson, M., Smith-Lovin, L., Cook, J.M.: Birds of a feather: homophily in social networks. Annu. Rev. Sociol. **27**, 415–444 (2001)
19. Mcauley, J.: Learning to discover social circles in ego networks. In: NIPS2012, pp. 1–9 (2012)
20. Tang, J., Tang, X., Xiao, X., Yuan, J.: Online processing algorithms for influence maximization. In: Proceedings of the ACM SIGMOD International Conference on Management Data, pp. 991–1005 (2018)
21. Tang, J., Tang, X., Yuan, J.: Profit maximization for viral marketing in online social networks: algorithms and analysis. IEEE Trans. Knowl. Data Eng. **30**(6), 1095–1108 (2017)

TLEF: Two-Layer Evolutionary Framework for t-Closeness Anonymization

Mingshan You[1], Yong-Feng Ge[1(✉)], Kate Wang[2], Hua Wang[1], Jinli Cao[3], and Georgios Kambourakis[4]

[1] Institute for Sustainable Industries and Liveable Cities, Victoria University, Melbourne, Australia
{mingshan.you,yongfeng.ge,hua.wang}@vu.edu.au
[2] School of Health and Biomedical Sciences, RMIT University, Melbourne, Australia
kate.wang@rmit.edu.au
[3] Department of Computer Science and Information Technology, La Trobe University, Melbourne, Australia
J.Cao@latrobe.edu.au
[4] Department of Information and Communication Systems Engineering, University of the Aegean, Karlovasi, Greece
gkamb@aegean.gr

Abstract. Data anonymization is a fundamental and practical privacy-preserving data publication (PPDP) method, while searching for the optimal anonymization scheme using traditional methods has been proven to be NP-hard. Some recent studies have introduced genetic algorithms (GA) into data anonymization to address this issue, revealing potential solutions. However, the discussions are restricted to a few privacy protection models and evolutionary algorithms (EAs). This paper extends this field by introducing differential evolution (DE) for the first time to optimize data anonymization schemes under the constraints of the t-closeness privacy model. To further enhance the algorithm's performance, this paper designs a two-layer evolutionary framework (TLEF) that effectively explores optimal solutions by leveraging the unique properties of both GA and DE in a balanced manner. Experimental evaluations conducted on 16 test datasets highlight the advantages of DE in addressing optimal t-closeness anonymization and validate the effectiveness of the TLEF.

Keywords: t-closeness anonymization · Genetic algorithm · Differential evolution

1 Introduction

In today's digital age, where data plays a crucial role in driving innovation and decision-making, the issue of privacy has become increasingly pertinent [8,22–26]. Privacy-preserving data publication (PPDP) has emerged as a paramount

F. Zhang et al. (Eds.): WISE 2023, LNCS 14306, pp. 235–244, 2023.
https://doi.org/10.1007/978-981-99-7254-8_18

concern, seeking to strike a delicate balance between sharing valuable information and safeguarding individuals' sensitive data [2,17–19]. This practice entails the dissemination of datasets that have been carefully anonymized or transformed to protect the privacy of individuals while still allowing researchers and organizations to extract meaningful insights [1,15,21].

Data anonymization is one of the widely employed privacy-preserving techniques, involving the alteration or removal of identifying information from datasets to safeguard individual privacy. Methods such as generalization, suppression, perturbation, and data synthesis are utilized to mitigate re-identification risks while preserving data utility for analysis [6,16]. Various models grounded in data anonymization have emerged to quantify data privacy post-anonymization, with classic examples being k-anonymity, l-diversity, and t-closeness [10,12,20]. Initially, k-anonymity ensures record indistinguishability, mandating a minimum of $k - 1$ similar records. l-diversity accentuates this by emphasizing diverse sensitive attributes within groups. Going further, t-closeness aligns sensitive attribute distributions in equivalence classes with the overall dataset. These seminal privacy models find widespread use, yet a central challenge remains-their optimization is NP-hard [11], rendering exact solutions infeasible within reasonable time frames and posing significant computational hurdles.

Evolutionary algorithms (EAs) have emerged as potent tools for optimizing NP-hard problems in data anonymization [9,13]. For instance, Kohlmayer et al. [7] propose Flash, which leverages EAs to achieve optimal k-anonymity. Ge et al. [5] employed a genetic algorithm (GA) based method to optimize k-anonymity anonymization. Despite advancements, only a subset of EAs and privacy models are covered. The use of EA to solve the optimal solutions under t-closeness privacy constraints is unaddressed. In addition, currently, only GAs' performance on this problem has been discussed, and other EAs' performance remains unverified. Hence, this paper introduces differential evolution (DE) to optimize the data anonymization scheme under t-closeness constraint.

This paper makes contributions to data privacy optimization, specifically in the context of the t-closeness privacy model. It introduces DE for the first time to tackle optimal data anonymity under t-closeness constraint, demonstrating its effectiveness. Additionally, a novel two-layer evolutionary framework (TLEF) is proposed, seamlessly integrating DE and GA, yielding a more stable and efficient solution for searching optimal data anonymization. The paper validates the approach using real data, offering insights into convergence behavior.

The paper's structure is as follows: Sect. 2 defines the t-closeness optimal anonymization problem. Section 3 outlines the TLEF approach. Sections 4 and 5 cover the experimental setup, results analysis, and conclusion, respectively.

2 Problem Formulation

Data Anonymization. In a general data anonymization practice, the data publisher converts the original dataset D to an anonymous dataset T using appropriate data anonymization means. The dataset D (typically a table) usually includes Explicit Identifiers, Quasi Identifiers ($QIDs$), Sensitive Attributes (SA), and Non-Sensitive Attributes. Explicit Identifiers directly identify record owners, while QID attributes can potentially reveal their identity. Sensitive Attributes contain private information, and Non-Sensitive Attributes include other attributes.

$$D\{QID, SA\} \xrightarrow{\mathcal{M}} T\{QID', SA\} \tag{1}$$

To ensure privacy, as shown in Eq. 1, a data publisher uses methods denoted as M to create an anonymous table, T. Explicit Identifiers are typically removed as they directly identify individuals. Non-Sensitive Attributes are irrelevant and need no special handling. Sensitive Attributes are usually not processed because of their significance. The primary goal of M is to transform QID into anonymized QID', making it difficult or impossible to link data back to individuals.

Data anonymization methods M involve approaches like generalization, suppression, perturbation, and data synthesis. Generalization replaces precise attribute values with less specific ones to prevent re-identification [4]. Suppression removes some records entirely to safeguard sensitive data [4]. Perturbation adds controlled noise while preserving utility. Data synthesis generates synthetic datasets mimicking original statistics without disclosing individual details.

Following the representation in the study [5], this paper employs suppression and generalization techniques to anonymize the original data table D. Record suppression removes individual records, using a one-dimensional numerical vector as the operator. This vector consists of "0" for data deletion and "1" for retention. Correspondingly, record generalization uniformly generalizes QID attribute values to specific levels on the taxonomy tree [3]. This paper uses a binary tree representation for simplicity. The process employs a one-dimensional vector of natural integers, matching the QID dimension. The vector's values signify binary tree depth, ranging from 0 to the tree's height.

Privacy and Utility Metrics. t-closeness measures the privacy of published data T by ensuring proximity between the distribution of sensitive attributes in the original and anonymized datasets.

Definition 1 (t-closeness). *An equivalence class is said to have t-closeness if the distance between the distribution of a sensitive attribute in this class and the distribution of the attribute in the whole table is no more than a threshold t. A table is said to have t-closeness if all equivalence classes have t-closeness.*

Numerous approaches exist for quantifying the "closeness" of distributions. This study chooses the Euclidean distance:

$$d(p,q) = \sqrt{(p_1 - q_1)^2 + (p_2 - q_2)^2 + \cdots + (p_n - q_n)^2} \tag{2}$$

where $(p_1, p_2, \ldots, p_n)$ and $(q_1, q_2, \ldots, q_n)$ denote the proportions of distinct values for sensitive attributes in the original dataset and the subtables categorized based on QID' after anonymization.

The utility of anonymized dataset T is quantified by its transparency degree (TD) [3], indicating the retained valuable information after applying suppression and generalization.

$$TD(T) = \sum_{r \in T} TD(r) = \sum_{r \in T} \sum_{v_g \in r} TD(v_g) \qquad (3)$$

where r is the retained record in dataset T; v_g is the generalized value in record r. The TD value of v_g is calculated by:

$$TD(v_g) = \frac{1}{|v_g|} \qquad (4)$$

where $|v_g|$ is the number of domain values that are descendants of v_g.

Optimal Anonymization. Optimal anonymization involves choosing the most effective suppression and generalization that strike a balance between safeguarding privacy and preserving data utility. In the context of t-closeness anonymization, given a t-closeness threshold t, its definition is as follows:

Definition 2 (Optimal anonymization). *For T, an optimal anonymization solution can satisfy the privacy requirement $(d(p, q) < t)$ and achieves the highest utility degree $(Max(TD(T)))$.*

3   Two-Layer Evolutionary Framework

TLEF, introduced in this study, synergizes the benefits of DE and GA. By harnessing their respective optimization strengths, TLEF aims to excel in resolving optimal t-closeness anonymization challenges.

DE is particularly proficient at rapidly converging towards promising solutions, especially when dealing with smooth optimization landscapes. It excels in scenarios where optimization landscapes are relatively uncomplicated or when swift convergence is a priority. In contrast, GA is notable for its adeptness at exploring diverse segments of the solution space using crossover and mutation. GA's adaptability extends to a broad spectrum of optimization challenges, making it suitable for scenarios characterized by either complexity or ruggedness in the landscape. DE brings exploration capabilities and a robust search mechanism, while GA incorporates the principles of natural selection and genetics to exploit promising solutions. The fusion of DE and GA in TLEF offers a synergistic effect, enhancing the optimization process by effectively exploring the solution space and exploiting the best solutions. This combination allows for a more comprehensive and efficient search for optimal solutions, making TLEF a promising approach for tackling challenging optimization problems.

Algorithm 1 outlines the structure of TLEF. Input parameters encompass population size N, maximum iterations G, DE process (crossover rate CR_{DE} and scaling factor F), and GA process (crossover rate CR_{GA} and mutation rate

MR_{GA}). During the initialization phase, the algorithm establishes an initial population P_0 of size N and defines the maximum iteration count G. Each individual within the population P_0 undergoes a fitness evaluation to quantify its quality. The input parameters for the DE process, including the crossover rate CR_{DE} and scaling factor F, as well as parameters for the GA process, such as the crossover rate CR_{GA} and mutation rate MR_{GA}. Lastly, a two-dimensional selector [5], involving the assessment of both privacy and utility metrics, identifies the most promising individuals from the initial generation to serve as the foundation for subsequent iterative evolution.

Algorithm 1 Pseudo-code of TLEF

1: **Input:** N, G, CR_{DE}, F, CR_{GA}, MR_{GA}
2: Initialize population P_0 with size N
3: Evaluate fitness for each individual in P_0
4: Select the $Individual_{best}$ in P_0
5: Set generation counter $g = 0$
6: **while** $g \leq G$ **do**
7:    **if** g is even **then**
8:       Update P with DE
9:       Evaluate fitness for each individual in P_g
10:       Select the $Individual_{best}$ in P_g
11:    **end if**
12:    **if** g is odd **then**
13:       Update P with GA
14:       Evaluate fitness for each individual in P_g
15:       Select the $Individual_{best}$ in P_g
16:    **end if**
17:    $g = g + 1$
18: **end while**
19: **Output:** $Individual_{best}$

The algorithm then initiates a while loop, incrementing the generation counter by 1 for each iteration. It updates the population using the DE layer for even counters and the GA layer for odd counters until the maximum specified generations are reached.

This paper applies basic DE and GA principles in their respective layers. DE employs "DE/best/1" strategy, while GA aligns with IDGA [5], reproducing with the best current individual and all contemporaneously generated individuals. DE and GA share a fitness function with two values: t-closeness and TD. The selection criteria for both are consistent: choosing individuals with higher TD values among those exceeding the t-closeness threshold.

The algorithm halts at the maximum generation limit. The best anonymization solution, labeled as $Individual_{best}$, is chosen from population P_G, representing the optimal configuration derived by TLEF for the dataset.

4   Experimental Results

4.1   Experiment Setting

Dataset and Test Cases. This study uses the Hospital Inpatient Discharges 2015 dataset[1], a real dataset released by the New York State Department of Health. Four data publishing examples are considered based on the original dataset to verify the proposed scheme, each focusing on a single sensitive attribute. These examples involve queries related to hospitalizations in 'Emergency' situations, mental diseases and disorders, patients with HIV infections, and respiratory system diseases. The attribute categories are simplified to true or false to facilitate the analysis. The experiment consists of 16 test cases randomly sampled from four sub-tables. Table 1 provides an overview of these test instances, including the number of QID attributes ($nQID$), sensitive attributes (nSA), and the number of records (nR) in each test case.

Table 1. Properties of 16 test cases

Sub-table	Sub-table 1				Sub-table 2				Sub-table 3				Sub-table 4			
Test Case	D_1	D_2	D_3	D_4	D_5	D_6	D_7	D_8	D_9	D_{10}	D_{11}	D_{12}	D_{13}	D_{14}	D_{15}	D_{16}
nQID	6	6	10	10	6	6	10	10	5	5	9	9	6	6	10	10
nSA	1	1	1	1	1	1	1	1	1	1	1	1	1	1	1	1
nR	300	600	300	600	300	600	300	600	300	600	300	600	300	600	300	600

Comparison with Other Approaches. To verify the effectiveness of the proposed TLEF, GA [13] and IDGA [7] and DE [14] are utilized for comparison.

- GA: The design and configuration of this scheme are consistent with the GA layer in TLEF, serving as a benchmark in the comparison.
- IDGA: This is a state-of-art algorithm in the k-anonymity PPDP field.
- DE: This algorithm serves as another baseline method, with its design and configuration matching the DE component of TLEF, to validate the effectiveness of TLEF.

Algorithm Implementation and Parameter Settings. The studied algorithms are executed on a Windows 10 Pro workstation. The workstation features an AMD Ryzen Threadripper PRO 3995WX CPU with 64 cores, 2.70 GHz clock speed, and 256 GB RAM.

A population size of 30 is used for all four algorithms. Maximum fitness evaluations are set at $10 \times nQID \times nR$. GA, IDGA, and TLEF share a crossover rate of 0.5 and a mutation rate of 0.2. DE and TLEF both utilize a scaling factor of 1.3 and a crossover rate of 0.3. These choices ensured consistent assessment of each algorithm's performance and behavior.

---

[1] https://health.data.ny.gov/Health/Hospital-Inpatient-Discharges-SPARCS-De-Identified/82xm-y6g8.

Table 2. TD comparison when t-closeness threshold t = 0.2

Case	GA		IDGA		DE		TLEF	
	Avg	Std	Avg	Std	Avg	Std	Avg	Std
D_1	5.16E+02	5.98E+00	5.70E+02	0.00E+00	**6.81E+02**	1.03E+01	**6.81E+02**	6.87E+00
D_2	9.43E+02	1.16E+01	1.14E+03	0.00E+00	**1.33E+03**	8.02E+01	1.31E+03	9.30E+01
D_3	5.02E+02	2.46E+01	6.54E+02	0.00E+00	6.56E+02	3.81E+01	**6.57E+02**†	3.35E+01
D_4	1.04E+03	2.74E+01	1.30E+03	0.00E+00	1.43E+03	1.65E+02	**1.55E+03**†	8.14E+01
D_5	4.12E+02	1.60E+01	5.32E+02	0.00E+00	5.42E+02	3.29E+01	**5.53E+02**	3.08E+01
D_6	8.84E+02	4.36E+01	9.89E+02	0.00E+00	1.20E+03	9.72E+01	**1.22E+03**	8.43E+01
D_7	5.36E+02	1.99E+01	6.54E+02	0.00E+00	7.16E+02	6.10E+01	**7.57E+02**†	1.79E+01
D_8	1.06E+03	1.39E+01	1.51E+03	7.63E+01	1.49E+03	8.51E+01	**1.52E+03**†	5.38E+00
D_9	5.30E+02	1.05E+01	**7.15E+02**†	0.00E+00	7.12E+02	3.21E+00	7.03E+02	3.05E+01
D_{10}	1.06E+03	1.38E+01	1.18E+03	1.03E+02	1.44E+03	5.19E+01	**1.54E+03**†	5.70E+01
D_{11}	5.85E+02	1.14E+01	6.54E+02	0.00E+00	7.74E+02	5.37E+01	**8.01E+02**†	4.21E+00
D_{12}	1.14E+03	1.51E+01	1.61E+03	0.00E+00	1.60E+03	9.64E+01	**1.66E+03**	6.90E+01
D_{13}	9.01E+02	1.63E+02	8.36E+02	2.14E+01	9.54E+02	1.43E+01	**1.13E+03**†	2.73E+02
D_{14}	1.54E+03	9.46E+01	1.66E+03	1.29E+00	2.21E+03	1.48E+02	**2.30E+03**†	1.22E+02
D_{15}	1.90E+03	3.01E+01	1.08E+03	3.37E+01	2.74E+03	3.16E+02	**2.76E+03**†	3.09E+02
D_{16}	2.95E+03	6.16E+02	2.29E+03	0.00E+00	3.04E+03	5.95E+02	**3.52E+03**	1.06E+03

4.2 Result and Analysis

TD **Comparison.** The experimental results are summarized in Table 2, which present the final TD values achieved by each algorithm at t-closeness thresholds of 0.2. It includes TD's mean and standard deviation based on 25 independent runs. Our proposed method outperformed other algorithms by achieving the best TD values on 14 test cases when t = 0.2.

Moreover, to investigate the advantage of TLEF in a statistical sense, the Wilcoxon rank-sum test with a 0.05 level is utilized. In Table 2, the symbol † shows that the corresponding result is significantly better than the compared results. TLEF can obtain significantly better results in 9 out of 16 test instances when $t = 0.2$.

Convergence Curves. Figure 1 shows convergence curves for TLEF and three other algorithms on 16 test cases, with unique symbols and colors in the legend. The horizontal axis represents the number of fitness evaluations (NFEs), while the vertical axis shows transparency degree (TD) values.

After analyzing all 16 convergence curves, a clear pattern emerges: IDGA achieves the fastest convergence, followed by DE, and GA demonstrates the slowest convergence. TLEF's convergence rate falls between DE and GA, leaning closer to DE. This trend persists across all test cases, irrespective of record count or QID length.

IDGA's rapid convergence is hindered by a notable drawback-it often converges prematurely to local optima in most test cases, posing challenges for attaining a global optimal solution. This limitation is particularly evident in multiple subgraphs (a, b, d, f, g, j, k, m, etc.). In contrast, TLEF frequently

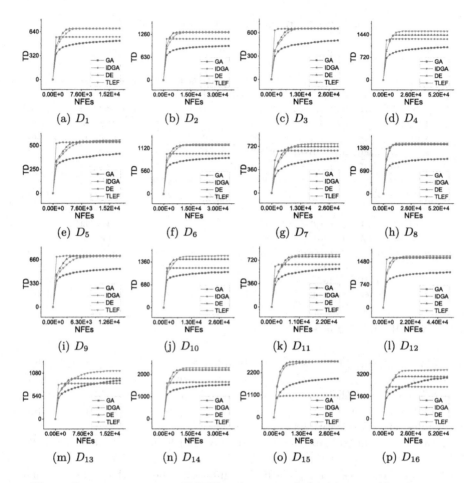

Fig. 1. Convergence curves of TLEF and compared algorithms on 16 test cases

attains optimal solutions while preserving algorithmic efficiency, exemplified in instances like (d, g, j, m, p, etc.). TLEF excels in efficiently searching for optimal solutions, surpassing GA and generally outperforming the optimal solutions derived from DE.

Discussion. In terms of both attaining optimal solutions and convergence speed, TLEF performs well in the experiments. It consistently achieves global optimal solutions within the specified iterations and surpasses DE without compromising search efficiency. This underscores TLEF's advantage in generating anonymization schemes that retain more useful information in published data under the t-closeness privacy constraint.

However, acknowledging limitations, our study mainly targets single sensitive attributes and binary values, potentially affecting its applicability to multi-attribute scenarios. Future research should conduct varied experiments to better understand TLEF's strengths and limitations across diverse settings.

5 Conclusion

In conclusion, this paper introduces, for the first time, the optimization problem of privacy preservation under the t-closeness privacy model and proposes the DE approach to address it. Furthermore, the TLEF is presented, which combines DE and GA, yielding a more effective and stable approach to searching for the optimal solution. Despite GA's inferior search efficiency and effectiveness compared to DE, their combination within TLEF enables them to achieve the global optimal solution collaboratively. Experimental results across multiple test datasets demonstrate DE's superior effectiveness over GA for this problem and validate the efficacy of TLEF. Nonetheless, this study's scope is confined to a single sensitive attribute, and analysis is limited to binary attribute value. Subsequent research should extend to comprehensive experimentation within intricate scenarios and explore multi-sensitive attribute contexts for a more thorough appraisal of the proposed methodology.

References

1. Cheng, K., et al.: Secure k-NN query on encrypted cloud data with multiple keys. IEEE Trans. Big Data **7**(4), 689–702 (2017). https://doi.org/10.1109/tbdata.2017. 2707552
2. Fatima, M., Rehman, O., Rahman, I.M.: Impact of features reduction on machine learning based intrusion detection systems. EAI Endorsed Trans. Scalable Inf. Syst. **9**(6), e9 (2022)
3. Fung, B.C.M., Wang, K., Chen, R., Yu, P.S.: Privacy-preserving data publishing: a survey of recent developments. ACM Comput. Surv. **42**(4) (2010). https://doi. org/10.1145/1749603.1749605
4. Ge, Y.F., Orlowska, M., Cao, J., Wang, H., Zhang, Y.: MDDE: multitasking distributed differential evolution for privacy-preserving database fragmentation. VLDB J. (2022). https://doi.org/10.1007/s00778-021-00718-w
5. Ge, Y.F., Wang, H., Cao, J., Zhang, Y.: An information-driven genetic algorithm for privacy-preserving data publishing. In: Chbeir, R., Huang, H., Silvestri, F., Manolopoulos, Y., Zhang, Y. (eds.) Web Information Systems Engineering – WISE 2022. WISE 2022. LNCS, vol. 13724, pp. 340–354. Springer, Cham (2022). https:// doi.org/10.1007/978-3-031-20891-1_24
6. Ge, Y.F., et al.: Distributed memetic algorithm for outsourced database fragmentation. IEEE Trans. Cybern. **51**(10), 4808–4821 (2021). https://doi.org/10.1109/ tcyb.2020.3027962
7. Kohlmayer, F., Prasser, F., Eckert, C., Kemper, A., Kuhn, K.A.: Flash: efficient, stable and optimal k-anonymity. In: 2012 International Conference on Privacy, Security, Risk and Trust and 2012 International Conference on Social Computing. IEEE (2012). https://doi.org/10.1109/socialcom-passat.2012.52
8. Kong, L., Wang, L., Gong, W., Yan, C., Duan, Y., Qi, L.: LSH-aware multitype health data prediction with privacy preservation in edge environment. World Wide Web, pp. 1–16 (2021)

9. Li, J.Y., Zhan, Z.H., Wang, H., Zhang, J.: Data-driven evolutionary algorithm with perturbation-based ensemble surrogates. IEEE Trans. Cybern. **51**(8), 3925–3937 (2021). https://doi.org/10.1109/tcyb.2020.3008280

10. Li, N., Li, T., Venkatasubramanian, S.: t-closeness: privacy beyond k-anonymity and l-diversity. In: 2007 IEEE 23rd International Conference on Data Engineering, pp. 106–115. IEEE (2006)

11. Liang, H., Yuan, H.: On the complexity of *t*-closeness anonymization and related problems. In: Meng, W., Feng, L., Bressan, S., Winiwarter, W., Song, W. (eds.) DASFAA 2013. LNCS, vol. 7825, pp. 331–345. Springer, Heidelberg (2013). https://doi.org/10.1007/978-3-642-37487-6_26

12. Machanavajjhala, A., Kifer, D., Gehrke, J., Venkitasubramaniam, M.: l-diversity: privacy beyond k-anonymity. ACM Trans. Knowl. Discov. Data (TKDD) **1**(1), 3-es (2007)

13. Mirjalili, S.: Evolutionary Algorithms and Neural Networks. Springer, Cham (2018). https://doi.org/10.1007/978-3-319-93025-1

14. Pant, M., Zaheer, H., Garcia-Hernandez, L., Abraham, A., et al.: Differential evolution: a review of more than two decades of research. Eng. Appl. Artif. Intell. **90**, 103479 (2020)

15. Patil, D.R., Pattewar, T.M.: Majority voting and feature selection based network intrusion detection system. EAI Endorsed Trans. Scalable Inf. Syst. **9**(6), e6 (2022)

16. Sarki, R., Ahmed, K., Wang, H., Zhang, Y., Wang, K.: Convolutional neural network for multi-class classification of diabetic eye disease. EAI Endorsed Trans. Scalable Inf. Syst. **9**(4), e5 (2022)

17. Shalini, R., Manoharan, R.: Trust model for effective consensus in blockchain. EAI Endorsed Trans. Scalable Inf. Syst. **9**(5), e7 (2022)

18. Sun, X., Wang, H., Li, J.: Injecting purpose and trust into data anonymisation. In: Proceedings of the 18th ACM Conference on Information and Knowledge Management, pp. 1541–1544 (2009)

19. Sun, X., Wang, H., Li, J., Zhang, Y.: Satisfying privacy requirements before data anonymization. Comput. J. **55**(4), 422–437 (2012). https://doi.org/10.1093/comjnl/bxr028

20. Sweeney, L.: k-anonymity: a model for protecting privacy. Int. J. Uncertain. Fuzziness Knowl.-Based Syst. **10**(05), 557–570 (2002)

21. Venkateswaran, N., Prabaharan, S.P.: An efficient neuro deep learning intrusion detection system for mobile Adhoc networks. EAI Endorsed Trans. Scalable Inf. Syst. **9**(6), e7 (2022)

22. Wang, H., Yi, X., Bertino, E., Sun, L.: Protecting outsourced data in cloud computing through access management. Concurr. Comput. Pract. Exp. **28** (2014). https://doi.org/10.1002/cpe.3286

23. Yin, J., Tang, M., Cao, J., Wang, H.: Apply transfer learning to cybersecurity: predicting exploitability of vulnerabilities by description. Knowl.-Based Syst. **210**, 106529 (2020)

24. Yin, J., Tang, M., Cao, J., Wang, H., You, M., Lin, Y.: Vulnerability exploitation time prediction: an integrated framework for dynamic imbalanced learning. World Wide Web, pp. 1–23 (2022)

25. You, M., Yin, J., Wang, H., Cao, J., Miao, Y.: A minority class boosted framework for adaptive access control decision-making. In: Zhang, W., Zou, L., Maamar, Z., Chen, L. (eds.) WISE 2021. LNCS, vol. 13080, pp. 143–157. Springer, Cham (2021). https://doi.org/10.1007/978-3-030-90888-1_12

26. You, M., et al.: A knowledge graph empowered online learning framework for access control decision-making. World Wide Web **26**(2), 827–848 (2023)

A Dual-Layer Privacy-Preserving Federated Learning Framework

Wenxuan Huang$^{(\boxtimes)}$ ⓘ, Thanassis Tiropanis, and George Konstantinidis ⓘ

Electronics and Computer Science, University of Southampton, Southampton, UK
{wh1g19,t.tiropanis,g.konstantinidis}@soton.ac.uk

Abstract. With the exponential growth of personal data use for machine learning models, significant privacy challenges arise. Anonymisation and federated learning can protect privacy-sensitive data at the cost of accuracy but there is lack of research on hybrid approaches. This paper uses federated learning and traditional centralised machine learning to evaluate the effectiveness of different anonymization strategies in environments with independent and identically distributed data. It considers the two layers of data collection (layer one) and model training (layer two) on three scenarios: (i) local data collection and local anonymisation for federated model training, (ii) central data collection before anonymisation for centralised model training, and (iii) central aggregation of locally anonymised data for centralised model training. Our assessment shows that the performance of the models generally decreases with increasing anonymity constraints, but the extent of decrease varies across different scenarios. In addition, we propose a dual-layer federated learning framework that applies differential privacy to ensure privacy during both data collection and model training stages. Evaluation on real-world datasets demonstrates that our framework achieves both acceptable data anonymization and model accuracy.

Keywords: Privacy preservation · Machine Learning · Federated learning · Anonymisation

1 Introduction

In the era of big data, the amount of data generated by humans is exponentially increasing. A significant portion of this data is inherently personal and includes various types of patient data collected and stored in electronic health records within the electronic health systems. This data encompasses laboratory test results, demographic information, age and weight statistics, as well as medication information [12]. Similarly, in social networks, data such as user names, addresses, email addresses, personal photos, and notes are collected [20]. This data can be used for numerous scientific or commercial purposes, such as data-driven research and product development, relying on the analysis of personal information to generate knowledge-based decisions or provide personalised services. However, due to the presence of personal information in the data, it may

F. Zhang et al. (Eds.): WISE 2023, LNCS 14306, pp. 245–259, 2023.
https://doi.org/10.1007/978-981-99-7254-8_19

face threats from inference attacks, where attackers can infer sensitive or private information that has not been explicitly disclosed by utilising patterns, correlations, or statistical characteristics present in the available data [20,30]. Therefore, privacy protection is crucial in the publication and utilisation of personal data. The "privacy by design" paradigm [14] emphasises minimising the use of sensitive information. The General Data Protection Regulation (GDPR) [24] introduced by the European Union provides a strict and mandatory framework for safeguarding personal and sensitive information.

To address the threats posed by privacy attacks, anonymization techniques and federated learning are widely employed to protect the publication and usage of privacy-sensitive data [2,18]. In the data collection phase, privacy-preserving data publishing (PPDP) offers a set of models, tools, and methods to mitigate privacy threats when releasing data. Data owners protect users' private information by applying anonymization techniques, including generalisation, suppression, microaggregation, to prevent inference attacks while preserving the utility of the anonymised data. In the data processing phase, the application of machine learning is becoming increasingly widespread. With the explosive growth of data and the rapid generation of information, traditional methods of data processing and analysis are no longer able to meet the demands of mining and insights from massive data. The development of machine learning technology enables people to harness the valuable information hidden in big data and extract profound insights and patterns, providing more accurate and efficient solutions. However, considering most real-world scenarios, personal data is often scattered across data islands, such as different healthcare institutions or banking systems. However, most traditional machine learning algorithms operate in a centralised manner, requiring data aggregation on data servers. This introduces a single point of failure and significant risks of data breaches, leading to a lack of trust among end users and challenges in complying with GDPR requirements. To overcome these challenges, Google researchers introduced federated learning as a promising solution [21], which has gained attention from both industry and academia. Unlike traditional machine learning, federated learning is a framework that enables machine learning algorithms to be implemented in a decentralised collaborative learning setting. In federated learning, models are executed on multiple local datasets stored on various local nodes, such as smartphones, tablets, personal computers, and Internet of Things (IoT) devices [15]. Each device uses its own local data to train the model, and after the local training is complete, each device sends the updated model parameters to the central server. The central server aggregates all received model parameters to generate new global model parameters [2]. This allows local nodes to collaboratively train a shared machine learning model, exchanging only the trained parameters (e.g., weights and biases of deep neural networks) periodically, without the need to centrally collect and process training data on a central data server. As a result, federated learning possesses a natural advantage in preserving data privacy. Furthermore, the parameter update and aggregation processes between local nodes and the central coordinating server can be enhanced with privacy protection techniques, such as differential privacy, to further strengthen data privacy protection [9,29].

However, despite the individual achievements of anonymization and federated learning in privacy protection during different stages of data processing, combining both techniques into a comprehensive privacy protection framework poses challenges. Previous research introducing anonymization algorithms often overlooked the relationship between anonymization and machine learning, partially due to the distinct origins of these two methods. It has been noted that information loss resulting from the generalisation and suppression algorithms in anonymization methods may lead to performance degradation in machine learning models [1,4,26]. Additionally, as a distributed machine learning framework, federated learning distributes data across local nodes instead of aggregating it on a central server. Currently, there is no research that discusses the relationship between anonymization in distributed data collection and the performance of machine learning models. Intuitively, With an increasing number of data holders, each holder possesses a smaller amount of data, resulting in lower levels of anonymity. To achieve anonymity constraints equivalent to those in centralised data sets, the data sets used in federated learning require a greater degree of anonymization transformation, which may further compromise model performance. Therefore, this study first investigates the impact of general anonymization strategies on three different training modes (federated learning, centralised machine learning, hybrid mode), addressing a gap in the existing literature. Subsequently, we propose a novel dual-layer federated learning framework that achieves privacy protection in both the data collection and data processing stages while maintaining acceptable model performance.

The main contributions of this paper are as follows:

- A dual-layer privacy-preserving federated learning framework to explore privacy protection in both the data collection and model training stages while maintaining acceptable model performance.
- Comparison of anonymisation techniques between federated learning on distributed data sets and centralised machine learning on centrally collected data sets using a real-world data set.
- Assessing the impact of different privacy-preserving anonymisation strategies on 3 training scenarios: anonymisation on federated learning, anonymisation on centralised learning, and centralised learning on datasets anonymised before aggregation.
- Evaluation of the proposed framework on a real-world data set, demonstrating improvements in both data anonymity and model performance.

Through these contributions, we provide a comprehensive understanding of the impact of anonymization strategies on federated learning, filling a gap in the field of privacy protection. Moreover, we introduce an innovative federated learning framework that simultaneously enhances data privacy and improves model performance in big data applications. This work is of significant importance in advancing privacy protection and the application of big data, providing valuable guidance for future research and practical implementations.

2   Background

2.1   Challenges in Data Publishing

As more and more personal information is used for data-driven research or product development, the protection of private personal information is becoming increasingly important. PPDP is a process of sharing data while protecting individual privacy. It involves techniques that aim to prevent unauthorised access to sensitive data and protect the anonymity of individuals in the dataset. It is particularly important in industries such as healthcare, finance, and government, where sensitive data needs to be shared for research or analysis purposes while maintaining the privacy of individuals. Table 1 shows the different attributes of the data in the PPDP.

Table 1. The types of attributes in privacy-preserving data publishing.

Type	Description
Identifier	Attributes in the data that are used to uniquely identify individuals' identities
Quasi-identifier	Attributes Combinations of attributes in a dataset that are linked with an Identifying Attribute
Sensitive Attribute	Attributes in the data that are related to individuals' sensitive information
Non-sensitive Attribute	Attributes in the data that are not sensitive attributes, identifying attributes, or quasi-identifier attributes

In the publishing of personal data, there are three types of privacy threats [8]:

- **Identity disclosure**: An attacker can correctly associate an individual with a personal record in a published dataset.
- **Attribute disclosure**: Attackers can obtain individuals' sensitive information through inference attacks. This type of threat is more likely to occur in datasets with low anonymity.
- **Membership disclosure**: Attackers can infer with a high probability whether an individual's record exists or does not exist in a published dataset [22, 28].

2.2   Privacy Paradigms

To protect user privacy in the published dataset, data publishers can apply anonymization techniques to enhance the dataset's resilience against attacks. The aim of anonymisation is to ensure that a person's data record can no longer be traced explicitly back to that particular person. To this purpose, various complementary privacy paradigms have been defined:

k-Anonymity. K-anonymity [27] is a privacy protection concept that requires each record in a dataset to be indistinguishable from at least K-1 other records in terms of their attributes, thereby hiding the specific identity information of individuals. K-anonymity is achieved by generalising or suppressing attributes, which increases the similarity between records and ensures anonymity. Specifically, for a dataset D with attribute set A, if for every record d in the dataset, there exist at least K-1 other records d' such that they have the same values for the attributes in set A, then the dataset D satisfies K-anonymity.

l-Diversity. L-diversity [19] is a measure of the richness of information in an anatomised dataset. It quantifies the number of different attribute values within each equivalence class in the dataset. The goal of L-diversity is to increase the diversity of attribute values in the economised dataset, thereby enhancing its utility. A higher L-diversity value indicates a greater diversity of attribute values in the dataset.

L-Diversity is measured by:

$$L - diversity(D) = \min_{q \in Q} \left(\frac{1}{n} \sum_{i=1}^{n} f(q, D_i) \right)$$

where D is the anonymised dataset, Q is the set of all possible values for the sensitive attribute, n is the number of equivalence classes, D_i is the $i - th$ equivalence class, and $f(q, D_i)$ is the proportion of records in the equivalence class D_i with a sensitive attribute value of q.

t-closeness. t-closeness [16] aims to protect against attribute disclosure attacks by minimising the likelihood of inferring sensitive information based on background knowledge. In t-closeness, the notion of closeness refers to the similarity between the distribution of sensitive attributes in the original data and their distribution in the published data. The parameter "t" represents a threshold value that determines the acceptable level of similarity. A smaller value of t indicates a higher degree of privacy protection. t-closeness can be measured by Kullback-Leibler [10] Divergence. Kullback-Leibler divergence, also known as relative entropy, is a measure used to quantify the difference between two probability distributions. KL divergence measures the information loss when using one probability distribution Q to approximate another distribution P, given that

P is the true distribution. Specifically, for two probability distributions P and Q, the KL divergence is defined as follows [7]:

$$KL(P \parallel Q) = \sum P(x) \log \left(\frac{P(x)}{Q(x)} \right)$$

Where P(x) and Q(x) represent the probabilities of event x under probability distributions P and Q, respectively.

To enhance privacy paradigms, common data anonymization operations include] [5]:

- **Generalisation** [25]: In this operation, the original values of quasi-identifiers are transformed into less specific but semantically consistent values. For example, age or income can be generalised into intervals.
- **Suppression** [25]: This operation hides the original values of quasi-identifiers by replacing them with a special value. For instance, the value "20" of an individual's age can be anonymised. The value "0" can be replaced with "*", resulting in "2*" as the suppressed value of the quasi-identifier.
- **Perturbation** [25]: In this operation, random noise is added to the data to obscure the true values of individuals. This can be achieved by adding random numbers to numerical data or introducing randomisation processes in categorical data.
- **Microaggregation** [3]: This operation involves aggregating the data by combining multiple individuals' data into representative values, thus concealing specific individual information.

These anonymization techniques aim to balance the privacy protection and data utility in the published dataset. By applying these operations, data publishers can enhance the privacy of the dataset while preserving its usefulness for analysis and research purposes.

2.3   Federated Learning

Federated Learning [13,21] is a distributed machine learning approach that aims to train models without the need to send data from local devices to a central server. In traditional machine learning approaches, data is typically centralised at a single location for training, which involves data transmission and storage, posing security and privacy risks. The main idea of federated learning is to move the training process of models to local devices such as smartphones, tablets, or IoT devices. Each device locally stores its data and performs the model training process locally. Only the updated model parameters are sent to a central server for aggregation to update the global model. This approach keeps individual data locally without the need to share it with third parties or store it centrally, thereby enhancing data privacy and security. Federated learning offers several advantages. It can handle distributed, sensitive, and large-scale datasets while preserving user privacy. It is applicable in various scenarios such as healthcare,

IoT, mobile devices, and edge computing. Through federated learning, individual devices can contribute their data to improve the performance of the global model while maintaining data confidentiality and privacy [11]. However, federated learning also poses several key challenges, such as inferred attacks on gradients, expensive communication costs between servers and clients, and device variability [6,17,31].

3   Methodology and Framework

This section first describes our proposed framework for privacy-preserving federated learning, followed by a description of dataset and methods for anonymisation. Our approach aims to improve the anonymity of data and to evaluate the impact of unionisation on the performance of federated learning and centralised machine learning models.

3.1   Data Description

In our study, we want to evaluate the impact of our framework on the performance of anonymity and federated learning models from a real, distributed dataset. Thus we utilise the Aposemat IoT-23 dataset [23] which aims to provide researchers with a large-scale, labelled dataset of IoT traffic to facilitate the development of machine learning algorithms. With 23 sub-datasets, the IoT-23 dataset covers a wide range of scenarios where network data was collected. These sub-datasets consist of network traffic data in pcap format, accompanied by labels indicating instances of malicious behaviour.

The dataset consists of 23 features, among which 'proto', 'orig_p' and 'ts' are selected as quasi-identifiers, and 'detailed-label' is sensitive data. 'proto' represents the protocol used in the network traffic packets, including 'tcp', 'udp', and 'icmp'. 'orig_p' represents the port used in the network traffic and 'ts' denotes the timestamp of the network connections, which has been standardised and retained with 4 significant digits. 'detailed-label' refers to the type of attack the system is subjected to.

3.2   Anonymisation Methods

In order to enhance data anonymity, we employ two strategies: generalisation and microaggregation.

Generalisation. Starting from the highest level of generalisation for the quasi-identifiers, we recursively specialise the partitions using multi-dimensional cuts until no further cuts can be made. In each iteration of the algorithm, a dimension (attribute) is selected for cutting. A common approach is to choose the dimension with the widest value range. Then, using the median split, we determine the splitting value and perform the cut based on that value.

Microaggregation. Initially, we create clusters with at least k similar records. We then choose a representative value to replace all the quasi-identifiers within each group. The selection of the representative value can be done using different methods, such as the mean, median, or random selection.

3.3   A Dual-Layer Privacy-Preserving Federated Learning Framework

Given that anonymization and federated learning achieve privacy protection at different stages of data processing, we propose a dual-layer framework(shown in Fig. 1 and Algorithm 1) that combines these two techniques to achieve comprehensive privacy protection from data collection to data utilisation.

The framework divides data processing into two stages: privacy data collection and privacy data usage.

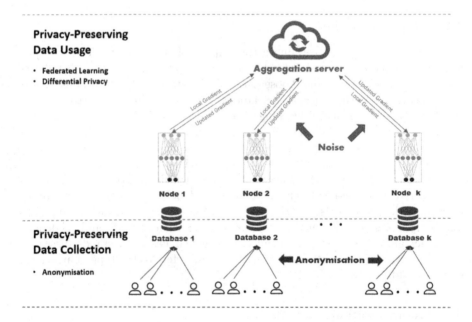

Fig. 1. Framework of the Dual-Layer Privacy-Preserving Federated Learning Framework.

1. In the first stage, after collecting individual information, the framework assesses the privacy metrics of the raw data and performs anonymization operations, such as generalisation and microaggregation, to ensure that data collection meets the requirements of Privacy-Preserving Data Publishing (PPDP).

2. In the second stage, through federated learning, the model is executed on multiple local datasets stored on various local nodes, utilising a central server to coordinate the training process. Additionally, the parameter update and aggregation processes between local nodes and the central coordinating server can be enhanced with differential privacy to strengthen data privacy protection. We add artificial noise to the parameters on the clients before aggregation to prevent inference attacks against the model gradients.

3.4 Privacy Against Centralisation

We generated two types of datasets, namely multiple distributed datasets and a single centralised dataset. First we sample 23 datasets from each of the 23 nodes as datasets $D\{a_1, a_2.....a_{23}\}$ for distributed scenario; then we aggregate all the datasets from $\mathbf{D}$ into a single dataset $\mathbf{C}$ as the centralised scenario.

To explore the performance of data anonymization and federated learning, we consider the following scenarios:

Algorithm 1. Dual-Layer Privacy-Preserving Federated Learning

---

Stage 1: Privacy Data Collection
Input : Original datasets $D\{d_1, d_2, ...\}$.
Output: Anatomised datasets $D'\{d'_1, d'_2, ...\}$.
for each dataset d in D **do**   Identify the quasi-identifiers in d
  Measuring privacy metrics k-anonymity
  for each quasi-identifier
    Apply generalisation or suppression to achieve k-anonymity
Return the anatomised data set D'

Stage 2: Privacy Data Usage
Input : Anatomised datasets D', Mini-batch size (B),
Participants per epoch (m), Total epochs (E), noise multiplier n.
Output: Global model W_{GM}.
Aggregation Service Execution:
Initialise W_{GM} :
for each epoch =1,2,3 . . . E **do**
  $D'_t \leftarrow$ (random set of m clients from C)
  for each participant d' in D' **do**
    $w_{GM}d'^{t+1} \leftarrow$ Update $\left(d', w_{GM}d'^t, n\right)$
  $w_{t+1} \leftarrow \sum_1^{d'} \frac{m_{d'}}{m} w_{GM}d'^{t+1}$ (Averaging Aggregation)
Client Update:
$\beta \leftarrow$ mini-batches creates through splitting local datasets D_L
for each epoch =1,2,3 . . . E **do**
  for local mini-batch $b \in \beta$ **do**
    $w_{GM} \leftarrow w - \eta \triangle l(w,b)$
    ($\triangle l$ is the gradient of l on b and η is the learning rate

---

1. Calculating different privacy parameters (k-anonymity, l-diversity, t-closeness) for a real-world dataset, IoT-23, in both centralised and federated learning distributed settings.
2. Comparing the effects of different privacy-preserving anonymization strategies on federated learning and centralised machine learning models. To test the impact of data anonymization on the performance of federated learning and centralised machine learning models, firstly, we established three experimental scenarios:
   (a) Federated Learning scenario: Anonymisation of the distributed datasets **D** followed by federated learning.
   (b) Centralised scenario: Anonymisation of the centralised dataset **C** followed by centralised machine learning.
   (c) Hybrid scenario: Anonymisation of the distributed datasets **D** followed by aggregation of the datasets into a single consolidated dataset for centralised machine learning.
   And then different levels of anonymization were implemented in each scenarios using generalisation and aggregation. Specifically, we tested anonymization with different degrees of k-anonymity (k-anonymity = 5, 10, 50, 100, 150, 200).
3. Exploring the trade-off between data privacy and model performance in the proposed dual-layer privacy-preserving federated learning framework. We first selected the anonymization technique that resulted in the least performance loss for the federated learning model from the previous experiment. Then, we tested the performance of the models by varying the levels of anonymization in the data collection and the levels of noise in the federated learning to find a balance between data privacy and model performance.

4 Experiments

4.1 Privacy Metrics

First, we measured the privacy metrics (K-anonymity, l-diversity, t-closeness) of the federated learning dataset and the centralised machine learning dataset on IoT-23. A higher value of K-anonymity and l-diversity and a lower value of t-closeness indicate a higher level of anonymization and better privacy of the data. Table 2 presents the results of the privacy metrics, and we can observe that the federated learning distributed dataset has lower values for each privacy metric compared to the centralised machine learning dataset.

Table 2. Anonymity metrics of distributed datasets and centralised dataset

	distributed dataset	Centralised dataset
k-anonymity	4	93
l-diversity	2	7
t-closeness	5.9	0.34

4.2   The Impact of Anonymization on Model Performance

We then compare the impact of different privacy-preserving anonymisation strategies on federated and centralised machine learning models, using generalisation, microaggregation, and increasing the k-anonymity of the data to 5, 10, 50, 100, 150 and 200. Figure 2 shows the accuracy of the models for each combination, where each bar chart represents a type of anonymization operation. The blue colour represents the accuracy of federated learning, the orange colour represents the accuracy of the hybrid scenario, and the green colour represents the accuracy of the centralised scenario.

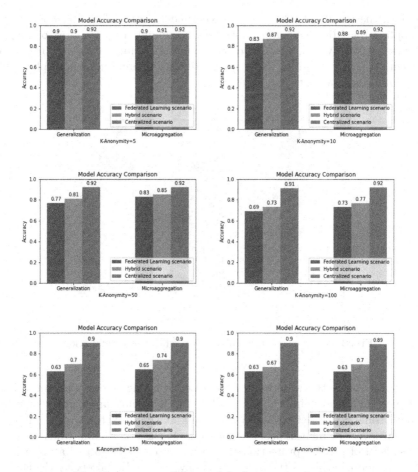

Fig. 2. Accuracy of the model after anonymisation

The results show that under the anonymity constraints we tested, regardless of the anonymization method used, the performance of centralised machine learning only slightly decreases from an initial accuracy of 92% to a minimum of 89%. For federated learning and the hybrid scenario, as the anonymity constraints increase, the model's accuracy continuously decreases, with federated learning experiencing a larger decrease. Specifically, when the k-anonymity is less than or equal to 50, the Microaggregation operation incurs the least performance loss, with accuracy of 83% for federated learning and 85% for the hybrid scenario, which are still within an acceptable range. However, when the k-anonymity is greater than 100, the accuracy of federated learning drops significantly, reaching a minimum of 63%.

4.3 Trade-Off in the Dual-Layer Framework

Based on the results of the previous experiment, in the data collection phase, we applied the Microaggregation strategy to anonymise the data to different levels (k-anonymity = 5, 10, 15). In the federated learning phase, we introduced differential privacy by adding Gaussian noise with different noise multipliers (0.5, 1.0, 1.5) during gradient computation.

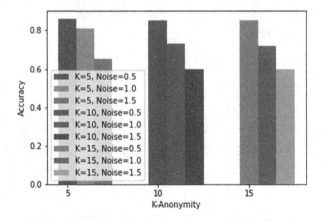

Fig. 3. Accuracy of different privacy strategies combinations.

Figure 3 shows the accuracy of federated learning under different privacy strategies. The results indicate that when the minimum anonymity constraint for data collection is set to 5 and the minimum noise factor is set to 0.5, the model achieves the highest accuracy of 85%. On the other hand, when using the highest level of privacy protection with a k-anonymity of 15 and a noise factor of 1.5, the model achieves the lowest accuracy of 61%. By observing the changes in accuracy, we can see that when the anonymity constraint for data collection is low, increasing data anonymity has less impact on the model's accuracy. However, during the model training process, the noise factor of differential privacy has a significant impact on the model's accuracy.

4.4 Evaluation and Discussion

In our work, we compared the privacy metrics (k-anonymity, l-diversity, t-closeness) between centralised machine learning datasets and distributed federated learning datasets. The results showed that the anonymity of centralised machine learning datasets was better than that of federated learning datasets. This is because in federated learning, each node only stores local data, resulting in a smaller dataset with fewer quasi-identifiers, thus leading to lower anonymity.

Additionally, we applied different anonymization techniques to federated learning, centralised machine learning, and hybrid scenarios. We found that anonymization operations had a minor impact on centralised machine learning models, while significantly affecting the accuracy of federated learning models and hybrid scenario, with the greatest impact observed on federated learning models. This is because the initial anonymity of the distributed data is lower, and achieving the same level of anonymity requires a more significant transformation of the distributed dataset, which further complicates the training of federated learning models. Among the tested anonymization techniques, microaggregation resulted in the least loss of model accuracy.

Finally, we combined privacy protection in data collection with differential privacy support in federated learning, resulting in a new dual-layer privacy protection framework. The results confirmed that within a certain range of anonymization operations (k-anonymity < 15) and the introduction of small noise perturbation (noise factor < 1), the framework could achieve dual-layer protection for data collection and utilisation while still maintaining an acceptable level of accuracy.

5 Conclusions and Future Work

This paper first compares the anonymity matrices between federated learning distributed datasets and centralised machine learning datasets using real-world datasets. It is found that the federated learning datasets have lower anonymity compared to the centralised machine learning dataset. Furthermore, the impact of different privacy-preserving anonymization strategies on federated learning and centralised machine learning models is evaluated. The results indicate that each anonymization operation leads to a decrease in the accuracy of the federated learning models compared to the centralised machine learning models. When the anonymity constraints are relatively large, the model accuracy can drop to below 70%. This is because the initial anonymity of the federated learning data is low, and a greater degree of data transformation is required to achieve the same level of anonymity. Among the tested anonymization techniques, Microaggregation exhibits the least loss in model accuracy.

Moreover, a dual-layer privacy-preserving federated learning framework is proposed. In the data collection phase, the Microaggregation strategy is applied for anonymising the data, while in the federated learning phase, differential privacy is achieved by adding Gaussian noise with different noise multipliers during the gradient computation. Evaluation on real-world datasets demonstrates the improvement in data anonymity and model performance achieved by this framework. Through these contributions, a comprehensive understanding of the impact of anonymization strategies on federated learning is gained, filling a gap in the field of privacy protection.

In the future, we will explore the impact of other anonymization strategies on federated learning, such as Top-Down Greedy Anonymisation and k-NN Clustering-Based Anonymisation. Additionally, we will compare various privacy metrics to select and apply them based on specific privacy protection requirements and scenarios, aiming to optimise the effectiveness of privacy protection measures.

References

1. Ayala-Rivera, V., McDonagh, P., Cerqueus, T., Murphy, L., et al.: A systematic comparison and evaluation of k-anonymization algorithms for practitioners. Trans. Data Priv. **7**(3), 337–370 (2014)
2. Bonawitz, K., et al.: Towards federated learning at scale: system design. Proc. Mach. Learn. Syst. **1**, 374–388 (2019)
3. Domingo-Ferrer, J., Mateo-Sanz, J.M.: Practical data-oriented microaggregation for statistical disclosure control. IEEE Trans. Knowl. Data Eng. **14**(1), 189–201 (2002)
4. Fung, B.C., Wang, K., Chen, R., Yu, P.S.: Privacy-preserving data publishing: a survey of recent developments. ACM Comput. Surv. (Csur) **42**(4), 1–53 (2010)
5. Gkoulalas-Divanis, A., Loukides, G., Sun, J.: Publishing data from electronic health records while preserving privacy: a survey of algorithms. J. Biomed. Inform. **50**, 4–19 (2014)
6. Hao, M., Li, H., Xu, G., Liu, S., Yang, H.: Towards efficient and privacy-preserving federated deep learning. In: ICC 2019–2019 IEEE International Conference on Communications (ICC), pp. 1–6. IEEE (2019)
7. Hershey, J.R., Olsen, P.A.: Approximating the Kullback-Leibler divergence between gaussian mixture models. In: 2007 IEEE International Conference on Acoustics, Speech and Signal Processing-ICASSP'07, vol. 4, pp. IV-317. IEEE (2007)
8. Jayabalan, M., Rana, M.E.: Anonymizing healthcare records: a study of privacy preserving data publishing techniques. Adv. Sci. Lett. **24**(3), 1694–1697 (2018)
9. Ji, Z., Lipton, Z.C., Elkan, C.: Differential privacy and machine learning: a survey and review. arXiv preprint arXiv:1412.7584 (2014)
10. Joyce, J.M.: Kullback-Leibler divergence. In: Lovric, M. (eds.) International Encyclopedia of Statistical Science, pp. 720–722. Springer, Berlin, Heidelberg (2011). https://doi.org/10.1007/978-3-642-04898-2_327
11. Kairouz, P., et al.: Advances and open problems in federated learning. Found. Trends® Mach. Learn. **14**(1–2), 1–210 (2021)
12. Kanwal, T., Anjum, A., Khan, A.: Privacy preservation in e-health cloud: taxonomy, privacy requirements, feasibility analysis, and opportunities. Clust. Comput. **24**, 293–317 (2021)
13. Konečný, J., McMahan, H.B., Yu, F.X., Richtárik, P., Suresh, A.T., Bacon, D.: Federated learning: strategies for improving communication efficiency (2017)

14. Langheinrich, M.: Privacy by design — principles of privacy-aware ubiquitous systems. In: Abowd, G.D., Brumitt, B., Shafer, S. (eds.) UbiComp 2001. LNCS, vol. 2201, pp. 273–291. Springer, Heidelberg (2001). https://doi.org/10.1007/3-540-45427-6_23

15. Li, L., Fan, Y., Tse, M., Lin, K.Y.: A review of applications in federated learning. Comput. Ind. Eng. **149**, 106854 (2020)

16. Li, N., Li, T., Venkatasubramanian, S.: t-closeness: privacy beyond k-anonymity and l-diversity. In: 2007 IEEE 23rd International Conference on Data Engineering, pp. 106–115. IEEE (2006)

17. Li, T., Sahu, A.K., Talwalkar, A., Smith, V.: Federated learning: challenges, methods, and future directions. IEEE Signal Process. Mag. **37**(3), 50–60 (2020)

18. Liu, B., Ding, M., Shaham, S., Rahayu, W., Farokhi, F., Lin, Z.: When machine learning meets privacy: a survey and outlook. ACM Comput. Surv. (CSUR) **54**(2), 1–36 (2021)

19. Machanavajjhala, A., Kifer, D., Gehrke, J., Venkitasubramaniam, M.: l-diversity: privacy beyond k-anonymity. ACM Trans. Knowl. Discov. Data (TKDD) **1**(1), 3-es (2007)

20. Majeed, A., Lee, S.: Anonymization techniques for privacy preserving data publishing: a comprehensive survey. IEEE Access **9**, 8512–8545 (2020). https://doi.org/10.1109/ACCESS.2020.3045700

21. McMahan, B., Moore, E., Ramage, D., Hampson, S., y Arcas, B.A.: Communication-efficient learning of deep networks from decentralized data. In: Artificial Intelligence and Statistics, pp. 1273–1282. PMLR (2017)

22. Nergiz, M.E., Atzori, M., Clifton, C.: Hiding the presence of individuals from shared databases. In: Proceedings of the 2007 ACM SIGMOD International Conference on Management of Data, pp. 665–676 (2007)

23. Parmisano, A., Garcia, S., Erquiaga, M.J.: A labeled dataset with malicious and benign IoT network traffic. Stratosphere Laboratory, Praha, Czech Republic (2020)

24. Regulation, P.: Regulation (eu) 2016/679 of the european parliament and of the council. Regulation (eu) 679, 2016 (2016)

25. Samarati, P.: Protecting respondents identities in microdata release. IEEE Trans. Knowl. Data Eng. **13**(6), 1010–1027 (2001)

26. Slijepčević, D., Henzl, M., Klausner, L.D., Dam, T., Kieseberg, P., Zeppelzauer, M.: k-Anonymity in practice: how generalisation and suppression affect machine learning classifiers. Comput. Secur. **111**, 102488 (2021)

27. Sweeney, L.: k-anonymity: a model for protecting privacy. Int. J. Uncertain. Fuzziness Knowl.-Based Syst. **10**(05), 557–570 (2002)

28. Vedangi, A., Anandam, V.: Data slicing technique to privacy preserving and data publishing. Cancer **4790**(4790), 4790 (2013)

29. Wei, K., et al.: Federated learning with differential privacy: algorithms and performance analysis. IEEE Trans. Inf. Forensics Secur. **15**, 3454–3469 (2020)

30. Wieringa, J., Kannan, P., Ma, X., Reutterer, T., Risselada, H., Skiera, B.: Data analytics in a privacy-concerned world. J. Bus. Res. **122**, 915–925 (2021)

31. Yang, H.H., Arafa, A., Quek, T.Q., Poor, H.V.: Age-based scheduling policy for federated learning in mobile edge networks. In: ICASSP 2020–2020 IEEE International Conference on Acoustics, Speech and Signal Processing (ICASSP), pp. 8743–8747. IEEE (2020)

A Privacy-Preserving Evolutionary Computation Framework for Feature Selection

Bing Sun[1], Jian-Yu Li[1(✉)], Xiao-Fang Liu[1], Qiang Yang[3], Zhi-Hui Zhan[4(✉)], and Jun Zhang[1,2]

[1] Nankai University, Tianjin, China
jianyulics@foxmail.com, junzhang@ieee.org
[2] Hanyang University, Ansan, South Korea
[3] Nanjing University of Information Science and Technology, Nanjing, China
mmmyq@126.com
[4] South China University of Technology, Guangzhou, China
zhanapollo@163.com

Abstract. Feature selection is a crucial process in data science that involves selecting the most effective subset of features. Evolutionary computation (EC) is one of the most commonly-used feature selection techniques and has demonstrated good performance, which can help find the suitable feature subset based on training data and fitness information. However, in real-world scenarios, the exact fitness information and privacy-protected data cannot be directly accessed due to privacy and security issues, which leads to a great optimization challenge. To solve such privacy-preserving feature selection problems efficiently, this paper proposes a novel EC-based feature selection framework that balances data privacy and optimization efficiency, together with three contributions. First, based on the rank-based cryptographic function that returns the rank of solutions rather than the exact fitness information, this paper proposes a new fitness function to guide the EC algorithm to approach the global optimum without knowing the exact fitness information and the dataset, thereby preserving data privacy. Second, by integrating the proposed method and EC algorithms, this paper develops a new differential evolution and particle swarm optimization algorithms for efficient feature selection. Finally, experiments are conducted on public datasets, which demonstrate that the proposed method can maintain feature selection efficiency while preserving data privacy.

Keywords: Data Science · Evolutionary Computation · Privacy Preservation · Feature Selection · Differential Evolution · Particle Swarm Optimization

1 Introduction

Feature selection is a fundamental step in the process of data science and machine learning, aiming to reduce the dimensionality of data while retaining the most informative features [1]. The importance of feature selection lies in its ability to remove redundant or irrelevant features, thus improving the efficiency and effectiveness of learning algorithm (LA) [2]. In many real-world applications, feature selection plays a crucial

F. Zhang et al. (Eds.): WISE 2023, LNCS 14306, pp. 260–274, 2023.
https://doi.org/10.1007/978-981-99-7254-8_20

role in extracting valuable information from vast amounts of data [3–6]. However, the increasing need for privacy preservation in these applications poses a major challenge to traditional feature selection methods. Privacy preservation, also known as privacy protection or data privacy preservation [7–9], refers to technology that protects personal and sensitive information from unauthorized access, disclosure, or misuse [10–13]. As feature selection algorithms require fetching original data for enhancing selection results, achieving both data privacy and good algorithm performance has become a challenging issue for researchers, impeding progress in the advancement of related fields [14].

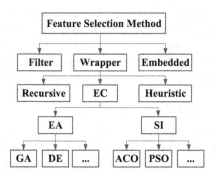

Fig. 1. The classification of feature selection algorithms.

In recent years, scholars have proposed many methods to solve feature selection problems. In general, the methods for feature selection can be categorized into three main groups: filter-based method [15], wrapper-based method [16], and embedded method [17]. Filter-based methods evaluate the relevance of features independently of the learning algorithm, using statistical measures such as correlation or mutual information [18]. Wrapper-based methods, on the other hand, utilize the learning algorithm itself to assess the quality of different feature subsets, often through a search strategy such as greedy search or evolutionary computation (EC) [16]. Embedded methods combine both feature selection and model learning, typically by incorporating a regularization term in the objective function [17].

Among these approaches, EC-based methods have attracted considerable attention due to their global search capability and adaptability to different problem domains [19], such as large-scale optimization [20–23], multi-objective optimization [24–28], data-driven optimization [29, 30], expensive optimization [31–34], and multi-task optimization [35, 36]. Evolutionary computation is a type of algorithm that simulates the evolutionary process to find the optimal solution to a problem [37–40]. Compared with traditional algorithms, EC has the advantages of global search capability, problem adaptability, and inherent parallelism. Nowadays, EC has various applications in solving optimization problems and can provide effective solutions to complex practical problems [41–44]. The EC algorithms mainly include the genetic algorithm [45], differential evolution (DE) [46–48], and particle swarm optimization (PSO) [49–53]. Among the above, the feature selection EC (FS-EC) algorithms are widely used in the field of data science and have been shown to be effective in identifying optimal or near-optimal feature subsets in a variety of applications [54].

In general, EC-based feature selection methods often require access to the complete dataset and accurate fitness information, which might not be feasible in privacy-sensitive applications. Because in fields that emphasize information security, the information required by these EC methods is not available, such as information on personal privacy and national security, which hinders the feature selection process [55]. To address this limitation, researchers have proposed alternative methods, such as the data obfuscation method [56], secure multiparty computation method [57], and homomorphic encryption method [58], which enable computation on encrypted data without revealing the underlying information.

However, existing privacy-preserving optimization methods often suffer from reduced optimization efficiency or increased computational complexity. Recently, Zhan *et al.* [59] proposed a privacy-preserving EC framework with a rank-based cryptographic function for efficiently solving continuous optimization problems in privacy-preserving environments. Inspired by this, we propose a novel EC-based feature selection framework that strikes a balance between data privacy and feature selection efficiency. Specifically, our contributions are as follows:

(1) We propose a new fitness function based on the rank-based cryptographic function that returns the rank of solutions rather than the exact fitness information, enabling the EC algorithm to approach the global optimum without knowing the exact fitness information and the dataset, thereby preserving data privacy and enhancing feature selection results.
(2) Based on the proposed rank-based cryptographic fitness function, we propose feature selection DE (FS-DE) and PSO (FS-PSO), and develop a new EC-based privacy-preserving methods.
(3) Extensive experiments are conducted on benchmark datasets, and the experimental results prove that the proposed algorithm can effectively accomplish the feature selection task while ensuring privacy protection.

The rest of this paper is organized as follows. Section 2 reviews the development of FS-EC and the privacy preservation problem. Section 3 presents a framework for privacy-preserving and feature selection ECs based on this framework. Section 4 demonstrates the effectiveness of the proposed algorithm through experiments. Finally, conclusions are given in Sect. 5.

2 Related Work

Feature selection is an important problem in machine learning. The algorithms for solving the feature selection problem can be mainly divided into three categories, which are filtering method, wrapping method, and embedding method, as shown in Fig. 1. Among these methods, the wrapping method can consider the interaction and complex relationship between features and adapt to different types of machine learning models, which has strong generality and been studied by many scholars. The feature selection methods based on evolutionary computation usually belong to the wrapping method, which guides the evolutionary direction of the algorithm through the fitness function [60]. Features selection-oriented EC can be divided into two categories, one is evolutionary algorithm

[61] and the other is swarm intelligence [16], both have shown excellent performance in feature selection.

Nowadays, FS-EC researchers mainly focus on the improvement of EC algorithms [20]. For example, Zhou et al. [62] improved the feature selection efficiency of GA by introducing a clustering algorithm to partition the data, which led to a more accurate classification of the support vector machine (SVM). To address the large-scale feature selection problem, Jia et al. [16] proposed a novel PSO with fuzzy learning for large-scale feature selection, which employs N-base encoding for particle representation, incorporates Hamming distance and fuzzy learning into the particle update process for discrete optimization, and includes a dynamic dimension skipping local search strategy to reduce search space and runtime. Yang et al. [20] proposed a bi-directional feature fixation (BDFF) framework for PSO to address the challenge of large-scale feature selection in Big Data environments. BDFF employs two opposite search directions to guide particles in exploring feature subsets of different sizes, effectively reducing the search space, and the self-adaptive strategy enhances the balance between exploration and exploitation. Meenachi et al. [63] employed fuzzy rough evaluation as fitness function to guide the feature selection process of DE and ant colony optimization (ACO). Experiments show that the accuracy, efficiency, and precision of FS-ECs are all improved by fuzzy rough set.

The privacy preservation problem can be defined as selecting a subset of features from a given dataset while ensuring the privacy of sensitive information contained in the dataset, and the objective is to identify a minimal set of features that maximizes the utility and performance of a specific data analysis, or machine learning task, while minimizing the disclosure risk of sensitive information, such problems can involve feature selection, data analysis, or computation while preserving privacy [64]. The privacy preservation has a wide use in social ethics [65], data science [66], cybersecurity [67], and other fields. Therefore, the study of privacy preservation is valuable for protecting sensitive information, addressing ethical concerns, ensuring legal compliance, and enabling secure data analysis and innovation.

Although ECs have achieved great success in feature selection problems, there is little research related to ECs for privacy-preserving feature selection problems [59]. Because if an EC cannot obtain either the original data or the fitness of the population, the evolutionary algorithm without fitness guidance will degenerate into a random algorithm. Therefore, solving the problem of privacy-preserving feature selection is important for the development of EC and data science.

3 Proposed Method

3.1 General Framework

Evolutionary computation is a powerful and widely used feature selection technique, the users only need to provide fitness information on the selection results without concern for the specific implementation process. However, in privacy-preserving feature selection problems, fitness information cannot be directly provided, which results in a lack of guidance for the evolutionary process of EC and makes it difficult to obtain an optimal solution. Therefore, this section proposes a rank-based cryptographic function to conceal fitness information and enable its encrypted information to guide the evolutionary process of EC.

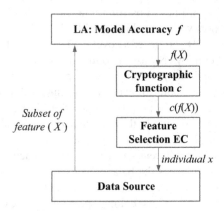

Fig. 2. The framework of EC for privacy-preserving feature selection.

During the optimization process, EC needs to perform multiple generations of evolution to select the optimal solution, and each evolution requires the user to evaluate the evolution results. As shown in Fig. 2, in the generation, EC sends the individuals x to the data owner, and subsequently, the data owner provides the feature-selected data X to the LA model for learning and testing. Then, the results of the feature selection are derived in the form of prediction accuracy $f(X)$. However, due to the need for privacy-preserving, $f(X)$ needs to be encrypted. Therefore, the cryptographic function encrypts $f(X)$ as $c(f(X))$, which retains only information about the relative merits of the data and hides the actual accuracy values. Finally, EC adjusts the evolutionary process after obtaining $c(f(X))$ to produce better results with fewer features and higher accuracy. The formula of the cryptographic function is as follows:

$$c(f(X)) = rank(f(X)) \tag{1}$$

where X is the feature subset of the original features, c is the cryptographic function that returns the rank of $f(X)$ according to ascending order.

The encryption function hides the true accuracy value by ranking, which may cause the duplicate evaluation of the same X, which led to the waste of computational resources. Therefore, this paper uses a local cache database on the LA model side, where all evaluated X are recorded. If a new X' is the same as X in the database, the value of $f(X)$ will be directly assigned to $f(X')$, thereby preventing the LA from re-evaluating. When the ranking is obtained, EC will combine the ranking information and the size of the feature subset for a comprehensive evaluation, to select the most representative feature subset.

In feature selection, the effectiveness of selected features should be evaluated by two main metrics, which are the size of the feature subset *dim* and the ranking given by the cryptographic function *rank*. Therefore, the proposed fitness function can be calculated as follows:

$$F(x_i) = \frac{c(f(X_i))}{N} + \frac{dim_i}{D} \tag{2}$$

where X_i is the feature subset obtained from the individual x_i, $f(X_i)$ is the model accuracy, $c(f(X_i))$ is the accuracy rank of i-th individual, which is obtained by the cryptographic function, N is the population size, D is the dimension of the features, and dim_i is the dimension of feature subsets.

3.2 Feature Selection DE with Privacy-Preserving

The pseudo-code of feature selection DE (FS-DE) with privacy-preserving is presented in Fig. 3. Which also includes the feature selection of data source, training of the LA model, and the processing of cryptographic function.

Essentially, FS is a selection of features in each dimension, the selection results should consist of a sequence of Boolean values. However, the original DE is designed for continuous problems, where the individual is encoded as a sequence of continuous values. Therefore, this algorithm encodes individuals with continuous values when performing evolutionary operations, and binarizes them when feature selection is performed. Specifically, in the beginning, each dimension of the individual is initialized to a value within $[0, 2]$, and when the evolution is over, the individual needs to be binarized as follows:

$$d_i = \begin{cases} 1 & d_i \geq 1 \\ 0 & d_i < 1 \end{cases} \tag{3}$$

where d_i is the value of i-th dimension of the individual, "1" means the feature of the dimension is selected, and "0" means it is not selected.

Evolutionary operations generate new individuals by changing the genetic combinations of individuals in a population and gradually optimize the fitness of these individuals. In FS-DE, the evolutionary operation mainly contains two parts: mutation, and crossover. Specifically, the i-th individual produces its offspring v_i by mutation, as shown in formula (4):

$$v_i = x_{r_1} + F \cdot (x_{r_2} - x_{r_3}) \tag{4}$$

where r_1, r_2, and r_3 are indexes of individuals randomly selected from the population, and F is a scaling factor to control the degree of selection of the difference vector, which is a real number between 0 and 1. Then, the crossover operation as shown in formula (5):

$$u_{i,d} = \begin{cases} v_{i,d} & \text{if } rand() < Cr \text{ or } d = d_{rand} \\ x_{i,d} & \text{else} \end{cases} \tag{5}$$

where $rand()$ is a random function that returns a value between 0 and 1, Cr is a parameter that controls the crossover probability for each individual to introduce external information, d is the dimension of $u_{i,d}$, and d_{rand} is the random dimension.

Next, individuals x and their offspring u need to be evaluated. However, the results of the LA model are private to FS-DE, which needs to send the results of feature selection (binarized x and u) to the data source. Based on the received information, the data source sends feature subsets to the model for training and testing to obtain the accuracy of the model. Finally, the cryptographic function ranks the accuracy and returns it to the FS-DE, which then performs the fitness calculation according to formula (2). After the fitness evaluation, if u_i has a better fitness, x_i will be replaced, otherwise, x_i will be retained.

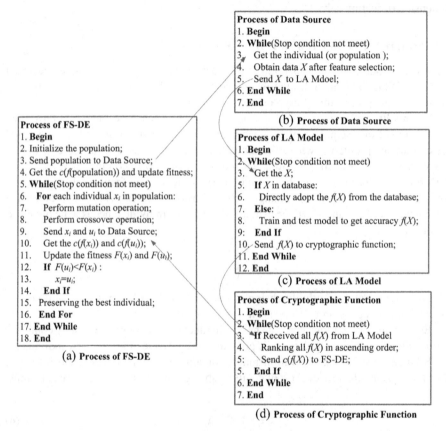

Fig. 3. Pseudo-code of feature selection DE with privacy-preserving.

Through the above process, FS-DE completes feature selection with the assistance of cryptographic functions, and the efficiency of the evolution results are also verified in the LA model, satisfying the privacy and feature selection requirements.

3.3 Feature Selection PSO with Privacy-Preserving

The pseudo-code of feature selection PSO (FS-PSO) with privacy-preserving as shown in Fig. 4. Since the various modules of the framework proposed in this paper are generic, the feature selection, training of LA model, and processing of cryptographic functions of FS-PSO are the same as those in FS-DE.

```
Process of FS-PSO
1. Begin
2. Initialize the population;
3. Send population to Data Source;
4. Get the c(f(X)) and update fitness F;
5. Update the gbest and pbest;
6. While(Stop condition not meet)
7.    For each particle pᵢ in population:
8.       Update speed vᵢ and position xᵢ;
9.       Send pᵢ and pbestᵢ to Data Source;
10.      Get the c(f(pᵢ)) and c(f(pbestᵢ)));
11.      Update the fitness F(pᵢ) and F(pbestᵢ);
12.      If F(pᵢ)<F(pbestᵢ) :
13.         pbestᵢ=pᵢ;
14.         If F(pbestᵢ)<F(gbest):
16:            gbest=pbestᵢ;
17:         End If
18.      End If
19.   End For
20. End While
21. End
```

Fig. 4. Pseudo-code of feature selection PSO with privacy-preserving n.

FS-PSO updates the velocity and position of each particle in each generation, where the velocity of each particle is affected by its personal best solution *pbest* and the global best solution *gbest* found by the swarm. This collaborative behavior ensures that all particles search toward the direction of the global best solution, thereby endowing the algorithm with global search capability.

The FS-PSO adopts a string of floating-point data encoded in a continuous search space for the particles, however, different from the traditional PSO, the extraction results and evaluation of the particles require the conversion of the floating-point data to binary, with the same conversion rules as formula (3). Due to the same optimization objective, the FS-PSO and FS-DE use the same fitness function, as formula (2).

At the beginning of the algorithm, each dimension of the position x in the particle is initialized to a random value between 0 and 1. Subsequently, *gbest* and *pbest* are selected by evaluating the population, and then, the velocity v and position x of each particle is updated, and the velocity and position of the particle is updated as follows:

$$v_i^d = w v_i^d + c_1 rand_1^d (gbest_i^d - x_i^d) + c_2 rand_2^d (pbest_i^d - x_i^d) \tag{6}$$

$$x_i^d = x_i^d + v_i^d \tag{7}$$

where w is the inertia weight, c_1 and c_2 are learning factors to control the effect of *pbest* and *gbest* on particle velocity, $rand_1$ and $rand_2$ are uniform random numbers that take values between 0 and 1.

Table 1. Basic Information about the Test Sets.

Test Set ID	Test Set Name	#All Features	KNN Accuracy
1	Dry Bean	16	0.685
2	Image Segmentation	19	0.813
3	German Credit Data	24	0.766
4	Dermatology	33	0.907
5	Ionosphere	34	0.863

When the positions of all the particles are updated, the particles, along with the personal best solution *pbest* and the global best solution *gbest*, are sent to the data source, which decodes particles to Booleans according to formula (3), to derive the selected feature subsets X and send them to the LA model. Next, the LA model evaluates the received X and wants to send the $f(X)$ to the encryption function $c()$. Finally, the cryptographic function ranks the accuracy and returns $c(f(X))$ to FS-PSO for calculating fitness as formula (2). The whole process will be repeated until the stopping condition is reached.

4 Experiments

4.1 Experimental Settings

In order to test the effectiveness of the privacy-preserving evolutionary computation framework proposed in this paper, we select public test sets from the fields of biology, medicine, image recognition, finance, and meteorology (marked as, Dry Bean [68], Image Segmentation [69], German Credit Data [70], Dermatology [71], and Ionosphere [72]), for comparison of the feature selection effects under privacy protection. We compare FS-DE and FS-PSO without privacy-preserving, and FS-DE and FS-PSO with the introduced privacy-preserving framework (marked as PPFS-DE and PPFS-PSO, respectively). To evaluate the accuracy of the selected feature subset, we first randomly shuffled the original data and used the first 80% of the data as the training set and the remaining 20% as the test set. We select KNN as the LA model, to compare the accuracy before and after feature selection, all settings of KNN are the default settings of Scikit-learn. Because different problems have different dimensions, we adopt the maximum fitness evaluation times as the stopping condition of the algorithm. If the fitness evaluation reaches $1000 \times D$, the algorithm stops, where D is the dimension of the feature. In this paper, the mutation strategy used in FS-DE is DE/rand/1, the scaling factor F is set to 0.9, the crossover probability Cr is set to 0.5, and the population size is 100. The inertia weight w of FS-PSO is 0.9, the values of c_1 and c_2 are both 0.5, and the population size is 100. To ensure generality, each experiment is independently run 30 times and the average value is taken. Table 1 lists the basic information of the test set selected in this paper.

4.2 Experimental Results of FS-EC with Privacy-Preserving Framework

The experimental results of FS-DE and PPFS-DE are shown in Table 2, where "Accuracy" indicates the average accuracy of the KNN model in 30 runs, "#Feature" denotes the average size of the selected feature subset after feature selection, for cases where the mean is not an integer, we take 10^{-1} precision. The experimental results show that FS-DE and PPFS-DE perform well on most of the test sets, not only extracting smaller feature subsets but also improving the accuracy of the model. Although the accuracy obtained in test 3 is slightly lower than the original data, the DE also significantly reduces the number of features. In summary, compared with FS-DE, PPFS-DE adds privacy protection, but the performance of the algorithm does not weaken as a result, thus proving the performance of the proposed privacy-preserving framework.

The experimental results of FS-PSO and PPFS-PSO are shown in Table 3. The experimental results show that FS-PSO and PPFS-PSO have excellent performance on most test sets and can complete the feature selection work efficiently, and the performance of PPFS-PSO is not weakened by the addition of privacy-preserving. Moreover, by comparing the experimental results in Table 2 and Table 3, we can find that the PSO-based feature selection algorithm proposed in this paper works better than the DE-based feature selection algorithms.

Table 2. Experimental Results of FS-DE and PPFS-DE on the Test Sets.

Test Set ID	FS-DE		PPFS-DE	
	Accuracy	#Feature	Accuracy	#Feature
1	0.864+	2	0.865+	2
2	0.850+	2	0.852+	2
3	0.716−	3	0.718−	3
4	0.950+	5.6	0.946+	5.3
5	0.917+	3.2	0.912+	3

Table 3. Experimental Results of FS-PSO and PPFS-PSO on the Test Sets.

Test Set ID	FS-PSO		PPFS-PSO	
	Accuracy	#Feature	Accuracy	#Feature
1	0.887+	2	0.887+	2
2	0.891+	2	0.877+	2
3	0.735−	2	0.734−	2
4	0.956+	6.2	0.945+	6
5	0.917+	2.2	0.916+	2.1

Notes: " +" indicates better than the accuracy of the original model, and "−" indicates lower than the accuracy of the original model without feature selection

5 Conclusion

This paper explores the application of EC in the field of feature selection with privacy protection, designs a privacy-preserving framework for feature selection using EC, and develops the feature selection DE and PSO based on this framework. Experimental results show that our algorithm and framework can efficiently perform feature selection while preserving privacy. In future work, we plan to design additional EC algorithms based on the privacy-preserving framework. Moreover, we aim to enhance the privacy-preserving framework to address other feature selection problems, including the privacy of the number of features, the privacy of ranking information in selection results, and a series of other privacy-related concerns.

Acknowledgment. This work was supported in part by the National Natural Science Foundation of China (NSFC) under Grant 62176094, and in part by the National Research Foundation of Korea under Grant NRF-2022H1D3A2A01093478 and Grant NRF-2020R1C1C1013806.

References

1. Li, J., et al.: Feature selection: a data perspective. ACM Comput. Surv. **50**(6), 1–45 (2017)
2. Cai, J., Luo, J., Wang, S., Yang, S.: Feature selection in machine learning: a new perspective. Neurocomputing **300**, 70–79 (2018)
3. Gao, M., Li, J.Y., Chen, C.H., Li, Y., Zhang, J., Zhan, Z.H.: Enhanced multi-task learning and knowledge graph-based recommender system. IEEE Trans. Knowl. Data Eng. **35**(10), 10281–10294 (2023)
4. Zhan, Z.H., Li, J.Y., Zhang, J.: Evolutionary deep learning: a survey. Neurocomputing **483**, 42–58 (2022)
5. Xiao, H., Huang, G., Xiong, G., Jiang, W., Dai, H.: A NOx emission prediction hybrid method based on boiler data feature subset selection. World Wide Web **26**(4), 1811–1825 (2023). https://doi.org/10.1007/s11280-022-01107-1
6. Li, Y., Zheng, Z., Dai, H.N., Wong, R.C.W., Xie, H.: Profit-based deep architecture with integration of reinforced data selector to enhance trend-following strategy. World Wide Web **26**(4), 1685–1705 (2023). https://doi.org/10.1007/s11280-022-01112-4

7. Mahanan, W., Chaovalitwongse, W.A., Natwichai, J.: Data privacy preservation algorithm with k-anonymity. World Wide Web **24**(5), 1551–1561 (2021). https://doi.org/10.1007/s11 280-021-00922-2

8. Muhammad, T., Ahmad, A.: A joint sharing approach for online privacy preservation. World Wide Web **24**(3), 895–924 (2021). https://doi.org/10.1007/s11280-021-00876-5

9. Jia, D., Yang, G., Huang, M., Xin, J., Wang, G., Yuan, G.Y.: An efficient privacy-preserving blockchain storage method for internet of things environment. World Wide Web (2023). https://doi.org/10.1007/s11280-023-01172-0

10. You, M., et al.: A knowledge graph empowered online learning framework for access control decision-making. World Wide Web **26**(2), 827–848 (2023). https://doi.org/10.1007/s11280-022-01076-5

11. Kong, L., et al.: LSH-aware multitype health data prediction with privacy preservation in edge environment. World Wide Web **25**(5), 1793–1808 (2022). https://doi.org/10.1007/s11 280-021-00941-z

12. Ge, Y.-F., Orlowska, M., Cao, J., Wang, H., Zhang, Y.: MDDE: multitasking distributed differential evolution for privacy-preserving database fragmentation. VLDB J. **31**(5), 957–975 (2022). https://doi.org/10.1007/s00778-021-00718-w

13. Vimalachandran, P., Liu, H., Lin, Y., Ji, K., Wang, H., Zhang, Y.: Improving accessibility of the Australian My Health Records while preserving privacy and security of the system. Health Inf. Sci. Syst. **8**(1), 1–9 (2020). https://doi.org/10.1007/s13755-020-00126-4

14. Braun, T., Fung, B.C.M., Iqbal, F., Shah, B.: Security and privacy challenges in smart cities. Sustain. Cities Soc. **39**, 499–507 (2018)

15. Santana, L.E.A.S., Canuto, A.M.P.: Filter-based optimization techniques for selection of feature subsets in ensemble systems. Expert Syst. Appl. **41**(4, Part 2), 1622–1631 (2014)

16. Yang, J.Q., Chen, C.H., Li, J.Y., Liu, D., Li, T., Zhan, Z.H.: Compressed-encoding particle swarm optimization with fuzzy learning for large-scale feature selection. Symmetry **14**(6), 1142 (2022)

17. Liu, H., Zhou, M., Liu, Q.: An embedded feature selection method for imbalanced data classification. IEEE/CAA J. Autom. Sin. **6**(3), 703–715 (2019)

18. Siddiqi, M.A., Pak, W.: Optimizing filter-based feature selection method flow for intrusion detection system. Electronics **9**(12), 1–18 (2020)

19. Zhan, Z.H., Wang, Z.J., Jin, H., Zhang, J.: Adaptive distributed differential evolution. IEEE Trans. Cybern. **50**(11), 4633–4647 (2020)

20. Yang, J.Q., et al.: Bi-directional feature fixation-based particle swarm optimization for large-scale feature selection. IEEE Trans. Big Data **9**(3), 1004–1017 (2023)

21. Zhang, X., et al.: Graph-based deep decomposition for overlapping large-scale optimization problems. IEEE Trans. Syst. Man Cybern. Syst. **53**(4), 2374–2386 (2023)

22. Li, J.Y., Zhan, Z.H., Tan, K.C., Zhang, J.: Dual differential grouping: a more general decomposition method for large-scale optimization. IEEE Trans. Cybern. **53**(6), 3624–3638 (2023)

23. Du, K.J., Li, J.Y., Wang, H., Zhang, J.: Multi-objective multi-criteria evolutionary algorithm for multi-objective multi-task optimization. Complex Intell. Syst. **9**(2), 1211–1228 (2023). https://doi.org/10.1007/s40747-022-00650-8

24. Yang, Q., et al.: A distributed swarm optimizer with adaptive communication for large-scale optimization. IEEE Trans. Cybern. **50**(7), 3393–3408 (2020)

25. Ge, Y.F., et al.: DSGA: a distributed segment-based genetic algorithm for multi-objective outsourced database partitioning. Inf. Sci. **612**, 864–886 (2022)

26. Yang, Q.T., Zhan, Z.H., Kwong, S., Zhang, J.: Multiple populations for multiple objectives framework with bias sorting for many-objective optimization. IEEE Trans. Evol. Comput. **27**(5), 1340–1354 (2023)

27. Jiang, Y., Zhan, Z.H., Tan, K.C., Zhang, J.: Block-level knowledge transfer for evolutionary multitask optimization. IEEE Trans. Cybern. (2023). Early Access. https://doi.org/10.1109/TCYB.2023.3273625
28. Li, J.Y., et al.: A multipopulation multiobjective ant colony system considering travel and prevention costs for vehicle routing in COVID-19-like epidemics. IEEE Trans. Intell. Transp. Syst. 23(12), 25062–25076 (2022)
29. Li, J.Y., Zhan, Z.H., Wang, C., Jin, H., Zhang, J.: Boosting data-driven evolutionary algorithm with localized data generation. IEEE Trans. Evol. Comput. 24(5), 923–937 (2020)
30. Li, J.Y., Zhan, Z.H., Wang, H., Zhang, J.: Data-driven evolutionary algorithm with perturbation-based ensemble surrogates. IEEE Trans. Cybern. 51(8), 3925–3937 (2021)
31. Li, J.Y., Zhan, Z.H., Zhang, J.: Evolutionary computation for expensive optimization: a survey. Mach. Intell. Res. 19(1), 3–23 (2022). https://doi.org/10.1007/s11633-022-1317-4
32. Wu, S.H., Zhan, Z.H., Zhang, J.: SAFE: scale-adaptive fitness evaluation method for expensive optimization problems. IEEE Trans. Evol. Comput. 25(3), 478–491 (2021)
33. Wang, Y.Q., Li, J.Y., Chen, C.H., Zhang, J., Zhan, Z.H.: Scale adaptive fitness evaluation-based particle swarm optimization for hyperparameter and architecture optimization in neural networks and deep learning. CAAI Trans. Intell. Technol. 8(3), 849–862 (2022)
34. Wei, F.F., et al.: A classifier-assisted level-based learning swarm optimizer for expensive optimization. IEEE Trans. Evol. Comput. 25(2), 219–233 (2021)
35. Li, J.Y., Zhan, Z.H., Tan, K.C., Zhang, J.: A meta-knowledge transfer-based differential evolution for multitask optimization. IEEE Trans. Evol. Comput. 26(4), 719–734 (2022)
36. Wu, S.H., Zhan, Z.H., Tan, K.C., Zhang, J.: Transferable adaptive differential evolution for many-task optimization. IEEE Trans. Cybern. (2023). Early Access. https://doi.org/10.1109/TCYB.2023.3234969
37. Zhan, Z.H., Li, J.Y., Kwong, S., Zhang, J.: Learning-aided evolution for optimization. IEEE Trans. Evol. Comput. (2022). Early Access. https://doi.org/10.1109/TEVC.2022.3232776
38. Zhan, Z.H., et al.: Matrix-based evolutionary computation. IEEE Trans. Emerg. Top. Comput. Intell. 6(2), 315–328 (2022)
39. Kumar, D., Baranwal, G., Shankar, Y., Vidyarthi, D.P.: A survey on nature-inspired techniques for computation offloading and service placement in emerging edge technologies. World Wide Web 25(5), 2049–2107 (2022). https://doi.org/10.1007/s11280-022-01053-y
40. Yang, Q., Chen, W.N., Li, Y., Chen, C.L.P., Xu, X.M., Zhang, J.: Multimodal estimation of distribution algorithms. IEEE Trans. Cybern. 47(3), 636–650 (2017)
41. Zhou, H., Song, M., Pedrycz, W.: A comparative study of improved GA and PSO in solving multiple traveling salesmen problem. Appl. Soft Comput. 64, 564–580 (2018)
42. Zhang, X., Zhan, Z.H., Fang, W., Qian, P., Zhang, J.: Multipopulation ant colony system with knowledge-based local searches for multiobjective supply chain configuration. IEEE Trans. Evol. Comput. 26(3), 512–526 (2022)
43. Wang, C., et al.: A novel evolutionary algorithm with column and sub-block local search for sudoku puzzles. IEEE Trans. Games (2023). Early Access. https://doi.org/10.1109/TG.2023.3236490
44. Guo, F., Tang, B., Tang, M.: Joint optimization of delay and cost for microservice composition in mobile edge computing. World Wide Web 25(5), 2019–2047 (2022). https://doi.org/10.1007/s11280-022-01017-2
45. Mirjalili, S., Song Dong, J., Sadiq, A.S., Faris, H.: Genetic algorithm: theory, literature review, and application in image reconstruction. In: Mirjalili, S., Song Dong, J., Lewis, A. (eds.) Nature-Inspired Optimizers. SCI, vol. 811, pp. 69–85. Springer, Cham (2020). https://doi.org/10.1007/978-3-030-12127-3_5
46. Wang, Z.J., Jian, J.R., Zhan, Z.H., Li, Y., Kwong, S., Zhang, J.: Gene targeting differential evolution: a simple and efficient method for large-scale optimization. IEEE Trans. Evol. Comput. 27(4), 964–979 (2023)

47. Li, J.Y., Du, K.J., Zhan, Z.H., Wang, H., Zhang, J.: Distributed differential evolution with adaptive resource allocation. IEEE Trans. Cybern. **53**(5), 2791–2804 (2023)
48. Zhang, J., et al.: Proximity ranking-based multimodal differential evolution. Swarm Evol. Comput. **78**, 101277 (2023)
49. Wang, D., Tan, D., Liu, L.: Particle swarm optimization algorithm: an overview. Soft. Comput. **22**(2), 387–408 (2018). https://doi.org/10.1007/s00500-016-2474-6
50. Yang, Q., Chen, W.N., Deng, J.D., Li, Y., Gu, T., Zhang, J.: A level-based learning swarm optimizer for large-scale optimization. IEEE Trans. Evol. Comput. **22**(4), 578–594 (2018)
51. Yang, Q., et al.: An adaptive stochastic dominant learning swarm optimizer for high-dimensional optimization. IEEE Trans. Cybern. **52**(3), 1960–1976 (2022)
52. Li, J.Y., et al.: Generation-level parallelism for evolutionary computation: a pipeline-based parallel particle swarm optimization. IEEE Trans. Cybern. **51**(10), 4848–4859 (2021)
53. Guo, Y., Li, J.Y., Zhan, Z.H.: Efficient hyperparameter optimization for convolution neural networks in deep learning: a distributed particle swarm optimization approach. Cybern. Syst. **52**(1), 36–57 (2020)
54. Bhandari, S., Pathak, S., Jain, S.A.: A literature review of early-stage diabetic retinopathy detection using deep learning and evolutionary computing techniques. Arch. Comput. Methods Eng. **30**(2), 799–810 (2023). https://doi.org/10.1007/s11831-022-09816-6
55. Osia, S.A., Taheri, A., Shamsabadi, A.S., Katevas, K., Haddadi, H., Rabiee, H.R.: Deep private-feature extraction. IEEE Trans. Knowl. Data Eng. **32**(1), 54–66 (2020)
56. Xu, C., Ren, J., Zhang, D., Zhang, Y.: Distilling at the edge: a local differential privacy obfuscation framework for IoT data analytics. IEEE Commun. Mag. **56**(8), 20–25 (2018)
57. Gao, C., Yu, J.: SecureRC: a system for privacy-preserving relation classification using secure multi-party computation. Comput. Secur. **128**, 103142 (2023)
58. Yang, H., Huang, Y., Yong, Yu., Yao, M., Zhang, X.: Privacy-preserving extraction of hog features based on integer vector homomorphic encryption. In: Liu, J.K., Samarati, P. (eds.) Information Security Practice and Experience, pp. 102–117. Springer, Cham (2017). https://doi.org/10.1007/978-3-319-72359-4_6
59. Zhan, Z.H., Wu, S.H., Zhang, J.: A new evolutionary computation framework for privacy-preserving optimization. In: International Conference on Advanced Computational Intelligence, pp. 220–226 (2021)
60. Xue, B., Zhang, M., Browne, W.N., Yao, X.: A survey on evolutionary computation approaches to feature selection. IEEE Trans. Evol. Comput. **20**(4), 606–626 (2016)
61. Tao, J., Zhang, R.: Intelligent feature selection using ga and neural network optimization for real-time driving pattern recognition. IEEE Trans. Intell. Transp. Syst. **23**(8), 12665–12674 (2022)
62. Zhou, T., Lu, H.L., Wang, W.W., Yong, X.: GA-SVM based feature selection and parameter optimization in hospitalization expense modeling. Appl. Soft Comput. **75**, 323–332 (2019)
63. Meenachi, L., Ramakrishnan, S.: Differential evolution and ACO based global optimal feature selection with fuzzy rough set for cancer data classification. Soft. Comput. **24**(24), 18463–18475 (2020)
64. Bhuyan, H.K., Kamila, N.K.: Privacy preserving sub-feature selection in distributed data mining. Appl. Soft Comput. **36**, 552–569 (2015)
65. Usynin, D., et al.: Adversarial interference and its mitigations in privacy-preserving collaborative machine learning. Nat. Mach. Intell. **3**(9), 749–758 (2021)
66. Iezzi, M.: Practical privacy-preserving data science with homomorphic encryption: an overview. In: IEEE International Conference on Big Data, pp. 3979–3988 (2020)
67. Vakilinia, I., Tosh, D.K., Sengupta, S.: Privacy-preserving cybersecurity information exchange mechanism. In: International Symposium on Performance Evaluation of Computer and Telecommunication Systems, pp. 1–7 (2017)

68. UCI Machine Learning Repository: Dry Bean Dataset. https://doi.org/10.24432/C50S4B. Accessed 19 June 2023
69. UCI Machine Learning Repository: Image Segmentation Dataset. https://doi.org/10.24432/C5GP4N. Accessed 19 June 2023
70. Hofmann, H.: Statlog (German Credit Data). https://doi.org/10.24432/C5NC77. Accessed 19 June 2023
71. Ilter, N.A.G., Dermatology. https://doi.org/10.24432/C5FK5P. Accessed 19 June 2023
72. Sigillito, V., Wing, S., Hutton, L., Baker, K.: Ionosphere. https://doi.org/10.24432/C5W01B. Accessed 19 June 2023

Local Difference-Based Federated Learning Against Preference Profiling Attacks

Qian Zhou[1,2]($\boxtimes$) (ID), Zhongxu Han[1], and Jiayang Wu[1]

[1] Nanjing University of Posts and Telecommunications, Nanjing 210003, China
`zhouqian@njupt.edu.cn`
[2] Key Laboratory of Safety-Critical Software (NUAA), Ministry of Industry and Information Technology, Nanjing 210016, China

Abstract. The recommendation system based on federated learning has become one of the most popular distributed machine learning technologies, which to some extent protects the privacy and security of users. However, personal privacy information can still be disclosed through privacy inference attacks. In order to resist preference profiling attack (PPA), we propose a differential privacy federated learning recommendation method based on federated neural collaborative filtering. We construct a neural collaborative filtering recommendation method based on federated learning with local differential privacy, which can achieve the effect similar to that of federal neural collaborative filtering recommendation. First, we compared three instances of neural collaborative filtering, i.e., Multi-Layer Perceptron (MLP), Generalized Matrix Factorization (GMF), and Neural Matrix Factorization (NeuMF) combined with federated learning, under the same conditions, in order to select the optimal instance. And then the training parameters varied using Gaussian noise of the gradient of the uninteracted items and Laplace noise of the interacted items. Under the same evaluation indicators, the training loss rate has decreased by 1.61%, and the recommendation hit rate hit_ratio@10 was improved by 3.05%, normalize discounted cumulative gain ndcg@10 was reduced by 2.55%. The experimental results validated the feasibility of this method, indicating that the improvement of the algorithm is effective.

Keywords: Differential Privacy · Federated Learning · Neural Collaborative Filtering · Preference Profiling Attack

1 Introduction

In recent years, due to the popularization of mobile devices such as mobile phones, China's mobile Internet industry has developed rapidly. According to the "Statistical Report on Internet Development in China" released by the China Internet Network Information Center for the 50th time, as of June 2022, the

F. Zhang et al. (Eds.): WISE 2023, LNCS 14306, pp. 275–288, 2023.
https://doi.org/10.1007/978-981-99-7254-8_21

Internet penetration rate in China has reached 74.4%. The report shows that the number of Internet users in China has reached 1.051 billion, and this scale is still growing steadily. It is particularly worth noting that the number of short video users has shown the most significant growth, reaching 962 million, an increase of 28.05 million compared to December 2021, accounting for 91.5% of the entire Internet user population [1]. In addition to short videos, there are many industries similar to it, such as news. With the rapid development of various industries, massive amounts of information are generated on the Internet every day, and users wanting to find their favorite information among them is tantamount to finding a needle in a haystack. Therefore, a recommendation system emerged as the times require. Through the recommendation system, massive data can be integrated and accurately pushed to users, reducing the cost of data screening for users.

With the promulgation and implementation of the General Data Protection Regulation [2] and other privacy data protection laws and regulations, as well as the enhancement of people's awareness of privacy protection, the privacy security of personal data has been paid more and more attention [3]. However, most of the current recommendation systems run on a central server, and the users' personal information and the interaction information between users and items are also stored on the central server, so the recommendation system faces the problem of user privacy leakage.

In order to solve the problem of privacy leakage faced by the recommendation system, Google proposed the federated learning paradigm [4] so that the user's original data is kept locally, and various privacy protection technologies can be comprehensively used locally on the user side to achieve better the purpose of protecting user privacy [5]. However, the application of the federated learning framework has many limitations, and it is not absolutely safe in practical applications. There are many attack methods that can threaten the data security in the federated learning process [6]. For instance, Li et al. [7] trained a poisoned model with a poisoned data set and replaced the neural pathways of the target model with its neural pathways to achieve poisoning attacks; Wang et al. [8] used toxic adversarial samples for model training and improved learning rate to accelerate the generation of poisoning models, thus improving the attack performance of poisoning attacks. The above two examples are poisoning attacks. In addition, reasoning attacks are the most typical attack methods faced by federated learning, threatening the privacy of users [9]. The difference can be divided into attribute reasoning attack and member reasoning attack [10]. Recently, some scholars have studied various inference attacks that federated learning may suffer, and proposed a new inference attack method, that is, preference profiling attack (PPA) [11]. This attack can analyze the local model gradient uploaded from each user's end thus obtaining private information such as user's preference for items [12], which is a serious threat to the user's privacy and security [13]. Therefore it is important to find a way to defend against the preference PPA of federated learning in practical applications.

To address the above issues, based on the above research ideas, the specific work completed in this paper is as follows:

*Contribution*1. A neural matrix factorization recommendation model based on federated learning is designed. The training efficiency and recommendation effect of three instances of federated neural collaborative filtering are compared and analyzed through experiments.

*Contribution*2. An improved differential privacy federated learning recommendation method that resists PPA is designed, and Laplace noise and Gaussian noise are added to the gradient of the local model for processing. The training efficiency and recommendation effect before and after adding differential privacy are compared and analyzed through experiments.

2   Related Works

2.1   Federated Recommendations Face Various Gradient Attacks

Federated learning is not absolutely safe. In order to build a global model for federated learning, users still need to upload local model parameters or gradients. These parameters or gradients are essentially a mapping of the user's local data and contain almost all information about the user's data. Multiple attack models show that by analyzing the parameters or gradients of local models, partial or complete information of the original data used by users for training can be obtained [14].

Truc et al. [15] proposed an Active Membership Inference, in which the server forges malicious parameters and embeds them into the global model to infer whether the target data samples are included in clients' private in the training data. Hu et al. [16] proposed Source Inference Attack (SIA), after determining which data instances are training members in membership inference attack, the attacker can further conduct SIA to identify which client it came from. Chen et al. [16] combined membership inference attack with double threshold function to improve the efficiency of distinguishing members from non-members. Peng et al. [17] combined principal component analysis with membership inference attack in the black-box membership attack scenario to suppress the low migration behavior caused by over-reliance on the model and improve attack efficiency.

In addition, Zhou et al. [18] proposed PPA. Through this attack, the attacker can obtain the user's privacy preferences, such as the favorite or least favorite when shopping online. Products and selfie expressions of photos you like to use, etc.

2.2   Federated Recommendations Face Various Gradient Attacks

The above-mentioned attack methods obtain users' private information by analyzing the gradient. The existing protection gradient research can be divided into gradient protection methods based on homomorphic encryption, gradient protection methods based on secret sharing, and gradient protection methods based on the gradient protection method of differential privacy and the gradient protection method of mixing multiple strategies.

Chen et al. [19] combined federated learning and homomorphic encryption algorithm for the training of electric power data prediction model, so as to protect the gradient of the local model; similarly, Yuan [20] used homomorphic encryption technology to encrypt the vertical federation Local model gradients during learning to avoid privacy leaks. Chen et al. [33] combined additive secret sharing technology to enhance the secrecy of gradient parameters on the basis of using compressed sensing to reduce the communication overhead of the federated learning framework; Wang et al. [21] used secret sharing to a reusable security parameter mask is generated in a way, and a mask is added to the model in the uplink communication of the training process to protect the security of the model gradient.

Liu et al. [22] proposed a secure federated transfer learning framework for neural network models, using homomorphic encryption and secret sharing to preserve privacy. Gao et al. [23] proposed a heterogeneous federated transfer learning method for logistic regression and support vector machine models, also using homomorphic encryption and secret sharing to protect privacy. Since there is no guarantee that the third-party server will not collude with the central server, there is still a risk of privacy leakage.

Xu et al. [24] proposed a federated learning method based on differential privacy-protected knowledge transfer, using differential privacy technology to add noise to the gradient that needs to be transmitted during the knowledge transfer process, realizing privacy-preserving knowledge transfer, thereby reducing privacy indirect leakage possibility. Wang et al. [25] proposed an adaptive tailoring differential privacy federated learning framework, which adds dynamic Gaussian noise to the uploaded model parameters, and then uploads the noise-added model parameters to the server for global model parameter update, ensuring data privacy security during parameter transmission is ensured.

Lin et al. [26] proposed a privacy-preserving federated recommendation algorithm based on data perturbation in order to protect user privacy in federated learning. Collection of ratings. During training, the algorithm improves privacy protection during transmission by mixing real and generated sets and uploading them. Although this method protects the interaction history of user items, it does not do any processing on the gradient in the real interaction set. Attackers can still obtain the user's real ratings for some items through the gradient, and there is a risk of privacy leakage.

It can be seen that the above strategies of federated learning to protect user privacy have certain limitations, and they cannot well defend against preference profiling attack. In order to better protect user privacy and prevent them from being attacked by preference analysis, this paper will combine differential privacy and data perturbation Technology Improvement Based on Federated Learning Neural Collaborative Filtering Recommendation Algorithm.

2.3   Attack Model

The PPA is a white-box attack, which assumes that the central server is malicious and selects samples in each item category and retrains the local model for a specific user to obtain the local model gradient sensitivity for each item category. The attack uses a selective aggregation mechanism to improve the gradient sensitivity by aggregating a subset of user-side of interest to the central server. It utilizes the attack model as a meta-classifier to predict the target user data preference by taking the extracted sensitivity information of the user uploaded and aggregated models as input.

The process of PPA is shown in Fig. 1. It mainly includes four steps. The first step is that the user trains the model locally and uploads the local model gradient to the central server. The second step is that the central server retrains the model using auxiliary datasets to obtain model sensitivities for each item class. The third step is to use the meta-classifier to predict the user's preferred items. The fourth step is selective aggregation. For users who are interested in the server, select other pairs of preference classes The model parameters of the most sensitive users are aggregated and sent to the target users.

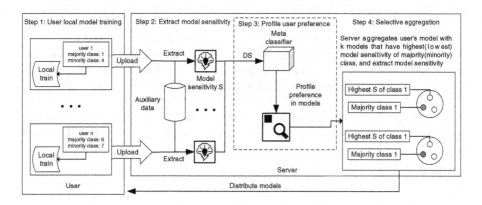

Fig. 1. Preference Profiling Attack Flow

In general, the PPA is an attack against users uploading gradients, and the capture of information such as gradients may lead to privacy leaks has been proved by Li et al. [27] privacy breach.

3   Recommendation Method Based on Improved Differential Privacy Federated Learning

3.1   Neural Matrix Factorization Recommendation Algorithm Based on Federated Learning

Neural Collaborative Filtering (NCF) is a general framework for collaborative filtering based on neural networks proposed by He et al. [28], which consists of five layers. Its input layer is composed of two feature vectors describing users and items respectively, and the embedding layer above the input layer is a fully connected layer, which projects the sparse representation to the dense vector. By feeding the embedding layer into the hidden layer, which maps the latent vector to the predicted score of the item. Each hidden layer can be different from the previous ones to discover specific latent structures in user-item interaction information. The performance of the model depends on the dimension of the last hidden layer.

He et al. [29] proposed three instances based on NCF, the first is Multi-Layer Perceptron (MLP), the second is Generalized Matrix Factorization (GMF) and the third is Neural Matrix Factorization (NeuMF) which fuses Multi-Layer Perceptron and Generalized Matrix Factorization. The main difference between these three instances is that they have different implementations of the neural collaborative filtering layer. NeuMF embeds user and item features independently for MLP and GMF at the embedding layer, thus avoiding the problem of consistent input matrices leading to poor results. In the collaborative filtering layer, MLP and GMF are mapped separately, and the results of the two models are merged in the last layer of the hidden layer and the predicted scores are output.

The framework of the neural matrix decomposition recommendation algorithm based on federated learning is shown in Fig. 2. The architecture adopted by the federated neural matrix decomposition is the client-central server architecture. A client can be one user or several users, and each client can train a local recommendation model independently. The central server is used to update the parameters of the global model and coordinate and control the entire training process. The aggregation of local model parameters is its core function. The local model parameters of each client are aggregated into new global model parameters.

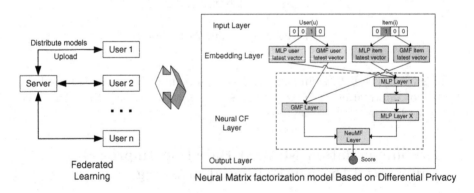

Fig. 2. Neural Matrix Factorization Framework Based on Federated Learning

3.2   Gradient Transfer Model Based on Differential Privacy

Common privacy protection technologies include differential privacy, homomorphic encryption, and secure multi-party computation [32]. Since Zhou [8] and

Algorithm 1. Improved Federated Learning Algorithm based on Differential Privacy

---

Input: Client c
Output: Local model parameters ω_{t+1}^c
Server execution:
1: Initialize global model parameter;
2: **for** every epoch $t = 1, 2, 3, \cdots$ **do**
3:     $m = \max(p * c, 1)$;
4:     $S = $ Randomly selected m users;
5:     **for** every client c belongs to S_t **do**
6:         $\omega_{t+1}^c = $ Clients update function $ClientUpdate(c, \omega_t)$;
7:     $\omega_{t+1} = \sum_{c \in S_t} \frac{n_c}{n} \omega_{t+1}^c$;

Clients update function $ClientUpdate(c, \omega_t)$:
1: $B = $ Divide D_c into batches of size B;
2: **for** every client's epoch $i = 1, 2, 3, \cdots, E$ **do**
3:     **for** batch **do**
4:         $\omega_{t+1}^c = \omega_c - \eta \nabla \vartheta(\omega_t; b)$;
5: Adding Laplace noise to non-zero parameters:
6:     $\omega_{t+1}^c = Laplace(\omega_{t+1}^c, \varepsilon)$;
7: The model parameter for this iteration is $params = \omega_{t+1}^c$;
8: **if** $last_params == $ None **then**
9:     The previous iteration's parameter is equal to the current iteration's:
10:         $last\_params = params$;
11: **else**
12:     Calculate the standard deviation sigma between $last\_params$ and $params$;
13:     Generate $fake\_params$ of pseudo interactive items using sigma as the standard deviation of Gaussian noise;
14:     Add Gaussian noise $\omega_{t+1}^c = \omega_{t+1}^c + fake\_params$;
15:     $last\_params = params$;
16: **return** Local model parameters ω_{t+1}^c to server;

---

others proved that after the introduction of differential privacy technology, federated learning can reduce the accuracy of PPA to a certain extent, thereby achieving the purpose of protecting user privacy. Differential privacy can be applied to various machine learning algorithms and optimization techniques. In federated learning, differential privacy can be combined with optimization methods such as gradient descent and stochastic gradient descent to provide privacy protection for gradient updates on each device. Therefore, this paper chooses to use differential privacy technology to improve the federated learning algorithm so as to resist PPA and protect user privacy.

Differential privacy generates a series of perturbed data with privacy-preserving properties by randomly perturbing the original data, so as to achieve the purpose of privacy protection [29]. In federated learning, noise can be added on the user's local device, and then only the noised gradients are shared. In this way, even if the malicious server in the PPA obtains this gradient information, it cannot accurately restore the real gradient of the entire data set, thereby protecting the privacy of individual data. The most common types of differential privacy are Laplace noise and Gaussian noise. These two types of noise have their own advantages. Therefore, this paper comprehensively uses the two types of noise to protect user privacy in gradients.

Because PPA can collect private information such as through interaction history records by the gradient analysis, we employ Laplace noise for numerical queries to prevent PPA from obtaining user-side preferred item information; Gaussian noise with better smoothness and continuity is used to generate random pseudo-interaction item information to prevent the leakage of user item interaction history information. The specific algorithm is shown in Algorithm 1.

Where C is the total number of participant ends, P is the proportion of randomly selected participant ends, S_t the set of randomly selected participant ends, n_c is the number of local training instances, n is the total number of training instances, ω_{t+1}^c the local weight update generated by participant ends, B is the local training minimum batch size, E is the number of rounds of local training, D_c is the data of the participant end, and η is the learning rate of training.

The algorithm is modified on the basis of FedAvg. First, after the training of each client end, a Laplace noise is added to the model parameters to resist PPA and obtain user preference information. The privacy budget of the Laplace noise ε is 0.1; then record the model parameters of each round of local training, if it is the first round of training, record the model parameters of this round as the model parameters of the previous round, and upload it to the central server, otherwise calculate the parameters of this round and the previous round The standard deviation of the parameters is used as the standard deviation of the Gaussian distribution to randomly generate the parameters of the pseudo-interaction items to resist the PPA and obtain the user item interaction history.

3.3   Privacy Analysis

Definition 1. *For a function $f : D \to R^d$, its maximum Manhattan distance output conditional on two neighboring datasets D_1 and D_2 denotes the sensitivity, as shown in Eq. 1 [30]:*

$$\Delta f = \max_{(D_1, D_2 \in Q)} \|f(D_1) - f(D_2)\| \tag{1}$$

In the above equation, R denotes the real number space of the mapping and d denotes the query dimension of the function f. The sensitivity Δf is independent of the dataset and related to the function f.

Definition 2. *Given neighboring datasets D_1 and D_2, assume that there is a privacy algorithm F and $Range(F)$ is all possible outputs of F. Any output of algorithm F on datasets D_1 and D_2 is O ($O \in Range(F)$), which satisfies the following inequality $\Pr(F(D_1) = 0) \leq e^\varepsilon \Pr(F(D_2) = 0)$, then Algorithm F is said to satisfy the ε-differential privacy mechanism, where ε is the differential* *privacy budget, and the smaller the value, the higher the probability that $F(D_1) = 0$ is equal to $F(D_2) = 0$, and the higher the level of privacy preservation of Algorithm F is.*

Theorem 1. *For any function $f : D \rightarrow R^d$, if the output result of algorithm F satisfies $F(D) = f(D) + \left\langle Lap_1(\frac{\Delta f}{\varepsilon}), \cdots, Lap_d(\frac{\Delta f}{\varepsilon}) \right\rangle$, then it is said that the algorithm F satisfies ε-differential privacy [31].*

Theorem 2. *Postprocessing Resistance Theorem. If $G : N^{|X|} \rightarrow R$ satisfies ε-differential privacy and $H : R \rightarrow R'$ is an arbitrary function, then $H \circ F : N^{|X|} \rightarrow R$ still satisfies ε-differential privacy.*

Proof. We know from the Laplace noise mechanism that the gradient after adding Laplace noise in Algorithm 1 is $\omega_{t+1}^{c} \leftarrow \omega_{t+1}^{c} + Lap(\frac{\Delta \omega_{t+1}^{c}}{\varepsilon})$, which satisfies Theorem 1, and therefore it satisfies ε-differential privacy. From Theorem 2, post-processing the result for ε-differential privacy does not weaken its differential privacy protection. Therefore, the gradient after adding Gaussian noise in Algorithm 1 is $\omega_{t+1}^{\ddot{c}} = \omega_{t+1}^{\ddot{c}} + fake\_params$, and it still satisfies ε-differential privacy.

In summary, Algorithm 1 satisfies the ε-differential privacy-preserving mechanism and realizes the privacy-preserving function for the gradient in federated learning.

4   Simulation

4.1   Lab Environment

This experiment is carried out under Windows 10 operating system, Intel(R) Core(TM) i5-8250U CPU@ 1.60 GHz 1.80 GHz, no GPU. The software environment is Python3.6, PyTorch1.10.2.

4.2   Evaluation Index

In this experiment, the loss rate loss is used as the evaluation index of training efficiency, and the two classic recommendation system evaluation indexes of Hit Ratio (HR) and Normalized Discounted Cumulative Gain (NDCG) are used to measure the recommendation effect. The formula for calculating the hit rate is as follows:

$$hit\_ratio@k = \frac{Number\_of\_hits@k}{GT} \tag{2}$$

In the formula, the denominator is the sum of the test set, and the numerator is the number of the first k recommended items in the recommendation list of each client that belong to the test set. The higher the value, the better the effect of the recommendation system. The calculation formula of $NDCG@k$ is as follows:

$$DCG@k = \sum_{i}^{k} \frac{r(i)}{\log_2(i+1)} \tag{3}$$

$$IDCG@k = \sum_i^{|REL|} \frac{r(i)}{\log_2(i+1)} \tag{4}$$

$$NDCG@k = \frac{DCG@k}{IDCG@k} \tag{5}$$

In the formula, $r(i)$ is the correlation score of each item in the data set, DCG is the recommendation effect for a certain user, IDCG is the real recommendation effect score for a certain user, and $|REL|$ represents the items in the recommendation list from large to small according to the recommendation score. Arranged in sequence, a collection of the first k items. The normalized score NDCG is obtained by dividing IDCG by each user's DCG. The higher the value of NDCG, the better the effect of the recommendation system.

4.3 Experimental Dataset

In this experiment, we used the MovieLens-1M dataset as the experimental data. The dataset contains personal information of 6040 users, information of 3952 movies and ratings of the movies by these users. Among them, the number of movies rated by each user is more than 20. In order to facilitate subsequent operations, we serialize and map the IDs of users and movies. This experiment only uses the data in the rating file ratings.dat. More specifically, we only use the rating data of the top 250 users on the movie. The data format is "UserID::MovieID::Rating::Timestamp", and the specific meanings are shown in the Table 1:

Table 1. MovieLens-1M Data Fields

Field Name	Meaning
UserID	ranging from 1 to 6040
MovieID	ranging from 1 to 3952
Rating	Movie rating, five-point scale, ranging from 1 to 5, all integers
Timestamp	Point in time for user ratings

4.4 Superiority Analysis

The purpose of this experiment is not to present more effective recommendations, but to compare three instances of NCF after federated learning, and thus to show the advantages of choosing neural matrix decomposition over the other two instances. The specific comparison models are:

FedGMF (Federated Generalized Matrix Factorization): Uses user-item data for matrix decomposition, transform the high-dimensional rating matrix into the product of the status feature matrix, then use the SGD method to converge the model to obtain the user's local model, and finally obtain the global model through the FedAvg method Model.

FedMLP (Federated Multi-layer Perceptron): Uses user-item data to train the interaction between the user and the latent features of the item, and then predicts it through the activation function ReLU.

FedNeuMF (Federated Neural Matrix Factorization): Through generalized matrix factorization and multi-layer perceptron fusion to jointly train user-item linear and nonlinear interactions for prediction. The experimental results are shown in Table 2 and Fig. 3 below:

Table 2. Indicators of the Three Federated NCF Models Under the Movielens-1M Dataset

Recommendation Model	loss	hit_ratio@10	ndcg@10
FedGMF	0.0962	0.7565	0.6960
FedMLP	0.0289	0.8881	0.9272
FedNeuMF	0.0186	0.8955	0.9325

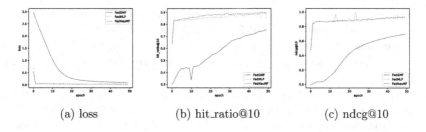

(a) loss (b) hit_ratio@10 (c) ndcg@10

Fig. 3. Changes of Three Instances under Movielens-1M

4.5 Effectiveness Analysis

This experiment was carried out on the MovieLens-1M dataset, and the recommendation effect and training efficiency of the FedNeuMF algorithm before and after adding differential privacy were compared. The experimental results are shown in Table 3:

Table 3. Indicators Before and After Adding Differential Privacy under The Movielens-1M

Recommendation Model	loss	hit_ratio@10	ndcg@10
FedNeuMF	0.0186	0.8955	0.9325
DP-FedNeuMF	0.0183	0.9228	0.9087

The privacy budget epsilon for this experiment was 0.1 and the rest of the parameters were the same as in the previous experiment. Compared with the final value of training, it can be seen from Table 3 that on the Movielens-1M dataset, the loss of DP-FedNeuMF is lower than that of FedNeuMF The hit rate hit_ratio@10 of DP-FedNeuMF is 3.05% higher than that of FedNeuMF; the cumulative gain of normalized loss ndcg@10 of DP-FedNeuMF is 2.55% lower than that of FedNeuMF.

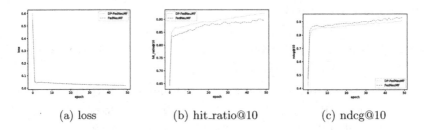

(a) loss   (b) hit_ratio@10   (c) ndcg@10

Fig. 4. Changes in Indicators Before and After Adding Differential Privacy

From Fig. 4, we can see that with the increase of training times, the hit_ratio@10 and ndcg@10 of DP-FedNeuMF and FedNeuMF models are different, but they will continue to increase, and then gradually stabilize, while the loss rate loss is different. The same, but both keep decreasing and then gradually stabilize.

To sum up, after adding differential privacy, we add noise to the data on the basis of ensuring the recommendation effect and training efficiency, which preserves the user's privacy and causes PPA more difficult. It can be considered that the algorithm after adding differential privacy has achieved our expected goal.

5   Conclusion

In this paper, a neural matrix factorization recommendation model based on federated learning and a gradient transmission model based on differential privacy are designed. The training efficiency and recommendation effect of three examples of federated neural collaborative filtering are compared and analyzed through experiments. The experimental results show that the federated neural matrix factorization algorithm has better training efficiency and recommendation effect than the other two algorithms. The training efficiency and recommendation effect of federated neural matrix decomposition before and after adding differential privacy are compared and analyzed through experiments. The experimental results show that the training efficiency and recommendation effect of the algorithm after adding differential privacy are not greatly affected. The improved algorithm is feasible.

Of course, there is still room for improvement in the current work. For example, the recommendation algorithm in this paper uses neural matrix decomposition, one of the examples of neural collaborative filtering. This paper only compares it with the federation of the other two examples, and does not compared with some more advanced recommendation algorithms that currently exist; secondly, although this paper can reduce the probability of being successfully attacked by preference analysis by adding differential privacy, it also increases the computing cost of the client and the communication between the client and the central server. These are not considered at present; in addition, there are many types of attack threats faced by federated learning, and this article only considers one of them, the PPA.

Therefore, in future work, the author will conduct further research on how to choose a recommendation algorithm to improve the recommendation effect, how to improve the algorithm to resist PPA while reducing computing and communication costs, and how to resist more types of attacks.

References

1. China Internet Network Information Center: 50th statistical report on the development of internet in China. Natl. Libr. J. **31**(05), 12 (2022)
2. Qiang, Y., Yang, L., Chen, T., Tong, Y.: Federated machine learning: concept and applications. ACM Trans. Intell. Syst. Technol. **10**(2), 1–19 (2019)
3. Zhou, Q., Dai, H., Sheng, W., et al.: EVSS: an efficient verifiable search scheme over encrypted cloud data. World Wide Web **26**, 1459–1479 (2023). https://doi.org/10.1007/s11280-022-01097-0
4. Konečný, J., McMahan, H.B., Yu, F.X., et al.: Federated learning: strategies for improving communication efficiency. arXiv preprint arXiv:1610.05492 (2016)
5. Zhou, Q., Dai, H., Hu, Z., et al.: Accuracy-first and efficiency-first privacy-preserving semantic-aware ranked searches in the cloud. Int. J. Intell. Syst. **37**(11), 9213–9244 (2022)
6. Xiao, X., Tang, Z., Xiao, B., et al.: A survey on privacy and security issues in federated learning. Chin. J. Comput. **46**(5), 1019–1044 (2023)
7. Li, X., Zheng, H., Chen, J., et al.: A neural pathway poisoning attack method for federated learning. J. Chin. Comput. Syst. 1–9 (2023)
8. Wang, B., Dai, X., Wang, W., et al.: Anti-sample poisoning attacks for federated learning. Sci. Sinica (Informationis) **53**(3), 470–484 (2023)
9. Zhu, C.: Research on defense methods for poisoning and reasoning attacks in federated learning. Doctoral dissertation, Anhui University (2022)
10. Zhou, Q., Sun, Z., Wu, J., et al.: A location privacy preservation scheme based on consortium blockchain in VANET. J. Nanjing Univ. Posts Telecommun. **42**(6), 86–98 (2022)
11. Zhou, C., et al.: PPA: preference profiling attack against federated learning. arXiv preprint arXiv:2202.04856 (2022)
12. Zhou, Q., Zhang, T., Wu, J., et al.: An adaptive path planning algorithm for local delivery of confidential documents based on blockchain. J. Data Acquisition Process. **37**(06), 1314–1322 (2022)
13. Zhou, Q., Dai, H., Hu, Z., Liu, Y., Yang, G.: SAPMS: a semantic-aware privacy-preserving multi-keyword search scheme in cloud. In: Li, B., Yue, L., Tao, C., Han, X., Calvanese, D., Amagasa, T. (eds.) APWeb-WAIM 2022. LNCS, vol. 13421, pp. 251–263. Springer, Cham (2023). https://doi.org/10.1007/978-3-031-25158-0_20

14. Yang, G., Wang, Z.: Survey on privacy preservation in federated learning. J. Nanjing Univ. Posts Telecommun. (Nat. Sci.) **40**(5), 204–214 (2020)
15. Nguyen, T.D.T., et al.: Active membership inference attack under local differential privacy in federated learning. arXiv preprint arXiv:2302.12685 (2023)
16. Hu, H., et al.: Source inference attacks in federated learning. In: Proceedings of the 2021 IEEE International Conference on Data Mining (ICDM), pp. 1102–1107 (2021)
17. Chen, D., Liu, X., Cui, J., et al.: A member inference attack method based on dual threshold function. Netinfo Secur. **23**(2), 64–75 (2023)
18. Peng, C., Gao, T., Liu, H., et al.: PCA-based membership inference attack for machine learning models. J. Commun. **43**(1), 149–160 (2022)
19. Chen, J., Sun, C., Zhou, X., et al.: Local protection of power data prediction model based on federated learning and homomorphic encryption. J. Inf. Secur. Res. **9**(3), 228–234 (2023)
20. Yuan, L.: Research on key technologies of vertical federated learning based on homomorphic encryption. Doctoral dissertation, East China Normal University (2022)
21. Wang, H., Fan, Y.: Local multi-node federated learning algorithm based on secret sharing. J. Guangzhou Univ. (Nat. Sci. Ed.) **21**(3), 1–13 (2022)
22. Liu, Y., Kang, Y., Xing, C., et al.: A secure federated transfer learning framework. IEEE Intell. Syst. **35**(4), 70–82 (2020)
23. Gao, D., Liu, Y., Huang, A., et al.: Privacy-preserving heterogeneous federated transfer learning. In: Proceedings of the 2019 IEEE International Conference on Big Data, p. 1 (2020)
24. Xu, C., Ge, L., Wang, Z., et al.: A federated learning method based on differential privacy protection knowledge transfer. Appl. Res. Comput. 1–9 (2023)
25. Wang, F., Xie, M., Li, Q., et al.: Adaptive tailored differential privacy federated learning framework. J. Xidian Univ. 1–11 (2023)
26. Lin, G., Liang, F., Pan, W., et al.: FedRec: federated recommendation with explicit feedback. IEEE Intell. Syst. **36**(5), 21–30 (2020)
27. Li, Q., Wen, Z., Wu, Z., et al.: A survey on federated learning systems: vision, hype and reality for data privacy and protection. IEEE Trans. Knowl. Data Eng. **35**(4), 3347–3366 (2023)
28. He, X., Liao, L., Zhang, H., et al.: Neural collaborative filtering. In: International World Wide Web Conferences Steering Committee, pp. 173–182 (2017)
29. Chen, X., Han, B., Huang, S.: An anonymized data privacy protection method based on differential privacy. Comput. Technol. Dev. **28**(7), 99–102+107 (2018)
30. Dwork, C.: Differential privacy. In: Bugliesi, M., Preneel, B., Sassone, V., Wegener, I. (eds.) ICALP 2006. LNCS, vol. 4052, pp. 1–12. Springer, Heidelberg (2006). https://doi.org/10.1007/11787006_1
31. Dwork, C., McSherry, F., Nissim, K., et al.: Calibrating noise to sensitivity in private data analysis. J. Priv. Confidentiality **7**(3), 17–51 (2017)
32. Zhou, Q., Dai, H., Liu, Y., et al.: A novel semantic-aware search scheme based on BCI-tree index over encrypted cloud data. World Wide Web 1–21 (2023). https://doi.org/10.1007/s11280-023-01176-w
33. Chen, L., Xiao, D., Yu, Z., et al.: Communication-efficient federated learning based on secret sharing and compressed sensing. J. Comput. Res. Dev. **59**(11), 2395–2407 (2022)

Empowering Vulnerability Prioritization: A Heterogeneous Graph-Driven Framework for Exploitability Prediction

Jiao Yin[1]([⊠])[iD], Guihong Chen[2,3][iD], Wei Hong[1][iD], Hua Wang[1][iD], Jinli Cao[4][iD], and Yuan Miao[1][iD]

[1] Institute for Sustainable Industries and Liveable Cities, Victoria University, Melbourne, VIC 3011, Australia
{jiao.yin,hua.wang,yuan.miao}@vu.edu.au, wei.hong2@live.vu.edu.au
[2] School of Automation Science and Engineering, South China University of Technology, Guangzhou 510641, Guangdong, China
[3] School of Cyber Security, Guangdong Polytechnic Normal University, Guangzhou 510000, Guangdong, China
chenguihong@gpnu.edu.cn
[4] Department of Computer Science and Information Technology, La Trobe University, Melbourne, VIC 3086, Australia
j.cao@latrobe.edu.au

Abstract. With the increasing number of software vulnerabilities being disclosed each year, prioritizing them becomes essential as it is challenging to patch all of them promptly. Exploitability prediction plays a crucial role in assessing the severity of vulnerabilities and determining their prioritization. Most existing works on exploitability prediction focus on building predictive models based on features extracted from individual vulnerabilities, neglecting the relationships between vulnerabilities and their contextual information. Only a few studies have explored using homogeneous graph-based techniques to enhance performance in this domain. This paper proposes a novel heterogeneous graph-driven framework for enhancing vulnerability exploitability prediction. The framework comprises two heterogeneous graph feature extraction technique streams: topological feature concatenation and node embedding based on heterogeneous graph neural networks (HGNN). Experimental results demonstrate that both streams, leveraging heterogeneous graph-based features, significantly improve the performance of exploitability prediction compared with using features extracted from individual vulnerabilities. Specifically, the two streams achieve 5.44% and 2.06% improvement in the F1 score, respectively. The data and codes are available on GitHub (https://github.com/happyResearcher/HG-VEP) to facilitate reproducibility and further research in this field.

Keywords: Software vulnerability · Exploitability prediction · Heterogeneous graph · Graph neural networks

The work reported in this paper was partly supported by the Australian Research Council (ARC) Linkage Project LP180101062.

F. Zhang et al. (Eds.): WISE 2023, LNCS 14306, pp. 289–299, 2023.
https://doi.org/10.1007/978-981-99-7254-8_23

1 Introduction

People rely heavily on various software and applications in today's digital era, concealing significant risks to privacy protection and data security [20,23]. As of June 2023, the National Vulnerability Database (NVD) has documented and published over 204,485 software vulnerabilities[1]. These vulnerabilities present substantial cybersecurity risks to the security and integrity of contemporary information systems [5,12,17].

Software vulnerability refers to "a security flaw, glitch, or weakness found in software code that could be exploited by an attacker (threat source)" [3,4]. Due to the continuous discovery of new vulnerabilities and large-scale existing unpatched software vulnerabilities, it is virtually impossible to patch all identified vulnerabilities in a timely manner [15,19]. On the other hand, not all identified vulnerabilities need to be immediately patched, as only a small portion of them, approximately 20%, have proof-of-concept exploits based on the records in the Exploit Database (EDB)[2] [16,30]. Therefore, exploitability prediction has emerged as a prominent research topic, aiming to prioritize vulnerabilities based on their likelihood of being exploited, enabling cybersecurity resources to be efficiently allocated toward patching vulnerabilities with a higher probability of exploitation [8,32].

Given the substantial amount of historical data available on vulnerabilities, including descriptions, CVSS metrics and scores, gained access details, affected products, and more, numerous machine learning (ML) and deep learning (DL) algorithms have been adopted in this field [2,6,7,22]. In 2010, Bozorgi M. et al. trained support vector machine (SVM) classifiers to predict whether and how soon a vulnerability is likely to be exploited [1]. More recently, Suciu O. et al. investigated exploitability as a time-varying process and adopted supervised classification techniques to update expected exploitability continuously [18]. These works often extracted features from individual vulnerabilities and built ML and DL models, neglecting connections between vulnerabilities and context.

Though some researchers began constructing vulnerability knowledge graphs from unstructured data and semi-structured data for vulnerability analysis and reasoning, most focused on data processing, entity extraction and recognition, and graph modelling and question answering [13,26]. A few explored using homogeneous graph-based methods for exploitability analysis. For example, Yin J. et al. proposed a homogeneous modality-aware graph convolutional network for coexploitation behavior prediction [31]. However, in the real world, vulnerability graphs are heterogeneous, with multiple node and relationship types. To the best of our knowledge, no existing works have applied heterogeneous graph-based feature extraction techniques for software vulnerability exploitability prediction.

This paper proposes a heterogeneous graph-based exploitability prediction framework that contains two heterogeneous graph feature extraction technique streams for enhancing vulnerability exploitability prediction to fill the gap.

---

[1] https://nvd.nist.gov/.

[2] https://www.exploit-db.com/.

Stream 1 is a topological feature concatenation method, and Stream 2 is heterogeneous graph neural network (HGNN) based node embedding. We further construct a heterogeneous graph containing 47,320 vulnerabilities to verify the effectiveness of the proposed framework. Experimental results verify that both heterogeneous-based feature extraction technique streams can improve the performance of exploitability prediction compared with using features from individual vulnerabilities only.

2 Related Works

When allocating resources to remediate, mitigate, and patch vulnerabilities, the exploitability of vulnerabilities is one of the most crucial factors that must be considered. Formulated exploitability prediction as a binary classification problem, Yin J. et al. proposed a transfer learning-based framework to extract features from vulnerability descriptions [30] in a balanced dataset. They further investigated this problem in an online learning setting and proposed an online learning framework to deal with the dynamic concept drift and imbalance problem [30]. Since exploitation time also influences vulnerability assessment and prioritization, some research also developed algorithms for exploitation time prediction [28]. However, it is difficult to predict the exact exploitation time due to limited historical data, incomplete information, and a wide value range of outputs. Therefore, in practice, researchers tried to predict the possible exploitation period in a coarse-grained manner. Although promising results were reported with the best performance of 91.12% on accuracy, it is hard to reproduce the results due to unpublished data and codes. Moreover, most of them assess vulnerabilities individually and fail to leverage the various relationships across vulnerabilities [24].

   In reality, data or knowledge can be easily represented as a graph, where nodes represent entities or concepts, and edges represent relationships or connections between them [25]. In cybersecurity, graph-based intelligence offers a powerful framework for modeling and analyzing complex systems by capturing and leveraging the rich relationships and dependencies in software, networks, systems, or user behaviors [11,14,27]. For example, You M. et al. built a knowledge graph for an access control system and developed graph-based algorithms for decision-making [33]. Hong W. et al. utilized organizational connections such as a shared supervisor or e-mail interactions to improve the overall performance of insider threat detection [9,10]. Regarding vulnerability assessment, researchers also built vulnerability knowledge graphs for analysis and reasoning [13,26]. For example, paper [21] constructed a vulnerability ontology based on multi-source heterogeneous databases, and an accuracy of 89.76% was reported for entity recognition of extracting vendor names.

3 Methodology

As a typical binary classification problem, vulnerability exploitability prediction also follows the general paradigm of ML tasks, including data collection, feature extraction, classifier training and testing, and performance evaluation. The structure of the proposed heterogeneous graph-driven framework for vulnerability exploitability prediction is shown in Fig. 1. It starts by collecting raw data on vulnerabilities from open-source repositories, including CVE Details[3], Common Weakness Enumeration (CWE)[4], NVD and Exploit Database (EDB)[5]. The collected information is integrated based on cveID, a unique Common Vulnerabilities and Exposures (CVE) number assigned to each vulnerability. Then, a heterogeneous vulnerability graph, G, is constructed, containing different nodes, relationships, and their attributes. The VHG details will be introduced in Sect. 4. We design two streams to extract features from G in the following feature extraction step.

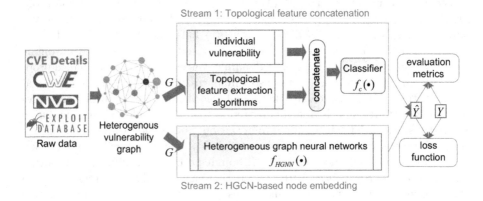

Fig. 1. Illustration of the proposed heterogeneous graph-driven framework

Stream 1: Topological Feature Concatenation Method. On the one hand, features are extracted from individual vulnerability information, denoted as X_{ind}. On the other hand, multiple topological feature extraction algorithms extract features from the VHG G and then concatenate these features as X_{top}. A classifier, $f_c(\cdot)$, is trained and evaluated on the concatenated features from X_{ind} and X_{top}. The predicted exploitability, $\hat{Y}$, can be calculated as (1),

$$\hat{Y} = f_c((X_{ind} \oplus X_{top}), \theta_c) \tag{1}$$

where, $\oplus$ stands for the concatenation operation and θ_c is the trainable parameter of the classifier $f_c(\cdot)$. A loss function is used to quantify the difference between the predicted result $\hat{Y}$ and the true label Y. General metrics for the binary classification problem, such as accuracy, precision, recall, and F1 score, can be used to evaluate the performance of Stream 1.

---

[3] https://www.cvedetails.com/.
[4] https://cwe.mitre.org/.
[5] https://www.exploit-db.com/.

Specifically, stream 1 adopts eight algorithms in total to extract heterogeneous graph features, i.e., PageRank, ArticleRank, Degree centrality (DC), Harmonic centrality (HC), Louvain, Label propagation (LP), Weakly connected components (WCC), and Modularity optimization (MO), based on Neo4j Graph Data Science (GDS)[6] library.

Stream 2: HGNN-Based Node Embedding. This end-to-end strategy uses HGNNs that directly work as a feature extractor and classifier. The individual vulnerability features X_{ind}, as the node attributes are embedded together with graph connection information using an HGNN model. The predicted result of Stream 2 can be calculated as (2),

$$\hat{Y} = f_{HGNN}(G, \Theta) \tag{2}$$

where the $f_{HGNN}(\cdot)$ denotes the mapping function between the output $\hat{Y}$ and the input G and Θ in the trainable parameter matrix set of the HGNN model. The loss function and evaluation metrics setting are the same as Stream 1.

HGNNs are designed explicitly for graphs with diverse types of nodes and edges, where nodes and edges can have different attributes or meanings. Compared with standard homogeneous message-passing GNNs, HGNNs create GNNs and implement message and update functions individually for each edge type to handle the differences in feature types. HGNNs need to iterate over edge-type dictionaries during message computation and node-type dictionaries during node updates. Also, HGNNs allow flexibly defining different operators for different edge and relationship types.

4   Experiment Results

4.1   Data Collection and Prepossessing

We collect vulnerabilities disclosed between 1999 and 2022 from NVD and CVE Details to verify the enhancement of heterogeneous graph connections on exploitability prediction. The cveID, description, and affected products are collected for each vulnerability. The description information works as the attributes of individual vulnerabilities, and the product information is used to create a Product node type and build relationships between Vulnerability and Product nodes, denoted as R1. The exploitability of a Vulnerability node is labeled as 1 if a proof-of-concept exploit is available at EDB. Otherwise, it is labeled as 0. Common Weakness Enumeration is a community-developed list of software & hardware weakness types independent from CVE records. We then collect weakness items from CWE, creating a Weakness node type and building relationships

---

[6] https://neo4j.com/docs/graph-data-science/current/algorithms/.

between Vulnerability and Weakness nodes, denoted as R2. Finally, we down-sample Vulnerability nodes with exploitability equal to 0 to build a balanced heterogeneous vulnerability graph, as shown in Fig. 2.

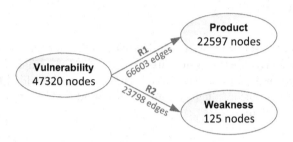

Fig. 2. Details of the constructed heterogeneous vulnerability graph

4.2   Performance Evaluation of Stream 1

Comparison Study. We compared the exploitability prediction performance of using individual vulnerability features and String 1 features on six widely-used ML algorithms, i.e., AdaBoost Classifier (ABC), Decision tree (DT), K nearest neighbors (KNN), Multi-layer perceptron (MLP), Random forest (RF) and XGBoost (XGB), implemented by scikit-learn[7] library.

Following the same method in [29], we extract features from individual vulnerability descriptions, denoted as X_{ind}, which work as both features that are extracted from individual vulnerabilities and attributes of the Vulnerability nodes. Next, we deploy the heterogeneous vulnerability graph on the Neo4j[8] graph database platform and use the implementation of Neo4j GDS library to extract X_{top}.

The experiment results are shown in Table 1. Features extracted from Stream 1 perform better than features extracted from individual vulnerabilities on all classifiers. For example, the F1 score of the ABC algorithm increases from 0.7041 to 0.7593. Among all classifiers, RF performs best with both X_{ind} and Stream 1, achieving 0.7667 and 0.8085 in the F1 score, respectively. By contrast, DT performs the worst in both situations, with 0.6801 and 0.7324 in the F1 score, respectively. It also verifies that weak classifiers, like DT, can be combined into a powerful classifier, like RF.

The comparison study results verify the effectiveness of concatenating topological features extracted from the heterogeneous graph for exploitability prediction.

---

[7] https://scikit-learn.org/stable/.
[8] https://neo4j.com/.

Table 1. Comparison between individual vulnerability feature and Stream 1

Classifier	Features	Acc	Pre	Rec	F1 score
ABC	X_{ind}	0.7058	0.7119	0.7065	0.7041
	Stream 1	0.7593	0.7593	0.7593	0.7593
DT	X_{ind}	0.6801	0.6801	0.6801	0.6801
	Stream 1	0.7324	0.7324	0.7324	0.7324
KNN	X_{ind}	0.7455	0.7468	0.7458	0.7453
	Stream 1	0.7740	0.7763	0.7744	0.7737
MLP	X_{ind}	0.7585	0.7586	0.7584	0.7584
	Stream 1	0.7887	0.7891	0.7889	0.7887
RF	X_{ind}	0.7671	0.7680	0.7668	0.7667
	Stream 1	0.8085	0.8085	0.8085	0.8085
XGB	X_{ind}	0.7562	0.7562	0.7561	0.7561
	Stream 1	0.8010	0.8012	0.8011	0.8009

Ablation Study. The number of nodes and edges for all entity and relationship types in the constructed heterogeneous vulnerability graph are shown in Fig. 2. Obviously, the sub-graph "Vulnerability - R1 - > Product" is much denser than the sub-graph "Vulnerability - R2 -> Weakness". Therefore, we compare the performance of applying sub-graphs with different relationships in Stream 1.

The results are shown in Table 2, where ΔF1 score are compared with the same classifier when using X_{ind} only. Table 2 shows all sub-graphs positively affect the exploitability prediction results, with only one exception. A -0.87% of ΔF1 score is recorded by MLP on stream 1: R2.

The ablation study shows that adding the graph's complexity does not necessarily improve the performance. It depends on the quality of the increased parts and the classifier's capability to capture the patterns from the extracted topological features.

4.3 Performance Evaluation of Stream 2

The HGNN is implemented based on a generic wrapper for computing graph convolution on heterogeneous graphs, HeteroConv, provided by the PyTorch Geometric[9] library. We define a two-layer HGNN with the SAGEConv as the basic GNN module and named it as HSAGE. The training process of HSAGE is controlled by an early stopping mechanism, with patience = 10, delta = 0.000001, and metric = Accuracy. Figure 3 shows the training process of the HSAGE model.

Comparison Study. We compare the best results achieved by X_{ind}, Stream 1 and Stream 2 in Table 3. Stream 1 achieves the best F1 score at 0.8085 with the RF classifier. It is 5.44% higher than X_{ind}. Stream 2 also performs 2.06% better than X_{ind} in the F1 score, reaching 0.7825.

[9] https://pytorch-geometric.readthedocs.io/en/latest/index.html.

Table 2. Ablation study result of Stream 1

Classifier	Features	Acc	Pre	Rec	F1	Δ F1
ABC	Stream 1: R1	0.7645	0.7648	0.7647	0.7645	8.58%
	Stream 1: R2	0.7137	0.7144	0.7134	0.7133	1.30%
	Stream 1: R1+R2	0.7593	0.7593	0.7593	0.7593	7.84%
DT	Stream 1: R1	0.7394	0.7395	0.7394	0.7393	8.72%
	Stream 1: R2	0.6825	0.6825	0.6825	0.6825	0.36%
	Stream 1: R1+R2	0.7324	0.7324	0.7324	0.7324	7.70%
KNN	Stream 1: R1	0.7796	0.7820	0.7800	0.7793	4.56%
	Stream 1: R2	0.7471	0.7487	0.7474	0.7469	0.21%
	Stream 1: R1+R2	0.7740	0.7763	0.7744	0.7737	3.81%
MLP	Stream 1: R1	0.7904	0.7904	0.7904	0.7904	4.21%
	Stream 1: R2	0.7518	0.7518	0.7518	0.7518	-0.87%
	Stream 1: R1+R2	0.7887	0.7891	0.7889	0.7887	3.99%
RF	Stream 1: R1	0.8064	0.8064	0.8064	0.8064	5.17%
	Stream 1: R2	0.7730	0.7740	0.7728	0.7727	0.78%
	Stream 1: R1+R2	0.8085	0.8085	0.8085	0.8085	5.44%
XGB	Stream 1: R1	0.7993	0.7995	0.7994	0.7993	5.70%
	Stream 1: R2	0.7608	0.7608	0.7608	0.7608	0.62%
	Stream 1: R1+R2	0.8010	0.8012	0.8011	0.8009	5.93%

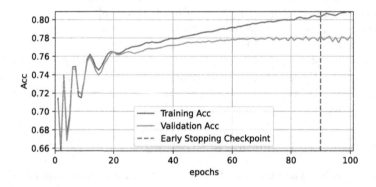

Fig. 3. The training process of the defined HSAGE model

Table 3. Comparison between description feature, Stream 1 and Stream 2

Classifier	Features	Acc	Pre	Rec	F1	Δ F1
RF	X_{ind}	0.7671	0.7680	0.7668	0.7667	0%
RF	Stream 1	0.8085	0.8085	0.8085	0.8085	5.44%
HSAGE	Stream 2	0.7827	0.7833	0.7825	0.7825	2.06%

Ablation Study. Similar to Stream 1, we also conduct an ablation study for Stream 2 as shown in Table 4. HGT has the same structure as HSAGE, but uses the heterogeneous graph transformer (HGT) operator as the basic GNN module. HSAGE can achieve equivalent performance when using Stream 2: R1 and Stream 2: R2, and gets the best result on Stream 2: R1+R2. However, HGT only sees the performance increase on Stream 2: R1 and Stream 2: R1+R2. Using Stream 2: R2 causes a 1.2% F1 score to decrease on HGT. This is similar to Stream 1: R2 on the MLP classifier. The ablation studies on both streams illustrate that the graphs' quality and the classifiers' capability play a role in determining the final performance.

Table 4. Ablation study result of Stream 2

Classifier	Features	Acc	Pre	Rec	F1	Δ F1
HSAGE	Stream 2: R1	0.7797	0.7812	0.7794	0.7793	1.63%
	Stream 2: R2	0.7717	0.7717	0.7717	0.7717	0.65%
	Stream 2: R1+R2	0.7827	0.7833	0.7825	0.7825	2.06%
HGT	Stream 2: R1	0.7724	0.7730	0.7722	0.7722	0.71%
	Stream 2: R2	0.7577	0.7583	0.7575	0.7575	−1.20%
	Stream 2: R1+R2	0.7707	0.7716	0.7705	0.7704	0.48%

5 Conclusion

In conclusion, this paper contributes to the field of vulnerability prioritization by introducing a heterogeneous graph-driven framework that enhances exploitability prediction. We propose a novel heterogeneous graph-driven framework for enhancing vulnerability exploitability prediction. By considering the relationships between vulnerabilities and their contextual information, the framework improves upon existing approaches that focus solely on individual vulnerability features. The framework incorporates two streams: topological feature concatenation and node embedding using heterogeneous graph neural networks. Experimental results demonstrate significant performance improvements in exploitability prediction, with F1 scores increasing by 5.44% and 2.06% for the two streams, respectively. Ablation studies reveal that denser graphs tend to yield superior performance than sparser ones. In further, we will further explore the effectiveness of heterogeneous graph-based features on more complicated graphs and more vulnerability prioritization tasks.

References

1. Bozorgi, M., Saul, L.K., Savage, S., Voelker, G.M.: Beyond heuristics: learning to classify vulnerabilities and predict exploits. In: Proceedings of the 16th ACM SIGKDD International Conference on Knowledge Discovery and Data Mining, pp. 105–114. ACM (2010)

2. Chen, Y., Han, S., Chen, G., Yin, J., Wang, K.N., Cao, J.: A deep reinforcement learning-based wireless body area network offloading optimization strategy for healthcare services. Health Inf. Sci. Syst. **11**(1), 8 (2023). https://doi.org/10.1007/s13755-023-00212-3

3. Cheng, K., et al.: Secure kk-NN query on encrypted cloud data with multiple keys. IEEE Trans. Big Data **7**(4), 689–702 (2017)

4. Dempsey, K., Takamura, E., Eavy, P., Moore, G.: Automation support for security control assessments: software vulnerability management. Technical report, National Institute of Standards and Technology (2020)

5. Fatima, M., Rehman, O., Rahman, I.M.: Impact of features reduction on machine learning based intrusion detection systems. EAI Endorsed Trans. Scalable Inf. Syst. **9**(6), e9 (2022)

6. Ge, Y.F., Cao, J., Wang, H., Chen, Z., Zhang, Y.: Set-based adaptive distributed differential evolution for anonymity-driven database fragmentation. Data Sci. Eng. **6**(4), 380–391 (2021). https://doi.org/10.1007/s41019-021-00170-4

7. Ge, Y.F., Orlowska, M., Cao, J., Wang, H., Zhang, Y.: MDDE: multitasking distributed differential evolution for privacy-preserving database fragmentation. VLDB J. **31**(5), 957–975 (2022). https://doi.org/10.1007/s00778-021-00718-w

8. Ge, Y.F., Wang, H., Cao, J., Zhang, Y.: An information-driven genetic algorithm for privacy-preserving data publishing. In: Chbeir, R., Huang, H., Silvestri, F., Manolopoulos, Y., Zhang, Y. (eds.) WISE 2022. LNCS, vol. 13724, pp. 340–354. Springer, Cham (2022). https://doi.org/10.1007/978-3-031-20891-1_24

9. Hong, W., et al.: Graph intelligence enhanced bi-channel insider threat detection. In: Yuan, X., Bai, G., Alcaraz, C., Majumdar, S. (eds.) NSS 2022. LNCS, vol. 13787, pp. 86–102. Springer, Cham (2022). https://doi.org/10.1007/978-3-031-23020-2_5

10. Hong, W., et al.: A graph empowered insider threat detection framework based on daily activities. ISA Trans. (2023, in press). https://doi.org/10.1016/j.isatra.2023.06.030

11. Kong, L., Wang, L., Gong, W., Yan, C., Duan, Y., Qi, L.: LSH-aware multitype health data prediction with privacy preservation in edge environment. World Wide Web **25**, 1793–1808 (2022). https://doi.org/10.1007/s11280-021-00941-z

12. Patil, D.R., Pattewar, T.M.: Majority voting and feature selection based network intrusion detection system. EAI Endorsed Trans. Scalable Inf. Syst. **9**(6), e6 (2022)

13. Qin, S., Chow, K.P.: Automatic analysis and reasoning based on vulnerability knowledge graph. In: Ning, H. (ed.) CyberDI/CyberLife -2019. CCIS, vol. 1137, pp. 3–19. Springer, Singapore (2019). https://doi.org/10.1007/978-981-15-1922-2_1

14. Sarki, R., Ahmed, K., Wang, H., Zhang, Y., Wang, K.: Convolutional neural network for multi-class classification of diabetic eye disease. EAI Endorsed Trans. Scalable Inf. Syst. **9**(4), e5 (2022)

15. Shalini, R., Manoharan, R.: Trust model for effective consensus in blockchain. EAI Endorsed Trans. Scalable Inf. Syst. **9**(5), 1–8 (2022). https://doi.org/10.4108/eai.1-2-2022.173294

16. Han, S., Chen, Y., Chen, G., Yin, J., Wang, H., Cao, J.: Multi-step reinforcement learning-based offloading for vehicle edge computing. In: 2023 15th International Conference on Advanced Computational Intelligence (ICACI), pp. 1–8. IEEE (2023)

17. Singh, R., et al.: Antisocial behavior identification from twitter feeds using traditional machine learning algorithms and deep learning. EAI Endorsed Trans. Scalable Inf. Syst. **10**(4), e17 (2023)

18. Suciu, O., Nelson, C., Lyu, Z., Bao, T., Dumitraş, T.: Expected exploitability: predicting the development of functional vulnerability exploits. In: 31st USENIX Security Symposium (USENIX Security 2022), pp. 377–394 (2022)
19. Sun, X., Wang, H., Li, J.: Injecting purpose and trust into data anonymisation. In: Proceedings of the 18th ACM Conference on Information and Knowledge Management, pp. 1541–1544 (2009)
20. Sun, X., Wang, H., Li, J., Zhang, Y.: Satisfying privacy requirements before data anonymization. Comput. J. **55**(4), 422–437 (2012)
21. Sun, Y., Lin, D., Song, H., Yan, M., Cao, L.: A method to construct vulnerability knowledge graph based on heterogeneous data. In: 2020 16th International Conference on Mobility, Sensing and Networking (MSN), pp. 740–745. IEEE (2020)
22. Venkateswaran, N., Prabaharan, S.P.: An efficient neuro deep learning intrusion detection system for mobile adhoc networks. EAI Endorsed Trans. Scalable Inf. Syst. **9**(6), e7 (2022)
23. Vimalachandran, P., Liu, H., Lin, Y., Ji, K., Wang, H., Zhang, Y.: Improving accessibility of the Australian my health records while preserving privacy and security of the system. Health Inf. Sci. Syst. **8**, 1–9 (2020). https://doi.org/10.1007/s13755-020-00126-4
24. Wang, H., Yi, X., Bertino, E., Sun, L.: Protecting outsourced data in cloud computing through access management. Concurr. Comput. Pract. Exp. **28**(3), 600–615 (2014). https://doi.org/10.1002/cpe.3286
25. Wang, W., Wang, W., Yin, J.: A bilateral filtering based ringing elimination approach for motion-blurred restoration image. Curr. Opt. Photonics **4**(3), 200–209 (2020)
26. Wang, Y., Zhou, Y., Zou, X., Miao, Q., Wang, W.: The analysis method of security vulnerability based on the knowledge graph. In: 2020 The 10th International Conference on Communication and Network Security, pp. 135–145 (2020)
27. Yang, Y., Guan, Z., Li, J., Zhao, W., Cui, J., Wang, Q.: Interpretable and efficient heterogeneous graph convolutional network. IEEE Trans. Knowl. Data Eng. **35**(2), 1637–1650 (2023)
28. Yin, J., Tang, M.J., Cao, J., Wang, H., You, M., Lin, Y.: Adaptive online learning for vulnerability exploitation time prediction. In: Huang, Z., Beek, W., Wang, H., Zhou, R., Zhang, Y. (eds.) WISE 2020. LNCS, vol. 12343, pp. 252–266. Springer, Cham (2020). https://doi.org/10.1007/978-3-030-62008-0_18
29. Yin, J., Tang, M., Cao, J., Wang, H., You, M., Lin, Y.: Vulnerability exploitation time prediction: an integrated framework for dynamic imbalanced learning. World Wide Web **25**, 401–423 (2022). https://doi.org/10.1007/s11280-021-00909-z
30. Yin, J., Tang, M., Cao, J., You, M., Wang, H.: Cybersecurity applications in software: data-driven software vulnerability assessment and management. In: Daimi, K., Alsadoon, A., Peoples, C., El Madhoun, N. (eds.) Emerging Trends in Cybersecurity Applications, pp. 371–389. Springer, Cham (2023). https://doi.org/10.1007/978-3-031-09640-2_17
31. Yin, J., Tang, M., Cao, J., You, M., Wang, H., Alazab, M.: Knowledge-driven cybersecurity intelligence: software vulnerability co-exploitation behavior discovery. IEEE Trans. Ind. Inform. **19**(4), 5593–5601 (2023)
32. You, M., Yin, J., Wang, H., Cao, J., Miao, Y.: A minority class boosted framework for adaptive access control decision-making. In: Zhang, W., Zou, L., Maamar, Z., Chen, L. (eds.) WISE 2021. LNCS, vol. 13080, pp. 143–157. Springer, Cham (2021). https://doi.org/10.1007/978-3-030-90888-1_12
33. You, M., et al.: A knowledge graph empowered online learning framework for access control decision-making. World Wide Web **26**(2), 827–848 (2023). https://doi.org/10.1007/s11280-022-01076-5

ICAD: An Intelligent Framework for Real-Time Criminal Analytics and Detection

Raed Abdallah[1], Hassan Harb[2], Yehia Taher[3(✉)], Salima Benbernou[1], and Rafiqul Haque[4]

[1] LIPADE, Université de Paris, Paris, France
{raed.abdallah,salima.benbernou}@u-paris.fr
[2] College of Engineering and Technology, American University of the Middle East, Kuwait City, Kuwait
hassan.harb@aum.edu.kw
[3] DAVID Lab, UVSQ - Université Paris-Saclay, Versailles, France
yehia.taher@uvsq.fr
[4] Intelligencia, R&D Department, Paris, France
rafiqul.haque@intelligencia.fr

Abstract. Criminal investigation plays a vital role nowadays where the law enforcement agencies (LEAs) carry out this critical mission thoroughly and competently. However, such complicated mission involves a broad spectrum of tasks including collecting evidences from various data sources, analyzing them, and eventually identifying the criminals. Particularly, data may be collected by LEAs from telecommunication companies, online money transfer agencies, social media networks, video surveillance systems, bank transactions, and airways companies. LEAs confront various challenges from different fronts regarding criminal investigation. Thus, handling such big and heterogeneous data coming from different sources and recognizing potential suspects in a real-time is becoming a major challenge for LEAs in criminal investigation. In this paper, we propose an end-to-end Intelligent framework, called as ICAD, to help LEAs in Criminal Analytics and Detection. Mainly, ICAD uses cutting-edge technologies (data science and big data tools) as well as ontological models and inference rules to automatically identify suspects and reduce the human intervention in the investigation process. Furthermore, ICAD consists of four phases. The data sources phase in which we take benefits of various data collection sources that are essential in the crime investigation process. The data acquisition phase where data are collected, preprocessed, and stored using data science tools. The model phase in which a criminal-based ontology is defined that semantically integrates and enriches real-time data into useful information. The last phase is the knowledge extraction where a set of inference and reasoning rules are defined and applied over the ontology to detect criminals according to their activities.

Keywords: Crime Investigation · Heterogeneous Data Sources · Data Science · Ontology · Inference Rules

F. Zhang et al. (Eds.): WISE 2023, LNCS 14306, pp. 300–315, 2023.
https://doi.org/10.1007/978-981-99-7254-8_24

1   Introduction

Criminal investigation has become increasingly crucial in light of the growing prevalence of criminal acts and the formation of extremist radicalization groups in contemporary times. Traditionally, investigation processes were primarily conducted manually by law enforcement agencies (LEAs). However, a significant transformation has taken place in recent years with the advent of advanced technologies such as Big Data, the Internet of Things (IoT), and Artificial Intelligence (AI). These cutting-edge technologies have empowered intelligence agencies to establish a smart ecosystem for criminal investigation. The Big Data-driven ecosystem allows LEAs to collect data from numerous sources of varying sizes and speeds, storing them in highly scalable data lakes, and processing and analyzing them in massively parallel computational environments.

Undoubtedly, the challenges associated with criminal investigations arise from the vast amount of data available in different formats and structures from various sources such as telecommunications, money transfers, banks, video systems, travel history, and social media. Managing and analyzing this data manually to extract the necessary information for the investigation process becomes increasingly difficult. However, dealing with such massive, heterogeneous, and rapidly changing data from diverse sources poses a challenge in providing semantically rich information. Combining separated data is often more beneficial than analyzing them in isolation. Consequently, there is a need to design intelligent frameworks that automate data analysis tasks and reduce human intervention, without compromising the quality of the analysis outcomes. Such frameworks are crucial for improving criminal investigations in the present day.

To address the diversity, heterogeneity, and velocity of data sources, we propose an intelligent framework called ICAD (Intelligent Framework for Real-Time Criminal Analytics and Detection). The ICAD framework collects data from potential crime sources, provides a standardized data storage structure, and applies reasoning rules generated by LEA experts to identify suspects and assist in solving crimes. The fundamental idea behind ICAD is to develop an automated end-to-end system that encompasses data acquisition, preprocessing, analysis, information extraction, and obtaining valuable insights while minimizing human effort and intervention. The proposed framework consists of four phases: data sources, data acquisition, data modeling, and knowledge extraction. It leverages various data science tools and data analytics models, particularly ontology and inference rules, to determine crime suspects and individuals involved in criminal activities.

The remainder of this paper is organized as follows: In Sect. 2, we provide an overview of different data sources and techniques found in the literature pertaining to criminal investigation. Section 3 introduces our intelligent framework, ICAD, while detailing the various tools and techniques employed in each phase. In Sect. 4, we discuss the implementation and evaluation of ICAD. Finally, we conclude the paper and provide some perspectives in Sect. 5.

2   Related Work

In recent times, the significance of crime investigation has gained considerable attention from governments and communities due to its profound impact on people's lives and society as a whole. In response, researchers have focused on developing systems that primarily rely on data science and data analytics to identify suspects and criminals by analyzing historical data from various sources. In this section, we will explore existing systems proposed in the literature, along with the data sources utilized and the techniques employed.

Several studies, such as those referenced in [5,9,10], have leveraged social media data analysis for crime investigation. For instance, in [5], the authors highlighted the importance of social media in detecting radicalization and employed semantic web and domain ontologies to automatically process messages and posts on these platforms. They introduced a radicalization-based ontology model that determines indicators of radicalization in social media users and employs inference rules to identify messages related to radicalization. Similarly, in [10], the authors used similar indicators to detect radicalized individuals based on their behavioral patterns. The patterns were extracted by analyzing the date and time of tweets written in multiple languages. For example, ISIS followers are proficient in several languages, primarily Arabic, and another secondary language such as Russian, Turkish, or English. The results showed that a significant proportion of tweets were published from accounts with time zones set to Riyadh and Pacific Time, which are geographical zones associated with ISIS.

In other studies, including those referenced in [4,11,13], researchers focused on analyzing video data obtained from surveillance systems used in crime investigations. In [4], a criminal detection system based on the Sombrero's Theory of Criminology was proposed. This theory aims to predict criminal tendencies based on facial traits. The system utilized deep learning facial recognition models applied to video surveillance data, along with coordinate measuring machine and support vector machine classifiers, to detect and predict whether a person is involved in criminal activities. In [13], the authors presented an approach that analyzed human positions and distances in video scenes, comparing them with trained data to detect criminal behaviors. The proposed approach combined machine learning techniques with coordinate-based methods to identify criminal activities based on various human poses and postures.

Furthermore, other studies, as mentioned in [7,8,12], focused on criminal documents and text analysis provided by law enforcement agencies (LEAs). In [12], AI techniques were integrated with manual criminal investigation methods to aid in the analysis and identification of different types of crimes. The authors introduced a Cognitive Computing enabled Convolution Neural Network (CC-CNN) approach, combined with various learning algorithms, to recognize crime types extracted from unstructured textual data. In [8], a graph-based clustering approach was proposed to extract relationships from criminal data documents. The approach employed natural language processing (NLP) techniques on crime data collected by LEAs to extract and represent crime-related information in a graph using named entities and relations. The graph was built based on a calculated similarity score, and an unsupervised clustering model was utilized to identify relations between criminological data and uncover criminal patterns. Similarly, in [7], a framework was introduced for the automatic extraction of information from criminal documents. The framework facilitated the discovery, extraction, and classification of reports and documents into named entities, which were then represented in a graph database tailored for the Portuguese language. The framework automated document processing and supported data representation in graphs.

Lastly, researchers in [1,3,6] utilized telecommunications data, specifically call detail records (CDR), to assist in criminal detection. In [3], an unsupervised data procedure was introduced to build a model that employed Neo4j for analyzing user behavior and identifying potential suspects. In [1], a method for tracking calls across multiple mobile networks was proposed to study, analyze, and link suspects to forensic crimes. The method took advantage of the spatio-temporal nature of CDR data to aid in forensic analysis. In [6], the authors employed a Bayesian Classifier to analyze CDR data collected from telecommunication companies in Pakistan and detect criminal or terrorist activities.

These studies demonstrate the diverse approaches employed in crime analytics and detection, utilizing social media data, video analysis, text mining, and telecommunications data. Each approach offers valuable insights and contributes to the overall objective of improving crime investigation techniques.

3 ICAD Framework

Despite the considerable efforts invested in criminal investigation, many of the techniques proposed suffer from several drawbacks. Firstly, they are often not fully automated systems and still require the intervention of law enforcement agencies (LEAs) to identify suspects recognized by the system. Secondly, these techniques typically focus on a single data source or multiple sources with similar data structures when investigating crimes. This limited scope restricts their ability to leverage diverse and heterogeneous data sources. Lastly, the real-time aspect and challenges posed by big data collection, including velocity, volume, and veracity, are not adequately addressed in most existing techniques.

To overcome these limitations, we propose the Intelligent Framework for Real-Time Criminal Analytics and Detection (ICAD). This framework aims to address the aforementioned challenges by enabling real-time data collection from various heterogeneous criminal data sources and identifying individuals potentially involved in criminal, radicalized, or terrorist activities. The general architecture of the ICAD framework is depicted in Fig. 1, which illustrates four distinct phases. Each phase utilizes a range of data science tools and techniques to achieve its objectives.

In the subsequent sections, we will present a motivation scenario that highlights the practical application of the ICAD framework. Additionally, we will provide detailed explanations of each proposed phase, outlining the methodologies and processes employed to enhance criminal analytics and detection capabilities.

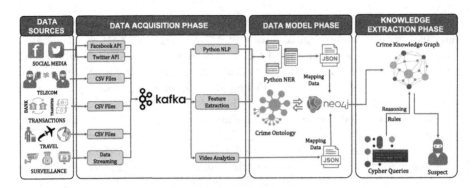

Fig. 1. ICAD architecture.

3.1   Motivating Scenario

Fig. 2 depicts a compelling scenario where our proposed framework can be effectively applied. Let's consider a typical individual named "Tom Harry", who, like many people, maintains multiple social media profiles across various platforms and frequently shares thoughts and ideas. However, authorities have recently discovered something alarming on one of Tom's accounts. Law enforcement agencies (LEAs) have come across posts that endorse the actions of "Al-Baghdadi" and express support for the ideologies of "Daech" (ISIS). This raises suspicions, prompting LEA analysts to delve deeper into Tom's activities to determine if any of them are connected to criminal, radicalized, or terrorist acts.

In their investigation, the LEA analysts stumbled upon a wealth of data about Tom in the transactions dataset of a well-known money transfer company, referred to as OMT. The data revealed that Tom has engaged in substantial financial transactions, both sending and receiving large sums of money to and from Syria, involving multiple individuals. Additionally, through the analysis of video data obtained from various surveillance systems strategically deployed in critical zones within Lebanon, Tom was identified in a region located between Lebanon and Syria. The video footage captured him holding a weapon and engaged in conversation with a suspected individual affiliated with a terrorist organization.

Furthermore, an examination of travel databases unveiled an extensive history of Tom's frequent trips to Syria, often for short periods of time. These recurring visits raised further suspicions and intensified the LEA's focus on investigating Tom. As part of their efforts, the LEA accessed Tom's telecommunications data and uncovered a substantial amount of call detail records (CDRs) indicating prolonged conversations with individuals residing in Syria.

The aforementioned findings have prompted the LEA to continue their comprehensive investigation into Tom's activities, using multiple sources of data such as social media, financial transactions, video surveillance, travel records, and telecommunications data. By meticulously analyzing these different data sets, the LEA aims to ascertain the extent of Tom's involvement and potential connections to criminal or terrorist activities, providing valuable insights for their ongoing investigation.

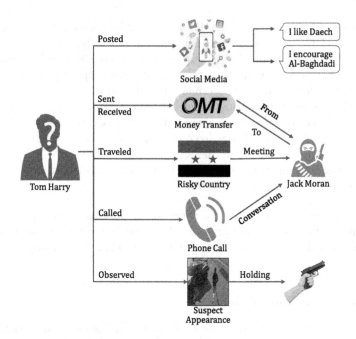

Fig. 2. Motivating scenario for ICAD application.

3.2 Data Sources Phase

ICAD offers several significant advantages, one of which is its comprehensive integration of various data sources in the crime investigation process. The primary objective of ICAD is to accurately identify suspects by tracking their activities in daily life. The following are the key data sources investigated in ICAD:

- **Social media:** In today's world, social media platforms have become crucial sources of data where individuals freely express their thoughts, ideas, locations, and more. As a result, social media platforms provide a wealth of information that can be invaluable in crime investigations.
- **Telecom:** Phone calls often serve as the initial means of communication among suspects involved in crimes, radicalized individuals, or members of terrorist organizations. Consequently, Law Enforcement Agencies (LEAs) can utilize Call Detail Records (CDR) to analyze the timing and content of calls, aiding in the crime analysis process.
- **Money transactions:** Money transactions, typically conducted through banks or global transfer companies, play a significant role in illegal activities. By collecting and analyzing data on financial transactions, LEAs can gain insight into the financial history of a person, detecting any suspicious or illicit activities.
- **Travel data:** Countries are often categorized as risky or non-risky, with the risky ones being prime targets for terrorists. By analyzing travel histories,

investigators can identify potential suspects who frequently travel to risky countries. This information becomes crucial in making informed decisions during the investigation. For example, in the aforementioned scenario, the extensive travel history of "Tom" to Syria to meet suspected individuals was instrumental for LEAs in their crime investigation process.

- **Surveillance systems:** Many cities have implemented surveillance systems for security purposes and to enhance various services such as traffic management and public health. The video data collected by these systems can assist LEAs in tracking suspect activities and movements. Additionally, surveillance footage can help identify the presence of weapons or other risky objects that may be relevant to the investigation.

By leveraging these diverse data sources, ICAD aims to provide a comprehensive and multi-dimensional approach to crime investigation, enhancing the ability of law enforcement agencies to effectively identify and apprehend suspects.

3.3   Data Acquisition Phase

The primary objective of this layer is to gather and consolidate semantically meaningful data from diverse data sources that may vary in format and structure. The purpose behind this data acquisition process is to provide law enforcement agencies (LEAs) with enhanced and valuable information. The data acquisition layer is carried out in two distinct stages, which are outlined below:

Data Collection. The data collection phase of the ICAD framework involves gathering data from various sources. The specific data collection methods employed depend on the format of the data stored in these sources. The following approaches are utilized:

- Facebook Graph and Twitter APIs: These APIs are used to collect data from social media platforms. This enables the retrieval of relevant information and activities from these platforms.
- CSV files: Data from telecommunication, transactions, and travel sources, which are typically structured, are gathered using CSV files. This allows for the extraction of data in a consistent and organized manner.
- Web Scraping: Streaming video data obtained from surveillance systems is handled using web scraping techniques. This enables the collection of real-time video data for further analysis.
- Textual data files: The content of police reports and other textual data is stored in text files. These files are accessed to retrieve and process relevant information.

Kafka, a messaging queue, is employed during this stage to store and manage the collected data from various sources. The data is produced into the Kafka messaging queue for subsequent analysis.

Data Analysis. Once the data is collected, the data analysis process begins. The Kafka consumer retrieves data from the message queue and performs the necessary analysis. The analysis techniques applied in ICAD can be categorized into three types:

1. Python NLP (Natural Language Processing): This technique is used to process and extract information from textual data obtained from social media and police reports. It enables the identification and extraction of relevant information from text-based sources.
2. Feature extraction: This technique involves selecting potential features (columns) from telecommunication, transactions, and travel databases. It helps identify relevant data points that are crucial for crime analysis.
3. Video analytics techniques: ICAD employs video analytics techniques, such as object detection (e.g., weapons) and human tracking, for analyzing video data obtained from surveillance systems. These techniques enable the detection and tracking of objects and individuals of interest.

ICAD has a flexible architecture that allows for the integration of existing or novel algorithms related to any type of data analysis. This ensures adaptability and the ability to incorporate new and advanced analysis techniques into the pipeline.

3.4   Data Model Phase

The Data Model Phase forms the core of the ICAD architecture and focuses on constructing a crime-based ontology. This ontology defines relevant concepts used by law enforcement agencies (LEAs) and establishes semantic relationships between them. The proposed ontology has the following characteristics:

1. Hybrid: The ontology takes into account information extracted from all data sources during the previous phase. It incorporates a comprehensive understanding of different aspects of crime analysis.
2. Scalability: The ontology is designed to accommodate the integration of new data sources and concepts developed by LEAs. This ensures that the ontology remains up to date and adaptable to emerging crime types.
3. Simplicity: The concepts and terminologies employed in the ontology are familiar to law enforcement investigators. This facilitates their ability to formulate queries and perform analyses without requiring extensive knowledge of the underlying data sources.

The ontology draws from existing ontologies in the literature and defines four main concepts: person, organization, location, and activity. Additionally, the following concepts and relationships are defined (Fig. 3):

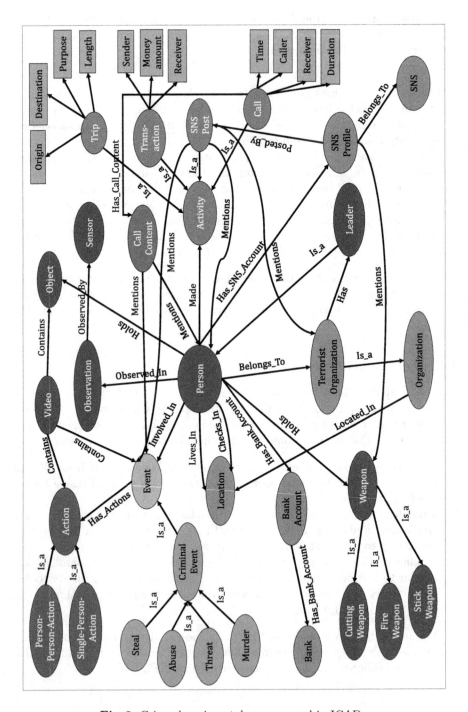

Fig. 3. Crime-domain ontology proposed in ICAD.

- A *person* can engage in various *activities*, such as traveling to another country, conducting financial *transactions*, posting on social media, or making *phone calls*.
- A person may be a member of a *terrorist organization* located in a particular country, which is managed by a *leader*.
- Individuals can be *observed* or detected by *sensors*, and the captured *video* footage may reveal *actions* that indicate a *criminal event*, such as *murder* or *threats*. The video may also provide evidence that the person *possesses* certain types of *weapons*.
- Regular *phone calls* between a person and members of an organization may indicate the occurrence of a *criminal event*.
- A person may have one or multiple *banking accounts* for performing various financial transactions.

3.5 Knowledge Extraction Phase

The process of extracting information from the data acquisition phase plays a vital role in generating a comprehensive knowledge graph by mapping the acquired information to various concepts defined within the ontology. This knowledge graph serves as a valuable resource for further analysis and decision-making. In the subsequent phase of knowledge extraction, semantic reasoning techniques are applied to the knowledge graph, enabling the retrieval of meaningful information and valuable insights.

The application of semantic reasoning adds an additional layer of intelligence to the system, empowering law enforcement agency (LEA) experts and analysts to define inference rules. These inference rules are designed to detect specific scenarios relevant to the criminal investigation process. By formulating these rules, LEA experts can uncover hidden connections, identify patterns, and make informed decisions based on the derived knowledge.

In the scope of this research work, several inference rules have been defined to enhance the effectiveness of the criminal investigation process. These rules are tailored to address distinct scenarios and contribute to the identification and understanding of complex criminal activities. The following inference rules have been established as part of this research:

- *Rule 1*: Person X posts about Terrorist Organization and have several calls to a Country C with a Person Y and X travels to C several times and made several transactions to C and has been observed holding weapon at Location L while meeting Person Y → X is a suspect.
- *Rule 2*: Person X calls several times Person Y and Y has been observed meeting X in videos holding weapons and (Y sends money to X and X send money to Y) and Person X is suspected → Y is a suspect.
- *Rule 3*: Person X is criminal and Person X supports Person X in a posts or call and Y posts about terrorist organization → Y is a suspect.
- *Rule 4*: Person X threats in a post or a call Person Y at Time T and Person Y lives in Place P and the Person X travels to Place P at Time T+1 and

[X observed by videos holding weapons at Place P and Time T+1] → X is a suspect.

- *Rule 5*: Person X threats in a post or call Person Y and been observed by video involved in a Criminal Event (for instance, Murder of Person Y) at Location L at Time T and holding weapon → X is a suspect.
- *Rule 6*: Person X threats by post or call Person Y at Time T and X sends money transaction to Person Z at Time T+1 then Person Z been observed meeting at same Location with Y at Time T+2 and Z was holding a weapon → X and Z are suspects.
- *Rule 7*: Person X threats by post or call Person Y and Person X checks-in at every location Y checked-in and X been observed holding weapons at the locations → X is a suspect.

4   Implementation and Evaluation

In this section, we provide a comprehensive overview of the implementation of each phase proposed within the ICAD framework.

4.1   Data Sources Phase Implementation

In our simulation phase, we employed a high-performance HPE ProLiant ML150 Gen9 Server equipped with a 64-bit 6-core Intel Xeon CPU operating at a clock speed of 1.7 GHz. The server boasted a substantial 64 GB RAM and had a storage capacity of 240 GB SSD (Solid State Drive) complemented by an 8 TB HDD (Hard Disk Drive). To support our simulation environment, we utilized the Windows Server 2012 R2 operating system.

To emulate the various data sources, we created dedicated virtual machines. Synthetic data was generated for three specific domains: telecom, transactions, and travel. For the telecom domain, we simulated telecommunications data reflecting call detail records (CDR), allowing us to analyze and investigate communication patterns. In the transactions domain, we generated artificial transactional data to mimic financial activities for investigative purposes. Lastly, in the travel domain, synthetic travel-related data was produced to simulate passenger itineraries and movements.

For the video surveillance aspect, we implemented a technique proposed in [2] that focused on the detection of knife-related crimes within public areas. This technique aimed to assist law enforcement agencies (LEAs) in minimizing the potential consequences of such incidents. By employing advanced algorithms and video analysis methods, the system could identify and alert authorities about suspicious activities involving knives captured by surveillance cameras.

By utilizing this robust server setup, virtual machines, and synthetic data generation techniques, we were able to simulate realistic scenarios and evaluate the effectiveness of our proposed approaches in crime analytics and detection.

4.2   Data Acquisition Phase Implementation

The implementation of this phase heavily relies on Apache Kafka and Python programming. Apache Kafka serves as the central component for data streaming, and Python is utilized for developing the necessary functionalities. Specifically, two Python-based Jupyter Notebooks are created: *DataProduce.ipynb* and *DataConsumer.ipynb*, each serving as a data producer and consumer, respectively.

In the data producer component, the Python code reads data from various data source files and sends it to the message queue implemented by Kafka. This enables the seamless flow of data from the different sources to the subsequent stages of processing.

On the other hand, the data consumer component receives the data from the message queue, leveraging Kafka's capabilities. Within the *DataConsumer.ipynb* Jupyter Notebook, different data analysis techniques are applied to the received data. These techniques include Natural Language Processing (NLP), feature extraction, and video analytics. All these data analysis techniques are implemented using Python libraries and frameworks.

By employing NLP, textual data can be processed and analyzed to extract meaningful insights and patterns. Feature extraction techniques enable the identification and extraction of relevant features from the data, enhancing subsequent analysis and modeling. Furthermore, video analytics techniques allow for the analysis and interpretation of video data, enabling the detection of specific events or actions of interest.

The combination of Apache Kafka and Python programming within these Jupyter Notebooks facilitates a smooth data flow, from data producers to data consumers, with intermediate processing and analysis steps. This enables efficient data processing, transformation, and extraction of valuable information before forwarding it to the next layer of the system for further processing or decision-making.

4.3   Data Model Phase Implementation

In this phase, the construction of the ontology involved utilizing the Neo4j Graph Database Desktop Application version 4.4.0. The data analysis process in the Kafka consumer generated two distinct types of data. Firstly, there were Named Entity Relationships (NER) derived from social media and CSV files as data sources. Secondly, there were objects detected through video analytics. To ensure compatibility and ease of integration, both types of data were initially converted into JSON format. Subsequently, a mapping process was performed, aligning the converted data with the various concepts defined within the ontology.

By leveraging the capabilities of the Neo4j Graph Database Desktop Application version 4.4.0, the ontology construction phase efficiently incorporated and processed the NER data originating from social media and CSV files, as well as the object data extracted from video analytics. This involved transforming the data into a JSON format, facilitating uniformity and standardization across different data sources. The subsequent mapping process ensured a seamless integration of the converted data with the defined ontology concepts, enabling comprehensive and meaningful analysis within the ontology framework.

4.4   Knowledge Extraction Phase Implementation

During this phase, we employed the Cypher Query language, which is available in Neo4j, to implement the predefined inference rules. These rules were applied to the knowledge graph generated in the data modeling phase, allowing us to determine if there were any matches with the real-time collected data. The results of these queries were organized and presented in a table format. In cases where matches were found, immediate notifications were sent to law enforcement agencies (LEAs) to ensure timely action.

To showcase the effectiveness of our framework in detecting real-life scenarios, we implemented the same scenario described in section III.A and visualized in Fig. 2 using Neo4j. All the predefined inference rules were applied during this implementation. As a result, we obtained a knowledge graph, as depicted in Fig. 4. This graph represents the synthesized data, integrating information from diverse data sources and mapping it to the specified ontology. The graph serves as a comprehensive representation of the interconnected relationships within the data.

Furthermore, Fig. 5 illustrates the outcomes of applying the inference rules within Neo4j to the motivating scenario. The visualization clearly demonstrates that our proposed framework successfully identified Tom Harry as a criminal suspect. This determination was based on his activities gathered from various data sources, which were integrated and analyzed by our framework.

By leveraging the capabilities of Neo4j and implementing the defined inference rules, our framework proves its efficacy in detecting and identifying potential criminal suspects in real-life situations. The seamless integration of data from multiple sources and the application of inference rules enable efficient and accurate crime detection, empowering law enforcement agencies to take appropriate actions in a timely manner.

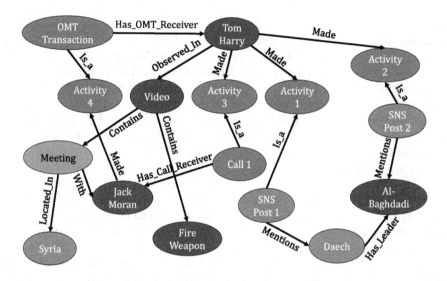

Fig. 4. Knowledge graph resulted from the motivating scenario.

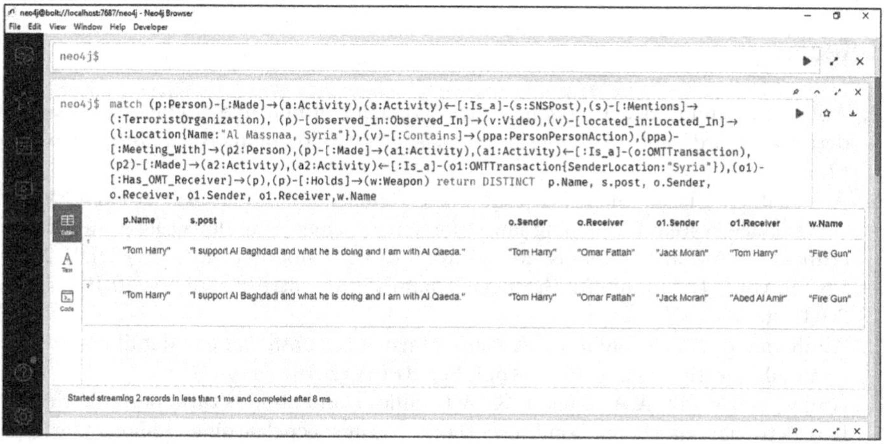

Fig. 5. Inference rules implemented in Neo4j.

5   Conclusion and Future Work

This research paper introduces the Intelligent Framework for Real-Time Criminal Analytics and Detection (ICAD), which offers a comprehensive solution for automating the crime investigation process and assisting law enforcement agencies (LEAs) in identifying suspects. The ICAD framework leverages ontological models and inference rules to enhance suspect recognition. To address various challenges associated with data collection and analysis, ICAD incorporates a range of data science tools and AI techniques across four key phases: data sources, data acquisition, data modeling, and knowledge extraction. Through the implementation of this proposed architecture, the efficiency of ICAD in detecting criminals has been successfully demonstrated across diverse scenarios.

There are two potential directions for enhancing ICAD. Firstly, the integration of additional data sources can significantly improve the accuracy of suspect identification. For example, incorporating police reports and court documents would provide valuable insights into a suspect's history and help predict their future intentions. These additional sources of information contribute to a more comprehensive and reliable suspect recognition process.

Secondly, studying suspect behaviors and body language can further enhance the effectiveness of ICAD in crime investigations. Criminals often exhibit common traits and physical gestures that can serve as valuable indicators. By incorporating the analysis of these behavioral cues, ICAD can provide deeper insights into suspect profiles and contribute to a more robust investigative process.

By expanding the scope of data sources and incorporating the study of suspect behaviors, ICAD has the potential to become an even more powerful and accurate tool for real-time criminal analytics and detection, thereby strengthening the capabilities of law enforcement agencies in combating crime.

References

1. Abba, E., Aibinu, A., Alhassan, J.: Development of multiple mobile networks call detailed records and its forensic analysis. Digit. Commun. Netw. **5**(4), 256–265 (2019)
2. Abdallah, R., Benbernou, S., Taher, Y., Younas, M., Haque, R.: A smart video surveillance system for helping law enforcement agencies in detecting knife related crimes. In: Awan, I., Younas, M., Bentahar, J., Benbernou, S. (eds.) DBB 2022. LNNS, vol. 541, pp. 65–78. Springer, Cham (2022). https://doi.org/10.1007/978-3-031-16035-6_6
3. Abuhamoud, N., Geepalla, E.: A study of using big data and call detail records for criminal investigation. J. Pure Appl. Sci. **18**(4) (2019)
4. Amjad, K., Malik, A.A., Mehta, S.: A technique and architectural design for criminal detection based on Lombroso theory using deep learning. Lahore Garrison Univ. Res. J. Comput. Sci. Inf. Technol. **4**(3), 47–63 (2020)
5. Barhamgi, M., Masmoudi, A., Lara-Cabrera, R., Camacho, D.: Social networks data analysis with semantics: application to the radicalization problem. J. Ambient Intell. Human. Comput. 1–15 (2018)
6. Burney, S.M.A., Arifeen, Q.U., Mahmood, N., Bari, S.A.K.: Suspicious call detection using Bayesian network approach. WSEAS Trans. Inf. Sci. Appl. 37–49
7. Carnaz, G., Nogueira, V.B., Antunes, M.: A graph database representation of Portuguese criminal-related documents. In: Informatics, vol. 8, p. 37. MDPI (2021)
8. Das, P., Das, A.K., Nayak, J., Pelusi, D., Ding, W.: A graph based clustering approach for relation extraction from crime data. IEEE Access **7**, 101269–101282 (2019)
9. Karpova, A., Savelev, A., Vilnin, A., Kuznetsov, S.: Method for detecting far-right extremist communities on social media. Soc. Sci. **11**(5), 200 (2022)

10. Lara-Cabrera, R., Gonzalez-Pardo, A., Barhamgi, M., Camacho, D.: Extracting radicalisation behavioural patterns from social network data. In: 2017 28th International Workshop on Database and Expert Systems Applications (DEXA), pp. 6–10. IEEE (2017)

11. Mushtaq, N., Ali, K., Moetesum, M., Siddiqi, I.: Impact of demographics on automated criminal tendency detection from facial images. In: 2022 International Conference on Frontiers of Information Technology (FIT), pp. 88–93. IEEE (2022)

12. Schiliro, F., Beheshti, A., Moustafa, N.: A novel cognitive computing technique using convolutional networks for automating the criminal investigation process in policing. In: Arai, K., Kapoor, S., Bhatia, R. (eds.) IntelliSys 2020. AISC, vol. 1250, pp. 528–539. Springer, Cham (2021). https://doi.org/10.1007/978-3-030-55180-3_39

13. Zaman, M., et al.: Execution of coordinate based classifier system to predict specific criminal behavior using regional multi person pose estimator. Ph.D. thesis, Brac University (2021)

Web Technologies

Web Page Segmentation:
A DOM-Structural Cohesion
Analysis Approach

Minh-Hieu Huynh[1], Quoc-Tri Le[1], Vu Nguyen[1,2,3]([✉]), and Tien Nguyen[1,4]

[1] Katalon Inc., Ho Chi Minh City, Vietnam
{hieu.huynh,tri.qle,vu.nguyen}@katalon.com
[2] University of Science, Ho Chi Minh City, Vietnam
[3] Vietnam National University, Ho Chi Minh City, Vietnam
nvu@fit.hcmus.edu.vn
[4] University of Texas at Dallas, Richardson, TX, USA
tien.n.nguyen@utdallas.edu

Abstract. Web page segmentation is a fundamental technique applied in information retrieval systems to enhance web crawling tasks and information extraction. Its objectives are to gain deep insights from crawling results and to extract the main content of a webpage by disregarding the irrelevant regions. Over time, several solutions have been proposed to address the segmentation problem using different approaches and learning strategies. Among these, the structural cue, which is a characteristic of the DOM tree, is widely utilized as a primary factor in segmentation models. In this paper, we propose a novel technique for web page segmentation using DOM-structural cohesion analysis. Our approach involves generating blocks that represent groups of DOM subtrees with similar tag structures. By analyzing the cohesion within each generated block and comparing detailed information such as types, attributes, and visual cues of web page elements, the approach can effectively maintain or reconstruct the segmentation layout. Additionally, we employ the Canny algorithm to optimize the segmentation result by reducing redundant spaces, resulting in a more accurate segmentation. We evaluate the effectiveness of our approach using a dataset of 1,969 web pages. The approach achieves 64% on the F_{B^3} score, surpassing existing state-of-the-art methods. The proposed DOM-structural cohesion analysis has the potential to improve web page segmentation and its various applications.

Keywords: Web Page Segmentation · Web Page Analysis · Tree Edit Distance

1 Introduction

Web page segmentation is the process of dividing a web page into smaller meaningful regions or segments such as the header, navigation menu, content area,

---

M.-H. Huynh and Q.-T. Le—Both authors contributed equally to this work.

F. Zhang et al. (Eds.): WISE 2023, LNCS 14306, pp. 319–333, 2023.
https://doi.org/10.1007/978-981-99-7254-8_25

sidebar, footer, and other elements. It is based on a web page's content, structure, and visibility that humans can perceive.

Web page segmentation has been applied for various purposes, with a prominent application in information retrieval systems to distinguish valuable content from irrelevant content on a web page. This segmentation process is utilized to enhance crawling (detecting templates [2,24,28], duplicates [18,20], and changes [7,15]) and for information extraction tasks (indexing [1], main content extraction [26,29], and entity mining [16]). For example, instead of extracting only an image, we consider extracting the region that contains the image, allowing us to combine additional relevant information and gain more insights from the crawling result [3]. In the field of information extraction, segmentation can be used for extracting main contents by ignoring regions that contain noise, such as advertisements, or unrelated parts like headers, menus, and navigation bars [23]. Furthermore, in other areas, such as test automation, dividing web pages into regions for page comparison plays a crucial role in generating reliable test oracles [27].

Over time, many solutions have been proposed to address the segmentation problem using different approaches and learning strategies. The most commonly used techniques fall into several categories: ad-hoc approaches [4,5,15,22,25] (which rely on manually-tuned heuristics and parameter-dependent methods), theoretically-founded approaches [1,7] (based on graph-theoretic and classical clustering algorithms), computer vision approaches [8,10], and others (as mentioned in [11]). In general, these approaches share three key elements: visual, textual, and structural cues found on web pages. Among other features, structural is most widely utilized in various approaches. The structural cue involves approaches that take the DOM (Document Object Model) tree as an input. Due to various information comprised in the DOM tree, several well-known approaches have employed DOM as the main feature of their works, including algorithms such as the VIsion-based Page Segmentation (VIPS) [5], Block-o-Matic (BoM) [22], Jiang et al. [12], and Xiang et al. [25]. However, most of these algorithms rely on hand-crafted parameters [5,22] or hard-configured rules [5].

These parameter-dependent or rule-based approaches have limitations in adaptability and robustness. They often require domain knowledge and fine-tuning, which is not fully automated and may not yield optimal results when applied on different web pages. Taking into account these limitations, our approach aims to overcome the reliance on human-tuning parameters by employing flexible techniques that adapt to the characteristics of each website being analyzed.

In this research, a novel DOM-structural analysis using a statistical method is proposed. The proposed method involves the following steps: (1) generating blocks that are DOM subtrees with similar tag structures, (2) analyzing the cohesion in each block to keep the block in segmentation layout or reconstruct it, the detailed information in the web page elements as type, attributes, and visual cues will be deeply compared to identify the block cohesion, and (3) applying the Canny algorithm [6] to reduce redundant spaces in the block for a more user-friendly layout.

We evaluate our method using a dataset of 1,969 web pages, which is based on the Webis-WebSeg-20 dataset [13]. The results show that our method achieves a 64% F_{B^3}, which is higher than VIPS and MMDetection evaluated on the same dataset by 19% and 10%, respectively.

2   Motivating Example

Modern websites undergo frequent changes in their display, such as updating information and responsive user interface. This poses a significant challenge for web page segmentation methods that rely heavily on visual characteristics. The following example shows a limitation of a vision-based method represented by VIPS.

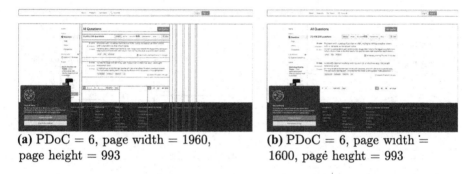

(a) PDoC = 6, page width = 1960, page height = 993

(b) PDoC = 6, page width = 1600, page height = 993

Fig. 1. Two VIPS segmentation results on different window sizes

Figure 1 showcases two VIPS segmentation results obtained using different window sizes with the red rectangles representing segments. The segmentation outcome is influenced by two primary factors: the extraction of visual blocks and the identification of horizontal and vertical separators within these blocks. In our investigation, we reduced the window size of the web page to observe a minor visual change. Surprisingly, the segmentation also changed, even though all other configurations remained the same. This limitation becomes apparent when performing information extraction tasks since the extracted contents are inconsistent, despite the web page's content remaining unchanged.

Based on this experiment, we have concluded that visual characteristics alone are not sufficient to solve the web page segmentation problem. Instead, we have shifted our focus toward DOM-structural analysis. Our approach integrates visual cues (text, visibility, etc.) for structural analysis under the DOM node's attributes, disregarding invisible elements on web pages. By taking this approach, we aim to overcome the limitations observed with purely visual-based methods.

3 Method

Our approach to site segmentation relies on identifying regions or segments that have structurally similar elements and highlighting them with corresponding zones on a snapshot of the webpage. The output of our proposed method is a list of DOM nodes (DOM-subtrees) extracted from the web page, referred to as a *DOM-driven layout*. This output is highly valuable for web information retrieval as the DOM tree represents the complete information of a web page, enabling us to extract all the relevant content. Similarly, each segment is represented by a DOM-subtree that contains all the necessary information that can be extracted from that specific segment. For result visualization, in some cases, the DOM node's visual block displays in an unexpected manner on the web page's screenshot. For example, it does not cover all inside elements' content or contains redundant spaces (i.e., borders, paddings). To tackle this problem, we perform a further task to create an *appearance-driven layout* by employing the Canny algorithm (Sect. 3.3).

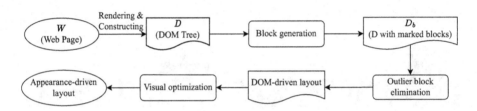

Fig. 2. Segmentation model

The segmentation process begins by taking the URL of a webpage (W) and generating a DOM tree (D) through rendering and constructing. By identifying DOM nodes with similar tag structures, we construct a modified DOM tree (D_b) that marks these nodes as blocks. To identify the desired regions within the *DOM-driven layout*, we analyze the cohesion or homogeneity of these blocks. Finally, we aim to optimize the geometry of each region on the webpage's screenshot, aligning it more closely with the human perspective in the *Appearance-driven layout* version.

3.1 Block Generation

In this section, we provide a detailed explanation of the *block generation* process mentioned in Fig. 2. The objective of this step is to identify the nodes that have children with similar structural characteristics and mark these nodes in the DOM tree (D_b).

Definition 1 (A DOM-block tree (D_b)) is the original DOM tree where each node is marked as a block or not.

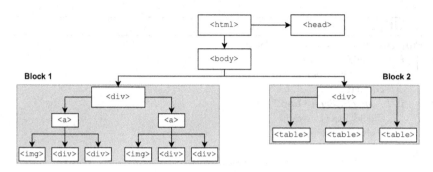

Fig. 3. Example of block generation. (Color figure online)

Figure 1(b) shows an example of how block nodes are identified. We define the blocks to be a DOM node that contains children with a similar structure, which is illustrated as the red zone in Fig. 3. For employing the breadth-first search traversal, we first initialize a queue with the root node of the tree (e.g., body node). For every element in the queue, we compare its structure to the left and right siblings. If its structure does not match, the children of the current element will be added to the queue. Otherwise, the current element is marked as a block node as it contains a similar structure and remove from the queue. This loop will be executed until the queue is empty.

In this stage, we aim to scan the whole tree to get all possible blocks. The output of this step is a *DOM-block tree*. It is possible that some blocks are either too large and contain other blocks or too small. The blocks that are of little importance are known as *outlying blocks* and will be dealt with in the upcoming phase called *outlying block elimination.*

3.2 Outlying Block Elimination

As mentioned earlier, we propose a statistical method to obtain desired blocks from a hierarchical block layout. The method is based on the cohesion of the blocks determined during the previous generation process. A larger block may internally contain more distinct structures, resulting in low homogeneity (high heterogeneity) in structure. In such cases, the corresponding blocks should be removed and replaced by their child blocks. Assuming that we have identified blocks with high heterogeneity in structure (referred to as *outlying blocks*), Algorithm 2 demonstrates how we eliminate outliers based on the result of their heterogeneity analysis.

Definition 2 (The segmentation block (S_{block})) is the set of blocks obtained after filtering out the outliers.

Before proceeding to the heterogeneity analysis process, we observe the hierarchical blocks represented as a flattened list of blocks. The objective of the analysis is to determine the heterogeneity score for each generated block.

Algorithm 1: Heterogeneity Analysis

---

1 **Function** GetHeterogeneity(*node*):
2 | Blocks, HMGs ← ∅
3 | **if** *! node* **or** *! node.isBlockNode* **then**
4 | | **return**
5 | **if** *! node.children* **then**
6 | | Blocks.insert(*node*)
7 | | HMGs.insert(0)
8 | **else**
9 | | H ← Heterogeneity (*node.children*)
10 | | Blocks.insert(*node*)
11 | | HMGs.insert(H)
12 | | **for** *child in node.children* **do**
13 | | | childAnalysis ← GetHeterogeneity(*child*)
14 | | | **if** childAnalysis *is not None* **then**
15 | | | | Blocks.insert(childAnalysis[0])
16 | | | | HMGs.insert(childAnalysis[1])
17 | | | **end**
18 | | **end**
19 | **end**
20 | **return** Blocks, HMGs

Definition 3 (The heterogeneity score (H)) of a block is derived by evaluating the dissimilarity in the structure of its children. To determine this score, the Tree Edit Distance (TED) algorithm [21] is utilized to compare each pair of children, and the resulting metric is represented by the standard deviation of the edit distance cost for these pairs.

$$\begin{cases} C_{i,j} = TED(Child_i, Child_j), \forall i,j \in \mathbb{N}; i, j \leq N; i \neq j \\ H_{block} = StandardDeviation(C) \end{cases} \tag{1}$$

– N: Number of block node's children.
– C: A edit distance cost matrix, where each value in the matrix represents the cost of the best sequence of actions to transform $Child_i$ to $Child_j$.

The higher H score of a block is, the more distinct structure inside that block, indicating an outlying block. Based on the result of the heterogeneity analysis (Algorithm 1), the question arises: How can we determine the threshold to identify outlying blocks by H scores? To address this research question, we propose a statistical method that is free from predefined thresholds. This method utilizes the Interquartile Range (IQR) to assess the heterogeneity score of each block. By employing the IQR, we can effectively identify outliers within the generated blocks.

Figure 4 shows a toy example of how H scores vary in different cases. The elements $\bigcirc, \square, \triangle$ belong to a block, and the edit distance cost between each pair of elements is different. In this case, B_1 contains only one type of element,

---

Algorithm 2: Outlying block elimination

```
 1  Function BlockEliminator(node):
 2  │   S_block = ∅
 3  │   if node.isOutlier then
 4  │   │   for child in node.children do
 5  │   │   │   if child.isBlockNode then
 6  │   │   │   │   S_block.insert(BlockEliminator(child))
 7  │   │   │   else
 8  │   │   │   │   S_block.insert(child)
 9  │   │   │   end
10  │   │   end
11  │   else
12  │   │   S_block.insert(node)
13  │   end
14  │   return S_block
15  Blocks, HMGs ← GetHeterogeneity(root)
16  MarkOutliers(Blocks, HMGs)
17  S_block ← BlockEliminator(root)
```

---

resulting in the minimum H score. Conversely, B_3 contains all types of assumed elements, leading to the maximum H score. In more complicated cases, the edit distance cost can be larger than in the example, depending on the differences between each pair of DOM subtrees within a block.

3.3 Visual Optimization

Definition 4 (A segmentation region (S_r)) is a segmentation block ($\in$ S_{block} (line 21 in Algorithm 2)) whose bounding box has been improved to be more suited for the screenshot of the web page. The bounding box's empty spaces will be removed, and the original bounding box will be cropped to match the screenshot's representation of the region's content.

Figure 5a demonstrates that practically all segmentation blocks in the DOM-driven layout version have additional vacant spaces (i.e., borders, paddings) inside, which, in our opinion, lowers the segmentation layout's quality even further. Canny Edge Detection is a computer vision technique that we employed to optimize the segmentation layout. The bounding box will be trimmed until it reaches an object inside the segmentation block. The optimized segmentation layout is more comprehensible and reduces redundant zones in each section, as shown in Fig. 5b.

4 Experiments and Results

4.1 Dataset

We conduct our evaluation on the Webis-WebSeg-20 [13] dataset, which is the largest publicly accessible set of data in terms of web segmentation. The dataset

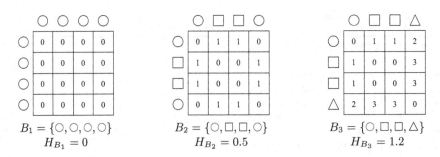

Fig. 4. The heterogeneity score (H) reflects the structural dissimilarity within each block (B). Assuming, $TED(\bigcirc,\bigcirc) = 0, TED(\bigcirc,\square) = 1, TED(\bigcirc,\triangle) = 2, TED(\square,\triangle) = 3$

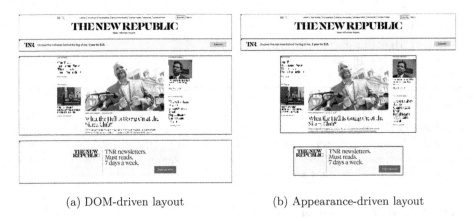

(a) DOM-driven layout   (b) Appearance-driven layout

Fig. 5. Example of a visually optimized layout segmentation

contains more than 8,000 web pages from more than 5,500 different domains. The websites are well distributed from top-ranked to low-ranked websites by Alexa ranking to ensure the diversity in data.

For each data instance, the authors provided an HTML file to store the DOM structure of the web page and a screenshot of the whole page. Theoretically, the position of every DOM node in the HTML file in the dataset is stored in another metadata file along with the respective absolute XPath. This is to make sure that we do not need to re-render the webpage and guarantee that the position of every node matches the corresponding position in the ground truth.

However, while reviewing the data, we realized that the XPaths in the metadata were constructed incorrectly. As they only count the index of visible siblings while ignoring the invisible ones. Therefore, in an HTML file, if there is a node that is invisible, the following sibling nodes would be mis-indexed. When reconstructing the XPath of nodes in the HTML file without rendering, we are unable to identify whether an HTML element is visible. As a result, it is impossible to map the nodes to the corresponding XPath in the dataset. To resolve this problem, we decided to filter out the data instances that are indexed XPath incorrectly.

Algorithm to Filter The Data: Let X represent the set of provided XPaths, and X^* denote the set of actual XPaths. We define P as the set of tuples (x, p) where x belongs to X and p is the rendered position of x on the page, $P = \{(x, p) \mid x \in X \}$. Our objective is to create a set $M = \{(x, x^*)\}$, which represents the one-to-one mapping between XPaths in the provided set X and their corresponding XPaths in the actual set X^*. Each element in M is a tuple (x, x^*), where x is an XPath from X, and x^* is the corresponding XPath from X^*. For each x in X, we aim to map it to the least greater-indexed x^* in X^* that possesses the same skeleton. As the index of x does not count the invisible nodes, it is always smaller than or equal to the actual index. Once all mappings are established, we check for any duplicated x^* values across all mappings. If duplicates are found, we eliminate the corresponding data instance as it fails to comply with the rules.

As a result, there are 1,969 data instances that are indexed correctly, and we use this set to evaluate our approach.

4.2   Metrics

We adopted a comprehensive framework for assessing the performance of web page segmentation algorithms [13]. This approach allows us to enhance the comparability and consistency of our method's performance with other evaluated models that have been tested on the same dataset.

Unlike other image segmentation problems, web segmentation might produce a tree-structured segmentation result with different granularity levels that make a segment bigger or smaller. As a result, a ground truth segment may contain several predicted segments and vice versa. Therefore, this evaluation framework considers web page segmentation as a clustering task where each web page element is clustered into a group.

In the context of clustering, defining a similarity function is essential as it allows us to quantify the distance or dissimilarity between elements within a cluster. In such a manner, Kiesel et al. [13] have introduced the *atomic element* concept; they are (1) pixels, (2) DOM nodes, and (3) characters. The authors adapt the extended BCubed measurement from clustering, which examines the P_{B^3} (Eq. 2), R_{B^3} (Eq. 3), and F_{B^3} (Eq. 4) for each data instance [13].

To recapitulate, in the same manner of common precision, P_{B^3} calculates the ratio of true positive segments (segments that are in both ground truth and predicted segmentation) to all of the positive segments (segments that are in the predicted segmentation). Likewise, R_{B^3} calculates the ratio of true positive segments to all of the positive segments in the ground truth. And F_{B^3} is the harmonic mean of P_{B^3} and R_{B^3}. F_{B^3} satisfies all the necessary criteria for a segmentation similarity measure. It effectively handles partial segmentations, overlapping segments, and even nested segments. Additionally, F_{B^3} is resilient against trivial segmentations, such as under-segmentation, which divides the whole page as a segment, or over-segmentation, which consider every atomic element as a segment.

$$P_{B^3}(S, S^*) = \frac{1}{|E^S|} \sum_{e \in E^S} \left(\frac{1}{|E_e^S|} \sum_{e' \in E^S} \frac{\min(|S_e \cap S_{e'}|, |S_e \cap S_{e'}^*|)}{|S_e \cap S_{e'}|} \right) \tag{2}$$

$$R_{B^3}(S, S^*) = P_{B^3}(S^*, S) \tag{3}$$

$$F_{B^3}(S, S^*) = \frac{2 \times R_{B^3}(S, S^*) \times P_{B^3}(S, S^*)}{R_{B^3}(S, S^*) + P_{B^3}(S, S^*)} \tag{4}$$

Let S, S^* be the set of prediction segments and ground truth segments respectively, S_e be the set of segments that contains element e, E_S be the set of elements that belong to at least one segment in S. In the mathematical terms, $S_e = \{s \mid s \in S \wedge e \in E\}$, $E_S = \{e \mid e \in E \wedge Se \neq \emptyset\}$, and $E_e^S = \{e' \mid e' \in E \wedge S_e \cap S_{e'} \neq \emptyset\}$. The set of element e is denoted by E. At the *pixels* atomic level, each pixel in the page's screenshot is represented by e. We may encounter two subatomic levels of *pixels* known as *edges-fine* and *edges-coarse*, which utilize the edge image generated by the Canny detector. Regarding *nodes*, E pertains to the collection of DOM nodes within the tree structure. As for *chars*, it represents the set of characters shown on the page.

4.3   Experimental Setup

We use the evaluation results from [13] to compare with our algorithm. The experiment and parameter setup for each algorithm will be summarized as follows.

- **Baseline:** To provide context, the performance of the algorithms is compared to a naive approach of segmenting a web page into a single segment, which always reaches a maximum recall of 1 but the lowest precision.
- **VIPS:** VIPS [5] creates a hierarchical tree of segments based on the DOM tree of the page. Segments are split based on their degree of coherence, determined by heuristic rules considering tag names, background colors, DOM node sizes, and visual separators. The single parameter that influences the algorithm is the permitted degree of coherence (PDoC). The higher PDoC is, the lower precision it be. After experimentation, it was determined that the optimal value for PDoC is 6.
- **HEPS:** HEPS [17] employs heuristic rules considering DOM tree position, tag name, font size, and weight to identify headings and their corresponding segments.
- **Cormier:** Cormier et al. [10] developed a visual algorithm for web page segmentation based on edge detection. It calculates the probability of significant edges and composes line segments. The algorithm recursively splits segments based on the most semantically significant lines. Cormier depends on two parameters which are tl (maximum line length) and smin (minimum segment size); the best setting (tl = 512, smin = 45) was used for further experiments.
- **Meier:** Meier et al.'s [19] convolutional neural network is cutting-edge in segmenting digitized newspaper pages. Kiesel et al. [14] re-implemented it using text node positions instead of OCR. Uniform height (4096 pixels) and

scaling (256×768 pixels) were applied. The training utilized 10-fold cross-validation, stopping after 20.8 epochs on average.

- **MMDetection:** MMDetection [9], one of the best algorithms for object segmentation tasks in images, is reused for web segmentation. Because the output of image segmentation is a pixel mask, which is not suitable for web segmentation, the authors conduct a further step to match to mask to the nearest DOM node. For those cases where MMDetection cannot recognize any segment, the whole page will be treated as a segment.

4.4   Results

Table 1. The result of evaluating seven algorithms, including six algorithms that we reuse the results from Kiesel et al. [14] and our algorithm. For each kind of atomic element, we provide four metrics, including F-bcubed (F_{B3}), Precision (P_{B3}), Recall (R_{B3}), and the harmonic mean of the averaged R_{B3} and R_{B3}. For every column, the bold figure shows the highest value among all (excluding the baseline).

Algorithm		Baseline	VIPS	HEPS	Corm.	MMD.	Meier	Ours
Pixels	P_{B3}	0.15	0.33	0.31	0.31	0.48	0.47	**0.60**
	R_{B3}	1.00	0.69	0.62	**0.89**	0.59	0.55	0.68
	F_{B3}	0.23	0.37	0.31	0.32	0.41	0.33	**0.51**
	F_{B3}^*	0.26	0.45	0.42	0.46	0.53	0.50	**0.64**
Chars	P_{B3}	0.44	0.81	0.72	0.56	0.80	0.61	**0.83**
	R_{B3}	1.00	0.73	0.56	**0.91**	0.60	0.66	0.71
	F_{B3}	0.57	**0.70**	0.53	0.61	0.61	0.53	0.68
	F_{B3}^*	0.61	**0.77**	0.63	0.70	0.68	0.63	0.76
Nodes	P_{B3}	0.32	0.72	0.61	0.47	**0.77**	0.53	0.75
	R_{B3}	1.00	0.72	0.52	**0.90**	0.52	0.63	0.67
	F_{B3}	0.45	**0.66**	0.46	0.52	0.54	0.46	0.62
	F_{B3}^*	0.49	**0.72**	0.56	0.62	0.62	0.57	0.71
Edges-fine	P_{B3}	0.33	0.67	0.58	0.48	0.73	0.55	**0.75**
	R_{B3}	1.00	0.71	0.61	**0.89**	0.55	0.59	0.70
	F_{B3}	0.46	0.61	0.49	0.51	0.55	0.43	**0.63**
	F_{B3}^*	0.50	0.69	0.59	0.62	0.63	0.57	**0.72**
Edges-coarse	P_{B3}	0.33	0.68	0.58	0.49	0.73	0.54	**0.75**
	R_{B3}	1.00	0.71	0.61	**0.89**	0.55	0.59	0.69
	F_{B3}	0.46	0.62	0.49	0.52	0.55	0.43	**0.63**
	F_{B3}^*	0.50	0.70	0.60	0.63	0.63	0.57	**0.72**

Table 1 illustrates the evaluation results of six algorithms mentioned in Sect. 4.3 and our method. Since the size of the dataset was reduced to nearly 1/4 as compared to the original one, we also filtered the evaluation data on those selected ones and recalculated the R_{B^3}, P_{B^3}, F_{B^3}, and $F_{B^3}^*$ for each atomic element type. Notably, we observed that the results for each metric exhibited only a slight variation, with changes of less than 5% for each of them, while the overall score distribution remained unchanged.

The baseline method gives the most trivial result, which considers a whole web page as a single segment. This segment covers all of the ground truth segments; Thus, it reaches the maximum R_{B^3} of 1. Obviously, the P_{B^3} achieves a fairly low score, resulting in lowest F_{B^3} and $F_{B^3}^*$ scores.

Considering the P_{B^3} score, our algorithm attains the highest figure for every atomic type except *nodes*. The character category reaches the highest P_{B^3} among all, which is 83%. About the F_{B^3} and $F_{B^3}^*$, our approach shows impressive improvements, especially for pixels, our algorithm is 11% higher than MMDetection, which is the best pixel-centric algorithm in this task.

Despite performing relatively well on character and node elements, VIPS exposes its shortcomings in the pixels category. This disadvantage can be explained by the fact that VIPS tends to leave unnecessary background regions in their segmentation.

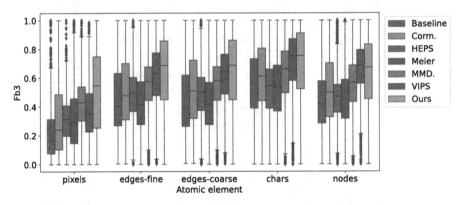

Fig. 6. The F_{B^3} score distribution for 1,969 data instances in the Webis-WebSeg-20 dataset [13]. Each box in the representation displays the median with a central mark, while the lower and upper edges of the box represent the 25th and 75th percentiles, respectively. The outliers are represented individually using the symbol ♦ on the plot.

Figure 6 illustrates the Fb3 distribution of our algorithm and the other six. Our algorithm's Fb3 median is higher than all other algorithms in every atomic type except for 'nodes.' Additionally, our upper quartiles for all five atomic levels reach the highest above all, showing that our algorithm generally produces higher accuracy.

Kiesel et al. [14] have pointed out a gap in previous works is the low F_{B^3} score on the *pixels* atomic level, where our algorithm makes a significant improvement and remains a competitive F_{B^3} and $F_{B^3}^*$ in other categories. The accompanying figure illustrates the remarkable proximity of our segmentation results to the human-annotated ground truth.

4.5 Discussion

To have a deeper insight, we conducted an investigation into cases where we achieved the highest and lowest F_{B^3} scores. Our goal was to gain a better understanding of the factors influencing the performance of our algorithm.

For the cases in which our algorithm was poorly performed, we see a common issue that the web page of these cases does not have a major dissimilarity in structure, such as the case that the whole page is full of a single tag name. As the main idea of our algorithm is to group similarly structured elements, our algorithm will consider the whole page as a single segment.

Conversely, our algorithm demonstrated remarkable performance in cases where web pages demonstrated easily distinguishable structures, with clear divisions for different functional areas such as the menu, navigation bar, content area, and footer. In these instances, the algorithm effectively identified and grouped elements based on their distinct structural patterns, enabling accurate segmentation and analysis.

In our approach, we specifically address the challenge posed by human-crafted parameters. We achieve this by incorporating an *outlying block elimination* step that is designed to be flexible and adaptive to the characteristics of each individual website. Moreover, our method takes the DOM tree as an input and returns the list of DOM nodes representing the segments; we thus are robust to the change of the relative position of elements as well as variations in element separators.

5 Related Work

There have been numerous approaches proposed for web page segmentation over the past two decades. One closely related approach, based on the Gestalt theory [25], applies the similarity law to group neighboring nodes under the same parent if their similarity measure exceeds 0.7, determined by their edit distance. BoM [22] consists of three phases: building a content structure from the DOM tree, mapping it to a logical structure based on a granularity parameter, and structuring it into a single representation that represents the segmented web page. VIPS method [5] extracts a hierarchical semantic structure by combining the DOM structure with visual cues through block extraction, separator detection, and content structure construction. In addition, the HEPS method [17], mentioned in the Webis-WebSeg-20 dataset [13] for comparison, utilizes text nodes and images to identify potential headings, corresponding blocks, and create a hierarchical segmentation. The DOM structure is also a vital component in other segmentation models [11,12], where additional factors like textual and visual cues are integrated to enhance performance.

A purely text-based approach, the Block Fusion (BF) algorithm [15], focuses on comparing the text density of adjacent blocks to determine whether they should be combined.

There are also approaches that treat a web page as an image and use computer vision techniques for segmentation. One such approach recursively splits segments into two by selecting the vertical and horizontal lines with the clearest edge pixels (detected through edge detection) from the entire page [10]. Another approach in this research direction fine-tuned the hybrid task cascade model from MMDetection for web page segmentation [8].

6   Conclusion

This paper proposes a novel method for web page segmentation using DOM-structural analysis. Our method overcame the limitations of parameter-dependent and rule-based methods by employing flexible techniques that adapt to the characteristics of each website being analyzed. The proposed method involves generating blocks, analyzing their cohesion, and applying the Canny algorithm for a more user-friendly layout. Results of evaluation on the dataset of 1,969 web pages show the efficacy of our method; with a score of 64% in F_{B^3}, it outperforms other approaches like VIPS and MMDetection by 19% and 10%, respectively. This study advances web page segmentation approaches and shows the potential to apply to information extraction and retrieval applications.

Future research will focus on improving our segmentation method to better analyze various type of applications. Better segmentation outcomes can be obtained by combining additional variables to provide multimodal cues, such as visual or textual features. Additionally, incorporating computer vision techniques can facilitate our method and produce a model that is more reliable.

References

1. Alcic, S., Conrad, S.: Page segmentation by web content clustering. In: Proceedings of the WIMS, pp. 1–9 (2011)
2. Bar-Yossef, Z., Rajagopalan, S.: Template detection via data mining and its applications. In: Proceedings of the 11th WWW, pp. 580–591 (2002)
3. Cai, D., He, X., Li, Z., Ma, W.Y., Wen, J.R.: Hierarchical clustering of www image search results using visual (2004)
4. Cai, D., Yu, S., Wen, J.-R., Ma, W.-Y.: Extracting content structure for web pages based on visual representation. In: Zhou, X., Orlowska, M.E., Zhang, Y. (eds.) APWeb 2003. LNCS, vol. 2642, pp. 406–417. Springer, Heidelberg (2003). https://doi.org/10.1007/3-540-36901-5_42
5. Cai, D., Yu, S., Wen, J.R., Ma, W.Y.: VIPS: a vision-based page segmentation algorithm (2003)
6. Canny, J.: A computational approach to edge detection. IEEE Trans. Pattern Anal. Mach. Intell. 6, 679–698 (1986)
7. Chakrabarti, D., Kumar, R., Punera, K.: A graph-theoretic approach to webpage segmentation. In: Proceedings of the 17th WWW, pp. 377–386 (2008)
8. Chen, K., et al.: Hybrid task cascade for instance segmentation. In: CVPR, pp. 4974–4983 (2019)
9. Chen, K., et al.: MMDetection: Open MMLab detection toolbox and benchmark. arXiv preprint arXiv:1906.07155 (2019)
10. Cormer, M., Mann, R., Moffatt, K., Cohen, R.: Towards an improved vision-based web page segmentation algorithm. In: 2017 14th CRV, pp. 345–352. IEEE (2017)

11. Jayashree, S.R., Dias, G., Andrew, J.J., Saha, S., Maurel, F., Ferrari, S.: Multi-modal web page segmentation using self-organized multi-objective clustering. ACM Trans. Inf. Syst. **40**(3) (2022). https://doi.org/10.1145/3480966

12. Jiang, Z., Yin, H., Wu, Y., Lyu, Y., Min, G., Zhang, X.: Constructing novel block layouts for webpage analysis. TOIT **19**(3), 1–18 (2019)

13. Kiesel, J., Kneist, F., Meyer, L., Komlossy, K., Stein, B., Potthast, M.: Web page segmentation revisited: evaluation framework and dataset. In: Proceedings of the 29th ACM CIKM, CIKM 2020, pp. 3047–3054. Association for Computing Machinery, New York (2020). https://doi.org/10.1145/3340531.3412782

14. Kiesel, J., Meyer, L., Kneist, F., Stein, B., Potthast, M.: An empirical comparison of web page segmentation algorithms. In: Hiemstra, D., Moens, M.-F., Mothe, J., Perego, R., Potthast, M., Sebastiani, F. (eds.) ECIR 2021. LNCS, vol. 12657, pp. 62–74. Springer, Cham (2021). https://doi.org/10.1007/978-3-030-72240-1_5

15. Kohlschütter, C., Nejdl, W.: A densitometric approach to web page segmentation. In: Proceedings of the 17th ACM CIKM, pp. 1173–1182 (2008)

16. Lu, C., Bing, L., Lam, W.: Structured positional entity language model for enterprise entity retrieval. In: 22nd ACM CIKM, pp. 129–138 (2013)

17. Manabe, T., Tajima, K.: Extracting logical hierarchical structure of html documents based on headings. Proc. VLDB Endow. **8**(12), 1606–1617 (2015). https://doi.org/10.14778/2824032.2824058

18. Manku, G.S., Jain, A., Das Sarma, A.: Detecting near-duplicates for web crawling. In: Proceedings of the 16th WWW, pp. 141–150 (2007)

19. Meier, B., Stadelmann, T., Stampfli, J., Arnold, M., Cieliebak, M.: Fully convolutional neural networks for newspaper article segmentation. In: 2017 14th ICDAR, vol. 1, pp. 414–419. IEEE (2017)

20. Narayana, V., Premchand, P., Govardhan, A.: A novel and efficient approach for near duplicate page detection in web crawling. In: 2009 IACC, pp. 1492–1496. IEEE (2009)

21. Pawlik, M., Augsten, N.: Tree edit distance: Robust and memory-efficient. Inf. Syst. **56**, 157–173 (2016). https://doi.org/10.1016/j.is.2015.08.004

22. Sanoja, A., Gançarski, S.: Block-o-matic: a web page segmentation framework. In: 2014 ICMCS, pp. 595–600 (2014). https://doi.org/10.1109/ICMCS.2014.6911249

23. Velloso, R.P., Dorneles, C.F.: Automatic web page segmentation and noise removal for structured extraction using tag path sequences. JIDM **4**(3), 173 (2013)

24. Vieira, K., Da Silva, A.S., Pinto, N., De Moura, E.S., Cavalcanti, J.M., Freire, J.: A fast and robust method for web page template detection and removal. In: 15th ACM CIKM, pp. 258–267 (2006)

25. Xiang, P., Yang, X., Shi, Y.: Web page segmentation based on gestalt theory. In: 2007 IEEE ICME, pp. 2253–2256. IEEE (2007)

26. Xie, X., Miao, G., Song, R., Wen, J.R., Ma, W.Y.: Efficient browsing of web search results on mobile devices based on block importance model. In: 3rd IEEE PerCom, pp. 17–26. IEEE (2005)

27. Yandrapally, R.K., Mesbah, A.: Fragment-based test generation for web apps. IEEE Trans. Softw. Eng. **49**(3), 1086–1101 (2023). https://doi.org/10.1109/TSE.2022.3171295

28. Yi, L., Liu, B., Li, X.: Eliminating noisy information in web pages for data mining. In: 9th KDD, pp. 296–305 (2003)

29. Yin, X., Lee, W.S.: Understanding the function of web elements for mobile content delivery using random walk models. In: Special interest tracks and posters of the 14th WWW, pp. 1150–1151 (2005)

Learning to Select the Relevant History Turns in Conversational Question Answering

Munazza Zaib[1]([⊠]), Wei Emma Zhang[2], Quan Z. Sheng[1], Subhash Sagar[1], Adnan Mahmood[1], and Yang Zhang[1,3]

[1] School of Computing, Macquarie University, Sydney, NSW 2109, Australia
munazza-zaib.ghori@students.mq.edu.au
[2] School of Computer and Mathematical Science, The University of Adelaide, Adelaide, Australia
[3] School of Information Management, Wuhan University, Wuhan, China

Abstract. The increasing demand for web-based digital assistants has given a rapid rise in the interest of the Information Retrieval (IR) community towards the field of conversational question answering (ConvQA). However, one of the critical aspects of ConvQA is the effective selection of conversational history turns to answer the question at hand. The dependency between relevant history selection and correct answer prediction is an intriguing but under-explored area. The selected relevant context can better guide the system so as to where exactly in the passage to look for an answer. Irrelevant context, on the other hand, brings noise to the system, thereby resulting in a decline in the model's performance. In this paper, we propose a framework, DHS-onvQA (*D*ynamic *H*istory *S*election in *C*onversational *Q*uestion *A*nswering), that first generates the context and question entities for all the history turns, which are then pruned on the basis of similarity they share in common with the question at hand. We also propose an attention-based mechanism to re-rank the pruned terms based on their calculated weights of how useful they are in answering the question. In the end, we further aid the model by highlighting the terms in the re-ranked conversational history using a binary classification task and keeping the useful terms (predicted as 1) and ignoring the irrelevant terms (predicted as 0). We demonstrate the efficacy of our proposed framework with extensive experimental results on CANARD and QuAC – the two popularly utilized datasets in ConvQA. We demonstrate that selecting relevant turns works better than rewriting the original question. We also investigate how adding the irrelevant history turns negatively impacts the model's performance and discuss the research challenges that demand more attention from the IR community.

Keywords: Dialogue systems · Conversational question answering · Natural language processing · Intelligent agents · Web retrieval

F. Zhang et al. (Eds.): WISE 2023, LNCS 14306, pp. 334–348, 2023.
https://doi.org/10.1007/978-981-99-7254-8_26

Table 1. An example of information-seeking conversation. The relevant terms in the conversational history are shown in boldface.

Topic: Jal-The band	
ID	Conversation
Q1	Who founded **Jal**?
A1	Goher Mumtaz and Atif Aslam.
Q2	Where was Atif Aslam born?
A2	Wazirabad
Q3	When was the **band** founded?
A3	2002.
Q4	What was their first **album**?
A4	Aadat.
Q5	When was **it** released?

1 Introduction

The long-standing objective of the IR community has been to design intelligent agents, whether web-based or mobile-based, that can engage in eloquent interaction with humans iteratively [1–3]. The IR community has come closer to the realization of the dream owing to the rapid progress in conversational datasets and pre-trained language models [3]. These advancements have resulted in the birth of the field of conversational question answering (ConvQA). ConvQA provides a simplified but strong setting for conversational search [4] where the user initiates the conversation with a specific information need in mind. The system attempts to find relevant information pertinent to the question at hand iteratively based on a user's response or follow-up questions [4–6]. When answering the follow-up questions, the model needs to take the previous conversational turns into account to comprehend the context [7,8]. Selecting the relevant context that helps the model in building a clear and strong understanding of the current question is, therefore, a very critical challenge in ConvQA [6,9,10]. Adding the entire conversational history may bring the noise to the system with irrelevant context. This hinders the model's capability to correctly interpret the context of the conversation [10,11], thus resulting in a decline in the accuracy of the predicted answer.

Limitations of State-of-the-Art. The process of selecting the relevant conversational turns and predicting the correct answer span is based on a number of factors. The flow of conversation keeps on changing because of the presence of dialog features like dialog shift, topic return, drill down, and clarification [12]. Therefore, prepending k immediate turns, as suggested in [4,13–15], won't be able to capture the gist of what the current question is about. Table 1 shows an example of a conversational excerpt. Q2 shows a *topic shift*, whereas, Q3 represents *topic return*. Q4 and Q5 are examples of topic drill. The topic of Q4 is related to the band. Adding Q2, which inquires about the singer, to it would introduce noise within the input.

Another factor is of incomplete or vague follow-up questions that impede the model from fully interpreting the conversation to be able to select the relevant conversational turns. The literature [16–19] suggests the task of question rewriting (QR) to address the issue where QR refers to rewriting the current question by adding missing information pieces or resolving co-references, thereby, making it context-independent [16]. However, taking questions out of the conversational context results in losing important cues from the conversational flow. Also, the rewritten questions might be lengthy and verbose which, in turn, adds difficulty in selecting relevant conversational history [20]. The model requires the resolution of 'it' and information about missing context (i.e., the band) to extract the correct answer span of Q4 from Table 1.

Approach. We study and propose a framework, DHS-ConvQA (*D*ynamic *H*istory *S*election in *C*onversational *Q*uestion *A*nswering), that focuses on selecting the relevant conversational turns by ensuring the changing conversational flow and incomplete information requirement expressed in the query in view. The model first generates the context entities and question entities for the entire conversational history using distant supervision learning. The *context entity* refers to the entity mentioned from the conversational context whereas *question entity* is the entity targeted in the current question. Once the entities are generated, the turns containing non-similar context entities and question entities as compared to the current question are pruned. The remaining conversational turns are then re-ranked on the basis of their relevance to the current question. Their relevance is measured via the weightage assigned to them using the history attention mechanism. In the end, to further aid the answer prediction process, we utilize a binary classification task to highlight the key terms within the conversation history as 1 and 0. This particularly helps the model with the incomplete questions by providing hints about what the current question is about. We also compare our proposed framework to the standard question rewriting module to evaluate its effectiveness.

Contributions: Our main contributions are as the following:

- We utilize a distant supervision approach to generate context and question entities for conversational turns. The turns that do not share similar context and question entities to the current question are pruned. The remaining turns are then re-ranked on the basis of their relevance to the question.
- We use binary term classification to highlight the important information from the conversational history. This helps in adding the missing information to the current incomplete question so that the model gets a better picture of the conversational flow.
- We demonstrate by our experimental setup that the dynamic history selection works better than question rewriting and that the presence of negative samples or irrelevant turns results in a decline in the model's performance. We conclude our paper with two possible research challenges for the IR community.

2 Related Work

2.1 Conversational Question Answering

The field of ConvQA has seen a rapid boom in terms of research works and development over the past few years mainly because of the increasing demands for digital assistants [3,21]. This development is further supported by the introduction of pre-trained language models and two large-scale ConvQA datasets, i.e., CoQA [7] and QuaC [8] resulting in many state-of-the-art ConQA models [4,6,10,13,22–26]. The task of ConQA can be utilized in three settings; extractive [7,8], retrieval [27], and knowledge graph-based QA [28–32]. We focus on extractive ConvQA in our paper. The input to any ConvQA model generally comprises a context passage, conversational history, and current question. The way the model selects and represents conversational history has a direct impact on the prediction of the correct answer span. This presents another research challenge for the IR community.

2.2 History Selection in ConvQA

ConvQA is still in its infancy and has a number of critical challenges that demand attention. One such challenge is the selection of the relevant history turns and how to utilize them within the framework [6,10]. The approaches within extractive ConvQA utilize static and dynamic methods to represent conversational history. In the case of the static history representation methods, the widely used approach involves prepending k history turns to the current question [7,8,14]. On the contrary, the dynamic selection can be further categorized as *hard history selection* and *soft history selection*. Hard history selection is a mechanism to select a subset of question-relevant conversational turns [4,9,10]. However, the more pervasive and reliable method is to generate question-aware contextualized representations of the conversational history [6,22]. The contextualized representations are, then, passed on to the neural reader to look for the answer span within the given context passage.

We utilize a combination of the two techniques (i.e., *soft and hard history selection*) to filter out the irrelevant turns and utilize only the relevant conversational history within the model.

2.3 Question Rewriting

A popular research direction that aims to address the challenges pertinent to an incomplete or ambiguous question is question rewriting (QR). The task of QR is recently adopted in the field of ConvQA to reformulate the ambiguous and incomplete questions, that relies on the conversational context for their interpretation and generate self-contained questions that can be answered from the given context [16–18,33–36]. However, the task of QR takes the conversational questions out of the context by transforming them into self-contained questions which does not fit well with the whole idea of ConvQA setting [37].

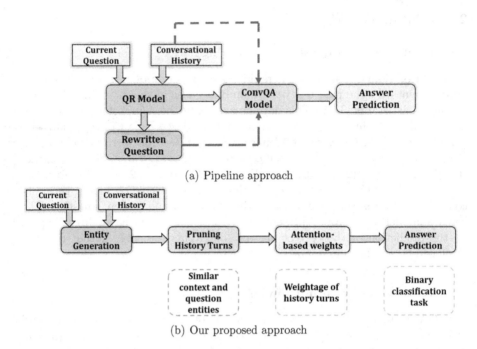

(a) Pipeline approach

(b) Our proposed approach

Fig. 1. In the traditional pipeline approach shown in (a), a context-independent question rewrite is generated by the QR module which is then answered by the QA module. The illustration of our proposed framework in (b) shows the dotted line modules which aid the respective process and help the model in finding relevant conversational turns that can help predict the correct answer span.

3   Methodology

3.1   Task Formulation

We take the traditional setting on ConvQA into consideration wherein a user instigates the conversation with a specific information need and the system attempts to provide a relevant and accurate answer after each of the user's questions [10]. To answer each question, the model needs to refer to the previous conversation turns to get the quintessence of the context of the conversation [4,9,10]. However, not all the previous turns contribute to aiding the model in understanding the current question. Thus, our model follows a four-step process to make sure that the most relevant terms are selected from the entire conversation and those selected turns maximize the probability of correct answer prediction by providing additional cues to the answer prediction module.

More formally, given a context passage C, current question Q_i, previous history turns H, the task of our proposed framework is to select the most relevant history turns H' based on different factors such as having similar context and question entities to the question at hand and the order based on their weightage which shows their relevance to the question. Once the conversational turns are selected, we further aid the answer prediction process by highlighting the relevant terms using the binary classification task.

3.2 Pipeline Approach

One of the most common techniques that have been in use to tackle the complexity of ConvQA tasks is by decomposing it into two sub-tasks of QR and QA [16,17,38,39]. The output from the QR module serves as an input to the QA module. The QR module is responsible for re-generating the question from scratch based on the provided context and the question at hand. Different techniques are in practice to produce these rewrites such as neural networks [38] and pre-trained language models [16,39,40].

The QR module can be trained on CANARD [33] dataset which consists of context-independent rewrites of the QuAC [8] dataset. The dataset contains 40K question-answer pairs produced by human annotators. Similar to [40], we utilize GPT-2 [41] to train the QR module. The conversational turns and the current question are passed on as input to the module during the training process and the module is required to generate a question rewrite that is to be answered by the QA module. Since it is assumed that all the dependencies and co-references have been resolved when rewriting the question, we use a traditional QA model instead of a ConvQA model to answer the question. We put together the process of predicting an answer as follows:

$$P(a_i \mid q_i, C, H) \approx P^{qa}(a_i \mid P^{qr}(q'_i \mid qi, H), C) \tag{1}$$

where P^{qa} and P^{qr} represent the probability of the two sub-task modules, respectively. q'_i represents the rewritten question by the QR module and will be provided as input to the QA module along with conversational history as shown in Fig. 1a.

3.3 DHS-ConvQA

The task of ConvQA heavily relies on conversational history. The more relevant and curated the conversational history is presented as input, the higher the chances of predicting the correct answer span. In our proposed method, we focus on utilizing different techniques to select the most relevant conversational turns to help the model better understand the question at hand. We emphasize addressing two issues. The first is to identify the relevance of turns to the current question. For this, we aim to generate context and question entities for each turn. To capture these entities for any incomplete question, we use the context and question entities from the last question. The underlying intuition is that the incomplete questions are usually the continuation of the conversation flow and it is safe to take the information from it to fill in the missing pieces. The context entity of Q4 in Table 1 is **band** and the question entity is **album**. These two can easily be added to incomplete Q5 and the resultant question would be **'When was the band's album released?'** To generate these entities, we employ a seq2seq pre-trained language model, BART [42]. The model takes the current question and the conversational history as input and is best utilized when the information is duplicated from the input but manipulated to produce the result [42]. Once the entities are generated, the next step is to prune all the history turns where there is no similarity of context and question entities with the current question. This comes under *hard history selection*.

Once the irrelevant turns are pruned, the next step is to calculate the attention weights for the remaining turns using the attention module. The attention module consists of a single-layer feed-forward network that learns an attention vector to map a sentence representation to a logit. Subsequently, the softmax probability function is utilized to calculate the probabilities across all the sequences. More formally, the computation of the weights can be shown as follows:

$$w_i = \frac{e^{D \cdot s_i^k}}{\sum_{i'=1}^{I} e^{D \cdot s_i^{k'}}} \tag{2}$$

where, D is an attention vector, s_i^k is a sentence representation, and w_i is the attention weight for s_i^k.

Once the weights are calculated, the vectorized turns are then passed on to the next module in a sequence where the turn with the highest weight is added next to the current question. This is how *soft history selection* is utilized within the framework. The output of the attention module is then passed on to RoBERTa [43] as an input. The next step is to introduce a term classification layer on top of the representations of the sub-token of each representation. The layer consists of a linear layer, a sigmoid function, and a dropout layer, and outputs a scalar value for each token. The terms relevant to the current question are highlighted as *'1'* and the remaining terms are set as *'0'*. The terms represented as 1 serve as a piece of missing information for incomplete questions. Finally, the decoder will generate the answer span for the current question based on context passage, conversational history, and the additional cues added to it.

3.4   Training of the Model

For the training of the entity generation module and binary term classification, we follow the strategy of distantly supervised labeling introduced in [20]. The idea behind the strategy is that if a piece of information is necessary for interpreting and answering the current question, it should be considered part of the current question. We start with the first question and gather all the context and question entities from it. For the incomplete or ambiguous follow-up questions, we keep on adding these entities to fill in the missing information. The entities are considered to be relevant for the incomplete question if an answer span is retrieved by adding them. For binary term classification, the relevant terms are tagged as 1 for being relevant and 0 for being irrelevant after passing through the term classification layer. For the task of answer prediction, the model is trained on the QuAC [8] dataset.

3.5   Configurations

We train the pipeline model on around 31K pairs of original questions and their respective rewrites, and validate it on a development set of 3K question pairs. The test set of the QR task consists of 5K question pairs from the CANARD [33] dataset. The DHS-ConvQA model is trained, validated, and tested on around 100K question-answer pairs from QuAC [8] dataset. The entire code was written in Python, making use of the popular PyTorch library[1].

Structured Representations: For generating the question and context entities, we utilize BART. The default hyperparameters were used from the Hugging Face library[2]. Early stopping was enabled with a batch size of 4. Adam optimizer with a learning rate of 0.00005 is used with a weight decay of 0.01.

Binary Term Classification: We utilize RoBERTa's PyTorch implementation by Hugging Face library[3] and introduce a term classification layer on top of it. Adam optimizer is used with a learning rate set in the range of {2e-5, 3e-5, 3e-6}. The dropout on the term classification layer lies in the range {0.1, 0.2, 0.3, 0.4}. The maximum answer length is set to 40 and the maximum question length is set to 64.

3.6   Dataset

CANARD: We utilize CANARD [33] dataset to train the QR module to generate the rewrites of the given question. The CANARD dataset is based on QuAC and yields the same answer as the original questions. We use the training and development sets to train and validate the QR model and the test set to evaluate the QA module.

QuAC: We have experimented with one of the widely utilized datasets that support the ConvQA setting–QuAC [8]. It comprises 100K question-answer pairs in a teacher-student setting. The reason for selecting this dataset is that it embodies more dialog features than the other datasets as proved in [12] and gives us more scope to experiment with our relevant history selection model.

3.7   Competing Methods

Since our proposed method is a combination of steps, we have, therefore, selected the models that more or less follow the part of our proposed technique in their models for a fair comparison. The chosen models are widely utilized and have been proven to perform remarkably well in ConvQA settings. These methods include:

---

[1] https://pytorch.org/.

[2] https://huggingface.co/facebook/bart-base.

[3] https://huggingface.co/docs/transformers/model_doc/roberta.

Table 2. Performance evaluation of the pipeline approach and our model using the QuAC and CANARD datasets. The best scores are highlighted in bold.

Models	Approach	F1	HEQ-Q	HEQ-D
BERT-HAE	Pipeline	62.3	58.2	5.5
	Ours	**63.1 (+0.8)**	**58.9 (+0.7)**	**6.0 (+0.5)**
BERT-HAM	Pipeline	63.4	60.1	6.1
	Ours	**65.4 (+2.0)**	**61.8 (+1.7)**	**6.7 (+0.6)**
BERT-CoQAC	Pipeline	63.1	59.2	5.9
	Ours	**64.4 (+1.3)**	**59.9 (+0.7)**	**6.9 (+2.0)**
CONVSR	Pipeline	66.1	62.2	6.0
	Ours	**67.5 (+1.4)**	**65.3 (+3.1)**	**7.5 (+1.5)**

- **BERT-HAE** [4]: The BERT-based model incorporates the conversational turns with history answer embedding (HAE) to predict the correct answer span. They experimented with different conversational turn settings and found optimal answers by including 5–6 history turns.
- **BERT-HAM** [6]: BERT-based history answer modeling (HAM) performs *soft selection* on the relevant conversational turns. The model conducts attentive history selection based on weights assigned to them. These weights signify how relevant the turn is in answering the current question.
- **BERT-CoQAC** [10]: Instead of prepending all the conversational turns to the current question, this model utilizes cosine similarity to select the relevant turns.
- **CONVSR** [44]: The model generates the intermediate structured representations to help the model in understanding the current question better.

3.8   Evaluation Metrics

For the sake of the evaluation, we follow the metrics suggested in [8] to assess our proposed model's performance. The metrics include not only the F1 score to evaluate the accuracy of the predicted answer but also the human equivalence score for questions (HEQ-Q) and human equivalence score for dialog (HEQ-D). HEQ-Q measures the model's ability to retrieve a more accurate (or, at least, similar) answer to the current question than the humans. HEQ-D represents the same performance measure, but instead of a question, it assesses the quality of the overall conversation.

4   Experimentation Results and Analysis

We conduct experiments on our proposed model using the QuAC [8] and CANARD [33] datasets and compare the results with the competing models.

Table 3. The evaluation results of our proposed model with the competing methods on the QuAC dataset. We also demonstrate the effect of each module on the model's performance.

Model	F1	HEQ-Q	HEQ-D
BERT-HAE	63.1	58.9	6.0
BERT-HAM	65.4	61.8	6.7
BERT-CoQAC	64.4	59.9	**6.9**
Ours (w/o pruning)	64.3	62.9	6.6
Ours (w/o re-ranking)	67.3	63.6	6.9
Ours (w/o term classification)	65.7	62.0	6.5
Ours (complete setup)	**67.5**	**65.3**	7.5

4.1 DHS-ConvQA Is Viable for Selecting Relevant Conversational Turns

Topic shift and topic return are two main challenges in the field of ConvQA. Adding k immediate turns as a part of the input to the ConvQA model fails to capture the essence of the conversational flow. Also, rewriting a question takes it out of the conversational context and focuses more on generating high-quality rewrites instead of improving the performance of a ConvQA model. Thus, the first and foremost takeaway from our experimental results is that selecting relevant history turns aids the model in better understanding the question at hand and then predicting the accurate answer span. Instead of rewriting the questions to fill in the missing gaps, which takes out the questions from the conversational context, selecting relevant turns after going through different stages works well in yielding higher accuracy as shown in Table 2.

4.2 Role of Relevant Conversational History in the ConvQA Setting

The existing works either opt for *soft history selection* or employ *hard history selection*. We propose a combination of both along with highlighting relevant terms to the current question as additional cues. From Table 3, we can clearly deduce that our proposed model consistently improves the model's performance, thereby, confirming the fact that our model works well in the ConvQA setting. We also conduct an in-depth analysis of the proposed model by studying the effect of each module it brings within the framework. Table 3 shows that omitting the pruning of the turns step results in a greater decline in the F1 score as compared to the other modules. The underlying reason is that without pruning, the model considers all the conversational turns as a part of input which brings in the noise in terms of irrelevant turns.

Table 4. The evaluation of the model's performance where the model receives Negative Samples (NS) as a part of input together with the relevant conversational turns.

Model	F1	Clarification	Topic Shift	Topic Return
Ours (complete setup)	**67.5**	**90.9**	**85.4**	**82.2**
Ours + 1NF	67.0	90.4	82.0	79.5
Ours + 3NF	64.3	89.4	78.4	77.3
Ours + 5NF	62.5	88.1	73.5	73.9
Ours + 7NF	60.7	86.7	70.9	70.3
Ours + 9NF	54.6	85.0	66.8	65.0
Ours + 11NF	52.4	83.8	63.0	62.1

Table 5. Effect of pruning (in %) on the rest of the modules

Pruning (%)	Re-ranking (%)	Binary-term Classification (%)	Answer Prediction (%)
100	100	92	90
70	95	86	80
50	89	70	65

4.3 Effect of Negative Samples on Model's Performance

For each question, we experiment by injecting negative samples together with the relevant turns identified by the proposed model. The negative samples are the questions related to the same topic but from different passages of the QuAC dataset. They are semantically closer to the relevant questions and, therefore, they can be considered a part of conversational history by the model. From Table 4, we can interpret that adding negative samples results in the decline of the model's F1 score. Also, the clarification questions are least impacted by the added noise as compared to the topic return and topic shift questions. The negative samples can easily be misleading for the model to capture the gist of the changing conversational flow.

4.4 Effect of Pruning on the Subsequent Modules In-Line

From Table 5, it is clearly evident that the pruning of irrelevant conversational history has a direct effect on the performance of the rest of the modules. The better the performance of the first module, the higher the chances of correct answer prediction. If the turns are pruned accurately (100%), the overall performance of all the components would be higher. The performance decreases as the number of correct pruned turns decreases. However, there are high chances of error propagation because the output of each module serves as an input to the next module.

5   Conclusion and Future Work

This paper discusses a significant point of view on the basic concept of the role of relevance in conversational question answering (ConvQA). We argue that many existing research works, even the popular ones, do not take into account the idea of relevant history selection and modeling. We propose a framework that combines the notion of both *hard history selection* and *soft history selection* to curate the input for the answer prediction module carefully. The model first generates context and question entities using distant supervision learning and selects the relevant terms using 'hard history selection'. After the pruning of irrelevant terms, the model assigns attention-based weightage to the remaining turns. The assigned score is based on how relevant they are to the current question and accessed in the same order. To further aid the answering prediction process, we utilize binary classification task to highlight the important terms with respect to the current question from the conversational history. Our experimental results depict that the proposed method has the potential to change how conversational history could be utilized more effectively.

We also highlight two significant future research challenges. The first challenge is that ConvQA is essentially a modular or cascading architecture that can be categorized as an information retrieval module responsible for selecting the relevant turns and the question answering module responsible for predicting the answer span. Any negative samples or turns selected during the history selection process would directly affect the model's performance in predicting the correct answer span. Thus, there is a need for a mechanism to minimize the retrieval of irrelevant conversational turns. The second challenge centers on the development of a framework that would eliminate the chances of error propagation within the modules.

References

1. Li, H., Gao, T., Goenka, M., Chen, D.: Ditch the gold standard: re-evaluating conversational question answering. In: Proceedings of the 60th Annual Meeting of the Association for Computational Linguistics, pp. 8074–8085 (2022)
2. Kotov, A., Zhai, C.: Towards natural question guided search. In: Proceedings of the 19th International Conference on World Wide Web, pp. 541–550 (2010)
3. Zaib, M., Zhang, W.E., Sheng, Q.Z., Mahmood, A., Zhang, Y.: Conversational question answering: a survey. Knowl. Inf. Syst. **64**, 3151–3195 (2022)
4. Qu, C., Yang, L., Qiu, M., Croft, W.B., Zhang, Y., Iyyer, M.: BERT with history answer embedding for conversational question answering. In: Proceedings of the 42nd International ACM SIGIR Conference on Research and Development in Information Retrieval, pp. 1133–1136 (2019)
5. Zaib, M., Sheng, Q.Z., Emma Zhang, W.: A short survey of pre-trained language models for conversational AI-A new age in NLP. In: Proceedings of the Australasian Computer Science Week, pp. 11:1–11:4 (2020)
6. Qu, C., et al.: Attentive history selection for conversational question answering. In: Proceedings of the 28th ACM International Conference on Information and Knowledge Management, pp. 1391–1400 (2019)

7. Reddy, S., Chen, D., Manning, C.D.: CoQA: a conversational question answering challenge. Trans. Assoc. Comput. Linguist. **7**, 249–266 (2019)
8. Choi, E., et al.: QuAC: question answering in context. In: Proceedings of the 2018 Conference on Empirical Methods in Natural Language Processing, pp. 2174–2184 (2018)
9. Qiu, M., et al.: Reinforced history backtracking for conversational question answering. In: Proceedings of the 35th AAAI Conference on Artificial Intelligence, AAAI 2021, Thirty-Third Conference on Innovative Applications of Artificial Intelligence, pp. 13718–13726 (2021)
10. Zaib, M., Tran, D.H., Sagar, S., Mahmood, A., Zhang, W.E., Sheng, Q.Z.: BERT-CoQAC: BERT-based conversational question answering in context. In: Ning, L., Chau, V., Lau, F. (eds.) PAAP 2020. CCIS, vol. 1362, pp. 47–57. Springer, Singapore (2021). https://doi.org/10.1007/978-981-16-0010-4_5
11. Sauchuk, A., Thorne, J., Halevy, A., Tonellotto, N., Silvestri, F.: On the role of relevance in natural language processing tasks. In: Proceedings of the 46th International ACM SIGIR Conference on Research and Development in Information Retrieval, pp. 1785–1789 (2022)
12. Yatskar, M.: A qualitative comparison of CoQA, SQuAD 2.0 and QuAC. In: Proceedings of the 2019 Conference of the North American Chapter of the Association for Computational Linguistics: Human Language Technologies, vol. 1, pp. 2318–2323 (2019)
13. Zhu, C., Zeng, M., Huang, X.: SDNet: contextualized attention-based deep network for conversational question answering. arXiv:1812.03593 (2018)
14. Seo, M., Kembhavi, A., Farhadi, A., Hajishirzi, H.: Bidirectional attention flow for machine comprehension. In: Proceedings of the 5th International Conference on Learning Representations (ICLR), pp. 01–13 (2017)
15. Ohsugi, Y., Saito, I., Nishida, K., Asano, H., Tomita, J.: A simple but effective method to incorporate multi-turn context with BERT for conversational machine comprehension. In: Proceedings of the 57th Annual Meeting of the Association for Computational Linguistics, pp. 11–17 (2019)
16. Raposo, G., Ribeiro, R., Martins, B., Coheur, L.: Question rewriting? Assessing its importance for conversational question answering. In: Hagen, M., et al. (eds.) ECIR 2022. LNCS, vol. 13186, pp. 199–206. Springer, Cham (2022). https://doi.org/10.1007/978-3-030-99739-7_23
17. Kim, G., Kim, H., Park, J., Kang, J.: Learn to resolve conversational dependency: a consistency training framework for conversational question answering. In: Proceedings of the 59th Annual Meeting of the Association for Computational Linguistics and the 11th International Joint Conference on Natural Language Processing (ACL-IJCNLP), pp. 6130–6141 (2021)
18. Vakulenko, S., Longpre, S., Tu, Z., Anantha, R.: Question rewriting for conversational question answering. In: Proceedings of the 14th ACM International Conference on Web Search and Data Mining, (WSDM), 2021, pp. 355–363 (2021)
19. Yu, S., et al.: Few-shot generative conversational query rewriting. In: Proceedings of the 43rd International ACM SIGIR Conference on Research and Development in Information Retrieval, pp. 1933–1936 (2020)
20. Christmann, P., Saha Roy, R., Weikum, G.: Conversational question answering on heterogeneous sources. In: Proceedings of the 45th International ACM SIGIR Conference on Research and Development in Information Retrieval, pp. 144–154 (2022)
21. Gao, J., Galley, M., Li, L.: Neural approaches to conversational AI. Found. Trends Inf. Retr. **13**, 127–298 (2019)

22. Huang, H.Y., Choi, E., Yih, W.T.: FlowQA: grasping flow in history for conversational machine comprehension. In: Proceedings of the 7th The International Conference on Learning Representations, pp. 86–90 (2019)

23. Chen, Y., Wu, L., Zaki, M.J.: GraphFlow: exploiting conversation flow with graph neural networks for conversational machine comprehension. In: Proceedings of the Twenty-Ninth International Joint Conference on Artificial Intelligence, pp. 1230–1236 (2020)

24. Yeh, Y.T., Chen, Y.N.: FlowDelta: modeling flow information gain in reasoning for conversational machine comprehension. In: Proceedings of the 2nd Workshop on Machine Reading for Question Answering, pp. 86–90 (2019)

25. Qu, C., Yang, L., Chen, C., Qiu, M., Croft, W.B., Iyyer, M.: Open-retrieval conversational question answering. In: Proceedings of the 43rd International Conference on Research and Development in Information Retrieval, pp. 539–548 (2020)

26. Qu, C., Yang, L., Chen, C., Croft, W.B., Krishna, K., Iyyer, M.: Weakly-supervised open-retrieval conversational question answering. In: Hiemstra, D., et al. (eds.) ECIR 2021. LNCS, vol. 12656, pp. 529–543. Springer, Cham (2021). https://doi.org/10.1007/978-3-030-72113-8_35

27. Dalton, J., Xiong, C., Callan, J.: CAst 2019: the conversational assistance track overview. Technical report (2019)

28. Christmann, P., Saha Roy, R., Abujabal, A., Singh, J., Weikum, G.: Look before you hop: conversational question answering over knowledge graphs using judicious context expansion. In: Proceedings of the 28th ACM International Conference on Information and Knowledge Management, pp. 729–738 (2019)

29. Saha, A., Pahuja, V., Khapra, M., Sankaranarayanan, K., Chandar, S.: Complex sequential question answering: towards learning to converse over linked question answer pairs with a knowledge graph. In: Proceedings of the 32nd Conference on Artificial Intelligence, pp. 705–713 (2018)

30. Guo, D., Tang, D., Duan, N., Zhou, M., Yin, J.: Dialog-to-action: conversational question answering over a large-scale knowledge base. In: Proceedings of the 32nd International Conference on Neural Information Processing Systems, pp. 2946–2955 (2018)

31. Shen, T., et al.: Multi-task learning for conversational question answering over a large-scale knowledge base. In: Proceedings of the Conference on Empirical Methods in Natural Language Processing and the 9th International Joint Conference on Natural Language Processing, pp. 2442–2451 (2019)

32. Kacupaj, E., Plepi, J., Singh, K., Thakkar, H., Lehmann, J., Maleshkova, M.: Conversational question answering over knowledge graphs with transformer and graph attention networks. In: Proceedings of the 16th Conference of the European Chapter of the Association for Computational Linguistics, pp. 850–862 (2021)

33. Elgohary, A., Peskov, D., Boyd-Graber, J.: Can you unpack that? learning to rewrite questions-in-context. In: Proceedings of the 2019 Conference on Empirical Methods in Natural Language Processing and the 9th International Joint Conference on Natural Language Processing (EMNLP-IJCNLP), pp. 5918–5924 (2019)

34. Li, H., Gao, T., Goenka, M., Chen, D.: Ditch the gold standard: re-evaluating conversational question answering. In: Proceedings of the 60th Annual Meeting of the Association for Computational Linguistics (ACL), pp. 8074–8085 (2022)

35. Chen, Z., Zhao, J., Fang, A., Fetahu, B., Rokhlenko, O., Malmasi, S.: Reinforced question rewriting for conversational question answering. arXiv preprint arXiv:2210.15777 (2022)

36. Ishii, E., Wilie, B., Xu, Y., Cahyawijaya, S., Fung, P.: Integrating question rewrites in conversational question answering: a reinforcement learning approach. In: Proceedings of the 60th Annual Meeting of the Association for Computational Linguistics: Student Research Workshop, pp. 55–66 (2022)
37. Christmann, P., Saha Roy, R., Weikum, G.: Conversational question answering on heterogeneous sources. In: Proceedings of the 45th ACM SIGIR International Conference on Research and Development in Information Retrieval, pp. 144–154 (2022)
38. Vakulenko, S., Longpre, S., Tu, Z., Anantha, R.: Question rewriting for conversational question answering. In: Proceedings of the 14th ACM International Conference on Web Search and Data Mining (WSDM), pp. 355–363 (2021)
39. Vakulenko, S., Longpre, S., Tu, Z., Anantha, R.: A wrong answer or a wrong question? An intricate relationship between question reformulation and answer selection in conversational question answering. In: Proceedings of the 5th International Workshop on Search-Oriented Conversational AI (SCAI), pp. 7–16 (2020)
40. Lin, S.C., Yang, J.H., Nogueira, R., Tsai, M.F., Wang, C. J., Lin, J.: Conversational question reformulation via sequence-to-sequence architectures and pretrained language models. CoRR, abs/2004.01909 (2020)
41. Radford, A., Narasimhan, K., Salimans, T., Sutskever, I.: Improving language understanding by generative pre-training (2018)
42. Lewis, M., et al.: BART: denoising sequence-to-sequence pre-training for natural language generation, translation, and comprehension. In: Proceedings of the 58th Annual Meeting of the Association for Computational Linguistics, pp. 7871–7880 (2020)
43. Liu, Y., et al.: RoBERTa: a robustly optimized BERT pretraining approach. CoRR, abs/1907.11692 (2019)
44. Zaib, M., Sheng, Q.Z., Zhang, W.E., Mahmood, A.: Keeping the questions conversational: using structured representations to resolve dependency in conversational question answering. arXiv preprint arXiv:2304.07125 (2023)

A Methodological Approach for Data-Intensive Web Application Design on Top of Data Lakes

Devis Bianchini[✉] and Massimiliano Garda

Department of Information Engineering, University of Brescia,
Via Branze 38, 25123 Brescia, Italy
{devis.bianchini,massimiliano.garda}@unibs.it

Abstract. Data exploration and decision making may benefit from the availability of data-intensive web applications, that enable domain experts to navigate across massive, dynamic and heterogeneous data sources, stored in the so-called Data Lakes. However, traditional design strategies for this kind of applications require in the background well-defined and cleaned data structures. Conceptual modelling may be fruitfully employed to provide web developers with a comprehensive vision over Data Lake sources, on which web applications are designed. Nevertheless, the cumbersome nature of Data Lakes turns the conceptual model into a dynamic entity, which must be properly managed. In this paper, we propose a methodological approach to design data-intensive web applications on top of a Data Lake. A conceptual data model, weaved over Data Lake sources, is leveraged to identify the relevant information to be included in the web application. The methodology makes the model evolve both with new data sources content emerging from the Data Lake, through a zone-based operations pipeline that prepares a curated version of the raw data (bottom-up), and with additional domain knowledge provided by web developers derived from the data-intensive web application design (top-down). The approach, independent from any specific implementation technology, is declined in the context of a real case study regarding an ongoing research project in the cultural heritage domain.

Keywords: Data-intensive web applications · Data Lakes · zone-based architecture · conceptual model · methodological approach

1 Introduction

Nowadays, data exploration and decision making may benefit from the availability of data-intensive web applications, that enable domain experts to navigate across massive, dynamic and heterogeneous data collected from the physical world. Let us consider, for example, Alice, a museum operator who is in charge of creating thematic paths of artworks for different target visitors (e.g., students, artworks experts, incidental visitors). To accomplish her task, Alice can exploit

© The Author(s), under exclusive license to Springer Nature Singapore Pte Ltd. 2023
F. Zhang et al. (Eds.): WISE 2023, LNCS 14306, pp. 349–359, 2023.
https://doi.org/10.1007/978-981-99-7254-8_27

all data available about artworks, such as structured data (e.g., author, period, type, location), social media contents (e.g., opinions about artworks) and statistics about visits. By exploring all this information (that may dynamically and frequently change over time) through a proper web application, Alice can take decisions on how artworks can be properly combined within thematic paths. Data Lakes have been recently adopted to gather loosely structured collections of data at large scale, postponing data preparation until its actual consumption [11], according to a schema-on-read approach. However, the design of traditional data-intensive web applications follows a schema-on-write paradigm, assuming the clear identification of core entities for web-based data exploration [2]. Therefore, when dealing with heterogeneous and highly dynamic data sources, development of web applications requires to separate the application design (in charge of web developers) from the data preparation pipeline (managed by data engineers). In this landscape, conceptual modelling may be fruitfully employed to provide web developers with a comprehensive vision over Data Lake sources. The advantages descending from the availability of the conceptual schema of Data Lake sources has recently been envisioned in a preliminary study [3], suggesting a principled approach to capitalise on the knowledge enclosed in the conceptual model of data to strengthen data curation tasks. Nevertheless, approaches like the one described in [3] have not been applied for data-intensive web application development yet.

In this paper, we propose a hybrid methodological approach, that contributes to the state of the art by: (i) propagating changes occurring on Data lake sources towards the conceptual model underlying the data-intensive web application (bottom-up); (ii) combining changes with requirements engineering updates descending from the web application design (top-down). The methodology leverages conceptual modelling to identify relevant information to be included in the web application and manage the transformation of data from raw data sources in the Data Lake up to their integration in the web application as web-based digital objects. The feasibility of the approach is demonstrated through its application in a real case study in an ongoing research project in the cultural heritage domain. The approach separates the data management pipeline across the Data Lake from the design of the web application. The methodology, independent from any specific implementation technology, assumes a *zone-based* architecture for the Data Lake [6].

The paper is organised as follows: Sect. 2 presents the case study and provides the approach overview; methodological steps are detailed in Sects. 3 and 4. Implementation and a preliminary evaluation for the case study are described in Sect. 5. Related work are discussed in Sect. 6. Finally, Sect. 7 closes the paper, suggesting future research directions.

2   Case Study and Approach Overview

The approach described in this paper has been investigated in the scope of the "Data Science for Brescia - Arts and Cultural Places" research project (in brief,

DS4BS). The DS4BS project is one of the initiatives organised for the nomination of Brescia and Bergamo (Northern Italy, Lombardy Region) as Italian Capitals of Culture in 2023. The main objective of the project is to increase knowledge about the way people visit the cultural places (e.g., museums, theatres, monuments), to support institutions and decision makers to organise cultural initiatives in presence of large groups of people, with the lesson learnt during recent pandemic events. In the project, several use cases are envisaged, targeted to different actors (e.g., the foundation that manages the museums, curators, citizens). Amongst them, in this paper we will focus on the following three use cases to support curators: (a) *exploration* of artworks and associated information; (b) *creation of thematic paths* of artworks for different categories of visitors; (c) *statistical analysis* about the history of visits to the museums, to plan new expositions both in the short and medium-long period. Use cases have been elicited starting from the research line of the project and are aimed at providing a holistic vision of artworks, conceived as aggregations of heterogeneous information.

Design Challenges. The requirements of the use cases of the DS4BS project are based on information collected from multiple heterogeneous sources, highly dynamic in nature. The Data Lake is apt to cope with data variety and heterogeneity, but web developers do not have specific skills for Data Lake management. Therefore, in the DS4BS project, the development of the web application upon a Data Lake has raised the following motivating challenges:

(1) requirements and use cases specification may frequently change over time, being influenced by new data sources added to the Data Lake;
(2) the conceptual data model underlying the web application is continuously enriched both with newly added data (emerging in a bottom-up way from Data Lake sources) and with new emerging design requirements (introduced in a top-down manner by web developers during web application design);
(3) all the information for the execution of the use cases should be easily accessible through the web application, abstracting from the inner dynamic nature of the Data Lake.

Approach Overview. Our aim is to demonstrate that Data Lakes can be leveraged to build a data-intensive web application for exploration and decision making purposes. With respect to approaches focused on the creation of APIs to expose Data Lake contents [1,7], the methodology described here also includes the integration of front-end web components in the final application and the management of changes on Data Lake sources, properly combined with requirements updates descending from the web application design. Furthermore, we remark that, unlike OBDA (Ontology-Based Data Access) approaches [12], the focus here is not on obtaining from the Data Lake sources the results of a query formulated on the conceptual schema. The methodology tackles the design of a web application on top of the Data Lake leveraging conceptual modelling under a two-fold perspective: (i) a *use case independent perspective*, conceived for data engineers, to guide the data management pipeline across the Data Lake zones, being independent from the web application use cases; (ii) a *use case dependent*

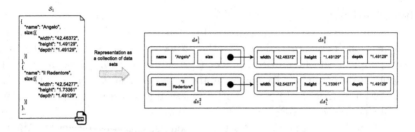

Fig. 1. Example of JSON data source representation as a collection of data sets.

perspective, where conceptual modelling is fostered to identify core entities from the domain to be explored and visualised (e.g., digital representation of artworks), within the web application. We foster a Data Lake organised over four zones, encapsulating data management operations, namely: (i) *Raw Zone*, containing the heterogeneous data sources in their original format; (ii) *Standardised Zone*, where data is abstracted through data sets, upon which data standardisation operations are applied; (iii) *Curated Zone*, where data sets are shaped into a tabular structure; (iv) *Application Zone*, containing the representation of web-based digital objects, obtained by mapping the tabular structures from the previous zone with core entities of the E-R conceptual model and associating them with front-end web components. The E-R model is built and enriched over time by the web developer: (a) exploiting knowledge from data sources content, in a semi-automatic way, with the support of well-consolidated techniques (e.g., devoted to discover type and domain of columns from the tabular structures in the Curated Zone [10]); (b) leveraging domain knowledge, to provide additional metadata (e.g., to identify hierarchies between entities and the definition of cardinality in relationships).

3   Use Case Independent Data Sources Management

Following existing approaches in literature [5,8], we model the Raw Zone of the Data Lake as a set of *data sources* (an example of data source containing information regarding artworks is illustrated in Fig. 1). A data source $\mathcal{S}_i$, for $i = 1 \ldots N$ (where N is the number of data sources in the Raw Zone), is modelled as a triple $\langle \mathcal{A}_i, \mathcal{DS}_i, \mathcal{M}_i \rangle$, where: (i) $\mathcal{A}_i$ is a set of *attributes*; (ii) $\mathcal{DS}_i$ is a collection of *data sets*, each one representing a record of the data source regardless its nature (i.e., structured, semi-structured, unstructured); (iii) $\mathcal{M}_i$ is a set of attribute-value pairs containing metadata apt to access the source (e.g., username, password, URL) and other source-specific metadata (e.g., in the case of a relational database, tables names and relationships between tables). In turn, each data set in $\mathcal{DS}_i$ is formalised as follows.

Definition 1 (Data set). *Given a data source $\langle \mathcal{A}_i, \mathcal{DS}_i, \mathcal{M}_i \rangle$, a data set $ds_i^j \in \mathcal{DS}_i$, for $j = 1 \ldots N_i$ (where N_i is the number of data sets in $\mathcal{DS}_i$), is defined*

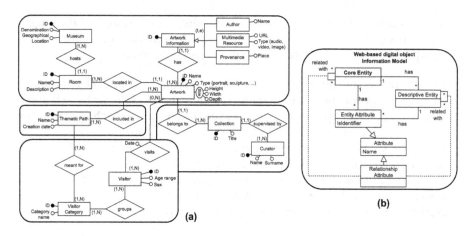

Fig. 2. E-R model for the data in the cultural heritage use cases enriched with Core Entities (a). Meta-model for the identification of Core Entities (b).

over a set of attribute-value pairs, considering the attribute set $\mathcal{A}_i^j \subseteq \mathcal{A}_i$. For an attribute $a_k \in \mathcal{A}_i^j$ in the data set ds_i^j, we use the notation $ds_i^j.a_k$ or, if not ambiguous, simply a_k, for $k = 1 \ldots |\mathcal{A}_i^j|$. An attribute $a_k \in \mathcal{A}_i^j$ can be either: (i) a simple attribute or (ii) an attribute referencing a nested data set in a recursive way (denoted with $\rightsquigarrow$ symbol), that is $a_k \rightsquigarrow ds_i^m$, with $ds_i^m \in \mathcal{DS}_i, \mathcal{A}_i^m \neq \mathcal{A}_i^j$.

Baseline elaboration operations (e.g., application of a standard format for fields, data type conversions, criteria to identify missing data values and actions to apply) are applied on data in the Standardised Zone with the aim of progressively converging towards a common data format. We will not delve into the details of this process, as this is out of the scope of the approach. Once baseline elaboration of data has been performed on the data sets, data sources are translated into a tabular representation from the Standardised to the Curated Zone. Then, the web developer builds the E-R conceptual model starting from the tabular representation of data sources in the Curated Zone with the support of tools and techniques from the literature [10], and enriches it with additional metadata and constraints (e.g., regarding relationships and their cardinality, hierarchies between entities). In this respect, mappings between the tabular data in the Curated Zone and the E-R model are established with the purpose of supporting the use case dependent perspective of our approach, as explained in the following section.

4   Use Case Dependent Digital Objects Modelling

Identification and Refinement of Core Entities. After the mapping between data sources and conceptual entities has been established in the Curated

Zone of the Data Lake, the web developers identify Core Entities and their ancillary information in the E-R model, according to the meta-model illustrated in Fig. 2(b). The meta-model is based on three pivotal elements:

- **Core Entity** (highlighted in red), which represents a pivotal informative entity, relevant for the execution of one or more use cases from the web application (in the example in Fig. 2(a), `Artwork`, `Thematic Path`, `Collection` and `Visitor` have been marked as Core Entities);
- **Descriptive Entity**, directly or indirectly connected through a relationship with a Core Entity, used to provide additional information regarding the Core Entity (e.g., `Room`, `Museum` and `Artwork Information` are used to provide details about the `Artwork` Core Entity);
- **Attribute**, regarding a Core Entity, a Descriptive Entity or a relationship.

Inherently, the identification of Core Entities and related Descriptive Entities and Attributes in the E-R model form the *Information Model* of the web-based digital object (rounded boxes in Fig. 2(a)), grouping together the conceptualisation directly ascribable to the digital object.

Web-Based Digital Object Model. From a conceptual viewpoint, a web-based digital object abstracts an object of interest in the considered domain, corresponding to a Core Entity identified in the E-R model and its corresponding Information Model. For example, in the case study presented in Sect. 2, a web-based digital object corresponds to an artwork, a thematic path or a collection. Beyond the Information Model, a web-based digital object is also associated with a *front-end web component*, which can be integrated in the web application to explore and manage digital objects. A web-based digital object can be formalised as follows.

Definition 2 (Web-based digital object). *A web-based digital object $do_i \in \mathcal{DO}$ (being $\mathcal{DO}$ the set of all the digital objects) is a tuple $\langle M_i, D_i, w_i \rangle$, where:*

(i) M_i *is the Information Model, composed of the Core Entity associated with do_i, along with the entities, relationships and attributes encompassed by the Information Model;*

(ii) $D_i = \{ds^j\}$ *are the data sets, belonging to different data sources in the Data Lake, mapped to the entities in M_i;*

(iii) $w_i = \langle T_i, I_i \rangle$ *is the front-end web component associated with do_i, to be included in the web application; w_i is characterised by a set of technical features T_i, and exposes an interface I_i containing methods with two different goals, that is $I_i = SI_i \cup CI_i$: (a) a self-interface SI_i, built upon M_i; (b) an inter-component interface CI_i, enabling the interaction of w_i with the components (and, by extension, with the Information Models) of other digital objects.*

Web Component Design. In the web component w_i, the set T_i contains pairs feature-value(s) apt to qualify the component (e.g., the protocol to be used for interaction). The methods constituting the interface I_i of w_i have a *signature* which can be automatically obtained by leveraging M_i, thus preparing a skeleton for the methods of the web component, in order to be used as a starting point for web application development, which is generic enough for not being constrained to any specific programming language and deployment environment for web components. The self-interface $I_i.SI_i$ provides CRUD methods rooted on the Information Model, enabling to read/write the data sets in D_i, whereas the inter-component interface $I_i.CI_i$ concerns the methods ensuring the interaction of w_i with other web components.

Example. The Information Model $M_{artwork}$ of the digital object $do_{artwork}$ is identified around the Artwork Core Entity in Fig. 2(a). The corresponding front-end web component $w_{artwork}$ presents feature-value(s) pairs in $T_{artwork}$ such as $\langle protocol, HTTP \rangle$, $\langle HTTP\_method, \{GET, POST\} \rangle$. As an example, the interface of $w_{artwork}$ would contain CRUD methods leveraging $M_{artwork}$ (e.g., getName(), for obtaining the values, backed by the Artwork.Name, from the data sets in $D_{artwork}$). Furthermore, the interface will contain methods for exchanging information with the other digital objects $do_{thematic\_path}$, $do_{visitor}$ and $do_{collection}$. For instance, the method setCollection(Artwork.ID, Collection.ID) would assign the artwork identified by Artwork.ID to the collection identified by Collection.ID ($w_{artwork}$ sends the identifier of the artwork to $w_{collection}$, whilst the identifier of the collection is an input from the web application).

Advantages for the Web Application Design. Web-based digital object modelling ensures to decouple the mapping of the digital object over the Data Lake (the data sources and their tabular representation) from the web application perspective (the web component and the underlying Information Model). In this respect, the interaction with the digital object is performed always through the web component, thus hiding the underlying changes on D_i to the web developer and ensuring a proper level of flexibility. On the other hand, modifications to the Information Model may be due to changes to the use cases requirements, which compel the web designer to modify the E-R model accordingly (e.g., by attaching new entities with attributes and relationships) and refine Core Entities, since new Core Entities, with their owns Information Models, emerge. Moreover, mappings between conceptual entities and data sources have to be revised as well; however, this task is decoupled from the data pipeline management.

5   Implementation and Preliminary Evaluation

Museum Data Lake and Web Application. To implement the Data Lake infrastructure, Apache Hadoop Distributed File System (HDFS) has been chosen, due to its capability of managing structured and unstructured data. On the top of HDFS, the Apache Spark framework (with PySpark Python library) and Apache Spark SQL module have been used to manipulate and query the data sets (implemented as Apache Spark DataFrames). The zones of the Museum

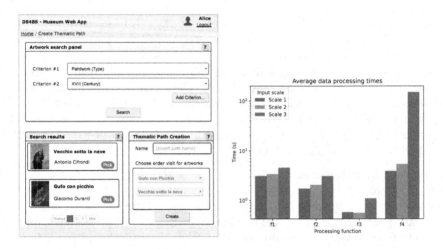

Fig. 3. Thematic paths creation web page mockup (left side). Data processing functions average times (right side).

Data Lake have been organised as follows: (i) *Raw Zone*, collecting the raw museum data sources, which are assigned a unique path in HDFS; (ii) *Standardised Zone*, wherein baseline elaboration operations (e.g., data format conversion, upper/lowercase conversion) are applied on the data sets, loaded into Spark DataFrames and then persisted in HDFS; (iii) *Curated Zone*, where a DataFrame for each entity of the E-R model, containing data related to that entity only, is derived, persisting in HDFS only entities involved in the execution of use cases; (iv) *Application Zone*, where the DataFrames associated with the entities of an Information Model are joined together, in order to be available for querying from the methods of the front-end web component. Downstream the Data Lake, a web application is used by curators to explore the content of the Data Lake, wherein the web components are leveraged to access data associated with the digital representation of artworks in the Application Zone. A representative page of the web application is depicted on the left side of Fig. 3, where data of $do_{artwork}$ and $do_{thematic\_path}$ digital objects (obtained through the respective web components) is exploited to let the curator create a new thematic path. Through the page, the curator may incrementally add a series of combo boxes to set parameters apt to limit the list of displayed artworks. Then, the curator selects the artworks and their order in the thematic path (reflecting the order that a visitor should adhere to while visiting the museum) and finalises the creation of the thematic path by assigning a name.

Experiments on Data Processing Times. Tests on data processing times have been performed by considering four different Python functions, invoked within the zones of the Data Lake to process data from real data sources, properly filled for tests with randomly generated records of three different scales (10^3, 10^4 and 10^5 records). Specifically: (i) f_1 loads artworks data and handles the execution of baseline transformations to save artworks data in the Standardised Zone; (ii) f_2 promotes data from the Standardised to the Curated Zone, checking for missing values in the attributes of an artwork; (iii) f_3 handles the migration of the DataFrames about museum visits, visitors and artworks from the Standardised the Curated Zone; (iv) f_4 joins the DataFrames that have been loaded through f_3 to establish the interconnection relationships Artwork-Collection, Artwork-Visitor and Artwork-ThematicPath. The plot on the right side of Fig. 3 evidences, as expected, that the highest execution times are obtained with f_1 (which both reads data from data sources and applies transformations functions) and f_4, the latter reporting critical processing times in case of hundreds of thousands records. Nevertheless, considering the exploratory nature of the museum web application, processing time is on average acceptable.

6   Related Work

In the recent years, a particular attention has been devoted to two major issues in the Data Lake field: (i) address data integration issues, to cope with the heterogeneity of Data Lake sources [8,9], also with the support of conceptual modelling [3]; (ii) guide the creation of APIs, to expose Data Lake content to application layers interconnected with the Data Lake [1,7]. Nonetheless, to the best of our knowledge, approaches to support web applications development on the top of Data Lakes are still under-investigated. The KAYAK framework [8] focuses on the optimisation of data preparation tasks, proposing the construction of pipelines of primitives to be applied on data sources content. Similarly, the approach in [9] fosters a UML conceptual data model to point out concepts and relationships from the analysed domain, as a support for the definition and organisation of data processing pipelines. Instead, in the Constance system [7], proper APIs are in charge of querying the Data Lake and feeding the user interface. The CoreKG Data Lake service [1] offers developers a single REST API with a set of functionalities to organise, curate, index and query the content of the Data Lake. The approach in [4] aims at proposing a solution to fruitfully organise, analyse and share heterogeneous cultural heritage data, through a web-based application. The aforementioned approaches do not consider a strategy to separate the model for the exploration of the main informative elements of the domain from the management of data stored in the Data Lake. Even though [9] somehow paves the way to a model-driven approach for applications design, the focus is more on leveraging such model for deploying a scalable ETL workflow for processing data. The approach in [4] is the only one grounded on a museum context, but issues related to the interaction between the web application and the Data Lake are not treated. A visionary approach highlighting the benefits of using conceptual modelling in Data Lakes has been proposed in [3] to pursue data quality improvement. However, the use of conceptual modelling there is not targeted to the design of an application layer on the top of the Data Lake.

7   Conclusions and Future Work

In this paper, we proposed a methodological approach to support the design of data-intensive web applications on top of a Data Lake. Conceptual modelling is adopted to abstract domain entities from their raw representation within the Data Lake. Front-end web components leveraging the core entities in the conceptual model are integrated in the target web application for visualisation and exploration purposes. A hybrid methodology based on conceptual modelling is provided to identify relevant information to be included in the conceptual model and, with respect to traditional data-intensive web applications, to manage data evolution across Data Lake zones, separating the data management pipeline from the design of the web application. The methodology has been declined in the context of a real case study in an ongoing research project in the cultural heritage domain. Future research efforts will be devoted to provide further support and a CASE tool to make each step of the methodology automatic. For instance, heuristics to suggest the most promising candidate core entities within the conceptual model will be introduced. Additionally, further investigation will regard how to optimise the data management pipeline in the Data Lake, for instance adapting the evidences described in the KAYAK approach [8].

References

1. Beheshti, A., Benatallah, B., Nouri, R., Tabebordbar, A.: CoreKG: a knowledge lake service. Proc. VLDB Endow. **11**(12), 1942–1945 (2018)
2. Ceri, D., Fraternali, P., Bongio, A., Brambilla, M., Comai, S., Matera, M.: Designing Data-Intensive Web Applications. Morgan Kaufmann, Burlington (2002)
3. Ciaccia, P., Martinenghi, D., Torlone, R.: Conceptual constraints for data quality in data lakes. In: Proceedings of the 1st Italian Conference on Big Data and Data Science (ITADATA 2022), Milan, Italy, vol. 3340, pp. 111–122 (2022)
4. Deligiannis, K., Raftopoulou, P., Tryfonopoulos, C., Platis, N., Vassilakis, C.: Hydria: an online data lake for multi-faceted analytics in the cultural heritage domain. Big Data Cogn. Comput. **4**(2), 7 (2020)
5. Diamantini, C., et al.: An approach to extracting topic-guided views from the sources of a data lake. Inf. Syst. Front. **23**, 243–262 (2021)
6. Giebler, C., et al.: A zone reference model for enterprise-grade data lake management. In: 2020 IEEE 24th International Enterprise Distributed Object Computing Conference (EDOC 2022), Eindhoven, The Netherlands, pp. 57–66 (2020)
7. Hai, R., Geisler, S., Quix, C.: Constance: an intelligent data lake system. In: Proceedings of the 2016 International Conference on Management of Data (SIGMOD/PODS 2016), San Francisco, California, pp. 2097–2100 (2016)
8. Maccioni, A., Torlone, R.: KAYAK: a framework for just-in-time data preparation in a data lake. In: Krogstie, J., Reijers, H.A. (eds.) CAiSE 2018. LNCS, vol. 10816, pp. 474–489. Springer, Cham (2018). https://doi.org/10.1007/978-3-319-91563-0_29
9. Martínez-Prieto, M.A., et al.: Integrating flight-related information into a (big) data lake. In: Proceedings of the IEEE/AIAA 36th Digital Avionics Systems Conference (DASC 2017), St. Petersburg, Florida, USA, pp. 1–10 (2017)

10. Ota, M., Mueller, H., Freire, J., Srivastava, D.: Data-driven domain discovery for structured datasets. Proc. VLDB Endow. **13**(7), 953–967 (2020)
11. Ravat, F., Zhao, Y.: Data lakes: trends and perspectives. In: Hartmann, S., Küng, J., Chakravarthy, S., Anderst-Kotsis, G., Tjoa, A.M., Khalil, I. (eds.) DEXA 2019. LNCS, vol. 11706, pp. 304–313. Springer, Cham (2019). https://doi.org/10.1007/978-3-030-27615-7_23
12. Xiao, G., et al.: Ontology-based data access: a survey. In: 27th International Joint Conference on Artificial Intelligence (IJCAI 2018), Stockholm, Sweden, pp. 5511–5519 (2018)

ESPRESSO: A Framework for Empowering Search on Decentralized Web

Mohamed Ragab[1($\boxtimes$)], Yury Savateev[1], Reza Moosaei[2], Thanassis Tiropanis[1], Alexandra Poulovassilis[2], Adriane Chapman[1], and George Roussos[2]

[1] School of Electronics and Computer Science, University of Southampton, Southampton, UK
`{ragab.mohamed,y.savateev,t.tiropanis,adriane.chapman}@soton.ac.uk`
[2] School of Computing and Mathematical Sciences, Birkbeck, University of London, London, UK
`{r.moosaei,a.poulovassilis,g.roussos}@bbk.ac.uk`

Abstract. The centralization of the Web has led to significant risks to privacy, security, and user autonomy, prompting the need for decentralization. *Solid* is a set of standards, protocols, and technologies that seeks to enable Web *re-decentralization* based on the existing W3C recommendations. In *Solid*, users store their data in *personal online data stores* (pods) with full control and sovereignty over which individuals and applications get access to them. However, the current state of the Web and Web-based applications rely heavily on search functionality using *centralized* indices. This poses significant challenges when it comes to searching or querying large-scale data stored in *decentralized* user-controlled pods, where different individuals and applications have varied access to data. To address this gap, we propose the *ESPRESSO* framework, which aims to enable individuals or applications to search Solid pods at a large scale while pod owners maintain control over access to their data. *ESPRESSO* considers *access rights* and *caching needs* while facilitating the performance of distributed queries. Our framework offers a vision for empowering search utilities in the decentralized Web, utilizing the Solid framework, and opens up new research directions for future decentralized search applications.

Keywords: Web Search · Decentralized Web · Linked Data · Personal Online Data Stores (pods) · Solid Framework

1 Introduction

The Internet has become an integral part of our daily lives, enabling us to access vast amounts of information and connect with people all around the world [18]. However, the current state of the Web is highly centralized, with a few large corporations (e.g., Google, Facebook, Amazon etc.) controlling a significant portion of online activity and user data. This centralization poses significant risks to privacy, security, and user autonomy [7]. Moreover, data stored in such centralized data silos are not readily available to other application providers to offer further added-value services [3].

F. Zhang et al. (Eds.): WISE 2023, LNCS 14306, pp. 360–375, 2023.
https://doi.org/10.1007/978-981-99-7254-8_28

Given these concerns, there have been several proposals for decentralizing the Web [3,7]. Decentralization refers to the distribution of control and ownership of data and infrastructure, enabling individuals to manage access to their online activity and data. Decentralized technologies aim to create a more equitable and transparent online environment that empowers users to maintain control over access to their data, rather than relying on third parties to centrally store it and manage access to it. This will foster data-driven advancements such as sharing and synchronizing data across various applications [3,7]. Decentralization requires the nature of applications to evolve from data in silos to *shared views* of data by decentralized applications. Last but not least, web decentralization encourages healthy competition and diversity of development by application providers [16].

One such decentralized technology that has gained significant attention in recent years is the Solid[1] technology suite [7,8,17]. Solid has been proposed as a solution to enable Web *re-decentralization* by empowering users to maintain their data in personal online data stores, also known as pods. Solid incorporates elements of the W3C *Linked Data Platform* (LDP) recommendation to enable *read/write* access to pod-stored resources, with special provisions for managing Linked Data. Solid provides standards and technologies for deploying pods with full sovereignty of users (identified by *WebID* specifications[2]) over their data, rather than having it stored in several separated data silos each controlled by third parties, such as Web platforms and applications. Application providers are required to acquire the consent of pod owners before accessing and utilizing their data [17]. Specifically, a third-party application can access data in a user's pod only if its *WebID* is associated with specific access rights recorded by the user in the *Access Control Lists* (ACLs[3]) associated with each of their resources.

While the concept of a decentralized Web holds great promise, there are still significant challenges to overcome, particularly in the area of search and query processing [20]. The development of the Web has been significantly aided by *search* as a key component, allowing more engagement from ever-growing numbers of users [18]. Search engines have always been an essential part of the Web, enabling users to access relevant information quickly and efficiently. However, most modern search engines only offer *centralized* search services, while emergent decentralized search engines do not provide search over resources where different users and applications can have different access rights. Therefore, we argue that the data search over pods is a challenging and essential problem to investigate. Empowering applications that access personal data (subject to users' stated access control permissions) with search capabilities is crucial for a successful decentralized Web [20]. However, the current search utilities across Solid applications [8] and other current distributed, federated, or Linked Data query processing systems [15] do not yet provide adequate solutions to this problem. Indeed, there is a lack of an efficient system in decentralized Web ecosystems that enables search capabilities while ensuring the privacy and security of search queries and results.

---

[1] https://solidproject.org.

[2] WebID specification https://www.w3.org/2005/Incubator/webid/spec/identity/.

[3] Web Access Control specifications: https://www.w3.org/wiki/WebAccessControl.

To fill in this research gap, this paper presents *Efficient Search over Personal Repositories - Secure and Sovereign (ESPRESSO)*, a novel framework that aims to enable large-scale data search across Solid pods while respecting individuals' data sovereignty, considering individuals' different *access rights* and *caching needs*. The ESPRESSO framework takes into consideration the requirements of the various Solid stakeholders, i.e., pod users, pod providers, search issuers, as well as information regulating entities. It aims to enable *privacy-respecting* data discovery for applications relating to domains such as healthcare, social networking, and education, with an initial emphasis on health and wellness. It will allow research, development, and testing of new indexing algorithms and query optimization techniques for search in decentralized ecosystems. Last but not least, it will foster experimentation and benchmarking of various search scenarios across large-scale decentralized Solid pods.

The remainder of the paper is organized as follows. Section 2 presents the design and implementation of the ESPRESSO framework. Section 3 provides a preliminary evaluation of the ESPRESSO system with a description of the experimental setup. Section 4 presents and discusses the results of the experiments. Section 5 provides an overview of related work. Section 6 discusses the prospective challenges ahead for the ESPRESSO project. Finally, Sect. 7 concludes the paper and discusses future research directions.

2   *ESPRESSO* Framework Architecture

This section discusses the design principles of the *ESPRESSO* framework together with implementation details for each core component of the framework. We believe that building an efficient search system within the Solid framework requires exploring the following challenges:

C.1 How to index users' data in a way that respects the access control requirements and does not jeopardize privacy.

C.2 How to effectively search a large amount of distributed indices across Solid servers' pods.

C.3 How to ensure that the search results only contain the data the search party is allowed to access.

C.4 How to efficiently route and propagate search queries across Solid servers.

ESPRESSO aims to establish a clear understanding of the challenges and requirements for enabling decentralized search across Solid pods. It also aims to provide an efficient distributed system that can facilitate the routing of both *keyword-based* searches and *declarative* more complex queries, e.g. SPARQL queries, across Solid pods for both *exhaustive* and *top-k* search scenarios while ensuring the privacy and security of the search queries and results.

The *ESPRESSO* framework needs to work with different deployment settings (ranging from online cloud-based Solid servers with thousands of pods, to a personal Solid server with a single pod) and to handle large-scale data. This requires designing distributed indexing mechanisms and query optimization techniques

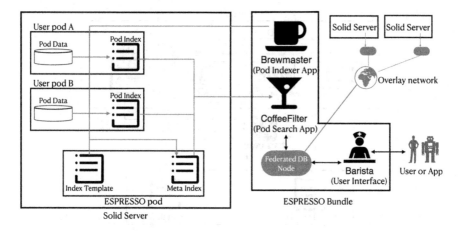

Fig. 1. *ESPRESSO* framework architecture.

for improving search performance. ESPRESSO also aims to build a decentralized search prototype implementation that enables experimentation and benchmarking on the search utilities, scenarios, and styles across Solid pods. This includes developing tools and frameworks for testing and validating the proposed search approach and ensuring its scalability and efficiency.

The *ESPRESSO* framework is built on several design principles that are summarized below alongside the specific challenges they address:

1. **Ensuring data sovereignty.** ESPRESSO should build and maintain *distributed* indices inside Solid pods rather than centralized ones, and maintain also Metadata indices to describe information on index access that can be used by search optimization algorithms (**C.1, C.3**).
2. **Respecting access control.** Enabling distributed keyword-based search and also supporting decentralized SPARQL querying while ensuring access control rights (**C.1, C.3**).
3. **Scalability.** Empowering search scenarios based on Solid servers that range from a few machines to hundreds/thousands of machines for implementing a diversity of applications (**C.2**).
4. **Decentralization.** We use a federated overlay network to propagate the queries and retrieve the search results. The search can be initiated from any node of the network (**C.4**).
5. **Privacy over efficiency.** Use of metadata for guiding query routing, and other search optimization techniques, should not compromise data privacy (**C.1, C.4**).

Figure 1 shows the abstract architecture of the ESPRESSO framework, depicting the core components that enable an end-to-end vision of how to empower search over pods. The online search functionality offered by the ESPRESSO system enables search for data stored in pods on Solid servers. First, a pod indexing application (called "*Brewmaster*") within the system creates a local index for each pod's data on a Solid server. These local indices are stored in the pods themselves

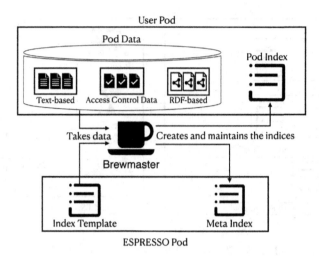

Fig. 2. Espresso pod indexing using the *Brewmaster* application.

and reflect not only the data but also users' access control assertions about it; that way, they differ from traditional indices since they include such access control information for each keyword and indexed resource. ESPRESSO allows users (or software applications/agents) to execute keyword-based search and SPARQL queries over indices through a querying user interface (called *"Barista"*). The system propagates a user query through an *overlay network* that connects the Solid servers, and returns aggregated and ranked search results retrieved from the Solid servers' pods to the user. This process of query answering passes by local indices filtering and a look-up process managed by another component (called *"CoffeeFilter"*) that provides search capabilities over the indices in a pod.

Both the pod indexer application (Brewmaster) and the pod search application (CoffeeFilter) need to get access for their webIDs from the pod owners. Only if pod owners have given that consent for these two applications are the applications' *WebIDs* stored in the access control list of the pods. At this point, Brewmaster has access to all data while CoffeeFilter has access only to the index files. Thus, Brewmaster can index the data and CoffeeFilter can search the resulting indices. Without the pod owners' consent, Brewmaster and CoffeeFilter cannot access the pods' data or the indices, respectively.

Below, we describe the functionality of the core components of the ESPRESSO framework that aims to effectively support search across a large number of Solid-compliant servers. We follow the design of each component with the details of our current prototype implementation.

2.1 Brewmaster (Pod Indexer App)

ESPRESSO provides a Solid indexing application called *Brewmaster* that builds and maintains indices for the Solid pods. Figure 2 shows the process of indexing in the ESPRESSO framework. The indexing process works as follows: on a Solid server, a special pod is created called the *ESPRESSO pod* that contains (1)

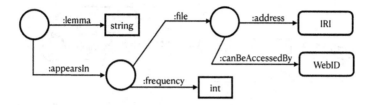

Fig. 3. Pod index format.

an *Index Template* which is an *RDF-graph* indexing template that serves as a blueprint for the pod indices, and (2) a *Meta Index* that is used for storing information about the pod indices such as index files' location and other metadata that is used by the search application for subsequent optimization and filtering purposes. Brewmaster accesses user pods for which permission is obtained by the owner for its WebID and creates a *local* index of the data stored there (pod data resources are organized hierarchically in containers) according to its type (e.g. RDF-based, or non-RDF text files) and the access control requirements provided, using the Index Template. The newly constructed pod index is saved in the pod itself. Then, Brewmaster adds the relevant information about the created local indices to the Meta Index. In the simplest case, the Meta Index maintains a list of all the addresses of the pod indices.

Figure 3 shows an example of an Index Template for *keyword-based* search and Fig. 4 shows a sample index built from this template. This RDF graph includes a node for each keyword and each of its appearances, that are connected to the relevant files (as *IRIs*), information about how many times it appears in the file, and who can access it (WebIDs). In this example, the word *"likes"* has the *lemma* *"like"*. It *appearsIn* with a *frequency* of 15 times in a *file* with the *address* `http://solidserver/pod1/file1.txt` and can be accessed by one WebID: `https://bob.example/profile#me`. It also appears with a *frequency* of 3 times in a *file* with the *address* `http://solidserver/pod1/file2.txt` and can be accessed by two WebIDs: `https://alice.example/profile#me` and `https://bob.example/profile#me`.

2.2 Barista (User Interface)

Barista serves as the ESPRESSO *User Interface* (UI) application to facilitate end user search operations. Once an input query and valid login credentials are submitted, Barista leverages a *QueryBuilder* interface to construct and prepare the query for execution. Barista allows not just human users to conduct search operations, but also applications and services that can have their own WebIDs or can borrow a user's WebID when needed (through delegation [16]).

After constructing the query, Barista passes it on to a federated database (DB) node, which in turn propagates the query to other federated DB nodes within the overlay network. The results are then collected and aggregated across these nodes before being sent back to the Barista interface through the federated DB node where the query was initiated. Barista then presents the results to the user in a format that is easy to read and understand.

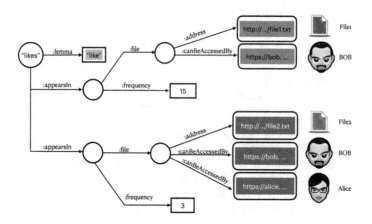

Fig. 4. An example of a pod index.

In our first prototype implementation of ESPRESSO, the search query is transformed into a GaianDB query (details on GaianDB are given in the following section), which is typically an *SQL* query. This transformation takes place in *step (1)* "Query Preparation" as shown in Fig. 5.

2.3   The Overlay Network

ESPRESSO uses an overlay network to propagate user queries to relevant data resources across Solid servers. Each solid sever in the ESPRESSO framework is connected to a federated DB node in the overlay network. The objective of query propagation is to execute the user's query while minimizing the volume of data transferred between various data sources.

The first prototype of ESPRESSO uses a data federation platform called *GaianDB*[4] for propagating user queries and aggregating search results from Solid servers [2] (as shown in *step (2)* in Fig. 5). *GaianDB* is a dynamic, distributed federated database that combines the principles of large distributed databases, database federation, and network topology. It works as a P2P overlay network that runs on a wide range of devices, addressing query propagation optimization and endpoint access restrictions. GaianDB also allows for data to be stored and accessed from multiple locations (i.e., *Store Locally and Query Anywhere*), increasing resilience and reducing the risk of data loss. Additionally, GaianDB supports query propagation across the GaianDB nodes, and result sets will be received over the *shortest paths* from nodes that can satisfy the query. Therefore, the query can be triggered at any of the GaianDB nodes and automatically propagated to the other nodes in the network. GaianDB then handles the composition of the results and sends the aggregated result back to the initiating GaianDB node. In the interests of search optimization, GaianDB also provides cache mechanisms for the preprocessed results.

---

[4] IBM GaianDB https://github.com/gaiandb/gaiandb.

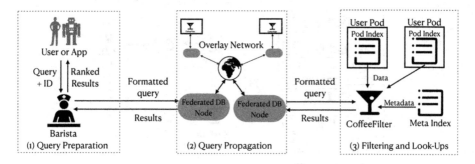

Fig. 5. Search, index look-ups, and query propagation pipeline in ESPRESSO.

In our ESPRESSO prototype, we have built a *Solid-to-GaianDB* connector component that establishes a connection between a GaianDB node and a Solid server. This connector stores the data obtained from the Solid server within a CSV file. Then, the connector generates a *logical table* (named *LTSOLID*) and maps the data from the CSV file onto the LTSOLID logical table. The Solid-to-GaianDB connector utilizes the concept of logical tables [2] for building an abstract federation layer in the GaianDB network for all data sources across solid servers' pods. Users can access all relevant data distributed across pods in different Solid servers through GaianDB nodes according to their access rights.

2.4 CoffeeFilter (Pod Search App.)

ESPRESSO provides a pod search application called *CoffeeFilter* to be installed on each Solid server. After receiving a query from the federated DB node, the *CoffeeFilter* accesses the Meta Index (created by the *Brewmaster* application) and gets the addresses of the pod indices and the relevant metadata. Then, CoffeeFilter performs a search against the relevant pod indices and sends the results back to the federated DB node.

In our first prototype of ESPRESSO, *CoffeeFilter* consists of two components, a *RESTful*[5] API and a query processing component. The API component receives the user query from a federated DB node (a GaianDB node), validates it, and then forwards it to the query processing component. The API component is also responsible for reformatting search results and returning them to that federated DB node. The query processing component accesses the Meta Index, transforms the user query into a SPARQL query, and runs it on the relevant pod indices (as shown in *step (3)* in Fig. 5). For the purpose of running a query against the indices, CoffeeFilter uses the *Comunica*[6] [19] search engine library. Comunica is a flexible SPARQL and GraphQL JavaScript library for querying decentralized knowledge graphs on the Web. Finally, the CoffeeFilter returns a ranked list of search results in JSON format to the federated DB node.

---

[5] https://aws.amazon.com/what-is/restful-api/.
[6] https://comunica.github.io/comunica/.

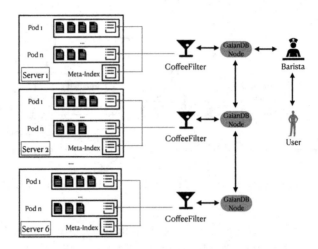

Fig. 6. Experimental architecture.

3   Preliminary Evaluation and Experimental Setup

This section outlines our experimental methodology for stress testing of the initial prototype implementation of the ESPRESSO framework. Our objective is to assess the viability and efficiency of ESPRESSO's underlying components in delivering efficient search utilities. The stress testing aimed to identify potential performance bottlenecks of our system at this early stage of development. Specifically, we evaluated the following:

– **The suitability of GaianDB** as an overlay network for propagating and routing the search queries across Solid servers. Specifically, we focused on testing the default GaianDB *query flooding* mechanism in the initial prototype implementation.
– **The efficiency of query processing** of the *CoffeeFilter* search application, which is powered by the *Communica* search engine. Our evaluation concentrated on the current implementation of keyword-based search, using a diverse set of keywords with varying frequencies across the dataset.
– **The scalability of the system** by increasing the dataset size, altering the data distribution over pods, and adjusting the number of data pods for each Solid server.

We now provide an overview of the dataset and experimental setup employed in our experiments, as illustrated in Fig. 6.

Dataset: In our evaluation, we used the *Medical Text*[7] *text-based* dataset from *Kaggle*. This dataset comprises medical abstracts that provide descriptions of various patient conditions. The original dataset has a size of 36 MB. We split

---

[7] https://www.kaggle.com/datasets/chaitanyakck/medical-text.

it into 100 files of roughly equal size, which we refer to as *Dataset-1*. For the scalability stress tests, we duplicated this dataset, resulting in a *72-MB* dataset of 200 files of roughly equal size (*Dataset-2*).

Environment Setup: Our experiments were executed on a cluster of 6 virtual machines with a Red-Hat Enterprise Linux 8.7 OS, running on 2.4 GHz per node processor, and 8 GB of memory per node, alongside a high-speed 125 GB drive for each node. The CoffeeFilter App. uses the Communica search engine V2.0.1 to support SPARQL query capabilities on RDF indices. We also used GaianDB V2.1.8.

Experiment Setup: We ran our experiments both on a single server and on the 6-machine cluster. For the experiments that involve multiple pods, we distributed the dataset files evenly (i.e., a uniform distribution) to reflect environments where each party has comparable contributions, or with a *Power-law* distribution (i.e., according to the *Zipf's* law) to reflect real-world scenarios where the majority of the data is contributed by few parties. The Brewmaster removes *stop words* and creates an inverted index of the dataset files with the keywords and their frequencies in each pod (Section 2.1).

For our tests, we chose *three* keywords – *Kwd1: disease*, *Kwd2: corona*, and *Kwd3: hemoproteins* – which appear in the dataset files *frequently*, *moderately* and *rarely*, respectively. We submit a keyword query from one machine and wait for the search results (c.f. Figure 6).

Performance Evaluation Measure (Response Time): We used the response time as a metric to measure the *latency* of query searches. Specifically, we recorded the time taken by the slowest search application instance in the cluster and the total time of the search operation. Thus, we were able to estimate the time taken to federate the query and results across the servers by GaianDB. For each experiment, we conducted tests using the three different keywords. For each experiment, we ran the query *five* times. We excluded the *first* run to avoid *warm-up* bias and computed an average of the other *four* run times.

4 Experiment Results and Discussion

In this section, we present and discuss the experimental results of our preliminary evaluation of the current implementation of ESPRESSO. We also share our experience dealing with querying decentralized indices in the Solid ecosystem.

Tables 1 and 2 show the results of our experiments on *Dataset-1* and *Dataset-2*, respectively. For each experiment, the tables show the search *keyword* (*Kwd*) and the number of rows fetched (*Res*). For each setup, we show the number of servers used (S), the average total response time (TT), including the CoffeeFilter search time (ST), and GaianDB routing time (RT). The upper part in each table addresses the results of the single-server experiments ($S=1$), while the lower part shows the 6-servers results ($S=6$). Within each part in each table, we show the results of two different distributions, i.e., Zipf and Uniform. Notably, N/As shown in the tables represent the non-applicability of distributing the data on a single server using Zipf distribution.

Table 1. Experiment results on Dataset-1. Runtimes are in *ms*.

Dataset-1			1pod/server						24 pods total					
			Zipf			Uniform			Zipf			Uniform		
			N/A			Largest index 76.8 MB			Largest index 21.5 MB			Largest index 3.5 MB		
S	Kwd	Res	ST	RT	TT	ST	RT	TT	ST	RT	TT	ST	RT	TT
	Kwd1	100				9898	28	9926	8964	25	8989	9045	26	9071
	Kwd2	12		N/A		9372	19	9390	7562	21	7583	6026	17	6043
1	*Kwd3*	1				9463	17	9480	5431	17	5448	4468	16	4483
			Largest index 34.1 MB			Largest index 14.5 MB			Largest index 21.5 MB			Largest index 3.5 MB		
	Kwd1	100	4132	20	4152	3957	89	4047	4726	20	4746	5363	47	5410
	Kwd2	12	3928	16	3944	3087	61	3147	4277	15	4291	2780	34	2813
6	*Kwd3*	1	3988	16	4004	1883	39	1921	3482	16	3498	1911	40	1951

The results show that the single-server experiments (i.e., $S=1$, upper part of Tables 1 and 2) have longer runtimes compared to the decentralized distributed indices experiments with 6 servers (i.e., $S=6$, lower part of the tables). We can also observe that in most cases the search becomes faster when data is spread across multiple pods on the same server (i.e., *24 pods total*) than when it is stored in just one pod (i.e., *1pod/server*). Indeed, the slowest search performance is seen in the case of a single server with one pod (i.e., $S=1$ and *1pod/server*). The reason behind this is that the more files a pod has, the bigger the pod index is, requiring a longer time for CoffeeFilter to load and query. To show that, we give information about the pod's *"Largest index"* size in the tables. This finding is supported also by the fact that in cases with the Zipf distribution (that puts more files into some pods, resulting in bigger index files) the search tends to perform slower compared to the cases with the uniform distribution. Comparing the results of the Dataset-1 (Table 1) and Dataset-2 (Table 2) experiments shows that the runtimes scale predictably with the dataset size.

Last but not least, it is evident that in all cases more than 99% of the total response time of ESPRESSO is taken by the search application (ST) and less than 1% is taken by the GaianDB routing (RT).

4.1 Results Discussion

In all cases, we have seen that in the keyword-based queries, most of the time for end-to-end search in the ESPRESSO prototype is taken by the search component that fetches results at each server. The time taken by GaianDB to propagate and route the query and aggregate the results is negligible by comparison. Indeed, the GaianDB overlay network shows a consistent stable performance for routing the queries and aggregating the results in our preliminary evaluations. On the other hand, the CoffeeFilter search application employs the *Communica* engine

Table 2. Experiment results on Dataset-2. Runtimes are in *ms*.

Dataset-2			1pod/server						24 pods total					
			Zipf N/A			Uniform Largest index 76.8 MB			Zipf Largest index 21.5 MB			Uniform Largest index 3.5 MB		
S	Kwd	Res	ST	RT	TT	ST	RT	TT	ST	RT	TT	ST	RT	TT
	Kwd1	200				23655	20	23675	19082	33	19115	20114	45	20159
	Kwd2	24		N/A		25064	11	25075	17085	18	17103	15599	19	15618
1	Kwd3	2				23160	12	23171	11785	15	11800	10078	18	10097
			Largest index 68.2 MB			Largest index 28.3 MB			Largest index 44.6 MB			Largest index 7 MB		
	Kwd1	200	8013	22	8035	7957	141	8098	10056	23	10079	4980	77	5057
	Kwd2	24	8306	18	8324	5921	88	6010	9903	16	9918	5971	83	6055
6	Kwd3	2	8085	16	8101	5294	44	5337	7467	18	7485	3439	48	3487

that requires loading index files into memory to run SPARQL queries on them. The size of the index files has a high impact on total response time.

The current implementation of the Solid ecosystem does not support *server-side* SPARQL executions [5]. Solid currently only provides authorization and LDP-style querying at the document level. Solid project maintainers encourage client-side SPARQL query engines for processing RDF pod data, such as Communica [19]. Thus, querying RDF resources on pods using SPARQL entails loading the entire document and delegating the query execution to the client-side engine. We believe that implementing a server-side querying paradigm will significantly enhance search component performance (i.e., only filtered search results will be transferred to client-side applications).

One more aspect to consider is that the current implementation of LDP-style querying in Solid may also violate the Solid principle of data sovereignty, retrieving and revealing more data than is necessary to answer the query. This opens up future research directions for the ESPRESSO project on how to search RDF resources (such as RDF indices), allowing only the necessary data to be retrieved to enhance search performance while respecting users' data sovereignty. This would further support application development on Solid, allowing apps to search data across pods to which they have access, without having to extract and aggregate such data on a central repository for search purposes.

Also, we are currently investigating alternative indexing schemes that do not require server-side SPARQL executions while enforcing data sovereignty. Our preliminary tests of a simple indexing scheme, where we create an index file for each keyword, and access only this small index file while querying, show at least *four-fold* improvement in search run-time.

5   Related Work

The decentralized web has received considerable attention in the academic and research literature [3, 7]. The challenge of performing a search within a decentralized data ecosystem is complex because it requires handling keyword or database queries that are dispersed across a vast network of thousands of data stores, each with varying accessibility and unique data governance constraints related to storage and migration. Different search parties may have distinct access rights, further complicating the search process [8,17]. A real example of the requirement to maintain decentralized data but facilitate queries arises in the health domain, in which health service providers must protect their patient information, yet wish to support research and cohort generation [11]. In this section, we review existing research efforts related to search over the decentralized web.

There has been extensive research in the domain of Distributed Database Systems. These works have explored various *distributed querying* techniques that enable querying of databases administered by different organizations with varying levels of autonomy [7]. Additionally, distributed indexing techniques have been proposed to support search across multiple databases, and distributed information retrieval techniques have been investigated to select datasets for search based on metadata [4].

Peer-to-Peer (P2P) data management and query routing have also been studied as potential solutions for decentralized search [9,12]. For instance, P2P protocols such as IPFS [1] leverage *Distributed Hash Tables* (DHTs) to enable keyword-based search. *Socio-aware* P2P search has also been explored for content sharing and community detection, with a distributed index used to support search within communities [12]. In personal data management, researchers have investigated distributed querying techniques to address security concerns related to storing all data in a single location. Additionally, access control policy enforcement has been studied in P2P environments.

Despite its potential benefits, decentralization poses substantial performance challenges when it comes to searching or querying *large-scale* data stored in decentralized pods. The current state-of-the-art research efforts in distributed database querying assume that the querying party has access to query endpoints, indices, and results caching options, which may not be the case in decentralized environments. Moreover, to support decentralized SPARQL querying, endpoint metadata would need to be created and maintained for each search party, access control would need to be implemented for resource selection, and caching control would need to be enforced for SPARQL *link-following* [6]. Therefore, the techniques required for data search over Solid pods go beyond the literature in distributed keyword-based search and distributed SPARQL Linked Data querying [10,14]. This is because *access rights* to pod data can vary for different search parties, and *caching restrictions* can apply to the propagation of search results across the network [20].

6   Challenges Ahead

Further development of the ESPRESSO framework must also address the following challenges:

1. The diverse nature of data stored in user-controlled pods makes efficient search challenging. Thus, ESPRESSO requires robust data indexing, meta-

data, and an efficient distributed indexing strategy that can accommodate the diversity of data types and access levels.

2. ESPRESSO must consider the access rights of users and applications as well as users' sovereignty over their data. This impacts performance since it restricts the use of standard optimization techniques such as caching.

3. ESPRESSO employs an overlay network that federates and propagates search queries. However, larger-scale experiments are required to analyze the need for optimizations on the level of query propagation, routing, and aggregation techniques.

4. ESPRESSO must address questions related to the scalability of Solid-based search applications and their ability to handle large-scale data.

5. To enable *top-k* search in ESPRESSO, decentralized ranking algorithms must be developed.

7 Conclusion and Future Directions

Solid proposed a set of standards and tools for building decentralized Web applications based on Linked Data principles. The development of search utilities in the decentralized Web is a vital step towards realizing the full potential of decentralized technologies such as Solid. The current distributed search techniques, including distributed and federated databases, as well as distributed SPARQL query processing, do not fully cover decentralized search requirements. In this paper, we present the *ESPRESSO* framework architecture that aims to enable distributed search across decentralized Solid pods. Specifically, *ESPRESSO* aims to address the challenges of search in decentralized environments, including varying access rights to pod data and caching restrictions that can apply to the propagation of search results across a network of multiple solid servers.

The roadmap of ESPRESSO includes the following future research directions:

1. Validating the architecture, proposing and implementing different real-world search scenarios that incorporate user-defined access control and data governance constraints in several application domains (e.g., healthcare, education, and well-being scenarios).

2. Performance and scalability evaluation via comprehensive experiments on the ESPRESSO framework against several baselines (e.g., fully centralized approaches, and other decentralized optimizations and caching mechanisms).

3. Performing extensive benchmarking experiments (using frameworks like [13]), testing various search scenarios and styles (i.e., exhaustive and top-k, for both keyword-based and SPARQL queries) as well as comparing different query propagation techniques.

4. Developing new decentralized search algorithms, metadata structures, indexing and query optimization techniques in existing or emergent ecosystems.

5. Investigating the integration of ESPRESSO with existing decentralized Web technologies, such as *IPFS*, and exploring the use of machine learning techniques to enhance search relevance and accuracy.

Achieving ESPRESSO's vision within this roadmap represents a significant step towards the development of a more decentralized and user-controlled Web.

Acknowledgements. This work was funded by EPSRC (EP/W024659/1).

References

1. Benet, J.: IPFS-content addressed, versioned, P2P file system. arXiv preprint arXiv:1407.3561 (2014)
2. Bent, G., Dantressangle, P., Vyvyan, D., Mowshowitz, A., Mitsou, V.: A dynamic distributed federated database. In: Proceedings of the 2nd Annual Conference International Technology Alliance (2008)
3. Berners-Lee, T.: Long live the web. Sci. Am. **303**(6), 80–85 (2010)
4. Crestani, F., Markov, I.: Distributed information retrieval and applications. In: Serdyukov, P., et al. (eds.) ECIR 2013. LNCS, vol. 7814, pp. 865–868. Springer, Heidelberg (2013). https://doi.org/10.1007/978-3-642-36973-5_104
5. Dedecker, R., Slabbinck, W., Hochstenbach, P., Colpaert, P., Verborgh, R.: What's in a Pod?-A knowledge graph interpretation for the solid ecosystem (2022)
6. Hartig, O.: An overview on execution strategies for linked data queries. Datenbank-Spektrum **13**, 89–99 (2013)
7. Kahle, B.: Locking the Web open: a call for a decentralized web. Brewster Kahle's Blog (2015)
8. Mansour, E., et al.: A demonstration of the solid platform for social web applications. In: Proceedings of the 25th International Conference Companion on World Wide Web, pp. 223–226 (2016)
9. Mislove, A., Gummadi, K.P., Druschel, P.: Exploiting social networks for internet search. In: 5th Workshop on Hot Topics in Networks (hotnets06). Citeseer, p. 79. Citeseer (2006)
10. Moaawad, M.R., Mokhtar, H.M.O., Al Feel, H.T.: On-the-fly academic linked data integration. In: Proceedings of the International Conference on Compute and Data Analysis, pp. 114–122 (2017)
11. Mork, P., Smith, K., Blaustein, B., Wolf, C., Sarver, K.: Facilitating discovery on the private Web using dataset digests. In: Proceedings of the 10th International Conference on Information Integration and Web-based Applications & Services, pp. 451–455 (2008)
12. Nordström, E., Rohner, C., Gunningberg, P.: Haggle: opportunistic mobile content sharing using search. Comput. Commun. **48**, 121–132 (2014)
13. Ragab, M., Awaysheh, F.M., Tommasini, R.: Bench-ranking: a first step towards prescriptive performance analyses for big data frameworks. In: 2021 IEEE International Conference on Big Data (Big Data), pp. 241–251. IEEE (2021)
14. Ragab, M., Tommasini, R., Eyvazov, S., Sakr, S.: Towards making sense of spark-SQL performance for processing vast distributed RDF datasets. In: Proceedings of The International Workshop on Semantic Big Data, pp. 1–6 (2020)
15. Sakr, S., et al.: The future is big graphs: a community view on graph processing systems. Commun. ACM **64**(9), 62–71 (2021)
16. Sambra, A., Guy, A., Capadisli, S., Greco, N.: Building decentralized applications for the social Web. In: Proceedings of the 25th International Conference Companion on World Wide Web, pp. 1033–1034 (2016)
17. Sambra, A.V., et al.: Solid: a platform for decentralized social applications based on linked data. MIT CSAIL & Qatar Computing Research Institute, Technical report (2016)
18. Spink, A., Jansen, B.J.: Web Search: Public Searching of the Web. Springer, Dordrecht (2004)

19. Taelman, R., Van Herwegen, J., Vander Sande, M., Verborgh, R.: Comunica: a modular SPARQL query engine for the web. In: Vrandečić, D., et al. (eds.) ISWC 2018. LNCS, vol. 11137, pp. 239–255. Springer, Cham (2018). https://doi.org/10.1007/978-3-030-00668-6_15

20. Tiropanis, T., Poulovassilis, A., Chapman, A., Roussos, G.: Search in a redecentralised web. In: Computer Science Conference Proceedings: 12th International Conference on Internet Engineering; Web Services (InWeS 2021) (2021)

Primary Building Blocks for Web Automation

Adrian Sterca(✉)[iD], Virginia Niculescu[iD], Maria-Camelia Chisăliţă-Creţu[iD],
and Cristina-Claudia Osman[iD]

Babeş-Bolyai University, Cluj-Napoca, Romania
{adrian.sterca,virginia.niculescu,
maria.chisalita,cristina.osman}@ubbcluj.ro

Abstract. Current RPA (Robotic Process Automation) platforms
increase the efficiency of business processes by automatically executing
them better and faster than the human users do. They require the human
user to analyze the UI of the target application, to identify important UI
controls and to program all these UI controls together with some control
instructions into an automatic workflow that can be later executed by
the RPA agent. We introduce a semi-automated tool based on a browser
plugin, which can be used to discover basic business processes in business web applications, construct more complex business processes based
on these and execute them automatically later. The central idea of our
tool is to map UI operations in the target business web application to
conceptual operations in a database. The advantage of our tool is that it
can be used by users without programming skills, in contrast to current
RPA platforms. Our web automation tool was successfully evaluated on
three commercial, business web applications.

Keywords: RPA · Web automation · Web User Interface analysis ·
DOM · CRUD operations

1 Introduction

Robotic Process Automation (RPA) is generally defined as the application of
specific methodologies and technologies that aim to automate repetitive tasks
achieved usually by human users [5,6]. Current RPA platforms allow an increase
of work efficiency and accuracy by automatizing business processes and executing them in a more robust way by avoiding possible human errors. RPA
refers to those tools that operate on the user interface (UI) aiming to perform
automation tasks using an "outside-in" approach. The information systems are
kept unchanged, compared to the traditional workflow technology, which allows
the improvement using an "inside-out" approach [10]. RPA frameworks (e.g.,
UiPath, Automation Anywhere, Blue Prism, Microsoft Power Automate, etc.)
operate (i.e. create automated business processes) in the following way: RPA
developers identify UI components of a software application like buttons, text

F. Zhang et al. (Eds.): WISE 2023, LNCS 14306, pp. 376–386, 2023.
https://doi.org/10.1007/978-981-99-7254-8_29

input controls, dropdown lists and tables, and then customize activities by writing code snippets in a programming language in order to act on these UI controls (e.g. click the selected button, write data in the text input, select all data from a table or a dropdown list etc.); this code that references the selected UI controls forms the automated business process which can be executed many times later with different input parameters.

Our paper introduces a semi-automated web tool that can be used to discover basic business processes and, based on these, construct more complex business processes that can be automatically executed later. This tool comes in the form of a Chrome browser extension and it is oriented on business web applications. The tool is semi-automatic, meaning that the human user must guide the tool through the various UI screens of the target web application (i.e. the human user navigates through the web application). Still, the user does not need to code for the automated business process execution, the tool handles all the understanding of the UI and the mapping of process parameters to UI controls.

The original contributions presented in the paper can be summarized as follows:

- a new approach for automating complex business processes from primary building blocks that represents the conceptual foundation of our web automation tool;
- a browser plugin that is able to extract primary building blocks from the UI of the target web application and is able to execute complex business processes composed from many primary blocks; this represents the implementation foundation of our web automation tool;
- verification and validation of the tool on three commercial business web applications.

In this paper, the term *concept* refers to the data stored in a database table, while *entity* refers to a row/record of a database table. A *concept* always describes a set of *entities*. The rest of the paper is structured as follows: Sect. 2 presents the methods used for discovering, representing and combining the *primary blocks* (into complex business processes). The evaluation of our tool is described in Sect. 3. Section 4 presents related work and the paper ends with conclusions and future work.

2   Primary Blocks Discovery, Construction and Composition

The central idea of this web automation tool is that all the UI functionalities/-operations of a business web application that uses a relational database in the backend can be of exactly two types:

1. UI operations that only affect the UI of the application and they do not use, expose or manipulate the data in the database; these may be various functionalities for navigation or for customizing the UI. These functionalities have no real value for business process automation.

2. UI operations that imply operations upon the associated database. Most UI operations translate into read or write operations in the database (CRUD operations) or in SQL terminology, they translate to 'Select', 'SelectAll', 'Insert', 'Update' or 'Delete' operations of various entities in the database; we denote them as *conceptual operations*. These are the UI functionalities that are important for business process automation and it makes sense to try to automate them.

In this sense, the proposed web automation tool automatically translates human user operations on the UI onto conceptual operations in the database. More specifically, the human user guides the automation tool (by navigating in the target business web application) such that it can discover what we call *primary blocks for process automation*.

A *primary block* or *primary navigation block* consists of a sequence of UI operations (i.e. clicks, input text fill in, mouse over, etc.) that correspond to conceptual operations for the entities in the database. The semantics of a *primary block* is given by the outcome of its final conceptual operation. For example, a *primary block* that represents a conceptual operation of *Update on an Account entity* for a business web application might include the sequence of the following conceptual operations on the database: first a *SelectAll Accounts* conceptual operation that displays in the UI a list of existing Account entities in the database, and then selecting the desired Account entity from this list and effectively updating it (i.e. the conceptual operation of *Update an Account entity*). This *primary block* also includes the corresponding UI events (i.e. click events) that facilitated the aforementioned conceptual operations on the database.

It should be noted that these UI operations that form a *primary navigation block* are either UI operations (i.e. clicks, text fills) on a single HTML content or they are UI operations that navigate from one HTML document to another (usually through click events) in the target web application. The *primary blocks for process automation* are similar to Lego blocks that we can use in order to build more complex automated business processes out of them; these complex business processes can be later executed automatically by the tool.

The browser plugin determines automatically the *primary blocks* corresponding to conceptual operations on all the concepts in the database of the applications. The human user still has to guide the plugin (i.e. the human user has to navigate) through the target web application, but there is no other required input from the human user except this navigation through the screens of the web application and the initial settings of the plugin for a target web application - which consists of the Data Model of the database used by the target web application. The human user mainly has to trigger click events in the targeted web application's UI in a logical order (so that the order of clicks on the UI describes the navigation through the web application from the first web page to the desired UI form, which allows the user to perform a specific conceptual operation in the database) and the browser plugin understands all the web content that is loaded in the browser like: identifying HTML elements/tags that the user clicked on, identifying entities or concepts from the database shown in the

HTML document loaded in the browser window, associating HTML text input fields with the data fields of an entity from the backend database, etc.

Conceptual Foundation

The actions executed during a conceptual operation may be organized into a pattern containing three sections, according to the particularity of each operation: *pre-operations* (operations required to identify the elements necessary for the main conceptual operation), *specific operations* (the main conceptual operation), and *post-operations* (the user final confirmations of the main operation).

For example, the *Insert* conceptual operation depicted in Fig. 1 requires achieving first the concept identification only, without any entity to operate on. Usually, the concept identification is achieved through a SelectAll and/or Select operations. Subsequently, the actions refer to choosing the UI element that allows entering new data (usually a New button), followed by the data entering step (filling in the input texts). The *Insert* operation finishes with the confirmation of adding new data into the database (e.g. clicking on a 'Save'-like button).

For all the other conceptual operations (Update, Delete, Select, SelectAll), similar patterns are defined (more details could be found in [9]).

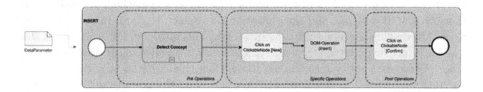

Fig. 1. *Insert* operation pattern representation

A *primary block* contains a sequence of pairs of the form: { "UI Click event", "Conceptual operation"}. Depending on its associated main conceptual operation (i.e. the last conceptual operation of the *primary block*) and on the target web application, as we have seen in the above pattern, usually a *primary block* ends with UI click events that are meant to confirm the operation by the user; for example, an Insert conceptual operation will usually end with a click on a 'Save' or 'Confirm' button; a Delete conceptual operation will usually end with a click on 'Are you sure ?' or 'Confirm' buttons. These click events form the *post-operations* and these steps have to be signalized as such to the plugin by checking the 'Finalization steps' checkbox of the plugin (so that when the plugin switches to the automatic execution of the *primary block*, it knows that the DOM(Document Object Model) that allows the main conceptual operation to be performed lies in the chain before these finalization steps). A *primary block* is tagged with the text [*concept: operation*], where *concept* and *operation* represent the associated main conceptual operation of the *primary block* (e.g. ["Account" : "Insert"]).

Web Automation Tool – Usage and Functioning

The Web Automation Tool is primarily based on a browser plugin. The user starts the process of recording a new *primary block* by clicking on the "Start recording primary block" button. Up to the point when the user clicks on the "End recording primary block" button , all actions happening on the UI of the target web application will be recorded by the plugin and at the end, they will be serialized in a JSON format and persisted to a database using a Rest API server or saved to the browser's local storage. But the plugin is not a record and replay tool for web UI actions, it is more than that - it abstracts UI actions to semantic/conceptual operations on the database.

During the time when the *primary block* is recorded/discovered, the plugin has two states: *idle* and *processing*. When the plugin is *idle* , it awaits for a UI operation (i.e. a click event) from the human user. After the user clicks on a button or other clickable element in the web page, the plugin saves to local storage the signature of the element that was clicked and then moves to the state of *processing*. In this new state, it waits until the result of the click event on the UI is finished (i.e. this would usually imply, for single-page applications, that one or more XHR requests are sent by the browser to the HTTP server and a part of the loaded document/DOM is updated). After the handling of the click event is complete, the plugin determines the *diffDOM* (i.e. the part of the DOM that was updated) and tries to identify the concept which is rendered in this *diffDOM*, if possible, and the operation (i.e. Select, Update, Insert, Delete or SelectAll) on this concept that is facilitated by this *diffDOM*. For example, if the user clicks a "New" button that constructs a web form allowing the user to insert a new "Account" entity into the database, then this *diffDOM* (the web form) is semantically defined by the concept "Account" and the operation "Insert".

So, actions happening on the UI of the target web application are recorded in pairs: a click event is first recorded (by saving the signature of the DOM element that was clicked - the signature is just its XPATH up to the document's <*body*>*tag*), and the resulted *diffDOM* is then saved in a semantically abstract form defined by: {*concept : operation*}. The *concept* is just a concept from the data model of the target web application (i.e. from the database) and *operation* is one of the following: *Insert, Update, Delete, Select* and *SelectAll*, although the human user can also annotate custom operations.

These operations correspond to the basic CRUD operations on a concept in the database; we distinguish *SelectAll* which basically means selecting several entities of a concept (not necessarily all entities in the database) from *Select* because the entities resulted from a *SelectAll* are usually displayed as a list or a table on the UI of a web application (which is different than the way a single entity resulted from a *Select* operation is rendered on the web UI). If the plugin does not identify any concept or entity from the database in the *diffDOM*, then this *diffDOM* will be represented as {*Concept:"" , Operation: "Generic DOM"*}.

When the user finally clicks the "End recording primary block" button, the recording of a *primary block* is complete and the user can tag this chain of UI actions / events with a custom string; by default, the tag/name of the *primary block* chain is the *concept : operation* pair discovered by the plugin at the end of recording of the primary block (e.g. {"Account" : "Update"} pair). For a full example of a *primary block* recorded in the CRM web application Microsoft Dynamics 2016 CRM, see [9]. The automation tool also allows the user to change this tag/name of the recorded *primary block* if he/she wants. The user can also change the attributes of the pre-recorded steps that form the *primary block*.

Configuration Settings for the Plugin. The initial settings of the plugin for a target web application are the following:

- URL of the target web application together with access credentials
- the Data Model of the database used by the target web application

The Data Model configuration does not need to match exactly the structure of the database used by the application, but it should match the text labels used for each concept of the database on the UI of the application. This is why, primary access to the database used by the target web application is not required in order to use the plugin.

A small snippet from a data model example used for the Microsoft Dynamics 2016 CRM application is given below in JSON format:

```
DataModel = {
    "Account" : ["Account Name","Phone","Fax","Website", "Parent Account","Ticker Symbol", "Address","Primary Contact",
    "Description","Industry", "SIC Code","Ownership"],

    "Contact" : ["Full Name","Job Title","Account Name","Email","Business Phone","Mobile Phone","Fax","Preferred Method of Contact",
    "Address", "Gender","Marital Status","Birthday", "Spouse/Partner Name","Anniversary","Personal Notes", "Company", "Originating
    Lead", "Last Campaign Date","Marketing Materials","Contact Method","Email","Bulk Email","Phone",
    "Fax","Mail"],

    "ForeignKeys" : [ {ForeignKey:"Company",ForeignTable: "Contact",PrimaryKey :"Account Name",PrimaryTable:"Account"} ]
    ...
};
```

The data model describes the concept *Account* with its associated attributes and the concept *Contact* with its associated attributes. It also describes that the *Company* attribute from *Contact* is a foreign key and refers to the primary key *Account Name* from the *Account* concept. Again, we emphasize that these attributes don't have to match exactly the attributes of the database tables, but instead they have to match the text labels for the respective entities on the UI of the target web application. The foreign key relation is used when for example the plugin tries to add a new (i.e. an Insert operation) entity of type *Contact* and the UI interface of the target web application only allows the input of values for the main attributes of *Contact* entity and assumes that the *Account* to which this new *Contact* entity is linked already exists in the database.

Composition of Complex Business Processes

In 2003, van der Aalst et al. defined a series of 20 workflow patterns [11]. Their initial goal was to use these patterns as qualitative criteria in workflow systems' assessment or standards' assessment. A comparison based on the workflow patterns, where BPMN models and UML Activity Diagrams are analysed, is depicted in [12]. Another similar approach that analyzes BPMN models, workflow patterns and YAWL models is presented in [3]. Wohed et al. studied the application of these patterns on BPMN models [13]. They do not focus only on control-flow perspective, but also resource and data perspectives are analyzed. A similar approach where business process models are built based on BPMN Workflow Patterns is treated in [14].

The *Sequence* pattern involves at least 2 tasks that should precede and succeed each other. This pattern requires tasks and sequence flows concepts. Modeling parallel tasks is performed using *Parallel Split* and *Synchronization* patterns, while the choice of one branch out of multiple branches is described by *Exclusive Choice* and *Merge* patterns. These patterns use tasks and gateways (exclusive of parallel gateways).

Complex processes could be obtained by combining *primary blocks* using the aforementioned control-flow patterns. To achieve this we may consider *primary blocks* as sub-processes and assimilate them to tasks. Sequencing the CRUD operations is a natural composition, but we may also allow discriminating composition based on some conditions (i.e. Insert or Update depending on the existence or not of the considered entities) or even parallel composition (e.g. several Insert operations executed in parallel). Parallel composition is achieved by operating on two or more browser tabs in which the target web application is loaded.

3   Evaluation

We have tested our tool on 3 commercial, business web applications: 1) Microsoft Dynamics 2016 CRM[1], 2) Microsoft Dynamics 365 Business Central[2] and 3) Atlassian Jira[3]. Although we tested our web automation tool on these 3 business web applications, we based our plugin implementation on common web design principles (like the fact that an input field is always placed in the web UI either on the right or below or in the south-east part of its corresponding text label), so it should work correctly on other business web applications. As shown in Fig. 1, we used general templates for the conceptual operations which are not specific to a particular web application, so our web automation tool should, in principle, work with any typical business web application that uses a relational database. The full code of our browser plugin is available at https://github.com/KiralyCraft/WAPlugin.

Automatic Detection of Primary Building Blocks. We evaluated the ability of our web automation tool to automatically discover *primary building blocks* of conceptual operations by going through use cases/functionalities of the three previous mentioned business applications. We considered all use cases that

---

[1] https://learn.microsoft.com/en-us/lifecycle/products/dynamics-crm-2016-dynamics-365.

[2] https://dynamics.microsoft.com/en-us/business-central/overview/.

[3] https://www.atlassian.com/software/jira.

involve (i.e. whose outcome is) a CRUD operation in the backend database. So, we ignored use cases that involve only UI modifications, without reading from or changing the data in the database. We ignored use cases that do not operate on the database (they operate just on the data that is shown in HTML documents in the browser) like for example: print current HTML document, draw reports, email a link/current document, import from Excel into the browser window, etc. On all these considered use cases, we tested whether our plugin is able to automatically detect the *primary block* (i.e. the main conceptual operation of the *primary block*). The results are summarized in Table 1.

Table 1. Automatic discovery of primary building blocks

Target application	Total number of use cases (i.e. primary blocks)	Number of primary blocks automatically discovered	Percentage of primary blocks automatically discovered
Atlassian Jira	39	26	67%
Microsoft Dynamics 2016 CRM	102	81	79%
Microsoft Dynamics 365 Business Central	135	70	52%

The second column in the table presents the number of use cases (i.e. potential *primary blocks*) we considered/tested in each of the 3 web applications. The third column presents the absolute number of *primary blocks* detected and the fourth column presents the percentage of this number of automatically detected *primary blocks* in the total number of potential *primary blocks* (i.e. the second column value). We can see in this table that our web automation tool was able to detect 67%, 79%, and respectively 52% of all the available *primary blocks* (i.e. all primary blocks employed by the target application). The rest of non-discovered *primary blocks* involve partial CRUD operations, i.e. operations that only change a single field or a couple of fields from a database entity (e.g. the operation "Fulfill Order" which only changes a field of the "Order" entity and does not perform a full-fledged Update operation of all fields).

Automatic Execution of Complex Business Processes. A complex, automatable business process is a sequence of *primary blocks* linked by the operators presented in the previous section. An example of such an automatable business process is presented in the following listing.

```
ComplexProcess=[
    {Operation:"Insert", Concept: "Account", Parameters:{"Account Name": "UBB", "Phone" : "000000000", "Fax" : "000000000",
    "Website" : "www.company.com", ...} }
    Operator,
    {Operation: "Insert", Concept: "Contact", Parameters:{"Full Name": "John Doe", "Job Title": "Professor",
    "Account Name" : "UBB", "Email" : "john.doe@company.com",
    ...} },
    Operator,
    ...
]
```

The complex process is given in the listing in a JSON representation. The Operator can be one of *"Sequence"*, *"Choice"* and *"Parallel"*. The *"Choice"* operator is implemented using *Exclusive choice* and *Merge* patterns, and the *"Parallel"* operator is implemented using the *Parallel Split* and *Synchronization* patterns. Each *primary block* in the listing is identified by the *Operation* and *Concept* pair and also contains the *Parameters* of the *primary block* (e.g. the { Operation: "Insert", Concept: "Account" } *primary block* specifies value parameters for each property of the Account entity that is to be inserted in the database). Of course, there can be more than two *primary blocks* linked by different operators in a complex automatable process.

The plugin's UI allows the user to specify a complex process for automatic execution in the above JSON format. We tested the automatic execution of complex processes functionalities of our plugin on the 3 aforementioned business web applications. We used similar complex processes as the one in the above JSON listing, having 2–3 operators. Our browser plugin was able to successfully discover the *primary blocks* and execute all tested complex processes in the 3 aforementioned business applications. Some screenshots and additional details of these experiments are presented in an extended report [9] and omitted here due to space constraints.

4   Related Work

Robidium [7] is a tool that discovers automatable routine tasks from the user interface (UI) logs and generates RPA scripts to automate these routines. This is a Software as a Service (SaaS) tool that implements the robotic process mining pipeline proposed in [8]. *Robidium* uses UI log files that consist of data and events that are not related to a specific task identified beforehand. Its architecture emphasizes a preprocessing step on UI logs, that allows the routine extraction and discovery of automatable routines that are compiled into a UiPath script.

SmartRPA [1] is a cross-platform tool that attempts to tackle the discovery and the automation of routine tasks, that current practice proves to be time-consuming and error-prone. The tool uses its own action logger to record UI actions on the actions system, Microsoft Office applications, or web browser into a log file, used as input for routine identification. The tool allows the generation of a high-level flowchart diagram that can be studied by expert users for potential diagnosis operations and to generate executable RPA scripts based on the most frequent routine variant. Some input fields of the selected routine variant can be personalized before executing the related RPA scripts, supporting those steps that require manual user inputs.

There are also tools that automate users' actions. Ringer is a web replayer developed as a Chrome extension. Based on the trace of DOM (i.e. Document Object Model) events performed by users, it provides a script replaying users' actions [2]. This tool is only used for recording users' actions. Rousillon uses Ringer to further develop complex web automation scripts using Helena web scripting language [4].

In contrast with *Robidium* [7] and *SmartRPA* [1], our tool does not use an external logging tool to record user actions. Instead, it uses the human user actions at UI level in order to compute a navigation flow in the target web application and it uses the web DOM itself and the data model of the target web application in order to identify the elements that are available on UI and can be included in future interactions. As a result, the tool allows the generation of the workflow blocks together with the inventory (or a map) of the UI elements the user may interact with (inputs, buttons, etc.). Robidium, SmartRPA and Ringer are all record-and-replay tools. Both *Robidium* and *SmartRPA* emphasize a particular type of routine, i.e., filling out a web form (Google Forms or other web application) with data taken from a desktop application (Microsoft Office Excel file), that is equivalent to inserting a new record into a database. These are very simple examples. Our tool is capable of discovering processes (i.e. *primary blocks*) on complex business web applications (e.g. CRM and ERP apps.) which imply complex browsing flows in the target web application. Also, our tool can automatically execute complex business processes that the human user didn't even recorded/executed (because complex automatizable business processes can be composed from individual *primary blocks* discovered by our tool and these complex business process can be automatically executed by our tool); i.e. our tool is not a simple record-and-replay tool. Also, our browser plugin is capable of *understanding the UI* using the data model of the target web application - so the human user does not need to indicate to the plugin relevant input fields or property controls on the UI.

5 Conclusions

We presented in this paper a web automation tool that detects basic business processes in business web applications, construct more complex business processes based on these and execute them automatically later.

Our tool maps UI operations in the target business web application to conceptual operations in a database. The user of our tool is not required to have any programming knowledge, all he/she needs to do is to provide a small startup configuration (like the URL of the target web application, credentials for accessing it and the concepts from the database with their properties) and to "guide" the plugin in the discovery of basic business processes (i.e. *primary blocks*) by browsing through the target web application. This is different than the current RPA platforms which function on a record-and-replay principle (i.e. they can only execute automatically what they have previously recorded in the UI) and also require the user to write code in order to program the automated process. We have shown that our idea is viable by experimenting on 3 commercial, business web applications.

Acknowledgement. The present work has received financial support through the project: *Integrated system for automating business processes using artificial intelligence*, POC/163/1/3/121075 - a Project Cofinanced by the European Regional Development Fund (ERDF) through the Competitiveness Operational Programme 2014–2020.

References

1. Agostinelli, S., Lupia, M., Marrella, A., Mecella, M.: Automated generation of executable RPA scripts from user interface logs (2020)
2. Barman, S., Chasins, S., Bodik, R., Gulwani, S.: Ringer: web automation by demonstration. In: Proceedings of the 2016 ACM SIGPLAN International Conference on Object-Oriented Programming, Systems, Languages, and Applications, pp. 748–764 (2016)
3. Börger, E.: Approaches to modeling business processes: a critical analysis of BPMN, workflow patterns and yawl. Softw. Syst. Model. **11**, 305–318 (2012)
4. Chasins, S.E., Mueller, M., Bodik, R.: Rousillon: scraping distributed hierarchical web data. In: Proceedings of the 31st Annual ACM Symposium on User Interface Software and Technology, pp. 963–975 (2018)
5. Hofmann, P., Samp, C., Urbach, N.: Robotic process automation. Electron. Mark. **30**(1), 99–106 (2020)
6. Institute for Robotic Process Automation. Introduction to robotic process automation. A primer, June 2015
7. Leno, V., Deviatykh, S., Polyvyanyy, A., Rosa, M.L., Dumas, M., Maggi, F.M.: Robidium: automated synthesis of robotic process automation scripts from UI logs. In: Proceedings of the Best Dissertation Award, Doctoral Consortium, and Demonstration & Resources Track at BPM 2020 co-located with the 18th International Conference on Business Process Management (BPM 2020), Sevilla, Spain, vol. 2673, pp. 102–106, 13–18 September 2020. CEUR-WS.org
8. Leno, V., Polyvyanyy, A., Dumas, M., Rosa, M.L., Maggi, F.M.: Robotic process mining: vision and challenges. Bus. Inf. Syst. Eng. Int. J. WIRTSCHAFTSINFORMATIK **63**(3), 301–314 (2021)
9. Sterca, A., Niculescu, V., Chisalita-Cretu, C., Osman, C.: Primary building blocks for web automation. Technical report, Babes-Bolyai University (2023). https://www.cs.ubbcluj.ro/~forest/research/papers/web-automation/waplugin-technical-report2023.pdf
10. Van-der Aalst, W.M.P., Bichler, M., Heinzl, A.: Robotic process automation. Bus. Inf. Syst. Eng. **60**, 269–272 (2018)
11. van der Aalst, W.M.P., ter Hofstede, A.H.M., Kiepuszewski, B., Barros, A.P.: Workflow patterns. Distrib. Parallel Databases **14**(1), 5–51 (2003)
12. White, S.A., et al.: Process modeling notations and workflow patterns. Workflow Handb. **2004**(265–294), 12 (2004)
13. Wohed, P., van der Aalst, W.M.P., Dumas, M., ter Hofstede, A.H.M., Russell, N.: On the suitability of BPMN for business process modelling. In: Dustdar, S., Fiadeiro, J.L., Sheth, A.P. (eds.) BPM 2006. LNCS, vol. 4102, pp. 161–176. Springer, Heidelberg (2006). https://doi.org/10.1007/11841760_12
14. Yamasathien, S., Vatanawood, W.: An approach to construct formal model of business process model from BPMN workflow patterns. In: 2014 Fourth International Conference on Digital Information and Communication Technology and its Applications (DICTAP), pp. 211–215. IEEE (2014)

A Web Service Oriented Integration Solution for Capital Facilities Information Handover

Elvismary Molina de Armas[1]($^{(\boxtimes)}$)(ID), Geiza Maria Hamazaki da Silva[2](ID),
Júlio Gonçalves Campos[1](ID), Vitor Pinheiro de Almeida[1](ID), Hugo Neves[1](ID),
Eduardo Thadeu Leite Corseuil[1](ID), and Fernando Rodrigues Gonzalez[3](ID)

[1] Instituto Tecgraf - Pontifícia Universidade Católica do Rio de Janeiro (PUC-RIO),
Rio de Janeiro, RJ, Brazil
{emolina,juliogcampos,valmeida,hugofn,thadeu}@tecgraf.puc-rio.br
[2] Universidade Federal do Estado do Rio De Janeiro (UNIRIO),
Rio de Janeiro, RJ, Brazil
geiza.hamazaki@uniriotec.br
[3] Petrobras S.A., Rio de Janeiro, RJ, Brazil
fernando.gonzalez@petrobras.com.br

Abstract. The potential to obtain the correct information, manage and interchange it are some of the keys to the success of a project. In the Oil and Gas industry context, the Capital Facilities Information Handover Specifications (CFIHOS) represents an initiative to improve how information is exchanged between companies that own, operate, and build equipment for the process and energy sectors. In that sense, CFIHOS proposes a data model and a library (Reference Data Library - RDL) with standard terms for data interchange. This work presents an implementation using a subset of the CFIHOS data model in the scope of Construction of Engineering Procurement (EPC) contracts. The use case was implemented over the INSIDE system, allowing dynamic integration between heterogeneous databases using an architecture based on web services. The knowledge of extracting the information from databases and generating a spreadsheet in the CFIHOS data model was encoded in INSIDE by defining data services in the knowledge base. There are no tools that verify how much the information contained in a file complies with the CFIHOS data model and RDL information. For this reason, a prototype of a validator was implemented to verify the challenges of using CFIHOS. The developed CFIHOS Validator complements the data extraction and data verification flows according to this standard.

Keywords: CFIHOS · Interoperability · Web Semantics

1 Introduction

Nowadays, the potential to get the correct information and how to manage and interchange are the fundamental keys to the success of large projects. It becomes

F. Zhang et al. (Eds.): WISE 2023, LNCS 14306, pp. 387–396, 2023.
https://doi.org/10.1007/978-981-99-7254-8_30

more critical with challenges such as complexity, variety, and a large volume of data, as seen in the Oil and Gas Industry.

It is known that 25% of employee time is spent searching for information [3]. The missing information during all phases of an Oil and Gas plant life-cycle directly influences the loss of millions of dollars. The data is commonly spread around heterogeneous databases, which complicates the situation. Each of these databases has its data model according to the software application, making necessary specific knowledge and understanding of the model of each one to get the correct data.

To allow dynamic interoperability between heterogeneous databases in the context of the Oil and Gas Industry was developed a system called INSIDE [1,2,4]. It allows to consult data over heterogeneous multi-model databases, integrating the results based on Polystore [6] and OBDA [17] architectures. Implemented using web services, INSIDE allows consulting data as a service without knowing the conceptual model of the databases. Furthermore, it is possible to compose new queries as composite services using a user-friendly interface.

CFIHOS is an initiative led by the International Association of Oil & Gas Producers (IOGP) [12] under Joint Industry Programme 36 (JIP36). Its goal is to standardize the data handover process between all companies that build, operate, maintain or decommission industrial facilities. It proposes a clear definition of information requirements to enable owners and contractors to agree on information for exchange. For this purpose, CFIHOS defines a data model and a dictionary with common terms (Reference Data Library - RDL). Also, it recommends templates that determine which data must be specified for each part depending on the contract type.

However, few applications of CFIHOS implementations are found. This work aims to implement data extraction from heterogeneous databases to accomplish the CFIHOS data model. We are proposing a validator for CFIHOS data model with the data generated as input.

Next, in Sect. 2, a brief explanation is presented with the main concepts related to CFIHOS, INSIDE, and the data source used in the case study, while Sect. 3 exposes the related works. Section 4 describes the case of use in detail, revealing the CFIHOS's template and entities selected. To follow, Sect. 5 presents the case study implementation, listing the mapping difficulties between the CFIHOS entities and the underlying data source. Moreover, this section details the additions in each component of INSIDE architecture, focusing on the CFIHOS Validator component. In Sect. 6, the validation of the implementation is shown. Finally, Sect. 7 presents the main points of our work are discussed, and some final considerations and contributions from this work are given.

2   Background

2.1   CFIHOS

The Capital Facilities Information Handover Specification (CFIHOS) [10] is an industry-standard developed to improve how information is exchanged between companies that own, operate, and build equipment for the process and energy sectors. CFIHOS v1.5 [11] includes a data model, a dictionary of common terms and definitions called Reference Data Library (RDL), a set of contractual specification documents, and implementation guides. To facilitate implementation, CFIHOS defines five Contract Scenario Templates reflecting typical contracting scenarios between the Owner, also called the Principal, and the Contractor. Template 1 describes the scope of Construction of Engineering Procurement (EPC) or Engineering Services Contractor (ESC), which is the most applicable according to our reality.

Once the information is extracted from the sources and represented in the CFIHOS data model, this information must be exchanged between the parties to the contract. Regardless of the source, it is essential to validate the accuracy of the information and its compliance with the CFIHOS data model before consuming and importing this information into the engineering software.

2.2   SPPID

SmartPlant P&ID software [8] allows piping and instrumentation diagrams (P& ID) management. It is focused on design quality and consistency in the context of the plant asset. SmartPlant P&ID Data Model is implemented in the Oracle database and organized under four schemes (called "SPPID database" for simplicity). It contains engineering information, such as tag, equipment, equipment characteristics, elements of the plant's physical structure, and the Process Diagrams. The SPPID Data Model is difficult to query because of its complex relational structure.

2.3   INSIDE

INSIDE [1,2,4] is a system developed to allow a Semantic Interoperability for Engineering Data Integration between data residing in heterogeneous databases. It enables consulting data as a service without knowing the conceptual model of the databases and allows composing new queries as composite services using a user-friendly interface.

The INSIDE's architecture comprises three main layers: the KB Manager, the Front-End, and the Engine. These layers intercommunicate through web services technologies. The KB Manager is responsible for accessing the Knowledge Base (KB) for generating INSIDE queries and saving in the KB the new services designed by the user in the Front-End. The KB contains three ontologies and one taxonomy: the upper ontology ISO15926, a data source ontology, a service ontology used to represent executable data services, and a vocable taxonomy for the domain. The INSIDE Front-End is a web application that provides the interface for the user. The INSIDE Front-End communicates with the KB Manager using HTTP REST and the Engine using Apache KafkaJS[1]. Finally, the Engine is responsible for executing the INSIDE query, gathering the results, and sending it to the Front-End in a scalable way.

3   Related Works

Kraken IM is a steering committee member of CFIHOS/JIP36 and is active in the standards' development. Phoenix and Halcyon software from Kraken IM are both available pre-configured for CFIHOS version 1.5. Halcyon [14] is a data collaboration platform that provides all stakeholders with a hub to supply, validate and approve engineering data. Phoenix [15] allows project owners to define their exact information requirements to contractors, suppliers, and sub-suppliers in a digital format.

Hexagon PPM [7] is another CFIHOS member and active participant. The HxGN SDx [9] is one of the products in the new Hexagon PPM Smart Digital Asset portfolio that is adopting this standard. It is a cloud-based asset life-cycle information management solution with two modules: HxGN SDx Projects and HxGN SDx Operations. A series of actions must be performed in HxGN SDx [9] to transform its native data model to CFIHOS-compliant elements (for example, PLANT, SITE, etc.), currently based on CFIHOS version 1.4. Once these transformations are executed, they are irreversible. HxGN SDx also presents the Exchange Data functionality that enables the data and documents exportation to CSV files using the CFIHOS format. Additionally, it is possible to validate and export these CSV files to a target system.

CFIHOS v1.5 is available in AVEVA Information Standards Manager (ISM) [3]. It imposes standards in class libraries that facilitate an effective information handover right from the start of the project and map data requirements to external systems.

According to what was explored in the study of the state-of-the-art, only proprietary license software have a kind of CFIHOS support. No open-source public domain software was found in our research. Generally, the public documentation of the tools that support CFIHOS is few, and the accomplished level to the standard needs to be better explained.

4   Use Case Description

The work aims to validate the idea of implementing CFIHOS v1.5. In that sense, our case study is focused on extracting data from data sources used in the Oil and Gas company and supporting the information handover that compliance the CFIHOS data model and RDL. For instance, we selected the SPPID database

---

[1] Apache KafkaJS: https://kafka.js.org.

and the following group of entities of CFIHOS that cover the plant breakdown structure: SITE, PLANT, PROCESS UNIT, AREA, COMMISSIONING UNIT, LEAF NODE COMMISSIONING UNIT, and TAG [11]. We also are concerned with the validation of the delivered information.

According to the CFIHOS Data Model, the SITE is related to a PLANT, so a PLANT is located in a SITE. A PLANT is functionally divided into PRO-CESSING UNIT(s), it is geographically divided into AREA(s), and is commissioned divided into COMMISSIONING UNIT(s). A TAG, as well as a PLANT, is related to these three entities, being that a PROCESSING UNIT can be functionally divided into TAG(s), an AREA locates TAG(s), and a COMMISSION-ING UNIT (LEAF NODE COMMISSIONING UNIT) groups TAG(s). Additionally, the CFIHOS model divides a TAG into classes and offers a list of properties for each class and pre-defined pick lists values for some properties. Therefore, the TAG CLASS, TAG OR EQUIPMENT CLASS, TAG CLASS PROPERTY, PROPERTY, PROPERTY PICKLIST, and PROPERTY PICKLIST VALUE entities also were included in our use case. We decided to restrict the scope of the case of study to "vessel" TAG CLASS. Following Template 1 for the EPC contracting scenario, the Principal must send the Contractor the information regarding the SITE and PLANT entities. In contrast, the Contractor must send the Principal the information on PROCESSING UNIT, AREA, COMMISSION-ING UNIT, and TAG.

5   Case Study Implementation

5.1   Data Flow

During the execution of the case study, see Fig. 1, the Owner can query and extract data from the data sources and export it as an Excel format that accomplishes the CFIHOS data model with the information specified for Template 1 (SITE and PLANT entities data). At that point, the data could be sent to the Contractor. Similarly, the Contractor could be able to extract the information specified in Template 1 related to the AREA, PROCESS UNIT, COMMIS-SIONING UNIT, TAG, TAG CLASS, and TAG PROPERTIES entities from data sources and send to the Owner that fulfills CFIHOS data model. This information flow is possible using the INSIDE engine with data services and the out-of-the-box services that express the sources' expert knowledge mapping to the CFIHOS model. The Owner and Contractor data flows are independent. The CFIHOS automatic validator is an autonomous component available to use from INSIDE. It could help to verify data consistency to the CFIHOS data model, regardless of how it was generated. The CFIHOS Validator acts at the final point to verify the data is ready for information handover (Fig. 1).

5.2   Mapping CFIHOS Entities in SPPID Database

One of the major difficulties during the implementation was the correct mapping between the CFIHOS entities and their attributes to corresponding values in the

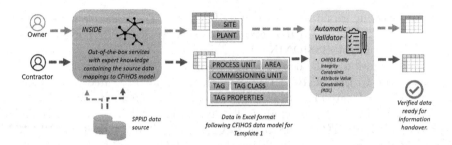

Fig. 1. Case use data flow. Owner flow using orange arrows, and Contractor flow in gray arrows. Finally, each output could be validated for information handover. (Color figure online)

SPPID data source. The main challenges were: (i) Lack of semantic description for the SPPID terms; (ii) SPPID attribute terms with equal syntactical of CFIHOS concepts and attributes, but with different semantics; (iii) SPPID changes the database location (table and column) used for the same part of information according to the project phase; (iv) Hierarchies of the entities presented in the SPPID model and CFIHOS data model are different; (v) Lack of the value in SPPID for many mandatory attributes in CFIHOS; and (vi) Lack of codes in SPPID for many entities in CFIHOS.

The main knowledge about of SPPID model was obtained from the IT specialists of Petrobras because of the lack of detailed documentation of it. The semantics of each term used in the software needs to be specified.

Since the SPPID model does not correspond in many aspects to the CFIHOS data model, it increases the complexity of extracting data regarding CFIHOS entities, forcing us to focus on mandatory attributes of CFIHOS, using alternative values in some cases and implementing complex and recursive queries.

5.3   INSIDE Architecture

The conceptual architecture of INSIDE had to change to support the generation and validation of files in the CFIHOS standard.

New services were modeled to obtain CFIHOS data over the INSIDE knowledge base, which uses UFO-S [16] as the core ontology. First, the CFIHOS entities used in our use case were modeled as a basic service containing the SQL queries obtained in the mapping process. Then, for entities that needed to add unmapped attributes (for example, null values), Rule Computations were added in the ontology to generate these additional values, generating composite services. In total, eight CFIHOS data services were included with its commitment specification, specifying the inputs and outputs of them. Each concept associated with a data service is also linked with a table and column in the data source and modeled in the relational database ontology. Given a known service, it is possible to know the association of its inputs and outputs with its localization in the data source.

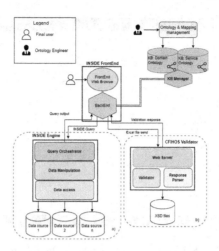

Fig. 2. INSIDE Architecture. Conceptual model for CFIHOS implementation.

It was necessary to add two new functional requirements (FR) to INSIDE: FR.1.Export CFIHOS data, with a FR.1.x sub-item for each CFIHOS entity (SITE, PLANT, AREA, COMMISSIONING UNIT, PROCESS UNIT, LEAF NODE COMMISSIONING UNIT, and TAG); and FR.2.Validate CFIHOS data, with a FR.2.x sub-item, one for Owner data and other for Contractor data.

To implement the FR.1, it was necessary to display the list of available data services. Then, users could select the entities corresponding to their role (Owner or Contractor) to generate the output containing data from SPPID following the CFIHOS data model.

The Query Orchestrator layer (Fig. 2.a) in the INSIDE Engine component was modified to generate files in the CFIHOS format. The Data Manipulation layer was updated to allow the INSIDE Engine to return the responses from executions of multiple independent sub-queries encapsulated in a single large query.

The INSIDE architecture had to be extended to use the new component: the CFIHOS Validator, to implement the FR.2. The Front-End had to be extended to include the logic to send data to validate by the new component and the logic to receive the validation result and show it to the user.

5.4   CFIHOS Validator

The CFIHOS Validator is a component responsible for validating whether files comply with CFIHOS standards. This component has three modules: the Web Server, the Validator, and the Response Parser (Fig. 2.b).

The Web Server module allows the CFIHOS Validator to receive files and send responses. The responses show the validation output so the client knows if the input file complies with the CFIHOS standard (see Fig. 3). The second module is the Validator, responsible for validating the files received by the Web

Fig. 3. GUI of the CFIHOS Validator. Validation of Owner and Contractor data. One error was identified.

Server. The Validator contains features that allow fully validating a file according to the CFIHOS standard. Finally, the third module is the Response Parser, which is liable for receiving the result of the file validation and traduce it to a language that the non-developer user understands.

6   Validation

We decided to use a workbook Excel format to support data in the CFIHOS model. The INSIDE allows the user to select the role (Owner or Contractor) before generating the Excel file with corresponding entities and the values for each attribute, following Template 1 of CFIHOS. Each entity is represented in a different sheet of the workbook. Entities entirely contained in the RDL, such as TAG CLASS, are not included in the result file. For instance, Fig. 4 illustrates the file generated for the Contractor with masked data.

Site code	Site name	Measurement system code							
PETROBRAS XX (P-XX)	PETROBRAS XX (P-XX)	SI							

| | | SITE | PLANT | PROCESS UNIT | AREA | COMMISSIONING UNIT | LEAF NODE COMMISSIONING UNIT | TAG | TAG PROPERTY |

Fig. 4. Data result from the extraction of SSPID for Contractor.

Finally, the CFIHOS Validator component can be used to check the file with CFIHOS data generated by INSIDE. It can show if the file has any irregularities concerning the standard or is in agreement. The validation covers the following items: a) entities, b) attributes associated with each entity, c) data type of each attribute, d) data mandatory, e) integrity constraints between attributes, f) data integrity constraints between attributes values and RDL.

We executed two test cases for the validation, one test with two artificial files with completed and corrected data, one for the Owner and another for the Contractor, and another test with real data extracted from SPPID. In each test case, the CFIHOS Validator returns the correct answer. In the first case, it checked and confirmed that the data was according to the CFIHOS model. For the second case, as some mandatory attributes could not be extracted from SPPID, the validation result showed a list of attributes with their corresponding issues. The files used to test are available in https://github.com/emolina85/CFIHOS-validor-test-data.

7   Discussion and Conclusions

The mapping process was one of the most significant difficulties due to the lack of defined terms' semantics and a formal guide of the SPPID database. Additionally, SPPID's custom attributes increase the data diversity and complexity. Even more critically, we found the same information saved in different attributes in the SPPID for the same project in different stages, challenging the mapping process. Although we used the SPPID data source, it is expected to observe the same characteristics in another data source in the Oil and Gas domain.

In our opinion, in further implementations of CFIHOS, the data sources should be modeled with the previous notion of the CFIHOS data model. However, for legacy systems, it is essential to have a system like INSIDE. The structure of the data sources underneath does not need to change according to CFIHOS, as is needed for other approaches, for instance, HxGN SDx [9], and it can be continued used for their proprietary software. Moreover, using ontologies, we are mapping the knowledge of specialists that will enable integration with other software and make tacit knowledge explicit.

This work presented a use case that offers a solution for CFIHOS based on a web service-oriented integration. The INSIDE solution for integrating heterogeneous databases was enriched to extract data and generate the result accomplishing the CFIHOS data model for contracting scenarios in Template 1. Finally, a CFIHOS validation solution was implemented and tested.

The use case implemented in this work proves the feasibility of INSIDE. In terms of validation, to the best of our knowledge, it is the first approach that validates CFIHOS data that can be generated from independent data sources. The availability of tools for validation significantly increases the standard's acceptance in the community. This result contributes to the development of a framework to extend the validation for other CFIHOS templates, that can be used as a reference for validating other patterns in the ecosystem in the process industry, such as DEXPI [5] and ISO [13].

In future works, we want to do a deep study and verify the best format to interchange CFIHOS data. The current implementation was done using an Excel workbook, but it could be better to use other formats like, for example, JSON. Also, we like to improve the CFIHOS Validator output. Finally, we expect to extend the scope of the current use case to cover other entities and templates.

References

1. Almeida, V., et al.: INSIDE: semantic interoperability in engineering data integration. In: Proceedings of the 25th International Conference on Enterprise Information Systems, ICEIS 2023, Prague, Czech Republic, 24–26 April 2023, vol. 1, April 2023. https://doi.org/10.5220/0011748700003467
2. Armas, E., et al.: Hybrid architecture to achieve semantic interoperability for engineering oil and gas industry process, pp. 176–182, November 2021. https://doi.org/10.1145/3487664.3487782
3. AVEVA: AVEVA Asset Information Management - Complying with a CFIHOS Handover Using Engineering Information Management Tools (2022). https://cdn.osisoft.com/osi/presentations/2022-AVEVA-Amsterdam/UC22EU-D3E1010-AVEVA-Parvin-AIM-Complying-with-a-CFIHOS-Handover.pdf
4. Campos, J.G., De Almeida, V.P., De Armas, E.M., Da Silva, G.M.H., Corseuil, E.T., Gonzalez, F.R.: Inside: an ontology-based data integration system applied to the oil and gas sector. In: Proceedings of the XIX Brazilian Symposium on Information Systems, pp. 94–101. SBSI '23, Association for Computing Machinery, New York, NY, USA (2023). https://doi.org/10.1145/3592813.3592893
5. DECHEMA: DEXPI - Data Exchange in the Process Industry (2020). https://dexpi.org
6. Gadepally, V., et al.: BigDAWG version 0.1. In: 2017 IEEE High Performance Extreme Computing Conference (HPEC), September 2017
7. Hexagon: CFIHOS, October 2022. https://hexagon.com/company/divisions/asset-lifecycle-intelligence/technology-compliance-standards/cfihos
8. Hexagon: Efficiently manage your process. Intergraph Smart P&ID. Product Brochure, October 2022. https://bynder.hexagon.com/m/b7635e6e2d4f7e2/original/Hexagon_PPM_Inter/graph/_Smart/_P-ID/_Brochure/_US/_2018.pdf
9. Hexagon: Hexagon Documentation. Administration and Configuration of HxGN SDx, October 2022. https://docs.hexagonppm.com/r/en-US/Administration-and-Configuration-of-HxGN-SDx/992388
10. IOGP: Capital Facilities Information HandOver Specification, October 2022. https://www.jip36-cfihos.org
11. IOGP: CFIHOS Standards Documents, vol. 1.5, October 2022. https://www.jip36-cfihos.org/wp-content/uploads/2023/04/CFIHOS-V.1.5.zip
12. IOGP: International Association of Oil & Gas Producers, October 2022. https://www.iogp.org
13. ISO: ISO15926 - Integration of life-cycle data for process plants, including oil and gas production facilities. https://15926.org
14. ltd, K.I.: Halcyon, October 2022. https://www.kraken.im/software/halcyon/
15. ltd, K.I.: Phoenix, October 2022. https://www.kraken.im/software/phoenix/
16. Nardi, J.C., de Almeida Falbo, R., et al.: A commitment-based reference ontology for services. Inf. Syst. **54**, 263–288 (2015). https://doi.org/10.1016/j.is.2015.01.012
17. Xiao, G., Ding, L., Cogrel, B., Calvanese, D.: Virtual knowledge graphs: an overview of systems and use cases. Data Intell. **1**(3), 201–223 (2019). https://doi.org/10.1162/dint_a_00011

Deep Neural Network-Based Approach for IoT Service QoS Prediction

Christson Awanyo$^{(\boxtimes)}$ and Nawal Guermouche

LAAS-CNRS, University of Toulouse, INSA, Toulouse, France
{kjbc.awanyo,nguermou}@laas.fr

Abstract. Building innovative and complex applications on top of the Internet of Things (IoT) services provided by huge connected devices and software while satisfying quality of service (QoS) parameters has become a challenging topic. Identifying suitable services according to their QoS parameters is one of the main underlying features to enable optimal selection, composition, and self-management of IoT systems. Checking each service to get its accurate QoS is not feasible. QoS prediction has been proposed these last years to try to cope with this issue. Mainly, the existing approaches rely on collaborative filtering methods, which suffer from scalability issues, that can considerably hamper the performance of QoS prediction. To overcome this limit, in this paper, we propose a deep-learning-based QoS prediction approach for IoT services. The approach we propose relies on Long Short-Term Memory (LSTM) to capture the service representation through a service latent vector and on Residual Network (ResNet) for QoS prediction. Unlike existing deep-learning-based approaches that assume a pre-defined static set of services, our approach addresses the QoS prediction problem for dynamic environments where the services are not necessarily fixed in advance.

Keywords: IoT · QoS prediction · Deep Learning · LSTM · ResNet · Smart City

1 Introduction

The Internet of Things (IoT) has emerged as a promising technology to build smart systems on top of distributed and connected physical devices. IoT is increasingly adopted across a broad range of domains, including healthcare, agriculture, transportation, factories, and in general smart cities. With IoT, real-time data can be collected, processed, and analyzed to enable smart decision-making. The Web of Things (WoT) has further propelled theses advances by enabling physical objects to be connected to the Web through their virtual representations [7], enabling them to be discovered and used as IoT services. Although WoT has brought great opportunities to provide new value added services that can leverage a wide range of potentially heterogeneous IoT devices to fulfill complex IoT needs, it also brings several challenges that remain open, such as IoT service discovery, selection and composition. Indeed, IoT environments are highly dynamic

F. Zhang et al. (Eds.): WISE 2023, LNCS 14306, pp. 397–406, 2023.
https://doi.org/10.1007/978-981-99-7254-8_31

where IoT devices can be mobile and can have limited resources. Moreover, the number of IoT devices is increasing rapidly and can exceed 70 billion by 2025 according to Gartner.

In this context, to select the suitable set of IoT services that meet awaited quality of service (QoS) requirements, it is crucial to get for each potential candidate IoT service its accurate QoS values. With the proliferation of IoT devices and their services, this remains a challenging concern. QoS prediction presents an interesting alternative to cope with this issue [9,14,18,21]. Mainly, the existing approaches use Collaborative Filtering (CF) method. CF-based approaches enable to predict QoS parameters of a given service for a given user based on previous historical QoS values of other services. Although CF-based approaches have shown interesting results to QoS prediction, they suffer from scalability issues [2], which limits their application in large scale IoT systems.

In recent years, Deep Neural Network (DNN) based models have been explored [5,17,18]. Mainly, they combine DNN with CF-based methods. Despite such hybrid methods enhance the efficiency of the classical CF-based approaches, they remain limited to making real-time QoS prediction for large-scale systems. The fully DNN-based models address these drawbacks [18]. Despite their advancements and performance, they require to inventory beforehand all the services for which it could be necessary to predict their QoS values. This assumption is very restrictive in IoT environments known for their inherently dynamic nature.

To tackle these limitations, in this paper, we propose a DNN-based approach that combines and leverages the power of Long Short-Term Memory (LSTM) [12] and Residual Network (ResNet) models [3]. LSTM network is a special kind of Recurrent Neural Network (RNN), able to learn long-term dependencies, which makes them well-suited to handle sequential data-based problems. In our work, LSTM is used to efficiently extract the underlying latent vector representation of services based on the history of their QoS values for a set of tasks they have performed. This provides valuable insights into the historical behavior of services, which overcomes the limits of existing DNN-based approaches which assume that the set of services must be fixed. Then, a ResNet model is used to predict QoS parameters according to the built latent vector. The main contributions of the paper can be summarized as follows:

1. We propose a new and efficient DNN-based approach that combines LSTM and ResNet models that outperforms the existing CF and DNN-based approaches.
2. Our approach enables to capture the services' representation automatically, which avoids the assumption of DNN-based existing approaches that rely on a predefined exhaustive list of services and their representation
3. The proposed approach has been implemented and evaluated against existing CF and DNN approaches. The results show significant improvements and demonstrate the effectiveness of our approach in terms of performance and accuracy.

The rest of the paper is organized as follows. Section 2 discusses the related works. The proposed approach is presented in Sect. 3. Experimental results are discussed in Sect. 4. Finally, Sect. 5 concludes the paper.

2   Related Work

The problem of QoS prediction has been widely studied in the literature [9,11,14,18,21]. We distinguish particularly two categories: 1- *CF-based* and 2- *DNN-based* approaches. CF methods are the most commonly used for QoS prediction [10]. A QoS value of a service for a given user is predicted based on the QoS values of similar users and services. These approaches can be classified into *neighborhood-based* and *model-based* methods. Neighborhood-based methods, also known as memory-based methods, assume a stable similarity relationship between users or services. Model-based approaches aim to build a predefined model to predict the required QoS values. Matrix factorization (MF) is the most popular model-based CF method that decomposes the user-item scoring matrix into a combination of several parts. The authors in [21] used MF to find the latent vector of every user and every service. Then Pearson Correlation Coefficient (PCC) has been applied to find the Top-K similar users and services. The desired QoS value is just the weighted average of the QoS values of similar users and services. The authors in [11] proved that adding a non-negative constraint may be suitable for the QoS prediction because almost all the QoS parameters are positive values. The authors in [14] used the non-parametric correlation coefficient Kendall's Tau to compute the similarity between users and services. It is worth noting that Kendall's Tau is less sensitive to outliers and it produces better accuracy. To improve the accuracy of QoS prediction, other works have integrated contextual information such as location and reputation into the proposed MF-based model [9,15]. In [6], the authors used a sequence of matrices for QoS experiences representation. Then, the prediction of the QoS values for each user on each service for a current time slice is computed based on the average of the precedent values. Although model-based approaches enhance QoS prediction compared to neighborhood-based approaches, they also suffer from scalability issues. This is due to the fact that the whole process operates at runtime, and the substantial volume of data that the model must handle directly impacts the performance of the approach.

More recently, new DNN-based models have been investigated. In [1], a time-aware QoS prediction based on a DNN with gated recurrent units (GRU) model has been proposed. This approach considers temporal slices of service invocations. In this context, QoS experiences are captured as a three-dimensional matrix. The binarization and neighborhood features are integrated to respectively represent the user's and service's features. GRU is used to mine temporal features among users and services so that QoS parameters can be predicted. In [13], the authors proposed a Recurrent Neural Network based collaborative filtering approach for QoS-prediction for the Internet of Vehicles (IoV). A matrix factorization model with Convolutional Neural Network has been proposed in

[17]. In [16], the authors provided an improved ARIMA model for QoS prediction in mobile edge computing. The QoS values are captured as a temporal sequence of QoS matrices, which are compressed using Singular Value Decomposition (SVD). Then, the values of the next temporal QoS matrice are predicted. In [18], the authors proposed a model based on ResNet. A user and a service are represented by a multidimensional vector through an embedding layer. Probabilistic distributions of user and service QoS values are added to form the input to the ResNet model.

This work operates on a fixed directory of services and tasks, which presents a serious limitation in open systems such as IoT-based systems.

Despite the advancements of DNN-based approaches in terms of accuracy and performance according to CF-based works, their effectiveness remains limited, especially in the context of open large-scale IoT systems. Indeed, on one side, the works that combine CF with DNN inherit partially the limits of CF-based models, and on the other side, fully DNN-based approaches require fixing the set of services for which QoS prediction could be necessary. To address these limitations, we propose an efficient novel LSTM and ResNet-based approach, in which the set of services is not fixed.

3   Neural Networks Based QoS Prediction Approach

As depicted in Fig. 1, the approach we propose involves three parts:

- *Input description*: corresponds to the representation of the required task to fulfill and the history of QoS values of a targeted service (i.e., service experience).
- *Latent Block*: generates the service latent vector representation from the given input data.
- *ResNet Block*: uses the generated latent vector to predict QoS value of the given service for the given task. Hereafter, we detail each step.

3.1   Input Description

The model's inputs are a task description and a service experience (i.e., QoS history). Tasks are identified through their unique identifier, which is a positive integer between 0 and the maximum number of given tasks. The representation of a service history s_j is in the form of a dictionary where each task performed by s_j is associated with the QoS value that has been recorded. It is in the form: $s_j = \{task\_id_1 : qos\_value_1, task\_id_2 : qos\_value_2, ..., task\_id_n : qos\_value_n\}$

Example 1. We consider for instance response time as a QoS parameter. If we suppose that, in past execution, a service s has taken 3.5 unit of time to execute a task t_1 and 1.2 unit of time to execute a task t_4 of a given abstract process, the experienced representation is $s = \{t_1 : 3.5, t_4 : 1.2\}$

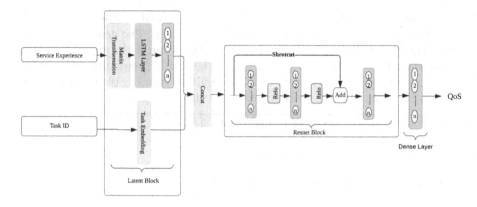

Fig. 1. DNN-based architecture of the proposed approach

3.2 Latent Block

As illustrated in Fig. 1, the latent block relies on task embedding, matrix transformation, and LSTM presented below.

Task Embedding. A task is represented by its *One-Hot-Encoding vector.* One-hot-encoding is used in machine learning as a method to quantify categorical data. In short, it produces a vector with a length equal to the number of abstract tasks to satisfy. All the components of the vector are assigned the value 0 except for the one which makes it possible to distinguish each task. The one-hot-encoding is then propagated through a dense layer to yield a more enriched and diversified representation of each task.

Example 2. If the number of task listed in our system is 5, the dimensionality of one hot encoding vector is set to five. For instance, the tasks t_1, and t_4 can be represented respectively as follows:

$$v_1 = \begin{bmatrix} 1, 0, 0, 0, 0 \end{bmatrix}, v_4 = \begin{bmatrix} 0, 0, 0, 1, 0 \end{bmatrix}$$

Matrix Transformation. The QoS record transformation aims to transform each service QoS history into a matrix. To do so, each pair of the QoS service history ($task\_id$: qos_value) is replaced by the vector: $qos\_value \times OneHotEncoding(task\_id)$.

Example 3. According to the history representation of the service $s = \{t_1 : 3.5, t_4 : 1.2\}$ given in Example 1, the vectors 3.5× OneHotEncoding(t_1) and 1.2× OneHotEncoding(t_4) are generated respectively as follows:

$$v_{t_1} = \begin{bmatrix} 3.5, 0, 0, 0, 0 \end{bmatrix}, v_{t_4} = \begin{bmatrix} 0, 0, 0, 1.2, 0 \end{bmatrix}$$

The final service representation is the matrix formed by the vectors of all the historical experiences of each service for each task. The generation of the representation of the services is depicted in Algorithm 1. Its input is a QoS history record Q. The algorithm starts with the transformation of each service experience for each task into a vector. The resulting vector is then added to the final matrix. This has a linear complexity calculus.

Algorithm   1 Services experience transformation

1: **Input:** QoS history Q
2: **Output:**   Service representation matrix
3: $service\_matrix \leftarrow []$
4: **for** each $id\_task : qos\_value \in Q$ **do**
5:      $vect \leftarrow qos\_value \times OneHotEncode(id\_task)$
6:      $service\_matrix.add(vect)$
7: **end for**

Example 4. If we consider the generated vectors given in Example 3, the service representation of s_1 is as follows:

$$\begin{bmatrix} 3.5 & 0 \\ 0 & 0 \\ 0 & 0 \\ 0 & 1.2 \\ 0 & 0 \end{bmatrix}$$

LSTM Layer. In our model, we handle the service matrix as a sequential data structure, where each column represents a time step. This sequential representation is then fed into an LSTM layer to generate a condensed and informative representation of the service QoS experience. The LSTM model will enable to capture long-term dependencies to extract and gather relevant information from the service's experiences into a vector. This vector is then passed to a Dense Layer to produce the final representation of the service as a vector based on its QoS history (i.e., service latent vector).

3.3   ResNet Block

Based on a given service and a given task representations, the aim is to identify their relationships with the expected QoS value to predict. The generated service latent and task representation vectors are concatenated and inputted into the Resnet block. This is performed through a Residual Network [3] which is a continuation of dense layers with a skip connection. Finally, the output of the Resnet block is then fed into one last Dense Layer, whose aim is to generate the final output which corresponds to the predicted QoS value of the execution of the given task by the given service.

Given that we are dealing with a regression problem, we have therefore opted for the use of Mean Absolute Error (MAE) as a loss function, given in Eq. 1. MAE is more stable for managing outliers which suits the prediction of QoS values we tackle.

$$MAE = \frac{\sum_{s,t}(|q_{s,t} - \hat{q}_{s,t}|)}{N} \tag{1}$$

where $\hat{q}_{s,t}$ and $q_{s,t}$ are the predicted and ground truth value of the target service when invoked for a specific task respectively, N is the number of the predicted QoS values.

It is worth noting that during the training phase, the *Adam (Adaptive Moment Estimation)* [8] optimization algorithm is used to update the parameters of the Dense Layers. This algorithm offers several advantages, such as the ability to achieve faster convergence with minimal hyperparameter tuning, which leads to enhancing the efficiency and effectiveness of the training.

4   Experimental Evaluation

The proposed approach has been implemented using Python 3.11. The experiments have been conducted on Windows 10 64-bit with 2.4 Ghz Intel(R) I7 processor and 16 GB RAM.

4.1   Used Dataset

We have conducted experiments using the WSDream dataset [19]. This dataset provides a matrix of the response time and throughput values collected from 5 825 services and 339 users. It gathers 1974675 historical records of service invocations. The response time values are concentrated between 0 and 2 ms and the throughput is between 0 and 200 kbps.

Data Transformation. The original dataset is in the form of a matrix $n \times m$ where missing values are represented by −1. We recorded each task by its identifier. For the services, the histories that correspond to the rows in the matrix are transformed into a dictionary *service_id : qos_value*. Thus we obtained an adapted version of the dataset.

4.2   Comparative Study

In order to evaluate and quantify the prediction quality of our approach, we use the two metrics: *Mean Absolute Error (MAE)* given above in Eq. 1 and *Root Mean Squared Error (RMSE)*. MAE is a linear score which means that all the individual differences are weighted equally in the average. MAE reflects the overall accuracy of QoS prediction, which averages absolute deviations to the ground truth QoS values.

RMSE, given in Eq. 2, measures the deviations between the predicted QoS and their corresponding observed QoS, which is then squared and averaged for calculating the square root. RMSE gives a relatively high weight to large errors due to the fact that errors are squared before they are averaged.

$$RMSE = \sqrt{\frac{\sum_{s,t}((q_{s,t} - \hat{q}_{s,t})^2)}{N}} \qquad (2)$$

A comparative study has been conducted to compare our approach with the following main existing approaches: *U-I-PCC (User-Item Pearson Correlation Coefficient)* [20], *NMF (Non-Negative Matrix Factorisation approach)* [11], *NeuMF (Neural Matrix Factorization)* [4], *PLRes (A Probability Distribution and Location-aware ResNet Approach for QoS Prediction)* [18].

Figure 2 and Fig. 3 show a comparison of our approach with the different approaches listed above based on MAE and RMSE respectively on four different matrix densities (5%, 10%, 15%, and 20%).

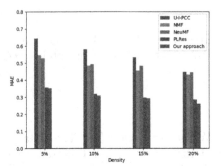

Fig. 2. MAE loss comparaison   **Fig. 3.** RMSE loss comparaison

The accuracy of all approaches increases as density increases. This is due to the fact that a higher density of data provides considerable information for models to learn, which leads to more accurate predictions. We note that our approach demonstrates enhanced results.

Figure 4 illustrates a comparison of the prediction time of our approach with the four approaches. As can be seen, our approach outperforms significantly CF-based approaches. However, PLRes shows a slight gain in terms of prediction time compared to our approach. This is directly related to the adopted service representation.

Specifically, the PLRes approach relies on a fixed static set of services. As mentioned earlier, this limitation restricts the applicability of the proposed approach in open IoT systems, as it cannot predict QoS values for services outside the fixed set. In contrast to this method, our approach automatically generates service representations from their histories using an LSTM model. This flexibility renders our approach highly suitable for open dynamic systems.

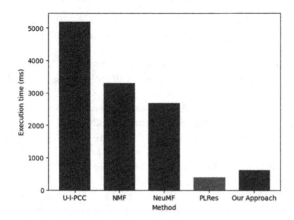

Fig. 4. Prediction time evaluation

5 Conclusion

In this paper, we have proposed a QoS prediction approach that combines the strengths of Long Short-Term Memory (LSTM) and Residual Network (ResNet) models. The LSTM model enables the generation of services latent vector by capturing relevant information from the service history. This latent vector is then fed into a ResNet which handles the underlying patterns and relationships to enable efficient QoS prediction. To evaluate and validate the effectiveness of the proposed approach, we conducted a series of comparative experiments with existing approaches. The results clearly demonstrate that our approach outperforms the existing works and offers better overall performance. In particular, it provides significant improvements in prediction time while guaranteeing a high level of accuracy. In addition, this approach avoids the limitations of DNN-based approaches that rely on a static set of services.

We plan to extend the proposed approach to tackle the challenging problem of predictive QoS-aware dynamic IoT service composition while considering other properties such as the mobility dimension and the spatio-temporal properties.

Acknowledgements. This work was supported by the ANR LabEx CIMI (grant ANR-11-LABX-0040) within the French State Programme "Investissements d'Avenir".

References

1. DeepTSQP: temporal-aware service QoS prediction via deep neural network and feature integration. Knowl.-Based Syst. (2022)
2. Al-Ghuribi, S., Noah, S.A.M.: Multi-criteria review-based recommender system - the state of the art. IEEE Access (2019)
3. He, K., Zhang, X., Ren, S., Sun, J.: Deep residual learning for image recognition (2015)

4. He, X., Liao, L., Zhang, H., Nie, L., Hu, X., Chua, T.S.: Neural collaborative filtering. In: Proceedings of the 26th International Conference on World Wide Web, pp. 173–182 (2017)
5. Huang, W., Zhang, P., Chen, Y., Zhou, M., Al-Turki, Y., Abusorrah, A.: QoS prediction model of cloud services based on deep learning. IEEE/CAA J. Autom. Sin. (2022)
6. Jin, Y., Guo, W., Zhang, Y.: A time-aware dynamic service quality prediction approach for services. Tsinghua Sci. Technol. (2020)
7. Khadir, K., Guermouche, N., Guittoum, A., Monteil, T.: A genetic algorithm-based approach for fluctuating QoS aware selection of IoT services. IEEE Access (2022)
8. Kingma, D.P., Ba, J.: Adam: a method for stochastic optimization. arXiv preprint arXiv:1412.6980 (2014)
9. Li, S., Wen, J., Luo, F., Cheng, T., Xiong, Q.: A location and reputation aware matrix factorization approach for personalized quality of service prediction. In: IEEE International Conference on Web Services (ICWS) (2017)
10. Lo, W., Yin, J., Deng, S., Li, Y., Wu, Z.: Collaborative web service QoS prediction with location-based regularization (2012)
11. Luo, X., Zhou, M., Xia, Y., Zhu, Q.: Predicting web service QoS via matrix-factorization-based collaborative filtering under non-negativity constraint. In: 2014 23rd Wireless and Optical Communication Conference (WOCC) (2014)
12. Schuster, M., Paliwal, K.: Bidirectional recurrent neural networks. IEEE Trans. Signal Process. 2673–2681 (1997)
13. Liang, T., Chen, M., Yin, Y., Zhou, L., Ying, H.: Recurrent neural network based collaborative filtering for QoS prediction in IoV. IEEE Trans. Intell. Transp. Syst. 2400–2410 (2022)
14. White, G., Palade, A., Cabrera, C., Clarke, S.: Iotpredict: collaborative QoS prediction in IoT. In: 2018 IEEE International Conference on Pervasive Computing and Communications (PerCom) (2018)
15. Xu, J., Zheng, Z., Lyu, M.R.: Web service personalized quality of service prediction via reputation-based matrix factorization. IEEE Trans. Reliab. (2016)
16. Yan, C., Zhang, Y., Zhong, W., Zhang, C., Xin, B.: A truncated SVD-based ARIMA model for multiple QoS prediction in mobile edge computing. Tsinghua Sci. Technol. (2022)
17. Yin, Y., Chen, L., Xu, Y., Wan, J., Zhang, H., Mai, Z.: QoS prediction for service recommendation with deep feature learning in edge computing environment. Mob. Netw. Appl. (2020)
18. Zhang, W., Xu, L., Yan, M., Wang, Z., Fu, C.: A probability distribution and location-aware ResNet approach for QoS prediction. CoRR (2020)
19. Zheng, Z., Zhang, Y., Lyu, M.R.: Investigating QoS of real-world web services. IEEE Trans. Serv. Comput. 32–39 (2014)
20. Zheng, Z., Ma, H., Lyu, M.R., King, I.: WSRec: a collaborative filtering based web service recommender system. In: IEEE International Conference on Web Services (2009)
21. Zheng, Z., Ma, H., Lyu, M.R., King, I.: Collaborative web service QoS prediction via neighborhood integrated matrix factorization. IEEE Trans. Serv. Comput. (2013)

Graph Embeddings and Link Predictions

Path-KGE: Preference-Aware Knowledge Graph Embedding with Path Semantics for Link Prediction

Liu Yang[1], Jie Zhao[1], Jun Long[2], Jincai Huang[2], Zidong Wang[1],
and Tingxuan Chen[1(✉)]

[1] School of Computer Science and Engineering, Central South University,
Changsha, China
{yangliu,zhaojie5,zdwang,chentingxuan}@csu.edu.cn
[2] Big Data Institute, Central South University, Changsha, China
{jlong,huangjincaicsu}@csu.edu.cn

Abstract. Knowledge graph embedding (KGE) aims to transfer entities and relations into low-dimensional vector space while preserving underlying semantics in knowledge graph (KG). Some existing models directly learn embeddings based on original triples, while others integrate external information to enhance the limited semantic information in KG. However, most of them ignore latent user preferences in their interactions with real-world KG applications, not even considering the relational semantics implied in historical interaction data, which are practical and essential for many downstream tasks like link prediction. To address these issues, we propose a novel preference-aware knowledge graph embedding with path semantics model Path-KGE, which learns semantic information of relation paths and integrates it into embedding process. First, we mine multi-hop relations with frequent and temporal characteristics as semantic relation paths in user interaction data, to obtain implicit user preference features. Second, we design a path importance function to distinguish the semantic impacts of user preferences on distinct relation paths. Finally, we utilize weight scores as long-term constraints to learn preference-aware embeddings, so that the representation vectors of entity pairs connected by preferred relation paths can remain close distances in vector space as in reality. The experimental results show that our model outperforms state-of-the-art translation-based models on link prediction and triple classification tasks.

Keywords: Knowledge Graph Embedding · Path Semantics · User Preference · Link Prediction

1 Introduction

As a structured semantic network, Knowledge Graphs (KGs) consist of numerous fact triples, in the form of (*head, relation, tail*) or (*subject, predicate, object*). Nowadays a great number of large-scale knowledge graphs have been proposed,

F. Zhang et al. (Eds.): WISE 2023, LNCS 14306, pp. 409–424, 2023.
https://doi.org/10.1007/978-981-99-7254-8_32

such as Freebase [6], NELL [7] and Wikidata [8], supporting many downstream applications like recommendation and question answering. Among them, link prediction is the most popular for providing accurate recommendations and search results for web applications [13]. Knowledge Graph Embedding (KGE), which maps entities and relations into continuous low-dimensional vector space, has been shown as a powerful tool for such link predictions [9].

Generally, the KGE models can be broadly divided into two categories: 1) Learning entity and relation representations based on original triples in KG. Among them, the translation-based models are the most popular for viewing the relation as a translation from head entity to tail entity $h + r \approx t$, and they can better capture potential semantic features of fact triples based on this assumption. 2) Knowledge representation learning methods that integrate external multi-source information. The original semantic information in KG is limited, so some studies introduce external information to obtain accurate knowledge representations [12]. For example, TKRL [17] integrates external entity type information, and Xie et al. [29] propose DKRL model to integrate entity description information from the entire text and get precise link prediction results.

Although the above methods capture underlying semantic information besides the inherent KG triples, most of them ignore user interaction data with KG applications in real-world scenarios, not even considering relational semantics implied in historical interaction data. There is a substantial amount of user interaction data with KG applications in real-world scenarios, like Wikidata [18], MovieLens [1] and LFM-1b [4]. User interaction data refers to the relationship between users and entities or relations within KG, reflecting the latent users' preferences and containing underlying relational semantics in KG. Some approaches integrate the mined user preference features into KGE model to enhance the reasoning ability in link prediction. He et al. [14] use a graph neural network to extract useful user preference features on items (entities) and input them in Adversarial Learning. KPRN [3] applies LSTM to model long-term sequence dependencies in user preferences, and further utilizes pooling operations to aggregate entity and relation representations.

However, the above methods ignore multi-hop relations with frequent and temporal features implied in user interaction data, which actually exhibit latent user preference features, e.g., $h \xrightarrow{ActedIn} e \xrightarrow{DirectedBy} t$. As shown in Fig. 1, we select query histories of some users in SPARQL query logs. Historical SPARQL logs store user query records on Wikidata, which are kinds of structured natural language questions executed on KG. The historical query data shows that users prefer to search the relation path of 'ActedIn-DirectedBy' over 'Cooperation - Nationality' and 'Husband-WorksIn'. This relation path is a typical query pattern in SPARQL queries, and it reflects that frequent combinations of relations (multi-hop relation paths) contain more relational semantics that exhibit user preference features, which cannot be learned from the original KG. At the same time, since the actor 'Kate Winslet' and director 'James Cameron' are more frequently associated together compared to the country 'United States' and the company 'Virgin Galactic ' in user queries, 'Kate Winslet' and 'James Cameron' connected by this path have a stronger semantic connection in contrast to others. Therefore, it is necessary to incorporate semantic impacts of user preferences on relation paths into KGE process, since it could help to learn preference-aware embeddings that exhibit user preferences, and entity pairs connected by preferred relation paths can also remain similarly close distances in vector space as in reality.

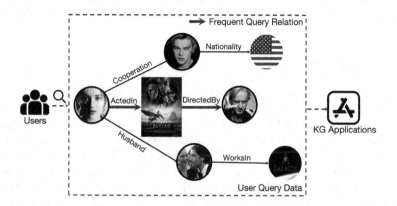

Fig. 1. The example of historical user query data in Wikidata.

In this paper, we aim to mine semantic paths that exhibit latent user preference features in historical SPARQL logs, which are actually multi-hop relations with frequent and temporal features, to analyze underlying semantics of relation paths. The implicit user preference can reflect explicit semantic importance of both relations and relation paths. By incorporating essential relational semantics of preferred relation paths into KGE process, the representations of entities and relations can externally preserve rich preference features and underlying semantic information in vector space as in reality.

To this end, we propose a novel preference-aware knowledge graph embedding model with path semantics(Path-KGE), to enhance practical relation path impacts on knowledge graph embedding. In our work, we first mine multi-hop query relations with frequent and temporal features as relation paths from historical SPARQL logs classified by time, and construct a preference feature matrix of relation paths to integrate statistical features of preferred multi-hop relations. Second, we construct a path importance function to calculate semantic weights of various relation paths with preference feature matrix as input. Finally, we further use the weight scores as long-term constraints to obtain preference-aware embeddings, so that entity pairs connected by preferred relation paths can remain close distances in vector space. Our contributions are summarized as follows:

- We introduce a frequent relation path mining method according to time series, which extracts user preference features of query paths by mining multi-hop relations in SPARQL logs, so as to obtain temporal and frequent features for each relation path.

- We propose a novel preference-aware knowledge graph embedding with path semantics model (Path-KGE), which encodes weight scores to measure various semantic impacts of user preferences on relation paths. Path-KGE learns the semantic weight scores of relation paths and incorporates them as long-term constraints into embedding process, so that entities connected by important relation paths have closer distance in vector space.
- We conduct extensive experiments on Wikidata datasets, and the results show that Path-KGE achieves excellent performance on link prediction and triple classification tasks.

2   Related Work

KGE models embed entities and relations into low-dimensional vector space in the form of vectors, preserving the inherent semantics of KG. Among them, translation-based embedding models are the most popular for their simplicity and efficiency. TransE [10] considers relation in the same vector space as the translation vector of head and tail entity in triple (h, r, t), but it has been long criticized for its over-simplified inference assumption [26]. Subsequently, TransH [21] and TransR [22] construct specific hyperplanes and use TransE-based triple translation constraints to learn representations of complex relations like 1-N, N-N relations. And bilinear models embedd entities and relations by comparing their meanings in vector space, like ComplEx [11] and DistMult [16]. PTransE [15] learns the vector embeddings of relation paths based on the translation assumption of TransE, and incorporates them into energy function.

External multi-source information provides knowledge besides the original triples in KG, which helps to learn more accurate knowledge representation. TKRL [17] incorporates constraint information between external entity types and relations into embedding, and uses TransR to fuse hierarchical entity category representations. Wang et al. [18] propose the KGE model that combines the knowledge graph and entity description text, which captures the underlying semantics of entities by learning entity features from unstructured text.

External information also includes rich interaction data between users and KG applications. Mining implicit user preference features helps to achieve recommendations or assist user decision-making in real-world scenarios, since it reflects user preferences and has practical meaning. To better understand user preferences on items (entities), Sun [2] employs a recurrent neural network to model relation paths linking the same entity pair. Different from the above work, Cao et al. [5] propose that learning user preferences on relations between items is also important because some relations play a critical role when users make their decisions. So they propose a new recommendation model based on TransH and jointly train it with a KG completion model by combining several transfer schemes.

The above KGE-based models mine valuable information from external information and user interaction data, but they ignore semantic impacts of user preferences on multi-hop relations with frequent and temporal characteristics, which can highly reveal the semantic features and importance of relation paths.

3 Methodology

In this section, we will introduce our Path-KGE model in detail. We introduce a couple of formal definitions:

Definition 3.1. KG. A KG consists of a set $K = (E, R, S)$, where E stands for the set of entities, R for the set of relations, and S for the set of facts.

Definition 3.2. Triple Fact. A triple fact is composed of a triple (h, r, t) or (s, p, o), where s represents the subject, p represents the predicate, and o represents the object.

Definition 3.3. Relation Path. A relation path is composed of multi relations, like $rp = (r_1, ..., r_l)$, and the vector representation of rp is composed by the sum of relation vectors $\boldsymbol{rp} = \boldsymbol{r_1} + ... + \boldsymbol{r_l}$.

Definition 3.4. SPARQL Query. A SPARQL query represents a mathematical set $Q = (V, L)$ described in SPARQL query language, where V represents the set of nodes and L represents the set of edges.

As relations are fundamental structure in KGs and naturally preserve important information for link prediction [28], our main design goals are, on one hand, learning semantic importance for distinct relation paths, so as to externally preserve essential semantic information in real-world KGs for link prediction, while on the other hand also modeling the semantic impacts of preferred relation paths on KGE process, in order to obtain preference-aware embeddings. We build Path-KGE with these goals to learn accurate embeddings from user preference features for link prediction in KGs.

Figure 2 illustrates our proposed model Path-KGE. It mainly contains three processes: 1) We first mine multi-hop relation paths in historical SPARQL logs to calculate frequency and temporal features of each relation path, and combine the statistical features to generate a preference feature matrix $M_{n \times n}$. 2) We construct a path importance function to calculate the semantic weight score w of each relation path and use $M_{n \times n}$ as input. 3) Finally, we use weight scores as long-term constraints in representation learning, so that entity pairs connected by important (preferred) relation paths maintain close distances in the vector space.

3.1 Learning User Preference Features of Relation Paths

We extract all multi-hop relations in SPARQL and calculate their frequent and temporal features respectively, in order to obtain user preferences features of distinct relation paths. Afterward, the statistical values are merged to build a preference feature matrix of relation paths.

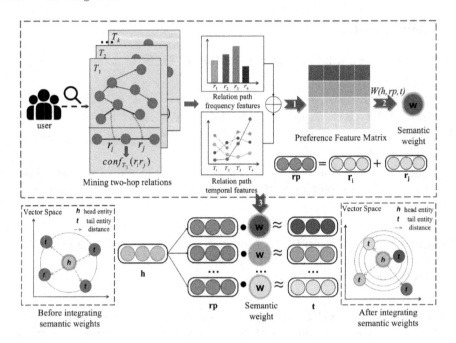

Fig. 2. Framework of preference-aware KGE with path semantics model.

Extracting Relation Paths in Historical SPARQL Logs. Given a sequence of historical SPARQL logs $\mathbb{Q} = \{Q_1, Q_2, ..., Q_w\}$, we fix the pattern of each query statement, while subjects and objects are variables in each query statement and only the predicates remain as constants, i.e., $v_1 \xrightarrow{p} v_2$, $v_1 \xrightarrow{p_1} v \xrightarrow{p_2} v_2$. We mine two expected predicate patterns: direct predicates as one-hop paths and predicate paths as two-hop paths in $\mathbb{Q}$ respectively. Here $DP = \{P_1, P_2, ..., P_n\}$ represents direct predicates set and $RP = \{P_1P_1, P_1P_2, ..., P_nP_n\}$ represents predicate paths set. In particular, we only mine direct relations and two-hop relation paths in this paper, since more than two hops would bring in redundant neighbors and lose meaningful semantic information [25].

Calculating the Frequent Features. We count the occurrence of relation paths, since it can significantly distinguish frequent predicate patterns from infrequent ones. Relation paths with higher occurrence frequencies are more preferred compared to others, which helps to better identify user preferences features and also facilitates machine learning of the implicit preference features from statistical perspective. We calculate the frequency of direct predicates and predicate paths using formulas (1) and (2).

$$Conf(P_i) = Conf(P_i \mid Q) = \frac{\sum_{m=1}^{w} count(Q_m, P_i)}{|Q|} \tag{1}$$

$$Conf(P_iP_j) = Conf(P_iP_j \mid Q) = \frac{\sum_{m=1}^{w} count(Q_m, P_iP_j)}{|Q|} \tag{2}$$

where $count(Q_m, P_iP_j)$ indicates whether the predicate path P_iP_j appears in query statement Q_m, and set to 1 if it exists, and 0 otherwise. $count(Q_m, P_i)$ is just the same for direct predicates. To distinguish users' preference levels for different relation paths, we use specific thresholds δ_1 and δ_2 to classify frequent statistical features for direct predicates and predicate paths, respectively. If $Conf(P_iP_j) \geq \delta_2$, we identify P_iP_j as frequent predicate path and add it to the set of frequent predicate paths FRP, otherwise, we add it to $\neg FRP$. If $Conf(P_i) \geq \delta_1$, we add predicate pattern P_i to the frequent predicate patterns set FDP, otherwise add to $\neg FDP$.

Calculating the Temporal Features. Since user query contents vary at different times, query preferences also dynamically change over time. We divide historical time into k segments to obtain distinct time periods. Given historical SPARQL queries $\mathbb{Q} = \{Q_{T_1}, ..., Q_{T_k}\}$ with timestamp $T = \{T_1, ..., T_k\}$, where Q_{T_k} denotes the set of query statements in the range of timestamp T_k. The predicate path pattern represented as $v_1 \xrightarrow{p_i/T_k} v \xrightarrow{p_j/T_k} v_2$ means that the entity variables in the query are connected by predicate path P_iP_j in timestamp T_k. We calculate temporal statistical features of direct predicates and predicate paths under different timestamps by formula (3) and (4) below.

$$Conf_{T_m}(P_i) = Conf(P_i \mid Q_{T_m}) = \frac{count(Q_{T_m}, P_i)}{|Q|} \qquad (3)$$

$$Conf_{T_m}(P_iP_j) = Conf(P_iP_j \mid Q_{T_m}) = \frac{count(Q_{T_m}, P_iP_j)}{|Q|} \qquad (4)$$

Learning Preference Feature Matrix of Relation Paths. Frequent query patterns closer to the current time can more precisely reflect recent user interests [24], so it is necessary to distinguish recent-frequent query patterns and remote-infrequent patterns. For this reason, we introduce temporal weights with the values gradually increasing over time, to represent the evolving temporal importance of user preferences at different times, as shown in Eq. (5). Moreover, the frequent predicate paths have greater semantic impacts on modeling user preference features. Therefore, for frequent relation paths $P_iP_j \in FRP$, we multiply temporal statistical features by temporal weights introduced above. For infrequent relation paths $P_iP_j \in \neg FRP$, we neglect the time influence since they reflect lower user preferences and contain less semantic information compared to frequent ones. We introduce β as a hyperparameter to balance preference feature values of infrequent predicate path patterns. The matrix calculation functions of direct predicate and predicate paths are shown in Eqs. (6), (7), respectively.

$$\sum_{i=1}^{k} \lambda_{T_i} = 1, \lambda_{T_1} < \lambda_{T_2} < ... < \lambda_{T_k} \qquad (5)$$

$$M(P_i) = \begin{cases} \sum_{m=1}^{k} \lambda_{T_m} \bullet Conf_{T_m}(P_i), P_i \in FDP \\ \beta \bullet Conf(P_i), P_i \in \neg FDP \end{cases} \qquad (6)$$

$$M(P_iP_j) = \begin{cases} \sum_{m=1}^{k} \lambda_{T_m} \bullet Conf_{T_m}(P_iP_j), P_iP_j \in FRP \\ \beta \bullet Conf(P_iP_j), P_iP_j \in \neg FRP \end{cases} \tag{7}$$

where $M(P_i)$ denotes the preference feature matrix of direct relations, and $M(P_iP_j)$ denotes the preference feature matrix of relation paths. $Conf_{T_m}(P_i)$ denotes the temporal statistical value of P_i at timestamp T_m, and similarly for $Conf_{T_m}(P_iP_j)$.

3.2   Learning Relation Paths Semantic Importance

We construct the path importance function, which learns the semantic importance (weight) scores of different relation paths, to model the semantic impacts of user preferences on multi-hop relations, and take the preference feature matrix $M_{n \times n}$ as input.

For each head entity h in KG, there are multiple direct relations r connected to it. We define $N(h) = \{r_1, r_2, ..., r_m\}$ as the set of direct relations connected to h, and multiple relation paths between h and t as the set $P(h,t) = \{rp_1, rp_2, ..., rp_t\}$. As various relation paths contain distinct semantic information, even the same relations or relation paths linked by different h still have varying importance. For example, Steve Jobs was the main founder of Apple Inc.: (*Steve Jobs*, FounderOf, *Apple Inc.*), and at the same time, Ron Wayne was one of the co-founders of Apple Inc: (*Ron Wayne*, FounderOf, *Apple Inc.*). Nevertheless, Steve Jobs is the most well-known among the public and thus is more frequently searched than Ron Wayne, so the semantic connection between Steve Jobs and Apple Inc. is closer than Wayne's, and the relation FounderOf connected to Steve Jobs is more important than the other. Therefore, we calculate the semantic importance scores of its direct relation and relation path for each h according to preference feature matrix M, as shown in Eqs. (8) (9).

$$w(h, r_i, t_{r_i}) = \frac{M(r_i)}{\sum_{j=1}^{m} M(r_j)} \tag{8}$$

$$w(h, rp_i, t_{r_n}) = \frac{M(rp_i)}{\sum_{j=1}^{t} M(rp_j)}, rp_i \in P(h, t_{r_n}) \tag{9}$$

where $w(h, r_n, t_{r_n})$ represents different importance scores of direct relations connected to h. $w(h, rp_i, t_{r_n})$ represents to the semantic importance score of relation path rp_i between h and t_{r_n}, and the high value means that user prefers rp_i over other relation paths. Meanwhile, a path importance expression with the same h and different relational path rp_i should satisfy the following constraint, as shown in Eq. (10).

$$\sum_{i=1}^{t} w(h, rp_i, t_{r_n}) = w(h, rp_1, t_{r_n}) + w(h, rp_2, t_{r_n}) + ... + w(h, rp_t, t_{r_n}) = 1 \tag{10}$$

3.3   Preference-Aware Embedding with Path Semantics

In this section, we incorporate semantic importance score w into the embedding process, so that entities connected by preferred relation paths can preserve close distances in vector space. Inspired by PTransE, we propose our preference-aware knowledge graph embedding model with path semantics and design the following energy function:

$$G(h, r, t) = E(h, r, t) * w(h, r, t) + E'(h, P, t) \tag{11}$$

$$E'(h, P, t) = \frac{1}{Z} \sum_{rp \in P(h,t)} R(rp \mid h, t) * E(h, rp, t) * w(h, rp, t) \tag{12}$$

here $G(h, r, t)$ consists of two parts: 1) $E(h, r, t) = ||h + r - t||$ calculates the similarity score under TransE assumption, and we integrate $w(h, r, t)$ to obtain the semantic importance of direct relations, where a higher score of $w(h, r, t)$ represents a more significant semantic weight of relation r ; 2) $E(h, P, t)$ models the inference correlations, where $R(rp \mid h, t)$ represents the confidence of rp connecting h and t, $Z = \sum_{rp \in P(h,t)} R(rp \mid h, t)$, and $E(h, rp, t) = ||rp - r|| = E(rp, r)$. The lower value of $E(h, rp, t)$ means that relation path rp is closer to the semantics of direct relation r, and vice versa. We also introduce $E'(h, P, t)$ to multiply $E(h, rp, t)$ by $w(h, rp, t)$ to increase the influence of path importance. The initial vector representations of entities and relations are randomly generated.

For rp with a higher score of $w(h, rp, t)$, it can clearly reflect user preferences and the entities connected by rp have practical and meaningful semantic connections in reality. Therefore, we set the preferred relation paths with higher semantic weights in embedding, so that h and t connected by rp can still have a closer distance in vector space. As the example in Sect. 3.2 demonstrates, the entity 'Steve Jobs' has a closer semantic connection with 'Apple Inc.' than 'Ron Wayne', so the vector distances between 'Steve Jobs' and 'Apple Inc.' should remain the same close distance. In the training process, our loss function is formulated as:

$$L(S) = \sum_{(h,r,t) \in S} [L(h, r, t) + \frac{1}{Z} \sum_{rp \in P(h,t)} R(rp \mid h, t) L(h, rp, t)] \tag{13}$$

We define $L(h, r, t)$ and $L(h, rp, t)$ are margin-based loss functions and employ stochastic gradient descent (SGD) to minimize the loss functions, which are formulated as:

$$L(h, r, t) = \sum_{(h',r',t') \in S'} [\gamma + E(h, r, t) - E(h', r', t')]_+ \cdot w(h, r, t) \tag{14}$$

$$L(h, rp, t) = \sum_{(h,r',t) \in S'} [\gamma + E(rp, r) - E(rp, r')]_+ \cdot w(h, rp, t) \tag{15}$$

where γ is the hyperparameter. $S = \{(h, r, t)\}$ represents the set of positive samples, and S' represents the set of negative samples. Here we add the path importance value w to determine the semantic weights of different direct relations and relation paths. The rule of extracting negative samples from the training set is expressed as follows:

$$S' = \{(h', r, t)\} \cup \{(h, r', t)\} \cup \{(h, r, t')\} \tag{16}$$

The set of negative samples is obtained by replacing one of the three constituent elements of the original (h, r, t).

4   Experiment

In this section, we conduct link prediction and triple classification tasks using our proposed Path-KGE model. Among them, link prediction is widely used by KG applications to evaluate the abilities of inference and recommendation. The experimental results show that our Path-KGE gains excellent performance on both tasks, which means it can effectively capture underlying relational semantics in KG and improve the accuracy of representation learning.

4.1   Datasets

We use Wikidata datasets and Wikidata subsets as knowledge graph datasets for our experiments. Natalia et al. [19] filter Wikidata datasets to obtain a subset where entities appear in more than two triples. We follow these two versions of Wikidata dataset called Wikidata-300k and Wikidata-1000k, containing 300k and 1M triples respectively. We divide these triples into train sets, validation sets and test sets. Table 1 shows the statistics of Wikidata datasets.

Table 1. Statistics of the used datasets.

Datasets	#Rel	#Ent	#Train	#Valid	#Test
Wikidata-300k	588	36001	240000	23310	23373
Wikidata-1000k	814	124050	950000	18912	18984

As for historical SPARQL queries, we use anonymous SPARQL logs provided by Wikipedia website [20], which provides historical query logs in six query periods, with each period containing 28 days of SPARQL logs. Malyshev et al. [23] count query logs for these six timestamps and divide the Total queries into Valid, Robotic and Organic queries, as shown in Table 2. Organic logs contain time information of historical queries, so we analyze Organic queries to better obtain temporal features of user preferences on paths.

4.2   Link Prediction

Link prediction is a typical task of knowledge graph completion, where the goal is to predict missing or future links between entities in KG, namely to predict r given h, t. It shows the expressiveness of embedding values learned by the model.

Table 2. Details of SPARQL logs.

NO.	Start-End	#Total	#Valid	#Robotic	#Organic
1	2017.06.12-2017.07.09	79,082,916	59,555,701	59,364,020	191,681
2	2017.07.10-2017.08.06	82,110,141	70,397,955	70,199,977	197,978
3	2017.08.07-2017.09.03	90,733,013	78,393,731	78,142,971	250,760
4	2018.01.01-2018.01.28	106,074,877	92,100,077	91,504,428	595,649
5	2018.01.29-2018.02.25	109,617,007	6,407,008	95,526,402	880,606
6	2018.02.26-2018.03.25	100,133,104	84,861,808	83,998,328	863,480

Evaluation Protocol. For each positive sample (h, r, t), we replace r with all relations in R to construct the negative sample triples. Then we calculate the score $S(h, r, t)$ using the same score function as in PTransE for every test sample, and sort the scores in ascending order so that we can obtain metrics based on ranking. We record the results in four dimensions of metrics, including MeanRank (MR), Hits@1, Hits@3, and Hits@10. MeanRank represents the mean rank of fact triples in the all test triples, and Hits@k represents the proportion of the fact triple in top k. A lower mean rank and a higher Hits@k mean better performance. Since the disrupted triples may also appear as positive samples in the original KG $(h, r', t) \in S$ and may not accurately show the embedding ability of the model, so we divide the test methods into *Raw* and *Filter*. We use *Raw* to represent the evaluation method of using the set S', and *Filter* to represent the set S' obtained by filtering out triples appearing in S.

Implementation. For all datasets, the optimal configuration is determined by monitoring MeanRank on the validation set. In the training phase, we use the following optimal configuration. The sample sizes of the mini-batch are 100, L1 regularization, learning rate $\lambda = 0.001$, and boundary distance value $\gamma = 1$. We limit the number of epochs over all training triples to 200. For Wikidata-300k, we set embedding dimension d = 100, and d = 200 for Wikidata-1000k dataset.

Results. Table 3 shows the link prediction results of Path-KGE and five baseline models on Wikidata-300k dataset, and the best results are highlighted in bold. Our Path-KGE model outperforms translation-based and bilinear models on all four metrics, and achieves the highest accuracy and effectiveness on Wikidata-300k. Compared to PTransE, the mean rank of factual links is significantly higher in our model, which indicates that Path-KGE has stronger inference ability than other models. Although there is only a slight improvement of about 1% at Hits@10, we observe an increase of nearly 4% at Hits@1 and almost 3% at Hits@3. Finally, our model achieves an accuracy rate of 98.94% at Hits@10, which indicates that user historical preferences on relation paths can reflect the semantic features of relation paths, and thus help to learn accurate embeddings.

Table 3. Link prediction results on Wikidata-300k

Datasets	Wikidata-300k							
Metric	Mean Rank		Hits@1		Hits@3		Hits@10	
	Raw	Filter	Raw	Filter	Raw	Filter	Raw	Filter
Path-KGE	**1.89**	**1.81**	**83.24**	**89.31**	**96.09**	**96.69**	**98.91**	**98.94**
PTransE	2.87	2.78	79.43	85.50	93.32	93.93	97.13	97.14
TransE	169.33	169.26	41.64	43.07	51.70	52.07	58.37	58.40
TransR	146.53	146.46	39.76	41.71	52.52	52.84	60.30	60.40
ComplEx	–	170.30	–	51.14	–	59.81	–	64.29
DistMult	–	79.0	–	76.01	–	82.52	–	84.77

Table 4 shows the link prediction results of Path-KGE and four baseline models on Wikidata-1000k. Our experimental results on Wikidata-1000k continue to outperform other models, demonstrating that our model can effectively capture semantic features of relation paths. Figure 3 and Fig. 4 below show the visualized embedding results of some entities in Wikidata-1000k using visualization model called t-SNE [27]. For entity embeddings learned by Path-KGE, the entity pairs belonging to 'actor' and 'movie' remain close distances in vector space since these two entity categories are frequently associated in reality. However, the entity vectors learned by PTransE fail to maintain these inherent semantic features, as shown in Fig. 3.

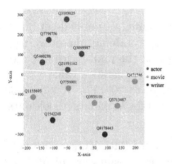

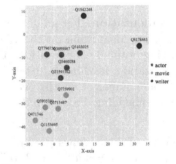

Fig. 3. Visualization results of entities learned by PTransE.

Fig. 4. Visualization results of entities learned by Path-KGE.

4.3   Triple Classification

Triple classification task aims to determine whether a given triple (h, r, t) is correct or not, and it is a typical binary classification problem. This task requires negative sample triples to be evaluated. Following the method in [21], we construct negative triples for Wikidata-300k and Wikidata-1000k separately, since the original datasets do not contain negative samples.

Table 4. Link prediction results on Wikidata-1000k

Datasets	Wikidata-1000k							
Metric	Mean Rank		Hits@1		Hits@3		Hits@10	
	Raw	Filter	Raw	Filter	Raw	Filter	Raw	Filter
Path-KGE	**1.71**	**1.64**	**83.21**	**88.80**	**96.01**	**96.69**	**98.89**	**98.92**
PTransE	2.33	2.24	82.56	88.72	95.81	96.41	98.45	98.47
TransE	153.25	153.19	49.89	51.08	59.47	59.75	67.04	67.08
ComplEx	–	20.8	–	74.32	–	91.68	–	95.75
DistMult	–	5.22	–	79.64	–	91.44	–	97.84

Evaluation Protocol. For each triple (h, r, t), if the dissimilarity score of the triple is below σ_r, this triple is classified as a positive triple, otherwise, it is classified as a negative triple. σ_r is determined by the threshold at which the verification set reaches the maximum classification accuracy.

Implementation. In the training phase, we select learning rate λ in $\{0.1, 0.01, 0.001\}$, boundary distance value γ in $\{1, 2, 4\}$, and vector dimension d in $\{20, 50, 100, 200\}$. According to the maximum classification accuracy of the learned model, we choose the ideal optimization with learning rate $\lambda = 0.001$, boundary distance value $\gamma = 1$, epoch = 200. We set d = 100 for Wikidata-300k and d = 200 for Wikidata-1000k.

Results. We conduct experiments of triple classification on Wikidata-300k dataset, and the results are shown in Table 5. We integrate path semantic importance mined in user preferences to knowledge graph embedding process in order to capture semantic information of multi-hop relations. The results show that our Path-KGE model outperforms other models on triple classification tasks. We enable entities connected by important paths to maintain close distances in embedding space by adding richer semantic information during the embedding, which in turn improves the triple classification performance.

Table 5. Triple classification results on Wikidata-300k

Datasets	Wikidata-300k	
Metric	Accuracy (%)	Precision (%)
Path-KGE	**74.37**	**74.73**
PTransE	73.58	73.62
TransE	72.63	72.45

5 Conclusion

We propose a novel preference-aware knowledge graph embedding with path semantics model (Path-KGE), which captures the semantic information of relation paths for embeddings. Actually, the implicit user preferences on relation paths contain explicit relational semantics, and entity pairs connected by preferred paths have stronger semantic connections. Specifically, we mine multihop relations with frequency and temporal features in historical SPARQL logs to capture practical semantic information in user preferences. Furthermore, we construct a path importance function to distinguish various semantic weights of distinct relation paths, and then use semantic weight scores as long-term constraints in embedding, so that entity pairs connected by preferred paths preserve close distances in vector space as in reality. The experimental results show that our model outperforms state-of-the-art models not only on link prediction task, but also on triple classification task.

Acknowledgements. This work is being supported by the National Natural Science Foundation of China under the Grant No. 62172451, and supported by Open Research Projects of Zhejiang Lab under the Grant No. 2022KG0AB01.

References

1. Harper, F.M., Konstan, J.A.: The movielens datasets: history and context. ACM Trans. Interact. Intell. Syst. (TIIS) **5**(4), 1–19 (2015)
2. Sun, Z., Yang, J., Zhang, J., Bozzon, A., Huang, L.-K., Xu, C.: Recurrent knowledge graph embedding for effective recommendation. In: Proceedings of the 12th ACM Conference on Recommender Systems, pp. 297–305 (2018)
3. Wang, X., Wang, D., Xu, C., He, X., Cao, Y., Chua, T.-S.: Explainable reasoning over knowledge graphs for recommendation. In: Proceedings of the AAAI Conference on Artificial Intelligence, vol. 33, no. 01, pp. 5329–5336 (2019)
4. Schedl, M.: The LFM-1B dataset for music retrieval and recommendation. In: Proceedings of the 2016 ACM on International Conference on Multimedia Retrieval, pp. 103–110 (2016)
5. Cao, Y., Wang, X., He, X., Hu, Z., Chua, T.-S.: Unifying knowledge graph learning and recommendation: towards a better understanding of user preferences. In: The World Wide Web Conference, pp. 151–161 (2019)
6. Bollacker, K., Evans, C., Paritosh, P., Sturge, T., Taylor, J.: Freebase: a collaboratively created graph database for structuring human knowledge. In: Proceedings of the 2008 ACM SIGMOD International Conference on Management of Data, pp. 1247–1250 (2008)
7. Carlson, A., Betteridge, J., Kisiel, B., Settles, B., Hruschka, E., Mitchell, T.: Toward an architecture for never-ending language learning. In: Proceedings of the AAAI Conference on Artificial Intelligence, vol. 24, no. 1, pp. 1306–1313 (2010)
8. Vrandečić, D., Krötzsch, M.: WikiData: a free collaborative knowledgebase. Commun. ACM **57**(10), 78–85 (2014)
9. Cao, Z., Xu, Q., Yang, Z., Cao, X., Huang, Q.: Geometry interaction knowledge graph embeddings. In: Proceedings of the AAAI Conference on Artificial Intelligence, vol. 36, no. 5, pp. 5521–5529 (2022)

10. Bordes, A., Usunier, N., Garcia-Duran, A., Weston, J., Yakhnenko, O.: Translating embeddings for modeling multi-relational data. In: Advances in Neural Information Processing Systems, vol. 26 (2013)
11. Trouillon, T., Welbl, J., Riedel, S., Gaussier, É., Bouchard, G.: Complex embeddings for simple link prediction. In: International Conference on Machine Learning, pp. 2071–2080. PMLR (2016)
12. Wang, H., Li, S., Pan, R.: An adversarial transfer network for knowledge representation learning. In: Proceedings of the Web Conference 2021, pp. 1749–1760 (2021)
13. Zhang, S., et al.: Page-link: path-based graph neural network explanation for heterogeneous link prediction. arXiv preprint arXiv:2302.12465 (2023)
14. He, G., Li, J., Zhao, W.X., Liu, P., Wen, J.: Mining implicit entity preference from user-item interaction data for knowledge graph completion via adversarial learning. In: Proceedings of The Web Conference 2020, pp. 740–751 (2020)
15. Lin, Y., Liu, Z., Luan, H., Sun, M., Rao, S., Liu, S.: Modeling relation paths for representation learning of knowledge bases. arXiv preprint arXiv:1506.00379 (2015)
16. Yang, B., Yih, W.-T., He, X., Gao, J., Deng, L.: Embedding entities and relations for learning and inference in knowledge bases. arXiv preprint arXiv:1412.6575 (2014)
17. Xie, R., Liu, Z., Sun, M. Luan, H., Sun, M.: Representation learning of knowledge graphs with hierarchical types. In: Proceedings of the 25th International Joint Conference on Artificial Intelligence 2016, pp. 2965–2971 (2016)
18. Wang, Z., Zhang, J., Feng, J., Chen, Z.: Knowledge graph and text jointly embedding. In: Proceedings of the 2014 Conference on Empirical Methods in Natural Language Processing (EMNLP), pp. 1591–1601 (2014)
19. Ostapuk, N., Yang, J., Cudré-Mauroux, P.: Activelink: deep active learning for link prediction in knowledge graphs. In: The World Wide Web Conference, pp. 1398–1408 (2019)
20. Spitz, A., Dixit, V., Richter, L., Gertz, M., Geiß, J.: State of the union: a data consumer's perspective on Wikidata and its properties for the classification and resolution of entities. In: Proceedings of the International AAAI Conference on Web and Social Media, vol. 10, no. 2, pp. 88–95 (2016)
21. Wang, Z., Zhang, J., Feng, J., Chen, Z.: Knowledge graph embedding by translating on hyperplanes. In: Proceedings of the AAAI Conference on Artificial Intelligence, vol. 28, no. 1 (2014)
22. Lin, Y., Liu, Z., Sun, M., Liu, Y., Zhu, X.: Learning entity and relation embeddings for knowledge graph completion. In: Proceedings of the AAAI Conference on Artificial Intelligence, vol. 29, no. 1 (2015)
23. Malyshev, S., Krötzsch, M., González, L., Gonsior, J., Bielefeldt, A.: Getting the most out of wikidata: semantic technology usage in Wikipedia's knowledge graph. In: Vrandečić, D., et al. (eds.) ISWC 2018, Part II. LNCS, vol. 11137, pp. 376–394. Springer, Cham (2018). https://doi.org/10.1007/978-3-030-00668-6_23
24. Bonifati, A., Martens, W., Timm, T.: An analytical study of large SPARQL query logs. arXiv preprint arXiv:1708.00363 (2017)
25. Sun, Y., Han, J., Yan, X., Yu, P.S., Wu, T.: PathSim: meta path-based top-k similarity search in heterogeneous information networks. Proc. VLDB Endow. 4(11), 992–1003 (2011)
26. Chen, X., Jia, S., Xiang, Y.: A review: knowledge reasoning over knowledge graph. Expert Syst. Appl. 141, 112948 (2020)
27. Van der Maaten, L., Hinton, G.: Visualizing data using t-SNE. J. Mach. Learn. Res. 9(11) (2008)

28. Rosso, P., Yang, D., Cudré-Mauroux, P.: Beyond triplets: hyper- relational knowledge graph embedding for link prediction. In: Proceedings of The Web Conference 2020, pp. 1885–1896 (2020)
29. Xie, R., Liu, Z., Jia, J., Luan, H., Sun, M.: Representation learning of knowledge graphs with entity descriptions. In: Proceedings of the AAAI Conference on Artificial Intelligence, vol. 30, no. 1 (2016)

Efficient Graph Embedding Method for Link Prediction via Incorporating Graph Structure and Node Attributes

Weisheng Li[1,3], Feiyi Tang[2(✉)], Chao Chang[1,3], Hao Zhong[1,3], Ronghua Lin[1,3], and Yong Tang[1,3]

[1] School of Computer Science, South China Normal University,
Guangzhou 510631, China
{liws,changchao,hzhong,rhlin,ytang}@m.scnu.edu.cn
[2] School of Information Engineering, Guangzhou Panyu Polytechnic,
Guangzhou 511483, China
tangfy@gzpyp.edu.cn
[3] Pazhou Lab, Guangzhou 510330, China

Abstract. Link prediction is a crucial task in graph analysis that aims to predict the existence of missing links in a graph. Graph embedding methods have gained popularity for link prediction by learning low-dimensional vector representations for nodes. However, most existing methods have not effectively utilized the graph structure and node attributes in attributed graphs. Additionally, higher-order neighborhood nodes that have high correlation with the source node are often disregarded. To address these issues, we propose an efficient graph embedding method called GSNA (**G**raph **S**tructure and **N**ode **A**ttributes), which effectively incorporates graph structure and node attributes to learn nodes representation for link prediction. Specifically, node sequences are generated using random walk, and then the nodes with high frequency are screened out. Then, the Top-N list of high-order neighborhood nodes with high correlation is obtained by calculating attribute similarities between nodes. Afterwards, a new graph is generated and passed through a multi-head attention mechanism to further learn the representations for link prediction tasks. Experiments conducted on several benchmark datasets demonstrate the effectiveness and efficiency of our proposed method for link prediction.

Keywords: Link Prediction · Graph Embedding · Graph Structure · Node Attributes

1 Introduction

An attributed graph is a graph data structure in which nodes are associated with attributes. Attributed graphs are widely used in various graph analysis tasks such as link prediction [1–3], node classification [4–6], and community detection [7–9]. Link prediction is a fundamental task in graph analysis that aims to predict

F. Zhang et al. (Eds.): WISE 2023, LNCS 14306, pp. 425–438, 2023.
https://doi.org/10.1007/978-981-99-7254-8_33

missing or future links in graphs. Graph embedding has become a effective way to tackle link prediction tasks due to its ability to capture complex relationships in a graph. Meanwhile, graph embedding is the process of transforming nodes and edges of a graph into low-dimensional vectors while preserving the structural and semantic information of graphs.

The development of graph embedding can be traced back to the early works on spectral graph theory, which leverage the eigenvalues and eigenvectors of the graph Laplacian matrix to embed nodes, such as Spectral Clustering [10]. However, the scalability of spectral methods is limited, and they can only handle small to medium-sized graphs. To overcome these limitations, researchers have proposed various methods based on random walk, matrix factorization, and deep learning. For example, methods based on random walk such as DeepWalk [11] and Node2Vec [12] have achieved promising results by using random walk to generate node sequences and then applying techniques such as Skip-Gram [13] to learn embeddings. Matrix factorization-based methods, such as LINE [14] and GraRep [15], factorize the graph adjacency matrix or higher-order proximity matrices to learn node embeddings. While these methods have achieved significant success, they also have certain limitations that need to be addressed. For example, random walk-based methods may fail to capture higher-order neighborhood information, and matrix factorization-based methods may not effectively capture the local graph structure. In recent years, with the rise of deep learning, graph embedding methods have also shifted towards utilizing deep learning techniques. Graph convolutional networks (GCNs) have gained popularity in the field of graph embedding. GraphSAGE [16] combines neighborhood aggregation with node features information to learn embeddings that capture both structural and attribute information. Graph Attention Network (GAT) [17] uses an attention mechanism to learn the importance of each node's neighbors for representation learning. Despite these advances, there is still room for improvement in graph embedding methods. One limitation is the computational cost of training deep learning-based methods on large-scale graphs. Another challenge is the need to balance the trade-off between capturing high-order structural information and efficiently learning embeddings.

In this paper, we propose an efficient method called GSNA (Graph Structure and Node Attributes) which incorporates graph structure and node attributes for link prediction. Firstly, to better preserve the proximity of the graph structure, we employ a biased random walk to generate node sequences and further sample highly correlated nodes by conducting frequency screening. Secondly, the attributes representation of nodes is trained by the BERT model. The similarity of attributes between nodes is calculated, and the Top-N nodes with high correlations to the source node in k-th order neighborhoods are selected. These nodes are then combined with the nodes obtained in the previous steps to merge a new graph, which not only effectively captures the high-order neighborhood information of nodes but also generates a more informative graph representation. Finally, an encoder approach is further performed to fuse representation learning of source and target nodes, and the existence of links between nodes is predicted by calculating the dot product similarity between the source node vector and its neighbors' vector representations.

In summary, the contributions of this paper mainly lie in three aspects:

- We propose an efficient method called GSNA for link prediction that effectively takes into account both local and global information of the graph. GSNA leverages random walk and frequency screening to obtain high-quality node sequences. Meanwhile, a Top-N nodes list through node attributes similarities is obtained to capture highly correlated nodes within k-order neighborhoods.
- We also design an encoder approach that employs a multi-head attention mechanism to learn the representations of the source node and its neighborhood nodes, which effectively captures the complex relationships between nodes and makes accurate link predictions.
- Experiments on publicly standard datasets demonstrate the effectiveness of our proposed method GSNA for link prediction tasks in attributed graphs.

The rest of this paper is organized as follows. The related work is briefly surveyed in Sect. 2. Then, the proposed method GSNA is detailed and the experimental results are reported in Sects. 3 and 4, respectively. Finally, we conclude our work in Sect. 5.

2 Related Work

Graph embedding can be categorized into two main categories: non-deep learning-based methods and deep learning-based methods. Non-deep learning-based methods include spectral methods, random walk-based methods, matrix factorization-based methods, and hybrid methods. Spectral methods aim to embed a graph into a low-dimensional space by performing matrix factorization on the graph's Laplacian matrix. Examples of spectral methods include Laplacian Eigenmaps [18], Local Linear Embedding [19] and Spectral Clustering [10]. Random walk-based methods, such as DeepWalk [11] and Node2Vec [12], generate node embeddings by simulating random walks on the graph and using the resulting node sequences as the input for a Skip-Gram [13] model. Matrix factorization-based methods aim to factorize the graph's adjacency or Laplacian matrix into low-rank matrices, and use the resulting factor matrices as node embeddings, such as GraRep [15] and HOPE [20]. Hybrid methods, such as LINE [14], combine multiple strategies to learn node embeddings. However, these methods have some limitations. Graph spectral theory-based methods can only handle undirected graphs, and the computation of the graph Laplacian is computationally expensive for large graphs. Matrix factorization-based methods can only handle simple graphs and do not account for node features. Random walk-based methods often fail to capture the global structure of the graph and may generate biased node sequences.

In recent years, deep learning-based methods aim to learn node embeddings through neural networks. GCN [21] utilizes convolutional layers to aggregate node features from its local neighborhood and propagate the features to its neighbors. GraphSAGE [16] uses a neighborhood aggregation approach to learn node embeddings by aggregating information from different levels of neighborhood structures. SDNE [22] learns node embedding preserving both local and global structures. HAN [23] adopts a hierarchical attention mechanism to learn embeddings that capture both structural and attribute information. However, these methods may suffer from over-smoothing and overfitting, especially on graphs with multiple scales of information diffusion. To address these issues, ARGA [24] utilizes an attention mechanism to selectively aggregate different levels of information from a node's neighbors. Linear GAE [25] uses a linear autoencoder to enforce smoothness and sparsity in the learned embeddings. These methods have demonstrated promising results on various graph-related tasks. By combining the strengths of both types of methods, they can achieve superior performance in graph embedding.

3   Methodology

In this section, we present a detailed description of the GSNA method, including problem definitions, structure-based graph random walk, attribute-based highly correlated neighborhood nodes, and encoder approach. The overall framework of the proposed GSNA method is shown in Fig. 1.

3.1   Problem Definition

Attributed Graph: An attributed graph G is defined as a tuple (V, E, A), where V is a set of nodes, E is a set of edges, and A is an attribute matrix where each row represents the attribute vectors of a node in V.

Graph Embedding: Given an attributed graph $G = (V, E, A)$, a graph embedding method aims to learn a low-dimensional vector representation z_i for each node $i \in V$ that preserves the graph structure and node attributes.

Link Prediction: Given a graph $G = (V, E)$ and a set of observed links $E_o \subset E$, the link prediction task is to predict the existence of missing links $E_u = E \setminus E_o$.

3.2   Structure-Based Graph Random Walk

Given an attributed graph $G = (V, E, A)$, the biased random walk is used in G to generate node sequences. Starting from a source node v_0, at each step t, the random walker moves to a neighbor node v_t of v_{t-1} with a probability $P(v_t|v_{t-1})$ calculated as follows:

$$P\left(v_t \mid v_{t-1}\right) = \begin{cases} \frac{\alpha(v_{t-1}, v_t)}{Z} & \text{if } (v_{t-1}, v_t) \in E \\ 0 & \text{otherwise} \end{cases} \tag{1}$$

where $\alpha(v_{t-1}, v_t)$ is a transition weight function between nodes v_{t-1} and v_t, Z is a normalization constant, and E is the set of edges in the graph.

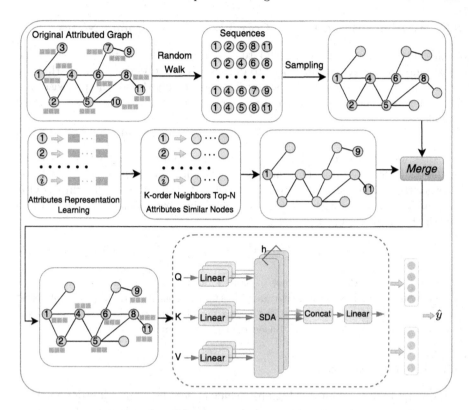

Fig. 1. Overall Framework of the proposed GSNA method.

Figure 1 shows an example of the biased random walk being used to generate node sequences in the original attributed graph. Assuming a walk length of 5, we can obtain a set of node sequences S such as $\{1, 2, 5, 8, 11\}$. We further utilize frequency screening to obtain a set of high-frequency nodes that appear in S. Specifically, we count the frequency of each node in S as follows:

$$\text{freq}(v, S) = \frac{\text{count}(v, S)}{\sum_{u \in S} \text{count}(u, S)} \tag{2}$$

where $count(v, S)$ represents the number of times node v appears in the set S, and the denominator represents the sum of the counts for all nodes in S. This score measures the relative frequency of node v appearing in S, and a set S' of the selected nodes using frequency screening can be denote as:

$$S' = F\left(|v \mid v \in S, \text{freq}(v, S) > \tau|\right) \tag{3}$$

where F is a function that selects the nodes with high frequency, and τ is a threshold value that controls the frequency of selected nodes.

3.3   Attribute-Based Highly Correlated Neighborhood Nodes

In this subsection, we first use BERT to train node attributes representation and then compute the cosine similarity to obtain a list of the Top-N nodes that are most similar to the source node within k-order neighborhood, the pairwise similarity between the learned attribute vectors of nodes in the graph is calculated as follows:

$$Sim(u, v) = cos(Attribute(u), Attribute(v)) \qquad (4)$$

After we obtain the similarity of k-order neighborhood nodes that are equal to the distance of k from the source node. We then select these nodes based on whether their cosine similarity to the source node is larger than the threshold ρ, and the Top-N nodes with the highest cosine similarity scores are selected in a set, the formula can be written as:

$$U_{top-N}^{K}(u) = \text{Top} -\text{N}(\{v \in V : dist(u, v) = k\}, Sim(u, v) > \rho) \qquad (5)$$

where $U_{Top-N}^{K}(u)$ denotes the set of Top-N nodes that are most similar to the source node u within its k-order neighborhood, and $dist(u, v)$ is the shortest distance between nodes u and v in the graph. The function Top-N(S, f) selects the Top-N elements from set S based on the function f.

3.4   Encoder Approach

After merging the sequence of high frequency nodes and similar k-order neighbor nodes from the above steps, we construct a new graph consisting of these nodes and their edges. Next, an encoder approach is used to learn the low-dimensional vector representation of each node in the new graph. Specifically, we concatenate the attributes representation of each node with its structural representation, a multi-head attention mechanism is further performed to fused representation learning of source and target nodes. The attention mechanism is defined as follows:

$$MultiHead(Q, K, V) = Concat\,(head_1, head_2, \ldots, head_h)\,W^O \qquad (6)$$

where Q, K, and V are the input queries, keys, and values, respectively, with dimensions of $n \times d$ (n is the number of nodes, d is the dimension of the representation). W^O is a weight matrix, and h is the number of attention heads. Each head i applies the scaled dot-product attention mechanism to Q, K, and V:

$$head_i = Attention\left(QW_i^Q, KW_i^K, VW_i^V\right) \qquad (7)$$

where W_i^Q, W_i^K, and W_i^V are learnable parameters for the i-th head, and the attention mechanism is defined as:

$$Attention(Q, K, V) = softmax\left(\frac{QK^T}{\sqrt{d_k}}\right) V \qquad (8)$$

where d_k is the dimension of the key vectors K.

The final node representation is obtained by concatenating the multi-head attention output with the original attributes representation of each node:

$$h_v = Concat\left(MultiHead\left(Q_v, K_v, V_v\right), Attribute(v)\right) \tag{9}$$

where Q_v, K_v, and V_v are the queries, keys, and values for node v, and x_v is the original attributes representation of node v.

Finally, the dot product similarity measurement between the nodes representations of a source node and its neighbor node is given by:

$$S_{i,j} = h_i^T h_j \tag{10}$$

where h_i and h_j are the vector representations of the source node i and its neighbor node j respectively.

The proposed method is trained using a binary cross-entropy loss function, which measures the difference between the predicted and true labels. The formula is defined as follows:

$$-\frac{1}{m} \sum_{i=1}^{m} [l_i \log \hat{p}_i + (1 - l_i) \log(1 - \hat{p}_i)] \tag{11}$$

where m is the number of training examples, l_i is the true label of the i-th example, $\hat{p}_i$ is the predicted label, and the sum is taken over all training examples. The loss function is optimized using gradient descent to find the optimal values for the model's parameters.

The specific procedure of GSNA is described as shown in Algorithm 1.

Algorithm 1 The GSNA Algorithm

Input: Graph $G = (V, E, A)$; walk length l; walk number n; window size w; embedding dimension d; threshold ρ; frequency τ; number of attention heads h; hidden dimension d; learning rate α; epochs number e.

Output: The probability $\tilde{y}_{ij}$ that v_i and v_j are connected.

1: **for** $t = 1$ to N **do**
2:     Generate node sequences S for each node using random walk;
3: **end for**
4: Count the frequency and screen a set of high-frequency nodes in S;
5: **for** $t = 1$ to N **do**
6:     Learn attributes representation by BERT and compute the similarities between each pair of nodes;
7: **end for**
8: Obtain high-correlated K-hop neighbor set $U_{top-N}^{K}(u)$;
9: Merge a new graph G';
10: Apply a multi-head attention mechanism to learn the fused embedding;
11: Obtain the predicted scores by dot production similarity measurement;
12: Return $\tilde{y}_{ij}$;

---

4   Experiments

In this section, experiments are conducted on benchmark datasets, and the effectiveness of the proposed method GSNA is compared with relevant baselines on link prediction tasks.

4.1   Datasets

To evaluate the effectiveness of the proposed method GSNA, we utilize three standard benchmark datasets from public real-world network datasets, including SCHOLAT, Cora, and Citeseer. SCHOLAT is an academic research platform that integrates scientific research management, academic social networking, and academic information. Cora and Citeseer are citation networks of academic papers, where nodes represent academic papers and each directed edge indicates the citation relationship between papers. For clarity, the details of the three datasets are listed in Table 1.

Table 1. Statistics of experimental datasets.

Statistics	SCHOLAT	Cora	Citeseer
# Nodes	10755	2708	3327
# Edges	168540	5429	4732
# Attributes	23172	1433	3703

4.2   Baselines Methods

We compare the efficiency of GSNA with three methods that consider graph structure only (Spectral, DeepWalk, and Node2Vec), and six methods that consider both graph structure and node attributes (GAE, VGAE, GCN, Graph-SAGE, ARGA, and Linear GAE). The descriptions of the baseline models are as follows:

Spectral [10]: spectral clustering is an effective graph representation method that uses the spectrum of the graph Laplacian to partition nodes into clusters.

DeepWalk [11]: a graph embedding method that learns node representations by generating random walks and treating them as sentences. The method uses the skip-gram model from natural language processing to learn embeddings that capture the local graph structure.

Node2Vec [12]: another graph embedding method that learns node representations by generating random walks, but it uses a biased random walk algorithm for efficiently exploring the neighborhood architecture.

GAE and **VGAE** [25]: graph embedding methods that learns a low-dimensional representation of the graph by training an autoencoder to reconstruct the graph structure.

GCN [21]: a neural network method that applies convolutional filters to the graph to learn node representations by aggregating features from its neighbors.

GraphSAGE [16]: another neural network method that learns node representations by aggregating features from its neighbors, but it uses a more flexible aggregator function that can incorporate different types of graph structures.

ARGA [24]: an extension of GAE that incorporates both the graph structure and node attributes to learn a low-dimensional representation of the graph.

Linear GAE [26]: is a simplified version of the GAE and VGAE methods with one-hop linear models.

4.3 Evaluation Metrics

In our experiments, we mainly select the most frequently-used metrics AUC and AP to evaluate the performance. These two above metrics are now widely used in problems of link prediction. The larger the two metrics are, the better the performance is.

AUC (Area under the ROC Curve) is a metric that measures the area under the Receiver Operating Characteristic (ROC) curve. The ROC curve is a graphical representation of the trade-off between the true positive rate and the false positive rate at different classification thresholds. The AUC ranges from 0 to 1, where a higher AUC value indicates better model performance in distinguishing between the two classes. Let n' represent the number of times that the edge score in the test set is larger than that in the non-existent edge set and n'' represents the number of times that the two edge scores are equal. The AUC is calculated as:

$$AUC = \frac{n' + 0.5n''}{n} \tag{12}$$

AP (The average precision) is a metric based on the area under a $P_r \times R_c$ curve that has been pre-processed to eliminate the zig-zag behavior. It summarizes this precision-recall trade-off dictated by confidence levels of the predicted bounding boxes. The AP is calculated as:

$$AP = \sum_{k=0}^{K} (R_r(k) - R_r(k+1)) Pr_{\text{interp}}(R_r(k)) \tag{13}$$

where $Pr_{\text{interp}}(R)$ is a continuous function, $R_r(k)$ is used to compute the Riemann integral.

4.4 Experimental Results

Throughout our experiments, the SCHOLAT dataset is divided into 80% training, 10% validation, and 10% testing sets, the Core and Citeseer datasets are divided into 85% training, 5% validation, and 10% testing sets. A pre-trained BERT with 12 layers, 768 hidden, 12 heads, and 110M parameters is applied for learning attributes representation of nodes. The proposed GSNA was trained for a maximum of 50 epochs with an early stopping mechanism and updated using the Adam algorithm with an initial learning rate of 0.001. All parameters of the baselines follow the settings described in the corresponding papers.

To verify the effectiveness of the proposed method GSNA for link prediction, we compare it with nine methods with respect to graph embedding. The experimental results are shown in Table 2, where the best results are marked in bold. As shown in Table 2, GSNA outperforms the selected baseline methods in terms of the metrics of AUC and AP. Due to the sparsity of the SCHOLAT dataset, the performance improvement of GSNA on SCHOLAT is more obvious. It suggests that GSNA can capture higher-order highly correlated nodes and thus can effectively learn local and global graph information. It can be observed that using deep learning-based methods generally achieves better results than not deep learning-based methods. Additionally, the methods that incorporate both graph structure and node attributes can achieve better performance compared with the methods that consider graph structure only. This shows that both the graph structure and node attributes are beneficial for graph representation learning, and illustrates the necessity and effectiveness of simultaneously incorporating structure and attribute for link prediction.

Table 2. The results of AUC and AP comparison with baseline methods on SCHOLAT, Cora, CiteSeer.

Model	SCHOLAT		Cora		CiteSeer	
	AUC	AP	AUC	AP	AUC	AP
Spectral	0.806	0.830	0.842	0.883	0.802	0.845
Deepwalk	0.811	0.835	0.831	0.850	0.805	0.836
Node2Vec	0.846	0.861	0.856	0.887	0.844	0.877
GAE	0.948	0.958	0.910	0.921	0.895	0.898
VGAE	0.950	0.962	0.914	0.925	0.906	0.918
GCN	0.936	0.947	0.907	0.918	0.881	0.890
GraphSAGE	0.921	0.941	0.865	0.898	0.853	0.886
ARGA	0.948	0.955	0.924	0.931	0.915	0.926
Linear GAE	0.952	0.968	0.921	0.933	0.915	0.930
GSNA	**0.959**	**0.970**	**0.928**	**0.939**	**0.922**	**0.931**

4.5   Ablation Study

To further investigate the effect of the various modules in our proposed method GSNA, an ablation study on the three datasets is conducted to compare the proposed GSNA model with two cases: WA (without attributes similar modes) and WF (without frequency screening). The ablation experimental results are presented in Table 3, GSNA has performance improvement compared to both WA and WF, it indicates the neighborhood nodes with higher correlation can be captured by attributes similar modes and frequency screening. We can also observe that the performance of WF is better than the performance of WA, it illustrates the necessity and effectiveness of simultaneously incorporating structure and attribute for link prediction. In essence, the incorporation of both structure and attributes facilitates the learning of graph representation. Overall, the results clearly validate that incorporating structure and attributes is conducive to the improvement of prediction performance.

Table 3. Comparison of the proposed GSNA, WA (without attributes similar nodes) and WF (without frequency screening) on SCHOLAT, Cora, CiteSeer. And the improvement percentage obtained by GSNA is defined as Imp. (%) = $\frac{\text{GSNA result-Best baseline result}}{\text{Best baseline result}} \times 100\%$.

Datasets	Metrics	WA	WF	GSNA	Imp. (%)	
					GSNA vs WA	GSNA vs WF
SCHOLAT	AUC	0.921	0.950	**0.959**	4.13%	0.95%
	AP	0.933	0.961	**0.970**	3.97%	0.94%
Cora	AUC	0.892	0.909	**0.928**	4.04%	2.09%
	AP	0.911	0.923	**0.939**	3.07%	1.73%
Citeseer	AUC	0.886	0.903	**0.922**	4.06%	2.10%
	AP	0.905	0.918	**0.931**	2.87%	1.42%

4.6   Parameter Sensitivity

In this subsection, the impact of parameters of on the proposed GSNA method is studied for the SCHOLAT dataset. As shown in Fig. 2, the proposed method GSNA shows the highest link prediction performance for l (walk length) = 10, n (walk length) = 8, w (window size) = 6, d (embedding dimension) = 64, ρ (threshold) = 0.5, τ (frequency) = 5.

We can find that increasing the number of wanderings, wandering steps or window size can collect more contextual information and thus learn more accurate graph representations, but too many wanderings, wandering steps or window size is also inappropriate because it tends to generate noisy data, which leads to a poorer network representation. For the embedding dimension, when the embedding dimension exceeds 64, the prediction performance tends to be stable, and we finally set the embedding dimension to 64 in order to save the limited computing power resources. For the similarity threshold, a lower threshold may screen out some relevant nodes, but a higher threshold will also discard some valuable nodes. For the frequency, we selected nodes with frequency over 5 as the final sequences, the number of nodes selected will be less if the frequency is

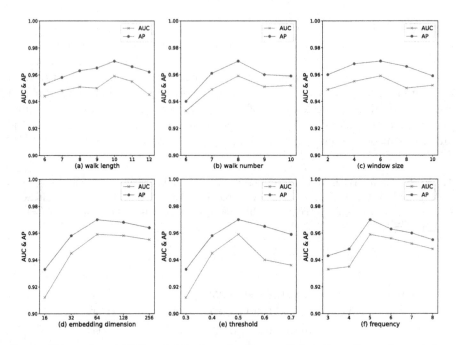

Fig. 2. The results of AUC and AP when changing walk length, walk number, window size, embedding dimension, threshold and embedding dimension on SCHOLAT dataset.

higher and cannot capture the comprehensive information, and some low correlation nodes will be selected if the frequency is higher, which affects the prediction performance.

5   Conclusion

In this paper, we propose a efficient graph embedding method to incorporate graph structure and node attributes for link prediction. We first generate node sequences using random walk on the original graph, and filter out low-frequency nodes to obtain high quality nodes. We then use a BERT model to learn node attributes representation and calculate attribute similarities to obtain the Top-N nodes with high correlation to the source node. These high-correlation nodes, together with the nodes selected in the first step, are used to construct a new graph. Our method effectively captures both structural and attributes information of nodes in a graph by generating a new graph. We design an encoder to learn the low-dimensional representations of nodes in this new graph. The encoder leverages the multiple-head attention mechanism to fuse both the structural and attributes representation of nodes. Finally, we utilize the learned node embeddings to predict the existence of edges using dot product similarity. Our experimental results on several benchmark datasets demonstrate that our proposed method outperforms several graph embedding methods. In the future, we plan to explore more advanced techniques to extend GSNA for link prediction in heterogeneous information networks with different types of entities and relationships.

Acknowledgements. This work was supported in part by the National Natural Science Foundation of China under Grant U1811263 and the Science and Technology Program of Guangzhou, China under Grant 2023A04J1728.

References

1. Halliwell, N.: Evaluating explanations of relational graph convolutional network link predictions on knowledge graphs. In: Thirty-Sixth AAAI Conference on Artificial Intelligence, pp. 12880–12881 (2022)
2. Wu, E., Cui, H., Chen, Z.: RelpNet: relation-based link prediction neural network. In: Proceedings of the 31st ACM International Conference on Information & Knowledge Management, pp. 2138–2147 (2022)
3. Baghershahi, P., Hosseini, R., Moradi, H.: Self-attention presents low-dimensional knowledge graph embeddings for link prediction. Knowl.-Based Syst. **260**, 110124 (2023)
4. Song, Z., Zhang, Y., King, I.: Towards an optimal asymmetric graph structure for robust semi-supervised node classification. In: The 28th ACM SIGKDD Conference on Knowledge Discovery and Data Mining, pp. 1656–1665 (2022)
5. Chen, C., et al.: Vertically federated graph neural network for privacy-preserving node classification. In: Proceedings of the Thirty-First International Joint Conference on Artificial Intelligence, IJCAI, pp. 1959–1965 (2022)
6. Lee, J., Oh, Y., In, Y., Lee, N., Hyun, D., Park, C.: GraFN: semi-supervised node classification on graph with few labels via non-parametric distribution assignment. In: The 45th International ACM SIGIR Conference on Research and Development in Information Retrieval, pp. 2243–2248 (2022)
7. Jin, D., et al.: A survey of community detection approaches: from statistical modeling to deep learning. IEEE Trans. Knowl. Data Eng. **35**(2), 1149–1170 (2023)
8. Ni, L., Xu, H., Zhang, Y., Luo, W.: Spatial-aware local community detection guided by dominance relation. IEEE Trans. Comput. Soc. Syst. **10**(2), 686–699 (2023)
9. Wu, X., et al.: CLARE: a semi-supervised community detection algorithm. In: The 28th ACM SIGKDD Conference on Knowledge Discovery and Data Mining, pp. 2059–2069 (2022)
10. Ng, A.Y., Jordan, M.I., Weiss, Y.: On spectral clustering: analysis and an algorithm. In: Advances in Neural Information Processing Systems 14 [Neural Information Processing Systems: Natural and Synthetic, NIPS 2001, Vancouver, British Columbia, Canada, 3–8 December 2001], pp. 849–856 (2001)
11. Perozzi, B., Al-Rfou, R., Skiena, S.: DeepWalk: online learning of social representations. In: Proceedings of the 20th ACM SIGKDD International Conference on Knowledge Discovery and Data Mining, pp. 701–710 (2014)
12. Grover, A., Leskovec, J.: node2vec: scalable feature learning for networks. In: Proceedings of the 22nd ACM SIGKDD International Conference on Knowledge Discovery and Data Mining, pp. 855–864 (2016)
13. Mikolov, T., Sutskever, I., Chen, K., Corrado, G.S., Dean, J.: Distributed representations of words and phrases and their compositionality. In: Advances in Neural Information Processing Systems 26: 27th Annual Conference on Neural Information Processing Systems 2013, pp. 3111–3119 (2013)

14. Tang, J., Qu, M., Wang, M., Zhang, M., Yan, J., Mei, Q.: LINE: large-scale information network embedding. In: Proceedings of the 24th International Conference on World Wide Web, WWW 2015, Florence, Italy, 18–22 May 2015, pp. 1067–1077 (2015)
15. Cao, S., Lu, W., Xu, Q.: GraRep: learning graph representations with global structural information. In: Proceedings of the 24th ACM International Conference on Information and Knowledge Management, CIKM 2015, Melbourne, VIC, Australia, 19–23 October 2015, pp. 891–900 (2015)
16. Hamilton, W.L., Ying, Z., Leskovec, J.: Inductive representation learning on large graphs. In: Advances in Neural Information Processing Systems 30: Annual Conference on Neural Information Processing Systems, pp. 1024–1034 (2017)
17. Velickovic, P., Cucurull, G., Casanova, A., Romero, A., Liò, P., Bengio, Y.: Graph attention networks. In: 6th International Conference on Learning Representations, ICLR (2018)
18. Belkin, M., Niyogi, P.: Laplacian eigenmaps and spectral techniques for embedding and clustering. In: Advances in Neural Information Processing Systems 14 [Neural Information Processing Systems: Natural and Synthetic, NIPS 2001, Vancouver, British Columbia, Canada, 3–8 December 2001], pp. 585–591 (2001)
19. Roweis, S.T., Saul, L.K.: Nonlinear dimensionality reduction by locally linear embedding. Science **290**, 2323–2326 (2000)
20. Ou, M., Cui, P., Pei, J., Zhang, Z., Zhu, W.: Asymmetric transitivity preserving graph embedding. In: Proceedings of the 22nd ACM SIGKDD International Conference on Knowledge Discovery and Data Mining, pp. 1105–1114 (2016)
21. Kipf, T.N., Welling, M.: Semi-supervised classification with graph convolutional networks. In: 5th International Conference on Learning Representations, ICLR (2017)
22. Wang, D., Cui, P., Zhu, W.: Structural deep network embedding. In: Proceedings of the 22nd ACM SIGKDD International Conference on Knowledge Discovery and Data Mining, pp. 1225–1234 (2016)
23. Wang, X., et al.: Heterogeneous graph attention network. In: The World Wide Web Conference, WWW, pp. 2022–2032 (2019)
24. Wang, H., et al.: A united approach to learning sparse attributed network embedding. In: IEEE International Conference on Data Mining, ICDM, pp. 557–566 (2018)
25. Kipf, T.N., Welling, M.: Variational graph auto-encoders. In: Advances in Neural Information Processing Systems, pp. 5591–5600 (2016)
26. Salha, G., Hennequin, R., Vazirgiannis, M.: Simple and effective graph autoencoders with one-hop linear models. In: Hutter, F., Kersting, K., Lijffijt, J., Valera, I. (eds.) ECML PKDD 2020. LNCS (LNAI), vol. 12457, pp. 319–334. Springer, Cham (2021). https://doi.org/10.1007/978-3-030-67658-2_19

Link Prediction for Opportunistic Networks Based on Hybrid Similarity Metrics and E-LSTM-D Models

Xiaoying Yang[1,2], Lijie Li[1,2], Gang Xu[1,2(✉)], Ming Song[1,2], and Feng Zhang[3]

[1] College of Computer Science, Inner Mongolia University, Hohhot 010021, China
csxugang@imu.edu.cn

[2] Inner Mongolia A.R. Key Laboratory of Data Mining and Knowledge Engineering, Inner Mongolia University, Hohhot 010021, China

[3] School of Computer and Information Technology, Shanxi University, Taiyuan 030000, China

Abstract. Link prediction is a crucial issue in opportunistic networks routing research. Static link prediction methods ignore the historical information of network evolution, which affects the prediction accuracy. In this paper, we propose a link prediction method (HS-LSTM) that combines hybrid similarity metrics and the E-LSTM-D model. The approach extracts structural features using hybrid similarity metrics, constructs a structural feature matrix, and applies the E-LSTM-D model to extract temporal features and predict the links that have not yet appeared in the network. Our experiments on three real datasets of opportunistic networks (Infocom5, MIT, and Haggle) shows that our proposed method outperforms the baseline method in terms of prediction accuracy.

Keywords: opportunistic networks · link prediction · similarity metrics · self-encoder · LSTM model · deep learning

1 Introduction

Opportunistic networks [1] rely on node encounters to establish communication and transmit messages in a "store-carry-forward" manner. They emerged from the development of DTN [2]. Thus, opportunistic networks are well-suited for scenarios or environments where infrastructure cannot be easily erected, including vehicular networking, drones, disaster area communication, satellite communication, wildlife tracking, and mobile edge computing [3–8].

Link prediction can support the development of efficient routing algorithms for opportunistic networks, which face challenges due to their dynamic nature. An effective link prediction method can uncover network evolution and provide valuable insights for designing routing protocols to improve network performance.

This paper proposes a link prediction method for opportunistic networks that considers node communication uncertainty and periodicity. By using hybrid similarity metrics and an E-LSTM-D model, it extracts both structural and temporal features for dynamic link prediction. The paper contributes in two main aspects.

© The Author(s), under exclusive license to Springer Nature Singapore Pte Ltd. 2023
F. Zhang et al. (Eds.): WISE 2023, LNCS 14306, pp. 439–450, 2023.
https://doi.org/10.1007/978-981-99-7254-8_34

(1) Extracting the structural features of the network using hybrid similarity metrics that leverage the interaction information of nodes. The network is divided into snapshots, weighted adjacency matrices are calculated, and structural features are extracted using hybrid similarity metrics to describe the network's topology.

(2) A link prediction model (HS-LSTM) for opportunistic network is proposed. The model compresses a sequence of structural feature matrices into a low-dimensional space using an encoder. LSTM captures temporal features, and a decoder reduces the dimensionality for output.

2 Related Work

Research on link prediction methods for opportunistic networks has gained significant attention in recent years. Existing methods can be classified into three categories: heuristic-based, latent feature-based, and deep learning-based approaches.

A. Heuristic-based methods

In static networks, various link prediction metrics are commonly used, such as the common neighbors (CN) algorithm and the resource allocation index (RA). Building on this approach, Sha C. et al. [10] proposed a hybrid similarity index that incorporates local network information and an influence fading factor for existing links. Rong Y. et al. [11] improved link prediction accuracy by using clustering and diffusion characteristics of edges as topological weights. Yong Y. et al. [12] combined degree, clustering coefficient, and node centrality to assess local information and node importance for link prediction.

B. Latent feature-based methods

Latent feature methods involve calculating node representations by factorizing matrices from the network, which are then used to predict links. Ahmed A. et al. [13] proposed a factorization technique for link prediction using learned embeddings from the network adjacency matrix. Xiaoke Ma et al. [14] introduced a graph regularized nonnegative matrix decomposition algorithm that characterizes each network subset. Perozzi B et al. [15] used random wandering and word2vec algorithm for learning hidden network information and node representation. Tang J et al. [16] developed a network embedding method that preserves both local and global network structure through an optimized objective function.

C. Deep learning-based methods

Deep learning-based models only require some preprocessing of the network and extract the features of the data in the network from certain perspectives to achieve link prediction. Chen J. et al. [18] proposed E-LSTM-D, a deep learning model for dynamic link prediction in networks of varying sizes and structures. Lei K. et al. [19] introduced GCN-GAN, a nonlinear model combining GCN, LSTM, and GAN for temporal link prediction in weighted dynamic networks. Shu J. et al. [20] developed a link prediction algorithm for opportunistic networks using 3D-CNNs to predict local link changes based on network evolution. Linlan L. et al. [21] proposed a link prediction method using network representation learning and a recurrent neural network with attention mechanism to capture dynamic network evolution and extract temporal features.

This paper proposes a method for link prediction in opportunistic networks, considering sparsity and time-varying topology. It combines similarity indices, constructs a structural feature matrix, and uses the E-LSTM-D model for predicting dynamic links.

3 Method Description

3.1 Representation of Opportunistic Networks

Definition 1: Opportunistic network. Let G denote opportunistic network topology. $G = \{V, E\}$, V is the set of nodes in the network, and $E(i, j)$ is the set of the edge of the node i and node j. $E(i, j) = 1$ when there is a link between the node i and j, else $E(i, j) = 0$. Let $G_s = \{G_1, G_2, ..., G_n\}$ denote the snapshot sequence of G divided by a fixed slice duration Δt. $G_t = \{V, E_t\}$ is the t-th snapshot graph of G and it is represented by the adjacency matrix $A_t \in N \times N$.

Figure 1 displays the appearance or disappearance of links in each snapshot topology diagram through the adjacency matrix.

Definition 2: Construction of the weighted adjacency matrix of the opportunistic network. Communication duration and frequency determine the weight of connected edges between node pairs. The weight W_t of an edge in the snapshot graph $G_{t\_weight} = \{V, E_t, W_t\}$ is calculated in the following equation:

$$W_{ij}^t = \{e^{\frac{w_{ij}^t}{\Delta t}} \mid \forall i \neq j \cap (i, j) \in E_t\} \tag{1}$$

where $w_{ij}^t = \frac{\sum d_{ij}}{f_{ij}}$, f_{ij} is the number of connections of node (i, j) in the t-th snapshot, $\sum d_{ij}$ is the total connection duration of node (i, j). Δt is the slice duration. Edge weights are normalized to the range [1, e] for improved computational efficiency.

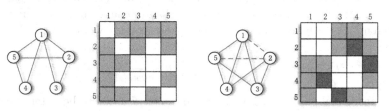

(a)When t=1, the link situation of nodes 1~5

(b) The links of nodes 1~5 when t=2,the dotted lines are the vanishing edges and the red lines are the newly generated edges

Fig. 1. Example diagram of opportunistic network link changes. (Color figure online)

The weighted adjacency matrix takes the following form:

$$W_t = \begin{bmatrix} 0 & \cdots & W_{1n}^t \\ \vdots & \ddots & \vdots \\ W_{n1}^t & \cdots & 0 \end{bmatrix} \tag{2}$$

3.2   Construction of Structural Feature Matrix

Given the social nature of nodes in opportunistic networks, this paper utilizes the common neighbor similarity metric and the preferential attachment similarity metric to extract the structural features of opportunistic network snapshot sequences.

1) Common neighbor similarity metric

The common neighbors heuristic measures link likelihood based on shared neighboring nodes. This paper utilizes the weighted Jaccard metric, considering both node degrees and the proportion of common neighbors, the weighted Jaccard metric is defined as follows:

$$Jaccard_{ij}^t = \frac{\sum_{z \in \Gamma_t(i) \cap \Gamma_t(j)} W_{zi}^t \times W_{zj}^t}{\sum_{b \in \Gamma_t(i) \cup \Gamma_t(j)} W_{bi}^t \times W_{bj}^t} \tag{3}$$

$\Gamma_t(i)$ and $\Gamma_t(j)$ are the neighboring node sets of nodes i and j, respectively, in the t-th snapshot of an opportunistic network. z represents their common neighboring nodes, b is the concatenation of their neighboring nodes, and W denotes the weights between nodes i, j, and their neighbors.

2) Preferential attachment similarity index

The preferential attachment heuristic measures the probability of link existence by the product of the degrees between nodes. It assumes that the probability of a new edge connecting to a node V_x is proportional to the degree k_x of that node. The formula for this is:

$$PA_{ij}^t = k_i^t \times k_j^t = \sum_{c \in \Gamma_t(i)} W_{ci}^t \times \sum_{h \in \Gamma_t(j)} W_{hj}^t \tag{4}$$

3) Local information hybrid similarity index

This paper presents a hybrid similarity index for analyzing node pairs in opportunistic network snapshot sequences. It combines common neighbor and preferential attachment similarity indices, as defined by Eq. (3) and Eq. (4).

$$HS_{ij}^t = \theta \frac{Jaccard_{ij}^t}{maxJaccard^t} + (1 - \theta) \frac{PA_{ij}^t}{maxPA^t} (0 \le \theta \le 1) \tag{5}$$

The specific value of the assignment parameter θ needs to be determined in the experiment, where $maxJaccard^t$, $maxPA^t$ represent the maximum value in the matrix formed with $Jaccard_{ij}^t$, PA_{ij}^t as elements.

4) Construction of structural feature matrix

Given an opportunistic network snapshot G_t, the hybrid similarity metric is calculated for each pair of nodes within the snapshot, and a structural feature matrix is constructed based on these metrics.

$$HS_t = \begin{bmatrix} 0 & \cdots & HS_{1n}^t \\ \vdots & \ddots & \vdots \\ HS_{n1}^t & \cdots & 0 \end{bmatrix} \tag{6}$$

3.3 Opportunistic Network Link Prediction Model

In this paper, an E-LSTM-D model [18] is used to extract the temporal features of the opportunistic network. The model includes an encoder, a decoder, and an LSTM network to predict the next network link, as depicted in Fig. 2.

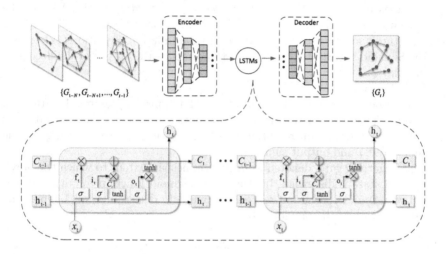

Fig. 2. The overall structure of the E-LSTM-D model.

Model Structure

(1) Self-encoder structure

A. Encoder: This component compresses the input into a low-dimensional feature space, which can be represented by the following equation.

$$y_i^{(0)} = ReLU(W^{(0)}x_i + b^{(0)}) \tag{7}$$

$$y_i^{(k)} = ReLU(W^{(k)}y_i^{(k-1)} + b^{(k)}) \tag{8}$$

$$Y^{(k)} = [y_0^{(k)}, y_1^{(k)}, ..., y_{N-1}^{(k)}] \tag{9}$$

Equation (7) defines x_i as the i-th graph in the input sequence X. Equation (8) uses $W^{(k)}$ and $b^{(k)}$ to represent the weight and bias matrices of the k-th layer encoder, respectively, and $y_i^{(k)}$ as the output produced by the k-th layer encoder for the i-th graph. Equation (9) defines $Y^{(k)}$ as the output generated by the k-th layer encoder for the entire sequence input. The encoder layers in this paper employ ReLU as the default activation function.

B. Decoder: The encoder and decoder components are mirror structures of each other. The decoder reconstructs the input from its low-dimensional feature space representation, which can be expressed by the following equation:

$$\hat{Y}^{(0)} = ReLU(\hat{W}^{(0)} H + \hat{b}^{(0)}) \tag{10}$$

$$\hat{Y}^{(k)} = ReLU(\hat{W}^{(k)} \hat{Y}^{(k-1)} + \hat{b}^{(k)}) \tag{11}$$

$$\hat{Y}^{(n)} = \sigma(\hat{W}^{(n)} \hat{Y}^{(n-1)} + \hat{b}^{(n)}) \tag{12}$$

Equation (10) defines H as the output of the LSTM structure, representing the extracted features. Equation (11) introduces $\hat{W}^{(k)}$ and $\hat{b}^{(k)}$ as the weight and bias matrices of the k-th layer decoder, respectively, with $\hat{Y}^{(k)}$ as the output of the k-th layer decoder. The decoder structure mirrors the encoder structure and utilizes ReLU as its activation function. Equation (12) applies the Sigmoid activation function (σ) to normalize the output of the decoder's final layer.

(2) LSTM structure

The autoencoder structure is insufficient for capturing temporal features in graph sequences. LSTM is used instead, with input, forget, and output gates regulating information retention and transmission. These gates impact the cell state C_t and output signal h_t.

The forgetting gate, denoted as σ, determines the extent to which the previous cell state is discarded. It utilizes the sigmoid function to output values between 0 and 1, where 0 represents complete discarding and 1 represents full retention of the previous state.

$$f_t = \sigma(W_f \cdot [h_{t-1}, Y^{(k)}] + b_f) \tag{13}$$

$Y^{(k)}$ is the input at time t, f_t is the output at time t, h_{t-1} is the previous hidden state, and W_f and b_f are the weight and bias matrices of the forgotten gate.

The input gate decides how much input information is stored in the cell state C_t. It uses a sigmoid layer to determine which information is updated and a tanh layer to generate a new state candidate vector $\widetilde{C}_t$ within the range of $[-1, 1]$.

$$i_t = \sigma(W_i \cdot [h_{t-1}, Y^{(k)}] + b_i) \tag{14}$$

$$\widetilde{C}_t = tanh(W_C \cdot [h_{t-1}, Y^{(k)}] + b_C) \tag{15}$$

To update the current memory C_t, the input gate value i_t and the new state candidate vector $\widetilde{C}_t$ are combined, merging past and present memories using a specific formula.

$$C_t = f_t * C_{t-1} + i_t * \widetilde{C}_t \tag{16}$$

W_i and W_C are the weight matrices associated with the input gates in the LSTM, while b_i and b_C are the corresponding bias matrices. By incorporating both forgetting and input gates, the LSTM cell is able to store long-term memory and filter out irrelevant information in a more effective manner.

The output gate uses the updated cell state to determine the next cell input, which generates the output. The formula for the output gate is:

$$o_t = \sigma(W_o \cdot [h_{t-1}, Y^{(k)}] + b_o) \tag{17}$$

$$h_t = o_t * tanh(C_t) \tag{18}$$

where W_o and b_o denote the weight matrix and bias matrix of the output gates in the LSTM.

Training Process

The loss function for link prediction typically involves calculating the L_2 norm between the true value $A^t_{(i,j)}$ and the predicted value $\hat{A}^t_{(i,j)}$. However, this paper addresses issues with sparse and imbalanced network data by improving the L_2 loss function through an increased penalty value p. This enhancement improves optimization. The calculation method for this is:

$$L_2 = \sum_{i=1}^{N} \sum_{j=1}^{N} ((A^t_{(i,j)} - \hat{A}^t_{(i,j)})^2 p) \tag{19}$$

For each training process, p takes a value of 1 if $A^t_{(i,j)} = 0$ and $p = \beta > 1$ if $\hat{A}^t_{(i,j)} = 1$. Here, β is a positive value that indicates the penalty coefficient. This penalty matrix imposes a greater penalty on the non-zero elements, thereby mitigating overfitting of the model to some extent.

To ensure uniform inter-layer inputs in the neural network, a regularized loss function L_{reg} is utilized. It computes the sum of squares of weight parameters in the prediction model, promoting weight regularization to prevent overfitting.

$$L_{reg} = \frac{1}{2} \sum_{k=1}^{K} (\| W^{(k)} \|_F^2 + \| \hat{W}^{(k)} \|_F^2) + \frac{1}{2} \sum_{l=1}^{L} (\| W_f^{(l)} \|_F^2 + \| W_i^{(l)} \|_F^2 + \| W_C^{(l)} \|_F^2 + \| W_o^{(l)} \|_F^2) \tag{20}$$

Finally, we use a hybrid loss function with the following equation:

$$L = L_2 + \alpha L_{reg} \tag{21}$$

where α is the proportion of the regularized loss in the loss function.

4   Experimental Procedure and Analysis of Results

4.1   Dataset

This paper analyzes three opportunistic network datasets, recording interactions between individuals. Nodes represent participants, while edges represent connections. Detailed dataset descriptions are provided, and summarized information is presented in Table 1.

Table 1. Basic information of the 3 datasets

Dataset	Infocom5	MIT	Haggle
Equipment Type	iMote	Phone	iMote
Network Type	Bluetooth	Bluetooth	Bluetooth
Number of nodes	41	97	274
Duration/d	3	246	4
Number of links	25459	102510	28202

4.2   Evaluation Indicators

This paper uses two evaluation metrics, namely, the area under the receiver operating characteristic curve (AUC curve) and error rate, which have different emphases.

$$AUC = \frac{n^{'} + 0.5n^{''}}{n} \tag{22}$$

$$ER = \frac{N_{false}}{N_{true}} \tag{23}$$

4.3   Baseline Methodology

To verify the effectiveness of our proposed method, we compare it with four baselines, namely, CN [9], Node2vec [17], DDNE [22], and DySAT [23].

Experiments on various datasets and prior research indicated that the optimal configuration involved 2 hidden layers with 256 nodes each. The input layer had 128 encoder nodes, and the decoder layer matched the output layer's shape to the dataset's participant count. Refer to Table 2 for detailed parameter settings.

Table 2. Hyperparameter setting

Dataset	Encoder layer	LSTMs layer 1, layer 2	Decoder layer
Infocom5	128	256,256	41
Mit	128	256,256	96
Haggle	128	256,256	274

4.4   Experimental Results

This paper compares the HS-LSTM model with four benchmark techniques by evaluating the AUC and ER metrics. The prediction performance comparison results can be found in Tables 3 and 4.

Table 3 shows that static link prediction methods such as CN and node2vec have lower accuracy in capturing link changes in dynamic networks. In contrast, DDNE and DySAT perform better by considering temporal characteristics. The proposed HS-LSTM algorithm achieves the highest AUC value on three datasets, demonstrating the importance of incorporating both network structure features and temporal characteristics in link prediction. This finding emphasizes the need to extract network structure features to improve prediction accuracy.

Table 4 compares the error rates of different link prediction algorithms by comparing predicted and actual link numbers. CN and Node2vec algorithms have higher error rates, likely due to their failure to consider temporal characteristics, resulting in over-prediction of links. DDNE and DySAT algorithms perform better by incorporating temporal features, resulting in lower error rates. The HS-LSTM model proposed in this study achieves the lowest error rate, indicating that considering both spatiotemporal characteristics simultaneously leads to superior performance in link prediction models.

Table 3. AUC Evaluation Metric

	CN	Node2vec	DDNE	DySAT	HS-LSTM
Infocom5	0.4821	0.7053	0.8112	0.8726	**0.9363**
Mit	0.6150	0.8331	0.9284	0.9330	**0.9745**
Haggle	0.6074	0.7938	0.8929	0.9244	**0.9746**

Table 4. ER Evaluation Metric

	CN	Node2vec	DDNE	DySAT	HS-LSTM
Infocom5	52.8164	45.6215	7.4357	5.3278	**3.7457**
Mit	50.9247	43.7313	5.5428	3.4312	**1.9128**
Haggle	50.8575	43.6544	5.4633	3.3791	**1.1047**

4.5 Experimental Parameter Setting

The experimental parameter settings include the number of snapshots, the assignment parameter θ, and the length of the model input sequence.

(1) Number of snapshots of opportunistic network

Determining the number of snapshots is essential for slicing network information in dynamic opportunistic network datasets. Our analysis on three datasets revealed varying snapshot requirements. Infocom5 and MIT datasets achieved optimal prediction performance with 500 and 450 snapshots respectively, balancing topology density. The Haggle dataset, with more nodes and uniform links, showed less sensitivity to the number of slices, ultimately settling on 300 snapshots. See Fig. 3 and Fig. 4 for visualization.

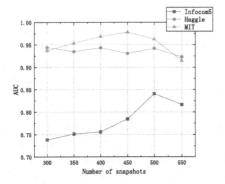

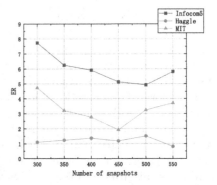

Fig. 3. Relationship between number of snapshots and AUC for Infocom5, MIT, Haggle dataset.

Fig. 4. Relationship between number of snapshots and ER for Infocom5, MIT, Haggle dataset.

(2) Assignment parameter θ

We experimented with different assignment parameter values to evaluate their impact on link prediction accuracy in the opportunistic network. Results in Fig. 5 and Fig. 6 show that accuracy increases with the time step, peaking in the range of [0.6, 0.8]. The mixed similarity metric performs better than the Jaccard metric (with parameter 1) and the PA metric (with parameter 0) in terms of prediction accuracy. This suggests that both common neighbor similarity and preferential attachment contribute to link prediction, with the range of [0.6, 0.8] providing the best results by considering both factors.

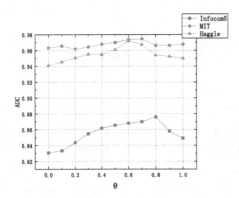

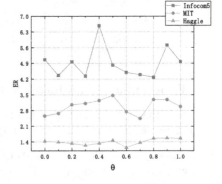

Fig. 5. Assignment parameters versus AUC graph.

Fig. 6. Assignment parameters versus ER graph.

(3) The length of the input graph sequence

As shown in Fig. 7 and Fig. 8, the length of the input graph sequence (X) had a varying impact on prediction accuracy. Increasing X initially improved performance, but beyond a certain point (X = 5 for Infocom5, X = 10 for MIT), accuracy declined due to irrelevant features. However, the model's performance on the Haggle dataset showed continuous improvement with increasing X, albeit at a slower rate after X = 10. Overall, finding the optimal X involved balancing relevant information and avoiding redundancy, potentially requiring additional computational training.

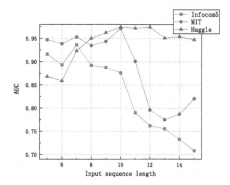
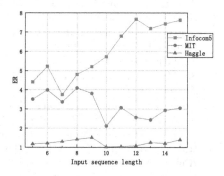

Fig. 7. Effect of input sequence length on AUC values.

Fig. 8. Effect of input sequence length on ER values.

5   Summary

Link prediction is crucial in network analysis, including opportunistic networks. Our proposed method combines hybrid similarity metrics and an E-LSTM-D model for accurate prediction. Experiments on real datasets show significant improvement. Future work will focus on optimizing the model and developing link prediction-based routing algorithms for efficient network routing.

Acknowledgements. This work was supported by the National Natural Science Foundation of China under Grants 62061036 and 62077032; The Self-Open Project of Engineering Research Center of Ecological Big Data, Ministry of Education; Natural Science Foundation of Shanxi Province under Grant 201901D111035.

References

1. Sachdeva, R., Dev, A.: Review of opportunistic network: assessing past, present, and future. Int. J. Commun Syst **34**(11), e4860 (2021)
2. Fall, K.: A delay-tolerant network architecture for challenged internets. In: Proceedings of the 2003 Conference on Applications, Technologies, Architectures, and Protocols for Computer Communications, pp. 27–34 (2003)
3. Yao, Z.: Trusted routing model based on opportunity network in vehicular networking environment. Comput. Syst. Appl. **30**(03), 214–220 (2021)

4. Pang, X., Liu, M., Li, Z.: Geographic position based hopless opportunistic routing for UAV networks. Ad Hoc Netw. **120**, 102560 (2021)
5. Juan, H.: Theoretical research related to the information triage mechanism of landslide disaster based on opportunity network. Guizhou University (2022)
6. Martínez-Vidal, R., Martí, R., Sreenan, J.C.: Measuring QoS in an aeronautical opportunistic network architecture with limited access to a satellite communications backhaul. Mob. Inf. Syst. **2016**, 7601316 (2016)
7. Wenhui, M.: Research on the application of wildlife location tracking technology based on wireless sensor network. Guizhou University (2018)
8. Zhang, H., Chen, Z., Wu, J.: FRRF: a fuzzy reasoning routing-forwarding algorithm using mobile device similarity in mobile edge computing-based opportunistic mobile social networks. IEEE Access **7**, 35874–35889 (2019)
9. Lorrain, F., White, H.C.: Structural equivalence of individuals in social networks. J. Math. Sociol. **1**(1), 49–80 (1979)
10. Sha, C., Fuxi, Z.: A dynamic link prediction method for networks based on hybrid similarity metrics. Small Microcomput. Syst. **37**(08), 1798–1801 (2016)
11. Rong, Y., Yurong, S., Fanrong, M.: A link prediction method based on weighted network topology weights. Comput. Sci. **47**(05), 265–270 (2020)
12. Yong, Y.: Link prediction algorithm based on clustering coefficients and node centrality. J. Tsinghua Univ. **62**(01), 98–104 (2022)
13. Ahmed, A.: Distributed large-scale natural graph factorization. In: Proceedings of the 22nd International Conference on World Wide Web, pp. 37–48 (2013)
14. Ma, X., Sun, P., Wang, Y.: Graph regularized nonnegative matrix factorization for temporal link prediction in dynamic networks. Phys. A **496**, 121–136 (2018)
15. Perozzi, B., Al-Rfou, R., Skiena, S.: DeepWalk: online learning of social representations. In: Proceedings of the 20th ACM SIGKDD International Conference on Knowledge Discovery and Data Mining, pp. 701–710 (2014)
16. Tang, J., Qu, M., Wang, M.: LINE: large-scale information network embedding. In: Proceedings of the 24th International Conference on World Wide Web, pp. 1067–1077 (2015)
17. Grover, A., Leskovec, J.: node2vec: scalable feature learning for networks. In: Proceedings of the 22nd ACM SIGKDD International Conference on Knowledge Discovery and Data Mining, pp. 855–864 (2016)
18. Chen, J., Zhang, J., Xu, X.: E-LSTM-D: a deep learning framework for dynamic network link prediction. IEEE Trans. Syst. Man Cybern. Syst. **51**(6), 3699–3712 (2019)
19. Lei, K., Qin, M., Bai, B.: GCN-GAN: a non-linear temporal link prediction model for weighted dynamic networks. In: IEEE INFOCOM 2019-IEEE Conference on Computer Communications, pp. 388–396. IEEE (2019)
20. Shu, J.: Link prediction based on 3D convolutional neural network. In: 2022 IEEE/CIC International Conference on Communications in China, pp. 156–161 (2022)
21. Linlan, L., Xiuyang, S., Yubin, C.: Opportunity network link prediction based on network representation learning. J. Beijing Univ. Posts Telecommun. **45**(04), 64–69+103 (2022)
22. Li, T., Zhang, J., Philip, S.Y.: Deep dynamic network embedding for link prediction. IEEE Access **6**, 29219–29230 (2018)
23. Sankar, A., Wu, Y., Gou, L.: DySAT: deep neural representation learning on dynamic graphs via self-attention networks. In: Proceedings of the 13th International Conference on Web Search and Data Mining, pp. 519–527 (2020)

FastAGEDs: Fast Approximate Graph Entity Dependency Discovery

Guangtong Zhou[1], Selasi Kwashie[2], Yidi Zhang[1], Michael Bewong[3],
Vincent M. Nofong[4], Junwei Hu[1], Debo Cheng[5], Keqing He[6], Shanmei Liu[1(✉)],
and Zaiwen Feng[1,7,8(✉)]

[1] College of Informatics, Huazhong Agricultural University, Wuhan, Hubei, China
{lsmei,Zaiwen.Feng}@mail.hzau.edu.cn
[2] AI & Cyber Futures Institute, Charles Sturt University, Bathurst, Australia
[3] School of Computing, Mathematics & Engineering, Charles Sturt University,
Wagga Wagga, Australia
[4] Department of Computer Science & Engineering,
University of Mines & Technology, Tarkwa, Ghana
[5] STEM, University of South Australia, Adelaide, Australia
[6] School of Computing Science, Wuhan University, Wuhan, Hubei, China
[7] Hubei Hongshan Laboratory, Huazhong Agricultural University,
Wuhan, Hubei, China
[8] Macro Agricultural Research Institute, Huazhong Agricultural University,
Wuhan, Hubei, China

Abstract. This paper studies the discovery of *approximate* rules in property graphs. First, we propose a semantically meaningful measure of error for mining graph entity dependencies (GEDs) that *almost* hold, to tolerate errors and inconsistencies that exist in real-world graphs. Second, we present a new characterisation of GED satisfaction, and devise a depth-first search strategy to traverse the search space of candidate GEDs efficiently. Further, we perform experiments to demonstrate the feasibility and scalability of our solution, FastAGEDs, with three real-world graphs. The results show FastAGEDs is effective and efficient for mining approximate GEDs in noisy and erroneous real-world graphs.

Keywords: graph entity dependency · approximate dependency · efficient algorithm · graph constraints

1 Introduction

In recent years, researchers have proposed integrity constraints (e.g., *keys* [7] and *functional dependencies* (FDs) [12]) for property graphs to specify various data semantics, and to address graph data quality and management issues. Graph entity dependencies (GEDs) [9,10] represent a new set of fundamental constraints that unify keys and FDs for property graphs. A GED φ over a property graph G is a pair, $\varphi = (Q[\bar{u}], X \to Y)$, specifying the dependency $X \to Y$ over *homomorphic matches* of the graph pattern $Q[\bar{u}]$ in G. Intuitively, since

F. Zhang et al. (Eds.): WISE 2023, LNCS 14306, pp. 451–465, 2023.
https://doi.org/10.1007/978-981-99-7254-8_35

graphs are schemaless, the graph pattern $Q[\bar{u}]$ identifies the set of entities in G over which the dependency $X \rightarrow Y$ should hold.

GEDs have various practical applications in data quality and management (cf. [9,10] for more details). For example, they have been extended for use in: fact checking in social media networks [24], entity resolution in graphs and relations [23,28], consistency checking [11], amongst others. Like other data integrity constraints, the automatic discovery of GEDs is paramount for their adoption and practical use. Indeed, there is a growing literature [2,8,25] on the discovery problems of keys [2], GFDs [8], and GEDs [25]. However, these existing works focus on the discovery of dependencies that fully hold. Unfortunately, the existence of errors, exceptions and ambiguity in real-world data inhibits the discovery of semantically meaningful and useful graph data rules.

Thus, in this paper, we investigate the automatic mining of GEDs that *almost* hold – a well-suited rule discovery problem for real-world property graphs. The main contributions of this paper are summarised as follows. First, we introduce and formalise the approximate GED discovery problem via a new measure of error for GEDs based on its semantics. Second, we propose a novel and efficient algorithm, FastAGEDs, to find approximate GEDs in large graphs. We introduce a new characterisation of GED satisfaction by extending the notions of *disagree* and *necessary sets* to graph dependencies; and we develop an efficient depth-first search strategy for effective traversal of the space of candidate GEDs, enabling fast discovery of both full and approximate GEDs. Third, we perform extensive experiments on real-world graphs to demonstrate the feasibility and scalability of our discovery solution in large graphs.

Related Works. The discovery of approximate data dependencies is not new in the database and data mining communities, particularly, in the relational data setting. Volumes of work exist on the discovery of approximate functional dependencies (FDs) [3,15,16,19,29–31] and its numerous extensions (e.g., conditional FDs [14,27,32], distance-based FDs [5,17,20–22,26], etc.). The general goal is to find a reduced set of valid dependencies that (almost) hold over the given input data. However, this is a challenging and often intractable problem for most dependencies, including GEDs. The difficulties, in the GED case, arise due to four factors: a) the presence of graph patterns as topological constraints; b) the LHS/RHS sets of GEDs have three possible literals; and c) the implication and validation analyses of GEDs are shown to be intractable (see [9] for details); and d) the data may contain errors and inconsistencies.

The closest works in the literature to ours are in [8] and [25]. However, both works consider the discovery of *fully satisfied dependencies* in property graphs. Indeed, [8] presents both sequential and parallel algorithms for mining graph functional dependencies [12] via a fix-parameterization; and [25] employs graph partitioning techniques to speed up its scope discovery. Contrary to our depth-first search strategy, [8] uses a vertical and horizontal spawning of generation trees whiles [25] uses a level-wise lattice search to model and search candidate rules. Furthermore, we adapt the notion of *necessary sets* to characterise validity of rules whereas the concepts of *partition and equivalence class* are used in [25], and computation of covers are used in [8].

2 Preliminaries

This section presents basic definitions and notions used throughout the paper, a recall of the syntax and semantics of GEDs, as well as an overview of approximate satisfaction of dependencies.

2.1 Basic Definitions and Notions

The definitions of *property graph, graph pattern* and *match* of graph patterns follow those in [9,10]. We use alphabets $\mathbf{A}, \mathbf{L}, \mathbf{C}$ to be denote the countably infinite universal sets of *attributes, labels* and *constants* respectively.

Graph. We consider a directed property graph $G = (V, E, L, F_A)$, where: (1) V is a finite set of nodes; (2) E is a finite set of edges, given by $E \subseteq V \times \mathbf{L} \times V$, in which (v, l, v') is an edge from node v to node v' with label $l \in \mathbf{L}$; (3) each node $v \in V$ has a special attribute *id* denoting its identity, and a label $L(v)$ drawn from $\mathbf{L}$; (4) every node v, has an associated list $F_A(v) = [(A_1, c_1), ..., (A_n, c_n)]$ of attribute-value pairs, where $c_i \in \mathbf{C}$ is a constant, $A_i \in \mathbf{A}$ is an attribute of v, written as $v.A_i = c_i$, and $A_i \neq A_j$ if $i \neq j$.

Graph Pattern. A graph pattern, denoted by $Q[\bar{u}]$, is a directed graph $Q[\bar{u}] = (V_Q, E_Q, L_Q)$, where: (a) V_Q and E_Q represent the set of pattern nodes and pattern edges respectively; (b) L_Q is a label function that assigns a label to each node $v \in V_Q$ and each edge $e \in E_Q$; and (c) $\bar{u}$ is all the nodes, called (pattern) variables in V_Q. All labels are drawn from $\mathbf{L}$, including the wildcard "$*$" as a special label. Two labels $l, l' \in \mathbf{L}$ are said to *match*, denoted $l \asymp l'$ iff: (a) $l = l'$; or (b) either l or l' is "$*$".

A **match** of a graph pattern $Q[\bar{u}]$ in a graph G is a homomorphism h from Q to G such that: (a) for each node $v \in V_Q$, $L_Q(v) \asymp L(h(v))$; and (b) each edge $e = (v, l, v') \in E_Q$, there exists an edge $e' = (h(v), l', h(v'))$ in G, such that $l \asymp l'$. We denote the set of all matches of $Q[\bar{u}]$ in G by $H(\bar{u})$[1]. An example of a graph, graph patterns and their matches are presented below in Example 1.

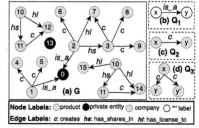

Fig. 1. Example: (a) graph; (b)–(d) graph patterns

Example 1 (Graph, Graph Pattern & Matches). Figure 1 (a) shows a simple graph; and in Fig. 1, (b)–(d) are examples of three graph patterns. We present the semantics of each graph pattern and its corresponding homomorphic matches in G as follows: i) $Q_1[x, y]$ describes an "is a" relationship between two generic

---

[1] simply H when the context is clear.

("*" labelled) nodes x and y. The list of matches of this pattern in the example graph is $H_1(x, y) = [\{1, 0\}, \{2, 0\}]$. ii) $Q_2[x, y]$ depicts a company node x with a create relation with a product node y, its matches in G : $H_2(x, y) = [\{1, 4\}\{1, 5\}\{2, 6\}, \{3, 7\}, \{3, 8\}, \{3, 9\}, \{11, 12\}, \{11, 14\}]$. iii) $Q_3[x, y, y']$ specifies a company node x with a create relation with two product nodes y, y'. Thus, matches in G are $H_3(x, y, y') = [\{1, 4, 5\}, \{3, 7, 8\}, \{3, 7, 9\}, \{3, 8, 9\}]$.   □

2.2   Graph Entity Dependencies (GEDs)

Here, we recall the definition of graph entity dependency (GED) [9,10].

GED Syntax. A GED φ is a pair $(Q[\bar{u}], X \to Y)$, where $Q[\bar{u}]$ is a graph pattern, and X, Y are two (possibly empty) sets of *literals* in $\bar{u}$. A literal w of $\bar{u}$ is one of the following three constraints: (a) $x.A = c$, (b) $x.A = y.A'$, (c) $x.id = y.id$, where $x, y \in \bar{u}$, are pattern variables, $A, A' \in \mathbf{A}$, are non-*id* attributes, and $c \in \mathbf{C}$ is a constant. $Q[\bar{u}]$, and $X \to Y$ are referred to as the *pattern/scope* and *dependency* of φ respectively.

GED Semantics. Given a GED $\varphi = (Q[\bar{u}], X \to Y)$, a match $h(\bar{u})$ of $Q[\bar{u}]$ in G *satisfies* a literal w of $\bar{u}$, denoted by $h(\bar{u}) \models w$, if: (a) when w is $x.A = c$, then the attribute $h(x).A$ exists, and $h(x).A = c$; (b) when w is $x.A = y.A'$, then the attributes $h(x).A$ and $h(y).A'$ exist and have the same value; and (c) when w is $x.id = y.id$, then $h(x).id = h(y).id$.

A match $h(\bar{u})$ satisfies a set X of literals if $h(\bar{u})$ satisfies every literal $w \in X$, (similarly defined for $h(\bar{u}) \models Y$). We write $h(\bar{u}) \models X \to Y$ if $h(\bar{x}) \models X$ implies $h(\bar{x}) \models Y$.

A graph G satisfies GED φ, denoted by $G \models \varphi$, if for all matches $h(\bar{u})$ of $Q[\bar{u}]$ in G, $h(\bar{x}) \models X \to Y$. A graph, G, satisfies a set Σ of GEDs, denoted by $G \models \Sigma$, if for all $\varphi \in \Sigma$, $G \models \varphi$.

In Example 2, we illustrate the semantics of GEDs with the sample graph and graph patterns in Fig. 1.

Example 2 (Semantics of GEDs). We define exemplar GEDs over the sample graph in Fig. 1(a), using the graph patterns in Fig. 1(b)–(d):
1) $\varphi_1 : (Q_1[x, y], \emptyset \to x.A = y.A)$ – this GED states that for any match $h(x, y)$ of the pattern $Q_1[x, y]$ in G (i.e., x is_a y), if the node $h(y)$ has property A, then $h(x)$ must have same values as $h(y)$ on A.
2) $\varphi_2 : (Q_2[x, y], \emptyset \to y.creator = x.name)$ – for every match $h(x, y)$ of Q_2 in G (i.e., company $h(x)$ create product $h(y)$), then $h(y).creator$ and $h(x).name$ must have the same value.
3) $\varphi_3 : (Q_3[x, y, y'], \emptyset \to y.creator = y'.creator)$ – this states for any match $h(x, y, y')$ in G (i.e., the company $h(x)$ create two products $h(y, y')$), then y, y' must have same value on their property/attribute *creator*.

2.3   Approximate Satisfaction of Dependencies

In the relational data model, there exists an extensive research on dependencies that almost hold due to their practical relevance in many real-world applications. For instance, several measures have been proposed to quantify the extent of dependence that exists between two sets of attributes/literals, using information theoretic ideas [13,18,35], probabilistic [34] and non-probabilistic approaches [16]. We refer interested readers to [37] for a recent comparative study of the subject.

This work attempts to present an intuitive, computationally efficient and effective measure of the degree of dependence for graph dependencies (GEDs, in particular). Thus, we extend the definition of an error measure in [16] based on the semantics of graph dependencies for approximating dependencies in graphs.

Error Measure for GEDs. Consider the set $H(\bar{u})$ of matches of the graph pattern $Q[\bar{u}]$ in a graph G. We say a match $h \in H$ *violates* a dependency $X \to Y$ over $Q[\bar{u}]$ if: $h \models X$, but $h \not\models Y$. However, intuitively, a dependency $X \to Y$ holds over $Q[\bar{u}]$ in G if and only if there are no violating matches in H. Hence we define an error measure e_3—*analogous to g_3 in* [16]—to be the minimum number of matches to be eliminated to obtain satisfaction.

Let E_3 be the number of matches that need to be eliminated from H for $X \to Y$ to hold, expressed as:

$$E_3(X \to Y, H) = |H| - max\{|J| \mid J \subseteq H, J \models X \to Y\}.$$

The e_3 error measure for graph dependencies is given in Eqs. 1 as:

$$e_3(X \to Y, H) = E_3/(|H| - |adom(X)|), \tag{1}$$

where $adom(X)^2$ is the active domain of literals over X. We remark that, the denominator of e_3 is different from that of g_3; and based on the observation in [13] that the numerator is upper bounded, it is consistent with the revised g_3' definition in [37]. e_3 ranges from 0 to 1; a value of 0 denotes full satisfaction of the dependency and a value of 1 shows an invalid dependency. Any value in between 0 and 1 indicates an approximate satisfaction of the dependency.

We define approximate GED w.r.t. e_3 and an error threshold $\epsilon \in [0,1]$ as follows in Definition 1.

Definition 1 (Approximate GED). *Let ϵ be a user-specified error threshold. A GED $\sigma : (Q[\bar{u}], X \to Y)$ is an approximate GED, iff: $e_3(X \to Y, H(\bar{u})) \leq \epsilon$.*

Suppose the pseudo-relational table in Fig. 2 represents the attribute values of matches of pattern Q_3 in G (from Fig. 1). We illustrate, in Example 3, examples of approximate GEDs based on e_3.

Example 3 (Measuring Error of Graph Dependencies). Consider the GEDs $\sigma_4 :$ $(Q_3[x, y, y'], X_1 \to X_2)$, and $\sigma_5 : (Q_3[x, y, y'], X_3 \to X_1)$, where X_1 is $\{y.\text{year} = y'.\text{released}\}$, X_2 is $\{y.\text{name} = y'.\text{name}\}$, and X_3 is $\{x.\text{name} = \text{EA}\}$. We compute $e_3(\sigma_4, H) = \frac{4-3}{4-2} = 0.5$ – requires removal of only match (h_1) and $|adom(X_1)| = 2$; and $e_3(\sigma_5, H) = \frac{4-2}{4-1} = 0.667$ – requires removal of two matches (h_3, h_4) and $|adom(X_3)| = 1$.   □

---

² the max. $|adom(X)|$ of variable literals is 2, whereas that of constant literals is 1.

Pattern variables	x		y					y'			
Attributes Matches	id	Name (A1)	id	Name (A2)	Genre (A3)	Year (A4)	Price (A5)	id	Name (A2)	Category (A3)	Released (A4)	Cost (A5)
h1	1	GL	4	AF9	Racing	2018	$50	5	AF11	Racing	2018	$55
h2	3	EA	7	F20	Soccer	2019	$55	8	F20	Soccer	2019	$60
h3	3	EA	7	F20	Soccer	2019	$55	9	F21	Soccer	2020	-
h4	3	EA	8	F20	Soccer	2019	$60	9	F21	Soccer	2020	-

Fig. 2. A pesudo-relation of matches of Q_3 in G (cf. Fig. 1)

3   Problem Formulation

The problem of mining GEDs is studied in [25]. In this section, we recall relevant notions and definition on the discovery of GEDs, and extend the problem to the approximate satisfaction scenario.

Given a property graph G, the general GED discovery problem is to find a *minimal cover* set of GEDs that hold over G. Thus, intuitively, the approximate GED discovery is to find a minimal cover set of GEDs that almost hold, based on a given error measure and error threshold. In the following, we formulate and present a more formal definition of the problem.

3.1   Persistent, Reduced, and Minimal GEDs

In rule discovery, it is paramount to return a succinct and non-redundant set of rules. Thus, in line with the data dependency discovery literature [5,8,25,27], we are interested in a cover set of *non-trivial* and *non-redundant* dependencies over *persistent* graph patterns.

Persistent Graph Patterns. Let $M = \{m_1, \cdots, m_k\}$ be the set of isomorphisms of a pattern $Q[\bar{u}]$ to a graph G; and $D(v) = \{m_1(v), \cdots, m_k(v)\}$ be the set containing the distinct nodes in G whose functions $m_1, \cdots, m_k$ map a node $v \in V$.

The minimum image based support[3] (MNI) [4] of Q in G, denoted by $mni(Q, G)$, is defined as:

$$mni(Q, G) = min\{x \mid x = |D(v)|, \ \forall \ v \in V\}.$$

We say a graph pattern $Q[\bar{u}]$ is *persistent* (i.e., *frequent*) in a graph G, if $mni(Q, G) \geq \tau$, where $\tau \in \mathbb{N}$ is a user-specified minimum MNI threshold.

Trivial GEDs. We say a GED $\varphi : (Q[\bar{u}], X \rightarrow Y)$ is *trivial* if: (a) the set of literals in X cannot be satisfied (i.e., X evaluates to `false`); or (b) Y is derivable from X (i.e., $\forall \ w \in Y$, w can be derived from X by transitivity of the equality operator). We are interested in mining only non-trivial GEDs.

---

[3] we adopt this metric due to its efficiency and anti-monotonic property.

Reduced GEDs. Given two patterns $Q[\bar{u}] = (V_Q, E_Q, L_Q)$ and $Q'[\bar{u}'] = (V'_{Q'}, E'_{Q'}, L'_{Q'})$, $Q[\bar{u}]$ is said to *reduce* $Q'[\bar{u}']$, denoted as $Q \ll Q'$ if: (a) $V_Q \subseteq V'_{Q'}$, $E_Q \subseteq E'_{Q'}$; or (b) L_Q upgrades some labels in $L'_{Q'}$ to wildcards. That is, Q is a less restrictive topological constraint than Q'.

Given two GEDs, $\varphi = (Q[\bar{u}], X \rightarrow w)$ and $\varphi' = (Q'[\bar{u}'], X' \rightarrow w')$. φ is said to *reduce* φ', denoted by $\varphi \ll \varphi'$, if: (a) $Q \ll Q'$; and (b) $X \subseteq X'$ and $w = w'$.

Thus, we say a GED φ is **reduced** in a graph G if: (a) $G \models \varphi$; and for any φ' such that $\varphi' \ll \varphi$, $G \not\models \varphi'$. We say a GED φ is **minimal** if it is both non-trivial and reduced.

3.2 Problem Definition

In this paper, we propose and study the approximate GED discovery problem.

Definition 2 (Approximate GED Discovery Problem). *Given a property graph, G, a user-specified MNI threshold, $\tau \in \mathbb{N}$, and e_3 error threshold, $\epsilon \in [0, 1]$. The approximate GED discovery is to find a set Σ of all minimal GEDs in G, such that for each $\sigma : (Q[\bar{u}], X \rightarrow Y) \in \Sigma$, we have: a) $mni(Q, G) \geq \tau$ and b) $e_3(X \rightarrow Y, H) \leq \epsilon$.* $\square$

4   Fast Approximate GED Mining

A GED specifies attribute dependencies over topological patterns in a graph. Thus, we first, examine the discovery of the graph patterns (Subsect. 4.1) which shall serve as the "scope" for the attribute dependencies discovery (Subsect. 4.2). A simplified pseudo-code of our solution, FastAGEDs, is presented in Algorithm 1.

Algorithm 1: FastAGEDs(G, τ, ϵ)

Data: Property graph, G
Input: MNI threshold, τ; error threshold, ϵ
Output: A minimal cover set $\Sigma \models G$ s.t.
$$\forall \, \sigma \in \Sigma : mni(\sigma.Q) \geq \tau \wedge e_3(\sigma) \leq \epsilon.$$
/* find & prune freq. graph patterns */
1 $\mathcal{Q} \leftarrow \mathsf{GraMi}(G, \tau)$
2 $\mathcal{Q}' \leftarrow reduce(\mathcal{Q})$
/* mine approx. GEDs over patterns */
3 **for** $Q \in \mathcal{Q}'$ **do**
4 $\quad H(Q, G) \leftarrow match(Q, G)$
5 $\quad \Sigma_Q \leftarrow mineDep(H(Q, G), \epsilon)$
6 $\quad \Sigma = \Sigma \cup \Sigma_Q$

7 **return** Σ

4.1   Graph Pattern (Scope) Discovery

Here, we present a brief discussion on the discovery of frequent graph patterns as the "scopes" or loose-schema over which we mine the attribute dependencies. We do not claim novelty of contribution on this task – which is a well-studied topic in the data mining and database literature, e.g., [1, 6, 36].

In this work, we adopt the efficient MNI-based technique, GRAMI [6], to find τ-frequent graph patterns as the scopes for our dependencies (line 1 of Algorithm 1); and employ the pruning strategies in [25] to return a set of reduced graph patterns (line 2). Next, for every reduced pattern Q, we find its homomorphic matches in G using the efficient worst-case optimal join based algorithm in [33] (i.e., line 4 in Algorithm 1). We then mine the dependencies over the set of matches of each reduced graph patterns in the following.

4.2 Dependency Mining

Let $\mathcal{Q}$ be the set of reduced τ-frequent graph patterns in a property graph G. We mine a minimal cover set, $\Sigma(Q, G, \epsilon)$, of approximate GEDs for each pattern $Q \in \mathcal{Q}$ in G based on a user-specified minimum threshold ϵ in G (lines 3–6 of Algorithm 1).

A Novel GED Characterisation. We present a novel characterisation of GEDs satisfaction based on the concept of *disagree set*, first introduced in [30,31] for relational functional dependency discovery.

Let $H(Q[\bar{u}], G)$ be the homomorphic matches of $Q[\bar{u}] \in \mathcal{Q}$ in the input graph G. We introduce the concepts of *item/itemset*, to map onto constant, variable, and id literals over the attributes of pattern variables $x, y \in \bar{u}$ in Q as follows.

Definition 3 (Item, Itemset, & Itemset Satisfaction). *Let an item-name, α, be an attribute of a pattern variable $x \in \bar{u}$ of a graph pattern Q. An item is a triple, consisting of item-name, pattern variable(s) $u \subseteq \bar{u}$, and constant $c \in \mathbf{C}$, denoted by $\alpha[u; c]$. An itemset, $X = \{\alpha_1[u_1; c_1], \cdots, \alpha_n[u_n; c_n]\}$, is a set of items with unique item-names. We say a match $h \in H$ satisfies an itemset X iff: $h(u_i) \models \alpha_i[u_i; c_i], \forall \alpha_i[u_i; c_i] \in X$.* □

An item $\alpha[u; c]$ over $\bar{u}$ of Q uniquely maps to constant, variable, and id literals of w of $\bar{u}$, respectively, as follows:

- when w is $x.A = c$, then its item is $\alpha[x; c]$
- when w is $x.A_1 = y.A_2$, then its item is $\alpha_{12}[x, y; \_]$
- when w is $x.\mathrm{id} = y.\mathrm{id}$, then its item is $\mathrm{id}[x, y; \_]$.

Thus, given a graph pattern $Q[\bar{u}] \in \mathcal{Q}$, we define constant items for all attributes of pattern variables $x \in \bar{u}$, and variable item over pattern variable pairs of the same kind $x, y \in \bar{u}$.

Definition 4 (Disagree and Necessary Sets). *Given the set of matches H of $Q[\bar{u}]$ in G:*

- *the disagree set, $D(h)$, of a match $h \in H$ is given by: $D(h) = \{\alpha[u; c] \mid h \not\models \alpha[u; c]\}$.*
- *the necessary set of an item, $\alpha[u; c]$, is defined as*

$$nec(\alpha[u; c]) = \{D(h) \setminus \alpha[u; c] \mid h \in H, \alpha[u; c] \in D(h)\}.$$ □

Let $\mathcal{I}$ denote the set of all items over a graph pattern $Q[\bar{u}]$, and $P(\mathcal{I})$ be the power set of $\mathcal{I}$. Given $M \subseteq \mathcal{I}, X \subseteq P(\mathcal{I})$, the set M **covers** X if and only if, for all $Y \in X$, we have $Y \cap M \neq \emptyset$. Furthermore, M is a minimal cover for X if there exists no $M' \subset M$ which covers X.

Pattern variables	x	y, y'				
Items Matches	$A_1[x; EA]$	$id[y, y'; \_]$	$A_2[y, y'; \_]$	$A_3[y; Soccer]$	$A_3[y, y'; \_]$	$A_4[y, y'; \_]$
h1	0	0	0	0	1	1
h2	1	0	1	1	1	1
h3	1	0	0	1	1	0
h4	1	0	0	1	1	0

Fig. 3. An example disagree table of items over Q_3

Lemma 1 (GED Characterisation). *Given the itemset $X \subseteq \mathcal{I}$ and an item $\alpha[u; c] \notin X$ over $Q[\bar{u}]$, $X \to \alpha[u; c]$ holds over H iff: X covers $nec(\alpha[u; c])$.* □

Thus, we reduce the minimal cover of GEDs discovery for a pattern $Q[\bar{u}]$ to the problem of finding the minimal covers for all $nec(\alpha[u; c])$, for every item $\alpha[u; c] \in \mathcal{I}$.

Construction of Disagree Sets. From the foregoing, a fast generation of the disagree and necessary sets is crucial. We construct a binary relation $\mathcal{B}(\mathcal{I}, H)$ of matches H over the set $\mathcal{I}$ of items over pattern variables in $Q[\bar{u}]$, based on the pseudo-relation of H. Given $\mathcal{I}$ and H, for each $h \in H$ and $\alpha[u; c] \in \mathcal{I}$

$$\mathcal{B}(h(\alpha[u; c])) := \begin{cases} 1, & \text{if } h \models \alpha[u; c] \\ 0, & \text{otherwise.} \end{cases} \tag{2}$$

We construct the disagree set $D(h)$ for all $h \in H$, and consequently, the necessary set $nec(\alpha[u; c])$ for all items $\alpha[u; c] \in \mathcal{I}$ with a single scan of the relation $\mathcal{B}(\mathcal{I}, H)$.

Example 4 (Disagree & Necessary Sets). Using the running example, the binary relation of Fig. 2 is presented in Fig. 3, for a select set of items, using Eq. 2. The ensuing disagree sets of the matches are as follows[4]:

$$D(h_1) = \{a_1, id, a_2, a_3^1\}; \qquad D(h_2) = \{id\};$$

$$D(h_3) = \{id, a_2, a_4\}; \qquad D(h_4) = \{id, a_2, a_4\}.$$

And, the necessary sets of the items are:

$$D(id) = \{\{a_1, a_2, a_3^1\}, \{a_2, a_4\}\}; \qquad D(a_1) = \{\{id, a_2, a_3^1\}\};$$

$$D(a_2) = \{\{a_1, id, a_3^1\}, \{id, a_4\}\}; \qquad D(a_3^1) = \{\{a_1, id, a_2\}\}$$

$$D(a_4) = \{\{id, a_2\}\}.$$

□

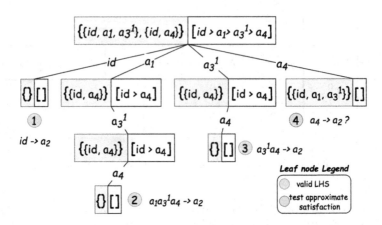

Fig. 4. FastAGEDs DFS Lattice for $A_2[y, y; \_]$

Search Strategy. The space of candidate itemsets for a given item $\alpha[u; c]$ is $P(\mathcal{I} \setminus \alpha[u; c])$, which is clearly exponential to the size $|\mathcal{I}|$ (i.e., $2^{|\mathcal{I}|-1}$). Thus, the necessary set, $nec(\alpha[u; c])$, reduces the candidate left hand sides (LHSs) of $\alpha[u; c]$. Specifically, to find all valid LHSs of a given item $\alpha[u; c]$, it suffices to find the set of all covers of $nec'(\alpha[u; c])$, where:

$$nec'(\alpha[u; c]) = \{D \in nec(\alpha[u; c]) \mid \nexists\, D' \subset D \in nec(\alpha[u; c])\}.$$

We construct and traverse the lattice of candidate itemsets for a given item $\alpha[u; c]$ with its minimal necessary set $nec'(\alpha[u; c])$ using a depth-first, left-to-right search strategy. Each node in the lattice consists of two elements: the necessary set (enclosed in "{}"), and its constituent items (in "[]"). We order constituent items at a node in decreasing order of appearance in the necessary itemsets, and break ties lexicographically. The root node of the search tree is set to $nec'(\alpha[u; c])$. Each node has up to the number of unique items in its constituent set, and an edge to a child node is labelled by its corresponding item. The necessary set of a child node is the set of itemsets in $nec'(\alpha[u; c])$ *not* covered thus far.

There are two possible cases of leaf nodes: (a) both node elements are empty; and (b) only the constituent items set is empty. The resulting branches of these cases correspond to valid LHS and invalid LHS respectively. For case (a), we check the minimality of the rules. For case (b), we will determine whether the error value of the rule is less than the specified error threshold. If it is, we will then check the minimality of the rule.

Example 5 (Find Minimum Cover). The depth-first search (DFS) tree for candidate RHS $A_2[y, y; \_]$ (i.e., a_2) is presented in Fig. 4. The leaf nodes $1, 2, 3$ produce valid GEDs with full satisfaction, whereas leaf node 4 results in an invalid GED.

---

[4] for brevity, we represent items by their lowercase letters, e.g. a_1 is $A_1[x; EA]$, a_3^1 is $A_3[y; Soccer]$.

Thus, we test such nodes for approximate satisfaction based on the specified error threshold. For instance, let $\epsilon = 0.25$; we compute $e_3(Q_3[x, y, y'], a_4 \rightarrow a_2) = \frac{1}{2}$. Thus, leaf node 4 does *not* produce an approximate GED – unless $\epsilon \geq 0.5$.   □

5 Experiments

We next present the experimental study of our algorithm FastAGEDs for discovering minimal GEDs. We conducted experiments under different error threshold and numbers of attributes to investigate the effects on the scalability and the number of minimal GEDs mined.

5.1 Experimental Settings

All the proposed algorithms in this work are implemented in Java; and the experiments were run on a 2.20GHz Intel Xeon processor computer with 128GB of memory running Linux OS.

Table 1. Summary of the data sets

Graph	#Nodes (N)	#Edges (E)	#N Types	#E Types
DBLP	300K	800K	3	3
IMDB	300K	650K	5	8
YAGO4	380K	800K	7764	83

We used three real-world property graphs in our empirical evaluation: a) IMDB[5] b) YAGO4[6] c) DBLP[7]. We sampled comparable sizes and properties of the three datasets, as summarised in Table 1.

5.2 Feasibility and Scalability of Proposal

We set the MNI threshold $\tau = 2$ in all experiments, corresponding to the worst case frequent graph pattern mining scenario.

Exp-a. We first evaluate the time performance of our algorithm for mining (approximate) GEDs in the three datasets, at different error rates (i.e., $\epsilon = 0.0, 0.15, 0.30$) and for varying number of attributes. The results are presented in Fig. 5 a) – c) for the DBLP, IMDB and YAGO4 datasets respectively. The results indicate that the time cost increases considerably as the number of attributes increases, regardless of the maximum error we set. Additionally, GED discovery in the DBLP data is the most efficient as it produces the least number of matches for its frequent patterns compared to the other data sets.

Exp-b. We next report the correlations between the error threshold and the number of mined GEDs for differing number of attributes (cf. Fig. 5d) – f)). In this group of experiments, we set a series of thresholds to conduct this experiments, with a range of threshold values from 0 to 0.3. In general, for a given error

---

[5] IMDB dataset. http://www.imdb.com/interfaces.
[6] YAGO4 dataset. https://www.mpi-inf.mpg.de/departments/databases-and-information-systems/research/yago-naga/yago/.
[7] DBLP dataset. https://dblp.uni-trier.de/xml/.

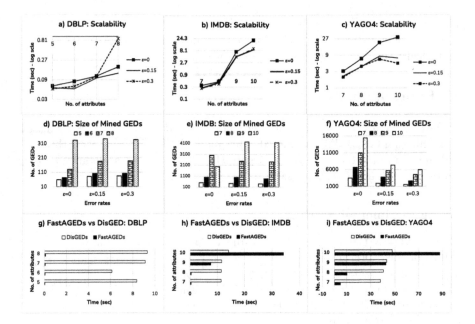

Fig. 5. FastAGEDs: Experimental Results

rate, the number of mined rules increase with increasing attribute size. However, the effect of an increased error rate for a fixed attribute size in any dataset differs. In exception of the YAGO4 data where there is a visible decreasing effect, the case is nuanced in the other datasets. The phenomenon in the YAGO4 datasets can be explained by its erroneousness – it is more dirty than the other datasets. Indeed, an increased error-rate returns more rules in principle, however, subsequent implication analysis results in pruning of more redundant rules. Thus, the resultant effect is a more succinct rule set.

Exp-c. Further, we fix the error threshold $\epsilon = 0$ and compare the performance of FastAGEDs to the only existing GED miner in the literature, DisGEDs [25]. Figure 5 g) – i) show the relative time performance of the two algorithms over the DBLP, IMDB, and YAGO4 datasets respectively, for varrying number of attributes. We observe that, in general, FastAGEDs significantly out-perform Dis-GEDs on all three datasets when number of attributes is less that 10. However, DisGEDs performs better when the number of attributes is 10.

5.3   Example of Mined Approximate GEDs: YAGO4

Here, we present examples of some approximate GEDs from the *YAGO4* dataset, with a discussion of their potential use in real-world data quality and data management applications. Figure 6 present the graph patterns of the exemplar rules.

Examples of rules in YAGO4. We present three (3) approximate GEDs:

- $\sigma_A : (Q_4[x_1, x_2], \emptyset \rightarrow x_1.\texttt{surname} = x_2.\texttt{surname}); \epsilon = 0.$
- $\sigma_B : (Q_5[x, y_1, y_2], y_1.\texttt{name} = y_2.\texttt{name} \wedge y_1.\texttt{dob} = y_2.\texttt{dob} \rightarrow y_1.\texttt{id} = y_2.\texttt{id}); \epsilon = 0.02.$
- $\sigma_C : (Q_6[x_1, x_2, y], y_1.\texttt{datePublished} = y_2.\texttt{datePublished} \rightarrow y_1.\texttt{id} = y_2.\texttt{id}); \epsilon = 0.12.$

The first GED, σ_A, is an example of a fully satisfied GED ($\epsilon = 0$). It simply states that for any match of Q_4 in the graph, the two person nodes, x_1, x_2, with parent-child relationships have the same **surname**. The rules, σ_B and σ_C, are examples of approximate GEDs (with non-zero errors). Both can be useful rules for de-duplication (or entity resolution) as they specify constraints for matching/linking **person** and **movie** nodes, respectively, in the YAGO4 graph.

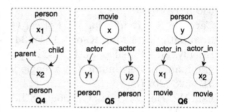

Fig. 6. Graph Patterns of Exemplar Approximate GEDs

6 Conclusion

This paper introduces and studies the approximate discovery problem for graph entity dependencies (GEDs). We propose a measure of error based on the semantics of GEDs, and characterise the satisfaction via the concepts of necessary and cover sets. The developed algorithm, FastAGEDs, uses a depth-first search strategy to traverse the candidate space of GEDs to find both full and approximate GEDs. Finally, we show that FastAGEDs is effective and scalable via an empirical evaluation over three real-world graphs.

Acknowledgment. This research project was supported in part by the following grant schemes: the Major Project of Hubei Hongshan Laboratory under Grant 2022HSZD031; the Innovation fund of Chinese Marine Defense Technology Innovation Center under Grant JJ-2021-722-04; the open funds of Hubei Three Gorges Laboratory, the Fundamental Research Funds for the Chinese Central Universities under Grant 2662023XXPY004, 2662022JC004; the open funds of the National Key Laboratory of Crop Genetic Improvement under Grant ZK202203, Huzhong Agricultural University; and the Inner Mongolia Key Scientific and Technological Project under Grant 2021SZD0099.

References

1. Aberger, C.R., Lamb, A., Tu, S., Nötzli, A., Olukotun, K., Ré, C.: Emptyheaded: a relational engine for graph processing. ACM Trans. Database Syst. (TODS) **42**(4), 1–44 (2017)
2. Alipourlangouri, M., Chiang, F.: Keyminer: discovering keys for graphs. In: VLDB Workshop TD-LSG (2018)

3. Bleifuß, T., et al.: Approximate discovery of functional dependencies for large datasets. In Proceedings of the 25th ACM International on Conference on Information and Knowledge Management, pp. 1803–1812 (2016)

4. Bringmann, B., Nijssen, S.: What is frequent in a single graph? In: Washio, T., Suzuki, E., Ting, K.M., Inokuchi, A. (eds.) PAKDD 2008. LNCS (LNAI), vol. 5012, pp. 858–863. Springer, Heidelberg (2008). https://doi.org/10.1007/978-3-540-68125-0_84

5. Caruccio, L., Deufemia, V., Polese, G.: Mining relaxed functional dependencies from data. Data Min. Knowl. Disc. **34**(2), 443–477 (2020)

6. Elseidy, M., Abdelhamid, E., Skiadopoulos, S., Kalnis, P.: GRAMI: frequent subgraph and pattern mining in a single large graph. Proc. VLDB Endowment **7**(7), 517–528 (2014)

7. Fan, W., Fan, Z., Tian, C., Dong, X.L.: Keys for graphs. Proc. VLDB Endowment **8**(12), 1590–1601 (2015)

8. Fan, W., Chunming, H., Liu, X., Ping, L.: Discovering graph functional dependencies. ACM Trans. Database Syst. (TODS) **45**(3), 1–42 (2020)

9. Fan, W., Lu, P.: Dependencies for graphs. In: Proceedings of the 36th ACM SIGMOD-SIGACT-SIGAI Symposium on Principles of Database Systems, pp. 403–416 (2017)

10. Fan, W., Ping, L.: Dependencies for graphs. ACM Trans. Database Syst. (TODS) **44**(2), 1–40 (2019)

11. Fan, W., Ping, L., Tian, C., Zhou, J.: Deducing certain fixes to graphs. Proc. VLDB Endowment **12**(7), 752–765 (2019)

12. Fan, W., Wu, Y., Xu, J.: Functional dependencies for graphs. In: Proceedings of the 2016 International Conference on Management of Data, pp. 1843–1857 (2016)

13. Giannella, C., Robertson, E.: On approximation measures for functional dependencies. Inf. Syst. **29**(6), 483–507 (2004)

14. Golab, L., Karloff, H., Korn, F., Srivastava, D., Bei, Yu.: On generating near-optimal tableaux for conditional functional dependencies. Proc. VLDB Endowment **1**(1), 376–390 (2008)

15. Huhtala, Y., Kärkkäinen, J., Porkka, P., Toivonen, H.: TANE: an efficient algorithm for discovering functional and approximate dependencies. Comput. J. **42**(2), 100–111 (1999)

16. Kivinen, J., Mannila, H.: Approximate inference of functional dependencies from relations. Theoret. Comput. Sci. **149**(1), 129–149 (1995)

17. Koudas, N., Saha, A., Srivastava, D., Venkatasubramanian, S.: Metric functional dependencies. In: 2009 IEEE 25th International Conference on Data Engineering, pp. 1275–1278. IEEE (2009)

18. Kramer, S., Pfahringer, B.: E cient search for strong partial determinations. In: Proceedings of the International Conference on Knowledge Discover and Data Mining, pp. 371–378. Citeseer (1996)

19. Kruse, S., Naumann, F.: Efficient discovery of approximate dependencies. Proc. VLDB Endowment **11**(7), 759–772 (2018)

20. Kwashie, S., Liu, J., Li, J., Ye, F.: Mining differential dependencies: a subspace clustering approach. In: Wang, H., Sharaf, M.A. (eds.) ADC 2014. LNCS, vol. 8506, pp. 50–61. Springer, Cham (2014). https://doi.org/10.1007/978-3-319-08608-8_5

21. Kwashie, S., Liu, J., Li, J., Ye, F.: Conditional differential dependencies (CDDs). In: Morzy, T., Valduriez, P., Bellatreche, L. (eds.) ADBIS 2015. LNCS, vol. 9282, pp. 3–17. Springer, Cham (2015). https://doi.org/10.1007/978-3-319-23135-8_1

22. Kwashie, S., Liu, J., Li, J., Ye, F.: Efficient discovery of differential dependencies through association rules mining. In: Sharaf, M.A., Cheema, M.A., Qi, J. (eds.) ADC 2015. LNCS, vol. 9093, pp. 3–15. Springer, Cham (2015). https://doi.org/10.1007/978-3-319-19548-3_1

23. Kwashie, S., Liu, L., Liu, J., Stumptner, M., Li, J., Yang, L.: Certus: an effective entity resolution approach with graph differential dependencies (GDDs). Proc. VLDB Endowment **12**(6), 653–666 (2019)

24. Lin, P., Song, Q., Yinghui, W.: Fact checking in knowledge graphs with ontological subgraph patterns. Data Sci. Eng. **3**(4), 341–358 (2018)

25. Liu, D., et al.: An efficient approach for discovering graph entity dependencies (GEDs). arXiv preprint arXiv:2301.06264 (2023)

26. Liu, J., Kwashie, S., Li, J., Ye, F., Vincent, M.: Discovery of approximate differential dependencies. arXiv preprint arXiv:1309.3733 (2013)

27. Liu, J., Li, J., Liu, C., Chen, Y.: Discover dependencies from data-a review. IEEE Trans. Knowl. Data Eng. **24**(2), 251–264 (2010)

28. Ma, H., Alipourlangouri, M., Yinghui, W., Chiang, F., Pi, J.: Ontology-based entity matching in attributed graphs. Proc. VLDB Endowment **12**(10), 1195–1207 (2019)

29. Mandros, P., Boley, M., Vreeken, J.: Discovering reliable approximate functional dependencies. In Proceedings of the 23rd ACM SIGKDD International Conference on Knowledge Discovery and Data Mining, pp. 355–363 (2017)

30. Mannila, H., Räihä, K.J.: Dependency inference. In Proceedings of the 13th International Conference on Very Large Data Bases, pp. 155–158 (1987)

31. Mannila, H., Räihä, K.-J.: Algorithms for inferring functional dependencies from relations. Data Knowl. Eng. **12**(1), 83–99 (1994)

32. Medina, R., Nourine, L.: A unified hierarchy for functional dependencies, conditional functional dependencies and association rules. In: Ferré, S., Rudolph, S. (eds.) ICFCA 2009. LNCS (LNAI), vol. 5548, pp. 98–113. Springer, Heidelberg (2009). https://doi.org/10.1007/978-3-642-01815-2_9

33. Mhedhbi, A., Salihoglu, S.: Optimizing subgraph queries by combining binary and worst-case optimal joins. Proc. VLDB Endowment **12**(11)

34. Piatetsky-Shapiro, G.: Probabilistic data dependencies. In: Machine Discovery Workshop (Aberdeen, Scotland) (1992)

35. Reimherr, M., Nicolae, D.L.: On quantifying dependence: a framework for developing interpretable measures (2013)

36. Teixeira, C.H., Fonseca, A.J., Serafini, M., Siganos, G., Zaki, M.J., Aboulnaga, A.: Arabesque: a system for distributed graph mining. In: Proceedings of the 25th Symposium on Operating Systems Principles, pp. 425–440 (2015)

37. Weytjens, S.: Approximate functional dependencies: a comparison of measures and a relevance focused tool for discovery (2021)

Topological Network Field Preservation for Heterogeneous Graph Embedding

Jiale Xu, Ouxia Du, Siyu Liu, and Ya Li[✉]

College of Computer and Information Science, Southwest University Chongqing,
Chongqing 400715, China
swu_yali@163.com

Abstract. Heterogeneous graph (HG) embedding, aiming to represent the nodes in the graph as a low-dimensional vector form for further reasoning to better implement downstream tasks, has attracted considerable attention in recent years. Most existing HG embedding methods use the meta-paths to preserve the proximity or adapt graph neural networks (GNNs) to facilitate the message-passing process. However, these methods neglect to analyze the shape properties of nodes and the influence of each node from a topological perspective, thus cannot fully explore the information on higher-order connectivity of HG and be effectively support more complex tasks of network analysis. In this paper, a novel HG embedding model (TNFE) is proposed to capture the topological link structure and the higher-order interactive information between nodes simultaneously. Specifically, persistent homology is used to reconstruct the connection between nodes in HG. Then the neighborhoods of the nodes are aggregated based on a graph convolutional network. Moreover, modular topology centrality is defined to sample the topological network field structure of each node. Finally, multi-task learning task is built to preserve the topology connectivity and the topological network field proximity simultaneously. The extensive experiments on three real-world datasets show that our method outperforms the state-of-the-art approaches on node classification and clustering task.

Keywords: Heterogeneous graph · Topological data analysis · Graph representation learning · Higher-order interaction · Graph neural network

1 Introduction

Graph embedding represents the nodes in a graph as low-dimensional, real-valued, and dense vector forms, so that the obtained vector can be used for further reasoning to better implement graph task analysis [6]. Graph embedding is widely used in various real-world scenarios, such as node classification, link prediction, node clustering, and node retrieval/recommendation [22], etc. Therefore, graph embedding has been commonly adopted in graph analysis tasks and has been a promising research field. The current graph embedding

F. Zhang et al. (Eds.): WISE 2023, LNCS 14306, pp. 466–480, 2023.
https://doi.org/10.1007/978-981-99-7254-8_36

methods can be divided into homogeneous graph embedding and heterogeneous graph(HG) embedding. However, real-world graphs are mostly heterogeneous in nature, involving a wide variety of node types and relationship types [5], making homogeneous graph embedding incapable of modeling graph tasks well. Thus, HG embedding has attracted considerable attention in recent years.

The earlier HG embedding methods learn the node representation by preserving network proximity. Specifically, the link-preserving methods [18,19] use first-order and second-order information of HG to preserve the proximity of nodes and link structures. The meta-paths preservation methods [3,4,29] define various meta-paths that represent the tiny sub-structure of a graph to capture the rich semantic information of nodes. However, these methods require larger memory spaces to store the parameters and only have the ability of transductive learning. Some recent results [7,22] suggest that heterogeneous graph neural networks (HGNNs) need less memory space and can work on inductive setting. So many existing HG embedding methods aggregate heterogeneous neighbor information of nodes based on GNNs. Specifically, unsupervised methods [1,24,28,31] use the information of multiple edges or node attributes to capture the heterogeneity of graph structures and can be well generalized to other tasks. Semi-supervised methods [5,9,13,30] prefer to use attention mechanism to learn task-specific node embedding and have better performance than unsupervised HGNNs.

Although GNNs have shown superior capacity on dealing with HG, these methods still remain a number of challenging problems. First, many existing HGNNs ignore the topological and geometric properties of nodes. Understanding such data characteristics from a topological perspective opens possibilities for mathematically rigorous integration of higher-order connectivity and its interplay to the analysis of complex networks [27], which is essential for extracting effective node information and learning edge relationships from high-dimensional data in a real complex system. Furthermore, these methods ignore the influence and importance of each node in a network. With the progress and development of society, the information contained in nodes and the relationship of edges between nodes become more complex, and the interactions between nodes are more abundant. This higher-order role of interplay is useful for solving complex problems in the real world, which leads to another challenging problem, i.e., how to accurately capture the interplay relation between nodes in a complex network.

To address the above key challenges, we observed that the machinery of topological data analysis (TDA) can extract effective information from high-dimensional data without causing information loss [25] by analyzing the topological features of the data. TDA offers a mathematically rigorous machinery for analysis of graph shape properties to sufficiently extract and preserve higher-order relations of HG. So TDA is introduced to study the topological and geometric features of complex heterogeneous networks and capture the higher-order connectivity in complex networks. Moreover, in physics, the concepts of fields and potentials can be used to describe the influence exerted on the outside and the energy possessed by an object. So the modular topology centrality is defined based on fields and potentials to quantify the interaction between nodes and a novel heterogeneous graph embedding model (TNFE) is proposed to learn the higher-order structural and semantic information in complex HG.

Specifically, persistent homology in TDA is leveraged to reconstruct heterogeneous weighted graphs for better preserving the topological connection between nodes. The basic principle is that the higher topological similarity between neighbors of nodes, the closer relationship between them. On this basis, the topology connectivity proximity is preserved. In addition, the heterogeneous subgraphs of each node are sampled by defining the modular topology centrality, i.e., the topological network field. Then the topological network field proximity is preserved to capture the higher-order interaction information in complex networks. Finally, the final representation of the nodes is learned through multi-task learning.

The major contributions of this work are as follows:

- We design a novel representation method for heterogeneous graph reconstruction based on persistent homology, which integrates the key persistent information from neighbors and connectivity of nodes and thus facilitates node classification tasks.
- We propose a novel heterogeneous graph embedding model, in which topological network field structure sampling and higher-order connection structures preservation are designed to improve heterogeneous representation learning performance.
- Our node classification and node clustering experiments demonstrate the effectiveness of the proposed method from various aspects compared with state-of-the-art approaches on three real-world datasets.

2 Related Work

In this section, the recent research related to heterogeneous graph embedding will be reviewed, including proximity preservation and message-passing methods.

2.1 Proximity Preservation

The current proximity preservation algorithm can be divided into link-preserving methods and random walk methods. For link-preserving methods, LINE [19] embeds the network by preserving first-order and second-order proximity. AspEm [18] divides HG into multiple aspects so that the semantic information in each aspect is preserved. For random walk methods, Metapath2Vec [3] designs a meta-paths guided random walk and a heterogeneous skip-gram to preserve the proximity between nodes. HIN2Vec [4] jointly conducts multiple prediction training tasks based on target relation sets specified in the form of meta-paths. More recently, SR-RSC [29] learns the relation-based embeddings based on an attentive fusion module and the correlation between nodes and neighbor-graphs.

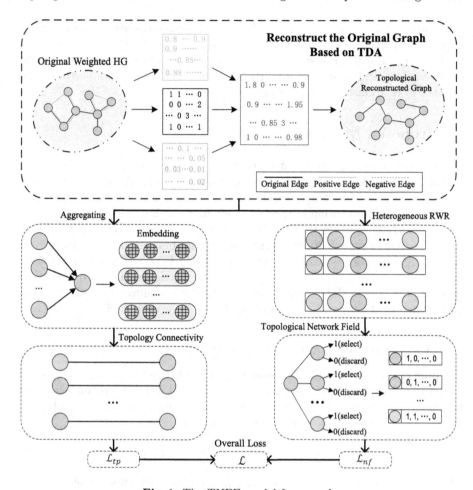

Fig. 1. The TNFE model framework

2.2 Message Passing

The current message-passing algorithms can be divided into unsupervised and semi-supervised methods. For unsupervised HGNNs, HetGNN [28] preserves the first-order and second-order proximity through the same and different types of aggregation. GATNE [1] utilizes multiple structures and attribute information of different nodes for embedding learning of multiple HG. HeCo [24] captures the information of meta-path and network schema based on contrastive learning. SELENE [31] designs a dual-channel embedding pipeline that encodes node information for learning on networks.

For semi-supervised HGNNs, MAGNN [5] utilizes attention mechanism for intra-metapath and inter-metapath aggregation. HCT [9] introduces an attention mechanism associated with node and edge types to handle graph heterogeneity. NSHE [30] samples network schema to depict the high-order structure information of different nodes. Meta-HGT [13] designs intra-hyperedge and inter-hyperedge aggregation to preserve high-order structures with diverse semantics.

However, these methods ignore the local topological properties of the observed data and cannot sufficiently mine the higher-order connectivity and interactive relationship in real complex networks.

3   Proposed Method

Given a heterogeneous weighted graph $\mathcal{G} = (\mathcal{V}, \mathcal{E})$ composed of a node set $\mathcal{V}$ and an edge set $\mathcal{E}$, the task of HG embedding is to learn the representation of nodes $h_{v_i} \in \mathbb{R}^{|\mathcal{V}| \times d}$ for all $v_i \in \mathcal{V}$. The representation dimension should be much smaller than the dimension of the adjacency matrix, that is, $d \ll |\mathcal{V}|$.

Figure 1 illustrates the framework of the proposed TNFE model. First, TNFE uses persistent homology to rewire the connectivity between nodes and preserves the topology relation proximity based on GNNs. Then the modular topology centrality of the node is defined to preserve the topological network field proximity. Finally, the model iteratively updates node embeddings via optimizing the aggregation of the topological connection loss and network field preserving loss.

3.1   Capturing the Topology Connectivity

Reconstruction of Heterogeneous Weighted Graphs. The first step of our model is to reconstruct the heterogeneous weighted graph based on persistent homology in TDA. For each node v_i, the weighted k-hop neighborhood subgraph $\mathcal{G}_{v_i}^k$ is used to generate the persistence diagram of nodes as:

$$PD\left(v_i\right) = \mathcal{D}\left(\mathcal{G}_{v_i}^k\right) = \mathcal{D}\left(\mathcal{N}_{v_i}^k, \, \mathcal{E}_{v_i}^k\right) \tag{1}$$

where $\mathcal{N}_{v_i}^k = \{v_j \mid \mathcal{P}_{ij} \le k, \forall v_j \ne v_i \in \mathcal{V}\}$ is the k-hop neighbor set of v_i, $\mathcal{P}_{ij}$ is the length of shortest path between v_i and v_j, k is the resolution threshold. Here we set $k = 2$. $\mathcal{E}_{v_i}^k = \{\mathcal{F}_s\left(u, v\right) \mid \forall u \ne v \in \mathcal{N}_{v_i}^k\}$ is the set of weights between nodes in $\mathcal{N}_{v_i}^k$, $\mathcal{F}_s\left(u, v\right) = \|f_u - f_v\|$ denotes the distance between node u and v, $\|\cdot\|$ is Euclidean distance, f_i is the feature vector of node i. There $\mathcal{D}(\cdot)$ denotes a function that converts a weighted k-hop neighborhood subgraph of the node to its corresponding persistence graph.

Then for local neighborhoods of all nodes, the p-Wasserstein distance [10, 25] is used to measure the topological shape similarity between the local neighborhoods of nodes as:

$$T_s\left(v_i, v_j\right) = W_p\left(v_i, v_j\right)^{-1} = W_p\left(PD\left(v_i\right), PD\left(v_j\right)\right)^{-1} \tag{2}$$

$$W_p\left(PD\left(v_i\right), PD\left(v_j\right)\right) = \left(\inf_{\gamma} \sum\nolimits_{x \in PD(v_i) \cup \Delta} \|x - \gamma(x)\|_{\infty}^p\right)^{1/p} \tag{3}$$

where $p \ge 1$, Δ denotes the set of all measures in $\mathcal{V} \times \mathcal{V}$ space, γ is taken over all bijective maps from $PD\left(v_i\right) \cup \Delta$ to $PD\left(v_j\right) \cup \Delta$. In our analysis we set $p = 1$.

Considering that the neighborhood of different types of nodes is quite different, the connection between nodes of the same type is reconstructed. The original heterogeneous weighted graph $\mathcal{G}_{topo} = (\mathcal{V}, \mathcal{E}^{tp})$ is reconstructed as:

$$
e_{v_i v_j}^{tp} = \begin{cases} e_{v_i v_j}^{ini} + \alpha_1 * T_s(v_i, v_j), & if\ W_p(v_i, v_j) \in [0, \mu_1] \\ e_{v_i v_j}^{ini} - \alpha_2 * T_s(v_i, v_j), & if\ W_p(v_i, v_j) \in [\mu_2, \infty] \\ e_{v_i v_j}^{ini}, & otherwise \end{cases} \tag{4}
$$

where $e_{v_i v_j}^{tp}$ is the element in $\mathcal{E}^{tp}$ for any $v_i, v_j \in \mathcal{V}$ with same type. $e_{v_i v_j}^{ini}$ is the weight between v_i and v_j in the original graph, α_1, α_2 are the topological balancing coefficient, and μ_1, μ_2 are the threshold that controls the topological relationship.

Note that if two nodes have no edge connected, but their neighbors have high shape similarity, then the edge between them is added, that is, $e_{v_i v_j}^{tp} = \alpha_1 * T_s(v_i, v_j)$. On the contrary, if they have edges connected, but the shape similarity of neighbors is so low, that is, $e_{v_i v_j}^{tp} = e_{v_i v_j}^{ini} - \alpha_2 * T_s(v_i, v_j) < 0$, then the edge between them is removed.

Preserving the Topological Relation Proximity. In this subsection, the topological relation proximity between nodes is captured in the new graph. It has been demonstrated that the pairwise similarity between nodes [2,19] is one of the most direct expressions in HG. We first update the feature representation of each node based on the topological side information, i.e.,

$$
f_{v_i}' = MLP\left(\psi\left(f_{v_i}, \sum_{v_j \in \mathcal{N}_{v_i}} \tau_{ij} \cdot f_{v_j}\right)\right) \tag{5}
$$

where f_{v_i} denotes the feature vector of nodes v_i. ψ is the aggregation function such as sum and mean. $\mathcal{N}_{v_i}$ is the set of neighbors of v_i in the reconstruction graph. τ_{ij} denotes the importance of different neighbors of v_i, which can be defined as:

$$
\tau_{ij} = \frac{exp\left(e_{v_i v_j}^{tp}\right)}{\sum_{v_k \in \mathcal{N}_{v_i}} exp\left(e_{v_i v_k}^{tp}\right)} \tag{6}
$$

where $e_{v_i v_j}^{tp}$ is the topological edge weight between v_i and v_j in $\mathcal{G}_{tp}$.

Then the graph convolution layer [11] can be defined as:

$$
H^{(l+1)} = \sigma\left(LH^{(l)}W^{(l)}\right) \tag{7}
$$

where $\sigma(\cdot)$ denotes the activation function. $L = D_{topo}^{-\frac{1}{2}}(A_{topo} + I)D_{topo}^{-\frac{1}{2}}$ is a Laplacian matrix, where A_{topo} is the topological reconstruction-based adjacency matrix, D_{topo} is a diagonal matrix where $(D_{topo})_{ii} = \sum_j (A_{topo})_{ij}$. For the first layer, $H^{(0)}$ is represented by the embedding of each node f_{v_i}'. Then the output of L-layer graph convolutional network h_{v_i} is the final embedding of node v_i.

The negative sampling [15] is leveraged to achieve efficient optimization and the loss can be defined as:

$$\mathcal{L}_{tp} = \frac{1}{|\mathcal{E}^{tp}|} \sum_{(v_i, v_j) \in \mathcal{E}^{tp}} [-log\delta(h_{v_j} \cdot h_{v_i}) - \sum_{m=1}^{N_s} \mathbb{E}_{v_{j'} \sim P_n(v)} log\delta(-h_{v_{j'}} \cdot h_{v_i})] \quad (8)$$

where $\delta(x) = 1/(1 + exp(-x))$, $P_n(v)$ is the noisy distribution, and N_s is the negative edge sampling rate.

3.2   Capturing Topological Network Field Structure

Modular Topology Centrality. In the real world, it can be considered that the influence and importance of each node are distinct due to the heterogeneity of different node features. Inspired by topology in mathematics and field theory in physics, we describe the interplay between nodes based on the node topological potential [12]. Then the modular topology centrality of a node in the network can be defined as:

$$C(v_i) = \frac{1}{n} \sum_{j=1}^{n} pro(v_j) \times e^{-\left(\frac{dt_{ij}^{net}}{\mathcal{I}}\right)^2} \quad (9)$$

$$dt_{ij}^{net} = \frac{\mathcal{P}_{ij}}{T_s(v_i, v_j)} \quad (10)$$

where n is the number of nodes in the specified network, $pro(v_j)$ denotes the inherent properties of v_j with rich physical meanings, and it can be defined by the degree centrality of v_j in this paper. $\mathcal{I}$ is the impact factor, which controls the range of influence of nodes in the network. dt_{ij}^{net} is the network distance between v_i and v_j, which reflects the intimacy between nodes. In a real network, it is not only related to the distance between nodes but also is affected by the topological similarity between nodes.

Topological Network Field Structure Sampling. Generally, the higher-order interaction information between nodes in the global network is richer and more comprehensive than the local neighborhoods of nodes. However, due to the uneven number of neighbors of each node, it is complex and time-consuming to save the interaction information of all node pairs in the entire network environment, and only focusing on local neighbors of nodes may lose some important information. Therefore, to preserve the higher-order interaction information between nodes, it is necessary to consider the role of nodes in both global and local networks.

Here a novel heterogeneous neighbor sampling strategy is proposed to sample all types of neighbors of nodes. We first design a type-based node sampling strategy based on the random walk with restart (RWR) [20]. The node v_i returns to the previous node with probability r and moves to neighbor nodes with probability $1 - r$. To ensure that all types of neighbors of v_i are selected, the probability from node v_i to the next node v_j can be defined as:

$$Pr\left(v_j|\mathcal{N}_{v_i}\right) = (1 - r)\lambda_{type}M^{type}\left(v_i, v_j\right) \tag{11}$$

where λ_{type} is the weight parameter that defines the probability when a certain type of neighbor is selected. The function $M^{type}(*)$ measures the attractiveness of v_j to v_i, which is defined as:

$$M^{type}\left(v_i, v_j\right) = \frac{e_{v_i v_j}^{tp}\,log\left(ID\left(v_j\right) + 1\right)}{\sum_{u \in N_{v_i}^{type}} e_{v_i u}^{tp}\,log\left(ID(u) + 1\right)} \tag{12}$$

where $ID(*)$ denotes the in-degree value of the node, $\mathcal{N}_{v_i}^{type}$ is the certain type of neighbor set of v_i.

Through running RWR iteratively, the set of heterogeneous neighbors of nodes for all types can be obtained, denoted as $S\left(v_i\right)$. Then the heterogeneous neighbors are filtered to obtain the topological network field set of nodes according to certain rules. We calculate the modular topology centrality of nodes in the global and local networks, respectively, and then constantly adjust the neighbor set by minimizing the centrality difference between nodes in the global and local networks. The objective function can be formulated as:

$$\min_{S_{new}(v_i)}\left|C_{global}\left(v_i\right) - C_{local}\left(v_i\right)\right| \tag{13}$$

where $S_{new}\left(v_i\right)$ is the topological network field set of v_i updated by the minimization function. $C_{global}(*)$ and $C_{local}(*)$ represent the modular topology centrality of nodes in the global and local network, respectively, and are calculated by Eq. 9. Our goal is to screen $S_{new}\left(v_i\right)$ from $S\left(v_i\right)$, so that the topological influence of nodes in $S_{new}\left(v_i\right)$ and global network is the closet.

The above situation can be regarded as a knapsack problem, which is a typical combinatorial optimization problem. To solve the above objective function, the particle swarm optimization algorithm [17] is used to get the best combination of node neighbors. By capturing the topological network field structure of nodes, not only the resulting neighbor set is topologically like the target node and highly attractive to the target node, but also we can better capture the higher-order interaction information between the target node and its neighbors.

Preserving Topological Network Feild Proximity. In this subsection, our aim is to preserve the topological network field proximity based on the previously sampled heterogeneous neighbor sets. The rationale is to predict whether a local network structure exists in a weighted heterogeneous graph [30].

Specifically, for set S_{new} with all the node types $\mathcal{A}$, we keep adding a new node to structure instance set $\mathcal{S}$ until $|\mathcal{S}| = |\mathcal{A}|$, where the type of the new node is different from the node types in $\mathcal{S}$. Assume the structure instance $\mathcal{S} = \{v_i, v_j, v_k\}$, for target node v_i, $\{v_j, v_k\}$ is the context nodes of v_i. By predicting

Table 1. Statistics of datasets

Datasets	Nodes	Edges	Labels
DBLP	Paper(P):9556, Author(A):2000, Venue(V):20	278,60	4
ACM	Paper(P):4019, Author(A):7167, Venue(V):60	174,26	3
IMDB	Movie(M):3676, Actor(A):4353, Director(D):1678	147,04	3

the multi-tasks of the structure instances S sampled from $S_{new}(v_i)$ for all $v_i \in \mathcal{V}$, the corresponding loss function can be described as:

$$\mathcal{L}_{nf} = -\frac{1}{|\mathcal{A}||S_{new}|} \sum_{S \in S_{new}} \sum_{v_i \in S} (\omega \cdot log y_S^{v_i} + (1-\omega) \cdot log(1 - y_S^{v_i})) \quad (14)$$

where $\omega = 1$ if a positive structure instance is sampled, otherwise $\omega = 0$. $y_S^{v_i} = MLP^{\phi(v_i)}(h_S^{v_i})$ is the probability of S with target node v_i, where $MLP^{\phi(v_i)}$ is the classifier for the node type $\phi(v_i)$. $h_S^{v_i} = h_{v_i}||c_{v_j}||c_{v_k}$ is the structure instance embedding with v_i. c_{v_j} and c_{v_k} are the context embeddings that can be obtained by a fully connected layer of neural network.

Then the overall loss can be defined as:

$$\mathcal{L} = \mathcal{L}_{tp} + \eta \cdot \mathcal{L}_{nf} \quad (15)$$

where η is the balancing coefficient. At last, minimizing the loss function can preserves the topology connectivity proximity and the topological network field proximity simultaneously.

4   Experiments

4.1   Experimental Setup

The experiments were performed on three publicly available HG datasets, including DBLP[1], ACM[2] and IMDB [23]. The basic information is summarized in Table 1. The proposed method is compared with 8 state-of-the-art heterogeneous graph embedding methods. The first category is two pairwise proximity preservation baselines, specifically DeepWalk [16] and LINE [19]. The second category is three meta-paths preservation baselines, specifically Metapath2Vec [3], HIN2Vec [4], and KNCA [26]. The third category is three message-passing baselines, specifically DHNE [21], HeGAN [8] and HeCo [24].

---

[1] https://dblp.uni-trier.de/.
[2] http://dl.acm.org/.

Table 2. Experiment results on three datasets for node classification task

Datasets	Metrics	DeepWalk	LINE	Metapath2Vec	HIN2Vec	KNCA	DHNE	HeGAN	HeCo	TNFE
DBLP-P	Micro-F1	0.9012	0.8476	0.9286	0.8381	0.8944	0.8571	0.8879	0.9174	**0.9512**
	Macro-F1	0.8945	0.8345	0.9244	0.8385	0.8759	0.8467	0.8381	0.9123	**0.9451**
DBLP-A	Micro-F1	0.8944	0.8876	0.8936	0.9030	0.8716	0.7330	0.9048	0.9083	**0.9181**
	Macro-F1	0.8848	0.8735	0.8795	0.8946	0.8675	0.6761	0.8927	0.8912	**0.9113**
ACM	Micro-F1	0.8217	0.8221	0.8361	0.5430	0.8177	0.6527	0.8309	0.8245	**0.8371**
	Macro-F1	0.8182	0.8132	0.8277	0.4859	0.8125	0.6231	0.8294	0.8137	**0.8315**
IMDB	Micro-F1	0.5652	0.4054	0.5190	0.4802	0.5448	0.3899	0.5856	0.5748	**0.5870**
	Macro-F1	0.5524	0.3306	0.5021	0.4624	0.5346	0.3053	0.5712	0.5644	**0.5777**

Table 3. Experiment results on three datasets for node clustering task

Datasets	Metrics	DeepWalk	LINE	Metapath2Vec	HIN2Vec	KNCA	DHNE	HeGAN	HeCo	TNFE
DBLP-P	NMI	0.4675	0.4683	0.5689	0.3047	0.4096	0.3533	0.6078	0.6290	**0.6581**
DBLP-A	NMI	0.6625	0.6111	0.6874	0.6579	0.3548	0.2100	0.6895	0.6781	**0.6933**
ACM	NMI	**0.4881**	0.4108	0.4271	0.4228	0.4389	0.2025	0.4335	0.4475	0.4479
IMDB	NMI	0.0041	0.0003	0.0009	0.0004	0.0055	0.0005	0.0656	0.0647	**0.0706**

Then the experimental settings are described. The feature dimension and embedding dimension are set to 128. The random walk restart probability r is 0.5, the walk length is 30, and the number of walks for each node is 10. The topological balancing coefficient $\alpha_1 = 10$, $\alpha_2 = 0.1$. The node influence range parameter is set to $\mathcal{I} = 1.5203$. The negative edge sampling rate is set to $N_s = 4$. Two-layer MLPs is used for structure instance classification. The node features are generated via DeepWalk [16]. The code and dataset are publicly available on Github[3].

4.2 Results Analysis

Node classification is usually utilized to evaluate the performance of graph embedding. To evaluate comprehensively, 80% of the labeled data is selected to train a logistic regression classifier and then 20% of the labeled data is used to test. To measure the performance of the model, Micro-F1 and Macro-F1 scores are used as the metrics. Based on the results in Table 2, it can be observed that the performance of TNFE is better than other baselines in all cases. Compared with meta-paths based methods, TNFE uses the topological network field to obtain the higher-order semantic dependencies between nodes and achieve better performance even if it does not need domain-specific knowledge. This indicates the utility of capturing the interplay relations between nodes.

---

[3] https://github.com/ahao-0324/TNFE.git.

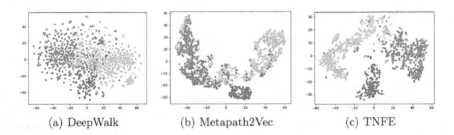

(a) DeepWalk   (b) Metapath2Vec   (c) TNFE

Fig. 2. Embedding visualization of different methods on DBLP-A

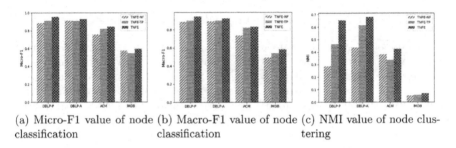

(a) Micro-F1 value of node (b) Macro-F1 value of node (c) NMI value of node clus-
classification   classification   tering

Fig. 3. Ablation Study of TNFE

Node clustering is another widely used method to evaluate the performance of the embedding learned by our model. We adapt normalized mutual information (NMI) to assess the quality of the clustering results. The results are reported in Table 3 and the best results are marked in bold. As can be seen, the proposed method significantly outperforms the baselines listed in most cases, which further demonstrates the effectiveness of TNFE.

To provide a more intuitive evaluation of network embedding, the t-SNE method [14] is used to conduct embedding visualization on DBLP dataset. Here DeepWalk and Metapath2Vec are chosen as the baselines for comparison with our method, and the results are shown in Fig. 2. From the plots, it can be found that the DeepWalk method, which preserves the basic connection between nodes, has poor results and does not aggregate the four types of nodes well. TNFE method outperforms Metapath2Vec method and separates the nodes with distinct boundaries, which further proves the effectiveness of preserving both topology connectivity proximity and topological network field proximity.

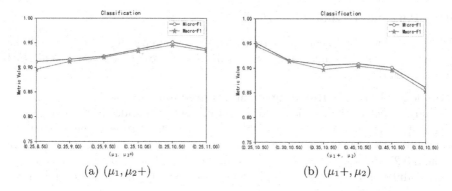

(a) (μ_1, μ_2+) (b) (μ_1+, μ_2)

Fig. 4. Hyperparameters μ_1, μ_2 impact of TNFE model

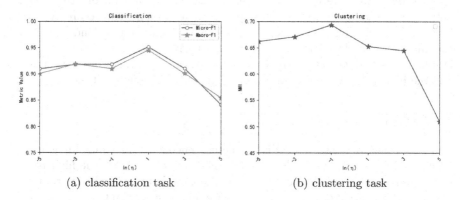

(a) classification task   (b) clustering task

Fig. 5. Balancing coefficient η impact of TNFE model

4.3 Variant Analysis

In this section, two variants of TNFE are designed as follows:

- **TNFE-TP**: We only consider the topological connection of nodes, and therefore do not preserve the topological network field structure of nodes that contain high-order interaction information between nodes.
- **TNFE-NF**: We only leverage the topological network field proximity, and therefore do not involve the topological connection of nodes in the network.

The experiments are conducted on node classification and clustering, and the results are shown in Fig. 3. It can be observed that TNFE outperforms two variants in most cases. By utilizing the topological properties and impact of nodes, TNFE obtains a significant performance improvement over TNFE-TP and TNFE-NF, indicating the necessity of considering both topological connectivity and topological network field proximity. All the components are indispensable.

4.4 Parameter Analysis

In this section, the effects of parameters are systematically analyzed. All the parameter analysis is performed on DBLP, the Micro-F1, Macro-F1, and NMI are used as the indicators.

Topological Graph Reconfiguration Threshold. μ_1, μ_2. Hyperparameters μ_1 and μ_2 control the topological relationship between nodes in the new graph. Figure 4 shows the performances with respect to different threshold combinations on classification tasks. As we can see, the corresponding values of μ_1 and μ_2 are around 0.25 and 10.50 respectively to achieve optimal performance. The optimal results differ among datasets and depend on sparsity, label rates, and graph higher-order properties.

Balancing Coefficient η. The balance coefficient η controls the balance between topological connection and topological network field structure. As shown in Fig. 5, the value of F1 score and NMI reach a peak with $\eta = e$ and $\eta = e^{-1}$ for classification and clustering respectively. Similarly, optimal η differs in different graphs, which indicates that the importance of the topology properties of nodes and the higher-order interaction information varies in different tasks.

5 Conclusion

A novel framework called TNFE for heterogeneous graph embedding is proposed in this paper. The TNFE model can effectively capture the higher-order graph information and the interaction relationship between nodes. Particularly, TNFE performs topology reconstruction graph representation through persistent homology, making similar nodes in the new graph closer, thereby facilitating the entire classification process. On this basis, TNFE simultaneously preserves topological connection proximity and topological network field proximity to better preserve the higher-order coupling and interaction information in complex networks. In experiments, TNFE outperforms the state-of-the-art approaches in the node classification and node clustering tasks on three real-world datasets. Variant analysis also demonstrates the effectiveness of the two major components of TNFE in boosting embedding performance. The major limitation of our model is the probable existence of bias in the unbalanced node neighborhoods. Since the analyzed node neighbors tend to be largely formed by nodes similar to the target node, such bias caused by diverse node neighborhoods may induce incorrect high-order interactive information. Our future work will focus on expanding the proposed approach to the modeling of datasets with unbalanced groups.

References

1. Cen, Y., Zou, X., Zhang, J., Yang, H., Zhou, J., Tang, J.: Representation learning for attributed multiplex heterogeneous network. In: Proceedings of the 25th ACM SIGKDD International Conference on Knowledge Discovery & Data Mining, pp. 1358–1368 (2019)

2. Chen, Y., Coskunuzer, B., Gel, Y.: Topological relational learning on graphs. In: Advances in Neural Information Processing Systems, vol. 34, pp. 27029–27042. Curran Associates, Inc. (2021)

3. Dong, Y., Chawla, N.V., Swami, A.: metapath2vec: scalable representation learning for heterogeneous networks. In: Proceedings of the 23rd ACM SIGKDD International Conference on Knowledge Discovery and Data Mining, pp. 135–144 (2017)

4. Fu, T.Y., Lee, W.C., Lei, Z.: Hin2Vec: explore meta-paths in heterogeneous information networks for representation learning. In: Proceedings of the 2017 ACM on Conference on Information and Knowledge Management, pp. 1797–1806 (2017)

5. Fu, X., Zhang, J., Meng, Z., King, I.: MAGNN: metapath aggregated graph neural network for heterogeneous graph embedding. In: Proceedings of The Web Conference 2020, pp. 2331–2341 (2020)

6. Goyal, P., Ferrara, E.: Graph embedding techniques, applications, and performance: a survey. Knowl.-Based Syst. **151**, 78–94 (2018)

7. Hou, S., et al.: αcyber: enhancing robustness of android malware detection system against adversarial attacks on heterogeneous graph based model. In: Proceedings of the 28th ACM International Conference on Information and Knowledge Management, pp. 609–618 (2019)

8. Hu, B., Fang, Y., Shi, C.: Adversarial learning on heterogeneous information networks. In: Proceedings of the 25th ACM SIGKDD International Conference on Knowledge Discovery & Data Mining, pp. 120–129 (2019)

9. Hu, Z., Dong, Y., Wang, K., Sun, Y.: Heterogeneous graph transformer. In: Proceedings of the Web Conference 2020, pp. 2704–2710 (2020)

10. Kerber, M., Morozov, D., Nigmetov, A.: Geometry helps to compare persistence diagrams (2017)

11. Kipf, T.N., Welling, M.: Semi-supervised classification with graph convolutional networks. arXiv preprint arXiv:1609.02907 (2016)

12. Li, Z., Wang, X., Li, J., Zhang, Q.: Deep attributed network representation learning of complex coupling and interaction. Knowl.-Based Syst. **212**, 106618 (2021)

13. Liu, J., Song, L., Wang, G., Shang, X.: Meta-HGT: metapath-aware hypergraph transformer for heterogeneous information network embedding. Neural Netw. **157**, 65–76 (2023)

14. Van der Maaten, L., Hinton, G.: Visualizing data using t-SNE. J. Mach. Learn. Res. **9**(11) (2008)

15. Mikolov, T., Sutskever, I., Chen, K., Corrado, G.S., Dean, J.: Distributed representations of words and phrases and their compositionality. In: Advances in Neural Information Processing Systems, vol. 26 (2013)

16. Perozzi, B., Al-Rfou, R., Skiena, S.: DeepWalk: online learning of social representations. In: Proceedings of the 20th ACM SIGKDD International Conference on Knowledge Discovery and Data Mining, pp. 701–710 (2014)

17. Shen, X., Wang, W., Zheng, B., Li, Y.: Modified particle swarm optimization for 0–1 knapsack problems. Comput. Eng. **32**(18), 23–25 (2006)

18. Shi, Y., Gui, H., Zhu, Q., Kaplan, L., Han, J.: ASPEM: embedding learning by aspects in heterogeneous information networks. In: Proceedings of the 2018 SIAM International Conference on Data Mining, pp. 144–152. SIAM (2018)

19. Tang, J., Qu, M., Wang, M., Zhang, M., Yan, J., Mei, Q.: LINE: large-scale information network embedding. In: Proceedings of the 24th International Conference on World Wide Web, pp. 1067–1077 (2015)

20. Tong, H., Faloutsos, C., Pan, J.Y.: Fast random walk with restart and its applications. In: Sixth International Conference on Data Mining (ICDM 2006), pp. 613–622. IEEE (2006)

21. Tu, K., Cui, P., Wang, X., Wang, F., Zhu, W.: Structural deep embedding for hyper-networks. In: Proceedings of the AAAI Conference on Artificial Intelligence, vol. 32 (2018)
22. Wang, X., Bo, D., Shi, C., Fan, S., Ye, Y., Philip, S.Y.: A survey on heterogeneous graph embedding: methods, techniques, applications and sources. IEEE Trans. Big Data 9(2), 415–436 (2022)
23. Wang, X., et al.: Heterogeneous graph attention network. In: The World Wide Web Conference, pp. 2022–2032 (2019)
24. Wang, X., Liu, N., Han, H., Shi, C.: Self-supervised heterogeneous graph neural network with co-contrastive learning. In: KDD 2021, pp. 1726–1736. Association for Computing Machinery, New York, NY, USA (2021)
25. Wasserman, L.: Topological data analysis. Ann. Rev. Stat. Appl. 5, 501–532 (2018)
26. Xu, H., Wang, W., Liu, H., Zhang, M., Tian, Q., Jiao, P.: Key nodes cluster augmented embedding for heterogeneous information networks. In: Yang, H., Pasupa, K., Leung, A.C.-S., Kwok, J.T., Chan, J.H., King, I. (eds.) ICONIP 2020. LNCS, vol. 12533, pp. 499–511. Springer, Cham (2020). https://doi.org/10.1007/978-3-030-63833-7_42
27. Yuvaraj, M., Dey, A.K., Lyubchich, V., Gel, Y.R., Poor, H.V.: Topological clustering of multilayer networks. Proc. Natl. Acad. Sci. 118(21), e2019994118 (2021)
28. Zhang, C., Song, D., Huang, C., Swami, A., Chawla, N.V.: Heterogeneous graph neural network. In: Proceedings of the 25th ACM SIGKDD International Conference on Knowledge Discovery & Data Mining, pp. 793–803 (2019)
29. Zhang, R., Zimek, A., Schneider-Kamp, P.: A simple meta-path-free framework for heterogeneous network embedding. In: CIKM 2022, pp. 2600–2609. Association for Computing Machinery, New York, NY, USA (2022)
30. Zhao, J., Wang, X., Shi, C., Liu, Z., Ye, Y.: Network schema preserving heterogeneous information network embedding. In: International Joint Conference on Artificial Intelligence (IJCAI) (2020)
31. Zhong, Z., Gonzalez, G., Grattarola, D., Pang, J.: Unsupervised network embedding beyond homophily. Trans. Mach. Learn. Res. (2022)

Predictive Analysis and Machine Learning

Federated Learning Performance on Early ICU Mortality Prediction with Extreme Data Distributions

Athanasios Georgoutsos[1], Paraskevas Kerasiotis[1], and Verena Kantere[2(✉)]

[1] School of Electrical and Computer Engineering (ECE), National Technical University of Athens (NTUA), 15772 Athens, Zografou, Greece
pkerasiotis@mail.ntua.gr
[2] School of EECS, University of Ottawa, Ottawa, Canada
vkantere@uottawa.ca

Abstract. Federated Learning (FL) is a novel machine learning technique that allows multiple parties to collaboratively train a global model without sharing their local data, thus addressing data privacy and security concerns. These issues are of paramount importance to the healthcare domain, due to strict regulations regarding patient data. By utilizing data from multiple medical institutions, FL could lead to generalizable models for one of the most prominent medical tasks, the early prediction of mortality risk in the ICU setting, where patients in critical condition are treated. This paper evaluates the performance of various FL algorithms in a realistic FL scenario and, also, in the presence of FL clients with 'extreme' data distributions, using real world data from a collaborative research database. Overall, the FL models perform, in general, substantially better than the local models of the participating hospitals and slightly worse than the 'ideal' model, which is trained on the centralized data. FedProx, a client-side optimization FL algorithm, regulates more effectively the contribution of a large FL client, with 'extreme' bias against the underrepresented class, while the server-side optimization FL algorithms incorporate the beneficial information of a smaller FL client into the global model more efficiently.

Keywords: Deep Federated Learning · ICU Mortality · Extreme Data Distributions

1 Introduction

In the digital age, the wide adoption of electronic health records by medical institutions has led to significant advancements within the healthcare domain. An electronic health record (EHR) is the collection of patient health information, capturing the patients' condition across time, and its storage in a digital format [4]. By effectively utilizing EHR data, healthcare professionals could improve healthcare delivery, enhance clinical decision-making support and advance medical research [5]. In order to gain a better insight into the overall patient population, EHRs from multiple sources ideally could be aggregated and analyzed as a single dataset.

In pursuit of these objectives, the rapid progress in the field of Machine Learning (ML) has led to high-quality solutions for various clinical tasks. Nevertheless, traditional ML approaches face several limitations, especially regarding privacy concerns. The Centralized Machine Learning (CML) approach, where multi-sourced patient data are centralized, does not strongly guarantee data privacy, even with the use of standard data anonymization and de-identification techniques [15]. Then, the privacy-preserving Local Machine Learning (LML) approach, where each medical center trains its own model on its local data, often cannot solely produce generalizable ML models due to limited size and bias of its local dataset. In response to these limitations, a novel ML approach, named Federated Learning (FL), has been proposed. FL enables participants to collaboratively train a robust ML model in a privacy-preserving manner, with regard to their local data [9]. The integration of the FL framework into the healthcare domain has led to tremendous opportunities. For instance, motivated by the recent COVID-19 outbreak, Vaid et al. [16] employed FL, utilizing real-world data from 5 hospitals to address 7-day mortality prediction for hospitalized COVID-19 patients.

The need for effective predictive models is imminent in the Intensive Care Unit (ICU) setting, where patients typically exhibit a critical health condition. In response to this, numerous traditional ML works focus on vital signs and lab test results, collected during patients' ICU stay in the form of Multivariate Time Series (MTS), to utilize their rich temporal dynamics for mortality prediction. Awad et al. [1] conducted a thorough time-series analysis on the performance of different mining methods and showed that ML classifiers with data from the first 6 h of an ICU stay outperformed conventional scoring systems with data from the first 48 h of an ICU stay, namely Apache and SAPS. Then, Pattalung et al. [11] proposed a data-driven framework with time-series and Recurrent Neural Network (RNN) models, achieving an AUROC score of 0.87–0.91 on three public critical care databases.

Recently, inspired by the aforementioned framework from [11], Mondrejevski et al. [10] proposed FLICU, a FL workflow for ICU mortality prediction, using clinical MTS data and deep sequential neural networks. Their FL approach, using the standard FedAvg algorithm [9], showed comparable performance to the 'ideal' CML approach and outperformed the privacy-preserving LML approach with various numbers of FL participants (2, 4 and 8). Randl et al. [13] adjusted FLICU to the first hours of the ICU stay, therefore enabling the use of their models for clinical decision-making support. They confirmed the results of [10] on a similar scenario, by using vital signs and lab test results from the first 24 h of the ICU stays to estimate the mortality risk during the next 48 h. However, for their experimental scenarios, they use the MIMIC-III database, containing real-world data from a single medical center, which they split in a stratified manner to the FL participants. As a result, their results correspond to an independently and identically distributed (IID) dataset, therefore to a non-realistic scenario.

A non-IID dataset poses a major challenge to the FL framework, as the statistically heterogeneous federated network may fail to develop an effective global model or it may lead to convergence issues. For the mortality prediction task, some FL works concentrated on the evaluation of the FL framework in a federated environment with imbalanced datasets, in terms of size, showing that the performance of their final model was scarcely affected [2,7]. In a more realistic non-IID scenario, with FL participants varying both in dataset size and class distribution, Dang et al. [3] evaluated various FL algorithms on hospital mortality prediction with the multi-center eICU database [12]. Utilizing static clinical variables and a simple neural network, they showed that FL models performed considerably well and proposed the use of time-series data and more complex neural network architectures as a future research direction.

Motivated by these recent works, we initially explore the performance of different FL algorithms with a non-IID dataset, using MTS data and a deep RNN model, on the early prediction of ICU mortality task. Apart from this basic experimental scenario, we aim to explore the performance of these FL algorithms in the presence of divergent FL clients, who significantly alter the properties of the federated network. Through our experiments, we compare the effectiveness of the implemented FL methods by constructing artificial hospitals with extreme data distributions and adding them to our FL setting.

2   Federated Learning Framework

Federated Learning. The basic FL workflow involves a centralized server, which orchestrates the overall training process, and the participating nodes, which locally compute updates to a global model. Before the training process commences, the central server selects the ML model and the training method, with regard to the specific parameters of the studied problem. Each iteration of the training process constitutes a FL round. During a FL round, the central server selects a group of clients to participate in the training process and broadcasts them the current global model parameters. Then, each client computes its own update to the current global model, after training it on its local data. Once the clients have computed their local updates, they are communicated and aggregated to the central server. Afterwards, the global model, maintained by the server, is updated according to the aggregated client updates [9].

Federated Averaging (FedAvg), introduced by McMahan et al. [9], constitutes one of the most widely used FL algorithms. This method allows the participants to train their models locally, optimizing their local objective functions, while the server aggregates their local updates by computing their weighted average to update the global model:

$$w^t = \Sigma_{h=1}^{H} p_h w_h^t, \tag{1}$$

where, for FL round t with H participating hospitals, w is the set of weights of the global model, p_h the fraction of training data of hospital h over the total training data and w_h the set of local model weights from hospital h. Based on this workflow of FedAvg, the objective function that the central server aims to optimize is the following:

$$F(\cdot) = \Sigma_{h=1}^{H} p_h F_h(\cdot), \tag{2}$$

where $F_h(\cdot)$ is the local objective function for hospital h. FedAvg is a fairly simple and comprehending FL algorithm, performing well with IID datasets. However, its effectiveness and convergence rate are not guaranteed in statistically heterogeneous scenarios, where the final global model may under-perform or fail to converge, leading to several optimization algorithms.

Client-Side FL Optimization. The former category of these optimization algorithms addresses a phenomenon called *client drift*, that is the detrimental effect of statistical heterogeneity on local updates, in terms of performance and convergence rate, causing them to drift away from the respective global update. In FL settings with non-IID datasets, the optimization of a local objective function for a client does not necessarily correspond to the optimization of the global objective function. One of these FL algorithms is FedProx [8], which introduces a proximal term μ to restrict the local updates to remain closer to the latest global model. The aggregation of the local model weights remains the same as in Eq. 1, however a participating hospital h, with the FedProx algorithm, aims to optimize the following function:

$$F_h'(\cdot) = F_h(\cdot) + \frac{\mu}{2} ||w_h^t - w^{t-1}||^2, \tag{3}$$

where, for FL round t, $F_h(\cdot)$ is the original objective function for hospital h, w_h^t are the local model weights that are being calculated by hospital h and w^{t-1} are the latest global model weights, computed at the previous FL round.

Server-Side FL Optimization. On the other hand, the latter category of these optimization algorithms focuses on the weight aggregation and the global model update at the server. The weight updates from FL participant h at FL round t can be expressed as:

$$\Delta w_h = w_h^t - w^{t-1}, \tag{4}$$

corresponding to the difference between the current local model weights of hospital h and the latest global model weights of the previous FL round. Then, we may provide a different expression for Eq. 1, by adding the Δw_h for every hospital h and using this total divergence of local models to update the global model:

$$\Delta w = \Sigma_{h=1}^{H} p_h \Delta w_h, \tag{5}$$

$$w = w - \Delta w \tag{6}$$

As a result, Δw acts as a *pseudo-gradient* to the above weight aggregation equation, in the form of a gradient-based optimization step. Motivated by the efficiency of adaptive optimization techniques to tackle convergence issues in non-FL settings, Reddi et al. [14] proposed an adjustment of these techniques to the federated setting. They suggested the application of the Adam, Adagrad and Yogi adaptive optimization methods on the server-side of the FL setting, naming these FL algorithms FedAdam, FedAdagrad and FedYogi respectively. Apart from these, Hsu et al. [6] proposed the use of momentum β to the server optimization step, referring to this approach as FedAvgM. As a result, Eq. 6 is expressed as:

$$w = w - u, \tag{7}$$

where $u = \beta u + \Delta w$, adding momentum to the contribution of the previous Δw values and, then, updating the global model.

3 Experimental Methodology

In this section, we re-formulate the early prediction of ICU mortality risk for this work and select the hospital cohorts for our experimental scenarios. Afterwards, we prepare our selected MTS data for ML training and discuss the model architecture and the parameters of our training procedure.

3.1 Problem Formulation

We formulate the task of predicting ICU mortality as a binary classification problem, with MTS data, where the patients who died during their ICU stay constitute the positive group (output = 1) and the patients who got discharged constitute the negative group (output = 0). The time point indicating the mortality event or discharge is defined by the *ICU discharge offset* variable, while the beginning of the ICU stay is defined as the first vital signs measurements after the official ICU admission record. Since this study focuses on *early* prediction, we consider an observation window during the first hours of a patient's ICU stay. It consists of 24 h of vital signs (7 variables) and lab test results (16 variables) after the beginning of the ICU stay. The MTS data from this observation window are extracted and utilized for training and evaluation of the predictive models. The resulting algorithm indicates the mortality likelihood of a patient during the 48-h period after the prediction time, which is at the 24-h mark of the ICU stay.

3.2 Cohort Selection

The experiments of this study were conducted with the eICU public critical care database [12], which contains data for more than 200,000 ICU admissions across the United States between 2014 and 2015. It includes demographics, medications, diagnosis and treatment information, vital signs and lab test results. Initially, we need to filter the ICU stays according to our problem's parameters. For an ICU stay to be relevant to our mortality prediction task, the patient outcome should be available, the length of the stay should be between 24 and 72 h and at least a vital signs measurement and a lab test result should be recorded. Following these filtering steps, and keeping only the first ICU stay for each unique patient to reduce our dataset's complexity, we end up with 55,147 ICU stays.

Table 1. Data distributions for the selected FL dataset of the basic scenario

Datasets	Total	Survival	Death
Hospital A	1,018	977	41 (4.0%)
Hospital B	1,041	972	69 (6.6%)
Hospital C	1,788	1,714	74 (4.1%)
Hospital D	773	746	27 (3.5%)
Hospital E	1,129	1,088	41 (3.6%)
Hospital F	1,344	1,244	100 (7.4%)
Hospital G	930	878	52 (5.6%)
Hospital H	1,316	1,248	68 (5.2%)
FL Dataset	9,339	8,867	472 (5.1%)

Table 2. Data distributions for the foreign test set of the basic scenario

Datasets	Total	Survival	Death
Hospital I	421	398	23 (5.5%)
Hospital J	477	456	21 (4.4%)
Hospital K	420	397	23 (5.5%)
Hospital L	485	460	25 (5.2%)
Test Set	1,803	1,711	92 (5.1%)

For our basic experimental scenario, we select 8 hospitals to participate in FL training, which are shown in Table 1. We ensure that the datasets of these hospitals vary in terms of both size and mortality ratio, so that we recreate a federated environment with non-IID data. This training cohort contains data for 9,339 ICU stays and it is characterized by a 5.1% mortality ratio. As a way to evaluate the FL models' performance on unseen data, we assemble a test set of 1,803 ICU stays, deriving from 4 hospitals that do not participate in FL training, which are shown in Table 2.

Then, we construct two hospitals with 'extreme' data distributions, in regard to the FL training dataset. Hospital X1 contains 1,900 ICU stays, more than the largest hospital of the FL dataset, however it is characterized by a meagre 0.5% mortality ratio. On the other hand, hospital X2 contains only 300 ICU stays,

Table 3. Data distributions for 'extreme' hospitals X1 and X2

Datasets	Total	Survival	Death
Hospital X1	1,900	1,890	10 (0.5%)
FL Dataset + X1	11,239	10,757	482 (4.3%)
Hospital X2	300	225	75 (25.0%)
FL Dataset + X2	9,639	9,092	547 (5.7%)

less than half of the smallest hospital of the FL dataset, but it corresponds to a 25% mortality ratio. By adding each of these hospitals to the FL dataset and increasing the degree of statistical heterogeneity, we aim to explore how FL training is affected. Hospitals X1 and X2, as well as their respective incorporation into the FL dataset, are shown in Table 3.

3.3   Data Preparation

For each ICU stay, we extract 7 vital signs (*heart rate, respiratory rate, mean blood pressure, systolic blood pressure, diastolic blood pressure, oxygen saturation (spO2) and temperature*) and 16 laboratory results (*albumin, blood urea nitrogen (BUN), bilirubin, lactate, bicarbonate, band neutrophi (bands), chloride, creatinine, glucose, hemoglobin, hematocrit, platelet count (platelet), potassium, partial thromboplastin time (PTT), sodium and white blood cells (WBC)*) in the form of MTS, from the first 24 h after ICU admission. Following the procedure described in related works [10,11], we re-sample vital sign measurements into 1-h intervals and lab test results into 8-h intervals, using *mean* as our aggregation function (we also used *max* and *min* on heart rate, respiratory rate and oxygen saturation, which are the most informative vital signs for mortality risk prediction in the eICU database [11]). We use forward and backward imputation successively to deal with missing values, while non-observed values are replaced with –1.

3.4   Model Architecture and Training Parameters

The vital signs and the lab test results are initially processed by two parallel channels, each consisting of 3 recurrent GRU layers of 16 units. After batch normalization, the outputs of these channels are concatenated and, then, pass through two fully-connected layers of 16 nodes each. After applying a sigmoid layer on the final outputs, we produce an estimation of the patient mortality risk in the ICU setting, in the range [0, 1]. This model is trained for a maximum of 100 rounds with the binary cross-entropy loss function, the Adam optimization method and a starting learning rate of 10^{-3}, which drops by 50% every 5 rounds.

During training, we monitor the F1-Score on the validation set through an early stopping mechanism, with a patience of 30 rounds. According to the size of the datasets for each approach, we set the batch size to 256 for CML and to 32 for LML and FL, while we address the high class imbalance of our datasets with the use of class weights on gradient updates. Moreover, for the FL approach, we assume full participation of the federated network at each FL round, where each participant trains its model for 1 epoch on its local data. For all experiments, we use 5-fold cross-validation to obtain a robust estimation of the model's performance, either on the train-validation splits of the basic scenario, or on the test set splits on the FL dataset for the scenarios with hospitals X1 and X2 (Fig. 1).

Table 4. Test Performance with the basic experimental scenario

Method	AUROC	AUPRC	F1-Score
CML	0.895 ± 0.002	0.539 ± 0.004	0.541 ± 0.020
LML	0.807 ± 0.032	0.360 ± 0.021	0.413 ± 0.024
FedAvg	0.890 ± 0.007	0.499 ± 0.020	0.489 ± 0.023
FedProx	0.891 ± 0.006	**0.507 ± 0.016**	0.472 ± 0.042
FedAdam	0.891 ± 0.005	0.505 ± 0.014	0.480 ± 0.046
FedAdagrad	**0.892 ± 0.006**	0.502 ± 0.018	**0.512 ± 0.032**
FedYogi	0.887 ± 0.007	0.500 ± 0.021	0.475 ± 0.030
FedAvgM	0.889 ± 0.008	0.502 ± 0.020	0.466 ± 0.039

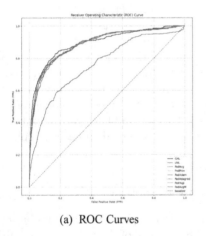

(a) ROC Curves

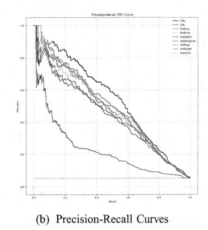

(b) Precision-Recall Curves

Fig. 1. Comparison of ROC and PR curves for CML, LML and FL approaches, with the basic experimental scenario

4   Results and Discussion

4.1   Basic Experimental Scenario

Initially, we measure the performance on the foreign test set, shown in Table 2, with models trained with data from 8 collaborating hospitals, shown in Table 1.

As reported in Table 4, the CML model obtains the best scores for every metric, while the LML models report the worst scores, since most participating hospitals do not contain sufficient data locally to train a robust, generalizable model. Overall, the FL models have similar performance, in terms of AUROC and AUPRC, while the model trained with the FedAdagrad algorithm reports the best F1-Score among them. Compared to the conventional ML approaches, the FL models show a comparable performance to the CML model, mostly regarding AUROC and AUPRC, and their metric scores are considerably better than those of the LML models. These results indicate that the FL algorithms are not heavily affected by a federated network with naturally-induced statistical heterogeneity, while the standard FedAvg algorithm has almost equivalent performance to the FL optimization algorithms. The comparison with the CML and LML models validates FL as an effective, privacy-preserving ML approach.

Table 5. Test Performance with 'extreme' hospital X1

Method	AUROC	AUPRC	F1-Score
CML	0.870 ± 0.004	0.461 ± 0.046	0.498 ± 0.042
LML	0.689 ± 0.030	0.185 ± 0.028	0.289 ± 0.046
FedAvg	0.852 ± 0.008	$\mathbf{0.405 \pm 0.055}$	0.407 ± 0.058
FedProx	$\mathbf{0.854 \pm 0.008}$	0.402 ± 0.044	0.413 ± 0.47
FedAdam	0.851 ± 0.012	0.392 ± 0.056	0.400 ± 0.072
FedAdagrad	0.848 ± 0.007	0.390 ± 0.049	0.426 ± 0.060
FedYogi	0.850 ± 0.008	0.399 ± 0.051	$\mathbf{0.433 \pm 0.050}$
FedAvgM	0.851 ± 0.006	0.392 ± 0.042	0.395 ± 0.074

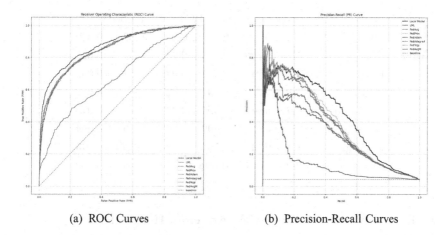

(a) ROC Curves   (b) Precision-Recall Curves

Fig. 2. Comparison of ROC and PR curves for CML, LML and FL approaches, with 'extreme' hospital X1

4.2   Experimental Scenario with 'extreme' Hospital X1

Table 5 shows the models' performance after including hospital X1 in the federated network, with the test set deriving from this cohort of hospitals. First, we observe that all models report worse scores than those of the basic experiment above, mainly because the statistical properties of the cohort of FL participants have largely changed. Again, the CML model performs the best in every metric category, followed by the FL models and, then, the LML models. However, we observe that the best scores by the FL models in every metric category diverge more from the respective scores of the CML model than for the previous experimental scenario. This can be interpreted as an effect of hospital X1, which contributes approximately 17% during the weight aggregation process, but it contains a extremely biased local dataset with a mortality ratio of 0.5%, in contrary to the average 4.3% of all participating hospitals.

Regarding the FL algorithms, we observe that FedProx reports the best AUROC score and the second best AUPRC score, behind FedAvg. However, after observing Fig. 2b, one can see that the FedProx model (*yellow line*) obtains better precision than other FL methods for most recall values, except for high recall, where they all have a similar performance, and low recall, where they display erratic behavior. As a result, we may say that the FedProx overall exhibits the best behavior for regulating hospital X1. As the proximal term restricts the local updates by hospital X1, it also restricts its contribution to the global model, preventing it from overpowering the contributions from other hospitals. Regarding AUROC and AUPRC, the server-side FL optimization algorithms perform worse than FedProx and FedAvg, with the exception of FedYogi.

Table 6. Test Performance with 'extreme' hospital X2

Method	AUROC	AUPRC	F1-Score
CML	0.871 ± 0.012	0.537 ± 0.029	0.526 ± 0.032
LML	0.728 ± 0.032	0.288 ± 0.037	0.390 ± 0.025
FedAvg	0.859 ± 0.011	0.481 ± 0.038	0.447 ± 0.062
FedProx	0.859 ± 0.013	0.492 ± 0.027	0.405 ± 0.052
FedAdam	0.857 ± 0.013	0.495 ± 0.032	0.452 ± 0.048
FedAdagrad	0.857 ± 0.013	0.492 ± 0.034	0.463 ± 0.054
FedYogi	0.854 ± 0.012	0.501 ± 0.036	$\mathbf{0.477 \pm 0.038}$
FedAvgM	$\mathbf{0.860 \pm 0.011}$	$\mathbf{0.503 \pm 0.026}$	0.463 ± 0.052

4.3   Experimental Scenario with 'extreme' Hospital X2

Table 6 shows the models' performance after including hospital X2 in the federated network, with the test set deriving from this cohort of hospitals. In this scenario, the models' performance resembles more their respective performance

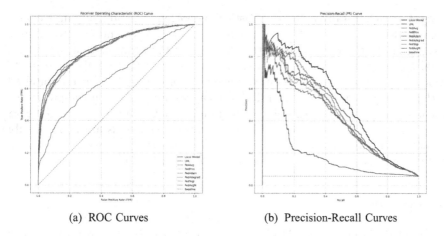

(a) ROC Curves   (b) Precision-Recall Curves

Fig. 3. Comparison of ROC and PR curves for CML, LML and FL approaches, with 'extreme' hospital X2

in the basic scenario. The reason is that hospital X2 is a smaller hospital, which does not alter significantly the overall structure of the federated network. Again, the FL models outperform the LML models, while they are not far behind the best scores of the CML model. As hospital X2 contributes only 3% during weight aggregation, but with an informative dataset with a 25% mortality ratio, we should observe how each FL algorithm utilizes this information.

Observing the results, it is evident that the server-side FL optimization algorithms are more effective in this scenario, with FedAvgM reporting the best AUROC and AUPRC scores, and FedYogi reporting the best F1-Score. As one can see at Fig. 3b, FedAvg and FedProx methods lead to worse precision for most recall values, outperformed by the other FL algorithms. The reason behind this is that FedAvg does not address explicitly the data heterogeneity of this federated environment, while the proximal term of FedProx actually reduces even more the minor contribution of hospital X2 to the global model, failing to effectively utilize its information and reporting a significantly lower F1-score than the other methods. By moving optimization to the weight aggregation and the global model update, server-side optimization algorithms are capable to utilize information from smaller FL participants. We repeat that FedYogi led to the development of a high-performing model, close to FedAvgM in terms of AUPRC.

5   Conclusion

We implement and evaluate various FL algorithms on the early prediction of ICU mortality risk, using MTS data. We recreate a realistic, statistically heterogeneous environment to explore the performance of each FL algorithm. Our results indicate that the FL algorithms are robust to a scenario using a non-IID dataset, with naturally-induced statistical heterogeneity, and maintain a comparable performance to the CML approach. However, in the presence of hospital X1, which contributes greatly to the final model, the FL algorithms are considerably affected, since they cannot easily regulate its effect on the final model. Among them, FedProx stands out as the best approach to deal with hospital X1, with the use of a proximal term during local training. Then, in the presence of a smaller hospital X2, with rich information about the under-represented class, we observe that the server-side FL optimization algorithms are more suitable to incorporate its update into the final model, outperforming both the standard FedAvg and the local-side FL optimization method FedProx.

References

1. Awad, A., Bader-El-Den, M., McNicholas, J., Briggs, J., El-Sonbaty, Y.: Predicting hospital mortality for intensive care unit patients: time-series analysis. Health Inform. J. **26**(2), 1043–1059 (2020). https://doi.org/10.1177/1460458219850323, pMID: 31347428
2. Budrionis, A., Miara, M., Miara, P., Wilk, S., Bellika, J.G.: Benchmarking PySyft federated learning framework on mimic-iii dataset. IEEE Access **9**, 116869–116878 (2021). https://doi.org/10.1109/ACCESS.2021.3105929
3. Dang, T.K., Lan, X., Weng, J., Feng, M.: Federated learning for electronic health records. ACM Trans. Intell. Syst. Technol. **13**(5) (2022). https://doi.org/10.1145/3514500
4. Gunter, T.D., Terry, N.P.: The emergence of national electronic health record architectures in the united states and Australia: models, costs, and questions. J. Med. Internet Res. **7**(1), e3 (2005)
5. Hong, N., et al.: State of the art of machine learning-enabled clinical decision support in intensive care units: literature review. JMIR Med. Inform. **10**(3), e28781 (2022)
6. Hsu, T.M.H., Qi, H., Brown, M.: Measuring the effects of non-identical data distribution for federated visual classification (2019)
7. Lee, G., Shin, S.Y.: Federated learning on clinical benchmark data: performance assessment. J. Med. Internet Res. **22**, e20891 (2020)
8. Li, T., Sahu, A.K., Zaheer, M., Sanjabi, M., Talwalkar, A., Smith, V.: Federated optimization in heterogeneous networks (2020)
9. McMahan, H.B., Moore, E., Ramage, D., Hampson, S., y Arcas, B.A.: Communication-efficient learning of deep networks from decentralized data. In: International Conference on Artificial Intelligence and Statistics (2016)
10. Mondrejevski, L., Miliou, I., Montanino, A., Pitts, D., Hollmén, J., Papapetrou, P.: FLICU: a federated learning workflow for intensive care unit mortality prediction (2022)
11. Na Pattalung, T., Ingviya, T., Chaichulee, S.: Feature explanations in recurrent neural networks for predicting risk of mortality in intensive care patients. J. Personal. Med. **11**(9), 934 (2021). https://doi.org/10.3390/jpm11090934
12. Pollard, T.J., Johnson, A.E.W., Raffa, J.D., Celi, L.A., Mark, R.G., Badawi, O.: The eICU collaborative research database, a freely available multi-center database for critical care research. Sci. Data **5**(1), 1–13 (2018)

13. Randl, K., Armengol, N., Mondrejevski, L., Miliou, I.: Early prediction of the risk of ICU mortality with deep federated learning (2022). https://doi.org/10.48550/arXiv.2212.00554
14. Reddi, S., et al.: Adaptive federated optimization (2021)
15. Sweeney, L.: Simple demographics often identify people uniquely, January 2000
16. Vaid, A., et al.: Federated learning of electronic health records to improve mortality prediction in hospitalized patients with COVID-19: machine learning approach, February 2021

TSEGformer: Time-Space Dimension Dependency Transformer for Use in Multivariate Time Series Prediction

Yuan Feng[1,2] and Qing Yu[1,2(✉)]

[1] Tianjin University of Technology, TUT, Tianjin 300382, China
[2] Tianjin Key Laboratory of Intelligence Computing and Novel Software Technology, Tianjin, China
1250918264@qq.com

Abstract. Multivariate time series (MTS) prediction has always been an important part of sequence prediction. Recently, many researchers have proposed many deep learning models for multivariate time series prediction. Transformer-based models have shown great potential in this regard, as they can better capture the long-term dependencies between sequences, which has great advantages in sequence prediction tasks. However, many existing models focus on encoding and embedding time positions when processing time series, ignoring the dependencies between different dimensions at different times. MTS is not only related in the temporal dimension, but also in the spatial dimension, therefore we propose the TSEG-former. This is a transformer-based model that considers not only temporal and positional information, but also information between different dimensions in the sequence embedding section. Dimension Segment Mean Fusion (DSMF) is proposed, and the input MTS is embedded into a new 2D vector matrix by a module containing temporal and spatial information. Two Part Attention (TPA) layer has also been proposed to effectively capture the relationships between sequences across time and space dimensions. We established the Encoder-Decoder framework and conducted experiments on 5 real datasets, which yielded impressive results.

Keywords: Multivariate time series · prediction · transformer

1 Introduction

Multivariate time series (MTS) [1] are time series with multiple dimensions, where each dimension represents a specific univariate time series. MTS forecasting based on using historical information to predict the information contained in future transactions(including finance [2], energy [3], Weather [4] etc.), which is important for long-term planning and future warning. With the development of deep learning, many transformer-based models have shown great ability in long-term prediction, such as LogTrans [5], Transformer [6], Informer [7], Autoformer [8], Pyraformer [9], FEDformer [10], Reformer [11] etc. Thanks to the attention mechanism, these models have achieved good results in long-term time forecasting.

F. Zhang et al. (Eds.): WISE 2023, LNCS 14306, pp. 496–508, 2023.
https://doi.org/10.1007/978-981-99-7254-8_38

Many transformer-based models only consider the embedding of temporally encoded information when embedding information, ignoring the fact that time series also contain a lot of information in spatial locations. This makes a lot of information lost when capturing attention.

To improve this situation, we propose TSEGformer, a transformer-based model. First, at the temporal processing level, we use Dimension Segment Mean Fusion (DSMF) to achieve embedding between different dimensions in spatial dimensions to compensate for the previous embedding only in temporal dimensions, specifically using segment [12] to partition data between different dimensions to achieve embedding in spatial dimensions, and using mean fusion to achieve dimensional uniformity when dimensions do not match. Then, at the attention level, Two Part Attention (TPA) is used, which includes FFT [10] for queries, keys to frequency domain conversion, removing most of the noise, and Time Delay Aggregation [8] is used to scroll based on the selected time delay, aligning similar subsequences with the same estimated period. This method not only reduces the time complexity, but also significantly improves on many benchmark models. The contributions are summarised as follows:

(1) To better exploit dimensional information, we not only incorporate temporal and positional encoding into information embedding, but also integrate information relationships between different dimensions.
(2) A new attention method is proposed that uses fast Fourier transform to capture information in time series through frequency domain mapping, and then aggregates similar sub-sequences through time delay aggregation. This improves computational efficiency and information utilization compared to the original self-attention mechanism.
(3) We developed TSEGformer, which is a transformer-based model that breaks the embedding in the temporal dimension and enables better use of spatial information. And good results were also achieved in long sequence prediction.

2   Relate Work

2.1   Multivariate Time Series Forecasting

Due to the rich application scenarios of time series forecasting [13], many models have emerged, such as the ARIMA statistical model [14], which transforms non-stationary processes into stationary processes by differentiation before making predictions. The recurrent neural network RNN [15] is very useful for modelling the time dependence of time series. TCN [16], based on time convolutional networks, and DeepAR [17], combining autoregressive and RNN, treat MTS data as vector sequences and use CNN/RNN [15,18] to capture time dependencies. The graph neural network GNN [13] clearly captures inter-dimensional dependencies. LSTNet [18] introduces a skip-connected convolutional neural network CNN [19] to capture time dependencies. MTGNN [13] uses time convolution and graph convolution to obtain temporal and dimensional dependencies, but it is difficult to improve prediction accuracy in long time series.

2.2   Transformer Based for MST Forcasting

Transformer based models initially achieved great success in the field of NLP (BERT [22] model in 2017), and also showed great potential in speech processing in the field of vision (CV) [20,21], reflecting the powerful ability of the modified model to handle sequence problems. Recently, there have been many transformer-based models such as LogTrans [5], Transformer [6], Informer [7], Pyraformer [9], FEDformer [10], Autoformer [8], etc. LogTrans proposed LogSparse autocorrelation attention and introduced local convolution, reducing the time complexity of the Transformer from $O(L^2)$ to $O(L \cdot log(L)^2)$. The Transformer proposed a method of local sensitive hashing attention, which also reduced the time complexity to $O(L \cdot log(L))$. Informer used a distillation-based attention mechanism and also reduced the time complexity to $O(L \cdot log(L))$. Pyraformer introduced a tree structure to perform self-attention, extracting features of different resolutions by connecting edges between scales, and modelling dependencies of different scales, greatly reducing the time complexity. FEDformer uses Fast Fourier Transform to achieve the transformation from time domain to frequency domain and has achieved good results. Autoformer introduces a sequence decomposition module to better apply the periodicity and trend of time series to time series prediction. These models ignore the cross-dimensional relationships and only embed the coding information and the dimensional information of the current time position together (Table 1).

Table 1. Computation complexity per layer of Transformer-based models. L denotes the length of past series, D denotes the number of dimensions, L_{seg} denotes the segment length of DSMF embedding in STEGformer.

Methods	Training		Testing
	Time	Memory	Steps
STEGformer	$O(\frac{D}{L_{seg}^2}L^2)$	$O(\frac{D}{L_{seg}^2}L^2)$	$\frac{D}{L_{seg}}$
FEDformer	$O(L)$	$O(L)$	1
Autoformer	$O(LlogL)$	$O(LlogL)$	1
Informer	$O(LlogL)$	$O(LlogL)$	1
Transformer	$O(L^2)$	$O(L^2)$	L
LogTrans	$O(LlogL)$	$O(L^2)$	1
Reformer	$O(LlogL)$	$O(LlogL)$	L
LSTM	$O(L)$	$O(L)$	L

3   Methodology

The task of multidimensional time series prediction is to use a past sequence $X_{:in,d}$ to predict the state of a future time series $Y_{:out,d}$. $X_{:in,d}$ represents the time information that has occurred in the past, $Y_{:out,d}$ represents the time that needs to be predicted in the future, and d represents the information dimensions contained in the time series (the information in these dimensions is not only relevant in the current time, but also in different spatial dimensions at different times). For example in transport processes, the number of vehicles entering the road during this period will affect the number of vehicles exiting the road in the future. Therefore, in Sect. 3.1 of this article, proposed to use DSMF to integrate the spatial dimensions of time series embedding. To effectively capture information between temporal positions and spatial dimensions. In Sect. 3.2, two-part attention was proposed, which differs from previous self-attention mechanisms in that temporal and spatial information are processed in different ways to extract dependencies. Finally, encoder-decoder structure is used in Sect. 3.3.

3.1   Dimension Segment Mean Fusion

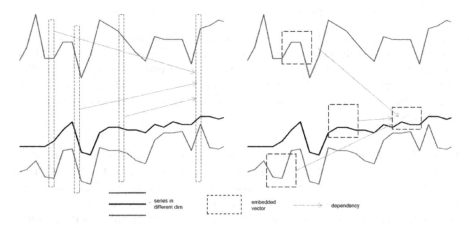

Fig. 1. The traditional transformer based model does not utilize the encoding method of spatial position information (left), utilizes spatial position information to divide the sequence into multiple segments and embed them in the vector (right)

In the past, much of the processing of multidimensional time series has involved concatenating information and position codes simultaneously (Fig. 1.), ignored searching for relationships between the encoded sequences. This results in a significant loss of dependency relationships in the spatial dimension. To make better use of spatial and temporal information, we propose DSMF to integrate information from different dimensions into embedded sequences. The approach is to embed information from different dimensions of a multidimensional time series into the same segment. The length of the multidimensional time series is N, the dimension is D, the selected segment size is L_{seg}, the expanded dimension is sampled using the fusion of the mean values of the sequence dimensions.

$$X_j = \frac{\sum_1^n x_{ij}}{n}(1 < n < N, 1 < j < D) \tag{1}$$

$$x_{seg}^{(s)} = \left\{ x_{i,d} \middle| 1 \le i \le \frac{D \cdot N}{L_{seg}} Padding(X_j), 1 \le d \le D, 1 \le X_j \le L_{seg} \right\} \quad (2)$$

where x_{ij} represent the elements of row i and column j of time series, $x_{seg}^{(s)}$ represents the features embedded in the spatial dimension

$$X_{in} = x_{seq}^{(s)} + x_{pos}^{(t)} \quad (3)$$

$x_{pos}^{(t)}$ represents the positional coding of time, X_{in} contains both temporal and spatial positional information. Crossformer [23] also used to segment the sequence and convert it into 2D vectors and embed them in the input part. However, they did not take well into account the stationarity of the input sequence. We incorporated stationary fusion into the segmentation idea to make the sequence smoother.

3.2   Two Part Attention

For X_{in} is a 2D vector [24] containing time and position information, which have different meanings in terms of length and width. Therefore, it is not possible to use self-attention mechanisms directly (Fig. 2.), and using self-attention mechanisms directly [25] can make the time complexity particularly high. Therefore, when dealing with X_{in}, we proposed Two Part Attention to process the input 2D vectors differently.

Cross-Time Part. For the time encoding part (Fig. 3.) we use Time_Attention which is a new method of attention that processes the obtained queries Q, keys K and values V [6] by Fourier transform and puts them into Time_delay_agg module, hereafter referred to as Tdg, using Tdg not only to reduce the time complexity but also to remove most of the noise caused by the encoding itself.

$$Time\_delay\_agg(R_{Q,K}) = softmax(argTopk(R_{Q,K})) \quad (4)$$

$$Time\_Attention(Q,K,V) = Tdg(\frac{IFFT(FFT(Q) \cdot FFT(K)^T)}{\sqrt{d_k}}) \cdot V \quad (5)$$

where argTopk(·) is to get the arguments of the Topk and let $k = \lfloor c \times logL \rfloor$, c is a hyper-parameter. $R_{Q,K}$ is series between series Q and K. The input Q, K, V represents the sequence that has been embedded in time and space in the previous stage, d_k represents the size of the data dimension, FFT is the Fast Fourier Transform, and IFFT is the Inverse Fast Fourier Transform.

$$time_{in}^1 = LayerNorm(X_{in} + Time\_attention(X_{in}, X_{in}, X_{in})) \quad (6)$$

$$time_{in}^2 = LayerNorm(time_{in}^1 + MLP(time_{in}^1)) \quad (7)$$

LayerNorm [26] stands for regularization, MLP [24] stands for feedforward neural network, and Attention is all your Need also adopts this approach. The final $time_{in}^2$ represents the encoder input at the time level.

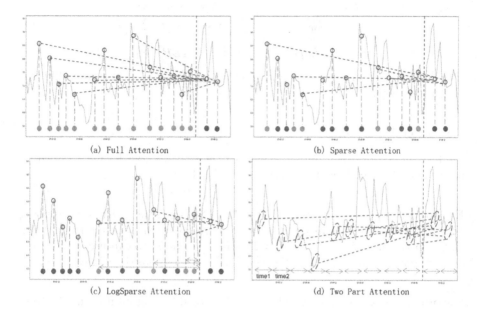

(a) Full Attention

(b) Sparse Attention

(c) LogSparse Attention

(d) Two Part Attention

Fig. 2. Two Part Attention compared to other Self-Attention families

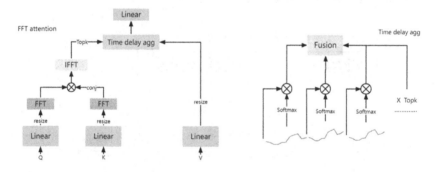

Fig. 3. FFT attention part (left) and Time delay agg (right). We first use Fast Fourier Transform to remove noise mixed in the temporal and spatial parts, and then use Time delay agg to capture information contained in the temporal part.

Cross-Dimension Part. In terms of spatial location information, we adopted the MSA [6] method, which uses a router mechanism to select a portion of the input vector and place it in the attention layer, greatly reducing time complexity.

$$dim_{in}^1 = MSA(R, time_{in}^2, time_{in}^2) \tag{8}$$

$$dim_{in}^2 = MSA(X_{in}, dim_{in}^1, dim_{in}^1) \tag{9}$$

where $R \in R^{l \times c \times d}$(1 is the batch size,c is a constant, d is the data dimensio) is the learnable vector arrayserving as routers., $time_{in}^2$ represents the embedded time series(), and the MSA layer represents multi-head self-attention,

$$dim_{in}^3 = LayerNorm(X_{in} + dim_{in}^2) \tag{10}$$

$$dim_{in}^4 = LayerNorm(dim_{in}^3 + MLP(dim_{in}^3)) \tag{11}$$

Ultimately, dim_{in}^4 involves extracting and fusing time information from different dimensions together.

3.3   Encoder-Decoder

We have added our own improvements to the original transformer to create a brand new Encoder-Decoder [6] structure (Fig. 4.).

Encoder. As is shown in Fig. 4, in the Encoder layer, the previously proposed DSMF results were used as input, containing temporal and spatial information, and then the attention section used Two part attention to capture information across temporal and spatial dimensions. The model contains three Encoder layers.

Decoder. For the input obtained from the Encoder, we output it in the Decoder, which uses a standard decoder structure consisting of two multi head attention mechanism layers stacked together.

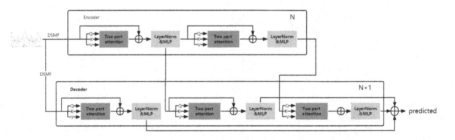

Fig. 4. An Encoder-Decoder architecture with two encoder layers, where the input is a multidimensional vector encoded by time and spatial positions. The encoder layer is used to capture features at two levels, and the output passing through the encoder layer is transmitted to the decoder layer as input. The decoder finally predicts by overlaying at each level.

Loss Function. We selected MSEloss [27] function as the prediction target sequence, and loss function was transferred from Decoder to the whole model. y represents the true result. $\hat{y}$ represents the predicted result.

$$MSEloss = \frac{\sum(\hat{y} - y)^2}{N} \tag{12}$$

4   Experiments

We conducted experiments on five real-world datasets, including five mainstream time series forecasting applications: electricity, transport, and disease, and compared them with five commonly used time series models.

4.1   Dataset

1) we build the benchmark on the two ETT datasets. which includes the hourly recorded ETTh1, 15-minutely recorded ETTm1. ETT dataset contains the data collected from electricity transformers, including load and oil temperature that are recorded every 15 min between July 2016 and July 2018. 2) ILI includes the weekly recorded influenza-like illness (ILI) patients data from Centers for Disease Control and Prevention of the United States between 2002 and 2021, which describes the ratio of patients seen with ILI and the total number of the patients. 3) ECL(Electricity Consuming Load): It collects the electricity consumption (Kwh) of 321 clients. Due to the missing data (Li et al. 2019), we convert the dataset into hourly consumption of 2 years and set 'MT 320' as the target value. The train/val/test is 15/3/4 months. 4) Traffic is a collection of hourly data from California Department of Transportation, which describes the road occupancy rates measured by different sensors on San Francisco Bay area freeways.

Table 2. Results of using 8 model times on 5 dataset and Selected input length of 96. The best results are indicated in bold font.

Models		LSTMa		LSTNet		MTGNN		Tranformer		Informer		Autoformer		Pyraformer		STEGformer	
Metric		MSE	MAE	MSE	MAE	MSE	MAE	MSE	MAE	MSE	MAE	MSE	MAE	MSE	MAE	MSE	MAE
ETTh1	24	0.650	0.624	1.293	0.901	0.336	0.393	0.620	0.577	0.577	0.549	0.439	0.440	0.493	0.507	**0.321**	**0.381**
	48	0.702	0.675	1.456	0.960	0.386	0.429	0.692	0.671	0.685	0.625	0.429	0.442	0.554	0.544	**0.371**	**0.420**
	168	1.212	0.867	1.997	1.214	**0.466**	**0.474**	0.947	0.797	0.931	0.752	0.493	0.479	0.781	0.675	0.531	0.524
	336	1.424	0.994	2.655	1.369	0.736	0.643	1.094	0.813	1.128	0.873	0.509	0.492	0.912	0.747	**0.622**	**0.580**
ETTm1	24	0.621	0.629	1.968	1.170	0.260	0.324	0.306	0.371	0.323	0.369	0.310	0.428	0.310	0.371	**0.252**	**0.321**
	48	1.392	0.939	1.999	1.215	0.386	0.408	0.465	0.470	0.494	0.503	0.465	0.464	0.465	0.646	**0.286**	**0.347**
	96	1.339	0.913	2.762	1.542	0.428	0.446	0.681	0.612	0.678	0.614	0.520	0.476	0.520	0.504	**0.327**	**0.380**
	288	1.740	1.124	1.257	2.076	0.469	0.488	1.162	0.879	1.056	0.786	0.729	0.522	0.729	0.657	**0.418**	**0.444**
ILI	24	5.914	1.734	6.026	1.770	4.265	1.387	3.954	1.323	4.588	1.462	3.101	1.238	3.970	1.338	**3.080**	**1.191**
	36	6.631	1.845	5.340	1.668	4.777	1.496	4.167	1.360	4.845	1.496	3.397	1.270	4.377	1.410	**3.611**	**1.232**
	48	6.736	1.857	6.080	1.787	5.333	1.592	4.746	1.463	4.865	1.516	2.947	1.203	4.811	1.503	**3.521**	**1.222**
	60	6.870	1.879	5.548	1.720	5.070	1.522	5.219	1.553	5.212	1.576	3.019	1.202	5.204	1.588	**3.580**	**1.220**
ECL	48	0.486	0.572	0.369	0.445	0.173	0.280	0.334	0.399	0.344	0.393	0.241	0.351	0.478	0.471	**0.115**	**0.214**
	168	0.574	0.602	0.394	0.476	0.236	0.320	0.353	0.420	0.368	0.424	0.299	0.387	0.452	0.455	**0.168**	**0.270**
	336	0.886	0.795	0.419	0.477	0.328	0.373	0.381	0.439	0.381	0.431	0.375	0.428	0.463	0.456	**0.182**	**0.281**
	720	1.676	1.095	0.556	0.565	0.422	0.410	0.391	0.438	0.406	0.443	0.377	0.434	0.480	0.461	**0.235**	**0.312**
Traffic	24	0.668	0.378	0.648	3.476	0.506	0.278	0.597	0.332	0.608	0.334	0.550	0.363	0.606	0.338	**0.495**	**0.268**
	48	0.709	0.400	0.709	4.476	0.512	0.298	0.658	0.369	0.644	0.359	0.595	0.376	0.619	0.346	**0.502**	**0.277**
	168	0.900	0.523	0.713	5.476	0.521	0.319	0.664	0.363	0.660	0.391	0.649	0.407	0.635	0.347	**0.516**	**0.308**
	336	1.067	0.599	0.741	6.476	0.540	0.335	0.654	0.358	0.747	0.405	0.624	0.388	0.641	0.364	**0.532**	**0.326**

4.2   Baseline

We selected 7 models for comparison, including 4 transformer based models: Transformer [6], Informer [7], Autoformer [8], Pyraformer [9], two RNN based models: LSTNet [18], LSTMa, and some well used models, MTGNN [13].

4.3   Setup

We used the same train/vali/test as Informer [7] to predict 24, 48, 96, 168, 336, etc. future series on each dataset. The Mean Square Error(MSE) and Mean Absolute Error (MAE) are used as evaluation metrics. The optimiser used Adam [28]. The experiments were run under the Pytorch [28] framework. We ran all experiments 5 times and took the average to ensure the stability of the results.

4.4   Main Result

As shown in Table 2, STEGformer has achieved good results in predicting sequences of different lengths in most datasets, with the first and second rankings being higher than the basic transformer model. As the predicted length gradually increases (Fig. 5), the improvement of MSE and MAE is also slow. Compared to Transformer, the prediction performance has greatly improved. It is worth noting that MTGNN [18] has also achieved good results in other models, and this model also uses cross-spatial dimensional information.

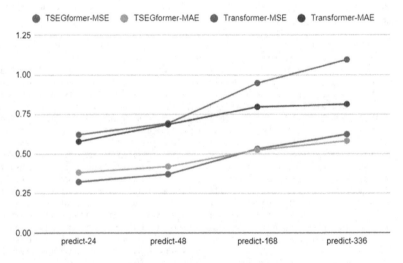

Fig. 5. MSE and MAE between TSEGformer and Transformer on ETTh1 datasets.

4.5 Ablation Study

In our approach, there are tow components: DSMF embedding, Two part attention (TPA). we perform ablation study on ETTh1 dataset. we use Transformer as the baseline and DSMF+TPA to denote TSEGformer without ablation. Three ablation versions are compared: 1) DSMF. 2) TPA. 3) DSMF+TPA.

Table 3. Predict-24 on ETTh1 dataset.

Models	Transformer		DSMF		TPA		DSMF+TPA	
Metric	MSE	MAE	MSE	MAE	MSE	MAE	MSE	MAE
24	0.620	0.577	0.435	0.420	0.356	0.391	**0.321**	**0.362**
48	0.692	0.671	0.493	0.510	0.436	0.493	**0.359**	**0.403**
168	0.947	0.797	0.926	0.766	0.863	0.703	**0.538**	**0.603**
336	1.094	0.813	0.996	0.753	0.983	0.695	**0.566**	**0.613**
720	1.241	0.971	1.081	0.865	0.963	0.806	**0.664**	**0.694**

We analysze the result shown in Table 3. 1) DSMF show better performes than Transformer on most settings. The difference between DSMF and Transformer is the enbedding method. The result shown in Table 3 indicates the usefulness of DSMF embedding and the importance of cross-dimension dependency. 2) TPA constantly improves the forecasting accuracy. This suggests that it is reasonable to treat time and dimension differently. Moreover, Adding only TPA is better than adding only DSMF. 3) Combining DSMF, TPA, TSEGformer yields best result on all settings. From Fig. 6, it is evident that DSMF+TPA has significantly improved the prediction results.

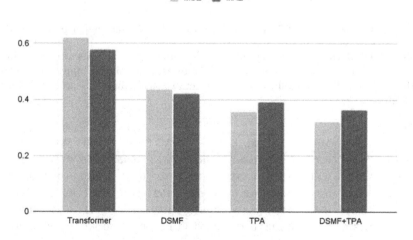

Fig. 6. The result about ablation study. The result of MSE and MAE on ETTh1 dataset under Preidct-24.

4.6 Hyper-Parameter Sensitivity

As is shown in Table 4, we can verify the model robustness with respect to hyper-parameter c (Eq. 4). To trade-off performance and efficiency. we set c to range of 1 to 5. It is also observed that datasets with periodicity tend to have a large factor c, such as ETTh1 and Traffic datasets. For ILI datasets without obvious periodicity, the large factor may bring noise. In Fig. 7, we conclude that hyper-parameter c has some impact on the experiment. In order to ensure the stability of the time results, we selected the same hyper-parameter c in the experiment.

As is shown in Table 5, we validated the impact of hyper-parameter L_{seg} (Eq. 2) on the experiment. It is related to both the model performance and computation efficiency. The general idea is to use small L_{seg} for short-term prediction and large L_{seg} for long-term prediction. Some priors about the data also help selete the L_{seg}. For example, if the hourly sampled data has a daily period, it is better to set $L_{seg} = 24$. Next we set different number of L_{seg} to explain the influence of hyper-parameters.

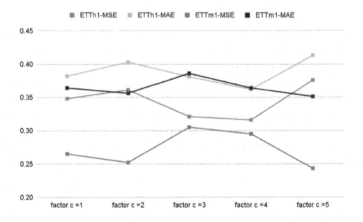

Fig. 7. Performance of ETTh1 and ETTm1 under different hyper-parameters

Table 4. STEGformer performance under different choices of hyper-parameter c in the Two part attention mechanism. we adopt the forecasting setting as input-12-predict-24 for the ETTh1, ETTm1, Traffic and ILI dataset. we choose input-24-predict-48 for the ECL dataset.

Dataset	ETTh1		ETTm1		ILI		ECL		Traffic	
Metric	MSE	MAE	MSE	MAE	MSE	MAE	MSE	MAE	MSE	MAE
c = 1	0.348	0.382	0.265	0.364	3.162	1.131	**0.095**	**0.206**	0.526	0.272
c = 2	0.361	0.403	0.252	0.356	3.264	1.152	0.165	0.256	**0.493**	**0.261**
c = 3	0.321	0.381	0.305	0.386	**3.062**	**1.102**	0.132	0.234	0.513	0.269
c = 4	**0.316**	**0.362**	0.295	0.364	3.364	1.216	0.116	0.214	0.534	0.283
c = 5	0.376	0.413	**0.243**	**0.351**	3.153	1.192	0.183	0.283	0.568	0.293

Table 5. MSE and MAE evaluation with difference segments on ETTh1 datasets and Traffic datasets.

Metric	MSE	MAE	MSE	MAE	MSE	MAE
Segment Length	5		6		7	
Input-24-Perdict-48	0.335	0.392	**0.321**	**0.381**	0.342	0.402
Segment Length	22		24		26	
Input-24-Perdict-48	0.506	0.283	**0.495**	**0.268**	0.516	0.293

5 Conclusion

This paper investigates the problem of multidimensional time series prediction, which is urgently needed in practical applications. Therefore, we propose a new transformer-based model. This model not only takes into account the time dependence of multidimensional time series, but also incorporates the dependence of spatial location information. Using DSMF, the time series is first divided into several segments to capture their different spatial dependencies, and then the temporal and spatial encodings are embedded together. The Two Part Attention (TPA) module was used to capture dependencies across time and space dimensions, and designed an Encoder-Decoder structure for prediction. The prediction achieved very good results.

References

1. Anderson, O., Kendall, M.: Time-series, 2nd edn. J. R. Stat. Soc. (Series D) (1976)
2. Patton, A.: Copula methods for forecasting multivariate time series. Handb. Econ. Forecast. (2013)
3. Demirel, O.F., Zaim, S., Caliskan, A., Ozuyar, P.: Forecasting natural gas consumption in Istanbul using neural networks and multivariate time series methods. Turk. J. Electr. Eng. Comput. Sci. (2012)
4. Angryk, R.A., et al.: Multivariate time series dataset for space weather data analytics. Sci. Data (2020)
5. Li, S., et al.: Enhancing the locality and breaking the memory bottleneck of transformer on time series forecasting (2019). arXiv:1907.00235
6. Vaswani, A., et al.: Attention is all you need. In: NeurIPS (2017)
7. Zhou, H., et al.: Informer: beyond efficient transformer for long sequence time-series forecasting. In: AAAI (2021)
8. Wu, H., Xu, J., Wang, J., Long, M.: Autoformer: decomposition transformers with auto-correlation for long-term series forecasting
9. Liu, S., et al.: PYRAFORMER: low-complexity pyramidal attention for long-range time series modeling and forecasting. In: International Conference on Learning Representations (ICLR) (2021a)
10. Zhou, T., Ma, Z., Wen, Q., Wang, X., Sun, L., Jin, R.: Fedformer: frequency enhanced decomposed transformer for long-term series forecasting. In: International Conference on Machine Learning (ICML) (2022)

11. Kitaev, N., Kaiser, L., Levskaya, A: Reformer: the efficient transformer. In: ICLR (2020)
12. Du, D., Su, B., Wei, Z.: Preformer: predictive transformer with multi-scale segment wise correlations for long-term time series forecasting (2022). arXiv preprint arXiv:2202.11356v1
13. Wu, Z., Pan, S., Long, G., Jiang, J., Chang, X., Zhang, C.: Connecting the dots: multivariate time series forecasting with grap neural networks. In: ACM SIGKDD International Conference on Knowledge Discovery Data Mining (KDD) (2020)
14. Ariyo, A.A., Adewumi, A.O., Ayo, C.K.: Stock price prediction using the ARIMA model. In The 16th International Conference on Computer Modelling and Simulation, pp. 106–112. IEEE (2014). cating Backpropagation Through Time to Control Gradient Bias. arXiv:1905.07473
15. Hochreiter, S., Schmidhuber, J.: Long short-term memory. Neural Comput. (1997)
16. Lea, C., Flynn, M.D., Vidal, R., Reiter, A., Hager, G.D.: Temporal convolutional networks for action segmentation and detection. In: IEEE Conference on Computer Vision and Pattern Recognition (CVPR) (2017)
17. Sen, R., Yu, H.F., Dhillon, I.S.: Think globally, act locally: a deep neural network approach to high-dimensional time series forecasting. In: NeurIPS (2019)
18. Lai, G., Chang, W.C., Yang, Y., Liu, H.: Modeling long- and short-term temporal patterns with deep neural networks. In: International ACM SIGIR Conference on Research Development in Information Retrieval (SIGIR) (2018)
19. Devlin, J., Chang, M.W., Lee, K., Toutanova, K.: Bert: pre-training of deep bidirectional transformers for language understanding. In: NAACL-HLT (2019)
20. Dosovitskiy, A., et al.: An image is worth 16×16 words: transformers for image recognition at scale. In: International Conference on Learning Representations (ICLR) (2021)
21. Li, S., et al.: Enhancing the locality and breaking the memory bottleneck of transformer on time series forecasting. In: NeurIPS (2019)
22. Yunhao, Z., Junchi, Y.: Autoformer: decomposition transformers with auto-correlation for long-term series forecasting
23. Zhang, Y., Yan, J.: Crossformer: transformer utilizing crossdimension dependency for multivariate time series forecasting
24. Taylor, S.J., Letham, B.: Forecasting at scale. Am. Stat. (2018)
25. Shih, S.-Y., Sun, F.-K., Lee, H.-Y.: Temporal pattern attention for multivariate time series forecasting. Mach. Learn. (2019)
26. Song, H., Rajan, D., Thiagarajan, J., Spanias, A.: Attend and diagnose: clinical time series analysis using attention models. In: AAAI (2018)
27. Angryk, R.A., et al.: Multivariate time series dataset for space weather data analytics. Sci. Data (2020)
28. Paszke, A., et al.: Pytorch: an imperative style, high-performance deep learning library. In: NeurIPS (2019)

Fraudulent Jobs Prediction Using Natural Language Processing and Deep Learning Sequential Models

Jacob Dylan Pratley and Mohammad Masbaul Alam Polash[✉]

University of Sydney, Sydney, Australia
masbaul.polash@sydney.edu.au

Abstract. The increase of job postings being made available, particularly online, has led to an increase in fraudulent job postings, designed to trick applicants into offering up their money and personal information. Previous works that proposed solutions to this issue, typically avoid analyzing sentiment to do this and instead rely only on information that can be converted into a categorical form. This paper proposes a methodology using deep learning sequential models in conjunction with natural language processing techniques to solve the fraudulent job posting issues. We test several text pre-processing techniques and word vectorization models, and experiments are performed to identify which combination of these techniques/vectorization models achieve the best results on the chosen deep learning models. The dataset used suffers from an imbalance issue, thus several different over-sampling techniques as well as the use of class weightings were tested to mitigate this. Through this experimentation, we were able to achieve a best accuracy of 98%, with a precision of 93%, recall of 89% and an F1 Score of 91%, utilizing data balanced using class weightings, a pre-trained Word2Vec embedding model and a Bi-Directional LSTM as our deep learning sequential model.

Keywords: Natural Language Processing · Fraudulent Job Prediction · Deep Learning · Sequential Models

1 Introduction

With an increasing number of job postings being made available online, an increase in the number of fraudulent job postings has been observed. The intent of these fraudulent postings is to fool applicants into offering up personal information, such as their name, email, and address, as well as tricking them out of their money, for instance by asking them to pay for 'training fees'. Fraudulent job postings are a huge problem for social media platforms, as users are accustomed to receiving fast-paced information. [1] This benefits fraudulent job postings as details are typically quite scarce due to there being no legitimate offer behind the posting. No verification is required to make posts, so getting information onto the platform is already quite simple [15]. Once on these platforms, it is quite easy for these posts to gain traction, increasing the chances

© The Author(s), under exclusive license to Springer Nature Singapore Pte Ltd. 2023
F. Zhang et al. (Eds.): WISE 2023, LNCS 14306, pp. 509–519, 2023.
https://doi.org/10.1007/978-981-99-7254-8_39

of people falling victim to them. These postings can overall be detrimental to the platforms they are posted on, and may also make it harder for companies to post legitimate information due to the reputation of the platform.

This project's aim is to provide a solution using an abundance of Natural Language Processing (NLP) techniques as well as sentiment analysis. The dataset employed to solve this problem was The Employment Scam Aegean Dataset (EMSCAD), which contains roughly 17000–18000 and was retrieved from Kaggle [3]. We start by identifying which column(s) are the best indicators of whether or not a job is fraudulent. Next, different combinations of text pre-processing techniques are compared and contrasted, followed by a comparison of different word embedding models. A series of imbalance mitigation techniques also needed to be tested. The dataset used is highly imbalanced in favour of legitimate job postings, with a ratio of around 95%–96% of all entries being legitimate. As a result, class weightings as well as three oversampling techniques; Random Oversampling (ROS), SMOTE, and ADASYN; were all tested to solve the imbalance. Finally, the best combination of text pre-processing, word embedding model, and weightings or oversampling technique were applied to three different deep learning sequential models; Long Short Term Memory (LSTM), Recurrent Neural Network (RNN) and Gated Recurrent Unit (GRU). To evaluate the performance of the models the following metrics were used; accuracy, precision, recall and F measure (f1 score), and in the end we achieved a model that achieved 98%, 93%, 89% and 91% in these respective metrics.

2 Literature Review

Habiba et al. [8] proposed a method that utilizes a series of data mining techniques to predict fraudulent jobs. Their study tested a series of machine learning algorithms as well as a Deep Neural Network (DNN). In order to perform their study, they only made use of attributes that could be converted to a categorical form. Overall their DNN model achieved the best results, with an average accuracy of 97.7%. This does demonstrate the potential that deep learning models have for predicting fraudulent jobs, however, their method is likely not sufficient for performing sentiment analysis, as the sequential models they tested only achieved an average of 75% in all metrics.

Khandagale et al. [11] proposed a similar study to predict fraudulent jobs using machine learning. Their study also utilized the EMSCAD dataset and tested numerous different machine learning classifiers, making use of the entire dataset by converting the data into numerical form using Term Frequency-Inverse Document Frequency (TF-IDF). This study highlights the importance of text pre-processing, performing measures such as stop word removal, special character removal, and missing value replacement. They were overall able to achieve a best accuracy of 97%, however, they fail to test any deep learning models and instead only rely on machine learning classifiers.

Mahbub et al. [12] investigated the importance of contextual features in the prediction of fraudulent jobs. The study arose from a lack of similar studies considering contextual aspects of the organization offering the job, such as the organization's history, reputation, internet footprint, and instead just utilizing textual and structural information of the job postings. The study did make use of the EMSCAD dataset, however, most data was gathered online, by first extracting the name of the company from the 'company_profile' column of the EMSCAD dataset, and then using this to research the company and gather additional information. The results of the study are overall incomparable to our study as well as previous studies due to the differences in their data collection and overall methodology, however, their study highlights the importance of contextual information and indicates that the 'company_profile' column may be useful.

Ranparia et al. [18] proposed a different study that aimed to predict fake jobs using a Sequential Network. Also using the EMSCAD dataset, the paper wanted to utilize Natural Language Processing (NLP) techniques as opposed to popular machine learning classifiers such as those used by previously mentioned studies. Their study made use of the Glove embedding model in order to vectorize their data, and utilized a Sequential Neural Network in order to classify the job postings. Their model achieved a training accuracy of 97.94% and a testing accuracy of 99.28% on a test set constructed using job postings scraped from LinkedIn. The results initially seem high, however, they leave out other performance metrics and only display accuracy, which is not a solid indicator of overall performance. Seeing as the dataset is imbalanced, a high accuracy is guaranteed if the model can just learn to predict legitimate jobs. Thus, without these other metrics, we don't know if their model is able to correctly classify fraudulent jobs or if it is only able to classify legitimate job postings.

Amaar et al. [4] performed a study that tackled the task of fake job detection that utilized both ML and NLP approaches. Again using the EMSCAD dataset, this study places a heavier emphasis on NLP techniques than previous studies, performing numerous text pre-processing techniques using Bag-of-Words and TF-IDF for feature extraction. The study also proposes a solution to the imbalance issue by using the ADASYN oversampling technique and claims to have achieved 98% in all metrics using a Convolutional Neural Network (CNN) model in conjunction with oversampling. These results initially seem high, however, the study oversamples the entire dataset rather than just the training set, and thus it is highly likely that these high results are due to data leakage.

3   Proposed Methodology

3.1   Feature Reduction

We test 7 of the 17 attributes available within the dataset. The attributes utilized were title, location, department, company profile, description, requirements, and benefits, with the fraudulent column acting as the class. The aim was to determine which features were the best indicators of a job postings legitimacy. Using only the best features would not only lead to better results, but reducing the size of the input to the models would also reduce the computation time needed to train them. Once each column was tested and the results found, the best-performing columns were concatenated together and tested to see if better results could be achieved and they would be used for all testing going forward.

3.2 Pre-processing

Pre-processing methods such as punctuation removal, number removal, case normalization and stop word removal, stemming and lemmatization were all tested, and the best combination of these techniques were used in the final model.

3.3 Word Embedding Models

As we are utilizing deep learning models, we need a way of representing words in some numerical form. Word embedding models were utilised, as they map words to numerical vectors and still allow for word similarities to be represented. This study trains several of these embedding models on our own dataset and also utilizes several pre-trained models. We train a Word2Vec [14] as well as a FastText [5] model on our dataset, whilst utilizing two Glove [17] as well as one Word2Vec pre-trained model, those being the 'glove-wiki-gigaword-300', 'glove-twitter-200', 'word2vec-google-news-300' models, all of which are available online [2]. For the models trained on our own dataset, we utilized the Continuous Bag-of-Words (CBOW) approach for training.

3.4 Weightings

The first data imbalance mitigation method we test is adjusting the class weightings, which helps indicate how important the class is, where a higher weighting would indicate it being more important. Due to the imbalance in the dataset, a higher weighting was assigned to fraudulent job postings. For testing purposes, we start by making the weight of each class proportionate to the number of entries the class has in the dataset. The calculation for the weights would look as follows:

$$\text{Weight\_legitimate(WL)} = \frac{\text{number\_of\_entries}}{\text{number\_of\_classes} \times \text{number\_of\_legitimate\_entries}}$$

$$\text{Weight\_fraudulent(WF)} = \frac{\text{number\_of\_entries}}{\text{number\_of\_classes} \times \text{number\_of\_fraudulent\_entries}}$$

We then experiment using different weight values, which are all calculated by dividing weight_fraudulent by a given amount.

3.5   Oversampling

The other method we use to mitigate the imbalance issue is oversampling, where new samples of the minority class(es) are generated until the amount of minority class samples is equal to or close to the amount of majority class samples. This study has utilized and tested three different techniques of oversampling, those being SMOTE [6], ADASYN [9] and Random Oversampling (ROS) [13]. SMOTE [6] and ADASYN [9] both generate synthetic (new) samples for the minority class, whereas ROS [13] simply duplicates existing minority samples and adds them back into the set.

3.6   Performance Metrics

Definition 1. *Accuracy is the amount of correctly predicted examples over the number of total examples.*

Definition 2. *Precision of a class refers to the ratio of the class correctly predicted and the number of times the class was predicted in total.*

$$Accuracy = \frac{correctly\_predicted}{number\_of\_entries} \qquad Precision = \frac{correct\_class\_prediction}{total\_times\_class\_predicted}$$

Definition 3. *Recall of a class is the ratio of the class correctly predicted and the total amount of entries the class has.*

Definition 4. *F1 Score of a class is essentially the mean of both precision and recall.*

$$Recall = \frac{correct\_class\_prediction}{total\_entries\_of\_class} \qquad F1Score = \frac{2 \times (Precision \times Recall)}{Precision + Recall}$$

For our results, we show the average precision, recall and f1 rather than the scores for each individual class.

3.7   Deep Learning Models

This section describes the deep learning sequential models that the study has made use of. Deep learning sequential models are very commonly employed for NLP tasks such as the sentiment analysis performed in our study. The models utilized are Recurrent Neural Network (RNN) [16], Long Short Term Memory (LSTM) [10], and Gated Recurrent Unit (GRU) [7].

Model Hyperparameters. For each model used, we use an embedding layer with an input dimension equal to the size of our vocabulary (number of word embeddings generated) and an output size equal to the dimension of these embeddings (as a result these sizes will differ depending on which word embedding model is being tested). Each model is bi-directional, having an input size equal to the embedding dimensions and a hidden size of 5. Each model is compiled using binary cross entropy as the loss function and 'adam' as the optimizer. Finally, each model is trained with a batch size of 32, and uses 20 epochs for training unbalanced data and 2 epochs for training the balanced data.

Initial and Final Models. As mentioned, we test different combinations of features, pre-processing techniques, embedding models, oversampling techniques and sequential deep learning models. However, in order to test and generate results we still need a basic model that can be trained and produce results. Thus, we developed an initial model that utilizes all pre-processing techniques, a word2vec embedding model, and a bi-directional LSTM architecture. As we iterate through the testing stages, the techniques/models used will be trained using the best techniques/models from the previous stages. For example, at the embedding model testing stage, the best combination of features as well as the best combination of pre-processing techniques discovered prior will be utilized. Our final model will use the best techniques/models identified throughout all the testing stages.

4   Experimental Evaluation

4.1   Feature Selection

Table 1. Feature Reduction Results

Features	Accuracy	Precision	Recall	F1
Title	95	47	50	49
Location	95	47	50	49
Department	95	47	50	49
Company Profile	96	98	63	70
Description	97	92	71	78
Requirements	97	92	71	78
Benefits	95	95	55	58
Description + Requirements	97	88	75	80
Company Profile + Description + Requirements + Benefits	98	92	82	86

Analyzing Table 1, we first observe poor results achieved from using the Title, Location and Department columns. Since the accuracy is quite high whilst all other metrics are quite low, it is likely that the model is simply predicting all entries as legitimate. Notable improvements are observed when looking at the Company Profile, Description, Requirements and Benefits columns. These improvements indicate that using these columns the model is able to correctly classify some fraudulent jobs as opposed to just legitimate jobs, which is to be expected as this is a sentiment analysis task and thus long textual descriptions such as these columns would prove useful. The concatenation of columns was also tested to see if better results could be obtained. Of the concatenations we tested, we found that the combination of the Company Profile, Description, Requirements and Benefits achieved the best results, having the highest accuracy, precision and F1 observed thus far. It is likely that for this task analyzing the sentiment of all of these columns is more useful than only analyzing one of the columns. This concatenation of columns would thus be used for all testing/models going forward.

4.2   Pre-Processing Combinations

Table 2. Pre-Processing Combination Results

	Accuracy	Precision	Recall	F1
No pre-processing	96	86	80	82
Case Normalization + special character removal+ stop word removal	97	88	83	85
All techniques + stemming	97	87	84	85
All techniques + lemmatization	98	92	82	86

From Table 2, we first observe that the worst performance was achieved when no pre-processing occurred. This is due to noise being left in the dataset, providing no benefits when trying to analyze sentiment. We also observe that stemming did not lead to any improvements whilst lemmatization did. This is likely due to how the two techniques operate. Since stemming truncates words down to their root or most common form, words may be truncated to the point where it loses its meaning. Lemmatization mitigates this by converting words to their root dictionary form, thus not losing the meaning, which is likely why it led to an improvement in results. The combination of lemmatization and all other pre-processing techniques is what will be used in the final model as well as all future testing, due to this combination achieving the highest accuracy, precision and F1 score whilst only being slightly lower in recall than some other combinations.

4.3   Word Embedding Models

Table 3. (a) Word Embedding Model Results (b) Class Weightings Results

(a)

	Accuracy	Precision	Recall	F1
Word2Vec	98	92	82	86
FastText	96	83	76	79
Glove Wiki 300	98	90	84	87
Glove Twitter 200	98	91	81	85
Word2Vec Google News 300	98	91	85	88

(b)

	Accuracy	Precision	Recall	F1
No weightings	98	91	85	88
WL & WF	97	85	87	86
WL & WF/2	98	93	89	91
WL & WF/4	98	88	87	88
WL & WF/8	98	89	89	89

Observing Table 3(a), we see that the Word2Vec model trained on our own dataset outperformed the FastText model trained on our dataset. FastText proves beneficial when dealing with out-of-vocabulary words, however, if these words don't appear then there is no longer an Advantage to FastText, which is likely what has occurred here and why Word2Vec has achieved better results. As for our pre-trained models, we see that the Word2Vec model trained on the google news dataset obtained the best results. Whilst this might be attributed to the embedding model itself, it is more likely that the dataset used to train the model was more similar to our own dataset than the data used to train the other models. The Word2Vec model trained on the google news dataset led to the overall best performance, as it achieved the same accuracy as the model trained on our dataset, whilst improving in recall and F1. Thus, this model was selected for all testing going forward.

4.4   Class Weightings

From the results in Table 3(b), we see that overall, the best results were obtained by assigning a weighting of WF/2 to the fraudulent class. As discussed, class weightings are a way of assigning importance to a class and updating the loss function. Since the loss function is responsible for how the model learns, the results likely mean that out of the values tested, the model had the easiest time converging to a local optimum when using a value of WF/2. Increasing the weighting likely leads to the model being punished too much and trying to change too drastically, whilst decreasing the weighting from here likely leads to the loss not being updated enough. WF/2 was tied for the highest accuracy and recall whilst also achieving the best precision and F1 score, and was thus selected as the best weighting to use.

4.5   Oversampling Techniques

Table 4(a) shows the results of oversampling only the training data. Table 4(b) shows that whilst the accuracy is quite high for oversampling the dataset, the model performs poorly in all other metrics, which is a indication that the model is

Table 4. (a) Oversampling only the training Set (b) Oversampling the entire dataset

	(a) Accuracy	Precision	Recall	F1		(b) Accuracy	Precision	Recall	F1
ROS	97	60	55	57	ROSS	99	99	99	99
SMOTE	98	63	57	59	SMOTE	99	99	99	99
ADASYN	98	64	61	64	ADASYN	99	99	99	99

overfitting. ROS simply duplicates entries whilst SMOTE and ADASYN produce synthetic data which is similar to the original, and thus it is likely that the model becomes accustomed to seeing either the same entries or extremely similar entries every epoch, and thus can't generalize well to new data during testing. Oversampling the dataset is also tested, as results of [4] were achieved the same way. Whilst the results are much better, it is important to consider that the issue of data leakage arises when oversampling a dataset as opposed to the training set. Data leakage occurs when data from the training set ends up or "leaks" into the test set. When oversampling the dataset, the new samples generated bear similarities to everything in the dataset. Thus, once the data is split into training and testing sets, the entries in both sets are nearly identical, at least in regard to the oversampled entries. We know from Table 4(a) that the models can't generalize well to new data when trained on the oversampled data, thus the high results in Table 4(b) must mean that it isn't really seeing new data, which would be a result of data leakage. Due to this, oversampled results should not be considered and no oversampling is used in the final model.

4.6 Final Results

Table 5. (a) Sequential Model Results (b) Comparison with state-of-the-art models

	(a) Accuracy	Precision	Recall	F1	(b)	Accuracy	Precision	Recall	F1
LSTM	98	93	89	91	Our Model (Bi LSTM+)	98	93	89	91
RNN	95	81	81	81	Amaar et al. [4]	98	95	80	86
GRU	97	90	84	87	Ranparia et al. [18]	99	N/A	N/A	N/A
					Habiba et al. [8]	75	75	75	75
					Khandagale et al. [11]	97	N/A	N/A	N/A

Overall, the results in Table 5(a) indicate that the LSTM model has outperformed all other models in all metrics. The RNN ended up being the worst-performing model, likely due to RNNs suffering from the vanishing gradient problem; where they start to learn at a slower rate when the input sequences become too large. The GRU was the next best performing model as it's able to discard information, mostly avoiding the vanishing gradient problem, however, it lets go of more information than an LSTM would in order to train faster. The LSTM achieved the best results and was thus chosen as our final model.

The results in Table 5(b) show our final results as well as the bet results achieved by the studies analyzed in the Literature Review.

5   Conclusions and Future Work

Through this study, we have been able to predict fraudulent jobs using a sentiment analysis approach. Of the dataset's 17 features, 7 were tested and our results found that the combination of company profile, description, requirements and benefits information produced the best results. Different pre-processing techniques were tested in order to reduce noise in the dataset, and our results found that all special/numerical character removal, stop word removal, case normalization and lemmatization used in conjunction with each other led to the best overall results. We used several different word embedding models in order to vectorize the data, and found that overall the highest results were achieved when utilizing a Word2Vec architecture trained using the google news dataset. The dataset utilized for experimentation suffered from a class imbalance issue in which fraudulent job postings made up roughly 5% of the dataset, and thus class weightings and oversampling techniques were tested in order to mitigate this issue. We found that calculating the ratio of fraudulent and legitimate job postings in the dataset, assigning these as class weights, and then dividing the weight of fraudulent jobs by 2 led to the highest overall increase in results. Weightings with both higher and lower values were tested, none of which achieved greater results. We have concluded that higher weightings cause the model to focus too much on fraudulent postings and leads the model to incorrectly classify more legitimate job postings, whilst decreasing the size of the weightings leads the model to not place enough emphasis on fraudulent postings. As for oversampling, our results show that oversampling only the train set using either ROS, SMOTE or ADASYN causes the model to further overfit and leads to poor results on the test set. When oversampling the entire dataset, we see a significant increase in results, however, we have concluded that this increase in results is due to data leakage and thus should not be considered useful. Class weightings were thus deemed to be the best solution to the class imbalance problem. Bi-directional LSTM, RNN and GRU models were also tested, with the LSTM model achieving the greatest results. Overall, our final model was able to achieve an accuracy of 98%, precision of 93%, recall of 89% and an F1 score of 91% on the test set.

Future work for the study would primarily aim at further mitigating the class imbalance issue with the dataset. Adding weightings to the classes did lead to an increase in results, however overall the model still has some issues with predicting fraudulent jobs. Mitigation strategies could include gathering additional data and combining it with our own dataset to reduce the class imbalance. Different oversampling techniques that are better suited for text data may also be an option, as it's likely that the methods tested performed poorly as they were designed with machine learning tasks in mind as opposed to sentiment analysis tasks and text data. To further improve the results, different deep learning models could also be tested, and hyper-parameter tuning of the current model may also yield better results.

References

1. Market incentives that drive fraud: The truth behind reach vs. frequency. Accessed 6 Nov 2022
2. Rare-technologies gensim-data. https://github.com/RaRe-Technologies/gensim-data. Accessed 6 Nov 2022
3. Real/fake job posting prediction. https://www.kaggle.com/datasets/shivamb/real-or-fake-fake-jobposting-prediction. Accessed 6 Nov 2022
4. Amaar, A., Aljedaani, W., Rustam, F., Ullah, S., Rupapara, V., Ludi, S.: Detection of fake job postings by utilizing machine learning and natural language processing approaches. Neural Process. Lett. **54**(3), 2219–2247 (2022)
5. Bojanowski, P., Grave, E., Joulin, A., Mikolov, T.: Enriching word vectors with subword information. Trans. Assoc. Comput. Linguist. **5**, 135–146 (2017)
6. Chawla, N.V., Bowyer, K.W., Hall, L.O., Kegelmeyer, W.P.: Smote: synthetic minority over-sampling technique. J. Artif. Intell. Res. **16**, 321–357 (2002)
7. Cho, K., et al.: Learning phrase representations using RNN encoder-decoder for statistical machine translation. arXiv preprint arXiv:1406.1078 (2014)
8. Habiba, S.U., Islam, M.K., Tasnim, F.: A comparative study on fake job post prediction using different data mining techniques. In: 2021 2nd International Conference on Robotics, Electrical and Signal Processing Techniques (ICREST), pp. 543–546. IEEE (2021)
9. He, H., Bai, Y., Garcia, E.A., Li, S.: ADASYN: adaptive synthetic sampling approach for imbalanced learning. In: 2008 IEEE International Joint Conference on Neural Networks (IEEE World Congress on Computational Intelligence), pp. 1322–1328. IEEE (2008)
10. Hochreiter, S., Schmidhuber, J.: Long short-term memory. Neural Comput. **9**(8), 1735–1780 (1997)
11. Khandagale, P., Utekar, A., Dhonde, A., Karve, S.: Fake job detection using machine learning
12. Mahbub, S., Pardede, E.: Using contextual features for online recruitment fraud detection (2018)
13. Menardi, G., Torelli, N.: Training and assessing classification rules with imbalanced data. Data Min. Knowl. Discov. **28**, 92–122 (2014)
14. Mikolov, T., Chen, K., Corrado, G., Dean, J.: Efficient estimation of word representations in vector space. CoRR abs/1301.3781 (2013)
15. Olan, F., Jayawickrama, U., Arakpogun, E.O., Suklan, J., Liu, S.: Fake news on social media: the impact on society. Inf. Syst. Front. 1–16 (2022)
16. Pearlmutter, B.A.: Learning state space trajectories in recurrent neural networks. Neural Comput. **1**(2), 263–269 (1989)
17. Pennington, J., Socher, R., Manning, C.D.: Glove: Global vectors for word representation. In: Empirical Methods in Natural Language Processing (EMNLP), pp. 1532–1543 (2014). https://www.aclweb.org/anthology/D14-1162
18. Ranparia, D., Kumari, S., Sahani, A.: Fake job prediction using sequential network. In: 2020 IEEE 15th International Conference on Industrial and Information Systems (ICIIS), pp. 339–343. IEEE (2020)

Prediction of Student Performance with Machine Learning Algorithms Based on Ensemble Learning Methods

Israa Alqatow[1], Amjad Rattrout[1(✉)], and Rashid Jayousi[2]

[1] Arab American University, Ramallah, Palestine
{israa.alqatow,amjad.rattrout}@aaup.edu
[2] Alquds University, Ramallah, Palestine
rjayousi@staff.alquds.edu

Abstract. In recent years, there has been significant interest surrounding Educational Data Mining (EDM). Numerous data mining techniques have been proposed to uncover latent knowledge from educational data. The knowledge extracted through these techniques assists institutions in enhancing their teaching methods and learning processes. These enhancements ultimately result in improved student performance and overall educational outcomes. In this paper, we introduce a novel student performance prediction model that utilizes data mining techniques and incorporates a set of new data features known as student behavioral features. These specific features are directly associated with the learner's interaction and engagement with the e-learning management system. To assess the performance of the student's predictive model, a set of classifiers is employed, including Artificial Neural Network(ANN), Naïve Bayes(NB), Decision Tree(DT), Support Vector Machine(SVM), Logistic Regression and K-Nearest Neighbors (KNN). Furthermore, ensemble methods such as Stacking, Boosting, and Random Forest (RF) were applied to enhance the performance of these classifiers. These ensemble methods have been widely utilized in the literature for this purpose. The obtained results demonstrate a robust correlation between learners' behaviors and their academic achievement. Through testing the model with newcomer students, an accuracy rate of 87.5% was achieved.

Keywords: Educational Data Mining · Stacking · Boosting

1 Introduction

The application of data mining, statistics, and machine learning in EDM enables researchers and educators to analyze vast amounts of educational data, such as student performance records, learning behaviors, and instructional materials. By leveraging these techniques, valuable patterns, trends, and relationships can be identified within the data, leading to the extraction of meaningful knowledge [1]. In recent times, the utilization of Artificial Intelligence (AI) in teaching

© The Author(s), under exclusive license to Springer Nature Singapore Pte Ltd. 2023
F. Zhang et al. (Eds.): WISE 2023, LNCS 14306, pp. 520–529, 2023.
https://doi.org/10.1007/978-981-99-7254-8_40

and learning processes within the educational system has undergone a remarkable evolution. The introduction of new technologies in education has become increasingly favored, as they are seen as instrumental in facilitating enhanced educational achievements for individuals [2]. The analysis and prediction of student performance play a vital role in the educational environment. Educational data mining encompasses the application of various data mining techniques, including neural networks, decision trees, support vector machines, Naïve Bayes classifier, and K-nearest neighbor, to extract valuable insights from educational data [3]. The analysis of student performance plays a crucial role in enabling students to enhance their academic achievements. Furthermore, it assists in identifying students who may require additional support or intervention to prevent academic failure. By recognizing these students in a timely manner, appropriate actions can be taken to provide the necessary assistance and make informed decisions to support their educational journey. In this research, a novel approach is introduced that utilizes ensemble learning methods to combine two classification algorithms. The primary objective is to achieve improved prediction accuracy when compared to existing algorithms. By harnessing the individual strengths of both techniques and leveraging the power of ensemble learning, the proposed approach aims to enhance the accuracy of predictions within the specific context of the study. The paper is structured, to begin with an introduction that outlines several machine-learning techniques that are used in the educational data mining field. The subsequent section delves into a thorough review of existing literature about feature reduction, educational data mining, machine learning classifiers, and ensemble learning methods. The proposed model section elucidates the mathematical model, system model, methodology, design objectives, experiments and results, and evaluation measures. Finally, the conclusion and future work section summarizes the key findings as a conclusion then in the future we will improve the model explanation, address data imbalances, integrate temporal and extracurricular variables, and create adaptable systems.

2 Literature Review

2.1 Features Reduction

In [10], authors contribute a comparative study focusing on feature selection methods designed to pinpoint pivotal factors that significantly influence classification performance. The primary aim is to amplify the models' predictive capacities by concentrating on these influential features. Within this context, the paper introduces a novel feature selection approach, named CHIMI, which employs a ranked vector score. The study thoroughly analyzes the feature sets generated by each feature selection (FS) technique to identify the prevailing feature set. The investigation [11] employs student data encompassing both demographic and academic information. By utilizing feature subset selection algorithms, a systematic analysis of diverse attributes within the student data is conducted. Notably, this research proposes a concise attribute set termed the Student Data Feature Set (SDFS). The experimental findings unequivocally demonstrate that employing the learning model with SDFS leads to the most favorable outcomes, concurrently minimizing errors.

2.2   Educational Data Mining

Educational data mining has gained prominence recently, aiming to enhance education quality. Institutions strive for academic excellence by considering various factors like personal attributes and academic abilities. A study [5] predicts student performance in an Indian technical institution using the support vector regression linear algorithm. Another contribution, [6], offers a pioneering systematic review of educational data mining in classroom learning, identifying predictors and emphasizing temporal aspects. However, its focus on classroom settings could limit its applicability to other educational scenarios.

2.3   Machine Learning Classifiers

The application of data mining techniques assists in enhancing students' performance by leveraging their psychological features. This approach utilizes both linear kernel and radial basis kernel (RBK) methods to analyze and extract valuable insights. The paper [7] employs a multi-classifier Support Vector Machine (SVM) to categorize learners into high, average, and low categories based on their academic scores. The NN algorithm predicts with 69% of accuracy and the decision tree predicts with 65% of accuracy. The prediction accuracy of SVM was found to be 83%. The authors [8] introduce a novel performance prediction model for students, leveraging data mining techniques. This model incorporates a set of newly identified features, referred to as behavioral features, to enhance the accuracy of predictions. Among the evaluated classification algorithms, the Decision Tree algorithm demonstrated the highest accuracy of 90%. Following closely was the Random Forest algorithm, which achieved an accuracy of 85%. The Naïve Bayesian (NB) algorithm provided an accuracy of 84%, while the Rule Induction algorithm had the lowest accuracy of 82%. Other algorithms, such as K-Nearest Neighbor (KNN), Discriminant Analysis (Disc), Pairwise Coupling (PWC), ID3, and Support Vector Machine (SVM), were not mentioned in terms of accuracy.

2.4   Ensemble Learning Methods

In [9], data mining techniques enhance student performance prediction accuracy through ensemble methods. Authors introduce the Ad-aBoostM2 technique combined with Differential Evolution as "ADDE," effectively reducing weak learners and improving accuracy on the KalBoard 360 dataset. This approach contributes by demonstrating the potential of ensemble learning in student performance prediction. AdaBoost adapts instance weights based on accuracy, while stacking leverages logistic regression for interpretability, using base models' predictions as features. However, ensemble model complexity poses a limitation for clear interpretation.

3 Proposed Model

Our "Prediction of Student Performance with Machine Learning Algorithms Based on Ensemble Learning Methods" model employs ensemble techniques for accurate and robust predictions. Ensemble learning merges individual models to create a potent prediction model. Aggregating these diverse perspectives enhances accuracy and reliability. We compare two models: **AdaBoost with Random Forest**, using AdaBoost to ensemble Random Forest classifiers; and **Stacking with Random Forest and Neural Networks** combined via logistic regression, effectively leveraging both models' predictions.

3.1 Design Objectives

The objectives of the Prediction of Student Performance with Machine Learning Algorithms Based on Ensemble Learning Methods are to:

- Enhance prediction accuracy using ensemble learning, combining models for robustness.
- Create models with strong generalization to diverse student data for reliable predictions.
- Reduce data dimensionality and enhance prediction efficiency.
- Conduct comprehensive evaluations to pinpoint the most effective ensemble learning approach for student performance prediction.

3.2 Mathematical Model

AdaBoost with Random Forest

1. Initialize the weights: Let's denote the weight of each training sample as wi, where i ranges from 1 to N (N is the number of training samples). Initially, all weights are set to 1/N, meaning each sample is equally weighted.
2. Iterative training: For each iteration t (or round), a weak learner (Random Forest classifier) is trained on the training set using the current sample weights. Let's denote the weak learner as ht(x), which represents the prediction of the t-th weak learner for a given input sample x.
3. Weight update: After the t-th weak learner is trained, the weights of the training samples are updated based on their performance. Misclassified samples are given higher weights, while correctly classified samples are given lower weights. The weight update formula is as shown in *Eq.* 1 for misclassified sample i and *Eq.* 2 for correctly classified sample i.

$$w_{it+1} = w_{it} * e^{a} \tag{1}$$

$$w_{it+1} = w_{it} * e^{-a} \tag{2}$$

Here, e is the base of the natural logarithm and a is the weight update factor determined by the performance of the weak learner. The higher the misclassification error, the higher the value of a, meaning those samples will have more weight in the next iteration.

4. Ensemble creation: The weak learner's predictions are combined using weighted majority voting, where the weights are based on the performance of the weak learner. The prediction of the ensemble model for a given input sample x is calculated using *Eq. 3*.

$$H(x) = sign \sum_{t=1}^{N} a_t * h_t(x)$$ (3)

Here, a_t is the weight associated with the t-th weak learner, and $h_t(x)$ is the prediction of the t-th weak learner for the input sample x.

5. Iteration update: The weights and distributions are updated for the next iteration, giving higher importance to the samples that were misclassified in the previous iteration. The weight update formula is similar to step 3.
6. Repeat steps 2–5 for a predefined number of iterations or until a stopping criterion is met.
7. Final prediction: After all iterations are completed, the ensemble of weak learners (Random Forest classifiers) is used to make predictions on new, unseen data. The final prediction is determined by majority voting.

Staking with a Combination of Random Forest and Neural Networks

Assuming we have a dataset with inputs denoted as X and corresponding target labels denoted as y. Let's define the following:

– RF(X): Random Forest prediction builds multiple decision trees denoted by i during training and combines their predictions to provide more accurate and robust results. See *Eq. 4*

$$RF(X) = (1/N) * \sum RF_i(X)$$ (4)

– NN(X): feedforward neural network prediction composed of an input layer, one or more hidden layers, and an output layer. See *Eq. 5*.

$$NN(X) = foutput(W_2 * fhidden(W_1 * X + b_1) + b_2)$$ (5)

where:
  • W1 and W2: the weight matrices of the connections between the input layer and the hidden layer, and between the hidden layer and the output layer, respectively.
  • b1 and b2: the bias vectors for the hidden layer and output layer, respectively.
  • fhidden() and foutput(): the activation functions applied to the intermediate hidden layer and the output layer, respectively.
– Logistic linear regression prediction, see *Eq. 6*:

$$Staked(X) = w_1 * RF(X) + w_2 * NN(X) + b$$ (6)

where:

- w1 and w2: weights assigned to the Random Forest and Neural Network predictions, respectively
- b is the bias term.

The logistic linear regression model learns the optimal values for w1, w2, and b based on the training data. During training, you would have a labeled dataset with inputs X and corresponding target labels y. The Random Forest and Neural Network models are trained separately on the training dataset, and their predictions (RF(X) and NN(X)) are combined using the logistic linear regression model to compute the final prediction Staked(X).

3.3   System Model

Our proposed model is designed to use the Random forest machine learning algorithm with the Adaboost ensemble method and applied after features reduction to 10 features, this means that all features participate in this model but with newly defined features that depend on the dominant feature's effects. Also, we proposed another model that used the stack ensemble method to combine the prediction model results from Random Forest(RF) and Neural Networks(NN) together and compare the testing results from the two models. The educational dataset used in this study was obtained from the Kalboard 360 E-Learning management system. This platform facilitates the interaction between various stakeholders in the educational process, including students, teachers, parents, and school management teams. To collect the data, a learner activity tracker tool (xAPI) was utilized, which tracks and records the students' activities within the learning system. These activity records provide valuable insights into the students' learning experiences within the platform see Fig. 1.

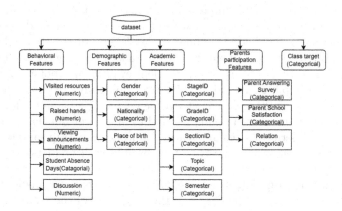

Fig. 1. Dataset features and target class

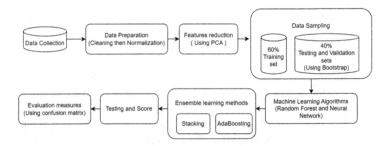

Fig. 2. Proposed model phases

3.4   Methodology

The methodology for developing a student performance prediction model involves the following steps see Fig. 2:

- **Data Collection**: Gather relevant data on student characteristics, Behavioral features, Demographic Features, Academic Background Features, and Parents' participation that might affect student performance.
- **Data Preparation**: Handling the missing values by removing records with missing values, then normalizing the data using Z-score to ensure consistency and compatibility for analysis.
- **Features reduction**: Select the most relevant features or variables that have a significant impact on student performance using principle component analysis (PCA).
- **Data Sampling**: We split the dataset into three separate sets: Training set (Fixed proportion 60%), the remaining records are also split into two subsets using Bootstrap; Test- ing set (unseen data) and Validation set (unseen data). The Trade-off between Training and Testing: The 60%–40% split strikes a balance between having enough data to train a competent model and having sufficient data for unbiased evaluation. With 60% of the data allocated to training, the model can benefit from a substantial training set, while the 40% held out for testing ensures an independent evaluation. Bootstrap data sampling is a resampling method that involves randomly selecting observations from a dataset, with replacement, to create multiple samples for analysis. Authors in [12] use this sampling method to build a model that predicts secondary school performance. By creating multiple bootstrap samples, you can assess the variability and uncertainty associated with predictions or analysis performed on the student performance dataset.
- **Machine learning Algorithm**: Choose an appropriate prediction model based on the nature of the data and the objectives of the study. Commonly used models include regression models (linear regression, logistic regression), decision trees, support vector machines, or artificial neural networks.
- **Ensemble learning methods**: Fine-tune the model by optimizing its parameters or exploring different algorithms to improve its predictive performance.

- **Testing and Score**: Once the model has been developed and optimized, it can be deployed to predict the performance of new or unseen student data. This allows for ongoing monitoring and support to help students improve their academic outcomes.
- **Model Evaluation**: Evaluate the trained model using the testing set to assess its performance and predictive accuracy. Common evaluation metrics include accuracy, precision, recall, and F1-score.

3.5   Experiments and Results

We compared the actual data and predicted data for both boosting and stacking approaches with and without features reduction see Fig. 3. First We notice that the False predicted class in the approach without features reduction for both methods is more than with features reduction. Second, the predicted results for AdaBoost are better than the Stacking method. We can also notice the distribution of data samples in clusters that spread between L: Low, M: Medium, and H: High where these categories represent the predicted class for each data sample.

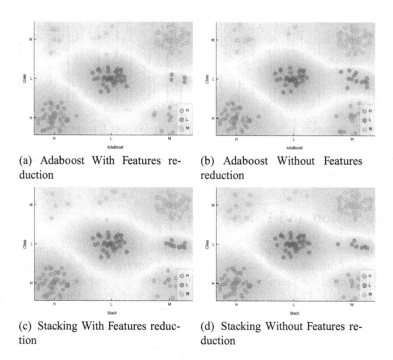

(a) Adaboost With Features reduction

(b) Adaboost Without Features reduction

(c) Stacking With Features reduction

(d) Stacking Without Features reduction

Fig. 3. Actual Class vs. predicted values for proposed model

3.6   Evaluation Measures

The evaluation measures are used to ensure that the prediction model works well by calculating a set of performance measures like Accuracy, F1 Score, precision, and Recall see Eqs. 7, 8, 9, and 10 respectively. Also, see Fig. 4.

$$Accuracy = \frac{TN + TP}{TN + FP + TP + FN} \tag{7}$$

$$F1Score = 2 * \frac{precision * Recall}{precision + Recall} \tag{8}$$

$$precision = \frac{TP}{TP + FP} \tag{9}$$

$$Recall = \frac{TP}{TP + FN} \tag{10}$$

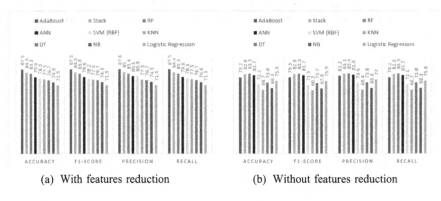

(a) With features reduction   (b) Without features reduction

Fig. 4. Comparison of evaluation measures between existing and proposed models (AdaBoost and Stack)

4   Conclusion and Future Work

Predicting student performance using machine learning algorithms based on ensemble learning methods can be a practical approach when compared with the previous machine learning methods like Artificial Neural Networks (ANN), Naive Bayes(NB), Decision Tree(DT), Support Vector Machine(SVM), Logistic Regression, and K-Nearest Neighbors (KNN). The accuracy of our proposed model using AdaBoost is 87.5%, which is greater than the accuracy of other machine learning algorithms when they worked individually. Ensemble learning combines multiple machine learning models to improve the predictive accuracy and robustness of the system. Including feature selection in the student's predictive model led to a slight improvement in accuracy across all classification algorithms. Notably, the Random Forest algorithm exhibited superior prediction results across all evaluation metrics so it was selected with Adaboost to make our proposed model. Future work should focus on accuracy enhancement, model interpretability, imbalanced data handling, temporal and non-academic factors inclusion, and adaptive systems for personalized interventions and decision-making.

References

1. Sultana, J., Rani, M.U., Farquad, M.A.H.: Student's performance prediction using deep learning and data mining methods. Int. J. Recent Technol. Eng. **8**(1S4), 1018–1021 (2019)
2. Sekeroglu, B., Dimililer, K., Tuncal, K.: Student performance prediction and classification using machine learning algorithms. In: Proceedings of the 2019 8th International Conference on Educational and Information Technology, pp. 7–11, March 2019
3. Francis, B.K., Babu, S.S.: Predicting academic performance of students using a hybrid data mining approach. J. Med. Syst. **43**, 1–15 (2019)
4. Romero, C., Ventura, S.: Data mining in education. Wiley Interdiscip. Rev. Data Min. Knowl. Discov. **3**(1), 12–27 (2013)
5. Dabhade, P., Agarwal, R., Alameen, K.P., Fathima, A.T., Sridharan, R., Gopakumar, G.: Educational data mining for predicting students' academic performance using machine learning algorithms. Mater. Today Proc. **47**, 5260–5267 (2021)
6. Khan, A., Ghosh, S.K.: Student performance analysis and prediction in classroom learning: a review of educational data mining studies. Educ. Inf. Technol. **26**, 205–240 (2021)
7. Burman, I., Som, S.: Predicting students academic performance using support vector machine. In: 2019 Amity International Conference on Artificial Intelligence (AICAI), pp. 756–759. IEEE, February 2019
8. Ajibade, S.-S.M., Ahmad, N.B., Shamsuddin, S.M.: A data mining approach to predict academic performance of students using ensemble techniques. In: Abraham, A., Cherukuri, A.K., Melin, P., Gandhi, N. (eds.) ISDA 2018 2018. AISC, vol. 940, pp. 749–760. Springer, Cham (2020). https://doi.org/10.1007/978-3-030-16657-1_70
9. Ajibade, S.S.M., Ahmad, N.B., Shamsuddin, S.M.: A novel hybrid approach of Adaboostm2 algorithm and differential evolution for prediction of student performance. Int. J. Sci. Technol. Res. **8**(07), 65–70 (2019)
10. Sokkhey, P., Okazaki, T.: Study on dominant factor for academic performance prediction using feature selection methods. Int. J. Adv. Comput. Sci. Appl. **11**(8), 492–502 (2020)
11. Chaudhury, P., Tripathy, H.K.: An empirical study on attribute selection of student performance prediction model. Int. J. Learn. Technol. **12**(3), 241–252 (2017)
12. Rebai, S., Yahia, F.B., Essid, H.: A graphically based machine learning approach to predict secondary schools performance in Tunisia. Socioecon. Plann. Sci. **70**, 100724 (2020)

Recommendation Systems

Counterfactual Explanations for Sequential Recommendation with Temporal Dependencies

Ming He[✉], Boyang An, Jiwen Wang, and Hao Wen

Beijing University of Technology, Beijing, China
heming@bjut.edu.cn, {anboyang,wangjiwen,bearwen}@emails.bjut.edu.cn

Abstract. Explanations can substantially enhance users' trust and satisfaction with recommender systems. Counterfactual explanations have demonstrated remarkable effectiveness in enhancing the performance of explainable sequential recommendation. However, existing counterfactual explanation models for sequential recommendation ignore temporal dependencies in a user's historical behavior sequence. Moreover, counterfactual histories must be as close as possible to the real history; otherwise, they will violate the user's real behavioral preferences. In this paper, we propose *Counterfactual Explanations with Temporal Dependencies* (CETD), a counterfactual explanation model based on a Variational Autoencoder (VAE) for sequential recommendation that handles temporal dependencies. When generating counterfactual histories, CETD uses a Recurrent Neural Network (RNN) to capture both long-term preferences and short-term behavior in the user's real behavioral history, which can enhance explainability. Meanwhile, CETD fits the distribution of reconstructed data in a latent space, and then uses the variance obtained from learning to make counterfactual sequences closer to the original sequence, which will reduce the proximity of counterfactual histories. Extensive experiments on two real-world datasets show that the proposed CETD consistently outperforms state-of-the-art methods.

Keywords: Recommender systems · Sequential recommendation · Counterfactual explanation

1 Introduction

Sequential recommendation predicts user preferences based on historical behaviors [8,13,17,24]. Recent years have seen effective models capturing sequential patterns. High-quality explanations enhance user understanding and satisfaction, making explainable sequential recommendation a current research focus.

Prior work has advanced explainable sequential recommendation. Current methods are categorized into deep learning and knowledge graph approaches. Deep learning methods employ various techniques for explanation [7,15]. Knowledge graph methods leverage user and item data for intuitive, tailored

F. Zhang et al. (Eds.): WISE 2023, LNCS 14306, pp. 533–543, 2023.
https://doi.org/10.1007/978-981-99-7254-8_41

explanations [10,12]. However, these approaches have limitations as they rely on correlated explanations. Extracting correlations from observed user behavior data without the foundation of causal inference may yield inaccurate explanations.

In the initial application of causal inference to explainable sequential recommendation [28,29], a perturbation model generates counterfactual histories as input sequences. These are then subjected to causal rule mining to derive explanations. Nevertheless, this approach inadequately addresses the following two counterfactual history generation challenges: (i) Given the sequential and chronological nature of a user's historical records, it becomes imperative for a model to account for temporal dependencies during counterfactual history generation. (ii) Proximity necessitates minimal perturbation magnitude for each historical sequence, aiming to maintain the closeness of counterfactual histories to the original input records, which proves most beneficial to users [18].

Addressing the mentioned challenges in explainable sequential recommendation, we propose the *Counterfactual Explanations with Temporal Dependencies* (CETD) model. CETD incorporates gated recurrent units (GRUs) when generating counterfactual histories. Unlike directly mapping a subset of the complete history to a latent space, CETD processes a subset of the historical sequence using GRUs, thereby capturing temporal dependencies within the user behavior sequence and enhancing interpretability. CETD fits the reconstructed data's distribution, comprising item embedding sequences produced by VAE with latent variational data. It generates counterfactual sequences using acquired latent variance, thus decreasing counterfactual history proximity. Our CETD counterfactual model strives to provide quality explanations for sequential recommendation, facilitating real-world application. Figure 1 exemplifies a counterfactual explanation output by CETD for item v_9.

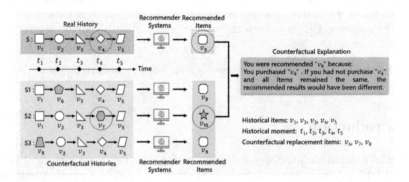

Fig. 1. An example of counterfactual explanation. In **S1** and **S3**, we use the counterfactual replacement items v_6 and v_8 to replace v_2 and v_1 in the historical sequence **S** respectively, and the recommended items are still v_9. However, in **S2**, after replacing v_4 in **S** with v_7, the recommendation result changes to v_{10}. Therefore, v_4 could be the true reason why the recommender systems recommend the original recommended item v_9.

The key contributions of this paper are summarized as follows:

- We proposed a VAE-based counterfactual explanation model for sequential recommendation that addresses temporal dependencies, effectively capturing both long-term preferences and short-term behavior to enhance explainability.
- By fitting the distribution of reconstructed data in a latent space and utilizing the acquired latent variance, CETD can produce counterfactual sequences with reduced proximity to the original sequence, thus mitigating the closeness of counterfactual histories.
- We have conducted extensive experiments to evaluate the effectiveness of our model on two real-world datasets. Results show that our model significantly outperforms state-of-the-art models.

2   Proposed Model

2.1   Notations

In this paper, we denote the set of users as $\mathcal{U} = \{u_1, u_2, ..., u_{|\mathcal{U}|}\}$ and the set of items as $\mathcal{V} = \{v_1, v_2, ..., v_{|\mathcal{V}|}\}$. Each user u is associated with a purchase history represented as a sequence of items $\mathcal{H}^u$. *In this paper, calligraphic $\mathcal{H}$ represents a user history and straight H represents an item in the user's history $\mathcal{H}$.* Function $\mathcal{F} : \mathcal{H} \rightarrow \mathcal{V}$ represents a black-box sequential recommendation model that takes a sequence of items as input and outputs recommended items.

2.2   The CETD Model

Perturbation Model. We adopt a perturbation-based approach to creating counterfactual histories by altering items in the original user history $\mathcal{H}^u$. Both VAE and GAN, prominent generative models, possess distinct attributes; VAE leverages hypothetical scenarios while GAN offers lower interpretability. Recognizing the non-random nature of user histories, we assume a definitive distribution and employ VAE to learn this distribution.

Assuming a given timestamp, item selection is influenced by a latent factor that encapsulates user trends and preferences. This latent factor is, in turn, shaped by user history to capture both enduring preferences and immediate actions. The foundational VAE framework proves valuable in accounting for time-sensitive user preferences. We assume the existence of timing information $T \in \mathbb{R}_+$, and introduce a temporal mark in the elements of H^u: The term $H^u_{(t)} \in \mathcal{V}$ (with $1 \leq t \leq T$) represents the t-th item in $\mathcal{H}^u$, whereas $H^u_{(1:t)}$ represents the sequence $H^u_{(1)}, ..., H^u_{(t)}$. Ideally, latent variable modeling when used to generate counterfactual histories must be able to express temporal dynamics. Within a probabilistic framework, we condition each event on previous events to model temporal dependencies. Therefore $H^u_{(1:T)}$ can be formulated as:

$$P(H_{(1:T)}^u) = \prod_{t=0}^{T-1} P(H_{(t+1)}^u | H_{(1:t)}^u). \tag{1}$$

Note that $H_{(1:0)}^u$ is an initialization when H^u is the first item in $\mathcal{H}$ as $H_{(1)}^u$. This specification implies two key points: (i) A recurrent relationship exists between $H_{(t+1)}^u$ and $H_{(1:t)}^u$ established by $P(H_{(t+1)}^u | H_{(1:t)}^u)$, which the modeling can leverage; and (ii) individual timesteps can be independently handled, especially through a conditional VAE. The proposed distribution introduces a dependence on the latent variable from a recurrent layer, enabling the retrieval of prior historical information. GRU, an advancement of the LSTM model, includes storage units for long-term historical data storage. In time series prediction, GRU's accuracy matches or exceeds LSTM's while boosting greater computational efficiency. We use GRU to learn the recurrent relationship between $H_{(t+1)}^u$ and $H_{(1:t)}^u$.

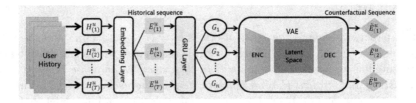

Fig. 2. Overall architecture of our proposed model CETD. E^u is the concatenation of the item embeddings of the user history. $\widetilde{E}^u$ is the perturbed embedding.

As shown in Fig. 2, we input users' real history $\mathcal{H}^u$ into the embedding layer, yielding embedding E^u. E^u then traverses a GRU layer, learning temporal dependencies from the prior history and generating enhanced long-term preference memory output G. Consequently, counterfactual sequence $\widetilde{E}^u$ can be derived for any historical sequence E^u using the VAE. This VAE incorporates a probabilistic encoder $(\mu, \sigma) = \text{ENC}(\cdot)$ and a decoder $\widetilde{E} = \text{DEC}(\cdot)$. We then transform $\widetilde{E}^u$ into the final counterfactual history $\widehat{\mathcal{H}}^u$ by dot product similarity. For each user, the perturbation will sample w times to obtain w different counterfactual histories. Finally, the generated counterfactual data $\widehat{\mathcal{H}}^u$ and the original $\mathcal{H}^u$ will be introduced into the black-box recommendation model $\mathcal{F}$ to obtain the recommendation results $\widehat{B}^u$ and B^u, respectively. For any user u, after completing this process, we will have w different counterfactual input-output pairs: $\{(\widehat{\mathcal{H}}_i^u, \widehat{B}_i^u)\}_{i=1}^w$, as well as the original pair $(\mathcal{H}^u, B^u)$. Here, the value of w is manually set but cannot exceed the number of all possible item combinations.

A counterfactual history formed after the perturbation is as relevant as possible to the user's interest. For a user, the proximity can be expressed as:

$$Proximity_u = mean\left(\sum_{\widetilde{B}_i^u \neq B^u} dist(\widetilde{\mathcal{H}}_i^u, \mathcal{H}^u) \right). \tag{2}$$

The distance is specified in the latent space. Each historical sequence can be represented by concatenating latent item representations. Sequence distance is defined as the Euclidean distance between sequences, with reported proximity as the user average. Model training's iterative objectives include fitting mean and variance distributions in potential space, while the second term reflects (negative) reconstruction error. Small variance during sampling maintains similarity to the original sequence. We train the model with the following loss function:

$$Loss = \frac{1}{|\mathcal{U}|} \sum_{u=1}^{|\mathcal{U}|} \left(-KL\Big(q(Z|G^u)\|p(Z)\Big) + \alpha \mathbb{E}_{q(Z|G^u)}\Big[log(p(G^u|Z))\Big] \right). \tag{3}$$

The first term is the KL divergence of the approximate $p(Z)$ from the true posterior $q(Z|G^u)$. We default $p(Z) \sim N(0,1)$, $q(Z|G^u) \sim N(\mu, \sigma^2)$. Z is the potential variance information. G^u is the input to the encoder. $p(G^u|Z)$ is output of the decoder. And α is a weight parameter.

Causal Rule Learning Model. Denoted as C^u, it combines counterfactual input-output pairs $\{(\widetilde{\mathcal{H}}_i^u, \widetilde{B}_i^u)\}_{i=1}^w$ and the original pair $(\mathcal{H}^u, B^u)$ for user u. $\hat{\mathcal{H}}_i^u = [\hat{H}_{i(1)}^u, \hat{H}_{i(2)}^u, \cdots, \hat{H}_{i(T)}^u]$ signifies the i-th input sequence record in C^u, with $\hat{H}_{i(t)}^u$ as the t-th item in $\hat{\mathcal{H}}_i^u$. $\hat{B}_i^u$ stands for the corresponding output. Our goal is a causal model, first extracting dependencies between input and output items from C^u, then selecting a causal rule based on these dependencies. We argue that modeling the occurrence of a single output involves a logistic regression of all input items' causal dependencies in the sequence. The model infers causal dependency $\theta_{\hat{H}_{i(t)}^u, \hat{B}_i^u}$ between input item $\hat{H}_{i(t)}^u$ and output item $\hat{B}_i^u$. In recommendation tasks, closer behaviors strongly influence future user behaviors, with earlier behaviors discounted. To represent this temporal effect, a weight growth parameter λ (positive value <1) is introduced. For an input-output pair in C^u, the occurrence probability is calculated as:

$$P(\hat{B}_i^u|\hat{\mathcal{H}}_i^u) = \sigma\left(\sum_{t=1}^T \theta_{\hat{H}_{i(t)}^u, \hat{B}_i^u} \cdot \lambda^{T-t} \right), \tag{4}$$

using the sigmoid function σ (scaling the score to $[0,1]$). The probability in Eq. (4) should closely approach 1. Causal dependencies θ are obtained by maximizing probability across C^u. All causal dependencies are gathered, selecting those with output as original B^u. Items with higher θ scores are then chosen for counterfactual explanations.

3   Experiments

3.1   Experimental Setup

Datasets. We assess our counterfactual explanation model against baselines using two datasets: MovieLens100k[1] and an office product dataset from Amazon[2]. The original dataset is 5-core. For sequential recommendation with an input length of 5, users with a minimum of 15 purchases and items with at least 10 interactions are selected.

Sequential Recommendation Models. We adopt the following methods to train the black-box sequential recommendation models, including FPMC [20], GRU4Rec [9], NARM [14] and Caser [24]. We adopt their best parameter selection in their corresponding public implementation.

Baselines. We extract traditional association rules, including AR-sup [19], AR-conf [19] and AR-lift [19] as comparative explanations. Meanwhile, we compare our model CETD with the state-of-the-art CR-VAE [29] that generates causal explanations for sequential recommendation.

Training Details. CETD comprises an embedding layer (size 256), a GRU recurrent layer (320 cells), two encoding layers (sizes 1024 and 512), and two decoding layers (sizes 512 and 1024). The VAE's latent factor number Z is set to 16. For optimization, Adam was employed with a weight decay of 0.01. The default weight parameter α is 0.003. On both datasets, the default number of counterfactual pairs is $m = 500$. The default time growth factor is $\lambda = 0.7$.

Evaluation Metrics. We assess our model from three angles. Initially, the model should provide explanations for a significant portion of recommendations, measured as the percentage of explainable recommendation outcomes (Fidelity). Secondly, we validate the pivotal role of our counterfactual explanations in endorsing the original item recommendation. This can be quantified using the average causal effect (ACE) on the model's outcomes [29]. Lastly, our model's ability to generate counterfactual history closely resembling real histories (Proximity) is evaluated.

3.2   Results

Fidelity. Table 1 presents the optimal outcomes achieved by all models across the two datasets. Analyzing the table, several observations can be made.

Our counterfactual explanation model CETD generates explanations for most recommendations on both datasets, while the association explanation approach

---

[1] https://grouplens.org/datasets/movielens/.
[2] https://nijianmo.github.io/amazon/.

Table 1. Results of model Fidelity. CR-VAE and our model CETD are tested under $k = 1$ (the number of candidate counterfactual explanations). The association explanation framework is tested at support, confidence and lift thresholds. The bold scores are the best in each column, whereas the underlined scores are the best results of the baseline.

Datasets	MovieLens100k				Amazon			
Models	FPMC	GRU4Rec	NARM	Caser	FPMC	GRU4Rec	NARM	Caser
AR-conf [19]	0.3160	0.1453	0.4581	0.1569	0.2932	0.1449	0.4066	0.2024
AR-sup [19]	0.2959	0.1410	0.4305	0.1569	0.2949	0.1449	0.4031	0.1885
AR-lift [19]	0.2959	0.1410	0.4305	0.1569	0.2949	0.1449	0.4031	0.1885
CR-VAE [29]	0.9650	0.9852	0.9714	0.9703	0.9511	0.9721	0.9791	0.9599
CETD	**0.9873**	**0.9968**	**0.9947**	**0.9915**	**0.9762**	**0.9906**	**0.9918**	**0.9831**

provides significantly fewer explanations due to limited input and output items, which restricts the flexibility of global association rules. In contrast, CETD creates multiple counterfactual histories to aid in causal rule learning, enabling it to extract counterfactual explanations beyond the original data. Moreover, CETD outperforms the CR-VAE baseline by capturing both long-term preferences and short-term behavior in a user's real history, resulting in more counterfactual sequences with temporal dynamics.

Average Causal Effect. The ACE values of CETD and CR-VAE are shown in Fig. 3, which verify that our counterfactual explanations are an important component for recommending the original item. Because the ACE value is used for related causal models, we cannot report it on the association rule baselines.

CETD achieves higher ACE values than CR-VAE for most sequential recommendation models on both datasets, which verify that the counterfactual explanations generated by CETD are a crucial component of the recommendation. CETD can capture temporal dependencies in users' real historical during training allows for more accurate extraction of causality and dependency between users' historical preferences when generating counterfactual histories, resulting in higher quality explanations. FPMC's Markov chain approach only considers the last behavior, resulting in a limited number of counterfactual histories when changing a small number of input items. This leads to a lower ACE value.

Proximity. As shown in Fig. 4, the proximity value reported is average across all users. Notably, the association rule model doesn't include counterfactual histories, so this metric is reported only for our CETD and CR-VAE.

CETD generates higher quality and more useful counterfactual histories than CR-VAE, as shown by its lower proximity values. It achieves this by fitting the distribution of reconstructed data to converge to a normal distribution, using the latent variance obtained from learning, and fitting the mean and variance distributions of variables.

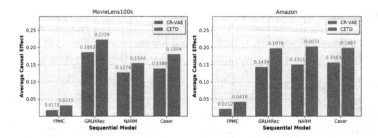

Fig. 3. Average Causal Effect results. CR-VAE and our model CETD are tested under $k = 1$ (the number of candidate counterfactual explanations).

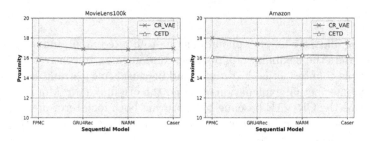

Fig. 4. Proximity results. The proximity value is calculated by Eq. (2).

4   Related Work

4.1   Sequential Recommendation

Sequential recommendation research focuses on extracting transitions between items within user-interacted sequences. Markov chains were used earlier to model item transition patterns [8,20]. Advances in neural networks prompted the adoption of RNNs [9,11,27], convolutional neural networks [24], transformers [13,21] and graph neural networks (GNNs) [2,16,17] for recommendation research. These approaches model high-order dependencies in historical interactions, such as GRU4Rec's [9] RNNs and Caser's [24] convolutions. SASRec [13] and BERT4Rec [21] leverage transformers' self-attention for item relation modeling. GNN-based models [16,17] capture intricate patterns beyond sequential ones. *Yet, these models often entail complex neural architectures, impeding interpretability. To address this, we intend to generate explanations for these enigmatic black box recommendation models.*

4.2   Explainable Recommendation

Explanations hold substantial importance in assisting users in evaluating recommender system outcomes [1,30]. A prevalent method involves utilizing knowledge graphs [4,5] to generate explanations. For instance, PLM-Rec [5] employs path language modeling to reason over knowledge graphs, capturing user behavior and item-side knowledge. Sentiments and opinions also contribute to an explainable recommendation. Wang et al. [26] introduced multitask learning for joint optimization of user preference and opinion-based content generation. However, these methods rely on correlations and lack a causal understanding of interactions. And they often require redesigning the original recommendation model, which may compromise the accuracy of the interpretation. *This paper takes a causal stance on explainable recommendation through counterfactual reasoning. Furthermore, our model is model-agnostic and interpretable, treating the underlying recommendation model as a black box without impacting its accuracy.*

4.3   Counterfactual Explanations

In the field of recommender systems, diverse efforts have been directed toward offering counterfactual explanations for recommendations via various approaches such as heterogeneous information networks [6,22], perturbation models [29], and influence functions [25]. PRINCE [6] employs an algorithm with polynomial-time optimization to pinpoint a minimal set of user actions by traversing dynamic graphs using random walks. ACCENT, proposed by Tran et al. [25], extends the influence function [3] to generate counterfactual explanations for neural recommender systems. CountER [23] produces explanations centered on counterfactual changes in item attributes. In contrast to obtaining counterfactual explanations by objectives, Xu et al. [29] extracted counterfactual explanations through a perturbation model and a causal rule mining model. *Different from the aforementioned works, our model considers temporal dependencies when generating counterfactual histories and reduces the proximity of counterfactual histories.*

5   Conclusions

In this paper, we propose CETD, a counterfactual explanation model based on a VAE for sequential recommendation, addressing temporal dependencies. CETD fits the reconstructed data's distribution in latent space using learned variance for closer counterfactual histories. Experiments on real-world datasets showcase its ability to generate high-quality explanations and reduce the proximity of counterfactual histories. However, observational user history data may have biases. Future work will explore counterfactual debiasing and advance counterfactual explanation research.

References

1. Cai, R., Wu, J., San, A., Wang, C., Wang, H.: Category-aware collaborative sequential recommendation. In: Proceedings of the 44th International ACM SIGIR Conference on Research and Development in Information Retrieval, pp. 388–397 (2021)
2. Chang, J., et al.: Sequential recommendation with graph neural networks. In: Proceedings of the 44th International ACM SIGIR Conference on Research and Development in Information Retrieval, pp. 378–387 (2021)

3. Cheng, W., Shen, Y., Huang, L., Zhu, Y.: Incorporating interpretability into latent factor models via fast influence analysis. In: Proceedings of the 25th ACM SIGKDD International Conference on Knowledge Discovery & Data Mining, pp. 885–893 (2019)

4. Fu, Z., et al.: Fairness-aware explainable recommendation over knowledge graphs. In: Proceedings of the 43rd International ACM SIGIR Conference on Research and Development in Information Retrieval, pp. 69–78 (2020)

5. Geng, S., Fu, Z., Tan, J., Ge, Y., De Melo, G., Zhang, Y.: Path language modeling over knowledge graphs for explainable recommendation. In: Proceedings of the ACM Web Conference 2022, pp. 946–955 (2022)

6. Ghazimatin, A., Balalau, O., Saha Roy, R., Weikum, G.: PRINCE: provider-side interpretability with counterfactual explanations in recommender systems. In: Proceedings of the 13th International Conference on Web Search and Data Mining, pp. 196–204 (2020)

7. Gholami, E., Motamedi, M., Aravindakshan, A.: PARSRec: explainable personalized attention-fused recurrent sequential recommendation using session partial actions. arXiv preprint arXiv:2209.13015 (2022)

8. He, R., McAuley, J.: Fusing similarity models with Markov chains for sparse sequential recommendation. In: 2016 IEEE 16th International Conference on Data Mining (ICDM), pp. 191–200. IEEE (2016)

9. Hidasi, B., Karatzoglou, A., Baltrunas, L., Tikk, D.: Session-based recommendations with recurrent neural networks. arXiv preprint arXiv:1511.06939 (2015)

10. Hou, H., Shi, C.: Explainable sequential recommendation using knowledge graphs. In: Proceedings of the 5th International Conference on Frontiers of Educational Technologies, pp. 53–57 (2019)

11. Hou, Y., Mu, S., Zhao, W.X., Li, Y., Ding, B., Wen, J.R.: Towards universal sequence representation learning for recommender systems. In: Proceedings of the 28th ACM SIGKDD Conference on Knowledge Discovery and Data Mining, pp. 585–593 (2022)

12. Huang, X., Fang, Q., Qian, S., Sang, J., Li, Y., Xu, C.: Explainable interaction-driven user modeling over knowledge graph for sequential recommendation. In: Proceedings of the 27th ACM International Conference on Multimedia, pp. 548–556 (2019)

13. Kang, W.C., McAuley, J.: Self-attentive sequential recommendation. In: 2018 IEEE International Conference on Data Mining (ICDM), pp. 197–206. IEEE (2018)

14. Li, J., Ren, P., Chen, Z., Ren, Z., Lian, T., Ma, J.: Neural attentive session-based recommendation. In: Proceedings of the 2017 ACM on Conference on Information and Knowledge Management, pp. 1419–1428 (2017)

15. Li, Y., Chen, H., Li, Y., Li, L., Philip, S.Y., Xu, G.: Reinforcement learning based path exploration for sequential explainable recommendation. IEEE Trans. Knowl. Data Eng. (2023)

16. Liu, Z., Chen, Y., Li, J., Yu, P.S., McAuley, J., Xiong, C.: Contrastive self-supervised sequential recommendation with robust augmentation. arXiv preprint arXiv:2108.06479 (2021)

17. Ma, C., Ma, L., Zhang, Y., Sun, J., Liu, X., Coates, M.: Memory augmented graph neural networks for sequential recommendation. In: Proceedings of the AAAI Conference on Artificial Intelligence, vol. 34, pp. 5045–5052 (2020)

18. Mothilal, R.K., Sharma, A., Tan, C.: Explaining machine learning classifiers through diverse counterfactual explanations. In: Proceedings of the 2020 Conference on Fairness, Accountability, and Transparency, pp. 607–617 (2020)

19. Peake, G., Wang, J.: Explanation mining: post hoc interpretability of latent factor models for recommendation systems. In: Proceedings of the 24th ACM SIGKDD International Conference on Knowledge Discovery & Data Mining, pp. 2060–2069 (2018)

20. Rendle, S., Freudenthaler, C., Schmidt-Thieme, L.: Factorizing personalized Markov chains for next-basket recommendation. In: Proceedings of the 19th International Conference on World Wide Web, pp. 811–820 (2010)

21. Sun, F., et al.: BERT4Rec: sequential recommendation with bidirectional encoder representations from transformer. In: Proceedings of the 28th ACM International Conference on Information and Knowledge Management, pp. 1441–1450 (2019)

22. Tan, J., et al.: Learning and evaluating graph neural network explanations based on counterfactual and factual reasoning. In: Proceedings of the ACM Web Conference 2022, pp. 1018–1027 (2022)

23. Tan, J., Xu, S., Ge, Y., Li, Y., Chen, X., Zhang, Y.: Counterfactual explainable recommendation. In: Proceedings of the 30th ACM International Conference on Information & Knowledge Management, pp. 1784–1793 (2021)

24. Tang, J., Wang, K.: Personalized top-n sequential recommendation via convolutional sequence embedding. In: Proceedings of the Eleventh ACM International Conference on Web Search and Data Mining, pp. 565–573 (2018)

25. Tran, K.H., Ghazimatin, A., Saha Roy, R.: Counterfactual explanations for neural recommenders. In: Proceedings of the 44th International ACM SIGIR Conference on Research and Development in Information Retrieval, pp. 1627–1631 (2021)

26. Wang, N., Wang, H., Jia, Y., Yin, Y.: Explainable recommendation via multi-task learning in opinionated text data. In: The 41st International ACM SIGIR Conference on Research & Development in Information Retrieval, pp. 165–174 (2018)

27. Xu, C., et al.: Recurrent convolutional neural network for sequential recommendation. In: The World Wide Web Conference, pp. 3398–3404 (2019)

28. Xu, S., Li, Y., Liu, S., Fu, Z., Chen, X., Zhang, Y.: Learning post-hoc causal explanations for recommendation. arXiv preprint arXiv:2006.16977 (2020)

29. Xu, S., et al.: Learning causal explanations for recommendation. In: The 1st International Workshop on Causality in Search and Recommendation (2021)

30. Yang, A., Wang, N., Cai, R., Deng, H., Wang, H.: Comparative explanations of recommendations. In: Proceedings of the ACM Web Conference 2022, pp. 3113–3123 (2022)

Incorporating Social-Aware User Preference for Video Recommendation

Xuanji Xiao[1]([✉]), Huaqiang Dai[2], Qian Dong[3], Shuzi Niu[4], Yuzhen Liu[5], and Pei Liu[5]

[1] Shopee, Shenzhen, China
charles.xiao@shopee.com
[2] Xiamen University, Xiamen, China
hqdai@stu.xmu.edu.cn
[3] Tsinghua University, Beijing, China
dq22@mails.tsinghua.edu.cn
[4] Institute of Software, Chinese Academy of Sciences, Beijing, China
shuzi@iscas.ac.cn
[5] Tencent Inc., Beijing, China
{yzhenliu,alexpliu}@tencent.com

Abstract. Modeling user interest accurately is crucial to recommendation systems. Existing works capture user interest from historical behaviors. Due to the sparsity and noise in user behavior data, behavior based models learn incomplete and sometimes inaccurate preference patterns and easily suffer from the cold user problem. In this work, we propose a social graph enhanced framework for behavior based models, namely **Social4Rec**. The social graph, involving multiple relation types, is extracted to find users with similar interests. It is challenging due to the trivial and sparse relations in social graph. To address the sparse relations issue, we first propose a Cluster-Calibrate-Merge network (CCM) to discover interest groups satisfying three properties: intrinsic self-organizing patterns through cluster layer, robustness to sparse relations through knowledge distillation of calibrator layer. We then use the averaged user interest representation within each group from CCM to complete each user behavior embedding and obtain relation specific interest aware embedding. To alleviate the trivial relation problem, relation specific interest aware embedding are aggregated among relation types through attention mechanism to obtain the interest aware social embedding for each user. It is combined with user behavior embedding to derive the matching score between the user and item. Both offline and online experiments on our video platform, which is one of the biggest video recommendation platforms with nearly one billion users over the world, demonstrate the superiority of our method, especially for cold users. The codes are available at https://github.com/xuanjixiao/onerec.

Keywords: recommendation · social net · distillation

F. Zhang et al. (Eds.): WISE 2023, LNCS 14306, pp. 544–558, 2023.
https://doi.org/10.1007/978-981-99-7254-8_42

1   Introduction

Recommendation systems play a vital role in contemporary content platforms, such as video streaming and news websites, by aiming to provide users with relevant and personalized content. The main challenge of recommendation systems is to identify user interest patterns for building effective recommendation models. Existing approaches mainly depend on capturing user interests from historical behaviors, such as clicks, views, and other interactions. Some examples of these approaches are Wide&Deep [5], DIN [40], and the classic video recommendation model YouTubeDNN [6].

However, user historical behaviors are frequently **sparse** and **noisy**. Users typically engage with a small subset of items they are truly interested in, leading to sparse behavior data. The sparsity of behavior data hampers the accurate capture of user interests and preferences [2,13,20,23,28,38]. The noise in historical behaviors arises from multiple biases that impact user actions. For example, users often click on items at the top of the recommendation list, resulting in a bias towards popular or highly ranked items. Since user interests are indirectly manifested in their behaviors, these behaviors alone do not sufficiently capture the complexity of user interests. This limitation arises from the homogeneity of information from a single source, resulting in the failure to capture the diverse and nuanced aspects of user preferences. Furthermore, behavior-based models frequently face challenges when serving **cold users**. Cold users refer to users who have recently joined the platform or have shown limited engagement with the content. Due to the limited or absence of behavioral data, traditional behavior-based models fail to effectively comprehend the preferences of cold users and offer accurate recommendations. However, it is crucial to address the needs and preferences of cold users for the continuous growth and development of content recommendation platforms.

Consequently, recommendation models that solely rely on historical behavior data often learn incomplete and inaccurate user interest patterns. These models are likely to face difficulties in delivering satisfactory recommendations, particularly for cold users. An approach that considers the A recommendation method that can incorporate multiple heterogeneous information sources is necessary, to alleviate the sparsity and noise limitation in user behavior data and tackle the challenges presented by cold user scenarios.

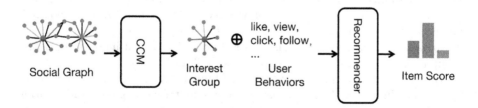

Fig. 1. The workflow of Social4Rec. (Color figure online)

To address the limitations of behavior based models mentioned above, we seek to utilize the social graph to help complete interest patterns from behavior based models. Social graphs on modern content platforms, such as Tencent, TikTok, and YouTube, are comprehensive and easily accessible. An social graph example in Fig. 1, is composed of different types of relations between users, such as friendship and following the same superstars, with different colors. The red and blue nodes represent target user and its neighbors respectively. The distance between nodes indicates the degree of interest consistency between users (i.e., the closer the more consistent of interests). Intuitively, similar interest preferences may exist among users when they are actual friends on our platform, follow the same superstars, subscribe to the same movie topics, follow the same uploaders, etc. Therefore, the social graph could be beneficial for RS. Despite the rich information contained in the social graph, it is difficult to take advantage of it directly for behavior based models due to the following two challenges:

– **Trivial Relation Challenge.** The social graph contains trivial relations, i.e., some neighbors are distant from the target user in Fig. 1, which hardly implies the interest characteristics of the target user. The inappropriate incorporation of the social graph could even jeopardize the RS performance. How to utilize the social graph with trivial relations in RS is remain a challenge in real RS.
– **Sparse Relation Challenge.** Despite the relations are abundant in the social graph, the types of edge (i.e. the types of relation between users) still suffer from the sparse issue. Most users only have one type of neighbor. How to learn interest preferences effectively from social data with sparse relation types is still a challenge.

To tackle the above challenges, we propose a novel social graph enhanced framework for behavior based recommendation, namely **Social4Rec**. The whole framework is composed of two modules in Fig. 1. One is to discover user interest groups from social graphs in face of these two challenges by the proposed Cluster-Calibrate-Merge network, namely CCM. The other is to refine user embedding based on learned interest groups from CCM, and matching it with item embedding, namely social enhanced recommendation.

Specifically, Cluster-Calibrate-Merge network is utilized to find user interest groups, which includes a cluster layer, calibrator layer and merge layer sequentially. The cluster layer is mainly based on self-organizing network [3,19,27], which discovers the intrinsic clustering patterns by competitively learning the network parameters. Taking the output of the cluster layer for initialization, a knowledge distillation technique is adopted to find a more robust and similar group assignment to the initialization through the calibrator layer in face of Sparse Relation Challenge. The merge layer is to find an interest consistent group assignment without too small groups by k-means.

Based on interest group assignments obtained from CCM, we further refine user embedding from behavior based models in terms of group and relation type. For the group level of each relation type, the user embedding is averaged to complete each user embedding in this group and obtain relation specific interest aware social embedding for each user. For the relation level, all the relation specific interest aware social embedding is aggregated through attention mechanism to tackle the Trivial Relation Challenge. Finally, the derived interest aware social representation and user behavior embedding are concatenated and fed into a vanilla recommender to calculate the matching score for each candidate item. Both offline and online experiments on our video platform, which is one of the biggest video recommendation platforms with nearly one billion users over the world, demonstrate the superiority of our work, especially for cold users.

Overall, our contributions can be summarized as follows:

- We propose a novel social graph enhanced paradigm to tackle limitations of behavior based models. As far as we know, it is the first attempt to introduce the social graph into large-scale online RS.
- In face of Sparse Relation Challenge, we design a Cluster-Calibrate-Merge network to discover intrinsic, robust and interest consistent groups. Base on learned group information, user behavior embedding is further refined through attention mechanism in face of Trivial Relation Challenge.
- Experimental results on both offline and online demonstrate the superiority of Social4Rec, especially for cold users, over the best baseline in our video recommendation platform.

2   Related Work

2.1   Behavior-Based Recommendation

Behavior-based recommendation, which is an emerging topic in RS, has attracted a wealth of researchers from both academia and industry. YouTubeDNN [6] is the most classic video recommendation model which has been deployed in many industrial video recommendation platforms. deepFM [14] and xdeepFM [22] jointly learn explicit and implicit feature interactions effectively without feature engineering. DIEN [39] and UBR4CTR [26] model the recommendation task from the perspectives of user behavior evolving and similar behaviors retrieval respectively.

2.2   Knowledge-Enhanced Techniques

Researchers have devoted substantial efforts to knowledge-enhanced techniques and benchmarks due to the superiority of diversified knowledge from different domain [9,29,30,35]. Both latent knowledge [8,10–12,21] and explicit knowledge [4,9,29] are explored by researchers. Recently, considerable knowledge-enhanced RS have been proposed for accurate interest modeling [16,32–34,37]. However, existing knowledge-enhanced RS mainly utilize knowledge graph of user-item, which is limited in the homogenized data. In this work, we propose a novel paradigm to enhance the RS with the interest knowledge distilled from social graph, i.e., user-user graph.

3　Preliminary

3.1　Self-organizing Neural Network

Through an unsupervised competitive learning mechanism, Self-organizing Neural Network (SoNN) could discover the intrinsic patterns from data by self-adjusting the network parameters [3,19,27]. Formally, given a user embedding, SoNN assigns him/her to an interest group j as follow

$$arg \min_{j} \|\mathbf{W}_j - f(X_u)\| \quad (j = 1, 2, \cdots, m),$$ (1)

where $X_u \in \mathbb{R}^d$ is the embedding of user u elaborated in the following section. $f(\cdot)$ are full-connected layers. The Eq. 1 measures the interest consistency between a user and an interest group by the Euclidean distance between the user X_u and the interest group $\mathbf{W}_j$, where $\mathbf{W} \in \mathbb{R}^{m \times d}$ and m is the number of interest group. After a user u is assigned to an interest group j, the embedding of the interest group $\mathbf{W}$ is updated as follows $\mathbf{W} = \mathbf{W} + d\mathbf{W}$. Despite the group embedding $\mathbf{W}$ are initialized randomly, the final embedding still reflects the intrinsic characteristics of the interest group properly after several iterations in SoNN.

Moreover, the user embedding X_u is updated through back propagation based on minimizing the following loss function

$$\mathcal{L}_u = \sum_{u \in \mathbb{U}} \|\mathbf{W}_j - f(X_u)\|^2,$$ (2)

where $\mathbb{U}$ is the user set in system. After multiple iterations, each interest group and user obtains a stable embedding, which can be employed for unsupervised user clustering accurately.

3.2　Recommendation

Given a user embedding F_u obtained from its historical behaviors, a qualified recommender calculates the relevant score between the target user u and candidate item set $\mathbb{T}$ in system, and returns top-relevant items that may be of interest to the user u. The embedding F_t of item $t \in \mathbb{T}$ is obtained from its features, such as the category item t belongs to, the number of item t has been liked, etc. The relevant score $\bar{y}_{u,t}$ between user u and item t is calculated by recommender as follow

$$\bar{y}_{u,t} = h(F_u) \cdot g(F_t),$$ (3)

where $h(\cdot)$ and $g(\cdot)$ are full-connected layers or other arbitrary neural network modules, and $\cdot$ means the inner product operation. This is a commonly used network backbone of commercial recommendation systems (Fig. 2).

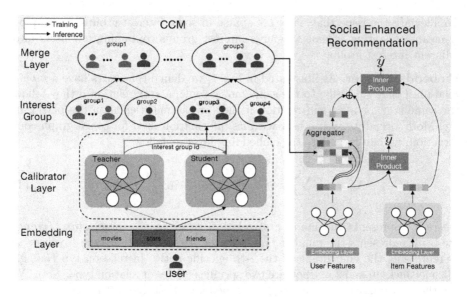

Fig. 2. The architecture of Social4Rec.

4 Methodology

In this section, we present our method in details, which introduces the **social** graph to enhance the user interest modeling **for** better video **re**commendation, namely **Social4Rec**. Social4Rec is mainly composed of two modules. The Cluster-Calibrator-Merge module is proposed to find intrinsic, robust and self-consistent social sub-graph (i.e., interest group) structures based on self-organizing, knowledge distillation and k-means techniques. The other is social graph enhanced recommender module, which refines the user behavior embedding based on group interest characteristic distilled from Cluster-Calibrator-Merge module. The overall framework of Social4Rec is depicted in Fig. 2.

4.1 Cluster-Calibrator-Merge Module

Birds of a feather flock together, and thus users with similar interests should be divided into one group. The potential interest of a user may be embedded in other users in his/her interest group. However, most neighbors of a user in the global social graph are trivial, as for example the interest preferences of users who subscribe to the same movie topics still vary greatly. Therefore, the global social graph should be carefully refined into an interest group, which is robust and self-consistent for the downstream user representation learning. In this section, we propose a Cluster-Calibrate-Merge module, which is utilized to unsupervised cluster the users in social graph into several interest groups. Specifically, the users in social graph are first encoded through the embedding layer. Then, each user is assigned a virtual interest group through a calibrator.

To alleviate the issue that users are sparse in some interest groups, we employ K-means clustering scheme to merge interest groups containing few users into adjacent interest group.

Embedding Layer. As illustrated in Fig. 1, we define that users have a *movie* relation if they subscribe to the same movie topic, a *star* relation if they follow the same star, or a *friend* relation if they are actual friends on the platform, etc. More formally, given a user with its information used for social graph construction, we can formulate the embedding layer as follow

$$X_u = \frac{1}{n_1^u} \sum_i^{n_1^u} e_i^1 \oplus \frac{1}{n_2^u} \sum_i^{n_2^u} e_i^2 \oplus \cdots \oplus \frac{1}{n_L^u} \sum_i^{n_L^u} e_i^L, \tag{4}$$

where L represents the number of relation types (e.g., *movie*, *star*, *friend*, etc.). n_l^u represents the number of specific entities in relation type l of user u. e_i^l represents the embedding of the i-th specific entity in relation type l (e.g., Michael Jackson and Jay Chou are two specific entities of relation type *star*). We use the concatenation operation $\oplus$ in embedding layer due to the heterogeneity of the specific entities between different relation types. Notably, the number of relation types is less than L for most users. For the absent relation types, we use zero to pad corresponding positions in X_u.

Cluster Layer. According to Self-organizing network, the group assignment $f(\cdot)$ is updated by optimizing Eq. 1 given user embedding and the user embedding X_u is updated by optimizing Eq. 2. Two steps are alternatively updated for each iteration. After multiple iterations, the process convergence and each interest group and user obtains a stable embedding. The learned group assignment $f(\cdot)$ serves as a guide for next layer.

Calibrator Layer. To mitigate the discrepancy introduced by the **Sparse Relation Challenge** in real social graph, we design a novel calibrator inspired by Masked Language Model (MLM) [7] in the community of natural language model. Meanwhile, with the light of distillation techniques [17,36], we utilize the well-trained $f(\cdot)$ from Sect. 3.1 which is trained on the subset $\overline{U}$ of users with all relation types as the teacher model, and then train a student model $k(\cdot)$ which is more robust on the social graph with sparse relations. Particularly, the input embedding X_u of teacher model is polluted as $\check{X}_u$ for the student model, where a small fraction of its relations in Eq. 4 are randomly replaced by zero. The goal of calibrator is to mimic the predicted distribution between teach $f(\cdot)$ and student $k(\cdot)$, where the loss can be measured by KL divergence as

$$\mathcal{L}_k = \sum_{u \in \overline{U}} f(X_u) \cdot log \frac{k(\check{X}_u)}{f(X_u)}. \tag{5}$$

Merge Layer. There is a trade-off between the number of interest group and the interest consistency of users within an interest group. To ensure that model can model accurate interest characteristics from social graph, we prioritize maintaining interest consistency within an interest group. Consequently, some interest groups have few users which also needs to be avoided. To address this issue, we employ the k-means clustering scheme to merge interest groups that contain few users with the nearest interest group.

Through the above modules, the CCM is empowered with the capability of modeling users with sparse relations in social graph and dividing users into several interest groups accurately.

4.2   Social Enhanced Recommendation Module

After obtaining the user's corresponding interest group, we first integrate the neighbors of target user u within its interest group by relation types, which can be formulated as

$$H_u^l = avg(\sum_{\mu \in N_u^l} X_\mu) + X_u, \tag{6}$$

where N_u^l is the neighbors with the relation type l to user u. Intuitively, different users have different interest consistency with neighbors of different relation types. To tackle the **Trivial Relation Challenge** in social graph, we employ the attention mechanism to finalize the overall interest-aware social representation of user u as follow

$$H_u = \sum_{l \in L} \alpha_{u,l} \times H_u^l, \tag{7}$$

where $\alpha_{u,l}$ is the attention score calculated by

$$\alpha_{u,l} = \frac{exp(\sigma(\beta_{u,l}))}{\sum_{\iota \in L} exp(\sigma(\beta_{u,\iota}))}, \tag{8}$$

where σ is an activation function and the logits $\beta_{u,\iota}$ is computed as

$$\beta_{u,\iota} = q(F_u \oplus H_u^\iota). \tag{9}$$

In Eq. 9, $q(\cdot)$ and $F(u)$ are full-connected layers and behavior-based embedding of user u respectively. Guided by the behavioral characteristics which are more accurate and easier to interest learning, a reliable social representation H_u could be obtained for the supplement of interest characteristics. With the interest-aware social representation H_u, the Eq. 3 could be enhanced by the social graph $\mathcal{G}$ as follow

$$\hat{y}_{u,t,\mathcal{G}} = h(F_u \oplus H_u) \cdot g(F_t), \tag{10}$$

where $\hat{y}_{u,t,\mathcal{G}}$ represents the relevant score that is aware of the interest characteristics extracted from $\mathcal{G}$.

Table 1. Statistics of social graph.

stars	movies	friends	uploaders
6M	63M	65M	25M

Table 2. Statistics of the recommendation datasets.

Dataset	user	video	impression	click	#impression/user	#click/user
FULL	68M	440M	340M	136M	5.0	2.0
COLD	2M	4M	3M	1M	1.5	0.5

5   Experiments

Our experiments are guided by the following research questions:

- **RQ1:** Whether the existing RS perform worse on cold users?
- **RQ2:** Does Social4Rec enhances the performance of existing RS significantly?
- **RQ3:** Does the deployment of Social4Rec contribute to the growth of our video platform's user base?

5.1   Experimental Setup

Dataset. Existing datasets [1,15,24,25,31] used for recommendations contain only user behavior data and no user corresponding social data, which is readily available in a mature content platform, such as Tencent, TikTok, and YouTube. Therefore, we conduct experiments in our video platform, which is a real-world video recommendation platform with nearly one *billion* users over the world. The detailed statistics of social graph and video recommendation datasets used in this work are reported in Table 1 and Table 2 respectively. For the *Social Graph*, we construct it from four relation types including *star*, *movie*, *friend* and *video uploader*. For the *FULL* dataset, we collect 15 consecutive days' online traffic log in our video recommendation platform, with the first 14 days for training and the last day for offline testing. For the *COLD* dataset, we process the *FULL* dataset by removing users with more than 30 historical behaviors in traffic log, as we find that users with less than 30 behaviors have a significant drop in impression of video items. In this dataset, 80% of users have less than two video clicks, and thus it is hard to mine interest preference from historical behaviors.

Baselines. The vanilla behavior-based RS achieved the best performance in our video platform is employed as a primary baseline in both offline and online experiments, which utilizes YouTubeDNN [6] as architecture backbone. The user and item features are mined by ourselves. It is worth noting that in real video recommendation systems, such as YouTube, TikTok, and Tencent, YouTubeDNN [6] is commonly selected as the backbone of the recommendation model due to its simplicity and effectiveness. These video platforms typically maintain their own user and item features to ensure adaptation to their respective platforms. To be consistent with the baseline, YouTubeDNN [6] is also utilized as the backbone of Social4Rec, i.e., $h(\cdot)$ and $g(\cdot)$ in Eq. 10. Social4Rec† and Social4Rec‡ represent the versions of Social4Rec without calibrator and merge layer respectively. Social4Rec$^-$ directly aggregates H_u by averaging without using the attention aggregator. The Eq. 6 of Social4Rec$^-$ could be redefined as

$$H_u = avg(\sum_{l \in L} H_u^l). \tag{11}$$

Parameter Setting. In our experiments, we have chosen to employ the Adam optimizer [18] with a fixed learning rate of 0.001. To improve the stability and convergence speed of our neural networks, we have applied batch normalization in each layer. Batch normalization normalizes the activations of each layer by subtracting the batch mean and dividing by the batch standard deviation. This technique helps to address the internal covariate shift problem and allows for smoother optimization, enabling faster training and better generalization performance. We have chosen the leaky ReLU activation function for all layers, except for the last layer, which utilizes the sigmoid activation function. The leaky ReLU activation function is an extension of the traditional rectified linear unit (ReLU) function, introducing a small slope for negative input values. This helps to mitigate the issue of "dying ReLUs" by allowing a small gradient to flow through when the neuron is inactive. The sigmoid activation function in the last layer is commonly used for binary classification tasks, as it squashes the output into the range of zero to one, representing the probability of the positive class. By adopting these settings as shared between all our baseline models, we aim to establish a consistent experimental setup, allowing us to focus on the impact of other variations or enhancements on the performance of our models.

Metrics. For the performance metrics, we resort to the widely used *AUC* (Area Under Curve) as the offline metric. AUC measures the quality of the ranking produced by the recommendation system, indicating the probability that a randomly chosen positive example (e.g., a clicked video) is ranked higher than a randomly chosen negative example (e.g., a non-clicked video). A higher AUC value implies better discrimination between positive and negative examples.

In addition to the offline metric, we have incorporated online metrics to capture the real-world performance of our method. One of the key online metrics we consider is the *CTR* (Click-Through-Rate). CTR measures the ratio of the number of clicks on recommended videos to the number of impressions (the times the recommendations are shown). A higher CTR signifies that our recommendations are attracting more user attention and engagement. To gain further insights into the user experience, we also track the *click number* and *view time*. The click number refers to the total number of clicks made by users on the recommended videos, providing an indication of user interest and engagement. The view time represents the total time spent by users watching the recommended videos. Analyzing these metrics helps us understand whether cold users, who may have limited interaction history with the platform, are benefiting from our recommendations and finding content that matches their preferences.

To ensure fair and consistent comparisons across our experiments, we have set the same configuration of evaluation throughout. By evaluating both offline and online metrics, we can gain a comprehensive understanding of the quality of our method, as well as the user engagement and satisfaction with our video recommendation platform.

5.2   Experimental Results

The offline experimental results on *FULL* and *COLD* datasets are illustrated in Table 3. We compare the performance of the Social4Rec model against the Vanilla RS (behavior-based RS) on both datasets. The results show that Social4Rec outperforms Vanilla RS in terms of performance, particularly on the cold user subset. This indicates that Social4Rec is more effective in handling the challenges posed by cold users.

From Table 3, we can draw the flowing findings:

- We observe a substantial performance difference between the two datasets, highlighting the significant challenge faced by recommendation systems when dealing with cold users (**RQ1**). The performance margin indicates that cold users, who have limited or no interaction history, pose a greater challenge in accurately recommending relevant items.
- Social4Rec could significantly enhances the performance of existing recommendation system (**RQ2**), even with a simple aggregation method for social graph (i.e., Social4Rec⁻).
- Comparing Social4Rec with Social4Rec⁻, the experimental results in Table 3 demonstrate the importance of the attention aggregator in Social4Rec for achieving overall better performance. The introduction of the social graph into the recommendation system is deemed appropriate. This suggests that social data, when guided by behavioral data, plays a crucial role in extracting interest characteristics and addressing the **Trivial Relation Challenge**.
- Among the variations of the Social4Rec model, Social4Rec† experiences the most significant performance drop. This indicates that users with sparse relations cannot be properly assigned to the desired interest group, thereby significantly compromising the model's performance. The **Sparse Relation Challenge** is effectively addressed through the inclusion of the calibrator layer, which helps mitigate the impact of sparse relations on the recommendation quality.

Overall, the results emphasize the superiority of the Social4Rec model over Vanilla RS, especially in handling cold users. The attention aggregator, the utilization of social graph data, and the calibration of sparse relations contribute significantly to the improved performance.

To provide a deeper analysis of the performance of Social4Rec in the online system, we conducted experiments on a real-world video recommendation platform that boasts nearly one billion users worldwide. The experimental results were reported for two types of users: all users and cold users, using the same settings as the offline dataset.

Table 3. Offline performance comparison on two datasets. The relative performance improvement is statistically significant with $p < 0.01$ in two-tailed paired t-test.

	FULL		COLD	
	AUC	Imp.%	AUC	Imp.%
Vanilla RS	0.765	–	0.729	–
Social4Rec[†]	0.767	0.26%	0.735	0.82%
Social4Rec[‡]	0.768	0.39%	0.741	1.65%
Social4Rec[−]	0.768	0.39%	0.739	1.37%
Social4Rec	**0.770**	0.65%	**0.746**	2.33%

Table 4 presents the mean performance gains of Social4Rec compared to the best online model over a span of seven consecutive days, which provides more statistically significant results. From Table 4, we can obtain the following conclusions:

- The overall Click-Through Rate (CTR) shows a remarkable improvement of 3.63% when using Social4Rec. This improvement is highly significant in the context of industrial recommendation systems, indicating the efficacy of Social4Rec in enhancing user engagement and interactions.
- Comparing the improvement in CTR for all users to that of cold users, we observe that Social4Rec achieves a performance gain of 2.00% specifically on cold users. This further emphasizes the challenges faced by recommendation systems in effectively catering to cold users (**RQ1**). Cold users, who lack sufficient interaction history, present a more demanding scenario for recommendation algorithms, and the significant improvement on cold user segment highlights the potential of Social4Rec in addressing this challenge.
- Despite the challenges associated with cold users, the metrics of click number and view time exhibit significant improvements compared to the online model. This indicates that integrating the social graph into the recommendation system through Social4Rec enables a better personalized experience for cold users and encourages their conversion into active users to a certain degree (**RQ3**). Active users exhibit a higher frequency of browsing video covers, clicking on and watching video content, which is observed in our video platform. This conversion of cold users into active users is vital for the continuous growth and development of the content platform.

Overall, the experiments conducted on the real-world video recommendation platform demonstrate the effectiveness of Social4Rec in improving the Click-Through Rate. By incorporating the social graph, the recommendation system provides a more personalized experience to cold users, facilitating their conversion into active users. These findings highlight the importance of Social4Rec in addressing challenges related to cold users and promoting the continuous growth and success of the content platform.

Table 4. Online performance gains over baseline model. The relative performance improvement is statistically significant with $p < 0.01$ in two-tailed paired t-test.

User type	CTR	click number	view time
All users	+3.63%	+2.94%	+0.78%
Cold users	+2.00%	+8.59%	+4.77%

6   Conclusion

In this work, we introduce Social4Rec, a recommendation model framework that utilizes a social graph to mitigate the issues of sparse and noisy user behavior encountered by vanilla RS. The main objective is to design a framework that offers a more accurate and comprehensive representation of users, especially for new and cold users.

To address the challenge of sparse relations that arises from the introduction of the social graph, we propose a cluster-calibrate-merge module. The objective of this module is to identify intrinsic, robust, and self-consistent interest groups within the user population. Through clustering users based on their behavioral patterns and calibrating the sparse relations, we can effectively identify interest groups that capture relevant user preferences.

To tackle the challenge of trivial relations, we enhance the user behavior embedding by incorporating the user's interest group. This refinement process improves the quality and relevance of the user behavior representation. Furthermore, we employ an attention mechanism to aggregate relation-specific refined embeddings, resulting in an interest-aware social embedding. This embedding captures the user's social preferences, which are then combined with the user behavior embedding to compute the relevance score for each candidate item.

Our model achieves a more accurate and comprehensive representation of users by incorporating interest preferences derived from the social graph. This is particularly advantageous for new and cold users with limited behavioral data. Experimental results demonstrate the superiority of our Social4Rec model over the best online model in our video platform. The performance improvements in user engagement metrics underscore the effectiveness of incorporating the social graph in the recommendation process.

References

1. Ben-Shimon, D., Tsikinovsky, A., Friedmann, M., Shapira, B., Rokach, L., Hoerle, J.: RecSys challenge 2015 and the YOOCHOOSE dataset. In: Proceedings of the 9th ACM Conference on Recommender Systems, pp. 357–358 (2015)
2. Bobadilla, J., Ortega, F., Hernando, A., Bernal, J.: A collaborative filtering approach to mitigate the new user cold start problem. Knowl.-Based Syst. **26**, 225–238 (2012)
3. Carpenter, G.A., Grossberg, S.: The ART of adaptive pattern recognition by a self-organizing neural network. Computer **21**(3), 77–88 (1988)

4. Cheng, A., et al.: Layout-aware webpage quality assessment. arXiv preprint arXiv:2301.12152 (2023)
5. Cheng, H.T., et al.: Wide & deep learning for recommender systems. In: Proceedings of the 1st Workshop on Deep Learning for Recommender Systems, pp. 7–10 (2016)
6. Covington, P., Adams, J., Sargin, E.: Deep neural networks for YouTube recommendations. In: Proceedings of the 10th ACM Conference on Recommender Systems, pp. 191–198 (2016)
7. Devlin, J., Chang, M.W., Lee, K., Toutanova, K.: BERT: pre-training of deep bidirectional transformers for language understanding. arXiv preprint arXiv:1810.04805 (2018)
8. Dong, Q., et al.: I^3 retriever: incorporating implicit interaction in pre-trained language models for passage retrieval. arXiv preprint arXiv:2306.02371 (2023)
9. Dong, Q., et al.: Incorporating explicit knowledge in pre-trained language models for passage re-ranking. arXiv preprint arXiv:2204.11673 (2022)
10. Dong, Q., Niu, S.: Latent graph recurrent network for document ranking. In: Jensen, C.S., et al. (eds.) DASFAA 2021. LNCS, vol. 12682, pp. 88–103. Springer, Cham (2021). https://doi.org/10.1007/978-3-030-73197-7_6
11. Dong, Q., Niu, S.: Legal judgment prediction via relational learning. In: Proceedings of the 44th International ACM SIGIR Conference on Research and Development in Information Retrieval, pp. 983–992 (2021)
12. Dong, Q., Niu, S., Yuan, T., Li, Y.: Disentangled graph recurrent network for document ranking. Data Sci. Eng. **7**(1), 30–43 (2022). https://doi.org/10.1007/s41019-022-00179-3
13. Gope, J., Jain, S.K.: A survey on solving cold start problem in recommender systems. In: 2017 International Conference on Computing, Communication and Automation (ICCCA), pp. 133–138. IEEE (2017)
14. Guo, H., Tang, R., Ye, Y., Li, Z., He, X.: DeepFM: a factorization-machine based neural network for CTR prediction. arXiv preprint arXiv:1703.04247 (2017)
15. Harper, F.M., Konstan, J.A.: The movielens datasets: history and context. ACM Trans. Interact. Intell. Syst. (TIIS) **5**(4), 1–19 (2015)
16. Huang, C., et al.: Knowledge-aware coupled graph neural network for social recommendation. In: 35th AAAI Conference on Artificial Intelligence (AAAI) (2021)
17. Huang, Z., Lin, Z., Gong, Z., Chen, Y., Tang, Y.: A two-phase knowledge distillation model for graph convolutional network-based recommendation. Int. J. Intell. Syst. **37**(9), 5902–5923 (2022)
18. Kingma, D.P., Ba, J.: Adam: a method for stochastic optimization. arXiv preprint arXiv:1412.6980 (2014)
19. Kohonen, T., Honkela, T.: Kohonen network. Scholarpedia **2**(1), 1568 (2007)
20. Li, D., et al.: User-level microblogging recommendation incorporating social influence. J. Am. Soc. Inf. Sci. **68**(3), 553–568 (2017)
21. Li, H., et al.: SAILER: structure-aware pre-trained language model for legal case retrieval. arXiv preprint arXiv:2304.11370 (2023)
22. Lian, J., Zhou, X., Zhang, F., Chen, Z., Xie, X., Sun, G.: xDeepFM: combining explicit and implicit feature interactions for recommender systems. In: Proceedings of the 24th ACM SIGKDD International Conference on Knowledge Discovery & Data Mining, pp. 1754–1763 (2018)
23. Lu, Y., Fang, Y., Shi, C.: Meta-learning on heterogeneous information networks for cold-start recommendation. In: Proceedings of the 26th ACM SIGKDD International Conference on Knowledge Discovery & Data Mining, pp. 1563–1573 (2020)

24. Meyffret, S., Guillot, E., Médini, L., Laforest, F.: RED: a rich epinions dataset for recommender systems. Ph.D. thesis, LIRIS (2012)
25. Ni, J., Li, J., McAuley, J.: Justifying recommendations using distantly-labeled reviews and fine-grained aspects. In: Proceedings of the 2019 Conference on Empirical Methods in Natural Language Processing and the 9th International Joint Conference on Natural Language Processing (EMNLP-IJCNLP), pp. 188–197 (2019)
26. Qin, J., Zhang, W., Wu, X., Jin, J., Fang, Y., Yu, Y.: User behavior retrieval for click-through rate prediction. In: Proceedings of the 43rd International ACM SIGIR Conference on Research and Development in Information Retrieval, pp. 2347–2356 (2020)
27. Seiffert, U.: Self-organizing neural networks: recent advances and applications (2001)
28. Sethi, R., Mehrotra, M.: Cold start in recommender systems-a survey from domain perspective. In: Hemanth, J., Bestak, R., Chen, J.I.Z. (eds.) Intelligent Data Communication Technologies and Internet of Things. LNDECT, vol. 57, pp. 223–232. Springer, Cham (2021). https://doi.org/10.1007/978-981-15-9509-7_19
29. Su, Y., et al.: CokeBERT: contextual knowledge selection and embedding towards enhanced pre-trained language models. AI Open **2**, 127–134 (2021)
30. Sun, Y., et al.: ERNIE: enhanced representation through knowledge integration. arXiv preprint arXiv:1904.09223 (2019)
31. Wan, M., McAuley, J.: Modeling ambiguity, subjectivity, and diverging viewpoints in opinion question answering systems. In: 2016 IEEE 16th International Conference on Data Mining (ICDM), pp. 489–498. IEEE (2016)
32. Xia, L., et al.: Knowledge-enhanced hierarchical graph transformer network for multi-behavior recommendation (2021)
33. Xia, L., Huang, C., Xu, Y., Pei, J.: Multi-behavior sequential recommendation with temporal graph transformer. IEEE Trans. Knowl. Data Eng. **35**(6), 6099–6112 (2022)
34. Xia, L., Xu, Y., Huang, C., Dai, P., Bo, L.: Graph meta network for multi-behavior recommendation. In: Proceedings of the 44th International ACM SIGIR Conference on Research and Development in Information Retrieval, pp. 757–766 (2021)
35. Xie, X., et al.: T2Ranking: a large-scale Chinese benchmark for passage ranking. arXiv preprint arXiv:2304.03679 (2023)
36. Yang, C., Pan, J., Gao, X., Jiang, T., Liu, D., Chen, G.: Cross-task knowledge distillation in multi-task recommendation. arXiv preprint arXiv:2202.09852 (2022)
37. Yang, Y., Huang, C., Xia, L., Li, C.: Knowledge graph contrastive learning for recommendation. arXiv preprint arXiv:2205.00976 (2022)
38. Zhang, C., Wang, H., Yang, S., Gao, Y.: A contextual bandit approach to personalized online recommendation via sparse interactions. In: Yang, Q., Zhou, Z.-H., Gong, Z., Zhang, M.-L., Huang, S.-J. (eds.) PAKDD 2019. LNCS (LNAI), vol. 11440, pp. 394–406. Springer, Cham (2019). https://doi.org/10.1007/978-3-030-16145-3_31
39. Zhou, G., et al.: Deep interest evolution network for click-through rate prediction. In: Proceedings of the AAAI Conference on Artificial Intelligence, vol. 33, pp. 5941–5948 (2019)
40. Zhou, G., et al.: Deep interest network for click-through rate prediction. In: Proceedings of the 24th ACM SIGKDD International Conference on Knowledge Discovery & Data Mining, pp. 1059–1068 (2018)

Noise-Augmented Contrastive Learning for Sequential Recommendation

Kun He[1], Shunmei Meng[2,3]([✉]), Qianmu Li[2], Xiao Liu[1], Amin Beheshti[4], Xiaoxiao Chi[4], and Xuyun Zhang[4]

[1] School of Cyber Science and Engineering,
Nanjing University of Science and Technology, Nanjing, China
hekun@njust.edu.cn
[2] School of Computer Science and Engineering,
Nanjing University of Science and Technology, Nanjing, China
mengshunmei@njust.edu.cn
[3] State Key Laboratory for Novel Software Technology, Nanjing University,
Nanjing, China
[4] School of Computing, Macquarie University, Sydney, Australia

Abstract. Recently, contrastive learning has been widely used in the field of sequential recommendation to solve the data sparsity problem. CL4Rec augments data through simple random crop, mask, and reorder, while DuoRec proposes a model-level data augmentation method. However, these methods do not take into account the issue of noisy data in sequential recommendation, such as false clicks during browsing. The noise may lead to poor representations of learned sequences and negatively affect the augmented data. Current sequential recommendation methods tend to learn the user's intention from their original sequences, but these methods have certain limitations as the user's intention for the next interaction may change. Based on the above observations, we propose Noise-augmented Contrastive Learning for Sequential Recommendation (NCL4Rec). Our NCL4Rec proposes sequential noise probability-guided data augmentation. We introduce supervised noise recognition during training instead of obtaining it from original sequences. Moreover, we design positive and negative augmentations of the sequence and design unique noise loss function to train them. Through experiments, it is verified that our NCL4Rec consistently outperforms the current state-of-the-art models.

Keywords: Sequential Recommendation · Contrastive Learning

1 Introduction

Sequential recommendation predicts potentially interesting items based on the user's historical behavior. In the internet age, the amount of user behavior data and available items has grown exponentially [1]. The deep neural network learns item representation through a large amount of data, and many classic models

F. Zhang et al. (Eds.): WISE 2023, LNCS 14306, pp. 559–568, 2023.
https://doi.org/10.1007/978-981-99-7254-8_43

emerge. For example, Caser [11] employs a convolutional neural network (CNN) as the backbone network, and GRU4Rec [4] uses a recurrent neural network (RNN) as the backbone network. In particular, the transformer [12] structure shines in sequential recommendation, such as SASRec [5], BERT4Rec [9].

However, due to the sparseness of sequence data, deep neural network cannot learn accurate item representations. The emergence of contrastive learning [6] solves the problem of sparse sequence data to a certain extent. CL4Rec [15] augments data through random crop, mask and reorder. DuoRec [8] utilizes a Dropout based approach to enhance sequence representation at the model level. On the other hand, it mines positive and negative samples using sequences of similar target items. But due to the noise in the sequence data, the augmented data is still disturbed by the noise in the original sequence.

But contrastive learning methods do not solve the problem of noise in the sequence. Noise has always been a major difficulty in representation learning and is no exception in sequential recommendation [13,14]. For example, in real online shopping, the user's mistaken click may not be the user's real intention behavior. The augmented data generated by randomly cropping, masking and reordering the original sequence may lack robustness due to the presence of noise data. Poor quality data augmentation can have negative effects on model training. Furthermore, most of current methods obtain the user's intent from the user's original sequence [3,7,10]. And it is easy to think of the user's recent behavior as the user's intention or query vector, but it may not be accurate due to the changing existence of the user's intention.

Based on the above observation, we propose a Noise-augmented Contrastive Learning for Sequential Recommendation (NCL4Rec) to address the noise problem in sequential recommendation. In our method, we use noise probabilities to guide the data augmentation process and mitigate the impact of noise in the original sequence. We introduce supervised noise recognition during training instead of relying on the original sequence, thereby eliminating the influence of noise in the original data. The noise probability is dynamically updated online after a certain number of training epochs. During training, we calculate the noise probability and design positive and negative sample augmentations based on it. Positive samples are generated by processing items with low noise probability, while negative samples are generated by processing items with high noise probability. Additionally, we design positive and negative loss functions to minimize the distance between positive samples and maximize the distance between positive and negative samples.

Our contributions:

- We propose a Noise-augmented Contrastive Learning for Sequential Recommendation (NCL4Rec), which addresses noise issues and data sparsity by unifying sequential recommendation and self-supervised contrastive learning methods.
- We propose novel noise-guided data positive and negative augmentations to better discriminate noisy data by exploiting the relevance of items to user intent. And a noise loss function is designed to better distinguish noise items from normal items.

- We conduct extensive experiments on three benchmark datasets, and our method consistently outperforms currently existing state-of-the-art models, with performance gains ranging from 3.37% to 7.10%.

2   Problem Formulation

Formally, let $S_u = (s_u^1, s_u^2, \ldots, s_u^n)$ be a sequence of items, and let s_u^{n+1} be the next item in the sequence to be predicted. We define the problem of sequence recommendation as follows:

Given a set of training sequences $D = (S_u, s_u^{n+1})$, where each training sequence S_u consists of n items, and the corresponding next item s_u^{n+1}, the goal is to learn a function f that maps a user's historical sequence S_u to the next item s_u^{n+1}. More formally, we seek a function f such that:

$$s_u^{n+1} = f(S_u) \tag{1}$$

where f is learned from the training set D. The learned function f can then be used to make predictions on new, unseen sequences.

3   Methods

The emphasis of this paper is on effective data augmentation, and there is no detailed description of the sequence encoding model. Instead, we use the backbone network that is commonly used in contrastive learning-based sequential recommendation models. It's important to note that the purpose of contrastive learning methods is to address the problem of sparse training data and help us obtain a more effective encoding model.

In this section, we describe in detail our proposed **Noise-augmented Contrastive Learning for Sequential Recommendation (NCL4Rec)**. The framework of our method is shown in Fig. 1. Our method mainly consists of four parts, **(1) the generation of sequence item noise probabilities; (2) data augmentation guided by noise probabilities, (3) user representation encoding model, (4) noise contrastive loss function.**

3.1   The Generation of Sequence Item Noise Probabilities

For our user sequence item, there are often a lot of noise data. Noise is an item that does not conform to the user's intention. Most current methods are based on the original sequence to enhance the data of the item. However, the user's sequence behavior will be transferred according to the user's next item, so we use the user's target item to calculate the user's noise probability. On the one hand, it can effectively eliminate the interference between the original sequences and grasp the user's intention more accurately. The user's intention transfer can be better learned. We define the user sequence as $S_u = s_u^1, s_u^2, s_u^3 \ldots s_u^n$, where n

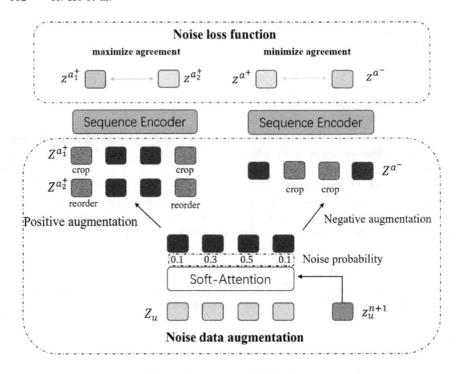

Fig. 1. Framework of NCL4Rec.

is the sequence length. s_u^{n+1} is the user's next interaction item, which is also the supervision signal in our training.

First our sequence passes through the embedding layer,

$$Z_u = Embedding(S_u) \tag{2}$$

$$Z_u = z_u^1, z_u^2, z_u^3...z_u^n \tag{3}$$

where z_u^i is the embedding space representation of the i-th item of user u. We calculate the similarity between the target item and the sequence item through the soft attention mechanism, which represents the noise probability of the item.

$$prob(z_u^i) = 1 - \frac{\exp(cor_i)}{\sum_{j=1}^n \exp(cor_j)} \tag{4}$$

where $cor_i = sim(z_u^i, z_u^{n+1})$, sim is our correlation calculation method. In this article, we use cosine similarity.

From the above method, we get the noise probability of each item of the user $Porb(Z_u) = prob(z_u^1), prob(z_u^2), prob(z_u^3), ..., prob(z_u^n)$, unlike all previous methods, we use the supervision signal to directly calculate the noise probability, because we only need to calculate the noise probability in the training set, and the supervision signal will not work in the test set.

Noise Update Strategy for Sequential Items. As our noise probabilities are calculated based on the embedding representation of items, after a certain number of training epochs, the noise probabilities of items may not be accurate enough and require updating. Our update interval epoch is a hyperparameter t, and every t epochs we recompute our noise probabilities for each item. Assuming that our total training round N is 50 and t is 20, we will update the sequence item noise update in the 20th and 40th epoch of training.

3.2 Data Augmentation Based on Noise Probability

According to the noise probabilities of the items in the sequence calculated in the previous section, we perform corresponding data augmentation. In this section, we design 5 sequence data augment methods. We perform positive data augmentation and negative data augmentation on the crop and mask in CL4Rec according to the noise probability. Our reorder operation will not change the element, so we only take positive data augmentation for it.

- **Crop or Mask for Noise reduction.** In order to reduce the noise data of the user behavior sequence, we select k items with the highest noise probability to crop or mask, so that the similarity between the behavior items in the sequence and the user's intention is higher, where k is calculated by our crop or mask coefficient α, $k = \alpha|Z_u|, 0 < \alpha < 1$.

$$Z_u^{crop+} = [\hat{v}_1, \hat{v}_2, ..., \hat{v}_{|Z_u|}] \tag{5}$$

$$\hat{v}_i = \begin{cases} z_u^i, prob(z_u^i) < Porb(Z_u).sort()[k] \\ \emptyset \ or \ [mask], prob(z_u^i) >= Porb(Z_u).sort()[k] \end{cases} \tag{6}$$

- **Crop or Mask for Noise augmentation.** In order to augment the noise data of the user behavior sequence, we select k items with the smallest noise probability to crop or mask, so that the items in the sequence are contrary to our user intentions as much as possible, where k is calculated by our crop or mask coefficient β, $k = \beta|Z_u|, 0 < \beta < 1$. The formulaic expression is as before
- **Reorder for Noise reduction.** In order to minimize the impact of noise items in users on user sequence intentions, we select k subsequences with the highest noise probability for random reorder. where k is calculated by our reorder coefficient γ, $k = \gamma|Z_u|, 0 < \gamma < 1$.

3.3 Sequence Encoder

Transformer has a good encoding ability for sequence data, and can overcapture the internal relationship between sequences through the self-attention mechanism. It is also widely used as the backbone network for sequential recommendation. Moreover, other sequence encoders are also valid, similar to GRU4Rec, Caser, BERT4Rec.

$$\hat{Z}_u = TranfomerEncoder(Z_u) \tag{7}$$

We follow the common approach of sequential recommendation models and use the last item representation z_u as the representation of the whole sequence.

$$z_u = \hat{Z}_u[-1] \tag{8}$$

3.4 Noise Contrastive Loss

In our data augmentation method, we differ from CL4Rec or DuoRec in that we introduce unique negative data augmentation, which is similar to our idea of contrastive learning by maximizing the difference between positive and negative samples.

Traditional Sequential Recommendation Loss Function. In this paper we adopt cross-entropy [2] as our supervised learning loss function.

$$\mathcal{L}_{seq}(s_u) = -\log \frac{\exp\left(\text{sim}\left(z_u, z_u^{n+1}\right)\right)}{\sum_{i=1}^{||V||} \exp\left(\text{sim}\left(z_u, z^{v_i}\right)\right)} \tag{9}$$

where z_u is the representation of the user sequence, z_u^{n+1} is the representation of our next item, z^{v_i} is the embedding of all candidate item sets, $||V||$ is the size of the item set.

Positive Contrastive Loss Function. We use a contrastive loss function [6] to calculate whether two positive samples come from the same user history sequence. We minimize positive samples from the same sequence with different augmentations, and maximize the difference between different sequences.

$$\mathcal{L}_{cl}^{+}(s_u) = -\log \frac{\exp\left(\text{sim}\left(z_u^{a_i}, z_u^{a_j}\right)/\tau\right)}{\exp\left(\text{sim}\left(z_u^{a_i}, z_u^{a_j}\right)/\tau\right) + \sum_{s^- \in S^-} \exp\left(\text{sim}\left(z_u^{a_i}, z^{s^-}\right)/\tau\right)} \tag{10}$$

where $z_u^{a_i}, z_u^{a_j}$ is the representation of user sequence from two noise reduction methods, S^- is the set of negative samples. This negative sample refers to a sample that is augmented from other sequences relative to the current sequence within the same batch.z^{s^-} is the negative sample. τ is temperature coefficient.

Negative Contrastive Loss Function. Our negative samples are the samples we generated by noise augmentations. Our goal is to make noise-augmented samples that are close to each other, and noise-augmented samples that are far from noise-reduced samples.

$$\mathcal{L}_{cl}^{-}(s_u) = -\frac{1}{|A^-|} \sum_{s_{u'}^a \in A^-} \log \frac{\exp\left(\text{sim}\left(z_u^{a^-}, z_{u'}^a\right)/\tau\right)}{\exp\left(\text{sim}\left(z_u^{a^-}, z_{u'}^a\right)/\tau\right) + \sum_{s \in A^+} \exp\left(\text{sim}\left(z_u^{a^-}, z\right)/\tau\right)} \tag{11}$$

where A^- is the set of sample generated by noise augmentations. A^+ is the set of sample generated by noise reduction. $z_u^{a^-}$ is the representation of user sequence from a noise augmentation method. $z_{u'}^a$ is a sample from noise augmentation and z is a sample from noise reduction.

Joint Training. Finally, the loss function of NCL4Rec is to jointly train the cross entropy with the positive loss function and the negative loss function.

$$\mathcal{L}_{NCL4Rec} = \mathcal{L}_{seq} + \lambda_{cl+}\mathcal{L}_{cl+}^{+} + \lambda_{cl-}\mathcal{L}_{cl}^{-} \tag{12}$$

where λ_{cl+} is the coefficient of positive loss function and λ_{cl-} is the coefficient of negative loss function.

4 Experiment

In order to better compare our experiments, we mainly focus on the following questions.

Q1: How does our NCL4Rec perform compared to other sequential recommendation models?
Q2: How does our NCL4Rec compare to other models in terms of representation learning?

4.1 Setup

Dataset. The datasets we use for sequential recommendation are widely used datasets, namely the Amazon and the MovieLens.

Baselines. The following methods are used for comparison:

- Sequential recommendation model: We use GRU4Rec [4] based on RNN, Caser [11] based on CNN, SASRec [5] based on Transformer.
- Contrastive learning model for sequential recommendation: We use CL4Rec [15] and DuoRec [8].

Metrics. We use top-K Hit Ratio (HR@K) and top-K Normalized Discounted Cumulative Gain (NDCG@K), where K is selected from 5, 10.

4.2 Overall Performance (Q1)

In general, NCL4Rec performs the best on all metrics and datasets. On ML-100K, it outperforms other algorithms by a significant margin in HR@5, HR@10, and NDCG@10, and achieves the highest NDCG@5. Similarly, on Beauty and Sports, NCL4Rec consistently achieves the best performance across all metrics, with improvements ranging from 3.47SASRec and DuoRec also show competitive performance on all datasets. SASRec performs well in HR@5 and NDCG@5 on ML-100K, while DuoRec excels in HR@10 and NDCG@10. Both algorithms perform well on Beauty and Sports. Caser and CL4Rec, however, exhibit relatively suboptimal performance compared to other algorithms across all datasets. Caser consistently performs poorly across all metrics, while CL4Rec has low rankings in HR@5, HR@10, and NDCG@10 on ML-100K and Beauty and Sports.

Overall, these results indicate that NCL4Rec is a promising recommendation algorithm that achieves superior performance across multiple datasets and evaluation metrics (Table 1).

Table 1. Overall performance. (The best results are bolded and the suboptimal ones are underlined. The last column represents the percentage improvement of our results compared to the best results.)

Dataset	Metrics	GRU4Rec	Caser	SASRec	CL4Rec	DuoRec	NCL4Rec	Improv.
ML-100K	HR@5	0.0710	0.0551	<u>0.0764</u>	0.0753	0.0742	**0.0806**	5.50%
	HR@10	0.1295	0.1007	0.1304	0.1326	<u>0.1400</u>	**0.1495**	6.79%
	NDCG@5	0.0384	0.0319	0.0431	0.0450	<u>0.0453</u>	**0.0471**	3.97%
	NDCG@10	0.0574	0.0463	0.0600	0.0631	<u>0.0663</u>	**0.0690**	4.07%
Beauty	HR@5	0.1640	0.0191	0.0365	0.0493	<u>0.0546</u>	**0.0569**	4.21%
	HR@10	0.0365	0.0335	0.0627	0.0807	<u>0.0831</u>	**0.0859**	3.37%
	NDCG@5	0.0086	0.0114	0.0236	0.0166	<u>0.0345</u>	**0.0357**	3.47%
	NDCG@10	0.0142	0.0160	0.0281	0.0312	<u>0.0436</u>	**0.0453**	3.90%
Sports	HR@5	0.0137	0.0121	0.0218	0.0280	<u>0.0310</u>	**0.0332**	7.10%
	HR@10	0.0274	0.0204	0.0336	0.0455	<u>0.0480</u>	**0.0505**	5.21%
	NDCG@5	0.0096	0.0076	0.0087	0.0167	<u>0.0190</u>	**0.0201**	5.79%
	NDCG@10	0.0137	0.0103	0.0224	0.0225	<u>0.0241</u>	**0.0254**	5.39%

4.3   Study of Ablation

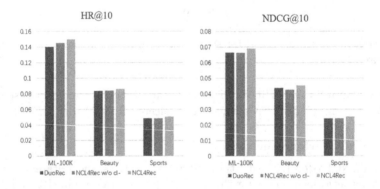

Fig. 2. Performance comparison on DuoRec, NCL4Rec w/o $\mathcal{L}_{cl}^{-}$, NCL4Rec on HR@10, NDCG@10.

To verify the effectiveness of our proposed method, we test the performance of NCL4Rec with different loss functions on three datasets. Additionally, we include DuoRec as a comparison for better observation. Figure 2 shows our results, and it can be seen that when we only use the positive loss function, our method outperforms DuoRec in terms of HR@10 on all three datasets. When using the full loss function, our method shows further improvement. However, on ML-100K, where only positive contrast is used, our method's performance is slightly lower than DuoRec.

ML-100K

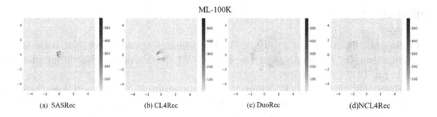

(a) SASRec   (b) CL4Rec   (c) DuoRec   (d)NCL4Rec

Fig. 3. Item embeddings on ML-100K dataset.

4.4 Discussion About Item Representation (Q3)

Representation learning is always the focus of deep recommendation systems. The embedded representation of items directly determines the performance of recommendation models. Figure 3 show the item embedding representations learned by the four methods of SASRec, CL4Rec, DuoRec, and NCL4Rec on the datasets ML-100K. These four methods all use the transformer as the backbone network. It can be seen that the embedded representations of SASRec are very clustered, followed by CL4Rec. DuoRec uses a contrast regularization method to enhance the uniformity of sequence representation distribution, which has a greater improvement compared to CL4Rec. Our NLC4Rec constructs positive and negative data augmentation to make it easier to distinguish the noise and normal items in the sequence. NCL4Rec can make the embedded representation of items more uniform and more discriminative, and our embedded representation is further improved.

5 Conclusion

In this paper, we investigate how to address the inherently noisy data present in sequence data to optimize our recommendation performance. We introduce supervisory signals to identify noise in raw sequence data, and then design positive and negative augmentations. By pulling in the distance between the positive sample data and widening the distance between the positive sample and the negative sample, we can better learn the representation of the item. Experiments demonstrate that NCL4Rec outperforms state-of-the-art sequence recommendation models on multiple datasets. In future research, we will explore more accurate noise identification methods, so that the inherent noise data in the sequence can be better identified, and the generated samples have better representation capabilities.

Acknowledgement. This work is supported in part by National Natural Science Foundation of China (61702264), the Open Research Project of State Key Laboratory of Novel Software Technology (Nanjing University, No. KFKT2022B28), the National Key R&D Program of China (No. 2020YFB1805503) and the Postdoctoral Science Foundation of China (2019M651835). Dr. Xuyun Zhang is supported only by ARC DECRA Grant DE210101458. Key Technologies and Industrialization of Industrial Internet Terminal Threat Detection and Response System.

References

1. Covington, P., Adams, J., Sargin, E.: Deep neural networks for YouTube recommendations. In: Proceedings of the 10th ACM Conference on Recommender Systems, pp. 191–198 (2016)
2. De Boer, P.T., Kroese, D.P., Mannor, S., Rubinstein, R.Y.: A tutorial on the cross-entropy method. Ann. Oper. Res. **134**, 19–67 (2005). https://doi.org/10.1007/s10479-005-5724-z
3. Duan, J., Zhang, P.F., Qiu, R., Huang, Z.: Long short-term enhanced memory for sequential recommendation. World Wide Web **26**(2), 561–583 (2023). https://doi.org/10.1007/s11280-022-01056-9
4. Hidasi, B., Karatzoglou, A., Baltrunas, L., Tikk, D.: Session-based recommendations with recurrent neural networks. arXiv preprint arXiv:1511.06939 (2016)
5. Kang, W.C., McAuley, J.: Self-attentive sequential recommendation. In: 2018 IEEE International Conference on Data Mining (ICDM), pp. 197–206. IEEE (2018)
6. Khosla, P., et al.: Supervised contrastive learning. In: Advances in Neural Information Processing Systems, vol. 33, pp. 18661–18673 (2020)
7. Li, J., Ren, P., Chen, Z., Ren, Z., Lian, T., Ma, J.: Neural attentive session-based recommendation. In: Proceedings of the 2017 ACM on Conference on Information and Knowledge Management, pp. 1419–1428 (2017)
8. Qiu, R., Huang, Z., Yin, H., Wang, Z.: Contrastive learning for representation degeneration problem in sequential recommendation. In: Proceedings of the Fifteenth ACM International Conference on Web Search and Data Mining, pp. 813–823 (2022)
9. Sun, F., et al.: BERT4Rec: sequential recommendation with bidirectional encoder representations from transformer. In: Proceedings of the 28th ACM International Conference on Information and Knowledge Management, pp. 1441–1450 (2019)
10. Sun, K., Qian, T., Zhong, M., Li, X.: Towards more effective encoders in pre-training for sequential recommendation. World Wide Web 1–32 (2023). https://doi.org/10.1007/s11280-023-01163-1
11. Tang, J., Wang, K.: Personalized top-n sequential recommendation via convolutional sequence embedding, pp. 565–573 (2018)
12. Vaswani, A., et al.: Attention is all you need. In: Advances in Neural Information Processing Systems, vol. 30 (2017)
13. Wang, G., Wang, H., Liu, J., Yang, Y.: Leveraging the fine-grained user preferences with graph neural networks for recommendation. World Wide Web **26**, 1371–1393 (2023). https://doi.org/10.1007/s11280-022-01099-y
14. Wang, W., Feng, F., He, X., Nie, L., Chua, T.S.: Denoising implicit feedback for recommendation. In: Proceedings of the 14th ACM International Conference on Web Search and Data Mining, pp. 373–381 (2021)
15. Xie, X., et al.: Contrastive learning for sequential recommendation. In: 2022 IEEE 38th International Conference on Data Engineering (ICDE), pp. 1259–1273. IEEE (2022)

Self-attention Convolutional Neural Network for Sequential Recommendation

Vadin James Sudarsan$^{(\boxtimes)}$ and Mohammad Masbaul Alam Polash

The University of Sydney, Sydney, NSW 2006, Australia
vadin.sudarsan@gmail.com

Abstract. Sequential recommendation uses user-interaction history of preferred items to predict which items a user is most likely to interact with in future. To tackle this prediction problem, over the years, many researchers have developed different approaches such as Convolutional Neural Networks (CNN) to identify patterns in interaction history, Self-Attention recommendation systems to find the similarity of items in a sequence with each other to model the connections between items etc. Although these approaches provide promising results, there are still a lot of scope for improvements. One limitation of such approaches for Top-N recommendation is the inability to capture long range dependencies in the sequence of interactions. Another issue is the inability for the network to model hierarchical information. To mitigate such limitations of existing approaches, in this paper, we propose a new approach called Self-Attention Convolutional (SACORec) network which combines both CNNs and Self-Attention. The idea is to take advantage of the effectiveness of various methods while mitigating their limitations. To find the effectiveness of our proposed model, we ran our model on several public data sets and collected a variety of evaluation metrics. The empirical study shows that our proposed model significantly outperforms state-of-art architectures that implement only one paradigm to the sequential recommendation. The efficiency of our model has led us to believe that it will open more pathways for future research in this area.

Keywords: Recommendation Systems · Self-Attention · Convolutional Neural Networks · Sequential Reccomendation

1 Introduction

The goal of sequential recommendation is that given user's history of interactions with items, predict the item(s) that users are most likely to interact in the near future. Items can be media i.e. movies/songs, retail products, webpages for search engine and browsing recommendation, and more. These predictions often influence business decisions such as adjusting the stock of items in warehouse. So, from an industry perspective, this is a very crucial problem to solve correctly and efficiently [2]. Sequential recommendation can be defined as the top-N problem, where given the user-item interaction history, predict the N most

F. Zhang et al. (Eds.): WISE 2023, LNCS 14306, pp. 569–578, 2023.
https://doi.org/10.1007/978-981-99-7254-8_44

likely items that a user will interact with. The simplest form of this is top-1 recommendation, where a recommendation system aims to predict the most likely item that a user will interact with given the interaction history. Considering various applications of sequential recommendation, there is a clear motivation to continuously improve the performance of recommendation systems.

Historically, the sequential recommendation problem is tackled with matrix factorization [10]. However, this method does not explicitly model the sequential element of recommendation. After that various models based on Markov chains were developed which model transition probabilities from one item to another. One such popular model is FPMC [12] which personalizes the transition probabilities for each user. More recently, state-of-the-art neural network based models have been proposed by several researchers. One of the most popular models, GRU4Rec [6], uses a recurrent neural network with Gated Recurrent Units to model user-item interaction chains and predict the next item. Another model, Caser [13] uses a convolutional neural network, with recent user-item interactions stacked to form an "image". Furthermore, another efficient model called SASRec [8] uses the self-attention mechanism to encode the historical sequence of interactions into the most recent interaction and use the augmented most recent interaction to predict the next item in the sequence.

Although the state-of-art models show promising results, our investigation reveals that there are still a lot of room for improvements. For example, convolutional neural networks (CNN) are limited to a fixed "image" size which is quite small; Caser [13] uses only the last 5 items. Self-attention based networks can encode sequences of much longer lengths (SASRec can encode sequence lengths of hundreds of items [8]), however patterns across recent items and features are not captured as in-detail as with a CNN. Thus, an opportunity exists to combine both convolutional and self-attention paradigms in network design.

In this paper, we propose a new approach called Self-Attention Convolutional (SACORec) network which combines both CNNs and Self-Attention. The idea is to take advantage of the effectiveness of various methods while mitigating their limitations. To find the effectiveness of our proposed model, we ran our model on several public data sets and collected a variety of evaluation metrics. The empirical study shows that our proposed model significantly outperforms state-of-art architectures that implement only one paradigm to the sequential recommendation. The efficiency of our model has led us to believe that it will open more pathways for future research in this area.

2   Related Work

Sequential recommendation systems seek to predict the next item a user will interact with. They do this by taking into account the order in which previous interactions have taken place.

2.1   Caser

The performance of CNN have been the gold standard across many applications, especially regarding computer vision and image processing [11]. Convolutional

Sequence Embedding Recommendation Model (Caser) is a neural model which uses convolutional operations to extract sequential information. It achieves state-of-the-art performance on top-N recommendation [13].

The first layer of Caser is the embedding layer, in which items are projected into a d dimensional representation. The next layers of Caser are the convolutional layers. The embeddings of L previous items are stacked to form an image. The order in which they are stacked captures sequential information. Convolutions along rows and columns are used to capture patterns at the sequential level and at the item feature level. These convolutions are fed into a fully connected layer. An embedding representing the user u is concatenated to the output of this layer and fed into a final fully connected layer which is normalized to output a probability distribution across all the items.

To generate training data, a sliding window of L previous items and T next items is used. It allows to capture higher order Markov chains and skip rules, where an item may be interacted with T steps after a previous item. Additionally, negative sampling is used to generate negative targets. The target vector is defined as the T targets encoded as 1 and N negative samples encoded as 0.

The loss of the network is calculated with Binary Cross Entropy (BCE). It compares the output with the target vector generated with negative sampling. The optimizer used here is Adaptive Movement Estimator (Adam) [9].

2.2 SASRec

Self-Attention based Sequential Recommendation model (SASRec) uses self-attention methods to encode sequences of user-item interactions and achieves state-of-the-art performance in sequential recommendation [8]. An embedding layer is used to encode the items in a d dimensional space. A sequence of embeddings is fed to the network. The similarity between items in the sequence is calculated, and the embeddings are weighted by the similarity with other items. This similarity-weighted encoding is then fed through a feed-forward of fully connected layers. This process is called self-attention which enriches the encoding of an item using information about other items in the sequence. The last item in the enriched sequence is used to predict the target item. Negative sampling is also used. The loss function is BCE and the optimizer is Adam [9].

2.3 Limitation of Existing Works

A limitation with Caser is the fixed size of the "image" used in convolution. For every prediction, Caser can only use the last L previous items to predict along with the user embedding. The user embedding may help in long range themes with the user, but long range sequential information is not captured. A limitation of SASRec is that only the last enriched item embedding is used for prediction. A limitation of both SASRec and Caser is that the loss function BCE is balanced between positive and negative samples. In many datasets, high sparsity means that there are a lot more negative samples than positive samples, especially in the case of top-1 recommendation where all the items except the target top-1 item are negative.

3   Methodology

In this chapter, the Self-Attention Convolution Recommendation (SACORec) architecture is proposed.

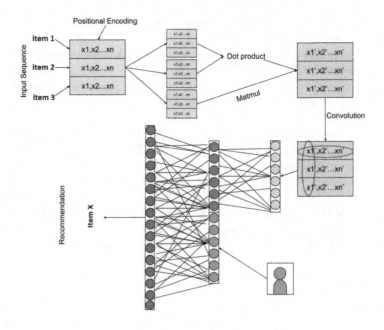

Fig. 1. SACORec architecture diagram

As shown in Fig. 1, the SACORec architecture has multiple layers. The first layer is an embedding layer, which transforms items into feature vectors. The next layer is a self-attention layer, which enriches the item embeddings with information from other item embeddings. The next layer is the convolution layer, which extracts information column-wise (feature) and row-wise (sequence). The final layers are fully connected and softmax layers. To generate the training data, a sliding window was used. L items were chosen in sequence (in this architecture, L is the input sequence length hyperparameter).The subsequent T items (in this architecture, T is a fixed hyperparameter 3) were taken as targets. The algorithm starts at the first L+T items, extracts an input-target pair, then shifts sequentially one and repeats the process until the end of the training data. Padding was used to ensure the same number of training samples were available regardless of the input sequence length. L-1 pad items were inserted at the beginning of every sequence.

3.1   Self Attention Layer

The embeddings of L items are stacked into a matrix S where $S \in \mathbb{R}^{L \times d}$, then fed into the self attention layer to cross-pollinate information from all the items in the sequence into each other. The input and output shapes are the same. The self-attention layer is based upon the Transformer network's encoder architecture. [14]

Positional Encoding. To allow the self-attention layer discern the items' position in the sequence, positional information was added to the embeddings [14]. A sine wave was added to even indexed items in the sequence and a cosine wave was added to odd indexed items.

For even elements:

$$PE(_{pos,2i}) = sin(pos/10000^{2i/d})$$

For odd elements:

$$PE(_{pos,2i+1}) = cos(pos/10000^{2i/d})$$

where i is the index of the dimension, d is the number of dimensions, and *pos* is the position in the sequence

3.2   Multi-headed and Multi-layered Attention

The item input embeddings can be split and the attention can be calculated separately for each split. For example, an embedding size of 50 and 2 heads, the input matrix is split in half, and one attention head will look at the similarity between the first 25 values in all item embeddings and the other attention head will attend to the last 25 values. Self attention heads learn different sub-elements of item embeddings [14], and some heads end up being more important than others for different predictions [15]. Practically, this operation can be parallelized.Furthermore, Multiple self-attention layers can be stacked. In this paper, we test 1,2, and 3 self-attention layers.

3.3   Convolution Layer

The information output from the self-attention layer(s) then goes through convolution operations.

Convolution Input. The last L item embeddings from the self-attention enriched sequence are taken (in this architecture, L is a fixed hyperparameter 5). These item embeddings are stacked to form a pseudo"image" as shown in Fig. 2.

Horizontal and Vertical Convolution. Convolution operations are performed to extract features. The convolution operations are horizontal to capture each embedding sequentially and vertical to capture the pattern in each feature. The output of the convolution will be $L \times D + D \times L$ values.

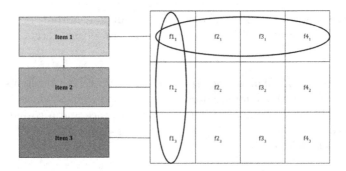

Fig. 2. Stacking of embeddings to form an "image"

3.4   Fully Connected Layers

Fully Connected Layer 1. The output of the convolution layer is fed into the first fully connected layer. This layer has an input size of $L \times D + D \times L$ and an output size d. The weights in this layer are learned.

User Embedding. The output of the first fully connected layer is concatenated with an embedding which represents the unique user. The embedding is d dimensional and randomly initialized.

Fully Connected Layer 2. The output of the first fully connected layer concatenated with the user embedding is fed into a final fully connected layer. This layer has an input size $d+d$ and output size of the number of items in the database.

3.5   Softmax, Backpropogation and Loss

To turn the output of the final fully connected layer into a probability distribution, the output of the layer is softmaxed.

The output of the network is compared to the target vector and the loss is calculated. The target vector consists of positive and negative targets. The positive targets were generated from the sliding window, and the negative targets were randomly sampled from the items the user has not interacted with in the training data. Negative sampling is a cheaper way to train the model without calculating the loss over every item for every training instance [4]. The loss used was balanced cross entropy.

$$\sum_{c=1}^{T+N} -(y \log(p) + b \cdot (1 - y) \log(1 - p))$$

where T is the number of positive targets, N is the number of negative targets, y is an indicator of whether the current observation should be 0(negative) or 1(positive)n and b is a hyperparameter biasing the loss function towards positive or negative loss. The loss was backpropogated through the network using the Adam optimizer, which is a variant of stochastic gradient descent [9].

3.6   Dropout

During training, dropout was used to capture information of multiple pathways and prevent overfitting [7]. Each node in the network was disconnected (fixed output 0) with a probability p and the remaining active nodes would have their output scaled by $1 + p$. Dropout rate is a hyperparameter.

4   Experiments

Two popular benchmark datasets were used - FoursquareNYC [16] and Movielens1M [5]. FoursquareNYC comes from Foursquare, an app which provides recommendations on places a user should visit based on a user's previous visited locations. The dataset contains 1083 users and 38333 locations, and the interaction history between users and locations. For sequential recommendation, only the user-item interactions sorted by time were used, without using any of the accompanying user and item metadata like venue category or geographic coordinates. Movielens1M contains 1 million ratings by 6000 users on 4000 movies. Again, no item or user metadata was used, only the user-item interactions sorted by time. In this case, we consider the interaction implicit feedback, where the act of rating a movie counted as an interaction regardless of how many stars a user gave an item.

4.1   Metrics

To compare SACORec with other recommendation systems, 2 standard metrics were used. The first metric is hit rate@10 (HR@10). Given a list of 101 items containing 100 randomly sampled negative items and the target item ranked by the recommendation system, HR@10 measures how often the target item appears in the top 10 ranked items. As there is only 1 target item, HR@10 is equivalent to recall@10. Metrics taking into account the discrete ranks of items like hit rate and NDCG make sense for a recommendation system over continuous metrics like mean squared error, prediction confidence, and testing loss due to the nature of the task; the internal state of the model is not important as the item is shown to the user [1]. A high loss or low confidence top-1 prediction is used the same as a low loss or high confidence top-1 prediction of the same item.

$$Recall = \frac{TP}{TP + FN}$$

The second metric assessed was normalized discounted cumulative gain @10 (NDGC@10). This metric assesses how highly the target item appears in the same list of 101 items containing 100 randomly sampled negative items and the target item discounted by the target's position in the list. The formula for NDCG@10 is

$$\sum_{i=1}^{10} \frac{relevance_i}{log_2(i + 1)}$$

In this case, the target being 1st in the list would return a NDGC of 1, 2nd a NDCG of 0.63, 3rd 0.5, all the way down to 10th returning a NDCG of 0.30. If the target is not within the top 10 ranked items, the NDCG would be 0. Both these metrics were used in the original SASRec paper.

4.2   Implementation Details of State of the Art Models

Caser and SASRec were implemented with code from the corresponding authors and implemented in the Pytorch package. An Nvidia K80 GPU was used through the Google Colab cloud computing service.

4.3   Performance Evaluation

SACORec was tested against the state-of-the-art models Caser and SASRec on the MovieLens1M and Foursquare NYC datasets. For MovieLens1M, the ideal hyperparameters except for latent dimension suggested by the paper's authors were used. The same hyperparameters were used on FoursquareNYC. A latent dimension of 100 was used for both MovieLens1M and Foursquare on all models, which performed the same or outperformed the suggested 50 dimensions. Caser and SACORec had a convolutional window of size 5. Caser and SACORec were both trained 5 times for 50 epochs, and testing set metrics of the epoch with the best validation NDCG@10 was taken. SASRec was trained for 400 epochs, also using the validation NDCG@10 to select the best epoch. All models had a learning rate of 0.001.

The remaining SACORec hyperparameters were found with grid search. SACORec had a loss bias of 20, a sequence length of 10, 1 attention layer, 1 attention head, and 0 dropout for MovieLens1M. SACORec had a loss bias of 50, a sequence length of 10, 1 attention layer, 1 attention head, and 0.5 dropout for Foursquare NYC.

Table 1. Performance Comparison

		State of the Art Models		Our Model
		Caser [18]	SASRec[9]	SACORec
MovieLens1M	NDCG@10	0.582 ±0.004	0.592 ±0.003	0.597 ±0.002
	HR@10	0.811 ±0.001	0.821 ±0.005	0.819 ±0.003
Foursquare NYC	NDCG@10	0.769 ±0.009	0.678 ±0.006	0.790 ±0.006
	HR@10	0.854 ±0.010	0.759 ±0.009	0.845 ±0.016

As shown in Table 1, SACORec had the best NDCG@10 on both datasets. This performance difference was statistically significant ($p<0.05$) against all models on all datasets. SASRec had the best HR@10 on MovieLens1M, however this result was not statistically significant against SACORec ($p=0.46$). Caser had the best HR@10 on Foursquare NYC, however this result was not statistically significant against SACORec ($p=0.37$).

5   Conclusion

Sequential recommendation is the usage of algorithms and models to predict, given a historical sequence of user-item interactions, the next item(s) that a user will interact with. A subset of this problem is top-1 recommendation, where the best next item is recommended to the user at every timestep. Practically, sequential recommendation systems are critical in industries like media recommendation, online shopping for product recommendation, webpage and information recommendation, and even tourism and point-of-interest recommendation.

Historically, the sequential recommendation problem has been solved with naive solutions like popularity recommendation, followed by matrix factorization models and Markov chain based models. Recent advances in the field use neural network models like recurrent neural networks, convolutional neural networks, and attention-based networks.

SACORec combines both self-attention based models and convolution based models. It does this by encoding a longer length sequence with self-attention, then feeding it through convolutional layers to extract patterns at the item and feature level. It then uses this information along with information learned about the user to suggest the next most relevant item. In top-1 recommendation, SACORec outperforms state-of-the-art models on benchmark datasets MovieLens1M and Foursquare NYC.

Some hyperparameters are more significant than others in improving performance. In particular, balanced cross-entropy provides a large part of the performance gain of SACORec compared to other models. More research could be conducted on applying balanced cross-entropy on other models. Additionally, as balanced-cross entropy is not a symmetrical loss function, testing could be done on noisy datasets where items are incorrectly labelled or not representative (for example, if a user lends their device to a child and contaminates the true user-item interaction history), as symmetric functions are known to be more stable with noisy data [3].

SACORec's model size depends on the number of items in the database. More work could be done to minimize the implementation of self-attention and convolution methods on real world data with much larger sizes and item counts.

References

1. Cremonesi, P., Koren, Y., Turrin, R.: Performance of recommender algorithms on top-N recommendation tasks, p. 39. ACM Press (2010). https://doi.org/10.1145/1864708.1864721
2. Fayyaz, Z., Ebrahimian, M., Nawara, D., Ibrahim, A., Kashef, R.: Recommendation systems: algorithms, challenges, metrics, and business opportunities. Appl. Sci. **10**, 7748 (2020). https://doi.org/10.3390/app10217748
3. Ghosh, A., Kumar, H., Sastry, P.S.: Robust loss functions under label noise for deep neural networks. In: Proceedings of the AAAI Conference on Artificial Intelligence, vol. 31 (2017). https://doi.org/10.1609/aaai.v31i1.10894

 4. Goldberg, Y., Levy, O.: word2vec explained: deriving Mikolov et al'.s negative-sampling word-embedding method (2014)
 5. Harper, F.M., Konstan, J.A.: The movielens datasets. ACM Trans. Interact. Intell. Syst. **5**, 1–19 (2016). https://doi.org/10.1145/2827872
 6. Hidasi, B., Karatzoglou, A., Baltrunas, L., Tikk, D.: Session-based recommendations with recurrent neural networks (2015). http://arxiv.org/abs/1511.06939
 7. Hinton, G.E., Srivastava, N., Krizhevsky, A., Sutskever, I., Salakhutdinov, R.R.: Improving neural networks by preventing co-adaptation of feature detectors (2012). http://arxiv.org/abs/1207.0580
 8. Kang, W.C., McAuley, J.: Self-attentive sequential recommendation (2018). http://arxiv.org/abs/1808.09781
 9. Kingma, D.P., Ba, J.: Adam: a method for stochastic optimization (2014). http://arxiv.org/abs/1412.6980
10. Koren, Y., Bell, R., Volinsky, C.: Matrix factorization techniques for recommender systems. Computer **42**, 30–37 (2009). https://doi.org/10.1109/MC.2009.263
11. Li, Z., Liu, F., Yang, W., Peng, S., Zhou, J.: A survey of convolutional neural networks: analysis, applications, and prospects. IEEE Trans. Neural Netw. Learn. Syst. 1–21 (2021). https://doi.org/10.1109/TNNLS.2021.3084827
12. Rendle, S., Freudenthaler, C., Schmidt-Thieme, L.: Factorizing personalized Markov chains for next-basket recommendation, p. 811. ACM Press (2010). https://doi.org/10.1145/1772690.1772773
13. Tang, J., Wang, K.: Personalized Top-N sequential recommendation via convolutional sequence embedding, vol. 2018-Febuary, pp. 565–573. Association for Computing Machinery, Inc (2018). https://doi.org/10.1145/3159652.3159656
14. Vaswani, A., et al.: Attention is all you need (2017). http://arxiv.org/abs/1706.03762
15. Voita, E., Talbot, D., Moiseev, F., Sennrich, R., Titov, I.: Analyzing multi-head self-attention: specialized heads do the heavy lifting, the rest can be pruned (2019)
16. Yang, D., Zhang, D., Zheng, V.W., Yu, Z.: Modeling user activity preference by leveraging user spatial temporal characteristics in LBSNS. IEEE Trans. Syst. Man Cybernet. Syst. **45**, 129–142 (2015). https://doi.org/10.1109/TSMC.2014.2327053

Informative Anchor-Enhanced Heterogeneous Global Graph Neural Networks for Personalized Session-Based Recommendation

Ronghua Lin[1,3], Luyao Teng[2], Feiyi Tang[2,3], Hao Zhong[1,3], Chengzhe Yuan[3,4(✉)], and Chengjie Mao[1,3]

[1] School of Computer Science, South China Normal University, Guangzhou 510631, China
{rhlin,hzhong,maochj}@m.scnu.edu.cn
[2] School of Information Engineering, Guangzhou Panyu Polytechnic, Guangzhou 511483, China
tangfy@gzpyp.edu.cn
[3] Pazhou Lab, Guangzhou 510330, China
[4] School of Electronics and Information, Guangdong Polytechnic Normal University, Guangzhou 510665, China
ycz@gpnu.edu.cn

Abstract. Due to the anonymity of user sessions, most existing session-based recommender systems (SBRSs) cannot effectively learn user features, leading to failure to make personalized recommendations. Besides, these SBRSs may neglect some similar items with common features if they are long-distance in the session graphs or global graphs. In this paper, we propose a novel SBRS based on heterogeneous graph neural network, which can effectively learn user and item embeddings for personalized recommendations. Furthermore, we find out the user and item informative anchors in the heterogeneous graph and propagate their features in the same type of nodes, which can help to explore those long-distance but similar items. We conduct extensive experiments on three real-world datasets and the experimental results demonstrate the effectiveness of our proposed method.

Keywords: Session-based recommendation · Heterogeneous graph · Informative anchor

1 Introduction

Due to the real-time nature of the recommendations, SBRSs have attracted more and more attention since they can predict the users' next clicks or interactions based on the short sessions. Conventional SBRSs can be roughly categorized into three types, including (1) association rule-based (AR-based) methods [4,7], (2)

F. Zhang et al. (Eds.): WISE 2023, LNCS 14306, pp. 579–593, 2023.
https://doi.org/10.1007/978-981-99-7254-8_45

k nearest neighbor-based (KNN-based) methods [6,9], and (3) Markov chain-based (MC-based) methods [14,22]. These methods mainly make recommendations by learning the association relationships, similarity, or transition probabilities between items in the sessions. With the development of deep learning, the capability of efficiently modeling the item features and session features makes a dramatic improvement in the performance of SBRSs.

As a branch of deep learning, graph neural network-based (GNN-based) methods have achieved huge success in SBRSs [17,19] because the users' sessions can be converted into different types of graphs and used GNN for item modeling. However, on the one hand, most existing GNN-based SBRSs assumed that the user sessions are anonymous and thus they cannot effectively utilize users' historical sessions and make personalized recommendations. For example, in Fig. 1, the current sessions of both users A and B contain the same clicking sequences, namely "basketball shoes → basketball socks". If we consider the session anonymity, we might recommend the same item "basketball" to both users A and B. In fact, user A might click the item "jersey" several times in historical sessions while not clicking "basketball". Therefore, it might be more suitable to recommend different "jerseys" to user A in the current session.

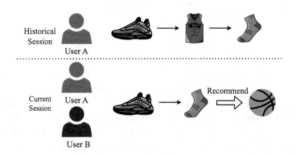

Fig. 1. The importance of users' historical sessions in SBRSs.

On the other hand, existing SBRSs mainly used the identifiers of the item (i.e., the item IDs) for item embedding training. It means that the item embeddings can only be initialized randomly or simply initialized using one-hot encoding. Besides, since the session graphs only record the item transitions according to the user clicking sequences in the sessions, some latent and similar features between items may be neglected if they are distant from each other in the same session graph, which means they are not connected. For example, users A and B might click on "basketball shoes" and "basketball socks", respectively. Although these two items do not exist in the same session, they both belong to the category of "basketball equipment", and shoes and socks are a pair of highly relevant items. Hence, the latent information of these two items should be shared in the session-based recommendation task.

In this paper, we propose a heterogeneous graph and multi-type informative anchor-based session-based recommender system (HASRS). It constructs a heterogeneous global graph based on the users' historical sessions and uses heterogeneous graph neural network HGNN to learn the user and item representations, respectively. By capturing the user features in their historical sessions, HASRS can make personalized recommendations for different users. Meanwhile, it mines multi-type informative anchors (including user anchors and item anchors) in the heterogeneous global graph and constructs the relationship matrices between user/item nodes and informative anchors. In this way, it propagates and shares the latent and similar features of these anchors with other nodes in the heterogeneous global graph.

We summarize the main contributions of this paper as follows.

1. In order to model user features, we construct a heterogeneous global graph by using users' historical sessions and utilize HGNN to learn the embedding representation of different types of nodes (including users and items).
2. Since most conventional GNN-based SBRSs will neglect the latent and similar features between distant nodes, we discover multi-type informative anchors and propagate their information with other nodes of the same type.
3. In order to make personalized recommendations, the session representation consists of two parts which are (1) the representation of clicking sequences in the sessions and (2) the representation of clicking sequences incorporating user embeddings.

2 Related Work

SBRSs have become a hot research field since it makes recommendations in time according to the user's current session. Traditional SBRSs use data mining or machine learning techniques to learn the transitions and dependencies between items and predict the next-clicked items, which include AR-based methods, KNN-based methods, and MC-based methods. AR-based methods try to capture the frequently occurring association rules from users' historical sessions and then match the current session with the association rules to generate a recommendation list [4,7]. KNN-based methods first find out the top-K sessions or items that are highly similar to the current session or the current clicking item and then make recommendations according to the similarity [6,9]. MC-based SBRSs mainly employ Markov chains to learn the item transition probabilities in the sessions and predict the next-clicked items according to the current session [14,22]. However, these traditional methods cannot effectively learn the item or session embedding representation, and thus fail to capture the potential dependencies among items.

With the arising of deep learning, more and more researchers attempted to develop SBRSs by using various neural networks, including recurrent neural network (RNN), convolutional neural network (CNN), graph neural network (GNN), and so on. RNN is widely used in the tasks of NLP since it can capture the context information of natural texts. Due to the temporal nature of interactions in user sessions, some researchers have used RNNs to capture user dynamic preferences in the current session [5,10]. CNN was first used in image processing due to its capacity to learn local features in images. Hence, some researchers have also applied CNN in session-based recommendations to learn the local features in user sessions and capture potential dependencies between items [16,20]. GNN-based SBRSs first construct different types of graphs according to users' sessions, then use GNN and its variants to learn item embeddings, and finally utilize them for session embedding and recommendations [12,19].

3   Our Proposed Method

The architecture of the proposed SBRS HASRS is shown in Fig. 2. It mainly follows five steps, which are (1) heterogeneous global graph construction, (2) informative anchor selection, (3) node representation learning, (4) session representation learning, and (5) next-clicked item probability prediction.

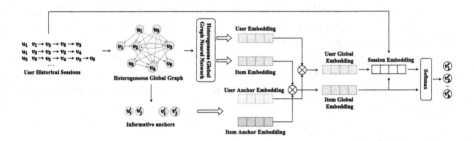

Fig. 2. The architecture of our proposed SBRS HASRS.

3.1   Heterogeneous Global Graph Construction

HASRS first constructs a directed heterogeneous global graph $\mathcal{G} =< \mathcal{V}, \mathcal{E} >$ based on the user session set S. The node set $\mathcal{V}$ contains user nodes $u_i \in U$ and item nodes $v_j \in V$. We define two types of meta-paths in $\mathcal{G}$, i.e., "user-item" and "item-item", which represent the relationship of users clicking on items and the transition relationship between items according to the clicking order in a session, respectively. Therefore, the edge set $\mathcal{E}$ of $\mathcal{G}$ also includes two types of edges which are the directed edges of "user $\rightarrow$ item" and "item $\rightarrow$ item". These two types of edges are represented as (u_i, r, v_j) and (v_i, r, v_j), respectively, where r is the type of edges.

The edges "item $\rightarrow$ item" includes the in-degree and out-degree relationships between items, denoted as r_{in} and r_{out}, respectively. Hence, the edges (v_i, r_{in}, v_j) and (v_j, r_{out}, v_i) both represent the transition from $v_i \rightarrow v_j$. The weight of the edge $v_i \rightarrow v_j$ is set as the number of times it appears in all sessions.

The relationship of "user-item" mainly includes two types which are clicking and being clicked, denoted as r_{click} and $r_{clicked}$. Therefore, the edges (u_i, r_{click}, v_j) and $(v_j, r_{clicked}, u_i)$ both represent that the user u_i has clicked on the item v_j. The weight of the edge $u_i \rightarrow v_j$ is set as the number of times the user u_i clicked on the item v_j in his/her historical sessions.

3.2   Informative Anchor Selection

In complex networks, informative anchors refer to significant nodes that contain crucial features of other similar nodes and play an important role in information propagation [1]. Hence, we propose to search for user and item informative anchors respectively in the heterogeneous global graph $\mathcal{G}$ to provide auxiliary features for other nodes.

There are several widely used methods to discover informative anchors in graphs, such as centrality algorithms [3], PageRank [11], HITS [8], etc. Specifically, common centrality algorithms include degree centrality, closeness centrality, betweenness centrality, and eigenvector centrality. In this paper, we simply use these methods to discover and select top-N significant user nodes and item nodes in $\mathcal{G}$ as user anchors and item anchors, denoted as $U_{IA} = \{u_{IA,1}, u_{IA,2}, \ldots, u_{IA,N}\}$ and $\text{IA}_v = \{v_{IA,1}, v_{IA,2}, \ldots, v_{IA,N}\}$, respectively.

3.3   Node Representation Learning

In this section, we detail the procedure of node representation learning, including user nodes and item nodes. Firstly, we use embedding layers and embed users and items into d-dimensional vectors by feeding the one-hot vectors of users and items, respectively, as shown in Eqs. (1) and (2).

$$\mathbf{e}_{u_i} = \text{Embed}(\text{one-hot}(u_i)), \tag{1}$$

$$\mathbf{e}_{v_i} = \text{Embed}(\text{one-hot}(v_i)), \tag{2}$$

where one-hot$(u_i) \in \mathbb{R}^{p \times 1}$ and one-hot$(v_i) \in \mathbb{R}^{q \times 1}$ are the one-hot vectors of user u_i and item v_i respectively with both the i-th element being 1 and others being 0.

We utilize HGNN to next learn the user and item embedding representation. Specifically, we use $\mathbf{u}_i^t$ and $\mathbf{v}_i^t$ to represent the embedding vectors of user u_i and item v_i after t update steps of HGNN. $\mathbf{u}_i^t$ and $\mathbf{v}_i^t$ are initialized as the user and item one-hot embedding vectors, respectively, i.e., $\mathbf{u}_i^0 = \mathbf{e}_{u_i}$ and $\mathbf{v}_i^0 = \mathbf{e}_{v_i}$. In HGNN, the node embedding vectors are updated by aggregating the features of neighbor nodes and propagating information along the directed edges. Taking item nodes as an example, the edges linking the item node to its neighbors include three types of relationships which are r_{in}, r_{out}, and $r_{clicked}$, where r_{in} and r_{out} are the edge relationships indicated that the neighbor nodes are items, and $r_{clicked}$ is the edge relationship indicated that the neighbor nodes are users. Therefore, the embedding representation of item v_i in HGNN is updated as shown in Eq. (3).

$$\mathbf{v}_i^t = f\left(\sum_{r \in \mathcal{R}} \sum_{v_j \in \mathcal{N}_i^r} \frac{1}{|\mathcal{N}_i^r|} \left(\mathbf{W}_r^t \mathbf{v}_j^{t-1} + \mathbf{b}_r^t\right)\right), \tag{3}$$

where $\mathcal{R} = \{r_{in}, r_{out}, r_{clicked}\}$, $\mathcal{N}_i^r$ is the neighbor node set of item v_i with the edge relationship being r, and $f(\cdot)$ is the activation function.

The embedding representation of user nodes is updated similarly to Eq. (3). Since the neighbors of user nodes are only items, the edge relationship of user nodes contains only one type, i.e., $\mathcal{R} = \{r_{click}\}$.

In Sect. 3.2, we have obtained top-N user and item anchors. In order to train the anchor embeddings, HASRS first initializes the embedding vectors of user and item anchors using the above trained embedding vectors in HGNN, denoted as $\mathbf{U}_{IA} \in \mathbb{R}^{d \times N}$ and $\mathbf{V}_{IA} \in \mathbb{R}^{d \times N}$. HASRS then leverages linear transformation layers to convert the user and item embedding vectors into anchor embedding matrices, as shown in Eqs. (4) and (5).

$$\mathbf{A}_u = \mathbf{W}_1 \mathbf{U}_{IA} + \mathbf{b}_1, \tag{4}$$

$$\mathbf{A}_v = \mathbf{W}_2 \mathbf{V}_{IA} + \mathbf{b}_2, \tag{5}$$

where $\mathbf{A}_u \in \mathbb{R}^{d \times N}$ and $\mathbf{A}_v \in \mathbb{R}^{d \times N}$ are user and item anchor embeddings, respectively.

In order to share and propagate the representative information of anchors with other nodes, it is necessary to construct the relationship matrices between other nodes with anchors. To this end, we use a feed-forward network and a softmax layer to train the "node-anchor" relationship matrices. Taking item nodes as an example, the "item node-item anchor" relationship matrix is updated following Eq. (6).

$$\mathbf{M}_v = \mathrm{softmax}\left(\sigma\left(\mathbf{W}_h^\top \mathbf{v}^t + \mathbf{b}_h\right)\right), \tag{6}$$

where $\mathbf{M}_v \in \mathbb{R}^{N \times q}$ is the "item node-item anchor" relationship matrix and $\sigma(\cdot)$ represents the sigmoid activation function. The "user node-user anchor" relationship matrix $\mathbf{M}_u \in \mathbb{R}^{N \times p}$ is updated similarly to Eq. (6).

The user and item global embeddings are multiplied by "node-anchor" relationship matrices and the anchor embeddings, as shown in Eqs. (7) and (8).

$$\mathbf{u} = \mathbf{A}_u \mathbf{M}_u, \tag{7}$$

$$\mathbf{v} = \mathbf{A}_v \mathbf{M}_v, \tag{8}$$

where $\mathbf{u} \in \mathbb{R}^{d \times p}$ and $\mathbf{v} \in \mathbb{R}^{d \times q}$ are the user and item global embeddings, respectively.

3.4   Session Representation Learning

The session representation consists of two parts. The first part only considers the clicking sequences of sessions. Specifically, given a current session $s_{u_i} = \{v_{u_i}^1, v_{u_i}^2, \ldots, v_{u_i}^t\}$ of user u_i, HASRS uses the corresponding item global embeddings to initial the session embeddings, which is denoted as $[\mathbf{v}_{u_i}^1, \mathbf{v}_{u_i}^2, \ldots, \mathbf{v}_{u_i}^t]$. HASRS subsequently utilizes the soft-attention mechanism to learn the representation of clicking sequences, as shown in Eqs. (9) and (10).

$$\gamma^1_{s_{u_i,j}} = \mathbf{c}_1^\top \sigma \left(\mathbf{W}_3 \mathbf{v}^t_{u_i} + \mathbf{W}_4 \mathbf{v}^j_{u_i} + \mathbf{d}_1 \right), \tag{9}$$

$$\mathbf{s}^1_{u_i} = \sum_{j=1}^{t} \gamma^1_{s_{u_i,j}} \mathbf{v}^j_{u_i}, \tag{10}$$

In order to make personalized recommendations, the second part of session embeddings combines the representation of clicking sequences and the user features. It is also trained by the soft-attention mechanism as shown in Eqs. (11) and (12).

$$\gamma^2_{s_{u_i,j}} = \mathbf{c}_2^\top \sigma \left(\mathbf{W}_5 \mathbf{u}_i + \mathbf{W}_6 \mathbf{v}^j_{u_i} + \mathbf{d}_2 \right), \tag{11}$$

$$\mathbf{s}^2_{u_i} = \sum_{j=1}^{t} \gamma^2_{s_{u_i,j}} \mathbf{v}^j_{u_i}, \tag{12}$$

where $\mathbf{u}_i$ is the user global embedding of user u_i.

To consider the above two parts of session embeddings, we leverage a balance factor $\alpha \in [0,1]$ to balance the weights of $\mathbf{s}^1_{u_i}$ and $\mathbf{s}^2_{u_i}$ in the session global embeddings, as shown in Eq. (13).

$$\mathbf{s}_{u_i} = \alpha \, \mathbf{s}^1_{u_i} + (1 - \alpha) \, \mathbf{s}^2_{u_i} \tag{13}$$

3.5   Next-Clicked Item Probability Prediction

After obtaining the session embeddings, the recommendation score can be calculated by the inner product of $\mathbf{s}_{u_i}$ and item one-hot embedding vectors, as shown in Eq. (14).

$$\hat{\mathbf{z}}_{s_{u_i,j}} = \mathbf{s}_{u_i}^\top \mathbf{e}_{v_j}, \tag{14}$$

where $\hat{\mathbf{z}}_{s_{u_i,j}}$ is the recommendation score of item v_j.

We then use the softmax function to calculate the probability of each item being clicked at the next timeslot and generate a top-k recommendation list, as shown in Eq. (15).

$$\hat{\mathbf{y}}_{s_{u_i}} = \mathrm{softmax}(\hat{\mathbf{z}}_{s_{u_i}}) \tag{15}$$

3.6   Model Training

For each session, the loss function is defined as the cross entropy loss between the predictive value and ground truth, as shown in Eq. (16).

$$\mathcal{L}(\hat{\mathbf{y}}_{s_{u_i}}) = -\sum_{j=1}^{n} \mathbf{y}_{s_{u_i,j}} \log(\hat{\mathbf{y}}_{s_{u_i,j}}) + (1 - \mathbf{y}_{s_{u_i,j}}) \log(1 - \hat{\mathbf{y}}_{s_{u_i,j}}), \tag{16}$$

where $\mathbf{y}_{s_{u_i}} \in \mathbb{R}^{q \times 1}$ is the one-hot vector of the ground truth, i.e., if v_j is the next clicked item in session s_{u_i}, then only the j-th element of $\mathbf{y}_{s_{u_i}}$ is 1, while others are 0.

4   Experimental Setup

4.1   Datasets

We use three real-world datasets to evaluate our proposed model HASRS, which are LastFM, Xing, and Reddit. For each dataset, 20% of the latest sessions in chronological order are selected as the test set, and the remaining sessions are used as the training set.

- LastFM: LastFM is a dataset for musician recommendation, which includes approximately 1,000 users and their historical music listening records.
- Xing: Xing is a recruitment post recommendation dataset, which includes about 770,000 user interaction records with recruitment posts on a social networking site.
- Reddit: Reddit is a forum comment dataset, which contains triples of (username, subreddit title, comment time).

4.2   Evaluation Metrics

In this paper, we use two metrics to measure the recommendation performance, which are **HR@k** and **MRR@k**. Both the larger values of **HR@k** and **MRR@k** indicate better recommendation performance.

- **HR@k**: Hit rate is a widely used metric to measure recommendation accuracy. It is calculated as shown in Eq. (17).

$$\text{HR@}k = \frac{\sum_{i=1}^{n} f(v_{i,t}, a_i)}{n}, \tag{17}$$

where n is the number of sessions in the test set, $v_{i,t}$ is the label of i-th session, a_i is the top-k recommendation list, and $f(v_{i,t}, a_i)$ indicates that whether the item $v_{i,t}$ appears in a_i as shown in Eq. (18).

$$f(v_{i,t}, a_i) = \begin{cases} 1, v_{i,t} \in a_i \\ 0, v_{i,t} \notin a_i \end{cases} \tag{18}$$

- **MRR@k** (Mean Reciprocal Rank): Mean reciprocal rank is used to calculate the mean reciprocal rank values of the target item (i.e., the session label) in the recommendation list. It is calculated as shown in Eq. (19).

$$\text{MRR@}k = \frac{1}{n} \sum_{i=1}^{n} \frac{1}{p_{v_{i,t}}}, \tag{19}$$

where $p_{v_{i,t}}$ represents the position of target item $v_{i,t}$ in the top-k recommendation list. Specifically, if the target item $v_{i,t}$ does not appear in the recommendation list, $\frac{1}{p_{v_{i,t}}}$ is set as 0.

4.3   Baselines

We adopt the following nine methods as baselines.

- Item-KNN [15]: Item-KNN is a conventional "item-to-item" model, which recommends the similar items according to users' historical sessions.
- GRU4REC [5]: GRU4REC utilized the gated recurrent unit (GRU) to learn item and session embeddings for session-based recommendations.
- NARM [10]: NARM is an SBRS based on recurrent neural network (RNN), which integrated GRU and the attention mechanism for user session representation.
- SR-GNN [19]: SR-GNN transforms the clicking sequences into session graphs and employs GNN to learn item embeddings.
- LESSR [2]: LESSR proposed a session lossless encoding scheme and established shortcuts between items to efficiently capture long-distance dependencies amongst them.
- GCE-GNN [18]: GCE-GNN is an SBRS based on global context-enhanced GNN. It captures user preferences within their current sessions by learning the embeddings of session graphs and global graphs.
- H-RNN [13]: H-RNN is a personalized recommender system based on RNN, which learns cross-session item transition patterns by a hierarchal RNN model.
- A-PGNN [21]: A-PGNN employed GNN to learn the item embeddings in session graphs and utilized the attention mechanism to capture the influence of users' historical sessions on the current sessions.
- HG-GNN [12]: HG-GNN is a personalized recommender system based on heterogeneous global graph neural network, which proposes a personalized session encoding layer to combine users' historical preferences with current preferences.

5   Experimental Results and Analysis

5.1   Recommendation Performance on Evaluation Datasets

In this section, we demonstrate the experimental results on LastFM, Xing, and Reddit datasets, respectively, as shown in Table 1. In Table 1, the highest value of each metric is bold and the second highest value is underlined.

As shown in Table 1, our proposed model HASRS is superior to the baseline methods on most metrics. Item-KNN underperforms since it simply makes recommendations based on item similarity. The GNN-based methods GRU4REC and NARM outperform Item-KNN because they take into account the clicking sequence information of user sessions. LESSR is superior to SR-GNN since LESSR further uses GRU for session lossless encoding and constructs the shortcuts between items, which is beneficial to discover the potential dependencies among items. Another GNN-based method GCE-GNN combines users' short-term preferences and long-term contextual preferences for making recommendations, so it also outperforms SR-GNN.

Table 1. Recommendation performance comparison on evaluation datasets.

Methods	LastFM				Xing				Reddit			
	HR@5	HR@10	MRR@5	MRR@10	HR@5	HR@10	MRR@5	MRR@10	HR@5	HR@10	MRR@5	MRR@10
Item-KNN	6.73%	10.90%	4.02%	4.81%	8.79%	11.85%	5.01%	5.42%	21.71%	30.32%	11.74%	12.88%
GRU4REC	8.47%	12.86%	4.71%	5.29%	10.35%	13.15%	5.94%	6.36%	33.72%	41.73%	24.36%	25.42%
NARM	10.29%	15.03%	6.09%	6.71%	13.51%	17.31%	8.87%	9.37%	33.25%	40.52%	24.56%	25.52%
SR-GNN	11.89%	16.90%	7.23%	7.85%	13.38%	16.71%	8.95%	9.39%	34.96%	42.38%	25.90%	26.88%
LESSR	12.96%	17.88%	**8.24%**	**8.82%**	14.84%	16.77%	11.98%	12.13%	36.03%	43.27%	26.45%	27.41%
GCE-GNN	12.83%	18.28%	7.60%	8.32%	16.98%	20.86%	11.14%	11.65%	36.30%	45.16%	26.65%	27.70%
H-RNN	10.92%	15.83%	6.71%	7.39%	10.72%	14.36%	7.22%	7.74%	44.76%	53.44%	32.13%	33.29%
A-PGNN	12.10%	17.13%	7.37%	8.01%	14.23%	17.01%	10.26%	10.58%	49.10%	58.23%	33.54%	34.62%
HG-GNN	13.09%	19.39%	7.35%	8.18%	17.25%	20.30%	12.23%	12.79%	51.08%	60.51%	35.46%	36.89%
HASRS	**13.58%**	**19.87%**	7.72%	8.34%	**18.14%**	**20.91%**	**12.57%**	**12.93%**	**52.23%**	**61.62%**	**36.21%**	**37.13%**

H-RNN and A-PGNN are different personalized SBRSs based on RNN and GNN, respectively. The recommendation performance of HG-GNN is further improved since it learns the global context features of users' historical interactions. Our proposed method HASRS outperforms HG-GNN since HASRS uses HGNN to capture user and item embeddings and mines informative anchors to explore long-distance items.

5.2 Analysis on Informative Anchor Selection Methods

In Sect. 3.2, we propose to mine the informative anchors in the heterogeneous global graph, which can be further utilized to explore those long-distance but similar items. In this section, we conduct experiments on LastFM dataset and analyze the effect of different anchor selection methods on recommendation performance. The results on the other two datasets are similar to that on LastFM dataset. The results are shown in Table 2.

Table 2. Experimental results on difference informative anchor selection methods on LastFM dataset.

Methods	HR@5	HR@10	MRR@5	MRR@10
Degree Centrality	**13.58%**	**19.87%**	**7.72%**	**8.34%**
Closeness Centrality	13.21%	19.05%	7.58%	8.11%
Betweenness Centrality	13.32%	19.41%	7.62%	8.19%
Eigenvector Centrality	12.90%	18.93%	7.46%	7.98%
PageRank	13.22%	19.13%	7.56%	8.15%
HITS	12.95%	18.94%	7.51%	7.97%

In Table 2, when using degree centrality to select informative anchors, HASRS can achieve the best performance, while using other methods, HASRS still performs satisfactorily. In fact, the differences in recommendation performance of these methods are not significant because the anchors selected using these methods are quite similar, especially item informative anchors. The differences in the recommendation performance of these methods mainly depend on the selection of user informative anchors. It can easily be inferred that the degree centrality method can select more accurate user informative anchors.

5.3   Analysis on the Number of Anchors

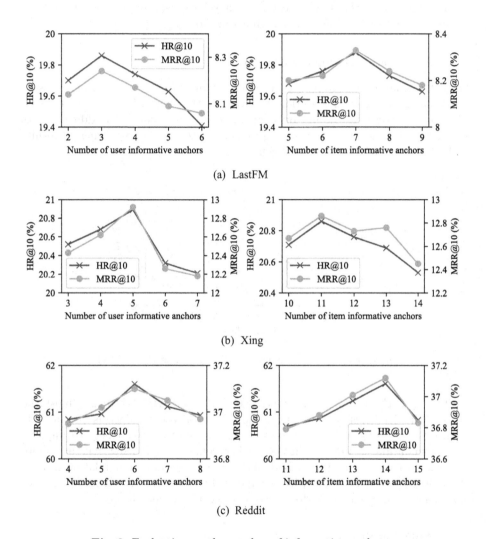

(a) LastFM

(b) Xing

(c) Reddit

Fig. 3. Evaluation on the number of informative anchors.

In this section, we analyze how the number of anchors (including user and item anchors) affects the recommendation performance. To this end, we change the number of informative anchors of one type while fixing the number of anchors of another type each time. For example, when we vary the number of item informative anchors, we fix the number of user anchors and record the experimental results.

Figure 3(a), 3(b) and 3(c) show the recommendation performance of evaluating the number of informative anchors on LastFM, Xing, and Reddit datasets. It can be easily seen that a too-small or too-large number of anchors is harmful to the recommendation performance. The reason is that an excessive number of anchors may introduce some noise and propagate meaningless information, while if too few anchors are selected, it may be impossible to consider all the important and similar information among anchors.

5.4   Analysis on Balance Factor α

In Sect. 3.4, we propose to fuse the user feature in session representation by using a balance factor α. In this section, we evaluate the effect of balance factor α on recommendation performance on LastFM, while the Xing and Reddit datasets can get similar results. By changing balance factor α, the experimental results of **HR**@10 and **MRR**@10 are shown in Fig. 4.

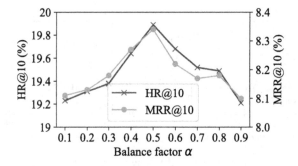

Fig. 4. Evaluation on balance factor α on LastFM dataset.

In Fig. 4, the trend of two curves (**HR**@10 and **MRR**@10) is almost the same. When α is set as 0.5, the recommendation performance is the best. It indicates that considering user embedding representation can help to improve recommendation accuracy. With a smaller value of α, HASRS will pay more attention to user embeddings and may ignore the transition relationships of items in the sessions, while with a larger value of α, HASRS tends to neglect user features and fails to perform personalized recommendations.

5.5   Ablation Study

In this section, we conduct ablation experiments to show the effectiveness of some crucial components in HASRS. Specifically, the ablation models include (1) **HASRS-non-HGNN** which uses naive GNN to learn item embeddings by constructing an isomorphic graph according to the user sessions, (2) **HASRS-non-Anchor** which learns the user and item embeddings without any anchors, and (3) **HASRS-FC** which employs the fully connected layers to learn the session representation instead of soft-attention mechanism. The ablation experimental results on LastFM are shown in Table 3 while can get similar results on the other two datasets.

Table 3. Ablation Study

Models	LastFM			
	HR@5	HR@10	MRR@5	MRR@10
HASRS-non-HGNN	11.74%	16.95%	7.01%	7.63%
HASRS-non-Anchor	11.96%	18.34%	7.18%	7.91%
HASRS-FC	12.93%	19.07%	7.29%	8.06%
HASRS	**13.58%**	**19.98%**	**7.72%**	**8.34%**

Since HASRS-non-HGNN only learns the item embeddings and cannot capture the user features, it fails to make personalized recommendations. HASRS-non-Anchor is inferior to HASRS because HASRS takes the pivotal information of anchors into account, which enriches the user and item embeddings. HASRS-FC outperforms HASRS-non-HGNN and HASRS-non-Anchor since it captures both user and item embeddings while incorporating the features of informative anchors. However, compared to HASRS-FC, HASRS utilizes the attention mechanism which can model the important clicks in the session and thus it is superior to HASRS-FC.

6   Conclusion

Most existing SBRSs only consider clicking sequences of sessions, so it is difficult to provide personalized recommendations. Meanwhile, since these SBRSs learn item embeddings through session graphs or global graphs, they may neglect some similar features due to the long distances between items. In this paper, we propose an HGNN-based SBRS HASRS integrating multi-type informative anchors. By constructing a heterogeneous global graph, it can learn the embedding representations of different types of nodes (users and items) and capture the user behavior patterns in users' historical sessions. HASRS further fuses the feature information of user and item anchors for enriching their embeddings, which helps to capture the long-distance dependencies among items. We evaluate the proposed model HASRS on three real-world datasets and the experimental results show that HASRS is superior to other baseline methods.

The drawback of our work is that we only consider topology information when selecting anchors and neglect their attribute information, which may introduce extra noise for recommendations. In the future, we will take the attribute-based features of anchors into account and explore other robust and effective anchor selection methods.

Acknowledgements. This work was supported in part by the National Natural Science Foundation of China under Grant U1811263 and the Science and Technology Program of Guangzhou under Grant 2023A04J1728.

References

1. Barabási, A.L.: Linked: the new science of networks. Am. J. Phys. **71**(4), 409–410 (2003)
2. Chen, T., Wong, R.C.W.: Handling information loss of graph neural networks for session-based recommendation. In: Proceedings of the 26th ACM International Conference on Knowledge Discovery & Data Mining (SIGKDD), pp. 1172–1180. KDD 2020, Association for Computing Machinery, New York, USA (2020)
3. Domingos, P., Richardson, M.: Mining the network value of customers. In: Proceedings of the 7th ACM International Conference on Knowledge Discovery and Data Mining (SIGKDD), pp. 57–66. KDD 2001, Association for Computing Machinery, New York, USA (2001)
4. Forsati, R., Meybodi, M., Neiat, A.G.: Web page personalization based on weighted association rules. In: Proceedings of the International Conference on Electronic Computer Technology, pp. 130–135 (2009)
5. Hidasi, B., Karatzoglou, A., Baltrunas, L., Tikk, D.: Session-based recommendations with recurrent neural networks. In: Proceedings of the 4th International Conference on Learning Representations (ICLR), Conference Track Proceedings. San Juan, Puerto Rico (2016)
6. Jannach, D., Ludewig, M.: When recurrent neural networks meet the neighborhood for session-based recommendation. In: Proceedings of the 11th ACM Conference on Recommender Systems (RecSys), pp. 306–310. RecSys 2017, Association for Computing Machinery, New York, USA (2017)
7. Jomsri, P.: Book recommendation system for digital library based on user profiles by using association rule. In: Proceedings of the 4th edition of the International Conference on the Innovative Computing Technology (INTECH), pp. 130–134 (2014)
8. Kleinberg, J.M.: Authoritative sources in a hyperlinked environment. J. ACM **46**(5), 604–632 (1999)
9. Latifi, S., Jannach, D.: Streaming session-based recommendation: when graph neural networks meet the neighborhood. In: Proceedings of the 16th ACM Conference on Recommender Systems (RecSys), pp. 420–426. RecSys 2022, Association for Computing Machinery, New York, USA (2022)
10. Li, J., Ren, P., Chen, Z., Ren, Z., Lian, T., Ma, J.: Neural attentive session-based recommendation. In: Proceedings of the ACM on Conference on Information and Knowledge Management (CIKM), pp. 1419–1428. CIKM 2017, Association for Computing Machinery, New York, USA (2017)
11. Page, L., Brin, S., Motwani, R., Winograd, T.: The PageRank citation ranking: bringing order to the web. Technical report, Stanford InfoLab (1999)
12. Pang, Y., et al.: Heterogeneous global graph neural networks for personalized session-based recommendation. In: Proceedings of the 15th ACM International Conference on Web Search and Data Mining (WSDM), pp. 775–783. WSDM 2022, Association for Computing Machinery, New York, USA (2022)

13. Quadrana, M., Karatzoglou, A., Hidasi, B., Cremonesi, P.: Personalizing session-based recommendations with hierarchical recurrent neural networks. In: Proceedings of the 11th ACM Conference on Recommender Systems (RecSys), pp. 130–137. RecSys 2017, Association for Computing Machinery, New York, USA (2017)

14. Rendle, S., Freudenthaler, C., Schmidt-Thieme, L.: Factorizing personalized markov chains for next-basket recommendation. In: Proceedings of the 19th International Conference on World Wide Web (WWW), pp. 811–820. WWW 2010, Association for Computing Machinery, New York, USA (2010)

15. Sarwar, B.M., Karypis, G., Konstan, J.A., Riedl, J.: Item-based collaborative filtering recommendation algorithms. In: Proceedings of the 10th International Conference on World Wide Web (WWW), pp. 285–295. ACM, Hong Kong, China (2001)

16. Tang, J., Wang, K.: Personalized Top-N sequential recommendation via convolutional sequence embedding. In: Proceedings of the 11th ACM International Conference on Web Search and Data Mining (WSDM), pp. 565–573. WSDM 2018, Association for Computing Machinery, New York, USA (2018)

17. Wang, N., Wang, S., Wang, Y., Sheng, Q.Z., Orgun, M.: Modelling local and global dependencies for next-item recommendations. In: Huang, Z., Beek, W., Wang, H., Zhou, R., Zhang, Y. (eds.) WISE 2020. LNCS, vol. 12343, pp. 285–300. Springer, Cham (2020). https://doi.org/10.1007/978-3-030-62008-0_20

18. Wang, Z., Wei, W., Cong, G., Li, X.L., Mao, X.L., Qiu, M.: Global context enhanced graph neural networks for session-based recommendation. In: Proceedings of the 43rd International ACM Conference on Research and Development in Information Retrieval (SIGIR), pp. 169–178. SIGIR 2020, Association for Computing Machinery, New York, USA (2020)

19. Wu, S., Tang, Y., Zhu, Y., Wang, L., Xie, X., Tan, T.: Session-based recommendation with graph neural networks. In: Proceedings of the 33rd AAAI Conference on Artificial Intelligence, vol. 33, pp. 346–353 (2019)

20. Xu, C., et al.: Recurrent convolutional neural network for sequential recommendation. In: Proceedings of the 28th International Conference on World Wide Web (WWW), pp. 3398–3404. WWW 2019, Association for Computing Machinery, New York, USA (2019)

21. Zhang, M., Wu, S., Gao, M., Jiang, X., Xu, K., Wang, L.: Personalized graph neural networks with attention mechanism for session-aware recommendation. IEEE Trans. Knowl. Data Eng. **34**(8), 3946–3957 (2022)

22. Zhang, Z., Nasraoui, O.: Efficient hybrid web recommendations based on Markov clickstream models and implicit search. In: Proceedings of the IEEE/WIC/ACM International Conference on Web Intelligence (WI), pp. 621–627 (2007)

Leveraging Sequential Episode Mining for Session-Based News Recommendation

Mozhgan Karimi[1]($\boxtimes$), Boris Cule[2], and Bart Goethals[1]

[1] University of Antwerp, Antwerp, Belgium
{mozhgan.karimi2,bart.goethals}@uantwerpen.be
[2] Tilburg University, Tilburg, The Netherlands
b.cule@tilburguniversity.edu

Abstract. News recommender systems aim to help users find interesting and relevant news stories while mitigating information overload. Over the past few decades, various challenges have emerged in developing effective algorithms for real-world scenarios. These challenges include capturing evolving user preferences and addressing concept drift during reading sessions. Additionally, ensuring the freshness and timeliness of news content poses significant obstacles.

To address these issues, we utilize an innovative sequential pattern mining approach known as MARBLES to capture user behavior. MARBLES leverages frequent episodes to generate a collection of association rules, where a frequent episode is a partially ordered pattern that occurs frequently in the input sequence. The recommendation process involves identifying relevant rules extracted from these patterns and weighting them. Subsequently, a heuristic procedure assesses candidate rules and generates a list of recommendations for users based on their most recent reading session. Notably, we conduct our evaluation in a streaming scenario, simulating real-world usage, where both our algorithm and baselines dynamically improve their models with each user click.

Through our empirical evaluation in this streaming-based scenario, which closely models real-world usage, we demonstrate the applicability of the MARBLES algorithm in session-based recommendation. Our proposed approach outperforms baseline algorithms on two real-world data sets, effectively addressing the challenges specific to the news domain.

Keywords: News Recommendation · Recommender System · Sequential Recommendation · Sessions · Clickstream · Evaluation

1 Introduction

Recommender systems are tools on online services that are principally designed to help users find relevant items by filtering incoming streams of information based on user preferences. News recommender systems are a particular application domain of recommender systems that pose a set of unique challenges. For example, one of the fundamental aspects of the news domain is the short time

© The Author(s), under exclusive license to Springer Nature Singapore Pte Ltd. 2023
F. Zhang et al. (Eds.): WISE 2023, LNCS 14306, pp. 594–608, 2023.
https://doi.org/10.1007/978-981-99-7254-8_46

frame in which new items can become outdated or replaced by newly published articles. Typically, over time, the number of clicks a given news story receives declines considerably. This issue can restrict the applicability of collaborative filtering methods, which are the most common approaches in the recommendation literature.

A shift in user preferences is another challenge in the news domain [3]. In contrast to other domains such as books and movies, user preferences are not consistent over time. Especially short-term user interests can be influenced by breaking news and contextual circumstances, such as election cycles. So-called stream-based recommender systems can be a solution to keep track of fast-changing trends, concept drifts, and continuously emerging new items. Academic stream-based recommender systems simulate real-time recommendations in an offline setting by replaying timestamped clickstreams. To this end, recommendation models are updated based on every new item or click. Despite the fact that stream-based recommender systems can be evaluated in offline settings, they are not well investigated in academic research [1,27].

In addition to the volatility of news stories and user interests, another problem in the news domain is the lack of long-term user profiles, as most visitors browse news websites anonymously. This issue—known as *user cold-start*—is also a common challenge in other domains. One possible solution to simultaneously tackle user cold-start and concept drift is to use session-based recommendation algorithms, in which a recommender system predicts the next actions of a user only based on a few recent interactions [22]. In this work, we focus on session-based recommender systems that only take the last few consumed news items into account, which would be hard with a number of traditional approaches such as matrix completion.

Although session-based recommender systems have recently been given attention in the literature [28], not many researchers have examined session-based algorithms in a streaming scenario. However, in the news domain with its inherent challenges of item freshness and lack of user profiles, such a combination seems promising. In addition, by analyzing sequential patterns of news streams across a large number of user interactions, sequential pattern mining (SPM) can quickly identify emerging trends or popular topics. This information can be valuable for news recommendation systems to highlight trending news articles or suggest timely content to users.

In the past, sequential pattern mining — a well-established field in data mining— has been extensively used in different application domains of recommender systems [2]. Recommender systems based on SPM capture user behavior by discovering (sub)sequences that occur often in the data. Then, frequent patterns extracted from these sequences can be used to predict users' next actions.

One of the potential reasons for the popularity of SPM methods in this field is the availability of existing algorithms used to efficiently determine frequent patterns in large amounts of data. For example, already in 2001, the Apriori algorithm was used to mine frequent patterns in newsletter click data so as to generate recommendation candidates [19]. The second advantage of using SPM

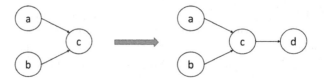

Fig. 1. An example of an episode association rule

algorithms in recommender systems is their simplicity, particularly in domains where users exhibit strong behavioral patterns in their click actions, such as music and e-commerce [22]. However, tuning of appropriate threshold values and the computational complexity of SPM approaches are the two main drawbacks of these methods. Our approach is based on a comparably novel SPM method, which tackles most of the above-mentioned issues of SPM intrinsically. In addition, our approach mines patterns from the incoming clickstream in a session-based manner, which improves accuracy by allowing it to react quickly to changes in the current user's behavior.

To the best of our knowledge, our approach is the first recommender system that utilizes this variety of SPM known as MARBLES [5]. Unlike most SPM methods, MARBLES mines *partially ordered* sequential patterns, and then generates association rules between them. An example of such a rule is shown in Fig. 1. We formally define the necessary concepts in Sect. 3.1. In this work, we show that MARBLES can be applied to session-based recommendations in a streaming scenario and cope with sparse sequential data and other challenges related to the news domain. Moreover, we introduce a heuristic weighting function that uses different scores from discovered rules in the training phase to calculate the significance of rules with respect to user behavior in the current session. Finally, we conduct an empirical experiment to evaluate the performance of our proposed model in the streaming scenario on two real-world data sets.

The rest of this paper is structured as follows. Section 2 reviews the related work. In Sect. 3, we describe our proposed approach, and in Sect. 4, the experimental setup is illustrated. We present the results of an empirical evaluation in Sect. 5 and the paper ends with concluding remarks in Sect. 6.

2   Related Work

In this section, we review the related work from two perspectives: session-based and stream-based recommender systems. Furthermore, we review a number of recent approaches in the news domain that are both stream- and session-based.

2.1   Session-Based Recommendations

In academia, many recommender systems have been developed with models that are based on extensive user profiles [9]. However, if visitors of a website are anonymous and their past interactions are not available, as discussed before, instead a session-based recommender system is a natural choice to predict the next items in the anonymous sessions. Although the main application of session-based approaches is when the recommender system focuses on the ongoing user session, they can be applied in a variety of settings of both long- and short-term user profiles. One common setting is to consider the last session of a user as the short-term interest and the whole user history as the long-term preference. In the news domain, for example, a hybrid approach based on Markov processes was proposed, which predicts the next news categories to be read from the current user session [7]. The experiments on combinations of three levels of user reading interests (short-, medium-, and long-term) show that recommendations based on augmenting short and long-term interests lead to higher accuracy. At the same time, news variety is increased when recommendations are based on a combination of short- and medium-term reading interests. Another approach models short-term and long-term user interests based on random walks where the short-term model consists of the most recent sessions of users via a sliding window [25]. The sliding time window promotes recent news articles. The results show that highlighting the last article in the session improves the accuracy, and that higher diversity was achieved in longer sessions. A similar perspective is adopted by Sottocornola et al., whose approach focuses on revealing users' last intentions via the last click of users [23]. To this end, a session-based recommender system using time-evolving graphs is developed that contains a novel type of node: a so-called session node, which stores information related to the last session of the user.

Recently, another data modeling approach for session-based recommendation has attracted attention in academia: Recurrent Neural Networks (RNN) [9,28,29]. For example, one RNN-based approach has been proposed that presents various changes to classic RNNs, including a ranking loss function, to adapt it for the recommendation task in a session-based scenario [9]. Other approaches leverage contextual features of the user session, such as the time of day or user location, or item features in their RNN models to improve session-based recommendations [29].

Over time, several other types of neural architectures such as attention mechanisms [17] and Convolutional Neural Networks (CNN) [28,31] have also been investigated in the context of recommendations. To capture the main purpose of users' sequential behavior in the ongoing session, a hybrid encoder with an attention mechanism has been proposed [17]. The session is represented by the combination of them. Based on this unified session representation, a bi-linear matching algorithm computes the recommendation score of each candidate item.

However, in a recent study focusing on sequential recommendation tasks, it was demonstrated that contemporary deep learning models can be outperformed by simple nearest-neighbor approaches [16]. Additionally, as approaches based on CNN are not able to update their models quickly, previous experiments have shown that they are not (yet) suited to be applied in the streaming scenario with a high item recency requirement [13,18].

2.2   Streaming Scenario in Recommender Systems

As mentioned in the introduction, due to the rapid and continuous user interactions on social media, e-commerce platforms, and news websites, it has become paramount to develop a recommender system that is able to deal with concept drift and data volatility [6]. To tackle these challenges, a number of approaches have been proposed, collectively called streaming recommender systems [1]. A simple variation of such a system can be a Bayesian approach that captures user interest drifts based on recent click data [4]. Over time, more and more sophisticated streaming recommenders have been proposed, e.g., based on item-based collaborative filtering [11] or neural memory networks that focus on both long- and short-term user preferences [27].

In general, not many recommender systems have been designed in both streaming and session-based settings simultaneously. However, open-source frameworks have been useful for prospective researchers to reproduce and replicate a recommender system in such scenarios. The FlowRec framework, for example, is built on *Scikit-Multiflow*, which is an open-source Python framework for learning from data streams [20,21]. The proposed approach consists of a wrapper for the Hoeffding Tree, which is an incremental decision tree learner implemented in Scikit-Multiflow. Similarly, another session-based news recommender system proposes an extension of the StreamingRec framework, which addresses concept drift and issues of the continuous data streams [13]. To accomplish that, the approach adopts a heuristic sequential pattern mining method on a tree-based model [14]. The algorithm incrementally mines patterns from a given session and updates the model accordingly, to make on-the-fly recommendations.

Although simulating real-time recommender systems by replaying click log data chronologically as a stream provides researchers with a proper evaluation method, results of offline evaluations are not always consistent with online evaluations in the real world. One approach to shorten the gap between academia and industry in terms of evaluation is a living lab. From 2014 to 2018, Plista, a data-driven company, provided an opportunity for both academia and industry to evaluate and optimize their recommendation algorithms in a live environment known as *CLEF NewsREEL*. During the contest, participants were supposed to generate news recommendations for millions of readers of online news articles within 100ms each. Click-through rate (CTR) was used as a metric of evaluation and participants received users' feedback after users had seen the recommendations, to optimize their proposed models accordingly [10].

In addition to the click logs, more and more researchers have taken advantage of contextual information about both users and items to not only boost the effectiveness of recommendations but also to capture potential user interest drifts [8,31]. In the news domain, a novel session-based deep learning approach uses contextual information to simulate streaming of user interactions and new published articles [8]. To that end, an open-source meta-architecture called CHAMELEON was designed, which models the sequence of user clicks by revealing clicks one by one to the recommender system. The RNN-based algorithm in this framework is updated every hour to provide recommendations for the next hour [24].

Our approach is designed to be similar to real-world recommender systems in terms of architecture and evaluation. To achieve that, our model is designed to be able to make recommendations without constituting user profiles, as there are always new or not registered readers on news websites. To this end, we propose a novel recommender system that uses MARBLES, as a form of SPM, to extract both users' sequential behavior and main intent in the current session. Therefore, the approach is flexible toward the number of interactions in a given session. In addition, to simulate a realistic evaluation scenario, we implement our approach in a session- and stream-based scenario.

3   Proposed Approach

In this section, we first introduce our underlying SPM method, MARBLES, in detail. Then, we discuss the training method and necessary adaptations for the streaming setting.

3.1   MARBLES

For the pattern mining stage of our method, we use a slightly adapted version of the MARBLES algorithm [5]. Unlike traditional pattern mining techniques that generate simple patterns such as itemsets or sequential patterns, MARBLES mines frequent episodes, i.e., patterns that can define a *partial order* between events, and then produces association rules between these episodes. We rely on the expressive power of episodes to discover patterns in users' histories that other methods would struggle to find.

MARBLES takes as input a single sequence of events, accompanied by time-stamps. As output, MARBLES produces a collection of association rules between frequent episodes. A frequent episode is a partially ordered pattern that occurs frequently in the input sequence.

Definition 1. *Given a set of symbols Σ, an episode G is represented by a directed acyclic graph with labeled nodes, that is, $G = (V; E; lab)$, where $V = (v_1, \ldots, v_k)$ is the set of nodes, E is the set of directed edges (v_i, v_j) connecting pairs of nodes, and lab is the function $lab : V \to \Sigma$, mapping each node v_i to its label.*

The set of edges E defines the partial order among the nodes and their labels. If the edges define a total order, we call the episode a *serial* episode. If the set of edges is empty, the episode is called *parallel*.

Definition 2. *Given two episodes G and H, we say that G is a subepisode of H, denoted $G \subset H$, if the DAG describing episode G is a subgraph of the directed acyclic graph DAG describing episode H.*

Definition 3. *Given two episodes G and H, such that $G \subset H$, we can express an association rule $G \Rightarrow H$. We call G the left-hand side of the rule (LHS), and H the right-hand side of the rule (RHS).*

In general, an association rule $G \Rightarrow H$ tells us that if pattern G occurs in the data, pattern H is also likely to occur. While the original MARBLES algorithm considers all possible association rules according to the definitions above, we are only interested in specific rules that can be used by a recommender system. Concretely, to be able to recommend a specific item $a \in \Sigma$, we need an association rule where the RHS differs from the LHS only by an introduction of item a, that does not precede any of the items in the RHS of the rule (i.e., that has no outgoing edges). In other words, our version of MARBLES produces only rules $G \Rightarrow H$, where $V(H) = V(G) \cup \{v\}$, with $lab(v) = a$, and $E(H) = E(G) \cup E'$, where E' is either empty or contains only edges of the form (v_i, v), with $v_i \in V(G)$. An example of such a rule is shown in Fig. 1.

There are three variants of MARBLES, all of which use three main parameters: a sliding window length ρ that defines the maximum interval within which two events may occur and still be considered part of the same pattern, a frequency threshold σ, and a confidence threshold ϕ. However, the three variants differ from each other in how they measure the frequency of an episode and the confidence of an association rule. MARBLES$_f$ defines the frequency of an episode X as the number of different time windows of length ρ that contain X, and the confidence of an association rule $X \Rightarrow Y$ as the proportion of windows that contain X that also contain Y. MARBLES$_m$ defines the frequency of an episode X as the maximal number of non-overlapping minimal windows that contain X, where a minimal window is a time window of length at most ρ, such that none of its subwindows also contains X. MARBLES$_m$ then defines the confidence of an association rule $X \Rightarrow Y$ as the proportion of minimal windows of X that are contained within a minimal window of Y.

Finally, MARBLES$_w$ defines the weight of a time window as the inverse of its length, and defines the frequency of an episode X as the maximal sum of weights of a set of non-overlapping minimal windows of X. To evaluate the confidence of an association rule $X \Rightarrow Y$, MARBLES$_w$ first defines the *extensibility* of each minimal window of X into a minimal window of Y as the ratio of their respective lengths (or 0 if the window of X is not contained within a window of Y), and then defines the confidence of the rule as the average extensibility of all minimal windows of X. Due to space limitations, we point the reader to the original paper for more details [5].

3.2 Training/Evaluation Framework

Before illustrating the specifics of the proposed model and how to adapt the MARBLES algorithm to our use case, we first discuss the framework we chose to evaluate our model. As far as we are aware, there are only a few frameworks that fulfill our requirements for a real-time simulation of news recommendations, such as FlowRec [21], Idomaar [10], and StreamingRec [13]. Among them, we selected the latter since it provides a light-weight evaluation environment with a large number of pre-implemented algorithms [15]. Additionally, its simplicity in terms of architecture and extension as well as the fact that it does not need any external dependencies make it a promising choice to test our model.

3.3 Training

To train the model based on incoming user sessions, we first employ a recency policy on the session data to pre-filter it using session timestamps. We apply a sliding recency window, referred to as δ_t, which is a hyper-parameter of our model. This allows us to adjust it according to a specific application and achieve the preferable results.

Algorithms implemented in the StreamingRec framework learn incrementally from each new click and immediately update their models accordingly as they are replayed by the framework in simulated real-time. Taking into account newly published items, new user clicks, and updating the model immediately could be the solution for the cold start problem and other challenges of the news recommendation domain discussed earlier. However, we cannot apply the MARBLES algorithm on each new click because the model has to be re-trained completely to update it.

Instead of training with each new click, we adopt a variant of incremental learning with a novel intermittent training method that alleviates computational load. To this end, the recommendation model is recomputed every k minutes (in simulation time) with the training data that has been aggregated up to this point. That is, during the recommendation phase of our evaluation, the timestamps of the incoming event stream are constantly evaluated. If the MARBLES model has last been (re-)trained at simulation timestamp t, and we encounter a user click that happened at simulation timestamp $t + k$ $min.$, then a model re-training is triggered.

3.4 Separating Training Data

Input data for the MARBLES algorithm is a single sequence of events, which are logically separated from each other by considering a time window. The data in our scenario consists of sessions of different users and multiple user histories. It is not possible to consider them as a single sequence by interleaving them using the original timestamps. As a result, we consider the user histories sequentially, one after the other, by offsetting the timestamps appropriately. To ensure that no pattern contains events from two different user sessions, we introduce a sufficient gap between the last event of one session and the first event of the next session. Concretely, this gap must be larger than ρ, the maximum length of the window within which patterns are discovered.

3.5 Recommendation Policies

As detailed in the previous section, we introduce gaps to separate sessions, and, thus, transform them into a readable format for the MARBLES algorithm. Then

Table 1. Examples of rules that are either applicable or not applicable when generating recommendations for the given user session: $\{A, B, C\}$. The column "Appl." indicates whether the rules can be applied during the recommendation process.

No	Rule	Appl	Explanation
1	$A \rightarrow B \rightarrow C \Rightarrow A \rightarrow B \rightarrow C \rightarrow D$	Y	This rule with serial episodes is a perfect candidate rule for s_1
2	$AB \rightarrow C \Rightarrow AB \rightarrow C \rightarrow D$	Y	This rule states that new item D always occurs after item C, while item C constantly occurs after A and B
3	$ABC \Rightarrow ABCD$	Y	Despite the parallel episode in the rule, it is still considered as a candidate rule for the user session
4	$B \rightarrow E \Rightarrow B \rightarrow E \rightarrow C$	N	The LHS of the rule does not match with items in the user session
5	$B \rightarrow AC \Rightarrow B \rightarrow ACD$	N	The LHS matches the items of the user session perfectly. However, item B occurs before item A, whereas the user first clicked on item A and then item B
6	$ABCD \Rightarrow ABCDF$	N	This rule's LHS includes all items in the current user session. However, it contains one extra item

our version of the MARBLES algorithm employs the episode mining approach described in Sect. 3.1 to extract association rules among sessions and generates candidate rules. At this stage, we have all candidate rules essential for the recommendation purpose. Subsequently, in order to predict the next items to click, a comparison is conducted between the items within the user's current session and the LHS of all rules derived from the model. Given a match, we use items from the RHS as recommendation candidates. Let the current session be s_1 where it contains clicks on items $\{A, B, C\}$. Table 1 reports a few examples of rules that either fulfill or do not fulfill the mentioned criteria to be a recommendation candidate for the session s_1.

For each candidate rule, we assign a score to the new item that only appears on the RHS, called the *candidate item*. To quantify how well the candidate item matches the user's current news reading session, we apply the following function to calculate the value of the candidate item x of the candidate rule r regarding the current session s:

$$V_x(s, r) = f(r) \cdot O(s, r_l) \tag{1}$$

Here, $f(r)$ is the so-called *confidence score* assigned by the MARBLES algorithm to the candidate rule r, and $O(s, r_l)$ is the overlap between the LHS of the rule r, denoted by r_l, and current session s of a user calculated as follows:

$$O(s, r_l) = \frac{|V(s) \cap V(r_l)|}{|V(s) \cup V(r_l)|} + \frac{|E(s) \cap E(r_l)|}{|E(s)|} \tag{2}$$

The first part of the overlap equation calculates the Jaccard similarity [12] between items in the current session of the user and the LHS of the candidate rule. The second part of the equation calculates the normalized similarity in terms of edges between the current session and the LHS of the rule including implicit edges resulting from transitive closure. In this way, we implicitly prioritize candidate rules with serial episodes rather than other types of episodes. For example, the first three rules in Table 1 contain the same items in their LHS's. However, the first rule is ranked higher by the second part of Eq. 2, because it has two serial edges that match the user's click pattern. Additionally, it shares an implicit edge between A and C with the user's session, obtained via transitive closure. The second rule in Table 1 is ranked lower because it shares only one common edge with the current user session s_1. Finally, because of its parallel episode, the third rule has a value of zero in terms of edge overlap.

The maximum score of each candidate item determines the item's recommendation score. Ultimately, the recommendation list consists of the top-N items in descending order of recommendation score.

4 Experimental Setup

In this section, we discuss the experimental design used to verify the hypothesis that the proposed approach can outperform state-of-the-art algorithms in both accuracy and ranking metrics in the news domain. We present our evaluation framework and describe the real-world data sets on which the experiments were conducted. We also illustrate metrics and baseline algorithms that were used in the comparison.

4.1 Evaluation Protocol

We design our experiments using the open-source benchmarking framework, StreamingRec, which enables rapid prototyping of a real-time recommender system for streaming data [13]. The evaluation scheme of this framework is specifically designed to simulate real-time recommendations by replaying chronologically ordered user-item interactions as a stream. To this end, algorithms receive data as it occurred in reality and they generate recommendations for each click. Therefore, they learn incrementally and consequently improve their models during the recommendation phase.

4.2 Data Sets and Evaluation Methodology

We perform experiments on two real-world data sets namely Plista and Outbrain, which are broadly used in academic research, particularly in the news domain. We select one medium-sized publisher each from the click logs of the two data sets. They consist of user interactions and information of published news articles. Statistics of the two data sets after pruning (e.g., of sessions with only one click) are as follows.

- *Outbrain data set:* This data set was obtained from the Outbrain Click Prediction challenge in 2017. The data set associated with the selected publisher (ID: 43) comprises 1,067,675 user interactions, 281,910 users, and 1,475 published news articles.
- *Plista data set:* This data set was collected during the CLEF-NewsREEL challenge in 2017, which comprises click logs, published news articles, and recommended items as well as a text snippet in the German language. For a selected publisher (ID: 418), it consists of 1,129,408 user clicks, 220,117 users, and 835 published news stories within one month.

The average number of clicks per session is 2.5 for Outbrain data set and 3.2 for the Plista data set. Per convention, the log data is divided into a training set and a test set using a time-based split criterion. In the subsequently described experiments, we placed 70% of the data into the training set and 30% into the test set. In the first step, the training set is provided to the algorithms to learn an initial model. Then, in the evaluation phase, the events are "replayed" in the test set in chronological order. For each click event, algorithms included in the comparison are requested to generate a recommendation list for the respective user. This list is then compared to the news articles that the user has visited during the remainder of their session in order to calculate the accuracy metrics.

4.3   Evaluation Metrics

We adopt two conventional metrics to evaluate the recommendation performance of all models namely F1-measure and Mean Reciprocal Rank (MRR). Both metrics are measured based on the top 10 recommended items.

The F1 metric [30] takes both Recall and Precision into account and, thus, gives a balanced view of how accurately a given recommendation list matches a respective user's future clicks. The MRR metric [26], on the other hand, measures how highly matching news articles are ranked in a given recommendation list. It, thus, focuses more on how far in a recommendation list a potential user might have to scroll to reach an interesting article.

4.4   Baselines

We compare the performance of our approach with five pre-implemented algorithms in the StreamingRec framework. Two of them are non-personalized baseline algorithms including POPULAR and RECENTLYPOPULAR. The latter ranks recommendations by the absolute number of user clicks for each news article within the recent past (for example, last 60 min). In contrast, as a session-based algorithm, the COOCCURRENCE approach is a variant of the association rule technique that counts the co-occurrences of news articles in the training sessions. Then, recommendation candidates are ranked based on the co-occurrence frequency of news articles with the given user session.

We additionally compare our proposed approach with the session-based variety of the k-nearest-neighbor approach called V-SKNN because it performed well in previous comparable experiments [16, 18]. This method selects neighboring sessions that have the most overlap with the current session. The V-SKNN approach also prioritizes recent candidate items as well as positional similarity of items in the candidate sessions with the current user session.

5 Performance Evaluation

In this section, we describe the algorithm configurations used in our empirical evaluation as well as its results.

5.1 Algorithm Configuration

The baseline algorithms POPULAR, COOCCURRENCE, and V-SKNN cannot be configured. The RECENTLYPOPULAR algorithm has only one configuration parameter: its recency filter threshold, which was set to 20 min. For our proposed approach, MARBLES, different configuration parameters exist that can be tweaked to fit the given data set. To this end, a validation subset (10%) of each data set was used to find the most suitable values.

As mentioned in Sect. 3.1 MARBLES has three major variants based on how the sliding window for finding frequent patterns is applied: $MARBLES_f$, $MARBLES_m$, $MARBLES_w$. For each of these three variants, the available configuration parameters (maximum window size ρ, frequency threshold σ, confidence threshold ϕ, and recency filter threshold δ_t) were adjusted to fit the data set. For ρ, σ, and δ_t, values of 5 items, 0.1 and 2000 sessions, respectively, yielded the best results on both data sets, and for all three variants of MARBLES. Lastly, as expected for sequential pattern mining approaches, the confidence threshold ϕ proved the most volatile with respect to the algorithm variant and data set. For the $MARBLES_f$, $MARBLES_m$, and $MARBLES_w$ algorithms, respectively, the most suitable values were 0.05, 0.1, and 0.07 for the Outbrain data set and 0.03, 0.05, and 0.03 for the Plista data set.

5.2 Results

Table 2 gives an overview of the results of our experimental evaluation. For both the Outbrain and Plista data sets, the results are mostly in line with each other.

Baselines. Simple methods that neither directly nor indirectly account for item "freshness" such as the POPULAR approach, perform very poorly. The RECENTLYPOPULAR algorithm, which takes item "freshness" into account, achieves decent results both in terms of F1 and MRR. Interestingly, the COOCCURRENCE approach, which tailors its recommendations to the current user session, while achieving better results in terms of F1, was only able to produce a better MRR for the Outbrain data set compared to RECENTLYPOPULAR. A possible interpretation is that for the item order in the recommendation list, an item's

Table 2. Empirical results for the Outbrain and Plista data sets. The best results for each metric and data set are underlined.

Algorithm	Outbrain		Plista	
	F1	MRR	F1	MRR
Popular	0.0032	0.0071	0.0046	0.0073
RecentlyPopular	0.1169	0.2090	0.1328	0.2160
CoOccurrence	0.1404	0.2957	0.1368	0.1981
V-SkNN	0.1581	0.3444	0.1626	0.3614
Marbles$_f$ (fixed window)	0.1893	0.3254	0.1972	0.3268
Marbles$_m$ (minimal window)	0.2037	0.3147	0.2026	0.3193
Marbles$_w$ (minimal weighted window)	0.2144	0.2986	0.2076	0.3092

recency is much more important than implicit relations between items. That is, placing breaking news high up in the list might be more effective than news stories with a strong relation to a user's current session. Lastly, among the baselines, the V-SkNN algorithm consistently delivers the best results in terms of F1 and MRR for both data sets.

Proposed Approach. In the empirical evaluation, all variants of Marbles were able to greatly improve upon the F1 performance figures of the V-SkNN baseline, both for the Outbrain and Plista data sets, partly confirming our hypothesis. The best results are consistently delivered by the minimal-weighted-window variant, followed by the minimal-window and fixed-window variants. At the same time, Marbles' performance with respect to the MRR metric fluctuates among its variants and falls slightly short of the level of the V-SkNN baseline. Interestingly, the comparably simple fixed-window variant of Marbles slightly outperforms the more complex Marbles variants in this metric and even comes close to the V-SkNN baseline, strongly surpassing all other simple baselines.

In summary, while at the same time not always ranking the respective "hits" as highly in the recommendation list as the V-SkNN approach, the proposed approach based on Marbles consistently generates recommendation lists that better align with users' tastes compared to all previous baselines. Further evaluations are necessary to determine if more optimized configuration parameter values or hybridizations with other algorithms could yield optimal results in all metric dimensions.

6 Conclusions

We have shown a novel way of applying an existing sequential pattern mining approach, Marbles, to the problem setting of news recommendation. To facilitate a realistic offline evaluation, we employed a replay scheme that simulates real-time recommendations in a streaming session-based setting.

Through an empirical evaluation, we were able to show superior recommendation accuracy of our proposed approach compared to state-of-the-art baselines for clickstream recommendations. In the future, we plan to hybridize our approach and apply it to other domains, such as music (playlist) recommendations.

References

1. Al-Ghossein, M., Abdessalem, T., Barré, A.: A survey on stream-based recommender systems. ACM Comput. Surv. **54**(5), 1–36 (2021)
2. Amatriain, X., Jaimes, A., Oliver, N., Pujol, J.M.: Data mining methods for recommender systems. In: Ricci, F., Rokach, L., Shapira, B., Kantor, P.B. (eds.) Recommender Systems Handbook, pp. 39–71. Springer, Boston, MA (2011). https://doi.org/10.1007/978-0-387-85820-3_2
3. Bogina, V., Kuflik, T., Jannach, D., Bielikova, M., Kompan, M., Trattner, C.: Considering temporal aspects in recommender systems: a survey. User Model. User-Adap. Inter. **33**(1), 81–119 (2023)
4. Chang, S., et al.: Streaming recommender systems. In: Proceedings of the 26th International Conference on World Wide Web (WWW 2017), pp. 381–389 (2017)
5. Cule, B., Tatti, N., Goethals, B.: Marbles: mining association rules buried in long event sequences. Stat. Anal. Data Min. ASA Data Sci. J. **7**(2), 93–110 (2014)
6. Diaz-Aviles, E., Drumond, L., Schmidt-Thieme, L., Nejdl, W.: Real-time Top-n recommendation in social streams. In: Proceedings of the 6th Conference on Recommender Systems (RecSys 2012), pp. 59–66 (2012)
7. Epure, E.V., Kille, B., Ingvaldsen, J.E., Deneckere, R., Salinesi, C., Albayrak, S.: Recommending personalized news in short user sessions. In: Proceedings of the 11th Conference on Recommender Systems (RecSys 2017), pp. 121–129 (2017)
8. de Souza Pereira Moreira, G., Jannach, D., Da Cunha, A.M.: Contextual hybrid session-based news recommendation with recurrent neural networks. IEEE Access **7**, 169185–169203 (2019)
9. Hidasi, B., Karatzoglou, A., Baltrunas, L., Tikk, D.: Session-based recommendations with recurrent neural networks. In: Conference Track Proceedings of the 4th International Conference on Learning Representations (ICLR 2016) (2016)
10. Hopfgartner, F., et al.: Benchmarking news recommendations: the clef newsreel use case. SIGIR Forum **49**(2), 129–136 (2016)
11. Huang, Y., Cui, B., Zhang, W., Jiang, J., Xu, Y.: TencentRec: real-time stream recommendation in practice. In: Proceedings of the 2015 International Conference on Management of Data (SIGMOD 2015), pp. 227–238 (2015)
12. Jaccard, P.: Nouvelles recherches sur la distribution florale. Bull. Soc. Vaud. Sci. Nat. **44**, 223–270 (1908)
13. Jugovac, M., Jannach, D., Karimi, M.: StreamingRec: a framework for benchmarking stream-based news recommenders. In: Proceedings of the 12th Conference on Recommender Systems (RecSys 2018), pp. 269–273 (2018)
14. Karimi, M., Cule, B., Goethals, B.: On-the-fly news recommendation using sequential patterns. In: Proceedings of the 7th International Workshop on News Recommendation and Analytics (INRA 2019) @ RecSys 2019, pp. 29–34 (2019)
15. Karimi, M., Jannach, D., Jugovac, M.: News recommender systems-survey and roads ahead. Inf. Proc. Manage. **54**(6), 1203–1227 (2018)

16. Latifi, S., Jannach, D., Ferraro, A.: Sequential recommendation: a study on transformers, nearest neighbors and sampled metrics. Inf. Sci. **609**, 660–678 (2022)
17. Li, J., Ren, P., Chen, Z., Ren, Z., Lian, T., Ma, J.: Neural attentive session-based recommendation. In: Proceedings of the 2017 on Conference on Information and Knowledge Management (CIKM 2017), pp. 1419–1428 (2017)
18. Ludewig, M., Mauro, N., Latifi, S., Jannach, D.: Empirical analysis of session-based recommendation algorithms. User Model. User-Adap. Inter. **31**(1), 149–181 (2021)
19. Mobasher, B., Dai, H., Luo, T., Nakagawa, M.: Effective personalization based on association rule discovery from web usage data. In: Proceedings of the 3rd International Workshop on Web Information and Data Management (WIDM 2001), pp. 9–15 (2001)
20. Montiel, J., Read, J., Bifet, A., Abdessalem, T.: Scikit-multiflow: a multi-output streaming framework. J. Mach. Learn. Res. **19**(1), 2914–2915 (2018)
21. Paraschakis, D., Nilsson, B.J.: FlowRec: prototyping session-based recommender systems in streaming mode. In: Lauw, H.W., Wong, R.C.-W., Ntoulas, A., Lim, E.-P., Ng, S.-K., Pan, S.J. (eds.) PAKDD 2020. LNCS (LNAI), vol. 12084, pp. 65–77. Springer, Cham (2020). https://doi.org/10.1007/978-3-030-47426-3_6
22. Quadrana, M., Cremonesi, P., Jannach, D.: Sequence-aware recommender systems. ACM Comput. Surv. **51**(4), 1–36 (2018)
23. Sottocornola, G., Symeonidis, P., Zanker, M.: Session-based news recommendations. In: Companion Proceedings of the 2018 The Web Conference (WWW 2018), pp. 1395–1399 (2018)
24. de Souza Pereira Moreira, G.: CHAMELEON: a deep learning meta-architecture for news recommender systems. In: Proceedings of the 12th ACM Conference on Recommender Systems (RecSys 2018), pp. 578–583 (2018)
25. Symeonidis, P., Kirjackaja, L., Zanker, M.: Session-aware news recommendations using random walks on time-evolving heterogeneous information networks. User Model. User-Adap. Inter. **30**(4), 727–755 (2020). https://doi.org/10.1007/s11257-020-09261-9
26. Voorhees, E.M.: The TREC-8 question answering track report. In: Proceedings of the 8th Text Retrieval Conference (TREC 1999), pp. 77–82 (1999)
27. Wang, Q., Yin, H., Hu, Z., Lian, D., Wang, H., Huang, Z.: Neural memory streaming recommender networks with adversarial training. In: Proceedings of the 24th International Conference on Knowledge Discovery & Data Mining (SIGKDD 2018), pp. 2467–2475 (2018)
28. Wang, S., Cao, L., Wang, Y., Sheng, Q.Z., Orgun, M.A., Lian, D.: A survey on session-based recommender systems. ACM Comput. Surv. **54**(7) (2021)
29. Wu, T., Sun, F., Dong, J., Wang, Z., Li, Y.: Context-aware session recommendation based on recurrent neural networks. Comput. Electr. Eng. **100** (2022)
30. Yang, Y., Liu, X.: A re-examination of text categorization methods. In: Proceedings of the 22nd Annual International Conference on Research and Development in Information Retrieval (SIGIR 1999), pp. 42–49 (1999)
31. Zhang, L., Liu, P., Gulla, J.A.: A deep joint network for session-based news recommendations with contextual augmentation. In: Proceedings of the 29th on Hypertext and Social Media (HT 2018), pp. 201–209 (2018)

Improving Conversational Recommender Systems via Knowledge-Enhanced Temporal Embedding

Chen Ji[1], Jilu Wang[1], Jie Xu[1(✉)], Wenxiao Liu[2], Zihong Yang[2],
Feiran Huang[2], and Chaozhuo Li[3]

[1] School of Information Science and Technology, Beijing Foreign Studies University,
Beijing, China
`jxu@bfsu.edu.cn`
[2] College of Cyber Security/College of Information Science and Technology,
Jinan University, Guangzhou, China
[3] Microsoft Research Asia, Beijing, China

Abstract. Conversational recommender systems are becoming increasingly popular due to their potential to facilitate personalized interactions between users. However, one major challenge lies in accurately representing the semantic meaning of the conversational history to make relevant recommendations. In this paper, we propose a knowledge-enhanced model KMTE to enhance conversational recommender systems. To achieve a more nuanced understanding of users' evolving interests and behaviors over time, a knowledge-enhanced temporal embedding is integrated into KMTE to facilitate the encoding of temporal aspects into the representation of user dialogues. Our proposal is extensively evaluated on a real conversational dataset, and the experimental results demonstrate the effectiveness and superiority of our proposals in improving the accuracy and relevance of conversational recommender systems. Our work sheds light on the potential of leveraging advanced language models to enhance the performance of conversational recommender systems.

Keywords: Conversational Recommender Systems · Pre-trained Language Models · Temporal Embedding

1 Introduction

Conversational recommender systems aim to tap into users' preferences and recommend items that they might like through multiple rounds of real-time interaction based on natural language. By capturing the user's dynamic preferences through multiple rounds of conversations, the intrinsic interests of users could be gradually modeled and refined, leading to the desirable recommendations. Conversational recommender systems have been widely employed in a myriad of real-life applications, which are capable of improving the user experience and driving revenue for the merchants.

© The Author(s), under exclusive license to Springer Nature Singapore Pte Ltd. 2023
F. Zhang et al. (Eds.): WISE 2023, LNCS 14306, pp. 609–618, 2023.
https://doi.org/10.1007/978-981-99-7254-8_47

Existing conversational recommender systems could be roughly classified into two categories: attribute-based conversational recommender systems and generation-based conversational recommender systems. Attribute-based conversational recommender systems are usually trained using reinforcement learning methods, which mainly focus on the design of strategy modules. The primary objective of these models is to achieve highly accurate recommendation outcomes within the fewest conversation rounds feasible. Consequently, they often employ a predetermined conversation template to present the recommendation results. Generative-based conversational recommender systems typically use a sequence-to-sequence model to construct dialogues, with a primary focus on the user interaction module. This category of methods places greater emphasis on delivering a seamless conversational experience to users and enhancing the interpretability of the generated results.

Despite the promising performance of existing conversational recommender models, they are still encountering numerous challenges in natural language understanding and generation. Due to the fluid and dynamic nature of natural language conversations and the inherent leaps in human thinking, it is challenging for dialogue-based systems to promptly capture the evolving user interests during a conversation. For instance, if a user's preference shifts from drama movies to comedy movies within a span of one minute, the system might still be focused on retrieving and recommending drama movies, failing to capture the transition in user interests. While humans are capable of comprehending and accommodating such shifts effortlessly, conversational recommender systems may become confused by this sudden change, ultimately leading to suboptimal recommendation quality.

In this paper, we propose a novel **K**nowledge-enhanced **M**odel via **T**emporal **E**mbedding based on pre-trained language models to enhance the ability of successfully recommending items, dubbed KMTE. To effectively capture the real-time shift of user interest, KMTE is integrated with a novel temporal embedding module, which contributes to capturing dynamic user preferences while incorporating domain-specific knowledge from downstream tasks to enhance the representation capability of sentence embeddings. Specifically, we assign time indices based on the user's historical interests in the conversation, organizing their timestamps into a sequential order that is incorporated into the input layer of the recurrent neural network. Additionally, we continuously pre-train the language models, allowing it to learn more relevant information and discriminative representations. Experimental results on the open dataset demonstrate the effectiveness of our approach in improving the performance of downstream tasks.

Our major contributions are summarized as follows:

- To capture the temporal dynamics of user-item interactions, we introduce a temporal embedding module into KMTE, which facilitates the capability of attending to the dynamic interests of users.
- By replacing the traditional word2vec with the SOTA pre-trained models, we propose a novel approach to incorporate the knowledge of downstream tasks into word embeddings. The experiments demonstrate that our approach significantly outperforms the baseline method on the downstream tasks.

– Through the incorporation of temporal embedding and integration of down-stream task knowledge, KMTE significantly boosts the recommendation quality of dialogue recommendation systems. Experimental results demonstrate that our proposal is capable of better understanding users' dynamic behavior patterns and generating more accurate recommendations.

2   Related Work

The conversational recommendation system is composed of two main modules: the recommendation component and the conversation component.

Recommender systems are intended to identify a subset of items from the item pool that satisfy the user's interests. Traditional approaches are highly reliable on historical user-item interactions, such as purchasing records [1,7]. To address problems of sparse data, conversational recommender systems pay more attention to information from conversations rather than historical interaction. In particular, it is well acknowledged that knowledge graphs can be used to improve recommendation performance and interpretability [5,14–16,20,21].

Conversation systems aim to generate appropriate responses based on multi-round contextual situations. The existing works can be divided into retrieval-based [6,12,17,19,23] and generation-based approaches [8,10,13,18].

Early conversational recommender systems mainly used predefined actions to interact with users [4]. Nowadays some research has started to integrate these two components for the purpose of better understanding the user's needs. In addition, follow-up studies [2,11,22] have adopted external KGs to improve CRS, with a focus mainly on enhanced item representation.

Based on previous studies, we design a novel conversational recommendation method that incorporates user preference, entity and temporal information, with downstream task knowledge injected.

3   Problem Definition

In our proposed approach, the user's historical information is transformed into a time sequence represented as $X = \{x_1, x_2, ..., x_N\}$ (x_i indicates a single token). This time sequence is then combined with other relevant features within the model. Moreover, we aim to generate word embeddings based on BERT, incorporating downstream task knowledge to enhance attention towards specific items during the recommendation process.

4   Methodology

4.1   Framework

Figure 1 demonstrates the framework of the proposed KMTE model. We integrate user interests, entity features, and time information to enhance the model's understanding of users' dynamic interests, filter out less relevant long-term hobbies, and generate personalized real-time recommendations for users, thereby improving the performance and effectiveness of the recommender system.

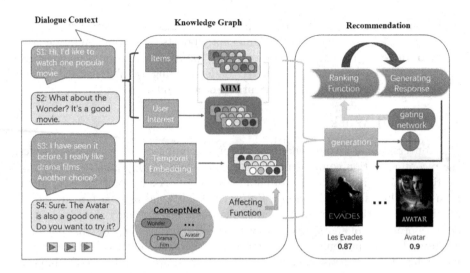

Fig. 1. Framework of the proposed KMTE model.

4.2 Knowledge Graph Encoder

We build a knowledge graph by mapping user interests and mentioned entities (movies) in the conversation to embedding vectors. Specifically, we define a user interest embedding vector $IU(u)$ and an entity embedding vector $IE(e)$, where u represents the user and e represents the movie entity:

$$IU(u) = Embedding(u), IE(e) = Embedding(e) \qquad (1)$$

Embedding(u) maps the user to their interest embedding vector while Embedding(e) maps a movie entity to its corresponding embedding vector.

By concatenating the user interest and movie entity embedding vectors, we construct a knowledge graph. This knowledge graph can be represented as a graph, where user interest vectors and entity embedding vectors serve as nodes, and the associations between them are represented by edges.

$$A(u, e) = Similarity(IU(u), IE(e)) \qquad (2)$$

In this graph, the association between users and movies can be measured by calculating the similarity between the user interest embedding vector $IU(u)$ and the entity embedding vector $IE(e)$. In this paper, we use cosine similarity to achieve that goal.

By building such a knowledge graph, we can leverage the graph structure and the associations between nodes to infer user interests and provide more accurate and personalized recommendations.

4.3 Dynamic Interest Module

We utilize temporal embedding to represent the relative time intervals between messages in a conversation. By calculating the difference in time offsets between messages and mapping it to the corresponding temporal embedding vector, we can capture the dynamic characteristics of the messages. Additionally, we combine user interest features with movie entity features to enable the model to better understand the evolving interests of users. Suppose the time offset of the i-th message is t_i, and the time offset of the previous message is t_{i-1}.

$$TE(t_i - t_{i-1}) = Embedding(t_i - t_{i-1}) \qquad (3)$$

Here, Embedding is a function that maps the relative time interval to the corresponding time embedding vector. By incorporating time information in this way, we can capture the temporal dynamics between messages and enhance the modeling capabilities of the recommendation system.

The temporal embedding vector $TE(t)$ is adjusted through the impact function g_{time}. t represents the given time. α is a tuning parameter that controls the rate of time decay. The exponential function $exp(-\alpha * t)$ represents the weight of time decay, indicating that the impact of time embedding vectors decreases as the distance from the current time increases:

$$g_{time}(TE(t)) = exp(-\alpha * t) \qquad (4)$$

By using such an exponential function, the time relevance calculation is further defined as:

$$S(u, e, t) = Similarity(IU(u), IE(e)) * g_{time}(TE(t)) \qquad (5)$$

$Similarity(IU(u), IE(e))$ represents the similarity calculation function between the user interest embedding vector $IU(u)$ and the entity embedding vector $IE(e)$. $exp(-\alpha * t)$ adjusts the time relevance based on the given time t. Obviously, the closer the time is to the present, the greater the influence it will have, while the impact of past events gradually diminishes. This approach allows the model to focus more on the user's recent interests and activities, improving the modeling capability for dynamic user interests.

4.4 Recommender Module

Unlike traditional recommender systems, which typically rely on previous interaction records, we assume that no prior interaction data is accessible. Our recommendation generation formula is as follows:

$$R(u) = weightedsum(S(u, e, t) * A(u, e))/weightedsum(S(u, e, t)) \qquad (6)$$

Table 1. Experimental results on different models.

Models	Metrics		
	R@1	R@10	R@50
Popularity	0.012	0.061	0.179
TextCNN	0.013	0.068	0.191
ReDial	0.024	0.140	0.320
KBRD	0.031	0.150	0.336
KGSF	0.037	0.181	0.372
KMTE	**0.044**	**0.236**	**0.456**

In this formula, we utilize a weighted sum operation *weightedsum* to calculate the recommendation result $R(u)$. We multiply $S(u, e, t)$ and $A(u, e)$, which represents the weighted combination of the user's dynamic interest and the relevance between the user and the entity. Then, we normalize the result by dividing it with the weighted sum of the time relevance.

This approach allows us to accurately capture the user's real-time interests rather than relying solely on historical preferences, thereby enabling the system to generate more precise recommendations.

4.5   Parameter Learning

Parameter learning plays a crucial role in the proposed model. To optimize the performance, we begin by calculating the loss function for the recommendation task, taking into account potential regularization terms. The resulting loss function is denoted as L, which encompasses the overall objective of the model:

$$L = L_{rec} + \lambda * L_{reg} \tag{7}$$

Next, we compute the gradients of the loss function with respect to the model parameters θ to determine the direction of parameter updates. The learning rate α determines the step size of parameter updates, controlling the magnitude of parameter changes during each update.

$$\theta_{new} = \theta_{old} - \alpha * \Delta L \tag{8}$$

By selecting an appropriate learning rate and balancing the weights of the regularization terms, we can effectively train the model and enhance its recommendation performance.

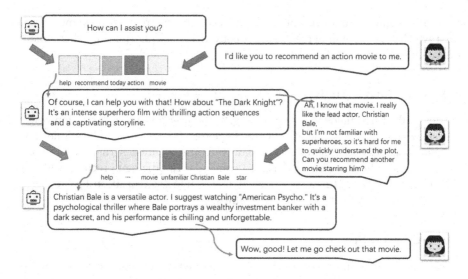

Fig. 2. A sampled conversation case for quantitative analysis.

5 Experiment

5.1 Experimental Settings

Dataset. We evaluate our model on DIALog (REDIAL) dataset, which is a conversational recommendation dataset published by Towards Deep Conversational Recommendations (2018). We filter out textual information in the dataset and replace the movie numbers with their real names to improve the completeness and readability of the text.

Baselines. We compare the proposed knowledge-intensive model with popular baselines for verifying the performance. Among these baselines, Popularity and TextCNN [3] are recommendation methods. We do not include other recommendation models, since there are no historical user-item interaction records except the text of a single conversation. Besides, REDIAL [9], KBRD [2] and KGSF [22] are all conversation recommendation methods.

5.2 Quantitative Analysis

Table 1 presents the performance of different proposed model. As we can see, Popularity and TextCNN perform evenly, but pale in comparison to the three CRS models Redial, KBRD and KGSF which are more independent by using entities only to make recommendations. Furthermore, KGSF performs more outstandingly because it achieves semantic fusion via knowledge graphs. It suggests that richer information is useful for enhancing data representation. Finally, our model KMTE outperforms the baseline by a large margin. KMTE fuses KG and valid temporal information while injecting downstream task knowledge to improve the system's understanding of conversational information, thus greatly improving recommendation quality.

5.3   Qualitative Analysis

In this multi-turn dialogue shown in Fig. 2, the user's interest transition occurs naturally through the association with the actor. This recommendation not only caters to the user's preference for Bale but also addresses their desire for a movie outside the superhero genre. To conclude, the dialogue recommendation system accurately captures the user's dynamic interest transition by leveraging the information from the user's timestamps.

5.4   Ablation Study

We conduct the ablation study based on three variations of our complete model, including: (1) using Word2Vec to generate word embeddings; (2) using pretrained BERT instead; and (3) injecting downstream task knowledge into the trained model. We evaluate the performance by calculating recall@k (k = 1, 10, 50) and visualize the results (See Fig. 3). As shown in the graph, the performance of using Word2Vec-generated embeddings is relatively poor in the recommendation system, while using pre-trained BERT embeddings shows performance enhancement. However, the best results are achieved when injecting downstream task knowledge into the model, further boosting the performance of the recommendation system.

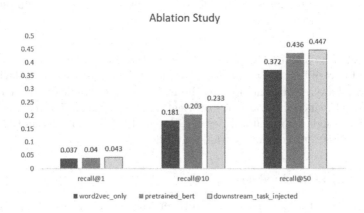

Fig. 3. Ablation Study.

6 Conclusion

In this study, we propose a new knowledge-intensive model based on BERT's masked language model and inject knowledge of downstream tasks to enable a better understanding of natural language. Our approach fully considers the characteristics of the conversational dataset and leverages the power of MLM to effectively train a model suitable for the conversational dataset and generate the corresponding embedding vector. Our experiments show that our approach outperforms state-of-the-art models, highlighting the effectiveness of incorporating temporal information into the model and generating text for the conversational dataset.

Acknowledgement. This work was supported by the Fundamental Research Funds for the Central Universities (No. 2021QD014) and in part by the National Natural Science Foundation of China (No. 62272200, 61932010, U22A2095).

References

1. Bobadilla, J., Ortega, F., Hernando, A., Gutiérrez, A.: Recommender systems survey. Knowl.-Based Syst. **46**, 109–132 (2013)
2. Chen, Q., et al.: Towards knowledge-based recommender dialog system. arXiv preprint arXiv:1908.05391 (2019)
3. Chen, Y.: Convolutional neural network for sentence classification. Master's thesis, University of Waterloo (2015)
4. Christakopoulou, K., Radlinski, F., Hofmann, K.: Towards conversational recommender systems. In: Proceedings of the 22nd ACM SIGKDD International Conference on Knowledge Discovery and Data Mining, pp. 815–824 (2016)
5. Huang, J., Zhao, W.X., Dou, H., Wen, J.R., Chang, E.Y.: Improving sequential recommendation with knowledge-enhanced memory networks. In: The 41st International ACM SIGIR Conference on Research & Development in Information Retrieval, pp. 505–514 (2018)
6. Ji, Z., Lu, Z., Li, H.: An information retrieval approach to short text conversation. arXiv preprint arXiv:1408.6988 (2014)
7. Koren, Y.: Factorization meets the neighborhood: a multifaceted collaborative filtering model. In: Proceedings of the 14th ACM SIGKDD International Conference on Knowledge Discovery and Data Mining, pp. 426–434 (2008)
8. Li, J., Galley, M., Brockett, C., Gao, J., Dolan, B.: A diversity-promoting objective function for neural conversation models. arXiv preprint arXiv:1510.03055 (2015)
9. Li, R., Ebrahimi Kahou, S., Schulz, H., Michalski, V., Charlin, L., Pal, C.: Towards deep conversational recommendations. In: Advances in Neural Information Processing Systems, vol. 31 (2018)
10. Li, R., et al.: House: knowledge graph embedding with householder parameterization. In: International Conference on Machine Learning, pp. 13209–13224. PMLR (2022)
11. Liao, L., Takanobu, R., Ma, Y., Yang, X., Huang, M., Chua, T.S.: Deep conversational recommender in travel. arXiv preprint arXiv:1907.00710 (2019)
12. Pang, B., et al.: Improving relevance modeling via heterogeneous behavior graph learning in Bing ads. In: Proceedings of the 28th ACM SIGKDD Conference on Knowledge Discovery and Data Mining, pp. 3713–3721 (2022)

13. Serban, I., Sordoni, A., Bengio, Y., Courville, A., Pineau, J.: Building end-to-end dialogue systems using generative hierarchical neural network models. In: Proceedings of the AAAI Conference on Artificial Intelligence, vol. 30 (2016)

14. Tian, Z., et al.: Multi-grained topological pre-training of language models in sponsored search. In: Proceedings of the 46th International ACM SIGIR Conference on Research and Development in Information Retrieval, pp. 2189–2193 (2023)

15. Wang, X., Wang, D., Xu, C., He, X., Cao, Y., Chua, T.S.: Explainable reasoning over knowledge graphs for recommendation. In: Proceedings of the AAAI Conference on Artificial Intelligence, vol. 33, pp. 5329–5336 (2019)

16. Wang, Y., et al.: An adaptive graph pre-training framework for localized collaborative filtering. ACM Trans. Inf. Syst. **41**(2), 1–27 (2022)

17. Zhang, P., et al.: Continual learning on dynamic graphs via parameter isolation. arXiv preprint arXiv:2305.13825 (2023)

18. Zhang, Y., et al.: Geometric disentangled collaborative filtering. In: Proceedings of the 45th International ACM SIGIR Conference on Research and Development in Information Retrieval, pp. 80–90 (2022)

19. Zhao, J., et al.: Learning on large-scale text-attributed graphs via variational inference. arXiv preprint arXiv:2210.14709 (2022)

20. Zhao, W.X., et al.: Kb4Rec: a data set for linking knowledge bases with recommender systems. Data Intell. **1**(2), 121–136 (2019)

21. Zhao, Y., et al.: Beyond the overlapping users: cross-domain recommendation via adaptive anchor link learning. In: Proceedings of the 46th International ACM SIGIR Conference on Research and Development in Information Retrieval, pp. 1488–1497 (2023)

22. Zhou, K., Zhao, W.X., Bian, S., Zhou, Y., Wen, J.R., Yu, J.: Improving conversational recommender systems via knowledge graph based semantic fusion. In: Proceedings of the 26th ACM SIGKDD International Conference on Knowledge Discovery & Data Mining, pp. 1006–1014 (2020)

23. Zhou, X., et al.: Multi-view response selection for human-computer conversation. In: Proceedings of the 2016 Conference on Empirical Methods in Natural Language Processing, pp. 372–381 (2016)

Natural Language Processing (NLP) and Databases

Multi-level Correlation Matching for Legal Text Similarity Modeling with Multiple Examples

Ting Huang[1], Xike Xie[1(✉)], and Xiufeng Liu[2]

[1] Suzhou Institute for Advanced Research,
University of Science and Technology of China, Suzhou, China
tinghuang1123@mail.ustc.edu.cn, xkxie@ustc.edu.cn
[2] Technical University of Denmark, Copenhagen, Denmark
xiuli@dtu.dk

Abstract. Legal artificial intelligence (LegalAI) is an emerging field that leverages AI technology to enhance legal services. Similar Case Matching (SCM), which calculates the relevance between a candidate and a target case, is a critical technique in LegalAI to enable diverse legal intelligences. Existing approaches mainly rely the on single query texts or specific keywords for retrieval, yet neglected the domain complexity and multi-faceted nature of queries. Thus, a multi-example matching paradigm is motivated where three inherent challenges reveal. 1) Relevance assessment across multiple examples is complex. 2) The inherent lengthy and structured property of legal documents. 3) Lacking datasets containing golden labels for multi-example-based legal text matching. To address these challenges, this paper develops a novel multi-example dataset, and a Multi-level Correlation Semantic Matching (MCSM) is devised to extract similarity between cases given multi-example inputs. The proposed multi-level scheme can be interpreted as two aspects. Firstly, we consider both content and structure correlations to evaluate the relevance. Secondly, by dividing legal documents into distinctive segments, we can hierarchically learn the intra- and inter-segment dependencies to model the long-term dependencies across components of legal documents. An attention mechanism is employed to capture the complex interconnections among these examples and enable an attentive matching aggregation of content and structure. With multiple examples, the MCSM tackles the intricate and diverse nature of legal queries, providing a comprehensive and multi-dimensional description view. Extensive experimental evaluations show that the proposed MCSM outperforms baseline methods.

Keywords: Semantic Matching · Legal Artificial Intelligence · Natural Language Processing

1 Introduction

Legal artificial intelligence (LegalAI) encompasses the use of AI technology to facilitate various legal tasks, including but not limited to legal judgement predic-

F. Zhang et al. (Eds.): WISE 2023, LNCS 14306, pp. 621–632, 2023.
https://doi.org/10.1007/978-981-99-7254-8_48

tion [4,8], legal question-answering [7,10], and legal summarization [1,9]. With the assistance of natural language processing (NLP), legal practitioners can be liberated from the burden of tedious and repetitive work, improving the efficiency, accuracy, and cost-effectiveness of legal services.

In LegalAI, Similar Case Matching (SCM) is a crucial task of determining the similarity between two given cases in a candidate pool, which enables diverse intelligent legal applications, such as question-answer and information retrieval. In common law systems, the principle of stare decisis guides the judicial decision-making process, where the past judicial decisions serve as authoritative precedents [17]. In the civil law systems, even though prior cases are not directly cited in the judgment, they can help legal practitioners gain insights in shaping the decision-making process by providing valuable information.

However, the traditional ad-hoc retrieval paradigm, which relies on specific keywords or a single query text, fails to effectively capture the complexity and ambiguity of a user's information needs, particularly in the legal domain. Firstly, queries in legal search can be highly intricate and multifaceted. Unlike simple keyword retrieval, legal cases require not only locating specific terms but also the consideration of the similarity of the factual background and legal consequences. Thus, solely relying on limited keywords, which yields simple combinations without contextual information, is insufficient for adequate legal search. Secondly, the precision and comprehensiveness of searching results are paramount in the realm of legal research, as legal practitioners heavily depend on these results for critical analyses and decision-making. Furthermore, conducting effective legal research highly requires the effective fusion between domain-specific expertise and technical proficiency of retrieval skills. Therefore, introducing a set of multiple examples for matching can be more useful for legal practitioners to conduct extensive analysis and decision-making. In particular, multiple examples can be exploited to fully capture the user's searching intents with diverse related examples and comprehensive contexts, thus the searching process becomes more intuitive and accessible.

For instance, it is often the case that legal practitioners may search for the concurrence of infringements and expressions related to infringements in the given cases [11]. In legal disputes or litigation, lawyers can make informed assessments and predictions by analyzing the similarities and patterns in the matched cases. In the process of drafting legal documents, employing a multi-example matching model enables them to comprehend legal implications and maintain language consistency. Even so, the surge of previous literature mostly focuses on the traditional retrieval paradigm with a single case, directly neglecting the retrieval techniques for multiple cases. To this end, we dissect three challenges that hinder the further development of multi-example-based matching.

Challenge 1. Judging the relevance between texts within multiple examples can be more complex. Actually, there are diverse dimensions considered, including fundamental legal concepts and document progression flow, there must be much more comparison dimensions between multiple examples.

Challenge 2. The inherent lengthy and structured property of legal documents poses great challenges to multi-example matching. For example, LeCaRD

[12], a Chinese law dataset containing case description with 6319 tokens on average, reveals difficulties in representing textual information in a limited vector space and modeling the structural relationships.

Challenge 3. There are no datasets containing golden labels for the research of multi-example-based legal text matching. On the one hand, access to legal documents is heavily restricted. Furthermore, labeling the relevance between legal documents requires substantial expert knowledge, especially in the civil law system. On the other hand, there is very little research related to the application scenarios of multi-example learning tasks, and the existing methods for generating such datasets are relatively coarse with only text topics considered [22].

In response to the aforementioned challenges, we propose to explore the multi-example correlation matching of legal cases, which empowers intelligent legal systems. To support this innovative research, we construct a multi-example legal text-matching dataset by leveraging the golden-label information from the LeCaRD dataset and enhancing dataset diversity through negative sampling techniques (**Challenge 3**). Then the Multi-level Correlation Semantic Matching (MCSM) model is devised. The proposed multi-level scheme can be interpreted as two aspects. First, instead of focusing on a single dimension, the proposed MCSM simultaneously considers both content and structure correlations to respectively model legal concepts and the successive document reasoning progression (**Challenge 1**). Second, the multi-level scheme is instantiated as the intra- and inter-segment sequence learning. Given a lengthy legal document, we hierarchically divide the document into distinct segments based on document progression flows. Thus, the dependencies within segments and across segments can be well captured (**Challenge 2**). Specifically, we employ Recurrent Neural Networks (RNNs) to capture structural reasoning logic and hybrid pooling strategies to get query-specific representations. The self-attention mechanism is utilized to thoroughly consider the interdependencies among multiple examples. Therefore, our techniques in a multi-level modeling scheme can cooperatively address the aforementioned long dependencies issue.

The main contributions of this paper are summarized as follows:

(1) We propose the first multi-example case matching in the intelligent legal system, which enables systematical case analysis and complements the lacking knowledge of legal practitioners. To support this research, a novel dataset based on LeCaRD [12] considering multiple examples is developed.
(2) We introduce MCSM, a novel semantic matching approach that effectively captures both content and structural correlations in legal documents. To the best of our knowledge, MCSM is the first semantic matching model to incorporate multi-level correlation for legal text modeling with multiple examples.
(3) We conduct extensive experiments to evaluate the performance of our proposed MCSM model. The results demonstrate that MCSM achieves strong performance compared to baseline methods.

2 Related Work

Legal Artificial Intelligence has recently emerged as a dynamic and rapidly growing area of research, with a wide range of studies exploring the potential of artificial intelligence techniques for diverse legal tasks that require a sophisticated
understanding of court documents and legal concepts. To evaluate the effectiveness of these techniques, a number of benchmark datasets have been proposed
in the field [20,21].

The emergence of pre-trained language models designed to benefit downstream NLP tasks has aroused a growing interest among AI researchers [2,6].
Given the success of PLMs, considerable efforts have been devoted to developing
legal-specific domain knowledge within these models [3,19].

In the realm of LegalAI, Similar Case Matching, which aims to determine
the similarity between given cases, plays a crucial role. Early attempts focus on
capturing case similarity from the term level, including TF-IDF [15], BM25 [14]
which are widely considered as baselines. Natural language processing techniques
have been employed to extract relevant information from legal documents and to
improve the efficiency and accuracy of legal search systems. For example, Tran et
al. [18] utilize legal summarization techniques to generate case summaries, which
are then used to measure the lexical overlap between a query case and its candidate cases. BERT-PLI [16] examines the interaction between the paragraphs
of a query case and candidate cases to infer their relevance.

However, these methods are limited to single query texts and fail to capture
the complexity and ambiguity of a user's information needs.

3 Method

3.1 Problem Formulation

The objective of similar case matching is to ascertain the relevance of a query case
to a given set of cases. Relevance is defined as the concurrence of infringements
and expressions related to infringements in the given cases. In this task, the
query case is considered to be relevant to the given set of cases only if it is a
noticed case for all of the cases in the set. A noticed case is a case that has been
cited by another case as a source of authority or considered relevant from the
legal perspective.

Formally, let q denote the query case and $T = t_1, t_2, ..., t_n | \forall 1 \leq i \leq n, t_i \in D$
denote the set of target cases. The task is to determine the relevance of q to T
using the following definition:

$$Relevance(q, T) = \begin{cases} 1, & noticed(q, t_1) \wedge ... \wedge noticed(q, t_n) \\ 0, & otherwise \end{cases}$$

Here, D represents the database of legal documents containing fact description, and $noticed(q, t)$ indicates that the query case q is relevant to the target
case t.

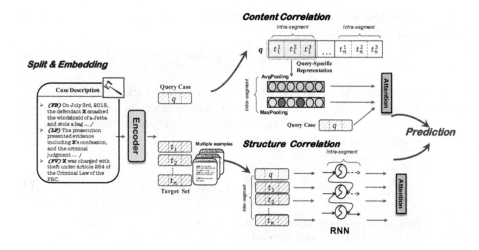

Fig. 1. Overview of MCSM Framework.

3.2   Framework

In general, texts are split and embedded by Text Segmentation and Representation Module, then forwarded to Content Correlation and Structure Correlation Modules for multi-level correlation modeling, as illustrated in Fig. 1.

Text Segmentation and Representation. The *Text Segmentation and Representation Module* is the initial component of the MCSM model, responsible for preprocessing the legal documents and representing them in a suitable format for further processing. Texts are segmented into three distinct parts: the case's factual background(FB), the complete legal proceedings(LP), and the final verdict(FV) due to the typical structure and logic of legal reasoning in court cases. Subsequently, each part is encoded into a vector representation using a pre-trained language model Lawformer [19], which has been fine-tuned on large scale legal corpora and can handle long texts efficiently. Each dataset sample is represented as a query case vector and a set of target vectors, where the number of target vectors is not fixed, and each vector consists of the three aforementioned segments, denoted as *query case* $q = (q_1, q_2, q_3)$ and *target set* $T = \{(t_1^1, t_1^2, t_1^3), (t_2^1, t_2^2, t_2^3), ..., (t_n^1, t_n^2, t_n^3)\}, where\ q_i,\ t_j^i \in \mathbb{R}^{H_i}$. By incorporating the structural characteristics of the legal document and leveraging the efficient attention mechanism of Lawformer, our method alleviates the pressure of information loss in handling long texts.

Content Correlation. To fully model the content correlation of query case and target set, we apply attention mechanism to get query-specific representation of the target case. Specifically, we construct a query-target interaction extraction, with embedding vectors as input.

The utilization of an attention mechanism enables the generation of a query-specific representation, which models the intra-segment relationship. Specifically, the attention weight of each case segmentation in relation to the query segmentation is computed as follows:

$$\alpha_{kji} = \frac{exp(q_k \cdot t_j^i)}{\sum_{k'} exp(q_{k'} \cdot t_j^i)} \tag{1}$$

Here, q_k denotes the k-th segmentation embedding of the query case, and t_j^i represents the i-th segmentation of the j-th case in the target set.

We can obtain a weighted representation of the target set based on the previously calculated attention score as follows:

$$\tilde{t}_j^i = \sum_k \alpha_{kji} \cdot q_k \tag{2}$$

For each case representation, we extract the most salient features via max-pooling and retain the overall information using the averaging-pooling strategy, then we get multi-view query-specific representation.

$$\tilde{t_{j_{avg}}} = AvgPool(\tilde{t}_j^1, \tilde{t}_j^2, \tilde{t}_j^3), t_{\tilde{j}_{avg}} \in \mathbb{R}^{H_i} \tag{3}$$

$$\tilde{t_{j_{max}}} = MaxPool(\tilde{t}_j^1, \tilde{t}_j^2, \tilde{t}_j^3), t_{\tilde{j}_{max}} \in \mathbb{R}^{H_i} \tag{4}$$

To comprehensively capture the information of the target cases, we utilize the attention mechanism to extract contextual representations of the given cases. The content correlation C is then computed using the following formula:

$$C = softmax(\frac{Q \cdot K^T}{\sqrt{d_k}}) \cdot V \tag{5}$$

Here, $Q = W_Q \cdot \oplus (q, \ \tilde{t}_{avg}, \ \tilde{t}_{max})$, $K = W_K \cdot \oplus (q, \ \tilde{t}_{avg}, \ \tilde{t}_{max})$, $V = W_V \cdot \oplus (q, \ \tilde{t}_{avg}, \ \tilde{t}_{max})$, where q represents the query case embedding, $\tilde{t}_{avg}$ and $\tilde{t}_{max}$ denote the average-pooled and max-pooled embeddings of the target set which applied to the weighted representation of all the target cases calculated previously. Notably, we use $\oplus$ to stand for the concat operation in the following.

Structure Correlation. Assuming that legal documents exhibit a certain logical structure, we use a *Text Segmentation and Representation Module* to partition the text into three segments. Meanwhile, to capture the inherent structural correlations within the documents, we employ a recurrent neural network to learn the sequential relations and temporal dependencies of each initial case vector. Furthermore, we utilize a self-attention mechanism to consider overall structure correlation. For the query case and target case set, hidden states generated by the RNN are as follows:

$$h_q = [h_{q1}, h_{q2}, h_{q3}], \ h_{qi} \in \mathbb{R}^{H_R} \tag{6}$$

$$h_{t_j} = [h_{t_j^1}, h_{t_j^2}, h_{t_j^3}], \ h_{t_j^i} \in \mathbb{R}^{H_R} \tag{7}$$

The attentive aggregation of structure correlation S is computed as follows:

$$S = softmax(\frac{Q' \cdot K'^T}{\sqrt{d_{k'}}}) \cdot V' \qquad (8)$$

Here, $Q' = W_{Q'} \cdot \oplus (h_q, h_{t1}, h_{t2}, ..., h_{tn})$, $K' = W_{K'} \cdot \oplus (h_q, h_{t1}, h_{t2}, ..., h_{tn})$, $V' = W_{V'} \cdot \oplus (h_q, h_{t1}, h_{t2}, ..., h_{tn})$, where h_q and h_{ti} are generated by the RNN.

Finally, the attentive matching representations of the content and structure correlations are concatenated and fed into a multilayer perceptron (MLP), followed by a softmax function for making predictions. We optimize the cross-entropy loss during the training process with the following objective function:

$$\mathcal{L}(\hat{y}, y) = -\sum_{r=1}^{|R|} y \cdot log(\hat{y}) \qquad (9)$$

where $R = \{0, 1\}$ denotes the relevance label of the query case with respect to the target set.

In the practice of multi-example semantic match task, we take the input format of a single query case and a set of target cases, without any restrictions on the number of target cases. And the model returns a binary label indicating the relevance of the query case to the provided set of cases.

4   Experiments

4.1   Dataset Construction

Due to the lack of exploration in the field of multi-example matching tasks, there is currently no existing multi-example matching dataset, especially for legal long-text data. Therefore, we rebuild existing datasets that fit this task.

The LeCaRD dataset [12], which has case relevance annotations based on expert judgment evaluations, provides golden labels for the query cases, which can greatly assist in building the target dataset. The label_top30.json file in the LeCaRD dataset provides relevance labels for all candidate cases with respect to each query case, and the rest unlabeled cases are considered irrelevant labeled as 0. Specifically, we consider the query case as a notice case that is related to all candidate cases that are deemed relevant. Therefore, there exists a relevant case set and an irrelevant case set with respect to each query case. In the process of sample generation, we adopt two strategies: random combination and negative sampling. For samples with ground truth, the relevant case combination and irrelevant case set combination are randomly extracted with the query case to generate 240,061 positive samples and 80,037 negative samples. To further diversify the dataset, we apply negative sampling by randomly selecting an irrelevant case from the corpus for the random combination of relevant cases, resulting in 36,054 negative samples. Statistics of the dataset are shown in Table 1.

Table 1. Dataset Attributes

Attributes	Number	Attributes	Number
Total documents	10,823	Average text length	6,261.05
Positive samples	240,061	Negative samples	116,091

4.2 Baseline Models

To verify the effectiveness of the proposed model, we compare MCSM with the following competitive baseline models:

- **Traditional Term-Matching Model.** Bag-of-words matching models are a widely used approach for text-matching tasks that impose no restrictions on text length. Among the various approaches, the TF-IDF model [15] and BM25 [14] have been extensively employed in current systems. For our experiments, we adopt them as baselines.
- **Deep Learning Models.** Deep learning methods have been proven effective in various semantic matching tasks. In this work, we compare our proposed model with three competitive deep learning models, namely TextCNN [5], BERT [6], BERT with attention mechanism, and SentenceBert [13]. It is worth noting that due to the processing limitation of BERT and its variations, we truncate the documents to 512 tokens for BERT-based methods.

4.3 Experimental Settings

Dataset Settings. Raw legal documents provide various information such as charged categories, court analysis, and judgments. However, this meta information may not always be available. To enhance the applicability of our method, we take the text body of legal documents as input. The dataset was partitioned into training, validation, and testing sets with 284,921, 35,615, and 35,616 samples, respectively, using a random split.

Hyperparameter Configurations. During the training process, we employed the Adam optimizer with a learning rate of 5×10^{-5} and weight decay of 10^{-7}. Considering the prescribed writing conventions for legal documents, the textual content is segmented into three distinct sections in accordance with a sentence distribution ratio of 0.2, 0.6, and 0.2, respectively. We take the last hidden state of case segmentation as the corresponding representation. To obtain the query-specific representation of the case, we simply adopt a single-head attention mechanism and get a 768-dimensional average-pooling and max-pooling vectors. The structure correlation module employs a vanilla RNN, which is applied uniformly across all cases, with H_R set to 768 to align with H_i.

Baseline Parameters. For the baseline methods, we employ a straightforward approach to respectively consider the target case set with the query case, given the absence of precedence in the multi-example text-matching task. In the TF-IDF baseline method, we calculate the similarity of the documents using the cosine measure. A threshold of 0.1 was chosen based on achieving an accuracy of more than 80% in single-case matching. In the BM25 baseline, we consider a query case relevant when it gets a score ranked within the top 20%.

Deep learning methods do not require a specific threshold, as the matching function is learned directly. Notably, the choice of which tokens to use is restricted by BERT, with only the first 512 tokens or the first 256 and last 256 tokens used depending on which approach yields the best performance. As for Sentence-Bert, we fine-tune based on the training dataset with the single text matching task and compute the cosine similarity between embeddings to measure the semantic similarity of two texts following the guideline. The kernel size of TextCNN, which simulates the N-gram language model specified as 2, 3, and 4 in the experiment.

4.4   Results and Analysis

Table 2. Experimental results.

Model	Accuracy	Recall	Precision	F1
TF-IDF	65.34	67.32	78.19	72.35
BM25	63.41	80.78	69.94	74.97
BERT	83.06	91.76	84.44	87.95
BERT+Attention	88.19	97.64	86.55	91.76
SentenceBert	73.55	89.82	80.40	84.85
TextCNN	86.60	94.77	86.59	90.50
MCSM	**98.81**	98.97	98.74	**98.85**
MCSM(GRU)	98.60	**98.99**	98.42	98.70
MCSM w/o MP	94.24	95.93	94.02	94.97
MCSM w/o AP	95.73	95.77	96.34	96.05
MCSM w/o SC	95.50	95.44	96.32	95.88

As mentioned in the introduction, datasets specifically designed for similar case matching with multiple examples are not readily available. Thus, we conduct our experiments on the synthetically developed dataset.

Table 2 shows all deep learning models outperform the traditional term-based statistical model and achieve comparable performance according. TF-IDF and BM25 serve as the baseline model, in which both target set documents and queries are represented as term vectors with term weighting. It is not surprising because the lexical overlap-based matching method merely captures the surface information of the text, neglecting the relevance of legal elements, semantics, and text structure. Compared with the baseline model BERT, the BERT model combined with the attention mechanism achieves the best performance, highlighting the effectiveness of attention mechanisms in capturing the overall contextual information of the cases, which is also applied in our proposed method. The truncation of documents significantly degrades the performance, as seen in the comparison between BERT-based models and MCSM. This indicates that on the semantic matching task, 512 tokens of truncated text or summarized content [16] fail to effectively convey the meaning of the text, as it may lead to a loss of essential information and complex reasoning patterns within a shorter length. The underperformance of SentenceBert can be primarily attributed to its limited training on a sizable Chinese corpus and the static cosine metric method in scalability. Even though TextCNN does not restrict the input length of text, its performance in modeling text semantics and contextual relations is slightly inferior to that of BERT-based models. There are improvements in models finetuned on the legal corpus.

In the experimental results, the proposed model outperforms the baseline models, demonstrating its superiority in similar case matching with multiple examples. Several factors contribute to the success of the proposed model and its improved performance compared to the baselines. Firstly, the proposed model leverages both content and structure correlations in legal documents with multiple examples to capture more comprehensive and nuanced information for matching. Secondly, the utilization of Lawformer as a pre-trained language model enhances the performance of the proposed model leading to better understanding and representation of legal concepts and language, thereby improving the model's matching capability. Furthermore, the proposed model handles long texts without the need for truncation or summarization. The model's attention mechanisms and segmentation embeddings enable it to capture and focus on relevant parts of the text, considering the fine-grained details necessary for accurate matching.

4.5   Ablation Study

The proposed MCSM outperforms all other models significantly, achieving a remarkable accuracy score of 98.81%, along with high recall, precision, and F1 scores. To further investigate the impact of individual components on the performance of our proposed MCSM model, we design two groups of variants for ablation study:1) MCSM with two types of RNN, i.e., MCSM and MCSM(GRU); 2) MCSM without the max-pooling representation, average-pooling representation, and structure correlation module, i.e., w/o MP, w/o AP, and w/o SC. The resulting models were then trained and evaluated under the same experimental conditions. The experimental results are illustrated in Table 2.

From the first group of variants, two types of RNN are employed: vanilla RNN and gated recurrent unit (GRU). We can observe that MCSM(GRU) shows relatively less improvement on the dataset, with only a marginal 0.02% increase in recall compared to MCSM. This may be a consequence of the relatively coarse granularity within intra-segments. Hence, the MCSM model utilizing RNN is deemed preferable due to its ability to achieve comparable performance to MCSM(GRU) while requiring fewer parameters.

Regarding the second group of variants, we can observe that these three components all make contributions to the model's performance, which validates the effectiveness of the modules. Besides, it is worth noting that the removal of max-pooling and average-pooling representation results in considerable deterioration. This explains that the content correlation module plays a critical role in enabling MCSM to effectively capture the semantic information of legal contextual concepts. The content correlation and structure correlation modules cooperatively model legal text similarity in the multi-example matching task.

5   Conclusions

In this research, we tackle the semantic matching problem in a novel scenario, the multi-example text-matching task, for lengthy legal documents. To this end, we established a new dataset using hybrid generating strategies based on the existing dataset [12]. To address the challenges of modeling lengthy legal documents and their complex interconnections, we propose a novel model, Multi-level Correlation Semantic Matching (MCSM) to hierarchically model the semantic content and structural correlations of the documents, enabling multi-dimensional text matching between multiple examples. Experimental results demonstrate that the proposed MCSM is efficient and effective to accommodate the multi-example text-matching problem in lengthy legal documents. The proposed model's approach can be extended to other domains, such as that healthcare, and finance, where the identification and analysis of similar cases or situations are crucial for decision-making. Furthermore, the availability of a more diverse and authoritative annotated dataset is crucial for the exploration, and the incorporation of legal knowledge such as legal ontologies, and legislation databases to support interpretable judgment into the model still need further research efforts.

References

1. Anand, D., Wagh, R.: Effective deep learning approaches for summarization of legal texts. J. King Saud Univ.-Comput. Inf. Sci. **34**(5), 2141–2150 (2022)
2. Beltagy, I., Peters, M.E., Cohan, A.: Longformer: the long-document transformer. arXiv preprint arXiv:2004.05150 (2020)
3. Chalkidis, I., Fergadiotis, M., Malakasiotis, P., Aletras, N., Androutsopoulos, I.: Legal-BERT: the muppets straight out of law school. arXiv preprint arXiv:2010.02559 (2020)
4. Chen, H., Cai, D., Dai, W., Dai, Z., Ding, Y.: Charge-based prison term prediction with deep gating network. arXiv preprint arXiv:1908.11521 (2019)
5. Chen, Y.: Convolutional neural network for sentence classification. Master's thesis, University of Waterloo (2015)
6. Devlin, J., Chang, M.W., Lee, K., Toutanova, K.: BERT: pre-training of deep bidirectional transformers for language understanding. arXiv preprint arXiv:1810.04805 (2018)
7. Fawei, B., Pan, J.Z., Kollingbaum, M., Wyner, A.Z.: A semi-automated ontology construction for legal question answering. N. Gener. Comput. **37**, 453–478 (2019)

8. Gan, L., Kuang, K., Yang, Y., Wu, F.: Judgment prediction via injecting legal knowledge into neural networks. In: Proceedings of the AAAI Conference on Artificial Intelligence, vol. 35, pp. 12866–12874 (2021)

9. Hachey, B., Grover, C.: Extractive summarisation of legal texts. Artif. Intell. Law **14**, 305–345 (2006)

10. Huang, W., Jiang, J., Qu, Q., Yang, M.: AILA: a question answering system in the legal domain. In: IJCAI, pp. 5258–5260 (2020)

11. Lissandrini, M., Mottin, D., Palpanas, T., Velegrakis, Y.: Multi-example search in rich information graphs. In: 2018 IEEE 34th International Conference on Data Engineering (ICDE), pp. 809–820. IEEE (2018)

12. Ma, Y., et al.: LeCaRD: a legal case retrieval dataset for Chinese law system. In: Proceedings of the 44th International ACM SIGIR Conference on Research and Development in Information Retrieval, pp. 2342–2348 (2021)

13. Reimers, N., Gurevych, I.: Sentence-BERT: sentence embeddings using Siamese BERT-networks. In: Proceedings of the 2019 Conference on Empirical Methods in Natural Language Processing. Association for Computational Linguistics (2019). https://arxiv.org/abs/1908.10084

14. Robertson, S.E., Walker, S.: Some simple effective approximations to the 2-Poisson model for probabilistic weighted retrieval. In: Croft, B.W., van Rijsbergen, C.J. (eds.) SIGIR 1994, pp. 232–241. Springer, London (1994). https://doi.org/10.1007/978-1-4471-2099-5_24

15. Salton, G., Buckley, C.: Term-weighting approaches in automatic text retrieval. Inf. Process. Manag. **24**(5), 513–523 (1988)

16. Shao, Y., et al.: BERT-PLI: modeling paragraph-level interactions for legal case retrieval. In: IJCAI, pp. 3501–3507 (2020)

17. Shulayeva, O., Siddharthan, A., Wyner, A.: Recognizing cited facts and principles in legal judgements. Artif. Intell. Law **25**(1), 107–126 (2017). https://doi.org/10.1007/s10506-017-9197-6

18. Tran, V., Nguyen, M.L., Satoh, K.: Building legal case retrieval systems with lexical matching and summarization using a pre-trained phrase scoring model. In: Proceedings of the Seventeenth International Conference on Artificial Intelligence and Law, pp. 275–282 (2019)

19. Xiao, C., Hu, X., Liu, Z., Tu, C., Sun, M.: Lawformer: a pre-trained language model for Chinese legal long documents. AI Open **2**, 79–84 (2021)

20. Xiao, C., et al.: CAIL 2018: a large-scale legal dataset for judgment prediction. arXiv preprint arXiv:1807.02478 (2018)

21. Yao, F., et al.: Leven: a large-scale Chinese legal event detection dataset. arXiv preprint arXiv:2203.08556 (2022)

22. Zhu, M., Xu, C., Wu, Y.F.B.: IFME: information filtering by multiple examples with under-sampling in a digital library environment. In: Proceedings of the 13th ACM/IEEE-CS Joint Conference on Digital Libraries, pp. 107–110 (2013)

GAN-IE: Generative Adversarial Network for Information Extraction with Limited Annotated Data

Ahmed Shoeb Talukder$^{(\boxtimes)}$, Richi Nayak◉, and Md Abul Bashar◉

Centre for Data Science, School of Computer Science,
Queensland University of Technology, Brisbane, Australia
ahmedshoeb.talukder@hdr.qut.edu.au

Abstract. Extracting valuable information from a large corpus of unstructured data poses a formidable challenge in many applications. Transformer-based architectures e.g. BERT, employing transfer learning techniques, have exhibited promising results across diverse NLP tasks. Nonetheless, the practical implementation of these models presents a significant hurdle given the substantial demand for annotated data during the training phase. In this paper, we present GAN-IE, a novel GAN-based model architecture, designed specifically for information extraction from unstructured textual data while accounting for limited annotated resources. In a generative adversarial setting, GAN-IE leverages BERT's rich semantic and contextual knowledge obtained from unlabelled data while fine-tuning. Experimental results show that GAN-IE achieves a level of accuracy that surpasses the current state-of-the-art models when trained using a fraction of labelled data ($\sim$100–200 annotated samples).

Keywords: Generative adversarial networks · Information extraction · Key-value extraction · Semi-supervised learning · Data scarcity

1 Introduction

Information extraction (IE) has emerged as a critical task in Natural Language Processing (NLP) to understand and semantically analyze unstructured textual information. IE is concerned with extracting essential details from text documents provided the application domain is well defined and the model is extensively trained on the target language [17]. However, queries can be complex, which may require the model to have in-depth knowledge of the subject matter and domain-specific terminology to comprehend the question within a broad context and then navigate accurately to extract the correct answer.

In the realm of IE, the prevailing deep learning methods rely upon hand-crafted rules, a large corpus of domain-specific data, and attention mechanisms [16] to address some of these issues. These techniques serve the purpose of capturing contextual and lexical representations pertaining to the desired domain.

F. Zhang et al. (Eds.): WISE 2023, LNCS 14306, pp. 633–642, 2023.
https://doi.org/10.1007/978-981-99-7254-8_49

However, constructing representative features becomes more challenging when the labelled data is sparse and fails to encompass diverse contextual meanings.

Transformer based architectures e.g. BERT (Bidirectional Encoder Representations from Transformers) [4] have exhibited remarkable efficacy in encapsulating domain-specific representations. Nevertheless, pre-training BERT model requires a significant amount of annotated data, thereby presenting computational burdens and time constraints. Danilo et al. [2] proposed an effective approach to address this issue by leveraging Semi-Supervised Generative Adversarial Networks (SS-GANs), with the objective of improving generalization capabilities when dealing with scarce annotated data.

This paper presents a novel method that aims to augment the process of IE by leveraging key-value pairs. Notably, the proposed model, GAN-IE demonstrates its efficacy even when confronted with limited labelled data by leveraging semi-supervised learning in a generative adversarial setting. The architecture of GAN-IE is designed to retrieve an answer span from a given context based on a keyword. Keywords allow the model to effectively capture semantic nuances and their associations with the desired information. We evaluate GAN-IE with a generated dataset consisting of geological mining reports, incorporating a wide range of query keywords aimed at retrieving relevant information. We assess the performance of GAN-IE against state-of-the-art deep learning models applicable to various NLP tasks. GAN-IE provides significantly improved results when trained with limited labelled data. These results ascertain that GAN-IE improves over conventional IE approaches by utilising adversarial training.

The main contributions of this paper are: 1) We propose a GAN-based method called GAN-IE to extract pertinent information from a given context, with a focus on a specific keyword. The task of capturing the essence of a question with a single keyword instead of expressing the complete question in NLP presents a considerable challenge. We argue that the adoption of semi-supervised learning using GAN enables the model to effectively encapsulate the surrounding context through a single keyword. 2) We present an innovative framework that enriches the BERT fine-tuning process by utilizing unlabelled data in a GAN framework for the IE task. Provided a key-context pair the model outputs a probability distribution of the start and end positions of the answer-span within the context. 3) We evaluate GAN-IE on a diverse dataset with limited labelled data in a generative adversarial setting. Our findings confirm that GAN-IE yields significantly superior outcomes, even when trained on a constrained dataset.

2   Related Works

Entity relationship extraction [12] and event extraction [17] are popular approaches of IE from unstructured text data. However, relation extraction models require prior knowledge of specific relation types, making them less adaptable to new domains. Supervised BI-LSTM models with attention mechanism [16] exhibited promising results in IE for entity relationship extraction, however many LSTM-based models lack higher-level linguistic feature encoding. Distant supervised learning [11] gained traction in IE for leveraging pre-existing knowledge bases, but suffers from assuming perfect alignment between these bases and the training data. Event extraction in IE identifies and extracts relevant events from unstructured text data. However, it often overlooks broader context, such as participants and temporal relations, resulting in inaccurate extraction.

BERT and similar transfer learning architectures are widely used in IE tasks for their ability to capture rich linguistic patterns and semantic information. BioBERT [9] trained in biomedical domain has shed light on the effectiveness of fine-tuned pre-trained models for domain-specific tasks. Nevertheless, embedding domain-specific vocabulary requires substantial computational resources and training data which can be challenging at times. In fact, experimental results show the accuracy of BERT based model significantly drops when fine-tuned with limited annotated data [2]. GAN-based semi-supervised learning approach [6] has exhibited considerable potential in addressing the sparse labelled data issue. Usually in GAN, the synthesized data generated by the "generator" serves as a valuable augmentation to the initially labelled dataset, offering supplementary instances and variations that enhance the model's capacity for generalization. In image processing, SS-GAN has shown promising outcomes in generating realistic images [3] and synthetic data [13].

GAN-IE leverages both rich contextual representation from BERT to produce high-quality synthetic data from the generator and semi-supervised learning with unlabelled data to improve the generalization capability of the network. GAN-IE primarily tackles two significant obstacles in IE - the limited availability of labelled data resulting in a lack of generalization, and the inadequate contextual representation of unseen data.

3   Proposed GAN-IE Model

GAN-IE incorporates semi-supervised learning within the BERT fine-tuning phase where the adversarial network focuses on learning the feature representation of the target domain based on the contextual embedding produced by BERT (Fig. 1). GAN is composed of i) a Generator $\mathcal{G}$ acting adversarially to produce fake samples where the hidden state h_{fake} resembles the data distribution of the BERT hidden-states h_{real}, and ii) a Discriminator $\mathcal{D}$, to discriminate between h_{fake} and h_{real}, coupled with a task-specific layer to predict the start and end positions of the answer span within the provided context.

Given a tokenised input sequence $\mathcal{S}$ consisting of a keyword and a context where $\mathcal{S} = (t_{CLS}, t_1^q, ...t_m^q, t_{SEP}, t_1^c...t_n^c)$, BERT produces an output vector of hidden representations for each token in each sequence at the last layer of the model. In BERT, the [CLS] token represents the whole input sequence for classification tasks, and the [SEP] token is used to separate different segments or sentences within the input [4]. In most BERT fine-tuning tasks, the pooled output representation (h_{CLS}) is utilised as an aggregated summary of the input sequence for classification tasks [4]. In contrast, the hidden states in each BERT layer represent the contextualized information of individual tokens, capturing information from both left and right contexts. GAN-IE adopts this representation for the downstream IE task as it is more beneficial in capturing dependencies and relationships within the text to predict the start and end position of the answer span. The hidden states are calculated using a combination of the word embeddings, the positional embeddings, and the segment embeddings [4]. During fine-tuning, BERT hidden states offer contextual embedding of each word within the input sequence along with sentence-level embedding that captures the semantics of the entire sentence.

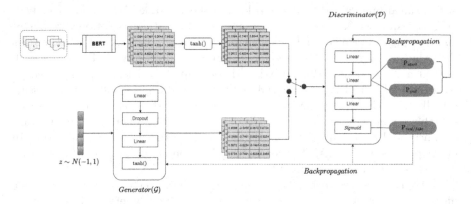

Fig. 1. GAN-IE architecture: A set of key-context embeddings is generated by $\mathcal{G}$ resembling the BERT hidden layer embeddings. These along with unlabelled U and labelled L datasets computed by BERT hidden layers are used as input for $\mathcal{D}$

The adversarial training process involves the interplay between the $\mathcal{G}$ and $\mathcal{D}$ models leveraging the contextual information extracted by BERT to enhance performance. $\mathcal{G}$ aims to minimise the Generator loss by learning input data patterns, generating fake samples that resemble the original dataset [1]. The training process "adversarially" depends on $\mathcal{D}$ to accurately classify real and fake samples, while learning the contextual embedding of the target domain to predict the start and end position of the given query. The unlabelled examples only contribute to minimizing the $L_{\mathcal{D}_{unsup}}$, which is the discriminative loss that determines whether the observed sample is real or fake. By including unlabelled examples in the training process, the $\mathcal{D}$ can learn from a more diverse set of data and improve its internal representation of domain-specific embedding.

A noise vector (768-dimensional) with uniform distribution $z \sim N(-1,1)$ is introduced as an input to $\mathcal{G}$, which produces an output vector h_{fake} resembling the final hidden states of the BERT output layer. This approach generates hidden representation that is more realistic and similar to the actual data. The $\mathcal{G}$ is optimised on i) a Mean Squared Error (MSE) loss $L_{G_{adv}}$ which measures the discrepancy between the generated samples and the real data ii) a binary cross-entropy loss $L_{G_{unsup}}$ which encourages the Generator to construct fake samples that can deceive the Discriminator into categorizing them as real. Each $\mathcal{G}$ loss component is determined as follows:

$$L_{G_{adv}} = ||\mathbb{E}_{x \sim p_r} f(x) - \mathbb{E}_{x \sim p_g} f(x)||_2^2 \tag{1}$$

$$L_{G_{unsup}} = -\mathbb{E}_{x \sim p_g} log[1 - P_d(y = real|x)] \tag{2}$$

Total $\mathcal{G}$ loss is computed by $L_{\mathcal{G}} = L_{G_{adv}} + L_{G_{unsup}}$, where p_r is Real data distribution and p_g is generator data distribution.

The Discriminator $\mathcal{D}$ receives input vector space $\mathcal{H}$, where $\mathcal{H}$ is composed of h_{fake} produced by the Generator and h_{real} generated by BERT from labelled or unlabelled examples. $\mathcal{D}$ is tasked with i) given a sample $\hat{h} \in \mathcal{H}$, distinguish whether $\hat{h}$ is real or fake, and ii) in case $\hat{h}$ is believed to be real, output a probability distribution P_{start} and P_{end} of start and end positions of the answer span within the input sequence $\mathcal{S}$, respectively. The loss function of $\mathcal{D}$ is formulated as $L_{\mathcal{D}} = L_{\mathcal{D}_{sup}} + L_{\mathcal{D}_{unsup}}$. $L_{\mathcal{D}_{unsup}}$ is a discriminative loss that determines whether the observed sample is generated from the Generator or the real distribution (including unlabelled data).

$$L_{\mathcal{D}_{unsup}} = -\mathbb{E}_{x \sim p_r} log[1 - P_d(y = real|x)] - \mathbb{E}_{x \sim p_g} log[P_d(y = real|x)] \tag{3}$$

whereas, $L_{\mathcal{D}_{sup}}$ is calculated as $L_{\mathcal{D}_{sup}} = L_{D_{start}} + L_{D_{end}}$. The loss $L_{D_{start}}$ for the start position $j \in \{1, 2, \ldots N\}$ and $L_{D_{end}}$ for end position $k \in \{1, 2, \ldots N\}$ are calculated as follows, where N is the length of the context.

$$L_{D_{start}} = -\mathbb{E}_{x \sim p_r} log[1 - P_d(j = start|x)] \tag{4}$$

$$L_{D_{end}} = -\mathbb{E}_{x \sim p_r} log[1 - P_d(k = end|x)] \tag{5}$$

Implementation Details: Several techniques are employed to tackle challenges pertaining to GAN training [5]. The Generator $\mathcal{G}$ applies the ReLU activation function after every linear layer, except for the output layer which utilizes Tanh to normalize the input to $\mathcal{D}$. LeakyReLU was used after every fully connected layer in $\mathcal{D}$ except for the final layer to address the vanishing gradient concern [5]. The intermediate layer in $\mathcal{D}$ is subsequently divided into two heads; one is processed by a Sigmoid layer for real/fake probabilities, while the other head is further processed by linear layers to generate the start/end positions probabilities. Employing a binary classification task enhances the Discriminator's capability to differentiate between real and fake samples. During inference, the input data is initially fed into the pre-trained BERT model, which generates the hidden representation, $\mathcal{H}$ that is subsequently forwarded to the $\mathcal{D}$ which generates two logits pertaining to the start (P_{start}) and end (P_{end}) positions of the answer. The $\mathcal{D}$'s real and fake prediction outputs are disregarded at this stage, as they are only advantageous during the adversarial training process. During the post-processing stage (P_{start}) and (P_{end}) logits goes through further analysis. We limit the selection to the top 10 most promising predictions for start and end positions. By carefully evaluating these combinations, we guarantee that the ultimate prediction remains within the length of the given context and the start position comes before the end position.

4   Experimental Setup and Analysis

The **dataset**, consisting of 367 Mining reports[1], was used to select 7 categories of key-value pairs, capturing diverse information. In Table 1 the keyword GROUND_ELEV will always resolve to a numeric value, while WELL_PU-
RPOSE potentially yield a multifaceted response. The selected pairs were used
to break down each mining report into smaller contextual chunks, serving the
purpose of training and testing. The unlabelled samples utilized in the semi-
supervised learning were also sourced from the same collection of 367 reports,
resulting in a total of 4000 unlabelled samples. We created an introductory
ground truth dataset[2] for training models in the geological mining domain, which
are annotated with key-value pairs. For instance, as shown in Table 1, the key
"WELL_NAME" denotes the name of the mining well (i.e. a straight hole dug in
the ground) and the corresponding value "Cameron 226" represent the well mentioned in the context. Figure 2 provides an overview of key-value pair category
distribution across training (2500 samples) and test ($\sim$2100 samples) datasets.

Table 1. Sample keyword-context pairs.

Keyword	Context	Ground Truth
WELL_NAME	A BG Group business Cameron 226 Well Completion Report 1 Well data card Well Name **Cameron 226** Well Type CSG Development	text: Cameron 226, answer_start: 82, answer_end: 93
WELL_PURPOSE	The aim of the well was to **target evaluate and produce** coal seam gas out of the Walloon Subgroup Coal Measures	text: target evaluate and produce, answer_start: 27, answer_end: 54
GROUND_ELEV	Summary for Woleebee Creek 171 On location 18 05 2015 Spud Date 18 05 2015 GL **372.12m** Proposed TD 954.00mRT	text: 372.12m, answer_start: 78, answer_end: 85

4.1   Experimental Settings

We choose 5 state-of-the-art models known for IE tasks, BERT [4], RoBERTa
[10], ALBERT [8], DistilBERT [15] and a Bi-LSTM model augmented with an
attention mechanism, as baseline models. These models excel in SQuAD (Stanford Question Answering Dataset)[3], achieving state-of-the-art performance.
SQuAD [14] is designed for the Question-Answering (QA) task where the goal
is to develop models that can read a passage and accurately answer questions
about it. Since our research objective of IE, is closely related to QA, these baseline models serve as ideal candidates for assessing the performance of GAN-IE.

---

[1] Mining reports were provided by the Queensland Department of Resources (DoR).
[2] We would like to acknowledge the DoR team, Frontier SI team and the Australian
   Spatial Analytics team for their assistance in obtaining the annotated reports.
[3] https://paperswithcode.com/sota/question-answering-on-squad20.

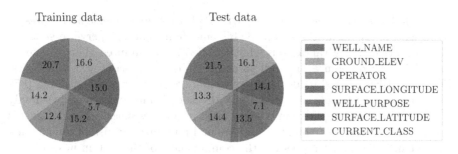

Fig. 2. Distribution of key-value pair categories in Training and Test dataset

To examine the performance of each method with limited labelled data, we train each model repeatedly with increasing sets of annotated data, starting with 1% (26 samples) of the training set, and eventually reaching a maximum of 2500 samples. Throughout this process, the size of the test set remains constant at ∼2100 samples. GAN-IE also utilizes around 4000 samples of unlabelled training instances. Following the training process, the Generator is disregarded, and solely the pre-trained BERT, together with the Discriminator, is utilized. Additionally, we conducted experiments involving early stopping and varying the learning rate during training. However, in the final experiment, we opted to maintain a consistent number of epochs and learning rate for simplicity.

We present F1 score performance, a common metric for information extraction tasks. To create distinct training and validation sets, we split the original training set into two subsets, maintaining a ratio of 7:3. To balance the ratio of labelled to unlabelled data in each training batch we augment the labelled data by a factor of $log()$. All the baseline models were implemented using pre-trained models and tokenizers from Hugging Face[4]. The baseline models also followed identical pre and post processing steps as that of GAN-IE.

4.2   Results and Discussion

Figure 3 shows a comparison of F1 scores between GAN-IE and baseline models where GAN-IE achieves improved performance when trained with only $5-40\%$ of the training dataset. GAN-IE achieves a 50% F1 score using 5% of the dataset (∼88 samples), while BERT struggled to achieve an accuracy of 35%. All the baseline models encountered challenges of overfitting when the amount of labelled data is scarce. However, GAN-IE successfully addressed this issue by effectively acquiring comprehensive contextual and sentence-level representations derived from BERT. The finest performance was witnessed by introducing a mere 122 (10% to 15%) annotated samples, which improved the F1 score from 60% to 85%. Under the same settings, the baseline models averaged around 58%. This trend is continued for the dataset using 40% of the labelled examples (∼700

---

[4] https://huggingface.co/docs/transformers/model_doc/bert.

samples). These results suggest that GAN-IE learns more diverse and representative feature representations from BERT embeddings in unsupervised settings. This is particularly advantageous when labelled data is limited. This is demonstrated by the difference in recall rates at 1% of the data in Fig. 4 (42% vs. 25%). The BERT-based model achieves recall of 85% when employing 50% (875 instances) of the training set, while GAN-IE yielded similar outcomes with only 262 samples. In our application domain, high recall is essential when the goal is to cover a wide range of potential answers and minimize the risk of missing any relevant information. It represents the completeness of the system in retrieving relevant information.

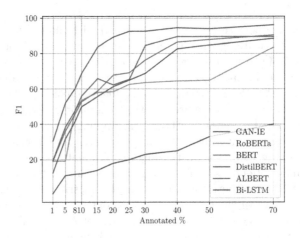

Fig. 3. F1 score comparison against baseline models.

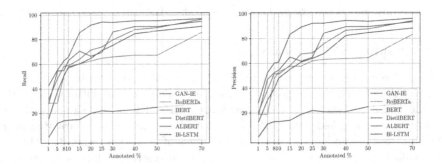

Fig. 4. Recall and Precision rates comparison against baseline models.

The baseline models start to compensate for the lack of generalization when using more than 40% (about 700 labelled examples) producing f1 score of 85%. GAN-IE provides an additional 10 points in the F1 score with respect to BERT (86% vs 94%) in identical settings. Using more annotated data leads to similar performance outcomes, with a slight advantage in using GAN-IE. With 1225 training samples which constitute 70% of the training set, our model reaches an F1 score of 96%, surpassing the 90% achieved by BERT.

Table 2 provides meaningful insights on GAN-IE's performance variability for each keyword. GAN-IE demonstrates high precision when the target information conforms to specific patterns within the given context. On the contrary, the model struggles when faced with keywords that elicit multifaceted responses, requiring complex comprehension of the context.

Table 2. Average F1 score of individual keywords

Keyword	F1 Score	Observation
SURFACE_LATITUDE	0.99808	If the target information follows a particular format,
SURFACE_LONGITUDE	0.9941	such as numeric values of coordinates represented as "150 14 36.99 E/S,"
GROUND_ELEV	0.95677	the retrieval performance of GAN-IE is notably satisfactory
WELL_NAME	0.88624	Situations where the desired information requires complex comprehension,
WELL_PURPOSE	0.84361	for example, well purpose changes across the lifecycle of a bore-hole, and also varies across different mining reports, can pose a challenge for GAN-IE
CURRENT_CLASS	0.97564	When the attribute has limited outcomes such as CURRENT_CLASS can only be either Development or Exploration, GAN-IE demonstrates commendable performance
OPERATOR	0.98139	If the keyword is present within the context, for example, operator names are often accompanied by the term "Operator", GAN-IE demonstrates high proficiency in extracting such pertinent information

We also conducted a thorough comparison between GAN-IE and a BI-LSTM model with attention, focusing on addressing over-fitting through techniques like dropout layers, pre-trained GloVe[5] embeddings, simplified architecture, and hyperparameter tuning. Despite our efforts, LSTM models (with pre-trained embeddings) performed poorly compared to the baseline settings (Fig. 4). Even with 70% of the training data, the LSTM models achieved only 40% F1 score, much lower than our model's impressive 96% (Fig. 3). The LSTM model struggles to capture domain-specific lexical representations, especially in the geological mining domain, and to exploit temporal dependencies with fewer training instances, leading to subpar performance.

5 Conclusion

Extracting meaningful information from voluminous texts can be a laborious task due to the lack of consistent patterns and the dispersed nature of the data within them. Our proposed GAN-IE model successfully extracted the relevant information with high precision from over 10,000 reports with limited annotated data. The exploitation of vast amounts of unlabelled data contributes to improved performance and generalization of the GAN-IE model. GAN-IE surpasses the current state-of-the-art models in terms of accuracy, achieving a

---

[5] https://nlp.stanford.edu/projects/glove/.

superior performance of 94% compared to 86%. Moreover, GAN-IE enhances the robustness of the BERT fine-tuning process, while incurring no additional inference costs. The results obtained highlight the potential of GAN in advancing the field of IE and its applicability across various domains. However, training GANs can be unstable and require careful hyperparameter tuning. In future work, we propose to adopt GAN-IE with advanced architectures such as Wasserstein GAN (WGAN) [7] or Self-Attention GAN (SAGAN) [18]. From an IE perspective, it is worth investigating domain adaptation and active learning techniques.

References

1. Brownlee, J.: A gentle introduction to generative adversarial networks (GANs). Mach. Learn. Mastery **17** (2019)
2. Croce, D., et al.: GAN-BERT: generative adversarial learning for robust text classification with a bunch of labeled examples. In: Proceedings of ACL 2020, pp. 2114–2119 (2020)
3. Denton, E.L., et al.: Deep generative image models using a Laplacian pyramid of adversarial networks. In: Advances in Neural Information Processing Systems, vol. 28 (2015)
4. Devlin, J., et al.: BERT: pre-training of deep bidirectional transformers for language understanding (2018)
5. Fang, W., et al.: A method for improving CNN-based image recognition using DCGAN. Comput. Mater. Others **57** (2018)
6. Goodfellow, I., et al.: Generative adversarial networks. Commun. ACM **63**(11), 139–144 (2020)
7. Gulrajani, I., et al.: Improved training of Wasserstein GANs. In: Advances in Neural Information Processing Systems, vol. 30 (2017)
8. Lan, Z., et al.: ALBERT: a lite BERT for self-supervised learning of language representations (2019)
9. Lee, J., et al.: BioBERT: a pre-trained biomedical language representation model for biomedical text mining. Bioinformatics **36** (2020)
10. Liu, Y., et al.: RoBERTa: a robustly optimized BERT pretraining approach (2019)
11. Mao, N., et al.: KGGCN: knowledge-guided graph convolutional networks for distantly supervised relation extraction. Appl. Sci. **11**, 7734 (2021)
12. McDonald, R., et al.: Simple algorithms for complex relation extraction with applications to biomedical IE. In: Proceedings of ACL 2005, pp. 491–498 (2005)
13. Mogren, O.: C-RNN-GAN: continuous recurrent neural networks with adversarial training (2016)
14. Rajpurkar, P., et al.: SQuAD: 100,000+ questions for machine comprehension of text (2016)
15. Sanh, V., et al.: DistilBERT, a distilled version of BERT: smaller, faster, cheaper and lighter (2019)
16. Vaswani, A., et al.: Attention is all you need. In: Advances in Neural Information Processing Systems, vol. 30 (2017)
17. Yang, Y., et al.: A survey of information extraction based on deep learning. Appl. Sci. **12**, 9691 (2022)
18. Zhang, H., et al.: Self-attention generative adversarial networks. In: International conference on machine learning, pp. 7354–7363. PMLR (2019)

An Integrated Interactive Framework for Natural Language to SQL Translation

Yuankai Fan[1]([⊠]), Tonghui Ren[1], Dianjun Guo[1], Zhigang Zhao[1,2],
Zhenying He[1], X. Sean Wang[1], Yu Wang[3], and Tao Sui[3]

[1] Fudan University, Shanghai, China
{fanyuankai,djguo20,zhenying,xywangcs}@fudan.edu.cn,
thren22@m.fudan.edu.cn
[2] Shandong Computer Science Center (National Supercomputer Center in Jinan),
Jinan, Shangdong, China
zgzhao21@m.fudan.edu.cn
[3] China UnionPay Merchant Services Co., LTD., Shanghai, China
{wangyu62,taosui}@chinaums.com

Abstract. Numerous web applications rely on databases, yet the traditional database interface often proves inconvenient for effective data utilization. It is crucial to address the significant demand from a vast number of end users who seek the ability to input their requirements and obtain query results effortlessly. Natural Language (NL) Interfaces to Databases (NLIDBs) with interactive query mechanisms make databases accessible to end users and simultaneously retain user confidence in the results. This paper proposes an approach called IKNOW-SQL for building interactive NLIDBs. IKNOW-SQL introduces a unified framework for translation models to improve accuracy and increase interactivity. Specifically, IKNOW-SQL first employs an underlying translation model to parse the semantics of a given NL query. By evaluating the model behavior, IKNOW-SQL then recognizes the parts of the model output that may require human intervention. Next, IKNOW-SQL presents clarifying questions to solicit and memorize user feedback until a polished result is obtained. Extensive experiments are performed to study IKNOW-SQL on the public benchmark. The results show that the translation models can be effectively improved using IKNOW-SQL with less user feedback.

Keywords: Interactive Semantic Parsing · Database System · NL2SQL

1 Introduction

In the modern digital landscape, web applications have become an integral part of our daily lives. These applications provide us with a wide range of functionalities, from social networking and e-commerce to productivity tools and content management systems. However, behind the scenes, the smooth functioning of these web applications often hinges on the effective utilization of databases for storing, managing, and retrieving data [9,15].

F. Zhang et al. (Eds.): WISE 2023, LNCS 14306, pp. 643–658, 2023.
https://doi.org/10.1007/978-981-99-7254-8_50

The concept of Natural Language Interfaces to Databases (NLIDBs) has emerged as a visionary approach to enhance database accessibility for a wide range of non-technical users. The ultimate goal is to enable users to interact with databases in a manner that closely resembles human conversation. Recent advancements in natural language processing technologies, particularly neural machine translation, have rekindled research interest in developing NLIDBs [3,4,19,20,26,28,33]. The main idea is to consider the NL to SQL translation (NL2SQL) problem as a translation task and train a generalized sequence-to-sequence (Seq2seq) model in a supervised manner.

Despite the significant gains in terms of translation accuracy, the translation may still exhibit inaccuracies or errors, particularly observed in some complex queries [8]. As a solution, *interactive NLIDBs* have been further proposed as a promising paradigm [14,36], which includes human users in the loop to resolve utterance ambiguity, boost system accuracy, and improve user confidence via human-machine collaboration [5,7,21]. While many recent studies successfully demonstrated the value of interactive NLIDB in practice, the interaction is for an individual prediction, and thus the feedback users provide is not preservable. Namely, if users input the same NL query again, a repeated interaction may be triggered with no change. Consider the example in Fig. 1 that shows two-way communication between an end-user and the NLIDB system during two interactive sessions. While the system has the capability to detect the confusion span (i.e., *"under age 30"*) in the input queries that need clarification, the two sessions request repeated feedback due to the same confusion span being recognized. This example shows that an inefficient interaction may be involved in the current interactive NLIDB system.

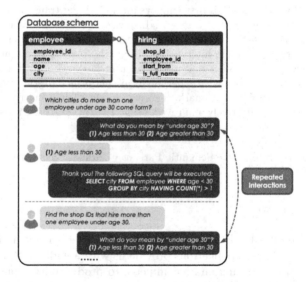

Fig. 1. An example of repeated interaction exists in the current interactive NLIDB. The database and queries are from the SPIDER benchmark [38].

In this paper, we present IKNOW-SQL, an Interactive **Know**ledge preservation approach for NL2**SQL** translation. IKNOW-SQL is inspired by the cache mechanism used in deep learning [12,31] and aims to minimize human feedback while maximizing translation accuracy by storing and recalling knowledge gained through human interactions.

Concrete speaking, IKNOW-SQL belongs to the field of *interactive semantic parsing* in natural language processing (NLP) and provides a **unified framework** for any back-end NL2SQL translation model that can interact with users. Given an NL query, IKNOW-SQL performs the following steps: ① uses an underlying translation model for semantic parsing and keeps track of its internal states during decoding; ② employs a confidence estimator to identify parts of the model output that may require human intervention based on probability mass at each decoding step; Assuming human intervention is needed, ③ IKNOW-SQL generates questions for user clarification using a question generator and memorizes user feedback through a knowledge collector until no low level of confidence is detected. Here, the mechanism for knowledge memorization in this context stores information from past interactions, which allows for a reduction in the number of user interactions needed over time.

To better demonstrate the advantages of IKNOW-SQL, we conduct our experiments on the popular NL2SQL benchmark SPIDER [38], by applying to three base NL2SQL models [4,20,28]. We empirically verified that with a small amount of targeted, test time user feedback, IKNOW-SQL can significantly improve the accuracy of base semantic parsers by 8.1% to 15.4% absolute.

To summarize, our contributions are three-fold:

- We propose a unified framework IKNOW-SQL for building interactive NLIDBs, which can be used for any existing NL2SQL translation models to improve the performance and efficiency.
- By incorporating a knowledge caching mechanism in IKNOW-SQL, a same run-time accuracy of a base semantic parser can be retained with soliciting less user feedback.
- We perform a series of experiments to evaluate IKNOW-SQL on the public NLIDB benchmark with three state-of-the-art Seq2seq-based translation models. The experimental results demonstrate the effectiveness of IKNOW-SQL for the NL2SQL problem.

The remainder of this paper is organized as follows. We first discuss the related works of IKNOW-SQL in Sect. 2. We then give an overview of IKNOW-SQL in Sect. 3. Next, we present the details of each key components used in IKNOW-SQL in Sect. 4. Finally, we presents the results of our experiments on IKNOW-SQL in Sect. 5 and conclude in Sect. 6.

2   Related Works

Natural Language Interface to Database. NLIDBs have been studied for several decades in database management and NLP communities. Early works [1,

2, 18, 25, 27, 29, 39] are rule-based approaches, which use handcrafted grammars and rules to map NL queries to SQL queries specific to a certain database.

The recent success of deep learning, notably in the realm of neural machine translation, have catalyzed the adoption of machine learning-based approaches to build NLIDB systems. These approaches treat the NLIDB challenge as a Seq2seq translation task and employ the encoder-decoder neural architecture to do the translation [3, 4, 13, 20, 33, 34, 37]. In addition, with the increasing attention given to large-scale language models (LLMs) [23, 24, 32] recently, they have emerged as a new approach for the NL2SQL task. In contrast to conventional end-to-end SQL query generation, IKNOW-SQL employs an interactive mechanism to achieve more precise NL2SQL translation, thereby enhancing the accuracy of the resulting SQL queries.

Interactive Semantic Parsing. Interactive natural language interfaces for databases are a promising solution to improve translation accuracy as well as user confidence in practical applications [6, 14, 16, 18, 30, 35]. However, current solutions are limited to specific formal languages and datasets, making them somewhat ad-hoc. The design of IKNOW-SQL centers around creating an interactive NLIDB framework independent of any specific model. Moreover, IKNOW-SQL is dedicated to integrating external knowledge into the system, aiming to minimize the extent of user feedback required.

3   IKNOW-SQL Overview

Figure 2 shows a high-level view of IKNOW-SQL. The main process unfolds as:

1. When a user query is fed into the base NL2SQL model, the model parses its semantics and then generates a corresponding raw SQL query initially.
2. The raw SQL query, along with the probability mass at each SQL token, is estimated by the confidence estimator to determine if any unconfidently-predicted target tokens exist.
3. If any uncertainties detect, the question generator is used to interact with users by generating a series of clarifying questions to solicit user input.
4. The user feedback is then used to update the states of the NL2SQL model and then generate a new polished SQL query for the user.
5. Meanwhile, the knowledge collector will also be incorporated to memorize the user feedback and sync with the underlying NL2SQL model.

Among these, incorporating the knowledge collection process into the semantic parsing is unique to our setup. We describe each above step below.

Semantic Parsing. This step in Fig. 2-① is to utilize an underlying NL2SQL model to parse the NL query that is given by the user to the SQL query counterpart. Mapping NL queries to their formal semantic representations (i.e., SQL queries), the mainstream models usually formulate the NL2SQL problem as a language translation task, and employ the Seq2seq framework to build the models [3, 4, 20, 28, 33]. These models can be recurrent neural network (RNN)-based simple encoder-decoder networks or the advanced attention-based encoder-decoder RNN or state-of-the-art transformer models. Concretely speaking,

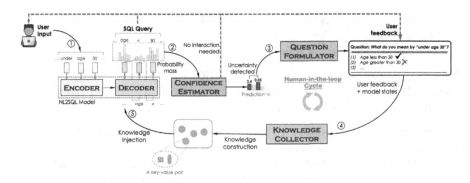

Fig. 2. A diagram illustrating the workflow of IKNOW-SQL.

taking a given NL query and a corresponding database schema, the model uses an encoder to compute a contextual representation by jointly embedding the NL utterance with schema information. Afterward, an auto-regressive decoder is used to compute a distribution over the SQL programs. Depending on different model designs, the learning target of the decoder can be raw SQL tokens [20,40], intermediate representations of SQL language [13], or SQL AST trees [4,28,33]. The NL2SQL model is generally trained with maximum likelihood estimation.

For example, assume the first NL query *"Which cities do more than one employee under age 30 come from?"* in Fig. 1 is given, an NL2SQL model may interpret it to a SQL query as below,

SELECT city **FROM** employee
WHERE age > 30
GROUP BY city **HAVING** count(*) > 1

The SQL query may be incorrect and will undergo subsequent processing steps.

Prediction Inspecting. The step in Fig. 2-② is an *inspection process* where IKNOW-SQL examines the state of each decoding step of the underlying NL2SQL model and determines if any error (i.e., unconfidently-prediction) exists in the SQL query output, and hence decides whether human intervention is needed. For example, after the underlying NL2SQL model outputs the above SQL query, IKNOW-SQL introspects its states at each decoding step and recognizes a lack of confidence in the prediction concerning the **WHERE** clause (i.e., **WHERE** age > 30). This prompts IKNOW-SQL to solicit user feedback on the unconfidently-prediction to refine the initial SQL query output.

User Interaction. If any unconfidently-prediction is detected, the step in Fig. 2-③ is triggered to generate the clarification question for the user. IKNOW-SQL formulates as an NL generation task and leverages a template-based method to customize the question. For example, by clarifying the unconfidently-prediction **WHERE** age > 30, IKNOW-SQL generates the following clarification question with two options accordingly,

Please select any options that the system needs to enforce as condition:
(1) Age of employee is large than 30.
(2) Age of employee is less than 30.

The type of the clarification questions in IKNOW-SQL are fixed (i.e., multichoice). However, it can be extended with more human-curated templates to accommodate more complex interactions.

Knowledge Memorization. To preserve the knowledge the interactions obtain from the users, we explore an approach at the step in Fig. 2-④ to memorize the knowledge properly. In IKNOW-SQL, each knowledge concept is modeled as a *key-value pair* (k, v), where the key k is the combination of both the predicted token and the input tokens that have top-K attention probabilities, and the value v is the answer that the user provides; All the knowledge concepts are then stored and managed in the knowledge bank (e.g., MongoDB). IKNOW-SQL therefore can leverage the knowledge to eliminate model uncertainties without human intervention. We posit that less human intervention can be avoided with more and more knowledge modeled and stored in the knowledge bank.

4   IKNOW-SQL

This section provides a detailed explanation of IKNOW-SQL design. We begin by explaining the confidence modeling technique, then describe the question generation process. Finally, we discuss the knowledge caching mechanism.

4.1   Difference-Based Confidence Modeling

The main observation of the inspection step is that a one-pass forward process while decoding may involve some uncertainties that the NL2SQL model likely makes mistakes. Therefore, an essential question for IKNOW-SQL is how to detect the potential errors a generated sequence has. We follow the confidence estimation techniques that appeared in the literature [10,17,22], and explore an approach to estimate model confidence at each token position.

Intuitively if the underlying NL2SQL model gives similar output values over several top predictions at a decoding step, the NL2SQL model is likely uncertain about the prediction (i.e., the low-confidence prediction). Without losing generality, we assume that the decoder of the base NL2SQL model is implemented with a vanilla recurrent neural network (RNN), and illustrate the process below.

During inference, the decoder employs the RNN network to unroll the target information. At the j-th step, the target hidden state h_j is given by

$$h_j = \mathbf{RNN}(e_{y_{j-1}}, h_{j-1}, c) \tag{1}$$

At the j-th step, a probability distribution P_j is created for all possible target vocabulary symbols. This is done by considering the embedding of the previously predicted symbol, the representation of the source context, and the hidden state,

$$t_j = g(e_{y-1}, h_j, c)$$
$$l_j = \mathbf{W}_o(t_j) \tag{2}$$
$$P_j = \mathrm{softmax}(l_j)$$

where g denotes a linear transformation, W_o is used to map t_j to logits l_j representing the raw (non-normalized) predictions for each target symbol. These logits are subsequently normalized into the output probabilities using a softmax function[1]. Thus, the 1-best symbol is selected as the predicted symbol,

$$y_j = \mathrm{argmax}(P_j) \tag{3}$$

Table 1. The templates used in IKNOW-SQL

TEMPLATES
Does the system needs to return all information about table? $\rightarrow$ KEYWORD[*]
Please select any options from the following list that the system needs to enforce as tables? $\rightarrow$ *table*
Please select any option that the system needs to enforce as conditions to join the two tables? $\rightarrow$ (*table.col*, OP, *table.col*)
Please select any option that the system needs to enforce as conditions? $\rightarrow$ (*table.col*, OP, *table.col*|VAL)
Please select any option that the system needs to enforce as conditions? $\rightarrow$ (*table.col*, OP, VAL)
Please select any option that the system needs to enforce group items with? $\rightarrow$ *table.col*
Please select any options that the system needs to enforce as a mathematical calculations when group items? $\rightarrow$ (AGG, *table.col*)
Please select any option that the system needs to enforce as conditions when group items? $\rightarrow$ (*table.col*, OP, *table.col*|VAL)
Please select any option that the system needs to enforce return information about? $\rightarrow$ *table.col*
Please select any option that the system needs to enforce as order when sort the results? $\rightarrow$ *table.col*
Please select any options from the following list that the system needs to enforce as order when sort the results? $\rightarrow$ KEYWORD[*desc*|*asc*]
Please select any options from the following list that the system needs to enforce as number of results to return? $\rightarrow$ VAL

Since the softmax probabilities are computed with the fast-growing exponential function, minor additions to the softmax inputs, i.e., the logits, can lead to substantial changes in the output distribution, the prediction probability from a softmax distribution has a poor direct correspondence to confidence [17]. Thus, to gauge confidence, we employ the raw predictions (i.e., logits) to estimate the j-th step output by using an indicator function $\mathbb{L}$,

$$\mathbb{L}_{y_j} = \begin{cases} 0 \text{ if } \mid l_j^{top_1} - l_j^{top_2} \mid < \omega \\ 1 \text{ otherwise} \end{cases} \tag{4}$$

where $l_j^{top_1}$ and $l_j^{top_2}$ are the 2-highest logits, and ω is a threshold. That is, if the difference between the 2-highest logits is less than the threshold, the prediction at the j-th step is modeled as low-confidence.

Probability-Based Confidence Modeling. In addition to the difference-based confidence measure, a more straightforward approach is to use the predicted probability to serve as the model confidence [17,36]. Namely, a prediction o_t needs user clarification if its probability is lower than a threshold p^*, i.e.,

$$p(o_t) < p^* \tag{5}$$

We also experiment IKNOW-SQL with this confidence measure in Sect. 5.

---

[1] In accordance with [11], model predictions are the weighted sum of target embeddings over output probabilities.

4.2   Template-Assisted Question Generation

The goal of the clarification question generation is to synthesize an NL expression corresponding to the generated SQL query, particularly the low-confidence situations that the confidence estimator detects. In order for users to better understand the potential error IKNOW-SQL needs to clarify, We follow the method introduced in [36] to design the question formulator in IKNOW-SQL. In this section, we provide a short description of the approach in [36] (we call the method RULE-QG in the rest of the paper) and then explain the improvements needed for the purpose of IKNOW-SQL.

The core idea of RULE-QG is to generate the clarification questions based on the SQL components that the unconfident-predictions belong to. Specifically, RULE-QG is a rule-based method, which pre-defines a seed lexicon and a set of templates for deriving questions. We adopt the idea and design our seed lexicon and templates, respectively:

- The seed lexicon defines NL descriptions for basic SQL elements in the form of $n \rightarrow t[p]$, where n is an NL phrase, t is a pre-defined syntactic category, and p is either an aggregator (e.g., avg) or an operator (e.g., >). For example, "*under* $\rightarrow$ OP[>]" defines the word "under" to describe the operator ">". RULE-QG considers four syntactic categories: AGG for aggregators, OP for operators, COL for columns and Q for generated questions.
- The templates define the production rules to derive clarification questions. Rules associated with each Q-typed item "$Q[v||$Clause$]$" constructs an NL question asking about v in Clause. The Clause represents a specific SQL component (e.g., **WHERE** age > 30), which is the necessary context to formulate meaningful questions.

IKNOW-SQL follows the methods introduced in RULE-QG but made some changes: (1) We categorize templates based on their associated Clauses, and simplify the derivation of questions by directly instantiating the NL expressions using Clause. (2) Instead of constructing simple binary questions, we leverage the pre-defined seed lexicon and the semantics of v to construct multi-choice questions. Table 1 shows the templates used in IKNOW-SQL.

4.3   Attention-Based Knowledge Acquisition

Once IKNOW-SQL received the user feedback from the interface of the question formulator, an important question for IKNOW-SQL is how to memorize the user feedback and make it preservable for the system.

Typically, storing the NL query that the user interacts with associates with the user feedback can effectively avoid repetitive interactions as shown in Fig. 1. Although intuitive, this hard one-one mapping memorization suffers from low generalizability and is extremely sensitive to language variations. Therefore, finding a more generalized way to memorize external knowledge is indispensable.

Motivated by recent works of the cache mechanism used in deep learning [12,31], we introduce an attention-based method to store the external knowledge obtained from users. The core idea of this method is to exploit the attention distribution over input tokens at a low-confidence step to define the knowledge. Without losing generality, we assume that the interaction is triggered when predicting t-th target token, in the sense that the user feedback is solicited for clarifying t-th prediction.

Specifically, we use key-value pairs to define each knowledge concept, in which the key is constructed with the following two parts,

- **Predicted token.** Since the underlying NL2SQL model is hesitant on predicting t-th token, we directly use the predicted token as part of the key.
- **Top-K input tokens.** Different token contributions vary for a specific prediction. Hence, we rank the input tokens based on the attention distribution over t-th prediction and select the tokens with top-K probabilities as another part of the key. For instance, Fig. 3 shows an example of the attention distribution of the predicted SQL query over the given input query (i.e., *Which cities do more than one employee under age 30 come from?*). For the specific ">" token, the corresponding top-5 input tokens are *"30"*, *"than"*, *"under"*, *"one"*, *"more"*.

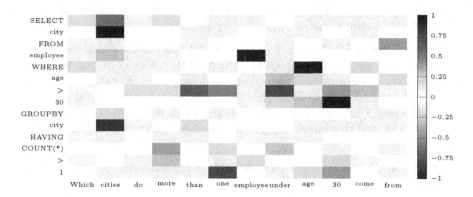

Fig. 3. An example of the attention distribution of BRIDGE model over the given NL query. The token with darker color indicates a higher probability. (Color figure online)

On the other hand, we use the answer that the user selects in the clarification question to serve as the value of the pair.

5   Experimental Evaluation

In this section, we evaluate the effectiveness of IKNOW-SQL by applying it to the state-of-the-art NL2SQL models and analyzing the experimental results.

5.1 Experimental Setup

Benchmark. We use the public SPIDER benchmark [38] to evaluate the performance of IKNOW-SQL. **Spider** is a state-of-the-art, large-scale benchmark for complex and cross-domain NL2SQL tasks. The benchmark includes 10,181 NL queries and 5,693 unique complex SQL queries on 206 databases with multiple tables covering 138 different domains. Based on the hardness levels it defined, SPIDER authors split the benchmark data into four types, namely *Easy*, *Medium*, *Hard*, and *Extra Hard*. Unlike other existing NLIDB benchmarks, SPIDER uses different databases in train and validation data sets. That is, a database schema is used exclusively for either training or validation, but not both.

Since the test set of SPIDER is hidden behind an evaluation server, the experiments we perform are on the validation set of the SPIDER benchmark.

Evaluation Metrics. We measure the query *exact-match accuracy (Acc$_{em}$)*[2] and the *effective interaction rate (Rate$_{ei}$)* in our experiments.

Exact-Match Accuracy. If the generated SQL query exactly matches the "gold" SQL after normalization, then the translation is said to be accurate. It is a performance lower bound since a semantically correct SQL query may differ from the "gold" SQL query syntactically. This metric is the same as the *Exact Match Accuracy* metric suggested by SPIDER.

Effective Interaction Ratio. To assess the efficiency of the confidence estimation (i.e., error detection) process in IKNOW-SQL, we measure the number of effective interaction rounds. This is done by determining the ratio of the actual number of errors detected by the error detection method to the total number of detected errors. Each time a false alarm is triggered, there will be an interaction with the user, and this metric reflects the number of such interactions.

NL2SQL Models. We apply IKNOW-SQL to the following three state-of-the-art machine learning-based NL2SQL models:

- BRIDGE [20] represents the question and schema in a tagged sequence where a subset of the fields are augmented with cell values mentioned in the question.
- GAP [28] is a pre-trained model that was built upon RAT-SQL [33]. The RAT-SQL model is a schema transformer-based model that is relation-aware, and it utilizes a self-attention mechanism to enhance the encoding capacity.
- LGESQL [4] a line graph enhanced text-to-SQL model to mine the underlying relational features without constructing metapaths.

5.2 Experimental Results

We first present the results of the simulation evaluation over the public benchmark, and then we report a user study to assess the effectiveness of IKNOW-SQL.

---

[2] We use the terms exact-match accuracy and translation accuracy interchangeably.

Table 2. The simulation evaluation of IKNOW-SQL on the validation set of SPIDER. "IKNOW-SQL$^{\omega=X}$" denotes IKNOW-SQL with difference-based confidence estimation approach (threshold at ω).

NL2SQL Model	BRIDGE [20]		GAP [28]		LGESQL [4]	
	Acc_{em}	$Rate_{ie}$	Acc_{em}	$Rate_{ie}$	Acc_{em}	$Rate_{ie}$
w/o interaction	70.0	–	71.8	–	75.0	–
IKNOW-SQL$^{\omega=2}$	74.3	67.7	73.2	63.2	84.9	66.7
IKNOW-SQL$^{\omega=3}$	76.0	**68.8**	75.8	64.3	86.4	67.2
IKNOW-SQL$^{\omega=4}$	78.1	68.2	77.1	64.1	88.3	62.8
IKNOW-SQL$^{\omega=6}$	**80.5**	67.2	79.9	60.8	90.4	49.2

Simulation Evaluation. In simulation evaluation, each model interacts with a simulated user, who always gives the correct answer based on the ground-truth SQL query for each clarification question. If the model fails to generate the ground truth in three consecutive interaction turns, then it is regarded as an error for that particular turn.

The results of all the models on the validation set of the SPIDER benchmark are presented in Table 2, both with and without the application of IKNOW-SQL. These results demonstrate that IKNOW-SQL can significantly enhance the overall performance of the three NL2SQL models, and the magnitude of this improvement becomes more noticeable as the threshold ω value increases. Notably, IKNOW-SQL provides a significant performance boost to the BRIDGE model, increasing its exact match accuracy from 70% to 80.5% at threshold 6, and obtaining 68.8% effective interaction rate at threshold 3.

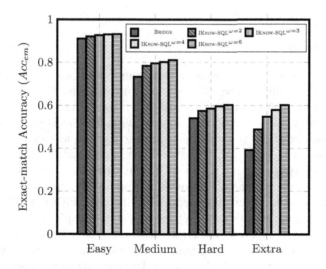

Fig. 4. Breakdown results of BRIDGE model on the validation set of SPIDER.

Next, we carry out further experiments on IKNOW-SQL by applying to BRIDGE. Figure 4 displays the translation accuracy breakdown for different SQL difficulties on the SPIDER validation set. The results reveal that the performance of BRIDGE has improved across all four categories. In particular, when using IKNOW-SQL with the "$\omega = 6$" setting, BRIDGE achieves an exact-match accuracy of 93.2% for the "Easy" queries (248 out of 1034), and a 60.2% accuracy for the "Extra Hard" queries (164 out of 1034 queries). We believe that since BRIDGE can perform well on simpler queries, IKNOW-SQL can significantly enhance its performance on more complex ones. However, there is only a minimal improvement observed when IKNOW-SQL is applied to BRIDGE. The reason behind this may be the fact that BRIDGE designs with a simple sequence decoder that does not inherently support nested queries. This issue is also evident in the nested queries within the "Extra Hard" category.

In order to assess the efficacy of the confidence estimator module in IKNOW-SQL, we compare the performance of IKNOW-SQL with BRIDGE with a probability-based approached, as we discussed in Sect. 4.1. The results are shown in Table 3, and they indicate that IKNOW-SQL's difference-based approach outperforms the probability-based method in terms of both translation accuracy and effective interaction rate. These findings illustrate the effectiveness of the difference-based approach within the interactive paradigm.

Table 3. Evaluation on two different confidence estimation methods.

Metrics	IKNOW-SQL				IKNOW-SQL$^{p=X}$	
	$\omega = 2$	$\omega = 3$	$\omega = 4$	$\omega = 6$	$p = 0.95$	$p = 0.8$
$Acc_{em}\%$	74.3	76.0	78.1	**80.5**	**77.1**	73.8
$Rate_{ei}\%$	67.7	**68.8**	68.2	67.2	52.7	**68.2**

5.3   User Study

In the rest of this section, we report a human user study to assess IKNOW-SQL. Our evaluation setting follows [36]: We randomly sampled 20 NL-SQL examples from the SPIDER validation set, and asked ten computer science students who have knowledge of SQL to task on each query with IKNOW-SQL. Firstly, participants were briefed about the study and then used a toy query to demonstrate the whole process. We recorded the results of each participant for the given queries.

Figure 5 illustrates that IKNOW-SQL can correctly translate most of the "Easy" queries (an average of 18 out of 20 queries) as reported by the participants. However, the participants reported difficulties with the "Hard" queries and the interactions with IKNOW-SQL were not very helpful in those cases. Furthermore, we conducted brief interviews with each participant, and one participant expressed confusion about certain words returned by IKNOW-SQL during the interactions, even though the natural language interface made it easier to query and interact with the underlying database.

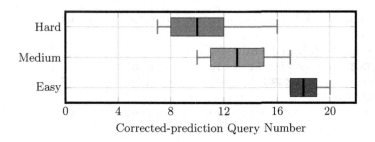

Fig. 5. Box plot of corrected-prediction count for different difficulties of queries.

The research findings indicate that an interactive natural language interface can enhance user interactions with databases. Nevertheless, additional improvements might be needed to effectively manage more intricate queries.

5.4   Error Analysis

To better understand IKNOW-SQL, we examine the failed cases and analyze the potential reason. We identify the following two major causes for the failures.

– **Clause Existence Problem.** One of the major failures is caused by the limitation of the implementation of the confidence estimator module. That is, IKNOW-SQL in the current setting can only detect the potential errors that occurred in a specific SQL clause, it is unable to detect if the potential error is for the existence of a certain clause. For instance, an example in SPIDER,

   NL Query: *Find name of the employee who got the highest one time bonus.*
   Predicted SQL of IKnow-SQL:
   ```
   SELECT employee.name
   FROM employee JOIN evaluation
   GROUP BY employee.name
   ORDER BY evaluation.bonus DESC LIMIT 1
   ```
   Gold SQL: `SELECT employee.name`
   ```
   FROM employee JOIN evaluation
   ORDER BY evaluation.bonus DESC LIMIT 1
   ```

   The **GROUP BY** clause is unnecessary for this prediction. Such failures may be avoided if finding a way to enhance the confidence estimator module to support the error detection on the existence (or nonexistence) of certain clauses.
– **Domain Knowledge Problem.** Other major failures are caused by the limited understanding of the underlying NL2SQL model over domain-specific semantics expressed in the NL queries. Since most of the existing NL2SQL models are based on pre-trained language models for semantic parsing work, it may not be possible to capture the semantics that is specific to certain databases. For example, following is an example from SPIDER validation set,

NL Query: *What is average, minimum, maximum age for all French singers?*

Predicted SQL of IKnow-SQL:

```
SELECT avg(age), min(age), max(age)
FROM singer WHERE is_male = 'French'
```

Gold SQL:

```
SELECT avg(age), min(age), max(age)
FROM singer WHERE country = 'France'
```

Since the model may fail to link the column "country" with the mentioned term "*French*" by token-level matching, the model mistakenly chooses the column "is_male" for the **WHERE** clause instead. To some extent, such failures can be mitigated by examining the data stored in databases for the schema linking process, but in the view of adapting to a new domain, providing some more external knowledge may be indispensable.

6 Conclusion

This paper presented IKNOW-SQL, a novel approach designed to facilitate seamless access to underlying databases for end users of web applications. IKNOW-SQL introduces a unified framework for any NL2SQL models to improve their translation accuracy through minimal interactions. IKNOW-SQL first leverages the NL2SQL model to get a raw prediction for a given user query. IKNOW-SQL then detects some potential errors in the prediction by measuring its confidence. Next, IKNOW-SQL synthesizes clarification questions to solicit user feedback. Finally, IKNOW-SQL memorizes the knowledge provided by the user for each interaction and outputs the final prediction until no low confidence is detected. Experimental results showed that IKNOW-SQL can significantly improve the performance of existing state-of-the-art NL2SQL models with less user feedback.

References

1. Androutsopoulos, I., et al.: Natural language interfaces to databases - an introduction. Nat. Lang. Eng. **1**(1), 29–81 (1995)
2. Baik, C., et al.: Bridging the semantic gap with SQL query logs in natural language interfaces to databases. In: ICDE (2019)
3. Bogin, B., et al.: Representing schema structure with graph neural networks for text-to-SQL parsing. In: ACL (2019)
4. Cao, R., et al.: LGESQL: line graph enhanced text-to-SQL model with mixed local and non-local relations. In: ACL (2021)
5. Castaldo, N., Daniel, F., Matera, M., Zaccaria, V.: Conversational data exploration. In: Bakaev, M., Frasincar, F., Ko, I.-Y. (eds.) ICWE 2019. LNCS, vol. 11496, pp. 490–497. Springer, Cham (2019). https://doi.org/10.1007/978-3-030-19274-7_34
6. Chaurasia, S., et al.: Dialog for language to code. In: IJCNLP, pp. 175–180 (2017)
7. Desolda, G., et al.: Rapid prototyping of chatbots for data exploration. In: BCNC, pp. 5–10 (2021)

8. Fan, Y., et al.: Gar: a generate-and-rank approach for natural language to SQL translation. In: ICDE (2023)
9. Feng, L., Lu, H.: Integrating database and world wide web technologies. WWWJ **1**(2), 73–86 (1998)
10. Gal, Y., Ghahramani, Z.: Dropout as a Bayesian approximation: representing model uncertainty in deep learning. In: ICML, vol. 48, pp. 1050–1059 (2016)
11. Goyal, K., et al.: Differentiable scheduled sampling for credit assignment. In: ACL, pp. 366–371 (2017)
12. Grave, E., et al.: Improving neural language models with a continuous cache. In: ICLR (2017)
13. Guo, J., et al.: Towards complex text-to-SQL in cross-domain database with intermediate representation. In: ACL (2019)
14. Gur, I., et al.: DialSQL: dialogue based structured query generation. In: ACL (2018)
15. He, H., et al.: Towards deeper understanding of the search interfaces of the deep web. WWWJ **2**, 133–155 (2007)
16. He, L., et al.: Human-in-the-loop parsing. In: EMNLP, pp. 2337–2342 (2016)
17. Hendrycks, D., Gimpel, K.: A baseline for detecting misclassified and out-of-distribution examples in neural networks. In: ICLR (2017)
18. Li, F., Jagadish, H.V.: Constructing an interactive natural language interface for relational databases. PVLDB **8**(1), 73–84 (2014)
19. Li, J., et al.: Graphix-T5: mixing pre-trained transformers with graph-aware layers for text-to-SQL parsing. In: AAAI, pp. 13076–13084 (2023)
20. Lin, X.V., et al.: Bridging textual and tabular data for cross-domain text-to-SQL semantic parsing. In: EMNLP (2020)
21. Nakatsuji, M., et al.: Knowledge-aware response selection with semantics underlying multi-turn open-domain conversations. In: World Wide Web, pp. 1–16 (2023)
22. Niehues, J., et al.: Modeling confidence in sequence-to-sequence models. In: INLG, pp. 575–583 (2019)
23. OpenAI: GPT-4 technical report. CoRR (2023)
24. Pourreza, M., Rafiei, D.: DIN-SQL: decomposed in-context learning of text-to-SQL with self-correction. CoRR (2023)
25. Saha, D., et al.: ATHENA: an ontology-driven system for natural language querying over relational data stores. PVLDB **9**(12), 1209–1220 (2016)
26. Scholak, T., et al.: PICARD: parsing incrementally for constrained auto-regressive decoding from language models. In: EMNLP (2021)
27. Sen, J., et al.: ATHENA++: natural language querying for complex nested SQL queries. PVLDB **13**(11), 2747–2759 (2020)
28. Shi, P., et al.: Learning contextual representations for semantic parsing with generation-augmented pre-training. In: AAAI (2021)
29. Simitsis, A., et al.: Précis: from unstructured keywords as queries to structured databases as answers. PVLDB **17**(1), 117–149 (2008)
30. Su, Y., et al.: Natural language interfaces with fine-grained user interaction: a case study on web APIs. In: SIGIR, pp. 855–864 (2018)
31. Sukhbaatar, S., et al.: End-to-end memory networks. In: NeurIPS, pp. 2440–2448 (2015)
32. Touvron, H., et al.: LLaMA: open and efficient foundation language models. CoRR (2023)
33. Wang, B., et al.: RAT-SQL: relation-aware schema encoding and linking for text-to-SQL parsers. In: ACL (2020)

34. Xu, X., et al.: SQLNet: generating structured queries from natural language without reinforcement learning. CoRR (2017)
35. Yao, Z., et al.: Interactive semantic parsing for if-then recipes via hierarchical reinforcement learning. In: AAAI, pp. 2547–2554 (2019)
36. Yao, Z., et al.: Model-based interactive semantic parsing: a unified framework and a text-to-SQL case study. In: EMNLP, pp. 5446–5457 (2019)
37. Yu, T., et al.: TypeSQL: knowledge-based type-aware neural text-to-SQL generation. In: NAACL (2018)
38. Yu, T., et al.: CoSQL: a conversational text-to-SQL challenge towards cross-domain natural language interfaces to databases. In: EMNLP (2019)
39. Zettlemoyer, L.S., Collins, M.: Learning to map sentences to logical form: structured classification with probabilistic categorial grammars. In: UAI (2005)
40. Zhang, R., et al.: Editing-based SQL query generation for cross-domain context-dependent questions. In: EMNLP, pp. 5337–5348 (2019)

Task-Driven Neural Natural Language Interface to Database

Yuquan Yang, Qifan Zhang, and Junjie Yao[✉]

East China Normal University, Shanghai, China
{51215901036,52194501005}@stu.ecnu.edu.cn, junjie.yao@cs.ecnu.edu.cn

Abstract. Natural language querying offers an intuitive and user-friendly interface. A Natural Language Interface over databases, often termed as "Text-to-SQL", involves translating a query posed in natural language into a corresponding SQL query for structured databases. A significant number of recent methodologies, anchored in the pre-trained language model and encode-decode paradigms, have been developed to address this task. Yet, existing approaches often grapple with generating accurate SQL queries, especially in scenarios that involve multiple values and intricate column calculations.

In this study, we present a task-driven Text-to-SQL model. This model breaks down the SQL prediction process into specific sub-tasks based on the unique task requirements of the query. Specifically, we amalgamate structure prediction, value extraction, and column relationship prediction into a cohesive workflow. The model is designed to construct target SQL queries incrementally, with each sub-task building upon the outcomes of its predecessors. Additionally, we introduce a novel filtering mechanism to refine and re-order candidates produced during the beam search phase. We substantiate the efficacy of our model using public datasets, showcasing its adeptness in both English and Chinese contexts.

Keywords: Text-to-SQL · Semantic Parsing

1 Introduction

The core concept of the Natural Language Interface to Database (NLIDB) is to enable users to retrieve pertinent data from relational databases without the necessity of understanding specific database languages like the Structured Query Language (SQL). Essentially, NLIDB serves as a bridge, converting general user inquiries into SQL queries and furnishing a seamless interface for user-database interactions. As the volume of stored data continues to surge, so does the demand for intuitive tools that empower non-specialist users to engage with these databases. NLIDB stands at the forefront of this trend, holding the promise of transforming user-database interactions and democratizing data analysis and retrieval for a broader audience.

Figure 1(a) depicts the Text-to-SQL task. Given a natural language question, denoted as N, and a relational database D, a seq-to-seq PLM is utilized to generate the target SQL query Q under the input information from N and D.

F. Zhang et al. (Eds.): WISE 2023, LNCS 14306, pp. 659–673, 2023.
https://doi.org/10.1007/978-981-99-7254-8_51

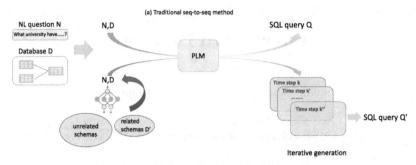

Fig. 1. Illustration of the Text-to-SQL tasks

There has been significant research in the field of Natural Language Interface to Databases (NLIDB) over the past few decades. The early approaches to building NLIDBs were based on rule-based systems [7,9,15], which used hand-crafted rules to map natural language queries to database queries. However, these systems had limited coverage and were difficult to maintain.

More recent approaches to NLIDB focus on neural machine translation approaches and pre-trained large language model. One such approach is the use of semantic parsing, which involves mapping natural language queries to structured representations that can be used to query databases. Several systems have been developed using this approach, including [1,2,5,22]. Although strategies mentioned above are effective for encoder-based pre-trained language models, recent studies have shown that the text-to-text PLM T5 [18] is highly effective in the text-to-SQL task. To improve the accuracy of text-to-SQL models, researchers have designed methods such as the constrained decoding process PICARD [19] and the injection of structural information of database into T5 [11].

In this study, we address the aforementioned challenges by introducing a task-guided enhanced transformer-based model. This model is equipped with modules for SQL keyword prediction, numeric value extraction, and column calculation generation. Our objective is to promote the model's acquisition of authentic SQL knowledge, deterring it from merely detecting pseudo-patterns. We simplify model training by segmenting the learning process into multiple manageable stages. Our approach is illustrated in Fig. 1(b). We employ schema pre-filtering prior to the seq-to-seq PLM. The initial relational database, denoted as D, is substituted with pertinent schemas D'. This substitution minimizes superfluous data, enabling the seq-to-seq PLM to hone in on schema items relevant to the natural language query N. Furthermore, our model utilizes a task-driven iterative generation, bolstering the quality of the SQL query Q' through multiple generative modules.

The contributions of this paper can be summarized as follows:

1. The introduction of an innovative training methodology that incorporates task-specific guidance, thereby amplifying the comprehension and decoding capacities of PLMs.
2. Enhancement of NLIDB model accuracy, particularly in intricate real-world computational contexts.
3. Comprehensive experimental evaluations across cross-domain benchmarks in both Chinese and English settings, underscoring the robustness and efficacy of our model.

2   Related Work

Natural Language Interface: NLIDB is a broader concept that encompasses all approaches to building natural language interfaces for databases. NLIDBs can use a variety of techniques, such as semantic parsing, machine learning, and rule-based systems, to translate natural language queries into structured queries that can be executed on a database. NLIDBs can generate SQL queries as well as other types of queries or actions, depending on the application [16].

Text-to-SQL is often regarded as a machine translation task, and seq2seq models are commonly used for this task, e.g., IRnet [5] adopts a neural model based on grammar to generate an intermediate representation, which connects natural language and SQL. Global-GNN [1], RAT-SQL [22], and LGESQL [2] utilizes graph neural network to encode various relations between the database schema and NL question. To achieve domain-generalization and greater robustness for NLIDB, some works explore the schema linking module. [8]re-exams the role of schema link in text-to-SQL. [23] and ISESL-SQL [13] leverage the rich knowledge in large-scale pre-trained language models to construct a schema linking graph, which enhances the robustness of the text-to-SQL model under challenging settings such as synonym substitution.

Benchmarks: Benchmarks for NLIDB have rapidly developed, GeoQuery [27] collects 880 natural language questions and constructs a relational database schema with related SQL queries for questions. The Spider [26] benchmark contains more than ten thousand natural language questions and thousands of distinct SQL queries over hundreds of databases. Additionally, Spider is a large-scale benchmark built from 138 different domains, which greatly promotes the development of cross-domain NLIDB. Other cross-domain datasets focus on particular aspects of the NLIDB task. Spider-Syn [3] challenges model's robustness to synonyms. Spider-DK [4] explores the capabilities of models at cross-domain generalisation. Furthermore, datasets such as DuSQL [24] are specifically designed for real-world scenarios, such as business intelligence and consulting, which can be extremely complex and involve numerical computations, column calculations and other elements not included in the Spider benchmark.

Matching Models: Graph-based encoders, as presented in works such as [1, 2, 22], are adept at delineating relationships between database schema components. Nevertheless, their efficacy is heavily contingent on the meticulous design of these relationships, necessitating domain-specific expertise for each unique database [10]. A salient challenge is the misalignment of representation spaces between graph neural networks and pre-trained language models. This discrepancy impedes the seamless integration of sophisticated pre-trained generative models, thereby constraining their expressive potential.

Decoders grounded in the principles of the abstract syntax tree, highlighted in studies such as [22,23], ensure the generation of syntactically coherent SQL queries. However, these methods demand bespoke transformation grammars. This specificity not only increases the overhead when accommodating new SQL structures but also precludes their compatibility with generative pre-trained language models.

A recent surge of interest has gravitated towards text-to-text pre-trained language models, with models like T5 demonstrating superior performance as noted in [10,11,19]. Yet, our investigations reveal an evident shortfall in these models. Specifically, they struggle to precisely extract numerical values and establish calculation relationships between columns, especially in intricate real-world scenarios, such as those prevalent in business intelligence contexts with multifaceted calculations.

3   Method

3.1   Problem Definition

Given a natural language question $Q = (q_1, q_2, \ldots, q_{|Q|})$ and a schema $S = <C, T>$ for a relational database D, our goal is to generate the corresponding SQL query y. Specifically, the schema includes multiple tables $T = (t_1, t_2, \ldots, t_{|T|})$, as well as multiple columns $C = (c_1^1, \ldots, c_1^{n_1}, \ldots, c_i^1 \ldots c_i^{n_i}, \ldots, c_T^1 \ldots c_T^{n_{|T|}})$ corresponding to each table, where n_i is the number of columns in the i_{th} table.

3.2   Overview

The framework of our approach is shown in Fig. 2. Our proposed model is built on the transformer-based framework, which has been widely used in natural language processing tasks. We adopt an encoder-decoder mechanism to generate the target SQL query. The input of encoder includes the natural language query as well as all schema items related to the natural language query. In order to get such related schema items, a cross-encoder is used to classify the schema items. At the decoder side, we do not directly generate the target SQL query but divide the learning process into several easily learnable stages, encouraging the model to first complete several subtasks such as SQL keyword prediction, value extraction, and column calculation prediction, before finally generating the complete SQL query.

3.3   Encoder

Previous works have shown that schema linking plays an important role in domain generalization [23]. Incorrect schema linking can further affect the

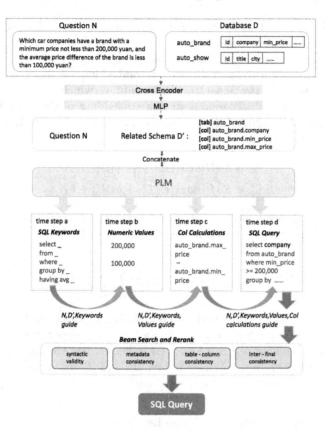

Fig. 2. Task-driven Text-to-SQL Framework.

performance of downstream tasks. Therefore, we transform explicit schema linking into implicit linking, which no longer links schema items with individual query tokens, but rather directly predicts the association between schema items and the entire query, implicitly allowing the model to learn the mapping between schema items and the query.

To achieve the aforementioned implicit linking, we adopted the setup used in RESDSQL [10] on the encoder side. Before feeding the encoder with the query and database schema inputs, a cross-encoder is used to classify the schema items, filtering out irrelevant table columns, and sorting relevant schema items according to the predicted probabilities. This approach allows the seq2seq model to implicitly learn the location information of the schema and the mapping between schema items and query tokens.

The NL query and schema items of database are concatenated as input X and fed into a pre-trained RoBERTa [14] encoder. It is arranged as:

$$X = [q_1, q_2, ..., q_{|Q|} | t_1 : c_1^1, ..., c_1^{n_1} | ... | c_T^1 ... c_T^{n_{|T|}}]$$
(1)

A two-layer BiLSTM [6] and a non-linear fully connected layer are used to aggregate each token corresponding to a table or column, obtaining a complete embedding for each corresponding schema item.

The embedding for the i_{th} table and the embedding for the k_{th} column in the i_{th} table are fed into two separate MLP modules, which output the predicted probabilities $\widehat{y}_i$ and $\widehat{y}_i^k$. T_i represents the embedding of the i_{th} table and C_i^k represents the embedding of the k_{th} column in the i_{th} table. U_1, b_1, U_2, b_2 are all trainable parameters.

$$\widehat{y}_i = Softmax((T_i U_1 + b_1)U_2 + b_2) \tag{2}$$

$$\widehat{y}_i^k = Softmax((C_i^k U_3 + b_3)U_4 + b_4) \tag{3}$$

To address the extremely imbalanced label distribution among schema items, focal loss [12] is applied as the loss function for the classifier:

$$L_1 = \frac{1}{|T|} \sum_{i=1}^{|T|} FL(y_i, \widehat{y}_i) + \frac{1}{|C|} \sum_{i=1}^{N} \sum_{k=1}^{n_i} FL(y_i^k, \widehat{y}_i^k) \tag{4}$$

The loss function is composed of the focal loss for tables and columns. Here, y_i represents the label for the i_{th} table and y_i^k represents the label for the k_{th} column of the i_{th} table, where a label of 1 indicates that the corresponding item is relevant to the natural language query. $|T|$ and $|C|$ represent the number of tables and the number of columns respectively.

3.4   Task-Driven Enhanced Decoder

Consider how humans write SQL, they often decompose complex SQL statements into multiple subtasks, such as filtering relevant columns, considering the SQL structure, and analyzing column calculations, rather than directly considering the entire SQL statement. However, traditional seq2seq models are mostly trained to directly output the target SQL, which makes it difficult for the model to achieve satisfactory results due to the significant gap between natural language and SQL expression. Additionally, the optimization objective of the seq2seq model is to maximize the conditional probability of the target sequence given the source sequence, which means that the model treats the prediction of key information and non-key information equally:

$$h = Encode_\gamma(x) \tag{5}$$

$$y = Decode_\delta(h) \tag{6}$$

$$\max_{\gamma, \delta} logp(\gamma, \delta)(y|x) = \sum_{i=1}^{|y|} logp\gamma, \delta(y_i|y_{1:i-1}, x) \tag{7}$$

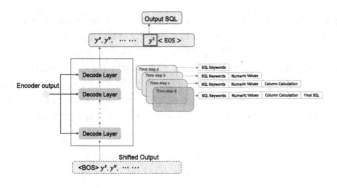

Fig. 3. The architecture of decoder.

Here, x represents input tokens and y refers to output tokens, $|y|$ is the max length of generation. γ, δ respectively refers to the parameters of the encoder and decoder. As a result, the model is easily trained to learn simple pseudo-patterns instead of learning the meta-knowledge of how to write SQL effectively.

Thus, we decompose the main task of generating SQL into several related subtasks: (1) generating the skeletal structure containing only SQL keywords based on the semantics of the question; (2) extracting values for the SQL query based on numerical expressions in the query; (3) predicting columns that have a computational relationship based on the query and skeletal structure; and (4) filling in the skeletal structure with data from the input sequence and the predicted results from the second and third stages. Hence, the output is composed of four parts:

$$y = y^s |y^v |y^r |y^t \tag{8}$$

y^s refers to skeletal structure containing only SQL keywords, y^v refers to numeric values in SQL, y^r refers to column calculations and y^t represents the final whole SQL query. Details are shown in Table 1.

Table 1. An example from DuSQL's training data

NL query	Which car companies have a brand with a minimum price not less than 200,000 yuan, and the average price difference between the highest and lowest prices of the brand is less than 100,000 yuan?
y^s	select _ from _ where _ group by _ having avg _
y^v	200000 100000
y^r	max_price - min_price
y^t	select company from auto_brand where min_price $\geq$ 200000 group by company having avg (max_price - min_price) < 100000

Considering the inherent characteristic of the Transformer decoder that the generation of the k_{th} token depends not only on the input but also on the previously generated $k-1$ tokens. We guide the decoder to generate the results of each task in sequence, starting with the first task and then proceeding to the second and third tasks, before generating the complete SQL statement. During this process, the results of each preceding task serve as guidance for the generation of the subsequent task. Thus, the final loss function of our seq2seq model is:

$$L_2 = \frac{1}{N} \sum_{i=1}^{N} p(y^s, y^v, y^r, y^t | x_i) \tag{9}$$

where N refers to the number of training samples and x_i refers to the i_{th} input.

To demonstrate the effectiveness of our model in an intuitive manner, Fig. 4 illustrates two examples taken from the DuSQL development set along with the corresponding SQL queries predicted by RESDSQL and our model, both of which are trained on the base scale. We can observe that both models can accurately predict the structure of SQL queries. However, when there are multiple numerical values in the SQL statements, our model can better capture each value and generate the correct SQL query. For example, in the first case, the natural language query contains two values that are associated with different schema items, and RESDSQL only captures the semantics of "the number of countries with a nut intake of 5 or more", but ignores "per capita nut intake is greater than 0.05 kg". In contrast, our model successfully captured the semantics related to both numerical values and generated the correct SQL query.

Moreover, in scenarios involving complex column calculations, our model can better predict the calculation relationship between columns. In the second case, the query requires to calculate the total number of students, including both undergraduate and graduate students. While RESDSQL understands the concept of the total number and predicts an addition relationship between columns, it generates a column calculation of "number of graduate students + number of graduate students". In contrast, our model successfully predicts that the total number of students is calculated as "num_undergraduate_students + num_graduate_students".

#Case1 NL Query	Which countries have a nut intake of 5 or more among the nut intake of more than 0.05 kg per capita, and what is the minimum per capita nut intake in the world for these nut intakes?
RESDSQL	select country , min (WorldPerCapita_Intake) from Nut_Intake group by country having count (*) >= 5 ✗
OUR'S	select country, min (WorldPerCapita_Intake) from Nut Intake where PerCapita _Intake > 0.05 group by country having count (*) >= 5 ✓
#Case2 NL Query	Which universities have a total student population not lower than the average population of all universities?
RESDSQL	select name from universities where Num_graduate_students + Num_graduate _students >= (select avg (Num_graduate_students + Num_graduate_students) from universities) ✗
OUR'S	select name from universities where Num_undergraduate_students + Num_graduate_students >= (select avg (Num_undergraduate_students + Num_graduate_students) from universities) ✓

Fig. 4. Case studies on the DuSQL dev set.

3.5   Filtering and Sorting Mechanism

Different from AST-based decoders, our model is better suited for generative pre-trained models but sometimes generates invalid SQL queries. To address this issue, some works propose the use of execution-guided SQL selection [10,21], which executes beam search during the decoding process and selects the first executable SQL query in the beam as the final result. However, some benchmarks do not support queries. To solve this problem, we propose a filtering and sorting mechanism that consists of four stages: syntax validity check, metadata consistency check, table-column consistency check and inter-final consistency check.

Before performing the four checks, we initialize the weights of candidate queries $\{W_i\}_{i=1}^n$ based on the results of beam search. Next, we conduct syntax parsing by tokenizing the predicted SQL statement into separate words, symbols, and other units. Through the application of a predefined set of grammar rules, we parse the tokenized statement to ascertain its structure and the relationships between its components.

In the first stage, we check the syntax and structure of each component to ensure that it is valid according to the SQL language specification. If it is invalid, the candidate query is filtered. Next, we check whether all tables and columns have corresponding database metadata and whether each column can be correctly mapped to its corresponding table. If it is invalid, the candidate query is filtered. Then, we check whether candidate query contains all numeric numbers and column calculations in the generation context of intermediate steps. If it contains, we increase its weight by adding β, β is a hyper-parameter representing the importance of inter-final consistency. Finally, we select the candidate SQL query that appears first after filtering and ranking. The overall process of filtering and sorting is illustrated in Algorithm 1.

Algorithm 1. Candidate SQL queries sorting

Input: Candidate SQL queries $Q\{q_1, q_2, ..., q_n\}$, Generation context of
      intermediate steps $P\{p_1, p_2, ..., p_n\}$
Output: One SQL query

1 Initialize the weights of SQL queries
  $W\{w_1, w_2, ..., w_n\} \leftarrow \{W_i\}_{i=1}^n := \{\alpha \cdot \frac{1}{i}\}_{i=1}^n;$
2 // α is a hyper-parameter representing the importance the
  initial sorting.;
3 **foreach** q_i, w_i *in* Q, W **do**
4 | Parse q_i with *sql_metadata* package;
5 | **if** *check syntax validity = false* **then**
6 | | $w_i := -\infty;$
7 | **end**
8 | **if** *check metadata consistency = false* **then**
9 | | $w_i := -\infty;$
10 | **end**
11 | **if** *check table-column consistency = false* **then**
12 | | $w_i := -\infty;$
13 | **end**
14 | **if** *check inter-final consistency = true* **then**
15 | | $w_i + = \beta;$
16 | **end**
17 | Rank Q according to W, and output the top SQL query;
18 **end**

---

4 Empirical Study

4.1 Experiment Setup

Datasets: We conduct extensive experiments on Two challenging public benchmarks.

1. **Spider** [26] is a large-scale cross-domain text-to-SQL benchmark, which contains 10,181 questions and 5,693 SQL queries, across 200 databases, covering 138 different domains. The training set of Spider contains 7,000 examples, and the development set contains 1,034 examples.
2. **DuSQL** [24] is a pragmatic and large-scale text-to-SQL dataset that contains 23,797 question-SQL pairs, 200 databases, and 813 tables belonging to more than 160 domains. For complex natural language queries, Chinese is more flexible and varied than English, making it more difficult for models to understand. Additionally, compared to the Spider, DuSQL includes more scenarios that are closer to real-world applications.

Baselines: We compare our model with several state of the art methods.

1. **IRNet** [5] proposes an intermediate representation called SemQL to bridge NL and SQL.

2. **RAT-SQL** [22] combines global reasoning over schema items and query words using relation-aware self-attention.
3. **T5** [18] is a pre-trained large-scale language model that unifies all tasks in an end-to-end manner and achieves good performance on Text-to-SQL task.
4. **T5+PICARD** [19] rejects inadmissible tokens to constrain the decoders to generate valid SQL utterances.
5. **RESDSQL** [10]decouples the schema linking and the skeleton parsing and achieves good performance.

Evaluation Metrics. Following [26], we apply Exact Match (EM) and Execution Accuracy (EX) to measure the performance of our model.

1. **Exact Match(EM)** The exact match accuracy is used to measure the consistency between the ground-truth SQL query and the predicted SQL query. Specifically, both the predicted SQL and the ground truth are parsed into normalized data structures, and the predicted SQL is considered correct only if every part of the SQL (excluding values) is predicted correctly. However, the EM metric does not consider whether the predicted values are correct, and it cannot handle cases where multiple SQL statements are valid for the same natural language expression [17].
2. **Execution Accuracy (EX)** The execution accuracy measures the effectiveness of the predicted SQL query by comparing the output results of executing it on the relational database with those of the ground-truth SQL query. It is deemed correct only when the predicted query produces identical output as the ground-truth query. The execution accuracy thus reflects the validity, executability, and ability to return desired results of the predicted SQL query. Since DuSQL benchmark does not support actual querying of databases, we replaced EX with EM (including value) as the standard for evaluation, which is more rigorous than EM (excluding value).

Implement Details. The effectiveness of our model is evaluated on the version of T5-Base with approximately 800M parameters. We set the max input length as 512 and the generation max length as 256. We fine-tune our model with Adafactor [20] with a cosine decayed learning rate of 1e-4, batch size of 32. During the decoding phase, we set the beam search size to 8, and the first executable SQL statement is selected as the predicted result. To adapt to the Chinese benchmark, DuSQL, we replace T5-base with multilingual T5-base [25]. Additionally, as DuSQL does not support querying the database directly, we propose a filtering and re-ranking mechanism to select suitable SQL queries, and the hyper-parameters α, β are set to 5. All of our experiments are conducted on one NVIDIA Tesla A100 GPU.

4.2 Results on DuSQL

Figure 5 shows the performance of our model and other competitive models on DuSQL benchmark. Upon observation of the results, our model achieves an EM (including values) of 77.2% and an EM (excluding values) of 85.8% on the development set of DuSQL, which represents a significant improvement over strong baselines. Moreover, our model achieves an improvement of 3% and 2.6% in EM (including values) and EM (excluding values) over the multilingual version of T5 [25] that also used the RESDSQL [10] encoder on base scale. This demonstrates the effectiveness of our proposed enhanced task-guided decoder.

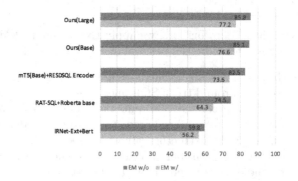

Fig. 5. Evaluation results on DuSQL.

4.3   Results on Spider

Table 2 displays EM and EX results on Spider dataset. First, we demonstrate that our model achieves great performance on the challenging large-scale cross-domain benchmark. Compared with T5-large, our model on base scale brings 4.9% EM and 7.8% EX absolute improvements, which indicates our method can better tap into the capability of a large-scale pre-trained language model. On the Spider dataset, our model shows only a slight improvement over RESDSQL, in contrast to the strong performance observed on DuSQL. This discrepancy may be attributable to the paucity of examples involving numerical and column calculations in the training and development sets of RESDSQL, whereas DuSQL comprises more intricate calculation tasks that are better aligned with real-world scenarios, including business intelligence and consulting. This suggests that our approach may have a stronger impact in real-world scenarios, particularly in business contexts involving complex calculations.

4.4   Component Analysis

To better analyze the function of each component of our model, we take an ablation study on DuSQL, the result of which is shown in Fig. 6 and Table 3. Figure 3 shows that removing all tasks will lead to a decrease of 2.94% EM (excluding values) and 2.46% EM(including values) and removing each subtask will result in a certain degree of performance degradation. Table 3 shows the impact of removing each subtask on the EM(including value) of different components of the SQL

Table 2. Evaluation results on Spider.

Approach	EM	EX
IRNet	61.9	–
RAT-SQL	69.7	–
T5-large	67.0	69.3
T5-large+PICARD	69.1	72.9
RESDSQL (base)	71.7	**77.9**
Ours (base)	**71.9**	77.1

statement. According to the results, it is observed that removing each subtask leads to a certain degree of performance degradation in different components of the SQL queries. Specifically, removing the column calculation prediction task has a relatively larger impact on the **WHERE** component, while removing the numerical extraction task affects the **ORDER** component more significantly. This may be attributed to the fact that column calculations appear more frequently in the **WHERE** module, and the numerical extraction task emphasizes the corresponding values in **ORDER**, preventing them from being overlooked when the SQL query contains multiple values.

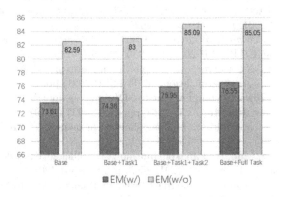

Fig. 6. Components validation on DuSQL.

Table 3. EM of component matching of DuSQL.

Model variant	All w/	All w/o	SELECT	WHERE	GROUP	ORDER	AND/OR	IUE
Ours-Base	**76.55**	**85.05**	**90.89**	**87.87**	94.43	96.98	**99.03**	**99.64**
-w/o t3	75.91	**85.05**	90.73	86.91	**95.16**	**97.22**	98.91	99.32
-w/o t3+t2	74.38	83.00	89.93	87.15	94.40	96.62	98.63	99.27
-w/o t3+t2+t1	73.61	82.59	88.15	86.50	92.87	96.94	98.75	99.27

5   Conclusion

In this paper, we propose an enhanced task-driven neural natural language interface to database. Specifically, on the decoder side, we decompose SQL prediction into several sub-tasks, including structure prediction, value extraction, and column relationship prediction, and generate them step-by-step, with the result of the previous sub-task guiding the generation of the next sub-task. This method boosts the decoding capability of T5. The results under extensive experiments on DuSQL and Spider demonstrate the performance of our model, proving that decomposing a complex task into smaller sub-tasks can improve the performance of current text-to-text pre-trained models in completing the main task more effectively.

Acknowledgement. This work is supported by National Natural Science Foundation of China (NSFC), 61972151. We thank the anonymous reviewers for their valuable comments and suggestions.

References

1. Bogin, B., Gardner, M., Berant, J.: Global reasoning over database structures for text-to-SQL parsing. In: EMNLP-IJCNLP 2019, pp. 3657–3662 (2019)
2. Cao, R., Chen, L., Chen, Z., Zhao, Y., Zhu, S., Yu, K.: LGESQL: line graph enhanced text-to-SQL model with mixed local and non-local relations. In: ACL/IJCNLP 2021, pp. 2541–2555 (2021)
3. Gan, Y., et al.: Towards robustness of text-to-SQL models against synonym substitution. In: ACL/IJCNLP 2021, pp. 2505–2515 (2021)
4. Gan, Y., Chen, X., Purver, M.: Exploring underexplored limitations of cross-domain text-to-SQL generalization. In: EMNLP 2021, pp. 8926–8931 (2021)
5. Guo, J., et al.: Towards complex text-to-SQL in cross-domain database with intermediate representation. In: ACL 2019, pp. 4524–4535 (2019)
6. Hochreiter, S., Schmidhuber, J.: Long short-term memory. Neural Comput. **9**(8), 1735–1780 (1997)
7. Hristidis, V., Gravano, L., Papakonstantinou, Y.: Efficient IR-style keyword search over relational databases. In: VLDB 2003, pp. 850–861 (2003)
8. Lei, W., et al.: Re-examining the role of schema linking in text-to-SQL. In: EMNLP 2020, pp. 6943–6954 (2020)
9. Li, F., Jagadish, H.V.: Constructing an interactive natural language interface for relational databases. Proc. VLDB Endow. **8**(1), 73–84 (2014)
10. Li, H., Zhang, J., Li, C., Chen, H.: RESDSQL: decoupling schema linking and skeleton parsing for text-to-SQL. CoRR abs/2302.05965 (2023)
11. Li, J., et al.: Graphix-T5: mixing pre-trained transformers with graph-aware layers for text-to-SQL parsing. CoRR abs/2301.07507 (2023)
12. Lin, T., Goyal, P., Girshick, R.B., He, K., Dollár, P.: Focal loss for dense object detection. In: ICCV 2017, pp. 2999–3007 (2017)
13. Liu, A., Hu, X., Lin, L., Wen, L.: Semantic enhanced text-to-SQL parsing via iteratively learning schema linking graph. In: KDD 2022, pp. 1021–1030 (2022)
14. Liu, Y., et al.: RoBERTa: a robustly optimized BERT pretraining approach. CoRR abs/1907.11692 (2019)

15. Luo, Y., Lin, X., Wang, W., Zhou, X.: SPARK: top-k keyword query in relational databases. In: SIGMOD 2007, pp. 115–126 (2007)
16. Ma, P., Wang, S.: MT-Teql: evaluating and augmenting neural NLIDB on real-world linguistic and schema variations. Proc. VLDB Endow. **15**(3), 569–582 (2021)
17. Qin, B., et al.: A survey on text-to-SQL parsing: concepts, methods, and future directions. CoRR abs/2208.13629 (2022)
18. Raffel, C., et al.: Exploring the limits of transfer learning with a unified text-to-text transformer. J. Mach. Learn. Res. **21**, 140:1–140:67 (2020)
19. Scholak, T., Schucher, N., Bahdanau, D.: PICARD: parsing incrementally for constrained auto-regressive decoding from language models. In: EMNLP 2021, pp. 9895–9901 (2021)
20. Shazeer, N., Stern, M.: Adafactor: adaptive learning rates with sublinear memory cost. In: ICML 2018. Proceedings of Machine Learning Research, vol. 80, pp. 4603–4611 (2018)
21. Suhr, A., Chang, M., Shaw, P., Lee, K.: Exploring unexplored generalization challenges for cross-database semantic parsing. In: ACL 2020, pp. 8372–8388 (2020)
22. Wang, B., Shin, R., Liu, X., Polozov, O., Richardson, M.: RAT-SQL: relation-aware schema encoding and linking for text-to-SQL parsers. In: ACL 2020, pp. 7567–7578 (2020)
23. Wang, L., et al.: Proton: probing schema linking information from pre-trained language models for text-to-SQL parsing. In: KDD 2022, pp. 1889–1898. ACM (2022)
24. Wang, L., et al.: DuSQL: a large-scale and pragmatic Chinese text-to-SQL dataset. In: EMNLP 2020, pp. 6923–6935 (2020)
25. Xue, L., et al.: mT5: a massively multilingual pre-trained text-to-text transformer. In: NAACL-HLT 2021, pp. 483–498 (2021)
26. Yu, T., et al.: Spider: a large-scale human-labeled dataset for complex and cross-domain semantic parsing and text-to-SQL task. In: EMNLP 2018, pp. 3911–3921 (2018)
27. Zelle, J.M., Mooney, R.J.: Learning to parse database queries using inductive logic programming. In: AAAI 1996, vol. 2, pp. 1050–1055 (1996)

Identification and Generation of Actions Using Pre-trained Language Models

Senthil Ganesan Yuvaraj[1(✉)], Boualem Benatallah[1,2],
Hamid Reza Motahari-Nezhad[3], and Fethi Rabhi[1]

[1] School of Computer Science and Engineering, University of New South Wales,
Sydney, Australia
senthily@cse.unsw.edu.au, f.rabhi@unsw.edu.au
[2] Dublin City University, Dublin, Ireland
boualem.benatallah@dcu.ie
[3] UpBrains AI, Inc., Reston, CA, USA

Abstract. Email is important in day-to-day communication and its volume is increasing rapidly in the workplace. Many tasks or actions that need to be tracked are contained in emails, but workers find this tracking difficult. An automatic way to find these actions would improve workplace productivity. We focused on the following problems in this paper: 1) identifying actions such as requests and commitments in emails, and 2) generating actionable text from the context of the emails. Recently, pre-trained language models trained on large unlabelled corpus have achieved state-of-the-art results in NLP tasks. In the present study, a combination of two pre-trained models, Bidirectional Encoder Representations from Transformers (BERT) and Text-to-Text Transfer Transformer (T5), is used to identify and generate actions from emails. In our method, the first step is to extract actions from emails using BERT sequence classification. The second step is to generate meaningful actionable text using T5 summarization. The Enron People Assignment (EPA) dataset is used for the evaluation of these methods on both large and small datasets. The BERT sequence classification model is evaluated against other language models and machine learning models. The results show that the BERT model outperforms other machine learning models for the action identification task, and the generated text from the summarization model shows significant improvement over the action sentence. Thus, the contribution of this paper is a state-of-the-art model for identifying actions and generating actionable text by leveraging pre-trained models.

Keywords: Action identification · Action generation · Text generation · BERT · Action extraction · Sequence classification

1 Introduction

Email and instant messages are used every day in the workplace as they are important communication tools in a virtual working environment. There has

F. Zhang et al. (Eds.): WISE 2023, LNCS 14306, pp. 674–683, 2023.
https://doi.org/10.1007/978-981-99-7254-8_52

been a rapid increase in the volume of text, and the difficulty of managing multiple tasks is referred to as information overload [17]. Actions such as requests and commitments can be missed due to this issue, which affects workplace productivity. An action in an email is a request or commitment in a natural language conversation [2,10]. The email may have one or more actions from the sender. For example, the sentence "Please review the below meeting notes" has a request from the sender. Identification of these actions from email is important to manage workplace activities. The action extraction methods [10,16] require labelled data to identify actions. However, it may not be possible to have labels for each action for a larger dataset. To solve the labelling problem, pre-trained language models [3] trained on large unlabelled data can be used for action identification.

In our approach, the action identification problem is formulated as a sequence classification. There are a few possible language models available for this, including the BERT pre-trained model [3]. Large unlabelled text corpus was used to train the model, and the outer layer of the model can be fine-tuned to achieve great results. We have fine-tuned the BERT model with large and small labelled datasets for action identification and compared the results. The performance of the BERT model is also compared with other pre-trained models: XLNet [18] is a bidirectional transformer that is trained on larger datasets and has better computation power; DistilBERT [13] is a distilled version of BERT with half of the parameters and can be trained with less effort. We evaluated the performance of BERT and both DistilBERT and XLNet pre-trained models in the action identification task. The Enron emails in the EPA dataset [12] are considered for the evaluation; these are a set of emails with labelled actions.

The classified sentences with actions do not always contain the details required to complete the action; they may have partial and irrelevant information. There is a need to read the entire email to complete the action even though the action is identified from one of the sentences. Text summarization can be used to create meaningful actionable text based on the context of the entire email. This provides the required details to users to perform the action. T5 [11] is one of several pre-trained models used for text summarization tasks. We have used the T5 model to generate actionable text from email content.

The key contributions of this paper are as follows: (i) Automatic action identification using a sequence classification model to extract actions, achieving state-of-the-art results with smaller datasets (ii) Comparison of different pre-trained models for action identification tasks and a recommendation on the models. (iii) An action generation method based on T5 summarization to generate meaningful actionable text

The remainder of the paper is arranged in the following order. Section 2 reviews related work on action identification and generation. Section 3 provides an overview of the action identification and generation framework. Section 4 explains the action identification method used to classify actions. Section 5 explains the action summarization method to generate actionable text, before the conclusion in Sect. 6.

2   Related Work

Action extraction from emails has been studied extensively. An action is defined as what is being performed (request and commitment). For example, the sentence "Steve will attend the annual meeting" is a commitment action. The speech act [2] classifies actions such as request, propose, amend, commit and deliver. The actions were identified manually in initial studies [1,7], which is a time-consuming task. Automatic extraction is important to identify actions such as request and commitment [6,10]. In the present study, we focus on automatic extraction of request and commitment actions from email.

In recent years, deep learning models have gained attention and been applied to the action extraction problem [14,16]. These methods use a bi-directional recurrent neural network model to extract actions such as request and promise. The method [16] outperformed Logistic Regression (LR) and Support Vector Machine (SVM) models. However, these neural network models train the model from scratch, and this can be expensive since a large dataset needs to be labelled for each task. This is the main factor limiting extension of these methods to multiple actions across various domains.

To counter this problem, a pre-trained model can be leveraged by fine-tuning it for multiple tasks. BERT [3] uses a masked language model and achieves better results in many NLP tasks [15]. We have fine-tuned BERT and other pre-trained models for the action identification task. These fine-tuned language models were evaluated against other machine learning models to evaluate their performance.

A recent paper [9] used text summarization to generate To-do items based on email content. It was focused on generating To-do items for commitment actions only, based on a BERT model. In our work, we summarize the text for both request and commitment actions. A request is an action requested by the sender and requires more details from the email to complete the action than a commitment action does. The generated text could have multiple sentences that contain information required for the action. The T5 architecture is used for our work as it is gaining attention and outperforms BERT on summarization tasks [4]. The T5 is fine-tuned to create separate models for request and commitment. The combined (request and commitment) summarization model is also developed for both request and commitment actions, and the results compared with individual models.

3   Action Identification and Generation Framework

The action identification and generation framework is illustrated in Fig. 1. The input stage extracts sentences from Enron emails using a pre-processor and then passes them to the sequence classifier. In the classification stage, the BERT tokenizer extracts tokens from each sentence and use an attention mask that considers the entire sentence while predicting the action. It classifies the sentences into request, commitment, and no-action sentences. It helps to identify the actions present in the email, but these sentences do not have all the information needed to perform the action. The emails and actions are passed to the text

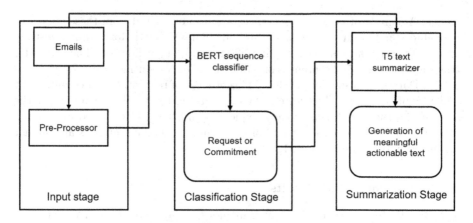

Fig. 1. Action identification and generation framework

summarizer. The summarization stage processes context of the email for actions. The relevant information for requests and commitments is extracted from email content to generate meaningful actionable text.

4 Action Identification

The action is identified using the classification method and compared against other language models and machine learning models. We discuss the methodology, experimental results, and performance improvements in this section.

4.1 Methodology

The classification method leverages a language model, BERT, which is a popular transformer model. This method uses the BERT pre-trained model "bert -base-uncased" [3], which is trained on a large corpus of lower-case English text from BooksCorpus (800M words) and Wikipedia (2500M words). The BERT model is fine-tuned with the EPA dataset to classify the actions. We want to fine-tune the model on both large and small datasets to understand the relative performance. The dataset with all the requests (5,711), commitments (894) and no-actions (5,405) is considered as Dataset 1. Dataset 2 is a subset of Dataset 1 and has 20% of Request (1,141) and 20% of No Action (1,080). All the commitment sentences (894) from Dataset 1 are considered, in order to have balanced data.

4.2 Data Preparation

Enron emails in the EPA dataset [12] are considered for this study. There are 6,733 sentences in this dataset coded as task sentences, which have requests from the sender of the email. Duplicates and sentences with less than three words are excluded from the study. The authors have annotated 894 commitments in these emails. A sample of no-action sentences are also extracted from these emails to be included in the data. The dataset is split in a 60:40 ratio for training/testing, and the training data is further split 80:20 for training/validation. The Dataset 1 training data has 2,740 sentences of request, 428 of commitment and 2,594 of no-action. Dataset 2 is smaller and has 547 sentences of request, 428 of commitment and 518 of no-action. The letters "[CLS]" are added to the beginning of the sentence as the first token of each sequence, and "[SEP]" is added at the end of each sentence to denote the end of the sequence. These sentences are further tokenized with a maximum of 128 tokens.

4.3   Experiment and Results

The BERT pre-trained model, which includes 12 layers of transformer encoder and 110 M parameters, is used for the sequence classification. The tokens are extracted from each sentence and assigned input IDs by the BERT tokenizer. The attention mask is used to determine if the token is a real word or just padding of the sentence. The BERT sequence classification transformer model is fine-tuned for the action identification. The model is trained with five epochs, a batch size of 16 and 2e-5 learning rate with an Adam optimizer.

Measures such as precision (P), recall (R) and F1-score (F1) are used for this evaluation. The results show that Dataset 1 achieves an F1-score above 97% for predicting requests and no-action. Dataset 2 achieves results that are good but slightly lower than those of Dataset 1. However, the commitment F1-score for Dataset 2 is higher as it has more balanced data. The results show that the smaller dataset (Dataset 2) can achieve results comparable to Dataset 1 using a BERT language model. Figure 2 shows the sequence classification results for each action.

BERT Model	Dataset 1			Dataset 2			Difference		
Actions	P	R	F1	P	R	F1	P	R	F1
Request	98.34%	98.69%	98.51%	98.04%	98.69%	98.36%	-0.30%	0.00%	-0.15%
Commitment	87.37%	94.69%	90.88%	97.72%	95.81%	96.76%	10.35%	1.12%	5.87%
No action	98.21%	96.48%	97.34%	95.87%	96.76%	96.31%	-2.34%	0.27%	-1.03%

Fig. 2. BERT Sequence classification results

4.4   Improving the Performance

The BERT model requires a large memory space and has a long execution time. It also consumes a large amount of space for storing the models. Thus we evaluate other pre-trained models for the action identification task and compare their performance with that of BERT. The XLNet and DistilBERT models are evaluated against the BERT model. The XLNet model is built on larger dataset with over 130 GB data and uses permutation language modelling to predict tokens in random order. DistilBERT is a distilled version of BERT and achieves 95% performance with half of the layers of BERT. The XLNet data preparation slightly differs by adding [SEP] [CLS] as the suffix of each sentence. The DistilBERT data is same dataset as used for the BERT model. We use the same batch size (16) and learning rate (2e−5) for both these models. Dataset 2 is used to evaluate these models since it achieved similar results to Dataset 1 and improvement in the commitment action.

The results show that XLNet improves the F1-score of commitment, but the request and no-action scores are slightly reduced. The XLnet training time has increased by about 60% and the model file size is almost double the BERT model size. The DistilBERT results are the same as BERT for commitment action and slightly lower for other actions. The DistilBERT training time is about 60% lower and model file size is around 50% lower than the BERT model. The DistilBERT model can be used to achieve similar results to BERT if there is limited memory or processing time. Figure 3 shows the comparison of XLNet and DistilBERT with the BERT model.

Comparison	XLNET			Diff - XLNET and BERT			DISTILBERT			Diff - DISTILBERT and BERT		
Actions	P	R	F1	P	R	F1	P	R	F1	P	R	F1
Request	99.10%	96.72%	97.90%	**1.06%**	-1.97%	-0.47%	98.68%	97.81%	98.24%	**0.63%**	-0.88%	-0.12%
Commitment	97.20%	96.93%	97.06%	-0.52%	**1.12%**	**0.31%**	97.72%	95.81%	96.76%	0.00%	0.00%	0.00%
No action	94.37%	96.99%	95.66%	-1.50%	**0.23%**	-0.65%	94.58%	96.99%	95.77%	-1.29%	**0.23%**	-0.54%

Fig. 3. XLNet and DistilBERT model results comparison

4.5   Comparison

We tested the techniques used in the action identification studies. The common machine learning techniques such as Decision Tree (DT), LR and SVM are used in this evaluation [2,16]. All actions - request, commitment and no-action - are considered. Dataset 2 is used for the evaluation to enable comparison with BERT model. In the training process, stop words are excluded, and words are changed to present tense. The sentence vector is calculated by averaging the word vectors of the sentence.

Another machine learning model, Long Short-Term Memory (LSTM), has achieved great results in natural language processing (NLP) tasks recently. The LSTM model [5] is a type of Recurrent Neural Network that is used for the text classification problem [14]. The embeddings are trained from the data using a Keras embedding layer. The stop words are excluded from sentences and there are assigned labels for each sentence. The sentences are tokenized and converted to sequences. The sequences are truncated to the same size for the model and SoftMax is used for the multi-class classification model. The model is trained with a 2e−3 learning rate with an Adam optimizer and five epochs, similar to the BERT model, for the purpose of comparison.

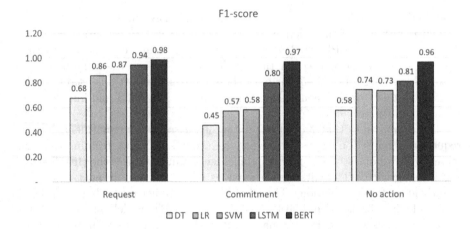

Fig. 4. Comparison of BERT with other machine learning models

The F1-score is calculated for all these techniques for comparison with the BERT model. The results show that DT achieved lower F1-score for all actions compared to the other models. The LR and SVM models have similar results for all actions that were better than those of DT, but lower than those of LSTM and BERT models. The LSTM model achieved a 94% F1-score for request but around 80% for commitment and no-action. The training sample of commitment is slightly smaller compared to request, and no-action data are noisy, which resulted in poor classification. The BERT model has better precision, recall and F1-score compared to LSTM for request, commitment, and no-action. This confirms that BERT can be fine-tuned with a smaller dataset and achieve better results than other machine learning models for action identification. Figure 4 compares the results of BERT with those of the other machine learning models for the action identification task.

5   Action Generation

The classification task detects actions contained in emails. However, the sentences with actions do not always contain the required information to complete the task. Text summarization can be used to generate meaningful actionable text based on the context of the entire email.

Email	Okay, I'm going to be gentle and send my complaints to you and let you ream the hourly people. Please check the following deals. They are all booked as Transalta Energy and should be Transalta Energy Marketing (US)Thanks
Action sentence	Please check the following deals.
Annotated text	Please check the following deals. They are all booked as Transalta Energy and should be Transalta Energy Marketing (US).
Generated text	please check the following deals. they are all booked as Transalta Energy . they should be transalta energy marketing (us).

Fig. 5. Examples of emails with annotated and generated text

5.1 Method

The purpose of text summarisation is to detect important words and reword and aggregate them into a meaningful summary. The T5 architecture has an encoder and decoder and has checkpoints with 60 million parameters. In the present study, the pre-trained T5 is fine-tuned for text summarization. We prepare T5 summarizer models separately for each action (request and commitment) as well as a combined model. The EPA dataset emails were annotated to obtain the details required to complete the action. The 139 emails with requests and 104 emails with commitments were considered for this evaluation. The dataset is split into training and testing in the ratio 70:30 for the purpose of modelling. The training data is further split into training and validation data in the ratio 80:20. The word "summarize:" needs to be added as a prefix to identify the data for the summarization task for the T5 architecture. Figure 5 shows examples of emails with actions and annotated text from the EPA dataset.

5.2 Experiment

The T5 tokenizer is used to tokenize the text and model "t5-small" is considered for this experiment. Our task is to produce a sequence of text and a data collator is used to pad the email and label to maximum length. The summarization models are trained with 3 epochs, a batch size of 8 and 2e-5 learning rate with an Adam optimizer. Rouge-L is a measure of longest common subsequence (LCS), which calculates difference between the prediction and actual text [8]. The F1-scores of Rouge-L are calculated to evaluate the results. In our work, overlap between generated text and annotated text is calculated and compared against the overlap of action sentence and annotated text. In the request model, the generated text has a Rouge-L F1-score of 0.73, higher than the action sentence score of 0.57. In the commitment model, the generated text has a Rouge-L F1-score of 0.78, which is better than the action sentence score of 0.56. The combined model generated text has a Rouge-L F1-score of 0.70, but slightly below the request and commitment model scores. The results show that the T5 summariser can pick important text for the actions and eliminate unnecessary text from emails. Figure 6 shows a comparison of action level models (request, commitment) and the combined model results.

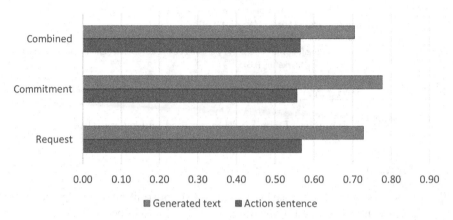

Fig. 6. Comparison of request, commitment and combined model results

6   Conclusion

We have explored the problem of action identification and the generation of actionable text. The proposed approach uses a classification model that identifies actions from emails first and then generates actionable text. The action identification problem is formulated as classification with the help of pre-trained models to identify actions. The classification method introduced in this paper leverages pre-trained models such as BERT, XLNet and DistilBERT. Large and small datasets are used for evaluation, and we show that a small dataset can achieve a higher accuracy. The sequence classification BERT model is compared with other machine learning models, and the results show that the BERT model outperforms them. Actionable text is generated using a T5 summarization model and it provides the required details to perform the action. The output shows that the combined model has a better Rouge-L F1-score than the action sentence and comparable to the individual action level model for summarization. In future work, we will be leveraging user feedback to continuously learn and improve the action identification.

References

1. Bellotti, V., Ducheneaut, N., Howard, M., Smith, I.: Taking email to task: the design and evaluation of a task management centered email tool. In: Proceedings of the SIGCHI Conference on Human Factors in Computing Systems, pp. 345–352. ACM (2003)
2. Cohen, W.W., Carvalho, V.R., Mitchell, T.M.: Learning to classify email into "speech acts". In: Proceedings of the 2004 Conference on Empirical Methods in Natural Language Processing (2004)

3. Devlin, J., Chang, M.W., Lee, K., Toutanova, K.: BERT: pre-training of deep bidirectional transformers for language understanding. arXiv preprint: arXiv:1810.04805 (2018)
4. Garg, A., et al.: NEWS article summarization with pretrained transformer. In: Garg, D., Wong, K., Sarangapani, J., Gupta, S.K. (eds.) IACC 2020. CCIS, vol. 1367, pp. 203–211. Springer, Singapore (2021). https://doi.org/10.1007/978-981-16-0401-0_15
5. Hochreiter, S., Schmidhuber, J.: Long short-term memory. Neural Comput. **9**(8), 1735–1780 (1997)
6. Lampert, A., Dale, R., Paris, C.: Detecting emails containing requests for action. In: Human Language Technologies: The 2010 Annual Conference of the North American Chapter of the Association for Computational Linguistics, pp. 984–992. Association for Computational Linguistics (2010)
7. Lampert, A., Dale, R., Paris, C., et al.: The nature of requests and commitments in email messages. In: Proceedings of the AAAI Workshop on Enhanced Messaging, pp. 42–47 (2008)
8. Lin, C.Y.: ROUGE: a package for automatic evaluation of summaries. In: Text Summarization Branches Out, pp. 74–81 (2004)
9. Mukherjee, S., Mukherjee, S., Hasegawa, M., Awadallah, A.H., White, R.: Smart to-do: automatic generation of to-do items from emails. arXiv preprint: arXiv:2005.06282 (2020)
10. Nezhad, H.R.M., Gunaratna, K., Cappi, J.: eAssistant: cognitive assistance for identification and auto-triage of actionable conversations. In: Proceedings of the 26th International Conference on World Wide Web Companion, pp. 89–98 (2017)
11. Raffel, C., et al.: Exploring the limits of transfer learning with a unified text-to-text transformer. J. Mach. Learn. Res. **21**(1), 5485–5551 (2020)
12. Rameshkumar, R., Bailey, P., Jha, A., Quirk, C.: Assigning people to tasks identified in email: the EPA dataset for addressee tagging for detected task intent. In: Proceedings of the 2018 EMNLP Workshop W-NUT: The 4th Workshop on Noisy User-Generated Text, pp. 28–32 (2018)
13. Sanh, V., Debut, L., Chaumond, J., Wolf, T.: DistilBERT, a distilled version of BERT: smaller, faster, cheaper and lighter. arXiv preprint: arXiv:1910.01108 (2019)
14. Shu, K., Mukherjee, S., Zheng, G., Awadallah, A.H., Shokouhi, M., Dumais, S.: Learning with weak supervision for email intent detection. In: Proceedings of the 43rd International ACM SIGIR Conference on Research and Development in Information Retrieval, pp. 1051–1060 (2020)
15. Sun, C., Qiu, X., Xu, Y., Huang, X.: How to fine-tune BERT for text classification? In: Sun, M., Huang, X., Ji, H., Liu, Z., Liu, Y. (eds.) CCL 2019. LNCS (LNAI), vol. 11856, pp. 194–206. Springer, Cham (2019). https://doi.org/10.1007/978-3-030-32381-3_16
16. Wang, W., Hosseini, S., Awadallah, A.H., Bennett, P.N., Quirk, C.: Context-aware intent identification in email conversations. In: Proceedings of the 42nd International ACM SIGIR Conference on Research and Development in Information Retrieval, pp. 585–594 (2019)
17. Whittaker, S., Sidner, C.: Email overload: exploring personal information management of email. In: Proceedings of the SIGCHI Conference on Human Factors in Computing Systems, pp. 276–283 (1996)
18. Yang, Z., Dai, Z., Yang, Y., Carbonell, J., Salakhutdinov, R.R., Le, Q.V.: XLNet: generalized autoregressive pretraining for language understanding. In: Advances in Neural Information Processing Systems, vol. 32 (2019)

GADESQL: Graph Attention Diffusion Enhanced Text-To-SQL with Single and Multi-hop Relations

Qinzhen Cao[1], Rui Xi[1(✉)], Jie Wu[1], Xiaowen Nie[1(✉)], Yubo Liu[2], and Mengshu Hou[1]

[1] University of Electronic Science and Technology of China, Chengdu, China
{qzcaoi,jiewu}@std.uestc.edu.cn, ruix.ryan@gmail.com,
{niexiaowen,mshou}@uestc.edu.cn
[2] China Jiuyuan Hi-tech equipment CORP, Beijing, China

Abstract. Text-To-SQL is crucial for enabling users without technical expertise to effectively extract important information from databases. The graph-based encoder has been successfully employed in this field. However, existing methods often adopt a node-centric approach, focusing on single-hop edge relations. This approach gives rise to two main issues: 1) failure to differentiate between single-hop and multi-hop relations among nodes; 2) ignoring the valuable multi-hop reasoning information between nodes. To tackle these challenges, we propose a **G**raph **A**ttention **D**iffusion **E**nhanced Text-To-**SQL**(GADESQL) model that enables multi-hop reasoning among nodes. With GAD, information can propagate efficiently through multi-hop paths, uniquely integrating single-hop and multi-hop relations during the graph iteration process. Furthermore, we employ Semantic Dependency Parsing for natural language analysis, constructing a semantic analysis tree for questions to enhance the effective connection between question tokens and Schema structures. Experiments on the cross-domain dataset Spider demonstrate that our model possesses strong generalization capabilities, achieving certain performance improvements over existing works.

Keywords: Text-To-SQL · Graph Attention Network · Attention Diffusion · Multi-hop Relations · Semantic Dependency Parsing

1 Introduction

Relational databases are widely utilized in diverse fields such as academia, finance, and entertainment, playing a crucial role in the era of big data. However, the complexity of structured query languages, such as SQL, poses a significant challenge for non-technical users when it comes to learning and using them effectively. To address this issue, the field of Text-To-SQL technologies have emerged [1,22], aiming to convert natural language questions into SQL queries based on the corresponding database schema. By bridging the gap between

© The Author(s), under exclusive license to Springer Nature Singapore Pte Ltd. 2023
F. Zhang et al. (Eds.): WISE 2023, LNCS 14306, pp. 684–698, 2023.
https://doi.org/10.1007/978-981-99-7254-8_53

non-technical users and relational databases, Text-To-SQL technologies have the potential to enhance data querying capabilities and facilitate information retrieval from databases. It has garnered considerable attention in both academics and industries, leading to extensive research and development efforts.

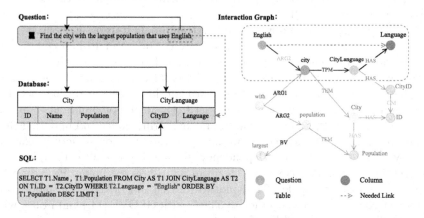

Fig. 1. A cross-domain Text-To-SQL challenge example. According to existing string matching rules, it is not possible to establish a connection between "English" and "Language". In this scenario, the problem can be solved by employing multi-hop reasoning via path patterns: (English $\xrightarrow{\text{ARG2}}$ city $\xrightarrow{\text{TPM}}$ CityLanguage $\xrightarrow{\text{HAS}}$ Language)

The ultimate goal is to enable non-technical users to interact with databases using familiar natural language queries, simplifying the process and making it more accessible for a broader range of individuals. However, improving the generalization ability of Text-To-SQL models poses a significant challenge, particularly in achieving domain generalization. That is, the model could accurately identify relationships and predict the correct SQL queries even in domains that it has not been previously trained on. It is crucial for the model to effectively handle new or unseen database schemas and natural language queries. As illustrated in Fig. 1, we hope the model can correctly recognize that "English" belongs to "Language".

Previous work, such as RATSQL [20], addressed the challenge of cross-domain generalization in Text-To-SQL by introducing path relationships like T-Has-C. These relationships establish a mapping between questions and the database schema, allowing the model to focus on tokens with similar relationships and improve generalization. However, RATSQL's approach of using the same relative position embedding [18] for all single-hop relationships overlooks multi-hop relationships and treats all nodes equally, leading to the over-smoothing problem [4]. To address these limitations, Graphix-T5 [10] introduced a Bridge Node that connects all nodes in the graph. This enables the model to capture multi-hop relationships and exchange information indirectly. However, the Bridge Node may introduce noise due to its connections with all other nodes.

Another challenging issue is the need for multi-hop reasoning in generating richly structured SQL queries [3,8,20]. That is, the model should consider explicit relationships (e.g., schema structural information) and implicit relationships (e.g., matching question tokens with tables) present in the input. By training the model's multi-hop reasoning ability based on these relationships, it is possible to improve prediction accuracy in cross-domain scenarios. As shown in Fig. 1 is an illustration of a multi-hop reasoning example in the context of cross-domain Text-To-SQL.

In this paper, we propose a **Graph Attention Diff-usion Enhanced** Text-To-**SQL**(GADESQL) model, which explicitly considers multi-hop connections between nodes. In each iteration process, the model first calculates the single-hop attention scores between nodes and then takes into account multi-hop connections based on a geometric distribution. Through this structure, during each iteration, every node in the graph will consider both single-hop and multi-hop connected nodes, collecting information from neighboring nodes and updating their feature representations. Moreover, we modified the question structure relationships by introducing Semantic Dependency Parsing [13] to analyze the questions, constructing a semantic parse tree to aid in multi-hop reasoning. Experimental results on benchmark Spider [24] demonstrate that our GADE-SQL model promotes the exact set match accuracy to 65.8%(with GLOVE [14]) and 71.9%(with pre-trained language model BERT [6]).

In summary, we make the following contributions to this paper:

- We develop a Multi-hop Attention Diffusion mechanism, combining single-hop and multi-hop connections for better focus on key information in Questions and Schema.
- We apply Semantic Dependency Parsing to questions, improving the model's understanding capabilities.
- We conduct some comparative experiments on the Spider dataset, and the results show that the proposed model achieves the optimal performance when considering node connections up to a hop count of 3.

2   Preliminaries

2.1   Problem Definition

Given a natural language question $Q = \left(q_1, q_2, \cdots, q_{|Q|}\right)$ and its corresponding table $S = \langle T, C \rangle$, where the database schema S consists of multiple tables $T = \left\{t_1, \ldots, t_{|T|}\right\}$ and columns $C = \left\{c_1^{t_1}, c_2^{t_1}, \ldots, c_{|C|}^{t_{|T|}}\right\}$, with each word phrase $c_j^{t_i}$ representing a column $c_j^{t_i} \in t_i$. The goal of Text-To-SQL is to generate an SQL query y that can be executed on the table structure S based on the question Q.

The practical approach for Text-To-SQL utilizes an encoder-decoder architecture. In this paper, we focus on improving the encoder component. The Entire heterogeneous graph centered on input nodes $G = (V, R)$ consists of all three types of nodes mentioned above, i.e., $V \in \{Q, T, C\}$, where the number of nodes $|V^n| = |Q| + |T| + |C|$, with $|T|$ and $|C|$ being the number of tables and columns, respectively.

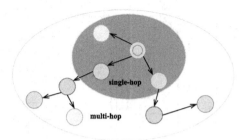

Fig. 2. Node Relation Graph

2.2 Path Pattern

A path pattern represents a path $\mathcal{V} \xrightarrow{r_1} \mathcal{V} \xrightarrow{r_2} \cdots \xrightarrow{r_l} \mathcal{V}_{l+1}$, where the target node of relation r_{i-1} is the source node of relation r_i. This statement describes the process of a node $\mathcal{V}_1$ in a graph structure being associated with node $\mathcal{V}_{l+1}$ through multi-hop edges.

In our model, $\mathcal{V}_i$ represents a node in a graph structure, with a value range of $\{Q, \mathcal{T}, \mathcal{C}\}$. At the same time, we define the relationships r_i between different graph nodes, the details of which will be explained in detail in Chap. 3. In our paper, we use single-hop edges to represent node relationships with a path length of 1, while multi-hop edges refer to node relationships with a path length longer than 1. Figure 2 introduced these two relationships: considering the dual elliptical nodes as starting points, the points within the dark blue range are regarded as single-hop nodes, while those within the light blue range are regarded as multi-hop nodes.

3   GADESQL

Our study adopts the classic encoder-decoder architecture as the core of the model [19]. The overview of GADESQL is depicted in Fig. 3, it consists of three key components: a graph input module, an attention diffusion-enhanced hidden module, and a Text-To-SQL decoding module.

The input to the model is the question Q, the database schema $\mathcal{S} = \langle \mathcal{T}, \mathcal{C} \rangle$, and necessary delimiters. In reference with the work of Shaw et al. [18], the input can be represented as Eq. 1:

$$X = Q|\mathcal{S}|t_1 : c_1^{t_1}, \cdots, c_{|t_1|}^{t_1} \mid t_2 : c_1^{t_2}, \cdots, \tag{1}$$

herein, t_i and $c_j^{t_i}$ represent the table name and the j-th column name of the i-th table, respectively. And we use | as the delimiter between the question and the tables. Within each table, we choose the colon symbol to separate the table name from the column names. Additionally, we use delimiters to differentiate between individual column names within a table.

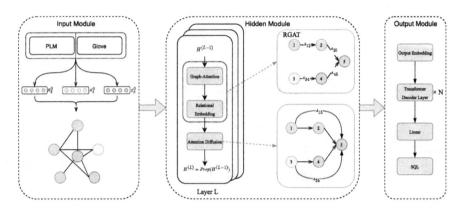

Fig. 3. Overall Model Framework

3.1   Graph Input Module

The joint input of text and tables can be represented as a heterogeneous graph $\mathcal{G} = (\mathcal{V}, \mathcal{R})$, which includes three types of nodes $\mathcal{V} \in \{\mathcal{Q}, \mathcal{T}, \mathcal{C}\}$ and multiple types of relations $\mathcal{R} = \{r_1, ..., r_{|\mathcal{R}|}\}$, where r_i represents the single-hop relationship between nodes. Additionally, we use $r^k = r_1 \circ r_2 \cdots \circ r_I$ to denote the multi-hop relations in the graph.

For the nodes, we can obtain their representations from word embeddings like GLOVE or pre-trained models like BERT by referring to works such as RATSQL [20] and LGESQL [3]. In this paper, we define the relations into the following three categories:

- **Schema structure.** It represents the organization and layout of the database, including tables, columns, primary keys, foreign keys, etc. For example, **Primary-Key** indicates which column serves as the primary key for a table, and **Foreign-Key** represents a column in one table pointing to the primary key of another table, establishing an association between the two tables.
- **Linking structure.** It involves aligning entity mentions in natural language with tables or columns in the database. We refer to the approach used in RATSQL, which utilizes n-gram matching to link the question with tables and columns. For example, **Table-Exact-Match** indicates a complete match between a question token and a table name, while **Column-Partial-Match** represents a partial match between a token and a column name.
- **Question structure.** It captures the relationship between two question tokens.

Previous graph-based Text-To-SQL models have primarily focused on the linking structure and schema structure, with limited research on the question structure. For example, S²SQL [8] is presented to construct syntactic parse trees for analyzing questions. Although they abstracted 55 complex syntactic relationships into 3 categories to reduce the number of model parameters, there

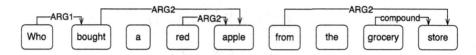

Fig. 4. SDP Analysis of the Problem

are still many unnecessary question linkings that can interfere with the model's performance.

To resolve it, we utilize the concept of Semantic Dependency Parsing (SDP) [13] and specifically the Dependency Mirs derived from Bi-Lexica Dependencies (DM). DM is a semantic representation pattern that emphasizes the predicate-argument relationships between sentence tokens. By using semantic dependency parsing, we filter out redundant token connections in the syntactic tree and select only the relevant connections that aid the model's semantic understanding. In this work, we select three types of relationships from SDP: ARG1, ARG2, and Compound. And Fig. 4 illustrates an example of dependency relationships in a specific question.

- ARG1: It represents the main argument or subject of a verb or predicate.
- ARG2: It represents the secondary argument or object of a verb or predicate.
- Compound: It represents a compound word composed of two or more individual words.

3.2 Graph Attention Diffusion Hidden Module

This module is designed to effectively compute attention scores between nodes that are multiple hops away from each other, thereby enhancing the representation and understanding of complex relational structures within the graph.

It consists of an N-layer Relational Graph Attention Network (RGAT). After the original RGAT computation, we introduced a multi-hop attention diffusion mechanism to directly calculate the attention between nodes after multiple hops. It operates on the attention scores computed by RGAT at each layer, obtaining the attention scores on single-hop edges and calculating the attention scores on multi-hop edges based on the diffusion process.

Relational Graph Attention Network(RGAT) [21] is a type of graph neural network that introduces relational embeddings to represent the relationships between nodes, thus modeling the relationships between nodes as a tuple (node, relation). RAGT then uses a multi-head attention mechanism to calculate the relationship strength between each node and its neighbor nodes, and to perform information propagation and aggregation on the graph.

Assuming an heterogeneous graph $\mathcal{G}$ is given, where $\mathbf{X}^l \in \mathbb{R}^{|V^n| \times d}$ represents the node encoding matrix of the graph at the l-th layer, with d denoting the hidden size of the graph, the attention $\mathbf{a}_{ij}$ and the node representation $\mathbf{z}_i$ of the l-th layer is calculated as follows:

$$e_{ij}^{(h)} = \left(\mathbf{x}_i \mathbf{W}_Q^{(h)}\right)\left(\mathbf{x}_j \mathbf{W}_K^{(h)} + \Psi\left(r_{ij}^K\right)\right)^{\mathrm{T}},$$

$$\alpha_{ij}^{(h)} = \mathrm{softmax}_j\left(e_{ij}^{(h)}/\sqrt{d/H}\right), \tag{2}$$

$$\mathbf{z}_i^{(h)} = \sum_{j=1}^{n} \alpha_{ij}^{(h)}\left(\mathbf{x}_j \mathbf{W}_V^{(h)} + \Psi\left(r_{ij}^V\right)\right),$$

$$\mathbf{z}_i = \mathrm{Concat}(\mathbf{z}_i^{(1)}, \cdots, \mathbf{z}_i^{(H)}), \tag{3}$$

Matrices $\mathbf{W}_Q^{(h)}, \mathbf{W}_K^{(h)}, \mathbf{W}_V^{(h)} \in \mathbb{R}^{d \times d/H}$, $\mathbf{W}_o \in \mathbb{R}^{d \times d}$ are trainable parameters, where H represents the number of attention heads, and FFN($\cdot$) denotes a feed-forward neural network. The function $\Psi\left(r_{ij}^K\right)$ returns the d-dimensional feature vector of relation r_{ij}^K, where r_{ij} encodes the known relationship between the two input elements x_i and x_j.

Inspired by the Graph Attention Diffusion mechanism in the work [12], we apply the attention diffusion process to calculate the attention scores $\mathcal{D}$ for multi-hop neighbors based on the single-hop attention scores $\mathcal{D}$:

$$\mathcal{D} = \sum_{i=0}^{\infty} \theta_i \boldsymbol{A}^i \text{ where } \sum_{i=0}^{\infty} \theta_i = 1 \text{ and } \theta_i > 0, \tag{4}$$

where θ_i is the attention decay factor, and $\theta_i > \theta_{i+1}$. The attention matrix $\boldsymbol{A}^i$ provides the number of paths between two nodes with a hop count of i. The attention bias between nodes with different hop numbers can be calculated based on θ and the path length. In the specific experimental process, we use the geometric distribution: $\theta_i = \alpha(1-\alpha)^i$ where $\alpha \in (0,1]$. This formula reflects the preference for the different path pattern lengths, with the distant target nodes being assigned smaller weights in the information aggregation process.

We consider $\mathcal{D}_{ij}$ as the attention score from node i to node j after applying the attention diffusion , since $\sum_{i=1}^{N_n} \mathcal{A}_{ij} = 1$. Following this, we introduce a feature aggregation method based on graph attention diffusion, which is formally defined as:

$$\boldsymbol{H}^{(l+1)} = \mathrm{AttDiff}\left(\mathcal{G}, \boldsymbol{H}^{(l)}, \boldsymbol{A}\right) = \mathcal{D}\boldsymbol{H}^{(l)}, \tag{5}$$

where $\mathcal{G}$ represents the encoded graph structure, $\boldsymbol{H}^{(l)}$ is the output from the previous encoding layer, $\boldsymbol{A}$ is the node attention scores computed by the RGAT.

We chose this mechanism to better capture the non-linear dependencies between nodes in graph data. Propagating information across multiple hops and capturing remote dependencies between nodes, this approach provides more accurate representation and understanding for semantic parsing and query generation in the Text-to-SQL task.

In the context of the Text-to-SQL task, generating SQL queries requires accounting for connections between multiple tables, logical relationships between conditions, and various aggregation operations. Often, these operations involve information propagation across multiple hops in the graph data. Thus, employing a multi-hop attention mechanism enables more effective modeling of these intricate relationships. By permitting information to propagate across multiple hops, our model better captures table connections, relationships between columns, and the logic between different conditions, ultimately resulting in SQL queries that more accurately reflect the intent of the original natural language instructions.

3.3   Text-To-SQL Output Module

We employed a grammar-based decoder [23] to generate the target query's abstract syntax tree(AST) in a depth-first search order. At each decoding time step, there are two possible outputs: 1) applying the APPLYRULE action to expand the current non-terminal node in the partially generated AST, and 2) selecting a SelectTable or SelectColumn operation, which is a schema element retrieved from the encoding memory. Mathematically, the probability of the sequence y given the input X is defined as $P(\hat{y} \mid \mathbf{X}) = \prod_j P\left(a_j \mid a_{<j}, \mathbf{X}\right)$ where a_j represents the action at the j-th time step.

For the decoder loss function, we utilize a conditional probability model to assess the discrepancy between the generated AST and the actual sequence:

$$\mathcal{L}_{\text{dec}} = \sum_{i=1}^{|Y|} y_i \log P\left(a_j \mid a_{<j}, \mathbf{X}\right), \tag{6}$$

where $y_i \in \left[y_1, \cdots, y_{|Y|}\right]$ represents the true labels encountered during the decoding process.

4   Experiments

4.1   Experiment Setup

Implementations. We utilize the Stanza toolkit [16] to preprocess questions, table names, and column names, for the purpose of tokenization and lemmatization. Our model implementation relies on Pytorch, and the creation of graphs is facilitated by the DGL library [21]. Inside the encoder, we employ GLOVE word embeddings with a 300-dimensional vector or pre-trained language models (PLMs) such as BERT. Our schema-linking approach draws inspiration from RATSQL, which serves as our baseline system.

Dataset. Our experiments employ the Spider dataset, a large-scale cross-domain zero-shot Text-To-SQL benchmark dataset that encompasses 8,659 training examples from 146 databases, including questions, involved database schemas, and corresponding SQL queries. Spider dataset covers various domains, with a total of 138 different domains. Specifically, the training set includes samples from domains such as Restaurants, GeoQuery, and Scholar, while the test set includes multiple domains such as real estate Properties, Musicians, and E-learning and others. Detailed statistics are shown in Table 1, The Nodes and relations data are created by our designed mapping algorithm. As a widely used benchmark with complex SQL queries and cross-domain multi-table databases, the Spider dataset was chosen for assessment in this study, aiming to explore the model's generalization capabilities in complex queries and cross-domain contexts. Moreover, the latest Text-To-SQL models are evaluated and compared on the Spider dataset, allowing for alignment with previous research and verification of the performance of the proposed model in this study.

Hyper-parameters. In the encoder, the GNN has hidden layer sizes of 256 (GLOVE) or 512 (BERT) and consists of 8 layers. The decoder features dimensions of 512 for hidden states, 128 for action embeddings, and 128 for node-type embeddings. The decoder's LSTM has a recurrent dropout rate of 0.2. With eight heads in the multi-head attention, both the encoder and decoder have a feature dropout rate of 0.2. We utilize the AdamW optimizer along with a linear warm-up scheduler, maintaining a warm-up ratio of 0.1. We set the learning rate for GLOVE at 7e-4 and the weight decay coefficient at 1e-4, while for BERT, we apply a lower learning rate of 1e-5 (bert-large) and a higher weight decay rate of 0.1. The GLOVE model uses a batch size of 20 with 200 training epochs, and the BERT model has a batch size of 24 with 300 training epochs.

4.2   Main Results

Overall Comparison. According to the main results on the test set presented in Table 2, our proposed attention-diffusion Text-To-SQL model (GADESQL) achieves a significant performance improvement compared to the original RAT-SQL. GADESQL, which utilizes GLOVE word embeddings as feature representations, improves the accuracy on the test set from 62.7% to 65.8%, achieving a performance gain of 3.1%.

Furthermore, by optimizing GADESQL with the pre-trained model bert-large-wwm, it achieves an accuracy of 71.9% on the test set. These experimental results demonstrate that our research has achieved remarkable progress in the Text-To-SQL task. The GADESQL mechanism effectively applies the attention-diffusion approach, accurately capturing the multi-hop relationships between the

Table 1. Statistics for the Spider dataset

Arguments	Train	Dev
count of samples	8501	1034
count of databases	146	20
Avg count of question nodes	13.8	14.2
Avg count of table nodes	9.6	7.2
Avg count of column nodes	29.5	25.8
Avg count of nodes	52.9	47.2
Avg count of relations	60.9	50.8

Table 2. Comparison with previous method

Model	Dev
Without PLM	
GNN	40.7
Global-GNN	52.7
IRNet	53.2
SADGA [2]	64.7
RATSQL	62.7
GADESQL(Ours)	65.8
With PLM: BERT	
BRIDGE + Ensemble	71.1
SmBoP [17]	69.5
ETA [11]	70.8
S^2SQL [8]	71.4
RATSQL	69.7
GADESQL(Ours)	71.9

Table 3. Detailed comparison with RATSQL model based on difficulty level

Split	Easy	Medium	Hard	Extra	All
RATSQL					
Dev	80.4	63.9	55.7	40.6	62.7
GADESQL					
Dev	83.3	66.5	59.2	**44.0**	**65.8**
RATSQL+BERT					
Dev	86.4	73.6	62.1	42.9	69.7
GADESQL+BERT					
Dev	87.7	74.9	66.5	**47.6**	**71.9**

question and the table structure, thereby improving the accuracy of generated SQL statements. Additionally, by incorporating the bert-large-wwm pre-trained model, GADESQL leverages its understanding capability of SQL statements, further enhancing its performance.

Detailed Comparison. To evaluate the performance of our model, we classify models according to the difficulty of the Spider dataset and conduct comparative studies, and the results are listed in Table 3. Experimental results show that GADESQL performs excellent in all difficulty levels, with or without pre-trained language models (PLMs). Particularly in the "HARD" level Text-to-SQL task, GADESQL shows a significant improvement. Specifically, without using PLMs,

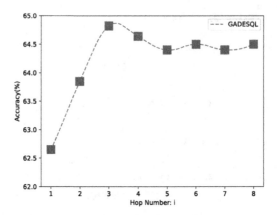

Fig. 5. Effect of Hop Number i on performance

GADESQL outperforms RATSQL by 3.5% in terms of performance. After using PLMs, the performance has been improved by 4.4%.

Interestingly, in the "Extra" difficulty level task, GADESQL even outperforms RATSQL+BERT with an improvement of 1.1%. In summary, by effectively applying PLMs and integrating attention diffusion mechanisms and information for SQL statement structure, GADESQL presents excellent performance and achieves satisfactory results.

Parameter Analysis. Table 4 shows our further exploration of graph attention diffusion. We compared the performance of the GADESQL in the experiment under different circumstances, where the maximum number of hops was 1(w/o GAD), 3, and 5. Considering the small size of the heterogeneous graph(Table 1), $i = 5$ has reached the distance of the farthest node in the entire graph. Therefore, we did not compare cases with higher values of i. The table shows that considering multi-hop relationships between nodes can improve the performance of the model. However, if distant multi-hop relationships are considered, it may have a negative impact on the model's performance. For example, when the maximum number of hops increased from 3 to 5, the model's accuracy decreased by almost 0.6%. Figure 5 report the effect of hop number i. Hence, in practice, both multi-hop relationships and computational costs should be considered when choosing the appropriate value of i.

Ablation Study. In order to better understand how our proposed GADESQL works, we conducted ablation studies and analysis with GADESQL on the Spider development set.

Semantic Dependency Parsing(SDP) aims to model information flow more effectively during a conversation, while Graph Attention Diffusion(GAD) aims to enhance node representations through the updating of information with single-hop and multi-hop mechanisms. We evaluate how they each influence overall

Table 4. Parametric analysis

Model	Accuracy(%)
GADESQL(i = 1)	63.5
GADESQL(i = 3)	65.8
GADESQL(i = 5)	65.1

Table 5. Ablation Study

Approach	Accuracy(%)
GADESQL	65.8
w/o SDP	64.2(−1.6)
w/o GAD	63.5(−2.3)

performance. We remove each of them and test the model's performance whose results are shown in Table 5. Significant performance decline is observed without either SDP or GAD. Specifically, in the absence of SDP, the accuracy drops by 1.6%, which demonstrates the effectiveness of explicitly modeling problem semantics. Furthermore, by omitting the GAD component in the encoding layer, which has the ability to integrate single-hop and multi-hop information, the accuracy drops by 2.3%. These results validate the critical importance of jointly considering single-hop and multi-hop information for achieving correct predictions.

SDP and GAD respectively contribute to enhancing Text-To-SQL models from the perspectives of natural language understanding and node information comprehension. Although neither of these approaches can significantly improve accuracy metrics alone, their combination leads to superior performance.

4.3   Case Studies

In Table 6, we conducted a detailed comparison of the SQL query statements generated by the GADESQL model with the reference baseline model RATSQL.

In the first case, RATSQL is unable to effectively deal with the matching requirements of new domains. It only recognizes "Onwer" as a resident but fails to recognize "Professional" as another identity of a resident, and instead mistakenly includes the "Dogs" table. In the second case, RATSQL struggles to properly associate the relatively close "before" and "after" phrases with the correct time points, leading to an incorrect prediction of "$singer.Birth\_Year > 1955$". In our GADESQL model, using SDP can easily derive the correct relationships: (before $\xrightarrow{\text{ARG2}}$ 1945) and (after $\xrightarrow{\text{ARG2}}$ 1945). With the help of these relationships, the correct SQL statements are predicted. In the third example, following the utilization of multi-hop reasoning, the second query statement, through its connection with both the country and language tables, is capable of more comprehensively considering the relationships among cities, countries, and languages. As analyzed in the third section, this results in a more enriched query outcome, capable of encompassing a greater depth of information across multiple levels.

Regrettably, in the last example, GADESQL mistakenly interprets "north america" as "country. Region". This phenomenon may be due to the negative impact of the distant "Region" nodes on multi-hop reasoning, causing the model to erroneously introduce the incorrect column.

5   Related Works

The fundamental principle of a cross-text Text-To-SQL parser is to construct an encoder that learns the representations and correlations of questions and schemas, while employing a decoder that generates SQL based on the learned information in the encoder. In particular, RYANSQL [5] employs a recursive neural network encoder to calculate attention-based representations for the question, tables, and columns, which are then integrated into a pooling layer. Its decoder utilizes the encoded intermediate representations to predict SQL. Later, graph-based encoders have been employed to demonstrate their effectiveness in

Table 6. Case study: the initial three cases represent positive samples, and the final case represents a negative sample.

HARD: Find the states where both owners and professionals live.

RATSQL: SELECT state FROM Owners INTERSECT SELECT state FROM Owners JOIN Dogs ON Owners.owner_id = Dogs.owner_id

GADESQL: SELECT Owners.state FROM Owners INTERSECT SELECT Professionals.state FROM Professionals

---
HARD: Show the citizenship shared by singers with birth year before 1945 and after 1955.

RATSQL: SELECT singer.Citizenship FROM singer WHERE singer.Birth_Year < 1945 INTERSECT SELECT singer.Citizenship FROM singer WHERE singer.Birth_Year < 1955

GADESQL: SELECT singer.Citizenship FROM singer WHERE singer.Birth_Year < 1945 INTERSECT SELECT singer.Citizenship FROM singer WHERE singer.Birth_Year > 1955

HARD: What are the names of cities in Europe for which English is not the official language?

RATSQL: SELECT city.Name FROM city WHERE city.CountryCode NOT IN (SELECT countrylanguage.CountryCode FROM countrylanguage WHERE countrylanguage.Language = 'English')

GADESQL: SELECT city.Name FROM city JOIN country ON city.CountryCode = country.Code WHERE country.Region = 'Europe' AND city.CountryCode NOT IN (SELECT countrylanguage.CountryCode FROM countrylanguage WHERE countrylanguage.Language = 'English')

Extra: Give the total population and average surface area corresponding to countries in North America that have a surface area greater than 300.

RATSQL: SELECT Sum(country.Population), Avg(country.SurfaceArea) FROM country WHERE country.SurfaceArea > 300 AND country.Continent = 'north america'

GADESQL: SELECT Sum(country.Population), Avg(country.SurfaceArea) FROM country WHERE country.SurfaceArea > 300 AND country.Region = 'north america'

Text-To-SQL, such as RATSQL and SDSQL [9], which construct graph patterns and enhance input representations. RASAT [15] and S^2SQL [8] improve the model's alignment ability by modeling the relationship between the question and schema in the graph structure. LGESQL [3] and Graphix-T5 enhance the model's reasoning ability by introducing new graph patterns. R^2SQL [7] enhance the structural reasoning from context-sensitive text to SQL parsing. In contrast to these previous studies, our work investigates the impact of semantic structures and multi-hop reasoning in the encoding phase.

In contrast, traditional single-hop attention mechanisms may be constrained by their locality and struggle to capture intricate semantic structures. By introducing attention diffusion, our GADESQL model comprehensively considers the interplay between text and schema, thus enhancing the grasp of problem semantics and the accuracy of SQL generation.

6 Conclusion

In this study, we employed Semantic Dependency Parsing (SDP) for deep semantic analysis of the questions to assist in constructing the heterogeneous graph, thereby revealing the connections between different nodes. We then introduced the Graph Attention Diffusion to enable multi-hop reasoning between nodes for the Text-To-SQL task. By performing attention diffusion based on the edges (node connections) in the heterogeneous graph, we effectively integrate features of multi-hop relationships and capture useful path patterns. This process allows our model to gather information from remote nodes, building upon the RGAT framework. It enables our model to maintain efficient solutions even when faced with complex questions. In future research, we plan to explore additional useful path patterns and investigate more efficient ways to handle neighbor nodes at different hop distances.

Acknowledgment. This work is supported by the National Science Fund of China under grant No. 62072075 and the Key research and development projects of Sichuan Provincial Science and Technology Plan Project under grant No. 2023YFS0420.

References

1. Cai, R., Xu, B., Yang, X., Zhang, Z., Li, Z., Liang, Z.: An encoder-decoder framework translating natural language to database queries. arXiv preprint: arXiv:1711.06061 (2017)
2. Cai, R., Yuan, J., Xu, B., Hao, Z.: SADGA: structure-aware dual graph aggregation network for Text-to-SQL. In: Advances in Neural Information Processing Systems, vol. 34, pp. –7676 (2021)
3. Cao, R., Chen, L., Chen, Z., Zhao, Y., Zhu, S., Yu, K.: LGESQL: line graph enhanced Text-to-SQL model with mixed local and non-local relations. arXiv preprint: arXiv:2106.01093 (2021)
4. Chen, D., Lin, Y., Li, W., Li, P., Zhou, J., Sun, X.: Measuring and relieving the over-smoothing problem for graph neural networks from the topological view. In: Proceedings of the AAAI Conference on Artificial Intelligence, vol. 34, pp. 3438–3445 (2020)

5. Choi, D., Shin, M.C., Kim, E., Shin, D.R.: RYANSQL: recursively applying sketch-based slot fillings for complex text-to-SQL in cross-domain databases. Comput. Linguist. **47**(2), 309–332 (2021)
6. Devlin, J., Chang, M.W., Lee, K., Toutanova, K.: BERT: pre-training of deep bidirectional transformers for language understanding. arXiv preprint: arXiv:1810.04805 (2018)
7. Hui, B., et al.: Dynamic hybrid relation exploration network for cross-domain context-dependent semantic parsing. In: Proceedings of the AAAI Conference on Artificial Intelligence, vol. 35, pp. 13116–13124 (2021)
8. Hui, B., et al.: S ˆ2 SQL: injecting syntax to question-schema interaction graph encoder for Text-to-SQL parsers. arXiv preprint: arXiv:2203.06958 (2022)
9. Hui, B., et al.: Improving Text-to-SQL with schema dependency learning. arXiv preprint: arXiv:2103.04399 (2021)
10. Li, J., et al.: Graphix-t5: mixing pre-trained transformers with graph-aware layers for Text-to-SQL parsing. arXiv preprint: arXiv:2301.07507 (2023)
11. Liu, Q., Yang, D., Zhang, J., Guo, J., Zhou, B., Lou, J.G.: Awakening latent grounding from pretrained language models for semantic parsing. arXiv preprint: arXiv:2109.10540 (2021)
12. Liu, Y., Guan, R., Giunchiglia, F., Liang, Y., Feng, X.: Deep attention diffusion graph neural networks for text classification. In: Proceedings of the 2021 Conference on Empirical Methods in Natural Language Processing, pp. 8142–8152 (2021)
13. Oepen, S., et al.: SemEval 2014 task 8: broad-coverage semantic dependency parsing. In: International Workshop on Semantic Evaluation (2014)
14. Pennington, J., Socher, R., Manning, C.D.: GloVe: global vectors for word representation. In: Proceedings of the 2014 Conference on Empirical Methods in Natural Language Processing (EMNLP), pp. 1532–1543 (2014)
15. Qi, J., et al.: RASAT: integrating relational structures into pretrained seq2seq model for Text-to-SQL. arXiv preprint: arXiv:2205.06983 (2022)
16. Qi, P., Zhang, Y., Zhang, Y., Bolton, J., Manning, C.D.: Stanza: a Python natural language processing toolkit for many human languages. arXiv preprint: arXiv:2003.07082 (2020)
17. Rubin, O., Berant, J.: SmBoP: semi-autoregressive bottom-up semantic parsing. arXiv preprint: arXiv:2010.12412 (2020)
18. Shaw, P., Uszkoreit, J., Vaswani, A.: Self-attention with relative position representations. arXiv preprint: arXiv:1803.02155 (2018)
19. Sutskever, I., Vinyals, O., Le, Q.V.: Sequence to sequence learning with neural networks. In: Advances in Neural Information Processing Systems, vol. 27 (2014)
20. Wang, B., Shin, R., Liu, X., Polozov, O., Richardson, M.: RAT-SQL: relation-aware schema encoding and linking for Text-to-SQL parsers. In: Annual Meeting of the Association for Computational Linguistics (2019)
21. Wang, K., Shen, W., Yang, Y., Quan, X., Wang, R.: Relational graph attention network for aspect-based sentiment analysis. arXiv preprint: arXiv:2004.12362 (2020)
22. Yaghmazadeh, N., Wang, Y., Dillig, I., Dillig, T.: SQLizer: query synthesis from natural language. Proc. ACM on Programm. Lang. **1**(OOPSLA), 1–26 (2017)
23. Yin, P., Neubig, G.: A syntactic neural model for general-purpose code generation. arXiv preprint: arXiv:1704.01696 (2017)
24. Yu, T., et al.: Spider: a large-scale human-labeled dataset for complex and cross-domain semantic parsing and Text-to-SQL task. In: EMNLP (2018)

An Ensemble-Based Approach for Generative Language Model Attribution

Harika Abburi[1]([envelope]), Michael Suesserman[2], Nirmala Pudota[1],
Balaji Veeramani[2], Edward Bowen[2], and Sanmitra Bhattacharya[2]

[1] Deloitte and Touche Assurance and Enterprise Risk Services India Private Limited,
Hyderabad, India
{abharika,npudota}@deloitte.com
[2] Deloitte and Touche LLP, New York, USA
{msuesserman,bveeramani,edbowen,sanmbhattacharya}@deloitte.com

Abstract. Recently, Large Language Models (LLMs) have gained considerable attention due to their incredible ability to automatically generate texts that closely resemble human-written text. They have become invaluable tools in handling various text-based tasks such as content creation and report generation. Nevertheless, the proliferation of these tools can create undesirable consequences such as generation of false information and plagiarism. A variety of LLMs have been operationalized in the last few years whose abilities are heavily influenced by the quality of their training corpus, model architecture, pre-training tasks, and fine-tuning processes. Our ability to attribute the generated text to a specific LLM will not only help us understand differences in the LLMs' output characteristics, but also effectively distinguish machine-generated text from human-generated text. In this paper, we study whether a machine learning model can be effectively trained to attribute text to the underlying LLM that generated it. We propose an ensemble neural model that generates probabilities from multiple pre-trained LLMs, which are then used as features for a traditional machine learning classifier. The proposed approach is tested on Automated Text Identification (AuTexTification) datasets in English and Spanish languages. We find that our models outperform various baselines, achieving macro F_{macro} scores of 0.63 and 0.65 for English and Spanish texts, respectively.

Keywords: Generative AI · Model Attribution · Large language models · Ensemble

1 Introduction

Recent advancements in machine learning and natural language processing research have paved the way for the development of sophisticated LLMs. The widespread availability and the ease with which they can generate coherent content are contributing to the production of massive volumes of automatically generated online content. LLMs have demonstrated remarkable performance in

F. Zhang et al. (Eds.): WISE 2023, LNCS 14306, pp. 699–709, 2023.
https://doi.org/10.1007/978-981-99-7254-8_54

producing human-like language, showcasing their potential use across a wide range of applications, such as domain specific tasks in legal [20] and financial services [23]. Foundation models such as OpenAI's GPT-3 [1] and Big Science's Bloom [19] are publicly available, and can generate highly sophisticated content with basic text prompts. This often presents a challenge to discern between human and LLM-generated text.

While LLMs demonstrate the ability to understand the context and generate coherent human-like responses, they do not have a true understanding of what they are producing [12]. This could potentially lead to adverse consequences when used in downstream applications. Generating plausible but false content (*hallucination* [10]), may inadvertently help propagate misinformation, fake news, and spam [9].

There is a considerable body of research available on detecting text generated by artificial intelligence (AI) systems [9,21]. However, the identification of a specific LLM responsible for generating such text is a relatively new area of research. We argue that attributing the generated text to a specific LLM is a vital research area, as the knowledge of the source LLM would enable one to be vigilant regarding potential known biases and limitations associated with that model and use the content appropriately in downstream applications with suitable oversight [21].

In this study, we focus on identifying the source of the AI-generated text (referred to as model attribution hereafter) in two different languages, English and Spanish. More specifically, given a piece of text, the goal is to determine which specific LLM generated the text. To address this problem statement, we propose an ensemble classifier, where the probabilities generated from various state-of-the-art LLMs are used as input feature vectors to traditional machine learning classification models to produce the final predictions. Our experiments show multiple instances of the proposed framework outperform several baselines using well-established evaluation metrics.

2   Related Work

The majority of research in this area is focused on differentiating between text authored by humans and text generated by AI [3,17].

The use of neural networks leveraging complex linguistic features and their derivatives is most prevalent in detecting AI-generated text. DetectGPT [15] generates minor perturbations of a passage using a generic pre-trained Text-to-Text Transfer Transformer (T5) model, and then compares the log probability of the original sample with each perturbed sample to determine if it is AI-generated. Deng *et al.* [4] build upon the DetectGTP model by incorporating a Bayesian surrogate model to select text samples more efficiently, which achieves similar performance as DetectGTP using half the number of samples. Mitrovic *et al.* [16] developed a fine-tuned Transformer-based approach to distinguish between human and ChatGTP generated text, with the addition of SHapely Additive exPlanations (SHAP) values for model explainability. This approach provides insight into the reasoning behind the model's predictions. Statistical methods have also been applied for detection of AI-generated text, such as the Giant Language model Test Room (GLTR) approach [6].

The increasing sophistication of generative AI models coupled with adversarial attacks make detection of AI-generated text especially challenging. Two forms of attacks that create additional complications are paraphrasing attacks and adversarial human spoofing [17]. Automatically generated text may also show factual, grammatical, or coherence artifacts [14] along with statistical abnormalities that impact the distributions of automatic and human texts [8]. The importance of detecting AI-generated text and the corresponding challenges will foster further research on this topic.

In addition to distinguishing between human and AI-generated text, identifying a specific LLM that generates the artificial text is becoming increasingly important. Uchendu et al. [21] explored the Robustly optimized BERT approach (RoBERTa) model to classify AI-generated text into eight different classes. Li et al. [11] developed a model for AI-generated multi-class text classification on Russian language using Decoding-enhanced BERT with disentangled attention (DeBERTa) as a pre-trained language model for category classification. These prior works focused on model attribution for only a single language, such as English or Russian. In contrast to the aforementioned research, and to the extent of our knowledge, our approach to model attribution is the first one to be applied across multiple languages, demonstrating the robustness of our approach across attributable LLMs, languages, and domains.

3   AuTexTification Dataset

The dataset used in the study comes from the Iberian Languages Evaluation Forum (IberCLEF)-AuTexTification shared task [18]. The data consists of texts from five domains, where three domains (legal, wiki, and tweets) are used for training, and two different domains are used for testing (reviews and news). It contains machine generated text from six text generation models, labeled as bloom-1b7 (A), bloom-3b (B), bloom-7b1 (C), babbage (D), curie (E), and text-davinci-003 (F) for two different languages, English and Spanish. The LLMs used to generate the text are of increasing number of neural parameters, ranging from 2B to 175B. The motivation here is to emulate realistic AI text detection approaches that should be versatile enough to detect a diverse set of text generation models and writing styles. The number of samples in each class for both languages is shown in Table 1. To showcase the complexity of the problem, we also present samples for each category from both the English and Spanish datasets in Tables 2 and 3.

4   Proposed Ensemble Approach

In this Section, we detail our approach for conducting the generative language model attribution. We first provide a description of the LLMs and machine learning models that we explored for model attribution. Next, we discuss the proposed

Table 1. Label distribution across the languages for model attribution task. Train and test splits for each language are also shown.

Category	Multiclass-English		Multiclass-Spanish	
	Train	*Test*	*Train*	*Test*
bloom-1b7 (A)	3562	887	3422	870
bloom-3b (B)	3648	875	3514	867
bloom-7b1 (C)	3687	952	3575	878
babbage (D)	3870	924	3788	946
curie (E)	3822	979	3770	1004
text-davinci-003 (F)	3827	988	3866	917

Table 2. Samples of English AI-generated text, with corresponding source models (labeled A-F).

Text	Label
The best songs are those that I can sing along with, and they're all there!	B
Summer Vacation time. That means we will have to get the kids in a school setting. We can look forward to all of that	C
Thanks @arohan and @MoneyEnergy I have heard this argument many times before. Im not going to get into it here, but suffice	E

Table 3. Samples of Spanish AI-generated text, with corresponding source models (labeled A-F).

Text	Label
¿En qué se parecen las ofertas de trabajo y los puestos laborales que están disponibles para el trabajador colombiano en este momento?. Las opciones	A
No se trata de ser una revolución, pero de que la gente sienta que ha visto un cambio y que quiere seguir segu	D
Los padres pueden negar la solicitud del niño y ofrecer alternativas saludables, como frutas, verduras o una bebida sin cafeína. Además, los padres pueden explicar por qué es importante que los niños consuman alimentos saludables y cuáles son los efectos negativos de comer alimentos poco saludables	F

Table 4. Models explored for English and Spanish datasets

Task	Large language models
English	xlm-roberta-large-finetuned-conll03-english, allenai/scibert_scivocab_cased, microsoft/deberta-base, roberta-large, allenai/longformer-base-4096, bert-large-uncased-whole-word-masking-finetuned-squad
Spanish	xlm-roberta-large-finetuned-conll03-english, PlanTL-GOB-ES/roberta-large-bne, hiiamsid/sentence_similarity_spanish_es, dbmdz/bert-base-multilingual-cased-finetuned-conll03-spanish, roberta-large

ensemble neural architecture, where we fine-tuned the LLMs and then passed their predictions to various traditional machine learning models to perform the ensemble operation.

4.1 Models

LLMs: We explored various state-of-the-art LLMs [22], such as Bidirectional Encoder Representations from Transformers (BERT), DeBERTa, RoBERTa, and cross-lingual language model RoBERTa (XLM-RoBERTa) along with their variants. Since the datasets are different for each language, and the same set of models will not fit across them, we fine-tuned different models for different languages. We investigated more than 15 distinct models for each language and selected the ones presented in this paper based on their performance on the validation data. This selection was made to ensure model diversity, which aids in generalisation and improved comprehension of context and semantics. Table 4 lists the different models that we selected for the two languages under consideration. We briefly describe each of the LLMs below.

- **microsoft/deberta-base** [7] is a transformer model which improves the BERT and RoBERTa models using disentangled attention and enhanced mask decoder.
- **xlm-roberta-large-finetuned-conll03-english** is XLM-RoBERTa based model [2] which is a large multi-lingual language model trained on 2.5TB of filtered Common Crawl data. The conll03-english model is fine-tuned on the XLM-RoBERTa model with conll2003 dataset in English.
- **roberta-large, PlanTL-GOB-ES/roberta-large-bne** are RoBERTa based models [13] which are pre-trained on a large corpus of English data in a self-supervised fashion using a Masked Language Modeling (MLM) objective. The roberta-large-bne model has been pre-trained using the largest Spanish corpus with a total of 570GB of text compiled from the web crawlings.
- **dbmdz/bert-base-multilingual-cased-finetuned-conll03-spanish, hiiamsid/sentence_similarity_spanish_es, allenai/scibert_scivocab_cased, bert-large-uncased-whole-word-masking-finetuned-squad, and allenai/longformer-base-4096** are BERT-based models [5]. The bert-basemultilingual model is pre-trained on 104 languages with the largest Wikipedia data using a MLM objective and further pre-trained on the CoNLL-2002 dataset in Spanish. The *sentence similarity* Spanish model is a sentencetransformer model where the base model is BETO which is trained on a large Spanish corpus. The scibert model is trained on papers taken from Semantic Scholars. The BERT-large SQuAD model is slightly different from other BERT models since it is trained with a whole word masking technique and further fine-tuned on the Stanford Question Answering Dataset (SQuAD). The Long-Document Transformer (Longformer) model is a BERT-like model stemmed from the RoBERTa checkpoint and pre-trained for MLM on long documents which supports sequences of lengths up to 4,096.

Machine Learning (ML) Models: We explored various traditional machine learning and ensembling models such as Bagging , Voting, OneVsRest, Error-Correcting Output Codes (ECOC), and LinearSVC [24].

4.2　Proposed Ensemble Neural Architecture

As shown in Fig. 1, an input text is passed through variants of the pre-trained LLMs such as, DeBERTa (D), XLM-RoBERTa (X), RoBERTa (R), and BERT (B). During the model training phase, these models are fine-tuned on the training data. For inference and testing, each of these models independently generate classification probabilities (P), namely P^D, P^X, P^R, P^B, etc. In order to maximize the contribution of each model, each of these probabilities are concatenated (P^C) or averaged (P^A), and this output is passed as a feature vector to train various traditional ML models to produce final predictions.

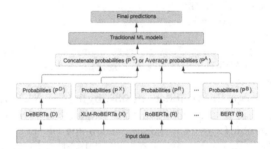

Fig. 1. Proposed ensemble neural architecture

5　Experiments

In this section, we discuss the evaluation of the proposed methods. We report model performance using well-established metrics such as accuracy (Acc), macro F1 score (F_{macro}), precision ($Prec$) and recall (Rec).

5.1　Baselines

We establish Linear Support Vector Classification (SVC), Logistic Regression (LR), and Random Forests (RF) as baselines, where each baseline model takes two distinct feature sets – word n-grams and character n-grams. We also explored other baselines like the Symanto Brain Few-shot and Zero-shot without label verbalization approaches[1], but due to their relatively low performance compared to the approaches presented in Table 5, we do not report those results.

---

[1] https://www.symanto.com/nlp-tools/symanto-brain/.

5.2   Implementation Details

During model training we set aside 20% from the training data for validation. However, for the held-out testing phase, the validation set is merged with the training set. The following hyper-parameters are used for model fine-tuning: batch size - 128, learning rate - $3e^-5$, max sequence length - 128, and number of epochs is set to 20. We also used a sliding window to prevent the truncation of longer sequences, allowing the model to handle longer sentences.

Table 5. Baseline results of model attribution for both English and Spanish.

Classifier	Features	English				Spanish			
		Acc	F_{macro}	$Prec$	Rec	Acc	F_{macro}	$Prec$	Rec
Linear SVC	word n-grams	0.360	0.355	0.354	0.357	0.464	0.459	0.457	0.463
	character n-grams	0.439	0.428	0.425	0.438	**0.505**	0.495	0.493	**0.505**
LR	word n-grams	0.374	0.368	0.366	0.371	0.482	0.475	0.473	0.481
	character n-grams	**0.451**	**0.440**	**0.438**	**0.450**	0.505	0.496	**0.495**	0.505
RF	word n-grams	0.339	0.330	0.330	0.337	0.425	0.407	0.409	0.425
	character n-grams	0.414	0.400	0.399	0.413	0.437	0.423	0.423	0.436

Table 6. Results of model attribution on the English dataset

Model	Acc	F_{macro}	$Prec$	Rec
xlm-roberta-large-finetuned-conll03-english	0.598	0.593	0.618	0.594
allenai/scibert_scivocab_cased	0.578	0.576	0.590	0.575
microsoft/deberta-base	0.564	0.558	0.602	0.558
roberta-large	0.581	0.568	0.611	0.574
allenai/longformer-base-4096	0.586	0.582	0.600	0.582
bert-large-uncased-whole-word-masking-finetuned-squad	0.581	0.581	0.597	0.579
Ensemble with P^C as an input feature				
Bagging	0.597	0.599	0.614	0.595
voting	0.607	0.603	0.650	0.603
OneVsRest	0.625	0.626	**0.651**	0.622
output code	0.624	0.625	0.649	0.621
Linear SVC	**0.629**	**0.630**	0.637	**0.626**

Table 7. Results of model attribution on the Spanish dataset

Model	Acc	F_{macro}	$Prec$	Rec
xlm-roberta-large-finetuned-conll03-english	0.632	0.629	0.661	0.628
PlanTL-GOB-ES/roberta-large-bne	0.614	0.615	0.630	0.612
hiiamsid/sentence_similarity_spanish_es	0.615	0.612	0.640	0.613
dbmdz/bert-base-multilingual-cased-finetuned-conll03-spanish	0.593	0.594	0.599	0.593
roberta-large	0.584	0.584	0.595	0.584
Ensemble with P^C as an input feature				
Bagging	0.616	0.615	0.637	0.613
voting	0.631	0.630	**0.691**	0.627
OneVsRest	0.648	0.648	0.677	0.645
output code	0.646	0.647	0.677	0.643
Linear SVC	**0.655**	**0.656**	0.669	**0.652**

5.3   Results

Table 5 shows results produced using three traditional ML methods (Linear SVC, LR, and RF) across two different feature sets (word n-grams and character n-grams) for both languages. LR with character n-grams outperforms other approaches on the macro $F1$ performance metric for both languages.

Tables 6 and 7 provide results on English and Spanish datasets respectively, with different variants of the proposed architecture. The first block in the table shows the results for individual LLMs. The second and third blocks show the ensemble results with P^C and P^A respectively, as input feature vector to several machine learning models.

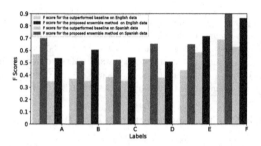

Fig. 2. Class-wise F-scores for the outperformed baseline (*LR with character n-grams*) and proposed ensemble method (*Linear SVC*) on English dataset

The results on the English test data are shown in Table 6. Out of all the combinations, Linear SVC with concatenated feature vector (P^C) as an input, outperforms other approaches for a majority of the evaluation metrics with an F_{macro} score of 0.63. Table 7 shows the results on the Spanish test dataset where the concatenated feature vector (P^C) is passed as an input to the Linear SVC classifier outperforms the other approaches with an F_{macro} score of 0.656.

Overall, we observed that the ensemble models performed well when compared to individual LLMs. Ensembling the models provides additional cues from each individual model, which helps enhance the performance. Furthermore, several variants of the proposed framework outperforms each of the baselines across the evaluated metrics.

Table 8. Samples form the English test dataset where the prediction from the ensemble model (Linear SVC) is accurate, that from the individual LLM is not.

Samples from test set	Ground truth
The Association is also a member of the European Federation for Transport and Environment (EFTE). The Association works closely with other associations that are active within the environmental sector such as the Environment Agency, Europe environment, EFTE and REACH.	B
@snedwan Oh shit We were like one of the most popular bands of the early 90 s and we have some of the best songs	D
But the second half was a completely different story, with the visitors responding with two tries from Andrew Conway and one from Chris Dickson. Conways score came just before the hour mark and gave the visitors a 2017 lead, with Lawrences second coming with just under 10 min to go. However, the Giants hit back with two tries in the dying moments, with Lawrences matchwinning effort on his first start since December making the difference	E

Figure 2 shows the class-wise performance comparison of our best ensemble method (*Linear SVC*) with that of the best baseline (*LR with character-n-grams*) on English and Spanish datasets. For all the classes in both datasets, the macro *F1* score of the proposed method outperforms the baseline macro *F1* scores. Even though the number of parameters for LLMs that we explore are not huge, our proposed ensemble approach performed very well on text generated using the large model with 175B parameters (text-davinci-003).

Tables 8 and 9 show a few samples from the test data for English and Spanish, respectively. In these samples, we demonstrate that while no individual LLM predict the ground truth label correctly, the ensemble Linear SVC classifier predicts the correct label. We also show the ground truth label associated with each sample.

Table 9. Samples form the Spanish test dataset where the prediction from the ensemble model (Linear SVC) is accurate, that from the individual LLM is not.

Samples from test set	Ground truth
La atención recibida por los responsables del Hotel siempre ha sido excepcional, así como la limpieza, calidad de los alimentos En definitiva un 10!	B
Hey seguidores! Sigan a @SoyElHazMeReir en Instagram para ver más contenido: ht t.co/QqJW3YhQ	C
Gracias a la actualización de Internet Explorer, el contenido de estas páginas se encuentra protegido por la ley de derechos de autor,	E

6   Conclusion

In this paper, we explored generative language model attribution for English and Spanish languages. We proposed an ensemble neural architecture where the probabilities of individual LLMs are concatenated and passed as input to machine learning models. Each of the variants of the proposed ensemble approach outperformed several traditional machine learning baselines and the individual LLMs for both languages. Our model results in macro F_{macro} scores of 63% and 65.6% on English and Spanish data, respectively, outperforming other baseline approaches. Our analysis showed that our proposed approach is also effective at classifying the samples that are generated using LLMs with large number of parameters. Our approach also performs well for out-of-domain themes since themes in the test dataset were different from the training dataset. Directions for future work include developing a multi-task approach for generative language model attribution as well as exploring other multilingual datasets.

References

1. Brown, T., et al.: Language models are few-shot learners. Adv. Neural. Inf. Process. Syst. **33**, 1877–1901 (2020)
2. Conneau, A., et al.: Unsupervised cross-lingual representation learning at scale. arXiv preprint arXiv:1911.02116 (2019)
3. Crothers, E., Japkowicz, N., Viktor, H.: Machine generated text: a comprehensive survey of threat models and detection methods. arXiv preprint arXiv:2210.07321 (2022)
4. Deng, Z., Gao, H., Miao, Y., Zhang, H.: Efficient detection of LLM-generated texts with a Bayesian surrogate model. arXiv preprint arXiv:2305.16617 (2023)
5. Devlin, J., Chang, M., Lee, K., Toutanova, K.: BERT: pre-training of deep bidirectional transformers for language understanding. CoRR abs/1810.04805 (2018). http://arxiv.org/abs/1810.04805
6. Gehrmann, S., Strobelt, H., Rush, A.M.: GLTR: statistical detection and visualization of generated text. arXiv preprint arXiv:1906.04043 (2019)
7. He, P., Liu, X., Gao, J., Chen, W.: DeBERTa: decoding-enhanced BERT with disentangled attention. In: International Conference on Learning Representations (2021). https://openreview.net/forum?id=XPZIaotutsD
8. Ippolito, D., Duckworth, D., Callison-Burch, C., Eck, D.: Automatic detection of generated text is easiest when humans are fooled. arXiv preprint arXiv:1911.00650 (2019)
9. Jawahar, G., Abdul-Mageed, M., Lakshmanan, L.V.: Automatic detection of machine generated text: a critical survey. arXiv preprint arXiv:2011.01314 (2020)
10. Ji, Z., et al.: Survey of hallucination in natural language generation. ACM Comput. Surv. **55**(12), 1–38 (2023)
11. Li, B., Weng, Y., Song, Q., Deng, H.: Artificial text detection with multiple training strategies. arXiv preprint arXiv:2212.05194 (2022)
12. Li, H., Moon, J.T., Purkayastha, S., Celi, L.A., Trivedi, H., Gichoya, J.W.: Ethics of large language models in medicine and medical research. Lancet Digit. Health **5**, e333–e335 (2023)
13. Liu, Y., et al.: RoBERTa: a robustly optimized BERT pretraining approach. CoRR abs/1907.11692 (2019). http://arxiv.org/abs/1907.11692
14. Massarelli, L., et al.: How decoding strategies affect the verifiability of generated text. arXiv preprint arXiv:1911.03587 (2019)
15. Mitchell, E., Lee, Y., Khazatsky, A., Manning, C.D., Finn, C.: DetectGPT: zeroshot machine-generated text detection using probability curvature. arXiv preprint arXiv:2301.11305 (2023)

16. Mitrović, S., Andreoletti, D., Ayoub, O.: ChatGPT or human? Detect and explain. explaining decisions of machine learning model for detecting short ChatGPT-generated text. arXiv preprint arXiv:2301.13852 (2023)
17. Sadasivan, V.S., Kumar, A., Balasubramanian, S., Wang, W., Feizi, S.: Can AI-generated text be reliably detected? arXiv preprint arXiv:2303.11156 (2023)
18. Sarvazyan, A.M., González, J.Á., Franco Salvador, M., Rangel, F., Chulvi, B., Rosso, P.: AuTexTification: automatic text identification. In: Procesamiento del Lenguaje Natural. Jaén, Spain (2023)
19. Scao, T.L., et al.: Bloom: a 176b-parameter open-access multilingual language model. arXiv preprint arXiv:2211.05100 (2022)
20. Sun, Z.: A short survey of viewing large language models in legal aspect. arXiv preprint arXiv:2303.09136 (2023)
21. Uchendu, A., Le, T., Shu, K., Lee, D.: Authorship attribution for neural text generation. In: Proceedings of the 2020 Conference on Empirical Methods in Natural Language Processing (EMNLP), pp. 8384–8395 (2020)
22. Wolf, T., et al.: Transformers: state-of-the-art natural language processing. In: Proceedings of the 2020 Conference on Empirical Methods in Natural Language Processing: System Demonstrations, pp. 38–45 (2020)
23. Wu, S., et al.: BloombergGPT: a large language model for finance. arXiv preprint arXiv:2303.17564 (2023)
24. Zhou, J.T., Tsang, I.W., Pan, S.J., Tan, M.: Heterogeneous domain adaptation for multiple classes. In: Artificial Intelligence and Statistics, pp. 1095–1103. PMLR (2014)

Knowledge-Grounded Dialogue Generation with Contrastive Knowledge Selection

Bin Wang[1], Fuyong Xu[1], Zhenfang Zhu[2], and Peiyu Liu[1(✉)]

[1] School of Information Science and Engineering, Shandong Normal University,
Jinan 250014, Shandong, China
liupy@sdnu.edu.cn
[2] School of Information Science and Electrical Engineering,
Shandong Jiaotong University, Jinan 250357, Shandong, China
zhuzf@sdjtu.edu.cn

Abstract. Knowledge selection is the key component in knowledge-ground dialogues, which aims to choice correct knowledge based on external knowledge for dialogue generation. The quality of knowledge selection depend on knowledge representation methods. However, the knowledge representation exploration is still challenging. We propose a knowledge-grounded dialogue model, which incorporates a knowledge-grounded module and a dialogue generation module, aiming to choose the most appropriate knowledge and fuse it into response generation. In addition, supervised contrastive knowledge representation signal is designed to obtain knowledge representation dynamically. Experiments on FoCus dataset show that our model outperforms the baseline models. The ablation study further demonstrates the effectiveness of each sub-modules.

Keywords: Dialogue Generation · Knowledge Selection · Contrastive Knowledge Representation · Knowledge-ground Dialogue · Encoder-decoder

1 Introduction

It has always been challenging to generate rich and consistent responses in dialogue systems. A great deal of previous works focus on the persona-based dialogue systems and yield some encouraging results. But in the actual conversation, users' persona information and factual information are equal significant. For example, when a person with a leg disability asks for suggestions about a trip to Changbai Mountain, the ski resort that most people prefer cannot be recommended. According to this human dialogue manner, Knowledge-grounded Dialogue Generation was proposed to improves the ability of the dialogue agent to generate rich and consistent responses based on knowledge. The knowledge include the user's persona information and customized knowledge about the topic

© The Author(s), under exclusive license to Springer Nature Singapore Pte Ltd. 2023
F. Zhang et al. (Eds.): WISE 2023, LNCS 14306, pp. 710–719, 2023.
https://doi.org/10.1007/978-981-99-7254-8_55

being talked about. Figure 1 depicts the informative and attractive response generated by considering both the user's persona and the customized knowledge.

Benefiting from the advance of dialogue datasets [1,2] and pre-trained models [3–5], human-machine dialogue research has made great achievements. However, most of exist datasets focus on the user's persona, which facilitates the construction of persona-based dialog agents. The lack of customized knowledge limits the ability of the agent to generate knowledge-grounded answers. Some researchers released several datasets with informative answers [6–8] to tackle this issue. Especially for the FoCus dataset [8], it provides each conversation with customized knowledge information that reflects the user preferences. The FoCus dataset makes knowledge-grounded dialogue possible.

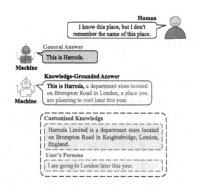

Fig. 1. Objective of knowledge-grounded dialogue generation. Compared with the general answer which can only generate basic information, the knowledge-grounded answer is richer and more attentive, reflecting the user's persona and customized knowledge.

Based on the FoCus dataset [8], some researchers have made efforts on knowledge-grounded dialogue generation. Saha et al. [9] create an end-to-end neural response generator to facilitate learning dependencies between knowledge and the context. Lee et al. [10] in order to alleviate the problem of overly stale knowledge in the dataset and to maximize the generative power of GPT3, propose a pipeline of creating diverse responses. However, these methods cannot obtain higher order embedding knowledge representation and do not consider clustering among the correct and incorrect answers in candidates. Therefore, we propose a knowledge-grounded dialogue generation model that incorporates knowledge-grounded module and dialogue generation module. The knowledge-grounded module pick out the persona and customized knowledge that fits the current context. And the dialogue generation module make knowledge-grounded dialogue and generate informative as well as attractive response. In addition, we introduce supervised contrastive learning into knowledge-grounded, by adjusting the embedding representation of persona and customized knowledge candidates. To be specific, the supervised contrastive learning make the distance between correct answers shrink and enlarge the distance between correct and incorrect answers, which significantly improve the ability of the model to select knowledge. To summarize, our main contributions can be concluded as follows:

- We propose a knowledge-grounded dialogue generation model, which can offer more correct and richer information for response generation.
- The supervised contrastive learning is introduced to acquire the high-order knowledge representation, significantly improving the model's ability to select knowledge.
- Automatic evaluations show that our model has better performance, and the ablation study proves the effectiveness of knowledge-grounded module in detail.

2 Related Work

2.1 Knowledge-Grounded Dialogue System.

There are currently two main approaches for persona-based dialogue systems, one mining the implicit persona information from dialogue history [11], and more researches focusing on understanding the pre-assigned persona [1,12]. Xu et al. [13] utilize a persona information memory network to pick out the persona that most relevant to context, and pre-trained model with reinforcement learning. Wang et al. [14] use the pre-trained model to encode the personas and conversation history independently and design a dynamic persona fusion mechanism to effectively mine the relevance of dialogue context and persona information. However, Due to lack of correct and customized knowledge, the dialogue agents merely answer the question without considering the user or specialized knowledge.

Some researchers have recognized this problem and released several datasets with persona and customized knowledge information, intending to enable dialogue agents to generate customized knowledge-grounded responses that reflect user's persona [8,15]. In this, the FoCus dataset provides factual information that reflect user's persona, allowing the model to retrieve the corresponding knowledge while considering the user's background information.

2.2 Contrastive Learning

In the field of computer vision, Chen et al. [16] use data enhancement methods in SimCLR to obtain image samples, which are from the same image as positive samples and from other images as negative samples, and then optimizing the contrastive loss. Thus they adjust the distance of the positive and negative samples in the vector space, achieving the unsupervised contrastive learning. Since cross-entropy loss may cause the pre-trained model to be unstable in training, and converge to a local optimum rather than a global optimum. Gunel et al. [18] introduce supervised contrast loss into the fine-tuning phase, which improves the overall performance of the pre-trained model. But it is difficult for contrastive learning that be applied in text generation task. To solve this problem, An et al.

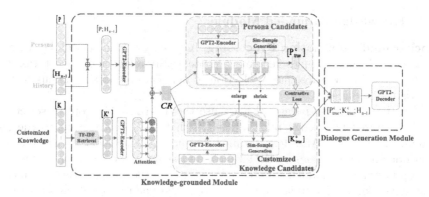

Fig. 2. The overview of model framework.

[19] propose a new Contrastive Neural Text generation frame-work, addressing bottlenecks that prevent contrastive learning from being widely adopted in generation tasks from three aspects. This allows contrastive learning to be applied to the field of text generation to alleviate the exposure bias problem.

3   Methodology

3.1   Problem Definition

The conversation history between user A and machine M consists of N dialogs, each dialog history having n-1 rounds, defined as $H_{n-1} = \{(u_1^A, u_1^M), \ldots, (u_{n-1}^A, u_{n-1}^M)\}$, and the question of user was defined as $H_n = \{(u_n^A)\}$. The known user persona is $P = \{P_1, P_2, \ldots, P_L\}$, prior customized knowledge of the topic being talked about is $K = \{K_1, K_2, \ldots, K_S\}$. The persona candidates and customized knowledge candidates that can be selected for response generation are $P^c = \{P_1^c, P_2^c, \ldots, P_I^c\}$, $K^c = \{K_1^c, K_2^c, \ldots, K_J^c\}$, respectively. Persona candidates and customized knowledge candidates comprise ground truth and distracting answer in which the correct answer is marked. To assist in generating rich and diverse responses, the task of the model is to extract the persona and customized knowledge from P^c and K^c that best fit the current context based on the existing P, K, and H_{n-1}. The overall framework of model is illustrated in Fig. 2.

In knowledge-grounded module, the customized knowledge is retrieved and encoded with history and persona, and the three are concatenated into contextually relevant representation (CR), which is used as the input of the grounding task. In the grounding task, the model uses CR as the foundation to select the correct candidate. Finally, P_{ture}^c, K_{ture}^c and H_{n-1} is concatenated and autoregressive decoding is performed to get the response.

3.2 Knowledge-Grounded Module

Background Information Processing. Inspired by Yoonna et al. [8], we first process P, K and H_{n-1} to generate a contextually relevant representation CR of the three for the subsequent selection of persona grounding and customized knowledge-grounded.

For the knowledge paragraphs, we use the TF-IDF [20] score to select the five customized knowledge paragraphs K', that are most relevant to the last utterance u_n^A of user. After transforming the chosen 5 knowledge paragraphs into embedded representations by GPT2 encoding, we using the attention mechanism [21] update the last hidden state representations of the special tokens from each customized knowledge paragraphs, then take the updated result as subsequent input.

For persona paragraphs and conversation history, we concatenate the two and encode them using GPT-2, taking the last hidden state of the last special token and concatenating it with customized knowledge to obtain a contextually relevant representation (CR) of the current conversation round.

Persona Grounding. The aim of the task is to select the most suitable persona based on the given CR representation to assist in generating rich and diverse responses. One of the persona candidate is the ground-truth. A special token is added to each candidate, after which the final hidden layer state of the special token is concatenated with the CR and used as input for classification. The loss function is defined as:

$$L_{PG} = -\sum_{j=1}^{J} \left(q_j^* log\ Prob\left([CR; h(p_j)]\right) \right.$$
$$\left. + (1 - q_j^*) log(1 - Prob\left([CR; h(p_j)]\right)\right), \tag{1}$$

when the $j-th$ candidate is ground-truth, q_j^* is 1, otherwise it is 0. $h(p_j)$ is the last hidden state representation of the special token of p_j. $Prob\left([CR; h(p_j)]\right)$ is the estimated probability of the models.

Customized Knowledge-Grounded. The model needs to select the customized knowledge that best fits the current context and most relate to the topic being talked about. The customized knowledge candidate, after encoding, is selected by concatenating the CR with the final hidden layer state to select the customized knowledge that can answer the question:

$$L_{KG} = -\sum_{s=1}^{S} q_s^* log\ Prob\left([CR; h(k_s)]\right), \tag{2}$$

with q_s^* denoting a label defined as 1 if $s-th$ knowledge paragraph is round-truth, 0 otherwise. $h(k_s)$ is the last hidden state representation of the special token of k_s. $Prob\left([CR; h(k_s)]\right)$ is the estimated probability of the models.

Supervise Contrastive Learning. To enable the model better select the most appropriate persona and customized knowledge, we introduced supervised contrastive learning [17], aiming to shrink the distance between positive samples and enlarge the distance between positive and negative samples.

However, in this task, only one candidate in each batch is positive sample, so clustering between positive samples is not possible. For this reason, we set up a similar sample generator to generate a pseudo-positive sample that is similar to the positive sample in the candidates, which can be used to achieve clustering of the positive samples in the supervised contrastive learning.

We concatenate the context-relevant representation CR with either persona candidates or customized knowledge candidates as input to the calculation of the contrastive loss. For one batch with N training samples, the supervised contrastive loss can be expressed by the following equation:

$$L_{SCL} = \sum_{i \in I} \frac{-1}{|P(i)|} \sum_{p \in P(i)} log \frac{exp((\boldsymbol{X_i} \cdot \boldsymbol{X_p})/\tau)}{\sum_{a \in A(i)} exp((\boldsymbol{X_i} \cdot \boldsymbol{X_a})/\tau)} \tag{3}$$

where $X \in \mathbb{R}^N$, $i \in I = \{1, 2, \ldots, N\}$ indicate the index of the samples, $\tau \in R^+$ denotes the temperature coefficient used to control the distance between instances, $P(i) = I_{j=i} - \{i\}$ represents samples with the same category as i while excluding itself, $A(i) = I - \{i, N+i\}$ indicates samples in a batch except itself.

3.3 Dialogue Generation Module

We use an auto-regressive decoding manner to model the utterance. The language modelling loss function is defined as follows:

$$L_{LM} = - \sum_{i=1}^{I} log \, Prob(x_i|v, \, x_1, \ldots, x_{i-1}), \tag{4}$$

where $Prob(\cdot)$ denotes a probability of the language model, x_i is i-th token of u^M, I is the number of tokens and v stands for the sequence $[P_{ture}^c, K_{ture}^c, H_{n-1}]$ with concatenation of P_{ture}^c, K_{ture}^c and H_{n-1}.

3.4 Model Training

The loss function is composed of 3 parts, language modeling loss, grounding loss and contrastive learning loss. We add the three parts of the loss in proportion to the sum, which like a muti-task learning method [?] [22], the full training objectives are defined as follows:

$$L = \alpha L_{PG} + \beta_{PG} L_{PG} + \beta_{KG} L_{KG} + \gamma_{PG} L_{SCL}^{PG} + \gamma_{KG} L_{SCL}^{KG}$$

where α, β_{PG}, β_{KG}, γ_{PG} and γ_{KG} are trainable parameters, which can self-adaptive adjust the weight of each loss.

4   Experiments

This section will elaborate on the experimental conditions, dataset, baseline models, and parameter settings adopt in the experiment. In addition, an ablation study is implemented to investigate the effect of persona grounding (PG) and customized knowledge-grounded (KG) tasks on the model.

4.1   Experimental Setup

The code framework and initial weight of $GPT - 2_{Small}$ come from Huggingface's Transformers [23]. The optimizer applied for model training is Adam [24], and the learning rate is set as 6.25e−5. Among the combinations, we choose the hyperparameters that showed the best performance. For the generation of the final response, we used nuclear sampling top-p decoding with a threshold of 0.9 and a sampling temperature of 0.7.

4.2   Dataset

In this work, we use the FoCus dataset for model training and testing. As the test set is not provided in its public release, we use the valid set for testing. The FoCus dataset supports knowledge-grounded answers that reflect user's persona. The main content of the dialog is a discussion of different geographical landmarks. The FoCus dataset contains not only background persona and customized knowledge information, but also persona candidates and customized knowledge candidates to each conversation and the corresponding index of ground-truth.

According to statistics of the FoCus dataset published by Yoonna et al. [8], there are 14,452 dialogs in the dataset, and approximately 6 rounds per-dialog on average. The average length of the machine's utterances is greater than 140. This suggests that machine-generated utterances contain more knowledge. In addition, the answer that contain only customized knowledge are 44,518 in total. And answers that include both customized knowledge and persona are 42,186.

4.3   Evaluation Metrics

To better evaluate the capability of the model, we divided it into two sub-tasks − Task 1 (*grounding*) and Task 2 (*generation*) to evaluate the generative and discriminative capability of the model respectively.

Task 1 - Grounding
The objective of this task was to evaluate the performance of the persona grounding and customized knowledge-grounded tasks we used in the model. In each dialogue set, we gave 5 persona candidates (P^c) and 10 customized knowledge candidates (K^c) with answer labels, where K^c contains the ground-truth sentence form Wikipedia and the distracting candidates with the same number of sentences as the grounding-truth but describing other landmarks. We used the selection accuracy as a measure of persona grounding and customized knowledge-grounded.

Task 2 - Generation. In evaluating the quality of generation, we used perplexity to measure the fluency of the generated sentences, using the chrF++ [25] score and the recall-oriented understudy (ROUGE-1, ROUGE-2, ROUGE-L) [26] for gisting evaluation to measure the similarity between the generated responses and the standard responses.

Table 1. The result in FoCus dataset. Above is the result of comparison with baseline, below is the result of the ablation study.

Models	Grounding (Acc.)		Generation				
	PG	KG	chrF++	R-1	R-2	R-L	PPL
Enc-Dec+PG+KG	**67.44%**	58.26%	0.1376	18.85	2.76	15.12	285.51
Baseline	67.41%	66.19%	0.2692	35.24	18.16	31.22	10.86
Ours	**67.44%**	**69.39%**	**0.32**	**37.39**	**20.35**	**33.11**	**10.79**
LM	32.56%	7.02%	0.22	29.96	11.91	25.98	12.31
LM+PG	**67.44%**	11.99%	0.20	27.31	10.36	23.89	15.39
LM+KG	63.63%	68.77%	**0.28**	34.95	18.33	31.22	10.93

4.4 Analysis

We chose the generative models proposed by Yoonna et al. as the baseline model. And we also measured the knowledge-grounded capability of the transformer-encdec [27] but no supervised contrastive representation. As shown in Table 1, the accuracy of our model on PG and KG is higher than that of baseline, which demonstrates that the supervised contrastive learning method we have introduced can shrink the distance between the same class samples and expand the distance between the different class samples, improving the performance of persona selection and customized knowledge selection. Our model also outperforms baseline in all generation metrics, and we use approximately the same generation method as baseline for the generation, which proves that the PG and KG subtasks are effective in assisting the model to generate fluent and rich responses. As for transformer-based model, the performance of all but PG is unsatisfactory, especially the generation part, which reflects the power of GPT2.

4.5 Ablation Study

In addition, in order to explore the effect of persona grounding and customized knowledge-grounded tasks on the performance of the model, this section conducts an ablation study on two tasks. The results are shown in Table 1.

In the generation task, there is no doubt that the language model trained with two grounding tasks achieved the best performance because of the relatively more correct customized knowledge. However, the language model trained with PG obtained the worst generative performance, even compared to the only language model. When the PG task is stacked with KG, the generation quality is further improved compared to language model trained with KG. In addition, thanks to the basic capabilities of GPT2, even with a language model only, the model can have a certain level of persona selection. After adding KG to the training to give the model more correct customized knowledge as hint, the persona grounding accuracy also improved accordingly.

5 Conclusion

We propose a unified framework with knowledge selection and contrastive representation for response generation in conversation. First, to filter the redundant information, the knowledge-grounded task is introduced to select the most appropriate persona and customized knowledge for the current context, making the generated responses more informative and attractive. In addition, we utilize supervised contrastive representation signal to reduce the intra-class distance, increase inter-class variance, and better select the correct answer from the candidates. The results of automatic evaluation compared with the baseline model demonstrate that the supervised contrastive representation signal can effectively improve the model's accuracy of knowledge selection. Furthermore, ablation studies show that the knowledge-grounded module facilitates the agent to generate higher-quality responses.

Acknowledgment. This work was supported in part Key R & D project of Shandong Province 2019JZZY010129, and in part by the Shandong Provincial Social Science Planning Project under Award 19BJCJ51, Award 18CXWJ01, and Award 18BJYJ04.

References

1. Zhang, S., et al.: Personalizing dialogue agents: i have a dog, do you have pets too?. In: ACL (Volume 1: Long Papers) (2018)
2. Kim, M., et al.: Dual task framework for improving persona-grounded dialogue dataset. In: AAAI, vol. 36, no. 10 (2022)
3. Brown, T., et al.: Language models are few-shot learners. In: NeurIPS, vol. 33, pp. 1877–1901 (2020)
4. Raffel, C., et al.: Exploring the limits of transfer learning with a unified text-to-text transformer. J. Mach. Learn. Res. **21**(1), 5485–5551 (2020)
5. Wang, P., et al.: OFA: unifying architectures, tasks, and modalities through a simple sequence-to-sequence learning framework. In: International Conference on Machine Learning. PMLR (2022)
6. Dinan, E., et al.: Wizard of Wikipedia: knowledge-powered conversational agents. In: ICLR (2018)
7. Smith, E.M., et al.: Can you put it all together: evaluating conversational agents' ability to blend skills. In: ACL (2020)
8. Jang, Y., et al.: Call for customized conversation: customized conversation grounding persona and knowledge. In: AAAI, vol. 36, no. 10 (2022)

9. Saha, S., Das, S., Srihari, R.K.: Proto-gen: an end-to-end neural generator for persona and knowledge grounded response generation. In: Proceedings of the 1st Workshop on Customized Chat Grounding Persona and Knowledge (2022)

10. Lee, Y.-J., et al.: PERSONACHATGEN: generating Personalized Dialogues using GPT-3. In: Proceedings of the 1st Workshop on Customized Chat Grounding Persona and Knowledge (2022)

11. Bak, J., Oh, A.: Variational hierarchical user-based conversation model. In: EMNLP-IJCNLP (2019)

12. Nakamura, K., et al.: HybriDialogue: an information-seeking dialogue dataset grounded on tabular and textual data. In: Findings of the Association for Computational Linguistics: ACL (2022)

13. Xu, F., et al.: Diverse dialogue generation by fusing mutual persona-aware and self-transferrer. In: APIN, pp. 1–14 (2022)

14. Wang, Y., et al.: Improving persona understanding for persona-based dialogue generation with diverse knowledge selection. In: ICPR. IEEE Computer Society (2022)

15. Smith, E.M., et al.: Can you put it all together: evaluating conversational agents' ability to blend skills. In: ACL (2020)

16. Chen, T., et al.: A simple framework for contrastive learning of visual representations. In: ICML. PMLR (2020)

17. Khosla, P., et al.: Supervised contrastive learning. In: NeurIPS, pp. 18661–18673 (2020)

18. Gunel, B., et al.: Supervised contrastive learning for pre-trained language model fine-tuning. In: ICLR (2020)

19. An, C., et al.: CoNT: contrastive neural text generation. In: NeurIPS (2022)

20. Salton, G., Buckley, C.: Term-weighting approaches in automatic text retrieval. IPM **24**(5), 513–523 (1988)

21. Bahdanau, D., Cho, K.H., Bengio, Y.: Neural machine translation by jointly learning to align and translate. In: ICLR (2015)

22. Zhang, Yu., Yang, Q.: A survey on multi-task learning. IEEE Trans. Knowl. Data Eng. **34**(12), 5586–5609 (2021)

23. Wolf, T., et al.: Transformers: State-of-the-art natural language processing. In: EMNLP: System Demonstrations (2020)

24. Kingma, D.P., Ba, J.: Adam: a method for stochastic optimization. arXiv preprint arXiv:1412.6980 (2014)

25. Popović, M.: chrF++: words helping character N-grams. In: Proceedings of the second conference on machine translation (2017)

26. Lin, C.-Y.: ROUGE: a package for automatic evaluation of summaries. In: Text Summarization Branches Out (2004)

27. Vaswani, A., et al.: Attention is all you need. In: NeurIPS (2017)

Data Analysis and Optimization

A Data-Driven Approach to Finding K for K Nearest Neighbor Matching in Average Causal Effect Estimation

Tingting Xu[1], Yinghao Zhang[1], Jiuyong Li[2], Lin Liu[2], Ziqi Xu[2],

Debo Cheng[2(✉)], and Zaiwen Feng[1,3,4(✉)]

[1] College of Informatics, Huazhong Agricultural University, Wuhan, China
Zaiwen.Feng@mail.hzau.edu.cn
[2] UniSA STEM, University of South Australia, Adelaide, Australia
Debo.Cheng@unisa.edu.au
[3] Macro Agricultural Research Institute, Huazhong Agricultural University, Wuhan, China
[4] Hubei Key Laboratory of Agricultural Bioinformatics, Huazhong Agricultural University, Wuhan, China

Abstract. In causal inference, a fundamental task is to estimate causal effects using observational data with confounding variables. K Nearest Neighbor Matching (K-NNM) is a commonly used method to address confounding bias. However, the traditional K-NNM method uses the same K value for all units, which may result in unacceptable performance in real-world applications. To address this issue, we propose a novel nearest-neighbor matching method called DK-NNM, which uses a data-driven approach to searching for the optimal K values for different units. DK-NNM first reconstructs a sparse coefficient matrix of all units via sparse representation learning for finding the optimal K value for each unit. Then, the joint propensity scores and prognostic scores are utilized to deal with high-dimensional covariates when performing K nearest-neighbor matching with the obtained K value for a unit. Extensive experiments are conducted on both semi-synthetic and real-world datasets, and the results demonstrate that the proposed DK-NNM method outperforms the state-of-the-art causal effect estimation methods in estimating average causal effects from observational data.

Keywords: Causal inference · Causal effects estimation · Matching methods · Confounding bias · K nearest neighbor method

1 Introduction

Most scientific research in fields like medicine, economics, and behavioral science aims to infer the causal effect of a treatment on an outcome of interest [1,2]. One of the key challenges in causal inference is how to eliminate confounding

---

T. Xu and Y. Zhang—These authors contributed equally to this work.

© The Author(s), under exclusive license to Springer Nature Singapore Pte Ltd. 2023
F. Zhang et al. (Eds.): WISE 2023, LNCS 14306, pp. 723–732, 2023.
https://doi.org/10.1007/978-981-99-7254-8_56

bias (bias caused by confounders) when estimating causal effects [3]. Confounding bias arises from unbalanced distributions in treatment and control groups among covariates. Randomized control trials (RCTs) are the most effective way to eliminate the bias [4]. However, due to limitations of time, cost, and ethical concerns, RCTs are often infeasible [2]. As a viable alternative, estimating causal effects from observational data has become increasingly popular [5].

Matching is a popular approach to eliminating confounding bias by balancing the distribution of covariates between the treatment and control groups in paired matching [6]. Some commonly used matching methods include nearest-neighbor matching, subclassification matching, and weighting-based matching [7].

K nearest-neighbor matching (K-NNM) is one of the most widely used matching methods [1]. However, it is challenging to determine the K value. Setting K too large can lead to underfitting and increased computational bias. Conversely, setting K too small can increase the number of false matches. Moreover, the traditional KNN method assigns a fixed K value to all units, it may lead to a biased estimation and impractical outcomes in real-world applications [8,9]. Thus, there is a need to develop a novel K-NNM method that can set an optimal K value for each unit for causal effect estimation from observational data.

In this paper, we propose a novel Data-driven K-Nearest Neighborhood Matching algorithm (DK-NNM) for causal effect estimation from observational data. We first reconstruct all units to obtain a sparse coefficient matrix by using sparse representation learning, and the matrix is used to obtain the optimal K value of each unit. We then perform K-NNM based on propensity and prognostic scores for reducing the dimension of the covariates to avoid the curse of dimensionality [10]. The main contributions of this paper are summarized as follows:

- We utilize a sparse representation learning method to reconstruct the covariates for obtaining an optimal K value of each unit for unbiased estimation of causal effects with observational data.
- We utilize propensity and prognostic scores to reduce the dimension of covariates, instead of using all covariates or only propensity scores for matching.
- We apply our proposed DK-NNM method to both semi-synthetic and real-world datasets for estimating causal effects. The results demonstrate that our proposed DK-NNM method has better performance and efficiency compared with the state-of-the-art causal effect estimation methods.

2   Related Work

In the following, we review previous papers related to our proposed method. In practice, matching methods are commonly used in causal inference to identify groups with comparable or balanced covariate distributions [7]. Rubin and Thomas [11] projected the entire set of variables into one dimension and proposed propensity score matching. Diamond and Sekhon [12] proposed Genetic matching (GenMatch) to improve covariate balance by learning covariate weights, which can be thought of as a broader version of propensity score matching and Mahalanobis distance matching. Additionally, Leacy and Stuart [13] demonstrated that using the combination of propensity and prognostic scores in matching methods had better performance than single-score-based matching methods in low-dimensional settings.

The most relevant work to ours is K-NNM. The exact K-NNM [1] is one of the most common methods. Luna et al. [14] adopted two resampling schemes to provide valid inference for K-NNM estimators. Additionally, Wager et al. [15] developed a random forest-based method to determine the weights for neighbor observations. However, these methods all use a fixed K value. When facing a more complicated scenario, it may lead to a huge deviation in the estimations.

3   Background

Under the potential outcome framework [2], we define the binary treatment variable T_i, which indicates whether a unit takes the treatment or not. The units that receive the treatment ($T_i = 1$) are treated units and the other units ($T_i = 0$) are control units. Let $\mathbf{X}$ denote the set of pre-treatment variables, i.e. covariates of T_i, which are variables that remain unchanged in the treatment process. Y_i represent the observed outcome for unit i, and we use $Y_i(1)$ to represent the potential outcome for unit i in treated group, and $Y_i(0)$ is the potential outcome of i in control group. However, in practice, each unit can only be assigned to either the treated or control group, so either $Y_i(1)$ or $Y_i(0)$ is unobserved for unit i. This is the fundamental challenge in causal effect estimation.

One of the basic tasks in causal inference is to estimate the causal effect of treatment T on outcome Y from observational data. In this paper, we would like to estimate the Average Treatment Effect (ATE) and the Average Treatment effect on the Treated group (ATT), as defined in the following:

$$ATE = E[Y_i(1) - Y_i(0)] \tag{1}$$

$$ATT = E[Y_i(1) \mid T = 1] - E[Y_i(0) \mid T = 1] \tag{2}$$

The propensity score $e(\mathbf{X})$ is defined as the conditional probability of a unit receiving the treatment conditioned on the full set of covariates $\mathbf{X}$ [16], i.e., $e(\mathbf{X}) = P(T = 1 \mid \mathbf{X})$. Furthermore, the prognostic score $p(\mathbf{X})$ is defined as the predicted outcome under the control condition [17], reflecting baseline "risk", i.e., $p(\mathbf{X}) = E[Y \mid \mathbf{X}]$. We use both the propensity and prognostic scores to construct a 2-dimensional space for conducting the matching process. For estimating causal effects from observational data, the following assumptions are required.

Assumption 1 (Stable Unit Treatment Value Assumption [2]). *The stability hypothesis has two implications: it first implies that the potential outcomes in different units are independent of each other. Besides, for each unit, there are no different forms of treatment levels that result in different potential outcomes.*

Assumption 2 (Overlap [2]). *For the covariates $\mathbf{X}$, every unit has a non-zero probability of receiving treatment 1 or 0. Formally, $0 < P(T = t \mid \mathbf{X}) < 1, t = 0, 1$.*

Assumption 3 (Unconfoundedness [18]). *The distribution of treatments is independent of the potential outcome conditioning on the set of covariates* $\mathbf{X}$, *i.e.* $T \perp\!\!\!\perp (Y(0), Y(1)) \mid \mathbf{X}$.

4   The Proposed DK-NNM Method

In this section, we introduce our proposed DK-NNM (Data-driven K-NNM) method. Specifically, we first explain the principle of selecting the K value for each unit through sparse representation learning. Then we present the specific process of our proposed DK-NNM method.

4.1   Sparse Representation Learning for the Optimal K Values

We propose to use sparse representation learning via self-representation for reconstructing the space of $\mathbf{X} \in \mathbb{R}^{n \times d}$, where n and d are the numbers of units and covariates, respectively.

We use a linear model to represent a sample (unit) x_j as $x_j = x_i z_i + \varepsilon_i$ where z_i and ε_i are the dictionary and error term of x_i, respectively. The self-representation makes the reconstruction error as small as possible [19,20], so as to obtain the sparse coefficient matrix $\mathbf{Z}$. We utilize the least squares loss function to reconstruct the self-representation learning process:

$$\min_z \sum_{i=1}^{n} (x_i z_i - x_j)^2 = \min_{\mathbf{Z}} \|\mathbf{XZ} - \mathbf{X}\|_F^2 \tag{3}$$

where $\mathbf{Z} \in \mathbb{R}^{n \times n}$ denotes the reconstruction coefficient matrix and is utilized to capture the correlations within the samples. Based on (3), we have $\mathbf{Z} = (\mathbf{X}^T \mathbf{X})^{-1} \mathbf{X}^T \mathbf{X}$. In real-world applications, $\mathbf{X}^T \mathbf{X}$ is not always invertible. The ℓ_2-norm regularization term is often added to avoid the invertible issue. Therefore, our loss function can be rewritten as follows:

$$\min_{\mathbf{Z}} \|\mathbf{XZ} - \mathbf{X}\|_F^2 + \mu \|\mathbf{Z}\|_2^2 \tag{4}$$

where $\|\mathbf{Z}\|_2^2$ is the ℓ_2-norm regularization term and μ is a tuning parameter. The optimal solution of the optimization problem in (4) can be represented in a close form, i.e., $\mathbf{Z} = (\mathbf{X}^T \mathbf{X} + \mu \mathbf{I})^{-1} \mathbf{X}^T \mathbf{X}$. However, the solution of $\mathbf{Z}$ does not have the sparsity. To obtain the optimal k value for each unit, we expect that each unit is represented by those units strongly correlated with it, and the coefficients of the units with weak correlations are compressed to zero. Therefore, ℓ_2-norm is replaced by ℓ_1-norm in our method, which has been proved to generate sparsity [21]. Hence, our objective function is rewritten as follows:

$$\min_{\mathbf{Z}} \|\mathbf{XZ} - \mathbf{X}\|_F^2 + \alpha \|\mathbf{Z}\|_1, \mathbf{Z} \geq 0 \tag{5}$$

where $\|\mathbf{Z}\|_1$ is the ℓ_1-norm regularization term and $\mathbf{Z} \geq 0$ means that each element of $\mathbf{Z}$ is non-negative. And α is a tuning parameter of ℓ_1-norm to control the sparsity of matrix $\mathbf{Z}$. The larger α is, the more sparse the resulting matrix.

Moreover, we consider a nonlinear dimensionality reduction method, Locality Preserving Projections (LPP) [22] to preserve the neighborhood structure of the data. The LPP regularization term is defined as $\varphi(\mathbf{Z}) = Tr(\mathbf{Z}^T \mathbf{X}^T \mathbf{L} \mathbf{X} \mathbf{Z})$, where $\mathbf{L} \in \mathbb{R}^{d \times d}$ is a Laplacian matrix, implying the correlative information between features. $\mathbf{L} = \mathbf{D} - \mathbf{S}$, where $\mathbf{D} \in \mathbb{R}^{d \times d}$ is a diagonal matrix and $\mathbf{S} \in \mathbb{R}^{d \times d}$ is a similarity matrix. Thus, our final objective function is defined as:

$$\min_{\mathbf{Z}} \frac{1}{2} \|\mathbf{X}\mathbf{Z} - \mathbf{X}\|_F^2 + \alpha \|\mathbf{Z}\|_1 + \beta \varphi(\mathbf{Z}), \mathbf{Z} \geq 0 \tag{6}$$

where β is a tuning parameter to adjust the structure of matrix $\mathbf{Z}$, and is used to balance the magnitude between $\varphi(\mathbf{Z})$ and $\|\mathbf{X}\mathbf{Z} - \mathbf{X}\|_F^2$.

After optimizing (6), the optimal solution $\mathbf{Z}^*$ can be obtained, which represents the weight matrix. The element z_{ij} of $\mathbf{Z}^*$ can be understood as the correlation between the ith sample and the jth sample. If $z_{ij} > 0$, the ith sample and the jth sample are positively correlated; if $z_{ij} < 0$, they are negatively correlated; and if $z_{ij} = 0$, they are independent. To predict, we only use those relevant samples, i.e., samples with nonzero coefficients, instead of using all samples. We take an example to illustrate the optimal K value for each sample. We assume that the optimal solution $\mathbf{Z}^* \in \mathbf{R}^{4 \times 4}$ is as follows:

$$\mathbf{Z}^* = \begin{pmatrix} 0.5 & 0 & 0 & 0.4 & 0.6 \\ 0 & 0.3 & 0.8 & 0 & 0 \\ 0 & 0 & 0.7 & 0 & 0.1 \\ 0.4 & 0.8 & 0 & 0.6 & 0 \\ 0.6 & 0 & 0.1 & 0 & 0.8 \end{pmatrix}$$

There are five samples, and assume that the first two samples are in the treated group ($T = 1$) and the last three samples are in the control group ($T = 0$). There are three nonzero elements in the first row of $\mathbf{Z}^*$, that is z_{11}, z_{14} and z_{15}. It means that the first treated sample is only related to the last two samples except itself, i.e., the fourth and fifth control samples. Then the corresponding optimal K value for the first sample is 2. Similarly, the corresponding optimal K value for the second sample is 1. In this way, the K value of each sample can be obtained. Therefore, our proposed sparse representation learning method takes the data distribution and prior knowledge into account to choose the optimal K value for each sample respectively.

4.2 Matching Based on the Propensity and Prognostic Scores

After learning the optimal K value for each unit, we can employ the K-NNM method to estimate the causal effect from observational data. The matched unit can be considered as the counterfactual outcome [23] for the unit.

In the matching algorithm, our DK-NNM algorithm employs the Mahalanobis distance to measure the distance between each pair of units. Additionally, we transform all covariates into two-dimensional covariates based on propensity score $e(\mathbf{X})$ and prognostic score $p(\mathbf{X})$, significantly reducing dimensionality compared to full matching on the complete covariates. Leacy et al. [13] suggested that matching method conditioning on the propensity and prognostic scores might help to decrease bias and enhance the accuracy of estimations. Hence, these two scores are utilized as the distance metric for our proposed DK-NNM method.

Formally, for the units i and j with estimated propensity scores $\hat{e}_i, \hat{e}_j$ and prognostic scores $\hat{p}_i, \hat{p}_j$, the score-based Mahalanobis distance between i and j can be defined as follows:

$$d(i,j) = \left[\begin{pmatrix} \hat{e}_i \\ \hat{p}_i \end{pmatrix} - \begin{pmatrix} \hat{e}_j \\ \hat{p}_j \end{pmatrix}\right]^{\top} \Sigma^{-1} \left[\begin{pmatrix} \hat{e}_i \\ \hat{p}_i \end{pmatrix} - \begin{pmatrix} \hat{e}_j \\ \hat{p}_j \end{pmatrix}\right], \tag{7}$$

where Σ indicates the variance-covariance matrix of $(\hat{e}, \hat{p})^{\top}$. The propensity score $\hat{e}$ can be estimated using logistic regression of the covariates $\mathbf{X}$ relative to the treatment variable T. For estimating the prognostic score, we restrict our analysis to the control group and perform an ordinary least squares regression of the outcome variable Y on the covariates $\mathbf{X}$. After conducting the K-NNM, we have a set of K-NNs for unit i, denoted as $\mathcal{J}_K(i)$. Then, we have

$$\tilde{Y}_i = (2T_i - 1)\frac{1}{K_i}\sum_{j \in \mathcal{J}_K(i)} Y_j \tag{8}$$

where K_i is the optimal k value for the ith unit, and $\tilde{Y}_i$ is the imputed outcome for unit i that is regarded as the unobserved potential outcome in this work.

5   Experiments

In this section, we conduct experiments on four datasets to evaluate the performance of our method, including IHPD, Jobs, Cattaneo2 and RHC. IHDP [24] is a semi-synthetic dataset, whose ground truth is generated by the synthetic process. The other three real-world datasets have empirical causal effects in the literature. We estimate ATT on the Jobs dataset, since the empirical ATT of this dataset is known. For experiments on the other datasets, we estimate ATE. To evaluate the performance of our proposed method, we use the root mean square errors (RMSE), and standard deviations (SD) as the evaluation metrics.

To demonstrate the superiority of our method, we take the following estimators for comparison: **NNM** (Nearest-Neighbor matching [11]), **PSM** (Propensity Score Matching [16]), **GenMatch** (Genetic Matching [12]), **BART** (Bayesian Additive Regression Trees [24]), **CF** (Causal Forest [25]), **BCF** (Bayesian Causal Forest [26]), and **S-LASSO** (S-learner using LASSO Regression [27]).

5.1   Experiment on Semi-synthetic Dataset IHDP

The dataset IHDP is a randomized experiment data [24] from the Infant Health and Development Program (IHDP). This program provided low-birth-weight, premature infants with high-quality child care and home visiting service. The IHDP dataset contains 747 units. There are 25 pre-treatment variables related to the study such as birth weight, twin status, first born, and sex. Following the procedures of Hill [24], the ground truth ATE of the IHDP dataset is 4.03.

Table 1. Experimental results on IHDP. The best performance is highlighted.

method	ATE	RMSE	SD
NNM	4.1300	0.1533	0.1645
PSM	3.8352	0.1945	0.1141
GenMatch	4.0002	0.0295	0.1874
BART	4.0180	3.5461	0.1192
CF	3.9733	2.7776	0.1019
BCF	3.9724	0.9369	0.9358
S-LASSO	3.8887	0.6956	0.6816
DK-NNM	4.0504	**0.0252**	**0.0145**

Table 2. Experimental results on Jobs. The best performance is highlighted.

method	ATT	RMSE	SD
NNM	198.16	683.34	1280.70
PSM	638.04	800.78	703.33
GenMatch	1098.50	212.54	1407.50
BART	966.60	2133.15	1024.00
CF	335.54	389.40	869.70
BCF	659.47	603.52	559.85
S-LASSO	277.24	2081.98	1992.62
DK-NNM	555.07	**331.41**	**88.94**

The experimental results of all estimators are listed in Table 1. We observe that DK-NNM achieves the best performance for ATE estimation, in particular, the standard deviation is extremely small against others. This demonstrates the competitiveness of DK-NNM with other state-of-the-art estimators.

Table 3. Experimental results on Cattaneo2 and RHC.

dataset	Cattaneo2		RHC	
method	ATE	SD	ATE	SD
NNM	−276.47	30.10	0.1006	0.0266
PSM	−303.97	18.63	0.0481	0.0143
GenMatch	−250.64	30.50	0.0671	0.0273
BART	−273.20	24.87	0.0389	0.0255
CF	−224.64	26.50	0.0229	0.0234
BCF	−227.08	79.81	0.0298	0.0176
S-LASSO	−240.55	87.95	0.0490	0.0810
DK-NNM	**−227.96**	**17.53**	**0.0656**	**0.0035**

5.2   Experiments on Three Real-World Datasets

Jobs. We adopt the Lalonde experiment dataset [28] and the control group data from the Panel Study of Income Dynamics(PSID) [29]. The pre-treatment variables include Age, Years of Education, and Proceeds in 1974 and 1975. The treatment variable represents whether the unit attends job training or not. We use the results of Imai's study as an experimental benchmark, the average causal effect on the treated group (ATT) is $886 with a standard error of $488 [29].

Table 2 shows the results for estimating ATT on the Jobs dataset. From Table 2, we see that the estimated ATT is close to the empirical ground truth and has the smallest SD. The results of BCF and BART are also close to the empirical ATT, but their estimated SDs are large. This indicates that the estimate of DK-NNM is consistent with the credible result and has a smaller SD.

Cattaneo2. The Cattaneo2 [30] is commonly used to study the effect of maternal smoking on birth weight. The mother's smoking status is used as the treatment variable. A variety of covariates are included, such as the Mother's marital status and Whether to drink alcohol or not. In a former paper, Almond et al. [31] studied the effect of maternal smoking on birth weight in pregnancy and they found a strong negative effect of about 200 g to 250 g lighter than normal birth.

The experimental results of all estimators on the Cattaneo2 dataset are listed in Table 3. The estimated ATE by DK-NNM is -227.96 g, which falls within the range of credible results obtained by [31]. And only the ATEs estimated by DK-NNM and CF fall within the empirical estimation interval $(-250$ g, -200 g), which further illustrates the competitiveness of our proposed DK-NNM method.

Right Heart Catheterization. The RHC dataset [32] was obtained from an observational study, which concerned the efficacy of Right Heart Catheterization (RHC) in the initial treatment of critically ill patients. The treatment is whether a patient received an RHC within 24 h. The covariates contain some physiological and clinical indicators. The existing evidence suggests that the use of RHC can result in higher 180-day mortality compared to not using RHC.

The experimental results of all estimators on the RHC dataset are described in Table 3. We can conclude that the causal effects obtained by PSM, GenMatch, BART, CF, BCF and DK-NNM are consistent. This indicates that the application of RHC leads to higher mortality rates within 180 days compared to not applying RHC. The consistent estimate of our method with the previous findings in the literature demonstrates the practicability of our DK-NNM method.

6   Conclusion

In this work, the key aspect of our proposed DK-NNM algorithm is to reconstruct the samples to obtain a sparse correlation matrix, allowing us to identify the best K value for each unit in the K-NNM method. To the best of our knowledge, this is the first study to incorporate data-driven K values into the K-NNM method in causal inference, while also considering the neighborhood structure of the data. Additionally, we employ dimensionality reduction techniques to improve the efficiency of our DK-NNM method. Experimental results on extensive datasets demonstrate that our method outperforms other matching methods, indicating its potential usefulness for causal effect estimation in various applications.

Acknowledgements. We wish to acknowledge the support from the Australian Research Council (under grant DP200101210). This research project was also supported in part by the Major Project of Hubei Hongshan Laboratory under Grant 2022HSZD031, and in part by the Innovation fund of Chinese Marine Defense Technology Innovation Center under Grant JJ-2021-722-04, and in part by the open funds of Hubei Three Gorges Laboratory, and in part by the Fundamental Research Funds for the Chinese Central Universities under Grant 2662023XXPY004, 2662022JC004, and in part by the open funds of the National Key Laboratory of Crop Genetic Improvement under Grant ZK202203, Huazhong Agricultural University, and in part by the Inner Mongolia Key Scientific and Technological Project under Grant 2021SZD0099.

References

1. Rubin, D.B.: Estimating causal effects of treatments in randomized and nonrandomized studies. J. Educ. Psychol. **66**, 688–701 (1974)
2. Imbens, G.W., Rubin, D.B.: Causal Inference for Statistics, Social, and Biomedical Sciences: An Introduction. Cambridge University Press, Cambridge (2015)
3. Cheng, D., Li, J., et al.: Data-driven causal effect estimation based on graphical causal modelling: a survey. arXiv preprint arXiv:2208.09590 (2022)
4. Deaton, A., Cartwright, N.: Understanding and misunderstanding randomized controlled trials. Soc. Sci. Med. **210**, 2–21 (2018)
5. Cheng, D., Li, J., et al.: Causal query in observational data with hidden variables. In: ECAI 2020, pp. 2551–2558. IOS Press (2020)
6. Stuart, E.A.: Matching methods for causal inference: a review and a look forward. Stat. Sci. Rev. J. Inst. Math. Stat. **25**(1), 1–21 (2010)
7. Stuart, E.A.: Matching methods for causal inference: a review and a look forward. Stat. Sci.: Rev. J. Inst. Math. Stat. **25**(1), 1–21 (2010)
8. Zhang, S., Li, X., et al.: Learning k for kNN classification. ACM Trans. Intell. Syst. Technol. (TIST) **8**(3), 1–19 (2017)
9. Wu, W., Parampalli, U., et al.: Privacy preserving k-nearest neighbor classification over encrypted database in outsourced cloud environments. World Wide Web **22**, 101–123 (2019)
10. Cheng, D., Li, J., et al.: Sufficient dimension reduction for average causal effect estimation. Data Min. Knowl. Disc. **36**(3), 1174–1196 (2022)
11. Rubin, D.B.: Matching to remove bias in observational studies. Biometrics **29**, 159–183 (1973)
12. Diamond, A., Sekhon, J.S.: Genetic matching for estimating causal effects: a general multivariate matching method for achieving balance in observational studies. Rev. Econ. Stat. **95**(3), 932–945 (2013)
13. Leacy, F.P., Stuart, E.A.: On the joint use of propensity and prognostic scores in estimation of the average treatment effect on the treated: a simulation study. Stat. Med. **33**(20), 3488–3508 (2014)

14. de Luna, X., Johansson, P., Sjöstedt-de Luna, S.: Bootstrap inference for k-nearest neighbour matching estimators (2010)
15. Wager, S., Athey, S.: Estimation and inference of heterogeneous treatment effects using random forests. J. Am. Stat. Assoc. **113**(523), 1228–1242 (2018)
16. Rosenbaum, P.R., Rubin, D.B.: The central role of the propensity score in observational studies for causal effects. Biometrika **70**(1), 41–55 (1983)
17. Aikens, R.C., Greaves, D., Baiocchi, M.: A pilot design for observational studies: using abundant data thoughtfully. Stat. Med. **39**(30), 4821–4840 (2020)
18. Ye, S.S., Chen, Y., Padilla, O.H.M.: 2D score based estimation of heterogeneous treatment effects. arXiv preprint arXiv:2110.02401 (2021)
19. Zhu, X., Suk, H.-I., Shen, D.: Matrix-similarity based loss function and feature selection for Alzheimer's disease diagnosis. In: Proceedings of the IEEE Conference on Computer Vision and Pattern Recognition, pp. 3089–3096 (2014)
20. Zhang, S., Cheng, D., et al.: Supervised feature selection algorithm via discriminative ridge regression. World Wide Web **21**, 1545–1562 (2018)
21. Zhu, X., Li, X., et al.: Robust joint graph sparse coding for unsupervised spectral feature selection. IEEE Trans. Neural Netw. Learn. Syst. **28**(6), 1263–1275 (2016)
22. He, X., Niyogi, P.: Locality preserving projections. In: Advances in Neural Information Processing Systems, vol. 16 (2003)
23. Chen, X., Wang, S., et al.: Intrinsically motivated reinforcement learning based recommendation with counterfactual data augmentation. World Wide Web 1–22 (2023)
24. Hill, J.L.: Bayesian nonparametric modeling for causal inference. J. Comput. Graph. Stat. **20**(1), 217–240 (2011)
25. Athey, S., Tibshirani, J., Wager, S.: Generalized random forests. Ann. Stat. **47**(2), 1148–1178 (2019)
26. Hahn, P.R., Murray, J.S., Carvalho, C.M.: Bayesian regression tree models for causal inference: regularization, confounding, and heterogeneous effects (with discussion). Bayesian Anal. **15**(3), 965–1056 (2020)
27. Nie, X., Wager, S.: Quasi-oracle estimation of heterogeneous treatment effects. Biometrika **108**(2), 299–319 (2021)
28. LaLonde, R.J.: Evaluating the econometric evaluations of training programs with experimental data. Am. Econ. Rev. **76**, 604–620 (1986)
29. Imai, K., Ratkovic, M.T.: Covariate balancing propensity score. J. Roy. Stat. Soc.: Ser. B (Stat. Methodol.) **76**, 243–263 (2014)
30. Ghosh, T., Ma, Y., De Luna, X.: Sufficient dimension reduction for feasible and robust estimation of average causal effect. Stat. Sin. **31**(2), 821 (2021)
31. Almond, D., Chay, K.Y., Lee, D.S.: The costs of low birth weight. Q. J. Econ. **120**(3), 1031–1083 (2005)
32. Connors, A.F., et al.: The effectiveness of right heart catheterization in the initial care of critically III patients. JAMA **276**(11), 889–897 (1996)

Processing Reverse Nearest Neighbor Queries Based on Unbalanced Multiway Region Tree Index

Liang Zhu[1]($\boxtimes$), Shilan Zhang[1], Xin Song[1]($\boxtimes$), Qin Ma[1], and Weiyi Meng[2]

[1] Hebei University, Baoding 071002, Hebei, China
{zhu,songx}@hbu.edu.cn
[2] State University of New York at Binghamton, Binghamton, NY 13902, USA

Abstract. In many applications and scenarios, there are opportunities for processing reverse nearest neighbor (RNN) queries, which are derived from and more complex than nearest neighbor (NN) queries. Generally, processing NN queries involves sophisticated data structures and methods, and has been very well addressed for low-dimensional data (usually less than 10); while efficiently processing exact NN or RNN queries for high dimensional data remains a challenging problem. This paper proposes an algorithm of evaluating RNN queries in higher dimensional l_p spaces. The main idea of our algorithm is that an RNN query can be processed efficiently based on relevant information easily available and retrievable from memory. The data space containing a finite dataset is divided into multiple small regions forming an unbalanced multiway region tree, then an index containing important information is created by using the tree and the sorted lists of tuples in the dataset. The algorithm consists of two pruning approaches and a verification method based on the index and the characteristics of l_p spaces. Extensive experiments are conducted to demonstrate the excellent performance of our algorithm over various datasets and to show that it outperforms existing state-of-the-art methods CSD, VR-RNN, SFT and TPL.

Keywords: Reverse Nearest Neighbor Query · Unbalanced Multiway Region Tree Index · Space Partitioning · Algorithm · n-Dimensional l_p Spaces

1 Introduction

The model of reverse nearest neighbor (RNN) query introduced by Korn and Muthukrishnan in 2000 is a variation of the nearest neighbor (NN) query [15]. Since then, techniques for processing RNN queries have received considerable attention in various communities, as they are useful in many fields such as database [14], data mining [12], artificial intelligence (AI) [10], machine learning [8], facility location [24], geographic information system [1], Geo-social network [13], etc. For instance, one of the essential tasks in decision support systems is to determine the influence of data points on the database, such as the influence of a new store on a housing estate or a newly created document on a repository, in which the concept of the influence set usually depends on the applications and is difficult to formalize. By defining RNN query, the influence set is described precisely in [15].

© The Author(s), under exclusive license to Springer Nature Singapore Pte Ltd. 2023
F. Zhang et al. (Eds.): WISE 2023, LNCS 14306, pp. 733–747, 2023.
https://doi.org/10.1007/978-981-99-7254-8_57

RNN queries and NN queries are not equivalent to each other, although the NN results and RNN results may be the same for some query points. In general, the efficient evaluation of RNN queries is more complex than that of NN queries, and the techniques for processing RNN queries and NN queries require different data structures and algorithms. Algorithms for evaluating RNN queries are generally classified into two categories: precomputation-based methods [15] (e.g., self-pruning techniques) and filter-refinement techniques [7, 22, 26] (e.g., regions-based pruning and half-space pruning approaches).

The evaluation of an RNN or NN query usually involves a small amount of data, e.g., the data in its neighborhood. Small data is an essential resource for many applications, and cannot be ignored in the era of big data [6]. For instance, small and wide data, as opposed to big data, solves a number of problems for organizations dealing with increasingly complex questions on AI and challenges with scarce data use cases [17]. Moreover, it is challenging to efficiently evaluate exact NN or RNN queries for high-dimensional datasets [27]. Generally, efficient processing of exact NN queries for low-dimensional datasets (usually < 10) has been well addressed [20]. To the best of our knowledge, the datasets used in evaluating the exact RNN queries had no more than 4 dimensions.

Motivated by the spirits of precomputation-based methods and filter-refinement techniques, we discuss the processing of exact RNN queries over datasets in n-dimensional l_p spaces. Our contributions are summarized below: (1) Using a space partition algorithm, we divide the data space containing a finite dataset into multiple small regions, and create an index with an unbalanced multiway region tree and sorted lists of tuples in the dataset. (2) Based on the index, we propose an algorithm to answer RNN queries by pruning useless regions in the tree, then pruning useless tuples in the sorted lists, and finally verifying the candidate tuples to obtain the RNN results. (3) We conduct extensive experiments to measure the performance of our algorithm over various datasets with dimensionality ranging from 2 to 50 and to compare with existing methods.

The rest of this paper is organized as follows. In Sect. 2, we briefly review some related work. In Sect. 3, the problem definition is introduced. Section 4 proposes our method URT-RNN. In Sect. 5, we present the experimental results. Finally, we conclude the paper in Sect. 6.

2 Related Work

As described in Sect. 1, there are two categories of methods for processing RNN queries. One is the class of precomputation-based methods. For instance, in 2000, Korn and Muthukrishnan introduced the concept of RNN queries and provided the algorithm KM based on precomputation by using two R-trees on the tuples and their nearest neighbor circles [15], while this algorithm has the trouble of dealing with updates to datasets [5].

The other is the family of filter-refinement techniques. For instance, in 2000, Stanoi et al. proposed the algorithm SAA using the six-regions pruning for processing RNN queries [21]. In 2007, based on half-space pruning, Tao et al. proposed the algorithm TPL, which prunes tuples according to the principle of the bisector [22]. In 2008, Wu et al. presented the algorithm FINCH using the bisectors to form a convex polygon to approximate the unpruned region [25]. In 2010, Sharifzadeh and Shahabi introduced the VoR-tree index consisting of Voronoi diagram and R-tree for their six-regions method VR-RNN [18]. In 2012, Cheema et al. introduced the concept of influence zone and provided the algorithm InfZone that optimizes the verification of candidates [7]. Yang et al. provided the algorithm SLICE by using more flexible approaches to prune a larger space than the six-regions method in 2017 [26]. In 2020, Li et al. proposed the method CSD based on the characteristics of the conic section by using the VoR-tree index and six-regions pruning [16]. As the dimension of the dataset increases, for the six-regions algorithms (e.g., SAA, VR-RNN and CSD), the number of regions to be retrieved increases exponential growth [19]; for the half-space methods (e.g., TPL, FINCH and InfZone), the complexity of half-space and hypergeometry increases, which lead to the performance diminish rapidly [5]. For example, the datasets used in [22] to measure TPL and SFT are no more than 4 dimensions.

It is a challenge to process exact RNN queries efficiently for both precomputation-based methods and filter-refinement techniques. Moreover, partitioning multidimensional spaces is challenging, and there are no obvious generalizations of practical techniques for more than one dimension [4].

3 Problem Definition

Consider an n-dimensional l_p space $(\mathfrak{R}^n, \|\cdot\|_p)$, where $\mathfrak{R}^n$ is a linear space (or a vector space) over the field $\mathfrak{R}$ of real scalars, and for $x = (x_1, \cdots, x_n) \in \mathfrak{R}^n$, its l_p-norm $\|x\|_p$ is

$$\|x\|_p = \left(\sum_{i=1}^n |x_i|^p\right)^{1/p} \text{ for } 1 \leq p < \infty \tag{1}$$

$$\|x\|_\infty = max_{1 \leq i \leq n}(|x_i|) \text{ for } p = \infty \tag{2}$$

Moreover, $\|x\|_p \to \|x\|_\infty$ when $p \to \infty$. The l_p-norm $\|\cdot\|_p$ will induce the distance function $d_p(x, y) = \|x - y\|_p$ for $x, y \in \mathfrak{R}^n$. When $p = 1, 2$, and ∞, $d_p(x, y)$ will be the *Manhattan distance $d_1(x, y)$, Euclidean distance $d_2(x, y)$,* and *Maximum distance $d_\infty(x, y)$*, respectively, which are useful in many applications. Without loss of generality, the Euclidean distance $d_2(\cdot, \cdot)$ will be used in the following discussion, and denoted by $d(\cdot, \cdot)$ for short. Notice that our approach can apply to any l_p-norm distance function $d_p(\cdot, \cdot)$.

Suppose $R \subset \mathfrak{R}^n$ is a finite dataset/relation and its schema is $R(tid, A_1, \cdots, A_n)$ with n attributes $(A_1, \cdots, A_n)$ corresponding to $\mathfrak{R}^n = \mathfrak{R}_1 \times \cdots \times \mathfrak{R}_n$, where the ith axis $\mathfrak{R}_i = \mathfrak{R}$ for every i. Each tuple $t = (tid, t_1, \cdots, t_n) \in R$ is associated with a *tid* (tuple *id*entifier). R is typically stored as a base table/relation in a relational database system. Let $|R|$ indicate the size of R (i.e., the number of tuples in R).

In this paper, an element (or a vector) will be called a *point* if it is in $\mathfrak{R}^n$, and called a *tuple* if we need to emphasize that it is in R. Now, we consider the $(\mathfrak{R}^n, d(\cdot, \cdot))$, dataset $R \subset \mathfrak{R}^n$ and a query point $Q = (q_1, \cdots, q_n) \in \mathfrak{R}^n$.

Definition 1. A nearest neighbor query NN(Q) is to find a tuple $t_{NN} \in R$ that is closest to Q (ties are broken arbitrarily); that is, NN(Q) = $\{t_{NN}\}$ is a singleton set satisfying

$$d(t_{NN}, Q) \leq d(t, Q) \text{ for all } t \in R - \{t_{NN}\} \tag{3}$$

While a reverse nearest neighbor query RNN(Q) is to find a set of tuples in $\boldsymbol{R}$ with Q as their nearest neighbor; that is,

$$\text{RNN}(Q) = \{t \in \boldsymbol{R} | \forall t' \in \boldsymbol{R}, d(t, t') \geq d(t, Q)\} = \{t \in \boldsymbol{R} | d(t, Q) \leq d(t, t_{NN})\} \quad (4)$$

where $t_{NN} \in \boldsymbol{R}$ is the nearest neighbor of tuple t.

Briefly, NN(Q) is to find "Who is my Nearest Neighbor", while RNN(Q) is to answer "Whose Nearest Neighbor am I", when the query point Q is me.

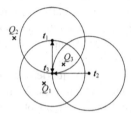

Fig. 1. NN and RNN queries for Q_1, Q_2 and Q_3.

In $(\Re^2, d(\cdot, \cdot))$, as an example shown in Fig. 1, considering $\boldsymbol{R} = \{t_1, t_2, t_3\}$ and three query points Q_1, Q_2 and Q_3, the NN results and RNN results for Q_1, Q_2 and Q_3 are below: NN(Q_1) = $\{t_3\}$ = RNN(Q_1), NN(Q_2) = $\{t_1\} \neq$ RNN(Q_2) = $\emptyset$, and NN(Q_3) = $\{t_3\} \neq$ RNN(Q_3) = $\{t_1, t_2, t_3\}$ = $\boldsymbol{R}$.

4 RNN Query Evaluation

4.1 UR-tree Index

For the dataset $\boldsymbol{R}(tid, A_1, \cdots, A_n)$, let $[a_i, b_i] = [min(A_i), max(A_i)]$ be the domain of attribute A_i ($1 \leq i \leq n$). Then $\boldsymbol{P} = \prod_{i=1}^{n} [a_i, b_i]$ ($\supset \boldsymbol{R}$) is the smallest n-dimensional rectangle containing all tuples in $\boldsymbol{R}$. We use the left-open and right-close interval $(a, b]$ to guarantee complete and disjoint space partitioning. Thus, the initial a_i needs to be replaced by $(a_i - \delta)$ with a small constant $\delta > 0$ ($1 \leq i \leq n$), let $\delta = 0.000001$ for simplifying in our experiments. Thus, $\boldsymbol{P} = \prod_{i=1}^{n} (a_i, b_i] \supset \boldsymbol{R}$.

Algorithm: DivideSpace(τ, $\boldsymbol{R}$, $\boldsymbol{P}$)
Input: the threshold τ, dataset $\boldsymbol{R}$, region $\boldsymbol{P} = \prod_{i=1}^{n}(a_i, b_i]$
Output: $\{\boldsymbol{P}_i: i = 1, \cdots, s\}$

1	**if** $\boldsymbol{P}.TupleNum \leq \tau$ //$\boldsymbol{P}$ is a leaf node
2	Sort the tuples in $\boldsymbol{R} \cap \boldsymbol{P}$ by List-attribute A;
3	**else**
4	Find the v longest edges $e_1, \cdots, e_v$ of $\boldsymbol{P}$, divide $e_1, \cdots, e_v$ into $n_1, \cdots, n_v$ equal-length segments respectively, and $\boldsymbol{P}$ is partitioned into $h = n_1 n_2 \cdots n_v$ cells $\{\boldsymbol{P}_j: j = 1, \cdots, h\}$;
5	**for** $j = 1$ to h
6	DivideSpace(τ, $\boldsymbol{R}$, $\boldsymbol{P}_j$); //recursively call itself
7	**end for**
8	**end if**
9	**return** $\{\boldsymbol{P}_i: i = 1, \cdots, h\}$

The unbalanced multiway region tree (UR-tree) in this paper is a tree, in which the number of tuples contained in each leaf-node does not exceed a fixed threshold τ. A *region* or *cell* in this paper is an n-dimensional rectangle with the form $\prod_{i=1}^{n} (x_i, y_i]$, which will be a node of our UR-tree Index. Let $P_0 = P$. Given a threshold τ, Algorithm DivideSpace is used to divide the region P_0 into multiple cells $\{P_i: i = 1, \cdots, s\}$, and the partitioning stops when the number of tuples in each leaf cell P_i is no more than τ. Let $R_i = R \cap P_i$ for each leaf cell P_i. Then $P = \cup_{i=1}^{s} P_i$ and $P_i \cap P_j = \emptyset$; meanwhile $R = \cup_{i=1}^{s} R_i$, $R_i \cap R_j = \emptyset$, and $|R_i| \leq \tau$. Moreover, $|R_u| = |R \cap P_u| > \tau$ for each non-leaf cell P_u.

The convergence of the Algorithm DivideSpace is very fast, in fact, it is not slower than $O(1/2^d)$, which is the slowest case with $v = 1$ and $n_1 = 2$, where d is the depth of the partitions in Algorithm DivideSpace. For example, let $P = \prod_{i=1}^{50} (a_i, b_i]$ be a 50-dimensional region, $v = 3$, and $n_1 = 3$, $n_2 = 2$ and $n_3 = 2$. In the first partition, we find the $v (= 3)$ longest edges e_1, e_2 and e_3 from all 50 edges of $P_0 = P$ are the 5th, 7th and 9th dimensions, respectively; thus, P is divided into $h = n_1 n_2 n_3 = 3 \times 2 \times 2 = 12$ cells $\{P_i: i = 1, \cdots, 12\}$. In the next partition, for a cell, say P_4, its three longest edges e_1, e_2 and e_3 may belong to other dimensions, e.g., the 7th, 20th and 39th dimensions, respectively.

Let A be an attribute with the maximum number of distinct values $t[A]$ for all $t \in R$. This attribute A is used to generate a sorted list with non-decreasing A-values in the UR-tree Index for each leaf cell P_i, and A is called the *List-attribute* in this paper.

The structure of the UR-tree Index consists of two parts: Part-I is a UR-tree in which each (non-leaf or leaf) node is a cell (i.e., region), and Part-II is a set of sorted lists in which each list is pointed to by a leaf node in the UR-tree.

Algorithm: BuildIndex(τ, R, *Root*)
Input: the threshold τ, dataset R, pointer *Root* to the UR-tree Index
Output: the UR-tree Index

1	DivideSpace(τ, R, *Root*);	//call Algorithm DivideSpace
2	**for each** *Leaf*	//find t_{NN} for each t in the *Leaf*
3	**if** *Leaf.TupleNum* = 0	
4	*Leaf.d_{max}* = 0;	//ignore this *Leaf*
5	**else**	//*Leaf.TupleNum* ≥ 1
6	**for each** $t \in Leaf$	
7	Find a candidate nearest neighbor t';	
8	Verify t' and get a nearest neighbor t_{NN};	
9	*Leaf.d_{max}* = max(*Leaf.d_{max}*, *t.d_{NN}*);	
10	**end for**	
11	**end if**	
12	**end for**	
13	**for each** *Node* in the UR-tree Index	
14	d_{max} = max$\{d_{NN} = d(t, t_{NN}) \mid t \in Node\}$;	
15	**end for**	
16	**return** UR-tree Index	

The node schema of the UR-tree Index is Node(*TupleNum*, x, y, c, r_{max}, d_{max}, *LP*, *CP*) for an n-dimensional non-leaf or leaf node $P_u = \prod_{i=1}^{n} (x_i, y_i]$, where *TupleNum* =

$|R_u| = |R \cap P_u|$; $x = (x_1, \cdots, x_n)$ and $y = (y_1, \cdots, y_n)$ are the min-point and max-point of P_u, respectively; $c = (c_1, \cdots, c_n)$ is the center-point of P_u with $c_i = (x_i + y_i)/2$ for $1 \leq i \leq n$; $r_{max} = d(c, y) = (\sum_{i=1}^{n} |c_i - y_i|^2)^{1/2}$ is the distance between the center-point c and the max-point y of P_u; $d_{max} = max\{d(t, t_{NN}) \mid \forall t \in R_u\}$; LP is the pointer to the sorted list of the tuples in R_u for leaf node P_u; while CP is the pointer to the sub-nodes of non-leaf node P_u.

The list schema of the UR-tree Index is List($tid, A_1, \cdots, A_n, NNtid, d_{NN}$) for a sorted list with the List-attribute, where tid is the identity of the tuple $t \in R_i \subset P_i$; $(A_1, \cdots, A_n)$ are the attributes of the tuple t; $NNtid$ is the identity of the nearest neighbor t_{NN} of the tuple t; d_{NN} is the distance $d(t, t_{NN})$ between the tuple t and its nearest neighbor t_{NN}.

Algorithm BuildIndex is used to build the UR-tree Index for the dataset $R \subset P$: (1) P is divided into small cells by Algorithm DivideSpace with a given threshold τ; (2) the nearest neighbor t_{NN} of the tuple $t \in R$ is searched; (3) d_{max} of non-leaf or leaf node P_u is recorded based on the nearest neighbors in Step (2).

4.2 Approach of RNN Query

Based on the UR-tree Index, we propose the algorithm URT-RNN to process RNN query, which includes two filters (i.e., FirstPrune and SecondPrune) and the verification of candidate tuples.

FirstPrune. Based on Lemma 1 below, we present Algorithm FirstPrune as follows, which is utilized to prune useless regions in the UR-tree Index and to obtain the set of candidate regions $CRSet$. Again, c is the center-point of P_i, y is the max-point of P_i, $r_{max} = d(c, y)$, and $d_{max} = max\{d(t, t_{NN}) \mid \forall t \in R_i\}$, which are used in Lemma 1 below.

Lemma 1. Consider the dataset R and its UR-tree Index with the region set $\{P_i: i = 0, 1, \cdots, s\}$. For a query point Q, a region P_i and $R_i = R \cap P_i$ ($0 \leq i \leq s$), if $d(c, Q) > r_{max} + d_{max}$, then $\forall t \in R_i, t \notin RNN(Q)$. The proof of Lemma 1 is given in Appendix.

Algorithm: FirstPrune($n, \tau, Node, Q$)
Input: the dimensionality n, threshold τ, region $Node$ in UR-tree, query point Q
Output: $CRSet$ //set of candidate regions {$Node$}

```
1    if Node.TupleNum ≠ 0
2        PruneDistance = Node.r_max + Node.d_max;
3        Calculate d(Node.c, Q);
4        if d(Node.c, Q) ≤ PruneDistance
5            if Node.TupleNum > τ
6                for each child∈Node
7                    FirstPrune(n, τ, child, Q);
8                end for
9            else
10                Insert the Node into CRSet;
11            end if
12        end if
13    end if
14    return CRSet
```

ScondPrune. Based on Lemma 2 below, Algorithm SecondPrune is provided as follows, which is used to prune the useless tuples in the set of candidate regions *CRSet*.

Lemma 2. Let two arbitrary points $x = (x_1, \cdots, x_n), y = (y_1, \cdots, y_n) \in \Re^n$, and a constant $\sigma > 0$. Then $d_p(x, y) > \sigma$ if $|x_i - y_i| > \sigma$ for some $1 \leq i \leq n$, where the distance function $d_p(\cdot, \cdot)$ is induced by $\|\cdot\|_p$.

The proof of Lemma 2 is presented in Appendix. Notice that Lemma 2 is not true for some distance functions, e.g., $d(x, y) = \left(\sum_{i=1}^{2} |x_i - y_i| / (1 + |x_i - y_i|) \right) / 2$ in $\Re^2$.

Given a query point $Q = (q_1, \cdots, q_n)$, according to Lemma 2, a tuple $t = (t_1, \cdots, t_n)$ $\in R$ is a candidate tuple of Q if and only if $|t_i - q_i| \leq d(t, t_{NN})$ for all $i = 1, \cdots, n$. The other tuple $t \in R$ will be pruned by Algorithm SecondPrune, when $|t_i - q_i| > d(t, t_{NN})$ for some $1 \leq i \leq n$.

Algorithm: SecondPrune(n, **P**, Q)
Input: the dimensionality n, node **P** in *CRSet*, query point Q
Output: *ctSet*   //set of candidate tuples $\{t\}$

---

1   Find the set of all tuples $T = \{t \in P \mid Q[A] - P.d_{max} \leq t[A] \leq Q[A] + P.d_{max}\}$ by using
        the Lists of UR-tree Index with binary search and sorted access;
                                                          //the others will be pruned
2   **for each** $t \in T$ **do** random access
3   Get its all attributes value $t_i = t[A_i]$;   //here $A_i \neq A$
4   **if** $|t_i - Q[A_i]| \leq t.d_{NN}$ for all such i
5   Insert t into *ctSet*;
6   **else**
7   **break**;   //it is pruned
8   **end if**
9   **end for**
10   **return** *ctSet*

Verification. For a query point Q, using the UR-tree Index, it is easy to know that its candidate tuple t will belong to RNN(Q) if $d(t, t_{NN}) \geq d(t, Q)$.

Algorithm: URT-RNN(n, τ, *Root*, Q)
Input: the dimensionality n, threshold τ, root node *Root* of UR-tree Index, query point Q
Output: RNN(Q)

---

1   FirstPrune(n, τ, *Root*, Q);   //Part-I
2   **for each** *Node* $\in$ *CRSet*   //Part-II
3   SecondPrune(n, *Node*, Q);
4   **end for**
5   **for each** $t \in ctSet$ // Part-III
6   Calculate the distance $d(t, Q)$;
7   **if** $d(t, Q) \leq t.d_{NN}$
8   Insert t into RNN(Q);
9   **end if**
10   **end for**
11   **return** RNN(Q)

Algorithm URT-RNN. Algorithm URT-RNN consists of three parts: Part-I obtains the set of candidate regions (i.e., *CRSet*) by Algorithm FirstPrune; Part-II obtains the set of candidate tuples (i.e., *ctSet*) by Algorithm SecondPrune; Part-III verifies the candidate tuple *t* in *ctSet* and retrieves the RNN tuples for a query point.

By Lemma 1, Lemma 2 and Definition 1 (of RNN), it is easy to see that the conclusion of following Theorem 1 holds true. The details of its proof are omitted due to space limitation.

Theorem 1. In an *n*-dimensional l_p space ($\mathfrak{R}^n$, $\|\cdot\|_p$), algorithm URT-RNN will correctly find the RNN tuple(s).

Cost and Optimality. The index with the UR-tree and sorted lists contains relevant information for processing RNN query efficiently. Moreover, this index can also be used to evaluate NN queries efficiently. It is easy to maintain the index by updating the tree and lists when the dataset has been changed. Its *time cost* consists of two parts, one is the time cost of dividing the space, and the other is the time cost of searching the nearest neighbor t_{NN} for a tuple $t \in R$, that is, $Time(Index) = Time(DivideSpace) + Time(SearchNN) \leq O(1/2^d) + |R| \cdot O(\tau^2)$. Its *space cost* is the sum of the space costs of its nodes and lists, that is, $Space(Index) = H \cdot Space(Node) + |R| \cdot Space(List) = O(H + |R|)$, where H is the number of nodes in the UR-tree, e.g., $H = 29{,}628$ and $|R| = 500K$ for the dataset B2D500K in our experiments.

The *execution cost* of URT-RNN is the sum of the execution costs of the algorithms FirstPrune, SecondPrune and Verification; that is,

$$cost(URT\text{-}RNN) = cost(FirstPrune) + cost(SecondPrune) + cost(Verification) \quad (5)$$

The execution cost of FirstPrune, $cost(FirstPrune)$, is the cost for accessing the nodes in the UR-tree. When the threshold $\tau = 100$, as an example, the dataset B2D500K in our experiments is divided into 29,628 cells. The average number of nodes accessed by FirstPrune is 114. Notice that all nodes may need to be accessed in the worst case.

The execution cost of SecondPrune, $cost(SecondPrune)$, includes the cost of the binary search, sorted access with the List-attribute and random access with other attributes for tuples in the sorted lists pointed to by the candidate leaf regions in *CRSet*. Ignoring the cost of the binary search, $cost(SecondPrune)$ will be *instance optimality*, according to the definition of instance optimality and Theorem 7.1 in [9]; that is, $cost(SecondPrune) \leq cost(TAz) + cost(Binary\text{-}search)$, where TAz is an algorithm with instance optimality in [9]. Continuing the example above, on the average, 33 tuples are seen by SecondPrune. In the worst case, however, about $\tau \cdot |CRSet|$ tuples may be seen by SecondPrune.

The execution cost of Verification, $cost(Verification)$, is the cost of verifying the tuples in the candidate tuple set *ctSet*. Continuing the above example again, the average number of tuples in *ctSet* is 1.5. Nonetheless, about $\tau \cdot |CRSet|$ tuples need to be verified in the worst case.

5 Experimental Results

The experiments are carried out using Microsoft's Visual C++ 2019 and Windows 10 on a PC with Intel(R) Core(TM) i5–9400 CPU @ 2.90 Hz and 16 GB memory.

5.1 Datasets and Preparations

The fifteen datasets we used include data of low-dimensionality (2, 3, 4, and 5 dimensions), medium- and high-dimensionality (10, 15, 20, and 50 dimensions). The dataset U2D50K is the US50000 dataset used in [16]. The datasets B2D100K, B2D200K, and B2D500K come from the dataset CABlock20 containing 519,723 tuples with the geographic information of California [23]. The datasets N2D569K, W3D60K and H4D65K are the datasets NA, Wave and Color used in [22]. The datasets C2D, C3D, C4D, C5D, C10D, C15D, C20D, and C50D come from the dataset CoverType with 581,012 tuples [2]. In the name of all datasets, the suffix "nD" indicates that the dataset has n dimensions or attributes $(A_1, \cdots, A_n)$ in addition to the tuple identifier tid, while the suffix "mK" (if any) indicates that the dataset has mK tuples. Each dataset B2DmK is obtained by a selection of the first mK tuples over the dataset CABlock20, e.g., B2D100K is a 2-dimensional dataset with 100,000 tuples. Each dataset CnD has 581,012 tuples obtained by a projection on the first n attributes from CoverType.

The UR-tree Index for an n-dimensional dataset is built with parameters $\tau = 100$, $v = 2$, $n_1 = 4$ and $n_2 = 3$ for $n = 2$; while $v = 3$, $n_1 = 3$, $n_2 = 2$ and $n_3 = 2$ for $n \geq 3$.

The following measures are used for each dataset. (1) *The elapsed time (millisecond, ms) used to obtain the RNN tuples*: It is the sum of the times of *Filters* (i.e., FirstPrune and SecondPrune) and *Verification*. (2) *The number of relevant tuples*: (i) The number of the tuples in the regions that are not pruned by FirstPrune (denoted by *#AFP*), (ii) that of the tuples being seen with SecondPrune (*#Seen*), and (iii) the size of the candidate set (*#ctSet*). Each dataset uses a workload with 1000 tuples randomly selected from respective dataset. We will present the average result for all queries in a workload.

5.2 Comparison with Existing Methods

As mentioned in Sect. 2, it is a challenge for both precomputation-based methods and filter-refinement techniques to process exact RNN queries efficiently over datasets with more than 4 dimensions. The experiments of methods VR-RNN [18] and CSD [16] were conducted for 2-dimentional datasets, and methods SFT [19] and TPL [22] are measured over datasets with no more than four dimensions in [22]. Consequently, we compare our algorithm URT-RNN against CSD and VR-RNN over 2-dimensional datasets, and against SFT and TPL over 2-, 3- and 4-dimensional datasets.

Figure 2 compares the performance of URT-RNN (i.e., the legend URT) and that of CSD and VR-RNN over four 2-dimensional datasets of different sizes. Figure 2(a) shows the average elapsed time. It can be seen that the size of the dataset has little impact on the elapsed time of the RNN query. The elapsed time of URT-RNN, VR-RNN and CSD are between 0.209ms and 0.356ms, between 2.720ms and 3.110ms, between 3.440ms and 3.840ms, respectively. Figure 2(b) illustrates the numbers of the candidate tuples found by the three algorithms, which are about 2.5 tuples for URT-RNN, 4.8 tuples for VR-RNN and 6 tuples for CSD, respectively, and are independent of the size of the datasets.

Figure 3 compares the performance of URT-RNN and that of SFT and TPL over three datasets of different dimensionality. Figure 3(a) shows the average elapsed time. The elapsed time of URT-RNN, SFT and TPL are between 0.361ms and 0.857ms, from

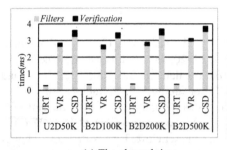
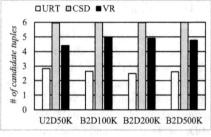

(a) The elapsed time.

(b) The number of candidate tuples.

Fig. 2. Comparison of CSD, VR-RNN and URT-RNN.

123ms to 2,954ms and from 75ms to 1,389ms, respectively. Figure 3(b) illustrates the numbers of the candidate tuples found by the three algorithms, which increases from 2.7 to 3.9 for URT-RNN, from 20 to 40 for SFT, and from 3.6 to 5.6 for TPL, respectively.

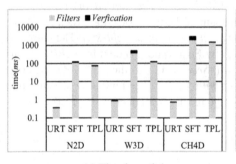
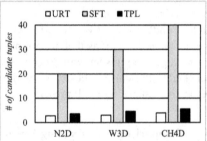

(a) The elapsed time.

(b) The number of candidate tuples.

Fig. 3. Comparison of SFT, TPL and URT-RNN.

5.3 Additional Experiments for URT-RNN

Effect of Threshold τ. For the two datasets B2D500K and C50D, and seven different thresholds $\tau = 50, 100, 200, 500, 1000, 2000,$ and 5000, Fig. 4(a) depicts the average elapsed time for processing an RNN query in each workload by the URT-RNN algorithm. Over the 2-dimensional dataset B2D500K, with the increase of threshold τ, the change of the elapsed time is small, which is between 0.344ms and 0.730ms, where *Verification* accounts for less than 1%. Over the 50-dimensional dataset C50D with 581,012 tuples, the elapsed time is between 3.620ms and 6.592ms with the increase of τ, where *Verification* accounts for less than 1%.

Figure 4(b) shows the numbers of relevant tuples for the seven values of τ. With the increase of τ, #AFP and #Seen increase from 51 to 4,370 and from 18 to 1,004 over B2D500K, respectively; while from 1,242 to 22,456 and from 564 to 9,433 over

C50D, respectively. However, #ctSet is independent of the change of τ. For the seven thresholds, the average #ctSet is 1.5 over B2D500K and 3.8 over C50D.

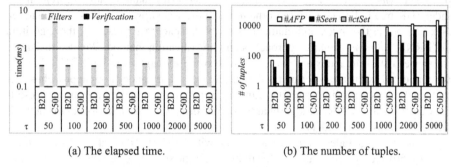

(a) The elapsed time.
(b) The number of tuples.

Fig. 4. The results over B2D500K and C50D.

Effect of Dimensionality n. Figure 5 reports the results over the eight datasets C2D, C3D, C4D, C5D, C10D, C15D, C20D, and C50D. In Fig. 5(a), the average elapsed time of the URT-RNN algorithm is between 0.492ms and 4.124ms (*Verification* accounts for less than 1%); that is, a larger dimensionality will lead to a longer elapsed time.

Figure 5(b) shows the number of relevant tuples over the eight datasets. With the increase of the dimensionality, #AFP changes between 127 and 2,027, and #Seen increases from 42 to 896, respectively, in which #Seen is less than 50% of #AFP. However, #ctSet, which ranges from 3.4 to 5.5, is independent of the dimensionality.

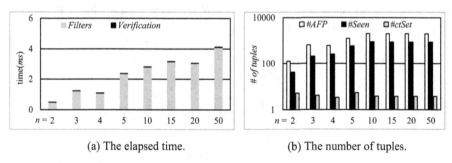

(a) The elapsed time.
(b) The number of tuples.

Fig. 5. The results over datasets CnD's with $2 \leq n \leq 50$.

For URT-RNN algorithm, the experiments mentioned in Sect. 5.3 use Euclidean distance as the sorting function, and we obtain similar experimental results using Manhattan distance and Maximum distance as sorting functions. In addition, we conclude through ablation experiments that the performance of FirstPrune is much better than that of SecondPrune. More detailed results are omitted due to space limitation.

6 Conclusion

We proposed an algorithm URT-RNN for processing exact RNN queries over a finite dataset in an n-dimensional l_p space. First, we created an unbalanced multiway region tree index (UR-tree Index) consisting of the tree and the sorted lists of tuples in the dataset. Next, based on the index and characteristics of l_p space, we presented the algorithm URT-RNN with two pruning approaches and a verification method. We also discussed the space cost of the index and the execution cost of the algorithm URT-RNN. Finally, we conducted extensive experiments to measure the performance of our approaches over various datasets with dimensionality ranging from 2 to 50, and the experimental results showed that our URT-RNN significantly outperforms several state-of-the-art methods CSD, VR-RNN, SFT and TPL.

Future work includes a study on RkNN(Q) with $k \geq 1$ over datasets in higher dimensions (> 50) and a consideration of the reduction in the space cost of index. Additionally, it would be interesting to consider the efficient evaluation of approximate RNN queries motivated by the spirit of the algorithms for approximate NN queries [11] that do not suffer from the "dimensionality curse" [3].

Appendix: Proofs for Lemmas

Lemma 1. Consider the dataset R and its UR-tree Index with the region set $\{\mathbf{P}_i: i = 0, 1, \cdots, s\}$. For a query point Q, a region $\mathbf{P}_i$ and $R_i = R \cap \mathbf{P}_i$ ($0 \leq i \leq s$), if $d(c, Q) > r_{max} + d_{max}$, then $\forall t \in R_i$, $t \notin$ RNN(Q), where c is the center-point of $\mathbf{P}_i$, $r_{max} = d(c, y)$, $d_{max} = max\{d(t, t_{NN}) \mid \forall t \in R_i\}$, and $y = (y_1, \cdots, y_n)$ is the max-point of $\mathbf{P}_i$.

Proof of Lemma 1:

For a query point Q, a region $\mathbf{P}_i$ and $R_i = R \cap \mathbf{P}_i$, as is shown in Fig.A, $d(c, Q) > r_{max} + d_{max} = d(c, y) + max\{d(t, t_{NN}) \mid \forall t \in R_i\}$, c is the center-point of $\mathbf{P}_i$, and $y = (y_1, \cdots, y_n)$ is the max-point of $\mathbf{P}_i$.

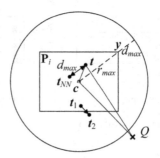

Fig. A. Illustration of the proof of Lemma 1.

For arbitrary $t \in R_i$, according to the triangle inequality of distance function, we have

$$d(c, t) + d(t, Q) \geq d(c, Q)$$
$$d(t, Q) \geq d(c, Q) - d(c, t)$$

Since $d(c, Q) > r_{max} + d_{max}$, we have.

$$d(t, Q) > r_{max} + d_{max} - d(c, t)$$
$$d(t, Q) - d_{max} > r_{max} - d(c, t)$$

Moreover, $d(c, t) \leq d(c, y) = r_{max}$ as y is the max-point of $\mathbf{P}_i$. Therefore,

$$d(t, Q) - d_{max} > 0$$
$$d(t, Q) > d_{max} = max\{d(t, t_{NN}) \mid \forall t \in \mathbf{R}_i\} \geq d(t, t_{NN})$$

Thus, query point Q is not the nearest neighbor of tuple t, that is, $t \notin \text{RNN}(Q)$.

We restate Lemma 2 that summarizes some characteristics of l_p spaces, and then we prove it.

Lemma 2. Let two arbitrary points $x = (x_1, \cdots, x_n), y = (y_1, \cdots, y_n) \in \Re^n$, and a constant $\sigma > 0$. Then.

(1°) $\|x\|_p \leq n^{(1/p-1/q)} \|x\|_q$, for $1 \leq p < q$.

(2°) $\|x\|_\infty \leq \|x\|_p \leq n^{1/p}\|x\|_\infty$, for $1 \leq p < \infty$.

(3°) $d_p(x, y) > \sigma$ if $|x_i - y_i| > \sigma$ for some $1 \leq i \leq n$, where the distance function $d_p(\cdot, \cdot)$ is induced by $\|\cdot\|_p$.

We will present the proof of (1°) by using Hölder's inequality.

Hölder's Inequality: Assume that r and s are in the open interval $(1, \infty)$ with $1/r + 1/s = 1$. Then, for arbitrary $a = (a_1, a_2, \cdots, a_n), b = (b_1, b_2, \cdots, b_n) \in \Re^n$,

$$\|ab\|_1 \leq |a|_r \|b\|_s$$

that is,

$$\sum_{i=1}^n |a_i b_i| \leq \left(\sum_{i=1}^n |a_i|^r\right)^{1/r} \left(\sum_{i=1}^n |b_i|^s\right)^{1/s}$$

Proof of Lemma 2:

(1°) Let $s = q/p$ and $r = q/(q-p)$. Then $s > 1, r > 1$ and $1/r + 1/s = 1$ since $1 \leq p < q$. Suppose that $a_i = 1$ and $b_i = |x_i|^p$, $i = 1, \cdots, n$. By Hölder's inequality, we have.

$$\sum_{i=1}^n |x_i|^p = \sum_{i=1}^n (1 \cdot |x_i|^p) = \sum_{i=1}^n |a_i b_i| \leq \left(\sum_{i=1}^n |a_i|^r\right)^{1/r} \left(\sum_{i=1}^n |b_i|^s\right)^{1/s}$$
$$= n^{1/r} \left(\sum_{i=1}^n |b_i|^s\right)^{1/s} = n^{(q-p)/q} \left(\sum_{i=1}^n |x_i|^{ps}\right)^{1/s} = n^{(q-p)/q} \left(\sum_{i=1}^n |x_i|^q\right)^{p/q}$$

Then,

$$\left(\sum_{i=1}^n |x_i|^p\right)^{1/p} \leq \left(n^{(q-p)/q} \left(\sum_{i=1}^n |x_i|^q\right)^{p/q}\right)^{1/p} = n^{(q-p)/qp} \left(\sum_{i=1}^n |x_i|^q\right)^{1/q}$$
$$= n^{(1/p-1/q)} \left(\sum_{i=1}^n |x_i|^q\right)^{1/q} = n^{(1/p-1/q)}\|x\|_q$$

That is, $\|x\|_p \leq n^{(1/p-1/q)}\|x\|_q$ by the definition $\|x\|_p = (\sum_{i=1}^n |x_i|^p)^{1/p}$.

(2°) By the definition of l_p-norm $\|\cdot\|_p$, (1°) and $\|x\|_q \to \|x\|_\infty$ when $q \to \infty$, we have.

$$\|x\|_\infty \leq \|x\|_p \, and \, \|x\|_p \leq n^{1/p}\|x\|_\infty$$

That is,

$$\|x\|_\infty \leq \|x\|_p \leq n^{1/p}\|x\|_\infty \, for \, 1 \leq p < \infty$$

(3°) If $|x_i - y_i| > \sigma$ for some $1 \leq i \leq n$, then $\|x - y\|_\infty \geq |x_i - y_i| > \sigma$. Thus, $d_p(x, y) = \|x - y\|_p \geq \|x - y\|_\infty > \sigma$ by using (2°).

References

1. Allheeib, N., Adhinugraha, K., Taniar, D., Islam, M.S.: Computing reverse nearest neighbourhood on road maps. World Wide Web **25**, 99–130 (2022)
2. Blackard, J.A., Dean, D.J., Anderson, C.W.: UCI repository of machine learning data-bases (1998). http://archive.ics.uci.edu/ml/datasets/Covertype. Accessed 10 Aug 2022
3. Borodin, A., Ostrovsky, R., Rabani, Y.: Lower bounds for high dimensional nearest neighbor search and related problems. In: Proceedings of the Thirty-First Annual ACM Symposium on Theory of Computing (STOC 1999), pp. 312–321 (1999)
4. Bruno, N., Chaudhuri, S., Gravano, L.: STHoles: a multidimensional workload-aware histogram. In: Proceedings of the 2001 ACM SIGMOD International Conference on Management of Data (SIGMOD 2001), pp. 211–222 (2001)
5. Casanova, G., et al.: Dimensional testing for reverse k-nearest neighbor search. Proc. VLDB Endowment **10**(7), 769–780 (2017)
6. Chahal, H., Toner, H., Rahkovsky, I.: Small data's big AI potential. Center for Security and Emerging Technology (2021). https://cset.georgetown.edu/publication/small-datas-big-ai-potential/. Accessed 26 July 2022
7. Cheema, M.A., Zhang, W., Lin, X., Zhang, Y.: Efficiently processing snapshot and continuous reverse k nearest neighbors queries. VLDB J. **21**(5), 703–728 (2012)
8. Das, R., Biswas, S.K., Devi, D., Sarma, B.: An oversampling technique by integrating reverse nearest neighbor in SMOTE: Reverse-SMOTE. In: 2020 International Conference on Smart Electronics and Communication (ICOSEC), pp. 1239–1244 (2020)
9. Fagin, R., Lotem, A., Naor, M.: Optimal aggregation algorithms for middleware. J. Comput. Syst. Sci. **66**(4), 614–656 (2003)
10. Guo, Y.-R., Bai, Y.-Q., Li, C.-N., Shao, Y.-H., Ye, Y.-F., Jiang, C.-Z.: Reverse nearest neighbors bhattacharyya bound linear discriminant analysis for multimodal classification. Eng. Appl. Artif. Intell. **97**, 104033 (2021)
11. Har-Peled, S., Indyk, P., Motwani, R.: Approximate nearest neighbor: towards removing the curse of dimensionality. Theory Comput. **8**(1), 321–350 (2012)
12. Hu, L., Liu, H., Zhang, J., Liu, A.: KR-DBSCAN: a density-based clustering algorithm based on reverse nearest neighbor and influence space. Expert Syst. Appl. **186**, 115763 (2021)
13. Jin, P., et al.: Maximizing the influence of bichromatic reverse k nearest neighbors in geo-social networks. World Wide Web **26**(4), 1567–1598 (2023)
14. Khedr, A.M., Raj, P.V.P.: DRNNA: decomposable reverse nearest neighbor algorithm for vertically distributed databases. In: 2021 18th International Multi-Conference on Systems, Signals & Devices (SSD), pp. 681–686 (2021)
15. Korn, F., Muthukrishnan, S.: Influence sets based on reverse nearest neighbor queries. ACM SIGMOD Rec. **29**(2), 201–212 (2000)

16. Li, Y., Liu, G., Bai, M., Gao, J., Ye, L., Ming, Z.: CSD: Discriminance with conic section for improving reverse k nearest neighbors queries. arXiv:2005.08483 (2020)
17. Panetta, K.: Gartner top 10 data and analytics trends for 2021 (2021). https://www.gartner.com/smarterwithgartner/gartner-top-10-data-and-analytics-trends-for-2021. Accessed 15 July 2022
18. Sharifzadeh, M., Shahabi, C.: VoR-tree: R-trees with voronoi diagrams for efficient processing of spatial nearest neighbor queries. Proc. VLDB Endowment **3**(1–2), 1231–1242 (2010)
19. Singh, A., Ferhatosmanoğlu, H., Tosun, A.Ş.: High dimensional reverse nearest neighbor queries. In: Proceedings of the Twelfth International Conference on Information and Knowledge Management (CIKM 2003), pp. 91–98 (2003)
20. Singh, V., Singh, A.K.: SIMP: accurate and efficient near neighbor search in high dimensional spaces. In: Proceedings of the 15th International Conference on Extending Database Technology (EDBT 2012), pp. 492–503 (2012)
21. Stanoi, I., Agrawal, D., Abbadi, A.E.: Reverse nearest neighbor queries for dynamic databases. In: ACM SIGMOD Workshop on Research Issues in Data Mining and Knowledge Discovery, pp. 44–53 (2000)
22. Tao, Y., Papadias, D., Lian, X., Xiao, X.: Multi-dimensional reverse kNN search. VLDB J. **16**(3), 293–316 (2007)
23. U.S. Census Bureau. https://www2.census.gov/geo/tiger/TGRGDB21/. Accessed 24 July 2022
24. Wang, S., Zhang, Y., Lin, X., Cheema, M.A.: Maximize spatial influence of facility bundle considering reverse k nearest neighbors. In: Database Systems for Advanced Applications, DASFAA 2018, pp. 684–700 (2018)
25. Wu, W., Yang, F., Chan, C.-Y., Tan, K.-L.: FINCH: Evaluating reverse k-nearest-neighbor queries on location data. Proc. VLDB Endowment **1**(1), 1056–1067 (2008)
26. Yang, S., Cheema, M.A., Lin, X., Zhang, Y., Zhang, W.: Reverse k nearest neighbors queries and spatial reverse top-k queries. VLDB J. **26**(2), 151–176 (2017)
27. Zheng, B., Zhao, X., Weng, L., Hung, N.Q.V., Liu, H., Jensen, C.S.: PM-LSH: A fast and accurate LSH framework for high-dimensional approximate NN search. Proc. VLDB Endowment **13**(5), 643–655 (2020)

Solving Injection Molding Production Cost Problem Based on Combined Group Role Assignment with Costs

Shaohua Teng[1], Yanhang Chen[1], Luyao Teng[2], Zefeng Zheng[1(✉)], and Wei Zhang[1]

[1] School of Computer Science and Technology, Guangdong University of Technology, Guangzhou 510006, China
2112005001@mail2.gdut.edu.cn
[2] School of Information Engineering, Guangzhou Panyu Polytechic, Guangzhou 511483, China

Abstract. Currently, scheduling plastic production is a big challenge. That is due to the emergence of complex features of small batches and more varieties. At present, two issues arise when it comes to production scheduling. The initial issue is that dissimilarities between previous and subsequent orders may result in extra expenses for order switching. For instance, a significant variation in the material or color of the product could increase scheduling time and production costs. The second issue is attaining greater profits within a limited time and resources. Unscientific scheduling techniques could decrease the production efficiency of plastic products and result in higher expenditures for companies. We suggest Combined Group Role Assignment with Costs (CGRAC) to address the mentioned issues. This technique is based on the theory of Role Based Collaboration (RBC). To solve the problem of high order switching costs, combine multiple roles and create a set of combined roles. Calculate the switching costs within each combination to minimize differences when scheduling orders. Calculate the total cost matrix and assignment matrix of the combined roles to minimize the overall cost and solve the problem of unscientific scheduling. Ultimately, a production schedule that fulfills all constraints is achieved. Evidence of the cost-reducing efficiency of CGRAC was demonstrated through experiments.

Keywords: Group Role Assignment · Injection molding production · Combined role · Production costs · Switching costs

1 Introduction

Plastic is widely used in numerous fields due to its advantages, such as variable shape, low cost, lightweight and ease of processing. In a few decades, plastics and their products have become ubiquitous in the national economy and social life. They play a significant role in agriculture, production, research, application,

F. Zhang et al. (Eds.): WISE 2023, LNCS 14306, pp. 748–762, 2023.
https://doi.org/10.1007/978-981-99-7254-8_58

materials and terminals. Currently, plastics have gained considerable prominence as an industrial material globally. China holds a crucial role in the global production of plastics as it is the world's largest manufacturer of plastic products. According to the records from January to December 2021, China's total production of plastic products was 80.04 million tons, witnessing a 5.9% year-on-year increase [16].

Injection molding is a crucial component of advanced manufacturing technologies. It is the primary approach used to produce plastic products in industrial production and serves as the core aspect of injection molding production [4,17]. Due to the rise of e-commerce platforms and the broader use of the internet, injection molding presents a complex form of manufacturing, with small batches and more varieties. This feature makes it difficult to schedule orders for plastic products. Variations in the color of raw materials and products occur during the production of plastic products between different customer orders. If two significantly different custom products are produced consecutively on the same injection molding machine, cleaning them to avoid cross-contamination. Ensuring tidy production facilities can be time-consuming. Furthermore, the unscientific planning of injection molding production will make the actual production less efficient and not give full play to the role of the injection molding machine. These two issues will necessitate increased operating costs for injection molding companies.

Therefore, the contribution of this paper is to propose a new approach to reduce the production cost of injection molding as follows:

1) We treat production orders as a role assignment problem and construct combined roles;
2) We achieve lower order switching costs by reducing the degree of order variation within the combination;
3) Considering the rationality of production scheduling, the total production cost is minimized by solving the allocation matrix with limited time and resources.

This paper is structured as follows. Section 2 reviews related work. Section 3 describes a scenario of production orders in an injection molding plant. Section 4 formalizes the problem by Combined Group Role Assignment with Costs (CGRAC). Section 5 performs performance testing and analysis of the model proposed in this paper. Section 6 concludes this paper and indicates the topics for future work.

2 Related Work

2.1 Production Optimisation

The issue of injection molding production costs is a commonly encountered problem with significant research conducted over several decades that has garnered increasing attention. Essentially, the optimal scheduling of injection molding production amounts to controlling production costs.

Various methods are available to optimize production and control costs in the injection molding process. A Lagrangian relaxation technique based on fuzzy optimization is employed to solve the suboptimal scheduling problem in the injection molding process [15]. A mixed integer formulation schedules parallel machines for multiple projects while minimizing total inventory, backlog, and setup costs under multiple capacity resource constraints [5]. In injection molding, a multi-objective approach based on a simulated annealing algorithm is proposed for efficient scheduling and energy consumption reduction [3]. A recurrent neural network is used to train a defect prediction model to improve the detection of defects in production parts and reduce the false alarm rate of part defects [9]. Using Simulation to Examine Production Scheduling Processes for Parallel Machines to enhance the sequence of work in the machines, optimizing the use of raw materials, meeting delivery deadlines and reducing total uptime [14].

Previous studies [1,3,5,9,12,14,15,19] have optimized plastic product manufacturing processes from various perspectives to achieve the core objective of cost reduction. However, more research needs to be done on the costs of raw material color switching and injection molding machine cleaning.

2.2 Role-Based Collaboration

The production scheduling of plastic products usually involves multi-person and multi-machine collaboration. Therefore, from the perspective of role collaboration, plastic product production orders can be viewed as role assignment problems.

H. Zhu proposed the 'Role-based Collaboration' (RBC) methodology and the 'Environments, Classes, Agents, Roles, Groups and Objects' (E-CARGO) model to facilitate the development of role-based collaboration systems [24,27,28].

RBC is a novel approach to organizing teamwork that provides mechanisms for role specification, assignment, transition, and negotiation [27]. It is a computational approach that uses roles as a core component, initially to support computer-supported collaborative work (CSCW) but has evolved into a generic approach to managing, organizing and supporting collaboration. It can also be seen as a generic approach to modeling, analyzing, designing and implementing artificial systems (including socio-technical systems). RBC can improve teamwork effectiveness and support more productive and flexible collaboration than face-to-face collaboration. The RBC process involves three steps: negotiating, assigning, and playing roles.

The E-CARGO model [27] is a formal model of RBC consisting of nine components, expressed as $\sum :: = <C, O, A, M, R, E, G, S_0, H>$. The symbols represent classes, objects, sets of agents, sets of information, sets of roles, sets of environments, sets of groups, the initial state of the system, and sets of users. The model conforms to RBC's fundamental principles and requirements and provides a precise specification of the components and their interrelationships.

Recently, some research has employed RBC theory and the E-CARGO model to formalize and obtain solutions for everyday problems in life. GRACCF [25] delivers solutions for forming high-performing teams by considering cooperation and conflict among agents. Formalize the exam scheduling problem as an extended Group Role Assignment with role-conflicting agents problem and solves it with a linear programming solver [26]. Solving the Tree-Structured Task Assignment Problem (TSTAP) with tree-structured relationships by implementing an efficient many-to-many assignment model to aid human resource officers in making rational plans based on the relationships among tasks [11]. Lastly, a Group Multi-Role Assignment (GMRA) based model, which employs the Agent Stability Assessment Method as a feedback mechanism, helps decision-makers quickly resettle refugees from multiple suffering countries [7].

The mentioned research [6–8, 10, 11, 13, 18, 20, 21, 23–28] provides a solid basis for the development of this paper. This paper employs RBC theory and the E-CARGO model to address scheduling orders for plastic products. Our approach combines the original roles, builds a combination of roles, and reduces the production cost by reducing the variation within the combination.

3   A Production Scenario

Factory A is a small to medium-sized manufacturer of plastic products. Its main business scope is the production of customized plastic products. For example, the custom production of anniversary plastic mugs for enterprises, personalized plastic luggage for e-commerce, etc. Due to the feature of custom production, there are usually orders with small batches and more varieties, and the number of pieces required to produce a product is small, but there is a diversity of shapes and colors.

Due to this feature, Factory A may incur huge costs due to the longer time required to clean the injection molding machine than that needed to produce a particular order. In addition to the time cost of cleaning, other costs such as resources and workforce are also included in the switching of the two orders before and after, and we call all the costs incurred during this period order switching costs.

To simplify the problem, on the order switching, we only calculate the cost in terms of the different colors of the ordered products. The actual situation can include but is not limited to colors. Table 1 provides an example of the switching costs for several colors.

Jack is the manager of this factory and is responsible for creating a production schedule for Factory A each day. Before arranging orders for production, Jack ensures that all pending orders can be completed within a specified time frame today. In addition to considering switching costs, Jack also considers the basic costs of orders. Basic costs include labor, water and electricity resources, material consumption, etc.

Table 2 shows some orders to be produced, and Jack needs to arrange injection molding machines for each of them for production.

To fulfill the seven orders listed in Table 2, Jack intends to employ two injection molding machines. The basic costs of the orders can be obtained according to Jack's experience, as shown in Table 3.

In addition, Jack knows that other constraints must be considered. Each injection molding machine can only produce one order at any given moment. Each order can be produced by only one injection molding machine and cannot be divided. Due to differences in machine models, aging levels, and order complexity, different injection molding machines may have different basic costs for the same order. The workload of injection molding machines should be balanced as much as possible.

Jack realizes that it is impossible for him to manually arrange a feasible schedule quickly with the increase in order quantity, color variety, machine input, and other tricky constraints in actual production.

Table 1. Switching costs

Color	Color	Cost
white	red	0.72
white	black	0.89
white	yellow	0.44
red	yellow	0.54
red	black	0.48
yellow	black	0.76

Table 2. Order information to be produced

Number	Name	Material	Color	quantity
1	lunch-box	PP	red	800
2	water cup	PC	black	500
3	washbasin	PP	white	730
4	toy	ABS	black	1200
5	water cup	PC	yellow	650
6	glasses case	ABS	red	680
7	glasses case	ABS	white	1000

Table 3. Basic costs

Order	1	2	3	4	5	6	7
Machine 1	0.3249	0.2872	0.2015	0.4988	0.3059	0.3522	0.4658
Machine 2	0.3976	0.1478	0.3191	0.5669	0.2899	0.3274	0.5866

4 Problem Formalizations

4.1 Using the Basic E-CARGO Model

The scheduling of production orders on injection molding machines can be seen as a Group Role Assignment (GRA) problem. In order to tackle Jack's issue, we employ the E-CARGO model to delineate the problem of assigning production orders in injection molding. The E-CARGO model [24,27,28] has been developed based on the RBC theory. The E-CARGO model allows the mapping of many real-world systems through abstraction. E-CARGO is achieved by identifying roles and agents and describing their relationships using constraints. After identifying roles and groups, assignments are made based on evaluation criteria to determine the final assignment scheme.

Definition 1. *R is a set of roles, where a role r is defined as* $r = <id, \circledR>$ *with "id" being the role's identifier and "$\circledR$" being the requirement for an agent to play the role. The size of the role set R is* $n = |R|$.

In order to differentiate from the subsequent combined roles, r is also called the original role. In this paper's scenario, an order serves as a role in the model.

Definition 2. *A is a set of agents, where an agent a is defined as $a = <id, ©>$, with "id" being the agent's identifier and "©" being the set of capabilities possessed by the agent. The size of the agent set A is $m = |A|$.*

In this paper's scenario, injection molding machines serve as agents in the model.

Definition 3. *The role demand vector L is an n-dimensional vector, where $L[j] \in N(0 \leq j < n)$ represents the number of agents required for a role, and N is a natural number.*

L represents the number of injection molding machines required to produce an order.

Definition 4. *The agent load vector L^a is an m-dimensional vector, where $L^a[i] \in N(0 \leq i < m)$ represents the minimum number of roles that an agent must play, and N is a natural number.*

L^a is used to ensure that each injection molding machine produces at least a certain number of orders.

Definition 5. *The cost matrix Q is an $m \times n$-dimensional matrix where $Q[i,j] \in [0,1]$ represents the cost incurred when agent $i \in N(0 \leq i < m)$ plays role $j \in N(0 \leq j < n)$.*

Definition 6. *The role assignment matrix T is an $m \times n$-dimensional matrix, where $T[i,j] \in \{0,1\} (0 \leq i < m, 0 \leq j < n)$ indicates whether agent i plays role j. $T[i,j] = 1$ means that agent i is assigned to role j and $T[i,j] = 0$ means the opposite.*

Definition 7. *The group's overall cost performance σ is defined as the sum of costs incurred by assigned agents. It can be obtained from the following equation: $\sigma = \sum_{i=0}^{m-1} \sum_{j=0}^{n-1} Q[i,j] \times T[i,j]$.*

Definition 8. *If there are enough agents assigned to role j, then role j in the group is workable: $\sum_{i=0}^{m-1} T[i,j] = L[j]$.*

Definition 9. *If there are enough roles for agent i to play, then agent i in the group is workable: $\sum_{j=0}^{n-1} T[i,j] \geq L^a[j]$.*

Definition 10. *If each agent and each role are workable, then the role assignment matrix T is workable. At the same time, if T is workable, then Group is workable.*

Based on the above definitions, we model the problem in Sect. 3 using GMRA with constraints and name it Group Role Assignment with Basic Costs (GRABC):

$$\min \sigma = \sum_{i=0}^{m-1} \sum_{j=0}^{n-1} Q[i,j] \times T[i,j] \tag{1}$$

subject to:

$$T[i,j] \in \{0,1\}\,(0 \le i < m, 0 \le j < n) \tag{2}$$

$$\sum_{i=0}^{m-1} T[i,j] = L[j] \tag{3}$$

$$\sum_{j=0}^{n-1} T[i,j] \ge L^a[j] \tag{4}$$

where (2) is the 0–1 constraint of the role assignment matrix T; (3) means that all roles must be workable; (4) means that all agents must be workable, i.e., meet the load requirements.

With the above modeling, it's easy to see that the group's overall cost performance σ only accounts for the basic cost in the injection molding process ($Q[i,j]$ only includes basic costs) and doesn't directly include the switching cost in $Q[i,j]$. That is because the switching cost is determined by the production order on the same injection molding machine, based on the assignment result T. However, T is unknown when calculating the switching cost, creating a contradiction.

4.2   CGRAC Model Based on E-CARGO

This paper presents an extended GRA methodology called Combined Group Role Assignment with Costs (CGRAC) to address the above problem and accurately calculate the costs associated with switching orders. CGRAC comprises the following definitions:

Definition 11. *F is the set of combined roles, the size of F is set to e, $F = [f_0, f_1, \ldots, f_{e-1}]$, and the combined role is defined as $f = \{r_a, r_b, \ldots, r_c\}\,(0 \le a \ne b \ne c < n)$, which represents a combined role as a set composed of several original roles.*

In this paper's scenario, the combined role consists of multiple plastic product orders.

Definition 12. *k is the number of roles contained in each combined role in the set F of combined roles.*

For example, for $F = \{\{r_1, r_2, r_3\}, \ldots, \{r_3, r_4, r_6\}\}$, k is equal to 3.

Definition 13. *D is the set of raw material color types, and its size is $d = |D|$. $D[i]\,(0 \le i < d)$ represents a color. Each color appears only once in D.*

Definition 14. *C is a $d \times d$-dimensional raw material color switching cost matrix. $C[i,j] \in [0,1]\,(0 \le i,j < d)$ represents the switching cost budget spent in the process of switching from an order with a product color of $D[i]$ to an order with a product color of $D[j]$ on the same injection molding machine, including cleaning costs, labor costs, resource consumption costs, etc.*

Definition 15. O *is the set of orders to be produced. According to Definition 1, an order is a role, so* $n = |O| = |R|$. $O[i](0 \le i < n)$ *represents an order and is associated with* r_i.

Definition 16. C' *is an* $n \times n$-*dimensional order switching cost matrix. Since each order has a definite raw material color,* C' *can be obtained by converting* C *matrix.*

C' can be obtained by Algorithm 1.

Algorithm 1: Obtain C'.

Input: An n-dimensional set of orders to be produced O
An d $\times$ d-dimensional raw material color switching costs matrix C.
Output: An $n \times n$ dimensional order switching costs matrix C'.

1 **begin**
2 | Initialize C'
3 | **for** $order_1 \in O$ **do**
4 | | $x \leftarrow$ index of $order_1$ in O
5 | | **for** $order_2 \in O$ **do**
6 | | | $y \leftarrow$ index of $order_2$ in O
7 | | | $D_{order_1} \leftarrow Colour(order_1)$
8 | | | $D_{order_2} \leftarrow Colour(order_2)$
9 | | | $i \leftarrow$ index of D_{order_1} in D
10 | | | $j \leftarrow$ index of D_{order_2} in D
11 | | | $C'[x, y] \leftarrow C[i, j]$
12 | | **end**
13 | **end**
14 | **return** C'
15 **end**

Definition 17. $Colour(x)$ *is a function that takes the raw material color of an order. The input of* $Colour(x)$ *is an order* $O_{input} \in O$ *and the output is a raw material color* $D_{output} \in D$.

Definition 18. C^+ *is an e-dimensional combined role switching cost vector, where e is the number of combined roles contained in* F. $C^+[i](0 \le i < e)$ *represents the minimum switching cost of the combined role* f_i.

In this paper's scenario, f_i consists of multiple orders. Therefore, $C^+[i]$ should represent the smallest switching cost generated by producing these orders in an optimal sequence on the same injection molding machine. Algorithm 2 can be used to calculate C^+.

Algorithm 2: Obtain C^+.

Input: An e-dimensional set of Combined roles F
An n × n-dimensional order switching costs matrix C'.
Output: An e-dimensional combined roles switching costs vector C^+.

1 **begin**
2   Initialize C^+
3   **for** $f \in F$ **do**
4        $cost \leftarrow 0$
5        $t \leftarrow$ index of f in F
6        $roles \leftarrow$ a set of all roles in f
7        $next \leftarrow$ the first element of $roles$
8   Remove $next$ from $roles$
9   **while** $roles$ is not empty **do**
10           $x \leftarrow$ index of $next$ in R
11           $min \leftarrow \infty$
12           $w \leftarrow -1$
13   **for** $r \in roles$ **do**
14              $y \leftarrow$ index of r in R
15              $z \leftarrow$ index of r in $roles$
16   **if** $min > C'[x,y]$ **then**
17                 $min \leftarrow C'[x,y]$
18                 $w \leftarrow z$
19   **end**
20   **end**
21           $cost \leftarrow cost + min$
22           $next \leftarrow$ element with an index value equal to w in $roles$
23   Remove $next$ from $roles$
24   **end**
25        $C^+[t] \leftarrow cost$
26   **end**
27   **return** C^+
28 **end**

Definition 19. C^- *is an* $m \times e$*-dimensional combined role basic cost matrix.* $C^-[i,j]$ *represents the sum of the basic costs of the original roles in* $f_j(0 \leq j < e)$ *when assigned to agent* $i(0 \leq i < m)$.

In this paper's scenario, $C^-[i,j]$ is the sum of the basic costs generated by the orders contained in f_j when assigned to injection molding machine i.

Definition 20. *The improved cost matrix* Q^+ *is an* $m \times e$*-dimensional matrix, where* $Q^+[i,j] \in [0,1]$ *represents the cost generated when agent* $i \in N(0 \leq i < m)$ *is assigned to combined role* $j \in N(0 \leq j < e)$, *including basic costs and switching costs.*

Q^+ can be obtained through C^+ and C^- :

$$Q^+[i,j] = \frac{C^+[j] + C^-[i,j]}{\sum_{x=0}^{m-1} \sum_{y=0}^{e-1} C^+[y] + C^-[x,y]}$$

Definition 21. *The improved role assignment matrix* T^+ *is an* $m \times e$ - *dimensional matrix.* $T^+[i,j] \in \{0,1\} \, (0 \leq i < m, 0 \leq j < e)$ *indicates whether agent* i *is assigned to combined role* f_j. *If* $T^+[i,j] = 1$, *it is assigned; if* $T^+[i,j] = 0$, *it is not.*

Definition 22. *Combined role conflict refers to the intersection of two combined roles being non-empty. That is:* $f_{j_1}, f_{j_2} \in F(0 \leq j_1 \neq j_2 < e)$ *and* $f_{j_1} \cap f_{j_2} \neq \emptyset$.

In this paper's scenario, a combined role contains k orders. If $f_1 = \{r_1, r_2, r_3\}$ and $f_2 = \{r_2, r_4, r_5\}$ exist, they have a duplicate element original role r_2. The order $O[2]$ corresponding to r_2 cannot appear in the switching cost calculation of both f_1 and f_2 at the same time, so these two combined roles are conflicting. Due to the constraints of combined role conflicts, the combined role set F should contain at least one set of combined roles that do not intersect. Each combined role in F contains k roles, so we have:

Theorem 1. *In the combined role set* F, *if each combined role comprises* k *roles, then a solution for non-conflicting combined roles implies that the number of original roles* n *is a multiple of* k.

Proof. Let the number of original roles be a. Let b and c be a positive integer. When $a < k$, it is not applicable because a combined role must contain k original roles. When $a = k$, a combined role containing a roles can be constructed, and at this time, a is a multiple of k. When $a > k$, the constraints are satisfied such that all roles have their own agents if and only if $a = bk$, due to conflict limitations. If $a = bk + c$ and a is not a multiple of k, then there will always be c roles that cannot be combined and do not satisfy the constraint.

In the scenario of Sect. 3, the original role corresponds to the order to be produced. In general, the order quantity is not a multiple of k. The solution is to supplement empty orders until the requirement is met. Empty orders are omitted when calculating basic costs and switching costs.

In summary, the CGRAC model can be expressed as:

$$\min \sigma^+ = \sum_{i=0}^{m-1} \sum_{j=0}^{e-1} Q^+[i,j] \times T^+[i,j] \tag{5}$$

subject to:

$$T^+[i,j] \in \{0,1\} \, (0 \leq i < m, 0 \leq j < e) \tag{6}$$

$$\sum_{i=0}^{m-1} T^+[i,j] \leq 1 \tag{7}$$

$$\sum_{j=0}^{e-1} T^+[i,j] \times k \geq L^a[j] \tag{8}$$

$$\sum_{i_1=0}^{m-1}\sum_{i_2=0}^{m-1} T^+[i_1, j_1] + T^+[i_1, j_2] \leq 1 \tag{9}$$

$$(j_1 < j_2 \ and \ f_{j_1}, f_{j_2} \in F \ and \ f_{j_1} \cap f_{j_2} \neq \emptyset)$$

where (6) is the 0–1 constraint of T^+; (7) indicates that a combined role can only be assigned to one agent; (8) indicates that the load requirements are met; (9) is the combined role conflict restriction constraint to ensure that two combined roles with intersections are not assigned at the same time.

5   Experimental Results and Analysis

5.1   Experimental Introduction and Setup

To verify the usability and performance of the CGRAC model, we used the IBM ILOG CPLEX Optimization Package to construct the model for testing [2,22,23].

It is worth noting that neither the σ obtained by GRABC nor the σ^+ obtained by CGRAC is the final total cost. σ does not include the switching cost of each injection molding machine during production; σ^+ does not include the switching cost between combined roles. Therefore, in order to calculate the final total cost, it is necessary to supplement the calculation after the experiment. In this paper, we use a greedy algorithm-like method to calculate all switching costs of GRA and switching costs between combined roles of CGRAC.

We observe the performance of CGRAC by comparing the cost reduction degree $u = \frac{\sigma_{final} - \sigma_{final}^+}{\sigma_{final}}$ of GRABC's final total cost σ_{final} and CGRAC's final total cost σ_{final}^+. Traditional permutation and combination forms are used to construct combined roles.

Since CGRAC mainly solves the problem of assigning small batches and more varieties, often the switching cost has a greater impact than the basic cost, and we set the random data in such a way that the cost is highlighted on the switching cost. The random range of switching costs is between 0.4 and 0.9, while the random range of basic costs is between 0.1 and 0.5.

5.2   Experiment and Analysis

In the first set of experiments, we explore the effect of order quantity on the results. We set $m = 4$ for machine numbers, $d = 6$ for material color types, $k = 2$, and n for order numbers increased from 5 to 25. Each will test 100 times per round to obtain an average value. The results are shown in Fig. 1(a). The horizontal coordinate indicates the number of orders, and the vertical coordinate indicates the degree of cost reduction.

As seen in Fig. 1(a), we can divide the curve into three stages by observation. In the first stage, when the number of orders is close to the number of machines, the cost reduction of CGRAC is slight and even worse than that of GRABC. That is because when the number of orders is small, the basic cost dominates the cost. The GRABC method can achieve the minimum basic cost, which is better than CGRAC. In the second stage, as the number of orders increases, CGRAC's performance gradually surpasses GRABC, reaching a cost reduction of nearly 30% at its highest. In the third stage, as the number of orders increases, CGRAC's cost reduction shows a slow downward trend.

In the second set of experiments, we explore the effect of the number of injection molding machines on the results. We set $m = 6$ and $m = 8$ for machine numbers and let n increase from 6 to 25 for $m = 6$ tests and from 8 to 25 for $m = 8$ tests. The other settings are consistent with the first group. We test the impact of machine numbers on results and combine Fig. 1(a) to obtain Fig. 1(b). The horizontal coordinate indicates the number of orders, and the vertical coordinate indicates the degree of cost reduction.

From Fig. 1(b), it can be seen that the trends of $m = 6$ and $m = 8$ also conform to the previous conclusion. At the same time, as the number of machines increases and the value of m becomes larger, the curve will be delayed in reaching the peak of the second stage. At the same time, the larger m is, the larger the cost reduction degree u when reaching the peak, that is, the more cost reduction.

In the third set of experiments, we explore the effect of material color type on the results. We set $m = 4$ for machine numbers, $n = 10$ for order numbers, $k = 2$, and d for material color types increased from 2 to 10. Each combination was tested 100 times per round to obtain an average value. The results are shown in Fig. 1(c). The horizontal coordinate indicates the number of material color and the vertical coordinate indicates the degree of cost reduction.

The number of material color types has little effect on CGRAC's cost reduction, as shown in Fig. 1(c).

In the fourth set of experiments, we explore the effect of the number of roles within the combined roles on the results. We randomly generated order data for the same group. When m, n, and d are fixed, we observed the impact on the experimental results by changing the number of roles k contained in the combined role group. Considering that the number of orders produced by small and medium-sized enterprises per day is not very large, the value of k does not need to be too large. We set $m = 4$, $n = 20$, $d = 6$, and k changed from 2 to 4. The results are shown in Fig. 1(d).

It can be clearly seen that for the same set of order data, when k is larger, the cost is reduced more. This is because when k becomes larger, CGRAC can select combinations with smaller switching costs within the group when selecting combined roles. However, it is not to say that the larger k is, the better. The increase of k value will cause the number of combinations to rise rapidly. The excessively considerable number of combinations will bring disaster to the time complexity and space complexity of solving. An improved method is to appropriately reduce the combinations, such as conflicting orders that cannot appear simultaneously in any combined. Another improved method is that each combined role in the combined role set F can have an inconsistent number of roles within the group and not fix k original roles.

(a) Impact of the number of orders(m=4, d=6, k=2)

(b) Impact of the number of injection molding machines(m=4/6/8, d=6, k=2)

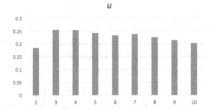

(c) Impact of the number of material colors(m=4, n=6, k=2)

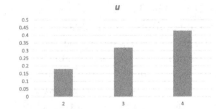

(d) Impact of the number of roles in the combination(m=4, n=20, d=6)

Fig. 1. CPLEX Experiment Results

In summary, GRABC reduces the total cost by using the basic cost as the evaluation value compared to random assignment. This can effectively reduce a part of the production cost. Furthermore, based on GRABC, CGRAC considers the switching cost, so that the total production cost can be further reduced. Based on the above experiments, selecting the appropriate number of injection molding machines and a suitable number k according to the actual usage scenario, and potentially implementing different strategies and constraints for building combinations and roles would be necessary.

6   Conclusion

In this paper, we propose the CGRAC model based on the RBC theory and the E-CARGO model for solving the basic cost and switching cost problems in the injection molding production process. We formalize the CGRAC model, implement the solution based on CPLEX, and test its performance. The test results demonstrate that CGRAC can combine several orders with slight differences in material color and reduce the switching cost. Simultaneously, CGRAC combines the base costs incurred by orders on different injection molding machines to generate a scheduling solution that minimizes the overall cost.

It is worth noting that CGRAC is suitable not only for injection molding machine production scenarios but also for other one-to-one (1-1) or one-to-many (1-m) assignment scenarios involving sequencing costs. For example, assigning a dispatcher for an express delivery, combining packages, picking the shortest distance within the combination to assign to the dispatcher.

Further research can be done on how to select a more suitable k value for different order quantities. Improve the combination of combined roles and appropriately filter out some combined roles.

References

1. Ayad, G., Fahim, I.S.: A practical scheduling optimizer for plastic injection molding facilities. In: 2020 International Conference on Decision Aid Sciences and Application (DASA), pp. 943–947. IEEE (2020)
2. Barros, M., Casquilho, M.: Linear programming with CPLEX: an illustrative application over the internet CPLEX in Fortran 90. In: 2019 14th Iberian Conference on Information Systems and Technologies (CISTI), pp. 1–6. IEEE (2019)
3. Dählmann, K., Sauer, J.: A multi-objective approach for both makespan- and energy-efficient scheduling in injection molding. In: Friedrich, G., Helmert, M., Wotawa, F. (eds.) KI 2016. LNCS (LNAI), vol. 9904, pp. 141–147. Springer, Cham (2016). https://doi.org/10.1007/978-3-319-46073-4_12
4. Dang, X.P.: General frameworks for optimization of plastic injection molding process parameters. Simul. Model. Pract. Theory **41**, 15–27 (2014)
5. Dastidar, S.G., Nagi, R.: Scheduling injection molding operations with multiple resource constraints and sequence dependent setup times and costs. Comput. Oper. Res. **32**(11), 2987–3005 (2005)
6. Ge, Y.F., Orlowska, M., Cao, J., Wang, H., Zhang, Y.: MDDE: multitasking distributed differential evolution for privacy-preserving database fragmentation. VLDB J. **31**(5), 957–975 (2022)
7. Jiang, Q., Zhu, H., Qiao, Y., Liu, D., Huang, B.: Refugee resettlement by extending group multirole assignment. IEEE Trans. Comput. Soc. Syst. (2021)
8. Jiang, Q., Zhu, H., Qiao, Y., Liu, D., Huang, B.: Extending group role assignment with cooperation and conflict factors via KD45 logic. IEEE Trans. Comput. Soc. Syst. **10**(1), 178–191 (2023)
9. Kim, S., Kim, S., Ryu, K.R.: Deep learning experiments with skewed data for defect prediction in plastic injection molding. In: 2018 IEEE/ACS 15th International Conference on Computer Systems and Applications (AICCSA), pp. 1–2. IEEE (2018)
10. Liang, L., Fu, J., Zhu, H., Liu, D.: Solving the team allocation problem in crowdsourcing via group multirole assignment. IEEE Trans. Comput. Soc. Syst. (2022)
11. Liu, D., Huang, B., Zhu, H.: Solving the tree-structured task allocation problem via group multirole assignment. IEEE Trans. Autom. Sci. Eng. **17**(1), 41–55 (2019)
12. Liu, J., Liang, R., Xian, J.: An ai planning approach to factory production planning and scheduling. In: 2022 International Conference on Machine Learning and Knowledge Engineering (MLKE), pp. 110–114. IEEE (2022)
13. Ma, H., Li, J., Tang, Y., Zhu, H., Huang, Z., Tang, W.: Universal optimization framework: leader-centered learning team formation based on fuzzy evaluations of learners and e-cargo. IEEE Syst. ManCybern. Mag. **9**(2), 6–17 (2023)
14. Panasri, J., Samattapapong, N., Sangthong, S.: Production scheduling for parallel machines using simulation techniques: case study of plastic packaging factory. In: 2022 Winter Simulation Conference (WSC), pp. 1876–1887. IEEE (2022)

15. Park, S.K., Sohn, K.M., Woo, K.B.: Suboptimal scheduling of injection molding process using fuzzy optimization technique. In: Proceedings of the 1996 IEEE IECON. 22nd International Conference on Industrial Electronics, Control, and Instrumentation, vol. 2, pp. 870–875 (1996)

16. Czech National Bank of Statistics: Plastic products production statistics. https:// data.stats.gov.cn/easyquery.htm?cn=A01&zb=A02090X&sj=202112

17. Tsou, H.H., Lee, K.D., Wang, Z.H., Huang, C.C.: The feature extraction modeling of product analysis in injection molding for intelligent manufacturing. In: 2020 International Computer Symposium (ICS), pp. 325–329 (2020)

18. Wu, S., et al.: Popularity-aware and diverse web APIs recommendation based on correlation graph. IEEE Trans. Comput. Soc. Syst. **10**, 771–782 (2022)

19. Yongqing, J., Fucheng, P.: Improved heuristic algorithm for modern industrial production scheduling. In: 2017 9th International Conference on Modelling, Identification and Control (ICMIC), pp. 1080–1084. IEEE (2017)

20. You, M., et al.: A knowledge graph empowered online learning framework for access control decision-making. World Wide Web **26**(2), 827–848 (2023)

21. Yu, Z., Yang, R., Liu, X., Zhu, H., Zhang, L.: Multi-group role assignment with constraints in adaptive collaboration. In: 2022 IEEE International Conference on Systems, Man, and Cybernetics (SMC), pp. 748–754. IEEE (2022)

22. Zhou, X., Li, G., Chen, C., Tian, M.: Research and implementation of printing and dyeing production process scheduling model based on ILOG OPL. In: 2008 Chinese Control and Decision Conference, pp. 1046–1051. IEEE (2008)

23. Zhu, H., Liu, D., Zhang, S., Teng, S., Zhu, Y.: Solving the group multirole assignment problem by improving the ILOG approach. IEEE Trans. Syst. Man Cybern.: Syst. **47**(12), 3418–3424 (2016)

24. Zhu, H., Liu, D., Zhang, S., Zhu, Y., Teng, L., Teng, S.: Solving the many to many assignment problem by improving the Kuhn-Munkres algorithm with backtracking. Theoret. Comput. Sci. **618**, 30–41 (2016)

25. Zhu, H., Sheng, Y., Zhou, X., Zhu, Y.: Group role assignment with cooperation and conflict factors. IEEE Trans. Syst. Man Cybern.: Syst. **48**(6), 851–863 (2016)

26. Zhu, H., Yu, Z., Gningue, Y.: Solving the exam scheduling problem with GRA+. In: 2020 IEEE International Conference on Systems, Man, and Cybernetics (SMC), pp. 1485–1490. IEEE (2020)

27. Zhu, H., Zhou, M.: Role-based collaboration and its kernel mechanisms. IEEE Trans. Syst. Man Cybern. Part C (Appl. Rev.) **36**(4), 578–589 (2006)

28. Zhu, H., Zhou, M., Alkins, R.: Group role assignment via a Kuhn-Munkres algorithm-based solution. IEEE Trans. Syst. Man Cybern.-Part A: Syst. Hum. **42**(3), 739–750 (2011)

CREAM: Named Entity Recognition with $\underline{C}$oncise query and $\underline{RE}$gion-$\underline{A}$ware $\underline{M}$inimization

Xun Yao[1], Qihang Yang[1], Xinrong Hu[1], Jie Yang[2(✉)], and Yi Guo[3]

[1] School of Computer Science and Artificial Intelligence, Wuhan Textile University, Wuhan, China
{yaoxun,hxr}@wtu.edu.cn
[2] School of Computing and Information Technology, University of Wollongong, Wollongong, Australia
jiey@uow.edu.au
[3] School of Computer, Data and Mathematical Sciences, Western Sydney University, Sydney, Australia
y.guo@westernsydney.edu.au

Abstract. Recent advancements in Machine Reading Comprehension (MRC) models have sparked interest in the field of Named Entity Recognition (NER), where entities are extracted as answers of given queries. Yet, existing MRC-based models face several challenges, including high computational costs, limited consideration of entity content information, and the tendency to generate sharp boundaries, that hinder their generalizability. To alleviate these issues, this paper introduces CREAM, an enhanced model leveraging $\underline{C}$oncise query and $\underline{RE}$gion-$\underline{A}$ware $\underline{M}$inimization. First, we propose a simple yet effective strategy of generating concise queries based primarily on entity categories. Second, we propose to go beyond existing methods by identifying **entire** entities, instead of just their boundaries (start and end positions), with an efficient continuous cross-entropy loss. An in-depth analysis is further provided to reveal their benefit. The proposed method is evaluated on six well-known NER benchmarks. Experimental results demonstrate its remarkable effectiveness by surpassing the current state-of-the-art models, with the substantial averaged improvement of 2.74, 1.12, and 2.38 absolute percentage points in Precision, Recall, and F1 metrics, respectively.

Keywords: Named Entity Recognition · Machine Reading Comprehension · Query Optimization · Region-Aware Loss

1 Introduction

Named Entity Recognition (NER) is a well-studied task in Natural Language Processing (NLP), which aims at identifying the span and classifying semantic category of mentioned entities from unstructured texts (input sequences). Neural based NER models have achieved remarkable performance, and also have been widely applied in many downstream tasks, including knowledge graph completion [22], question answering [10], *etc.*

F. Zhang et al. (Eds.): WISE 2023, LNCS 14306, pp. 763–777, 2023.
https://doi.org/10.1007/978-981-99-7254-8_59

Three mainstream approaches to tackle NER include sequence-to-sequence, hypergraph, and span-based models (detailed in Sect. 2). Sequence-to-sequence models treat NER as a sequence generation task, while hypergraph models leverage sequence structural information to recognize entities. Span-based models, on the other hand, enumerate possible spans and use them to classify entity categories. Recently, Machine Reading Comprehension (MRC)-based models have emerged as a promising approach to NER [9, 19]. These methods reformulate NER as a question-answering task, where a query (question) is constructed using descriptions of entity categories, and the input sequence is treated as the context. The model takes as input this query and context to identify answers (as entities). The advantage includes the capability of addressing overlapping or nested entities (as nested entities with different categories are recognized via answering independent questions), and encoding prior knowledge of the entity category.

However, previous MRC-based approaches face two main issues. Firstly, designing queries requires human effort, which introduces potential bias, noise, and ambiguity; lengthy queries also lead to increased computational costs. Secondly, existing methods primarily concentrate on learning boundaries (start and end tokens) of entities. Yet, boundary tokens are scarce and assigned full probability, while other tokens, including those intermediate tokens within the boundary, have zero probability. This sharpens the distinction between boundary and intermediate tokens, even though both are crucial for forming entities, potentially hindering neural network trainability.

To alleviate these issues, a MRC-enhanced NER model, termed **CREAM**, is proposed with two simple yet effective strategies of Concise query and REgion-Aware Minimization. Firstly, we uncover the characteristics of the query from the self-attention perspective. Then, by leveraging readily-available entity categories as queries, we eliminate the requirement for intricate query design. This streamlined strategy not only simplifies the process but also reduces computational costs significantly. Secondly, we explore the limitations associated with the conventional separation of start/end boundary detection. Instead, the model is improved via treating the entire entity as a region, encompassing both boundary and intermediate tokens. Deeply inside the core of this holistic approach lies the distinction between a single classifier (for the entire entity) and two classifiers (for the separated start/end detection). The former offers advantages including simplicity, a less severe data imbalance problem, and a reduced requirement for a complex model compared to the latter. Utilizing the proposed region-aware minimization, our approach effectively captures the holistic nature of entity context, as opposed to the atomistic assumption made in the existing boundary token identification. This holistic approach allows us to effectively utilize both the boundary and content information of entities, thereby overcoming the limitations of the previous boundary-centric approach. By considering the entity as a unified region, we successfully harness a comprehensive understanding of the entity context, enabling more accurate and robust entity detection.

Empirically, our proposed method is evaluated using six NER benchmarks, and achieves a substantial averaged improvement of 2.74, 1.12, and 2.38 absolute percentage points in Precision, Recall, and F1 metrics, respectively, compared to the previously reported best results. In addition, the effectiveness of the proposed approach is also validated in a series of ablation studies, including the encoder flexibility and the model breakdown. The proposed method also performs well with the low-resource training and cross-domain setting.

2 Related Work

Named Entity Recognition (NER) has attracted substantial attention due to its applicability of many downstream tasks. Various neural models have accordingly been proposed to investigate NER, and can be roughly categorized into three types, including sequence-to-sequence, hypergraph, and span based methods.

The first line of work conceptualizes NER as a sequence generation task in which an encoder-decode network is typically applied. Hang *et al.* [25] utilize three pointer-based entity representation to generate the entity index sequence. Tan *et al.* present a sequence-to-set (**S2S**) method [20], where the self- and cross-attention mechanism are adopted to capture the entity correlations, and a bipartite matching-based loss function is leveraged for scoring decoded results.

An alternative approach involves constructing hypergraphs from the input sequence and incorporating structural information to detect entities. For instance, **HiRe** is proposed in [12], which leverages the constituency tree to represent the input as a hierarchical region learning method. Adjacent regions are merged strategically using a predefined coherence measure, and then classified as entities using word and boundary representations. The work by Li *et al.* [7] traverses all candidate spans to create an entity fragment relation graph; then the fragment relation and type classification is performed for NER. In [23], a span-level heterogeneous graph (**SLHG**) is proposed by considering the lexical and semantic correlations of span-entity and entity-entity relationships. They then utilize a graph convolutional network to model the probability of span nodes being entities. **LLCP** is presented in [13] to formulate the input sequence as a (latent) lexicalized constituency tree, and to introduce the entity-head regularization and aware-labeling loss during the model training. Despite their success, hypergraph-based methods often rely on pre-defined structures (*i.e.*, nodes and connections), and they may encounter issues related to structural ambiguity [4, 16].

Span-based approaches in Named Entity Recognition (NER) typically involve a two-step process of span extraction and classification. Several notable approaches have been proposed in recent research. Fu *et al.* [3] introduce **Spanner**, a model that systematically investigates the strengths and weaknesses of span prediction models for NER. In the modularized interaction network (**MIN**) model presented by Li *et al.* [8], segment-level contents and word-level dependencies are extracted and encoded. Additionally, a multiple-level attention mechanism is adopted to combine and reinforce features. Shen *et al.* [18] propose **LAL**, a two-stage identifier for NER. It employs a span filter to eliminate unnecessary candidate spans and a boundary regressor to locate correct entities by adjusting the left and right boundaries of the candidates. Zhu *et al.* [28] introduce the boundary smoothing (**BS**) technique. In addition to the annotated entity, a soft label with a small probability is assigned to the surrounding spans to smooth the entity boundaries. Huang *et al.* [4] propose **Extract-Select**, a two-stage adversarial approach comprising an extractor and a discriminator. The extractor adopts type keywords and synonyms of entities to produce candidate spans, and the discriminator evaluates the correctness of these candidates. Wang *et al.* [24] present **MINER** that leverages information theory. By maximizing the mutual information between entity representations from two inputs with the same entity categories but different words, MINER encourages representations to be invariant to changes in entity mentions, while minimizing the divergence of input-specific information.

Another recent trend in span-based studies involves approaching NER as a Machine Reading Comprehension (MRC) task. In **NER-MRC** [9], a hand-crafted query related to a specific entity category is introduced. Entities are accordingly identified by answering this query as a question, given the original sequence as context. A similar approach of **NER-MQMRC** is presented in [19], where multiple queries are posed simultaneously instead of a single query in NER-MRC. This enables faster training as it could consider multiple entities in one single pass.

Our work is also under the MRC based NER framework. Yet, our method is characterized by (1) investigating the effective query design and (2) enhancing the model-learning objective to detect the entire entity (rather than only start/end tokens of entities), which in turn helps in avoiding the boundary sharpness, reducing the time complexity, and further learning better entity representation.

3　Proposed Method

3.1　Preliminary

Our approach formulates NER as a span classification task, for which the (single and/or multiple-adjacent) token is categorized with the corresponding label. Specifically, given the tokenized input sequence x (*i.e.*, $x = [\text{CLS}] x_1 \cdots x_{|x|} [\text{SEP}]$), where x_i represents the i-th token from x. The possible entity span $x_{s,e} = \{x_s, x_{s+1}, \cdots, x_{e-1}, x_e\}$ is a continuous sub-string from x, and $1 \leq s < e \leq |x|$. For the span classification task, we aim to map $x_{s,e}$ to a desirable entity type y ($y \in Y$, where Y is a predefined list of all entity categories including null, *i.e.*, non-entity). **NER-MRC** [9] is adopted as the baseline model in this paper, with the main core of the *query generation* and (start-end) *indexing and matching*.

For the query generation, each category y is assigned with one tokenized query (a natural question with descriptive words of entity categories), say q^y ($= q_1 \cdots q_{|q^y|}$). Then q^y is concatenated with x to form the model input, *i.e.*,

$$[\text{CLS}] x_1 \cdots x_{|x|} [\text{SEP}] q_1 \cdots q_{|q^y|} [\text{SEP}],$$

before feeding into the encoder to extract the latent representation. On the other hand, the indexing and matching entails fine-tuning the model with two label sequences l^{start} and l^{end}, with a length of $|x|$ (representing the ground-truth labels for the start/end tokens of entities). That is, the objective of indexing is to train the model to accurately identify individual start and end tokens for each entity. This is achieved by applying the standard cross-entropy loss between the predicted x_i and corresponding actual start or end token (using l^{start} or l^{end}). Additionally, the matching process aims to establish precise alignment on the pair level. It involves calculating another standard cross-entropy loss between predicted start-end pairs and ground-truth ones.

3.2 Concise Query

In the baseline model, the query q^y suffers from two serious weaknesses. First, q^y is hand-crafted to contain entity descriptions, where relevant memory usage and computational complexity comes at a quadratic cost of its length. The longer the query, the more computationally expensive. Second, q^y requires human efforts to carefully design its content. This manual design inevitably introduces noise and bias. Noticeably, queries for different entity categories may also contain same keywords, which further reduce query uniqueness and increase ambiguity. These issues can be found in all existing MRC based work [4, 19]. To alleviate this problem, we propose to utilize only one single token (say [PH]) as the query, to encourage the simplicity. Accordingly, the concatenated input becomes:

$$[\texttt{CLS}]\, x_1 \cdots x_{|x|}\, [\texttt{SEP}]\, [\texttt{PH}]\, [\texttt{SEP}],$$

where [PH] is a placeholder and can be replaced by one **unique token** for each entity category, such as [GPE] for geography, and [PER] for person, *etc.* Due to its length, the proposed query design has the innate ability to reduce the computational cost, and avoid ambiguity. Additionally, a discussion is further provided in the *Analysis* Section to justify the proposed concise query.

3.3 Region-Aware Loss

In this section, we further introduce a region-aware loss that optimizes the model fine-tuning. That is, in the baseline model, only *boundary* (either start or end) tokens are assigned full probability, whereas *intermediate* tokens (those inside the boundary) are assigned zero probability, resulting in a distinct boundary sharpness between two types of tokens. Yet, intermediate tokens are essential as auxiliary components in forming entities, since a single boundary token is insufficient to flag a complete entity. For instance, boundary tokens may appear multiple times in one sequence; yet, they can only be recognized as the entity boundary when accompanied by other intermediate tokens.

To better align both boundary and intermediate tokens, we employ one label sequence l^y (with a length of $|x|$), which indicates ground-truth indices for the entire entity (including both boundary and intermediate tokens) for this y category. Consequently, the encoder ($\mathbf{F}$) is applied to induce the following probability distribution:

$$p(\widehat{l_i^y} = l_i^y) \triangleq \frac{\exp(\mathrm{MLP}(\mathbf{F}(x_i)))}{\sum_j^{|x|} \exp(\mathrm{MLP}(\mathbf{F}(x_j)))}, \tag{1}$$

where $\widehat{l_i^y}$ is the model output label for x_i, $\mathbf{F}(x_i)$ represents its relevant feature, and MLP is a multilayer perceptron network (with one-hidden layer). Accordingly, the proposed region-aware loss (by accounting all entity types Y) is computed as follows

$$\mathcal{L}_{\text{region}} \triangleq - \sum_{y \in Y} \sum_i^{|x|} \mathbb{1}(\widehat{l_i^y} = l_i^y) \log p(\widehat{l_i^y} = l_i^y), \tag{2}$$

where $\mathbb{1}(\cdot)$ is the indicator function. The proposed loss function, as such, takes into account both boundary and intermediate tokens, treating them as equally important in aligning with the given query. This is in contrast to previous work, which only emphasized boundary tokens and neglected intermediate ones. By doing so, our region-aware loss encourages entity tokens to be more closely connected and avoids sharp boundaries between them.

3.4 Analysis

On the Concise Query. The impact of the query w.r.t. the MRC-based entity identification is under-explored from existing methods, while the following theoretical analysis serves this purpose. To assist the explanation, let x represent the input sequence, q^y is the query to be concatenated with x to identify entities for the category y, and $q^y = \{\mathcal{S}^u \cup \mathcal{S}^c\}$, where $\mathcal{S}^u$ is a set of **unique** tokens only for q^y, and $\mathcal{S}^c$ is the set of common tokens shared with queries of other types ($\neq y$).

With the concatenation input of $\{x, \mathcal{S}^u, \mathcal{S}^c\}$, its latent representation, computed using self-attention (from PLM encoders), is

$$\sigma\left(\begin{bmatrix} \widetilde{x_1} \\ \widetilde{\mathcal{S}_1^u} \\ \widetilde{\mathcal{S}_1^c} \end{bmatrix} [\widetilde{x_2}, \widetilde{\mathcal{S}_2^u}, \widetilde{\mathcal{S}_2^c}]^\top \right) \begin{bmatrix} \widetilde{x_3} \\ \widetilde{\mathcal{S}_3^u} \\ \widetilde{\mathcal{S}_3^c} \end{bmatrix},$$

where σ represents the operation of row-wise softmax, and $\widetilde{x_k}, \widetilde{\mathcal{S}_k^u}, \widetilde{\mathcal{S}_k^c}$ ($\forall k \in [1,3]$) are the result matrices of token embeddings projected by compatible weights. Accordingly, x', the representation of x, is derived by

$$x' = \sigma(\underbrace{[\widetilde{x_1}\widetilde{x_2}^\top}_{a_1}, \underbrace{\widetilde{x_1}\widetilde{\mathcal{S}_2^u}^\top}_{a_2}, \underbrace{\widetilde{x_1}\widetilde{\mathcal{S}_2^c}^\top}_{a_3}]) \begin{bmatrix} \widetilde{x_3} \\ \widetilde{\mathcal{S}_3^u} \\ \widetilde{\mathcal{S}_3^c} \end{bmatrix},$$

where a_k ($\forall k \in [1,3]$) is the source to calculate the self-attention coefficient of the input sequence, and unique and common tokens from q^y, respectively. Upon observation, it is evident that a_2 derived from unique tokens plays a crucial role in differentiating the latent representation of x across various queries. On the other hand, as $\mathcal{S}^c$ is shared across different queries, its non-decisive information tends to smear out within the reconstructed representation x' after the attention mechanism, thereby reducing the distinguishability. As such, the proposed CREAM completely eliminates the use of $\mathcal{S}^c$. By doing so, we ensure that the non-decisive information is not incorporated into the reconstructed representation, allowing for better differentiation between query-specific representations. Yet, including more $\mathcal{S}^u$ (unique tokens) would increase the computational cost. Thus, in our method, we consider only one unique token, and the potential benefit of incorporating additional $\mathcal{S}^u$ tokens is examined in the ablation study. Interestingly, experimental results reveal minimal performance variation, indicating that the inclusion of more $\mathcal{S}^u$ tokens does not significantly improve the overall performance.

On the Region-Aware Loss. We use the region-aware loss in Eq. (2) instead of simply detecting boundary tokens (only) as existing work [4,9,19], and detailed reasons are provided hereafter. Let us denote the final representation of the i-th token x_i as v_i. The entity identification is implemented as a binary classification problem where the logits are generated from a projection $\mathcal{P}$, *i.e.*, the final classification is performed on $\mathcal{P}v_i$ ($\mathcal{P}$ represents MLP weights in Eq. (1)). The classification can be rendered as a *decision boundary* separating various types of tokens, say boundary vs non-boundary or entities vs non-entities, as shown in Fig. 1 and 2, where we demonstrate in 2-dimensional linear space, *i.e.* for $v_i \in \mathbb{R}^2$, only for illustration purpose. The arrows in Fig. 1 and 2 indicate the projections associated with corresponding classifiers. Note that the decision boundaries are shown as linear because v_i's that we discuss here are final features immediately before the classifier in the model. When one projects them back to the original input space, the decision boundaries are most likely highly nonlinear.

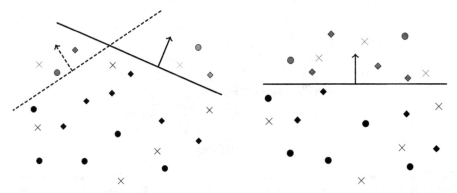

Fig. 1. Two classifiers for start and end tokens. The dashed and solid line show the classifier for boundary (start/end) tokens respectively. Red and green are corresponding start and end tokens. Different shapes show tokens from different instances (sentences). (Color figure online)

Fig. 2. Single classifier for entity tokens with the same meanings for the symbols. The red ones are identified entities tokens, including both boundary and intermediate tokens. (Color figure online)

Figure 1 shows the scenario of using traditional (binary cross entropy) loss for boundary tokens only, written as TBCE for short, where two classifiers are necessary for start/end positions respectively. Yet, there is a severe data imbalance problem that two classifiers face. Shown in Fig. 1, there are 3 entities in three instances (sentences) and hence 3 start tokens against all the rest tokens. The same situation for end tokens. It is well known that data imbalance biases the model towards the dominant class [5], *i.e.*, non-boundary tokens, and hence the sensitivity of correctly identification of boundary tokens becomes more difficult. By contrast, this problem is alleviated by the proposed region-aware (binary cross entropy) loss, written as RBCE for short, where a single classifier suffices leading to more balanced classes in general (shown in Fig. 2).

Furthermore, let us write the probability of mis-classification for TBCE as p_t and RBCE as p_r for any boundary token. Apparently, $p_t \leq p_r$. The final success rate for NER using TBCE and RBCE is $1-(1-p_t)^2$ and $1-p_r$ respectively, because TBCE has two boundary tokens and hence two classifiers. Figure 3 shows different success rates using TBCE and RBCE. When $p_r = p_t = p$, one can see the gap (blue region) between their success rates. As RBCE has the smaller error rate to begin with, its success rate is higher and can reach to the green region shown in Fig. 3. On the other hand, TBCE attracts larger error rate and can end up in the red region and hence lower success rate.

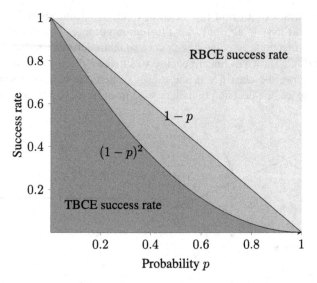

Fig. 3. The success rate comparison between TBCE and RBCE. The red/gree region shows the TBCE/RBCE success rate region on various probabilities of p_t/p_r. The blue region is the success rate gap between using TBCE and RBCE. Apparently RBCE has higher success rate. (Color figure online)

The decision to utilize the region-aware loss is also closely tied to the model complexity. Transformer-like encoders have been demonstrated the capability of approximating universal sequence-to-sequence functions [26]. Analogous to the proof of universal approximation property of feed-forward neural networks, the proof presented in [26] only establishes the transformer existence for the sequence-to-sequence function. However, the mere existence of such a model does not guarantee that a specific choice of transformer is sufficient for solving NER. Specifically, TBCE necessitates higher model complexity when compared to RBCE, due to the fact that the underlying transformer model in TBCE must reorganize the final token embeddings (v_i's) to accommodate two classifiers, whereas RBCE employs a single classifier that exploits the spatial smoothness property (tokens representing entities are consecutive within input sequences). Consequently, TBCE requires a greater degree of freedom from the encoder, whereas the proposed region-aware loss, with its reduced degree of freedom, offers a clear advantage.

On the Time Complexity. Let m and n be the length of input sequence and query, respectively. Existing span-based methods [3,24,28] need to enumerate almost all spans into corresponding categories, which leads to a high computational cost of $\mathbb{O}(cm^2)$ and c is the number of categories. Although some methods apply the span filter to eliminate candidates, the time complexity still reaches $\mathbb{O}(m^2 + ck)$ [18], where k is the number of entities from the input sequence. In contrast, CREAM performs a token-wise classification for c categories (queries) with the $\mathbb{O}(cm)$ time complexity (notably $m \gg c$). Moreover, compared to existing MRC-based models (such as NER-MRC or Extract-Select), CREAM also benefits from the concise query with $n = 1$, as the computation dilates due to the self-attention module at a quadratic cost of $(m + n)$.

4 Experiments

4.1 Experimental Settings

Datasets. Six highly-competitive NER datasets are employed, including **ACE2004** [2], **ACE2005** [15], **Conll2003** [21], **Twitter** [27], **GENIA** [17], and **JNLPBA** [1]. The standard data pre-processing is applied, such as the protocol from [6] for ACE2004/2005, GENIA, JNLPBA, [14] for Conll2003, and [19] for Twitter. Moreover, Table 1 summarizes adopted queries, which are simply individual tokens corresponding to entity categories.

Table 1. Summary of employed queries (*i.e.*, entity categories) for six benchmarks, where [GPE], [ORG], [PER], [FAC], [VEH], [LOC], [WEA], [MISC], [C_L], [C_T], [DNA], [RNA], and [PRO] represents geography, organization, person, facility, vehicle, location, weapon, miscellaneous, cell line, cell type, DNA, RNA, and protein,respectively.

	[GPE]	[ORG]	[PER]	[FAC]	[VEH]	[LOC]	[WEA]	[MISC]
ACE2004	✔	✔	✔	✔	✔	✔	✔	
ACE2005	✔	✔	✔	✔	✔	✔	✔	
Conll03		✔	✔			✔		✔
Twitter		✔	✔			✔		

	[C_L]	[C_T]	[DNA]	[RNA]	[PRO]
GENIA	✔	✔	✔	✔	✔
JNLPBA	✔	✔	✔	✔	✔

Baselines. Several baseline models are employed, including the sequence-to-sequence method of **S2S** [20], hypergraph based methods (**HiRe** [12], **LLCP** [13] and **SLHG** [23]), and span based ones (that is, **NER-MRC** [9], **MIN** [8], **Spanner** [3], **LAL** [18], **BS** [28], **Extract-Select** [4], **NER-MQMRC** [19], and **MINER** [24]). These methods are reviewed in Sect. 2, and results directly sourced from original papers are reported. BERT($base$) is adopted as the primary encoder for CREAM. The dropout rate for each layer is set as 0.1. The Adam optimizer is employed with a learning rate of 0.001. The training is performed with batches of 32 sequences of length 512. The maximal number of training epoch is 10. Meanwhile, 10% samples are randomly selected from the training set to form the validation set, and the training stops if the validation accuracy fails to improve for one epoch. At last, the proposed model is trained using a machine of the NVIDIA A100 GPU server. Three standard measurements are employed, including **Precision**, **Recall**, and **F1**, respectively.

4.2   Main Results

The proposed method is run for five trials (with randomly initialized seeds) and averaged results are shown in Table 2. Except the Recall metric from ACE2005, CREAM consistently improves the state-of-the-art models from six benchmarks for all three metrics. For instance, CREAM outperforms the strongest baseline by 1.79, 0.48, 0.35, 3.28, 3.48 and 4.88 absolute F1 points with respect to ACE2004 (Extract-Select), ACE2005 (Extract-Select), Conll2003 (MIN), Twitter (NER-MQMRC), GENIA (Extract-Select), and JNLPBA (MIN), respectively. In addition, we also implement the significance test (*i.e.*, the one-sample T-test). The p-values of our results being greater than relevant strongest baselines, from ACE2004/ACE2005 (Extract-Select), Conll2003 (MIN), Twitter (NER-MQMRC), GENIA (Extract-Select), and JNLPBA (MIN), are 1.6×10^{-4}, 9.3×10^{-4}, 1.3×10^{-5}, 3.7×10^{-4}, 6.1×10^{-6}, and 6.2×10^{-4}, respectively, which verifies the effectiveness and stability of our proposed method.

Table 2. Performance comparison between the proposed method with previous best reported results (ordered by the publication year) for six NER benchmarks. Statistically significant gains achieved by the proposed method at p-values < 0.01 are marked with †, and − represents no results reported from the original paper.

ACE2004	Precision	Rrecall	F1
NER-MRC [9]	85.05	86.32	85.98
S2S [20]	88.46	86.10	87.26
LAL [18]	87.44	87.38	87.41
LLCP [13]	87.39	88.40	87.90
BS [28]	88.43	87.53	87.98
Extract-Select [4]	88.26	88.53	88.39
CREAM	**90.67**†	**89.11**†	**90.18**†

ACE2005	Precision	Recall	F1
NER-MRC [9]	87.16	86.59	86.88
S2S [20]	87.48	86.63	87.05
LAL [18]	86.09	87.27	86.67
LLCP [13]	85.97	87.87	86.91
BS [28]	86.25	88.07	87.15
Extract-Select [4]	87.15	**88.37**	87.76
SLHG [23]	84.37	85.87	85.11
CREAM	**88.33**†	88.19†	**88.24**†

Conll03	Precision	Recall	F1
NER-MRC [9]	92.33	94.61	93.04
LAL [18]	92.13	93.73	92.94
MIN [8]	94.75	94.15	94.45
BS [28]	93.61	93.68	93.65
CREAM	**95.36**†	**94.72**†	**94.80**†

Twitter	Precision	Recall	F1
NER-MRC [9]	80.37	76.90	78.59
Spanner [3]	−	−	71.57
MINER [24]	−	−	75.26
NER-MQMRC [19]	77.79	79.96	78.86
CREAM	**83.58**†	**80.75**†	**82.14**†

GENIA	Precision	Recall	F1
NER-MRC [9]	85.18	81.12	83.75
HiRe [12]	77.40	73.90	75.60
S2S [20]	82.31	78.66	80.44
LAL [18]	80.19	80.89	80.54
LLCP [13]	78.39	78.50	78.44
SLHG [23]	77.92	80.74	79.30
Extract-Select [4]	83.64	84.41	84.02
CREAM	**87.91**†	**87.09**†	**87.50**†

JNLPBA	Precision	Recall	F1
HiRe [12]	72.50	75.60	74.00
Spanner [3]	−	−	73.78
MIN [8]	75.00	81.19	77.97
MINER [24]	−	−	77.03
CREAM	**81.83**†	**83.91**†	**82.85**†

4.3 Ablation Study

On the Encoder. To begin with, we assess the flexibility of CREAM with respect to the employed encoder, while keeping all other configurations constant. Specifically, we adopt the RoBERTa-base encoder [11] and re-implement three MRC-based baselines (NER-MRC, NER-MQMRC, Extract-Select) for the purpose of comparison. The F1 results presented in Table 3 demonstrate that our

Table 3. F1 comparison from MRC-based NER models using RoBERTa as the encoder.

	NER-MRC	NER-MQMRC	Extract-Select	CREAM
ACE2004	85.98	86.40	88.33	90.29
ACE2005	86.88	86.62	87.85	88.21
Conll2003	93.04	93.25	93.65	94.11
Twitter	79.20	78.86	77.73	82.67
GENIA	83.06	83.72	84.62	86.39
JNLPBA	79.21	80.05	78.68	83.23

CREAM method consistently achieves the highest scores across all datasets. These findings further confirm the stability of CREAM on different encoders, surpassing the performance of current leading models.

On the Breakdown. The following experiment examines the effectiveness of CREAM from two aspects: (1) concise query (CQ) and (2) region-aware loss (RAL). Specifically, the comparison is considered among the following variants:

- Base represents the model trained by long queries with the TBCE loss for start/end positions of entities; notably, this equivalents to the NER-MRC model;
- Base+CQ differs from Base by using concise (short) query but maintaining the TBCE for start/end positions;
- Base+RAL adopts the long query but to optimize the model using the proposed region-aware loss.

Comparison results are summarized in Fig. 4, which clearly show contributions from individual aspect to the final performance. Surprisingly, substituting the long query simply with concise (short) one does not compromise the F1 performance. For the benchmarks of ACE2004, Twitter, GENIA, JNLPBA, the Base+CQ variant even slightly improves the overall performance compared to the Base model, demonstrating the superiority of unique (no overlapping) queries. Additionally, we observe Base+RAL brings the biggest performance boost, that achieves the averaged improvement of 3.28 F1 points

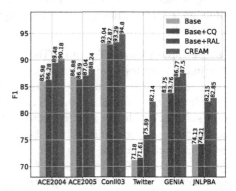

Fig. 4. Impact analysis of the proposed (1) concise query (CQ) and (2) region-aware loss (RAL) from employed benchmarks.

on top of Base. The result highlights the significance of treating the entire entity as a whole and imposing the region loss, instead of conceptually separating the detection for start/end tokens.

On the query. The following experiment validates the impact of the query length across all benchmarks, as illustrated in Fig. 5. The results demonstrate the stability of

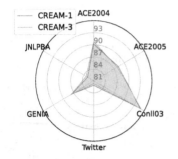

Fig. 5. F1 scores as the function of the number of unique tokens from the query.

Table 4. Computational efficiency for training one epoch (for the entire dataset) in terms of the GPU calculation time (minutes). Results within brackets represents the running time for 3 tokens as queries.

	NER-MRC	NER-MQMRC	Extract-Select	CREAM
ACE2004	28	20	35	10 (11)
ACE2005	32	22	40	11 (12)
Conll2003	28	21	32	13 (14)
Twitter	10	7	13	4 (4)
GENIA	37	26	46	16 (19)
JNLPBA	53	38	68	22 (23)

CREAM's performance regardless of the query length (whether it is 1 or 3 tokens), as evidenced by the minimal variation observed. Moreover, Table 4 further presents the computational complexity (the training time for one epoch) of existing MRC based methods. Comparatively, Extract-Select requires slightly more time than NER-MRC due to the additional fine-tuning of the discriminator. NER-MQMRC achieves lower training time compared to NER-MRC by simultaneously combining multiple queries. In contrast, CREAM exhibits the significantly lower computational complexity by utilizing a concise query, resulting in a reduced input length and further computational cost. Not surprisingly, with an increase in the query length (from 1 to 3 tokens), there is a slight increment for CREAM in the training time. However, this increase remains within an acceptable range and does not significantly impact the overall efficiency of the method.

On the Low-resource Training. This experiment validates CREAM from the aspect of the low-resource training. Accordingly, only a small amount, say m of samples (randomly selected from the training set) are utilized for the model fine-tuning, where $m = \{20\%, 40\%, 60\%, 80\%, 100\%\}$ ($m = 100\%$ represents the full dataset). Figure 6 shows the F1 score as a function of the sample size using ACE2004. Compared

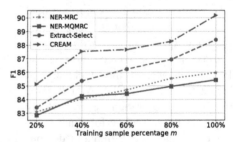

Fig. 6. F1 comparison as a function of different numbers of training samples.

to existing MRC-based baselines, CREAM consistently achieves the best performance with all percentages of the training samples. Specifically, with only 40% of labeled data, CREAM has achieved even higher results than that of NER-(MQ)MRC at the full dataset. Empirically, the result clearly demonstrates the spot-on advantage from the short query and the region-aware loss. The scarcity of the training data demands for more robust loss function to improve generalizability. The large performance gap between CREAM and NER-MRC best reflects our conclusion of RBCE in Sect. 3.4.

On Out-of-Domain Generalizability. Inspired by consistent entity categories (shown in Table 1) across various benchmarks (*e.g.*, ACE2004/2005 encompass seven identical categories), this experiment focuses on evaluating the model's ability to adapt to unseen datasets in a zero-shot manner. That is, the model is first trained on a single source dataset, and further evaluated on a different target dataset with matching entity categories. To facilitate the comparison, we employ the Extract-Select method as the overall best baseline. Results from Fig. 7 reveal that CREAM surpasses Extract-Select to demonstrate a robust cross-domain adaptation capability. Specifically, in terms of absolute F1 scores, CREAM consistently outperforms Extract-Select across all cases; yet, in a single instance (GENIA→JNLPBA), Extract-Select exhibits marginally better relative model adaptation scores (enclosed in brackets, %). Still, results underscore the advantage of leveraging the relationship among entity categories for NER, that leaves room for future investigations of CREAM in this domain.

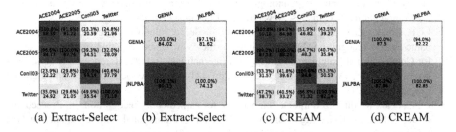

| (a) Extract-Select | (b) Extract-Select | (c) CREAM | (d) CREAM |

Fig. 7. F1 comparison of Extract-Select and CREAM on transferring the NER model, trained from one dataset, to other unseen benchmarks.

5   Conclusion

We introduce a novel Named Entity Recognition method that achieves a remarkable advancement surpassing previous state-of-the-art models. Specifically, the proposed method, termed CREAM, is characterized by the Concise query and REgion-Aware Minimization. First, the NER task is formulated as a question-answering task, where entities are identified by answering given queries (questions). Our method then introduces concise queries based solely on entity categories. Additionally, we further enhance the training loss by incorporating the identification of entire entities, rather than focusing primarily on their start or end positions. The theoretical analysis is provided to reveal compelling insights into its effectiveness. Furthermore, extensive experimental results on six benchmark datasets provide strong evidence of the superiority of our proposed algorithm over existing state-of-the-arts.

References

1. Collier, N., Ohta, T., Tsuruoka, Y., Tateisi, Y., Kim, J.D.: Introduction to the bio-entity recognition task at JNLPBA. In: Proceedings of the International Joint Workshop on Natural Language Processing in Biomedicine and its Applications (NLPBA/BioNLP), pp. 73–78. COLING, Geneva, Switzerland (2004)

2. Doddington, G., Mitchell, A., Przybocki, M., Ramshaw, L., Strassel, S., Weischedel, R.: The automatic content extraction (ACE) program - tasks, data, and evaluation. In: Proceedings of the Fourth International Conference on Language Resources and Evaluation (LREC'04). European Language Resources Association (ELRA), Lisbon, Portugal (2004)

3. Fu, J., Huang, X., Liu, P.: SpanNER: named entity re-/recognition as span prediction. In: Proceedings of the 59th Annual Meeting of the Association for Computational Linguistics, pp. 7183–7195. Association for Computational Linguistics (2021)

4. Huang, P., Zhao, X., Hu, M., Fang, Y., Li, X., Xiao, W.: Extract-select: a span selection framework for nested named entity recognition with generative adversarial training. In: Findings of the Association for Computational Linguistics: ACL 2022, pp. 85–96. Association for Computational Linguistics, Dublin, Ireland (2022)

5. Japkowicz, N., Stephen, S.: The class imbalance problem: a systematic study. Intell. Data Anal. **6**(5), 429–449 (2002)

6. Katiyar, A., Cardie, C.: Nested named entity recognition revisited. In: Proceedings of the 2018 Conference of the North American Chapter of the Association for Computational Linguistics: Human Language Technologies, Volume 1 (Long Papers), pp. 861–871. Association for Computational Linguistics, New Orleans, Louisiana (2018)

7. Li, F., Lin, Z., Zhang, M., Ji, D.: A span-based model for joint overlapped and discontinuous named entity recognition. In: Proceedings of the 59th Annual Meeting of the Association for Computational Linguistics and the 11th International Joint Conference on Natural Language Processing (Volume 1: Long Papers), pp. 4814–4828. Association for Computational Linguistics (2021)

8. Li, F., et al.: Modularized interaction network for named entity recognition. In: Proceedings of the 59th Annual Meeting of the Association for Computational Linguistics and the 11th International Joint Conference on Natural Language Processing (Volume 1: Long Papers), pp. 200–209. Association for Computational Linguistics (2021)

9. Li, X., Feng, J., Meng, Y., Han, Q., Wu, F., Li, J.: A unified MRC framework for named entity recognition. In: Proceedings of the 58th Annual Meeting of the Association for Computational Linguistics, pp. 5849–5859. Association for Computational Linguistics (2020)

10. Liu, J., Mei, S., Hu, X., Yao, X., Yang, J., Guo, Y.: Seeing the wood for the trees: a contrastive regularization method for the low-resource knowledge base question answering. In: Findings of the Association for Computational Linguistics: NAACL 2022, pp. 1085–1094. Association for Computational Linguistics, Seattle, United States (2022)

11. Liu, Y., et al.: RoBERTa: a robustly optimized BERT pretraining approach, vol. abs/1907.11692 (2019)

12. Long, X., Niu, S., Li, Y.: Hierarchical region learning for nested named entity recognition. In: Findings of the Association for Computational Linguistics: EMNLP 2020, pp. 4788–4793. Association for Computational Linguistics (2020)

13. Lou, C., Yang, S., Tu, K.: Nested named entity recognition as latent lexicalized constituency parsing. In: Proceedings of the 60th Annual Meeting of the Association for Computational Linguistics (Volume 1: Long Papers), pp. 6183–6198. Association for Computational Linguistics, Dublin, Ireland (2022)

14. Ma, X., Hovy, E.: End-to-end sequence labeling via bi-directional LSTM-CNNs-CRF. In: Proceedings of the 54th Annual Meeting of the Association for Computational Linguistics (Volume 1: Long Papers), pp. 1064–1074. Association for Computational Linguistics, Berlin, Germany (2016)

15. Medero, J., Maeda, K., Strassel, S., Walker, C.: An efficient approach to gold-standard annotation: decision points for complex tasks. In: Proceedings of the Fifth International Conference on Language Resources and Evaluation (LREC'06). European Language Resources Association (ELRA), Genoa, Italy (2006)

16. Muis, A.O., Lu, W.: Labeling gaps between words: recognizing overlapping mentions with mention separators. In: Proceedings of the 2017 Conference on Empirical Methods in Natural Language Processing, pp. 2608–2618. Association for Computational Linguistics, Copenhagen, Denmark (2017)

17. Ohta, T., Tateisi, Y., Kim, J.D.: The GENIA corpus: an annotated research abstract corpus in molecular biology domain. In: International Conference on Human Language Technology Research (2002)

18. Shen, Y., Ma, X., Tan, Z., Zhang, S., Wang, W., Lu, W.: Locate and label: A two-stage identifier for nested named entity recognition. In: Proceedings of the 59th Annual Meeting of the Association for Computational Linguistics and the 11th International Joint Conference on Natural Language Processing (Volume 1: Long Papers), pp. 2782–2794. Association for Computational Linguistics (2021)

19. Shrimal, A., Jain, A., Mehta, K., Yenigalla, P.: NER-MQMRC: formulating named entity recognition as multi question machine reading comprehension. In: Proceedings of the 2022 Conference of the North American Chapter of the Association for Computational Linguistics: Human Language Technologies: Industry Track, pp. 230–238. Association for Computational Linguistics, Hybrid: Seattle, Washington + Online (2022)

20. Tan, Z., Shen, Y., Zhang, S., Lu, W., Zhuang, Y.: A sequence-to-set network for nested named entity recognition. In: Proceedings of the 30th International Joint Conference on Artificial Intelligence, IJCAI-21 (2021)

21. Tjong Kim Sang, E.F., De Meulder, F.: Introduction to the CoNLL-2003 shared task: Language-independent named entity recognition. In: Proceedings of the Seventh Conference on Natural Language Learning at HLT-NAACL 2003, pp. 142–147 (2003)

22. Verlinden, S., Zaporojets, K., Deleu, J., Demeester, T., Develder, C.: Injecting knowledge base information into end-to-end joint entity and relation extraction and coreference resolution. In: Findings of the Association for Computational Linguistics: ACL-IJCNLP 2021, pp. 1952–1957. Association for Computational Linguistics (2021)

23. Wan, J., Ru, D., Zhang, W., Yu, Y.: Nested named entity recognition with span-level graphs. In: Proceedings of the 60th Annual Meeting of the Association for Computational Linguistics (Volume 1: Long Papers), pp. 892–903. Association for Computational Linguistics, Dublin, Ireland (2022)

24. Wang, X., et al.: MINER: improving out-of-vocabulary named entity recognition from an information theoretic perspective. In: Proceedings of the 60th Annual Meeting of the Association for Computational Linguistics (Volume 1: Long Papers), pp. 5590–5600. Association for Computational Linguistics, Dublin, Ireland (2022)

25. Yan, H., Gui, T., Dai, J., Guo, Q., Zhang, Z., Qiu, X.: A unified generative framework for various NER subtasks. In: Proceedings of the 59th Annual Meeting of the Association for Computational Linguistics and the 11th International Joint Conference on Natural Language Processing (Volume 1: Long Papers), pp. 5808–5822. Association for Computational Linguistics (2021)

26. Yun, C., Bhojanapalli, S., Rawat, A.S., Reddi, S.J., Kumar, S.: Are transformers universal approximators of sequence-to-sequence functions? CoRR abs/1912.10077 (2019)

27. Zhang, Q., Fu, J., Liu, X., Huang, X.: Adaptive co-attention network for named entity recognition in tweets. Proc, AAAI Conf. Artif. Intell. **32**(1) (2018)

28. Zhu, E., Li, J.: Boundary smoothing for named entity recognition. In: Proceedings of the 60th Annual Meeting of the Association for Computational Linguistics (Volume 1: Long Papers), pp. 7096–7108. Association for Computational Linguistics, Dublin, Ireland (2022)

Anomaly and Threat Detection:

An Effective Dynamic Cost-Sensitive Weighting Based Anomaly Multi-classification Model for Imbalanced Multivariate Time Series

Sibo Qi, Juan Chen, Peng Chen[✉], Jie Li, Wenyu Shan, and Peian Wen

School of Computer and Software Engineering, Xihua University,
Jinniu District 610039, China
chenpeng@mail.xhu.edu.cn

Abstract. Addressing imbalanced multivariate time series classification remains challenging due to skewed class distribution, resulting in suboptimal minority class classification. High dimensionality and temporal dependencies further complicate the task. We propose a novel model with dynamic cost-sensitive weighting to handle this. Our model employs multi-head self-attention and a transformer structure to capture dependencies. The proposed dynamic cost-sensitive weighting function enhances imbalanced multivariate time series handling with anomalies across classes. We comprehensively evaluated our model using KPI-monitored multivariate time series data via a microservice benchmark, comparing against baselines. Results underscore our model's efficacy, especially in cloud computing and deep learning contexts.

Keywords: Multivariate Time Series · Multiclass · Anomaly Detection · Imbalanced Data · Deep Learning · Cloud Computing

1 Introduction

The surge in microservice-based applications and cloud computing [1,3,10] has heightened the importance of monitoring and analyzing key performance indicators (KPIs) to ensure reliable system operation [15]. KPI and monitoring data are recorded as multivariate time series. Yet, analyzing KPIs poses challenges due to high-dimensional, complex, and heterogeneous time series data [8]. Hence, anomaly detection and classification are vital for understanding KPI behavior and identifying system issues [11]. Current approaches, including deep learning-based models [2,8,16], show promise in time series anomaly detection and classification. However, skewed class distribution hampers these methods [7]. Insufficient samples for rare categories lead models to favor more numerous ones,

This research was supported by the Science and Technology Program of Sichuan Province under Grant No. 2020JDRC0067, No. 2023JDRC0087, and No. 2020YFG0326, and the Talent Program of Xihua University under Grant No. Z202047 and No. Z222001.

F. Zhang et al. (Eds.): WISE 2023, LNCS 14306, pp. 781–790, 2023.
https://doi.org/10.1007/978-981-99-7254-8_60

causing poor classification and bias [9]. The high dimensionality and temporal dependencies further complicate classification [14].

This study introduces a dynamic, cost-sensitive multi-classification model employing self-attention and a multi-head mechanism for anomaly detection in imbalanced multivariate time series data. The model uses a weighting approach to enhance accuracy in microservice KPIs handling class imbalance. We term this model the Dynamic Cost-Sensitive Weighting-based Multi-head Self-Attention Anomaly Multi-Classifier (DCW-MSA-AMC). Our approach, utilizing the Transformer structure, captures sequence dependencies and aggregates key information via Self-Attention. Dynamic cost-sensitive function enhances imbalanced multivariate time series data containing multiple anomaly classes.

Our experiments on real-world microservice data showcase the superiority of our model over state-of-the-art methods. Key contributions include:

1. We tackle the challenge of feature extraction from high-dimensional data in imbalanced multiclassification problems by aggregating multivariate time series features and mapping them into latent space representations using a multi-headed self-attention mechanism.
2. We introduce a dynamic cost-sensitive function to address imbalanced data with multiple anomaly classes, enabling the multiclassification model to self-adapt to various data distributions.
3. We perform extensive experiments on a real-world microservice dataset to substantiate the effectiveness and superiority of our proposed model.

2   Related Work

The related work section surveys time series anomaly detection and classification approaches, including deep learning-based models and techniques for handling imbalanced datasets. Various deep learning models [11], have been proposed for time series anomaly detection and classification, showing promise across applications. However, these models face challenges with imbalanced datasets, high dimensionality, and other complexities. The Transformer, a seminal innovation in sequence-to-sequence modeling, employs self-attention mechanisms to facilitate comprehensive inter-token interactions, thereby revolutionizing the field of natural language processing and sequential data analysis. While the Transformer architecture excels in sequence tasks, its use for imbalanced multivariate time series data in microservices remains underexplored. The self-attention mechanism, a cornerstone in modern neural architectures, endows tokens with the capability to selectively integrate information from other tokens, fostering a contextually enriched representation within a sequence. Attention-based models, including self-attention mechanisms, have shown promise in tasks like forecasting [6], imputation [4], and detection [12]. However, they haven't specifically addressed imbalanced multi-classification in microservice KPI time series data. Cost-sensitive learning offers the potential to tackle imbalanced datasets by assigning distinct misclassification costs to classes [5]. While some works have explored cost-sensitive learning for time series classification [13], their application to imbalanced multivariate time series data with multiple class anomalies requires further exploration.

In summary, current approaches exhibit promise in time series anomaly detection and classification but may be limited in handling imbalanced multivariate data with multiple class anomalies. Our proposed self-attention-based classification model with dynamic cost-sensitive function aims to mitigate these challenges and enhance classification performance on microservice KPI time series data.

3 Proposed Methodology

We give the time series historical data collected by n sensors with length T, that is, $X = (x^1, ..., x^n)^T \in R^{n \times T}$, where T is the characteristic dimension of data at each input time point. Our time series anomaly detection task is to generate an output vector $Y = (y^1, ..., y^n) \in R^{n \times 1}$, where $y^i \in \{0, 1, 2, 3\}$ represents whether the i-th timestamp is a normal (marked as 0) or specific type of anomaly (CPU hog, memory leak, and network delay marked as 1,2,3, respectively). Since each dimension of the input time series data is not necessarily the same, we perform min-max normalization on all input data.

3.1 DCW-MSA-AMC Model Framework

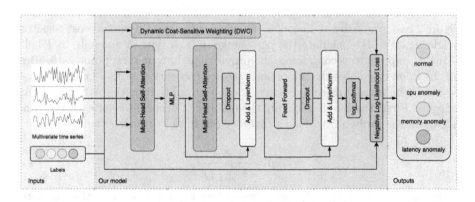

Fig. 1. DCW-MSA-AMC Framework.

Our novel DCW-MSA-AMC model is built upon the principles of supervised learning and is designed to tackle challenges in imbalanced multivariate time series classification. By integrating self-attention mechanisms and dynamic cost-sensitive learning, our model improves classification performance, particularly for minority classes. The model, shown in Fig. 1, processes input tensor

$\mathbf{X} \in \mathbb{R}^{N \times T \times D}$ with N batch size, T time steps, and D feature dimension. Initially, multi-head self-attention learns diverse temporal relationships. Aggregating attention output, an input layer with normalization follows. Next, a linear layer maps the aggregated output to a feature space. A Transformer encoder with multi-head self-attention and feed-forward networks uses normalization and residual connections for stability. The output tensor, normalized and input to an output layer, employs log-softmax activation. Cost-sensitive negative log-likelihood loss, incorporating class weights, improves minority class focus and overall performance.

3.2   Dynamic Cost-Sensitive Weighting

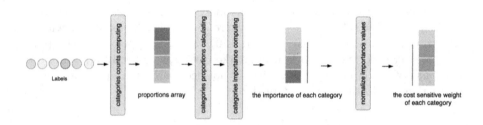

Fig. 2. Dynamic Cost-Sensitive Weighting Process.

Figure 2 and Algorithm 1 describe the whole process of dynamic cost-sensitive weighting. We first calculate the percentage of each type of anomaly by labels. Given an input array containing the proportions of four-time point categories, this function calculates the importance of each category. Let $\hat{\mathbf{X}} = (x_1, x_2, x_3, x_4)$ be the input array, where x_i represents the proportion of the i-th time point category. First, the function counts the number of occurrences of each type and calculates the probability of each category (cf. lines 1–2) using the formula :

$$\mathbf{p} = \frac{\hat{\mathbf{X}}}{\sum_{i=1}^{4} x_i} \qquad (1)$$

Here, $\mathbf{p} = (p_1, p_2, p_3, p_4)$, and p_i represents the probability of the i-th category. Next, the function computes the importance of each type of data (cf. lines 3–4), where a smaller importance value indicates a less important type of data. The importance values are calculated using the formula:

$$\mathbf{I} = 1 - \frac{\mathbf{p}}{\sum_{i=1}^{4} p_i} \qquad (2)$$

In this equation, $\mathbf{I} = (I_1, I_2, I_3, I_4)$, and I_i represents the importance of the i-th category. Finally, the function normalizes the importance values (cf. lines 5–8) to get the weights of cost sensitives using the following formula:

Algorithm 1. Dynamic Cost-Sensitive Weighting

Require: An input array $\mathbf{x} = (x_1, x_2, x_3, x_4)$ representing the proportions of four time point categories.

Ensure: An output array $\mathbf{I}$ containing the importance values for each time point category.

1: Compute the probability of each category:
2: $\mathbf{p} \leftarrow \dfrac{\hat{\mathbf{x}}}{\sum_{i=1}^{4} x_i}$
3: Calculate the importance of each type of data:
4: $\mathbf{I} \leftarrow 1 - \dfrac{\mathbf{p}}{\sum_{i=1}^{4} p_i}$
5: Normalize the importance values:
6: **for** $i \leftarrow 1$ to 3 **do**
7: $\quad W_i \leftarrow (1 - I_0) \dfrac{I_i}{\sum_{j=1}^{4} I_j - I_0}$
8: **end for**
9: **return** $\mathbf{W}$

$$W_0 = I_0, \quad W_i = (1 - I_0)\frac{I_i}{\sum_{j=1}^{4} I_j - I_0}, \quad i = 1, 2, 3 \tag{3}$$

In this equation, I_0 remains unchanged, while I_i is updated for $i = 1, 2, 3$. The normalization ensures that the important values are adjusted, to sum up to one. After normalization, the function returns an array with the calculated importance values for each time point category.

3.3 Multi-headed Self-attention Mechanism

Our model employs multi-headed self-attention to aggregate vital input sequence data, mapping it through an MLP layer to yield robust feature representation for improved multi-class anomaly detection. Multi-head self-attention extends the mechanism by conducting parallel attention operations, each focusing on distinct input facets, enabling joint information assimilation.

Multi-head self-attention involves three inputs: query matrix Q, key matrix K, and value matrix V. These matrices transform into h sets of matrices Q_i, K_i, and V_i, each with reduced dimensions. These sets undergo h self-attention layers, their outputs concatenated and linearly transformed.

The output of the multi-head self-attention mechanism is computed as follows:

$$\text{MultiHead}(Q, K, V) = \text{Concat}(h_1, \ldots, h_h) W^O \tag{4}$$

where W^O is a weight matrix used to linearly transform the concatenated output, and

$$h_i = \text{Attention}(Q_i, K_i, V_i) = \text{softmax}\left(\frac{Q_i K_i^T}{\sqrt{d_k}}\right) V_i \tag{5}$$

Here, softmax is the softmax function, d_k is the dimensionality of the key matrix K, and Concat is a function that concatenates the output of each attention head along the feature dimension. The main difference between multi-head attention and regular attention is that the query, key, and value matrices are transformed into multiple sets of matrices, each of which attends to a different subset of the input representation. This enables the model to capture more complex interactions between different input parts.

3.4 Transformer Multi-classification Module

The Transformer Anomaly Multi-Classification (TF-AMC) module is a model variant of our model that omits the initial multi-headed self-attention feature aggregation and MLP mapping layers. The Transformer model is renowned for handling sequence-to-sequence tasks by capturing long-range dependencies and facilitating parallelization. Its core component, self-attention mechanism, captures relationships between input sequence tokens.

The TF-AMC module's main components include transformer encoder layers and a linear output layer. TF-AMC module employs a stack of transformer encoder layers comprising multi-head self-attention and position-wise feed-forward layers. The multi-head self-attention layer computes self-attention multiple times with different linear input projections. It concatenates the results, allowing the model to focus on various aspects of the input sequence. Each transformer encoder layer follows the structure:

$$\text{LayerNorm}(x + \text{MultiHead}(x, x, x)) \rightarrow \text{LayerNorm}(x + FFN(x)) \qquad (6)$$

where $\text{MultiHead}(x, x, x)$ represents the multi-head self-attention mechanism, $FFN(x)$ denotes the position-wise feed-forward layer, and LayerNorm refers to the layer normalization operation.

TF-AMC utilizes a linear output layer to generate logits for classification, with the final activation function being the log-softmax function, converting logits into probabilities.

4   Performance Evaluation

4.1   Evaluation Methods

To assess the performance of DCW-MSA-AMC, considering that the applicable datasets fall within the imbalanced data category, we employ a combination of two evaluation metrics: accuracy (ACC) and Macro F1 score. We compare the proposed model and its variants with several baseline methods to demonstrate its effectiveness in addressing time series classification challenges for imbalanced data.

4.2   Dataset

In our study, we employ the Sock-Shop e-commerce website[1] as a benchmark to evaluate microservices and cloud-native technologies. This platform encompasses 13 services, ranging from functional ones, such as frontend, catalogue, carts, user, orders, payment, and shipping, to communication services that enable seamless interaction among different services.

We introduce three prevalent anomalies to mimic real-world application scenarios: CPU hog, memory leak, and network delay [2]. We employ Pumba, a tool designed to emulate network failures and stress-testing resources for Docker containers for anomaly injection. For the CPU hog anomaly, we consume each service's CPU resources; for the memory leak, we continuously allocate memory for each service; and for the network delay, we employ traffic control to delay network packets. For more information on the different service data we use, refer to Table 1.

Table 1. DATASET STATISTICS

Dataset	Size	Dimensions	Anomalies (%)
carts	4681	35	11.94
catalogue	4613	35	12.79
front-end	4927	36	14.43
orders	4676	35	13.15
payment	4401	36	13.95
user	4535	36	10.41
shipping	4425	36	13.11

4.3   Baseline Methods

In this section, we introduce four well-established classifiers used for comparative experiments. These classifiers include two machine learning algorithms, Support Vector Machines for Anomaly Multi-Classification (SVM-AMC) and Adaptive Boosting Anomaly Multi-Classification with Decision Trees (AdaBoost-AMC), as well as two deep learning-based models, Multi-Layer Perceptron Anomaly Multi-Classification (MLP-AMC) and Long Short-Term Memory (LSTM-AMC). SVM-AMC is a supervised learning model to classify data points into different classes by finding an optimal hyperplane. AdaBoost-AMC is an ensemble learning algorithm with decision trees as the base learners. MLP-AMC is a feedforward neural network with an input layer, one or more hidden layers, and an output layer. LSTM-AMC is an LSTM-based model that processes sequences and time-series data for multi-class classification.

---

[1] https://github.com/microservices-demo/microservices-demo.

4.4   Parameter Setting

We implemented our approach using PyTorch, normalizing multivariate time series data with MinMaxScaler and processing uniform batches of size 32 per time step. Our model and deep learning baselines employed Adam optimizer with a learning rate of 1e-3. Our LSTM classifier had two layers; our proposed model featured 4 TransformerEncoderLayer heads, 2 layers, and 0.5 dropout. The initial layer of DCW-MSA-AMC contained five self-attention heads. All models were trained for 10 epochs. Experiments were executed on an NVIDIA 2080Ti GPU, Intel Core i9-10900K CPU (3.70GHz), and 32GB RAM.

4.5   Experimental Results

This section presents a comprehensive analysis of experimental findings. As Table 2 indicates, our proposed DCW-MSA-AMC model consistently outperforms baselines in F1 scores, both overall and for various microservices. By scrutinizing accuracy (Acc) and F1 scores, our model stands out, achieving top-tier performance in most services. Notably, for "catalogue," "front-end," "orders," and the overall category, our model surpasses competitors in both metrics. This underscores our model's prowess in delivering precise and balanced classification outcomes across these domains. The DCW-MSA-AMC model attains an exceptional overall F1 score of 0.716, a testament to the substantial enhancement through self-attention and cost-sensitive integration. Particularly remarkable is its performance in "orders" and "shipping" microservices, with F1 scores respectively 0.238 and 0.89 higher than the second highest. It's worth noting that in the user category, DCW-MLP-AMC achieves prime performance, boasting highest accuracy and F1 score. Nevertheless, DCW-MSA-AMC remains competitive, securing a close second in Acc and third in F1.

Table 2. Experimental results of our model and the baseline methods.

Method	carts		catalogue		front-end		orders		payment		user		shipping		overall	
	Acc	F1	Acc	F1	Acc	F1	Acc	F1	Acc	F1	Acc	F1	Acc	F1	Acc	F1
SVM-AMC	0.898	0.463	0.910	0.442	0.882	0.468	0.903	0.462	0.897	0.468	0.903	0.237	**0.904**	0.237	0.900	0.397
AdaBoost-AMC	0.861	0.284	0.898	0.560	0.887	0.570	0.889	0.515	0.868	0.461	0.913	0.381	0.902	0.381	0.888	0.450
DCW-MLP-AMC	**0.910**	**0.601**	0.927	0.561	0.944	0.861	0.926	0.651	0.925	0.748	0.938	**0.636**	0.901	0.456	0.924	0.645
DCW-LSTM-AMC	0.864	0.335	0.922	0.545	0.834	0.325	0.922	0.573	0.845	0.324	0.938	0.631	0.851	0.279	0.882	0.430
DCW-MSA-AMC	0.908	0.581	**0.948**	**0.828**	**0.946**	**0.866**	**0.965**	**0.889**	0.924	0.665	0.930	0.573	0.903	0.545	**0.932**	**0.707**

We visualize the classification results of DCW-MSA-AMC and DCW-MLP-AMC, which has the second-best overall performance in macroF1, on the catalog microservices dataset through the confusion matrix graph shown in Fig. 3. The comparison shows that DCW-MLP-AMC fails to detect memory leak anomalies, indicating that DCW-MLP-AMC does not learn the feature representation of memory leak anomalies well. The darker the color of the squares with diagonal lines in the matrix, the more time points are correctly classified (98-time points that should have been categorized as memory leak anomalies were incorrectly

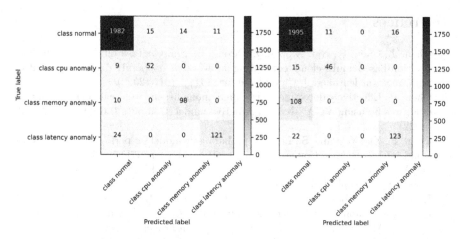

Fig. 3. Visualization of the confusion matrix of DCW-MSA-AMC (left) and DCW-MLP-AMC (right) on orders dataset on orders dataset.

categorized as normal points), which strongly suggests that DCW-MSA-AMC outperforms the other baselines. In conclusion, our proposed DCW-MSA-AMC model demonstrates superior performance over the baseline methods, proving its effectiveness in handling multi-class classification problems in the context of multivariate time series anomaly detection. The self-attention mechanism and the cost-sensitive function contribute to the model's improved performance, making it a promising approach for similar applications.

5   Conclusion and Future Work

In this paper, we introduce DCW-MSA-AMC, a pioneering anomaly detection model designed for multi-class classification within the realm of multivariate time series. Our model ingeniously integrates a self-attention mechanism with a cost-sensitive function, thereby capturing dependencies among time-series features and effectively addressing class imbalance challenges. Empirical results indicate that our proposed DCW-MSA-AMC model surpasses traditional machine learning methods as well as deep learning-based approaches . The integration of the self-attention mechanism and cost-sensitive function significantly bolsters the performance of the model, marking it as a promising solution for similar applications. Future work will explore integrating other cost-sensitive learning techniques and loss functions to better tackle class imbalance issues and further enhance the model's performance. Another prospective avenue for exploration is to assess the scalability and efficiency of our proposed DCW-MSA-AMC model when applied to larger, more complex microservice-based applications that feature a greater number of services and higher feature dimensionality.

References

1. Chen, J., Chen, P., Niu, X., Wu, Z., Xiong, L., Shi, C.: Task offloading in hybrid-decision-based multi-cloud computing network: a cooperative multi-agent deep reinforcement learning. J. Cloud Comput. **11**(1), 1–17 (2022)
2. Chen, P.: Effectively detecting operational anomalies in large-scale IoT data infrastructures by using a GAN-based predictive model. Comput. J. **65**(11), 2909–2925 (2022)
3. Chen, P., Xia, Y., Pang, S., Li, J.: A probabilistic model for performance analysis of cloud infrastructures. Concurr. Comput.: Pract. Exper. **27**(17), 4784–4796 (2015)
4. Du, W., Côté, D., Liu, Y.: SAITS: self-attention-based imputation for time series. Expert Syst. Appl. **219**, 119619 (2023)
5. Elkan, C.: The foundations of cost-sensitive learning. In: Proceedings of the 17th International Joint Conference on Artificial Intelligence - Volume 2, IJCAI'01, pp. 973–978. Morgan Kaufmann Publishers Inc., San Francisco (2001)
6. Gao, C., Zhang, N., Li, Y., Bian, F., Wan, H.: Self-attention-based time-variant neural networks for multi-step time series forecasting. Neural Comput. Appl. **34**(11), 8737–8754 (2022)
7. He, H., Garcia, E.A.: Learning from imbalanced data. IEEE Trans. Knowl. Data Eng. **21**(9), 1263–1284 (2009)
8. Ismail Fawaz, H., Forestier, G., Weber, J., Idoumghar, L., Muller, P.-A.: Deep learning for time series classification: a review. Data Min. Knowl. Disc. **33**(4), 917–963 (2019). https://doi.org/10.1007/s10618-019-00619-1
9. Khan, S.H., Hayat, M., Bennamoun, M., Sohel, F.A., Togneri, R.: Cost-sensitive learning of deep feature representations from imbalanced data. IEEE Trans. Neural Netw. Learn. Syst. **29**(8), 3573–3587 (2017)
10. Liu, H., et al.: Robustness challenges in reinforcement learning based time-critical cloud resource scheduling: a meta-learning based solution. Future Gener. Comput. Syst. **146**, 18–33 (2023)
11. Pang, G., Shen, C., Cao, L., Hengel, A.V.D.: Deep learning for anomaly detection: a review. ACM Comput. Surv. (CSUR) **54**(2), 1–38 (2021)
12. Pang, G., Shen, C., van den Hengel, A.: Deep anomaly detection with deviation networks. In: Proceedings of the 25th ACM SIGKDD International Conference on Knowledge Discovery & Data Mining, pp. 353–362 (2019)
13. Roychoudhury, S., Ghalwash, M., Obradovic, Z.: Cost sensitive time-series classification. In: Ceci, M., Hollmén, J., Todorovski, L., Vens, C., Džeroski, S. (eds.) ECML PKDD 2017. LNCS (LNAI), vol. 10535, pp. 495–511. Springer, Cham (2017). https://doi.org/10.1007/978-3-319-71246-8_30
14. Ruiz, A.P., Flynn, M., Large, J., Middlehurst, M., Bagnall, A.: The great multivariate time series classification bake off: a review and experimental evaluation of recent algorithmic advances. Data Min. Knowl. Disc. **35**(2), 401–449 (2021)
15. Sgueglia, A., Di Sorbo, A., Visaggio, C.A., Canfora, G.: A systematic literature review of IoT time series anomaly detection solutions. Future Gener. Comput. Syst. **134**, 170–186 (2022)
16. Song, Y., Xin, R., Chen, P., Zhang, R., Chen, J., Zhao, Z.: Identifying performance anomalies in fluctuating cloud environments: a robust correlative-GNN-based explainable approach. Futur. Gener. Comput. Syst. **145**, 77–86 (2023)

Multivariate Time Series Anomaly Detection Based on Graph Neural Network for Big Data Scheduling System

Shipeng Zhang and Jing Liu[(✉)]

College of Computer Science, Inner Mongolia University, Hohhot 010021, China
liujing@imu.edu.cn

Abstract. With the increasing complexity of tasks in a big data task scheduling system, how to effectively organize the data collected from each subtask of a big data task scheduling system and model the spatiotemporal dependence between them, and then perform the accurate anomaly detection of multivariate time series is of great significance. Existing methods always could not effectively capture the relationship between different time series clearly, which leads to the inevitable false alarm. To address this issue, we propose a new multivariate time series anomaly detection framework called GraphTransformerAD, which combines GraphTransformer and LSTM. Specifically, each univariate time series is an independent feature, and graph neural networks are introduced to learn the complex dependence of multivariate time series in both time and feature dimensions. Runtime performance data are collected from the actual big data workflow task scheduling system, which is used to demonstrate the effectiveness of our proposed method. The proposed method outperforms baseline models on real datasets.

Keywords: Graph neural network · Big data scheduling system · Multivariate time series · Anomaly detection · Transformer

1 Introduction

With the rapid development of big data technology, the complexity and scale of workflow task systems are increasing, which leads to frequent accidents and performance degradation of workflow task scheduling systems. To ensure the performance and reliability of the system, it is necessary to continuously monitor the status of tasks, including queue resource occupancy, CPU utilization, memory occupancy, and other indicators. These indicators can provide anomaly detection and fault removal for the running workflow task scheduling system. At present, how to solve the problem of capturing multivariate correlation in big data task scheduling system and catching anomalies in time has not been studied, which is a very challenging and important research problem with great practical application value.

In this paper, we propose GraphTransformerAD, a novel framework for multivariate time series anomaly detection based on graph attention networks, to address the

© The Author(s), under exclusive license to Springer Nature Singapore Pte Ltd. 2023
F. Zhang et al. (Eds.): WISE 2023, LNCS 14306, pp. 791–800, 2023.
https://doi.org/10.1007/978-981-99-7254-8_61

limitations of previous methods. This approach treats each univariate time series as an independent feature and tries to explicitly model the correlation between different features while modeling the temporal dependencies within each time series. It takes full advantage of GNN and LSTM by using two GraphTransformer layers. The first layer is used to capture the DAG graph features in the whole big data scheduling system, as well as the causal relationships between multiple nodes. The second layer is multiple features for a single node, emphasizing the dependence of multiple metrics in the time dimension. Compared with other models, our proposed model can effectively improve the accuracy of anomaly prediction.

2   Related Work

As an important practical problem, unsupervised time series anomaly detection has been widely studied. It can be divided into traditional methods and deep model-based methods. Traditional methods include statistical-based methods [1, 2]. Compared with traditional methods, deep learning-based models can better model complex dependencies in data [3, 4], so they have received extensive attention. For example, Deep Auto-Encoder [5] can achieve dimensionality reduction through multiple nonlinear transformations. Donut uses VAE [6] to model the reconstruction probability [7] of univariate time series, and performs anomaly detection based on this measure.

Recently, Transformers [8] have shown great power in sequential data processing. For time series analysis, Transformer is used to discover reliable long-term temporal dependencies thanks to the advantages of the self-attention mechanism [9]. For time series anomaly detection, GTA proposed by Chen [10] et al. utilizes graph structure to learn the relationship between multiple IoT sensors, as well as Transformer for time modeling and reconstruction criterion for anomaly detection. Although some of these approaches have addressed the problem of time dependence of complex modeling. For time series, continuously collected data from such graph structures as workflow in big data scheduling systems, an effective method for modeling spatiotemporal dependencies is still needed. This paper focuses on this issue to improve the performance of multivariate time series anomaly detection.

3   Method

3.1   The Overall Architecture of the Model

Figure 1 shows the overall structure of GraphTransformerAD. In the model training phase, the model is trained on historical data by offline batch processing. After the model is properly trained, the threshold selection module uses these anomaly scores to automatically select the anomaly threshold following the POT [11] approach. This trained model is then used to compute anomaly scores for new observations in the online anomaly detection phase. If the observed anomaly score is above our chosen threshold, an alert is triggered.

Figure 2 depicts the overall architecture of the proposed GraphTransformerAD model and the inference steps in the GraphTransformerLSTM EncoderDecoder reconstruction model for sequences with $L = 3$.

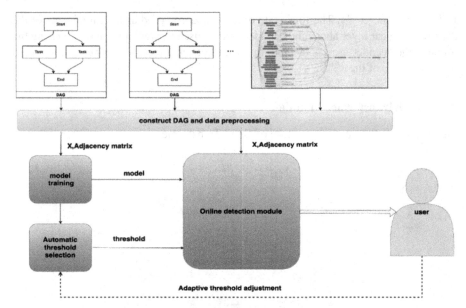

Fig. 1. The overall structure of GraphTransformerAD.

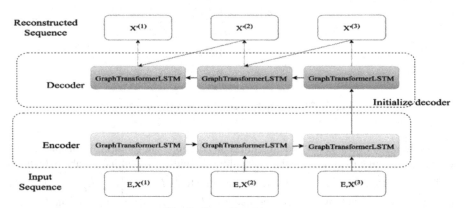

Fig. 2. Overall architecture.

Suppose the length of time series $X = \{x^{(1)}, x^{(2)}, \ldots, x^{(L)}\}$ is L, where each point $x^{(i)} \in R^m$ is at time t_i m dimensional vector of reads. This paper considers the case where more than one such time series is available on a larger time series or can be obtained by taking a window of length L. GraphTransformerLSTM is used as part of the encoder to capture spatiotemporal dependencies between tasks and over long periods of time. Likewise, similar architecture is adopted as the decoder to reconstruct the sequence in reverse order, and the states of the decoder are initialized using the final states of the encoder. For each point $x^{(i)}$ the anomaly score $a^{(i)}$ is obtained. The higher the outlier value, the more likely it is that the point is abnormal. The encoder and decoder are jointly trained to reconstruct the time series in reverse order, that is, the target time series is

$\{x^{(L)}, x^{(L-1)}, \dots, x^{(1)}\}$. The final state of the encoder is used as the initial state of the decoder. A linear layer above the decoder layer is used to predict the target. During the training, the decoder use $x^{(i)}$ as input to obtain state, and then predict corresponding to the target $x^{(i-1)}$ of the $x'^{(i-1)}$.

3.2 GraphTransformer Module

Figure 3 shows the internal structure of GraphTransformer.

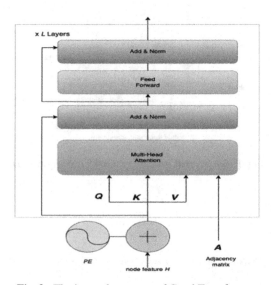

Fig. 3. The internal structure of GraphTransformer.

As shown in Fig. 3, given node feature H and the adjacency matrix A, this paper uses GraphTransformer to jointly use the embedding technique to combine the above features and label propagation. Specifically, given node features $H^{(l)} = \left\{ h_1^{(l)}, h_2^{(l)}, \dots, h_n^{(l)} \right\}$ In this paper, we compute the multi-head attention for each edge from j to i. The formula is as follows:

$$q_{c,i}^{(l)} = W_{c,q}^{(l)} h_i^{(l)} + b_{c,q}^{(l)}$$

$$k_{c,j}^{(l)} = W_{c,k}^{(l)} h_j^{(l)} + b_{c,k}^{(l)}$$

$$e_{c,ij} = W_{c,e} e_{ij} + b_{c,e}$$

$$\alpha_{c,ij}^{(l)} = \frac{\langle q_{c,i}^{(l)}, k_{c,j}^{(l)} + e_{c,ij} \rangle}{\sum_{u \in \mathcal{N}(i)} \langle q_{c,i}^{(l)}, k_{c,u}^{(l)} + e_{c,iu} \rangle} \tag{1}$$

$\langle q, k \rangle = \exp\left(\frac{q^T k}{\sqrt{d}}\right)$ is the dot product index scale function, and d is to hide the size of each head. For the *c-th* head attention, We first transform the source characteristics $h_i^{(l)}$ and the distance characteristic $h_j^{(l)}$ were converted to query vector $q_{c,i}^{(l)} \in R^d$ and key vector $k_{c,j}^{(l)} \in R^d$ respectively use different training parameters $W_{c,q}^{(l)}, W_{c,k}^{(l)}, b_{c,q}^{(l)}, b_{c,k}^{(l)}$. The edge features e_{ij} will be encoded and added to the key vector as additional information for each layer.

3.3 GraphTransformerLSTM Module

Specifically, we replace fully connected layers in LSTM with GraphTransformer layers to build a GraphTransformerLSTM cell. Figure 4 shows the internal structure of GraphTransformerLSTM.

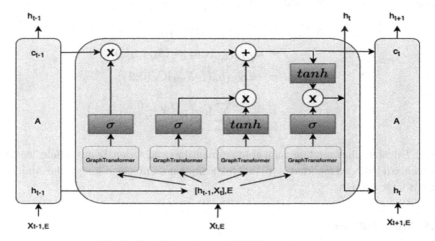

Fig. 4. GraphTransformerLSTM Internal structure

All states and gates in GraphTransformerLSTM are graph-based representations containing the features of each node and a DAG graph represented by an array E of input edge sets. When a new input X_t to time series X arrives at time t, GraphLSTM updates the cell state c_t^i and computes the new hidden state h_t^i for some node i in the topology. Consider input $X_t^{\mathcal{N}_j}$ and the state of its own and its neighbor nodes past $c_{t-1}^{\mathcal{N}_j}, h_{t-1}^{\mathcal{N}_j}$. The computation performed by GraphTransformerLSTM is shown in the following formula, where $*_G$ represents the graph neural operator and "*" represents the Hadamard product:

$$f_t = sigmoid\left(W_f *_G \left([h_{t-1}, x_t], E\right) + b_f\right)$$

$$i_t = sigmoid\left(W_i *_G \left([h_{t-1}, x_t], E\right) + b_i\right)$$

$$g_t = \tanh\left(W_g *_G \left([h_{t-1}, x_t], E\right) + b_g\right)$$

$$c_t = f_t * c_{t-1} + i_t * g_t$$

$$o_t = sigmoid\left(W_o*g\left([h_{t-1}, x_t], E\right) + b_o\right)$$

$$h_t = o_t * \tanh(c_t). \tag{2}$$

3.4 Model Training

Let ϕ denote the encoder network parameters and θ denote the decoder network parameters. Our model is trained by optimizing the variational lower bound on the marginal likelihood. Given a time series $X_{t_0:t}$, where $t_0 = t - W + 1$ denotes the beginning of the sliding window, the loss function is derived as follows:

$$
\begin{aligned}
\mathcal{L}(\theta, \phi; X_{t_0:t}) &= -D_{\mathrm{KL}}\left(q_\phi\left(z_t|X_{t_0:t}\right)|p_\theta\left(z_t\right)\right) \\
&+ \mathbf{E}_{\mathbf{q}_\phi(\mathbf{z_t}|\mathbf{X_{t_0:}})}\left(\log\left(p_\theta\left(X_{t_0:t}|z_t\right)\right)\right) \\
&= -D_{\mathrm{KL}}\left(q_\phi\left(z_t|X_{t_0:t}\right)|\mathcal{N}(0, I)\right) \\
&+ \frac{1}{L}\sum_{l=1}^{L}\sum_{j=t_0}^{t}\log\left(p_\theta\left(X_j|z_t^{(l)}, X_{j+1:t}\right)\right).
\end{aligned}
\tag{3}
$$

Here, L denotes the sampling number to estimate the expectation. In this article, we set $L = 1$ since it has been reported in [6] that one sample is sufficient as long as the minibatch size is large enough.

3.5 Model Inference

In calculating anomaly score phase, t_i reconstruction error vector for $e^{(i)} = |x^{(i)} - x'^{(i)}|$. The error vector at each time point in the series is estimated using maximum likelihood estimation to estimate the parameters μ and Σ of the normal distribution $\mathcal{N}(\mu, \Sigma)$. Then, for any point $x^{(i)}$, the anomaly fraction $a^{(i)} = \left(e^{(i)} - \mu\right)^T \Sigma^{-1}\left(e^{(i)} - \mu\right)$. In the supervised setting, if $a^{(i)} > \tau$, it is predicted as "abnormal", otherwise it is "normal". When there are enough abnormal sequences, a threshold τ on the likelihood is learned to maximize $F_\beta = \left(1 + \beta^2\right) \times P \times R/\left(\beta^2 P + R\right)$, where P is precision and R is recall. If the window contains outliers, the entire window is labeled as "abnormal".

We calculate an inference score s_i for each feature and take the summation of all features as the final inference score. We identify a timestamp as an anomaly if its corresponding inference score is larger than a threshold. We use Peak Over Threshold (POT) to choose the threshold automatically.

4 Experiment Design

4.1 Dataset

In this paper, the data collected by the big data scheduling system airflow is taken as an example. A DAG scheduling task in the current queue is selected as the experimental data, and the history data of nearly 60 days with a time interval of 5 min is used for the experiment. The dataset contains 53 DAGs, each DAG is composed of 29 subtasks, each subtask has 8 features, and a total of 93,064 data, with the anomaly rate is 7.23%.

To demonstrate the validity of our model, we also conducted experiments using a publicly available dataset [13] from an environment running a big data batch processing system (MBD), from a cluster containing five nodes with one master and four slaves. The MBD dataset monitors and collects 26 metrics at each node, including CPU idle, CPU I/O wait, CPU system, CPU user, etc. and a total of 8640 data, with the anomaly rate is 6.55%.

4.2 Evaluation Metrics

All anomaly detectors evaluated in this paper can return an anomaly score for each observation; therefore, we consider comparing them using the AP (Average Precision) of the anomaly points as a performance measure. In addition, the AUC(Area Under Curve) value is used as the evaluation criterion because in many cases the ROC curve does not indicate which anomaly detector performs better, and as a numerical value, the anomaly detector with a larger AUC performs better.

5 Results and Analysis

The GraphTransformerAD model is compared with eight baseline anomaly detectors. The evaluation metrics of the different models are then evaluated.

For the hyperparameter Settings, the same sliding window size n = 10 was used for all models, the hidden dim we set to 3, the number of recurrent layers per GraphTransformerLSTM unit was set to 2, the learning rate was set to 10^{-4}, the batch size was set to 16, the number of attention heads was set to 8, and the number of attention heads was set to 8. The dropout rate is set to 0.4. All experiments were performed on a PC server with 2.3 GHz dual-core Intel Core i5 with Intel Iris Plus Graphics 640 1536 MB graphics card, and 8 GB RAM.

Table 1 shows the performance of GraphTransformerAD and other methods. The results show that the GraphTransformerAD model has the highest AUC and AP.

5.1 AUC and AP Analysis

GraphTransformerAD has the highest *AUC* value and *AP* value among all anomaly detectors. The main reason why GraphTransformerAD performs better than LSTM-ED is that this paper uses graph neural networks to consider the spatial characteristics of nearby nodes, and propagates to nearby nodes according to the label propagation

Table 1. Performance of GraphTransformerAD and other baseline methods

Dataset	Airflow		MBD	
Metric	AUC	AP	AUC	AP
LOF	0.241	0.138	0.702	0.274
DAGMM	0.422	0.178	0.544	0.159
OC-SVM	0.459	0.190	0.712	0.325
Isolation-Forest	0.503	0.205	0.482	0.124
MLP-VAE	0.521	0.236	0.536	0.148
RecurrentEBM	0.549	0.242	0.574	0.185
AutoEncoder	0.639	0.376	0.727	0.345
LSTM-ED	0.689	0.429	0.738	0.369
Our Method	**0.724**	**0.478**	**0.771**	**0.458**

algorithm. When there is an anomaly in the nearby node, the current stage is more likely to have an anomaly, so it has a higher *AUC* value. LSTM-ED is a model based on reconstruction, but lacks the consideration of DAG graph structure as spatial features and abnormal training data can be propagated as labels.

Compared with Recent State-of-the-Art Multivariate Time Series Detection Models
We also compare with recent state-of-the-art multivariate time series detection models in the Airflow dataset of the big data scheduling system, including Anomaly Transformer [12], TopoMAD [13], MTAD-GATv2 [14], TadGan [15], and LSTM-VAE [16]. The results are shown in Table 2.

Table 2. AP of GraphTransformerAD and recent state-of-the-art models

Dataset	Airflow
Metric	AP
LSTM-VAE	0.338
TadGan	0.361
TopoMAD	0.395
Anomaly Transformer	0.459
MTAD-GATv2	0.481
Our Method	**0.478**

The results show that GraphTransformerAD performs almost the best, with nearly 4.14% improvement over Anomaly Transformer and only 0.63% difference with the highest performing MTAD-GATv2. We believe that the adoption of Gaussian distributions for prior associations proposed by Anomaly Transformer is not universally valid.

If there are multimodal anomalies in the window, there may not be a certain correlation difference between the unimodal prior correlation and the multimodal sequence correlation, which will have a negative impact on the detection effect. Compared with MTAD-GATv2, we think that this is mainly the dynamic graph attention mechanism proposed in GATv2, which will select different key nodes for each query node because it calculates the dynamic attention.

5.2 Effects of Major Components

In this section, we answer the question "How does GraphTransformerAD affect performance?". The results are shown in Table 3. We include LSTM-ED here because LSTM-ED ignores the DAG structure. As well as GCN + LSTM, GAT + LSTM and GATv2 + LSTM models. We will validate these models on the Airflow dataset, MBD dataset and the MSL (Mars Science Laboratory rover) public dataset [17] with 55 dimensions.

Table 3. AP of GraphTransformerAD and other methods

Dataset	Airflow	MBD	MSL
LSTM-ED	0.429	0.369	0.381
GCN-LSTM	0.395	0.434	0.433
GAT-LSTM	0.370	0.407	0.426
GATv2-LSTM	0.481	0.423	0.436
Our Method	**0.478**	**0.458**	**0.440**

From Table 3, we can see that the GraphTransformer module is optimal on most of the datasets. That is, explicit modeling of spatial dependencies between components in big data scheduling systems using graph neural networks is both beneficial and GraphTransformer performs better than GCN and GATv2.

6 Conclusion

Anomaly detection is the key to the operation of big data task scheduling systems. This paper integrates graph neural network, Transformer, and LSTM technology, and proposes a new multivariate time series anomaly detection method GraphTransformerAD. This method can effectively model the complex spatiotemporal dependence of data in big data task scheduling systems. The results show that the GraphTransformerAD algorithm is effective in analyzing large-scale workflow task scheduling systems. Experimental results on real datasets show that the proposed model outperforms other baseline anomaly detectors. In our future work, we will focus on the following aspects: 1. Select the metrics that can better expose the faults of the big data task scheduling system 2. Investigate how to combine other advanced deep anomaly detectors for better performance.

Acknowledgment. This work is supported in part by the Natural Science Foundation of Inner Mongolia of China (No. 2023ZD18), the Inner Mongolia Science and Technology Plan Project (No. 2020GG0187) and the Engineering Research Center of Ecological Big Data, Ministry of Education.

References

1. Schölkopf, B., Platt, J.C., Shawe-Taylor, J., et al.: Estimating the support of a high-dimensional distribution. Neural Comput. **13**, 1443–1471 (2001)
2. Breunig, M.M., Kriegel, H.-P., Ng, R.T., et al.: LOF: identifying density-based local outliers. In: ACM SIGMOD, pp. 93–104. ACM (2000)
3. Shen, L.F., Li, Z.C., Kwok, J.T.: Timeseries anomaly detection using temporal hierarchical one-class network. In: NeurIPS, pp. 9–20 (2020)
4. Li, Z.H., Zhao, Y.J., Han, J.Q., et al.: Multivariate time series anomaly detection and interpretation using hierarchical inter-metric and temporal embedding. In: ACMSIGKDD, pp. 3220–3230. ACM (2021)
5. Hawkins, S., He, H., Williams, G., et al.: Outlier detection using replicator neural networks. In: Proceedings of the 4th International Conference on Data Warehousing and Knowledge Discovery, pp. 113–123 (2002)
6. Kingma, D.P., Welling, M.: Auto-encoding variational Bayes. arXiv.org, pp. 1–14 (2014)
7. An, J., Cho, S.: Variational autoencoder based anomaly detection using reconstruction probability. Spec. Lect. **2**, 1–18 (2015)
8. Vaswani, A., Shazeer, N., Parmar, N., et al.: Attention is all you need. In: NeurIPS, pp. 1–15 (2017)
9. Kitaev, N., Kaiser, L., Levskaya, A.: Reformer: the efficient transformer. In: ICLR, pp. 1–12 (2020)
10. Chen, Z.K., Chen, D.S., Yuan, Z.X., et al.: Learning graph structures with transformer for multivariate time-series anomaly detection in IoT. IEEE Internet Things J. **9**, 1–10 (2021)
11. Su, Y., Zhao, Y., Niu, C., et al.: Robust anomaly detection for multivariate time series through stochastic recurrent neural network. In: 25th ACMSIGKDD, pp. 2828–2837. ACM (2019)
12. Chen, T., Xu, R., He, Y., Liu, X.: Anomaly transformer: learning to detect anomalous patterns with transformers. arXiv preprint arXiv:2010.04243 (2020)
13. Zhang, Y., Liu, J., Chen, Y., Liu, Y.: A spatiotemporal deep learning approach for unsupervised anomaly detection in cloud systems. In: ICONIP, vol. 11955, p. 48 (2019)
14. Zhao, H., Wang, Y., Duan, J., et al.: Multivariate time-series anomaly detection via graph attention network. In: ICDM (2020)
15. Geiger, A., Liu, D., Alnegheimish, S., et al.: TadGAN: time series anomaly detection using generative adversarial networks. IEEE (2020)
16. Lin, S., Clark, R., Birke, R., et al.: Anomaly detection for time series using VAE-LSTM hybrid model. In: ICASSP (2020)
17. Hundman, K., Constantinou, V., Laporte, C., et al.: Detecting spacecraft anomalies using LSTMs and nonparametric dynamic thresholding. In: KDD (2018)

Study on Credit Risk Control by Variational Inference

Kun Wang[1,4(✉)], Ang Li[5], Xiaokun Wang[2], and Lili Sun[3]

[1] Victoria University, Melbourne, Australia
lingling-1106@hotmail.com
[2] Hebei Normal University, Shijiazhuang 050024, China
[3] University of Southern Queensland, Toowoomba, Australia
[4] Texas A&M University, College Station, TX, USA
[5] University of Puerto Rico, Rio Piedras, San Juan, Puerto Rico

Abstract. This paper presents the development of an intelligent, machine learning-based Markov chain model to investigate loan risk and strategies for controlling credit risk. The model involves modeling state transitions of loan accounts using a Markov transition matrix and optimizing collection actions at each state and age for each consumer type to maximize the expected value for the lender. To enhance the performance of the minority class, we have designed some new algorithms and developed a consecutive incremental batch learning framework within the model. In addition, we use the variational inference method and logistic regression model to address the imbalanced data gap during the traditional machine learning process. We expect that the results of this study will lead to a more accurate and effective machine learning-based prediction method and make a significant contribution to the credit risk field.

Keywords: Credit Risk · Variational Inference · Markov Chain

1 Introduction

Loan risk control is an essential aspect of lending and banking operations. Lenders face the risk of loss from borrower default or non-payment, which can result in significant financial losses. As such, managing loan risk is critical to the success and stability of lending institutions.

Historically, loan risk control has been a key concern for banks and other lending institutions. In the early days of banking, lenders primarily relied on personal relationships and trust to manage loan risk. However, as lending institutions grew and loan portfolios became more complex, lenders began to develop more sophisticated methods for managing loan risk.

In this paper, we aim to investigate loan risk and control credit risk using a machine learning approach based on the Markov chain model [1,2,8,25]. Specifically, we will utilize both Variational Bayes and logistic regression methods to develop a more robust and precise model.

F. Zhang et al. (Eds.): WISE 2023, LNCS 14306, pp. 801–809, 2023.
https://doi.org/10.1007/978-981-99-7254-8_62

Markov Chain model have been applied in many research areas such as website access prediction [15–17,26,32]. It is applied to risk assessment in this paper. Let $\{X_n\}$ denote a Markov chain where X_n is the delinquency state of a loan in month n. Let $\pi(n)$ denote the unconditional probability distribution of a loan in month n, and is a vector whose entries correspond to the different Markov chain delinquency states. If the delinquency state for month n is known, then $\pi(n)$ is a row vector with a one indicating this month's delinquency state for loan i and zeros elsewhere. The transition matrix moving from month n to month $n+1$ of the Markov chain is denoted by $P(n, n+1)$, a matrix containing the probabilities of movement between delinquency states. If the transition matrix is known, a forecast of the delinquency state probability distribution for next month can be formed given the previous month's delinquency state probability distribution. That is, for loan i, the delinquency state probability distribution of month $n+1$ is computed from $\pi_i(n+1) = \pi_i(n)P_i(n, n+1)$ if $\pi_i(n)$ and $P_i(n, n+1)$ are known. Associated with loan i is an outstanding balance at month n denoted by $w_i(n)$. The 'one month ahead' forecast outstanding balance by delinquency state of loan i is the vector

$$w_i(n+1) = w_i(n) \cdot \pi_i(n+1).$$

Coefficients Limitation Problem. The logistic regression model is commonly employed to address various problems, and it provides a solid foundation for modeling. However, the traditional approach of estimating model coefficients may have limitations in terms of accuracy [3,5,10,20]. To address this concern, we propose the use of the inference variational method in our paper. This method bridges the gap by offering a more robust alternative. By employing this approach, we can now assign a segment or range to each coefficient, allowing for greater flexibility and providing valuable insights in practical applications.

By incorporating the inference variational method, our model gains the ability to capture the inherent uncertainty in the coefficient estimates. This not only enhances the accuracy of our predictions but also provides a more comprehensive understanding of the underlying data.

In summary, our paper introduces the inference variational method as a means to improve logistic regression models. By providing segments for each coefficient, we enhance the model's flexibility and offer valuable insights, resulting in more accurate and nuanced analyses [12,13,30].

2   Variational Bayes for Loan-Level Classification Modeling

Refining Markov Model Estimation with Loan-Level Models. Binary classification models, including logistic and probit regression, are among the most prevalent loan-level models in credit risk and loss forecasting [21,24,31]. Diggle *et al.* [7] outline a general methodology for modeling longitudinal categorical data as a Markov chain, where the transition matrices $P(n, n+1)$ feature multinomial logistic models for each row, using n as a covariate. Smith and Lawrence [27] model all transition probabilities, however, as previously mentioned, this approach is not essential for modeling loan repayment, as only a few key transition probabilities exhibit non-constant probabilities. Moreover, modeling all transition probabilities may be unwarranted in cases where there is insufficient data to construct a predictive model, such as when loans with a 'DPD120+' status in the current month transition to 'Current' the following month. In this paper, we outline the construction of loan-level models, incorporating essential explanatory variables within a Bayesian inference framework, to estimate transaction probabilities and integrate them into the transaction matrix.

Addressing Model Output Uncertainty with Variational Bayes Classification Models. Bayesian logistic or probit regression offers the advantage of providing a posterior distribution, as opposed to a single point estimate or a confidence interval found in the classical or frequentist approach. By integrating prior beliefs, we can quantify uncertainty surrounding point estimates of transaction probabilities. This enables us to gain insights into the potential ranges of outstanding balances for each delinquency state on a monthly basis.

Variational Bayes is a widely used approach for approximate Bayesian inference. However, straightforward methods are typically limited to specific model classes [23,29], particularly those with conditionally conjugate structures within an exponential family. Instead of using Gaussian priors, which are a common and popular choice in variational Bayes approximation, Li et al. [18] integrate the intrinsic priors [4] introduced by Berger and Pericchi into Variational Bayes to construct probit regression models.

However, models with logit components seem to be a significant exception to this class, primarily due to the lack of conjugacy between the logistic likelihood and the Gaussian priors for the coefficients in the linear predictor. To enable approximate inference within this widely used class of models, Jaakkola and Jordan [11] proposed a straightforward variational approach that leverages a family of tangent quadratic lower bounds for the logistic log-likelihood, thereby reestablishing conjugacy between these approximate bounds and the Gaussian priors. Durante and Rigon [9] offer insights into the effectiveness of this strategy by presenting a formal connection between the aforementioned bound and the Pólya-gamma data augmentation [22] for logistic regression.

Background on Variational Bayes Methods. Variational methods have their origins in the 18th century with the work of Euler, Lagrange, and others on the *calculus of variations* [6,14].[1] *Variational inference* is a body of deterministic techniques for making approximate inference for parameters in complex statistical models. Variational approximations are a much faster alternative to Markov Chain Monte Carlo (MCMC), especially for large models, and are a richer class of methods than the Laplace approximation [19,28,33].

---

[1] The derivation in this section is standard in the literature on variational approximation and will at times follow the arguments in Bishop (2006) and Jordan et al. (1999).

The iterative procedure is described in Algorithm 1.

Algorithm 1. Iterative procedure for obtaining the optimal densities under factorized density restriction.

1: Initialize $q_2^*(\boldsymbol{\theta}_2), ..., q_M^*(\boldsymbol{\theta}_M)$.
2: Cycle through

$$q_1^*(\boldsymbol{\theta}_1) \leftarrow \frac{\exp(\mathbb{E}_{i \neq 1}[\ln p(\mathbf{X}, \boldsymbol{\theta})])}{\int \exp(\mathbb{E}_{i \neq 1}[\ln p(\mathbf{X}, \boldsymbol{\theta})]) d\boldsymbol{\theta}_1}$$

$$\vdots$$

$$q_M^*(\boldsymbol{\theta}_M) \leftarrow \frac{\exp(\mathbb{E}_{i \neq M}[\ln p(\mathbf{X}, \boldsymbol{\theta})])}{\int \exp(\mathbb{E}_{i \neq M}[\ln p(\mathbf{X}, \boldsymbol{\theta})]) d\boldsymbol{\theta}_M}$$

until the increase in $\mathcal{L}(q)$ is negligible.

---

3 Modeling of Charge-Off and Repayment Probabilities

LendingClub, a pioneering enterprise in the financial technology sector, holds the title as the world's largest peer-to-peer lending platform. Founded with the mission of transforming the banking system to make credit more affordable and investing more rewarding, LendingClub has managed to connect thousands of borrowers with individual investors. This unique business model not only democratizes access to loans but also opens up a new avenue for investors to diversify their portfolios.

Predictive Modeling of Charge-off and Fully-Paid Probabilities - Target Variable and Sampling. LendingClub's publicly available data from the year 2016 provides a rich source of information for building predictive models. This comprehensive dataset consists of a total of 433,042 issued loans. Every loan in the dataset comes with a specific status: **Fully-paid**, **Charged-off**, or **Current**. These statuses carry crucial information about the loan repayment, and hence, serve as the target variable for our predictive models. In particular, we will construct models that can predict the probability of a loan being charged-off or fully paid.

The above mentioned models will employ a variety of loan-related features as covariates. These covariates, or input features, have been chosen for their potential relevance to loan repayment outcomes. Among these are:

- Loan Term in Months
- FICO Score
- Issued Loan Amount
- Debt-to-Income Ratio (DTI)
- Number of Credit Lines Opened in the Past 24 Months

- Employment Length in Years
- Annual Income
- Home Ownership Type.

By including these diverse and informative features as covariates in our predictive models, we aim to maximize the predictive power of our models. These models will provide valuable insights into the factors that influence the charge-off and full-paid rates of loans issued by LendingClub.

Addressing Uncertainty of Estimated Loan-level Models using Variational Inference

Specifying the Priors. To complete the two Bayesian logistic regression models that predict the likelihood of a loan being Charged-off or Fully-paid, it's imperative to set the prior models for our regression parameters, β_i. Since these parameters can take any value in the real line, Gaussian priors are appropriate choices.

To visually encapsulate our initial understanding and the extent of uncertainty around these variables, we've plotted 100 instances of plausible relationships for a selection of the input features. These can be observed in Fig. 1 (for charge-off) and Fig. 2 (for full-payment).

Our plots echo our initial assumptions about these relationships:

- The probability of a loan being charged-off seems to rise with both the loan term and the Debt-to-Income (DTI) ratio. This is likely because longer loan terms and higher debt compared to income could indicate greater financial strain and risk.
- Conversely, we find the likelihood of a loan being charged-off decreases with an increase in the FICO score and the borrower's annual income. Higher FICO scores and annual incomes suggest better creditworthiness and financial stability, reducing the risk of default.
- In contrast, the likelihood of a loan being paid off in full tends to increase with higher FICO scores and annual income. Again, these factors indicate a better financial standing, making full repayment more likely.
- However, the probability of full payment seems to decrease as the loan term and DTI ratio increase, mirroring the trends observed for charge-offs but in the opposite direction.
- Additionally, these plots encapsulate our initial uncertainty about the rate of these increases and decreases.

Simulating the Posterior. In constructing our Bayesian logistic regression models, a crucial step involves updating our prior models based on actual observed data. This step allows us to simulate the posterior models for our parameters, essentially refining our initial assumptions with the lens of empirical evidence. The posterior distribution encapsulates the adjusted uncertainty pertaining to the unknown parameter values after factoring in the observed data.

To illustrate this process, we provide visual representations in Figs. 1 and 2. These figures delineate the posterior distribution for the parameters of our model.

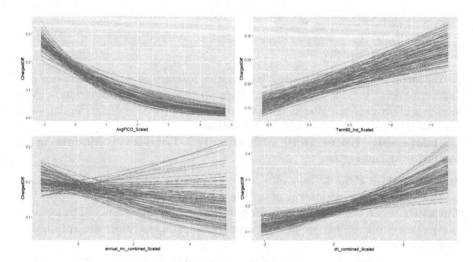

Fig. 1. Charge-off Model Priors

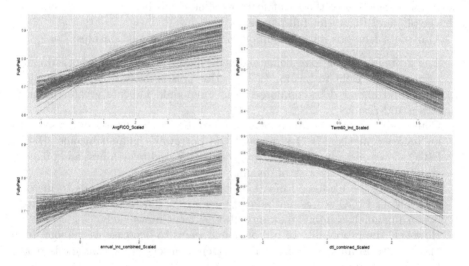

Fig. 2. Paid-off Model Priors

A difference between our prior and posterior models can be seen when comparing these figures with those in Figs. 1 and 2. It is evident that the posterior models, having been updated with the observed loan-level data, exhibit much less variability than their prior counterparts. This implies that the integration of actual data into the model has provided us with a higher level of certainty about the relationship between the probabilities of loans being charged-off or paid-off and the input features (Fig. 3).

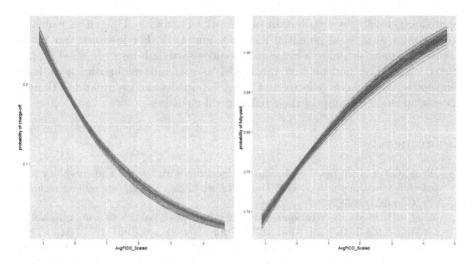

Fig. 3. Posterior plausible models for the probability of charged-off/fully-paid versus input features

In essence, by merging our initial understanding with observed data, we are able to effectively narrow down the plausible range of our model parameters, enhancing the precision of our predictions. This, in turn, underscores the value of leveraging Bayesian models in predictive analytics, as they allow us to continually refine our estimates as new data becomes available.

4   Conclusions

In this paper, we have proposed an innovative, comprehensive approach to predicting the movement of loans across different delinquency states. To address this complex task, we employed a Markov chain model which allowed us to characterize the transitions between different states of delinquency. By capturing these transitions, we gained deeper insight into the life-cycle of loans and the factors that influence their evolution.

A significant portion of this paper was devoted to explaining how to fit loan-level Bayesian logistic models using the Variational Bayes framework. This enabled us to estimate key transition probabilities. Specifically, we built two models that predict the probability of loans transitioning from the 'Current' status to either 'Charged-off' or 'Fully-paid'. This loan-level modeling provided us with a granular perspective on loan transitions, enabling us to estimate the likelihood of different outcomes with a higher degree of precision.

By combining the Markov chain delinquency matrix with the estimated loan-level models for key transition probabilities, we have developed a framework that has promising applications in risk management for lenders. A primary strength of our Bayesian model is its ability to quantify uncertainty associated with predictions. Unlike traditional models that provide single point-estimate, our Bayesian approach generates a distribution of potential outcomes. This offers lenders a more complete view of potential scenarios and risks. For instance, our model allows lenders to estimate a range for the necessary cash reserves based on predicted charged-off and paid-off rates. This is a significant benefit, as it helps lenders to prepare more effectively for potential risks and eventualities, thereby increasing the robustness of their risk control measures.

References

1. Wang, C., et al.: A novel evolutionary algorithm with column and sub-block local search for sudoku puzzles. IEEE Trans. Games (2023). https://api.semanticscholar.org/CorpusID:255879353
2. Yang, J.Q., et al.: Bi-directional feature fixation-based particle swarm optimization for large-scale feature selection. IEEE Trans. Big Data **9**, 1004–1017 (2023)
3. Alvi, A.M., Siuly, S., Wang, H.: A long short-term memory based framework for early detection of mild cognitive impairment from EEG signals. IEEE Trans. Emerg. Top. Comput. Intell. **7**, 375–388 (2023)
4. Berger, J.O., Pericchi, L.R.: The intrinsic bayes factor for linear models. Bayesian Stat. **5**, 25–44 (1996)
5. Bhargavi, B., Rani, K.S., Neog, A.: Finding multidimensional constraint reachable paths for attributed graphs. EAI Endorsed Trans. Scalable Inf. Syst. **10**, e8 (2022)
6. Bishop, C.M.: Pattern Recognition and Machine Learning. Springer, New York (2006)
7. Diggle, P., Diggle, P.J., Heagerty, P., Liang, K.Y., Zeger, S., et al.: Analysis of Longitudinal Data. Oxford University Press, Oxford (2002)
8. Du, J., Michalska, S., Subramani, S., Wang, H., Zhang, Y.: Neural attention with character embeddings for hay fever detection from twitter. Health Inf. Sci. Syst. **7**(1), 1–7 (2019). https://doi.org/10.1007/s13755-019-0084-2
9. Durante, D., Rigon, T.: Conditionally conjugate mean-field variational bayes for logistic models (2019)
10. Hu, H., Li, J., Wang, H., Daggard, G., Shi, M.: A maximally diversified multiple decision tree algorithm for microarray data classification (2006). https://api.semanticscholar.org/CorpusID:12168114
11. Jaakkola, T.S., Jordan, M.I.: Bayesian parameter estimation via variational methods. Stat. Comput. **10**(1), 25–37 (2000)
12. Li, J.-Y., et al.: Distributed differential evolution with adaptive resource allocation. IEEE Trans. Cybern. **53**, 2791–2804 (2022)
13. Yin, J., et al.: Knowledge-driven cybersecurity intelligence: software vulnerability coexploitation behavior discovery. IEEE Trans. Ind. Inform. **19**, 5593–5601 (2023)
14. Jordan, M.I., Ghahramani, Z., Jaakkola, T.S., Saul, L.K.: An introduction to variational methods for graphical models. Mach. Learn. **37**(2), 183–233 (1999)
15. Khalil, F., Li, J., Wang, H.: A framework of combining Markov model with association rules for predicting web page accesses. In: Australasian Data Mining Conference (2006). https://api.semanticscholar.org/CorpusID:6255653
16. Khalil, F., Wang, H., Li, J.: Integrating Markov model with clustering for predicting web page accesses (2007). https://api.semanticscholar.org/CorpusID:20151972
17. Lee, J., Park, J.S., Wang, K., Feng, B., Tennant, M., Kruger, E.: The use of telehealth during the coronavirus (covid-19) pandemic in oral and maxillofacial surgery - a qualitative analysis. EAI Endorsed Trans. Scalable Inf. Syst. **9**, 2 (2021)

18. Li, A., Pericchi, L., Wang, K.: Objective Bayesian inference in probit models with intrinsic priors using variational approximations. Entropy **22**(5), 513 (2020)

19. Ormerod, J.T., Wand, M.P.: Explaining variational approximations. Am. Stat. **64**(2), 140–153 (2010)

20. Pandey, D., Wang, H., Yin, X., Wang, K.N., Zhang, Y., Shen, J.: Automatic breast lesion segmentation in phase preserved DCE-MRIs. Health Inf. Sci. Syst. **10** (2022). https://api.semanticscholar.org/CorpusID:248924735

21. Pang, X., Ge, Y.F., Wang, K.N., Traina, A.J.M., Wang, H.: Patient assignment optimization in cloud healthcare systems: a distributed genetic algorithm. Health Inf. Sci. Syst. **11** (2023). https://api.semanticscholar.org/CorpusID:259277247

22. Polson, N.G., Scott, J.G., Windle, J.: Bayesian inference for logistic models using pólya-gamma latent variables. J. Am. Stat. Assoc. **108**(504), 1339–1349 (2013)

23. Qin, Y., Sheng, Q.Z., Falkner, N.J.G., Dustdar, S., Wang, H., Vasilakos, A.V.: When things matter: a data-centric view of the internet of things. arXiv abs/1407.2704 (2014)

24. Sahani, G., Thaker, C.S., Shah, S.M.: Supervised learning-based approach mining ABAC rules from existing RBAC enabled systems. EAI Endorsed Trans. Scalable Inf. Syst. **10**, e9 (2022)

25. Siddiqui, S.A., Fatima, N., Ahmad, A.: Chest X-ray and CT scan classification using ensemble learning through transfer learning. EAI Endorsed Trans. Scalable Inf. Syst. **9**, e8 (2022)

26. Singh, R., et al.: Antisocial behavior identification from twitter feeds using traditional machine learning algorithms and deep learning. ICST Trans. Scalable Inf. Syst. (2023). https://api.semanticscholar.org/CorpusID:258671645

27. Smith, L.D., Lawrence, E.C.: Forecasting losses on a liquidating long-term loan portfolio. J. Bank. Financ. **19**(6), 959–985 (1995)

28. Sun, X., Wang, H., Li, J., Zhang, Y.: Satisfying privacy requirements before data anonymization. Comput. J. **55**, 422–437 (2012)

29. Wang, H., Yi, X., Bertino, E., Sun, L.: Protecting outsourced data in cloud computing through access management. Concurr. Comput. Pract. Exp. **28**, 600–615 (2016)

30. Wang, H., Zhang, Y., Cao, J., Varadharajan, V.: Achieving secure and flexible m-services through tickets. IEEE Trans. Syst. Man Cybern. Part A **33**, 697–708 (2003)

31. Yin, J., Tang, M., Cao, J., Wang, H., You, M., Lin, Y.: Vulnerability exploitation time prediction: an integrated framework for dynamic imbalanced learning. World Wide Web **25**, 401–423 (2021)

32. You, M., Yin, J., Wang, H., Cao, J., Miao, Y.: A minority class boosted framework for adaptive access control decision-making. In: WISE (2021). https://api.semanticscholar.org/CorpusID:244852711

33. You, M., et al.: A knowledge graph empowered online learning framework for access control decision-making. World Wide Web **26**, 827–848 (2022)

Streaming Data

An Adaptive Drilling Sampling Method and Evaluation Model for Large-Scale Streaming Data

Zhaohui Zhang$^{(\boxtimes)}$ (iD), Yifei Tang, Peng Zhang, Pei Zhang, Dongxue Zhang, and Pengwei Wang

School of Computer Science and Technology, Donghua University, Shanghai 201600, China
zhzhang@dhu.edu.cn

Abstract. The sampling methods for real-time and high-speed changing streaming data are prone to lose a large amount of valuable discrete data. The SDDS (Streaming Data Dynamic Drilling Sampling) sampling method can obtain the value of a large amount of discrete data, but it retains too many discrete values in the sample set, resulting in inconsistent distribution with the original stream dataset and difficulty in describing the overall characteristics of the streaming data. Based on the SDDS sampling method, we propose an adaptive drilling sampling method SDADS (Streaming Data Adaptive Drilling Sampling), which adaptively adjusts various sampling rates in the well during the sampling process, caches all data in the current well, and then adaptively resamples the data in the well, ensuring consistency in data distribution before and after sampling. A new model SDVM (Streaming Data Valuation Model), is further proposed for evaluating the overall value characteristics of streaming datasets. Experiments show that the method proposed in the paper uses neural network training and testing with a small sampling rate to achieve accuracy, recall, and F1 scores above 90%, which is higher than that of the SDDS sampling method. In summary, the SDADS sampling method is beneficial to train neural network models and evaluate the overall value characteristics of streaming data, which has essential research significance in big data valuation.

Keywords: Streaming Data · Adaptive Sampling · Data Valuation · Big Data Evaluation · Neural Network

1 Introduction

In the era of big data, sampling is the core method of evaluating the value of big data, and how to obtain the value characteristics of big data through sampling has become an urgent problem. Hariharakrishnan J. et al. [1] proposed big data analysis has become much important, as more and more data is generated, there is an urgent need to manage the data and extract value from the data collected. Streaming data, characterized by real-time updates and rapid changes, is typically the prevalent form of big data. These characteristics make it a serious challenge to accurately and effectively sample the value

F. Zhang et al. (Eds.): WISE 2023, LNCS 14306, pp. 813–825, 2023.
https://doi.org/10.1007/978-981-99-7254-8_63

features of streaming data. For streaming data, there are currently two main types of sampling and evaluation methods. The first type is unbiased sampling: reservoir sampling [2, 3], and random sampling [4]. Unbiased sampling can effectively evaluate the overall value characteristics of streaming data, but it is subject to randomness. The sampled streaming data will lose some valuable discrete data, ultimately leading to low accuracy in evaluating the value of the streaming data. The second type is biased sampling [5–7]. Biased sampling solves the problem of sampling randomness, but removes valuable discrete data, ultimately resulting in low accuracy in evaluating the value of streaming data. To sum up, due to the inconsistent goals of unbiased sampling and biased sampling, existing methods find it difficult to include a large amount of valuable discrete data while efficiently and accurately evaluating the value of streaming data.

At present, there are still some difficulties: 1. When there are too many discrete data in the sample, it is difficult to evaluate the overall value characteristics of the streaming data. 2. It is difficult to evaluate the consistency of the distribution of streaming data distribution.

In response to the above issues, we propose the SDADS sampling method and an SDVM model. Overall, the contributions of this paper are summarized as follows:

1. We propose an adaptive sampling method SDADS for large-scale streaming datasets. This method is based on the dynamic drilling sampling method, which adaptively adjusts different sampling rates in the well during the sampling process, caches all data in the current well, and then adaptively resamples the data in the well to ensure consistency of data distribution before and after sampling.
2. We propose a sampling-based overall value evaluation model SDVM, which solves the problem of not being able to effectively describe the overall value feature distribution of stream data when many discrete values are retained in the sample set. Furtherly we proposes a sampling-based overall value evaluation model from three aspects: dense trend, sparse trend, and overall trend, which evaluates the SDADS sampling method from different perspectives.

The overall structure of this paper is as follows: The first section introduces the current research status; The second section introduces the relevant work; The third section introduces the SDADS sampling method; The fourth section introduces the evaluation model of the overall value characteristics of streaming data; The fifth section introduces the dataset and experimental analysis; The sixth section summarizes the research results of the paper and prospects for the future.

2   Related Work

In the field of big data, sampling methods can extract valuable data from datasets, so using efficient and accurate sampling methods to obtain high-quality samples is crucial for data valuation. However, streaming data presents challenges in sampling high-quality data. Cervellera C. et al. [8] to obtain high-quality sample sets, a recursive binary partitioning algorithm based on input space is proposed to obtain sample sets with similar features to the original dataset. Lin l. et al. [9] proposed a feature weight sampling method based on sliding windows, which is proposed to obtain a sample set consistent with the category proportion of the original stream dataset. Current sampling methods can effectively preserve the overall characteristics of the original stream data. However, if the proportion of categories in the raw stream data is unbalanced, the sampled sample set tends to lose a large amount of valuable discrete data, thereby reducing the quality of the sample set.

In response to the above situation, there are currently many sampling methods that can effectively collect unbalanced raw stream datasets, making the sample set a good training set for neural networks. Li L. et al. [10] proposed entropy-based oversampling method (EOS), entropy-based under sampling (EUS) method, and entropy-based hybrid sampling (EHS) method combining oversampling and under-sampling methods to balance data sets and improve classification accuracy. Zhang P. et al. [11] proposed a streaming data dynamic drilling sampling (SDDS) method and an overall feature evaluation model of streaming data sets. The main concept of the SDDS method is to dynamically adapt the size and position of the analysis unit as the well changes, and to accurately predict the position and range of discrete data. However, it preserves too many individual data points in the sample set, leading to an inconsistent distribution with the original streaming dataset and making it difficult to describe the overall features of the streaming data. Based on the SDDS method, we introduce the SDADS method which implements adaptive adjustments of sampling rates in the well during the sampling process, caches all data in the well, and resamples the data adaptively, ensuring consistent data distribution before and after sampling. Experiments show that the SDADS method attains higher sampling accuracy of the overall stream data features compared to the SDDS method. Additionally, the neural network model trained using the SDADS and SDDS sampling methods shows similar training effects.

In summary, sampling streaming data often fails to create a comprehensive sample set with enough discrete data and sufficient accuracy to capture the characteristics of streaming data. Moreover, current methods for evaluating sampling values are limited in scope, thus hindering a multi-dimensional characterization of streaming data.

3   Adaptive Drilling Sampling Method

3.1   Basic Concepts and SDADS Framework

Definition 1 (Streaming Data).   Streaming data can be defined as a quadruple comprising of data sequence number, data arrival time, data value, and data class, which can be represented as:

$$S = \left\{ (id_i, \ time_i, \ value_i, \ class_i) | 1 \leq i \leq N \ \ and \ \ i \in N^+ \right\} \tag{1}$$

where id_i is the order of the ith arrival data, $time_i$ is the arrival time of the ith data, $value_i$ is the data value of the ith streaming, N is the size of streaming data, and the size grows infinitely as time changes, $class_i$ is the class of the ith arrival data. Data values that are relatively high over a period of time are referred to as peaks whilst those that are relatively low are known as troughs. Data values in between are referred to as median data. Based on the above, in order to better analyse the distribution of streaming data, the data are categorized into three classes, troughs, peaks and medians, denoted as $class_i = 0, 1, 2$. The distribution of streaming data is shown in Fig. 1.

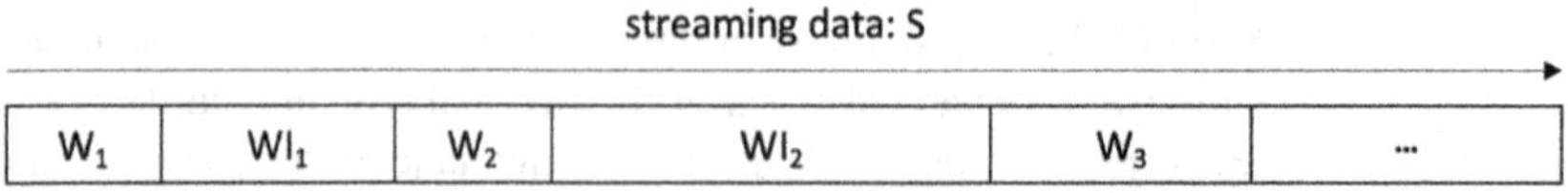

W_1	WI_1	W_2	WI_2	W_3	...

Fig. 1. Streaming data schematic diagram

Definition 2 (Well). Based on the concept of drilling sampling, the concept of well is introduced [11]. Here, the well is an analysis model for stream data containing N time periods. To adjust to changes in discrete values in stream data, we continuously modify the well's size during the sampling process to precisely predict the position and range of discrete values in streaming data. Surrounding. We refer to this type of well as dynamic drilling. The ith well is recorded as: W_i. The size of the ith well is denoted as: WS_i. The number of sampling wells in the original streaming dataset is denoted as WN. The data within W_i is represented as:

$$W_i = \left\{ (id_j,\ time_j,\ value_j,\ class_j) | 1 \le j \le WS_i\ and\ j \in N^+ \right\} (1 \le i \le WN) \quad (2)$$

Definition 3 (Well-Interval). In order to decrease the frequency of accessing streaming data samples, the interval between wells is adjusted. The ith well interval is recorded as: WI_i. The interval size of the ith well is recorded as: WIS_i. The ith well interval WI_i is represented as:

$$WI_i = \left\{ (id_j,\ time_j,\ value_j,\ class_j) | id_{wi\_max} + 1 \le id_j \le id_{wi+1\_min} - 1 \right\} \quad (3)$$

where id_{wi_max} is the maximum id of the arrival data in the ith well, id_{wi+1_min} is the smallest id of the arrival data in the $i + 1^{th}$ well.

Definition 4 (Class Imbalance Ratio). Class imbalance ratio refers to the proportion between different categories in the original stream dataset, denoted as CIR. Considering the characteristics of streaming data with troughs, peaks and intermediate values, divide the original stream dataset S into three parts according to category, denoted as C0, C1, and C2, and represent CIR as:

$$CIR = len(C0) : len(C1) : len(C2) \quad (4)$$

Definition 5 (Candidate Sample Set). The candidate sample set is the data in the well that has not been sampled, denoted as CSS. As with CIR, considering data characteristics, divide the unsampled data of the the streaming dataset S in the well into three parts based on the category, denoted as SC0, SC1, and SC2. Then, CSS is represented as:

$$CSS = (SC0, SC1, SC2) \quad (5)$$

SDADS Framework. To obtain valuable discrete data in streaming data, we introduce a large-scale streaming data sampling method SDADS for adaptive drilling. The method involves initially setting the well and well interval. The size of the well interval is then adaptively changed using skewness coefficients to predict the position of discrete data.

Furthermore, the sampling rate of each class in the well is adaptively changed based on skewness coefficients. Then, use Reservoir Sampling in the well and add the unsampled data to the candidate sampling set. Within the well interval, the use of equidistant sampling is recommended. Furthermore, by exploiting correlation coefficients and variation coefficients to forecast the range of discrete data, the size of the subsequent well is changed adaptively. Finally, the sample set should be dynamically adjusted to maintain consistency in data distribution before and after sampling. The specific sampling method is shown in Fig. 2.

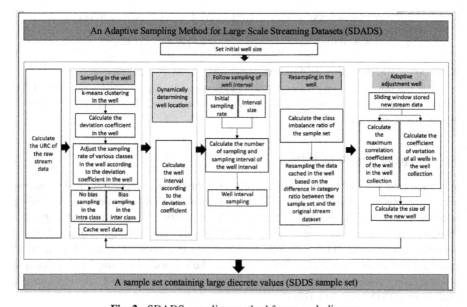

Fig. 2. SDADS sampling method framework diagram

3.2 Dynamic Adjustment of Wells

The method of dynamically adjusting well parameters in this paper is based on our previous work [11].To predict the location of discrete values in the streaming data and more discrete values in the sampling wells accurately, we dynamically adjust the sampling rate for each class, based on the initial sampling rate for each case. Here, we dynamically adjust the sampling rate and location in wells using the skewness coefficient, denoted SK, which becomes

$$SK_i = \frac{WS_i \times \sum_{j=1}^{WS_i}(value_j - \overline{value})^3}{(WS_i - 1) \times (WS_i - 2) \times [\sum_{j=1}^{WS_i}(value_j - \overline{value})^2]^{\frac{3}{2}}}, (1 \leq i \leq WN) \quad (6)$$

where SK_i is the skewness coefficient of the ith well, $value_j$ is the jth data in the ith well, and $\overline{value}$ denotes the mean value of the data in the ith well.

Once the skewness coefficients have been obtained, we present the sampling rate adjustment scheme as follows:

$$p_i = \begin{cases} 2 \times p_{init} \times |SK_i|, & SK_i \in (-1, -0.5) \cup (0.5, 1) \\ 1, & SK_i \in (-\infty, -1] \cup [1, \infty) \\ p_{init}, & SK_i \in [-0.5, 0.5] \end{cases} \quad (7)$$

where p_{init} is the initial sampling rate, and p_i is the sampling rate of the ith well.

Furthermore, the scheme for adjusting well interval is as follows:

$$WIS_i = \begin{cases} \left| \frac{WIS_{init}}{SK_i} \right|, & SK_i \in (-1, -0.5) \cup (0.5, 1) \cup (-\infty, -1] \cup [1, \infty) \\ 2 \times WIS_{init}, & SK_i \in [-0.5, 0.5] \end{cases} \quad (8)$$

where WIS_{init} is the initial well interval, and WIS_i is the ith well interval.

Last but not least, our previous work[11] proposed adaptive well sizing algorithm called AWS for dynamic well sizing based on Pearson's correlation coefficient as well as the coefficient of variation.

3.3 Sampling Algorithm (SDADS)

We propose an SDADS sampling method that uses the classic sampling algorithm: Reservoir Sampling (RS) in wells, and equidistant sampling within well intervals. According to the SDDS algorithm, the size of the well is dynamically adjusted to accurately predict the range of discrete data. Then, the well interval is dynamically adjusted based on the skewness coefficient, and the discrete data position is adaptively adjusted. Finally, to maintain consistency in the class imbalance ratio before and after sampling, the sample set adaptively removes data or adds data from the candidate sample set. The specific algorithm SDADS is shown below.

Algorithm . Adaptive drilling sampling for streaming data (SDADS)

Input: WS_{init} −Init Well Size; S −Streaming Data;WIS_{init} −Init Well Interval Size; p_{init} −Init Sample Rate; CSS−Candidate Sample Set.

Output: SS -Sample Set

1. Set initial well: W_{init}, length is WS_{init}
2. Set initial well interval: WI_{init}, length is WIS_{init}
3. Calculate the p for each class in W_{init} according to formula (7)
4. SS.add(Data obtained from three classes of reservoir sampling)
5. CSS.add(Data not obtained from sampling three types of reservoirs)
6. Equidistant sampling of well interval data
7. while S is generating:
8.   Get the size of the next well through Algorithm AWS: WS_{next}
9.   Set well: W_i, length is WS_{next}
10.   Calculate the SK_i of W_i according to formula (6)
11.   Calculate the p_i of three classes in W_i according to formula (7)
12. SS.add(Data obtained from three classes of reservoir sampling)
13.   Calculate the WIS_i of WI_i, according to formula (8)
14.   Set well interval: WI_i, length is WIS_i
15. SS.add(Data obtained from WI_i of equidistant sampling)
16. SS.sort()
17. Divide SS into three parts according to Class 0, 1, 2: SCZ, SCO, SCT
18. Divide CSS into three parts according to Class 0, 1, 2: CCZ, CCO, CCT
19. MC = The least number of SCZ, SCO, SCT
20. if MC == SCZ:
21.   NUM = $\left| (len(SCZ) + len(SCO)) \times \left(\frac{len(SCZ)}{len(SCO)} - \frac{len(C0)}{len(C1)} \right) \right|$
22.   SCO add or remove NUM data obtained from CCO by reservoir sampling
23.   NUM1 = $\left| (len(SCZ) + len(SCT)) \times \left(\frac{len(SCZ)}{len(SCT)} - \frac{len(C0)}{len(C2)} \right) \right|$
24.   SCT add or remove NUM1 data obtained from CCT by reservoir sampling
25. elseif MC == SCO:
26.   NUM = $\left| (len(SCZ) + len(SCO)) \times \left(\frac{len(SCO)}{len(SCZ)} - \frac{len(C1)}{len(C0)} \right) \right|$
27.   SCZ add or remove NUM data obtained from CCZ by reservoir sampling
28.   NUM1 = $\left| (len(SCT) + len(SCO)) \times \left(\frac{len(SCO)}{len(SCT)} - \frac{len(C1)}{len(C2)} \right) \right|$
29.   SCT add or remove NUM1 data obtained from CCT by reservoir sampling
30. else:
31.   NUM = $\left| (len(SCZ) + len(SCT)) \times \left(\frac{len(SCT)}{len(SCZ)} - \frac{len(C2)}{len(C0)} \right) \right|$
32.   SCZ add or remove NUM data obtained from CCZ by reservoir sampling
33.   NUM1 = $\left| (len(SCO) + len(SCT)) \times \left(\frac{len(SCT)}{len(SCO)} - \frac{len(C2)}{len(C1)} \right) \right|$
34.   SCO add or remove NUM1 data obtained from CCO by reservoir sampling
35. SS.sort()
36. return SS

---

4 Evaluation Model for Streaming Data (SDVM)

We propose a new overall features evaluation model for streaming data (SDVM), which evaluates the overall features of the original dataset using a sample set from three aspects: dense trend (mean), sparse trend (standard deviation), and overall trend (skewness coefficient, class imbalance ratio). The following evaluation indicators are provided above:

Definition 6 (Mean Similarity Accuracy). Refers to the accuracy of estimating the mean of the original streaming dataset RS using the mean of the sample set SS. The calculation formula for Mean Similar Accuracy (MSA) is as follows:

$$MSA = \left(3 - \frac{|\overline{SS_{C0}} - \overline{RS_{C0}}|}{\overline{RS_{C0}}} - \frac{|\overline{SS_{C1}} - \overline{RS_{C1}}|}{\overline{RS_{C1}}} - \frac{|\overline{SS_{C2}} - \overline{RS_{C2}}|}{\overline{RS_{C2}}} \right) \div 3 \times 100\% \qquad (9)$$

where $\overline{SS_{C0}}$ is the mean of data with class 0 in the sample set, $\overline{RS_{C0}}$ is the mean of data with class 0 in the original stream dataset; $\overline{SS_{C1}}$ is the mean of data with class 1 in the sample set, $\overline{RS_{C1}}$ is the mean of data with class 1 in the original stream dataset; $\overline{SS_{C2}}$ is the mean of class 2 data in the sample set, $\overline{RS_{C2}}$ the mean of class 2 data in the original stream dataset.

Definition 8 (Skewness Coefficient Similarity Accuracy). Refers to the accuracy of estimating the skewness coefficient of the original streaming dataset RS using the skewness coefficient of the sample set SS. The deviation coefficient similarity accuracy (DCSA) calculation formula is as follows:

$$DCSA = \left(3 - \frac{|SK(SS_{C0}) - SK(RS_{C0})|}{|SK(RS_{C0})|} - \frac{|SK(SS_{C1}) - SK(RS_{C1})|}{|SK(RS_{C1})|} - \frac{|SK(SS_{C2}) - SK(RS_{C2})|}{|SK(RS_{C2})|} \right) \div 3 \times 100\% \qquad (10)$$

where $SK(SS_{C0})$ is the skewness coefficient of the data with class 0 in the sample set, and $SK(RS_{C0})$ is the skewness coefficient of the data with class 0 in the original stream dataset; $SK(SS_{C1})$ is the skewness coefficient of the data with class 1 in the sample set, and $SK(RS_{C1})$ is the skewness coefficient of the data with class 1 in the original stream dataset; $SK(SS_{C2})$ is the skewness coefficient of the data with class 2 in the sample set, and $SK(RS_{C2})$ is the skewness coefficient of the data with class 2 in the original stream dataset.

Definition 9 (Class Imbalance Ratio Similarity Accuracy). Refers to the accuracy of estimating the RS class imbalance ratio of the original stream dataset using the class imbalance ratio of the sample set SS. We divide the sample set SS into three categories based on class: 0, 1, and 2: SS0, SS1, and SS2. The calculation formula for Class Imbalance Ratio Similar Accuracy (CIRSA) is as follows:

$$CIRSA = \left(\frac{len(SS0) \times len(C1)}{len(C0) \times len(SS1)} + \frac{len(SS2) \times len(C0)}{len(C2) \times len(SS0)} + \frac{len(SS2) \times len(C1)}{len(C2) \times len(SS1)} \right) \div 3 \times 100\% \qquad (11)$$

where $len(SS0)$ is the length of the divided sample set SS0, while $len(SS1)$ and $len(SS2)$ respectively represent the length of the set SS1 and SS2. Moreover, $len(C0)$ denotes the count of the data belonging to class 0 in the original stream dataset. Similarly, $len(C1)$ and $len(C2)$ denote the count of data which belong to either class 1 or class 2 in the original stream dataset.

5 Experiment and Analysis

To demonstrate that the SDADS algorithm proposed in this paper can effectively evaluate the quality and value of overall stream data, this section first introduces the dataset used in this experiment, and then uses the SDVM evaluation model to evaluate the sampling results. In conclusion, comparing the SDADS algorithm with the SDDS algorithm establishes that the sample set obtained by the new method can be useful for training deep learning models. Additionally, it can precisely characterize the significant characteristics of the original stream data.

5.1 Experimental Dataset

We select the real dataset HSI as the experimental streaming dataset, which is the 2014 Hong Kong Hang Seng Futures Index published in Kaggle. To demonstrate the universality of the new algorithm on different datasets, considering the characteristics of streaming data with peaks, troughs and intermediate values, first K-Means clustering with K = 3 was performed on HSI to obtain classification labels. Then, the classified HSI dataset was modified to obtain two datasets: as shown in Fig. 3(a), the class imbalance ratio of HSI1 was 47:1:17, with a total of 55736 pieces of data; As shown in Fig. 3(b), the class imbalance ratio of HSI2 is 94:1:35, with a total of 55442 pieces of data. Split the two stream datasets HSI1 and HSI2 in a 4:1 ratio, with the first 80% of the data being used as the training set and sampling object for the neural network model, and the last 20% as the testing set.

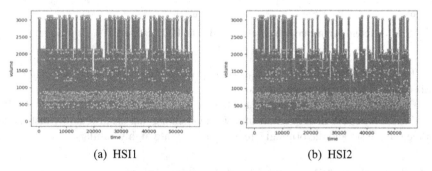

(a) HSI1   (b) HSI2

Fig. 3. Experimental Data Collection

5.2 SDVM Model Evaluation

To demonstrate that the AWS algorithm can accurately predict the position and range of discrete data, we use the SDADS algorithm to obtain a sample set that preserves the discrete data while reflecting the centralized and overall characteristics of the original streaming data. We then conduct experimental evaluations on the HSI1 and HSI2 datasets using the SDVM model under different parameters, a detailed analysis of parameters WS_{init}, WIS_{init} and p_{init} in the SDADS algorithm.

Firstly, WS_{init} and WIS_{init} are set as 20, 20 respectively, with the adjusted parameter p_{init}. The obtained experimental results are shown in Fig. 4.

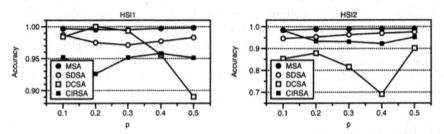

Fig. 4. Evaluation results of streaming data value under different parameters p_{init} of the HSI1 and HSI2 dataset

Then, we set up $WIS_{init} = 20$, $p_{init} = 0.3$ with adjusted parameter WS_{init}, and the experimental results obtained are shown in Fig. 5.

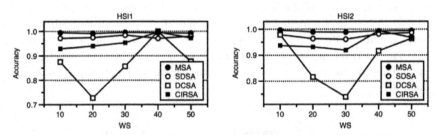

Fig. 5. Different parameters WS_{init} of the HSI1 and HSI2 dataset SDVM evaluation results

Then, we set up $WI_{init} = 20$, $p_{init} = 0.3$, with adjusted parameter WIS_{init}, and the experimental results obtained are shown in Fig. 6.

From Fig. 4, 5 and Fig. 6, MSA and SDSA are almost all above 95%, while CIRSA and DCSA is almost all above 90% and 80%, indicating that the probability distribution of the sample set and the original streaming dataset are highly similar.

5.3 Comparison of SDDS and SDADS Experiments

We conduct comparative experiments on SDADS and SDDS using datasets HSI1 and HSI2. The experimental results are shown in Fig. 7 and Fig. 8.

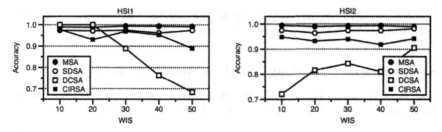

Fig. 6. Different parameters WIS_{init} of the HSI1 and HSI2 dataset SDVM evaluation results

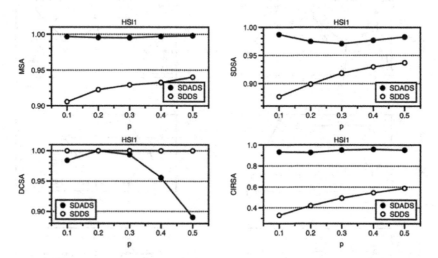

Fig. 7. Different parameters p of HSI1 dataset SDVM evaluation results

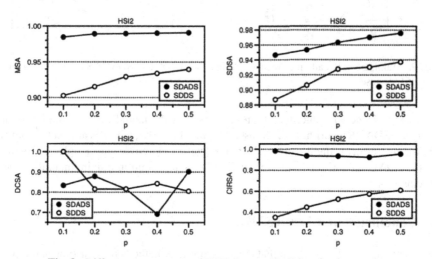

Fig. 8. Different parameters p of HSI2 dataset SDVM evaluation results

In Fig. 7 and Fig. 8, the SDADS algorithm has significant improvements in MSA, SDSA, and CIRSA evaluation metrics compared to the SDDS algorithm.

5.4 Comparison of Classification Effects of Neural Networks

We set $WS_{init} = 20$, $WIS_{init} = 20$, for the parameter p in the SDADS algorithm different adjustments and the experimental results obtained are shown in Fig. 9.

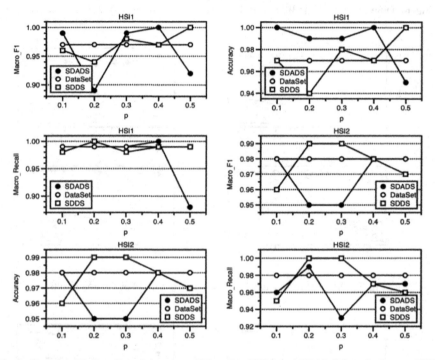

Fig. 9. Training F1, Recall, and Accuracy Values for SDDS and SDADS Sample Sets on HSI1 and HSI2 Datasets

In Fig. 9, the F1 value, recall, and accuracy of the neural network model trained using the SDADS algorithm are almost all higher than 90%, which is almost the same as the training effect using the original stream dataset. Moreover, the sample set obtained by the SDADS algorithm outperforms the SDDS algorithm in training neural network models.

6 Conclusion and Future Work

In order to address the problem that current sampling methods for real-time and rapidly changing streaming data are prone to losing large amounts of valuable discrete data, as well as the difficulty of efficiently and accurately evaluating the overall characteristics of the streaming data, we propose a large-scale imbalanced streaming data sampling method

SDADS for adaptive drilling, as well as a new overall evaluation model SDVM for streaming data. The SDADS sampling method takes wells as analysis units, adaptively changes the size and position of wells, accurately predicts the location and range of valuable discrete data, and evaluates the SDVM model from dense trends (mean) Starting from the three aspects of sparse trend (standard deviation) and overall trend (skewness coefficient, class imbalance ratio, and JS divergence), a sufficient and detailed analysis was conducted on the overall characteristics of the original streaming dataset using the sample set. In future work, we will further increase the dimensions of evaluating the value of streaming data and comprehensively evaluate its value.

Acknowledgement. This work was supported in part by the Shanghai Science and Technology Innovation Action Plan Project (22511100700).

References

1. Hariharakrishnan, J., Mohanavalli, S., Srividya, et al.: Survey of pre-processing techniques for mining big data. In: International Conference on Computer, Communication and Signal Processing (ICCCSP), Chennai, India, pp. 1–5 (2017)
2. Ke, Y.: Technical perspective: online model management via temporally biased sampling. SIGMOD Rec. **48**(1), 68 (2019)
3. Zhang, L., Jiang, H., Wang, F., et al.: T-sample: a dual reservoir-based sampling method for characterizing large graph streams. In: IEEE 35th International Conference on Data Engineering (ICDE), Macao, China, pp. 1674–1677 (2019)
4. Sengupta, N., Bagchi, A., Bedathur, S., Ramanath, M.: Sampling and reconstruction using bloom filters. In: 33rd IEEE Transactions on Knowledge and Data Engineering, San Diego, CA, USA, pp. 195–198 (2017)
5. Hu, Z., Ren, Y., Yang, X.: Data stream bias sampling algorithm based on sliding window density clustering. Comput. Sci. **40**(9), 254–256+269 (2013)
6. Hafeez, T., McArdle, G., Xu, L.: Adaptive window based sampling on the edge for internet of things data streams. In: 11th International Conference on Network of the Future (NoF), Bordeaux, France, pp. 105–109 (2020)
7. Li, S., Li, L., Yan, J., He, H.: SDE: a novel clustering framework based on sparsity-density entropy. IEEE Trans. Knowl. Data Eng. **30**(8), 1575–1587 (2018)
8. Cervellera, C., Macciò, D.: Distribution-preserving stratified sampling for learning problems. IEEE Trans. Neural Netw. Learn. Syst. **29**(7), 2886–2895 (2018)
9. Lin, L., Yu, Q., Ji, W., Gao, Y.: Feature-selected and -preserved sampling for high-dimensional stream data summary. In: 2019 IEEE 31st International Conference on Tools with Artificial Intelligence (ICTAI), Portland, OR, USA, pp. 1406–1411 (2019)
10. Li, L., He, H., Li, J.: Entropy-based sampling approaches for multi-class imbalanced problems. IEEE Trans. Knowl. Data Eng. **32**(11), 2159–2170 (2020)
11. Zhang, P., Zhang, Z., Hu, C., et al.: A dynamic drilling sampling method and evaluation model for large-scale streaming data. In: Proceedings of the 35th International Conference on Software Engineering and Knowledge Engineering (SEKE2023), USA, pp. 437–442 (2023)

Unsupervised Representation Learning with Semantic of Streaming Time Series

Chengyang Ye[1]([✉]) [iD] and Qiang Ma[2] [iD]

[1] Graduate School of Informatics, Kyoto University, Kyoto, Japan
ye@db.soc.i.kyoto-u.ac.jp
[2] Department of Information Science, Kyoto Institute of Technology, Kyoto, Japan
qiang@ieee.org

Abstract. Representation learning of time series is common in tasks like data mining and improves performance in downstream tasks. However, existing methods aren't appropriate for streaming time series due to two main limitations: first, The efficiency of representation learning methods can be a concern when dealing with streaming time series. Secondly, most of representation learning are designed for timestamp-level representation. They cannot reveal the semantic information in time series, which further reduces the efficiency and effectiveness of representation learning of streaming time series. This study introduces an unsupervised method tailored for streaming time series, considering semantic information. Specifically, it integrates recursive covariance estimation into a simplified transformer structure, PoolFormer, to enhance efficiency and reveal real-time semantic information. In addition, a novel unsupervised method is designed to learning the representation of streaming time series. The experiments show that this method outperforms other representation methods.

Keywords: Streaming time series · Unsupervised representation learning · Semantic information

1 Introduction

The proliferation of digital technologies and the Internet of Things has generated an unprecedented volume of time series. This wealth of information are collected from a wide range of domains, including finance [1] and healthcare [2]. With the increasing complexity of application scenarios and downstream tasks involving time series, representation learning has emerged as a powerful technique for advancing their analysis.

However, most representation learning are designed to represent each timestamp of time series. They cannot represent the state of subsequences, i.e., the semantic information. This makes these timestamp-level methods not suitable for certain downstream tasks, like retrieval. Therefore, semantic-based methods have been widely concerned in representation learning of time series [3]. Figure 1

© The Author(s), under exclusive license to Springer Nature Singapore Pte Ltd. 2023
F. Zhang et al. (Eds.): WISE 2023, LNCS 14306, pp. 826–835, 2023.
https://doi.org/10.1007/978-981-99-7254-8_64

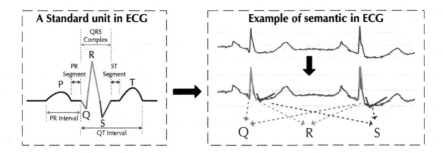

Fig. 1. Example of semantic information in ECG.

shows a typical example of semantic information in electrocardiograms (ECG). As shown in the left side of Fig. 1, a standard unit in ECG can be divided into several parts with different states. These different states can be regarded as the semantic in time series. And according to different semantic, a ECG time series data can be represented more efficiently (as shown in the right side of Fig. 1).

In addition, as more and more devices become smarter and ubiquitous, they generate streaming time series. It differs from traditional time series data in that it is constantly updated. The efficient analysis of streaming time series holds practical significance. For instance, the increasing popularity of smartwatches has enabled the collection and analysis of streaming ECG. It is benefit for detecting heart diseases more promptly and accurately. Nevertheless, the issue of representation learning in streaming time series remains a huge challenge.

In this study, a novel representation learning algorithm is designed for streaming time series. This proposed algorithm introduces the recursive covariance estimation in a simplified transformer structure, PoolFormer, and is named CPFormer. Some research has already proved that covariance can reveal the semantic information in time series [4]. Furthermore, a stochastic Pooling-based triplet network is designed specifically for streaming time series to generate positive and negative sample pairs for unsupervised training.

In summary, the main contributions of our work are as follows:

- A novel representation learning algorithm, CPFormer, is designed to learn the semantic-based representation of streaming time series (Sect. 3.2).
- Subsequently, a novel unsupervised method is designed to learning the representation of streaming time series (Sect. 3.3).
- We conducted extensive experiments on several public datasets from different fields (Sect. 4). In comparison with other baseline algorithms, the proposed CPFormer algorithm achieved an improved performance.

The rest of this paper is organized as follows. Section 2 outlines previous research on representation learning of streaming time series, as well as some variants of transformer architecture. Section 3 presents the architecture of the proposed algorithm CPFormer in detail. Thereafter, Sect. 4 discussed the experimental results. Finally, Sect. 5 gives conclusions and future work.

2   Related Works

2.1   Representation Learning of Streaming Time Series

Basically, there are three types of representation learning for streaming time series: traditional feature engineering methods, symbolic representation methods and neural networks-based methods.

Traditional feature engineering methods aim to extract relevant features from streaming data to represent the temporal patterns and variations (such as Fourier transform-based [5]). These traditional feature methods may not be able to capture complex patterns in streaming time series data, leading to sub-optimal representations.

Symbolic representation methods transform the data into a symbolic form using discrete symbols. Symbolic Aggregate Approximation (SAX) [6] represents a time series by mapping it to a sequence of symbols based on breakpoints derived from the data distribution. However, these methods often rely on human expertise to select relevant symbolic. This process can be time-consuming.

Neural networks-based methods leverage the power of deep learning to automatically learn meaningful representations from the raw data. However, most of these representation learning methods are focus on timestamp-level representation, which can not represent the state of subsequences and relationship between different semantic patterns.

2.2   Variants of Transformer Architecture

transformer architecture, initially introduced for natural language processing (NLP) tasks, has been adapted and extended for various domains. This famous architecture has already developed several variants, which demonstrate the versatility and adaptability of the original model.

Reformer [7] addresses the computational efficiency of transformer by introducing a set of optimizations. It leverages reversible layers, chunked processing, and locality-sensitive hashing to reduce memory requirements and enable training and inference on longer sequences.

Performer [8] is another variant of the transformer architecture that approximates the self-attention mechanism with a faster and more memory-efficient approach. It uses the kernelized self-attention to significantly reduce the computational complexity of the attention mechanism.

MetaFormer [9] proposed a token mixer component to replace the self-attention in original transformer architecture. In the paper of MetaFormer, a Pooling-based token mixer is applied in MetaFormer, which is named Pool-Former. MetaFormer architecture allows subsequent studies to develop different designs and studies for different application scenarios.

3   Methodology

3.1   Overview

In this section, the proposed CPFormer model structure and relevant algorithms are described. The structure of CPFormer is shown in Fig. 2.

CPFormer is designed for unsupervised representation learning with semantic of streaming time series. Firstly, the greedy Gaussian segmentation (GGS) method [11] is applied to generate subsequences with semantic. In addition, a widely used input normalization method is temporal pyramid pooling (TPP) [12], which is designed to generate regular inputs for time series subseries with unequal lengths.

It is worth noting that the incomplete subsequence does not go through the TPP normalization method. Because the length and Gaussian distribution of incomplete subsequence has not been determined, which means it can not join the subsequent learning processing.

3.2   Covariance-Based PoolFormer Mechanism

The original encoder architecture of PoolFormer, as depicted in Fig. 3(a), replaces the self-attention mechanism with the Pooling mechanism to address the challenges of trainable parameters and computational complexity. However, Pooling mechanism cannot represent subsequences with semantic information. It can only capture similarity information among different inputs.

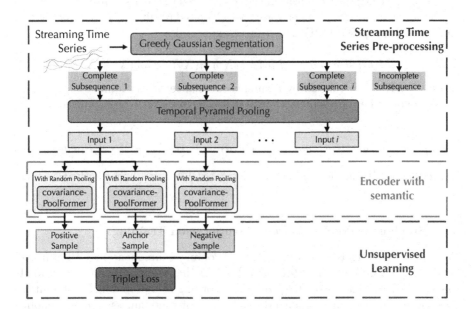

Fig. 2. Structure of unsupervised representation learning for streaming time series with semantic information.

(a)

(b)

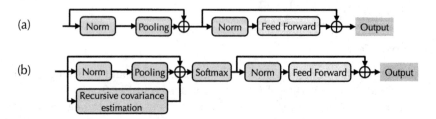

Fig. 3. Schematic of Pooling-based transformer architecture: (a) the architecture of PoolFormer; (b) the architecture of proposed CPFormer.

Covariance has already been proved to reveal the semantic information in time series. According to the characteristic of streaming time series, recursive covariance estimation is considered. The structure of proposed CPFormer is shown in Fig. 3(b). As same as PoolFormer, the encoder layer of CPFormer is consist of two sub-block. The first sub-block is designed to calculated the Interaction information of subsequences. The second sub-block is considered to generate the representation.

According to the expression in original PoolFormer paper, the calculated result $Y(PoolFormer)$ of first sub-block can be expressed as:

$$Y(PoolFormer) = Pooling(Norm(X)) + X \tag{1}$$

where X represents inputs of complete subsequences group. After adding recursive covariance estimation, covariance is considered in the first sub-block to reveal the semantic information. Therefore, the calculated result $Y(CPFormer)$ of first sub-block in proposed CPFormer can be expressed as:

$$Y(CPFormer) = Pooling(Norm(X)) + Cov(X) + X \tag{2}$$

where $Cov(X)$ is calculated by recursive covariance estimation.

Therefore, the representation output of CPFormer can be expressed as:

$$output = \sigma(Norm(Softmax(Y(CPFormer)))W_1)W_2 + Y(CFPormer) \tag{3}$$

where W_1 and W_2 are learnable parameters; $\sigma(\cdot)$ is a non-linear activation function.

3.3   Stochastic Pooling-Based Unsupervised Training

We employed stochastic Pooling [13] as Pooling component in CPFormer to generate training pairs. In Stochastic Pooling the pooling operation randomly samples values from the pooling window according to a probability distribution. This probabilistic sampling introduces a level of randomness into the pooling process, which meets the requirement of construction of training pairs in unsupervised representation learning.

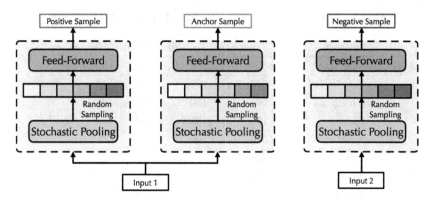

Fig. 4. Schematic of generating training pairs for triplet network in representation learning of streaming time series.

A diagram of stochastic Pooling in triplet network of proposed CPFormer is shown in Fig. 4. Positive sample pairs are constructed by two stochastic Pooling operation for one streaming time series subsequence. For negative sample pairs, subsequences are randomly chosen from different streaming time series in the dataset.

The original training objective of the triplet loss is calculated based on the distances between the positive, anchor, and negative samples. It can be expressed as follows:

$$max(d(a,p) - d(a,n) + margin, 0) \tag{4}$$

where $d(a,p)$ denote the distance between the anchor sample (a) and the positive sample (p), and $d(a,n)$ denote the distance between the anchor sample (a) and the negative sample (n). Margin is a hyperparameter that specifies the desired separation or margin between the distances of positive and negative samples. Specifically, based on the cosine distance, the training objective can be defined as follows:

$$\log\left(1 + \exp\left(margin - \cos(a,p) + \cos(a,n)\right)\right) \tag{5}$$

4   Experiments

We examined CPFormer with other algorithms of streaming time series in terms of downstream task of classification and retrieval. To generate streaming time series from offline public datasets of time series, we employed Spark streaming [14] to simulate streaming time series. Spark Streaming is a real-time stream processing framework. As for the time series datasets, we utilized datasets from the UEA&UCR time series classification archives [15], which offer an initial benchmark for existing models, providing valuable baseline information on their performance.

Table 1. Summary of UEA&UCR datasets in classification task.

Dataset	Train Size	Test Size	Length	Classes
CBF	30	900	128	3
FaceUCR	200	2050	131	14
GunPoint	50	150	150	2
Plane	105	105	144	7
SyntheticControl	300	300	60	6
TwoPatterns	23	1139	82	2
TwoLeadECG	1000	4000	128	4
Wafer	1000	6164	152	2

4.1   Classification

In the classification task, to obtain a distribution over classes from the model's output vector, we applied a Softmax function. The cross-entropy between this distribution and the categorical ground truth labels was then calculated as the sample loss.

Following eight datasets from UEA&UCR time series classification archives were chosen to evaluate model performance. These datasets were selected because they are also utilized in evaluation of some advanced algorithms of streaming time series [16]. Table 1 provides a summary of these datasets.

Meanwhile, we have selected the following three advanced models as our baseline: GP-HLS [4] uses semantic information to represent subsequences of time series. ODTW-NN [17] presents a online dynamic time warping (ODTW) for streaming time series. PED [16] introduces an active adaptation strategy for time series classifiers, which enables them to adjust in real-time to the evolving nature of streaming time series.

Table 2. Classification accuracy results of proposed and other methods.

Dataset	GP-HLS	ODTW-NN	PED	CPFormer
CBF	0.79	0.63	0.76	**0.81**
FaceUCR	**0.45**	0.20	0.39	**0.45**
GunPoint	0.73	0.53	0.74	**0.76**
Plane	0.77	0.47	0.73	**0.80**
SyntheticControl	0.81	0.30	**0.82**	0.74
TwoPatterns	**0.75**	0.68	0.69	0.68
TwoLeadECG	0.45	0.40	0.47	**0.50**
Wafer	**0.57**	0.51	0.55	0.55
Average Accuracy	**0.67**	0.46	0.64	0.66
Average Rank	1.8	3.8	2.2	**1.6**

Among these three baseline models, GP-HLS is proposed for offline time series. PED and ODTW-NN are designed for streaming time series. Table 2 presents the classification results for the streaming time series, where bold indicates best values.

In general, CPFormer model can hold best result in five datasets. Compared with GP-HLS, our model get a better rank, though GP-HLS has a better performance in accuracy. Comparing the experimental results of the four algorithms, we conclude that the representation considering semantic information, GP-HLS and our propose CPFormer, has a better performance than those general models. The results of the SyntheticControl and TwoPatterns data indicate a relative weakness of our model when dealing with shorter time series. Meanwhile, our model is relatively more advantageous for those datasets with longer length than baselines.

4.2   Retrieval

For the time series retrieval task, we evaluate the effectiveness of the proposed model for streaming time series retrieval tasks based on five different datasets. Same as described in the Sect. 6.2 of classification tasks, these five datasets were selected because they are utilized in evaluation of some advanced retrieval algorithms of streaming times [20]. Table 3 presents the details of these datasets.

We compared our model with three advanced baseline methods in streaming time series retrieval: multi-step filtering mechanism (MSM) [21]: MSM is used to perform similarity matching over streaming time series. This mechanism allows for the reduction of the search space, leading to faster response times. Multi-resolution search scheme (MRSS) [20]: This is a variants of MSM, which is based on multi-resolution filtering to perform the similarity search in streaming time series. Efficient multi-resolution representation (EMR) [22]: EMR proposes a multi-resolution filtering scheme for incrementally calculating the similarity distance among sequence patterns of streaming time series.

According to the descriptions in baseline research MRSS and EMR, for streaming time series, the objective of retrieval task is to rapidly identify all subsequences in the time series stream data that match the given query sequence. In this context, the retrieval time serves as a metric to evaluate the performance of the search. In addition, both the baseline model and our proposed model select

Table 3. Summary of UEA&UCR datasets in retrieval task.

Dataset	Train Size	Test Size	Length	Classes
ElectricDevices	8926	7711	96	7
ECG5000	500	4500	140	5
FordA	3601	1320	500	2
Worms	181	77	900	5
ShapesAll	600	600	512	60

Table 4. Retrieval time of proposed and other methods (millisecond).

Dataset	MSM	MRSS	EMR	CPFormer
ElectricDevices	4016	**1950**	2001	2011
ECG5000	1369	1224	1230	**1206**
FordA	4330	2745	2566	**2108**
Worms	1442	1452	1410	**1393**
ShapesAll	4125	2102	2527	**1993**

Euclidean distance for evaluating the similarity. The experimental results are shown in Table 4, where bold indicates shortest retrieval time. Obviously, compared with baselines methods, our CPFormer model has better performance in retrieval task of streaming time series.

5   Conclusions

Semantic information is indeed crucial in the representation learning of streaming time series. It allows the model to capture meaningful patterns and relationships within the data. In addition, the iterative training method has proven to be beneficial in the context of streaming time series representation learning. Our proposed CPFormer algorithm combines these two important aspects. In this study, a Covariance-based Pooling mechanism was introduced for representation learning of streaming time series. Meanwhile, stochastic Pooling-based triplet network is designed for unsupervised training of streaming time series. The experiments show that the proposed model demonstrates significant improvement in multivariate time series representation learning.

In future research, we will focus on developing a more comprehensive framework for streaming time series that addresses various aspects such as storage, management, and mining tasks. Our goal is to create an integrated solution that efficiently handles the challenges associated with streaming time series data.

References

1. Lawi, A., Mesra, H., Amir, S.: Implementation of long short-term memory and gated recurrent units on grouped time-series data to predict stock prices accurately. J. Big Data **9**, 1–19 (2022)
2. Tseng, K., Li, J., Tang, Y., Yang, C., Lin, F.: Healthcare knowledge of relationship between time series electrocardiogram and cigarette smoking using clinical records. BMC Med. Inform. Decis. Mak. **20**, 1–11 (2020)
3. Imani, S., Keogh, E.: Matrix profile XIX: time series semantic motifs: a new primitive for finding higher-level structure in time series. In: 2019 IEEE International Conference on Data Mining (ICDM), pp. 329–338 (2019)
4. Ye, C., Ma, Q.: GP-HLS: Gaussian process-based unsupervised high-level semantics representation learning of multivariate time series. In: Wang, X., et al. (eds.) DASFAA 2023. LNCS, vol. 13943, pp. 221–236. Springer, Cham (2023). https://doi.org/10.1007/978-3-031-30637-2_15

5. Lehman, E., Krishnan, R., Zhao, X., Mark, R., Li-Wei, H.: Representation learning approaches to detect false arrhythmia alarms from ECG dynamics. In: Machine Learning for Healthcare Conference, pp. 571–586 (2018)
6. Sun, Y., Li, J., Liu, J., Sun, B., Chow, C.: An improvement of symbolic aggregate approximation distance measure for time series. Neurocomputing **138**, 189–198 (2014)
7. Kitaev, N., Kaiser, Ł., Levskaya, A.: Reformer: the efficient Transformer. arXiv Preprint arXiv:2001.04451 (2020)
8. Choromanski, K., et al.: Rethinking attention with performers. arXiv Preprint arXiv:2009.14794 (2020)
9. Yu, W., et al.: Metaformer is actually what you need for vision. In: Proceedings of the IEEE/CVF Conference on Computer Vision and Pattern Recognition, pp. 10819–10829 (2022)
10. Li, G., Choi, B., Xu, J., Bhowmick, S., Chun, K., Wong, G.: Shapenet: a shapelet-neural network approach for multivariate time series classification. In: Proceedings of the AAAI Conference on Artificial Intelligence, vol. 35, pp. 8375–8383 (2021)
11. Hallac, D., Nystrup, P., Boyd, S.: Greedy Gaussian segmentation of multivariate time series. Adv. Data Anal. Classif. **13**, 727–751 (2019)
12. Chen, Y., Fang, W., Dai, S., Lu, C.: Skeleton moving pose-based human fall detection with sparse coding and temporal pyramid pooling. In: 2021 7th International Conference on Applied System Innovation (ICASI), pp. 91–96 (2021)
13. Zeiler, M., Fergus, R.: Stochastic pooling for regularization of deep convolutional neural networks. arXiv Preprint arXiv:1301.3557 (2013)
14. Bifet, A., Maniu, S., Qian, J., Tian, G., He, C., Fan, W.: Streamdm: advanced data mining in spark streaming. In: 2015 IEEE International Conference on Data Mining Workshop (ICDMW), pp. 1608–1611 (2015)
15. Bagnall, A., et al.: The UEA multivariate time series classification archive, 2018. arXiv Preprint arXiv:1811.00075 (2018)
16. Oregi, I., Pérez, A., Del Ser, J., Lozano, J.: An active adaptation strategy for streaming time series classification based on elastic similarity measures. Neural Comput. Appl. **34**, 13237–13252 (2022)
17. Oregi, I., Pérez, A., Del Ser, J., Lozano, J.A.: On-line dynamic time warping for streaming time series. In: Ceci, M., Hollmén, J., Todorovski, L., Vens, C., Džeroski, S. (eds.) ECML PKDD 2017. LNCS (LNAI), vol. 10535, pp. 591–605. Springer, Cham (2017). https://doi.org/10.1007/978-3-319-71246-8_36
18. Chen, Y., Hu, B., Keogh, E., Batista, G.: DTW-D: time series semi-supervised learning from a single example. In: Proceedings of the 19th ACM SIGKDD International Conference on Knowledge Discovery and Data Mining, pp. 383–391 (2013)
19. Yue, Z., et al.: Ts2Vec: towards universal representation of time series. In: Proceedings of the AAAI Conference on Artificial Intelligence, vol. 36, pp. 8980–8987 (2022)
20. Ding, Y., Luo, W., Zhao, Y., Li, Z., Zhan, P., Li, X.: A novel similarity search approach for streaming time series. J. Phys: Conf. Ser. **1302**, 022084 (2019)
21. Lian, X., Chen, L., Yu, J., Wang, G., Yu, G.: Similarity match over high speed time-series streams. In: 2007 IEEE 23rd International Conference on Data Engineering, pp. 1086–1095 (2006)
22. Luo, W., et al.: Multi-resolution representation for streaming time series retrieval. Int. J. Pattern Recognit. Artif. Intell. **35**, 2150019 (2021)

Miscellaneous

Capo: Calibrating Device-to-Device Positioning with a Collaborative Network

Kao Wan[1], Zhaoxi Wu[1], Qian Cao[2], Xiaotao Zheng[1], Ziwei Li[3],
and Tong Li[4(✉)]

[1] Peng Cheng Laboratory, Shenzhen, China
[2] Xi'an University of Posts and Telecommunications, Xi'an, China
[3] Tsinghua University, Beijing, China
[4] Renmin University of China, Beijing, China
tong.li@ruc.edu.cn

Abstract. Device-to-device relative positioning has been widely applied in modern Web-based systems such as COVID-19 mobile contact tracing, seamless access systems, mobile interactive gaming, and mobile e-Commerce. The legacy absolute positioning technologies are not suitable for device-to-device positioning attributed to their mobility and heterogeneity of devices. In this paper, we focus on the heterogeneity problem and propose Capo, the first calibration algorithm that enables the interaction among devices with different communication modes for relative positioning in heterogeneous systems. Capo optimizes the ranging results of low-precision devices in a collaborative network based on the ranging data from high-precision devices. The evaluation shows that Capo can significantly improve up to 26.56% of the positioning accuracy of the heterogeneous systems. Real use case study on COVID-19 contact tracing further shows that Capo significantly improves the accuracy of exposure notifications.

Keywords: Relative positioning · Heterogeneous devices · Web based tracing

1 Introduction

With the emergence of mobile devices and cloud computing, novel Web-based applications such as COVID-19 contact tracing [17], seamless access systems, mobile interactive gaming, robot navigation, and mobile e-Commerce have been widely promoted. The applications of mobile devices first collect positioning data and then interact with each other by connecting the cloud servers with Web services (e.g., HTTP, XML). The user experience is closely related to the precision of device-to-device positioning, the prerequisite stage of these applications.

Device-to-device positioning is a process by which mobile devices, such as smartphones or tablets, can determine their relative positions to one another without the use of external infrastructure like GPS. This is done through the exchange of wireless signals, which can be used to calculate the distances between devices and then be used to infer their relative positions. For example, Apple recently released Airtag [12] portable hardware to provide users with fast and accurate tracking and positioning through Ultra-Wide Band (UWB). The proposal of such positioning methods also provides new ideas for the development direction of motion-sensing mobile games such as Nintendo Switch, a game console that supports Bluetooth Low Energy (BLE) to connect its controller to play motion-sensing games. Nintendo Switch has reached 125 million units worldwide in 2023 and this number will continue to increase. This indicates the immense potential values for the device-to-device relative positioning systems.

Although many schemes [4,14,16] for object positioning using pre-deployed anchors have been proposed, they mostly focus on absolute object positioning. They are not suitable for device-to-device relative positioning because of the mobility and heterogeneity of devices. First, due to the mobility of devices, a large number of devices may continue to join or withdraw from the positioning system, and it might be impossible to pre-deploy a number of fixed anchors in all the spots. Second, devices with different modes cannot communicate with each other. For example, a UWB-only device cannot parse a message from a BLE-only device. Due to the heterogeneity of devices, the legacy positioning systems mainly focused on the interaction between devices with the same communication mode, the positioning accuracy is therefore decided by the lower bound achieved by the most compatible mode among a group of devices. In this case, the precision of device-to-device positioning is decided by the BLE-based technology, although some of the devices support the UWB-based technology with higher accuracy [3].

Modern UWB technology is a pulse communication technology that started in the 1960s. However, UWB is a kind of new communication mode for mobile devices compared with the widely-deployed modes such as Wi-Fi, Bluetooth, etc. Recently, several companies have been developing UWB chips and antenna manufacturers to provide out-of-the-box solutions, but most of them only sell chips or demo kits rather than consumer-oriented products. When revisiting the evolution of Near-field communication (NFC) in the past two decades [10], we can easily infer that it takes a long time for a new mode to be supported by most devices. We thus believe that UWB-based positioning technology will have to coexist with legacy positioning technologies in the next few decades. Generally, it will be a significant contribution if we find a way to use a "high-precision mode" (e.g., UWB) to calibrate the device-to-device positioning of a "low-precision mode" (e.g., BLE).

In this paper, we propose Capo [18], an algorithm that improves the accuracy of low-precision device-to-device positioning with the help of high-precision ones. To the best of our knowledge, Capo is the first calibration algorithm that enables the interaction among devices with different communication modes for relative positioning in heterogeneous systems. In particular, Capo optimizes the ranging results of low-precision devices in a collaborative network based on the ranging data from high-precision devices. First, it calculates the actual distance from the high-precision device to the target low-precision device. Then it calculates the standard deviation of the distribution according to the signal attenuation model and takes the actual distance as the mean to obtain the simulated ranging distance. Finally, the estimated coordinates of the target low-precision device are obtained by the least squares method, which greatly accurately locates the low-precision device. The evaluation shows that Capo can significantly improve 11.56%–26.56% of the positioning accuracy of the system.

The remainder of this paper is organized as follows. Section 2 discusses the background and motivation of the paper. Section 3 introduces the overall design of the scheme. Section 4 presents the performance evaluation and studies a real-world use case of COVID-19 contact tracing. Finally, concluding remarks are made in Sect. 5.

2 Background and Motivation

Device-to-Device Positioning Requires High Accuracy. Nowadays, there are many device-to-device applications, such as indoor navigation, and robotics that require centimeter-level high-precision positioning. However, only achieve meter-level positioning would lead to serious errors or even unavailability when running the application. Apple and Google have jointly proposed the Exposure Notification framework [1] in 2020 to help governments and public health authorities reduce the spread of COVID-19 through contact tracing applications. To improve framework capabilities, Huawei developed Contact Shield [2] to provide basic contact tracing services to detect the user's contact level with COVID-19 patients, ensuring the interoperability between Huawei phones and other Android/iOS phones.

Accuracy Varies with Different Communication Modes. Most works developing BLE-based [5] location systems use RSSI [11] to estimate location. And it was demonstrated that a scheme [7] using BLE as a location sensing medium is able to obtain 92% precision to within meters accuracy. The positioning accuracy of the Wi-Fi signal-based positioning method [15] is in the range of 2–10 m, and it has a serious problem of co-frequency interference. Aparicio et al. proposed a fusion method of BLE and Wi-Fi technologies for indoor positioning, which improved accuracy by 50 cm on average compared with the Wi-Fi positioning method. Due to the precision positioning potential of UWB technology with a centimeter scale and higher precision, it is the first choice for indoor high-precision positioning.

Low-Precision Devices Can be Enhanced by High-Precision Ones. Some interactions between high-precision devices and low-precision device, would have the potential to achieve better device-to-device positioning performance [13]. As shown in Fig. 1(a), from the perspective of device O, it adopts BLE to compute the distances (OA, OB, OC) to the devices A, B, and C, with an error denoted by an arc-shaped shaded region. From the perspective of devices A, B, and C, they adopt UWB to compute the distances (AB, AC, BC) between each other. As shown in Fig. 1(b), the relative positions of devices A, B, and C form a triangle. According to the constraint that devices A and C cannot be out of the scope of their shaded regions, we can infer that there might exist an unavailable location of device B in Fig. 1(b) when the triangle moves to a certain position.

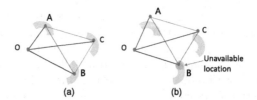

Fig. 1. Calibrating low-precision device using high-precision devices.

The relative position of the three high-precision devices adds a new position constraint to the ranging results of the low-precision devices, so as to narrow the margin of error of the low-precision devices.

3   The Capo Design

3.1   Design Rationale

Our goal is to calibrate device-to-device relative positioning for low-precision devices. To enable multiple high-precision devices to help the low-precision device in a collaborative network, inspired by the legacy absolute positioning technologies such as trilateral positioning, we give the design rationale of new solution. Theoretically, with only two high-precision devices, it might also be possible to enhance the position capability the low-precision devices, as detailed in Sect. 3.3. For ease of understanding and description, we mainly consider the situation of at least three high-precision devices. In this case, the calibration of low-precision can be achieved in four steps. In step 1, we measure the relative positions between high-precision devices via the high-precision communication mode and initialize the coordinates of all high-precision devices. In step 2, we measure the distances (D1) between the low-precision device and the high-precision device via the low-precision communication mode. In step 3, a trilateral positioning algorithm can be used to locate the coordinates of the low-precision device. In step 4, recalculate the distances (D2) between the low-precision device and the high-precision device via the measured coordinates of the low-precision device. The distance set of D2 is regarded as the calibration of D1.

Assume three high-precision devices A, B, and C, and one target low-precision device O that are non-collinear on the plane. For each ranging device, we regard its coordinates as the center of the circle and the distance to point O as the radius, then we obtain three circles. Ideally, the three circles intersect at one point, which is the coordinate of the target device O. Since the measurement variation is ubiquitous, it may result in these circles to intersecting in an area or even not intersecting. Based on the above analysis, we propose a new positioning algorithm Capo to calculate the coordinates of the target point. Capo adopts the least squares method to solve the approximate coordinates of the target, which is detailed in the next section.

3.2   The Capo Algorithm

Capo assumes the ranging of low-precision communication mode based on RSSI obeys Gaussian distribution. The simplified model [6] of wireless signal attenuation can be expressed as $RSSI_i = K_{dB} - 10\gamma \log_{10}(d_i)$, where $RSSI_i$ signifies the received signal strength of ith receiving end, and K_{dB} signifies the signal strength at a certain fixed distance from the signal source. For calculation convenience, this value is usually $1\,\text{m}$ [6].

Thus the ranging data can be generated based on the $RSSI_i$ equation mentioned above, γ represents the power falloff exponent, which is measured in practical applications and determined by the device type and its ranging accuracy. The lower the accuracy, the higher the value, and the greater the margin of error caused by the distance. If not specified, we set $\gamma = 5$. d_i represents the distance of the target away from the ith signal source.

According to [8], the relation of the distance d and the signal strength can be displayed as $(d = 10^{\wedge}\frac{K_{dB}-RSSI_i}{10*\gamma})$. Therefore, the signal value conforming to the signal attenuation model can be used to express the error caused by the signal strength at a certain point. Since a large number of experiments have shown that the signal strength of RSSI at a certain point conforms to the Gaussian distribution [9] as the form of $RSSI \sim N\left(\mu, \sigma^2\right)$, where $\mu = \frac{1}{m}\sum_{i=1}^{m} RSSI_i$, and $\sigma^2 = \frac{1}{(m-1)}\sum_{i}^{m}\left(RSSI_i - \mu\right)^2$, so we can construct the ranging data distance values d that obey the distribution through the above-mentioned signal attenuation model based on the $RSSI_i$ equation. Algorithm 1 demonstrates the process of generating ranging data d.

Algorithm 1. Ranging data generation

Input: Set of points of high-precision devices P, P_i represents the ith device $P_i(x_x.y_i)$. Measurement point $P_m(x_m, y_m)$. Power falloff exponent γ.

Output: Ranging data array d, d_i represents the ranging data obtained from i^{th} device.

1: $n \leftarrow 1$
2: $\sigma, error, distance \leftarrow 0$
3: **while** $n \leq i$ **do**
4:      $distance \leftarrow \sqrt{(x_n - x_m)^2 + (y_n - y_m)^2}$
5:      $\sigma \leftarrow \gamma * \log_{10}(distance)$
6:      $error \leftarrow$ Random number that follow the distribution $N(distance, \sigma^2)$
7:      $d_n \leftarrow distance + error$
8: **end while**
9: **send** d

Algorithm 2. The Capo

Input: A:i*2 matrix, B:i*1 matrix Ranging data array d, d_i represents the ranging data obtained from i^{th} device Set of points of high-precision devices P, P_i represents the ith device $P_i(x_x.y_i)$.

Output: X, the 2*1 matrix.

1: $n \leftarrow 1$
2: **while** $n \leq i$ **do**
3:      **if** $n = 1$ **then**
4:          $A_{11} \leftarrow 2(x_1 - x_i), A_{12} \leftarrow 2(y_1 - y_i)$
5:          $B_1 \leftarrow x_1^2 - x_i^2 + y_1^2 - y_i^2 + d_i^2 - d_1^2$
6:      **else**
7:          $A_{n1} \leftarrow 2(x_{n-1} - x_n), A_{n2} \leftarrow 2(y_{n-1} - y_n)$
8:          $B_n \leftarrow x_{n-1}^2 - x_n^2 + y_{n-1}^2 - y_n^2 + d_n^2 - d_{n-1}^2$
9:      **end if**
10: **end while**
11: $X \leftarrow (A^T A)^{-1} A^T B$
12: **send** X

To apply the least squares method to solve the approximate solution based on the ranging results, we first establish the system of equations using the information from each device. Each equation within this system is in the form of: $(x_i - x)^2 + (y_i - y)^2 = d_i^2$, where x_i, y_i as the coordinates of the ith device

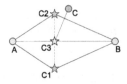

Fig. 2. Approximate target points measured under two high-precision devices.

obtained via the high-precision positioning technology[1]. Then we calculate the non-linear equations to obtain the linear equations. Algorithm 2 demonstrates the process of applying the least squares method by ranging data d to obtain the approximate coordinate of the target device.

Finally, we use the least squares method to solve the above equations and obtain a two-dimensional column vector $X^T = [x \ y]$, representing the approximate coordinate (x, y) of the target point we obtained.

3.3   Discussion: Two High-Precision Devices

We now discuss the effects of our algorithm for calibrating the coordinates of low-precision devices when there are only two high-precision devices. As shown in Fig. 2, when there are only two high-precision devices A and B in the two-dimensional space, in theory, there should be two feasible point coordinates of device C, i.e., nodes C1 and C2. However, the actual output of the least squares method is node C3 instead. As illustrated in Fig. 2, the ranging error between C3 and C might be much larger than that between C2 and C. In other words, applying Capo to a scenario with only two high-precision devices could potentially introduce extra biases.

The challenge here is that by applying the least squares method, we can only obtain a single approximate coordinate of the target point other than two. Thus, we infer that by adding a module of angle measurements, it is possible to indirectly compute the coordinates of C1 or C2 via the cosine function. However, we leave this for future work.

4   Evaluation

In this section, we first evaluate the overall performance of Capo with three high-precision devices. We then explore how Capo performs with different impact factors, such as a number of high-precision devices. We also investigate the extra overhead introduced by applying Capo. Finally, we give a case study of contact tracing, to further show the improvement of Capo in real-world scenarios.

---

[1] Since the centimeter-level error of high precision technology is negligible compared to the meter-level error of low precision technology, for the sake of simplicity, in this paper we assume a zero positioning error between high-precision devices, and d_i represents the ranging distance generated using the signal attenuation model mentioned above. The case of non-zero positioning error, however, we leave it as future work.

4.1   Overall Performance of Capo

For simplicity, we consider a heterogeneous system with three high-precision devices and one low-precision device in two-dimensional space. In this section, we conduct a simulation evaluation of the calibration performance of Capo, where three high-precision devices help the low-precision device achieve higher precision of device-to-device positioning. In practical implementation, we need the relative position of high-precision devices to conduct the calibration process. For these high-precision devices, the existing positioning methods (based on ToA, AoA, etc.) can be used to establish the relative coordinate relationship based on these high-precision devices. Since the calibration performance is independent of the absolute position of the devices, our experiment does not lose the general setting of the coordinates of the devices. The fixed coordinates of the three high-precision devices A, B and C are $(-50, 0)$, $(10, 40)$ and $(20, -30)$ respectively, and the coordinates of low-precision ranging target device O are $(5, 5)$ (if not specified, the coordinate units are meters). Noted that the coordinates of high-precision devices here are only for generating simulated ranging data, and absolute coordinates are not necessary for the practical implementation of Capo. The tests are conducted 3,000 times to explore the error distribution of the ranging results between the low-precision and high-precision devices.

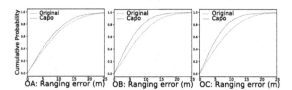 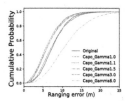

Fig. 3. Error distribution of the ranging result between device O and device A, B, C.

Fig. 4. Calibration performance of Capo in different γ values.

Figure 3 illustrates the calibration performance of Capo compared with the original way, which simply applies the wireless signal attenuation model. It is demonstrated that Capo can significantly calibrate the device-to-device positioning compared with the original way. Specifically, Capo improves the accuracy of the ranging between O and A by 11.56%, with the median ranging error decreasing from 6.9960 m to 6.1873 m. Similarly, it improves the ranging accuracy between O and B, and C by 24.76%, and 26.56%, respectively, leading to median ranging error reductions from 6.3081 m to 4.7461 m for O and B, and from 6.4972 m to 4.7715 m for O and C.

We further consider Capo's performance in the above scenario when the high-precision device has ranging errors in different γ values. The generation of high-precision device error values is also based on Sect. 3.2. Since Capo does not give a specific positioning algorithm for high-precision devices, when simulating the high-precision device error in this scenario, the coordinate offset of the high-precision device caused by ranging error will be simulated by using the error generated from Sect. 3.2. In particular, in this scenario, the algorithm employs the average distance among three high-precision devices for calculations.

Figure 4 illustrates the Capo's calibration performance when a high-precision device has ranging errors caused by different γ values compared with the original way (with γ being 1). It is demonstrated that when the high-precision device has a relatively small γ compared to the low-precision device, Capo maintains stable calibration performance even considering the error in high-precision devices.

To summarize, the positioning results obtained by the Capo algorithm have an optimization effect on each device in the system, which can improve the accuracy of the positioning results as a whole. This relies on Capo making full use of three high-precision devices to provide more calibration data for the ranging of the low-precision device.

4.2   Overhead Analysis of Capo

We further evaluate the communication overhead of running Capo among devices. We let C_h and C_l denote the ranging cost required by the high-precision device and the low-precision device respectively, noting that $C_h = 2C_l$. And assume n is the number of high-precision devices. We define the overhead of the system running Capo as follows: Cost $= n^*(n-1)^*C_h + n^*C_l$.

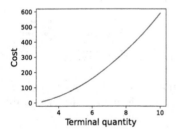
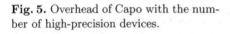
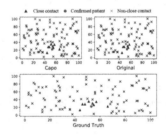

Fig. 5. Overhead of Capo with the number of high-precision devices.

Fig. 6. An example of exposure check results.

Figure 5 demonstrates that the cost of Capo rises with an increase in the number of devices, attributed to the heightened number of interactions leading to higher overhead. However, we believe the improved ranging accuracy will more than pay for the Capo overhead if we limit the maximum number of high-precision devices N_{max}, for instance, $N_{max} = 4$.

Based on the above observations, we find that 4 high-precision devices gain a considerable accuracy improvement with a slightly increased cost compared with 2, 3, 5, and 6 high-precision devices. We infer that the inclusion of a fourth high-precision device, if feasible, has the potential to substantially enhance the overall performance of the calibration system.

4.3   Case Study: Contact Tracing

We apply Capo in a COVID-19 Contact Tracing application to improve system-ranging performance for more accurate exposure notifications and Fig. 6 shows an example of exposure check results. We take the 100 m × 100 m space as the experimental scene, where 100 users are randomly distributed. One confirmed patient was randomly selected for each test and the test was repeated 1,000 times. Note that since scenes with several confirmed patients can be divided into multiple independent scenes with a single confirmed patient, repeating a single experiment can restore the practical situation.

Methodology. We assume that the confirmed patient uses a BLE-only device (i.e., a low-precision device with $\gamma = 5$)[2], and other users use both UWB and BLE enabled devices (i.e., high-precision devices). The safe distance is regarded as 1 m and by applying Capo, UWB ranging is used to assist in improving the ranging results of low-precision BLE devices. As concluded above, 4 high-precision devices are enough for calibration, and in this scenario, if there are more than four UWB devices in the scene, only 4 UWBs need to be selected to complete the calibration. After calibrating device-to-device ranging with Capo, a list of close contacts and non-close contacts is obtained by comparing the safe distance with the measured distance.

Performance Evaluation Metrics. For each test, we evaluate its accuracy, precision, and recall by calculating the classification results of Capo, Original (without Capo), and Ground Truth.

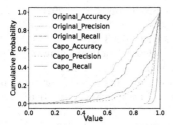
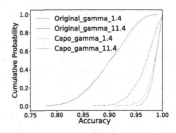

Fig. 7. Capo improves exposure notification in Contact Tracing system ($\gamma = 5$).

Fig. 8. Accuracy with different value of γ.

Results. The classification results of Capo and Original are illustrated in Fig. 7. The accuracy of contact tracing classification using Capo is obviously higher than that using Original. Specifically, the application of Capo has resulted in an increase in accuracy by over 60%, elevating it from 95% to 98%, and his improvement is attributed to Capo's ability to calibrate device-to-device ranging among low-precision BLE devices using high-precision UWB devices.

---

[2] According to the $RSSI_i$ equation, based on the scale of the distance and BLE's RSSI-based ranging error of 2–10 m, we set $\gamma = 5$ for BLE devices.

We further explore the impact of varying values of γ, and Fig. 8 shows that Capo's augmented benefit as γ increases. This reveals that the lower the precision of the device, the more benefit we can get by applying Capo.

5 Conclusion

In this paper, we proposed Capo for calibrating device-to-device positioning in heterogeneous systems. By applying Capo, the ranging accuracy of low-precision devices can be significantly improved according to the relative positioning of high-precision devices. Evaluation results further show that Capo with four high-precision devices can balance calibration performance and cost well, which is recommended. We studied a real-world use case of contact tracing, and the results show that Capo significantly improves the accuracy of exposure notifications.

Acknowledgements. This work is supported by NSFC Project (Grant No. 62202473, 62132011, 62132009), National Key R&D Program of China (Grant No. 2022YFB3105000), and PCL Future Regional Network Facilities for Large-scale Experiments and Applications (Grant No. PCL2018KP001).

References

1. Gaen (2022). https://www.google.com/covid19/exposurenotifications
2. Huawei contact shield (2022). https://developer.huawei.com/consumer/en/doc/development/system-Guides/contactshield-introduction-0000001057494465
3. Chen, Y.C., Alexsander, I., Lai, C., Wu, R.B.: UWB-assisted high-precision positioning in a UTM prototype. In: 2020 IEEE WiSNeT, pp. 42–45 (2020)
4. Cheng, L., Wang, Y., Xue, M., Bi, Y.: An indoor robust localization algorithm based on data association technique. Sensors **20**(22), 6598 (2020)
5. Ding, Y., Li, T., Liang, J., Wang, D.: Blender: toward practical simulation framework for BLE neighbor discovery. In: MSWiM, pp. 103–110 (2022)
6. Durgin, G., Rappaport, T.S., Xu, H.: Measurements and models for radio path loss and penetration loss in and around homes and trees at 5.85 GHz. IEEE Trans. Commun. **46**(11), 1484–1496 (1998)
7. Ho, Y.H., Chan, H.C.: BluePrint: BLE positioning algorithm based on NUFO detection. In: 2017–2017 IEEE GLOBECOM, pp. 1–6 (2017)
8. Jayakody, J.A., Lokuliyana, S., Chathurangi, D., Vithana, D., et al.: Indoor positioning: novel approach for bluetooth networks using RSSI smoothing. Int. J. Comput. Appl. **137**(13), 26–32 (2016)
9. Jianyong, Z., Haiyong, L., Zili, C., Zhaohui, L.: RSSI based bluetooth low energy indoor positioning. In: IPIN, pp. 526–533 (2014)
10. Lazaro, A., Villarino, R., Girbau, D.: A survey of NFC sensors based on energy harvesting for IoT applications. Sensors **18**(11), 3746 (2018)
11. Li, G., Geng, E., Ye, Z., Xu, Y., Lin, J., Pang, Y.: Indoor positioning algorithm based on the improved RSSI distance model. Sensors **18**(9), 2820 (2018)
12. Li, T., Liang, J., Ding, Y., Zheng, K., Zhang, X., Xu, K.: On design and performance of offline finding network. In: IEEE INFOCOM, pp. 1–10 (2023)
13. Li, T., et al.: TACK: improving wireless transport performance by taming acknowledgments. In: ACM SIGCOMM, pp. 15–30 (2020)

14. Li, Z., Xu, K., Wang, H., Zhao, Y., Wang, X., Shen, M.: Machine-learning-based positioning: a survey and future directions. IEEE Netw. **33**(3), 96–101 (2019)
15. Liu, F., Liu, J., Yin, Y., Wang, W., Hu, D., Chen, P., Niu, Q.: Survey on wifi-based indoor positioning techniques. IET Commun. **14**(9), 1372–1383 (2020)
16. Mayer, P., Magno, M., Schnetzler, C., Benini, L.: EmbedUWB: low power embedded high-precision and low latency UWB localization. In: WF-IoT, pp. 519–523 (2019)
17. Shen, M., Wei, Y., Li, T.: Bluetooth-based COVID-19 proximity tracing proposals: an overview. arXiv:2008.12469 (2020)
18. Wu, Z., Cao, Q., Zheng, X.: Capo's publication version with the implementation and experimental data(capo_rssp_python v2.1). zenodo (2023). https://doi.org/10.5281/zenodo.8246597

The Impact on Employability by COVID-19 Pandemic - AI Case Studies

Venkata Bharath Bandi[1]([✉]), Xiaohui Tao[1]([✉]), Thanveer Shaik[1],
Jianming Yong[2], and Ji Zhang[1]

[1] School of Mathematics, Physics and Computing, University of Southern
Queensland, Toowoomba, Australia
{VenkataBharath.Bandi,xiaohui.tao,thanveer.shaik,ji.zhang}@unisq.edu.au
[2] School of Business, University of Southern Queensland, Springfield, Australia
jianming.yong@unisq.edu.au

Abstract. The COVID-19 pandemic has had far-reaching effects on
society, the economy, and mental health. The service industry, particularly the hotel sector, has been severely impacted, leading to job insecurity and negative mental health outcomes, especially among women who
face heightened uncertainty and increased unemployment concerns. This
study aims to investigate the effect of economic challenges and job loss on
female workers during the pandemic, focusing on perceived job insecurity. Through a survey of hotel employees, we examine how these factors
interacted within the context of COVID-19. Our findings suggest that
job uncertainty moderates the relationship between anxiety stemming
from economic crises, unemployment, and mental health outcomes. The
fear of COVID-19 indirectly links economic distress and mental health
through the lens of employment instability. This study's results provide
insights for managers to better address job security and mental health
challenges faced by female employees during a global recession.

Keywords: Employability · Pandemic · Economy

1 Introduction

The changing landscape of public employment policy, focusing on skills-based
solutions to economic competition and work-based solutions to social challenges,
along with the perceived end of traditional 'careers' and lifelong job security
(which have historically applied to a minority of the workforce), has heightened employer concerns about the quantity and types of future employment.
This has led to increased anxiety among employers about the need to cultivate
new links with employability, which is centered around employment and work
capability. These encompass the ability to secure initial employment, essential
skills, caregiver oversight, and being able to comprehend and function within a

F. Zhang et al. (Eds.): WISE 2023, LNCS 14306, pp. 850–864, 2023.
https://doi.org/10.1007/978-981-99-7254-8_66

work environment. Employability also encompasses the ability to sustain employment and not only transition within the same organization to meet changing job requirements, but switch jobs if necessary. These employability attributes enable self-sufficiency in the labor market through managing one's own employment transitions within and across organizations.

This paper delves into the realm of employability for women in the hospitality sector and explores its correlation with mental health. It does so through assessing existing research, examining the relationship between COVID-19, employment, and various factors influencing this relationship. Furthermore, it delves into the selection of appropriate models for analysis and evaluates their impact on the subject matter. The discussion also extends to the concept of the "new normal" and how it relates to the recession, followed by a consideration of the effects of pandemics on employee well-being and productivity. From the analysis, it becomes evident that employee mental health holds a significant sway over their attitude and service quality. This study emphasizes the need for organizations to prioritize the mental health of their employees, especially women, in the current and future pandemic situations.

To gain a comprehensive understanding of the pandemic's long-term implications, it is crucial to make gender-based comparisons. The decision to leave a job may lead to financial setbacks and reentry difficulties, potentially causing long-lasting scars. Additionally, offering wage subsidies might alleviate short-term losses. A proactive approach to enhancing women's employability involves adapting childcare facilities, which could significantly boost women's participation in the workforce. Furthermore, in a post-pandemic scenario, certain industries might experience decline while others may flourish. Quick reemployment and the effective reallocation of affected women across industries could mitigate long-term employment repercussions. Novel research suggests that closing gender gaps in the workforce could potentially benefit both the labor market and productivity [4].

This study aims to shed light on how the unpredictability brought about by COVID-19 impacts the mental health and employability of women, with specific focus on the hospitality sector. By addressing this gap in the literature, this research provides insights that can enhance managerial decision-making. It delves into how job insecurity is linked with economic crises, unemployment, and mental health, and assesses the state of employees' mental health in the context of the pandemic. The study primarily contributes to a deeper understanding of the hospitality industry and its unique vulnerabilities. Furthermore, given the recurrent nature of pandemics, the study's implications extend to preparing for future health crises. In this regard, the study explores the interplay between economic crises, unemployment, women's work insecurity, and health.

Several challenges, including those related to the "new normal" skills and training, are addressed. A case study aids in comprehending the dynamics of recession and the decline in women's employment in certain sectors. This case study is instrumental in analyzing the social impact of COVID-19 on women. The findings from this research are valuable in gauging the impact of the global catastrophe on women's employability and mental health. By manipulating one variable, the same concepts can be applied to various challenging scenarios. Building on the literature review, the study proceeds to define employability and its associated variables, particularly in the context of a COVID-induced recession. The study also delves into the role of the recession as a moderator in the context of employability and mental health.

Drawing on Llosa's research and considering the comprehensive analysis carried out, employees' uncertainty about their future careers can significantly impact both their mental and financial well-being. This is especially true for women, who are more likely to suffer from diminished life satisfaction, weaker professional networks, and a range of mental and psychological issues [37]. The findings emphasize the fact that when employees perceive their job security as precarious, it has a cascading negative effect on their overall mental and financial health. The study's insights highlight the importance of considering employee mental health, given its direct impact on overall company success. This underscores the need to examine how macro-level economic uncertainties, such as the current economic crisis, affect employee mental and financial well-being. In light of these findings, it becomes evident that women's employability and mental health are closely interconnected within the broader economic landscape. The study proceeds to explore these assumptions through various methodologies, allowing for a comprehensive assessment of their validity:

1. Hypothesis 1a (H1a): The perception of workplace instability, magnified by the current economic conditions, has a negative impact on the mental and financial well-being of women. This effect is further exacerbated by the disproportionate likelihood of women experiencing job losses compared to men.
2. Hypothesis 1b (H1b): Non-employability acts as a mediator between employees' perceptions of employment uncertainty and their actual levels of job insecurity, significantly affecting workers' mental health and financial well-being.

This study lays the foundation for a comprehensive exploration of the complex interplay between employability, mental health, and economic dynamics, particularly within the context of the pandemic and its widespread implications for the workforce. It underscores the necessity of holistically considering relevant factors to inform strategies and interventions that support employees' well-being and resilience.

2   Related Works

Numerous studies have previously investigated the intricate relationship between economic downturns, employment, and mental health outcomes. Llosa et al. [31] conducted a study that explored the effects of economic instability on individuals' mental and financial well-being. Their findings highlighted the connection between perceptions of job insecurity during times of economic uncertainty and reduced life satisfaction, impaired professional networking, and heightened risk of psychological disorders. Similarly, De et al. [15] highlighted the repercussions of job instability on employee well-being, emphasizing the adverse effects of unemployment-related fears on mental health. Otterbach and Sousa-Poza [32] unearthed a substantial correlation between employment uncertainty and mental health, underscoring the significance of job stability for overall well-being.

Singh et al. [41] conducted a study that delved into social behavior patterns using location-based data, using a Melbourne-based case study. Their investigation harnessed location-based data to decipher the dynamics of social behaviors, offering insightful observations into the way people's interactions and movements were influenced during the pandemic. This type of analysis not only provides nuanced insights into human behavior during crises, but also provides a foundation for grasping the societal implications of such events.

The emergence of telehealth as a pivotal tool during the pandemic was significant, allowing healthcare services to continue with minimal physical contact. Lee et al. [28] undertook a qualitative analysis of telehealth's application in oral and maxillofacial surgery during the COVID-19 pandemic. By exploring the experiences of healthcare professionals and patients, the study highlighted the effectiveness of telehealth in sustaining essential medical services, while mitigating the risk of virus transmission. This underscores the importance of technology-driven solutions in confronting the challenges posed by global crises.

2.1   Gender Disparities in the Labor Market

Recent research has brought to light the disproportionate impact of economic downturns on women's employment [44]. A recurring pattern known as "she-cession" has been identified, wherein women encounter greater employment setbacks compared to men during economic downturns [5,7,17]. Klammer [25] explored the distinct challenges that women face in the labor market, especially during periods of recession, which emphasizes the vulnerabilities of women's career trajectories in times of disruptions. The recession brought about by the pandemic further exacerbated these disparities, leading to a significant decline in labor force participation by women [29]. Remote work opportunities presented both advantages and challenges for women's employment [26].

The impact of economic challenges on broader development objectives has been explored in various contexts. Kaur and Tao [23] delved into the relationship between information and communication technologies (ICTs) and the attainment of Millennium Development Goals. Their research underscored the significance of leveraging technology to address socio-economic challenges, a lesson further accentuated by the accelerated adoption of digital solutions during the pandemic.

2.2   Employability and Skill Adaptation

Researchers have long been intrigued by the concept of employability in the face of evolving economic landscapes. Hussain et al. [22] highlighted the dynamic nature of employability, which encompasses a wide array of competencies that contribute to an individual's ability to secure and retain employment. As industries evolve, the adaptation of skills becomes paramount in sustaining employability [22]. Peeters et al. [33] underscored the importance of enhancing employability through skill development, particularly in the context of economic challenges. The COVID-19 pandemic triggered discussions about the necessity for individuals to cultivate "new normal" skills to navigate the evolving employment landscape [27].

2.3   Mediating Factors: Job Insecurity and Mental Health

Numerous studies have explored the mediating role of job insecurity between economic crises and mental health [13,14,45]. Reisel & Banai [36] extended the concept of job instability to encompass organizational uncertainty, shedding light on its detrimental effects on employees' mental health. Chirumbolo [10] delved into the impact of job insecurity on mental health and underscored its relevance for overall business performance. De et al. [12] explored how job insecurity contributes to mental health issues, thus influencing employee well-being and productivity.

The analysis of social media data has also proven invaluable in understanding public sentiment and the dynamics of opinion. Zhou et al. [47] coupled topic modeling with opinion mining to analyze social media content. Through the fusion of text analysis and data mining techniques, their study provided insights into the expression of opinions and emotions on Online platforms, contributing an enhanced understanding of societal responses during crises [47].

Even in the realm of mental health, technology-driven approaches have exhibited promise. Tao et al. [42] developed an ensemble classifier based on the Quality of Life scales to detect depression. Their research showcased the potential of harnessing data and machine learning (ML) to identify mental health challenges, a relevance that becomes particularly pronounced as the psychological impacts of the pandemic continue to emerge [42].

While existing research has delved into the intricate connections between economic challenges, job insecurity, mental health, and employability, a gap remains in comprehending the nuanced interplay of these factors within the context of the COVID-19 pandemic. This study endeavors to bridge this gap by investigating the specific influence of economic challenges and job loss on female workers, especially in the hospitality sector. The study aims to elucidate how these factors interrelate with perceived job insecurity and mental health outcomes.

3   Research Derivations

3.1   Hypotheses

We are particularly interested in research that addresses employability prediction using data-driven and artificial intelligence technologies, motivated by the need to explore and forecast emerging employability issues [4]. This survey compiles all published works on predicting employability using ML methods from several academic libraries, including the Web of Science, Scopus, and Google Scholar databases, that are relevant to the ML-based employability prediction issue [11]. Twenty relevant publications were chosen that demonstrate the use of ML approaches to address employability prediction challenges. Several research studies were reviewed and compared using terms from the phases of the data mining process [21]. Additionally, we suggested scenarios for employability prediction research using ML and discussed their common needs and primary problems. The remainder of this article will begin with a synopsis of chosen papers in chronological sequence. The study is then initiated with a background section in which generally used definitions of employability are given, along with the literature's major issues. We summarize the major ML algorithms employed, along with information on their associated datasets. In the end, we discuss the limitations and difficulties inherent in forecasting employment.

3.2 Theoretical Derivations

Ramelli and Wagner [35] found that the global economic crisis during COVID-19 was exceptional. The hotel business absorbed the brunt of the economic devastation. Globally, hotels are growing as entities, and have far-reaching effects on national economies and the service industry. This industry was impacted across numerous nations: tourism stopped (thus hotels and restaurants couldn't welcome visitors), employees were laid off, and those who remained risked job loss. In light of this, the pandemic gives the hotel industry a chance to grow by using creative techniques and enhancing consumer safety [11].

Current employment patterns don't show the COVID-19 recession's long-term, disproportionate negative impacts on women's labor chances. According to a recent survey, women are more inclined to re-evaluate their professional choices in light of the pandemic, which might herald a future decline in the number of women in the labor market and have a bad influence on their mental health. COVID-19 may affect women's long-term income, career prospects, and mental health owing to professional interruptions [11].

By studying these links, we can better understand the origins of the pandemic's detrimental consequences on women's employment prospects and mental health. This research analyses micro- and macro-level factors on women's employability and mental health in the hotel business [19].

4   Defining Employability and Its Perception

Employability is a person's (perceived) ability to find and retain employment. Employability is a 'set of accomplishments - abilities, understandings, and personal attributes - that boosts graduates' prospects of obtaining employment and thriving in their professions'. All of these competency qualities are impacted by attitudes; thus, they should be evaluated [9]. Competency combines knowledge (formal and informal education, training, and experience), abilities (practical application of knowledge), and attitudes (like honesty, loyalty, and styles of action: perfectionism and independence). Attitudes are a crucial part of competence, especially in conditions of sudden environmental change like COVID-19, where uncertainty is the norm. Educational institutions must promote employability competency attitudes that fit with the unpredictable economy. Any labor market competitor preparing for the "new normal" should be proactive and prepared [9].

Employability competencies includes generic competencies, generic capabilities, key competencies, core competencies, common competencies, necessary skills, workplace competencies, know-how competencies, critical enabling competencies, transferable competencies, trans-disciplinary goals, key qualifications, and emotional competency [35]. As a key concept, employability ha utility for policymakers and researchers in that it helps train people for jobs that don't exist yet and solves problems that can't be handled now. In the "new normal", employability competence is comprised of more than just the ability to find a job; it also encompasses the ability to maintain that employment in tough, trying times, and handle work-related hurdles. Educational and training institutions must examine graduates' abilities to find jobs and function at the level for which they are prepared [9]. Socioeconomic realities emphasize integrating educational and social inputs to develop competencies. Education, skills, training, and experience will likely undergo a paradigm change. Skill is the ability to do a job; employability is the ability to find and keep work [33].

Competence is conceptual and operational. Competence-based models also consider employability as a multifaceted notion, including knowledge and understanding, applied psychomotor skills, behavior and attitudes, and the ability to learn how to learn. It is a time-consuming process to acquire and maintain such skills, but this effort can help people find and keep the best jobs in today's competitive economy [34].

5   Defining Recession

Not only do economists question whether the global economy, regions, or countries are in a recession, but the news media and the general public fear a recession. Recession is a definitional problem that isn't routinely handled in academic literature or international organizations' practices [18]. Record-low productivity, investment, and consumption marked the Great Recession of 2008–2009. Per capita employment and labor force participation have dropped and show little prospect of improvement. Since the Great Recession's heights, unemployment has fallen. This drop is mostly attributable to a loss in labor force participation, rather than a labor market rebound. Job opportunities have recovered to pre-recession levels, but employment has not. Inflation remains steady despite the economic slump.

The concepts of recession duration, depth, and diffusion are considered the "important dimensions" that characterize it. These "three Ds" are used by business cycle researchers to explain periods of slow economic growth. Recessions are known to significantly reduce economic activity and have long-lasting impacts.

The National Bureau of Economic Research's (NBER) Business Cycle Dating Committee is responsible for dating US economic cycles[1] NBER defines a recession as "a long-term fall in economic activity that affects all sectors of the economy". This definition by NBER is not rigid, allowing for interpretation when determining whether an economy is in a recession, thus leading to frequent delays in NBER's conclusions. Since Julius Shiskin published his idea in The New York Times in 1974[2], it has been widely accepted among economic experts in the U.S. and globally. Shiskin characterized a recession as a decline in real GDP over two consecutive seasons and calendars, and it typically lasts at least six months. However, not all approaches to defining recession adhere to the rule of recognizing recessions as two or more consecutive quarters of decreasing real GDP, and some methods deviate from this two-quarter guideline [43].

6   The Mediating Factor Between Recession and Employability

Pandemic and Great Recession employment losses differ. Figure 1 depicts the employment-to-population ratio during the 2020 recession and the Great Recession. There were two modifications per session. According to the NBER's Business Cycle Dating Committee, the Great Recession ran from March 2007-November 2007 through December 2007-June 2009. The post-recession recovery period lasted from July 2009 to July 2012. The 2020 pandemic recession adjustment affects both. We analyzed March - May 2020, when the pandemic started and the tightest mitigation efforts were in place, and June to November 2020, when the least rigorous measures were in place. Each adjustment is categorized by family status: single, single with children, married, or married with children. Within each family type, women's advancement is inside, and men's is outside [1].

Men's employment declined in this and earlier recessions, but women's remained steady. Men's employment dropped by six percentage points, while women's dropped by two. Males decreased by 6.1% points, and lone parents dropped by 2.7% points. Married males without kids' employment rate fell by 2% points. Men with children have a lower employment-to-population ratio than women. Women lost half to a third of men's employment during the recession [8].

Women lost more jobs during the recessions in every family category. In Phase 1, single men without children had 15% lower unemployment than women. Single males with kids lost 10%, single women with kids lost 15%. Unmarried men lost 10% points, while women lost 12.5 points. Married men with children had their employment-to-population ratio decline by 8.5%, and women by 13%. Second, employment is lower than before the pandemic. Since the outbreak, men's employment has declined by 8 to 3 points, and women's by 11 to 8 points. Married women with children have seen a 50% drop in employment from pre-pandemic levels.

---

[1] NBER. (2022) National Bureau of Economic Research https://www.nber.org/.
[2] https://www.nytimes.com/1974/12/01/archives/the-changing-business-cycle-points-op-view.html.

Job insecurity is both the fear of losing and the inability to retain a job. Greenhalgh and Rosenblatt [20] widened job instability to include organizational unemployment. Job insecurity hurts. Career instability may lead to mental illness, apathy, and work dissatisfaction. The recession has increased women's job insecurity fears. Workers no longer value long-term firm relationships due to the recession and job loss. Elman and O'Rand [16] said no one is immune to job unpredictability. Unemployment hurts individuals. Studies link job-finding skills to job instability. Otterbach and Sousa-Poza [32] linked mental health to employment uncertainty. This research considers work insecurity as a mediator between unemployment and mental health to fill information gaps. Uncertainty regarding work harms mental health [46].

Llosa [31] says job insecurity harms mental health. Women who perceive employment uncertainty are more likely to have low life satisfaction, inadequate professional networking, and mental and psychological disorders. Layoffs make employees more apprehensive about job security. Current research explains how an economic crisis affects employees' mental health. We can't ignore mental health due to its impacts on business [6].

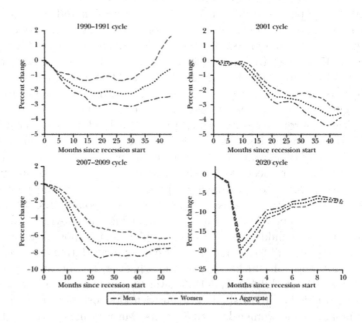

Fig. 1. Percentage Change in the Employment-to-Population Ratio since the Start of Each Recession for the Four Most Recent Business Cycles. Recession dates based on the National Bureau of Economic Research business cycle dates [3]

First Measurement: Frequent, manual, and abstract task inputs index (DOT). RTIs highlight automation risk. Four jobs are covered. The pre-pandemic percentage of jobs with above-median RTI was 9.22%. Inflexible/low-contact women held high-RTI jobs. Most victims had high-contact, rigid occupations.

Flexible/low-touch jobs include office, sales, and administrative work. Low-tech vocations include teaching and librarianship. Women occupy 0.2% of automatable jobs. Once the pandemic ends, the healthcare and personal services sectors may recover. Pandemic employment losses may harm women long-term. Mothers lose pay and lifetime wages.

Human capital deterioration accounts for 13% of the gender income difference, according to Dustmann and Stevens [2]. Fear of career disruptions affects human resources and women's careers. The pandemic threatens to undo decades of improved female labor force participation. While the epidemic may hinder remote work for some due to various challenges, such as technology limitations or workplace policies, women in certain situations may benefit from working remotely throughout the pandemic as child care needs stabilize. It was discovered that remote work increases fathers' child care share. Given parents' greater nonparticipation during the outbreak, this is unlikely to help. During the outbreak, more women worked remotely than males. Remote workers risk stigmatization and career advancement, particularly in professional and managerial fields.

Second Measurement: The fear of an economic crisis among employees is assessed using Giorgi's five-question approach [19]. Nonemployability is defined as a perception among employees that their talents hinder them from working. Five parameters from Giorgi were utilized. After re-coding negative categories, anxiety related to economic crises and unemployment scored the highest, with scores of 0.925 and 0.096, respectively. Among women, the concern regarding "work uncertainty" was measured using Kinnunen and Malmi's [24] 7-step approach, with high scores on "perceived job insecurity" being interpreted as pessimistic. This approach has a reliability of 0.922% and a factor load range of 0.720–0.901. In the context of COVID-19, fears were measured using Reznik and Satici's 7-point scale, where higher scores indicate more fear of the coronavirus pandemic, with 0.941% reliability. Additionally, the Adult Mental Health Questionnaire GHQ-12 will be used to assess other aspects.

7   Case Study

7.1   Case Study 1: Analyzing the Impact of Pandemic-Induced Recessions on Female Employability and Mental Health Using Data-Driven Insights

The COVID-19 pandemic has triggered widespread economic challenges, with a particularly pronounced impact on the service industry, leading to significant job insecurity. This case study employs data-driven insights with NLP, ML [47], and statistical analysis, to investigate the latent relationship between economic downturns, employability, and mental health among women during the pandemic-induced recession. The data driven approach is designed based on the techniques explored in the education feedback analysis [38,39]. The primary focus is to explore how women's perceptions of job insecurity act as a mediating factor in the complex interplay between economic uncertainty and mental health.

To systematically uncover this multifaceted relationship, a comprehensive mixed-methods approach was undertaken. A meticulously designed survey was administered to female employees across diverse sectors, collecting both quantitative and qualitative data. This dataset was subjected to NLP techniques to gauge women's perceptions of job insecurity and fears linked to economic crises, alongside self-reported mental health indicators. Additionally, ML algorithms were employed to identify patterns and correlations within the data.

The survey results exhibited a significant correlation between perceived job insecurity and adverse mental health outcomes among women. The exacerbation of economic uncertainties due to the pandemic-induced recession intensified women's anxieties about the stability of their employment, resulting in elevated stress levels and heightened anxiety. Qualitative interviews further contextualized these findings, offering insights into the emotional toll of job insecurity on personal well-being.

Furthermore, the research unveiled the mediating role of job insecurity in the nexus between economic distress and mental health outcomes. Women who perceived their job security as precarious were more vulnerable to experiencing the detrimental impacts of economic downturns on their mental health. This study underscores the importance of recognizing employability as a dynamic factor significantly influenced by economic conditions and individual perspectives.

This case study provides a data-driven exploration of the intricate interplay between economic challenges, job insecurity, and mental health among women during times of recession. The findings emphasize the necessity for targeted interventions that address the intertwined concerns of employability and mental health. Stakeholders, ranging from employers to policymakers and support networks, are encouraged to leverage these insights to cultivate job security, facilitate skill development initiatives, and offer mental health resources. Such measures aim to mitigate the adverse consequences of economic uncertainties on the mental health of women.

7.2 Case Study 2: Deep Learning Insights into Women's Empowerment and Skill Adaptation Amidst Recession and Pandemic

The advent of the COVID-19 pandemic has ushered in a "new normal" characterized by economic uncertainties and transformative employability dynamics. This case study harnesses the power of deep learning techniques [40] to probe into the adaptability of women's employability skills and their resilience in the face of the challenges spawned by recession. The primary objective is to elucidate how deep learning can unveil the dynamics of women's skill adaptation and empowerment, contributing to both employability enhancement and mental health resilience.

To comprehensively investigate this subject, a rigorous longitudinal study was conducted, enrolling women from various industries that bore the brunt of the recession's impact. Employing cutting-edge deep learning models, quantitative data extracted from the surveys was analyzed to assess alterations in employment status, endeavors to acquire new skills, and self-reported mental health indicators. Additionally, deep learning algorithms were applied in sentiment analysis of the qualitative interviews, offering insights into individual experiences and coping strategies.

The research findings unveil a robust connection between proactive skill development, employability enhancement, and mental health resilience among women. Those who actively embrace upskilling and seize opportunities to diversify their skill repertoire demonstrate superior adaptability in navigating the evolving job landscape during economic downturns. This adaptability mitigates job insecurity and results to a bolstered mental health.

Furthermore, deep learning insights drawn from sentiment analysis of qualitative interviews underscore the pivotal role of personal agency in mitigating the adverse impacts of economic uncertainties. Women who proactively pursue skill enhancement report heightened confidence, diminished anxiety surrounding job loss, and heightened emotional resilience. Moreover, the study underscores the significance of networking and mentorship in supporting women's career transitions and employability endeavors.

This case study underscores the criticality of proactive skill development and cultivating a resilient mindset to counteract the repercussions of economic challenges triggered by recession. The findings highlight the necessity for a holistic approach involving individuals, employers, and educational institutions to facilitate skill adaptation, employability enhancement, and mental health resilience among women. As a whole, the study underpins a call for strategic interventions that empower women to confidently navigate the "new normal", fostering enduring career sustainability and overall well-being.

8   Conclusion

Due to the unique characteristics of the pandemic recession, including widespread economic lockdowns, school closures, and significant impacts on contact-intensive sectors, concerns arose regarding its disproportionate negative impact on women. According to a panel of 38 experts from major economies and developing markets, "she-cessions", where women experience greater employment losses than men, are expected to occur in over half to two-thirds of the countries was analyzed till the second quarter of 2020. She-cessions refer to a decrease in the percentage of women in the labor force compared to men during economic downturns. She-cessions tend to be relatively short-lived, and it was anticipated that most countries will recover from this state by 2020 [33].

There is a significant correlation between the rise of she-cessions and the decline in the proportion of women employed in certain industries. The observation for this phenomenon is highest in professions where women constitute a disproportionately large portion of the workforce. The phenomenon is more directly related to the broader labor market (employment) due to a widening gender wage gap and an increase in average work hours. This is because the average work hours have increased (i.e., women who retained their jobs experienced smaller reductions in work hours compared to men). Additionally, a larger proportion of women chose to stop working altogether instead of just losing their jobs and looking for new ones. This is influenced by the fact that women have lower labor force participation rates, which can be attributed to factors like childcare costs and educational disparities [30].

As the pandemic comes to an end, a major concern is whether the jobs lost during the crisis will be reinstated and if employment levels will recover to pre-crisis levels. The term "jobless recovery" refers to a scenario where GDP and aggregate demand rebound from cyclical troughs, but labor market indicators remain sluggish, and employment as a whole struggles to return to pre-crisis levels. This phenomenon was observed after the end of the 1991 recession, where employment did not fully recover until 1993. Similarly, following the 2009 Great Recession, it took until 2014 for total employment rates to reach pre-recession levels.

References

1. Abberger, K., Nierhaus, W.: How to define a recession? In: CESifo Forum, vol. 9, pp. 74–76. München: ifo Institut für Wirtschaftsforschung an der Universität München (2008)
2. Adda, J., Dustmann, C., Stevens, K.: The career costs of children. J. Polit. Econ. **125**(2), 293–337 (2017)
3. Albanesi, S., Kim, J.: Effects of the COVID-19 recession on the us labor market: occupation, family, and gender. J. Econ. Perspect. **35**(3), 3–24 (2021)
4. Alghamlas, M., Alabduljabbar, R.: Predicting the suitability of it students' skills for the recruitment in Saudi labor market. In: 2019 2nd International Conference on Computer Applications & Information Security (ICCAIS), pp. 1–5. IEEE (2019)
5. Alon, T., Coskun, S., Doepke, M., Koll, D., Tertilt, M.: From mancession to shecession: women's employment in regular and pandemic recessions. NBER Macroecon. Annu. **36**(1), 83–151 (2022)
6. Bilan, Y., Lyeonov, S., Stoyanets, N., Vysochyna, A.: The impact of environmental determinants of sustainable agriculture on country food security. Int. J. Environ. Technol. Manage. **21**(5–6), 289–305 (2018)
7. Bluedorn, J., Caselli, F., Hansen, N.J., Shibata, I., Tavares, M.M.: Gender and employment in the COVID-19 recession: cross-country evidence on "she-cessions". Labour Econ. **81**, 102308 (2023)
8. Buheji, M., Founding, I.: Future foresight of post COVID-19 generations. Int. J. Youth Econ. **4**(1), 1–11 (2020)
9. Casuat, C.D., Festijo, E.D., Alon, A.S.: Predicting students' employability using support vector machine: a smote-optimized machine learning system. Int. J. **8**(5), 2101–2106 (2020)
10. Chirumbolo, A.: The impact of job insecurity on counterproductive work behaviors: the moderating role of honesty-humility personality trait. J. Psychol. **149**(6), 554–569 (2015)
11. Cole, D., Tibby, M.: Defining and developing your approach to employability: a framework for higher education institutions. The Higher Education Academy, Heslington (2013)
12. De Angelis, M., Mazzetti, G., Guglielmi, D.: Job insecurity and job performance: a serial mediated relationship and the buffering effect of organizational justice. Front. Psychol. **12**, 3781 (2021)

13. De Spiegelaere, S., Van Gyes, G., De Witte, H., Niesen, W., Van Hootegem, G.: On the relation of job insecurity, job autonomy, innovative work behaviour and the mediating effect of work engagement. Creat. Innov. Manage. **23**(3), 318–330 (2014)

14. De Witte, H., Pienaar, J., De Cuyper, N.: Review of 30 years of longitudinal studies on the association between job insecurity and health and well-being: is there causal evidence? Aust. Psychol. **51**(1), 18–31 (2016)

15. De Witte, H., Vander Elst, T., De Cuyper, N.: Job insecurity, health and well-being. Sustainable working lives: managing work transitions and health throughout the life course, pp. 109–128 (2015)

16. Elman, C., Angela, M.: Perceived job insecurity and entry into work-related education and training among adult workers. Soc. Sci. Res. **31**(1), 49–76 (2002)

17. Fabrizio, M.S., Gomes, D.B., Tavares, M.M.M.: COVID-19 She-Cession: The Employment Penalty of Taking Care of Young Children. International Monetary Fund (2021)

18. Friedland, D.S., Price, R.H.: Underemployment: consequences for the health and well-being of workers. Am. J. Community Psychol. **32**, 33–45 (2003)

19. Giorgi, G., et al.: Fear of non-employability and of economic crisis increase workplace harassment through lower organizational welfare orientation. Sustainability **12**(9), 3876 (2020)

20. Greenhalgh, L., Rosenblatt, Z.: Job insecurity: toward conceptual clarity. Acad. Manag. Rev. **9**(3), 438–448 (1984)

21. Hillage, J., Pollard, E.: Employability: developing a framework for policy analysis (1998)

22. Hussain, S., Singh, A.M., Mohanty, P., Gavinolla, M.R.: Next generation employability and career sustainability in the hospitality industry 5.0. Worldwide Hospit. Tour. Themes **15**(3), 308–321 (2023)

23. Kaur, H., Tao, X.: ICTs and the Millennium Development Goals. Springer, Heidelberg (2014). https://doi.org/10.1007/978-1-4899-7439-6

24. Kinnunen, P., Malmi, L.: Problems in problem-based learning-experiences, analysis and lessons learned on an introductory programming course. Inform. Educ. **4**(2), 193–214 (2005)

25. Klammer, U.: The ambivalent trajectory of the German gender regime: are female breadwinner families an indicator of a shift towards a public gender regime? In: Women's Studies International Forum, vol. 99, p. 102783. Elsevier (2023)

26. Kooli, C.: Challenges of working from home during the COVID-19 pandemic for women in the UAE. J. Public Aff. **23**(1), e2829 (2023)

27. Krammer, S.M.: Navigating the new normal: which firms have adapted better to the COVID-19 disruption? Technovation **110**, 102368 (2022)

28. Lee, J., Park, J.S., Wang, K.N., Feng, B., Tennant, M., Kruger, E.: The use of telehealth during the coronavirus (COVID-19) pandemic in oral and maxillofacial surgery-a qualitative analysis. EAI Endors. Trans. Scalable Inf. Syst. **9**(4) (2021)

29. Lim, K., Zabek, M.: Women's labor force exits during COVID-19: differences by motherhood, race, and ethnicity. J. Family Econ. Issues 1–24 (2023)

30. Livingstone, D., Pankhurst, K.: Chapter one prior concepts and theories of the relationship between workers and jobs. Educ. Jobs: Explor. Gaps 11 (2009)

31. Llosa, J.A., Menéndez-Espina, S., Agulló-Tomás, E., Rodríguez-Suárez, J.: Job insecurity and mental health: a meta-analytical review of the consequences of precarious work in clinical disorders (2018)

32. Otterbach, S., Sousa-Poza, A.: Job insecurity, employability and health: an analysis for Germany across generations. Appl. Econ. **48**(14), 1303–1316 (2016)

33. Peeters, E., Nelissen, J., De Cuyper, N., Forrier, A., Verbruggen, M., De Witte, H.: Employability capital: a conceptual framework tested through expert analysis. J. Career Dev. **46**(2), 79–93 (2019)

34. Perkins, D.N., Salomon, G., et al.: Transfer of learning. Int. Encycl. Educ. **2**, 6452–6457 (1992)

35. Ramelli, S., Wagner, A.F.: Feverish stock price reactions to COVID-19. Rev. Corp. Financ. Stud. **9**(3), 622–655 (2020)

36. Reisel, W.D., Banai, M.: Job insecurity revisited: reformulating with affect. J. Behav. Appl. Manag. **4**(1), 1063 (2016)

37. Schrage, M.: Don't let metrics critics undermine your business. MIT Sloan Manag. Rev. **23** (2019)

38. Shaik, T., Tao, X., Dann, C., Xie, H., Li, Y., Galligan, L.: Sentiment analysis and opinion mining on educational data: a survey. Nat. Lang. Process. J. **2**, 100003 (2023)

39. Shaik, T., et al.: A review of the trends and challenges in adopting natural language processing methods for education feedback analysis. IEEE Access **10**, 56720–56739 (2022)

40. Singh, R., et al.: Antisocial behavior identification from twitter feeds using traditional machine learning algorithms and deep learning. EAI Endors. Trans. Scalable Inf. Syst. **10**(4), e17–e17 (2023)

41. Singh, R., Zhang, Y., Wang, H., Miao, Y., Ahmed, K.: Investigation of social behaviour patterns using location-based data-a Melbourne case study. EAI Endors. Trans. Scalable Inf. Syst. **8**(31) (2020)

42. Tao, X., Chi, O., Delaney, P.J., Li, L., Huang, J.: Detecting depression using an ensemble classifier based on quality of life scales. Brain Inform. **8**, 1–15 (2021)

43. Vasiljeva, M., et al.: A predictive model for assessing the impact of the COVID-19 pandemic on the economies of some eastern European countries. J. Open Innov.: Technol. Mark. Complexity **6**(3), 92 (2020)

44. Williams, C.L.: Still a Man's World: Men Who Do Women's Work, vol. 1. University of California Press (2023)

45. Wilson, J.M., Lee, J., Fitzgerald, H.N., Oosterhoff, B., Sevi, B., Shook, N.J.: Job insecurity and financial concern during the COVID-19 pandemic are associated with worse mental health. J. Occup. Environ. Med. **62**(9), 686–691 (2020)

46. Zamarro, G., Prados, M.J.: Gender differences in couples' division of childcare, work and mental health during COVID-19. Rev. Econ. Household **19**(1), 11–40 (2021)

47. Zhou, X., Tao, X., Rahman, M.M., Zhang, J.: Coupling topic modelling in opinion mining for social media analysis. In: Proceedings of the International Conference on Web Intelligence, pp. 533–540 (2017)

A Semi-automatic Framework Towards Building Electricity Grid Infrastructure Management Ontology: A Case Study and Retrospective

Abdelhadi Belfadel[1(✉)], Maxence Gagnant[1], Matthieu Dussartre[2], Jérôme Picault[2], Laure Crochepierre[2], and Sana Tmar[1]

[1] IRT SystemX, 2 Bd Thomas Gobert, 91120 Palaiseau, France
`{abdelhadi.belfadel,maxence.gagnant,sana.tmar}@irt-systemx.fr`
[2] RTE Réseau de transport d'électricité, 7C place du Dôme, 92073 Paris La Defense Cedex, France
`{matthieu.dussartre,jerome.Picault,laure.crochepierre}@rte-france.com`

Abstract. Thanks to their extensive use in Internet-based applications, ontologies have gained significant popularity and recognition within the semantic web domain. They are widely regarded as valuable sources of semantics and interoperability in artificial intelligence systems. With the exponential growth of unstructured data on the web, there is a pressing need for automated acquisition of ontologies from unstructured text. This research area has seen the emergence of various methodologies that leverage techniques from machine learning, text mining, knowledge representation and reasoning, information retrieval, and high level natural language processing. These new techniques represent an opportunity to introduce automation into the process of ontology acquisition from unstructured text. To this end, this contribution offers a semi-automatic framework with a concrete usage of a tooled NLP-based approach to design an application ontology in a real-world industrial context. We discuss the state of the art analysis, the challenges met and the technological choices for the realization of this approach. Specifically, we explore its application in the real-world scenario of RTE's power grid event management.

Keywords: Ontology · NLP · Information Extraction · Power grid

1 Introduction

In the modern age of big data, vast amounts of diverse, unstructured information are generated daily across various professions. Adapting this data for real-time decision-making, while integrating expert knowledge and external sources, is a challenge. The semantic web, with ontologies, addresses this by providing meaningful information representation for humans and computers.

F. Zhang et al. (Eds.): WISE 2023, LNCS 14306, pp. 865–874, 2023.
https://doi.org/10.1007/978-981-99-7254-8_67

An ontology formally structures knowledge in a specific domain, including concepts, relations, attributes, and hierarchies. Building ontologies manually is time-intensive, requiring extraction of instances from unstructured text via ontology population. However, creating large ontologies manually is challenging [2], prompting a shift toward automated ontology population. This shift promotes exploring automatic ontology learning as an alternative to manual design.

This work introduces a semi-automated approach to build an application ontology for power grid event management. It addresses the lack of practical NLP-based ontology learning experiments and shares insights from the ongoing implementation and results. The following sections cover the conceptual framework, technical decisions, current progress, and encountered limitations in this real-world industrial context.

2 Industrial Case Study: Electricity Grid Infrastructure Management

RTE (Réseau de Transport d'Électricité) is the electrical transmission system operator (TSO) in France. It is an independent public company in charge of ensuring the smooth operation, safety and reliability of the French high-voltage electricity network. As a transmission system operator, RTE plays a crucial role in the coordination and management of electricity flows in France. In this context, electricity network operators handle critical documents for reporting grid operations and incident management. These reports enhance internal communication and inform decision-making, but they lack standardization in content and structure. Ontologies provide coordination among operators. Similarly, machine-generated documents like real-time monitoring data, archives, forecasts, network models and simulations play a crucial role in the efficient management and forecasting of power flows. Using ontology to model these documents bridges the gap between machines and operators, enhancing reliability and power system performance.

In order to meet RTE's ambitions, the proposed method involves four objectives: i) The generation of a Knowledge Graph (KG) from operating reports; ii) KG enrichment from information contained in the real-time (monitoring) or anticipatory databases; iii) The design of an application ontology allowing to represent RTE specific knowledge in a formal way; iv) The ultimate objective is to automatically generate operating reports, while allowing AI assistants to offer communication adapted to the operators' vocabulary.

The results of this research will benefit power grid operators by facilitating optimized decision making, refining the understanding of network phenomena and ensuring good continuity of service. The rest of this paper will focus on objectives (i) and (iii) to elaborate on these crucial steps.

3   State of the Art

In recent decades, there has been significant interest in ontology engineering [18], resulting in a multitude of studies exploring methodologies, guidelines, tools, resources, and ongoing research in various related areas such as ontology learning topic.

To shift from a handcrafting development process to a (semi)-automatic process, several techniques emerging from the fields of machine learning, natural language processing, data mining or information retrieval have been proposed. Authors in [2] summarizes the various steps required for ontology learning from an unstructured text. It starts by extracting terms and synonyms using linguistic techniques, then relations between these concepts are found based on statistical techniques such as co-occurrence analysis or clustering. Finally, axioms are extracted thanks to inductive logic programming techniques such as [4,17].

Named Entity Recognition (NER) is a core NLP method that leverages machine learning and linguistic patterns to identify and categorize specific elements like people, organizations, places, and dates in text, offering insights into document structure. NER aids ontology development by extracting entities that can be mapped to ontology concepts [7]. In order to predict relations between entities in a given sentence, relation extraction techniques are of high value. Early rule-based methods [1] had difficulty generalizing as relation syntax differ within situations. Therefore deep learning models were introduced, in particular the max-pooling CNN model [20] which has long remained the most efficient structure at classifying relations. More recently, large language models [11,22] proved to be better at capturing semantics in sentences. They achieve state-of-the art results on all benchmark datasets. However, training large supervised models typically requires huge amounts of data examples.

Using knowledge bases for extensive training sets, [16] introduced distant supervision for relation extraction. Graph neural networks perform well in such cases [3]. Yet, this supervision can be noisy, as it relies on the strong assumption that the relation to extract is the same as the one found in the knowledge base. Semi-supervision addresses data scarcity: self-training models [9] generate artificial examples, and self-ensembling models [13] jointly label and generate. Despite notable progress in relation classification and improved results on benchmarks, limited research targets extracting unknown relation types. Unsupervised models constitute a decent alternative as they do not require prior knowledge. They first represent sentences in specific semantic spaces then apply clustering to extract different relation types [10]. Further works integrate hierarchy information which appears to be useful to relation clustering [21].

4   Overview of the Framework and Implementation Steps

4.1   Framework for Ontology Learning

To achieve our objectives, we have established the following steps (Fig. 1):

- *Pre-processing*: It involves syntactic analysis of unstructured text (example in Fig. 2). It uses NLP techniques like part-of-speech tagging, French lemmatization, and sentence parsing to label words, normalize terms, and reduce data dimension.

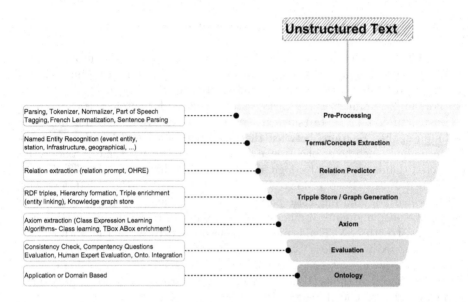

Fig. 1. Framework for ontology learning

- *Terms/Concepts Extraction*: This relies on the use of linguistic techniques for the extraction of important terms/concepts of a domain in the unstructured text, and the relations between them. This is achieved by using NER techniques to recognize important information in the text that refer to key subjects in our context, such as transmission lines, stations, infrastructures, as well as geographical locations, electrical grid events,...
- *Relation Predictor*: This important step helps identify the relation between the extracted terms/concepts, and enables during the next steps the creation of a knowledge graph. This step relies on language models which capture the semantics of sentences. More details about the chosen algorithms from the literature are described in the workflow of Fig. 3.
- *Triple Store/Graph Generation*: This step uses previous results to form an initial data graph. Each term and relation becomes an atomic data entity in the Resource Description Framework (RDF) [6] data model, a W3C standard for web data interchange. Entity linking enhances resources with syntactic and semantic details from broad or domain-specific ontologies like DBpedia[1] or the Common Grid Model Exchange Standard (CGMES) ontology[2]. This establishes initial class expressions, concepts, and hierarchy. Ontology learning then constructs, learns, and enriches the graph by identifying class expressions and axioms, laying the foundation for the application ontology.
- *Axiom*: This step employs logic programming to uncover patterns among concepts in the knowledge graph, extracting axiom schemata and general axioms.

---

[1] https://www.dbpedia.org/.

[2] https://www.entsoe.eu/data/cim/cim-for-grid-models-exchange/.

Techniques like supervised learning can identify expressed OWL classes using positive and negative examples [12]. Alternatively, a class learning approach employs class instances as positive examples, learning about the class and its relations in the graph.

- *Evaluation*: Evaluating ontology acquisition is vital to assess concept coverage, correctness, and suitability. It refines learning processes, aligning with user needs. Literature offers techniques like golden standard, application-based, data-driven, and human evaluation, outlined in [2].

The remainder of this paper focuses on the results of the framework's initial steps, including pre-processing, term/concept extraction, relation extraction, and RDF triple generation. It discusses the chosen algorithms and the lessons learned from analyzing existing methods. Figure 3 presents a workflow that depicts the implemented technical tasks.

Evénement(s) réseaux

• **Evénement(s) sur le réseau électrique avec impact clientèle (Coupure Longue)**

Date et heure	Centre	Ouvrage(s) concerné(s)	Impact(s)
29/01/22 à 10h02	Centre	Coupure longue du client Client XYZ (3 MW non encore réalimentés) suite au déclenchement de ligne Ligne XYZ 63kV et au retrait définitif de la conduite du réseau de la ligne Ligne XYZ 63kV, sans retour possible. Cf. MIN du CE-SQY	3 MW non rétablis

Fig. 2. Anonymized unstructured text example from a PDF file. Each PDF contains diverse event descriptions in various formats (tables, figures, paragraphs, etc.).

4.2 NLP Pipeline

The blue and yellow NLP tasks in Fig. 3 are implemented using the Spacy framework [8], an open-source, flexible software library for advanced natural language processing, written in Python. Given the input documents specificity (technical french content in a specialized field), our NLP pipeline entails: 1) standard Spacy components, 2) third-party components, and 3) custom RTE components. Noteworthy design choices for components include:

- *Tokenization level*: in the RTE corpus, documents mention power grid equipments, including voltage levels like "le poste 400 kV" or "le poste 400 kV". When using the standard Spacy tokenizer for French, "400 kV" becomes separate tokens, which is not intended. Specific components in our NLP pipeline handle this situation.
- *Part-of-Speech (POS) tagging level*: the default Spacy French component provides quite poor performance for POS tagging, this is why we decided to replace the default component with a component based on LEFFF [19], developed by INRIA, which is superior by far.

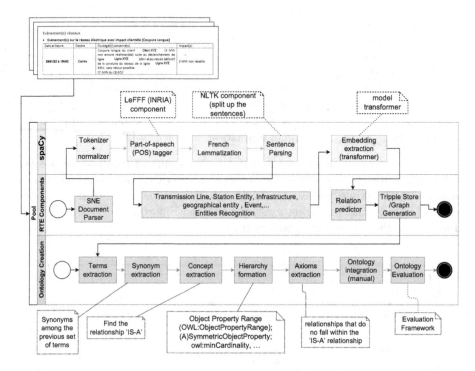

Fig. 3. Proposed Workflow for a semi-automatic construction of an application Ontology

– *Sentencizer level*: similarly, the Spacy sentencizer component has a rather strange behaviour, which considers soft punctuation marks (such as ";", "_") as delimiters for sentences. This behaviour is not the one we expect, we used instead a component based on NLTK [14].

– *Entity level*: we targeted operations-related entities in the power grid, such as substations, lines, transformers, and associated grid events. Spacy's NER lacks the necessary specificity, therefore we developed custom components to detect a wider array of pertinent entities. Figure 4a depicts an output of this step.

– *Embeddings*: RTE documents contain a lot of technical vocabulary and even French terms meaning may diverge from common language usage. Thus, a specific transformation of tokens and entities is required to obtain meaningful numerical vectors (embeddings) describing accurately the documents. This is achieved by fine-tuning a language model, CamemBERT [15] (a French transformer model), with 5000+ technical documents.

– *Relation predictor*: a new component is designed to establish meaningful links between entities, forming the foundation for semi-automated ontology creation. In the unique context of power grid management, this involves extracting highly specific relation types. While traditional relation extraction models like [11] seemed promising at first, they didn't deliver the expected real-case

RTE results. This led to the exploration of open relation extraction models, in particular [10] and [21]. However, their unsupervised approach, while suitable for new relations and limited data, was discarded due to its tendency to produce relation clusters instead of labels. For automated knowledge graph and ontology creation, relation labeling is vital. Existing solutions lacked adaptability to specific contexts, relying on initial datasets. Therefore, the Relation Prompt solution [5] gained prominence. This dual relation extraction method consists of a powerful BART-based model operating the extraction, coupled with a generative model. Below, we outline the relation prompt process shown in Fig. 4b.

(a) Named Entity Recognition result (anonymized extract)

(b) Workflow of the Relation Prompt solution

Fig. 4. NER result example and Workflow of relation prompt solution

Figure 4b illustrates the relation prediction step. The generator provides artificial sentences depicting a given relation. Then, the extractor is fine-tuned with these synthetic sentences in order to adapt classification to the desired relation types. This flexible approach only requires a very small amount of training sentences which fitted well to the context. Providing quality annotations and specific relations for our business data is indeed costly in terms of time and thus money. Table 1 shows the details of the RTE dataset and some targeted relations. Indeed, some very specific relations such as a relation between an Event and Event Criticality or Event Type are difficult to extract through this NLP process due to the absence of this knowledge in the unstructured text. In addition, only a very small amount of sentences was available with very specific relation types which constitutes a real challenge to training.

Results presented in Table 1 show that some relations such as occurred at date, occurred at time, or of voltage were effectively classified, even though there was very few training examples. Meanwhile, others are very bad classified. Several reasons can explain poor result: some relations involving proper nouns such as locations, infrastructures or clients are tougher to perceive as proper names inherently bear very little resemblance to each other. Also, some relations such as geographical proximity are rare in the set and thus not learnt enough. Finally, the ending time relation is more ambiguous than others and appears in very different ways which explains why it is harder to classify.

Table 1. Composition and results on RTE dataset

Entities	Relation types	Training examples	Test examples	Precision
Event ; Datetime	occurred at date	18	6	100%
Event ; Datetime	occurred at time	17	4	100%
Event ; Geo. Region	occurred in geographical region	21	6	17%
Event ; Client	with participation of client	4	2	0%
Event ; Power	of electrical power	18	6	33%
Event ; Datetime	ending time	23	6	0%
Geo. Region ; Geo. Region	geographical proximity	4	2	0%
Infrastructure ; Voltage level	of voltage	39	3	100%
Event; Infrastructure;	occurred on infrastructure	16	2	0%
−	Total	160	37	43%

4.3   Knowledge Graph Generation

The transformation of NLP entities and relations into a knowledge graph is depicted in (Fig. 5). It involves two steps: 1) Entity Linking: this associates entity types with targeted RDF classes. A straightforward match currently based on existing ontology drafts, for instance, the "outage" extracted as an "event" type has to appear in RDF as an instance of an "Event" class. 2) Instance Uniqueness: in the knowledge graph, identical entities from different relation triples appear only once, grouped by textual similarity within a paragraph. However, dealing with different instances mentioned in different ways and in various contexts would require more extensive analysis.

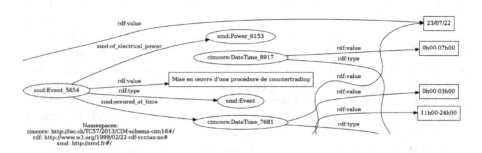

Fig. 5. Excerpt from a generated knowledge graph

5   Conclusion

This paper presents a framework that introduces automation into the process of ontology acquisition from unstructured text. We provide, as a retrospective in each step, the challenges met, the methodologies and technological choices for the realization of this approach on a real-world industrial context applied for power grid events management. In terms of implementation, our efforts were primarily directed towards the upper levels of the suggested framework. Our objective was to transform domain-specific unstructured text into a knowledge graph representation, with the aim of generating an initial draft of an application ontology as a subsequent step. To accomplish this, we employed a NLP-based approach that utilizes syntactic and linguistic techniques. Additionally, we employed a specialized language model that generates synthetic training data to support low-resource relation extraction methods.

As for the work to come in the next few months, our aim is twofold. Firstly, we intend to implement the OWL class expression learner algorithm to construct class expressions and relevant axioms using the extracted and observed dataset. This effort strives to create an initial and formal application ontology, capitalizing on the specified steps detailed in this paper, along with technical insights and subsequent assessment. Additionally, our ultimate objective is to develop a system that can automatically generate feedback documents and enable AI assistants to provide communication that is tailored to the operators' vocabulary. This will enhance the effectiveness and adaptability of RTE communication process.

Acknowledgement. This work has been supported by the French government under the "France 2030" program, as part of the SystemX Technological Research Institute.

References

1. Aone, C., Halverson, L., Hampton, T., Ramos-Santacruz, M.: SRA: description of the IE2 system used for MUC-7. In: Seventh Message Understanding Conference (MUC-7): Proceedings of a Conference Held in Fairfax, Virginia, 29 April–1 May 1998 (1998). https://aclanthology.org/M98-1012
2. Asim, M.N., Wasim, M., Khan, M.U.G., Mahmood, W., Abbasi, H.M.: A survey of ontology learning techniques and applications. Database 2018 (2018)
3. Bastos, A., et al.: Recon: Relation extraction using knowledge graph context in a graph neural network (2021)
4. Bühmann, L., Lehmann, J., Westphal, P.: Dl-learner-a framework for inductive learning on the semantic web. J. Web Semant. **39**, 15–24 (2016)
5. Chia, Y.K., Bing, L., Poria, S., Si, L.: Relationprompt: leveraging prompts to generate synthetic data for zero-shot relation triplet extraction (2022)
6. Cyganiak, R., Wood, D., Lanthaler, M., Klyne, G., Carroll, J.J., McBride, B.: RDF 1.1 concepts and abstract syntax. W3C Recommendation **25**(02), 1–22 (2014)
7. Elgamal, M., Abou-Kreisha, M., Elezz, R., Hamada, S.: An ontology-based name entity recognition NER and NLP systems in Arabic storytelling. Al-Azhar Bull. Sci. **31**, 31–38 (2020). https://doi.org/10.21608/absb.2020.44367.1088
8. Honnibal, M., Montani, I.: spaCy 2: Natural language understanding with Bloom embeddings, convolutional neural networks and incremental parsing (2017). https://spacy.io/
9. Hu, X., Zhang, C., Ma, F., Liu, C., Wen, L., Yu, P.S.: Semi-supervised relation extraction via incremental meta self-training (2021)

10. Hu, X., Zhang, C., Xu, Y., Wen, L., Yu, P.S.: Selfore: Self-supervised relational feature learning for open relation extraction. arXiv preprint arXiv:2004.02438 (2020)
11. Huguet Cabot, P.L., Navigli, R.: REBEL: relation extraction by end-to-end language generation. In: Findings of the Association for Computational Linguistics: EMNLP 2021, pp. 2370–2381. Association for Computational Linguistics, Punta Cana, Dominican Republic (2021). https://aclanthology.org/2021.findings-emnlp. 204
12. Lehmann, J., Auer, S., Bühmann, L., Tramp, S.: Class expression learning for ontology engineering. J. Web Semant. **9**(1), 71–81 (2011)
13. Lin, H., Yan, J., Qu, M., Ren, X.: Learning dual retrieval module for semi-supervised relation extraction (2019)
14. Loper, E., Bird, S.: NLTK: the natural language toolkit (2002). https://arxiv.org/abs/cs/0205028
15. Martin, L., et al.: Camembert: a tasty French language model. CoRR abs/1911.03894 (2019). http://arxiv.org/abs/1911.03894
16. Mintz, M., Bills, S., Snow, R., Jurafsky, D.: Distant supervision for relation extraction without labeled data. In: Proceedings of the Joint Conference of the 47th Annual Meeting of the ACL and the 4th International Joint Conference on Natural Language Processing of the AFNLP, pp. 1003–1011. Association for Computational Linguistics, Suntec, Singapore (2009). https://aclanthology.org/P09-1113
17. Muggleton, S., et al.: ILP turns 20: biography and future challenges. Mach. Learn. **86**, 3–23 (2012)
18. Poveda-Villalón, M., Fernández-Izquierdo, A., Fernández-López, M., García-Castro, R.: Lot: an industrial oriented ontology engineering framework. Eng. Appl. Artif. Intell. **111**, 104755 (2022)
19. Sagot, B.: The Lefff, a freely available and large-coverage morphological and syntactic lexicon for French. In: 7th International Conference on Language Resources and Evaluation (LREC 2010). Valletta, Malta (2010). https://inria.hal.science/inria-00521242
20. Zeng, D., Liu, K., Lai, S., Zhou, G., Zhao, J.: Relation classification via convolutional deep neural network. In: Proceedings of COLING 2014, the 25th International Conference on Computational Linguistics: Technical Papers, pp. 2335–2344. Dublin City University and Association for Computational Linguistics, Dublin, Ireland (2014). https://aclanthology.org/C14-1220
21. Zhang, K., et al.: Open hierarchical relation extraction. In: Proceedings of the 2021 Conference of the North American Chapter of the Association for Computational Linguistics: Human Language Technologies, pp. 5682–5693 (2021). https://doi.org/10.18653/v1/2021.naacl-main.452
22. Zhou, W., Huang, K., Ma, T., Huang, J.: Document-level relation extraction with adaptive thresholding and localized context pooling (2020)

Word-Graph2vec: An Efficient Word Embedding Approach on Word Co-occurrence Graph Using Random Walk Technique

Wenting Li[1], Jiahong Xue[1], Xi Zhang[1], Huacan Chen[1], Zeyu Chen[1], Feijuan Huang[2(⊠)], and Yuanzhe Cai[1(⊠)]

[1] Shenzhen Technology University, Shenzhen, Guangdong, China
`caiyuanzhe@sztu.edu.cn`
[2] Shenzhen Institute of Translational Medicine, Shenzhen Second People's Hospital, The First Affiliated Hospital of Shenzhen University, Shenzhen, Guangdong, China
`fjhuang@email.szu.edu.cn`

Abstract. Word embedding has become ubiquitous and is widely used in various natural language processing (NLP) tasks, such as web retrieval, web semantic analysis, and machine translation, and so on. Unfortunately, training the word embedding in a relatively large corpus is prohibitively expensive. We propose a graph-based word embedding algorithm, called Word-Graph2vec, which converts the large corpus into a word co-occurrence graph, then takes the word sequence samples from this graph by randomly traveling and trains the word embedding on this sampling corpus in the end. We posit that because of the limited vocabulary, huge idioms, and fixed expressions in English, the size and density of the word co-occurrence graph change slightly with the increase in the training corpus. So that Word-Graph2vec has stable runtime on the large-scale data set, and its performance advantage becomes more and more obvious with the growth of the training corpus. Extensive experiments conducted on real-world datasets show that the proposed algorithm outperforms traditional Word2vec four to five times in terms of efficiency and two to three times than FastText, while the error generated by the random walk technique is small.

Keywords: Word co-occurrence Graph · Random walk · Word embedding

1 Introduction

Word embedding is widely used in modern natural language processing (NLP) tasks, including sentiment analysis [2], web retrieval [7]and so on. Current word

The authors acknowledge funding from 2023 Special Fund for Science and Technology Innovation Strategy of Guangdong Province (Science and Technology Innovation Cultivation of College Students), the Shenzhen High-Level Hospital Construction Fund (4001020), and the Shenzhen Science and Technology Innovation Committee Funds (JSGG20220919091404008).

embedding methods, such as Word2vec [9] and Glove [12], rely on large corpora to learn the association between words and obtain the statistical correlation between different words so as to simulate the human cognitive process for a word. The time complexity of these two approaches is $O(|N|log(|V|))$, where $|N|$ is the total corpus size, and $|V|$ is the size of vocabulary, which clearly indicates that the runtime of these two training approaches increases linearly as the size of corpus increases.

In the era of big data, how to speed up these existing word embedding approaches becomes increasingly essential.

In this paper, we address the problem of efficiently computing the word embedding on a large-scale corpus. Our solution is also established on a word co-occurrence graph, Then text sampling by random walk traveling on the graph. In detail, we intend to go one step further and propose a graph-based word embedding method called Word-Graph2vec. This approach contains three steps. First, Word-Graph2vec uses word co-occurrence information to construct a word graph whose each word as a node, whose edges represent co-occurrences between the word and its adjacency node, and whose edge direction represents word order. Second, Word-Graph2vec performs random walk traveling on this word graph and samples the word sequences. Third, skip-gram [9] has been applied to these sampling word sequences to gain the final word embedding.

The main advantage of Word-Graph2vec is the performance on the large-scale corpus. Because of the limited vocabulary[1], the number of nodes and density of the word co-occurrence graph change slightly with the increase of training corpus. So that Word-Graph2vec has stable runtime on the large-scale data set, and its performance advantage becomes more and more obvious with the growth of the training corpus. Parenthetically, noted that adding more training corpus only results in adjusting the edge weights. Therefore, the time consumed by training the model increases slowly as the corpus increases.

2   Related Works

We categorize existing work related to our study into two classes: word embedding approaches and graph embedding approaches.

Word Embedding Approaches: One of the most prominent methods for word-level representation is Word2vec [9]. So far, Word2vec has widely established its effectiveness for achieving state-of-the-art performances in various clinical NLP tasks. GloVe [12] is another unsupervised learning approach for obtaining a single word's representation. Different from Word2vec and GloVe, Fast-Text [15] considers individual words as character n-grams. Words actually have different meanings in different contexts, and the vector representation of the two model words in different contexts is the same. However, the structure of these pre-training models is limited by the unidirectional language model (from left

---

[1] The vocabulary of the New Oxford Dictionary is around 170,000, but some of the words are old English words, so that in actual training, the word co-occurrence graph contains about 100,000 to 130,000 nodes.

to right or from right to left), which also limits the representation ability of the model so that it can only obtain unidirectional context information.

Word-Graph2vec model makes the training time in a stable interval with the increasing of the size of the corpus and also ensures the accuracy for various NLP tasks.

Graph Embedding Method: In graphical analysis, traditional machine learning methods usually rely on manual design and are limited by flexibility and high cost. Based on the idea of representational learning and the success of Word2vec, Deepwalk [13], as the first graph embedding method based on representational learning, applies the Skip-Gram model to the generated random walk. Similarly, inspired by Deepwalk, Node2vec [3] improves the random walking mode in Deepwalk. Node2vec introduces a heuristic method, second-order random walk. Considering the difference between the linear structure of the text and the complex structure of graphics, our model adopts the idea of Node2vec for node learning.

3   Word-Graph2vec Algorithm

3.1   Motivation

Word graphs, extracted from the text, have already been successfully used in the NLP tasks, such as information retrieval [1]and text classification [4]. The impact of the term order has been a popular issue, and relationships between the terms, in general, are claimed to play an important role in text processing. For example, the sentence *"Lily is more beautiful than Lucy"* is totally different from the sentence *"Lucy is more beautiful than Lily"*. This motivated us to use a word co-occurrence graph representation that would capture these word relationships.

Training the word embedding on a word co-occurrence graph is an efficient approach. First, the number of nodes in this word co-occurrence graph is not large. According to lexicographer and dictionary expert, Susie Dent, "the average active vocabulary of an adult English speaker is around 20,000 words, while his passive vocabulary is around 40,000 words." Meanwhile, even for the large En-Wikipedia data set, the total number of word graph nodes is around 100,723, and these word graphs are highly sparse(see Table 1).

As the size of the training corpus increases, the weight on edges will change a lot, but the size of nodes and graph density do not have significant alterations. Thus, this pushes us to propose our approach, Word-Graph2vec, to address word embedding issue.

3.2   Framework of Word-Graph2vec

Figure 1 shows the framework of Word-Graph2vec.

Generate Word Co-occurrence Graph. A textual document is presented as a word co-occurrence graph that corresponds to a weighted directed graph whose vertices represent unique words, whose edges represent co-occurrence between

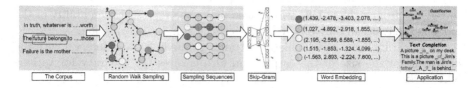

Fig. 1. The overall framework for Word-Graph2vec algorithm.

the words, and whose edge direction represents word order. An example of graph creation is given in Fig. 2(a). The source text is an extract of a sentence from Philip Dormer Stanhope's letter, "In truth, whatever is **worth doing at** all, is **worth doing well**; and nothing can be done well without attention."

Figure 2(b) corresponds to the resulting weighted directed graph where each vertex represents a unique word, and each edge is a co-occurrence of the two words.

Weight on Edges: The number of simultaneous occurrences of these two words in the text is used as the weight on edge. A weighted adjacency matrix W is used to store the edge weights, and $W_{v,x}$ is the weight from node v to node x.

$$W_{v,x} = \sum co\text{-}occurrence(v, x) \tag{1}$$

where $co\text{-}occurrence(v, x)$ is the number of times that the words v and x appear together from left to right in the same order.

Weight on Nodes:

The weight of the node is used to determine the sampling times in the random walk process. We take probability PW_v as a representation of the importance of the word v in the whole corpus, that is, the weight of nodes in the graph. This paper uses the terms frequency(TF) and inverse document probability(TF-IDF) to set the word weights PW.

Sampling Word Sequences by Random Walk. This random walk sampling process [16] iteratively explores the global structure network of the object to estimate the proximity between two nodes. Generate a random walk from the current node, and select the random neighbors of the current node as a candidate based on the transition probability on the word co-occurrence graph.

First, the different nodes, as distinct from the same selection probability for graph embedding, should have different probabilities to be selected as the starting point. We use the probability sampling method based on the word weight to select the rooted node. For example, the sampling times of node v as the starting node are shown in Eq. 2:

$$number\_walks(v) = \lfloor total\_walks \times PW_v \rfloor \tag{2}$$

Where $total\_walks$ is the total number of random walk sampling, and PW_v is the weight of word v.

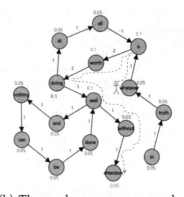

In truth, whatever is worth doing at all, is

worth doing well; and nothing can be done

well without attention.

(a) An example sentence. A solid arrow represents a new directed edge while a dashed arrow an already existing one in the graph. The edges are drawn from or to word "doing".

(b) The word co-occurrence graph. The red dotted line describes a random walk with "whatever" as the starting node and "attention" as the endding node.

Fig. 2. An example of word co-occurrence graph creating from a sentence in Philip Dormer Stanhope's letter.

Second, considering the shuttle between two kinds of graph similarities (homophily and structural equivalence), Node2vec [3] is selected as the graph sampling approach.

Then, according to the 2nd order random walk transfer probability of the Node2vec model, the random neighbours of the current node is selected as the candidate node. The sampling sequence of a node is determined by simulating several biased random walks of fixed length l.

Learning Embedding by Skip-Gram Model. After obtaining a much smaller set of walking sequences compared to the original corpus, we used the Skip-Gram model to learn the final word embedding.

3.3   Word-Graph2vecAlgorithm

Word-Graph2vec algorithm is presented in Algorithm 1.

The algorithm first initializes variables (Lines 1–2). We scan all the corpus once and build the word co-occurrence graph (Lines 1–3). The adjacency matrix W and node's weight PW have been calculated in this scanning.

Line 4 is to calculate the transitive matrix using the 2nd transfer probability formula provided by Node2vec. Line 6–7 introduces how to generate the word sequences SC by traveling on the word co-occurrence graph. The node on the graph is scanned one by one, and the number of times in which each node is traversed as the rooted node is equal to $n \frac{PW_u}{\sum_k PW_k}$.

Algorithm 1: *Word-Graph2vec Algorithm*

---

1 **Input:** A processed corpus C, The number of sampling n, Walk length l, p, q
  Context size k, Dimension d

2 **Output:** Word vector representations Φ

  1: $W \leftarrow \emptyset$ // `Adjacency Matrix` ;

  2: $PW \leftarrow \emptyset$ // `Weight on nodes` ;

  3: **for** $i = 1$ **to** $Size(C)$ **do**

     for *word* **to** C_i **do**

         $W_{word,word+1} \leftarrow W_{word,word+1} + 1 \quad PW_{word} \leftarrow PW_{word} + 1$

  4: $\pi \leftarrow$ PreprocessModifiedWeights(W, p, q) ;

  5: $G' = (V, E, \pi, PW)$;

  6: $SC \leftarrow \emptyset$ // `SC is the result set of random walk sampling.`

  7: **for** *all nodes* $u \in V$ **do**

     for $iter = 1$ **to** $n\frac{PW_u}{\sum_k PW_k}$ **do**

         word_sequence $\leftarrow \emptyset$ RandomWalkSampleProcess (G', u, l);

         Append *word_sequence* to SC

  8: $\Phi =$ Skip-Gram(k, d, SC);

  9: **return** Φ;

3.4 Time and Space Complexity Analysis

Denoting N as the total corpus size and V as the unique word vocabulary count.

In Word-Graph2vec, the training corpus for Skip-Gram is our sampling corpus whose size is nl, where n is the number of random walks and l is the walk length. The time complexity is reduced to $O(nllog(V))$, since nl is smaller than N ($nl \approx 1.9e^8$ for both 1 GB and 4 GB data set).

As for the space complexity, Word-Graph2vec needs to store the word graph, the generated word corpus, and the final word embedding. So, the space complexity of the word graph is $O(m|V|)$, m is the average degree of the graph; the space complexity of generated word corpus is $O(nl)$; the word embedding is $O(d|V|)$. Therefore, the space complexity of Word-Graph2vec is $O(m|V| + nl + d|V|)$.

4 Experimental Analysis

4.1 Experimental Setting

We use various data sets to test our approaches. The processed dataset information can be found in Table 1.

Text8[2]: Text8 [10] contains 100M processed Wikipedia characters created by changing the case to lower of the text and removing any character other than the 26 letters a through z. Meanwhile, PyDictonary, as in the English language dictionary, Wordnet lexical database, and Enchant Spell Dictionary, is applied to filter the correct English words.

---

[2] http://mattmahoney.NET/dc/text8.zip.

One Billion Words Benchmark (1b Words Banchmark)[3]: This is a new benchmark corpus with nearly 1 billion words of training data, which is used to measure the progress of statistical language modeling.

Enlish Wikipedia Data Set (En-Wikipedia)[4]: This is a word corpus of English articles collected from Wikipedia web pages.

Concatenating Data Set: To test the scalability of our approach, we also process several En-Wikipedia data sets successively as a single sequential data set. We use Con-En-Wikipedia-i to denote the concatenating data set with *i-th* data sets merged together. By the way, Con-En-Wikipedia-2 is 16.4G, and Con-En-Wikipedia-3 is 24.6 G.

Table 1. Statistics of Datasets

Data sets	Size	$|V|$	$|E|$	Density
Text8	95.3M	135,317	3,920,065	0.02%
1b words benchmark	2.51G	82,473	54,125,475	0.80%
En-Wikipedia	8.22G	100,723	64,633,532	0.64%

Baseline Method: Word2vec and Fasttext are two standard methods for training static word embedding, so we use them as our baseline to compare with Word-Graph2vec. For these two baselines, all parameters are the default values provided by the original function.

All our experiments are conducted on a PC with a 1.60GHz Intel Core 5 Duo Processor, 8GB memory, and running Win10, and all algorithms are implemented in Python and C++. Meanwhile, instead of using Node2vec, the Pecanpy model [6], which uses cache optimized compact graph data structure and precomputing/parallelization to improve the shortcomings of Node2vec, is applied in our experiment.

4.2   Evaluation Criteria

We adopted the three evaluation tasks mentioned in [14]: Categorization, Similarity, and Analogy, and we tested them with the method proposed in [5].

Categorization: The goal here is to restore word clusters to different categories. Therefore, the corresponding word embedding of all words in the data set are clustered, and the purity of the cluster is calculated according to the marked data set.

Similarity: This task requires calculating the cosine similarity of paired words calculated using word vectors and comparing it with the relevant human judgment similarity.

---

[3] https://www.kaggle.com/datasets/alexrenz/one-billion-words-benchmark.
[4] https://dumps.wikimedia.org/enwiki/latest/enwiki-latest-pages-articles.xml.bz2.

Analogy: The goal is to find a term x for a given term y so that $x : y$ is most like the sample relationship $a : b$. It requires predicting the degree to which the semantic relations between x and y are similar to those between a and b.

The word similarity prediction effectiveness is measured with the help of Spearman's rank correlation coefficient ρ [11]. For the analogy and the concept categorization tasks, we report the accuracy [8] in predicting the reference word and that of the class, respectively[5]

4.3   Parameters Study

Study of P, Q: We explored the best combination of parameters p and q on $[(0.001, 1), (1, 1), (1, 0.001)]$. Table 2 shows the evaluation results of the three tasks. It can be seen from the results that the (p, q)combination of $(1, 0.001)$ can obtain better accuracy.

Node's Weight Study: Table 2 shows a comparison of the evaluation results of word embedding obtained by setting various word weight. Method 1 (Pecanpy+TF) uses TF value as the weight of the node; Method 2 (Pecanpy+TF-IDF) uses $TF\text{-}IDF$ value; Method 3 (Pecanpy) do not set the node's weight. The results show that using TF-IDF to set weights is the best, so we will use this method in the following experiments.

Table 2. Evaluation results of different p , q combinations and word weight setting

Tasks	Data set	Different (p, q) Combimations			Different Word Weight Setting Method		
		(0.001, 1)	(1, 1)	(1, 0.001)	Pecanpy+TF	Pecanpy+TF-IDF	Pecanpy
Categorization Tasks	BLESS	48.0	59.5	**66.0**	60.5	**61.0**	60.0
(Accuracy*100)	Battig	25.1	30.0	**32.2**	32.1	**34.3**	30.1
Word Similarity	MEN	37.7	52.4	**56.0**	**54.5**	54.4	54.1
(Spearman's ρ *100)	SimLex999	20.6	18.1	**21.5**	21.3	**21.7**	20.4
Word Anology	MSR	4.0	**15.7**	11.9	**12.9**	12.3	12.1
(Accuracy(P@1)*100)	SemEval2012_2	8.4	**13.5**	10.4	11.0	**11.5**	10.3

Due to space limitations, we have only reported test results for some important parameters. Our final experiment used the best performing values for each parameter in the test.

4.4   Accuracy Experiments

We compared the performance of Word-Graph2vec, Word2vec, and FastText on three tasks. Table 3 show the experimental results of the categorization task, word similarity task and word analogy task. The experimental results show that: On the three tasks, the quality of word embedding trained by Word-Graph2vec,

---

[5] The detailed information and the source code shows on this website https://github.com/kudkudak/word-embeddings-benchmarks.

Word2vec, and FastText will improve with the increased data set. We can see that the performance of Word-Graph2vec is gradually close to Word2vec and FastText, or even better. This shows that a random walk has a certain probability to capture marginal words that appear relatively few times. Thus, this makes the sampled corpus closer to the real text and even can follow the similar word's distribution in advance. Moreover, this may be the reason to explain that the word embedding obtained by Word-Graph2vec performs better in some test tasks.

Table 3. Precision Experiments Results

Tasks		Categorization Tasks		Word Similarity		Word Anology	
Datasets	Method	Accuracy*100		Spearman's ρ *100		Accuracy(P@1)*100	
		BLESS	Battig	MEN	SimLex999	MSR	SemEval2012_2
Text8	Word2vec	58.0	35.2	**63.0**	26.3	27.6	**13.2**
	FastText	50.5	**36.2**	61.1	**27.5**	**41.4**	10.1
	Word-Graph2vec	**66.0**	32.2	56.0	21.5	11.9	10.4
1b Words Benchmark	Word2vec	77.0	30.8	68.6	**33.0**	34.8	13.9
	FastText	72.5	**32.3**	70.0	30.3	**37.5**	12.2
	Word-Graph2vec	**83.5**	31.6	**70.1**	31.6	24.8	**15.7**
En-Wikipedia	Word2vec	70.5	35.4	67.7	28.6	30.8	13.8
	FastText	77.0	**37.3**	**69.0**	28.4	**42.8**	15.6
	Word-Graph2vec	**83.5**	36.5	66.5	**29.7**	28.8	**15.9**

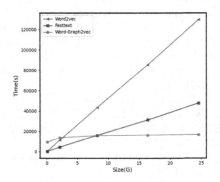

Fig. 3. Times (h) vs. Size (G)

4.5   Efficiency of Proposed Algorithm

In order to observe the time trend more intuitively, we generated two more extensive data sets (Con-En-Wikipedia-1, 16.4 G; Con-En-Wikipedia-2, 24.6 G) for testing using the En-Wikipedia. As shown in Fig. 3, we have plotted the experimental results on four data sets of different sizes (2.51 G, 8.22 G, 16.4 G, 24.6 G) into time curves (including 1b Words Benchmark and En-Wikipedia). Figure 3 indicates that the runtime of Word2vec and FastText increase almost linearly. But Word-Graph2vec 's runtime increases slowly (the slight increase of runtime is due to loading the word corpus).

5   Conclusion

We propose the Word-Graph2vec algorithm to improve the performance of word embedding, which converts the large corpus into a word co-occurrence graph, then takes the word sequence samples from this graph by randomly walking and trains the word embedding on these sampling corpora in the end. We argue that due to the stable vocabulary, relative idioms, and fixed expressions in English, the size and density of the word co-occurrence graph change slightly with the increase of the training corpus. Thus, Word-Graph2vec has a stable runtime on the large-scale data set, and its performance advantage becomes more and more obvious with the growth of the training corpus. Experimental results show that the proposed algorithm outperforms traditional Word2vec in terms of efficiency and two-three times than FastText.

References

1. Blanco, R., Lioma, C.: Graph-based term weighting for information retrieval. Inf. Retrieval **15**(1), 54–92 (2012)
2. Faruqui, M., Dodge, J., Jauhar, S.K., Dyer, C., Hovy, E., Smith, N.A.: Retrofitting word vectors to semantic lexicons. arXiv preprint arXiv:1411.4166 (2014)
3. Grover, A., Leskovec, J.: node2vec: scalable feature learning for networks. In: Proceedings of the 22nd ACM SIGKDD International Conference on Knowledge Discovery and Data Mining, pp. 855–864 (2016)
4. Hassan, S., Mihalcea, R., Banea, C.: Random walk term weighting for improved text classification. Int. J. Semant. Comput. **1**(04), 421–439 (2007)
5. Jastrzebski, S., Leśniak, D., Czarnecki, W.M.: How to evaluate word embeddings? on importance of data efficiency and simple supervised tasks. arXiv preprint arXiv:1702.02170 (2017)
6. Liu, R., Krishnan, A.: Pecanpy: a fast, efficient and parallelized python implementation of node2vec. Bioinformatics **37**(19), 3377–3379 (2021)
7. Manning, C., Raghavan, P., Schütze, H.: Introduction to information retrieval. Nat. Lang. Eng. **16**(1), 100–103 (2010)
8. Metz, C.E.: Basic principles of roc analysis. In: Seminars in Nuclear Medicine, vol. 8, pp. 283–298. Elsevier (1978)
9. Mikolov, T., Chen, K., Corrado, G., Dean, J.: Efficient estimation of word representations in vector space. arXiv preprint arXiv:1301.3781 (2013)
10. MultiMedia, L.: Large text compression benchmark (2009)
11. Myers, J.L., Well, A.D., Lorch, R.F., Jr.: Research Design and Statistical Analysis. Routledge, Milton Park (2013)
12. Pennington, J., Socher, R., Manning, C.D.: Glove: global vectors for word representation. In: Proceedings of the 2014 Conference on Empirical Methods in Natural Language Processing (EMNLP), pp. 1532–1543 (2014)
13. Perozzi, B., Al-Rfou, R., Skiena, S.: Deepwalk: online learning of social representations. In: Proceedings of the 20th ACM SIGKDD International Conference on Knowledge Discovery and Data Mining, pp. 701–710 (2014)
14. Schnabel, T., Labutov, I., Mimno, D., Joachims, T.: Evaluation methods for unsupervised word embeddings. In: Proceedings of the 2015 Conference on Empirical Methods in Natural Language Processing, pp. 298–307 (2015)

15. Si, Y., Wang, J., Xu, H., Roberts, K.: Enhancing clinical concept extraction with contextual embeddings. J. Am. Med. Inform. Assoc. **26**(11), 1297–1304 (2019)
16. Wang, Z.W., Wang, S.K., Wan, B.T., Song, W.W.: A novel multi-label classification algorithm based on k-nearest neighbor and random walk. Int. J. Distrib. Sens. Netw. **16**(3), 1550147720911892 (2020)

Meta-learning for Estimating Multiple Treatment Effects with Imbalance

Guanglin Zhou[1]([⊠]), Lina Yao[1,2], Xiwei Xu[2], Chen Wang[2], and Liming Zhu[2]

[1] University of New South Wales, Sydney, Australia
{guanglin.zhou,lina.yao}@unsw.edu.au
[2] Data 61, CSIRO, Eveleigh, Australia
{xiwei.xu,chen.wang,liming.zhu}@data61.csiro.au

Abstract. Ascertaining counterfactual questions, for instance, "Would individuals with diabetes have exhibited better if they had opted for a different medication?", is a frequent pursuit in research. Observational studies have become increasingly significant in addressing such queries due to their extensive availability and ease of acquisition relative to Randomized Control Trials (RCTs). Recently, approaches based on representation learning and observational data have gained attention for counterfactual inference. Nevertheless, current techniques mainly concentrate on binary treatments and do not tackle the problem of imbalance, whereby data examples in specific treatment groups are relatively limited owing to inherent user preference. In this paper, we present a pioneering model-agnostic framework for counterfactual inference, namely, MetaITE, which stands for **Meta**-learning for Estimating **I**ndividual **T**reatment **E**ffects, that resolves these research gaps. Furthermore, we introduce two complementary modules that are closely related to the problem set. The first module employs supervisory signals from multiple source treatments, while the second aligns latent distributions among treatment groups to minimize discrepancies. We assess the inference accuracy and generalization ability of MetaITE on two real-world datasets and illustrate that it surpasses state-of-the-art methods.

Keywords: Counterfactual inference · Meta-learning · Multiple imbalanced treatments

1 Introduction

Counterfactual questions, such as "Would individuals with diabetes experience an improvement in their condition had they opted for a different medication?", are prevalent in research. Representation learning, particularly when fused with domain adaptation, has exhibited its efficacy in estimating counterfactual effects from observational data.

However, current methods typically overlook the issue of imbalanced treatments, which is a significant limitation. According to [2], the issue of imbalance is recognized in the literature, but a solution to this challenge continues to remain

© The Author(s), under exclusive license to Springer Nature Singapore Pte Ltd. 2023
F. Zhang et al. (Eds.): WISE 2023, LNCS 14306, pp. 886–895, 2023.
https://doi.org/10.1007/978-981-99-7254-8_69

elusive. The aforementioned study [2] draws attention to the Infant Health and Development Program (IHDP) as a real-world example, where the number of individuals in the treated group is substantially smaller than those in the control group (139 treated and 608 control). It is contended that the settings that involve multiple imbalanced treatments are more reflective of realistic situations, thereby emphasizing the practical significance of the findings.

In this study, we address common but often overlooked issues by focusing on the scenario of multiple imbalanced treatments, where certain groups possess sufficient samples while others are limited. To address this challenge, we propose a *meta-learning* framework for counterfactual inference. This approach is chosen due to its model-agnostic nature, flexibility in integrating multiple learning tasks, and high performance in supervised classifications. Specifically, we treat the control groups with abundant samples as source domains, and the treated groups with limited examples as target domains. Note that our framework differs from MAML [10] in several aspects: (1) we transfer knowledge across groups (domains) instead of tasks; (2) Our label space remains consistent while meta-learning requires the ability to handle various tasks; (3) While MAML focuses on few-shot learning, we aim to address imbalance resulting from covariate bias, such as the price of medicine drugs. To account for distinctions (1) and (3), we incorporate the *Maximum Mean Discrepancy* (MMD) measure to align the distributions among different treatment groups, thus mitigating the effects of covariate disparity. To address difference (2), we leverage supervised information from the source groups, which we expect to yield superior performance in each group as opposed to a new one.

The key contributions are summarized as follows.

- To the best of our knowledge, this may be the first work that investigated the issue of multiple imbalanced treatments in the context of counterfactual inference.
- We design a novel model-agnostic framework MetaITE for estimating individual treatment effects, which incorporates a meta-learning paradigm, as illustrated in Fig. 1.
- Additionally, we leverage the supervised information available from the source samples and implement discrepancy measures to mitigate the distribution disparity among treatment groups.
- The superiority of our proposed approach is demonstrated through extensive experiments on two real-world datasets, where it outperforms state-of-the-art methods.

2   Related Work

Counterfactual inference is vital across various domains, with early research relying on regression methods like OLS/LR and k-NN [15]. The advent of representation learning sparked significant enhancements, introducing frameworks that combine domain adaptation [1], balanced representation [2], and GANs for treatment effects [6]. Further developments include local similarity consideration

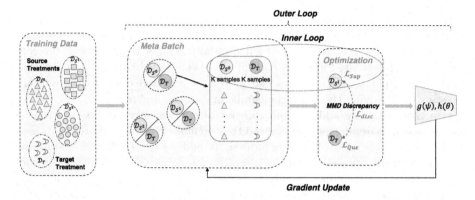

Fig. 1. The overview of our proposed model, MetaITE. We begin by collecting data, denoted as $\{\mathcal{D}_{S^j}, \mathcal{D}_T\}$, from a randomly selected source treatment group S^j, and a target treatment group T. The model parameters are updated locally on the support set within the inner loop, while in the outer loop, three losses are utilized to update the parameters globally. Moreover, to address distribution disparity among treatment groups, we incorporate the MMD discrepancy as a regularization technique.

[3], adversarial training [4], and information preservation [5]. Despite progress, challenges remain in handling multiple and imbalanced treatments.

Simultaneously, meta-learning or learning to learn has emerged as a promising field, focusing on learning across multiple data episodes. It has found application in diverse areas, including few-shot learning [10], and recently in causality [13,14]. The MAML framework [10] is prominent, with extensions like CFRNet integration for counterfactual outcomes [16]. Some works also explore small data challenges and causal directionality, differing from counterfactual inference [14].

3   Problem Setup

Let $\mathcal{X}$ denote the p-dimensional feature space, and $\mathcal{Y}$ represent the space of potential outcomes. We consider a set of observational data $\{\mathbf{x}_i, \mathbf{t}_i, \mathbf{y}_i\}_{i=1}^n$, where $\mathbf{x}_i \in \mathcal{X} \subseteq \mathbb{R}^p$ represents the vector of covariates associated with each user. Here, $\mathbf{t}_i$ signifies the treatment assigned to the respective unit, and is an element of the set of $\mathcal{T} \in \{0,1\}^k$. Meanwhile, $\mathbf{y}_i \in \mathcal{Y} \subseteq \mathbb{R}$ corresponds to the factual outcome observed.

For each unit i, a set of covariates $\{x_i^{(0)}, x_i^{(1)}, ..., x_i^{(p-1)}\}$ are obtained, together with the treatment $\mathbf{t}_i$ and factual outcome $\mathbf{y}_i$. In contrast to prior studies, we extend the treatment from binary to multiple settings, where $k \geq 2$. According to the potential outcome framework [9], each sample has k potential outcomes. We explicitly distinguish between the observed outcome, referred to as factual outcome $\mathbf{y}_i^F$, and unobserved outcomes, known as counterfactual outcomes $\mathbf{y}_i^{CF}$. Note that users only select one treatment for the factual outcome, while a collection of outcomes associated with the remaining $k-1$ treatments are all called $\mathbf{y}_i^{CF}$. Our objective is to accurately estimate both $\mathbf{y}_i^F$ and $\mathbf{y}_i^{CF}$ for each sample, given the covariates $\mathbf{x}_i$ and the treatment $\mathbf{t}_i$.

4   The Proposed Method

4.1   Base Learner Regularized with Maximum Mean Discrepancy (MMD)

The base learner f, a composite function $f = g \circ h$, consists of the feature extractor $g(\psi) : \mathcal{X} \to \mathcal{Z}$ and the inference network $h(\cdot|\theta) : \mathcal{Z} \to \mathcal{Y}$. The former embeds input space $\mathcal{X}$ into latent representation space $\mathcal{Z}$, while the latter predicts the outcome using these features. The inference network operates on latent features, enabling complex relationship capture.

In iterations, the base model is fed with source treatment $\mathcal{D}_{S^j}$ and target treatment $\mathcal{D}_T$, promoting a treatment-invariant model. We employ a fully connected neural network, denoted by $g(\mathbf{X}; \psi)$, to obtain a latent feature matrix $\mathbf{Z} = g(\mathbf{X}; \psi)$, with $\mathbf{Z}$ being a vector of real values of dimension d_z.

We enhance transferability and generalization across domains by incorporating discrepancy measures such as Maximum Mean Discrepancy (MMD), an integral probability metric. In our case, we consider distributions from the source domain S^j and target domain T, obtaining latent representations $\mathbf{Z}_{S^j}$ and $\mathbf{Z}_T$, and compute the squared MMD as:

$$\widehat{MMD}^2(\mathcal{D}_{S^j}, \mathcal{D}_T) = \left\| \sum_{n=1}^{N} \frac{k(\cdot, \mathbf{Z}_{S^j})}{N} - \sum_{m=1}^{M} \frac{k(\cdot, \mathbf{Z}_T)}{M} \right\|_{\mathcal{H}_k}^2 \tag{1}$$

$\ldots$

where $k(\cdot, \cdot)$ measures distance using a Gaussian kernel.

Through MMD, we employ $\mathcal{L}_{disc} = \widehat{MMD}^2(g(\mathbf{X}_{S^j}), g(\mathbf{X}_T))$ to gauge distribution discrepancy, promoting balanced embeddings by $g(\mathbf{X}; \psi)$. Optimization of $\mathcal{L}_{disc}$ and the objective loss $\mathcal{L}_{inf}$ is achieved by stochastic gradient descent (SGD). The network is optimized using cross-entropy loss or mean-squared error for classification and regression problems, respectively.

4.2   The MetaITE Architecture

The MetaITE framework consists of three main components: episodic training, local update, and global update, which are implemented to partition data, optimize model parameters, and update parameters, respectively.

Episodic Training. In this study, the training data originated from a collection of $k - 1$ domains, denoted by $\mathcal{D}_S = \{\mathcal{D}_{S^j}\}_{j=1}^{k-1}$, and one target domain, $\mathcal{D}_T$. To prepare the data for meta-train and meta-test, we split training data into support sets and query sets, as illustrated in Fig. 1. In particular, one source domain, S^j, is uniformly sampled from the source sets for meta-train, and the data collection $\mathcal{D}_T$ is selected for meta-test. In each outer loop, we create a meta-batch, which includes two domains, one for the source and the other for the target. We randomly select K samples from the chosen source domain as the support set, denoted by $\{\mathbf{X}_i^{Sup}, \mathbf{y}_i^{Sup}\}_{i=1}^{K}$, for the local update. Additionally, we select K identities from the target domain as the query set $\{\mathbf{X}_i^{Que}, \mathbf{y}_i^{Que}\}_{i=1}^K$, for global update. Here, K denotes a hyper-parameter.

Local Update. Our approach is based on the model-agnostic meta-learning (MAML) paradigm, which facilities the acquisition of transferable internal representations across diverse domains [10]. Notably, our objective is to ensure that the base model generalizes well across multiple domains. We initiate the learning process by training the model on the source domain, leveraging the support set $\{\mathbf{X}_i^{Sup}, \mathbf{y}_i^{Sup}\}_{i=1}^K$. The corresponding loss function is formulated as follows:

$$\mathcal{L}_{Sup} = \sum_{i=1}^K \mathcal{L}_{inf}(\mathbf{y}_i^{Sup}, h(g(\mathbf{X}_i^{Sup}; \psi); \theta)) \tag{2}$$

The parameters ψ and θ are optimized using stochastic gradient descent (SGD):

$$(\psi', \theta') \leftarrow (\psi, \theta) - \alpha \nabla_{\psi, \theta} \mathcal{L}_{Sup} \tag{3}$$

where α is a fixed hyper-parameter that determines the rate of update. In practice, we compute the updated parameters ψ' and θ' using several iterations of gradient descent updates. To simplify the presentation, we only show one iteration in Eq. 3. The model parameters are trained and optimized based on the performance of $f(\cdot \, ; \psi', \theta')$. Consequently, the meta-objective can be expressed as follows:

$$\min_{\psi} \mathcal{L}_{Sup}(f_{\psi'}) = \min_{\psi} \sum_{\{\mathbf{X}, \mathbf{y}\} \sim p(\mathcal{D}_{Sj})} \mathcal{L}_{Sup}(\mathbf{y}, f(\mathbf{X}; \psi')) \tag{4}$$

$$\min_{\theta} \mathcal{L}_{Sup}(f_{\theta'}) = \min_{\theta} \sum_{\{\mathbf{X}, \mathbf{y}\} \sim p(\mathcal{D}_{Sj})} \mathcal{L}_{Sup}(\mathbf{y}, f(\mathbf{X}; \theta')) \tag{5}$$

where the number of sums is equal to the number of gradient updates in the inner loop.

Global Update. Once we have obtained updated parameters ψ' and θ' through local updates, we optimize the loss on the query set:

$$\mathcal{L}_{Que} = \sum_{i=1}^K \mathcal{L}_{inf}(\mathbf{y}_i^{Que}, h(g(\mathbf{X}_i^{Que}; \psi'); \theta')) \tag{6}$$

Subsequently, we update the model parameters with respect to the query set loss:

$$(\psi, \theta) \leftarrow (\psi, \theta) - \beta \nabla_{\psi, \theta} \mathcal{L}_{Que} \tag{7}$$

Here, β denotes the meta-learning rate, and it is treated as a hyper-parameter. By means of the local and global updates, the base model is trained on sufficient data from source domains, enabling it to adapt swiftly to the target domain. In this way, we attain a model that generalizes well across multiple treatments.

Meta Optimization. While the MAML paradigm is capable of learning transferable information across multiple domains through the aforementioned three steps, it falls short in providing precise outcomes related to each treatment domain in the context of counterfactual inference. In addition, the performance of the inference model is impacted by domain discrepancy. Therefore, to optimize the MetaTIE jointly, we propose incorporating $\mathcal{L}_{disc}$ in Eq. (1) alongside the aforementioned losses on the support and query sets. The $\mathcal{L}_{disc}$ term in the MetaITE objective is formulated as:

$$\mathcal{L}_{disc} = \widehat{MMD}^2(g(\mathbf{X}^{Sup};\psi), g(\mathbf{X}^{Que};\psi)) \tag{8}$$

where $\widehat{MMD}^2$, as given by Eq. (1), is utilized. By enforcing consistency in the latent distributions of the source and target domains, the discrepancy among various treatment groups is mitigated after the completion of the training iterations. The final objective loss function for meta optimization is concluded, and the optimization is performed using the Adam [11] optimizer.

$$\mathcal{L}_{obj} = \mu\mathcal{L}_{Que} + \epsilon\mathcal{L}_{Sup} + \gamma\mathcal{L}_{disc} + \|\omega\|_2 \tag{9}$$

The term $\|\cdot\|_2$ represents l_2 regularization, which is employed to constrain the model complexity. In the testing phase, we construct query sets by selecting test data and sample support sets iteratively from each domain. This process enables us to obtain estimated effect outcomes for each treatment, denoted by $\{\hat{\mathbf{y}}_i^{t_i=t}\}_{t=1}^k$. Algorithm 1 demonstrates the estimate process of MetaITE.

Algorithm 1: Training process of MetaITE

1: **Input:** Set of source domains $\mathcal{D}_S = \{\mathcal{D}_{Sj}\}_{j=1}^{k-1}$; Target domain $\mathcal{D}_T = \{\mathcal{D}_T\}$
2: **Require:** Hyperparameters $\alpha, \beta, \mu, \epsilon, \gamma$
3: **Output:** Feature Extractor $g(\psi)$, Inference Network $h(\theta)$
4: ▷ learning ψ, θ from training data
5: randomly initialize model parameters ψ, θ
6: **while** Outer-loop not done **do**
7:     Uniformly select one source domain S^j
8:     Sample a batch from $\{\mathcal{D}_{Sj}, \mathcal{D}_T\}$
9:     **while** Inner-loop not done **do**
10:         K samples in support set from $\mathcal{D}_{Sj}$: $\{\mathbf{X}_i^{Sup}, \mathbf{y}_i^{Sup}\}_{i=1}^K$
11:         K samples in the query set from $\mathcal{D}_T$: $\{\mathbf{X}_i^{Que}, \mathbf{y}_i^{Que}\}_{i=1}^K$
12:         Compute $\mathcal{L}_{Sup}$ using Eq.(2)
13:         Compute adapted parameters (ψ', θ') via Eq.(3)
14:     **end while**
15:     Compute $\mathcal{L}_{Que}$ with Eq.(6)
16:     Compute discrepancy $\mathcal{L}_{disc}$ by using Eq.(8)
17:     Update $(\psi, \theta) \leftarrow (\psi, \theta) - \beta\nabla_{\psi,\theta}\mathcal{L}_{obj}$
18: **end while**

---

5   Experiments

5.1   Datasets and Preprocessing

We evaluate our approach using two real-world benchmark datasets, namely Twins and News. **Twins.** This dataset is created from all twins birth[1] that occurred in the USA between 1989–1991. We focus solely on twins who weighed less than 2kg and had no missing features [7]. For binary treatments, this dataset is the same as that used in [5,6]. **Preprocessing:** We introduce selection bias by selectively choosing one twin and hiding the other, based on the following distribution: $t_i | x_i \sim Bern(Sigmoid(w^T x_i + n))$, where $w^T \sim \mathcal{U}((-0.1, 0.1)^{30 \times 1})$ and $n \sim \mathcal{N}(0, 01)$. Moreover, we note that the mortality rate for the lighter twin is 17.7%, while that for the heavier twin is 16.1%. Concerning multiple treatments, we follow the procedure proposed in [6,7] and shape the four treatments as follows: (1) $t = 0$: lower weight and female sex, (2) $t = 1$: lower weight and male sex, (3) $t = 2$: higher weight and female sex, (4) $t = 3$: higher weight and male sex. The dataset consists of 11984 samples and 50 covariates, and the outcome is the same as that for binary treatments.

News. We employ the News dataset introduced by [1], which simulates the opinions of a media consumer who is exposed to multiple news items. The News dataset originates from the NY Times corpus[2]. **Preprocessing:** We utilize an LDA topic model [12] to characterize the topic distribution of each news item. Specifically, we select 5000 samples and learn 50 LDA topics from the corpus. The topic distribution of each news item is denoted by $z(\mathbf{X})$. To simulate multiple viewing devices, we randomly select k centroids in topic space $\{z^0, \cdots, z^{k-1}\}$ and set z^m as the mean centroid of the entire topic space. The centorids are chosen as different devices. We introduce a random Gaussian distribution with mean $\mu \sim \mathcal{N}(0.45, 0.15)$ and standard deviation $\sigma \sim \mathcal{N}(0.1, 0.05)$. We generate potential outcomes for each sample with $\tilde{y} \sim \mathcal{N}(\mu, \sigma) + \epsilon$, where $\epsilon \sim \mathcal{N}(0, 0.15)$. For each sample, we provide k potential outcomes, given by $y_i^j \sim C(\tilde{y} \mathbf{D}(z(\mathbf{X}_i), z^j) + \mathbf{D}(z(\mathbf{X}_i), z^m)), j = 0, \cdots, k - 1$, where C is a scaling factor and $\mathbf{D}$ is the Euclidean distance metric. The observed treatment is modeled as $\mathbf{t}_i | \mathbf{X}_i \sim \text{softmax}(\kappa \mathbf{y}_i)$ with a treatment assignment bias κ. The values of C and κ are set to 50 and 10, respectively, following previous work [8]. Two variants of this dataset are created with $k = \{2, 4\}$ viewing devices.

5.2   Experimental Settings

Baselines. In this work, we consider several state-of-the-art models that have demonstrated superior performance in counterfactual inference. Specifically, the model include: **OLS/LR$_1$, OLS/LR$_2$**, **k-NN** [15], **BNN** [1], **CFR-Wass**, **CFR-MMD** [2], **TARNet** [2], **GANITE, SITE, ABCEI, CBRE.**

---

[1] http://data.nber.org/data/linked-birth-infant-death-data-vital-statistics-data. html.

[2] https://archive.ics.uci.edu/ml/datasets/bag+of+words.

Evaluation Metrics. For binary treatments, we measure performance using Rooted Precision in Estimation of Heterogeneous Effect ($\sqrt{\epsilon_{PEHE}}$) and Mean Absolute Error on ATE (ϵ_{ATE}). In multiple treatments scenarios, the root mean square error ($RMSE$) is used; a smaller metric value indicates better performance.

Implementation. Baselines are conducted using parameters from respective sources, trained with Adam optimizer. MetaITE's maximum iteration is 15000. Datasets are partitioned into $80\% : 20\%$ for training and testing, with ten repetitions to compute mean and standard deviation of results.

5.3   Performance Evaluation

This section evaluates MetaITE against baselines on Twins and News datasets. For Twins_bin, the control group for $t = 0$ consists of 4594 samples, and the treated group has 80 samples. In Twins_4, $t = 0$ and $t = 2$ contain 6058 and 5926 samples; $t = 1$ and $t = 3$ each have 160 samples. MetaITE outperforms other models in both binary and four treatments, with learning-based models excelling over regression-based methods. Simpler models like CFR-Wass perform better in imbalanced settings due to limited samples. News_2 and News_4 consist of 1634 and $\{860, 80, 80, 80\}$ samples. MetaITE performs best in $\sqrt{\epsilon_{ATE}}$ for News_2 and $RMSE$ for News_4. GANITE is reported as n.r. for regression tasks. MetaITE's consistent performance and alignment with dataset imbalance show its promise. Models with higher complexity may not suit small data settings, while MetaITE addresses few-show settings through meta-learning and discrepancy measures like MMD distance (Table 1).

Table 1. Performance Evaluation of **MetaITE** in comparison with other state-of-the-art methods on the Twins and News datasets. The best performing method is highlighted in bold. A lower value corresponds to better performance. In some cases, a value of n.r. is reported due to null values or failure to achieve convergence.

Methods	Twins_bin		News_2		Twins_4	News_4
	$\sqrt{\epsilon_{PEHE}}$	ϵ_{ATE}	$\sqrt{\epsilon_{PEHE}}$	ϵ_{ATE}	$RMSE$	$RMSE$
OLS/LR$_1$	0.310 ± 0.0	0.008 ± 0.0	16.179 ± 0.0	16.977 ± 0.0	0.227 ± 0.0	11.045 ± 0.0
OLS/LR$_2$	0.318 ± 0.0	0.010 ± 0.0	14.196 ± 0.0	12.693 ± 0.0	n.r.	16.334 ± 0.0
K-NN	0.310 ± 0.0	0.008 ± 0.0	27.347 ± 0.0	26.360 ± 0.0	0.236 ± 0.0	8.755 ± 0.0
BNN	0.318 ± 0.0	0.010 ± 0.0	$\mathbf{13.639 \pm 0.0}$	12.190 ± 0.0	1.494 ± 0.0	9.457 ± 0.0
TARNet	0.336 ± 0.0	0.010 ± 0.0	19.056 ± 0.0	19.055 ± 0.0	0.193 ± 0.0	9.259 ± 0.0
CFR-Wass	0.311 ± 0.0	0.008 ± 0.0	19.239 ± 0.0	19.238 ± 0.0	0.195 ± 0.0	9.458 ± 0.0
CFR-MMD	0.336 ± 0.0	0.010 ± 0.0	19.264 ± 0.0	19.263 ± 0.0	0.197 ± 0.0	10.784 ± 0.0
GANITE	0.323 ± 0.0	0.069 ± 0.0	n.r.	n.r.	0.228 ± 0.040	n.r.
SITE	0.318 ± 0.0	0.007 ± 0.0	20.592 ± 0.0	16.778 ± 0.0	0.200 ± 0.0	9.227 ± 0.0
ABCEI	n.r.	n.r.	n.r.	n.r.	0.209 ± 0.0	n.r.
CBRE	0.330 ± 0.0	0.011 ± 0.0	19.543 ± 0.0	19.542 ± 0.0	0.210 ± 0.0	11.945 ± 0.0
MetaITE	$\mathbf{0.309 \pm 0.0}$	$\mathbf{0.006 \pm 0.0}$	17.173 ± 0.4	$\mathbf{9.255 \pm 0.7}$	$\mathbf{0.192 \pm 0.0}$	$\mathbf{8.730 \pm 0.1}$

5.4 Ablation Study

We explore loss functions on News_2 and News_4, with l_2 regularization weight decay of 0.05, varying hyper-parameters $\{\mu, \epsilon, \gamma\}$ from 0 to 1 in steps of 0.1. Top three $\sqrt{PEHE}$ results for News_2: 17.1726 with $\{1.0, 0.9, 1.0\}$, 18.9048 with $\{1.0, 0.8, 1.0\}$, 19.1451 with $\{1.0, 0.7, 1.0\}$. For News_4 in terms of RMSE: 8.7303 with $\{1.0, 0.0, 1.0\}$, 8.9489 with $\{0.3, 0.0, 0.8\}$, 8.9807 with $\{0.8, 0.0, 1.0\}$. Discrepancy loss weight is crucial; source loss is less useful for News_4. Optimal values are $\{1.0, 0.0, 1.0\}$ for News_4 and $\{1.0, 0.9, 1.0\}$ for News_2.

5.5 Robustness Study of Imbalanced Treatments

We evaluate MetaITE's ability to handle imbalanced treatments, varying the treated group's sample size from 100% to 5% (imbalance from 1 to 20) with 4561 samples in the control group and 4464 in the treated group. Employing $\sqrt{PEHE}$ as the metric, Fig. 2 shows MetaITE outperforms four models in inference performance and robustness as imbalance grows.

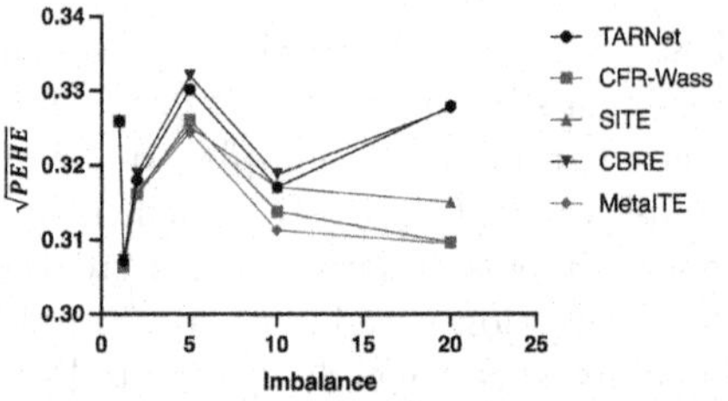

Fig. 2. Robustness Study of imbalanced treatments on Twins_bin. The term imbalance denotes the configuration of the proportion of control sizes to treated samples in the experiment.

6 Conclusion

This paper addresses the research gap in the area of multiple imbalanced treatments and introduces a novel model-agnostic framework for counterfactual inference. The proposed framework, MetaITE, builds on the flexbile MAML approach and introduces two additional regularizers to enhance inference performance. Specifically, it leverages distribution discrepancy measures and supervision signals from groups with sufficient samples. We evaluate the effectiveness of our model on two real-world benchmarks and report superior performance compared to eleven baseline models. In future work, we aim to scale up this framework to handle an even larger number of treatments.

References

1. Johansson, F., Shalit, U., Sontag, D.: Learning representations for counterfactual inference. In: International Conference on Machine Learning, pp. 3020–3029 (2016)
2. Shalit, U., Johansson, F., Sontag, D.: Estimating individual treatment effect: generalization bounds and algorithms. In: International Conference on Machine Learning, pp. 3076–3085 (2017)
3. Yao, L., Li, S., Li, Y., Huai, M., Gao, J., Zhang, A.: Representation learning for treatment effect estimation from observational data. In: Advances in Neural Information Processing Systems, vol. 31 (2018)

4. Du, X., Sun, L., Duivesteijn, W., Nikolaev, A., Pechenizkiy, M.: Adversarial balancing-based representation learning for causal effect inference with observational data. Data Min. Knowl. Disc. **35**(4), 1713–1738 (2021)
5. Zhou, G., Yao, L., Xu, X., Wang, C., Zhu, L.: Cycle-balanced representation learning for counterfactual inference. In: SDM (2022)
6. Yoon, J., Jordon, J., Van Der Schaar, M.: GANITE: estimation of individualized treatment effects using generative adversarial nets. In: International Conference on Learning Representations (2018)
7. Louizos, C., Shalit, U., Mooij, J., Sontag, D., Zemel, R., Welling, M.: Causal effect inference with deep latent-variable models. ArXiv Preprint ArXiv:1705.08821 (2017)
8. Schwab, P., Linhardt, L., Bauer, S., Buhmann, J., Karlen, W.: Learning counterfactual representations for estimating individual dose-response curves. Proceedings Of The AAAI Conference On Artificial Intelligence. **34**, 5612–5619 (2020)
9. Rubin, D.: Causal inference using potential outcomes: Design, modeling, decisions. J. Am. Stat. Assoc. **100**, 322–331 (2005)
10. Finn, C., Abbeel, P., Levine, S.: Model-agnostic meta-learning for fast adaptation of deep networks. In: International Conference on Machine Learning, pp. 1126–1135 (2017)
11. Kingma, D., Ba, J.: Adam: A method for stochastic optimization. ArXiv Preprint ArXiv:1412.6980 (2014)
12. Blei, D., Ng, A., Jordan, M.: Latent dirichlet allocation. J. Mach. Learn. Res. **3**, 993–1022 (2003)
13. Bengio, Y., et al.: A meta-transfer objective for learning to disentangle causal mechanisms. ArXiv Preprint ArXiv:1901.10912 (2019)
14. Ton, J., Sejdinovic, D., Fukumizu, K.: Meta learning for causal direction. Proc. AAAI Conf. Artif. Intell. **35**, 9897–9905 (2021)
15. Crump, R., Hotz, V., Imbens, G., Mitnik, O.: Nonparametric tests for treatment effect heterogeneity. Rev. Econ. Stat. **90**, 389–405 (2008)
16. Sharma, A., Gupta, G., Prasad, R., Chatterjee, A., Vig, L., Shroff, G.: Metaci: Meta-learning for causal inference in a heterogeneous population, ArXiv Preprint ArXiv:1912.03960 (2019)

SML: Semantic Machine Learning Model Ontology

Lara Kallab[1]([✉]), Elio Mansour[2], and Richard Chbeir[3]

[1] Open Group, 92300 Levallois Perret, France
lara.kallab@open-groupe.com
[2] Scient Analytics, Paris, France
elio.mansour@scient.io
[3] Univ Pau & Pays Adour, E2S UPPA, LIUPPA, EA3000, Anglet, France
richard.chbeir@univ-pau.fr

Abstract. Artificial Intelligence is a set of technologies that simulate human-like cognition, using computer software and systems, to perform tasks associated with intelligent beings. One method of doing so, is Machine Learning (ML), which enhances system efficiency based on learning algorithms that create models from data and its underlying patterns. Nowadays, many ML models are being generated with different characteristics (e.g., type of the algorithm used, data set used to train it, resulting model performance), thus making the selection of a suitable model for a given use case a complex task, especially for non-expert users (with no or limited knowledge in ML). In this paper, we propose SML, an ontology-based model for Semantic Machine Learning description. SML allows, mainly, to describe and store ML models' characteristics with their operational specifications, related data features, contextual usage, and evaluation metrics/scores to facilitate and improve ML model selection. The conducted experiments show promising results on both the efficiency and the performance levels.

Keywords: Machine Learning Model · Supervised Learning · Ontology · Data Set · Context Description · Model Evaluation

1 Introduction

Today, Artificial Intelligence (AI) has become a major player in a wide range of fields (e.g., social, commercial, industrial), such as speech recognition, medical diagnosis, autonomous vehicles and building automation [5]. It is basically a computer system designed to mimic human intelligence by accessing data from numerous sources and systems, allowing to make decisions and learn from the outcomes. Machine Learning (ML) is an implementation of the AI that enables computers to learn from data without specific programming [12]. It is focused on building models that can learn from historical data, to identify meaningful data relationships and patterns [6], and make logical decisions with little or no human intervention. ML automates the construction of analytical models using data that encompasses various forms of numerical information including numbers, words, images, etc.

In ML, there are a plethora of models that a user can adopt and reuse (without the need to create new models every time), all having their own specifications and uses. Each model has different characteristics, such as the type of algorithm the model relies on (e.g., Linear Regression and Bayes Classifier [8]), the data set used to train it, the application domain (e.g., finance, travel and transportation), its performance, etc. All this makes the task of selecting a suitable model, for a given use case, a complex one especially for non-expert users (having limited or no ML knowledge). Choosing the right model for a specific use case is essential. In fact, the better the machine learning model fits a given case, the more accurately it can find features and patterns in the data. This means better decision-making, with more accurate analysis and forecasts. For example, using a regression model trained on a winter season data, to predict data related to a summer season, will more likely cause poor quality in the predicted results, since the learning of the model is applied on a different data set pattern (in terms of season). Therefore, it is necessary to describe ML models and represent their main characteristics, in a semantic form, to know how and where each model ca be better used/adopted, and understand their operating context. This allows to compare, evaluate and propose the most appropriate model(s) for a specific application scenario.

In the literature, there are several models, approaches, and reviews that describe machine learning models' characteristics, applicability, and performance. However, these works have several limitations. For instance, most of them, [1,2,7,10,14], do not describe well the data sets used to train and test the models. In addition, the majority of the works, [7,10,11,14], does not take into account model application domain and model operational performance. Also, none of them describes well the model usability or its context (e.g., temporal context, spatial context), and neglects considering model metadata on several levels (e.g., ML model metadata, algorithm metadata, data set metadata). The aforementioned criteria are important to consider in order to facilitate the usability and the selection of the ML models. Given the limitations of the existing solutions in representing machine learning models, which is essential for understanding their functioning, their applications, evaluating them, and comparing them, we propose, in this paper, **SML**: an ontology-based model for **S**emantic **M**achine **L**earning description. SML describes machine learning models through a human and a machine understandable vocabulary, to ease the comprehension, the evaluation and the selection of the convenient ML model to be used in a given context. As it is based on an ontology model [9], SML gives the same meaning to the specified and exchanged ML models characteristics and operating specifications. This makes it easier for systems, from various organizations and platforms, to store, integrate, and share ML knowledge, enabling both syntactic and semantic interoperability, and allowing for future extensibility and adaptation.

The rest of the paper is organized as follows. Section 2 presents a scenario to motivate the usability and applicability of our work. Section 3 reviews the related work and highlights the added value of our model. Section 4 details the specifications of our proposed semantic machine learning model ontology. Section 5 evaluates the efficiency and the performance of the solution. Finally, Sect. 6 summarizes the work and discusses future research directions.

2   Motivating Scenario

In order to show the motivation behind our proposal, consider the following Smart City scenario illustrated in Fig. 1. The environment is densely covered by an extensive Wireless Sensor Network (WSN) that collects a wide variety of data from the city (e.g., CO_2 emissions, lighting conditions, noise levels, energy consumption, temperature). The city has appointed a team of experts to help monitor, analyze, and forecast elements from within the city, in an effort to make it a smart, proactive, safe, and healthy environment for its occupants. The team members have different expertise and are interested in forecasting and analyzing data related to their respective fields. Figure 1 illustrates some examples: (i) environmental experts are interested in predicting noise, air, and water pollution levels, to make the city a more healthy space; (ii) road safety experts are interested in predicting traffic congestion, risky traffic hours/conditions, and road deterioration to avoid deadly accidents; (iii) weather experts are interested in predicting rising temperatures and extreme weather conditions, in order to disseminate important information to the city occupants, in a proactive manner; and (iv) energy experts are interested in analyzing and predicting energy consumption, and production levels/patterns in the city, to help make it a greener more eco-friendly place.

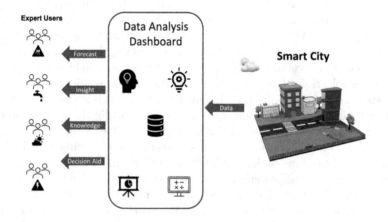

Fig. 1. Smart City Scenario

The aforementioned team members often need to collaborate with each other on cross-field projects. More importantly, they all need to generate, train, test, and deploy prediction models that ingest the collected data on one end, and provide the required forecasts on the other. In such a dynamic and collaborative environment, it is easy to quickly end up with a huge number of machine learning models each: (i) covering a specific need; (ii) relying on a specific algorithm; (iii) using a specific data set for training; (iv) having a specific level accuracy; and (v) deployed in a specific application domain/field of interest.

In order to sustain this collaborative workspace, prevent isolated analysis, and provide a decision-making process based on collective intelligence and shared insights, the team members require a system capable of storing, and recommending ML models for each new application use case. This will enable model re-usage instead of creating slightly different models every time one needs to make a prediction, and will ensure reproducibility of experiments in the context of open science. The system would suggest and retrieve a model that best fits the user's need if such model already exists. Otherwise, the user can always generate a new model from scratch. This will significantly prove useful when considering the growing number of ML models that will be generated over time. Moreover, such a recommendation system would increase users' understanding of the existing models, improve result explain-ability, and allow the team to collaborate in a more productive manner. In order to deliver this ML model recommendation engine, one needs to address two main sets of challenges related to: **(i) Model Representation**: this entails the challenges related to the description of the models, as well as their metadata, technical aspects (i.e., algorithmic specifications), used data sets (i.e., training, testing features/data specifications), the application domains in which the models are eventually deployed, and the evaluation metrics/scores; and **(ii) Model Recommendation:** this entails a whole different set of challenges related to model similarity measures, model recommendation processes, and model recommendation optimization. In this work, we solely focus on the first set of challenges related to the model representation. We will consider model recommendation in a future dedicated work. As a result, we specifically focus here on the following challenges:

Challenge 1. How to extensively represent the machine learning models and their various descriptive metadata? This helps users to easily search, version, and retrieve the existing ML models (e.g., describing when, where, and by whom a model was generated and for which purpose/application domain).

Challenge 2. How to cover technical aspects and map models to the algorithms that generated them? How to categorize technical specifications to allow easy search and retrieval of ML models? This helps clustering and filtering models based on their underlying technical features (e.g., separating classification from regression, linear from nonlinear, statistical from deep learning).

Challenge 3. How to cover the different intricacies of the training and testing data sets in the modeling? How to capture the context (i.e., spatial, temporal, or feature-based) of the data sets that help build and evaluate the ML models in the representation? This allows comparing model similarity from a data perspective, as well as discovering the usage context of the models based on their training/testing data set features (e.g., differentiating an indoor from an outdoor temperature prediction model since their contexts differ).

Challenge 4. How to include the application domains where the models are eventually deployed in the description? This allows a higher level clustering/categorization of the ML models based on their field of application, which will consequently improve model suggestion to users based on their expertise (e.g., to provide team members from various fields with the useful models that are applicable in their application domain).

Challenge 5. How to include model evaluation metrics and scores in the representation? The evaluation is crucial for ranking and presenting adequate models for user needs (e.g., to provide energy experts with the most accurate model for energy prediction in a smart building).

Existing works focus mainly on data set similarity or some performance metrics when trying to suggest an adequate model for a specific task. In this work, we aim to extend existing solutions by considering a more complete set of concepts (e.g., application domains, usage scenarios/contexts, technical algorithmic aspects) that could impact a ML model recommendation. However, before detailing our proposal, we review, next, related works about Machine Learning model representation and evaluate the state of the art based on the challenges/requirements of our motivating scenario.

3   State of the Art

In this section, we study several ML description models, approaches, and reviews, that are defined to mainly, give knowledge about ML techniques and algorithms (e.g., categories, advantages, to mention a few), and to describe their performance and applicability. We compare these solutions according to the following different criteria, grouped into two categories:

1. *ML representation criteria*: which include the criteria used to represent ML models, their generation/building process, their behavior, their performance, and useful metadata descriptors:
   - **Criterion 1.A. Algorithm representation:** denoting the ability to describe and link the models to the corresponding ML algorithms that generated them, thus allowing the inference of their usability, and technical limitations.
   - **Criterion 1.B. Data representation:** denoting the representation of the data sets used to train and test the ML models including their characteristics (e.g., the features, their values, and statistical descriptors).
   - **Criterion 1.C. Performance representation:** denoting the ability to include accuracy and performance metrics/descriptions for each ML model, to give insights on the quality of the obtained results and allow for ML models comparisons.

    – **Criterion 1.D. Metadata representation:** denoting the ability to include meta descriptors that enrich the ML modeling and include various high-level features/information (e.g., data set metadata, algorithm metadata, model metadata).

2. ***ML usability and compatibility criteria:*** which hold the criteria used to describe the application domain and the context of each ML model:

    – **Criterion 2.A. Application-domain representation:** denoting the ability to cover a keyword-based representation of various application domains and link ML models to these domains (e.g., linking a temperature prediction model to environmental monitoring application domain).

    – **Criterion 2.B. Usability representation:** denoting the ability to specify several ML models contexts (i.e., defining the environment constraints) in each application domain, to know where each ML model can be more convenient to be applied for more accurate results (e.g., when using a regression prediction model trained on a winter season data in a summer season, the quality of the results will be negatively affected).

3.1 Ontology-Based ML Description Models

MLOnto [2], Machine Learning Ontology, is an ontology that represents knowledge about the Machine Learning discipline. It consists of 7 main classes: Algorithms, Applications, Dependencies, Dictionary, Frameworks, Involved, and MLTypes. Despite representing different ML types (i.e., AutoML, Reinforcement Learning, Semi-supervised Machine Learning, Supervised Learning, and Unsupervised Learning), the representation of the model is very high level and limited, as it neglects several criteria, e.g., Data sets representation (training sets and testing sets), model performance, and usability.

In [4] an ontology-based approach is proposed for making Machine Learning systems accountable. The approach is based on three phases: (1) the creation of the predictive models and their deployment for availability, (2) the annotation of pertinent information derived from the predictive models and forecasts by using ontological-based terms, and (3) the storage of the annotated data while providing means to exploit them for accountability. The second phase is based on two areas. In the first one, the forecasts produced by the predictive model are represented, by using three ontologies models: the AffectedBy ontology (https://iesnaola.github.io/AffectedBy), the Execution-Executor-Procedure (EEP) (https://iesnaola.github.io/EEP), and the Result Context (RC) (https://iesnaola.github.io/RC). In the second one, the predictive procedures used for achieving the forecasts are modeled via the ML-Schema ontology [13]. Despite that these ontologies' models cover many aspects of Machine Learning models, including model performance and training data sets representation, they lack in considering several criteria, such as the model context (other than the temporal and the spatial ones) with its constraints (whenever it is necessary) and the model application domain.

Authors in [1] define an ontology-based IML (Interpretable Machine Learning), OnML, for generating semantic explanations, by using interpretable models, ontologies, and information extraction techniques, in order to generate semantic explanations. This is done by identifying and including ontology-based tuples into a sampling strategy, where the semantic relationships between terms, words, and ideas, are sampled and captured in training the interpretable model, rather of using each of them separately. To reduce the search space for semantic explanations, an anchor learning method is also proposed. The work mainly focuses on using ontologies models for semantic explanation of the predicted ML results, without representing or describing the ML data sets, their behavior, context, etc. However, by relying on the ontologies' models, the approach gives some hints regarding the application domain of the used ML, as well as their usability.

3.2   Context-Aware ML Description Approaches

The work in [11] describes an approach that uses contextual information to train ML models. It mainly consists of training ML models to maximize a specific scoring function for each operating context. In the experiments, the context-aware approach results, obtained from specialized models that were trained for each particular context, were compared against the use of a general model that was trained using all contexts. The results demonstrate that the suggested approach lessens bias toward a strategy that employs a special general model, however, the error difference is considered to be low. Therefore, an evaluation is needed to identify which strategy fits more application needs. Nonetheless, the context-aware approach should be taken into consideration, depending on how crucial the application resources needs are (such as connectivity and memory). Comparing the proposed approach to our work, the contexts of the ML models are manually defined and used, without being represented (nor other aspects, e.g., data sets, application domains, etc.) via a machine understandable form, which allows for the correct and the automatic usage of ML models in the right contexts.

3.3   Reviews and Surveys-Based ML Description

In [14], a review is given to provide definitions and a foundational understanding of the ML categories (i.e., Supervised, Unsupervised, and Reinforcement Learning). It discusses methods for the design of supervised ML studies, and introduces the bias-variance trade-off, as a key theoretical underpinning for supervised Machine Learning. The work provides an overview and a description of common supervised ML algorithms (Linear Regression, Logistic Regression, Naive Bayes, etc.), however, it does not represent them (i.e., data sets, applications domains, etc.) through a comprehensive model to machine, allowing for their correct usage in the required cases.

In [10], a survey is given to discuss the strength and the weakness of different ML algorithms: Logic basic algorithms (e.g., Decision Trees and Learning Set of Rules), Statistical learning algorithms (e.g., Bayesian Networks), Instance-based Learning, Support Vector Machines, and Deep Learning. Despite describing the scope of the usage of each ML algorithm, such a description is dedicated to users that should have some expertise to know how and where these MLs' are better

Table 1. Evaluation of existing ML description models and approaches w.r.t. the identified criteria

	1. ML Representation Criteria				2. ML Usability & Compatibility	
	Algorithm	Data	Performance	Metadata	Application domain	Usability
MLOnto, 2020 [2]	+	-	-	Limited	+	-
ML-Schema, 2021 [4]	+	+	+	Limited	-	Limited
OnML Approach, 2022 [1]	-	-	-	-	Limited	Limited
Context-aware ML-based Approach, 2018 [11]	-	-	-	-	-	Limited
Review, 2019 [14]	Limited*	-	Limited*	-	Limited*	Limited
Survey, 2015 [10]	Limited*	-	Limited*	-	Limited*	Limited
Study, 2020 [7]	Limited*	-	Limited*	-	Limited*	Limited

used. Our work goes further beyond by describing ML models, in terms of the data sets used, the corresponding application domain, etc., through an understandable machine form that facilitates ML use, based on different contexts.

The study in [7] gives an overview of ML classifications (i.e., Unsupervised, Semi-supervised, and Reinforcement), and presents three different ways (i.e., Clustering, Classification, and Prediction) that ML is used in enterprises. The work also includes a process model for choosing ML algorithms based on the type of data, intended interpretability, and desired accuracy. Although the study helps in comprehending the state of ML techniques, and their applicability in enterprise applications, along with the trade-off between their interpretability and their accuracy, it misses several aspects that are important to consider, to know what ML model is better to use in particular cases, e.g., describing ML data sets, their corresponding contexts, etc. This is apart from neglecting ML models description using a comprehensible machine format, reducing, thus, users expertise and knowledge.

In Table 1, we show the comparative study of the ML description models, approaches and reviews previously described, based on the criteria outlined at the beginning of this section. We utilized the "+" symbol to indicate a criterion's positive coverage, the "-" symbol to indicate a criterion's lack of coverage, "Limited" to denote partial coverage of a criterion, and "Limited*" to indicate partial coverage of a criterion with a lack of implementation/proposed model.

4 Semantic Machine Learning Model Ontology

To describe and store the characteristics and the operational specifications of ML models, which are necessary to facilitate ML models comprehension behavior, and ease their selection in the right contexts, we present, in this section, an ontology-based model entitled SML, for Semantic Machine Learning description. SML, which is represented in Fig. 2 via entities an relationships between these entities, is based on a vocabulary that can be used by different environments and/or platforms to describe ML models in a normalized manner. We note that attributes of each entity are not shown in Fig. 2 for the sake of clarity.

4.1   SML Ontology Features

SML Model' Representation and Application. As shown in Fig. 3, a semantic Machine Learning Model, is a model that is designed to recognize patterns or behaviors in some collected data, based on previous or historical data, referred to as training data set (*SML:TrainingDataSet*). A training data set is a data set (*SML:DataSet*) that is used during the learning process to fit (train) a model for prediction or classification of values that are known in the training set, but unknown in other (future) data. Each SML model has some metadata (*SML:MetaData*), e.g., Creation Date, Model Developer, etc., and is applicable in specific application domains (*SML:ApplicationDomain*), such as smart buildings, healthcare, transportation, etc.

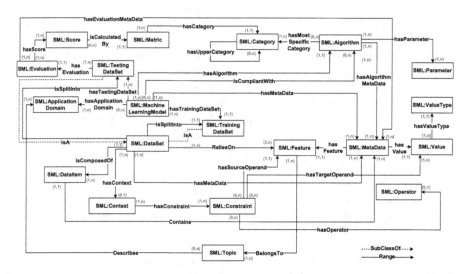

Fig. 2. Overview of the proposed Semantic Machine Learning (SML) model ontology

SML models are based on specific algorithms (*SML:Algorithm*), e.g., Naïve Bayes, Support Vector Machines, Decision Trees, etc., having, each, some metadata (e.g., Creation Date, Description), and some parameters (i.e., key-value pairs). An algorithm belongs to a specific category (*SML:Category*), such as Classification and Regression, which might have, if necessary, subcategories through the relation "hasUpperCategory". Some SML models that are based on particular algorithms (e.g., Linear Regression) can be compliant, through the relation "isCompliantWith", with other algorithms (e.g., Lasso Regression). This can be known by applying several calculations and studies on the training data set used for each SML model, along with their contexts (see subsection below).

SML Data Set Modeling and Context. As represented in Fig. 4, a data set, *SML:DataSet*, can be splitted into either: (1) a training data set

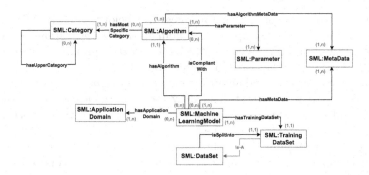

Fig. 3. SML model' representation and application

(*SML:TrainingDataSet)* that is used to train the SML model, or (2) a testing data set (*SML:TestingDataSet*), which is used to test and evaluate the SML model after being trained (see Fig. 5). It is composed of data items (*SML:DataItem*). A data item has some metadata (*SML:MetaData*). Each metadata has a feature, *SML:Feature* (e.g., Creation Date, Description, Temperature, Location), and a value, *SML:Value*, linked to a value type, *SML:ValueType*. We defined concepts for each of the features, values and type of values, to be able to apply on some features values, specific constraints (see below), which can be in many cases necessary to describe the context of ML models.

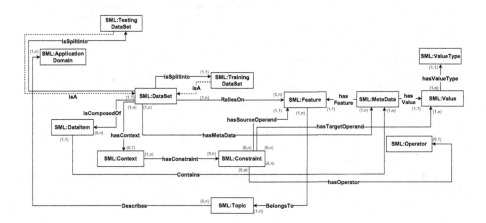

Fig. 4. SML data set' modeling and context

A data set, which has also some metadata, relies on, at least, two features, having, each, some attributes, such as a Name, a Type (e.g., categorical, textual, numerical), a Range, and a Boolean value (to check whether it is an independent feature or not). The independent feature is the cause. Its value is independent of other variables in the study. The dependent feature is the effect. Its value depends on changes in the independent feature. Features belong to topics (*SML:Topic*) that are used to describe the application domain (*SML:ApplicationDomain*) of a SML model. A data set has a context (*SML:Context*) represented by constraints (*SML:Constraint*), having, each, a source operand, i.e., *SML:Feature*, a target operand, i.e., *SML:Value*, and an operator (*SML:Operator*). For example, we can have a spatio-temporal context defined by the "Season" feature, with the value "Winter", and by a "Location" feature having "Paris" as a value. Such context allows to know that, for instance, the training data set of a specific ML model, is related to Paris in Winter. Contexts also enable to use some data sets for other ML models, depending on the matching or how closely their contexts are.

SML Model Evaluation. Once the machine learning model is built using the training data set, it needs to be tested using data, referred to as testing data set (*SML:TestingDataSet*). A testing data set is used to evaluate the performance and progress of the SML model training, which might need to be adjusted or optimized for improved results. As shown in Fig. 5, a testing data set has an evaluation (*SML:Evaluation*). Each evaluation has some metadata (*SML:hasEvaluationMetaData*), and a score (*SML:Score*) that is computed using some metrics (*SML:Metric*), e.g., MAPE (Mean Absolute Percentage Error) and MSE (Mean Squared Error) [3]. The metrics are grouped into categories (*SML:Category*), depending on the algorithm used to build the SML model.

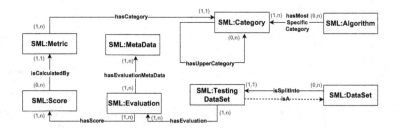

Fig. 5. SML model' evaluation

Next, we present the evaluation of the SML ontology model on two aspects: the efficiency and the performance, after being implemented.

5   Experimental Evaluation

In this section, we outline the experimental procedure that we used to evaluate SML ontology. It is founded on two types of evaluation:

1. *Evaluation of its efficiency:* This involves determining if the concepts and properties (objects and data properties) established in the SML ontology, are capable of overcoming the various challenges described in Sect. 2, and of meeting the criteria listed in Sect. 3.

2. *Evaluation of its performance:* This entails studying the response time of the SML ontology, by applying various simple and complex queries on different simulated SML model instances. Such instances are based on several configurations (e.g., increasing the number of SML models, their data-items, the used features in their training data sets, etc.).

5.1   Efficiency Evaluation

In this part, we define the most useful queries (see Table 2), which can be applied to the SML ontology, to help in facing the challenges identified and explained in Sect. 2. Also, we analyze the ability of these queries in meeting the criteria presented in Sect. 3. The following link: https://tinyurl.com/bdrudrtw, shows the list of queries that we used, expressed in SPARQL[1].

As shown in Table 2, different queries can be used to interrogate the SML ontology model. For instance, the Query *Q1*, where we require the algorithm of a given ML model, meets the challenge 2, which includes mapping models to the algorithms that generated them. The representation of a ML model algorithm is a criterion that is part of the ML representation, hence the relationship between the Query *Q1* and the ML representation criteria. Another example of a query is Query *Q7* that requires the description of the training data set context of a given ML model. The Query *Q7* takes up challenge 3, which covers the context of the data sets (training or testing data sets) features to help build and evaluate the ML models, and meets ML usability and compatibility criteria, as it specifies the ML context.

Table 2. List of useful queries overcoming the required challenges and meeting the needed criteria

	ML Representation Criteria	ML Usability and Compatibility Criteria
Challenge 1	Q5- Retrieve the metadata of a given ML model, with those related to its algorithm, its training data set, its testing data set, and to the evaluations applied to the testing data	
Challenge 2	Q1 - Retrieve the algorithm of a given ML model	
Challenge 3	Q2 - Describe the training data set of a given ML model Q3 - Describe the testing data set of a given ML model	Q7 - Describe the training data context of a given ML model
Challenge 4		Q6 - Find the application domain of each ML model, and give a clear description of this domain
Challenge 5	Q4 - Retrieve the performance of a given ML model (i.e., the scores and the metrics used to calculate the evaluation applied to the testing data)	

5.2   Performance Evaluation

In this part, we took into consideration five different scenarios, to evaluate the performance of the SML ontology model, in terms of the response time, while

---

[1] A standard query language that is able to retrieve and manipulate data stored in Resource Description Framework (RDF) format.

applying several queries on the SML model. The scenarios were made by simulating different SML models using "Protégé" tool https://protege.stanford.edu/,
through which all information about data sets for instance were filled, and varying their criteria: (1) their number (the number of SML model instances), (2)
the number of the data items used in their training data set, (3) the number of
the used features in their training data set, (4) the number of metrics used to
compute the score of their testing data set, and (5) the number of their metadata. We display the query response time (ms) in the experiments based on
an average of 10 sequential executions for each query. The tests have been carried out using "Stardog" (https://www.stardog.com/), a platform for enterprise
knowledge graph, run on a Windows 10 Professional machine having an Intel
i7-8665U CPU @ 1.90 GHz 2.11 GHz processor and 1 GB RAM.

Impact of ML Models Instances and Their Metadata. In the first scenario
(see Fig. 6-(a)), we studied the impact of varying the number of ML models
instances, when requiring the set of models having a given algorithm (i.e., Linear
Regression). In the scenario, we fixed the number of algorithms to 50, linked every
ML model (between 100 and 10000 models) to a single algorithm (as defined in
the SML ontology), and measured the corresponding query response time. As
per the resulted graph curve, the query run time increases quasi-linearly with the
increased number of ML models instances. The time evolution is more important
between the first two tests, as the number of ML models was increased from 100
to 1000 (with a difference of 900 models), contrary to the rest of the other tests,
where the increased number of ML models was more constant (with a difference
of 2000/3000 models).

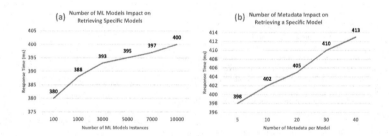

Fig. 6. Number of ML models instances vs ML models metadata impact

In the second scenario (see Fig. 6-(b)), we studied the impact of varying the
number of metadata related to each ML model instance, when requesting the
set of the metadata related to a specific model. In the scenario, we fixed the
number of ML models to 500, varied the number of their data items (from 5 to
40), and measured the corresponding query response time. The resulted curve
shows that the query execution time evolves linearly with the increased number
of metadata defined for each ML model.

Impact of Data Items and Features Used in ML Training Data Sets. In Fig. 7-(a), we looked at the effect of varying the number of data items included within the training data sets of ML models, while demanding the set of the data items of a specific model. We limited the number of ML models in the tests to 100, varied the numbers of data items used in the training data sets of the ML models (from 100 to 1000), and then, calculated the query response time. The resulted graph demonstrates that as more metadata are defined for each ML model training data set, the query run time increases linearly.

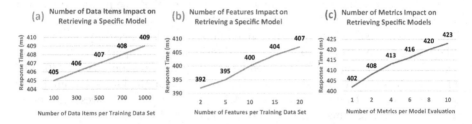

Fig. 7. Training data set data items vs Training data set features vs ML evaluation metrics impact

In Fig. 7-(b), we investigated the impact of increasing the number of features used in the training data sets of the ML models, while requesting the set of the features used for a particular model. We set a cap of 1000 ML models for each test, distributed different number of features (from 2 to 20) to each ML model training data set, and then retrieved the corresponding query response time. The resulted graph shows that the run time evolves linearly with the increased number of features used for each ML model training data set.

Impact of ML Evaluation Metrics. In the last scenario, we looked into the impact of adding metrics in the evaluation score related to the testing data set of ML models (see Fig. 7-(c)). In the tests, where we requested the top 3 ML models having the best evaluation score, we fixed the number of ML models to 1000 and varied the number of score metrics from 1 to 10 (e.g., MAPE and MSE [3]), and got the corresponding query response time. From the resulted graph, we can see that as the number of metrics used in the score (to evaluate ML models testing data sets) increases, the run time evolves linearly.

Discussion. In the experimental scenarios, the resulted graphs reveal promising and positive linear curves, indicating that the query execution response time increases linearly with the growing number of ML models instances, their metadata, their data items and features used in their training data, as well as the number of the metrics used to compute the score of their testing data set. This shows a proportionate relation, with almost a constant growth between the various variables employed and the query execution time. The findings also highlight that the curves of the graphs, in which we increased the number of ML models instances (see Fig. 6-(a)), where the time jump is equal to 20 ms, and the number of the score metrics of the ML models evaluation (see Fig. 7-(c)), where the time jump is equal to 21 ms, are more important than the others, as the time jumps are equal to 15 ms, 4 ms and 15 ms, respectively, in Fig. 6-(b), Fig. 7-(a) and Fig. 7-(b). In Fig. 6-(a), the time jump is explained by the huge number of ML models instances we used (10000), and in Fig. 7-(c), the time jump can be dedicated to the fact that there were more concepts to reach in the query (*SML:MachineLearningModel*, *SML:TestingDataSet*, *SML:Evaluation*, *SML:Score*, and *SML:Metric*). Moreover, we can see that the increased number of metadata, and the number of features used in ML models training data sets, have the same resulted curve with a time jump equal to 15 ms, despite of varying different variables: from 5 to 40 for metadata number, comparing to 2 to 20 for features number. This can be justified by the very close response times (405 and 407 ms) when the two variables are equal to 20. As for the increased number of data items in the training data sets of ML models, it has the lowest impact on the query response time, with a time jump equal to 4 ms.

6   Conclusion

In this paper, we propose a Semantic Machine Learning Model ontology (SML) that describes and stores ML models' characteristics and operational specifications (e.g., their used algorithms, their metadata, their training and testing data sets, their evaluation, etc.). SML allows to share ML knowledge across different platforms and environments, enabling to ease the comprehension of ML models, as well as their selection in various use cases. After implementing SML, we have evaluated its efficiency and performance in different scenarios, where we varied the number of ML instances models, their metadata, the number of data items and features used in their training data sets, and the number of metrics used to compute their testing data evaluation scores. Our experimental results are promising and encouraging.

As part of our ongoing evaluation of the ontology, we aim to check its consistency, to see if the defined concepts and properties cause any inconsistencies in the ontology's structure. This can be done by running different reasoners. We also seek to evaluate its clarity, to check whether the names or labels of the concepts and properties are clear to users (experts and/or non-experts), and see how easy it is for users to use/understand the ontology. Finally, we aim to use SML ontology in real environments or projects to evaluate further how the ontology can be exploited in practice, and work on the recommendation engine, which will use SML ontology to suggest the most suitable ML model(s) that can be applied in specific contexts and different scenarios.

References

1. Ayranci, P., et al.: OnML: an ontology-based approach for interpretable machine learning. J. Comb. Optim. 1–24 (2022)
2. Braga, J., Dias, J.L., Regateiro, F.: A machine learning ontology (2020)
3. Chicco, D., Warrens, M.J., Jurman, G.: The coefficient of determination R-squared is more informative than SMAPE, MAE, MAPE, MSE and RMSE in regression analysis evaluation. PeerJ Comput. Sci. **7**, e623 (2021)
4. Esnaola-Gonzalez, I.: An ontology-based approach for making machine learning systems accountable. Semant. Web J. (2021)
5. Hassani, H., Silva, E.S., Unger, S., TajMazinani, M., Mac Feely, S.: Artificial intelligence (AI) or intelligence augmentation (IA): what is the future? AI **1**(2), 8 (2020)
6. Janiesch, C., Zschech, P., Heinrich, K.: Machine learning and deep learning. Electron. Mark. **31**(3), 685–695 (2021). https://doi.org/10.1007/s12525-021-00475-2
7. Lee, I., Shin, Y.J.: Machine learning for enterprises: applications, algorithm selection, and challenges. Bus. Horiz. **63**(2), 157–170 (2020)
8. Lindholm, A., Wahlström, N., Lindsten, F., Schön, T.B.: Supervised machine learning. Department of Information Technology, Uppsala University: Uppsala, Sweden, p. 112 (2019)
9. Mishra, S., Jain, S.: Ontologies as a semantic model in IoT. IJCA **42**(3), 233–243 (2020)
10. Muhammad, I., Yan, Z.: Supervised machine learning approaches: a survey. ICTACT J. Soft Comput. **5**(3) (2015)
11. Nascimento, N., Alencar, P., Lucena, C., Cowan, D.: A context-aware machine learning-based approach. In: Proceedings of the 28th Annual International Conference on Computer Science and Software Engineering, pp. 40–47 (2018)
12. Ngiam, K.Y., Khor, W.: Big data and machine learning algorithms for health-care delivery. Lancet Oncol. **20**(5), e262–e273 (2019)
13. Publio, G.C., et al.: ML-schema: exposing the semantics of machine learning with schemas and ontologies. arXiv preprint arXiv:1807.05351 (2018)
14. Rashidi, H.H., Tran, N.K., Betts, E.V., Howell, L.P., Green, R.: Artificial intelligence and machine learning in pathology: the present landscape of supervised methods. Acad. Pathol. **6**, 2374289519873088 (2019)

Explainability and Scalability in AI

A Comprehensive Survey of Explainable Artificial Intelligence (XAI) Methods: Exploring Transparency and Interpretability

Ambreen Hanif[1]([✉]), Amin Beheshti[1]([✉]), Boualem Benatallah[2], Xuyun Zhang[1], Habiba[1], EuJin Foo[1], Nasrin Shabani[1], and Maryam Shahabikargar[1]

[1] Macquarie University, Sydney, Australia
{ambreen.hanif,eujin.foo,nasrin.shabani,
maryam.shahabi-kargar}@hdr.mq.edu.au,
{amin.beheshti,xuyun.zhang}@mq.edu.au, habibah@gmail.com
[2] Dublin City University, Dublin, Ireland
boualem.benatallah@adaptcentre.ie

Abstract. Artificial Intelligence (AI) is undergoing a significant transformation. In recent years, the deployment of AI models, from Analytical to Cognitive and Generative AI, has become imminent; however, the widespread utilization of these models has prompted questions and concerns within the research and business communities regarding their transparency and interpretability. A primary challenge lies in comprehending the underlying reasoning mechanisms employed by AI-enabled systems. The absence of transparency and interpretability into the decision-making process of these systems indicates a deficiency that can have severe consequences, e.g., in domains such as medical diagnosis and financial decision-making, where valuable resources are at stake. This survey explores Explainable AI (XAI) techniques within the AI system pipeline based on existing literature. It covers tools and applications across various domains, assessing current methods and addressing challenges and opportunities, particularly in the context of Generative AI.

Keywords: Explainable Artificial Intelligence · Artificial Intelligence · Transparency · Interpretability

1 Introduction

The rapid development of Artificial Intelligence (AI) and the supporting domain including Big Data and high-performing computational infrastructure has triggered a tectonic shift. The substantial refinement of deep learning-based systems including foundation models(e.g. Transformer, GPT-4, Bard, DALL-E, RoBERTa, etc.) has equipped the AI-based systems to penetrate high-stake applications. These applications span across various critical domains, including

F. Zhang et al. (Eds.): WISE 2023, LNCS 14306, pp. 915–925, 2023.
https://doi.org/10.1007/978-981-99-7254-8_71

healthcare, finance, law enforcement, and agriculture [35,39]. This speedy penetration has sociotechnical, privacy, and safety implications associated with these
intelligent systems and is categorized as an existential threat to the human race.
One of the key contributions to the scepticism is the non-transparent nature of
these models. The opaqueness of the ML algorithms restricts trust and resists
deployment in vulnerable domains.

AI is defined as a set of approaches to mimic human behaviour in general
whereas by and large, Machine Learning (ML) algorithms are predictive models
using existing data features to build class mapping during the learning phase.
This learning phase is based on the data retrieved from the usual user activities (e.g. online shopping, medical history, social interactions, customer profiles, etc.). This enormous amount of data is liable to contain human biases
and predispositions. So the decision models also have the innate ability to have
presumptions on the learning which can lead to wrong decisions. As black box
models are extensively developed and tested on huge datasets, numerous stakeholders emphasize system transparency [23,24]. In general, people are restrained
from using techniques that are not justifiable and transparent, which results
in demanding ethical AI [38]. The increasing complexity of these opaque systems enhances performance, yet they still lack transparency. While designing
and developing the ML model, keeping transparency as a design consideration
drive impartial decision-making and can guarantee to use of important variables
to generate the model predictions.

As a consequence, Explainable Artificial Intelligence (XAI), an emerging frontier of AI, is pertinent due to its ability to help answer the raised concerns and
mitigate the associated risks. XAI gives a suite of ML techniques to generate
an explainable model and develop a trustworthy human-understandable system.
Various communities are using explanations for Model decisions. The objectives
and perspectives of the developed various XAI system vary as per the need for
explanations. The contribution of this paper is summarized below. This paper
begins by providing an overview of the key requirements in the field and subsequently conducts a comprehensive review of explainable artificial intelligence
(XAI) approaches for the machine learning (ML) pipeline. The review specifically focuses on different stages of the ML lifecycle to analyze and evaluate the
effectiveness of XAI techniques. This is an extension of our previous survey on
XAI techniques [16].

The paper is organized as follows. In Sect. 2, we discuss the terminology of
the domain. Following that, Sect. 3 contributes to providing the overview of the
approaches in XAI, and the evaluation and discussion on these approaches are
presented in Sect. 4. Lastly, the conclusion is highlighted in Sect. 5.

2   Desiderata for Explainable Artificial Intelligence

As the domain is emerging and we don't have enough context, some research
works [6,21], are using the terms interpretability and explainability interchangeably, preventing the creation of common grounds. There is communal agreement

Table 1. This table elucidates essential terminology within the XAI literature, serving as a reference for clarifying the concepts explored in this study.

Terms	Definition
Domain	
Artificial Intelligence	It refers to a branch of computer sciences focusing on developing the machines capable of mimicking human intelligence.
Machine Learning	It is the subset of AI techniques focused on learning from Experience with respect to some classes of tasks and performance measures.
Explainable Artificial Intelligence	The capacity of the system to explain the results generated by the AI system [15]
Interpretable Machine Learning	The ability of the models to be fundamentally human understandable due to simpler nature [21].
Explainability	It refers to the capacity of the AI system to cater to the specific requirements of the audience in the explanations [28].
Explanation	This term is defined as the outcome of the model to explain or clarify its internal functionalities [5,20].
Interpretability	It defines as a tendency of the system to produce the human-intelligible understanding of the model decision making [21].
Ethical Terms	
Fairness (unbiased)	It refers to the ethical principle to treat individuals and groups equitable [27].
Model Evaluation Measures	
Transparency	The degree to which a model can explain the route to reach the decision [8].
Robustness	The capacity of the model to be persistent in the model decision with the minor input perturbations [2].
Trustworthy	It defines the confidence in a system's performance when facing a given problem [35]
Completeness	The system is complete when the system behavior can be anticipated in more situations [13].

on the necessity for a formal definition of the nomenclature [1,14]. In this section, we will outline the definitions that we adopt to comprehend the techniques within the domain. This understanding will allow us to assess the capabilities of the explanation system and evaluate its alignment with the responsible AI framework.

Explainability has varying definitions; for this study, we refer to the definition: "Explainability aims to bridge the gap between the algorithm and human interpretation of the decision-making process. It is capable of enhancing trust by answering the how and why of the system" [28].

Interpretability from a user-centric view, is the human-intelligible explanation of the model system output [7]. For different users understanding of the system varies. A point of caution is reliance on human evaluations can lead to persuasive systems rather than transparent systems. This limits the ability to define the appropriate scope of interpretation. The selected terminology and the definitions are listed in Table 1.

3   Explainable Artificial Intelligence Methods

These days ML tends deep learning systems are complex and comprise many more layers and huge training data and have achieved high accuracy [28]. Despite these successes, the associated risks are a reluctance to adopt these models. The challenge of the hour is to develop trustworthy systems with these complex systems with escalating performance to help the user to understand the why of the decision to mitigate the associated risks. Now the next challenge is building trustworthy systems. So now with this development, we have achieved high accuracy. There are numerous surveys on XAI [1,5,7,13,14,21] and explainable deep learning [25,41]. All of these surveys cover a large body of work in different dimensions. A standard ML pipeline consists of several phases as shown in Fig. 1. In this paper, We will analyze each phase and will discuss the XAI approaches in the literature to address the various problems of each stage. As various stakeholders are involved in the different stages of the pipeline. The appropriate explanation to answer the various questions associated with the different phases of the ML pipeline.

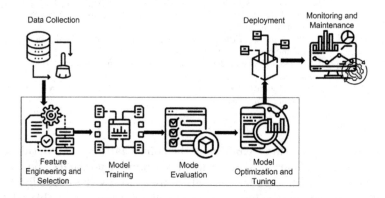

Fig. 1. A snapshot of a standard machine learning lifecycle.

3.1   Data Collection and Preparation

The foremost and most crucial stage of the ML lifecycle. It refers to the process of gathering and organizing data for utilization in machine-learning applications. This is a multi-step phase to ensure data relevance, reliability, and accuracy of the data using data cleaning, transformation, and integration techniques. The generation of explanations for data sources can address different aspects. We will classify these aspects into two categories: i) Detection of Data Bias, and iii) Annotation and Labeling of Data.

Detection of Data Bias. Counterfactual explanations often take the form of statements such as, "You were denied a loan due to an annual income of X. If your income had been X+Y, you would have been approved for the loan" [37].

The goal of a counterfactual statement is to identify the smallest modification in feature values that can yield the desired prediction.

Annotation and Labeling of Data. XAI can play a role in data annotation by providing transparency and interpretability to the annotation process. Forward Propagation-Based study [10] retrieved the feature importance with perturbation and identified the accountable mask for the results. Altering or blurring these salient features directly impacts the original classification outcome. These predictions can then be analyzed and interpreted using various XAI techniques to gain insights into the decision-making process of the model and understand the factors influencing the predictions.

3.2   Feature Engineering and Selection

Feature Interaction Analysis. Saliency Based Approaches highlight the importance of the region in the systems. These methods employ saliency maps to comprehend the contribution and significance of features in specific decisions. Visualization support aids in facilitating the comprehension of a diverse audience, allowing them to discern which feature influenced the decision. Prominent approaches proposed to calculate salience maps includes Integrated Gradients [34], SmoothGrad [32].

Outlier Detection. Automatic rule extraction Decompositional approaches work on the neurons to mimic the rules from the network architecture. Studies on transforming the neural network to the fuzzy rule are also available, the main work is on the extraction of approximation from the neurons [43]. Rule extraction techniques are valuable for identifying behavioural patterns, despite not being completely faithful to the models. As a result, there's a requirement for further research on explainability to address this limitation. Adversarial Examples will provide the interpretable model understanding. Most approaches suggest reducing the gap between the antagonistic example and the instance to be controlled while adjusting the prognosis to the desired outcome of the system. This method allows for diagnosing the outlier in the data [40].

3.3   Model Training

Propagation Based Approaches supports the identification of important regions. The output of the model is feedback to the system. The robustness of the system helps to understand the stability of the decision. *Backpropagation-based* methods take derivatives of the output w.r.t. input and the system gradients. These approaches are intrinsic as they are based on the important regions and rely on the model structure to understand the important region. DeepLift [31], an example approach assigns the positive and negative contributions to the features based on the actual and retrieved output difference.

3.4   Model Evaluation

One of the accepted convenient ways to explain networks is to develop proxy models that can approximate the behavior of these networks, such methods are referred to as 'model-agnostic' approaches. Ribeiro et al. have exemplified the proxy model by developing LIME(Local Interpretable Model-agnostic Explanations) [26]. Whereas SHAP(SHapely Additive exPlanations) method [18] supports interpretability by assigning feature scores to each attribute. The underlying mechanism of these models is to use the input to generate the linear proxy model to predict the behaviour by probing and perturbation. These models can be evaluated for their faithfulness to the original models. Decision Trees, another accepted type of proxy model, generate insights of Neural networks in equivalent Decision Trees [4]. The tree equivalence holds for fully connected, convolution, recurrent, and activation layers to satisfy the faithfulness. Although the generated trees are faithful these computations are computationally expensive and take substantial computational resources and time to develop.

Attention Mechanisms are neural networks that learn to assign weights to inputs or internal features, enabling them to focus on relevant information. These approaches have demonstrated incredible success in various complex tasks [36]. While attention units are not explicitly trained to generate human-readable explanations, they inherently provide a map of the information flow within the network, which can be interpreted as a form of explanation.

Knowledge Infused Explanations are general knowledge and knowledge-based methods. *General Knowledge* is generally referred to as a body of information or facts acquired through intellectual processes and diversity is the key trait. In this section, we will analyze the XAI techniques employing general knowledge for enrichment. Kim et al. [17] utilize the Concept Activation Vector(CAV) and analyze the importance of a concept in the task.

Knowledge-base (KB) Methods are deployed to enrich the model with human knowledge using available corpora explanations, which are suitable for specific situations. The KBs are generally represented as Knowledge Graphs(KG). The knowledge graph can be employed in the model design to enrich the feature entities and system rules to improve the model performance and explain the decisions. This is a known strategy for the recommender systems [19] to enrich the relation to identifying the similarity. A knowledge-based system can be employed after modeling to enhance reasoning, potentially through abductive reasoning, by utilizing its knowledge base to provide richer explanations [12,29].

3.5   Model Optimization

Gradient-based explanation helps to understand the vector representation at the system and the intermediate layer level. These layer-based vector representations support the 'transfer learning' mechanism for the other problems to learn from the underlying vector representation. These are not the real explanation of the system, these are intermediate vectors for the system to understand and resolve similar problem understanding and learning patterns. CAM [42], and GradCAM [30] are to name a few.

Explanation Generation Systems are designed to generate their own explanation units. The primary working principle is to generate the 'because' part with the model decision-making. These explanations are not directly interpretable and need proper evaluation to have faith in the model-generated answers. TEXTVQA [22], an extension of VQA a system that generates the multimodel explanation for the image captioning system can be visual as well as textual to help to understand why a certain caption is generated for the visual.

3.6 Deployment

The explanation without the training data can be categorized into human collaboration and policy abstraction-based binary categories.

Human Alliance: The studies [3,9] proposed methods to automatically build the explanation corpus for the system agents to guide humans. The network learns to translate the action to the natural language generation. These beginning steps to experiential studies and exploring the machine learning pattern leads to a formal evaluation of the explanations to provide the information related to the events based on the experience gained throughout the processes.

Policy Abstraction highlights the policy information from the experience of the player. The generated summary is capable to enrich the context to understand the explanation of a specific action in the circumstances. A few relevant studies are [3,33] the former study proposes the framework for abstraction and the latter support various abstraction levels for the same to be used in the system for the following action plan generation.

3.7 Monitoring and Maintenance

XAI can help detect and understand data drift by supplying explanations for model predictions, identifying changes in feature importance, and monitoring shifts in underlying patterns, enhancing the model's adaptability. *incremental Permutation Feature Importance(iPFI)* on the interpretation of the complex feature is proposed by [11].

4 Discussion

The utilization of XAI techniques is crucial for algorithm transparency and interpreting model decisions, leading to improvements in the machine learning lifecycle. These techniques aid in understanding the decision-making process of models at different stages of the pipeline and enable achieving transparency objectives based on system requirements. We will summarize the approaches at the various stages of the ML pipeline in Table 2. Applying XAI techniques can indeed provide numerous benefits across various aspects of machine learning models.

Table 2. An overview of selective XAI approaches across various stages of the ML pipeline.

ML Pipeline	XAI Methods	Type of Explanation	Inter.	Trans.	Data Type			
					T	I	Te	G
Data Collection	Counterfactual	Instance-Based	o	o	✓	✓	✓	✓
	Forward Prop.	Prop. Based	o	x	✓	✓	✓	✓
Feature Engineering and Selection	Van. Grad	Saliency Based	o	o	✓	✓	✓	✓
	Integ. Grad.	Saliency Based	o	o	✓	✓	✓	✓
	SmoothGrad	Saliency Based	x	o	✓	✓		
	DeepRed	Autom. Rule Extr.	o	o	✓			
	DIFFI	Isolation Forest	o	o	✓			✓
	FuzzyRules	Autom. Rule Extr.	o	o	✓			
	Advers.Ex.	Insatnce Based	o	o	✓	✓	✓	✓
Model Training	LRP	Gradient Based	o	o	✓	✓	✓	✓
	DeepLift	Gradient Based	o	o	✓	✓	✓	
	Atten. Rollouts	Attention Based	o	x	✓		✓	
	SHAP	(Game Theory)	o	x	✓	✓	✓	✓
	LIME	MA Perturb. based	o	x	✓	✓	✓	
	Decision Trees	Intr. Rule Based	o	o	✓	✓	✓	
	Capture attention	Self-atten. Net.	o	o	✓			✓
Model Eval.	CAV/TCAV	Knowledge Based	o	x	✓	✓	✓	
Model Optimization and Tunning	Semantically corr.	Knowledge Based	o	x	✓	✓	✓	
	GradCAM	Gradient Based	o	o			✓	
	TEXTVQA	Multimodel Expla.	o	x			✓	
Deployment	Human Alliance	Experience Based	o	x	-	-	-	-
	Policy Abstraction	Experience Based	o	x	-	-	-	-
Monitoring	PFI	Feature Importance	o	o	✓		✓	

Through XAI, data quality can be evaluated, quantified, and remedied. Explanations aid in data selection, identifying valuable information for improvement, and enabling adjustments to ensure fairness and equity in the model's performance. XAI techniques have the tendency to support data discretization and feature interaction analysis. The integration of XAI with data discretization and feature interaction analysis enhances our understanding and enhances the reliability of the machine learning models. Moreover, XAI techniques contribute to privacy protection. XAI techniques allow for the interpretation of models without compromising individual privacy. In conclusion, applications of XAI techniques bring several benefits to machine learning models. XAI techniques enhance transparency, fairness, and reliability. By leveraging XAI, organizations can make informed decisions, address ethical concerns, and build robust and trustworthy AI systems.

5   Conclusion and Future Directions

In this paper, a comprehensive and systematic review of the development of XAI approaches for the machine learning pipeline is presented. XAI posed several challenges, from complex infrastructure to computational cost, but the strategic choices of the explanation techniques with the defined objective are beneficial and can mitigate the risks associated with the high-stake application. Deploying the right approach for the explanation of the model decisions can not only enrich the business processes but help to build faith in the system results. In these times of generative AI and the foundation models, systems are suffering from the inaccessibility to system understanding, and XAI can fill the gap in human understanding and model decision-making in high stake decisions. The explanation generation and evaluation framework for the machine learning pipeline can strengthen the downstream applications even derived from the foundation models. Appropriate XAI techniques with the relevant metrics for computational and cognitive evaluations of the model are a key step to proceed.

Acknowledgement. We acknowledge the Centre for Applied Artificial Intelligence at Macquarie University, Sydney, Australia, for funding this research.

References

1. Adadi, A., et al.: Peeking inside the black-box: a survey on Explainable Artificial Intelligence (XAI). IEEE Access **6**, 52138–52160 (2018)
2. Alvarez-Melis, D., et al.: On the Robustness of Interpretability Methods. arXiv preprint arXiv:1806.08049 (2018)
3. Amir, O., et al.: Summarizing agent strategies. Auton. Agent. Multi-Agent Syst. **33**(5), 628–644 (2019)
4. Aytekin, C.: Neural Networks are Decision Trees. arXiv preprint arXiv:2210.05189 (2022)
5. Arrieta, A.B., et al.: Explainable Artificial Intelligence (XAI): concepts, taxonomies, opportunities and challenges toward responsible AI. Inf. Fusion **58**, 82–115 (2020)
6. Cabitza, F., Campagner, A., Ciucci, D.: New frontiers in explainable AI: understanding the GI to interpret the GO. In: Holzinger, A., Kieseberg, P., Tjoa, A.M., Weippl, E. (eds.) CD-MAKE 2019. LNCS, vol. 11713, pp. 27–47. Springer, Cham (2019). https://doi.org/10.1007/978-3-030-29726-8_3
7. Doshi-Velez, F., et al.: Towards A Rigorous Science of Interpretable Machine Learning. arXiv preprint arXiv:1702.08608 (2017)
8. Došilović, F.K., Brčić, M., Hlupić, N.: Explainable artificial intelligence: a survey. In: 2018 41st International Convention on Information and Communication Technology, Electronics and Microelectronics (MIPRO), Opatija, Croatia, 2018, pp. 0210–0215 (2018). https://doi.org/10.23919/MIPRO.2018.8400040
9. Ehsan, U., et al.: Automated rationale generation: a technique for explainable AI and its effects on human perceptions. In: Proceedings of IUI. ACM (2019)
10. Fong, R.C., et al.: Interpretable explanations of black boxes by meaningful perturbation. In: Proceedings of the IEEE ICCV, pp. 3429–3437 (2017)
11. Fumagalli, F., et al.: Incremental Permutation Feature Importance (iPFI): Towards Online Explanations on Data Streams. arXiv preprint arXiv:2209.01939 (2022)
12. Gaur, M., et al.: Semantics of the black-box: can knowledge graphs help make deep learning systems more interpretable and explainable? IEEE Internet Comput. **25**(1), 51–59 (2021)

13. Gilpin, L.H., et al.: Explaining explanations: an overview of interpretability of machine learning. In: IEEE 5th International Conference on DSAA (2019)
14. Guidotti, R., et al.: A survey of methods for explaining black box models. ACM Comput. Surv. (CSUR) **51**(5), 1–42 (2018)
15. Gunning, D., et al.: XAI-Explainable Artificial Intelligence. Sci. Robot. 4(37), 7120 (2019)
16. Hanif, A., et al.: A survey on explainable artificial intelligence techniques and challenges. In: IEEE 25th EDOCW, pp. 81–89. IEEE (2021)
17. Kim, B., et al.: Examples are not enough, learn to criticize! criticism for interpretability. In: Advances in NIPS, vol. 29 (2016)
18. Lundberg, S.M., et al.: A unified approach to interpreting model predictions. In: Advances in NIPS, Long Beach, CA, vol. 30 (2017)
19. Ma, W., et al.: Jointly learning explainable rules for recommendation with knowledge graph. In: Proceedings of the WWW, pp. 1210–1221 (2019)
20. Markus, A.F., et al.: The role of explainability in creating trustworthy artificial intelligence for health care: a comprehensive survey of the terminology, design choices, and evaluation strategies. JBI **113**, 103655 (2021)
21. Miller, T.: Explanation in artificial intelligence: insights from the social sciences. Artif. Intell. **267**, 1–38 (2019)
22. Rao, V.N., et al.: A first look: towards explainable TextVQA models via visual and textual explanations. In: Proceedings of the Third MAI-Workshop, pp. 19–29. ACL (2021)
23. Pouriyeh, S., et al.: A comprehensive investigation and comparison of machine learning techniques in the domain of heart disease. In: IEEE ISCC, pp. 204–207 (2017)
24. Raju, C., et al.: A survey on predicting heart disease using data mining techniques. In: ICEDSS, pp. 253–255 (2018)
25. Ras, G., et al.: Explainable deep learning: a field guide for the uninitiated. J. Artif. Intell. Res. **73**, 329–397 (2022)
26. Ribeiro, M.T., et al.: "Why should I trust you?" Explaining the predictions of any classifier. In: Proceedings of the ACM SIGKDD, KDD 2016, pp. 1135–1144 (2016)
27. Romei, A., et al.: A multidisciplinary survey on discrimination analysis. KER **29**(5), 582–638 (2014)
28. Saeed, W., et al.: Explainable AI (XAI): a systematic meta-survey of current challenges and future opportunities. KBS **263**, 110273 (2023)
29. Sarker, I.H.: Deep learning: a comprehensive overview on techniques, taxonomy, applications and research directions. SNCS **2**(6), 420 (2021)
30. Selvaraju, R.R., et al.: Grad-CAM: visual explanations from deep networks via gradient-based localization. IJCV **128**(2), 336–359 (2017)
31. Shrikumar, A., et al.: Learning important features through propagating activation differences. In: 34th ICML, vol. 7, pp. 4844–4866 (2017)
32. Smilkov, D., et al.: SmoothGrad: removing noise by adding noise. arXiv (2017)
33. Sridharan, M., et al.: Towards a theory of explanations for human-robot collaboration. KI Künstliche Intell. **33**(4), 331–342 (2019)
34. Sundararajan, M., et al.: Axiomatic attribution for deep networks. In: 34th ICML 2017, vol. 7, pp. 5109–5118 (2017)
35. Tjoa, E., et al.: A survey on explainable artificial intelligence (XAI): towards medical XAI. IEEE Trans. Neural Netw. Learn. **14**(8), 1–21 (2019)
36. Vaswani, A., et al.: Attention is all you need. In: Advances in NIPS (2017)
37. Wachter, S., et al.: Counterfactual explanations without opening the black box: automated decisions and the GDPR. Harvard JOLT **31**, 841 (2017)

38. Wang, Y.-X., et al.: Using data mining and machine learning techniques for system design space exploration and automatized optimization. In: ICASI, pp. 1079–1082 (2017)
39. Wells, L., et al.: Explainable AI and reinforcement learning-a systematic review of current approaches and trends. Front. Artif. **4**, 550030 (2021)
40. Yuan, X., et al.: Adversarial examples: attacks and defenses for deep learning. IEEE Trans. Neural Netw. Learn. **30**(9), 2805–2824 (2018)
41. Zhang, Z., et al.: Deep learning on graphs: a survey. IEEE Trans. Knowl. Data Eng. **34**(1), 249–270 (2022)
42. Zhou, B., et al.: Learning deep features for discriminative localization. In: IEEE CVPR, pp. 2921–2929 (2016)
43. Zilke, J.R., Loza Mencía, E., Janssen, F.: DeepRED – rule extraction from deep neural networks. In: Calders, T., Ceci, M., Malerba, D. (eds.) DS 2016. LNCS (LNAI), vol. 9956, pp. 457–473. Springer, Cham (2016). https://doi.org/10.1007/978-3-319-46307-0_29

Scaling Machine Learning with an Efficient Hybrid Distributed Framework

Kankan Zhao[1], Youfang Leng[1], Hui Zhang[1]([✉]), and Xiyu Gao[2]

[1] Shandong Inspur Database Technology Co., Ltd., Beijing, China
{zhaokankan,lengyoufang,zhanghui}@inspur.com
[2] XiDian University, Xi'an, China
xygao@xidian.edu.cn

Abstract. Hybrid distributed frameworks combine the advantage of data parallelism and model parallelism, thus achieving better model performance and training efficiency. However, the existing hybrid architectures still suffer from low efficiency caused by the high communication cost and global barriers problem. In this paper, we propose a more efficient hybrid distributed framework that trains sub-models asynchronously and predicts in an ensemble learning way. To divide a global model into multiple independent sub-models, we propose a general model partition approach which constructs the unique sub-model by aggregating feature sets of training data into multiple independent feature subsets. To further improve the performance of our framework, we design a pruning strategy that stops the poor sub-model early and assigns the idle computation resource to active model training groups. The experimental results show that the proposed algorithm achieves significantly better performance (1.82%–4.58% RMSE) than the state-of-the-art baselines and also achieves a 3.7×–7.9× speedup when reaching a comparable RMSE performance.

Keywords: Hybrid Distributed Framework · Machine Learning · Model Partition · Factorization Machine

1 Introduction

Distributed frameworks employ two key parallel mechanisms for machine learning tasks: data parallelism and model parallelism. While data parallelism improves training efficiency by partitioning large-scale datasets into multiple workers, it suffers from low convergence due to conflicting updates. On the other hand, model parallelism [1,5,8] accelerates training by splitting the model into several workers to prevent concurrent updates of the same parameter. However, it has low parallelism and requires synchronous updates of all model partitions. To avoid the drawbacks of both parallel mechanisms, hybrid parallel methods [5,8] are proposed. Although the existing hybrid frameworks achieve better performance within less time, problems remain largely unsolved. First, some of them focus on deep learning model training. Second, although the drawbacks of data and model parallelism are alleviated, they have not been resolved fundamentally.

In this paper, we first propose a novel hybrid framework to learn most of the ML models. In our framework, we divide all workers into multiple groups. Different from the existing solutions, we remove the global model stored in the global server and use the sub-models partitioned in all worker groups to predict the new instance with the ensemble learning method. Secondly, to split a complex global model into multiple sub-models, we design a general model partition approach which clusters the features in the dataset to unrelated feature subsets and then applies independent sub-models on them. Last, we design a model pruning strategy that can identify and terminate the model with bad performance early and assign idle workers to other active model training groups. Thus, the training efficiency and model accuracy of proposed framework can be further improved.

The main contributions of this paper can be listed as:

- We present a novel hybrid framework that can learn a variety of ML models by eliminating the global model and updating sub-models asynchronously. As a result, communication costs is reduced and training efficiency is accelerated. To enhance model performance, ensemble learning is incorporated.
- To automatically divide a complex model into independent sub-models, we design a general model partition approach which can evaluate the strength of features and feature interactions. By removing unnecessary features and feature pairs, we can then group the remaining features into several independent sets on which the sub-models are learned.
- To further improve model performance and training efficiency, we propose a model pruning strategy which can pre-stop the poorly performing models and reallocate the available computational resources to other active groups.
- The experimental results demonstrate that our proposed framework compares RMSE performance (1.82%–4.58%) favorably against the state-of-the-art methods, and achieves a 3.7×–7.9× speedup.

2 Preliminary

2.1 Factorization Machine

Factorization Machine (FM) [9] combines feature engineering with factorization models and achieves competitive performance [3,7,10,11]. Suppose the training set of a prediction problem is formulated by $D = \{(\mathbf{x}, y)\}$, where each pair $(\mathbf{x}, y)$ represents an instance $\mathbf{x}$ with p-dimension variables and its target value (or label) y, then an FM model of order $d = 2$ is defined as:

$$\hat{y}(\mathbf{x}) = w_0 + \sum_{j=1}^{p} w_j x_j + \sum_{j=1}^{p} \sum_{j'=j+1}^{p} \langle \boldsymbol{v}_j, \boldsymbol{v}_{j'} \rangle x_j x_{j'}, \tag{1}$$

From the equation, we can see that FM is a generic approach. On one hand, it can mimic most factorization models, such as linear regression, matrix factorization, pairwise interaction tensor factorization [12], SVD++, timeSVD++,

FPMC [15], just by feature engineering. On the other hand, many recent studies try to extend FM with deep learning [2,14,17]. Therefore, we use the FM model to model the strength of feature interaction and test our proposed framework.

2.2   Permutation Feature Importance

The general idea of the permutation variable importance method is that the importance of a feature can be represented as the increase of the model's prediction error when permuting the feature's values. Keep using the dataset in Sect. 2.1, the prediction error in the regression setting can be defined as:

$$R(\hat{f}, D) = \frac{1}{|D|} \sum_{(\mathbf{X}_i, Y_i) \in D} (Y_i - \hat{f}(\mathbf{X}_i))^2 \tag{2}$$

After permuting the value of j-th variable, the permuted prediction error is:

$$R(\hat{f}, D^j) = \frac{1}{|D^j|} \sum_{(\mathbf{X}_i^j, Y_i) \in D^j} (Y_i - \hat{f}(\mathbf{X}_i^j))^2 \tag{3}$$

where D^j denotes the validation data which shuffled the feature j's value and X_i^j is the ith instance with the value of jth feature changed.

Then the permutation importance of the j-th variable is given by

$$I(X_j) = R(\hat{f}, D^j) - R(\hat{f}, D^j) \tag{4}$$

In general, a feature is considered 'important' if alterations to its values result in a higher model error. This occurs because shuffling the feature values causes the previously learned relationship between the feature and target variable Y to be disrupted. Conversely, a feature is deemed 'unimportant' if alterations to its values do not have a substantial effect on the model error.

3   Our Hybrid Distributed Framework

In this section, we introduce the general framework of our hybrid framework.

Figure 1 depicts the general framework of our system, which consists of three types of nodes. **Global server** is responsible for global model partitioning, cluster resource scheduling, and ensemble learning prediction. **Server** is in charge of keeping the latest sub-model of the current group. **Worker** is used to storing the training data, updating the sub-model and predicting.

The hybrid framework splits the nodes into several groups and keeps a unique sub-model and training data replica in each group. Under this design, the new instances are predicted in an ensemble learning manner. From the perspective of parallelism, we implement model parallelism among groups and achieve data parallelism within a group.

The detail algorithm can be outlined as follows. The Global Server initially splits a complex global model into independent sub-models and then assigns them to servers in different groups. Within each group, the server initializes its own sub-model, while each worker reads a portion of training data from the distributed file system. During the training process, workers sample a mini-batch of data, pull necessary model parameters from the server, update the parameters, and push the new parameters back to the server. Once the server receives these parameters, it replaces the old ones in the sub-model. When reaching the maximal iterations, all training actions are complete. In the prediction process, each group reads a replica of the test data and predicts with their own sub-model. Predicted values are then pushed to the global server. Ultimately, the global server uses an ensemble learning method to calculate the final predicted result.

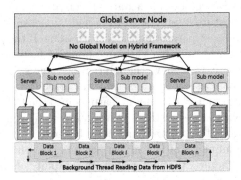

Fig. 1. The architecture of Our proposed hybrid framework

Compared to existing hybrid solutions, our framework offers several advantages. Firstly, we reduce the communication cost between the global server and each group. Secondly, we remove the synchronous updating global barrier in model parallelism by learning each sub-model asynchronously. As such, our training efficiency is superior to that of existing systems. Thirdly, our framework achieves a better model performance because the sub-models are diverse and predictions take place in an ensemble learning manner.

4   Model Partition Strategy

In this section, we present a general model partition approach capable of dividing a complicated model into several independent sub-models.

It is generally believed that the training process of machine learning models is to learn the impact of the features and feature interactions of the training data on the model. With this theory, we categorize features into three types:

- **Strong feature:** feature with a significant impact on the model.
- **Weak feature:** feature with little impact on the model.
- **Irrelevant feature:** feature with no impact on the model.

Generally, strong features have a greater impact on the model, so it is generally advised to retain them, while irrelevant features should be discarded since they do not impact the model. However, weak features may be retained if they can form strong feature pairs through interactions with other features. A summary theory can be formulated: strong feature interactions are retained, while weak feature interactions are discarded. Our model partition method is based on this theory, allowing us to aggregate the features in the training data into several independent subsets for generating different sub-models.

To estimate the strength of feature interactions, we propose a new method called PFI-FM that integrates PFI with FM models. The general idea of PFI-FM is to train the FM model on a dataset containing all features and then evaluate whether a feature interaction is retained by measuring how the model's performance changes after permuting the feature value. If the permuted version's performance is better, we consider the corresponding feature interaction strong and keep it. Conversely, we believe the interaction is noise and filter it out.

To address the bias issue caused by feature correlations in the original PFI method, we introduce "noise" or random features into the training data and then use a greedy approach to select the feature interaction, which performs better than other interactions that contain any noise features.

To mitigate the influence of FM model performance on the feature selection process, we define a factor s that determines the stability of the feature selection results. Given the feature pair set A selected in previous iterations and the new feature pair set B generated in the current iteration, we can define s as follows.

$$s = |A \cap B|/|A \cup B| \tag{5}$$

where the values of $s \in [0,1]$. When $s = 0$, the selected features in sets A and B are totally different. Conversely, when s reaches 1, A and B are the same. In such a case, we can further define a threshold ξ. When $s > \xi$, we consider that the model performance is good and can generate a stable feature selection sets.

After discussing the technical details for estimating the strength of feature interaction. We now propose a method to aggregate the selected feature interactions into independent feature subsets. The idea behind our proposed feature aggregation method is straightforward: we consider each selected feature pair as an initial feature group and then combine feature groups into larger ones if any feature pairs in the big group can be found in the initial feature group.

To better understand the process of feature aggregation, we give an example to explain how the method works. Suppose that we have two sets of feature groups: $\{a, b, c, d\}$ and $\{a, b, c, e\}$. Our aim is to ascertain whether these sets can be merged into a larger feature group set, $\{a, b, c, d, e\}$. Initially, we execute a set difference operation for the sets. Consequently, we obtain the features, d and e, respectively. We then pair them up as (d, e), and verify whether the feature pair is available in the strong feature interaction set. If it is, we can merge the feature groups, $\{a, b, c, d\}$ and $\{a, b, c, e\}$, into a larger feature set, $\{a, b, c, d, e\}$.

5   Sub-model Pruning and Final Implementation

5.1   Sub-model Pruning

To prevent any weak model from affecting the final performance and further improve the training efficiency, we introduce a sub-model pruning strategy into our hybrid distributed framework. The approach involves terminating sub-models whose performance significantly lags behind other models and reallocating their workers to other active groups.

The general idea is to terminate the model whose performance significantly lags behind other models and reallocating their corresponding workers to other active groups. To detect which model is underperforming and should be removed, we define an adaptive threshold which is derived by taking the average of all sub-model performance as the base value and decreasing it by a certain percentage φ (a hyper-parameter defined by the user). During training process, all groups predict on the same validation set every t iterations and record model performance on the global server. The global server computes the threshold and terminates the underperforming models and reallocates idle workers to other active groups.

5.2   Final System Implementation

From a training process perspective, the entire framework can be categorized into two stages: model partitioning and sub-model training. In the model partitioning stage, the system functions as a classic parameter server framework to train the FM model. After a fixed number of iterations, the PFI-FM approach runs and generates the latest feature interaction set in a distributed manner. We determine whether the set is stable by comparing it with the set generated previously. If the set is stable, the feature aggregation method begins to split all features into several independent groups. At this point, the system enters the sub-model training stage. The global server divides all workers into multiple groups and assigns a feature group to the server in each group. During the sub-model training process, the sub-model with poor performance is terminated and its corresponding idle nodes are assigned to other active groups.

6   Experiments

6.1   Experimental Setup

Datasets. We perform experiments on two datasets shown in Table 1.

Comparison Methods. The details of comparison algorithms are as follows:

- **FM:** Implemented with SGD and on a single machine.
- **FM-AsynSGD-PS:** Implemented with asyn-SGD on Parameter Server [5].
- **NFM:** Implemented with neural network and GPU-based tensorflow [2].
- **AFM:** Implemented with attention network and GPU-based tensorflow [14].
- **Hybrid-FM (our approach):** Implemented on the proposed framework.

Table 1. Datasets

dataset	ratings	users	items	# of features	purpose
Books	5.8 million	53,424	58,077	15	book recommendation
TMDB	20 million	138,000	27,000	16	movie recommendation

Evaluation Measures. We consider the following performance measurements:

- **Accuracy & Efficiency Performance.** We use RMSE and the runtime to evaluate the accuracy and efficiency performance of all methods respectively.
- **Parameter Analysis.** We analyze the effect of different factors in our method including the ensemble learning of sub-models, the different number of feature groups, and do feature groups make sense.

Platform and Implementation. Among all these algorithms, FM, FM-AsynSGD-PS and Hybrid-FM are implemented using Scala, while NFM and AFM are implemented with Python. FM, NFM and AFM are performed on a computer that contains 20 CPU cores and 250G memory and 40G GPU memory. FM-AsynSGD-PS and Hybrid-FM are run on a cluster containing 20 machines which shares the configurations of 2 CPU cores and 16G memory. For the datasets, we split them into the training set, validation set, and testing set, each of which is 80%, 10%, and 10% of the total dataset, respectively. Due to the limited resources, we set the maximum number of groups as 9 by default.

6.2   Accuracy and Efficiency Performance

We compare RMSE performance and the corresponding elapsed time of all the comparison methods on the two datasets. To present the learning details of each method, we plot all the (RMSE, time) pairs for each algorithm in Fig. 2 and give the final stable test error and the corresponding runtime in Table 2.

Table 2. Test error and run-time of different methods.

Method	Books		Movielens	
	Runtime(sec)	RMSE	Runtime(sec)	RMSE
Hybrid-FM	**5,933.0**	**0.8095**	**12,027.0**	**0.7945**
FM	6,696.0	0.8282	20,134.0	0.8093
FM-AsynSGD-PS	6,815.0	0.8338	25,131.0	0.8197
NFM	12,553.0	0.8256	20,221.0	0.8327
AFM	5,680.0	0.8141	14,018.0	0.8005

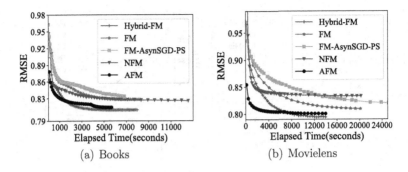

Fig. 2. Performance of all the comparison methods.

From Fig. 2 and Table 2, we can see that Hybrid-FM achieves better performance and training efficiency than the state-of-the-art baselines. Specifically, when comparing with FM, Hybrid-FM achieves better performance (1.82%–2.25%) within less time (3.7×–4.2× speedup for the comparable performance). The reason is that Hybrid-FM filters out the useless feature interactions and trains under the distributed environment. Compared to FM-AsynSGD-PS, Hybrid-FM improves RMSE performance by 2.91%–3.07% and achieves 5.4×–6.0× speedup. The main reason is that Hybrid-FM trains multiple sub-models without global barriers not only within each group but also between different groups and predicts with ensemble learning. When comparing with NFM, Hybrid-FM gets 1.95%–4.58% performance improvement and 6.0×–7.9× efficiency improvement on both datasets. The reasons are as follows: firstly, although NFM can model the high-order interactions, not all the interactions are helpful and some noise features even cause bad effect to the final model. In contrast, Hybrid partition the model by selecting good feature interactions. Secondly, our hybrid distributed framework is more efficient. As for the AFM, we can find that the performance of Hybrid-FM is slightly better than AFM within a comparable time. The main reason is that AFM distinguishes the interactions with different weights by attention network and speeds up its training process with GPU.

6.3   Parameter Analysis

The Ensemble Learning. We study how the ensemble learning affects the RMSE performance of the proposed Hybrid-FM in Fig. 3(a). In such a case, FM-Max and FM-Min denotes the best sub-model and the worst sub-model on movielens dataset respectively. We can see that the performance of both FM-Max and FM-Min are comparable than the FM model based on all features even though each sub-model only captures part of the information contained in the data. And with the ensemble learning, Hybrid-FM achieves significantly better performance than the FM model. The reason is that we abandon the useless and noise interactions and combine good interactions at the model level.

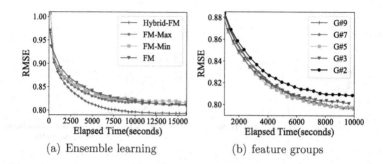

(a) Ensemble learning   (b) feature groups

Fig. 3. Effect of ensemble learning and feature groups.

The Number of Feature Groups. We study how the number of groups affects the final model performance in Fig. 3(b). In this context, G#n denotes the Hybrid-FM with n groups on movielens dataset. With the increase of feature groups, the performance of Hybrid-FM achieves significant improvement and better than the FM model. When the number of groups reaches 7, the improvement of performance is close to 0. Because almost all the information contained in the data is captured when the feature group exceeds a certain number.

Are Feature Groups Reasonable. We take TMDB dataset as an example to study whether the generated feature groups are reasonable in Table 3. In this case, G#n denotes the n-th feature group. And the feature index from 0 to 15 represents *uid, mid, isadult, genres, originallanguage, countries, releaseyear, spokenlanguage, actors, crews, budget, revenue, runtime, rating, votecounts* and *popularity*, respectively. We can see that *uid, mid, actors* and *crews* are contained in almost all the groups. The reason is that people always like to watch the movies performed by the favorite actors or the movies directed by the favorite directors. In summary, our approach can select good interactions and generate reasonable feature groups effectively.

Table 3. Selected Feature Interactions on Movielens Dataset.

	0	1	2	3	4	5	6	7	8	9	10	11	12	13	14	15
G#1	✓	✓			✓				✓	✓						
G#2	✓	✓				✓			✓	✓						
G#3	✓	✓							✓	✓					✓	
G#4	✓	✓							✓	✓			✓			✓
G#5	✓		✓						✓	✓	✓					
G#6	✓			✓					✓	✓	✓					
G#7	✓			✓					✓	✓						✓
G#8	✓								✓	✓		✓	✓			
G#9	✓	✓						✓	✓	✓			✓			

7   Related Work

Due to the growth of data scale and model complexity, the memory and time cost of the stand-alone version of ML models become infeasible in practice. Some research efforts have been made to train the models on distributed framework. Data parallelism and model parallelism are two common strategies that are widely adopted to the distributed ML applications. Compared with model parallelism, data parallel method is easier to be implemented. Most of existing distributed solutions support data parallelism, such as Hadoop, Spark, Parameter Server [6,13,16], TensorFlow [1], Angel [5], Singa [8] and pyTorch FSDP. However, as the model has to be replicated and synchronized among workers, data parallel methods incur significant network and memory overheads. In addition, data parallelism damages the statistical efficiency due to the conflicting updates on parameters. Different from data parallel methods, model parallelism [1,4,5,8] partitions the global model to all workers. Although it can achieve good statistical efficiency, the performance still be harmed by the synchronous update rule and it also suffer from the small degree of parallelism.

To avoid the drawbacks in both of them, Angel [5] and Singa [8] propose hybrid distributed frameworks which combine these two types of parallel methods into a unified system. Take angel as an example, it divides workers into multiple groups, and adopts data parallelism inside each group, and applies model parallelism among the groups. The updates generated by different groups are merged through the global parameter servers. Although the problems of data parallelism and model parallelism are alleviated, the high communication cost and synchronized model parallelism still limit their training efficiency. To address above problems, we propose a novel hybrid architecture.

8   Conclusion and Future Work

In this work, we introduce an efficient hybrid distributed framework to train ML models. Firstly, we propose a novel distributed architecture which can speed up the training efficiency by reducing the global barriers and high communication cost, and improve model performance by predicting in an ensemble learning manner. Secondly, we propose a model partition algorithm to split the common global model into independent sub-models. Thirdly, we design a sub-model pruning mechanism to further improve the model performance and training efficiency. The experimental results on two different real-world datasets show that our framework achieves better performance (1.82%–4.58%) within less time (3.7×–7.9× speedup). In future work, we aim to further optimize this hybrid distributed framework for more efficient learning of general ML models.

References

1. Abadi, M., Barham, P., et al.: Tensorflow: a system for large-scale machine learning. In: OSDI 2016, pp. 265–283 (2016)
2. Guo, H., Tang, R., et al.: DeepFM: a factorization-machine based neural network for CTR prediction. In: IJCAI 2017, pp. 1725–1731. AAAI Press (2017)
3. Hong, L., Doumith, A.S., et al.: Co-factorization machines: modeling user interests and predicting individual decisions in twitter. In: WSDM 2013, pp. 557–566 (2013)
4. Huang, Y., Cheng, Y., et al.: GPipe: Efficient Training of Giant Neural Networks Using Pipeline Parallelism. Curran Associates Inc., Red Hook (2019)
5. Jiang, J., Yu, L., et al.: Angel: a new large-scale machine learning system. Natl. Sci. Rev. **5**(2), 216–236 (2017)
6. Li, M., Andersen, D.G., et al.: Scaling distributed machine learning with the parameter server. In: OSDI 2014, vol. 14, pp. 583–598 (2014)
7. Loni, B., Shi, Y., Larson, M., Hanjalic, A.: Cross-domain collaborative filtering with factorization machines. In: de Rijke, M., et al. (eds.) ECIR 2014. LNCS, vol. 8416, pp. 656–661. Springer, Cham (2014). https://doi.org/10.1007/978-3-319-06028-6_72
8. Ooi, B.C., Tan, K.L., et al.: SINGA: a distributed deep learning platform. In: MM 2015, pp. 685–688. ACM (2015)
9. Rendle, S.: Factorization machines. In: ICDM 2010, pp. 995–1000 (2010)
10. Rendle, S.: Learning recommender systems with adaptive regularization. In: WSDM 2012, pp. 133–142. ACM (2012)
11. Rendle, S., Gantner, Z., et al.: Fast context-aware recommendations with factorization machines. In: SIGIR 2011, pp. 635–644 (2011)
12. Rendle, S., Schmidt-Thieme, L.: Pairwise interaction tensor factorization for personalized tag recommendation. In: WSDM 2010, pp. 81–90 (2010)
13. Song, Z., Gu, Y., et al.: DRPS: efficient disk-resident parameter servers for distributed machine learning. Front. Comput. Sci. **16**, 1–12 (2022)
14. Xiao, J., et al.: Attentional factorization machines: learning the weight of feature interactions via attention networks. In: IJCAI 2017, pp. 3119–3125 (2017)
15. Xiong, L., Chen, X., et al.: Temporal collaborative filtering with Bayesian probabilistic tensor factorization. In: SDM 2010, pp. 211–222 (2010)
16. Zhao, W., Xie, D., et al.: Distributed hierarchical GPU parameter server for massive scale deep learning ads systems. In: MLSys 2020, vol. 2, pp. 412–428 (2020)
17. Zheng, L., Noroozi, V., et al.: Joint deep modeling of users and items using reviews for recommendation. In: WSDM 2017, pp. 425–434. ACM (2017)

Domain Adaptation with Sample Relation Reinforcement

Shaohua Teng[1], Wenjie Liu[1], Ruixi Guo[2], Wei Zhang[1], Zefeng Zheng[1], Luyao Teng[3(✉)], and Tongbao Chen[4]

[1] School of Computer Science and Technology, Guangdong University of Technology, Guangzhou 510006, China
[2] School of Electrical Engineering, Xi'an Jiaotong University, Xi'an 710049, China
[3] School of Information Engineering, Guangzhou Panyu Polytechnic, Guangzhou 511483, China
`luna.teng@qq.com`
[4] School of Advanced Manufacturing, Guangdong University of Technology, Guangzhou 510006, China

Abstract. Domain adaptation transfers knowledge from the source domain into the target domain by minimizing the distribution discrepancy between two domains. Recently, existing approaches ignore the position differences between samples within the same class. However, there are still two problems that need to be resolved. Firstly, marginal samples and central samples may interact with each other, which leads to samples within the same class aggregate toward the margin (loss common knowledge) or toward the center (loss specific knowledge). Secondly, large distribution differences may result in degraded performance in classification. To solve these two problems, we propose a domain adaptation method called Sample Relation Reinforcement (SRR). To mitigate the interaction between marginal samples and central samples, marginal samples detection (MSD) and central samples detection (CSD) are proposed. Specifically, MSD propose a triple distances metric among the sample pairs and class centers to detect the marginal samples and learn specific knowledge. CSD utilizes the nearest and second-nearest centroid of samples to detect the central samples and learn common knowledge. In addition, dual centroid detection (DCD) is proposed to alleviate the negative effects of distribution differences, which utilizes the class centers of the source and target domains to classify the target samples. Finally, the experimental results on four datasets demonstrate that the proposed method outperforms other competing approaches significantly.

Keywords: Domain adaptation · Common knowledge · Specific knowledge · Distribution shift

1 Introduction

Due to a shortage of labeled data, it is difficult to train a learning model in emerging industrial domains. Fortunately, certain well-established domains possess an ample supply of labeled data that is suitable for training purposes [1].

© The Author(s), under exclusive license to Springer Nature Singapore Pte Ltd. 2023
F. Zhang et al. (Eds.): WISE 2023, LNCS 14306, pp. 937–952, 2023.
https://doi.org/10.1007/978-981-99-7254-8_73

Yet, domain discrepancies arise from the presence of marginal and conditional distributions between the well-established and the emerging domains (so called the source and target domains, respectively) [27]. They affect the training model, which uses the source knowledge to classify the target domain.

Domain adaptation (DA) is proposed to solve the problems caused by domain discrepancies [24]. In particular, DA projects the source and target domains into a common subspace which reduces the difference in distribution between the two domains. On such common subspace, the source knowledge is reused, while the target samples can be classified effortlessly [12].

Domain adaptation should properly handle the relationship between samples to improve performance of classifier [20]. For example, there are some methods that effectively handle samples from each class by incorporating comprehensive processing of the entire class [16,22,23,25]. However, these methods use the same weights to process all samples within the same class, which ignores the positional variability of the samples. Specifically, the samples within the same class can be divided into central samples (samples near the class center) and marginal samples (samples far from the class center). If marginal samples are particularly remote, this may cause the central sample to be pulled to the margin. Since the central and marginal samples can interact with each other, a strategy that acts fairly to all samples may cause the samples to aggregate toward the margin (resulting in a loss of common knowledge) or toward the center (resulting in a loss of specific knowledge). In addition, there are some methods that learn specific knowledge by preserving the local geometric structure [5,9,10]. However, these methods often rely on a single classifier for classification, which can make the marginal samples vulnerable to misclassification. Specifically, when the similarity between the source and target domain data is not obvious enough, it indicates that their distributions are highly dissimilar. The source domain samples may deviate from the target domain samples in the common subspace, making it difficult for a single classifier to reflect the probability of marginal samples. When the dense central samples are biased towards the marginal samples on one side, the marginal samples on the other side may out-of-control. To better illustrate this, an example is shown in Fig. 1. As a result, the marginal samples in the middle of two neighboring classes are easily misclassified.

To address the aforementioned challenges, we propose a domain adaptation method called Sample Relation Reinforcement (SRR). The primary focus of this paper is to differentiate the handling of marginal and central samples, so that both common and specific knowledge can be maintained. Therefore, two methods are proposed, marginal samples detection (MSD) for detecting marginal samples and central samples detection (CSD) for detecting central samples. MSD utilizes a triple distance metric among the sample pairs and class centers to detect the marginal samples within the same class. By MSD, larger weight is assigned with the increase of the triple distance metric, so that the specific knowledge of marginal samples is well retained. CSD utilizes the nearest and second-nearest centroids of samples to detect the central samples within the same class. By CSD, the closer to the nearest center and the farther from the second closest center,

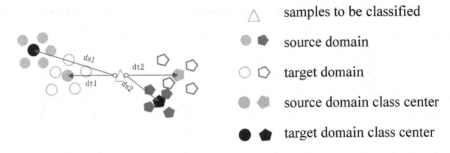

Fig. 1. The class centered classifier involves labeling samples in the target domain with their nearest class centers. When the marginal sample is out of control and is in the middle of two classes, the distance from the sample to the two class centers of target domain is the same (dt1 = dt2), which makes it difficult to determine the class of this sample. At this time, the distance from the sample to the two class centers in source domain is different (ds1 > ds2). If the class centers of source domain are used, it is easy to determine the class of the sample.

the more weight is given to the sample, so that the common knowledge of central samples can be greatly preserved. In addition, dual centroid detection (DCD) categorizes the target samples which are closest to both the source and target class centers. By DCD, the effect of sample deviation is mitigated, ensuring a high confidence level for the target samples across two domains.

The contributions of the paper are as follows, and the flowchart of SRR is shown in Fig. 2.

1) Sample Relation Reinforcement (SRR) is proposed, which consists of three parts: marginal samples detection (MSD); central samples detection (CSD); and dual centroid detection (DCD). SRR learns marginal-specific knowledge and central-common knowledge respectively, ensuring high confidence in the target domain sample labels.
2) MSD try to retain the specific knowledge of marginal samples, while CSD try to preserve the common knowledge of central samples.
3) To mitigate the effect of sample deviation, source domain class centers and target domains class centers are used to classify target samples by DCD.
4) Extensive experiments tested on four datasets and several algorithms demonstrate the superior performance of SSR.

2   Related Work

As there are extensive prior work on domain adaptation, this section focuses on the manipulation of whole class of samples and the improvement of the classifier.

There are some methods that samples within the same class are processed equally to learn common and specific knowledge together [20,22]. Xiao et al. explicitly incorporate class label information into the least squares regression framework to enlarge the distances between different classes [22]. The label

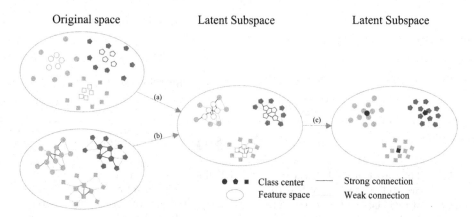

Fig. 2. SRR process is depicted in the flow chart, which applies the same process to both the source and target domains. (a) MSD projects samples into a common subspace to detect marginal samples and learn specific knowledge of marginal samples (represented by solid samples). (b) CSD detects central samples when projecting into a common subspace (represented by strong connection). (c) DCD is applied in the common subspace to classify the target domain samples.

regression in source domain is used to learn common knowledge within each class. To extract the common knowledge between different classes, Li et al. reduce the distance between every pair of samples from the same class, which the weights of samples are adjusted dynamically based on the number of samples in each class [6]. Liang et al. learn the discriminative common knowledge among different classes by bringing samples closer to the class center in a common subspace [8]. In doing so, the distances from the intra-class samples to the corresponding clusters are reduced. Similarly, Li et al. pull each sample closer to the center of its respective class to reduce the intra-class distance [7].

To mitigate the influence of sample deviation on classifiers, several previous studies are conducted [9,10]. Lu et al. propose a circular validation strategy to iteratively exchange information between two domains in a circular manner, so that the impact of sample deviation between domains is eased [10]. Liang et al. assign labels to samples by matching them with the nearest cluster centers, which are dependent on the cluster centers of source domain [21]. Du et al. consider that the classifier trained with the source domain has the error caused by the sample deviation, and propose a method to train the classifier with target domain [3]. To achieve this, they utilize source class centers to cluster the target domain data and tag labels accordingly. In addition, Chang et al. use the K-means clustering algorithm to gather the source and target domains separately, and then matching the class centers of the two domains [2].

To address the issues, SRR differs from previous work in two key aspects. Firstly, MSD and CSD are proposed to learn specific knowledge and common knowledge respectively, while other methods utilize same approach to learn specific and common knowledge concurrently. In addition, DCD utilizes both the source and target domains class centers to classify, while other methods only employ either the source or target domain signal classifier for this purpose.

3   Proposed Method

This section provides a detailed account of Sample Relationship Reinforcement (SRR). A common method along with its potential drawbacks is given, and SRR is then introduced to overcome the shortcomings.

3.1   Symbol Description and Problem Definition

Domain adaptation refers to the scenario where two datasets share the same label space and are similar in nature [13,17]. The labeled dataset is referred to as the source domain, while the unlabeled dataset is referred to as the target domain. Specifically, n_s and n_t are the number of source and target samples respectively, let $X_s = \{x_{s,i}\}_{i=1}^{n_s}$ denotes the samples from the source domain, $X_t = \{x_{t,i}\}_{i=1}^{n_s}$ denotes the samples from the target domain, and $Y_s = \{y_i\}_{i=1}^{n_s} \in R^{n_s}$ denotes the labels associated with the source domain. $Y_t = \{y_i\}_{i=1}^{n_t} \in R^{n_t}$ is the ground-truth label set of the target domain, which are unavailable during the training process and are only used to evaluate the performance of the model.

3.2   Distribution Alignment and Inter-class Dispersion Expansion

Domain discrepancies causes degradation of classification effectiveness, and DA is proposed to address this problem [4]. According to previous studies, distribution alignment and inter-class dispersion expansion are used as common solutions for DA. In particular, distribution alignment aims to reduce the differences in marginal and conditional distributions. It involves projecting both domains onto a common subspace that minimizes the distributional differences through maximum mean difference (MMD) metric [19]. Specifically, we seek to minimize

$$\min \Omega_{MMD} = \alpha \left\| \frac{1}{n_s} \sum_{i=1}^{n_s} W^T x_{s,i} - \frac{1}{n_t} \sum_{j=1}^{n_t} W^T x_{t,i} \right\|_F^2$$

$$+ \beta \sum_{c=1}^{C} \left\| \frac{1}{n_s^c} \sum_{i=1}^{n_s^c} W^T x_{s,i} - \frac{1}{n_t^c} \sum_{j=1}^{n_t^c} W^T x_{t,i} \right\|_F^2$$

$$= Tr \left(W^T X M X^T W \right)$$

$$s.t. W^T X H X^T W = I \tag{1}$$

where $W \in R^{m \times d}$ is the projection matrix, m is the dimension of the domain, d is dimension after projection, $X = [X_s, X_t]$ is a dataset for the source and target domains, M is a MMD matrix that calculates the marginal and conditional distributions, $H = I_{n \times n} - \frac{1}{n} 11^T$ is a center matrix, and $I_{n \times n} \in^{n \times n}$ is an identity matrix. $1_{m \times n}$ is a matrix with all one elements. Let $M = \alpha M_0 + \beta M_c$ denotes the joint probability distribution. M_0 and M_c are two matrices that measure the marginal and conditional distributions, respectively, i.e.,

$$
(M_0)_{i,j} = \begin{cases} \frac{1}{n_s^2} & \text{if } x_i, x_j \in X_s \\ \frac{1}{n_t^2} & \text{if } x_i, x_j \in X_t \\ -\frac{1}{n_s n_t} & \text{otherwise} \end{cases} \tag{2}
$$

$$
(M_c)_{i,j} = \begin{cases} \frac{1}{(n_s^c)^2} & \text{if } x_i, x_j \in X_s^c \\ \frac{1}{(n_t^c)^2} & \text{if } x_i, x_j \in X_t^c \\ -\frac{1}{n_s^c n_t^c} & \text{otherwise} \end{cases} \tag{3}
$$

Though Eq. (1) can align the distributions, it may not make the discriminatory nature between different classes evident. Therefore, inter-class dispersion expansion is proposed to amplify the distance between different classes. Specifically, in the source domain, the distance between any two samples from different classes can be increased using the following formula:

$$
\max \Sigma_s = \sum_{y_{s,i} \neq y_{s,j}} \left\| W^T x_{s,i} - W^T x_{s,j} \right\|_F^2
$$
$$
= Tr \left(W^T X_s G_s X_s^T W \right) \tag{4}
$$

where

$$
G_s = \begin{cases} n_s - n_s^c, & \text{if } i = j, y_{s,i} = c \\ -1, & \text{if } i \neq j, y_{s,i} \neq y_{s,j} \\ 0, & \text{otherwise} \end{cases} \tag{5}
$$

Similarly, in the target domain, the distance between any two samples from different classes can be calculated using the following formula:

$$
\max \Sigma_t = \sum_{\hat{y}_{s,i} \neq \hat{y}_{s,j}} \left\| W^T x_{t,i} - W^T x_{t,j} \right\|_F^2
$$
$$
= Tr \left(W^T X_t G_t X_t^T W \right) \tag{6}
$$

When we define $G = \text{diag}(G_s, G_t)$, Σ can define as:

$$
\max \Sigma = \Sigma_s + \Sigma_t
$$
$$
= Tr \left(W^T X G X^T W \right) \tag{7}
$$

Eq. (1) aligns the distribution as well as Eq. (7) amplifies the inter-class dispersion, which are just some of the basic operations in DA. In this case, there is further work need to be completed. Therefore, our proposed approach is described in detail in Sects. 3.3, 3.4 and 3.5.

3.3   Marginal Samples Detection

Many methods try to learn specific and common knowledge together, but they often treat the entire class of samples equally, ignoring the potential distinctions and interaction between marginal and central samples. As a result, samples within the same class may be aggregated toward the margin or toward the center, resulting in the loss of specific or common knowledge. In contrast, we propose two methods to deal with marginal samples and central samples respectively. Therefore, MSD is proposed to detect marginal samples which uses a novel ternary distance metric to assign weights to marginal samples. Specifically, each pair of samples in the same class are closer to each other, taking the source domain as an example:

$$
\begin{aligned}
\min \varGamma_s &= \sum_{c=1}^{C} \sum_{y_{s,i}, y_{s,j}=c} \left\| W^T x_{s,i}^c - W^T x_{s,j}^c \right\|_F^2 f_{i,j}^c \\
&= Tr\left(W^T X_s F_s X_s^T W \right)
\end{aligned}
\tag{8}
$$

where $f_{i,j}^c$ is the weight between sample pairs within the class. Specifically, it can be calculated using the following formula:

$$
f_{i,j}^c = \frac{n_s}{n_s^c} \exp \sqrt{\frac{e_{i,j}^c{}^2}{\sum_{k=1}^{n_s^c} e_{i,k}^c{}^2}}
\tag{9}
$$

where $\frac{n_s}{n_s^c}$ indicates the penalty coefficients of different classes, which is introduced to balance the influence of different classes during training [6]. If x_i and x_j share the same label c, and $e_{i,j}^c$ denotes the sum of the side lengths of the triangle consisting of x_i and x_j and $\overline{x}_s^c$. The formula is calculated as follows:

$$
e_{i,j}^c \Big|_{y_{s,i}, y_{s,j}=c} = \left\| W^T x_{s,i}^c - W^T x_{s,j}^c \right\|^2 + \left\| W^T x_{s,i}^c - W^T \overline{x}_s^c \right\|^2 + \left\| W^T x_{s,j}^c - W^T \overline{x}_s^c \right\|^2
\tag{10}
$$

Similar to the above, using pseudo-labels, the formula of target domain can be written as follows:

$$
\min \varGamma_t = Tr\left(W^T X_t F_t X_t^T W \right)
\tag{11}
$$

If we define $F = diag\left(F_s, F_t \right)$, we can combine the Eq. (8) and (11) as follows:

$$
\begin{aligned}
\min \varGamma &= \varGamma_s + \varGamma_t \\
&= Tr\left(W^T X F X^T W \right)
\end{aligned}
\tag{12}
$$

By Eq. (12), the marginal samples are aggregated toward the class center and specific knowledge is learned. At this time, the marginal samples are emphasized, which may lead to the samples being biased toward the margin and the common information being destroyed.

3.4   Central Samples Detection

To avoid focusing on the marginal samples and ignoring the central samples, CSD is proposed to identify the central samples and learn common knowledge between different class. Specifically, the central affinity is the position of the sample with respect to the class center, which is determined by the distance of this sample to the nearest class center and the second nearest class center. The closer the sample is to the nearest class center and the farther it is from the second nearest class center, the higher central affinity of that sample. Specifically, in source domain, CSD aggregates sample pairs of local connection through the following formula:

$$\min Z_s = \sum_{i=1}^{n_s} \sum_{j=1}^{n_s} \left\| W^T x_{s,i}^c - W^T x_{s,j}^c \right\|_F^2 s_{i,j}^c \tag{13}$$

where $s_{i,j}^s = e^{v_i v_j} a_{i,j}^s$ is the weight of sample $x_{s,i}$ and $x_{s,j}$, $e^{v_i v_j}$ represents the central affinity. Respectively, v_i can be calculated by the following formula:

$$v_i = 1 - \frac{d_i^{c1}}{d_i^{c1} + d_i^{c2}} \tag{14}$$

where $d_i^{c1} = \left\| x_i - \bar{x}^{c1} \right\|^2$ denotes the distance between x_i and the nearest class center, $d_i^{c2} = \left\| x_i - \bar{x}^{c2} \right\|^2$ denotes the distance between x_i and the second nearest class center. $\bar{x}^{c1}$ represents the class center closest to sample x_i, $\bar{x}^{c2}$ represents the class center second closest to sample x_i.

The local structure allows the selection of appropriate samples and facilitates better information mining of the central sample. We refer to the previous studies to establish the local structure using the following formula [18]:

$$a_{i,j}^s = \begin{cases} \frac{\widehat{d}_{i,k+1}^s - d_{i,j}^s}{k \widehat{d}_{i,k+1}^s - \sum_1^k \widehat{d}_{i,j}^s}, & \text{if } y_i = y_j, x_i \in KNN\left(x_j\right), x_j \in KNN\left(x_i\right) \\ 0, & \text{otherwise} \end{cases} \tag{15}$$

where k is the neighborhood number, $\hat{x}_{s,j}$ are the j th-nearest samples with $x_{s,i}$, and $\widehat{d}_{i,j}^s$ represents the distance between $x_{s,i}$ and $\hat{x}_{s,j}$.

Similarly to the source domain, we can obtain the following formula in the target domain:

$$\min Z_t = \sum_{i=1}^{n_t} \sum_{j=1}^{n_t} \left\| W^T x_{t,i}^c - W^T x_{t,j}^c \right\|_F^2 s_{i,j}^c$$
$$= Tr\left(W^T X_t F_t X_t^T W\right) \tag{16}$$

If we define $S = diag\left(S^s, S^t\right)$, CSD combined with Eq. (13) and (16) can be expressed as the following formula:

$$\min Z = \sum_{i=1}^{n} \sum_{j=1}^{n} \left\| W^T x_i^c - W^T x_j^c \right\|_F^2 s_{i,j}^c$$
$$= Tr\left(W^T X F X^T W\right) \tag{17}$$

where $L = D-S$ is the Laplace matrix, D is a diagonal matrix and calculated by $D_{i,i} = \sum_{j=1}^{n} S_{i,j}$. By Eq. (17), CSD emphasizes the central sample and extracts common knowledge between different classes. A common subspace for domain adaptation is searched, so that the target domain samples can be classified.

3.5   Dual Centroid Detection

Many methods utilize a single classifier to classify target domain samples. However, the source domain samples and target domain samples may be biased due to distribution differences and the interaction between marginal and central samples. As a result, the marginal samples in the middle of the two classes are easily misclassified. DCD method is proposed to mitigate this impact and guarantee high confidence in the sample labels of the target domain. To obtain the class centers of the target domain, we employ the Structural Risk Minimization (SRM) classifier to get the initial labels [5]. Respectively, the class centers of source domain and target domain are calculated. To categorize the target domain samples with the nearest class centers from two domains, we use the following formula:

$$\widehat{y}_i = arg \min_{j} \delta \frac{1}{n_t} d_{s,i}^{c_j} + (1 - \delta) \frac{1}{n_s} d_{t,i}^{c_j} \tag{18}$$

where $d_{s,i}^{c_j} = \left\| W^T x_{t,i} - W^T \hat{x}_{s,i}^{c_j} \right\|^2$ denotes the distance between $x_{s,i}$ and $\bar{x}_{s,i}^{c_j}$, $d_{t,i}^{c_j} = \left\| W^T x_{t,i} - W^T \hat{x}_{t,i}^{c_j} \right\|^2$ denotes the distance between $x_{t,i}$ and $\bar{x}_{t,i}^{c_j}$, δ is the tradeoff parameter. $\frac{1}{n_s}, \frac{1}{n_t}$ are the tradeoff parameters for different domains, so that the domain with more samples can have more significant impact.

3.6   Overall Objective Function

We combine the ideas discussed above and get the following general formula:

$$\min_{W} \quad \Omega_{MMD} + \sigma\Gamma - \omega\Sigma + \gamma Z + \lambda\|W\|^2$$
$$= Tr\left(W^T X \left(M + \sigma F - \omega G + \gamma L\right) X^T W\right) + \lambda\|W\|_F^2$$
$$s.t. W^T XHX^T W = I \tag{19}$$

where $\sigma, \omega, \gamma, \lambda$ are trade-off parameters, $\|W\|_F^2$ is regularization term.

Obviously, Eq. (19) is a nonlinear optimization problem with constraints that we can solve by the Lagrange method. The partial derivative of Eq. (19) with respect to W is obtained as follows:

$$\Psi(W, \Theta) = Tr\left(W^T \left(X\Phi X^T + \lambda I_m\right) W\right) + Tr\left(\left(I_d - W^T XHX^T W\right)\Theta\right) \tag{20}$$

where $\Phi = M + \sigma F - \omega G + \gamma L$, and $\Theta = diag(\theta_1, \theta_2, \ldots, \theta_d) \in R^{d \times d}$ is the diagonal matrix of Lagrange multipliers. Finally, let $\psi(W, \Theta) = 0$ and obtain:

$$\left(X\Phi X^T + \lambda I_m\right) W = XHX^T W\Theta \tag{21}$$

Eq. (21) is a classical generalized eigen-decomposition problem, it can be obtained by computing eigenvectors corresponding to d smallest eigenvalues. To better illustrate the process of whole algorithm, we summarize in Algorithm 1:

Algorithm1:	Domain adaptation with Sample Relation Reinforcement
Input:	X_s and X_t: the source and target samples
	Y_s: the source label;
	$\sigma, \omega, \gamma, \lambda, d$ the hyperparameters;
	T: the number of iterations;
Output:	W: the projection matrix;
	$\hat{Y}_t$ the pseudo label matrix for target samples X_t
Initialize:	$\widetilde{T} = 0$, $\Gamma = 0$, $S^t = 0$
While $\widetilde{T} < T$	
	1) $\widetilde{T} = \widetilde{T} + 1$
	2) The projection matrix W is calculated by the Eq. (21)
	3) Update the pseudolabel $\hat{Y}$ by Eq. (18)
	4) Update the matrix $\Phi = M + \sigma F + \omega G + \gamma S$
End while	
Output:	Projection matrix W and final classification label $\hat{Y}$

4 Experiments

In this chapter, we focus on presenting the results of experiments. We conducted experiments on four widely used datasets: Office+Caltech10, Office31, Office-Home and ImageCLEF-DA. Office+Caltech10 is widely used in domain adaptation, which consists of four different parts: A(Amazon), W(Webcam), C(Caltech) and D(DSLR). Office31 is a popular dataset of real-world images, which is composed of three sub-domains: A(Amazon), D(DSLR), W(Webcam). Office-Home contains the following four different subdomains, i.e., Ar(Art), Cl(Clipart), Pr(Product) and Re(Real-World). ImageCLEF-DA is a dataset consisting of three public datasets that share 12 classes, including C (Caltech256), I (ImageNet ILSVRC2012), P (Pascal VOC2012). These datasets not only have different dimensions and different amounts of image data, but also consist of several different subdomains that can constitute cross-domain tasks. Then, we conduct a comparative analysis with other experiments to evaluate the performance. Additionally, we perform parameter sensitivity analysis and ablation experiments.

4.1 Comparison Method

To evaluate our proposed approach more broadly, we compare SRR with seven machine learning-based domain adaptation methods: DICD [6], JPDA [26], GPDA [14], PDALC [7], ICSC [15], CMFC [2], DLAD [11]. These methods focus on learning specific and common knowledge together, and classifier based on target domain. This has similar ideas to the proposed SRR methods to some extent, and comparative experiments with them can better evaluate our method.

4.2 Experimental Setting

To ensure a fair comparison with other methods, we cite the best results reported in the original paper. Based on our experience, we find that using values $\alpha = 0.4$ and $\beta = 1.1$ yields excellent results, and fixed $T = 15$, $k = 5$, and $\delta = 0.2$, $\alpha = 0.4$, $\beta = 1.1$. Then, we grid-search the tradeoff parameter σ in $[0.5, 0.6, 0.7, 0.8, 0.9, 1]$, the tradeoff parameter ω in $[0.01, 0.05, 0.1, 0.2]$, the similarity parameter γ in $[0.001, 0.01, 0.02, 0.03, 0.04, 0.05, 0.06, 0.07, 0.08, 0.09, 0.1]$, the dimension d in $[10, 20, 30, 40, 50, 60, 70, 80, 90, 100]$, and the regularization parameter λ in $[0.01, 0.05, 0.1, 0.2, 0.3, 0.4, 0.5]$.

4.3 Comparison Experiments

To visually describe the experimental results, we present the results in Table 1, 2, 3 and 4. SRR is higher than the other methods in terms of average classification accuracy on the four datasets. The results achieved may be attributed to three main factors. First, MSD identifies marginal samples and learns specific knowledge. Second, CSD identifies central samples and learns common knowledge. Finally, DCD balances the weights between the class centers of the source and target domains, leading to improved robustness of the classifier.

Table 1. Classification accuracies (%) of office-caltech (SURF)

Source	Target	DICD	JPDA	GPDA	PDALC	ICSC	CMFC	DLAD	SRR
C	A	47.29	47.60	43.70	58.10	55.53	58.50	57.60	**62.42**
C	W	46.44	45.76	42.40	56.60	59.32	57.30	52.90	**61.36**
C	D	49.68	46.50	52.20	52.20	54.14	47.10	44.00	**57.32**
A	C	42.39	40.78	40.80	47.90	42.21	42.50	46.80	**48.98**
A	W	45.08	40.68	41.40	54.60	54.24	45.80	47.10	**57.29**
A	D	38.85	36.94	40.10	44.60	**50.96**	43.30	49.00	50.32
W	C	33.57	34.55	31.90	**39.90**	36.69	36.90	37.90	39.72
W	A	34.13	33.82	35.60	**47.20**	40.08	39.70	41.00	46.24
W	D	89.81	88.54	87.30	**94.30**	75.80	87.30	85.40	92.99
D	C	34.64	34.73	32.50	34.00	34.19	32.80	35.20	**40.78**
D	A	34.45	34.66	35.70	42.70	40.50	40.70	39.90	**50.21**
D	W	91.19	91.19	84.80	**91.90**	85.42	85.10	81.00	84.07
		48.96	45.09	47.37	55.33	52.42	51.42	51.48	**57.64**

Table 2. Classification accuracies (%) of office-31 (RESNET50)

Source	Target	DICD	JPDA	GPDA	PDALC	ICSC	CMFC	DLAD	SRR
A	D	82.13	82.13	85.80	81.12	87.80	85.14	<u>92.37</u>	**94.58**
A	W	84.28	86.04	87.40	81.51	87.80	87.55	<u>93.58</u>	**96.10**
D	A	73.48	71.07	70.60	71.64	74.10	73.34	**74.65**	<u>74.58</u>
D	W	**99.12**	97.74	98.40	95.97	95.00	97.36	<u>99.12</u>	98.99
W	A	71.57	68.51	72.80	70.11	**74.30**	73.59	73.34	<u>74.19</u>
W	D	<u>99.80</u>	99.20	99.40	97.79	97.40	99.60	**100.00**	**100.00**
		85.06	84.12	85.73	83.02	86.07	86.10	<u>88.84</u>	**89.74**

Table 3. Classification accuracies (%) of office-home (RESNET50)

Source	Target	DICD	JPDA	GPDA	PDALC	ICSC	CMFC	DLAD	SRR
Ar	Cl	53.00	46.35	52.90	54.70	51.70	55.30	**57.70**	<u>55.97</u>
Ar	Pr	73.60	60.60	73.40	76.10	71.30	<u>78.33</u>	78.10	**78.98**
Ar	Re	75.70	67.62	77.10	79.50	75.70	<u>81.29</u>	80.70	**81.57**
Cl	Ar	59.70	50.52	52.90	63.20	62.00	<u>63.70</u>	60.90	**67.16**
Cl	Pr	70.30	62.81	66.10	75.40	70.70	**78.98**	73.40	<u>78.01</u>
Cl	Re	70.60	62.59	65.60	75.10	70.70	<u>79.00</u>	74.00	**79.46**
Pr	Ar	60.90	51.79	52.90	63.70	62.40	**65.47**	63.10	<u>64.94</u>
Pr	Cl	49.40	47.72	44.90	52.60	50.00	**53.95**	<u>53.10</u>	53.08
Pr	Re	77.70	72.09	76.10	79.80	76.00	**81.20**	80.30	<u>80.61</u>
Re	Ar	67.90	59.99	65.60	69.30	68.20	<u>69.88</u>	**70.30**	69.34
Re	Cl	56.20	49.99	49.70	56.00	52.40	57.30	**59.50**	<u>58.28</u>
Re	Pr	79.70	74.34	79.20	82.60	79.00	<u>83.22</u>	82.60	**83.40**
		66.23	58.87	63.03	69.00	65.84	<u>70.64</u>	69.48	**70.90**

Table 4. Classification accuracies (%) of ImageCLEF-DA (RESNET50)

Source	Target	DICD	JPDA	GPDA	PDALC	ICSC	CMFC	DLAD	SRR
C	I	90.00	88.33	92.33	<u>93.83</u>	91.30	87.67	92.80	**94.50**
C	P	78.17	72.42	78.51	<u>80.71</u>	78.70	75.13	78.80	**80.71**
I	C	93.33	90.83	96.33	<u>96.00</u>	94.70	94.33	95.70	**96.33**
I	P	80.03	75.97	79.53	<u>80.88</u>	**80.90**	78.34	79.80	<u>80.88</u>
P	C	89.00	82.00	91.17	94.33	94.70	93.33	<u>95.30</u>	**96.50**
P	I	83.50	78.83	85.67	<u>93.00</u>	92.70	88.50	92.80	**95.00**
		85.67	81.40	87.26	<u>89.79</u>	88.83	86.22	89.20	**90.65**

4.4   Parameter Sensitivity

To verify the generalisation of the proposed method, the parameters involved in the model are subjected to sensitivity analysis in the tuning interval. As shown in Fig. 3, the method achieves stable and excellent classification accuracy curves for different hyperparameters $\omega, \gamma, \sigma, \lambda, d, T$. These parameters have minimal impact on the model's performance and exhibit good generalization ability.

4.5   Ablation Experiment

Our proposed method performs ablation experiments on four data sets. SRR is based on DICD method and SRM classifier with three new components: marginal samples detection (MSD), central samples detection (CSD), and dual centroid detection (DCD). The specific ablation methods are as follows:

DICD+SRM: the method that DICD method with the SRM classifier;

SRR-MSD: SRR method without MSD;

SRR-CSD: SRR method without CSD;

SRR-DCD: SRR method without DCD.

The results of the ablation experiment are shown in Table 5. The results reveal that SRR achieves the highest classification accuracy across all four datasets. Additionally, the performance of SRR-MSD, SRR-CSD, and SRR-DCD is significantly improved compared to DICD+SRM, but slightly lower than that of complete SRR. SRR exhibits superior effectiveness over SRR-MSD and SRR-CSD, as SRR utilizes two methods to learn specific and common knowledge respectively, which avoid the loss of specific or common knowledge. SRR demonstrates greater effectiveness compared to DCD as it achieves a balance

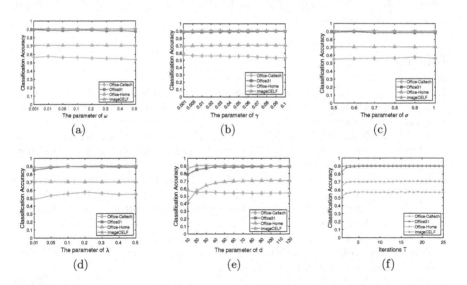

Fig. 3. The sensitivity of hyper-parameters of $\omega, \lambda, \sigma, \gamma, d$ and the iteration T.

Table 5. The ablation experiment of SRR on four datasets

	DICD+SRM	SRR-MSD	SRR- CSD	SRR- DCD	SRR
Office-Caltech	50.67	56.6	57.27	52.38	**57.64**
OFFICE-31	85.76	89.43	88.32	87.55	**89.74**
OFFICE-HOME	66.89	70.79	67.57	67.39	**70.90**
ImageCLEF-DA	87.95	90.54	90.48	88.34	**90.71**

between the source and target domain class centers, effectively serving as classifiers and enhancing the robustness of the classifier. Overall, the ablation experiments demonstrate that the three proposed improvements are effective.

5   Conclusion

This paper proposes a domain adaptation method that strengthens the relationship between samples to better extract the knowledge between the source and target domains. SRR uses different methods to learn the specific knowledge of marginal samples and the common knowledge of central samples respectively. Additionally, the approach explores a dual centroid detection method which improve the robustness of the class center classifier. The experimental results demonstrate that our proposed method significantly outperforms existing methods in four datasets. However, the detection of marginal and central samples as well as classifiers are based on class centers, and performance is affected by class centers. In the future, we will explore a more accurate way to compute class centers and also introduce additional metrics to detect marginal and central samples, such as density.

References

1. Cao, Y., Long, M., Wang, J.: Unsupervised domain adaptation with distribution matching machines. In: Proceedings of the AAAI Conference on Artificial Intelligence, vol. 32 (2018)
2. Chang, H., Zhang, F., Ma, S., Gao, G., Zheng, H., Chen, Y.: Unsupervised domain adaptation based on cluster matching and fisher criterion for image classification. Comput. Electr. Eng. **91**, 107041 (2021)
3. Du, Y., Chen, Y., Cui, F., Zhang, X., Wang, C.: Cross-domain error minimization for unsupervised domain adaptation. In: Jensen, C.S., et al. (eds.) DASFAA 2021. LNCS, vol. 12682, pp. 429–448. Springer, Cham (2021). https://doi.org/10.1007/978-3-030-73197-7_29
4. Gong, B., Shi, Y., Sha, F., Grauman, K.: Geodesic flow kernel for unsupervised domain adaptation. In: 2012 IEEE Conference on Computer Vision and Pattern Recognition, pp. 2066–2073. IEEE (2012)
5. Li, J., Jing, M., Lu, K., Zhu, L., Shen, H.T.: Locality preserving joint transfer for domain adaptation. IEEE Trans. Image Process. **28**(12), 6103–6115 (2019)

6. Li, S., Song, S., Huang, G., Ding, Z., Wu, C.: Domain invariant and class discriminative feature learning for visual domain adaptation. IEEE Trans. Image Process. **27**(9), 4260–4273 (2018)
7. Li, Y., Li, D., Lu, Y., Gao, C., Wang, W., Lu, J.: Progressive distribution alignment based on label correction for unsupervised domain adaptation. In: 2021 IEEE International Conference on Multimedia and Expo (ICME), pp. 1–6. IEEE (2021)
8. Liang, J., He, R., Sun, Z., Tan, T.: Aggregating randomized clustering-promoting invariant projections for domain adaptation. IEEE Trans. Pattern Anal. Mach. Intell. **41**(5), 1027–1042 (2018)
9. Liang, J., He, R., Sun, Z., Tan, T.: Distant supervised centroid shift: a simple and efficient approach to visual domain adaptation. In: Proceedings of the IEEE/CVF Conference on Computer Vision and Pattern Recognition, pp. 2975–2984 (2019)
10. Lu, H., Shen, C., Cao, Z., Xiao, Y., van den Hengel, A.: An embarrassingly simple approach to visual domain adaptation. IEEE Trans. Image Process. **27**(7), 3403–3417 (2018)
11. Meng, M., Lan, M., Yu, J., Wu, J., Liu, L.: Dual-level adaptive and discriminative knowledge transfer for cross-domain recognition. IEEE Trans. Multimedia (2022)
12. Patil, D.R., Pattewar, T.M.: Majority voting and feature selection based network intrusion detection system. EAI Endorsed Trans. Scalable Inf. Syst. **9**(6), e6 (2022)
13. Saenko, K., Kulis, B., Fritz, M., Darrell, T.: Adapting visual category models to new domains. In: Daniilidis, K., Maragos, P., Paragios, N. (eds.) ECCV 2010. LNCS, vol. 6314, pp. 213–226. Springer, Heidelberg (2010). https://doi.org/10.1007/978-3-642-15561-1_16
14. Sun, J., Wang, Z., Wang, W., Li, H., Sun, F.: Domain adaptation with geometrical preservation and distribution alignment. Neurocomputing **454**, 152–167 (2021)
15. Teng, S., Zheng, Z., Wu, N., Fei, L., Zhang, W.: Domain adaptation via incremental confidence samples into classification. Int. J. Intell. Syst. **37**(1), 365–385 (2022)
16. Vascon, S., Aslan, S., Torcinovich, A., van Laarhoven, T., Marchiori, E., Pelillo, M.: Unsupervised domain adaptation using graph transduction games. In: 2019 International Joint Conference on Neural Networks (IJCNN), pp. 1–8. IEEE (2019)
17. Venkateswara, H., Eusebio, J., Chakraborty, S., Panchanathan, S.: Deep hashing network for unsupervised domain adaptation. In: Proceedings of the IEEE Conference on Computer Vision and Pattern Recognition, pp. 5018–5027 (2017)
18. Wang, H., Yang, Y., Liu, B.: GMC: graph-based multi-view clustering. IEEE Trans. Knowl. Data Eng. **32**(6), 1116–1129 (2019)
19. Wang, J., Chen, Y., Hao, S., Feng, W., Shen, Z.: Balanced distribution adaptation for transfer learning. In: 2017 IEEE International Conference on Data Mining (ICDM), pp. 1129–1134. IEEE (2017)
20. Wang, J., Chen, Y., Yu, H., Huang, M., Yang, Q.: Easy transfer learning by exploiting intra-domain structures. In: 2019 IEEE International Conference on Multimedia and Expo (ICME), pp. 1210–1215. IEEE (2019)
21. Wang, Q., Bu, P., Breckon, T.P.: Unifying unsupervised domain adaptation and zero-shot visual recognition. In: 2019 International Joint Conference on Neural Networks (IJCNN), pp. 1–8. IEEE (2019)
22. Xiao, T., Liu, P., Zhao, W., Liu, H., Tang, X.: Structure preservation and distribution alignment in discriminative transfer subspace learning. Neurocomputing **337**, 218–234 (2019)
23. You, M., et al.: A knowledge graph empowered online learning framework for access control decision-making. World Wide Web **26**(2), 827–848 (2023)
24. Zhang, L., Gao, X.: Transfer adaptation learning: a decade survey. IEEE Trans. Neural Netw. Learn. Syst. (2022)

25. Zhang, L., et al.: Unsupervised domain adaptation using robust class-wise matching. IEEE Trans. Circuits Syst. Video Technol. **29**(5), 1339–1349 (2018)
26. Zhang, W., Wu, D.: Discriminative joint probability maximum mean discrepancy (DJP-MMD) for domain adaptation. In: 2020 International Joint Conference on Neural Networks (IJCNN), pp. 1–8. IEEE (2020)
27. Zhuang, F., et al.: A comprehensive survey on transfer learning. Proc. IEEE **109**(1), 43–76 (2020)

Author Index

© The Editor(s) (if applicable) and The Author(s), under exclusive license
to Springer Nature Singapore Pte Ltd. 2023
F. Zhang et al. (Eds.): WISE 2023, LNCS 14306, pp. 953–956, 2023.
https://doi.org/10.1007/978-981-99-7254-8

Printed in the United States
by Baker & Taylor Publisher Services